Book Publishing Resource Guide

Marie Kiefer

FIFTH EDITION

COMPLETE LISTINGS FOR MORE THAN 7500 BOOK MARKETING CONTACTS AND RESOURCES

AdLiB

Ad-Lib Publications, Fairfield, IA 52556

Dedication

I cannot take full credit, or for that matter, any blame, for the finished product, putting together this directory has not been a one-person job. Many people have contributed to the collection of information, verification of data, and formatting of the printed directory. Here are the names of the people who have helped over the years (in alphabetical order): Mary Adam, Barb Anderson, Carol Anderson, Melinda-Carol Ballou, Jeanette Beasley, Lynelle Chalupa, Judy Cooper, Sue Cummings, Sandy Johnson, Annette Kiefer, Pam Kiefer, John Kremer (the original author), Sue Lowe, Barb Martin, Bob McIlvride, Jane Nicolson, Joan Sirdoreus, Jean Smith, Karen Stacy, Carol Stansberry, and Suzette Striegel, Janet Whitten, and Shawn Wilson.

I also want to thank all the readers of the previous *Book Marketing Opportunities* directories who have let us know of changes in the listings. I hope readers of this directory will be as vigilant. You can send changes you come across to me at the following address: Marie Kiefer, Attn: Directory Changes, Ad-Lib Publications, 51½ West Adams, PO Box 1102, Fairfield IA 52556-1102. Please send changes in writing. Thanks!

> Published by:
> Ad-Lib Publications
> 51 West Adams
> PO Box 1102
> Fairfield, IA 52556-1102
> (515) 472-6617
> Toll-free: (800) 669-0773
> Fax: (515) 472-3186

Printed and bound in the USA by Walsworth Publishing, Marceline MO

Preliminary cataloging information:
Kiefer, Marie, 1945
Book Publishing Resource Guide
 Bibliography: p.
 1. Book industries and trade--United States--Directories. 2. Book--Marketing--Directories.
1996
ISBN 0-912411-46-5 (pbk.)

Copyright © 1996 by Marie Kiefer. **ALL RIGHTS RESERVED.** No part of this publication maybe reproduced or transmitted in any form or by any means, electronic or mechanical, including photocopying or by any information storage or retrieval system, without written permission from the publisher.

Every effort has been made to find reliable and up-to-date information for inclusion on this directory. Ad-Lib Publications makes no representation that the information is accurate or complete, does not assume, and hereby disclaim, any liability to any party for any loss or damage caused by errors or omissions in this publication, whether such errors or omissions result from negligence, accident or any other cause.

Introduction: How to Make Best Use of This Book

The *Book Publishing Resource Guide* is a directory of key contacts for marketing and promoting books. Not only does it list almost all book wholesalers and distributors in North America, but it also lists many other book marketing channels, print media that feature books, and many other book marketing services. Here are just a few of the services it features:

Distribution Channels and Services
- 127 book distributors, both exclusive and non-exclusive
- 191 publishers who also distribute books
- 710 wholesalers who service bookstores, libraries, schools, and other retail outlets
- 294 local independent distributors (magazine and paperback jobbers)
- 240 sales representatives for books and related items
- 39 fulfillment services which will warehouse your books and fulfill orders for you
- 50 foreign sales services and international distributors

Book Markets
- 285 bookstore chains, including national, regional, and specialized chains
- 483 top independent booksellers (largest, best known, or most influential)
- 119 book clubs, the majors and well as the smaller special-interest clubs
- 823 mail order catalogs that feature books as their major product
- 45 book remainder dealers and organizations that will accept donations of books

Magazines and Newspapers
- 77 magazines that feature reviews for booksellers, librarians, and the book trade
- 412 book reviews at general and special-interest magazines, both large and small
- 842 business trade magazines and marketing magazines
- 1949 major daily newspapers, with more than 3000 editors and book reviewers

Publishing and Marketing Services
- 260 publicity and marketing services
- 241 card packs in which publishers have advertised their books
- 648 sources of mailing lists, including list brokers as well as list managers
- 114 book fairs and conventions, as well as other trade shows
- 273 associations for authors, booksellers, and publishers

Directories and Other Resource Books
- 117 directories of authors, books (bibliographies), and publishers
- 315 directories of booksellers, librarians, schools, other retail outlets, media, and more
- 250 reviews of books on publishing, marketing, publicity, graphics, printing, and more

How can you make best use of these 5000 plus listings?

Begin by mailing an information packet to those people you want to contact. Depending on the company or service you are contacting, this packet might include some of the following items: your book catalog, a news release, a brochure, a fact sheet, an order form, a cover letter, and whatever else you feel is necessary to convey your message.

Once they have received the information packet, you will probably want to follow up with a phone call. Give them time to receive the packet. Then, when you call, ask them if they require any further information. Tell them you'd be happy to send them more information or answer their questions over the phone right then or whenever it would be convenient.

Keep it low key, but be sure to let them know what action you want them to take — whether to stock your book or books, buy them (and in what quantities), review a particular title, feature it in a news story, or provide some other service for you.

Ron Gold, author of *The Personal Computer Publicity Book*, asserts that the three most important PR jobs are: 1) followup calls, 2) followup letters, and 3) followup calls. These three basic steps are important in any marketing program. You must be persistent — not obnoxious, but pleasantly and reasonably persistent. If you knock on enough doors enough times, you're bound to get through.

Besides following up the initial mailing with a phone call, mail to your key marketing contacts whenever you have new developments. Repetition is a key to getting recognition. I recommend mailing some sort of communication to your key wholesalers, distributors, bookstore accounts, and media contacts at least four times a year. Keep them informed of any new publicity your books have received, any recognition from celebrities, any special sales (such as book club rights, foreign rights, or catalog sales), any upcoming tie-ins to other events or special days, and whatever other news that might be appropriate.

To keep up-to-date on the many changes that occur in the addresses, phone numbers, and contact people at the various media, distributors, and book markets, subscribe to the bimonthly *Book Marketing Update* and/or the bi-weekly *Book Promotion Hotline* newsletters (for more details, see the next page). The major purpose of these newsletters is to keep book publishers up-to-date on the changes taking place among the key book marketing contacts.

If you want to mail to an entire category, such as all wholesalers or all travel editors at the major newspapers, contact Ad-Lib Publications. We can supply you with mailing labels for any list selected from the *Book Marketing ProfitCenter*tm *and PRProfitCenter*tm *Data Files*, from which this directory was created.

Finally, if you want to locate a book marketing company or service not listed in this Directory but which you know exists, write to me in care of Ad-Lib Publications. I'll try to locate the company for you and let you know as soon as possible. And, last but not least, if you know of a book marketing company or service that is not listed in this Directory but should be, again please send me a note with whatever details you have regarding the company. I'll be sure to add it to our database and share it with other publishers through the newsletters and future editions of this Directory. Meanwhile, thank you for your continued interest and support.

Marie Kiefer, Publisher
Ad-Lib Publications
51½ W Adams
PO Box 1102
Fairfield, IA 52556-1102
(515) 472-6617
Fax: (515)472-3186
E-mail: Adlib100@aol.com

Other Books from Ad-Lib Publications

Directory of Printers 1994-95 Edition

Special Reports from Ad-Lib Publications

How to Sell to Mail Order Catalogs (with listings of 823 mail order catalogs)
Radio Phone Interview Shows: How to Do an Author Tour from Home
The Top 200 National TV News / Talk / Magazine Shows

Other Products and Services from Ad-Lib Publications

Book Marketing ProfitCenter$_{tm}$ data files 7000+ key book marketing contacts)

PRProfitCenter Data Files$_m$ (10,500+ national media)

Book Promotion Hotline (a bi-weekly newsletter)

Mailing Lists of Booksellers, Wholesalers, Magazines, Newspapers, and More

Ad-Lib Books Catalog

Table of Contents

Section I: Distribution Channels

Distributors — Exclusive and Non-Exclusive 3
Publishers Who Also Distribute Books 11
Wholesalers 21
Independent Distributors (Paperback Jobbers) 55
Sales Representatives 69
Fulfillment Services 81

Section II: Book Marketing Channels

Bookstore Chains and Other Chain Stores 87
Top Independent Booksellers 97
Book Clubs 119
Rights Buyers 125
Mail Order Catalogs that Feature Books 129
Book Remainder Dealers 169

Section III: Magazines and Newspapers

Magazines 173
Newspapers 273

Section IV: Marketing Services

Publicity Services 365
Marketing Services and Publishing Consultants 373
Speakers Bureaus 377
Cooperative Marketing Services 379
Card Decks or Card Packs 383
Mailing List Brokers and Managers 393
Trade Shows, Book Fairs, and Conventions 415
Publishing Associations 421
Publishing Insititutes, Courses, and Conferences 432
Miscellaneous Marketing Resources 434

Section V: Bibliography

Bibliographies and Publishing Directories 444
Marketing Directories 449
An Annotated Review of Books on Publishing 463

Index 485

Section I:

Distribution Channels

3	Distributors — Exclusive and Non-Exclusive
11	Publishers Who Also Distribute Books
21	Wholesalers
	51 Canadian Wholesalers
55	Independent Distributors (Jobbers)
	67 Canadian Jobbers
69	Sales Representatives
81	Fulfillment Services

Section I: Distribution Channels

Section I lists the major distribution channels for books: distributors, wholesalers, jobbers, sales representatives, and fulfillment services. Section II, which follows, lists the major book marketing channels such as bookstore chains, independent booksellers, book clubs, catalogs that feature books, and book remainder dealers.

In preparing the lists for this section, we chose to distinguish between distributors and wholesalers, a distinction which is not always easy to make in the book business. Nonetheless, here are the definitions we used in making the distinction for this directory:

A **distributor** stocks books, represents the books to its accounts (usually in person), handles all fulfillment and collection, and pays for the books on consignment (that is, only when the books are actually sold). Many also require an exclusive for their territory and/or market.

A **wholesaler**, on the other hand, functions essentially as an order taker for its accounts. Wholesalers generally do little promotion outside of a catalog. They order books as the need arises or in small stock quantities and pay for the books under normal terms (usually net 30 or net 90). None of these require any kind of exclusive.

Unfortunately, many distribution companies do not easily fit either category. More and more wholesalers are beginning to require consignment of books from smaller publishers.

Anyway, when in doubt, we tended to list companies under the Wholesaler section rather than the Distributor section. But, please note, we often relied on the distribution companies self-report. Hence, if they called themselves a distributor, we listed them as a distributor.

If you are looking for a specific company (for example, Ingram) and you are not sure how they would be classified, you should refer to the Index in the back of the book.

We have divided Section I into six subsections, as follows:

- **Distributors**, both exclusive and non-exclusive
- **Publishers** who also act as distributors for other publishers
- **Wholesalers**
- **Independent distributors** (otherwise known as paperback jobbers or I.D.s)
- **Sales representatives** for book, toys, and other items
- **Fulfillment services** (these companies generally handle no marketing functions; they simply take orders from you, warehouse and ship books, and, in some cases, also handle collections.)

Book Publishing Resource Guide Page 3

Distributors — Exclusive and Non-Exclusive

The following companies distribute books, magazines, audiotapes, videotapes, and other products. Besides their names and addresses, we also list their phone numbers, subject interests, territories covered, items marketed and markets served. Items listed are those they distribute beside books. If no markets are listed, they serve the book trade (bookstores, libraries, and schools).

A

ABC School Supply
Steve Barber, Mdse Dir
3312 N Berkeley Lake Rd
Duluth GA 30136
770-497-0001; Fax: 770-497-1407
Subjects: 21-31-76-89
Territory: US; 26 reps
Markets: SC
Items: HC-PB-CR-MA-PO-SB-TA-TV-OT
Memo: 900 titles; 75 publishers represented.

Active Home Video
12121 Wilshire Blvd #200
W Los Angeles CA 90025
310-447-6131
Subjects: 29-69-99
Territory: US
Markets: RO-JB
Items: TV
Memo: Tapes only.

AIMS International Books Inc
Georgia Crowell, Pres
7709 Hamilton Ave
Cincinnati OH 45231
513-521-5590; Fax: 513-521-5592
Subjects: 21-45(Spanish)-78-80-99
Territory: US-CN-OT(Puerto Rico)
Markets: BK-SC-PL-JB-CO-SL-MM-R0
Items: HC-PB-MM-RM
Memo: Foreign language books ONLY. No English please. # of publishers represented = 100.

Amcam Inc
Joe Greco, Mgr
462 Broadway #4000
New York NY 10013
212-966-8400; Fax: 212-966-9366
Subjects: 35S-37
Territory: Distributor to jobbers only
Markets: JB
Items: HC-PB-MM
Memo: Very selective. Must fit with the books they already carry. Titles: 26. They represent 20 publishers.

American Intl Distribution Corp
Peter A Miller, Pres/Buyer
2 Winter Sport Ln
PO Box 80
Williston VT 05495-0080
802-862-0095; Fax: 802-864-4672
800-678-2432
Subjects: 99
Territory: US-CN-S AM; 23 reps
Markets: BK-PL-SC-CO-MM(direct mail)
Items: HC-PB-TX-CA-MA-PO-RC-TA-TV
Memo: 40,000 accounts served; 25,000 titles; 20+ publishers represented.

Associated Publishers Group
Sandra Hall, Mktg Dir
1501 County Hospital Rd
Nashville TN 37218
615-254-2450; Fax: 615-254-2456
800-327-5113
Subjects: 21-23-27-28-43-63-76
Territory: US
Markets: BK-RO
Items: HC-PB

Atrium Publishing Group
Deborah Fremont Smith
Aquisitions Review Committee
3356 Coffey Ln
Santa Rosa CA 95403
707-542-5400; Fax: 707-542-5444
800-275-2606
Subjects: 11-27-39H-49A-53-54-57-63E-99
Territory: US-CN
Markets: ALL
Items: HC-PB-MM-CA
Memo: Formerly known as **The Great Tradition**, this company now distributes all types of books (not just new age). Dawson Church, President. Recently published a new health & cooking catalog to be distributed to health food stores.

B

Bay to Bay Dist Inc
Gina Chiotti, Buyer
453 Rovendale Dr #A
Mt View C^ 94043
Subjects: 27-39
Territory: US-CN
Markets: SL
Items: Maureen Salaman books

Beijing Book Company Inc
Dongsan Guan, VP
701 E Linden Ave
Linden NJ 07036-2495
908-862-0909; Fax: 908-862-4201
Subjects: 23-24-39-67-99
Territory: IT(exports to China)
Markets: BK-JB
Items: HC-PB-MG-NP
Memo: Book forwarder for China National Publications Import and Export Corporation. They do not represent publishers, they buy from the publishers (1000 of them).

Bernan
Rebecca Zahn, Promotions Mgr
4611-F Assembly Dr
Lanham MD 20706
301-459-7666; Fax: 800-865-3450
800-274-4447
Subjects: 55G
Territory: US-CN-IT(US government titles)
Markets: BK-JB-PL-SL-SC-CO
Items: TX-reports

Beyda & Associates
Jay Beyda, Audio Buyer
Ruth Beyda, Bookstore Buyer
Mal Beyda, Gen Mgr
6943 Valjean Ave
Van Nuys CA 91406
818-988-3102; Fax: 818-994-8724
Subjects: 21-49A-27(cookbooks/zoo)
Territory: US; 7 reps
Markets: BK-SC-PL-RO-RO(drug stores/zoo)
Items: HC-PB-MM-TA-TV

Bilingual Publications
Linda E Goodman, Pres/Buyer
270 Lafayette St
New York NY 10012
212-431-3500; Fax: 212-431-3567
Subjects: 10-21-31-44-45(Spanish)-71-47-99
Territory: US-CA(books are Spanish imports)
Markets: SC-PL-OT(other institutions)
Items: HC-PB-MA-TA
Memo: Latin American literature.

Blue Sky Marketing Inc
Vic Spadaccini, Owner
1568 Ashbury Ct
PO Box 21583
St Paul MN 55121
612-456-5602
Subjects: 29
Territory: US
Markets: RO(Hallmark)
Items: HC-PB

Books & Bytes Inc
Eric Gavin, Mdse Dir/Buyer
815 E Odgen
Naperville IL 60563
708-416-2460; Fax: 708-416-0375
E-Mail: Eric@bytes.com
Subjects: 23-23T
Territory: US-IT; 1 rep
Markets: BK-CO-PL-SL-SC-RO
Items: HC-TX-SW-MG
Memo: 200+ accounts served; 5,000 titles; 20 publishers represented.

Books Nippan USA
John P Whalen, Mktg Dir
1123 Dominguez St #K
Carson CA 90746
310-604-9701; Fax: 310-604-1134
Subjects: 11-12(professional art design)
Territory: IT-US-CA-Mexico-Latin America; 28 reps
Markets: BK-PL-CO-SC-MU-RO
Items: HC-PB-CA-MG-TA-TV
Memo: 2,000 titles; Japanese books and magazines; Japanese animation; Japanese animation books.

BookWorld Services
Ron T Smith, Pres
1933 Whitfield Park Loop
Sarasota FL 34243
941-758-8094; Fax: 800-777-2525
800-444-2524
E-mail: Bookw@aol.com
WWW: http://www.bookworld.com
Subjects: 99
Territory: US
Markets: BK-RO
Items: HC-PB-CA
Memo: Catalog on the World Wide Web. They can also provide editing, design, and production services as well as book promotion and marketing.

Bright Horizons Specialty Dist
Becky, Faye, or Mike
138 Springside Rd
Asheville NC 28803
800-437-3959; Fax: 704-681-1790
Subjects: 21-27-29-41-43G-51N-61(SE-US) 49A
Territory: Southern Appalacians; 2 reps
Markets: BK-CO-SC-PL-SL-RO
Items: HC-PB
Memo: Number of accounts: 1,000; number of titles: 7,000.

C

Center City News
Yoel Wulfhart, Gen Mgr
202-208 Cecil B Moore Ave
Philadelphia PA 19122
215-423-3173; Fax: 215-423-3175
Subjects: 99
Territory: Mid-Atlantic; 1 rep
Markets: JB-MM
Items: MG-NP
Memo: Titles carried: over 100; Publishers represented: over 100+.

Cheng & Tsui Company
Anson Joyce
25 West St
Boston MA 02111
617-426-6074; Fax: 617-426-3669
Subjects: 11-19-27-41-44-45(Chinese/Japan)
Territory: US-CN-IT
Markets: BK-JB-SC-CO-PL-SL-RO
Items: HC-PB-TX-MM-CA-PO-SW-MA-RC-TA
Memo: 2,000 titles; 50 publishers represented.

Chicago Law Book Company
Bernadine Dziedzic, Buyer
4814 S Pulaski Rd
Chicago IL 60632-4116
312-376-1711; Fax: 312-376-1110
800-628-1160
Subjects: 19L-55C-55L-59
Territory: US
Markets: BK-CO-SL
Items: HC-TX-PB-RM-MM-GI-PO-SB-US

Childrens Small Press Collection
Kathleen Baxter
Trade Dept
719 N Fourth Ave
Ann Arbor MI 48104-1003
313-668-8056; Fax: 313-668-6308
800-221-8056
Subjects: 21-31-76-89
Territory: US-IN
Markets: BK-MU-(see memo)
Items: HC-PB-TA
Memo: Other markets: museums, school supply stores, childrens bookfairs, and homeschool markets; no reps, all done by phone marketing.

Cinema Guild
Gary Crowdis, Acquisitions Mgr
1697 Broadway #506
New York NY 10019
212-246-5522; Fax: 212-246-5525
Subjects: 11-14-31-47-65-67-99
Territory: US; 4 reps
Markets: SC-CO-PL-SL-RO
Items: TV
Memo: Educational videos, & how-to videos; 500 titles; 2-300 independent publishers represented.

CJR Periodical
Nancy Murphy, Book Buyer
237 Washington Ave
Hackensack NJ 07601
201-488-9490; Fax: 201-488-9496
Subjects: 99
Territory: US-IT
Markets: BK-CO-PL-SL
Items: MG-(all types of journals)

Compton's NewMedia
Steven Marder, Dir of Business New Products
2320 Camino Vida Roble
Carlsbad CA 92009-1504
619-929-2500; Fax: 619-929-2511
Subjects: 23C-99
Territory: US; 25 reps
Markets: BK-RO-PL
Items: CD-ROM products
Memo: Steven's title: Director of Entertainment Business Development; titles: 15.

Consortium Book Sales & Dist
Randall Beek, Pres
1045 Westgate Dr
St Paul MN 55114-1065
612-221-9035; Fax: 612-221-0124
800-283-3572
Subjects: 11-13-47-55-65-73-83-90-95
Territory: US; 27 reps
Markets: BK-RO
Items: HC-PB(literary distibutor)
Memo: Distributes 40 literary presses. 4000+ titles. They represent 45 publishers.

Corinth Films
Peter Meyer
Video & Film Acquisitions
34 Gansevoort St
New York NY 10014
212-463-0305; Fax: 212-910-0010
Subjects: 14-14M(opera)-14T-33M
Territory: US; 2 reps
Markets: RO(videos only)-CO-SC-PL-SL
Items: TV
Memo: Extensive list of videos carried; no publishers represented.

Crescent Imports & Publications
Ashfag Ibrahim, Owner
1952 D South Industrial
Ann Arbor MI 48104
313-665-3492; Fax: 313-677-1717
Subjects: 27-29-39-45-49B
Territory: US; 1 rep
Markets: Institutions
Items: HC-PB-GI
Memo: Arabic/Asian/African. Number of titles: 375; number of publishers they represent: 25.

Cultural Hispana
Jose M Guerricagoitia, Owner
PO Box 7729
Silver Spring MD 20907
301-585-0134; Fax: 301-585-0134
Subjects: 29-39-41-45-49-78-80-84-99-55
Territory: US(Washington DC metro area); 1 rep
Markets: BK-PL-SL
Items: HC-PB-MM-CO-MA
Memo: 50-100 accounts served; 3,150 titles; 50 publishers represented.

Book Publishing Resource Guide

CUP Services
Chris Quinlan, Business Mgr
750 Cascadilla St
PO Box 6525
Ithaca NY 14850
607-277-2696; Fax: 607-277-6292
800-666-2211
Subjects: 11-12-19E-31-39-41-44-47-54-55
Territory: US(university presses)
Markets: CO-BK-RO-PL
Items: HC-PB-TX
Memo: Represent 12 publishers.

D

D D L Books
Justo Rey
Distribuidora del Libro
6521 NW 87th Ave
Miami FL 33178
305-592-5929; Fax: 305-477-5632
800-63-LIBRO
Subjects: 45(Spanish)-78-80-21
Territory: US; 12 reps
Markets: BK-PL-SL-CO-MM-RO
Items: HC-PB
Memo: 250 accounts served; 100 titles; 2 publishers represented.

D Robbins & Company
Paul Fried, Book Buyer
70 Washington St
Brooklyn NY 11201
718-625-1804; Fax: 718-858-2351
Subjects: 33C-33H(magic/novelty)
Territory: US-CN(foreign also)
Markets: BK-RO(novelty shops)
Items: HC-PB-GI
Memo: 1000 titles; they represent 25 publishers including themselves.

Diamond Comic Distributors
Dena Cusick, Book Buyer
Mark Herr, Book Buyer
1966 Greenspring Dr #300
Timonium MD 21093
410-560-7100; Fax: 410-560-7148
Subjects: 33C-69G-82-86
Territory: US-CN-IT
Markets: BK-MM-RO(toy/comic stores)
Items: MM-PB-CO
Memo: 9 warehouses: 301-298-2981. Thousands of titles and publishers represented.

Dot Gibson Distributors
Dot Gibson
PO Box 117
Waycross GA 31502-0117
912-285-2848; Fax: 912-285-0349
Subjects: 27
Territory: US(community cookbooks); 3 reps
Markets: BK-RO(gift stores)
Items: HC-PB
Memo: 6,000 accounts served; 500 titles; they represent a lot of publishers.

E

Eastern News Distributors Inc
Lisa Scott, VP
250 West 55th St
New York NY 10019
212-649-4484; Fax: 212-265-6239
800-221-3148
Subjects: 11-12-14-16-19-23-29-33-41-57-69
Territory: US
Markets: MG-NS-RO
Items: MG-NP
Memo: 1130 Cleveland Road, Sandusky, OH 44870(warehouse and customer service), 600 titles.

Electronic Arts Intermix
Stephen Vitiello
Distribution Dir
536 Broadway 9th Fl
New York NY 10012
212-966-4605; Fax: 212-941-6118
Subjects: 11 (experimental art)
Territory: US-CN-W Europe-Japan-Latin Amer
Markets: PL-SL-MM-SC-CO
Items: TV
Memo: 1,850 video titles; 150 video artists represented.

Empire Publishing Service
Joseph Witt, Dir
PO Box 1344
Studio City CA 91614
818-784-8918
Subjects: 11-14-17-33(entertainment)
Territory: US-INT; 62 reps worldwide
Markets: BK-PL-RO-CO-SC-JB-WH-MM
Items: HC-PB-PO-TV-TA
Memo: 400+ titles; 40+ publishers represented.

F

Filmmakers Library
Linda Gottesman
Acquisitions Manager
124 East 40th #901
New York NY 10016
212-808-4980; Fax: 212-808-4983
Subjects: 31-98(documentary)
Territory: US-CA-N Zealand-Australia; 3 reps
Markets: SC-PL-SL-CO
Items: TV
Memo: 10,000 accounts served; 600 titles; 100+ producers represented (independent producers).

Fine Print Distributors
Mr Chris Parkman, Buyer
500 Pampa Dr
Austin TX 78752
512-452-8709; Fax: 512-452-8716
Subjects: 13-14-33-35S-37-73-86-99
800-874-7082
Territory: US
Markets: BK-RO-NS
Items: MG(magazines only)
Memo: 1500 publishers represented; 2,000 accounts served.

Forsyth Travel Library Inc
Stephen F Forsyth, Owner
9154 W 57th St
PO Box 2975
Shawnee Mission KS 66201
913-384-3440; Fax: 913-384-3553
Subjects: 45(travel guides)-71-99
Territory: US-CN; 13 reps
Markets: SC-CO-PL-SL-OT(travel industry)
Items: HC-MG-NP-PB-MA-TV
Memo: Basically a bookstore.

Forty-Eight States News Dist Co
Diane Roe
PO Box 1389
Grants Pass OR 97526-0327
541-476-7828; Fax: 541-474-6910
Subjects: 99
Territory: US-CN
Markets: NS
Items: MG(only)
Memo: 500 accounts served; 400 titles;150 publishers represented.

G

Genealogical Sources Unlimited
George K Schweitzer, Owner
407 Ascot Ct
Knoxville TN 37923
615-690-7831
Subjects: 41G
Markets: BK-Individuals
Items: PB
Memo: Distributes books he writes.

GLP International
Angelika Koops, Dir/Marketing
153 S Dean St
Englewood NJ 07631
201-871-1010; Fax: 201-871-0870
E-Mail: ADL:GLPNEWS
  COMPUSERVE:75557,105
Subjects: 99
Territory: US-CN
Markets: BK-MM-NS-PL-SL-CO-SC
Items: MG (400 titles)

Grace Company
Grace Adams, Pres
829 Langdon Court
Rochester Hills MI 48307
810-650-9450; Fax: 810-650-9450
Subjects: 99; 3 reps
Territory: US
Markets: BK-PL-RO
Items: HC-PB
Memo: 2,500 titles; 20 smaller publishers and 15 major publishers represented.

I

ICD/Hearst Corporation
Debra Delmar, Exec Dir
Magazine Sales
250 West 55th St 11th Fl
New York NY 10019-5288
212-649-4447; Fax: 212-262-1239
Subjects: 99
Territory: US-CN(foreign sales)
Markets: BK-JB-MM
Items: MM-HC-TA-PB-MG
Memo: Debra's whole title is: Exec Director Business Development; 172 titles; 8 book lines/publishers represented.

Independent Publishers Group
Curt Mathews, Pres
Chicago Review Press
814 N Franklin Ave
Chicago IL 60610
312-337-0747; Fax: 312-337-5985
800-888-4741
Subjects: 99
Territory: US
Markets: BK-PL-SL-JB
Items: HC-PB
Memo: Mark Suchomel, Sales Manager. Distributor for 40 publishers.

Independent Publishers Marketing
Donna Montgomery, Pres/Buyer
6824 Oaklawn Ave
Edina MN 55435
612-920-9044; Fax: 612-920-7662
800-669-9044
Subjects: 17-19-27-29-31P-69-99
Territory: US; 80 reps
Markets: BK
Items: HC-PB
Memo: This company has a separate division that markets books to the gift market. Several major New York publishers, plus many small publishers are represented by IPM in the gift market.

Ingram Distribution Group Inc
Wanda Smith, Buyer
One Ingram Blvd
Box 3006
LaVergne TN 37086-1986
615-793-5000; Fax: 615-793-3825
800-937-8100
Subjects: 39-53-54-99
Territory: US;
Markets: BK-SC-CO-PL-SL-RO-MM
Items: HC-PB
Memo: Wanda is main contact for new publishers. Her FAX: 615-793-5655. General frontlist & backlist; CD-ROM's; access to more than 300,000 titles.

International Book Distrib Inc
Frank Ringuette, Sales Dir
674 Via de la Valle #200
Solana Beach CA 92075
619-481-5928; Fax: 619-259-9409
800-793-7931
Subjects: 23(computer books)
Territory: US-IT
Markets: BK-RO
Items: HC-PB

International Periodical Dists
Jaime Parker, New Publ Accts
674 Via de la Valle #200
Solano Beach CA 92075
619-481-5928; Fax: 619-481-5848
800-793-7931
Subjects: 23-59(bks & mags)-99
Territory: US; 15 reps
Markets: BK-JB-CO-SC-PL-SL
Items: HC-PB-MG
Memo: 2,000 titles; thousands of publishers represented. Magazines are their primary market.

International Specialized Books
Ms Giselle Karam, Mktg Adm
5804 NE Hassalo St
Portland OR 97213-3644
503-287-3093; Fax: 503-280-8832
800-944-6190
Subjects: 48-44-67-65-47-75-63-51-43G-71
Territory: North America & US
Markets: BK-CO-JB-PL-SL-SC-RO
Items: TX(academic and scholarly)
Memo: 10,000 titles; 54 publishers represented.

J

Jackman Music Corporation
Jerry Jackman, Pres
PO Box 1900
Orem UT 84059-1900
801-225-0859; Fax: 801-225-0851
800-950-1900
Subjects: 19(music anthologies)
Territory: US-CA
Markets: BK-RO(music stores)
Items: PB-CD-TA
Memo: Catalog 4x/year. No books.

K

Kable News Company
William McCollough, Dir of Mktg
Magazine Division
641 Lexington Ave 6th Fl
New York NY 10022
212-705-4600; Fax: 212-705-4666
Subjects: 99
Territory: US; 100 reps
Markets: MM-MG-CO
Items: MG-CA

L

Library Book Selection Service
Larry Efaw, Mgr
2714 McGraw Dr
PO Box 277
Bloomington IL 61704-0277
309-663-1411; Fax: 309-664-0059
Subjects: 21-76-79-89
Territory: US; 12 reps
Markets: SC-PL
Items: HC-PB-SW-TV
Memo: 500 titles.

Libros de Espana Y America
Angel Capellan, Owner
170-23 83rd Ave
Jamaica NY 11432-2101
718-291-9891; Fax: 718-291-9830
Subjects: 45-47-57-80
Territory: IT; 2 reps
Markets: BK-NS-SC-CO-MM-PL-SL
Items: HC-TX-RM-SW-PB-TV
Memo: Exports US books to Spain; also imports Spanish books to the US.

Ling's International Books
David Ling, Mgr
7531 Convoy Ct
PO Box 82684
San Diego CA 92138-2684
619-292-8104
Subjects: 45(Fr/Sp)-47-83(Fr & Sp mainly)
Territory: US-CA
Markets: BK-SC-CO-PL
Items: HC-PB-TX

LPC Group, Login Trade Div
Dominique Raccah
1436 W Randolph St 2nd Fl
Chicago IL 60607
312-432-7650; Fax: 312-432-7603
Subjects: 19-21-27-59-69-71-99
Territory: US-IT
Markets: BK-CO-PL-SL-JB
Items: HC-PB
Memo: Call Dominique at 708-961-3900 or Mitch Rogatz: 312-939-3330; FAX: 708-961-2168.

M

Magic City
Chuck Kirchner, Book Buyer
15528 Illinois Ave
Paramount CA 90723
310-531-1991; Fax: 310-531-4516
Subjects: 33C-33H(magic/novelty)
Territory: US; 4 reps
Markets: BK-RO(novelty shops)
Items: HC-PB-GI

Major Video Concepts
Mike Davis, Buyer
7998 Georgetown Rd #1000
PO Box 6800
Indianapolis IN 46268
317-875-8000; Fax: 317-872-7067
800-365-0150
Subjects: 99(videos only)
Territory: IN
Markets: BK-RO(video stores)-MM-PL
Items: TV
Memo: 160 reps; 15,000 titles; 40 vendors

Merisel Inc
Mike Pickett, Pres
200 Continental Blvd
PO Box 984
El Segundo CA 90245
310-615-3080; Fax: 310-615-1234 or 310-615-6819.
Subjects: 23C
Territory: US-CN-IT
Markets: RO(computer stores)
Items: HC-PB-SW
Memo: New Products submission line: 310-615-1211

Micro United
Mike Goldfarb, Mktg Projects Mgr
2200 East Golf Rd
Des Plaines IL 60016
708-297-1200; Fax: 708-297-7885
800-755-8800
Subjects: 23
Territory: US:
Markets: RO(computer stores)
Items: HC-PB
Memo: Markets: office product dealers, computer supplies, computer furniture, and computer hardware. Not very many books.

Mill City Music Record Dist
Jay Danz, Buyer
3820 East Lake St
Minneapolis MN 55406
612-722-6649
Subjects: 14
Territory: US; 50+ reps
Markets: BK-RO-SL-PL-SC-CO-SP(state parks)
Items: CD-TA
Memo: 2,000 titles.

Modern Books & Crafts Inc
Alex M Yudkin, Pres
147 McKinley Ave
Bridgeport CT 06606
203-366-5494
Subjects: 28-11-41-61
Territory: US; 3 reps
Markets: BK
Items: HC-PB
Memo: 25 titles; 3 publishers represented.

Morris Costumes
Phyllis Blackman, Buyer
3108 Monroe Rd
Charlotte NC 28205
704-333-4653; Fax: 704-332-4443
Subjects: 33C-33H(costumes/novelty)
Territory: US; 20 internal reps
Markets: BK-RO(novelty/costume shops)
Items: HC-PB-GI
Memo: 200 titles.

N

National Book Co Inc
Barb Macca, Office Mgr
800 Keystone Industrial Park
Scranton PA 18512
717-346-2020; Fax: 800-458-6515
Subjects: 99
Territory: US-CA-UK
Markets: BK-CO-JB-MM-NS-PL-RO-SC-SL
Items: TX-SW-HC-PB

National Book Network
Jed Lyons, Pres
4720 Boston Way
Lanham MD 20706
301-459-3366; Fax: 301-459-2118
Subjects: 19-27-33-41-44-48-55-57-61-71-99
Territory: US
Markets: BK-JB-WH-CO
Items: HC-PB
Memo: Distributes 70 publishers. Miriam Bass, Director of Marketing; Richard Freese, VP of Sales & Marketing.

New and Unique Videos
Mark Schulze, Pres
2336 Sumac
San Diego CA 92105
619-282-6126; Fax: 619-283-8264
Subjects: 99(videos); 5 reps plus several sub distributors
Territory: US-Canada
Markets: BK-RO-CH(bike stores)
Items: TV
Memo: Video distribution and production of home videos and TV shows; sales reps: varies, 48 titles, 20 producers represented.

New Era Publications
Donna Barancewicz, Mgr
PO Box 130109
Ann Arbor MI 48113-0109
313-663-1929; Fax: 313-747-8414
Subjects: 45-63(Islam and Middle East)
Territory: US-CN
Markets: OT(direct order)-BK-SL-PL
Items: HC-TX-PB
Memo: 1 rep; 1,000 titles.

Newsouth Distributor
Gil Brechtel, Pres
5638 Commonwealth Ave
PO Box 61297
Jacksonville FL 32236-1297
904-783-2350; Fax: 904-786-6026
Subjects: 75-77-81-82-84-85-86-87-88-89
Territory: Northern FL & Southern GA
Markets: BK-CO-SC-PL-SL-RO
Items: HC-PB-MM-TX-MG-ML-NP

Nightengale-Conant Corporation
Judy Durham, Production Mgr
7300 N Leigh
Niles IL 60714
312-588-6217; Fax: 708-647-7145
Subjects: 39-54-57-57S
Territory: US-IT; 13 reps
Markets: SC-PL-SL-BK
Items: TV-HC-PB

P

Paperbacks for Educators
Dave Craig, Pres
426 W Front St
Washington MO 63090
314-239-1999; Fax: 314-239-4515
800-227-2591
Subjects: 21
Territory: US
Markets: SC-CO
Items: HC-PB-MM
Memo: 11,000 titles; several hundred publishers represented.

Paul & Company Publishers
Robert Paul, Owner
PO Box 442
Concord MA 01742
508-369-3049; Fax: 508-369-2385
Subjects: 31-99
Territory: US-CN; 17 reps
Markets: BK-CO-PL-SL(universities)
Items: HC-TX-PB
Memo: 1,000 titles; 45 publishers represented. They publish 200 books a year.

Pendar Book Company
S R Akbarian, Buyer or Joni L Stump, Buyer
PO Box 6385
Salt Lake City UT 84106
801-947-0970; Fax: 801-947-0970
Subjects: 19-57S
Territory: US-CN-IT(Europe & Far East); 2 reps
Markets: BK-JB-SL-RO
Items: HC-PB-TA-TV
Memo: 500 titles; 100 publishers represented.

Periodical Brokers
Sam Solana, Pres
7060 Convoy Ct
San Diego CA 92111
619-278-9080; Fax: 619-278-9081
800-333-9345
Subjects: 23
Territory: US
Markets: RO-BK-NS-MM-CO-SC
Items: MG
Memo: 1 sales rep; 32 titles; 8 publishers represented.

Phoenix Films & Video Inc
Leonard Feldman, Acquisition Mgr
Robert Dunlap, VP Sales
2349 Chaffee Dr
St Louis MO 63146
314-569-0211; Fax: 314-569-2834
Subjects: 11-14-31
Territory: US-CN-IT; 69 reps
Markets: SC-PL-SL
Items: TV-HC-PB
Memo: 1200-1300 titles.

Prima Publishing
John McCarthy, Dir of Sales
3875 Atherton Rd (95765)
PO Box 1260
Rocklin CA 95677-1260
916-632-4400; Fax: 916-632-4405
Subjects: 99
Territory: US-IT; 15 reps
Markets: BK-LI-WH
Items: HC-PB
Memo: 250 titles per year; Prima Publishing puts out a quarterly catalog.

Publisher Resources Inc
Steve Authur, Buyer
1224 Heil Quaker Blvd
LaVergne TN 37086
615-793-5090; Fax: 615-793-2706
800-937-5557
Subjects: 99
Territory: US-CA
Markets: BK-SC-CO-PL-SL-RO-MM
Items: HC-PB-MM-CA
Memo: Ms Chris DiGiovanna, Publisher Liason Dept.

Publishers Distributing Company
Greg Constante, Sales Mgr
PO Box 4371
Los Angeles CA 90078-4371
213-871-1225; Fax: 213-957-9219
Subjects: 37(gay & lesbian issues only)
Territory: US; 2 reps
Markets: JB-NS-RO
Items: MG-HC-PB
Memo: 25 titles; 3 publishers represented.

Publishers Distribution Service
John Lindberg, CEO
6893 Sullivan Rd
Grawn MI 49637
616-276-5196; Fax: 616-276-5197
800-345-0096
Subjects: 99
Territory: US-CN-IT
Markets: BK-PL-RO-SC
Items: HC-PB-TA-TV
Memo: 400 titles from 100 small publishers - single titles a specialty.

Publishers Group West
Karla Simmons, Acquisitions Ed
4065 Hollis St (94608)
PO Box 8843
Emeryville CA 94662
510-658-3453; Fax: 510-658-1934
Subjects: 19-25-27-29-35-39-43-53-54-71-99
Territory: US
Markets: BK-JB-SC-CO-PL-SL
Items: HC-PB-MM-TA-SW(CD ROM)
Memo: Distributes 150 publishers. Charlie Winton, President. Warehouse: 2724 W Winton Ave, Hayward, CA 94545. 510-786-6528.

Pyramid Film & Video
Patricia Hamada, Distribution
PO Box 1048
Santa Monica CA 90406
310-828-7577; Fax: 310-453-9083
Subjects: 19(training)-21-27-31-39-57
Territory: CO-SC-PL-SL-BU-ID
Markets: US-IT-CN; 6 reps
Items: TA-TV
Memo: Randy Wright, President.

Q

Quality Books Inc
Michael Huston/T Relations Mgr
Product Development Specialist
1003 W Pines Rd
Oregon IL 61061-9680
815-732-4450; Fax: 815-732-4499
Subjects: 11-99(non-fiction only)
Territory: US-CN; 18 reps
Markets: PL-SL
Items: HC-TX-PB-RM
Memo: Michael Huston's title: Thunder Relations Manager.

R

REI America
Frank Castro, Owner
6355 NW 36th St
Virginia Gardens
Miami FL 33166
305-871-4829; Fax: 305-871-8032
Subjects: 99-31(educational)
Territory: US(all Spanish titles); 4-6 reps
Markets: CO-PL-SC-SL(libraries)
Items: HC-PB
Memo: This distributor carries books published by its mother company in Spain; 1,000 titles; 12 publishers represented.

S

SCB Distributors
Aaron Silverman, Dir
15612 S New Century Dr
Gardena CA 90248
310-532-9400; Fax: 310-532-7001
Subjects: 39H-51-53-54-63E-71-99
800-729-6423
Territory: US; 20 reps
Markets: BK-JB-PL-RO-SC-CO(universities)
Items: HC-PB-MA-TA-TV-SW(CD-rom)-OT(cloth)
Memo: General distributor; represents 40 to 50 publishers.

School Products Company
William Klein
1201 Broadway
New York NY 10001
212-679-3516; Fax: 212-679-3519
Subjects: 29
Territory: US; 12 reps
Markets: RO(needlework/craft)-BK-CO-SC
Items: TV-PB-HC
Memo: 45 titles; 10 publishers represented.

Seven Hills Book Distributors
Ion Itescu, Pres
49 Central Ave #300
Cincinnati OH 45202-3409
513-381-3881; Fax: 513-381-0753
800-545-2005
Subjects: 11-17-28-45-48-71-29C-99
Territory: US-CN-IT; 26 reps
Markets: BK-PL-SL-RO(camera/antique)-WH
Items: HC-PB-SW-RM-GC
Memo: 5,000 titles; 50 publishers represented.

Silo Inc
Bill Fishman, Purchaser
S Main St
PO Box 429
Waterbury VT 05676
802-244-5178; Fax: 802-244-6128
Subjects: 14-53-99(music only)
Territory: US-CN(music sidelines); 7 reps
Markets: BK-RO
Items: TA-TV-CD-BT
Memo: 6-7 titles.

Social Studies School Service
Weiner & Levin, Owners
10200 Culver Blvd
PO Box 802
Culver City CA 90232-0802
310-839-2436; Fax: 310-839-2249
Subjects: 10-21-31-76-99(educational)
Territory: US-IT
Markets: SC-CO-PL-SL
Items: HC-PB-MM-MA-PO-SW-TV-TA

Source Books
Jane and Denis Clarke, Owners
PO Box 794
Trabuco Canyon CA 92678
800-695-4237; Fax: 714-858-1420
Subjects: 63C-63P(Orthodox)
Territory: US; 2 reps
Markets: BK-RO(religious)
Items: HC-PB-TA
Memo: 75 titles; 4 publishers represented.

Speedimpex USA Inc
Carmine Castellano, Natl Sls Mgr
35-02 48th Ave
Long Island City NY 11101
718-392-7477; Fax: 718-361-0815
Subjects: 11-45(Spanish/Italian)-47-61-80
Territory: US importer (Spanish/Italian)
Markets: BK-CO-PL-SL-RO
Items: HC-PB-MG-NP
Memo: Regional offices: 1000 W Hillcrest Blvd, Inglewood, CA 90301; 400 titles.

Spring Arbor Distributors
Robert Stone, Bible Buyer
Rufas Walsh, Book Buyer, Adult Religious Books
Phyllis Hedges, Buyer, Adult Trade Books
Susan Heuser, Children's Books
Bill Washburn, Music Buyer
Lyn Brown, Product Purchasing Department
10885 Textile Rd
Belleville MI 48111-2398
313-481-0900; Fax: 313-481-0179
800-395-7234
Subjects: 63C-63P
Territory: US-CN-IT
Markets: BK-MM-RO
Items: HC-PB-MM
Memo: Distribution centers: Newport TN, Portland OR, Grand Prairie TX, Belleville MI. They serve 12,000+ stores, mostly in the religious marketplace.

Starlite Inc
C Green, Exec Asst
PO Box 20004
Saint Petersburg FL 33742
813-392-2929; Fax: 813-392-6161
Subjects: 99
Territory: US-CA-Europe-Austrailia; 26 reps
Markets: BK-PL-CO-SC(doctors-legal prof)
Items: HC-PB(by direct mail only)
Memo: 50,000+ accounts served; 152 titles; 30 publishers represented.

Story House Corporation
Sigurd Rahmas, Pres
Bindery Ln
Charlotteville NY 12036-0010
607-397-8725; Fax: 607-397-8282
Subjects: 41-47
Territory: US
Markets: BK-SC-CO-PL-SL-(military bases)
Items: PB-HC
Memo: 25+ publishers represented.

T

Talman Company
Marilee Talman, Pres
131 Spring St #201E-N
New York NY 10012
212-431-7175; Fax: 212-431-7215
800-537-8894
Subjects: 21-27-39-53-54-69-71-73-76-99
Territory: US-CN; 30 reps
Markets: BK-PL-CO-RO-MM
Items: HC-PB-MA-TA-TV
Memo: 3,000 titles; 26 publishers represented.

Book Publishing Resource Guide

Theatre Communications Group
Terry Nemeth, Book Buyer
355 Lexington Ave
New York NY 10017
212-697-5230; Fax: 212-983-4847
Subjects: 14T
Territory: US-CN-IT; 30 reps
Markets: BK
Items: HC-PB
Memo: 100 titles in print; 3 publishers represented.

Thomas Reed Publications
Jerald Knops, Pres
13 A Lewis St
Boston MA 02113
800-995-4995
617-248-0700; Fax: 617-248-5855
Subjects: 70N(nautical almanacs)
Territory: US-Carribean-CN
Markets: BK-PL(marina chandlers/marinas)
Items: PB
Memo: 700 accounts served; 4 titles carried. They only represent themselves.

Total Circulation Services
Jan Zucker, Pres
83 Myers St
Hackensack NJ 07601
201-342-6334
Subjects: 99
Territory: US
Markets: JB-BK-MM-RO
Items: MG-ML

TransAmerican & Export News Co
Dennis Tynes, National Dist Mgr
591 Camino de la Reina #200
San Diego CA 92108-3104
619-297-8032; Fax: 619-297-5353
Subjects: 21-29-41-43-33-59-67-69-71-75
Territory: US-CN-IT(Australia/New Zealand); 8 reps
Markets: BK-SC-CO-SL-PL-RO-MM-NS
Items: HC-PB-RM-MM-MG-CA-SO-MA-SB-TV-SW
Memo: MAGAZINES ONLY! 16 titles; 6 publishers represented.

U

Ubiquity
Joe Massey, Pres
607 Degraw St
Brooklyn NY 11217
718-875-5491; Fax: 718-875-8047
Subjects: 13-14-47-44-51-55-65
Territory: US
Markets: BK-CO-NS-MM-SL(universities)
Items: MG
Memo: 1,800 titles.

Unique Books
Richard Capps, Product Mgr
4230 Grove Ave
Gurnee IL 60031
847-623-9171; Fax: 847-623-7238
800-553-5446
Subjects: 10(small press titles)-21-76-99
Territory: US
Markets: PL
Items: HC-PB-TV

Memo: This library distributor now offers a Cataloging in Publication program. Cost: $25.00 per title for 30-day turnaround or $40.00 per title for 10-day turnaround.

University of Washington Press
Pat Sodden, Gen Mgr
Associate Director
PO Box 50096
Seattle WA 98145-5096
206-543-4050; Fax: 206-543-3932
Subjects: 11(museum publications)
Territory: US-IN-CA
Markets: BK-PL-SL-JB
Items: HC-PB
Memo: 115 titles.

W

The Wright Group
James Cahill, Pres/CEO
19201 120th Ave NE
Bothell WA 98011
206-486-8011; Fax: 206-486-7868
Subjects: 31
Territory: US-IT
Markets: PL-SC
Items: HC-PB-TA-TV
Memo: 50-60 reps.

Y

Yellowstone Art Center
Linda Ewart, Buyer
Regional Writers Project
401 N 27th St
Billings MT 59101
406-256-6804; Fax: 406-256-6817
Subjects: 75-83-90-95(regional small press)
Territory: MT-SD-ND-WA-ID-WY-OR
Markets: MU
Items: HC-PB
Memo: 130 fiction & non-fiction titles; 12 publishers represented.

Canada

B Broughton Company
Brian Boughton, Owner
2105 Danforth Ave
Toronto ON Canada M4C 1K1
416-690-4777; Fax: 416-690-5357
Subjects: 21-31-35-61-63-65
Territory: CN offers direct mail; 3 reps
Markets: BK-RO
Items: HC-PB-TA-TV
Memo: 5,000 titles carried; number of publishers represented: 15.

Centax Books and Distribution
Leanne Ochitwa
Sales & Marketing Manager
1150 8th Ave
Regina SK Canada S4R 1C9
306-359-7580; Fax: 306-757-2439
Subjects: 27-99(best sellers)
Territory: CN-US; Reps: 20 CN, 10 US
Markets: BK-SC-CO-MM
Items: MM-PB
Memo: # of titles: 95.

Cheren Canada
Paul Lessard, Pres
Box 698 Route 3
Markdale ON Canada N0C 1H0
519-986-4353; Fax: 519-986-3103
800-263-2408
Subjects: 39H-39R-49A-53-54-57
Territory: CN
Markets: BK-RO
Items: HC-PB-MM
Memo: Distributes for 230 publishers. Books on new age, metaphysical, Native American, recovery, holistic health, herbalism, and self-help.

Christie & Christie
David or Nancy Christie
261 Alice St
Kincardine ON Canada N2Z 2P9
519-396-9553; Fax: 519-396-9554
FAX: 800-458-0025
Subjects: 99
Territory: US-CN; 1 rep
Items: HC-PB
Memo: US address: 1575 Military Rd #13-203, Niagara Falls, NY 14304-4706.

Claude M Diffusion Ltd
Claude Meissonnier
1544 Villeray
Montreal PQ Canada H2E 1H1
514-376-9723; Fax: 514-727-0899
Subjects: 99
Territory: US & CN; 2 reps
Markets: BK-SC-CO-PL-SL(religious bksts)
Items: HC-PB
Memo: 1,000 accounts served; 18,000 titles; 60 publishers represented.

Firefly Books Ltd
Lionel Koffler, Pres
250 Sparks Ave
Willowdale ON Canada M2H 2S4
416-499-8412; Fax: 416-499-8313
Subjects: 11-21-27-29-39-76-99(small press)
Territory: CN-US; 22 reps
Markets: BK-PL-SC-CO-JB-MM
Items: HC-PB-CA

HB Fenn & Company
Michael Fenn, Book Buyer
1090 Lorimar Dr
Mississauga ON Canada L5S 1R7
800-267-3366
Subjects: 21T-43-71-86-99
Territory: CN; 5 in-house reps, 10 out
Markets: BK-RO-SC-CO-PL-SL
Items: HC-PB-MM-CA
Memo: 15 publishers represented.

MHW Distribution
Marshall Hrycink
836 Bloor St W
Toronto ON Canada
416-5334-6942; 800-216-2985;
   Fax: 800-216-2987
Subjects: 27-41-47-61-99
Territory: CN
Markets: BK-JB-NS-SC-CO-MM-PL-RO(gift)
Items: HC-PB-RM-MM-CA-CO-GI-MA-RC-TA-TV

Negev Importing Company Ltd
Morty Kaplan, Buyer
3509 Bathurst St
Toronto ON Canada M6A 2C5
416-781-9356; Fax: 416-781-0071
Subjects: 63-99(Israel/Jewish)
Territory: CN; 2 reps
Markets: BK-SC-CO-MM-PL-SL
Items: HC-TX-PB-RM-TA-TV-GI-GC
Memo: 31,000 titles.

Prologue Inc
Guy Saint-Jean, Chairman
1650 Lionel-Bertrand Blvd
Boisbriand PQ Canada J7H 1N7
514-434-0306; Fax: 514-434-2627
Subjects: 11-21-27-17B-99
Territory: CN; 10 reps
Markets: BK-RO-MM
Items: HC-PB-MG

Raincoast Book Distribution
Allan MacDougall, Executive VP
Director of Sales and Marketing
8680 Cambie St
Vancouver BC Canada V6P 6M9
604-323-7100; Fax: 604-323-7109
Subjects: 21-71-99
Territory: CN-US
Markets: BK-PL-SL-RO
Items: HC-PB-CA-ST-TA
Memo: Marketing Manager, Wendy Bond: 604-323-7114.

Scholarly Book Service
Brian Donat, Pres
77 Mowat Ave #403
Toronto ON Canada M6K 3E3
416-533-5490; Fax: 416-533-5652
Subjects: 11-12A-19-23-24-31-39-41-45-47-99
Territory: CN-US-UK-IT; 4 reps
Markets: SC-CO-BSK-RO-PL-SL
Items: HC-PB-TX
Memo: 15,000 accounts served; 12,000 titles; 40+ publishers represented.

Sandhill Book Marketing
Nancy Wise, Owner
#99-1270 Ellis St
Kelowna BC Canada V1Y 1Z4
604-763-1406; Fax: 604-763-4051
Subjects: 99(small press/self-publishers)
Territory: CN; 1 rep
Markets: BK-SC-RO-PL-SL
Items: HC-PB
Memo: 600 titles; 100 publishers represented.

International Distributors

Airlift Book Company
Don Skirving or Beth Grossman
26/28 Eden Grove
London N7 8EF England
071-607-5792; Fax: 071-607-6714
Subjects: 19C-25-27-39-53-54-57-65-73-75
Territory: IT(England) small press titles
Markets: BK-PL-JB
Items: HC-PB-MM-TX
Memo: Currently distributing for 150 small presses.

Charles E Tuttle Company
Robert Self, Buyer
21-13 Seki 1-chome
Tama-ku
Kawasaki 214 Japan
044-833-0225; Fax: 044-833-7559
Subjects: 99
Territory: IT(Japan); 25 reps
Markets: BK-PL-SL-SC-CO-MM
Items: HC-PB-MM-RM-TX-CA-MG-CR-TA
Memo: Haruhiko Oguchi, also a Buyer; 400 accounts served; 10,000 titles; 500 publishers represented.

Cordee
Ken Vickers
3a De Montfort St
Leicester LE1 7HD England
Subjects: 69(mountaineering)-71
Territory: IT(UK & Europe); 7 reps
Markets: BK-SL-RO(recreation trade)
Items: HC-PB-TX-RM-CA-MA-TV-OT
Memo: 4,000 accounts served; 5,000+ titles; 60 publishers represented. Phone: 0116-2543579; FAX: 0116-2471176.

Toppan Company Ltd
Moto Sekino
3-1 Kanda Ogawamachi
Chiyoda-Ku
Tokyo 101 Japan
03-3295-3461; Fax: 03-3293-5963
Subjects: 51-67S(natural science)
Territory: IT(Japan); 5 reps
Markets: BK-SL-CL-MM-RO(PC shops)
Items: HC-PB-TX
Memo: Hiroshi Yuri, Mdse Director. 450 accounts served; 13,000 titles; 60 publishers represented.

Memo: As you have already noticed abbreviations are used in the entries. Here is a list of the abbreviations used.

Abbreviations Used

Territory

CN	Canada
IT	International
MX	Mexico
OT	Other
US	United States with some state abbreviations for the different states

Markets

BK	Bookstores
CO	Colleges
JB	Jobbers
MM	Mass Markets
NS	Newsstands
OT	Other
PL	Public Libraries
RO	Retail Outlets
SC	Schools
SL	Special Libraries

Items

CA	Calendars
CO	Comics
CR	Craft Items
GA	Games
GC	Greeting Cards
GI	Gifts
HC	Hardcovers
MA	Maps and Atlases
MG	General / Special Magazines
ML	Literary Magazines
MM	Mass Market Books
NP	Newspapers
OP	Out of Print Books
OT	Other Items
PB	Trade Paperbacks
PO	Posters
RC	Records
RM	Remainders
SB	Stickers/Bookmarks
ST	Stationery
SW	Software
TA	Tapes, Audio
TO	Toys
TV	Tapes, Video
TX	Textbooks
US	Used books

Publishers Who Also Distribute Books

The following publishers not only distribute their own books, but they also distribute books from other publishers. Besides their names and addresses, we also list their subject interests, territories covered, and markets served. Items listed are those they distribute.

A

A R E Press
Joseph W Dunn, Publisher
PO Box 656
Virginia Beach VA 23451
804-428-3588; Fax: 804-422-6921
800-723-1112
Subjects: 53-54
Territory: US-CN
Markets: BK
Items: HC-PB
Memo: Mail order business.

Acropolis Books
Alphons Hackl, Publisher
415 Wood Duck Dr
Sarasota FL 34236
813-953-5214; Fax: 813-366-0745
Subjects: 19-51
Territory: US-IT
Markets: BK-PL-SC-CO-SL-RO
Items: HC-PB

Adams Media Corporation
Bob Adams, Publisher
260 Center St
Holbrook MA 02343
617-767-8100; Fax: 617-767-0994
Subjects: 99
Territory: US
Markets: BK
Items: HC-PB

Adventure Publications
Gordon Slabaugh, Pres
PO Box 269
Cambridge MN 55008
612-689-9800; Fax: 612-689-9039
800-678-7006
Subjects: 27-29-43G-51-61(MN/WI)
Territory: US-MN; 25 - 30 reps
Markets: BK-PL-RO
Items: HC-PB-CA

Agincourt Press
David Rubel
270 Lafayette St #903
New York NY 10012
212-334-0907; Fax: 212-431-3251
Subjects: 17-21-41-67S
Territory: US
Markets: BK-PL
Items: TA-TV
Memo: Expertise in creating books for the trade & library markets.

Alamo Square Distributors
Bert Herrman, Owner
Alamo Square Press
PO Box 14543
San Francisco CA 94114
415-863-7410; Fax: 415-863-7456
Subjects: 37-73(see memo)
Territory: US-CN-IT
Markets: BK-PL-CO
Items: HC-PB
Memo: Category also to include cross dressing & trans gender books. Stores in Australia and South Africa.

Alan C Hood & Company
Alan C Hood Jr, Pres
PO Box 775
Chambersburg PA 17201
717-267-0867; Fax: 717-267-0572
Subjects: 15-51-69R-99
Territory: US-CN
Markets: BK-SC-PL-RO(sporting goods)
Items: HC-PB
Memo: Distributes for 8-9 other various publishers. Although Alan is in PA, the VT address is still in service which is: 28 Birge St, Brattleboro VT, 05301. Phone: 802-254-2200.

Alyson Publication
Karen Cole
PO Box 4371
Los Angeles CA 90078
213-871-1225
Subjects: 37
Territory: US
Markets: BK-PL-SC-CO
Items: HC-PB-CA

American Cooking Guild
Karen Perrino, Mktg Dir
6-A East Cedar Ave
Gaithersburg MD 20877
301-963-0698; Fax: 301-963-1910
800-367-9388
Subjects: 27
Territory: US
Markets: RO(gourmet/kitchenware)
Items: PB

American Nurseryman Pub
Kathy Valduga, Dir of Book Dist
77 West Washington St #2100
Chicago IL 60602
312-782-5505; Fax: 312-782-3232
Subjects: 43-51-12A(horticulture, landscape)
Territory: Nursery-related items
Markets: BK-SC-PL-SL-RO-CO
Items: HC-PB-TA-TV
Memo: Catalog mailed twice a year to 100,000.

Amherst Media
Craig Alesse, Owner
418 Homecrest Dr
Amherst NY 14226
716-874-4450; Fax: 716-874-4508
Subjects: 11P-67A
Territory: US-CA-IT
Markets: BK-RO(photo stores)
Items: HC-PB-TV

Apollo Books
Kimberly Ann Rentz, Mgr
5 School House Ln
Poughkeepsie NY 12603-4907
914-473-6560
Subjects: 33-59
Territory: US-CN-IT; 1 rep
Markets: BK-JB-NS-SC-CO-MM-PL-SL
Items: HC-PB-RM
Memo: Glenn B Opitz, Owner.

Archtype Press Inc
Diane Maddex, Pres
4201 Connecticut Ave NW #407
Washington DC 20008
202-364-4201; Fax: 202-966-6733
Subjects: 11P-12A-14-27-28-41-43G
Territory: US
Markets: BK
Items: CA-HC-OT
Memo: Specializes in illustrated books, calendars, & sidelines on American culture.

Ariel Books
Susan Feuer
112 Cat Rock Rd
Cos Cob CT 06807
203-661-2237; Fax: 203-661-2294
Subjects: 99
Territory: US
Markets: BK-MM
Items: HC
Memo: High-quality books for adults & children.

Armenian Reference Books Co
Hamo Vassilian, Buyer
PO Box 231
Glendale CA 91209
818-504-2550; Fax: 818-504-2550
Subjects: 27-45-78-80
Territory: US-IT(mail order only)
Markets: BK-RO-SC-PL
Items: HC-PB-TV

Ashgate Publishing Company
James W Gerard, Pres
Ashgate Publishing
Old Post Road
Brookfield VT 05036-9707
802-276-3162; Fax: 802-276-3837
Subjects: 19-47-49-55-57-59-63-65-67-19E
Territory: US-CN-IT
Markets: BK-JB-SC-CO-PL-SL
Items: HC-TX-PB
Memo: Category: chemical references and law. Parent company in England.

Augsburg Fortress Publishers
Rod Olson, Book Selector
426 S 5th St
PO Box 1209
Minneapolis MN 55440-1209
612-330-3300; Fax: 612-330-3455
800-328-4648
Subjects: 63P-14M-57-63
Territory: US
Markets: BK-CO-PL
Items: HC-PB-MM(religious goods)GC-TA

B

Baron Barclay Bridge Supplies
Randy Baron, Pres
3600 Chamberlain Ln #230
Louisville KY 40241
502-426-0410; Fax: 502-426-2044
800-274-2221
Subjects: 69G(exclusively bridge)
Territory: IT(worldwide)
Markets: BK-SC-CO-MM-RO(and individuals)
Items: PB-HC

Bascom Communications Company
Betsy Ryan
399 East 72nd St
New York NY 10021
212-988-4212; Fax: 212-988-4212
Subjects: 99
Territory: US
Markets: BK
Items: HC-TA-TV
Memo: Also acts as literary agent for a selected list of writers of adult nonfiction.

BDK Books Inc
Barbara DuPree Knowles, Pres
127 West 56th St
New York NY 10019-3809
212-262-4489
Subjects: 27-99
Territory: US
Markets: BK
Items: HC-PB

Beekman Publishers
Stuart Ober, Owner
Mill Hill Rd
PO Box 888
Woodstock NY 12498-0888
914-679-2300; Fax: 914-679-2301
Subjects: 19-39-41
Territory: US-CA
Markets: BK-SC-CO-PL-SL(and individuals)
Items: HC-RM

The Benjamin Company Inc
Ted Benjamin, Pres
21 Dupont Ave
White Plains NY 10605
914-997-0111; Fax: 914-997-7214
Subjects: 99
Territory: US
Markets: BK
Items: HC-PB-TA-TV
Memo: Publishes items to be used in premium, promotion, advertising, PR, public service & incentive programs.

Bhaktivedanta Book Trust
Stuart Kadetz, Mgr/Buyer
3764 Watseka Ave
Los Angeles CA 90034
310-559-4455; Fax: 310-837-1056
Subjects: 53-54
Territory: IT
Markets: Worldwide distributor/publisher
Items: HC-PB-MM-CA-GC-PO-TA-TV

BiblioFile
Glenn A Hauman
1130 Willow Ave 3rd Fl
Hoboken NJ 07030-3222
201-222-1600; Fax: 201-216-0544
Email: info@bb.com or comment@bb.com
Internet: http://www.bb.com
Subjects: 99-86-84(classic literature)
Territory: IT
Markets: Internet
Items: 300 titles
Memo: English lang only; art/photos with special circumstances only; electronic publishing & distribution.

Booklink Distributors
Karen L Reinecke, Owner
1715 Bee Canyon Rd
PO Box 840
Arroyo Grande CA 93420-0840
805-473-1947
Subjects: 27-51-61(Western)-69
Territory: CA-NV(Western states); 3 reps
Markets: BK-SC-CO-PL-RO-SL-RO
Items: HC-PB

Breakthrough Publications
Peter Ognibene, Owner
310 N Highland Ave
Ossining NY 10562
914-762-5111; Fax: 914-762-4818
Subjects: 15(horses)-19
Territory: US-CN-IT
Markets: SC-BK-PL
Items: HC-PB

Bridge Works Publishing Co
Barbara & Warren Phillips, Owner
Bridge Lane
Box 1798
Bridgehampton NY 11932
516-537-3418; Fax: 516-537-5092
Subjects: 99(original fic/non-fiction)
Territory: US
Markets: SC-PL-MM-CO
Items: HC only (PB rights)

Burns Archive Productions Ltd
Stanley B Burns, MD
140 East 38th St
New York NY 10016
212-889-1938; Fax: 212-481-9113
Subjects: 99
Territory: US
Markets: BK
Items: HC
Memo: Archive of 250,000 original vintage prints.

Byron Preiss Visual Publ Inc
Clarice Levin
24 West 25th St
New York NY 10010
212-645-9870; Fax: 212-645-9874
Subjects: 21-21T-67-99
Territory: US
Markets: BK
Items: HC-PB

C

Charles E Tuttle Company
Michael Kerber, VP/Gen Mgr
153 Milk St 5th Fl
Boston MA 02109
617-951-4080; Fax: 617-951-4045
Subjects: 44-45-80-99-11-27-76
Territory: US
Markets: BK-SC-RO-PL-CO
Items: HC-PB-MM

China Books & Periodicals Inc
Lisa Ryan, Mgr
2929 24th St
San Francisco CA 94110-4196
415-282-2994
Subjects: 11-19-44-45(Chinese)-55-80
Territory: US-IT
Markets: BK-SC-CO-PL-SL
Items: HC-PB-MG-CA-GI-GC-MA-SW-TA-TV-NP-PO-SB

Consulting Psychologists Press
Lee Langhammer-Law, Contact
3803 E Bayshore Rd
PO Box 10096
Palo Alto CA 94303
415-969-8901; Fax: 415-969-8608
Subjects: 19C-31-35-57
Territory: US-IT
Markets: BK-SC-CO
Items: HC-PB-TA-TV

Contemporary Arts Press
Anna Couey, Asst Dir
70 12th St
PO Box 193123 Rincon Annex
San Francisco CA 94119-3123
415-431-7524
Subjects: 11-14-23-33-47
Territory: US-CN-IT
Markets: BK-SC-CO-PL-SL
Items: HC-PB-SW-TV-OT-PB-MM-HC-SW-TV

Craftsman Book Co
Bill Grote
6058 Corte del Cedro
Carlsbad CA 92009
619-438-7828; Fax: 619-438-0398
800-829-8123
Subjects: 12B
Territory: US
Markets: BK-PL-SL-CO-MM
Items: PB-TA
Memo: 80 titles; 3 publishers represented.

Creative Homeowner Press
Ted Marcus, Contact
24 Parkway
Upper Saddle River NJ 07458-9960
800-631-7795
201-934-7100; Fax: 201-934-8971
Subjects: 29-43
Territory: US
Markets: BK-RO
Items: PB
Memo: Related to HB Fenn & Company in Canada, a book distributor.

Curtis Circulation Company
James H Moon, Sales Mgr
433 Hackensack Ave
Hackensack NJ 07601
201-907-5500; Fax: 201-836-7622
Subjects: 99
Territory: US
Markets: BK-NS-CO-MM-RO
Items: CA-MA

Cypress House
John Fremont
155 Cypress St
Fort Bragg CA 95437
707-964-9520; Fax: 707-964-7531
800-773-7782
Subjects: 99
Territory: US
Markets: BK-PL-SL-CO-GI(stores)
Items: HC-PB-TX
Memo: Primarily produce, promote, and market books by & for independent publishers. We sell through our catalogs and line up distributors for our clients.

D

Dearborn Trade
Charles Lilly, Sales Mgr
155 N Wacker Dr #900
Chicago IL 60606-1719
312-836-4400; Fax: 312-644-0644
800-245-book
Subjects: 19-19H-19A-19E
Territory: US-CA-IT
Markets: BK-PL-CO
Items: HC-PB
Memo: 25 years in business. Dearborn Financial Publishing Inc.

DeVorss Book Distributors
Gary Peattie, Audio Buyer
Hedda G Lark, Book Buyer
1046 Princeton Dr
PO Box 550
Marina Del Rey CA 90294-0550
310-870-7478; Fax: 310-821-6290
US:800-843-5743; CA:800-331-4719
Subjects: 27-39H-53-54-57-63
Territory: US
Markets: BK-JB-MM-OT(churches)
Items: HC-PB-MM-CA-TA-OT(Tarot cards)

Distributed Art Publishers
Marcus Ratliff, Sales Mgr
D.A.P.
636 Broadway #1200
New York NY 10012
212-473-5119; Fax: 212-673-2887
Subjects: 11-11P(art history)
Territory: US-CN
Markets: BK-PL-CO-RO-MU-OT
Items: HC-PB-CA

DreamHaven Books & Art
Atom Wolff
1309 Fourth St SE
Minneapolis MN 55414-2029
612-823-6070; Fax: 612-823-6062
Subjects: 82-86
Territory: US-IT
Markets: BK-PL-individuals-RO
Items: HC-PB-CO
Memo: 4 locations.

Dufour Editions
Christopher May, Pres/Publisher
PO Box 7
Chester Springs PA 19425-0007
610-458-5005; Fax: 610-458-7103
Subjects: 44(Irish)-45(Irish)-80(Irish)
Territory: US-CN
Markets: BK-PL-SL-RO
Items: HC-PB

Durkin Hayes Publishing Ltd
Patrick Hayes, CEO
One Colomba Dr
Niagara Falls NY 14305
716-298-5150; Fax: 716-298-5607
Subjects: 21-75
Territory: 20 reps
Markets: BK-SC-PL-SL-MM-RO
Items: PB(children)-BT(spoken word)-CD

E

Eagle's View Publishing
Denise Knight, Book Buyer
6756 North Fork Rd
Liberty UT 84310
801-393-4555; Fax: 801-745-0903
Subjects: 17-21-29-41-45-49-51-99
Territory: US-IT(American Indian)
Markets: BK-JB-SC-CO-PL
Items: HC-PB-RM-CA-GC

Eleanor Friede Books Inc
Eleanor Friede, Pres
Rte 1 Box 175V
Faber VA 22938
804-361-9050; Fax: 804-361-1125
Subjects: 70A(books about better living)
Territory: US
Markets: BK
Items: HC

Ettlinger Editorial Projects
Stephen R Ettlinger, Pres
225 East 28th St
New York NY 10016
212-683-0355; Fax: 212-683-0502
Subjects: 59-99
Territory: US
Markets: BK
Items: HC-SW
Memo: Produces popular "niche" reference books, authoritative nonfiction, interactive CD-ROM projects, and high-quality photojournalism books.

Event Horizon Press
Joseph Cowles, Publisher
PO Box 867
Desert Hot Springs CA 92240
619-329-3950; Fax: 619-329-1720
Subjects: 99
Territory: US(mail order sales)
Markets: BK and direct to consumers
Items: HC-PB
Memo: Not accepting manuscripts at this time. Formerly **Best Books Distribution.**

Eye On Education
Robert Sickles, Pres
PO Box 3113t
Princeton NY 08543
609-395-0005; Fax: 609-395-1180
Subjects: 31E
Territory: US
Markets: SC-PL(individuals/direct mail)
Items: HC-TX

F

Fair Street Productions
Susan Wechsler
127 West 26th St
New York NY 10001
212-633-2266; Fax: 212-633-2069
Subjects: 11-41-99
Territory: US
Markets: BK
Items: HC
Memo: A division of Photosearch, Inc.

Falcon Press Publishing
Byron Parnell, Sales Dir
PO Box 1718
Helena MT 59624
406-442-6597; Fax: 406-442-2995
Subjects: 51-61
Territory: US-CN
Markets: RO-BK-JB
Items: HC-PB
Memo: A select group of regional and nature books.

Fantaco Enterprises Inc
Thomas D Skulan, Pres
21 Central Ave
Albany NY 12210-1391
518-463-1400; Fax: 518-463-0090
Subjects: 33-82
Territory: US-CN-IT
Markets: BK-CO-PL
Items: PB-CO

Far Corner Books
Tom Booth, Editor
PO Box 82157
Portland OR 97282
503-230-1900
Subjects: 99
Territory: US-IT
Markets: BK
Items: HC-PB
Memo: Formerly a sales rep to bookstores.

Farrar Straus & Giroux
Joy Isenbergh, Office Mgr
19 Union Square West
New York NY 10003
212-741-6900; Fax: 212-633-9385
Subjects: 99
Territory: US-CN-IT
Markets: BK-PL
Items: HC-PB

First Glance Books
Neil Panico, Pres
PO Box 960
Cobb CA 95426
707-928-1994; Fax: 707-928-1995
Subjects: 11-27(cookbooks)-53-54-76-99
Territory: US-CA-Asia/Europe/Austrailia
Markets: BK
Items: HC-PB-RM

Forum Publishing Company
Ray Lawrence, Contact
383 E Main St
Centerport NY 11721
516-754-5000; Fax: 516-754-0630
Subjects: 19
Territory: US(mail order/retail/export)
Markets: RO
Items: HC-PB

Free Spirit Publishing
Judy Galbraith, Owner
400 1st Ave North #616
Minneapolis MN 55401
612-338-2068; Fax: 612-337-5050
Subjects: 21-31-57
Territory: US; 7 reps
Markets: BK-SC-PL-MM-RO
Items: MM-PB-PO-TA-GA-HC(few)

Gem Guides Book Company
Judy Irvine, Buyer
Al Mayerski, General Mgr
315 Cloverleaf Dr #F
Baldwin Park CA 91706
818-855-1611; Fax: 818-855-1610
Subjects: 28(gems/minerals)-61(SW)-71
Territory: SW US/local SW books-NW also
Markets: BK-RO-PL-JB
Items: HC-PB

General Publishing Company
Helen Butchart, Buyer
30 Lesmill Rd
Don Mills ON Canada M3B 2T6
416-445-3333; Fax: 416-445-5967
Subjects: 99
Territory: CN-US
Markets: BK-JB-NS-SC-CO-MM-PL-SL
Items: HC-PB-RM

Gessler Publishing Company
Seth C Levin, Pres
10 E Church Ave
Roanoke VA 24011
540-345-3798; Fax: 540-342-7172
Subjects: 31-45(Fr,Sp,Gm,It)
Territory: US-CN-IT; 3 reps
Markets: SC-CO-PL-SL(individuals)
Items: HC-PB-CD-TX-MA-PO-SW-TA-TV-GA

Girol Books Inc
Leslie Roster, Mgr
120 Somerset St W
PO Box 5473 Sta F
Ottawa ON Canada K2C 3M1
613-233-9044; Fax: 613-233-9044
Subjects: 45(Spanish/Portuguese)-80-99
Territory: US-CN-IT Spanish/Portuguese only; 2 reps
Markets: BK-JB-SC-CO-PL-SL
Items: HC-TX-PB-MM-MG-NW-GC-CD-TA

Gleason Group Inc
Gerald Gleason
12 Main St
Norwalk CT 06851
203-854-5895; Fax: 203-838-5452
Subjects: 23(college-level texts)
Territory: US
Markets: BK
Items: HC-PB

Globe Pequot Press Inc
Hugh Shiebler, Sales Mgr
6 Business Park Rd
PO Box 833
Old Saybrook CT 06475
860-395-0440; Fax: 860-395-0312
800-243-0495
Subjects: 27(cookbooks)-69R-44-61-71
Territory: US-IT
Markets: BK-PL-SL-SC-CO-RO
Items: HC-PB
Memo: International and regional travel guides.

Granary Books
Steven Clay
568 Broadway #403
New York NY 10012
212-226-5462
Subjects: 11
Territory: US
Markets: BK
Items: HC-US(specializes artists books)

Green Gate Books
Karen M Nester, Buyer
1162 Latham Ave
PO Box 934
Lima OH 45802-0934
419-222-3816; Fax: 419-227-3816
Subjects: 28
Territory: US
Markets: RO(antique trade)
Items: HC-PB-RM

Greene Bark Press
Thomas J Greene, Owner
PO Box 1108
Bridgeport CT 06601-1108
203-372-4861; Fax: 201-371-5856
Subjects: 21(illustrated children's books)
Territory: US-IT
Markets: BK
Items: HC

Gryphon House Inc
Larry Rood, Pres
10726 Tucker St
PO Box 207
Beltsville MD 20797-0207
301-595-9500; Fax: 301-595-0051
800-638-0928
E-Mail: LRood@GryphonHouse.Com
Subjects: 21-31C-31E-31P-76
Territory: US
Markets: BK-SC-PL-RO(school)-OT(child care)
Items: HC-PB-TV-TA

H N Miller Books
Harold & Phyllis Miller, Owners
12142 E Front St
Norwalk CA 90650
310-864-4116
Subjects: 41W-48(large research section)
Territory: US
Markets: BK-SC-CO-MU
Items: HC-TA-TV-CD

Hancock House Publishers
David Hancock, Pres
1431 Harrison Ave
Box 959
Blaine WA 98231-0959
800-938-1114; Fax: 800-983-2262
E-Mail: HANCOCK@UNISERVE.COM
Subjects: 27-43-51-61-69-75-99
Territory: US-CN; 2 reps
Markets: BK-JB-NS-SC-CO-MM-PL-SL
Items: HC-PB-RM-CA

Harper Collins
Geoff Hannell, VP Sales/Mktg
10 East 53rd St
New York NY 10022
212-207-7000; Fax: 212-207-7145
800-242-7737
Subjects: 99
Territory: US-IT
Markets: BK-PL
Items: HC-PB

Harsand Financial Press
8565 Wholeseth Rd
PO Box 515
Holmen WI 54636
608-526-3848; Fax: 608-526-3848
Subjects: 19-25-29-31-35-39-57-61(WI)-99
Territory: US
Markets: MO
Items: PB-TV-TA-MM-HC-CA-GI

Harvard Associates Inc
Andre Rossi
10 Holworthy St
Cambridge MA 02138
617-492-0660; Fax: 617-492-4610
E-Mail: PCLOGO@HARVASSOC.COM
Subjects: 23(relating to software)
Territory: US
Markets: BK-RO
Items: HC-PB-SW
Memo: Offers a 22 page catalog.

Heart Of The Lakes Publishing
Walter Steesy, Owner
2989 Lodi Rd
PO Box 299
Interlaken NY 14847-0299
607-532-4997; Fax: 607-532-4684
Subjects: 41(NY history & family history)
Territory: NY
Markets: Direct market
Items: HC-PB

I

Images Media Corporation
Peter Gould, Publisher
89 Fifth Ave
New York NY 10003-3020
212-675-3707; Fax: 212-243-2308
Subjects: 11P
Territory: US-IT-CN
Markets: BK-PL-SC-RO
Items: HC-PB(photo supplies)

Independent Music Association
Don Kulak
10 Spruce Rd
Saddle River NJ 07458
201-812-6789; Fax: 201-818-6996
Subjects: 14(music/acoustics)
Territory: US; 3 reps
Markets: RO(music stores)
Items: PB-RC-TA
Memo: 300 accounts served.

Ink Projects
Lynne Arany
56 West 11th St #4FW
New York NY 10011
212-979-6212; Fax: 212-979-7379
Subjects: 99
Territory: US
Markets: BK
Items: HC

Iranbooks Inc
Farhad Shirzad, Owner
8014 Old Georgetown Rd
Bethesda MD 20814
301-986-0079; Fax: 301-907-8707
Subjects: 44A-45-80(Persian)
Territory: US(books from & about Iran)
Markets: BK-PL
Items: HC-PB

Irvington Publishers Inc
Irving B Naiburg, Jr
522 East 82nd St
New York NY 10028
212-861-1501; Fax: 212-861-0998
Subjects: 39-57B
Territory: US
Markets:BK
Items: HC

Irwin Professional Publishing
Wayne McGuirt, Sr VP
1333 Burr Ridge Pky
Burr Ridge IL 60521
708-789-4000; Fax: 708-789-6933
Subjects: 19
Territory: US-IT
Markets: WH-PL-BK
Items: HC-PB

Irwin Publishing
Michael Davis, VP
1800 Steeles Ave W
Concord ON Canada L4K 2P3
416-660-0611
Subjects: 99
Territory: CN; 6 reps
Markets: CO-SC-SL
Items: HC-PB-TX

J

James L Evers Associates
James L Evers, Owner
10 Rockland Ave
Nanuet NY 10954
800-753-7429
Subjects: 19-57S
Territory: US-CA-Europe
Markets: BK-SC-CO-PL-SL(direct)
Items: HC-PB

John Benjamins Publishing Co
Paul Peranteau, Mgr
821 Bethlehem Pike (19038)
PO Box 27519
Erdenheim PA 19118-0519
215-836-1200; Fax: 215-836-1204
Subjects: 11-47(liguistics)
Territory: US-CN-MX
Markets: PL-wholesale & individuals
Items: TX

K

Kazi Publications Inc
L Ali, Pres
3023-27 W Belmont
Chicago IL 60618
312-267-7001; Fax: 312-267-7002
Subjects: 21(Islamic)-45(Arabic/Urdu)-63
Territory: US-CN-IT; 5 reps
Markets: BK-JB-SC-CO-MM-PL-SL-RO(Islamic)
Items: HC-TX-PB-CA-GI-GC-MA-PO-SW-TA-TV
Memo: Other phone: 312-267-7031.

Kenet Media
70 Perry St
New York NY 10014
212-727-7496; Fax: 212-691-8874
Subjects: 39M
Territory: US
Markets: BK
Items: HC-PB-SW

Ketab
Bijan Khalili, Book Buyer
6742 Van Nuys Blvd 1st Fl
Van Nuys CA 91405
818-908-8976Subjects:
 45(Persian)-99(Persian only)
Territory: US-CN
Markets: BK-SC-CO-PL-SL
Items: HC-TX-PB-MG-CA-GI-ML-MA-PO-NW-TA

KJ21 Bible Publishers
Kathy Almos, Mgr
PO Box 40
Gary SD 57237
605-272-5575; Fax: 605-272-5306
Subjects: 63
Territory: US-CA
Markets: BK-RO(religious)
Items: HC-PB(bonded leather)

L

L & W Book Sales
Neil Wood/Jane Conder, Buyers
Box 69
Gas City IN 46933
317-674-6450; Fax: 317-674-3503
Subjects: 11-28(antique/collectible books)
Territory: US
Markets: BK-JB-PL-RO(antique dealers)
Items: HC-PB
Memo: Store location: 5243 S Adams, Marion, IN 46953, 317-674-6450.

Lamppost Press Inc
Roseann Hirsch, Pres
1172 Park Ave
New York NY 10128
212-876-9511; Fax: 212-289-6908
Subjects: 17-21T-33H-73-75
Territory: US
Markets: BK
Items: HC

Larry Flynt Publications
Jeff Hawkins
8484 Wilshire Rd #900
Beverly Hills CA 90211
213-651-5400; Fax: 213-651-0522
Subjects: 99
Territory: US
Markets: MM-RO
Items: MG
Memo: Division of Flynt Distributing Co.

Lifetime Books
Donald L Lessne, Pres
2131 Hollywood Blvd
Hollywood FL 33020
305-925-5242; Fax: 305-925-5244
800-771-3355
Subjects: 29H-99
Territory: US-CN-IT
Markets: BK-PL-SC(how-to books)
Items: HC-TX-PB
Memo: Formerly **Frederick Fell Publishers Inc**; Orders only: 800-462-6420; el-hi market in life management skills.

Llewellyn Publications
Carl Weschke, Pres
PO Box 64383
Saint Paul MN 55164-0383
612-291-1970; Fax: 612-291-1908
Subjects: 53-54
Territory: US-IT
Markets: BK-RO
Items: HC-PB-TA-TV(few hardcover)

Lushena Books
Luther Warner, Gen Mgr
1804-06 West Irving Park Rd
Chicago IL 60613
312-975-9945; Fax: 312-975-0045
Subjects: 44F(Africa)-49B-80(African)-99
Territory: US-CA(Carribean)
Markets: BK-LI-SC
Items: HC-PB

M

MacRae's Indian Book Distributor
Ken MacRae, Owner
PO Box 652
Enumclaw WA 98022-0652
360-825-3737
Subjects: 49(American Indian)-78-79
Territory: US
Markets: SC-CO-PL-SL-OT(museums)
Items: HC-PB(3000 titles)

Marquand Books Inc
Ed Marquand, Dir
506 Second Ave #1201
Seattle WA 98104
206-624-2030; Fax: 206-624-1821
Subjects: 11-41-49
Territory: US
Markets: BK
Items: HC

Marshall Cavendish Corporation
Albert Lee
99 White Plains Rd
PO Box 2001
Tarrytown NY 10591
914-332-8888; Fax: 914-332-1888
Subjects: 59
Territory: US-CN-IT; 120 reps
Markets: PL-SL
Items: HC(young readers K-8)
Memo: Wholesaler & publisher.

Media Projects Inc
Carter Smith, Pres/Editorial Dir
305 Second Ave
New York NY 10003
212-777-4510; Fax: 212-475-6409
E-Mail: Media Proj@aol.com
Subjects: 11-21-27-75
Territory: US
Markets: BK
Items: HC-SW

Mega-Books Inc
Pat Fortunato, Pres
116 East 19th St #2
New York NY 10003
212-598-0909; Fax: 212-979-5074
Subjects: 21-21T-75
Territory: US
Markets: BK
Items: HC
Memo: Direct-mail continuity projects including book and card programs.

Menasha Ridge Press Inc
R W Sehlinger, Pres/Publ
3169 Cahaba Heights Rd
PO Box 43059
Birmingham AL 35243
205-967-0566; Fax: 205-967-058
Subjects: 69-71
Territory: US
Markets: BK-RO-PL-SC
Items: HC-PB

Metamorphous Press
David Balding
2663 NW Saint Helens Rd
PO Box 10616
Portland OR 97210
503-228-4972

Subjects: 19-21-31-57
Territory: US-CA-IT(worldwide)
Markets: BK-CO-JB-SL-SC-MM-PL-SL
Items: PB-RM-TX-MM(paperback only)

MGA Ltd
Michel Goldberg, Pres
30 West 63rd St
New York NY 10023
212-333-5453; Fax: 212-333-5453
Subjects: 11-11P-21-27-61
Territory: US
Markets: BK
Items: HC-PB

Michael Wolff & Co Inc
Michael Wolff, Pres
1633 Broadway 27th Fl
New York NY 10019
212-841-1572; Fax: 212-841-1539
Subjects: 99
Territory: US
Markets: BK
Items: HC-PB-SW

Milton Simpson Design
Milton Simpson, Pres
529 W 42nd St
New York NY 10036
212-868-3465
Subjects: 99
Territory: US
Markets: BU-MU
Items: PB-HC

Morris Inc
Dawn Morris, Owner
2707 Plaza De Lamo
Torrance CA 90503
310-533-4800
Subjects: 39-43-57-69-71
Territory: US-IT
Markets: BK-RO-OT
Items: TV-GI

Motorbooks International
Brad Siqueiros, Book Buyer
729 Prospect Ave
PO Box 1
Osceola WI 54020
715-294-3345; Fax: 715-294-4448
800-458-0454
Subjects: 16A-48-70A
Territory: US-IT; 2 reps
Markets: BK-PL-SL
Items: HC-PB-RM

Mountain Lion Inc
John J Monteleone, Pres
PO Box 257
Rocky Hill NJ 08553
609-924-8363; Fax: 609-924-9262
Subjects: 99
Territory: US
Markets: BK
Items: HC-PB-CA-SW

Mountain N'Air Books
Gilberto d'Urso
PO Box 12540
La Crescenta CA 91214
818-951-4150
800-446-9696
Subjects: 16-51-69-70-71
Territory: US-CN-MX
Markets: RO
Items: HC-PB

Mountain Press
PO Box 2399
Missoula MT 59806
406-728-1900; Fax: 406-728-1635
Subjects: 61
Territory: US
Markets: BK-PL-JB-SC-CO
Items: HC-PB-RM

N

Native American Distribution
James Bruchac, Dir
Greenfield Review Press
2 Middle Grove Rd PO Box 308
Greenfield Center NY 12833
518-584-1728; Fax: 518-583-9741
Subjects: 49(Native American)-78-83-95
Territory: US
Markets: BK-PL-OT(pow wows/book fairs)
Items: HC-PB
Memo: 450 titles from 100 publishers-all books by Native American authors. Distributed to pow wows, book fairs, and by direct mail.

Naturegraph Publishers
Barbara Brown
3543 Indian Creek Rd
PO Box 1075
Happy Camp CA 96039-1075
916-493-5353
Subjects: 15-27-29-39-41-43-49A
Territory: US-IT
Markets: BK-SC-RO-PL-CO
Items: PB

New Century Communications
Peggy Schmidt, Pres
30 Bear Gulch Dr
Portola Valley CA 94027
415-851-9455; Fax: 415-851-9229
Subjects: 19-23
Territory: US
Markets: BK
Items: HC-SW

North Country Books Inc
Sheila Orlin, Book Buyer
311 Turner St
Utica NY 13501
315-735-4877; Fax: 315-738-4342
Subjects: 17-41(NY)-61(NY)-71-79
Territory: US-NY; 3 reps
Markets: BK
Items: HB-PB

Northwestern University Press
Nick Weir-Williams, Dir
625 Colfax St
Evanston IL 60208
708-491-5313; Fax: 708-491-8150
Subjects: 47-99
Territory: US
Markets: BK
Items: HC-PB

O

O'Reilley & Associates Inc
Jill Berlin, Mdse Dir/Buyer
103A Morris St
Sebastopol CA 95472
707-829-0515; Fax: 707-829-0104
800-998-9938
E-Mail: jill@ora.com
Subjects: 23
Territory: US-CN; 7 reps
Markets: BK-JB-PL-SL-MM
Items: PB-SW
Memo: 4500 accounts served; 200 titles; 2 publishers represented.

Orbis Books
Robert J Gormly, Exec Dir
PO Box 308
Maryknoll NY 10545-0308
914-941-7636; Fax: 914-941-0670
Subjects: 63C(theology, missionology, ethics)
Territory: US
Markets: BK-PL-SL-CO-SC
Items: HC-PB

Original Products DBA Jamil
Milton Benezra, Owner
2486 Webster Ave
Bronx NY 10458
718-367-9589; Fax: 718-367-3613
Subjects: 45(Spanish)-53(occult)-54-63O
Territory: US-CN
Markets: BK-SL
Items: HC-PB

Original Publications
PO Box 236
Old Bethpage NY 11804-0236
516-454-6809; Fax: 516-454-6829
Subjects: 39H-53-54-57-63E
Markets: BK-RO(New Age)
Items: HC-PB-MM-CA-PO-TA-TV-GI
Memo: They stock all related titles from both major & special interest publishers.

Ottenheimer Publishers Inc
Allan T Hirsh, III
10 Church Ln
Baltimore MD 21208
410-484-2100; Fax: 410-486-8301
Subjects: 10-21-27
Territory: US
Markets: BK
Items: HC-OT

Oxford University Press
Vera Plummer
198 Madison Ave
New York NY 10016
800-334-4249; Fax: 212-726-6446
Subjects: 99
Territory: 5+ commission reps
Markets: BK-JB-PL-SL-SC-CO
Items: HC-PB-TX-MA
Memo: Thousands of accounts served; 17,000+ titles; publishers represented: not many other than themselves.

P

Parachute Press Inc
Jane Stine, Exec VP
156 Fifth Ave Rm 325
New York NY 10010
212-691-1421
Subjects: 21
Territory: US
Markets: BK-SC
Items: HC-PB

Pearl Publishing House
Muhammad Al-Akili
PO Box 28870
Philadelphia PA 19151
215-877-4458; Fax: 215-877-7439
Subjects: 63(Islamic inner traditions)
Territory: US/CN/Europe/Far East
Markets: BK
Items: HC-PB
Memo: Translation of orig manuscripts.

Pen Notes
Lorette Konezny, Owner
61 Bennington Ave
Freeport NY 11520
516-868-1966; Fax: 516-868-8441
Subjects: 11-21-29-31
Territory: US-CN-IT(Europe)
Markets: BK-SC-CO-MM-PL-SL-RO-OT
Items: HC-OT(calligraphy pens & kits)
Memo: Emphasis on art.

Penfield Press
Joan Liffring-Zug, Publisher
215 Brown St
Iowa City IA 52245
319-337-9998; Fax: 319-351-6846
800-728-9998
Subjects: 44-80(ethnic titles)
Territory: US
Markets: BK-RO(gift)
Items: HC-PB
Memo: Wholesales 700 ethnic titles with Eastern European, German, Scandinavian, and Italian subjects to the gift industry.

Penguin USA
375 Hudson St
New York NY 10014
212-366-2000; Fax: 212-366-2666
Subjects: 99
Territory: US-IT
Markets: BK-PL
Items: HC-PB

Plough Publishing House
Manager
Spring Valley
Rt 381 N Box 446
Farmington PA 15437
412-329-1100; Fax: 412-329-0914
Subjects: 31-35-63-98(community life)
Territory: US-CN-IT
Markets: BK-JB-SC-CO-PL-SL-RO
Items: HC-PB-TA-TV

Prairie House Inc
Cindy Weishaar, Sales Mgr
1335 2nd Ave N #G
Fargo ND 58102
701-235-0210; Fax: 701-237-4662
Subjects: 61(Midwest)-99
Territory: ND-MN-SD-IA-MT-WY-WI-KS-NE
Markets: BK-RO-SC-PL
Items: HC-PB
Memo: 1000 titles from 150 Upper Midwest small publishers.

Princeton Book Company
Charles Woodford, Pres
PO Box 57
Pennington NJ 08534-0057
609-737-8177; Fax: 609-737-1869
Subjects: 14(dance)
Territory: US-CN
Markets: BK-PL-SL-CO-RO-JB
Items: HC-PB-TV

Professional Book Center
Jennifer Ballentine
2050 South St Paul St
PO Box 102650
Denver CO 80250
303-756-5222; Fax: 303-756-5374
Subjects: 19-23T-39-59-61-67S
Territory: US
Markets: BKB
Items: HC

Pudding House
Jennifer Bosveld, Publ
60 N Main St
Johnstown OH 43031
614-967-6060
Subjects: 47-83-90-95 (Poetry only)
Territory: US(applied poetry)
Items: PB(only) 40 titles
Memo: Publishes a magazine "The International Journal of Applied Poetry".

R

Random House Inc
201 East 50th St
New York NY 10022
212-751-2600; Fax: 212-572-8700
Subjects: 99
Territory: US-IT
Markets: BK-PL
Items: HC-PB

RECAP: Publications Inc
Brian A Padol, Pres
273 Columbus Ave #6
Tuckahoe NY 10707
914-337-6454; Fax: 914-337-6582
Subjects: 14T-23-31-44A-86
Territory: US
Markets: BK
Items: HC-PB

Red Sea Press
Kassahun Checole, Pres
Africa World Press
11-D Princes Rd
Lawrenceville NJ 08648
609-844-9583; Fax: 609-844-0198
Subjects: 44A-49-49B-78-80-99 (Black and Third World books)
Territory: US
Markets: BK-PL(African-Americans)
Items: HC-PB-TA
Memo: Also some Latin American books. Distributes for 60 publishers.

Regina Ryan Publ Enterprises Inc
Regina Ryan, Pres
251 Central Park West
New York NY 10024
212-787-5589; Fax: 212-787-0243
Subjects: 11-39-41-51-69-73
Territory: US
Markets: BK
Items: HC
Memo: Literary agent for a selected list of writers of adult & juvenile books.

Riverside Book Co Inc
Brian Eskenazi, Owner/Mgr
250 W 57th St
New York NY 10107
212-765-2680
Subjects: 11(Italian Renaissance art)
Territory: 45 titles
Markets: BK-PL-SL-SC-CO
Items: PB

Rockport Publishers
Stan Patey, Buyer
146 Granite St
Rockport MA 01966
508-546-9590; Fax: 508-546-7141
Subjects: 11-12(graphic design)
Territory: US-IT
Markets: WH-RO
Items: PB-HC

Roundtable Press Inc
Susan E Meyer, Dir
80 Fifth Ave
New York NY 10011
212-691-0500
Subjects: 99
Territory: US
Markets: BK
Items: HC-PB-SW

S

Samuel Weiser Inc
Karen Caldwell, Buyer
PO Box 612
York Beach ME 03910-0612
207-363-4393; Fax: 207-363-5799
800-423-7087
Subjects: 39-53-54-57
Territory: US-IN
Markets: BK-PL-SL-RO
Items: HC-PB-MM-CA-GI-PO-TA-OT(games)
Memo: 3,000 items from 200 publishers.

Sandra Taylor Literary Ent
Sandra J Taylor, Pres
38 Fairfield Rd
Hancock NH 03449
603-525-4436; Fax: 603-525-4654
Subjects: 27-39-43G-51N
Territory: US
Markets: BK
Items: CA-HC

Saraband
Sara Hunt
8 Ensign Rd
Rowayton CT 06853
203-853-7980; Fax: 203-853-7980

Subjects: 11-41-73
Territory: US-IT
Markets: BK
Items: HC

Scholium International
Authur A Candido, Mgr
14 Vanderventer Ave
Port Washington NY 11050
516-767-7171; Fax: 516-944-9824
Subjects: 19-23-27-39-51-59-67
Territory: US-CN; 3 reps
Markets: BK-JB-SC-CO-PL-SL
Items: HC-PB-TX

School Works
Louise Colligan
200 Riverview Ave
Tarrytown NY 10591
914-332-0316; Fax: 914-332-7839
Subjects: 10-31E-59-75
Territory: US
Markets: BK-SC
Items: HC

Self-Esteem Publishing
Pamela Kirk, Mdse Mgr
14252 Culver Dr #A-801
Irvine CA 92714
714-835-5550; Fax: 714-838-8212
800-717-1997
Subjects: 57S
Territory: US-CN; 2 reps
Markets: BK-PL-MM-SC
Items: PB-PO-CD-TA
Memo:. 6 accounts served; 1 title; 1 publisher represented.

Shelter Publications Inc
Lloyd Kahn, Pres
PO Box 279
Bolinas CA 94924-0279
415-868-0280; Fax: 415-868-0280
Subjects: 12-19-29-39-40
Territory: US-IT
Markets: BK-SC-RO-PL-CO
Items: HC-PB-TV
Memo: Random House distributes; publisher not a distributor.

Silver Visions Publishing
Betty Kaufman, Pres
PO Box 610415
Newton MA 02161
617-787-2939
Subjects: 11-99
Territory: US; 80 reps
Markets: BK-CO-MM-MU-NS-RO(gift stores)
Items: PB-CA-CR-GI-GC-ST (novelty items)
Memo: 35 titles; 4 publishers represented.

Simon & Schuster Distribution
Marilyn Allen, Dir/Direct Sales & Marketing
1230 Ave of the Americas
New York NY 10020-1586
212-698-7430; Fax: 212-698-7276
800-223-2336
Subjects: 99
Territory: US-CN-IT
Markets: BK-JB-MM-RO
Items: HC-PB-MM
Memo: Main #212-698-7400.

Smallwood & Stewart Inc
Sarah Stewart
9 West 19th St
New York NY 10011
212-620-8144; Fax: 212-727-9616
Subjects: 27-43
Territory: US
Markets: BK
Items: HC
Memo: Also consultants for publishers and magazines.

Sourcebooks Inc
Bob Lester, Sales Mgr
121 N Washington #2
Naperville IL 60540
708-961-2161; Fax: 708-961-2168
Subjects: 21-31P-19S-19-73-99
Territory: Gift oriented books
Markets: RO(gift stores)
Items: HC-PB
Memo: A test program. Reps to catalogs as well.

SporTradition Publications
Bob Moon, Pres
798 Linworth Rd E
Columbus OH 43235
614-785-0641; Fax: 614-793-2314
Subjects: 69
Territory: US
Markets: BK
Items: HC-PB-CA-SW

St Martin's Press
Karen Deutchman
175 Fifth Ave
New York NY 10010
212-674-5151; Fax: 212-995-2584
800-221-7945
Subjects: 99
Territory: US-CN-IT; 38 reps
Markets: BK-PL-JB-CO-SC-SL-MM-NS-RO
Items: HC-PB-MM-TX-RM-CA-GI-GC-MA-TA-OT

Staples & Charles Ltd
Barbara Fahs Charles
225 North Fairfax St
Alexandria VA 22314-2646
703-683-0900; Fax: 703-683-2821
Subjects: 11-41-43D
Territory: US
Markets: BK
Items: HC

Statford Publishing
Hope Daly
1259 El Camino Real #1500
Menlo Park CA 94025
800-647-5749; Fax: 415-854-5779
Subjects: 27-39
Territory: US
Markets: BK
Items: HC
Memo: Maureen Kennedy Salaman bks.

Stearn Publishers Ltd
Dorothy Stearn, Pres
500 East 77th St #1204
New York NY 10162
212-737-9304
 E-Mail: spubl@aol.com
Subjects: 99
Territory: US
Markets: BK-BU-PL-SC
Items: HC-PB

The Stonesong Press Inc
Paul Fargis, Pres
211 East 51st St #11D
New York NY 10022
212-750-1090; Fax: 212-486-9123
Subjects: 10-59
Territory: US
Markets: BK
Items: HC

Storey Communications Inc
Patricia Nestork, Special Sales
Schoolhouse Road
Pownal VT 05261
800-451-3522; Fax: 802-482-3555
Subjects: 15-27(beer brewing)-43G
Territory: US
Markets: RO(garden retailers)
Items: HC-PB
Memo: Primarily garden books. They distribute their own and selected other garden titles.

Sue Katz & Associates Inc
Eliza Booth
126 Fifth Ave #803
New York NY 10011
212-242-6499; Fax: 212-242-6799
Subjects: 14T-19-21
Territory: US
Markets: BK
Items: HC-PB

T

Taylor Publishing Co
Jim Green, Distribution Mgr
1550 W Mockingbird Ln
Dallas TX 75235
800-759-8120; Fax: 214-819-8580
Subjects: 99
Territory: US-IN
Markets: BK-PL-SC(libraries)
Items: HC-PB
Memo: 200+ titles. Publish in-house non fiction only. Distributes all types.

Thinkers' Press
Robert B Long, Pres
PO Box 8
Davenport IA 52805-0008
319-323-7117; Fax: 319-323-0511
Subjects: 69G (chess books)
Territory: US
Markets: BK-CO-PL-RO
Items: PB-SW-HC-TV

Treasure Chest Books
John Helder, Distribution
1802 W Grant Rd #101
Tucson AZ 85745
602-623-9558; Fax: 601-624-5888
Subjects: 76-33H-43-39-51-69-71G-75-12-41
Territory: 71-11-29C-49A-27(cookbooks)
Markets: US-IT
Items: MA-TV-TA-HC-PB
Memo: Ross Humphreys, Publisher. Mostly distributes, publishes four times a year.

V

Visual Education Corporation
Paula McGuire
Box 2321
Princeton NJ 08543
609-799-9200; Fax: 609-799-1591
Subjects: 59
Territory: US
Markets: BK
Items: HC-TX-TV

VKH
Victoria Houston
3201 Bray Ave
Columbia MO 65203
314-446-4089; Fax: 314-446-4177
Subjects: 23-35-39
Territory: US
Markets: BK
Items: HC

Volcano Press
Ruth Gottstein, Publ
PO Box 270
Volcano CA 95689
209-296-3445; Fax: 209-296-4515
Subjects: 21-73
Territory: US-IT
Markets: BK-CO-PL
Items: HC-PB-TA

W

W W Norton & Co
500 Fifth Ave
New York NY 10110
212-354-5500; Fax: 212-869-0856
800-223-2584
Subjects: 99
Territory: US-IT
Markets: BK-PL
Items: HC-PB

Warner Publisher Services
Charles Raab Jr, Exec VP Bk Div
Time Life Building
1271 Ave of Americas
New York NY 10020
212-522-8900; Fax: 212-522-7161
Subjects: 99
Territory: US-CN-IT
Markets: BK-JB-MM-RO
Items: HC-PB-MM

Welcome Enterprises Inc
Ellen Mendlow
575 Broadway
New York NY 10012
212-343-9430; Fax: 212-343-9434
Subjects: 99
Territory: US
Markets: BK
Items: HC
Memo: Specializes in illustrated books of all kinds.

Wellton Books
109 Baldwin Lake Cir
Folsom CA 95630-1517
916-988-4116
Subjects: 27(cook books)
Territory: US-CN
Markets: RO(gift/gourmet shops)
Items: PB

Western Marine Enterprises
Book Buyer
PO Box 67944
Los Angeles CA 90067-0944
310-287-2830; Fax: 310-287-2834
Subjects: 70N(how-to)
Territory: US-CA-IN
Markets: BK-RO-GI
Items: HC-PB-GI

Whitaker House
Delores Vargo, Book Buyer
580 Pittsburgh St
Springdale PA 15144-1498
412-274-4440; Fax: 412-274-4676
800-444-4484
Subjects: 21-31-35-63(Christian)
Territory: US
Markets: BK-PL-RO
Items: HC-PB-CO-TA-CD-TV-GC-GA-TO-Bible
Memo: 250+ vendors.

White Dove International
1017 Dea Ln
PO Box 1000
Taos NM 87571
505-758-0500; Fax: 505-758-7100
Subjects: 39H-53-54
Territory: US-IT: 800-962-4457
Markets: BK-GI
Items: TA-TV
Memo: Not actively seeking titles.

Wilderness Books
Erin Sims Howarth, Mgr
PO Box 217
Davisburg MI 48350
810-634-1595; Fax: 810-634-0946
Subjects: 29H-51E-51N-71-81(adventure)
Territory: US-CN; 22 reps
Markets: BK-SC-CO-PL-RO(outdoor stores)
Items: HC-PB-TV

Wilderness Press
Thomas Winnett, Pres
2440 Bancroft Way
Berkeley CA 94704
510-843-8080; Fax: 510-548-1355
800-443-7227
Subjects: 51-69R(camping/backpacking)-71
Territory: US:
Markets: BK-JB-PL-SC-RO (camping/outdoor)
Items: HC-PB-MA

Wimmer Cookbook Distribution
Mary Margaret Ragland
4210 B F Goodrich Blvd
Memphis TN 38118
901-362-8900; Fax: 800-794-9806
800-727-1034
Subjects: 27(cookbooks)
Territory: US
Markets: BK-JB-PL-MM-RO
Items: HC-PB

Publishers Who Also Distribute Books

Wine Appreciation Guild
Maurice Sullivan, Dir
155 Connecticut St
San Francisco CA 94107-2414
415-864-1202; Fax: 415-864-0377
Subjects: 27(wine)
Territory: US-IT; 18 reps
Markets: BK-CO-SC-PL-SL
Items: HC-PB-MA-PO-SW-TV-TX
Memo: Distributor in London and in Sidney. (Worldwide)

Wingra Woods Press
Anne Matthews
3 Witherspoon St #3
Princeton NJ 08542
609-683-1218
Subjects: 10-11-41A-51N
Territory: US
Markets: BK
Items: HC

Winston-Derek Publ Group Inc
Dr James W Peebles, Pres, or Kimberly Turner, Mdse Dir
1722 West End Ave
Nashville TN 37203
615-321-0535 or 615-321-0537; Fax: 615-329-4824
800-826-1888 or 800-225-2256
Subjects: 21-49-63-75-76-78-80-95
Territory: US-CN-IT; 5 reps
Markets: BK-PL-SC-CO-SL-JB-MM (churches)
Items: PB-HC-PO
Memo: 10,000+ accounts serviced; 400 titles; 6 publishers represented.

Woodland Books
Dan Jackson, Mgr
295 W 200 South
PO Box 160
Pleasant Grove UT 84602
801-785-8100; Fax: 801-785-8511
800-777-2665
Subjects: 39H
Territory: US-CA
Markets: BK-RO
Items: HC-PB
Memo: Mark Lisonbee, President.

World Literature Ministries
Jeff Stam, Managing Editor
Div of CRC Publications
2850 Kalamazoo Ave SE
Jenison MI 49560
616-246-0773; Fax: 616-246-0834
Subjects: 63(religious material in 6 languages)
Territory: US-IT
Markets: BK-CO-PL-SL-churches
Items: HC-PB

Y

Yellow Moon Press
Robert Smyth
PO Box 381316
Cambridge MA 02238
617-776-2230; Fax: 617-776-8246
800-497-4385
Subjects: 21-47-76-79-83-90(storytelling)
Territory: US
Markets: PL-SC
Items: HC-PB-RC-TA
Memo: Carries 175 titles and represents 25 publishers.

Canada

Breakwater Books Ltd
Clyde Rose, Pres
100 Water St
PO Box 2188
St John's NF Canada A1C 6E6
709-722-6680; Fax: 709-753-0708
Subjects: 11P-21-27-31-33H-55-79-95
Territory: CN; 3 reps
Markets: BK-SC-CO-PL-SL
Items: HC-PB-TX-SW(educational)

Brimar Publishing Inc
Guy Briere, Mgr
338 Saint Antoinne St E
Montreal PQ Canada H2Y 1A3
514-954-1441; Fax: 514-954-1443
Subjects: 21-27
Territory: US
Markets: BK-CO-PL-SL(door-to-door)
Items: HC

Can-Ed Media Ltd
185 Spadina Ave #1
Toronto ON Canada M5T 2C6
416-593-0737
Subjects: 11-14D-43-69(physical education)
Territory: US-CN
Markets: SC-CO-PL-SL-BK
Items: HC-TX-PB-PO-RC-SW-TA-TV

Carter & Carter
Hugh Carter
277 Lakeshore Rd E #218
Oakville ON Canada L6J 5J8
905-842-8102; Fax: 905-844-8460
Subjects: 11-11P-12A-27-43G-67S-61(regional pictorial books)
Territory: CN
Markets: BK
Items: HC-MA

Gordon Soules Book Publishers
Gordon Soules, Owner
1354-B Marine Dr
West Vancouver BC Canada V7T 1B5
604-922-6588; Fax: 604-688-5442
Subjects: 13-39-51-61-69(regional/intl)
Territory: CN-US
Markets: BK-PL-RO-SC-CO
Items: HC-PB

International Press Publications
Bali Sethi, Buyer
90 Nolan Ct Unit 21
Markam ON Canada L3R 4L9
905-946-9588; Fax: 905-946-9590
Subjects: 45-59-99
Territory: CN
Markets: CO-PL-SL-BK-(library sales/intl suppliers)
Items: HC-PB-MM-RM-OT

Les Editions Francaises
Daniel Johnson, Book Buyer
1411 rue Ampere
Boucherville PQ Canada J4B 5Z5
514-641-0514; Fax: 514-641-4893
Subjects: 76-90-95-59(dictionary)
Territory: CN-US; 7 reps
Markets: BK-SC-CO-MM-PL-SL
Items: HC-TX-PB-MM-MA-TA-TV

Life Cycle Books
Paul Broughton, Owner
2205 Danforth Ave
Toronto ON Canada M4C 1K4
416-690-5860; Fax: 416-690-8532
Subjects: 99
Territory: CN
Markets: PL-SL
Items: PB-MM-TV-(brochures/pamphlets)
Memo: American address: PO Box 420, Lewiston, NY 14092-0420.

Milestone Publications
PO Box 35548 Sta E
Vancouver BC Canada VGM 4G8
604-251-7675; Fax: 604-738-5135
Subjects: 99
Territory: CN
Markets: BK-PL
Items: HC-PB

Prentice Hall - Canada
Laura Pearson
1870 Birchmount Rd
Scarborough ON Canada M1P 2J7
416-293-3621; Fax: 416-299-2539
Subjects: 99
Territory: CN
Markets: BK-SC-CO-PL
Items: HC-PB-TV

Somerville House Books Ltd
Jane Somerville, Pres
3080 Yonge St #5000
Toronto ON Canada M4N 3N1
416-488-5938; Fax: 416-488-5506
Subjects: 11P-33H-21-27
Territory: CN
Markets: BK
Items: HC-PB

White Cap Books
Peter Clark
351 Lynn Ave
North Vancouver BC Canada V7J 2C4
604-980-9852; Fax: 604-980-8197
Subjects: 27-31P-41(regional)-43G
Territory: CN-IT
Markets: BK-RO(book clubs)
Items: HC-PB-CA-GC-MG-OT

International Publishers

Peaceful Living Publications
Attn: Book Buyer
PO Box 300
Tauranga BOP NewZealand
07-571-8105; Fax: 07-571-8513
Subjects: 39H-53-54
Territory: IT(New Zealand)
Markets: BK-GI; Items: HC-PB-TA

Wholesalers

The following companies wholesale books, magazines, and/or tapes. Besides their names and addresses, we also list their phone numbers, subject interests, territories covered, markets served, and items carried. If no subject interest is listed, they are probably interested in almost any subject. If no territory is listed, their primary territory is the United States. If no markets are listed, they serve the book trade (bookstores, libraries, and schools).

21st Century Publications
Anthony Kainauskas
PO Box 702
Fairfield IA 52556-0702
515-472-5105; Fax: 515-472-8443
Subjects: 99
Territory: 7 reps
Markets: BK-CO-PL-SC
Items: MM-PB

A

A & B Distributors
Book Buyer
1000 Atlantic Ave
Brooklyn NY 11238
718-783-7808; Fax: 718-783-7267
Subjects: 49B-78-80 (Afro American literature)
Territory: N/A
Markets: BK-RO
Items: HC-PB

A & B Smith Co
Martin Smith
4250 Old Wm Penn Hwy
Monroeville PA 15230
412-242-5400; Fax: 412-372-3734
Subjects: 29
Territory: 6 reps
Markets: MM-RO
Items: HC-PB
Memo: PO Box 1776, Pittsburg, PA 15230.

A & M Church Supplies
Patrick Klopp, Owner
220 E Genesee Ave
Saginaw MI 48607-1228
517-753-4672; Fax: 517-753-4799
Subjects: 21-63
Territory: 1 rep
Markets: SC-PL-SL-RO
Items: PB-GC-PO-SB-TA-TV

A M Pierson
Patsy Dow
545 Front St
PO Box 1236
Binghamton NY 13902
607-723-3561; Fax: 607-723-8537
Subjects: 99
Territory: 100-mile radius of Binghamton
Markets: BK-NS-MM-RO
Items: HC-MM-MG-PB

Abel Love Inc
Abraham Leiss, Buyer
20 Lakeshore Dr (23608)
PO Box 2250
Newport News VA 23609
804-989-0188; Fax: 804-877-2939
800-520-2939
Subjects: 11-21-23 (Civil war/military/aerospace/airplanes)
Territory: 6 reps
Markets: BK-SC-CO-PL-RO
Items: HC-RM-TA-TV-GA-GI-SW
Memo: Warehouse: 935 Lucas Creek Dr, Newport News, VA 23608.

Abranovic Associates
Mary Hritz, Hardcover Book Buyer
Cally Smith, Paperback Buyer or
Mark Abranovic
161 S McKean St
Kittanning PA 16201
412-543-2005; Fax: 412-543-3477
Subjects: 99
Territory: PA; 4 reps
Markets: MM-BK-SC-PL-SL-RO-NS
Items: HC-PB-MM-MG-NP

Academi-Text Medical Wholesalers
Daryl Yourist, Dir
330 N Superior
Toledo OH 43604
419-255-9755; Fax: 419-255-9606
800-552-8398
Subjects: 39M
Territory: 2 reps
Markets: CO-hospitals/institutions
Items: HC-TX

Academic Book Center
Jackie Thompson
5600 NE Hassalo St
Portland OR 97213-3640
503-287-6657; Fax: 503-284-8859
800-547-7704
Subjects: 39-67-99(academic titles)
Territory: US
Markets: CO-PL-SL
Items: HC-TX-PB-SW
Memo: Customers: medical, professional, and academic. Daniel P Halloran, President. Affiliated with the Professional Book Center which sells to corporate and special libraries.

Academic Book Services Inc
Alan Castro, Pres
5490 Fulton Blvd
Atlanta GA 30336
404-344-8317; Fax: 404-349-2127
Subjects: 99
Territory: US
Markets: SC-CO
Items: HC-MM-PB

Accents Publications Service Inc
Nadav Katz, Dir
721 Ellsworth Dr #203
Silver Spring MD 20910
301-588-5496; Fax: 301-588-5249
Subjects: 39M-55-67
Territory: IT
Markets: PL-SL-SC-CO
Items: HC-PB

Adams Book Company
Paul Davidson, Book Buyer
537 Sackett St
Brooklyn NY 11217-3099
718-875-5464; Fax: 800-FAX-ADAM
800-221-0909
Subjects: 99
Territory: NY; 6 reps
Markets: BK-SC
Items: TX-PB-SW-MM
Memo: Electronic catalog on-line Internet.

Adler's Foreign Books
8220 N Christiana
Skokie IL 60076-2911
708-676-9944; Fax: 708-676-9909
Subjects: 45
Territory: US
Markets: BK-CO-PL-MM(individuals)
Items: HC-TX(Gr/Sp/Fr)MG-TA(Gr & Fr)

ADS Publisher Services Inc
Irwin Krimke, Natl Sales Mgr
3400 Dundee Rd
Northbrook IL 60062
847-498-5014; Fax: 847-498-1190
Subjects: 99
Territory: Peter Walsh, another contact
Markets: MM-NS
Items: PB-MG-NP

Advanced Marketing Services
Roxanne DeGennaro, Purchaser, Audio/Video
Robert Davis, Purchaser, Computer
Doug Rierdan, Purchaser, Gifts/Books
Kevan Lyon, VP Merchandising
5880 Oberlin Dr #400
San Diego CA 92121
619-457-2500; Fax: 619-452-2237
Subjects: 99
Territory: US
Markets: MM-BK-RO
Items: TA-TV
Memo: Wholesale book distributor to membership warehouse clubs and office superstores.

AKJ Book Fare Inc
Edward S Mandel
5609-2A Fishers Ln
Rockville MD 20852
301-770-4030; Fax: 301-770-2338
Subjects: 99
Territory: US
Markets: SC-PL
Items: MM-PB

Alan Gordon Enterprises
Grant Loucks, Pres
1430 Cahuenga Blvd
Hollywood CA 90028
213-466-3561; Fax: 213-871-2193
Subjects: 99
Territory: US
Markets: BK-SC-CO
Items: HC-PB-SW-TV
Memo: Services film industry.

All America Distributors Corp
Mitchell Neal
8431 Melrose Pl
Los Angeles CA 90069
213-651-2650; Fax: 213-655-9452
Subjects: 41-49B-99
  (Multi-cultural/African-American)
Territory: 3 reps
Markets: BK-JB-SC-PL-SL-MM
Items: MM-CA-GC-MG-PO
Memo: 400 accounts served; 400 titles; 11 publishers represented.

Alpen Books
Robert Koch, Owner
3616 South Rd #C-1
Mukilteo WA 98275
206-290-8587; Fax: 206-290-9461
Subjects: 51-69R-71
Territory: US
Markets: RO(outdoor recreation stores)
Items: HC-PB-MM
Memo: 3000+ titles, Linda Harder, Book Buyer. Robert makes the initial decision to buy from new publishers. Send books to him. Linda buys books from continuing suppliers.

Alpha 10 Cycles Bookstore
Marcelino Alcala, Owner
Car No 21 San Jose Shopping Ctr
GPO Box 363924
San Juan PR 00936-3924
809-751-3800; Fax: 809-767-7092
Subjects: 57
Territory: 1 rep
Markets: BK
Items: HC-PB-TA

Ambassador Book Service Inc
Kay Manson
42 Chasner St
Hempstead NY 11550
516-489-4011; Fax: 800-431-8913
800-431-8913
Subjects: 19-23-41-47-55-57-59-63-65-67-9
Territory: US; 5 reps
Markets: CO-PL-SL
Items: HC-PB-MM-TX-SW-TV
Memo: Gary Herald, President.

Amcorp Ltd
Mr Chandru Mahtani
10 Norden Ln
Huntington Station NY 11746
516-271-0548; Fax: 516-549-8849
Subjects: 99
Territory: US
Markets: IT
Items: HC-PB-TX-MM
Memo: Export to India, Singapore, etc.

America's Hobby Center
Peter Winston, Mgr
146 W 22nd St
New York NY 10011
212-675-8922; Fax: 212-633-2754
Subjects: 99
Territory: 3 reps
Markets: Hobby stores only
Items: HC-MM-PB-TV

American Buddhist Shim Gum Do
Mary Stackhouse, Mgr
203 Chestnut Hill Ave
Brighton MA 02135
617-787-1506
Subjects: 99
Territory: US
Markets: BK-CO-SC-PL
Items: HC-MG-OT(newsletter)

American Eagles Inc
George Edwards
2220 NW Market St
Seattle WA 98107
206-782-8448; Fax: 206-783-8978
Subjects: 29H
Territory: US
Markets: Hobby shops
Items: PB-RM-MG

American Econo-Clad Services
Mike Printz, Libr Serv Coord
2101 N Topeka Blvd (66608)
PO Box 1777
Topeka KS 66601-1777
913-233-4252; Fax: 913-233-3129
800-255-3502
Subjects: 21-76-79
Territory: 70 reps
Markets: SC-CO-PL
Items: PB-MM-SW-OT(tapes/CD-ROM bks)
Memo: 15,000 titles.

American Media Corporation
Laurence Compton
Library Book Division
219 N Milwaukee St
Milwaukee WI 53202
414-287-4600; Fax: 414-287-4602
Subjects: 21-31-76-79
Territory: US Media Source: telemarketing
Markets: PL-SC
Items: HC-PB-OT(puppets)-TA-TV

American Opinion Book Services
David Martin, Mgr
770 Westhill Blvd
PO Box 8040
Appleton WI 54913
414-749-3780; Fax: 414-749-3785
Subjects: 19E-21-41-51B-55
Territory: US
Markets: BK-CO-SC-PL-SL
Items: HC-PB-MM-NP-TA-TV-OT(shirts/hat)

American Overseas Book Co
Donna Gallagar or Janine Casella
550 Walnut St
Norwood NJ 07648-1393
201-767-7600; Fax: 201-784-0263
Subjects: 99-39-67-19-23T-19G
Territory: US-CN-IT; 2 reps
Markets: BK-SC-CO-PL-SL(US & overseas)
Items: HC-TX-PB-MM-MG-ML-MA-SW-NP-TV
Memo: H R Jaffney, Owner.

American Society of Agronomy Inc
677 S Segoe Rd
Madison WI 53711-1048
608-273-8080; Fax: 608-273-2021
Subjects: 19(agriculture)
Territory: US
Markets: BK(members)
Items: HC(scientific)-TX-PB-MM

Ancestry Inc
John C Sittner, Pres/Owner
440 S 400 W #D
Salt Lake City UT 84101
801-531-1790; Fax: 801-531-1798
Subjects: 41G
Territory: US
Markets: BK-SC-PL(individual mail order)
Items: PB-MG

Ancient Healing Ways
Aradhana Singh Khalsa
RR 3 Box 259
Espanola NM 87532
800-359-2940; Fax: 505-747-2868
Subjects: 27-39H-53-54-63(Kundalini yoga/ayurveda/vegetarian cooking)
Territory: US
Markets: BK-RO
Items: HC-PB-GI

Anderson Merchandisers
Buyer
421 E 34th St
Amarillo TX 79103-1799
806-376-6251; Fax: 806-374-0010
800-999-09804
Subjects: 21-31-61-76-99
Territory: SW & NW US; 80 Reps
Markets: MM-(Walmart)
Items: HC-MM-TV-PB-TA-TV

Anderson News
Greg Davis, Book Buyer
5035 Galley Rd
Colorado Springs CO 80915
719-380-1400
Subjects: 99
Territory: US
Markets: BK-RO-CO-MM
Items: HC-MM-MG-PB-TA-CA-CO-SB
Memo: Formerly: **A & A Periodical Services.**

Andrzejewski's Religious Goods
Tom Klopp, Buyer
220 E Genesee
Saginaw MI 48607
517-753-4672; Fax: 517-753-4799
Subjects: 63C
Territory: US(Michigan)
Markets: RO(churches)
Items: HC-PB-GC-SB-TA-TV

Annex Book Distributor
Carole Libster, Buyer
335A Main St
Farmingdale NY 11735
516-249-9803; Fax: 516-249-0830
800-544-4583
Subjects: 21-31-59-76-99
Territory: Metro NYC-US
Markets: BK-PL-SL-SC-RO
Items: HC-PB-CA-MA-SB

Answers Period Inc
Susie Hart
PO Box 72666
Corpus Christi TX 78472
512-852-8927
Subjects: 99
Territory: Sells whls to corps/non-profit
Markets: BK-CO-SC-SL
Items: HC-GI
Memo: Prefer to use PO box only, but street address is: 823 S Water, Corpus Christi, TX 78401. Sells to non-profit org, corporations,& direct to the public.

Appalachian Bible & Books
Robbie Edger, Purchasing Mgr
506 Princeton Rd
PO Box 1573
Johnson City TN 37601
423-282-9947; Fax: 423-282-9110
800-289-2772
Subjects: 25-27-35-63-99
Territory: US
Markets: BK-SC
Items: HC-PB-MM-TA-TV-CD-OT

Apple Book Co
Alan James Boyko, Pres
5901 Northwoods Bus Pky #N
Charlotte NC 28209
704-596-6641; Fax: 704-599-1738
Subjects: 21
Territory: Sales area restricted; 2 reps
Markets: SC
Items: PB

ARA Services SBW-Mag & Book Div
Flora Belford, Mgr
520 Industrial Ave
San Bernardino CA 92408
909-799-1042
Subjects: 99
Territory: US
Markets: BK-MM-RO
Items: HC-CA-CO-MA-MM-MG-NP-TA

Arabic & Islamic Univ Press
Ben Chaban, Mgr
4283 Fountain Ave
Los Angeles CA 90029-2223
213-665-1000
Subjects: 45(Arabic)-63(Islam)-80
Territory: 7 reps
Markets: BK-CO-SC-PL
Items: MM-PB-TX-TA-TV-SW(coming)

Arbit Books Inc
Bruce Arbit, Pres
8050 N Port Washington Rd
Milwaukee WI 53217
414-352-4404; Fax: 414-352-3994
Subjects: 99
Territory: 2 reps
Markets: BK-CO-SC-PL-SL
Items: MA(Hebrew letters)

Arkansas Book Services Corp
Whitney Morgan, Mgr
1936 North Shiloh Dr
Fayetteville AR 72703
501-443-9205; Fax: 501-442-3064
Subjects: 99
Territory: 12 reps
Markets: BK(college)-CO-SC
Items: HC-PB-TX-SW

Arrowhead Magazine Co Inc
Jack Merrell, Owner
1055 Cooley Ave
PO Box 5947
San Bernardino CA 92408
909-799-8294; Fax: 909-799-3774
Subjects: 99
Territory: Sales area restricted; 16 reps
Markets: BK-PL-SL-CO-SC-RO
Items: MM-PB-MG-NP

Art Sales Company
Earl Howard, Mdse Buyer
4801 W Jefferson
Los Angeles CA 90016
213-731-2531; Fax: 213-735-3753
Subjects: 29
Territory: US
Markets: RO
Items: Needlework, and quilting supplies

Arthur Vanous Company
Allan Benz, Owner or Carolyn Wyatt
PO Box 650279
Vero Beach FL 32965-0279
407-562-9186; Fax: 407-562-3221
Subjects: 45-59-71
Territory: US(European imports only)
Markets: BK-JB-SC-CO-PL-SL-MA(mail order)
Items: TX-MM-MA-HR-PB
Memo: Imports from Scandinavia & Eastern Europe to the entire US.

Aspen West Publishers
Kent Frandsen, Pres
8385 Sandy Pky #129
Salt Lake City UT 84070
801-565-1370; Fax: 801-565-1373
Subjects: 27
Territory: 2 reps
Markets: BK-RO(gift shops)
Items: HC-PB-TX-OT(textiles)

Associated Libraries Inc
Robert J Cahill Jr, Pres/Buyer
229-33 N 63rd St
Philadelphia PA 19139-1199
215-476-3200; Fax: 215-476-3207
Subjects: 21-31-76
Territory: PA-NJ; 38 reps
Markets: SC-PL
Items: Pre-bound children's reference books.

Astran Inc
Rene Navarro, Pres
591 SW 8th St
Miami FL 33130
305-858-4300; Fax: 305-858-0405
Subjects: 49O(Spanish)-99
Territory: Spanish markets
Markets: BK-CO-SC-PL-SL
Items: MM-PB-MG

Auromere Books & Imports
Vishmu Eschner
2621 W Highway 12
Lodi CA 95242
209-339-3710; Fax: 209-339-3715
800-735-4691
Subjects: 21-39-54
Territory: 2 reps
Markets: BK-CO-SC-PL-SL-RO
Items: HC-PB-GI

Ausio Diversions
Frank Johnson
6639 Madison-McLean Dr
McLean VA 22101-2902
703-442-4855; Fax: 703-442-9344
800-628-6145
Subjects: 99(spoken word audiobooks)
Territory: US
Markets: BK-RO
Items: TA

Austin Management Group
Nancy Galloway, Corp Ret Mgr
PO Box 3206
Paducah KY 42002-3206
502-442-1052; Fax: 502-444-6450
Subjects: 99
Territory: US
Markets: BK-NS-MM-RO(chain stores)
Items: HC-PB-MM-MG

Auto-Bound Inc
Andrew DeFrancesco, Book Buyer
2313 Santa Clara Ave
Alameda CA 94501-4521
510-521-8630; Fax: 510-521-8755
Subjects: 16(auto/motorcycles)
Territory: Western US ; 3 reps
Markets: BK-JB-SC-CO-PL-OT(auto parts)
Items: HC-PB-MM-CA-PO-TV

Aviation Book Company
Nancy Griffith
7201 Perimeter Rd S #C
Seattle WA 98108
206-767-5232; Fax: 206-763-3428
Subjects: 70A
Territory: US-IT
Markets: BK-SC-PL
Items: HC-PB-GI-CA-GC-MA-ST-SW-TV

Awareness & Health Unlimited
Phil Wilson, Buyer
3509 N High St
Columbus OH 43214
614-262-7087; Fax: 614-262-0532
800-533-7087
Subjects: 39H-53
Territory: US
Markets: US-RO
Items: PB-HC-GI(mainly sidelines)
Memo: Wallet cards, charts & posters, massage tools, & trade paperbacks.

B

B B Kirkbride Bible Co Inc
Ann Alhand
335 W Ninth St
PO Box 606
Indianapolis IN 46206-0606
317-633-1900; Fax: 317-633-1444
Subjects: 59-63(Bibles)
Territory: US
Markets: BK-CO-PL-SL
Items: SW

Badger Periodical
Bill Streur
2420 W 4th St
Appleton WI 54914
414-731-9521; Fax: 414-731-3671
Subjects: 99
Territory: US
Markets: BK-NS-MM-PL-RO
Items: HC-PB-MG-CA-CO-SW-SB-TA

Baker & Taylor
Kathy McDevitt, Book Buyer (promotional
   & academic/univ)
Julia Quinones, Buyer
   (religious/academic/some independent
   presses)
Karen Perry-Lewis, Calendars
Joel Primer, Computer Books
Juilia Witteman, New Presses
Mary Imperials, Religious Buyer
Bonnie Shafer, Senior Buyer (mass
   market books/audiotapes)
H David Hogue, Trade Book Buyer
652 E Main St
PO Box 734
Bridgewater NJ 08807-0734
908-722-8000; Fax: 908-722-0184
Subjects: 99
Territory: IT
Markets: BK-PL-SC-CO
Items: HC-PB-TX-MM-RM
Memo: 220,000 titles from 18,600+
   publishers.

Baker & Taylor Company
Sales Director
Western Division
380 Edison Way
Reno NV 89564-0001
702-856-6700; Fax: 702-856-0526
Subjects: 99
Territory: Western US
Markets: BK-SC-CO-PL-SL
Items: PB-MM-TX-RM-TA

Baker & Taylor Company
Sales Director
Eastern Division
50 Kirby Ave
Somerville NJ 08876
908-722-8000; Fax: 908-722-0184
Subjects: 99
Territory: Eastern US
Markets: BK-SC-CO-PL-SL
Items: HC-PB-MM-TX-RM-TA

Baker & Taylor Company
Buyer
Midwest Division
501 S Gladiolus St
Momence IL 60954-1799
815-472-2444; Fax: 815-472-4141
Subjects: 99
Territory: Midwest
Markets: BK-SC-CO-PL-SL
Items: HC-PB-MM-TX-RM-TA

Baker & Taylor Company
Sales Director
Southeastern Division
251 Mount Olive Church Rd
Commerce GA 30599-9988
706-335-5000; Fax: 706-335-2027
Subjects: 99
Territory: SE US
Markets: BK-SC-CO-PL-SL
Items: HC-PB-MM-TX-RM-TA

Baker & Taylor International
1200 US Hwy 22
Bridgewater NJ 08807
908-427-4073; Fax: 908-429-4037
Subjects: 99
Territory: IT
Markets: BK-PL-SC-CO
Items: HC-PB-TX-MM-RM

Balzekas Museum
Stanley Balzekas, Pres
6500 S Pulaski Rd
Chicago IL 60629
312-582-6500; Fax: 312-582-5133
Subjects: 99
Territory: US
Markets: BK-CO-SC-PL
Items: HC-PB-TV(demonstrating only)

Banner of Truth
James B Eshelman, Mgr
63 East Louther St
Carlisle PA 17013
717-249-5747; Fax: 717-249-0604
Subjects: 99
Territory: Sales area restricted; 1 rep
Markets: BK-churches
Items: HC-PB-MM

Baptist Spanish Publishing House
Jose Amezaga
7000 Alabama St
PO Box 4255
El Paso TX 79914
915-566-9656; Fax: 915-562-6502
Subjects: 45-63
Territory: US
Markets: BK-SL-RO(churches)
Items: MA-GC
Memo: Books in Spanish, religious books.

Beechwood Global Publications
Paul Kennedy, Pres
71 Amory St
Roxbury MA 02119
617-522-5771; Fax: 617-522-7127
Subjects: 11-99
Territory: US
Markets: BK-RO
Items: GC-art prints

Best Continental Book Co Inc
James Lawson
PO Box 615
Merrifield VA 22116
703-280-1400
Subjects: 21
Territory: US
Markets: SC-CO
Items: HC-PB-MM-TX

Beverly Books Inc
Ilene Schaffzin
19 Meridian Rd
Edison NJ 08820
908-906-8500; Fax: 908-906-9526
Subjects: 19-23-24-39-47-51-67
Territory: US-IN
Markets: PL-SL
Items: HC-TX-PB-MA-MG
Memo: Customers: primarily corporate,
   medical, and public libraries.

Bible Truth Publishers
Don Rule, Mgr
59 Industrial
Addison IL 60101
708-543-1441; Fax: 708-543-1476
Subjects: 99
Territory: IT
Markets: BK-CO-SC
Items: CA-GI-MM-MG-NP(periodicals)

Big Horn Booksellers
Jim Skellet, Pres
1019 Fox Hills Dr
Fort Collins CO 80526
303-226-8701; Fax: 303-226-4418
800-433-5995
E-mail: BHBS@aol.com
Subjects: 51-61-(Rocky Mountain)-69R-71D
Territory: Rocky Mountain
Markets: BK-RO
Items: HC-PB

Bilingual Educational Services
Jeff Penichet, Owner
2514 S Grand Ave
Los Angeles CA 90007-2688
213-749-6213; Fax: 213-749-1820
Subjects: 31-45(Spanish)-71-80-99
Territory: US; 10 Reps
Markets: SC-CO-PL-SL-BK-RO
Items: HC-TX-PB-TV-RC

Black Magazine Agency
Melanie McGuin
PO Box 1018
Logansport IN 46947
219-753-2429; Fax: 219-753-5480
Subjects: 99
Territory: US
Markets: CO-SC-PL-SL
Items: MG

Blackstone Audio
Craig W Black, Owner
PO Box 969
Ashland OR 97520
541-776-5179; Fax: 541-734-2537
Subjects: 99
Territory: US
Markets: PL-MM-SC-RO
Items: BT-TA

BMI Educational Services
Jerry Wagner, Pres
Hay Press Rd
PO Box 8000
Dayton NJ 08810-0707
908-329-6991
Subjects: 21-31-76-89(childrens textbooks)
Territory: US
Markets: SC-CO-PL-SL
Items: TX-PB-SW-TV

Book Distribution Center
Harvey D Eluto, Pres
4617 N Witchduck Rd (23455)
PO Box 64608
Virginia Beach VA 23467
804-456-0005; Fax: 804-552-0837
Subjects: 21-31-59-76-99
Territory: Mid-Atlantic; 2 reps
Markets: SC-SL-Govt/Corp-PL-RO
Items: HC-PB-MM
Memo: Formerly Paperback Books Inc. Educational, reference, and general books.

The Book House
James Marsh, VP
208 W Chicago St
Jonesville MI 49250-1125
517-849-2117; Fax: 517-849-9716
800-248-1146
Subjects: 23-67-99(any book in print)
Territory: US; 4 reps
Markets: PL-SL-CO
Items: HC-PB-TX-SW-TV
Memo: John F Ansett, President.

Book Jobbers Hawaii
287 Kalihi St
Honolulu HI 96819-3938
808-845-2656; Fax: 808-841-4674
Subjects: 61(HI)-99
Territory: HI
Markets: SC-CO-PL
Items: HC-TX-PB-MG-NP

Book Marketing Plus
Laura Schneider
406 Post Oak Rd
Fredericksburg TX 78624
800-356-2445; Fax: 210-997-9752
Subjects: 21-61-71-76
Territory: South Central states
Markets: BK-RO
Items: HC-PB-CA-GI(books)-GC-MA-TA

Book Sales Inc
Melvin Shapiro, Pres
114 Northfield Ave
Edison NJ 08837
908-225-0530; Fax: 908-225-2257'
800-526-7257
Subjects: 21-76-99
Territory: 17 reps
Markets: BK-CO-SC-PL-SL(specialty shops)
Items: HC-RM

Book Service of Puerto Rico Inc
Felix A Mattei, Pres
102 De Diego Ave
Santurce PR 00907
809-728-5000; Fax: 809-726-6131
Subjects: 11-21-47-49H-59
Territory: 3 reps
Markets: BK-CO-SC-PL-SL-RO(some)
Items: HC-PB-MM-TA-TV

Book Tech Distributing Inc
Ed Mash, Book Buyer
5961 East 39th Ave
Denver CO 80207
303-329-0300; Fax: 303-329-3117
800-541-5542
Subjects: 23-39-51-53
Territory: US; 5 reps
Markets: BK-CO
Items: PB-MM-MG-RM

Memo: They distribute bargain computer books and magazines, CD-ROMS, and specialty magazines:

Book Wholesalers Inc
Jennifer Carrico, Buyer or John Welch, Sales Mgr
1847 Mercer Rd
Lexington KY 40511
606-231-9789; Fax: 800-888-6319
800-888-4478
Subjects: 21-21T-31-76-79-89
Territory: US; 5 reps
Markets: SC-PL-SL
Items: HC-PB

Bookazine Company
Dan Sado, Buyer
Stu Carter, Buyer, Paperbacks/Computer Books
Fran Stone, Dir of Purchasing
Mr Chris Avena, Hardcover Buyer
Kate Hubert, Juvenile Buyer, Paperbacks/Computer Books
Mary Flanders, Small Press Buyer
75 Hook Rd
Bayonne NJ 07002
201-339-7777; Fax: 201-339-7778
800-221-8112
Subjects: 11-19-27-29-39-41-57-67-69-71-9
Territory: US-IT
Markets: BK-SC-CO-PL-SL-MM
Items: HC-TA

Bookcraft
Russell B Orton, Owner/Pres
1848 W 2300 S
Salt Lake City UT 84119
801-972-6180; Fax: 801-972-6184
Subjects: 99
Territory: 2 reps
Markets: BK-CO
Items: HC-PB-PL-RO(chain stores)

Bookfairs By Toad Hall
Adele Gully
5609-C Adams Ave
Austin TX 78756
512-452-1700
Subjects: 21
Territory: 99
Markets: SC(preschool to middle school)
Items: HC-PO-TV
Memo: School fundraisers.

The Booklegger
Kent C Noye, Purchasing Mgr
13100 Grass Valley Ave
Grass Valley CA 95945-9019
916-272-1556; Fax: 916-272-2133
Subjects: 69(golf)
Territory: US-IT-CN
Markets: MM-RO(sporting goods/golf shops)
Items: HC-PB-CA-GC-SW-TV-TA

Booklines Hawaii
Claudia Cannon or Jeffrey Swartz, Gen Mgr
94-527 Puahi St
Waipahu HI 96797
808-676-0116; Fax: 808-676-0634
Subjects: 61-71
Territory: Hawaii and Pacific Rim
Markets: BK-RO
Items: HC-PB-MM

Bookmargins
David Hathaway, Gen Mgr
65 Richards Rd
Ivyland PA 18974
215-672-5150; Fax: 215-672-5460
Subjects: 21
Territory: 16 reps
Markets: BK-MM-RO
Items: PB-RM-ST

The Bookmen Inc
Bill Mockler, Adult/Juv Buyer
John Kudrle, Paperback Buyer
525 N Third St
Minneapolis MN 55401-1296
612-341-3333; Fax: 800-BOOKMEN
800-328-8411
Subjects: 21-31-76-89-99(regional)
Territory: US-Midwest
Markets: BK-SC-PL-CO-SL
Items: PB-MM-CA-PB-RM
Memo: Norton Stillman & Ned Waldman, Co-Owners. More than 50,000 titles.

Bookpeople
Jeff Scott, Buyer
Sheridan McCarthy, Mdse Dir
7900 Edgewater Dr
Oakland CA 94621
510-632-4700; Fax: 510-632-1281
800-999-4650
Subjects: 13-51-75-83-95-99(small press)
Territory: US-CN-IT
Markets: BK-RO
Items: HC-PB-MM
Memo: 2 field reps; 6,000 accounts served; 30,000 titles; 3,500 publishers represented.

Books and Research Inc
Naseem Jamali, Pres
250 West 57th St #2028
New York NY 10107
212-333-7772; Fax: 212-315-3604
E-Mail: BRINC.@1X.netcom.com
Subjects: 59-99(science-technology)
Territory: US-IT
Markets: SL
Items: HC-PB-SW

Books Etc
Jean Cuce, Mgr
268 N Ridge Ave
Ambler PA 19002
215-646-3363; Fax: 215-885-4935
Subjects: 21-89
Territory: US (Book fairs & fund raisers)
Markets: SC-PL(all non-profit)
Items: HC-PB-CA

Books to Grow On
Marilyn Hollinshead, Owner
826 S Aiken Ave
Pittsburgh PA 15232
412-621-1323; Fax: 412-621-5324
Subjects: 21-31P-45-79-86
Territory: 99
Markets: SC(preschool to 12)
Items: HC-PB-MM-TV
Memo: Branch: 5815 Ellsworth Ave, Rear.

Booksmith Promotional Co
Annette Kaye, Mgr
100 Paterson Plank Rd
Jersey City NJ 07307
201-659-2768; Fax: 201-659-3631
Subjects: 11-21
Territory: 12 reps
Markets: BK-SC-CO-PL-RO
Items: HC-PB-TX-RM

The Booksource
Vickie Sence or Shari Nelson Faulkner,
    Buyer, Trade Hardcover Books
Cindy Clausen, Juvenile Buyer
Sandy Jaffe, Owner
Tim Hand, Regional Books Buyer
1230 Macklind Ave
St Louis MO 63110
314-647-0600; Fax: 314-652-1635
800-444-0435
Subjects: 99
Territory: US
Markets: BK-CO-SC-PL-Midwest
Items: HC-PB-MM

Bookwise
Rebecca Parsons
2931 Melanie Ln
Oakton VA 22124
703-631-9042; Fax: 703-631-6398
Subjects: 21-31E-31P-76
Territory: 2 reps
Markets: SC
Items: HC-PB

Bookworm
Herbert Nelson, Owner/Buyer
417 Monmouth Dr
Cherry Hill NJ 08002
609-667-5884
Subjects: 21
Territory: US
Markets: SC(high school only)
Items: HC-PB-MM

Bound to Stay Bound Books
Bill Early, Sales/Mktg Mgr
1880 W Morton Rd
Jacksonville IL 62650
217-245-5191; Fax: 217-245-0424
Subjects: 21-99
Territory: US
Markets: SC-PL-SL
Items: HC-OT(CD-ROM)
Memo: Pre-bound juv library books.

Bowers & Merena Galleries Publ
John Babalis, Oper Mgr
S Main St
Wolfeboro NH 03894-1224
603-569-5095; Fax: 603-569-5319
Subjects: 99
Territory: US
Markets: BK-PL-RO
Items: HC-PB-MM

Brewer Sewing Supplies
Flo Perk
3800 West 42nd St
Chicago IL 60632
312-247-2121; Fax: 312-247-6154
Subjects: 29
Territory: US
Markets: SC-RO
Items: HC-PB-TV-TX-OT(sewing machine
    parts)

Brodart
Kathy Johnson, Book Buyer, Hardcover
    Books
Wendy Beatty, Juvenile Buyer
Christy Dawson, Video Buyer
500 Arch St
Williamsport PA 17705-0001
717-326-2461; Fax: 717-326-6769
800-233-8467
Subjects: 99(videos)
Territory: US-CN-IT
Markets: BK-RO-SC-CO-MM-PL-SL
Items: TV
Memo: 12,000 publishers, 80,000 titles.
    Richard Black, General Manager. For
    books for schools and juveniles, send
    catalogs and info to Mike Puma; for
    public and governmental libraries,
    send to Marc Steiger.

Brotherhood of Life Inc
Richard E Buhler, Pres
110 Dartmouth SE
Albuquerque NM 87106
505-873-2179; Fax: 505-873-2423
Subjects: 39-53-54
Territory: US
Markets: SC-CO-NS-PL-SL-RO
Items: HC-PB-PO-GC

Bryant Altman Map Inc
Mark Linnane
Norwood Commerce Ctr
Endicott St Bldg 26
Norwood MA 02062
617-762-3339; Fax: 617-769-9080
Subjects: 99
Territory: US
Markets: BK-NS-CO-MM-RO
Items: MA(travel/local/regional)

Buckeye News
Tony Neely, Book Buyer
PO Box 1012
Toledo OH 43697
419-243-2161; Fax: 419-243-2207
Subjects: 99
Territory: Northern OH
Markets: BK-CO-SC-PL-SL-RO
Items: HC-PB-MG

Budget Book Service Div of LDAP
Lawrence D Alexander, President
386 Park Ave S #1913
New York NY 10016
212-679-4200; Fax: 212-679-4234
Subjects: 99
Territory: US
Markets: BK-SC-CO-SL-MM-RO
Items: PB-RM(some)-GI
Memo: Full name: Budget Book Service
    Inc, Div of LDAP.

Business Books Network
Spencer Smith and Jean Kerr
Smith/Kerr Associates
163 Central Ave #4
Dover NH 03820
603-749-9171; Fax: 603-749-6155
Subjects: 19-57
Territory: US-IN
Markets: BK-SC-CO-OT
Items: HC-PB
Memo: They sell business books only to
    the educational market (nonexclusive),
    special markets (exclusive), and in
    1996, bookstore market (exclusive). In
    the educational market, they sell to
    colleges, jr colleges, and adult
    education programs via catalogs,
    telemarketing, and travelling reps.

Byrrd Enterprises Inc
Willard Williams, Pres
7964 Ft Hunt Rd
Alexandria VA 22308
703-765-5626; Fax: 703-768-4086
Subjects: 48-55-61
Territory: 3 reps
Markets: BK-RO
Items: HC-PB-MM(military books)

C

C & W Zabel Company
Andrew Zabel, Book Buyer
345 Commercial Ave
Palisades Park NJ 07650-1211
201-947-3300; Fax: 201-947-9790
Subjects: 11-59
Territory: 4 reps
Markets: SC-CO-PL-SL
Items: HC

C W Associates
C T Williams, Mgr
PO Box 34099
Bethesda MD 20827
301-340-9399; Fax: 301-309-6428
Subjects: 99
Territory: US
Markets: BK-CO-SC-PL-SL
Items: HC

Cajun Country Distributors
David & Sandra Longmire, Owners
8956 Trudeau Ave
Baton Rouge LA 70806
504-924-1275; Fax: 504-924-1275
Subjects: 27-41A-61(South)-71
Territory: Southern culture/humor
Markets: BK-RO(gift/gourmet)
Items: HC-PB
Memo: Titles of South & Civil War,
    cookbooks & X-mas books.

Canyonlands Publications
Brian A Billideau, Owner/Buyer
4860 N Ken Morey Dr
Bellemont AZ 86015
520-779-3888; Fax: 520-779-3778
Subjects: 61(Southwest)
Territory: 3 reps
Markets: BK-RO(specialty whls)
Items: HC-CA-MA-MM-PB-TA-TV

Capital City Comics
Pat Allen, Owner
900 Market St
Lemoyne PA 17043
717-737-5716
Subjects: 99
Territory: US
Markets: BK(comic dealers)
Items: HC(selected)-PB-CO

Capital City Distribution
Tom Flinn, Lead Buyer
2537 Daniels St
PO Box 8156
Madison WI 53708
608-223-2000; Fax: 608-223-2010
Subjects: 28(cards)-33C-69-86
Territory: US(comics are their specialty)
Markets: BK-RO(game stores)
Items: PB-MM-CO-GA-GI-PO-SB-TV
Memo: They distribute trading cards, art, media, pop culture products, t-shirts, role-playing games, and novelty items.

Carl B Noelke Co
Jane Kerbaugh
529 Main Box 563
La Crosse WI 54602
608-782-8544; Fax: 608-782-0844
Subjects: 63
Territory: US
Markets: SC-RO-(some)-churches
Items: PB-OT(rel articles/supplies)

Carl Fischer Music Distributor
Tomas Mormile, VP/Mgr
62 Cooper Square
New York NY 10003
212-777-2550; Fax: 212-477-4129
Subjects: 14
Territory: US-CN-IT
Markets: JB-SC-CO-MM-SL-RO(music stores)
Items: HC-TX-PB-MG-CA-GI-PO-RC-ST-TA

Carolina Biological Supply Co
T E Powell III, Pres
2700 York Rd
Burlington NC 27215
919-584-0381; Fax: 800-222-7112
Subjects: 23-39-51-67
Territory: US
Markets: SC-CO-MM(some)
Items: HC-PB-TA-TV-GA-MA-PO-SW

Catholic Book & Supply Co
Francis J Mahsem, Owner/Mgr
PO Box 43
South Milwaukee WI 53172
414-762-1087; Fax: 414-762-4323
Subjects: 63-99
Territory: 1 rep
Markets: CO-SC(K-12)
Items: HC-PB-TX

Catholic Bookrack Service
Mary McMahon, Mgr
700 E Elm
La Grange IL 60525
708-482-0044
Subjects: 17-41-47-49-57-59-63-76-77-81-8
Territory: Chicago IL
Markets: SC-CO-SL
Items: PB-MM

Cedar Fort Inc
Lyle Mortimer, Pres
925 N Main
Springville UT 84663
801-489-4084; Fax: 801-489-9432
Subjects: 29-51-69
Territory: 2 reps
Markets: BK-PL
Items: HC-PB-TV

Checkers Distributors
Jenny Brockman, Crafts Buyer
400-B W Dussel Dr
Maumee OH 43537
419-893-3636; Fax: 419-893-2422
Subjects: 29
Territory: US
Markets: RO
Items: Notions/fabric/quilting/crafts

Cheng & Tsui Co
Anson Joyce
25 West St
Boston MA 02111
617-426-6074; Fax: 617-426-3669
Subjects: 11-19-27-41-44-45(Chinese/Japan)
Territory: US-CN-IT
Markets: BK-JB-SC-CO-PL-SL-RO
Items: HC-PB-TX-MM-CA-PO-SW-MA-RC-TA
Memo: 2,000 titles; 50 publishers represented.

China Cultural Center
Hou-Luan Chung, Owner/Mgr
970 N Broadway #103
Los Angeles CA 90012
213-489-3827; Fax: 213-489-3080
Subjects: 11(art/acupuncture supplies)
Territory: US
Markets: BK-CO-PL-SL-SC
Items: HC-PB

Chinese Christian Mission
Walter Leung
PO Box 750759
Petaluma CA 94575-0759
707-762-1314; Fax: 707-762-1713
Subjects: 63
Territory: Mail-order
Markets: BK-churches
Items: HC-PB-CA-TA-TV

Choice Books
John M Bomberger
1251 Virginia Ave
Harrisonburg VA 22801-2497
703-434-1827; Fax: 540-434-5556
Subjects: 21-45-51B
Territory: US-CN; 19 reps
Markets: RO
Items: PB-MM-OT(note cards)
Memo: Branch - Choice Books of Ontario, Kitchener, ON.

Christian Literature Crusade
Willard Stone, Mgr
701 Pennsylvania Ave
PO Box 1449
Fort Washington PA 19034-8449
215-542-1240; Fax: 215-542-7580
Subjects: 21-63
Territory: 2 reps
Markets: BK-PL(mail order ministries)
Items: HC-PB

Christian Publications Inc
Pam Taylor
3825 Hartzcale Dr
Camp Hill PA 17011-8070
717-761-7044; Fax: 717-761-7273
Subjects: 31P-59- 63P-76
Territory: US
Markets: BK-CO-SC-PL
Items: HC-PB-MM-GI-GC-TA-TV(a few)

Christine Pegram Main Bookshop
Christine Pegram, Owner/Mgr
1502 Main St
Sarasota FL 34236
813-365-0586
Subjects: 99
Territory: US
Markets: BK-CO-PL
Items: HC-OP-RM-US-OT(prints/postcards)

Circa Publications Inc
Donald Cerasi, VP
415 Fifth Ave
Pelham NY 10803-1203
914-738-5570; Fax: 914-738-6460
Subjects: 19-23-39-59-67
Territory: US - 2 reps
Markets: SC-PL-SL(govt)
Items: HC-PB

Circle Book Service
Mary Ann Dumond, Buyer
PO Box 626
Tomball TX 77377-0626
713-255-6824; Fax: 800-227-1591
Subjects: 99
Territory: 3 reps
Markets: SC-CO-PL-SL
Items: HC-PB-TA-TV

Classic Gift Shoppe
John Magee
1950 E Greyhound Pass #152
Carmel IN 46032
317-767-4003
Subjects: 57S
Territory: US
Items: HC-PB-CD-TA

Classroom Reading Service Inc
C J Pappas, Owner
9830 Norwalk Blvd #174
PO Box 2708
Santa Fe Springs CA 90670
310-906-1366; Fax: 310-906-1370
Subjects: 99
Territory: 2 reps
Markets: SC-PL-SL
Items: HC-PB-SW-TV

Cogan Books
Nancy Cogan, Mgr (415-453-6174)
Annette Cogan, Mdse Dir
15020 Desman Rd
La Mirada CA 90638
714-523-1569
Subjects: 21-27-43G-59-61
Territory: US
Markets: RO(gift/gourmet)
Items: HC-PB-CA-OT

Colonial Williamsburg Foundation
Marina Ashton
PO Box 1776
Williamsburg VA 23187-1776
804-220-7340; Fax: 804-221-8968
Subjects: 41-99
Territory: VA
Markets: BK-CO-SC-PL-RO(gift shops)
Items: HC-PB-TA-TV

Colorado Springs Fine Arts Ctr
Ellen Jeffers
30 W Dale St
Colorado Springs CO 80903-3210
719-634-5583; Fax: 719-634-0570
Subjects: 99
Territory: CO
Markets: BK-SC-PL-RO(museum shops)
Items: HC-PB-GI-PO

Connemara Trading Co
R Davis, Owner
PO Box 657
Chapel Hill NC 27514
919-967-1157
Subjects: 39-53-54-57
Territory: US; 3 reps
Markets: BK-PL-SL
Items: HC-PB-MM-SW-CD

Continental Book Co
A Hayat, Mgr
80-00 Cooper Ave Bldg 29
Glendale NY 11385
718-326-0560; Fax: 718-326-4276
Subjects: 31-45
Territory: 5 reps
Markets: BK-SC-CO-PL-SL
Items: HC-PB-TX

The Cookbook Collection
Larry L Eveler, Owner
2500 East 195th St
Belton MO 64012
816-322-2122; Fax: 816-322-8086
Subjects: 27
Territory: US(community cookbooks)
Markets: BK-PL-CO-SL-MM-RO
Items: HC-PB

Cookbook Warehouse Div-Booklink
Carol Coelen, Mdse Mgr
PO Box 671011
Dallas TX 75367
214-480-9987; Fax: 214-480-8443
800-413-3300
Subjects: 27
Territory: US; 8 reps
Markets: BK-PL-SC-RO(gift and gourmet)
Items: HC-PB(all kinds of cookbooks)
Memo: John Hervey, Pres. 2,000+ accounts served; 900+ titles; 800+ publishers represented. Largest wholesaler in cookbooks. Junior League, non-profit & small press cookbooks.

Corporate Book Resources
John Weigen
305 Main St
PO Box 65
Sutton WV 26601
304-765-3365; Fax: 304-765-3374
Subjects: 19-99 (books of interest to business)
Territory: US
Markets: CO-SL-OT(corporations)
Items: HC-PB-MM-SW-TA-TV

Countryside Books
R W Morey
3023 Eastland Blvd #103
Clearwater FL 34621-4106
813-796-7337; Fax: 813-791-4126
E-Mail: 72627,3436@compuserve
Subjects: 43
Territory: US
Markets: BK-SC(some)-RO
Items: PB

Coutts Library Services Inc
Ron Morse, Mdse Dir
1823 Maryland Ave
Niagara Falls NY 14302
716-282-8627; Fax: 716-282-3831
800-772-4304
Subjects: 99
Territory: US-CN-IT
Markets: CO-SC-SL-PL
Items: HC-TX-PB-MM-TV

Covenant Communications
Paul Lee, Gen Mgr
920 E State Rd
American Fork UT 84003-0416
800-662-9545
Subjects: 14M-75
Territory: 2 reps
Markets: BK-CO-SL-RO
Items: HC-PB-SW-TA-TV

Craft Wholesalers
Farley Piper, Craft Buyer
987 Claycraft Rd
Blacklick OH 43004
614-863-3125; Fax: 614-863-3234
OH:800-633-2828; US:800-248-6112
Subjects: 11-29
Territory: US
Markets: RO(craft stores)
Items: PB-CA-CR(supplies)-GI-TA-TV

Crafts Americana Group
Jennifer Gilge, Quiltery Div
13118 NE 4th St
Vancouver WA 98684
360-260-8900; Fax: 360-260-8877
Subjects: 11-29
Territory: US
Markets: Direct mail
Items: HC-PB-OT(supplies for quilting & decorative painting)

Creative Crafts Distributor
Andy Babiana, Contact
PO Box 134
Manville RI 02838-0134
401-769-4010; Fax: 401-769-4212
Subjects: 11-29
Territory: US
Markets: RO(craft stores)
Items: PB-CR(craft supplies)

Crescent International Inc
Jim Khatib, Mgr
2238 Otranto Rd
North Charleston SC 29406
803-797-6363; Fax: 803-797-6367
Subjects: 99
Territory: IT
Markets: Exporter- no US sales
Items: HC-PB-MM-RM

Cromland
Keith Miller, Sales Mgr
2200 Irving St
Allentown PA 18103
215-266-8900; Fax: 215-266-7244
Subjects: 23C-67
Territory: US-CN-IT(computer bks overseas)
Markets: BK-RO(computer)
Items: HC-TX-PB-SW
Memo: Lars Cromsjo, President. They are "very interested in small press titles".

Cuban Boy's Spanish Books
Luis Tigera, Owner
1225 W 18th St
Chicago IL 60608
312-243-5911; Fax: 312-243-8405
Subjects: 45(Spanish)-78-80
Territory: All Midwest; 4 reps
Markets: RO(grocery stores)
Items: MG

Cypress Book Co Inc
Xiao Jing Zhang
3450 Third St Unit 4-B
San Francisco CA 94124
415-821-3582; Fax: 415-821-3523
Subjects: 65-67
Territory: IT
Markets: BK(overseas)-PL-CO-SL
Items: HC-PB-TA-GC

D

D & J Book Distributors
Mr Reves or Robbie Garrison, Sales & Mktg
229-21B Merrick Blvd
Laurelton NY 11413
718-949-5400; Fax: 718-949-6161
Subjects: 11-19-21-27-39-49B-63-76-99
Territory: US
Markets: BK-PL-SC-RO-(giftshops, day care centers, church organizations, and preschools
Items: HC-PB

D Young & Associates
Don L & Dorothy Young, Owners
1025 N Stemmons Fwy #400
Dallas TX 75207
214-742-2665; Fax: 214-742-2666
Subjects: 28
Territory: 99
Markets: BK-CO-SC-PL
Items: OP

Daedalus Books Inc
Tamara Stock, Sales Mgr
4601 Decatur St
Hyattsville MD 20781
301-779-4102; Fax: 800-289-9635
Subjects: 11-14-41-43-47-54-71-75
Territory: 11 reps
Markets: BK-CO-PL-SL
Items: HC-PB-RM-MA(atlas)-TA

Darcy Williamson/South Cross Pub
Darcy Williamson, Owner
PO Box 717
Donnelly ID 83615-1528
208-325-8606
Subjects: 13-27-51-61
Territory: US; 1 rep
Markets: BK-RO(health food/gift/co-ops)
Items: Booklets-PO
Memo: Darcy Williamson for South Cross Publications.

Darlin Library Book Services
Darryl DiNoto, Mgr
353 Buffalo Ave
Niagara Falls NY 14303-1223
716-285-2665; Fax: 716-285-5864
Subjects: 99
Territory: US
Markets: PL-SL
Items: HC-PB-MM-MG-NP-RM-TA-TV

Dawn Sign Press
Joe W Dannis, Pres
9080 Activity Rd #A
San Diego CA 92126
619-549-5330; Fax: 619-549-2200
Subjects: All sign language-related
Territory: 2 reps
Markets: BK-CO-SC-PL-SL
Items: PB-TX-GC-GI-PO-ST

De Ru's Fine Art Books
Kenneth F Jones, Mgr
9100 E Artesia Blvd
Bellflower CA 90706-6205
310-920-1312; Fax: 310-920-3077
Subjects: 11
Territory: US
Markets: BK-PL-SL-SC
Items: HC

Dehoff Publications
Marie T Dehoff
749 NW Broad St
Murfreesboro TN 37129
800-695-5385
615-893-8322; Fax: 615-896-7447
Subjects: 99
Territory: US-IT; 3 reps
Markets: BK-SL
Items: HC-GI-GC-CD-TA-TV(church supp)

Derry Dale Press
Douglas C Mauldin, Owner
226 Sunflower Ave
PO Box 411
Lyon MS 38645
601-624-5514; Fax: 601-627-3131
Subjects: 15-69H
Territory: US
Markets: BK-CO-PL-RO(mail order)
Items: HC

Deseret Book Distribution Center
Pat Harrison, Mgr
2150 W 1500 South Whse
Salt Lake City UT 84104
801-534-1515; Fax: 801-578-3338
Subjects: 21-45-75-76-79(self-help)
Territory: US
Markets: BK-MM-PL-SL-RO
Items: MM-CA-GC-MA-CD-SW-NP-ST-TA-TV

Desert Moon Periodicals
Antonio Lopez
1226A Calle de Comercio
Santa Fe NM 87501
505-474-6311; Fax: 505-474-6317
800-547-0182
Subjects: 11-13-14-23-33-39H-53-69-71-99 (alternative, counter-culture magazines)
Territory: US
Markets: BK-CO-NS-RO(chain stores)
Items: MG(magazines only)

Diamond Art & Crafts
Roger Hutchins
2207 Royal Ln
Dallas TX 75229
800-234-2787; Fax: 214-484-3540
Subjects: 11-29
Territory: US-IT
Markets: MO-RO(art and craft stores)
Items: HC-PB-CR(supplies)
Memo: Formerly: C & S Distributors.

Distributors Nueva Vida
Tony Mendoza, Owner
3725 Montana Ave
El Paso TX 79903
915-565-6215; Fax: 915-751-4228
Subjects: 45(FR, Port, SP, IT)-63
Territory: US
Markets: BK-RO(gift stores, religious)
Items: HC-PB-GI-Bibles

the distributors
Samantha Arnold, Buyer, Small Press Books
Linda Raymond, Buyer, Trade Books
702 S Michigan
South Bend IN 46601
219-232-8500; Fax: 219-233-3607
800-348-5200
Subjects: 99
Territory: US; 3 reps
Markets: BK-CO
Items: HC-PB-MM-MG-ML-NP--SW

DMR International
Melvin Morris, Pres
5748 Commerce Ln
South Miami FL 33143-3641
305-661-8950; Fax: 305-661-5454
Subjects: 11-29
Territory: 2 reps
Markets: SC-MU RO(frame shops/galleries)
Items: Art/framing supplies

Don Olson Distribution
Don Olson
2645 16th Ave S
Minneapolis MN 55407
612-724-2976
Subjects: 13-27(vegetarian)-39H-55-65
Territory: Twin Cities
Markets: BK-NS-SC-CO-MU-RO
Items: HC-PB-MG-CA-TA

Dover News Agency
Thomas P Miller, Owner
619 E Iron Ave
Dover OH 44622
216-343-2134
Subjects: 99
Territory: Sales area restricted: 3 reps
Markets: BK-NS
Items: MG-NP

Downtown Book Center Inc
Jose M Rabade, Pres/Mgr
245 SE First St
Suites 236-237
Miami FL 33131
305-377-9941; Fax: 305-371-5926
Subjects: 99
Territory: US
Markets: CO-SC-PL-SL
Items: HC-PB-MA-CA-MM-MG-TA (language)

E

E C S Publishing
Robert Schuneman, Pres
138 Ipswich St
Boston MA 02215-3534
617-236-1935; Fax: 617-236-0261
Subjects: 14M
Territory: US
Markets: BK
Items: HC-PB-RC-TA

Eaglecrafts Inc
Sue Smith, Mdse Mgr
168 W 12th St
Ogden UT 84404
801-393-3991; Fax: 801-745-0903
800-547-3364
Subjects: 29
Territory: US
Markets: BK-SC-PL-SL-CO
Items: HC-PB-MM-CA-GI-GC-TV-OT

Eas'l Publications
Jerry Klein, Book Buyer
11150 Lindbergh Business Ct
St Louis MO 63123
314-892-9222; Fax: 314-892-9607
Subjects: 11-29
Territory: US-CA-IT
Markets: WH (only)
Items: HC-PB(craft how-to books)

East West Room
Myrna Bloom, Owner
3139 Alpin Dr
Dresher PA 19025
215-657-0178; Fax: 215-657-6685
Subjects: 99
Territory: 1 rep
Markets: BK
Items: HC-PB-RM

Eastern Book Company
David Foshey
131 Middle St
PO Box 4540
Portland ME 04112-4540
207-774-0331; Fax: 207-774-4678
Subjects: 23-99
Territory: East Coast; 2 reps
Markets: BK-SC-CO-PL-SL
Items: HC-TX-PB-SW
Memo: Richard J Coyne, VP.

Eastwind Books & Gallery
Doroteo Ng
633 Vallejo St
San Francisco CA 94133
415-772-5899; Fax: 415-772-5885
Subjects: 11-44-45(Chinese)-80-99
Territory: US
Markets: BK-SL-PL-CO-SC
Items: HC-PB
Memo: Another location: Chinese only: 1435A Stockton St, San Francisco, CA 94133.

EBS Book Service
Preston D Treiber, Pres
290 Broadway
Lynbrook NY 11563
516-593-1195; Fax: 516-596-2911
Subjects: 19-23-39-55-59-99
Territory: US; 5 reps
Markets: CO-PL-Government
Items: HC-PB-MM
Memo: Primary customer: college libraries.

Economical Wholesale Co
Joseph J Fortier, Owner
Six King Phillip Rd
Worcester MA 01606
508-853-3127
Subjects: 21-27-29-51
Territory: 2 reps
Markets: BK-CO-PL-RO
Items: HC-CA-MA

Ediciones Universal
Martha Salvat
390 SW 8th (33135)
PO Box 450353
Miami FL 33245-0353
305-642-3234; Fax: 305-642-7978
Subjects: 41-45(Spanish)-57P-59-78-80-99
Territory: US-IN
Markets: BK-PL-SL-CO-SC-RO
Items: HC-PB

Editorial Cernuda Corp
Ramon Cernuda, Owner
1040 SW 27th Ave
Miami FL 33135
305-649-4600; Fax: 305-649-1049
Subjects: 45X(books to learn English)
Territory: US
Markets: BK
Items: PB-HC

Edna Hibel Studio
Theodore Plotkin, Owner
1530 W 53 St
PO Box 99967 Riviera Beach
Mangonia Park FL 33419
407-848-9633; Fax: 407-848-9640
Subjects: 11-21-27
Territory: 70 reps; 15 primary reps
Markets: BK-RO
Items: GI-TV-PO

Edu-Tech Corporation
Miriam Caston, Sales Mgr
65 Bailey Rd
Fairfield CT 06432-2607
203-374-4212; Fax: 203-374-8050
Subjects: 99
Territory: 2 reps
Markets: PL-SL-SC
Items: HC-PB-RM-TA-TV
Memo: Two catalogs per year.

Educational Book Distributors
Robert Thoms, Pres
PO Box 551
San Mateo CA 94401-0551
415-344-8458
Subjects: 21-31-76
Territory: West US; 6 reps
Markets: BK-CO-RO(teacher supply stores)
Items: HC-PB-TX-TV

Educational Development Corp
Randall White, Pres
10302 E 55th Pl
Tulsa OK 74146
918-622-4522; Fax: 918-665-7919
Subjects: 21-23-24-(activity kits)-41-67
Territory: 45 reps
Markets: BK-SC-PL-RO
Items: HC-PB
Memo: Wholesale publishing division & home business division.

Edward Weston Graphics Inc
Edward Weston, Pres
19355 Business Ctr Dr
Northridge CA 91324
818-885-1044; Fax: 818-885-1021
Subjects: 99
Territory: 3 reps
Markets: CO-SL-SC
Items: PO-TV

El Qui-Jote Book Inc
Jose Obelleiro, Owner
12651 Monarch
Houston TX 77047
713-433-3388; Fax: 713-433-4650
Subjects: 46H(Spanish textbooks)
Territory: US
Markets: CO-SC-PL-SL
Items: HC-PB-TX

Elder's Bookstore
Charles & Randy Elder, Owners
2115 Elliston Pl
Nashville TN 37203
615-327-1867
Subjects: 41
Territory: 1 rep
Markets: SC-PL
Items: HC-PB

Ellis Distributors
Richard Seifert, Mgr/Buyer, or Jerome Colwell, Buyer
130 E Grand Ave
San Francisco CA 94080
415-873-2094; Fax: 415-873-4222
Subjects: 99
Territory: Sales area restricted; 6 reps
Markets: BK-CO-SC-PL-SL-MM
Items: HC-MG-PB-BT-CA-TA
Memo: 30,000 titles.

Emery-Pratt Company
Kathi Witte, Book Buyer
1966 W Main St
Owosso MI 48867-1372
517-723-5291; Fax: 517-723-4677
Subjects: 23-59-99
Territory: US-CN; 9 reps
Markets: PL-SL-CO-SC
Items: HC-TX-PB-MM-SW-TV

Eric Chaim Kline Bookseller
E H Kline, Owner/Mgr
2221 Benedict Canyon Dr
Beverly Hills CA 90210
310-395-4747
Subjects: 63
Territory: US
Markets: BK-PL-SC-CO
Items: OP

ETD Mid-Atlantic Distributors
Stephen Becker, Gen Mgr
3rd Ave & Cherry St
PO Box 1182
West Reading PA 19603
610-376-2851; Fax: 610-376-2333
Subjects: 27
Territory: 6 reps
Markets: BK-CO-NS-RO
Items: MM-PB-MG-NP
Memo: Berkshire News Book Shop, Reading, PA. 610-375-1345.

Eugene Chernin Company
Mike Epstein, Book Buyer
1401 Germantown Ave
Philadelphia PA 19122-3799
215-235-2700; Fax: 215-236-1290
US: 800-523-0115; PA: 800-233-9276
Subjects: 11-29
Territory: US
Markets: RO(craft & needlework stores)
Items: PB(needlework/quilt supplies)

European Book Company
Sara Gabriel, Book Buyer
925 Larkin St
San Francisco CA 94109-7198
415-474-0626; Fax: 415-474-0630
Subjects: 44-45-80 (How-to books for English)
Territory: US
Markets: BK-SC-PL-CO-SL
Items: HC-PB-MG-TA(Fr/Gr/Sp)

Excalibur Hobbies Ltd
William F Murphy, Pres
63 Exchange St
Malden MA 02148-5523
617-322-2959; Fax: 617-322-7910
Subjects: 29-48
Territory: 2 reps
Markets: BK-RO
Items: HC-PB-MG-NP

Executive Books
Charles Klinger
206 W Allen St
Mechanicsburg PA 17055
717-766-9499; Fax: 717-766-6565
Subjects: 19-35-63 (motivational, inspirational books)
Territory: US
Markets: RO
Items: HC-PB

F

F.E.P. Inc
John Martin, Mktg/Sales
5405 Boran Pl
Tampa FL 33610
813-621-6085; Fax: 800-543-5165
Subjects: 21-76
Territory: Southeastern US
Markets: BK-PL-SC-CO
Items: PB
Memo: 10,000+ titles.

Fairfield Book Service Inc
George A Smith, Owner/Buyer
150 Margherita Lawn Corner
Stratford CT 06497
203-375-7607
Subjects: 99
Territory: 1 rep
Markets: NS-RO
Items: PB(fiction)-MM

Far West Book Service
Katherine McCanna, Owner
3515 NE Hassalo
Portland OR 97232-2528
503-234-7664
Subjects: 21-27-51-61(Northwest US)
Territory: OR-WA
Markets: BK-PL-RM-CO-SL
Items: HC-PB

The Faxon Company
Publishers Service Dept
15 Southwest Park
Westwood MA 02090
617-329-3350; Fax: 617-329-9875
Subjects: 56M-59(subscription services)
Territory: US
Markets: PL
Items: HC-PB-MG(directories)

Flannery Company
13106 S Avalon Blvd
Los Angeles CA 90061-2794
310-324-1179
Subjects: 13-21-31-35-41-47-55-57-59-63-6
Territory: West US/Rocky Mountains; 4 reps
Markets: BK-SC-RO(religious)
Items: HC-TX-PB

Fleming Museum
Janet Daignault, Mgr
University of Vermont
Colchester Ave
Burlington VT 05405-0064
802-656-0750; Fax: 802-656-8059
Subjects: 11-65A
Territory: US
Markets: MU
Items: HC-PB-CA-GC-PO-TA

Florida Educational Paperbacks
John Michel, Pres
FEP Inc
5405 Boran Pl
Tampa FL 33610-0283
813-621-6085; Fax: 813-626-9782
Subjects: 21-31-76-89-99
800-543-0121; FL:800-227-0121
Territory: SE
Markets: BK-CO-SC-PL
Items: PB-TX

Memo: 20,000 titles from 250 publishers promoted to school boards, libraries, college bookstores, regular bookstores, and Reading Is Fundamental programs.

Florida School Book Depository
J Herbert Stanley
1125 N Ellis Rd
PO Box 6578
Jacksonville FL 32236
904-781-7191
Subjects: 21-31-99
Territory: FL
Markets: SC
Items: HC

Follett Library Resources
Patricia Hall, Purchasing Dir, or Lin Ertl, Buyer
4506 Northwest Hwy
Crystal Lake IL 60014
815-455-1100; Fax: 815-477-9303
800-435-6170
Subjects: 45(bilingual books)-99
Territory: US-IT; 29 reps
Markets: SC-PL
Items: HC-PB

Forest Sales & Distributing
Joseph A Arrigo, Pres
2616 Spain St
New Orleans LA 70117
504-947-2106; Fax: 504-947-2107
800-347-2106
Subjects: 11-17-27-41-61(LA)
Territory: LA-AR-AL-MS
Markets: BK-SC-RO-PL-SL-TV-TA
Items: HC-PB-MM-MA-GI
Memo: 2,000 titles; cookbooks & regional titles.

Four Winds Trading Company
Cat Carey
685 S Broadway #A
Boulder CO 80303
303-499-4484; Fax: 303-499-6640
800-456-5444
Subjects: 49A(Native American only)
Territory: US
Markets: BK-RO(museums/natl parks)
Items: HC-PB-TA-TV

Francis Kuykendall's Press
Francis Kuydendall, Owner
506 Chandler St
PO Box 627
Athens AL 35612
205-232-1754
Subjects: 63
Territory: US
Markets: BK-CO
Items: HC-TX

Franklin Book Company
Ed Merkel, Mgr
7804 Montgomery Ave
Elkins Park PA 19027
215-635-5252; Fax: 215-635-6155
Subjects: 19-23-67-99
Territory: US
Markets: CO-PL-SL-SC
Items: HC-DB-SW

Fraser Management & Publications
James L Fraser, Owner
309 S Willard St
Box 494
Burlington VT 05402
802-658-0322; Fax: 802-658-0260
Subjects: 19(finances/economy)
Territory: US
Markets: BK-CO-SC-PL(individuals)
Items: PB

Fred B Rothman and Co
Paul A Rothman, Pres
10368 West Centennial Rd
Littleton CO 80127-4205
303-979-5657; Fax: 303-978-1457
Subjects: 19-55(law)
Territory: US;
Markets: BK-SC-CO-PL(law firms)
Items: HC-PB
Memo: Also subscription agent; back issues of law reviews available.

Fred L Saddy Books
Fred Saddy
4965 E Acoma Dr
Scottsdale AZ 85254
602-996-3109
Subjects: 99
Territory: US
Markets: BK
Items: HC-MM-PB

French & European Publications
Emanuel Molho, Mgr
Rockefeller Ctr Promenade
610 Fifth Ave
New York NY 10020
212-581-8810; Fax: 212-265-1094
Subjects: 44-45(FR/SP)-59-80
Territory: US
Markets: BK-SC-CO-PL-SL
Items: HC-TX-PB-RM-MG-CA-CO-MA-TA-TV
Memo: French, Spanish, & imported titles; language and learning materials, dictionaries in more than 100 languages.

Frontline Distribution Intl
Ricardo Cunningham
Distributing Director
5937 W Madison Ave
Chicago IL 60644
312-626-1203
Subjects: 49B-78-80
Territory: US
Markets: BK-RO
Items: HC-PB-GI-African-American artifacts
Memo: Southside location: 751 East 75th St, Chicago, IL 60619; 312-651-9888.

G

Gannon Distributing Co
Ms Kenna Wood, Front List Buyer
Laurie Holmes, Backlist Buyer
2887 Cooks Rd
Santa Fe NM 87505
505-438-3430; Fax: 505-471-5916
800-442-2044
Subjects: 41A-61(Southwest)-71(regional)
Territory: US
Markets: BK-PL-MU-SC-CO
Items: HC-PB-CA-TA-CD's-TV
Memo: Specialty in Southwestern & Native American art booksellers.

Garrett Book Co
Lionel Garrett, Pres
130 E 13th
PO Box 1588
Ada OK 74820
405-332-6884; Fax: 405-332-1560
Subjects: 21
Territory: 19 reps
Markets: SC-PL
Items: HC

Gay Bowles Sales
Gay Bowles, Pres/Buyer
PO Box 1060
Janesville WI 53547-1060
608-754-9466; Fax: 608-754-0665
800-356-9438
Subjects: 11-29
Territory: US-WI: 800-362-8466
Markets: RO(craft stores)
Items: PB(craft supplies)

Gerard Hamon Inc
Gerard Hamon, Pres
525 Fenimore Rd
Mamaroneck NY 10543
914-381-4649; Fax: 914-381-2607
Subjects: 45
Territory: US
Markets: BK-CO-SC-PL-SL
Items: HC-PB

Gerold International Booksellers
Jane Farrell
35-23 Utopia Pkwy
Flushing NY 11358
718-358-4741; Fax: 718-358-3688
Subjects: 45
Territory: US
Markets: BK-CO-SC(on occasion)
Items: SW

Giovanni's Room
Edwin Hermence, Owner/Mgr
1145 Pine St
Philadelphia PA 19107
215-923-296
E-Mail: giophilp@netaxs.com
Subjects: 37-73(gay/lesbian/feminist)
Territory: US-IT
Markets: BK-PL
Items: HC-PB-MM-RM-US-GC-MG-PO-TA-TV-OT

GJ's Wholesale Hobbies/Crafts Inc
George Brooks, Buyer
200 Front St
Vestal NY 13850-1514
607-754-3351; Fax: 607-786-0640
Subjects: 29C-70(all airplanes)
Territory: US
Markets: RO(hobby and craft stores)
Items: PB(craft and hobby supplies)

Golden-Lee Book Distributors
Ron Ratoff, Buyer, Computer Books
Dennis Haritou, Buyer, Hardcovers & Trade Paperbacks
Tracy Dowd, Buyer, Mass Market/Audio/Paperbacks
Marcello Amari, Buyer, Regional Interests & Calendars
1000 Dean St
Brooklyn NY 11238
718-857-6333; Fax: 718-857-5997
800-473-7475
Subjects: 23C
Territory: US, 15 reps
Markets: BK-SC-CO-PL
Items: HC-PB-MM
Memo: One of 4 distributors used by Sam's Wholesale Clubs. Contact Dennis for Sam's books. Other branches buy separately: La Mirada CA, Norcross GA, Avon MA.

Good News Magazine Distributors
Ed Hurley, Owner
255 Washington St
Mount Vernon NY 10553
914-668-5949; Fax: 914-636-0441
Subjects: 99
Territory: US; 27 reps
Markets: BK-CO-NS-RO
Items: MM-PB-RM-US-MG-TA-TV

Gospel Mission
Pastor Henry Bouma
316 - 1st St NW
PO Box M
Choteau MT 59422-0318
406-466-2311; Fax: 406-466-2311
Subjects: 63(religious literature)
Territory: US
Markets: BK-CO-SC-PL-SL(individuals)
Items: HC-PB

Goyescas Corporation of Florida
Attn: General Manager
2155 NW 26th Ave
Miami FL 33142-7187
305-635-5321; Fax: 305-635-9037
Subjects: 45(Spanish)-99
Territory: US
Markets: BK-MM-RO
Items: HC-PB(in Spanish)

Graham Maughan Co
Steven G Hatch, Owner
50 East 500 S
Provo UT 84606-3203
801-377-3335
Subjects: 99
Territory: US; 3 reps
Markets: BK-CO-SC-PL
Items: HC-PB-TA-TV-OT

Grail Foundation of America
Richard Gehl, Mgr
2081 Partridge Ln
Binghamton NY 13903
607-723-5163; Fax: 607-722-4098
Subjects: 99
Territory: US; 100 reps
Markets: BK-CO-PL-SC
Items: HC-PB-TA

Grey Owl Indian Craft Sales
James E Feldman, Owner
132-05 Merrick Blvd
Jamaica NY 11434
718-341-4000; Fax: 718-572-6000
Subjects: 21-29-49A
Territory: US; 2 reps
Markets: SC-CO-PL-SL-MU
Items: HC-PB-CR

Guaranteed Irish
Donal Gallagher, Pres
Route 145
East Durham NY 12423
518-634-2392
Subjects: 45-80 (Irish & Irish-American)
Territory: US
Markets: RO(out of their store)
Items: HC-PB

Guardian Book Company
N Black, Owner
PO Box 6566
Toledo OH 43612-4231
419-476-7624; Fax: 313-854-7638
Subjects: 21-29
Territory: OH-MI; 4 reps
Markets: SC-PL-SL
Items: HC-PB-MM-RM-SW-TV

Gulf States Educational Books
Philip Smith, Owner
368 Laurel Dr
Satsuma AL 36572
334-679-0377; Fax: 334-679-1860
Subjects: 31E
Territory: US; 3 reps
Markets: SC(K-12)
Items: HC-MM-OT(school supplies)

H

H P Kopplemann Inc
Donald S Hauss MD, Owner
140 Van Block Ave
PO Box 145
Hartford CT 06141-0145
203-549-6210; Fax: 860-293-0279
800-243-7724
Subjects: 21-31-76-89
Territory: US
Markets: SC-PL-BK-CO
Items: PB-MM

Haley's Comics
Don Bettis (615-378-4818)
817 W Walnut St
Johnson City TN 37604
615-928-9327
Subjects: 99
Territory: US
Markets: RO
Items: CO-TV-OT(t-shirts/trading cards)
Memo: Other location: Kingsport, TN.

Hamilton News Co
Eitan Evan, Owner
Hannay Lane
Glenmont NY 12077
518-463-1135; Fax: 518-463-3154
Subjects: 99
Territory: 1 rep
Markets: BK-SC-CO-PL-SL
Items: TX-PB-MG-NP

Hammond Publishing Co Inc
Leo Flynn, Owner
G-7166 N Saginaw St
PO Box 279
Mount Morris MI 48458
810-686-8879; Fax: 810-686-0561
Subjects: 63
Territory: US
Markets: BK-CO
Items: GI(church supplies)

Handleman National Book Dist
Stuart Schaefer, Book Product Mgr
David McCarthy, Buyer, Hardcovers and Cookbooks
500 Kirts Blvd
Troy MI 48084
810-362-4400; Fax: 810-362-5160
Subjects: 27-17-75-99
Territory: 150 reps
Markets: RO-MM
Items: HC-MM-PB
Memo: One of 4 distributors used by Sam's Wholesale Club. Also distributes to Kmart.

Haranbee Books & Crafts
Kenneth Holley, Owner
1367 Fillmore Ave
Buffalo NY 14211
716-886-1399; Fax:
Subjects: 21(African-American interests)
Territory: US
Markets: Exhibitors/conferences/centers
Items: HC-PB-GC-TO-GA-MG(some)

Harvard University Art Musuem
Sales Dept
485 Broadway
Cambridge MA 02138
617-495-8286; Fax: 617-495-9936
Subjects: 11
Territory: US
Markets: BK-CO-SC-PL-SL
Items: HC-PB-PO-GC-GI

Hawaii Geographic Maps/Books
Willis Moore, Mgr
#49 South Hotel #218
PO Box 1698
Honolulu HI 96813
808-538-3952; Fax: 808-536-5999
Subjects: 61(HI & South Pacific)-99
Territory: US-IT
Markets: CO-SC-PL-RO
Items: PB-MA(hiking books)
Memo: Only mail-order house in Hawaii.

Heart of America Press
Roy Ehrhardt, Owner
10101 Blue Ridge Blvd
Kansas City MO 64134
816-761-0080; Fax: 816-763-9382
Subjects: 28
Territory: 2 reps
Markets: BK-CO
Items: PB-MM-OT(notebooks)

Herald House Publishing
James N Hough, Gen Mgr
3225 S Noland Rd
Independence MO 64055
816-252-5010; Fax: 816-252-3976
Subjects: 21-27
Territory: US
Markets: BK-CO-PL-RO
Items: HC-PB-SW-TA-TV

Herbko International
Jeff Sternberg or Leonard Traur, Buyer
301 W Hallandale Beach Blvd
Hallandale FL 33009
305-454-7771; Fax: 305-454-2825
Subjects: 33(crossword puzzles/companions)
Territory: US-CN-IT; 96 reps
Markets: BK-CO-RO(gift/department stores)
Items: GI-TO-OT
Memo: 5,000 accounts served; 54 titles; one publisher represented.

Herr's Inc
Book Buyer
70 Eastgate Dr
PO Box 630
Danville IL 61832-9361
217-442-4121; Fax: 217-442-4191
US: 800-637-2647;IL: 800-252-509
Subjects: 11-29(tole/dec painting/crosstitch)
Territory: US
Markets: RO(craft stores)
Items: HC-PB(craft supplies)

Hervey's Book Link
John Hervey, Pres
401 S Sherman #207
Richardson TX 75081
214-480-9987; Fax: 214-480-8443
800-413-3300
Subjects: 27-61-99
Territory: US-TX
Markets: BK-RO-CH-PL-SC
Items: HC-PB-MM-CA-TA
Memo: They sell to all the regional buyers at the major bookstore chains.Special regional books, gifts, bestsellers, African-American book market.

Hispanic Books Distributors Inc
Annettte Trejo, Book Buyer
1665 W Grant Rd
Tucson AZ 85745
602-882-9484; Fax: 602-882-7696
Subjects: 45(Spanish)-49-99
Territory: US
Markets: BK-PL-RO-SC
Items: HC-PB-MG-MM(few bilingual)

Historic Aviation Books
James B Horne, Owner
1401 Kingswood Rd
Eagan MN 55122
612-454-2493; Fax: 612-454-8554
Subjects: 70A
Territory: US
Markets: BK-SC-CO-PL-RO-SL
Items: HC-PB-TV(aviation only)

Historic Cherry Hill
Lauren Mastin, Mgr/Buyer
523 1/2 S Pearl St
Albany NY 12202
518-434-4806; Fax: 518-434-4806
Subjects: 11-41
Territory: 1 rep
Markets: BK-CO-PL-SL-MU
Items: PB-PO

Hobbyquest Marketing
Arlene Placer, Buyer
62 White St
Red Bank NJ 07701
908-842-6082; Fax: 908-747-3752
Subjects: 29
Territory: US
Markets: RO(hobby shops)
Items: HC-PB-OT

Hokulele Distributors
Ken Robinson
PO Box 809
Honakaa HI 96727
808-775-0150; Fax: 808-775-8262
Subjects: 99
Territory: HI
Markets: RO(health food stores)
Items: MG

Holiday Enterprises Inc
James Rochester, Mgr
3328 US Highway 123
Greenville SC 29611
803-269-4311; Fax: 803-269-4314
Subjects: 99
Territory: 2 reps
Markets: BK-SC-RO
Items: HC-PB-CA-GC

Homestead Book Company
Marlin Ayotte, VP
6101 22nd Ave NW
Seattle WA 98107-2496
206-782-4532; Fax: 206-784-9328
800-426-6777
Subjects: 13-14-27-29-33-39H-43-51-53-71
Territory: US; 10 reps
Markets: BK-NS-RO-CO
Items: HC-PB-MG-CA-CO-TA-TV-NP
Memo: 3000 titles from 150 publishers. Subjects: radical politics, underground economy, mysticism, tattoos, the sixties, rock music, etc.

Hope Farm Press & Bookshop
Richard Frisbie, Owner
1708 Rt 212
Saugerties NY 12477
914-679-6809
800-883-5778(orders)
Internet: HOPEFARM@MHV.NET
Subjects: 61
Territory: US
Markets: BK-RO
Items: HC-PB-MA
Memo: Specializes in NY state material.

Hotho & Co
Donna Hotho, Owner
916 Norwood
PO Box 9738
Fort Worth TX 76107
817-335-1833; Fax: 817-335-2300
Territory: 10 reps
Markets: SC-PL
Items: HC-RM-TA-TV-SW

Hubbard Co
E Keith Hubbard, Pres
612 Clinton St
Defiance OH 43512
419-784-4455; Fax: 419-782-1662
Subjects: 99
Territory: Sales area restricted; 5 reps
Markets: BK-SC-PL
Items: HC-TX

Hudson Valley News Dist Inc
Bryon Waters
175 Overlook Pl
Newburg NY 12550
914-562-3399; Fax: 914-562-6010
Subjects: 99
Territory: US
Markets: BK-SC-NS-RO(chain, drug, discount)
Items: HC-MM-MG-CO-MA-TA(X-mas)
Memo: Formerly: **Northeast News Dist**.

I

IBD Ltd
Freek Lankhof, Owner
24 Hudson St
PO Box 467
Kinderhook NY 12106
518-758-1411; Fax: 518-758-1959
Subjects: 59 (importer of dictionaries)
Territory: US
Markets: PL-BK-RO
Items: HC-PB

Ideal Foreign Books
Andre A Fetaya, Owner
132-10 Hillside Ave
Richmond Hill NY 11418-1926
718-297-7477; Fax: 718-297-7645
Subjects: 44-45(French)-80(Spanish)
Territory: US-IN
Markets: BK-SC-CO-PL-SL-MM-RO
Items: HC-PB

Ideal School Supply
Rita O'Toole, Buyer
5623 W 115th St
Alsip IL 60482
708-385-0400; Fax: 800-328-5131
Subjects: 21-31
Territory: US-IN
Markets: SC-MM-RO
Items: PB

Impact Books
Sue & William Banks, Owners
332 Leffingwell Ave #101
Kirkwood MO 63122
314-822-3309; Fax: 314-822-3325
Subjects: 63
Territory: Worldwide
Markets: BK-churches
Items: MM-PB

Imported Books
Robert Niell Jones, Owner
2025 W Clarendon
PO Box 4414
Dallas TX 75208
214-941-6497
Subjects: 44-45-80
Territory: US & territories
Markets: SC-CO-translators

Items: HB-PB-TA
Memo: Catalog 3x annually.

Incor Periodicals
Joseph H Meier, Owner
32150 Highway 34
Tagant OR 97389
503-926-8889; Fax: 503-926-9553
Subjects: 99
Territory: OR & Idaho Falls, ID; 4 reps
Markets: BK-CO-SC-PL
Items: HC-PB-MG-NP-TV

Ingham Publishing Inc
Dwight Byers, Pres
5650 First Ave N
PO Box 12642
St Petersburg FL 33733-2642
813-343-4811; Fax: 813-381-2807
Subjects: 39
Territory: US-IT; 6 reps
Markets: BK-SC-PL-SL
Items: HC-PB

Ingram Micro
Product Evaluation
1600 East St Andrew Pl
PO Box 5125
Santa Ana CA 92799-5125
714-566-1000; Fax: 714-566-7828
Subjects: 23(software only)
Territory: US
Markets: BK-RO
Items: MM-SW
Memo: FAX for product evaluation.

Ingram Periodicals Inc
1226 Heil Quaker Blvd
La Vergne TN 37086
615-793-5522; Fax: 615-793-6043
800-627-6247
Subjects: 23-75-83-99
Territory: US
Markets: BK-SC-CO-RO(computer)
Items: MG-ML-NP

Input Culture Company
Roger Williams
5937 Fausold Rd
Valois NY 14888
607-546-8576; Fax: 607-546-2277
Subjects: 19L-23-24-39-51-55L-67-99
Territory: 2 reps
Markets: CO-PL-SL
Items: TX-HC-PB(specialty books)

Intergalactic Trading Co Inc
Sandy Reid, Gen Mgr
1655 Timocuan Way
Longwood FL 32750
407-831-8344; Fax: 407-332-0142
Subjects: 86
Territory: US-IT
Markets: RO-mail order
Items: HC-PB-TA-TV

International Book Centre
Claude J Mukalla, Owner
2007 Laurel Dr
PO Box 295
Troy MI 48099-0295
810-879-8436; Fax: 810-879-8436
Subjects: 44-45-80
Territory: US-IT
Markets: SL-BK-CO-PL
Items: TV-HC-PB

International Imports
Martin Mayer, Owner/Pres
236 W Manchester Ave
Los Angeles CA 90003
213-778-2231; Fax: 213-750-7048
Subjects: 53-54
Territory: 1 rep; US-CN-IT
Markets: BK-PL
Items: HC-MM-PB-PO

Interstate Textbook Co
Tom Pike & Glen Davies, Owners
5689 New Peachtree
PO Box 80627
Atlanta GA 30366
770-451-4726; Fax: 770-458-3808
Subjects: 99
Territory: US only
Markets: BK-CO-SC-PL
Items: HC-PB-TX(college)

Irish Books and Media
Ethna McKiernan, Mgr Buyer
Franklin Business Ctr
1433 Franklin Ave E
Minneapolis MN 55404-2135
612-871-3505; Fax: 612-871-3358
Subjects: 45(Irish)-71
Territory: US-CN
Markets: BK-PL(consumers)RO(import shops)
Items: HC-PB-MA-MG-PO-TA-TV

Ironside International Publisher
Thomas B Nelson, Owner
800 Slaters Ln
3800 Fort Hill Dr
Alexandria VA 22313
703-684-6111; Fax: 703-683-5486
Subjects: 48
Territory: US-IT
Markets: BK-CO-PL-SL
Items: HC

Islamic Book Service
Abdul Slam
2622 E Main St
Plainfield IN 46168
317-839-8150; Fax: 317-839-2511
Subjects: 63(Islam)
Territory: US
Markets: BK-CO-PL-SL
Items: HC-PB-TV-TA

J

J & L Book Company
Terry L Smith, Owner
E 124 Sinto Ave (99202)
PO Box 3548
Spokane WA 99220
509-327-6364; Fax: 509-327-6364
Subjects: 21(K-9)-89
Territory: NW US-CN; 1 rep
Markets: SC-PL-SL-(book fairs)
Items: HC-PB-RM-MM-CA

J A Majors Company
Mr Van Vick, Purchaser
1851 Diplomat Dr
Dallas TX 75234
214-247-2929; Fax: 214-888-4800
800-633-1851
Subjects: 39-67
Territory: US; 12 reps
Markets: BK-CO-PL-SL
Items: HC-TX-PB
Memo: Formerly J A Majors Medical Book Company. Monthly catalog; 57,000 medical, scientific, and multimedia titles from more than 300 publishers.

J A Majors Scientific Books
9464 Kirby Dr
Houston TX 77054
713-662-3984
800-458-9077
Subjects: 39-67
Territory: US
Markets: BK-CO-PL-SL
Items: HC-TX-PB

J C Strelow Christian Media Int
James Strelow, Owner
9440 El Blanco Ave
Fountain Valley CA 92708
714-962-3697; Fax: 714-968-1703
Subjects: 63(Christian)
Territory: 1 rep
Markets: BK
Items: PB(songbooks)-TA-TV
Memo: Children's videos & Christian music tapes.

J G Sieve Periodicals Inc
Joseph G Sieve, Owner
5378 Westwood Dr
St Charles MO 63304
314-441-1490
Subjects: 99
Territory: Sales area restricted; 2 reps
Markets: BK-CO
Items: MM-PB-MG-NP

J L M Remainders
John Lynch, Owner
2370 E Little Creek Rd
Norfolk VA 23518
804-588-0699; Fax: 804-587-7421
Subjects: 99
Territory: US; 5 reps
Markets: BK-CO-PL
Items: HC-PB-RM

J Levine Religious Supplies Inc
Dan Levine, Pres
5 W 30th St
New York NY 10001
212-695-6888; Fax: 212-643-1044
Subjects: 14M-21-45-63J
Territory: US-IT
Markets: BK-RO
Items: HC-PB-TX-GI-PO-TA-TV

J S Canner & Co Inc
Marshall Lebowitz, VP/Mgr
10 Charles St
Needham Heights MA 02194
617-449-9103; Fax: 617-449-1767
Subjects: 99
Territory: US-IT
Markets: BK-CO-SC-PL
Items: HC-PB

James & Law Company
David C Carpenter, Book Buyer
217 W Main St
PO Box 2468
Clarksburg WV 26302-2468
304-624-7401; Fax: 304-624-9331
Subjects: 61(WV)-99
Territory: WV; 6 reps
Markets: BK-SC-CO-PL-SL-RO
Items: HC-PB-RM-MM-CA-MA-CD-SB-TA-OT

Jay R Benford
Jay R Benford
605 Talbot St
PO Box 447
Saint Michaels MD 21663
410-745-3235; Fax: 410-745-9743
Subjects: 70N
Territory: US-IT
Markets: MM-RO(marine stores)
Items: HC-PB-RM
Memo: Publishing name is Tiller Publishing.

Jean Cohen Books
Jean Cohen, Owner
PO Box 654
Bonita Springs FL 33959
941-992-1262; Fax: 941-992-1284
Subjects: 99
Territory: US by mail
Markets: BK
Items: HC-OP-US

John Justice Book Wholesalers
John P Justice, Pres
600 W John
Martinsburg WV 25401
304-263-3399; Fax: 304-263-1134
Subjects: 10-17-41(military/Amer)-55-99
Territory: US
Markets: BK-JB-SL-MM-RO
Items: HC-PB-RM-OP-TV-TA

Joseph T Reilly Co Inc
Joseph T Reilly, Owner
120 Secatogua
Farmingdale NY 11735
516-756-0610 or 516-872-0805
Subjects: 21-45-63-99
Territory: US
Markets: SC-RO
Items: HC-PB-GI-GC

Junius Book Distributors Inc
Michael V Cordasco, Pres
168 Calvin St
Washington Townshp NJ 07675
201-868-7725
Subjects: 39-47-59-65
Territory: US-CN-IT
Markets: BK-individuals
Items: HC-OP-RM-US

K

Kabyn Books
Leif Fearn, Owner
1742 Garnet Ave #309
San Diego CA 92109
619-274-3306
Subjects: 99
Territory: US-IT; 1 rep
Markets: BK-CO-SC-PL
Items: PB

Kaplan School Supply Corp
Patricia Revelle, Purchasing Mgr
1310 Lewisville-Clemmons Rd
PO Box 609
Lewisville NC 27023-0609
910-766-7374; Fax: 910-766-5652
Subjects: 59-76
Territory: US-IT; 35 reps
Markets: CO-SC-PL-OT(day care)
Items: HC-PB-TX-TA-TV

Kaye Distributors
Attn: Book Buyer
46 Terminal Way
Pittsburgh PA 15219
412-481-8884
Subjects: 29
Territory: East US
Markets: RO
Items: Fabric/quilting/crafts

KC Publishing
700 W 47th St #310
Kansas City MO 64112
816-531-5730; Fax: 816-531-3873
Subjects: 29-39-43
Territory: US
Markets: BK-RO(groc stores)
Items: MG

Keith Distributors
Conrad & Carol Crane, Owners
1055 S Ballenger Hwy
Flint MI 48532-3875
810-238-9104; Fax: 810-238-9028
Subjects: 21
Territory: US; 3 reps
Markets: BK-SC-PL-RO
Items: HC-PB-MM-RM

KidsBooks Inc
Julie Chase, VP
Div of Scholastic Book Fairs
421 Fairfield Ave
Stamford CT 06902
203-323-1819
Subjects: 21-76
Territory: NE US
Markets: SC(school book fairs)
Items: HC-PB-CA-PO-SB-TA-TO

King Electronics Distributing
Jeanne Davis, Mgr
1711 Southeastern Ave
Indianapolis IN 46201-3990
317-639-1484; Fax: 317-639-4711
Subjects: 23-57-63
Territory: IN; 3 reps
Markets: SC-RO
Items: HC-PB-TV-OT(electronic parts)

Kinokuniya Bookstores of America
Tom Okagaki
1581 Webster St
San Francisco CA 94115
415-567-7625; Fax: 415-567-4109
Subjects: 45(Japanese books from Japan)
Territory: US; 4 reps
Markets: BK-CO-SC-PL-SL
Items: PB-TX

Kitrick Management Co
Bernard F Kitrick, Mgr
320 Whitthorne Dr
PO Box 15523
Cincinnati OH 45215
513-522-2339; Fax: 513-522-5192
Subjects: 31-63 (religious books)
Territory: Overseas distributor
Markets: Africa/Japan/Malasia/Asia
Items: HC-PB-MM-RC-TV-TA

Knowledge Industries Inc
Carl Conn, Owner/Buyer
405 Waukena Ave
Oceanside NY 11572
516-764-4900; Fax: 516-764-4958
Subjects: 31(K-12)-99
Territory: Sales area restricted; 5 reps
Markets: SC(ed materials)
Items: HC-TA-TV

Koen Book Distributors
Dina Ciquero, Asst Children's Book Buyer
Shelia Kowalsky, Buyer, Small Press Books
Bobbie Combs, Childen's Buyer
Mark Bove, Computer Books Buyer
Keith McCabe, Mass Market Buyer
Sally Lindsay, VP Merchandising
Shelia Kowalsky, Buyer, Small Press Books
10 Twosome Dr
PO Box 600
Moorestown NJ 08057
609-235-4444; Fax: 609-727-6914
800-257-8481
Subjects: 21-76-79
Territory: East US; 4 reps
Markets: BK-SC-PL-SL
Items: MM
Memo: Send catalogs to Sheila Kowalsky, Buyer.

L

L L Company
Arthur & Garn A Wallace, Owners
1647 Manning Ave
Los Angeles CA 90024
310-640-6815; Fax: 310-640-6863
Subjects: 41G-44F-63
Territory: 1 rep
Markets: Individuals
Items: HC

L-S Distributors
Richard Seifert, Buyer, Calendars/Periodicals
Ronald Shoop, Buyer, Mass Market & Small Press Books
Judy Kennedy, Juvenile Buyer
Jerome Colwell, Trade Book Buyer
130 E Grand Ave
S San Francisco CA 94080
415-873-2094; Fax: 415-873-4222
800-654-7040
Subjects: 99
Territory: CA
Markets: BK
Items: CA-MG-ML-NP
Memo: 30,000 titles. Lots of California regional and children's books.

La Moderna Poesia
Mike Alvarez, Mgr
5246 SW 8th St
Miami FL 33134-2375
305-446-9884; Fax: 305-445-1635
Subjects: 41-45(Spanish)-47-78-80-99
Territory: US
Markets: BK-CO-SC
Items: HC-PB

Lacis Books
Jules Kliot, Book Buyer
3163 Adeline St
Berkeley CA 94703
510-843-7178; Fax: 510-843-5018
Subjects: 29(textile arts)
Markets: BK-RO(needlework stores)
Items: HC-PB(supplies)

Lacite
L Plauzoles, Pres
2306 Westwood Blvd
Los Angeles CA 90064-2110
310-475-0095; Fax: 310-470-0610
Subjects: 45(French)-80
Territory: US; 1 rep
Markets: BK-CO
Items: PB(in French)
Memo: Importers from France.

Ladyslipper Inc
Reggae Dodson, Buyer
PO Box 3124
Durham NC 27715
919-683-1570; Fax: 919-383-3525
800-634-6044
Subjects: 14-53-73(music tapes)
Territory: US
Markets: BK-RO
Items: PB-TA-CD-RC-TV
Memo: Music by women recording artists.

Lambert Book House Inc
Billy Banks, Mgr
4139 Parkway Dr
Florence AL 35630
205-764-4098
Subjects: 63-99 (Christian books)
Territory: US
Markets: BK-CO-SC-RO
Items: PB-MG

Larry Laster Old & Rare Books
Larry Laster, Owner
2416 Maplewood Ave
Winston-Salem NC 27103
910-724-7544
Subjects: 99
Territory: US
Markets: BK
Items: HC-US-OP-MA

Las Americas
Sergio Jiminec, Mgr
911 Faile St
Bronx NY 10709
718-893-4445; Fax: 718-378-6961
Subjects: 99 (all in Spanish)
Territory: US
Markets: BK-SC-PL-SL
Items: HC-MM-PB

Las Vegas News Agency
Cheryl Harrison, Book Buyer
3933 W Ali Baba Ln
Las Vegas NV 89118
702-795-4600; Fax: 702-795-4545
Subjects: 39-75-84-95-99
Territory: Las Vegas
Markets: BK-SC-PL-SL-RO-MM
Items: HC-MM-MG-RM-PB-SW

Last Gasp
Erick Gilbert, Book Buyer
777 Florida St
San Francisco CA 94110
415-824-6636; Fax: 415-824-1836
800-366-5121
Subjects: 13-14M-33C-33H-35S-39R (drugs)-99
Territory: US; 4 reps
Markets: BK-RO-CO-SC-PL-SL
Items: HC-PB-CO-MG-NP-TV-OT
Memo: Ronald Turner, Owner. Lots of counter-culture material including poetry, drug info, erotica, music, body art, and more. 75+ magazines, 700 music books, 70 t-shirts.

Latin American Book Source Inc
Edgardo Moctezuma Bender, Owner
48 Las Flores Dr
Chula Vista CA 91910
619-426-1226; Fax: 619-426-0212
Subjects: 47-78 (Spanish-American adult literature)
Territory: US
Markets: BK-PL-SL-SC
Items: MG-NP

Lauriat's
Julie Barton
10 Pequot Way
Canton MA 02021-2311
617-828-8300; Fax: 617-821-0167
Subjects: 99
Territory: US-IT(wholesale/retail)
Markets: BK-SC-CO-PL
Items: HC-PB-MM-MG

Law Pak Inc
Ted Swartz, Owner
PO Box 221
Terrace Park OH 45174
513-831-1620; Fax: 800-455-8522
Subjects: 19L(self-help)
Markets: BK-PL-RO
Items: MM-PB
Memo: Law Pak Publishing, 128 Wrenwood Ln, Terrace Park, OH 45172, 513-831-3900.

Lay Renewal Ministries
Bob Fenn, Mgr
3101 Bartold
St Louis MO 63143
314-647-0717; Fax: 314-647-7604
Subjects: 63(Christian bks & bibles)
Territory: US
Markets: MM-churches & individuals
Items: HC-PB-Bibles

Lectorum Publications
Carmen Rivera
111 8th Ave #804
New York NY 10011-5201
212-929-2833; Fax: 212-727-3035
800-345-5946
Subjects: 44-45(Spanish)-47-78-80
Territory: US
Markets: BK-JB-SC-CO-MM-PL-SL
Items: HC-TX-PB-MM

Leff Brothers
Marsha Landry
7202 Rampart
Houston TX 77081
713-541-2229; Fax: 713-541-2227
Subjects: 29-99
Territory: TX
Markets: RO
Items: Baby mdse only

Legacy Distributing
Tom Garinger, Book Buyer
Lone Star Industrial Park
811 Lone Star Dr
O'Fallon MO 63366
314-281-5700; Fax: 314-281-5750
Subjects: 29-48
Territory: US-IT
Markets: RO(hobby shops)-BK
Items: HC-PB-OT(models)

Leprechaun's Lair
Jack Hadden
926 Diamond Park
Meadville PA 16335
814-333-6527
Subjects: 99
Territory: 1 rep
Markets: BK
Items: HC-PB-US

Levy Home Entertainment
Ray Carolle, Book Buyer
4201 Raymond Dr
Hillside IL 60162-1786
708-547-4400; Fax: 708-547-4503
Subjects: 99(remainders)
Territory: US
Markets: RO (Serves discount retail market)
Items: HC-PB-RM

Liberation Distributors
Pat Sims, Mgr
PO Box 5341
Chicago IL 60680-5341
312-987-0004
Subjects: 13-41-47-49-73
Territory: US-CN; 1 rep
Markets: BK-CO-PL-SL
Items: HC-TX-PB-MG-NP

Liberty Hobby Distributors
C T Rigsby, Pres
1232 E Magnolia St
Lakeland FL 33802
941-688-5904; Fax: 941-683-5730
Subjects: 29C-29H
Territory: US
Markets: BK-RO(hobby stores)
Items: HC-PB-PO-GI(supplies)
Memo: Carries games, miniatures, railroads, airplanes, model rockets, paints, die-cast collectibles, diorama supplies, and other educational supplies for hobbysts.

Librairie Francaise Inc
Philippe Lahmani, Mgr
27 W 20th St
New York NY 10011
212-463-9644; Fax: 212-633-1571
800-255-3741
Subjects: 45
Territory: US
Markets: BK-SC-CO-PL
Items: HC-PB

Library Sales Inc
William Ewing, VP
2001 SW 31st Ave
Pembroke Park FL 33009
954-985-9400; Fax: 954-987-2200
Subjects: 99
Territory: US
Markets: SC-PL
Items: HC-PB
Memo: Formerly: **Intellabooks Inc.**

Libreria Bereana
Sigfredo Polanco
1825 San Alejandro
Urb San Ignacio
Rio Piedras PR 00927-6819
809-764-6175; Fax: 809-764-6175
Subjects: 45(Spanish)-78-80-99
Territory: 1 rep
Markets: BK-SC-SL
Items: HC-MM-PB-TA(few)

Light Impressions Corp
Lance Speer, Buyer
439 Monroe Ave
PO Box 940
Rochester NY 14603
716-271-8960; Fax: 716-442-7318
Subjects: 11(photography, graphic arts)
Territory: US - some retail
Markets: BK-CO-SC-PL-SL
Items: HC-PB-TX-TV

Lindsay News
Robert Lindsay, Buyer
3025 Niagara St MP0948
Niagara Falls NY 14302
716-284-0491; Fax: 716-284-0810
Subjects: 99
Territory: US
Markets: BK-SC-NS-RO
Items: PB-MG-NP

Literal Book Distributors
Jose M Valencia, Owner
1402 Caddington Ave
Silver Spring MD 20012
202-723-8688; Fax: 202-882-6592
800-366-8680
Subjects: 99
Territory: 3 reps
Markets: BK-CO-SC-PL-SL
Items: MM-PB(in Spanish)

Login Brothers Book Co
Doug Purington, Book Buyer
1436 W Randolph St
Chicago IL 60607-1436
312-432-7700; Fax: 312-432-7801
800-621-4249
E-Mail: sales@lb.com
Subjects: 39(primarily professional texts)
Territory: US
Markets: BK-CO-PL-SL
Items: HC-PB-TX

Long Beach Books Inc
Randy Bogash, Owner
17 E Park Ave
Long Beach NY 11561
516-432-2265; Fax: 516-432-0063
Subjects: 99
Territory: US
Markets: BK-SC-some retail
Items: HC-PB-MM-US

Looseleaf Law Publications Inc
Michael L Loughrey, Co-owner/Mgr
PO Box 650042
Fresh Meadows NY 11365-0042
718-359-5559; Fax: 718-539-0941
Subjects: 55L-59
Territory: Sales area restricted
Markets: BK-CO-PL-SL-RO
Items: Law books
Memo: 41-23 150th St, Flushing, NY

Lotus Light Distributing
Santosh Krinsky, Pres
Lotus Brands Inc
PO Box 2
Wilmot WI 53192
414-889-8501; Fax: 414-889-8591
800-548-3824
Subjects: 39H-53-54(Sri Aurobindo, etc)
Territory: US
Markets: BK-GI-RO(health food)
Items: HC-PB-TA-TV-GI(foods)

Luminary Distributing
Alex Wedmedyk, Book Buyer
2488 Nadine
Hinckley OH 44233
216-273-6260; 800-234-6260
Subjects: 39-53-54-57-63
Territory: US
Markets: BK-RO
Items: HC-PB-GI-TA-TV

M

M & M News Agency Inc
Joseph M Clancy, Owner
Civic Industrial Park
La Salle IL 61301
815-223-2754
Subjects: 99
Territory: 3 reps
Markets: BK-SC-CO-MM-RO
Items: MM-PB-MG

Ma'ayan Book Co
Robert Gersh, Owner
400 W Cummings Park #2650
Woburn MA 01801
617-938-6001; Fax: 617-938-6002
Subjects: 63(Jewish interest)
Territory: US
Markets: BK-CO-PL-SL-OT(gift stores)
Items: HC-PB-TX-MM-GA-SW

MacGregor News Agency
Charles MacGregor, Owner
1733 Industrial Park Dr
Mount Pleasant MI 48858-4698
517-773-3888
Subjects: 99
Territory: US; 5 reps
Markets: BK-PL-SL-CO-SC-RO
Items: MG-PB-TX
Memo: Magazine subscription agency.

Mackin Book Co
Randall Heise, Owner
615 Travelers Trail W
Burnsville MN 55337
612-895-9540; Fax: 612-894-8806
Subjects: 99
Territory: US
Markets: SC-CO-SL; Items: TX

Magazine Distributors
100 Canciague Rock Rd
Hicksville NY 11801
516-433-2300; Fax: 516-433-2327
800-691-1145
Subjects: 75-99
Territory: US
Markets: BK-RO(supermarkets)
Items: HC-NP-MG(school paperbacks)

Magee Publications
Peggy Magee, Owner
8175 E Loos
Prescott Valley AZ 86314
602-772-7957
Subjects: 41G(Ireland)
Territory: US
Markets: BK-PL-SL
Items: HC-PB

Magickal Childe Inc
Anthony Passaro
35 West 19th St
New York NY 10011
212-242-7182
Subjects: 53-54-57-79
Territory: US
Markets: RO
Items: HC-PB-RM-US

Mahoning Valley Distributors
Tim Kempe
2556 Rush Blvd
PO Box 2764
Youngstown OH 44507
216-788-9661; Fax: 216-788-9046
Subjects: 99
Territory: 2 reps
Markets: BK-CO-SC-PL-SL-NS-RO
Items: HC-PB(childrens)-MM

Maine Periodical Dist Inc
Allen Shaw
PO Box 849
Presque Isle ME 04769
207-764-5913; Fax: 207-764-4750
Subjects: 75-99
Territory: Maine
Markets: BK-CO-RO-MM
Items: MM-MG-PB

Maine Writers/Publ Alliance
Patricia Conn
12 Pleasant St
Brunswick ME 04011
207-729-6333; Fax: 207-725-1014
Subjects: 61(ME)-83-99(small press books)
Territory: US
Markets: BK-PL-SL-SC-RO
Items: HC-PB-ML

Majors Scientific Distributors
9464 Kirby Dr
Houston TX 77054
713-662-3984
800-458-9077
Subjects: 39-67
Territory: US
Markets: BK-CO-PL-SL
Items: HC-PB-TX(medical/scientific)

Mangelsen's
Suzanne Cameron, Mdse Mgr
9706 Mockingbird Dr
Omaha NE 68127
402-339-3922; Fax: 402-339-3296
800-228-2601
Subjects: 11-29
Territory: US
Markets: RO(craft stores)
Items: PB(soft-cover craft bk)

Manhattan Publishing Co
T A Johnson, Mgr
PO Box 850
Croton-on-Hudson NY 10520
914-271-5194; Fax: 914-271-5856
Subjects: 55
Territory: US
Markets: CO-SC-SL-PL
Items: HC-PB

Many Feathers Books & Maps
Michael Bayne, Book Buyer
2626 W Indian School Rd
Phoenix AZ 85017-4303
602-266-1043; Fax: 602-279-2350
800-279-7652; FAX: 800-279-7653
Subjects: 51-61(AZ/SW US)-69R-71-99
Territory: US-AZ
Markets: BK-SC-CO-PL-SL-RO(gift)
Items: HC-PB-MA-TV-GA-TA

Map Link
William Sargent, Whsl
25 E Mason St
Santa Barbara CA 93101
805-965-4402; Fax: 805-962-0884
Subjects: 99
Territory: US
Markets: BK-PL-SL-RO
Items: MA(travel guides)

Marco Co
M Penn, Owner
739 E New York Ave
PO Box 108 Rugby Sta
Brooklyn NY 11203
718-773-0005; Fax: 718-774-0380
800-842-4234
Subjects: 99
Territory: 7 reps
Markets: SC
Items: HC-PB-MM

Marshall-Mangold Distributing Co
Marsha Goldberg, Book Buyer
4805 Nelson Ave
Baltimore MD 21215
410-542-7214; Fax: 410-367-8080
800-972-2665
Subjects: 21-31-33-39-57-71
Territory: Mid-Atlantic; 3 reps
Markets: BK-MM-JB-RO
Items: PB-MM-TO-TA

Martin/Osa Johnson Safari Museum
Buyer
111 N Lincoln
Chanute KS 66720
316-431-2730
Subjects: 99
Territory: US
Markets: MU
Items: HC-PB-TV-OT(Items from South Seas/Africa)

Matthews Medical Books Co
John Marcus, Owner
11559 Rock Island
St Louis MO 63043-3596
314-432-1400; Fax: 314-432-7044
800-NEDBOOK; FAX: 800-421-8816.
Subjects: 39
Territory: MO-US: 10 reps
Markets: BK-CO-PL-SL
Items: HC-PB-SW
Memo: Medical & health sciences titles.

McCrory's Wholesale Books
Hilton McCrory, Mdse Dir
113 North Bolton
Alexandria LA 71301
318-448-8954; 800-734-3264
Subjects: 59-63
Territory: US
Markets: PL-SL-SC-RO(Christian bookstores)
Items: HC-TX-RM-TV
Memo: 3,000 titles.

McKnight Sales Inc
David P McKnight Sr, Pres
540 California Ave
PO Box 4138
Pittsburgh PA 15202
412-761-4443; Fax: 412-761-0122
Subjects: 99
Territory: US
Markets: BK-SL-RO
Items: PB-MG-NP

Meader Book Distributing Co
Jean Meader, Owner
1686 Gervais Ave
St Paul MN 55109-2199
612-777-8343; Fax: 612-777-3425
Subjects: 99
Territory: Midwest
Markets: BK-PB-SL-PL-RO-MM
Items: HC-PB-MM-RM-TA

Melton Book Co Inc
Randy Elliott, Gen Mgr
506 Nelson Pl
PO Box 22968
Donelson TN 37214
615-391-3917; Fax: 615-391-5225
800-441-0511
Subjects: 63
Territory: US
Markets: Churches, individuals
Items: HC-PB

Merle Distributing
John Buell, Book Buyer
Linda Ruelbach, Juvenile Buyer
27222 Plymouth Rd
Detroit MI 48239-2395
313-937-8400; Fax: 313-937-8380
800-233-9380
Subjects: 99
Territory: US: 5 reps
Markets: BK-SC-CO-MM-PL
Items: HC-PB-MM-CA-CO-MA-PO-ST-SB-TA-TV
Memo: 15,000 titles.

Metropolitan Museum of Art
Kennedy O'Grady, Mgr
66-26 Metropolitan Ave
Middle Village NY 11381
718-417-3633; Fax: 718-628-5485
Subjects: 11
Territory: US
Markets: BK-PL-SL-SC-CO
Items: HC-PB

Miami Books
Howard Rhoat, Buyer
17842 State Rd 9
Miami FL 33162-1008
305-652-3231; Fax: 305-652-2480
Subjects: 99
Territory: 3 reps
Markets: BK-SL
Items: MM-PB-MG-NP-RM-SW

Michigan Church Supply Co
Leo F Flynn, Pres
G 7166 N Saginaw
PO Box 279
Mount Morris MI 48458-0023
810-686-8877; Fax: 810-686-0561
Subjects: 63
Territory: US; 3 reps
Markets: BK-RO(religious stores)-SC
Items: HB-PB-GI-GC-TV

Mickler's Floridiana Inc
Sam Mickler, Owner
181 W Broadway
PO Box 621450
Oviedo FL 32762-1450
407-365-6425; Fax: 407-365-6425
Subjects: 61(Florida)
Territory: FL
Markets: BK-SC-PL-SL
Items: PB-TA-TV-RM-MA

Micronesia Media Dist Inc
Jacqueline M Calvo, Mgr
Jane Camacho, Buyer
PO Box 22319
G M F
Barrigada GU 96921
671-477-7174; Fax: 671-477-0361
Subjects: 99
Territory: US-Guam; 1 field rep
Markets: BK-NS-MM-CO-RO(bookstores)
Items: HC-PB-CA-GC-MG-MA-ST-TA-TV-TO-OT
Memo: 150 accounts served; 2,000 titles; 30 publishers represented.

Midtown Auto Books
M Ray, Owner
212 Burnet Ave
Syracuse NY 13203
315-422-2187; Fax: 315-476-9421
Subjects: 16A
Territory: Sales area restricted; 2 reps
Markets: BK-CO-SC-SL
Items: HC-PB-MM

Midwest European Publications
Hubert Mengin, School Division
915 Foster St
Evanston IL 60201-3199
708-866-6262; Fax: 708-866-6290
Subjects: 44-45(SP/IT/FR/GR)-80
Territory: US; 2 reps
Markets: BK-CO-SC-PL
Items: HC-PB(in foreign languages)
Memo: Trade division: Yves Mengin, Distribooks, 8220 N Christiana, Shaker, IL 60076; 708-676-1596. College div: Marie Ellen Geismer, Adler's Foreign Books, Skokie, IL; 708-676-9944.

Midwest Library Service
Regina Lows
11443 St Charles Rock Rd
Bridgeton MO 63044-2789
314-739-3100; Fax: 314-739-1326
Subjects: 23-39-59-65-67-99
Territory: Midwest; 7 reps
Markets: CO-PL-SL
Items: HC-PB-MM(academic)
Memo: Library jobbers.

Miller Harness Co
Gary Stull
235 Murray Hill Pky
East Rutherford NJ 07073-2114
201-460-1200; Fax: 201-460-7289
Subjects: 15(horses)-69(horse riding)
Territory: US; 7 reps
Markets: BK-RO(riding shops)
Items: HC-PB-TV

Mineral Land Publications
T Maley, Owner
790 Troutner Way
Boise ID 83712
208-343-9143
Subjects: Geology & mining law
Territory: US
Markets: BK-CO
Items: HC-PB

Mississippi Library & Media Sup
John C Conner, Owner
PO Box 108
Brandon MS 39042
601-824-1900; Fax: 601-824-1999
Subjects: 21
Territory: Sales area restricted, MS; 2 reps
Markets: SC
Items: HC-PB-SW(teacher resource matl)

MKS Inc
Maureen Salaman, Owner
1259 El Camino Real #1500
Menlo Park CA 94025
415-854-3922
Subjects: 27-39
Territory: US
Markets: BK
Items: HC-PB

MLES Inc
Wendell Johnson, Mgr
Lower Village
Gilsum NH 03448
603-357-0236; Fax: 603-357-2073
Subjects: 21-31
Territory: US; 21 reps
Markets: PL-SL
Items: HC-TX-MM-PB-TV

Montfort Publications
Roger Charest, Mgr
26 S Saxon Ave
Bay Shore NY 11706-8993
516-665-0726; Fax: 516-665-4349
Subjects: 99
Territory: US
Markets: BK
Items: HC-PB

Mook & Blanchard
Jerry J Mook, Pres
546 S Hofgaarden
PO Box 1295
La Puente CA 91749-1295
818-968-6424; Fax: 818-968-6877
Subjects: 21-31-76-89
Territory: US; 6 reps
Markets: SC-PL-SL
Items: HC-OT(prebound)-SW-TA-TV
Memo: Childrens trade wholesale, K-8.

Mother Lode News Company
Dave Munroe
119 E Theall St
Sonora CA 95370-5798
209-532-4224; Fax: 209-532-5070
Subjects: 99
Territory: Sales area restricted; 3 reps
Markets: BK-RO
Items: HC-MM-MG-NP-RM-PB

Moving Books Inc
Emily Blackington, Book Buyer
Allison Radke, Book Buyer
948 S Doris St
PO Box 20037
Seattle WA 98108
206-762-1750; Fax: 206-762-1896
800-777-6683
Subjects: 21-35-39H-39R-43-53-54-57-71-99
Territory: US-CN-IT; 1 rep
Markets: BK-PL-RO(health/self-help)-SL
Items: PB-RM-MM-CA-GC-PO-RC-TA-TV-HC
Memo: Frank Kroger, President. Primarily stock: new age, metaphysical, holistic health, recovery, environmental, feminism, and multicultural.

Mr Paperback
Lee Jovien, Mgr
2224 S 11th St
Niles MI 49120
616-684-1551; Fax: 616-684-8740
Subjects: 99
Territory: US
Markets: BK-RO
Items: MM-PB-MG

Mr Paperback/Publishers News Co
Mike Gilbert
2224 South 11th St
Niles MI 49120
616-684-1551; Fax: 616-684-0130
Subjects: 99
Territory: US
Markets: BK-CO-SC-PL-SL-RO
Items: HC-PB-MM
Memo: Formerly: **Publishers News Agency.**

Multicultural Distributing Ctr
Daniel Chen, Mgr
Greenshower Corp
800 N Grand Ave
Covina CA 91724
818-859-3133; Fax: 818-859-3136
800-537-4357
Subjects: 21-44A-49-78-80
Territory: US
Markets: SC-SL-PL
Items: HC-PB
Memo: Multicultural books and instructional materials for K-12.

Mumford Library Book Sales
Douglas McNamara, Owner/Pres
7847 Bayberry Rd
Jacksonville FL 32256
904-737-2649; Fax: 904-730-8913
800-367-3927
Subjects: 99
Territory: FL; 3 reps
Markets: PL-SC-CO(universities)
Items: HC-PB-MM-RM

Murdoch Magazine Dist Inc
Robert F Brassell, Dir Sls & Mkt
TV Guide Magazine
PO Box 500
Radnor PA 19088
610-293-8500; Fax: 610-293-6212
Subjects: 99
Territory: US
Markets: BK-CO-MM-NS-RO
Items: MG
Memo: Satellite office: Murdoch Magazines, 1099 W Wall, Lyndhurst, NJ 07071; 201-460-0222.

Murr's Library Service
John Murr, Owner
4045 E Palm Ln
Phoenix AZ 85008
602-273-1121; Fax: 602-273-1217
Subjects: 99
Territory: SW US-IT; 8 reps
Markets: SC-PL-SL
Items: HC-SW-TV-OT(library bound bk)-PB - reinforced bindings)

Music Book Service Corporation
Warren Hicks, Gen Mgr
16295 NW 13th Ave #B
Miami FL 33169
305-620-2626; Fax: 305-620-8484
800-555-2626
Subjects: 14M
Territory: US
Markets: BK-RO
Items: HC-PB-TA-TV-RC

Mustard Seed
Eugene & Louise Groves, Owners
55 West Rd
Ellington CT 06029
203-872-1225; Fax: 203-872-2705
Subjects: 63
Territory: Sales area restricted
Markets: SL-RO
Items: PB-GI-GC-TV-OT(music/figurines)

N

N L Associates
Judy Kay
PO Box 1199
Hightstown NJ 08520
609-448-8443
Subjects: 99
Territory: US
Markets: Teacher conferences/mail order
Items: PB-MM-RM

NACSCORP Inc
Susan Hiesser, Backlist Buyer, Mass Market Books
Liz Giamboi, Book Buyer, Childrens & Promotional Books
Dick Riley, Frontlist Buyer
528 E Lorain St
Oberlin OH 44074-1298
216-775-7777; Fax: 216-774-1335 or 800-344-5059
800-321-3883
Subjects: 99
Territory: US
Markets: BK-CO(college bookstores)
Items: MM-HC-PB-CA

Najarian Music Company
Robert Najarian, Pres
269 Lexington St
Waltham MA 02154-4690
617-899-2200; Fax: 617-899-0838
Subjects: 14M(music only)
Territory: New England
Markets: RO(music)
Items: PB-OT(sheet music)

Nash Finch
PO Box 2427
Rocky Mount NC 27802
919-446-6151; Fax: 919-985-1802
Subjects: 99
Territory: US
Markets: RO
Items: HC-PB-MG

National Association of Deaf
Donna Morris, Mgr
Book Distribution
814 Thayer Ave
Silver Spring MD 20910
301-587-6282; Fax: 301-587-4873
Subjects: 39-99(books for the deaf)
Territory: US
Markets: BK-CO-PL-SL(personal orders)
Items: TV

National Book Distributors
Book Distributors
500 Kirts Blvd
Troy MI 48084
810-362-2400; Fax: 810-362-5160
Subjects: 75-77-81-82-84-85-86-87-88-89-9
Territory: 150 reps
Markets: RO-MM
Items: HC-MM-PB

National Catholic Reading Dist
John Sheerins, RINS
997 MacArthur Blvd
Mahwah NJ 07430
201-825-7300; Fax: 201-825-8345
Subjects: 63(Catholic)
Territory: US
Markets: SL
Items: PB

National Learning Corp
M Peters, Mgr
212 Michael Dr
Syosset NY 11791-5379
516-921-8888; Fax: 516-921-8743
Subjects: 55(educational study guides)
Territory: US
Markets: SC-PL-OT(bus/gov't)-BK-CO-SL
Items: PB-MM

National Rifle Assn
Frank A Engelhart, Mgr
11250 Waples Mill Rd
Fairfax VA 22030
703-267-1000; Fax: 703-267-3957
Subjects: 28-31-69
Territory: US
Markets: PL-CO
Items: MG

New Concepts Book & Tape Distrib
Jacqueline Ellis, Owner
9722 Pine Lake
PO Box 55068
Houston TX 77055
713-465-7736; Fax: 713-465-7106

800-842-4807
Subjects: 57S(mental/phys/spiritual help)
Territory: US
Markets: BK-CO
Items: HC-PB-TA-TV
Memo: 1 catalog annually. 5000 tapes & videos.

New England Mobile Book Fair
Kent Rhodehamel, Buyer
PO Box 87
21 E Belcher Rd
Foxboro MA 02035
508-698-0626; Fax: 508-543-2740
Subjects: 21-31-76-99
Territory: US; 5 reps
Markets: BK-SC-CO-PL-SL
Items: HC-PB-RM-MM
Memo: Features wholesaler remainders.

New Jersey Book Agency
Linton Segal, Owner
59 Leamoor Dr
PO Box 144
Morris Plains NJ 07950-0144
201-267-7093; Fax: 201-292-3177
Subjects: 19-23-39-59-67(no stock/special
Territory: US-IT(Europe)
Markets: BK-SL(thru special orders)
Items: HC-PB

New Jersey Books Inc
Barry Skinner, Mgr
59 Market St
Newark NJ 07102
201-624-8070; Fax: 201-624-6945
Subjects: 31-99
Territory: 4 reps
Markets: BK-CO
Items: HC-PB-US-TX

New Leaf Distributing
Safiya Harrison, Book Buyer, Wellness and Afri-Centric Titles
Elizabeth Harrington, Buyer
Patrick Gaffney, Buyer, Gay/Lesbian & Recovery Books
Alim Provo-Thompson, Buyer, Major Publishers
Lisa Roggoco, Buyer, Metaphysical Books
Fran Holt-Underwood, Children's Books
Mary Grider, Music Buyer
401 Thornton Rd
Lithia Springs GA 30057-2323
770-948-7845; 800-326-2665;
    Fax: 800-326-1066
Subjects: 21-31E-31P-35-51E-76-79
Territory: US
Markets: BK-RO(metaphy)-OT (health/church)-home schooling
Items: HC-PB-MM

New Life Foundation
Joan Philips
PO Box 2230
Pine AZ 85544
520-476-3224; Fax: 520-476-4192
Subjects: 53-54-57
Territory: US
Markets: BK-mail order
Items: PB-MM-TA

New York Periodical Dist Inc
Ed Murphy
213 Main St
PO Box 29
Massena NY 13662
315-764-5512; Fax: 315-364-5543
Subjects: 99
Territory: US
Markets: BK-MM-RO
Items: MM-PB-MG

Newark Book Center
Norman B Lehrman, Pres/Owner
Ten Academy St
Newark NJ 07102
201-642-7956; Fax: 201-642-3345
Subjects: 19-39-59-67
Territory: US
Markets: SL
Items: HC-PB-SW

NG Hing Kee
NG Yan Wah, Owner
724 Jackson
San Francisco CA 94133
415-956-0432
Subjects: 99
Territory: US
Markets: BK-SC-PL
Items: MG-CD-TA-TV-NS(Chinese)

Noll's Educational Books
Ardiss Galvin, Buyer
1407 W Milwaukee Ave
Storm Lake IA 50588
712-732-2818
Subjects: 31(ages K-high school)
Territory: IA-School library supplier
Markets: SC-SL-PL
Items: HC-PB(Christian material)

North America Bookdealers Exchange
Al Galasso
PO Box 606
Cottage Grove OR 97424
503-942-7455; Fax: 503-942-7455
Subjects: 99
Territory: US
Markets: BK-SC-RO(gift shops)
Items: HC-PB-CA-TA-TV
Memo: A marketing association; 1,000+ members.

North Carolina School Book Dept
O W Overton, Mgr
811 W Hargett St
Raleigh NC 27603-1603
919-833-6615
Subjects: 21-31-76-89(textbooks)
Territory: US
Markets: SC(K-8)
Items: TX

North Cascades National Park
Wayne Waits
2105 State Rt 20
Sedro-Woolley WA 98284
360-856-5700
Subjects: 31-41-51
Territory: US
Markets: MU
Items: MA

North Central Book Distributors
Thomas J Ziegler, Owner/Mgr
N57 W13636 Carmen Ave
Menomonee Falls WI 53051
414-781-3299; Fax: 414-781-4432
Subjects: 31
Territory: 1 rep
Markets: SC-PL(bookstores in schools)
Items: MM-PB

North East Wholesale Services
Harold Paulsen, Mgr
27 Sheep Davis Rd
Pembroke NH 03275
603-225-9787
Subjects: 99
Territory: US
Markets: BK-RO
Items: HC-MG-MM

Northwest International Trading
David Vinson, Owner
96 E Broadway #8
Eugene OR 97401
541-484-7060; Fax: 541-484-7063
Subjects: 27(Chinese cookbooks)
Territory: 1 rep
Markets: Bk-individuals
Items: HC

O G Waffle Book Co
Nancy K Jennings, Owner
897 13th St
Marion IA 52302
319-373-1832
Subjects: 21
Territory: 1 rep
Markets: SC-PL-SL
Items: HC-OP-MM-PB-TV-TA

Ohio Periodical
Debbie Reese, Book Buyer
Scherer Co
777 W Goodale Blvd
Columbus OH 43212
614-224-4901; Fax: 614-224-4118
Subjects: US
Territory: 6 reps
Markets: BK-RO
Items: HC-PB-MG-NP(few)
Memo: Corporate office: 5131 Post Rd, Dublin OH 43017; 614-792-0777.

Ollis Book Corporation
Kenneth E Ollis, Pres
28 East 35th St
Steger IL 60475-1712
708-755-5151
Subjects: 76-79(children's storybooks)
Territory: Midwest; 10 reps
Markets: SC-PL
Items: RM and sets only

Orbit Books Corp
Olga Grilli, Pres/Mgr
43 Timberline Dr
Poughkeepsie NY 12603
914-462-5653; Fax: 914-462-8409
Subjects: 39-67
Territory: US
Markets: SL-RO(govt agencies)
Items: HC-PB

P

Pacific Books
PO Box 3562
Santa Barbara CA 93130
805-687-8340; Fax: 805-687-2514
Subjects: 51N-61(Central & Coastal CA)
Territory: CA
Markets: BK-RO(gift shops/missions)
Items: HC-PB

Pacific Crest
Gail Nelson
16149 Redmond Way
PO Box 380
Redmond WA 98073
206-885-2433; Fax: 206-861-5578
Subjects: 27
Territory: 2 reps
Markets: BK-CO-SC-PL
Items: MA
Memo: Formerly: **Mr Map**.

Pacific Northwest Books
PO Box 314
Medford OR 97501
503-664-5205;
Subjects: 41(NW US)-61
Territory: Pacific NW
Markets: PL(distribute to libraries)
Items: HC-PB-(highly specialized)
Memo: Seasonal closing: December 19 thru January 10.

Pacific Pipeline Inc
Vickie Andre, Asst Head Buyer
Marilyn Dahl, Buyer; Mass Market and Trade Books
John Henry, Buyer, Sidelines and Remainders
Bill Preston
8030 S 228th St
Kent WA 98001
206-872-5523; Fax: 206-244-6109
Subjects: 99
Territory: Western US-Western CN; 3 reps
Markets: BK-PL-MM
Items: HC-PB-MM-RM-CA-TA
Memo: 70,000 titles with strong emphasis on children's books, NW small presses, university presses, and Western Americana; 3,000 publishers represented.

Partners Book Distributing
Vicky Eaves, Children's/New Titles Buyer
Sam Speigel, Small Press Buyer
2325 Jarco Dr
Holt MI 48842
517-694-3205
800-336-3137
Subjects: 49A-49B-61-99
Territory: US
Markets: BK-CO
Items: HC-PB-MM
Memo: Eric Stahl buys for RIF, library and school accounts. 20,000 titles from 400 publishers. Besides major titles, also features Great Lakes regional, children's books, African-American and Native American.

Periodical Services Inc
Ernest B Bronsveld, Owner
PO Box 367
Stockton NJ 08559
908-782-2969; Fax: 908-782-2969
Subjects: 21-27-45
Territory: 99
Markets: BK
Items: HC-PB-RM-CA

Perma-Bound Hertzberg New Method
John Brosnahan, Buyer
617 E Vandalia Rd
Jacksonville IL 62650
217-243-5451; Fax: 217-243-7505
Subjects: 21-59
Territory: 115 reps
Markets: SC(K-12)-PL-SL
Items: HC-TA-TV

Polybook Distributors
Joshua H Makanoff, Owner
22 S 6th Ave
PO Box 109
Mount Vernon NY 10550
914-664-1633
Subjects: 21-99
Territory: US
Markets: RO
Items: MM

Professional Book Distributors
James E Dockter, Pres/CEO of Warehouse & Distributing
1650 Bluegrass Lakes Pky
Altharetta GA 30201
770-442-8633; Fax: 770-442-9742
Subjects: 99
Territory: 2 reps
Markets: CO-SC-BU
Items: TX
Memo: Professional textbooks; insurance, banking, etc.

Professional Media Service Corp
Dianne Noguera, Purchasing Mgr
In the Groove Selection Guide
19122 S Vermont Ave
Gardena CA 90248
310-532-9024; Fax: 310-532-0131
Subjects: 99(videos/audios)
US: 800-223-7672; Fax: 800-253-8853
E-Mail:promedia@class.org
Territory: US
Markets: PL-SL-SC-CO(military)
Items: TV-TA(laser discs)
Memo: Produces listing of audios and videos each month. Catalog titled "In the Groove".

Professional's Library
Michael Clarke, Owner/Mgr
Rt 55
PO Box 249
Poughquag NY 12570
914-724-3000; Fax: 914-724-3063
Subjects: 99
Territory: US
Markets: SC-CO-PL-SL
Items: HC-PB-MM-SW-TV-OP

Publisher's Intl Mktg Services
Cynthia L Zimpfer, Sales Dir
1350 Ave of the Americas
New York NY 10019
212-261-6770; Fax: 212-261-6795
Subjects: 99
Territory: US
Markets: BK-JB-RO(book chains)
Items: HC-PB-MM(graphics titles)

Publishers Distribution Center
Scott Beutler, Pres
PO Box 27734 (84127-0734)
805 West 1700 South
Salt Lake City UT 84104
801-972-6338; Fax: 802-972-6570
800-922-9681
Subjects: 27-35-39-57
Territory: US
Markets: BK
Items: HC-PB
Memo: Formerly **Publishers Wholesale**.

Publishers Media
Ed Thompson
1447 Valley View Rd
Glendale CA 91202-1716
818-548-1998
Subjects: 45-49-59-78-80
Territory: US; 3 reps
Markets: SC-CO-PL-SL
Items: HC-PB
Memo: Languages of the world; dictionaries & reference books.

Publishers Resources Inc
1224 Heil Quaker Blvd
LaVergne TN 37086
615-793-5072; Fax: 615-793-3915
Subjects: 99
Territory: US
Markets: BK
Items: HC-PB-MM
Memo: Distributes and fulfills. Ingram Book Co affiliate.

Pulley Learning Associates
Elizabeth Pulley, Mgr
215 Altamont Rd
Greenville SC 29609
803-271-8694
Subjects: 21
Territory: SC
Markets: SC
Items: HC-PB-MM-OT(science kits)

Puski-Corvin Hungarian Books
Istvan Puski, Owner
217 E 83rd St St
New York NY 10028-2766
212-879-8893; Fax: 212-734-3848
Subjects: 44-45(Hungarian)-80-99
Territory: US
Markets: BK-individuals-PL
Items: HC-PB
Memo: 13-14,000 titles; 14 Hungarian novels in English.

R

R & S Supply
John Jenks
1601 West 3rd
Amarillo TX 79106
806-376-4301; Fax: 806-379-8926
800-299-2637
Subjects: 11-29
Territory: US
Markets: RO
Items: HC-PB

R & W Distribution Inc
B Wartelsky, Owner
87 Bright St
Jersey City NJ 07302
201-333-1540; Fax: 201-333-1541
Subjects: 99
Territory: 2 reps
Markets: JB-wholesalers
Items: MG-CO-RM

Ralph Curtis Books
Ralph Curtis, Owner
PO Box 349
Sanibel FL 33957-0183
941-454-0010; Fax: 941-395-2727
Subjects: 15
Territory: US
Markets: RO
Items: HC-RM-US-pocket field guides
Memo: 30 titles marketed to 200 shops specializing in reptiles, birds, & animals. Located at: 16956 MacGregor Blvd, Ft Myers, FL 33908.

Ransom Hill Press
Polly Meyers
3601 Main St
PO Box 325
Ramona CA 92065
619-789-0620; Fax: 619-789-1582
800-423-0620
Subjects: 39
Territory: US
Markets: BK-CO-PL-SC
Items: PB

Raritan Periodicals Sales Co
Authur Gelfand, Owner
125 Clearview Ave
PO Box 4076
Edison NJ 08818
908-225-6060; Fax: 908-417-0595
Subjects: 99
Territory: 5 reps
Markets: BK
Items: MM-MG-NP

Reading Circle
Jack Davis, Chief Exec Officer
1456 N High St
Columbus OH 43201-0458
614-299-9673
Subjects: 75
Territory: 2 reps
Markets: BK-SC-PL-SL
Items: HC

Reading Peddler Book Fairs
Sharon Hearn, Mgr
10580 3/4 W Pico Blvd
Los Angeles CA 90064
310-559-2665
Subjects: 21-31-76-89
Territory: S CA
Markets: SC
Items: HC-PB-RM-CA-GC-RC-TA-TV-TO

Reading's Fun Ltd
Jill Weiss, Main Buyer
123 N Main
Fairfield IA 52556-2804
515-472-8301; Fax: 515-472-8079
Subjects: 21-31-76-89-99
Territory: US
Markets: SC
Items: HC-PB
Memo: Sells through Book Fairs.

Readmore Academic Services
Dorothy Collins
700 Black Horse Pike #204-208
Blackwood NJ 08012
609-629-2500; Fax: 609-227-8322
Subjects: 99
Territory: 10 reps
Markets: SC-CO-PL-SL
Items: MG-NP
Memo: B H Blackwell is the parent company.

Readmore Inc
Dan Tonkery, Pres
22 Cortlandt St
New York NY 10007
212-349-5540; Fax: 212-233-0746
Subjects: 56M-99(subscription service)
Territory: Medical clients; 18 reps
Markets: SL-PL(hospitals)
Items: MG-HC-PB-SW
Memo: B H Blackwell is the parent company. Magazine subscription service.

Redwing Book Company
Martha Fielding, Pres
44 Linden St
Brookline MA 02146
617-738-4664; Fax: 617-738-4620
Subjects: 39H-53-54
Territory: New England
Markets: BK-RO
Items: HC-PB

Regent Book Company Inc
Morton & Doris Levin, Mgrs
101 A Route 46
Saddlebrook NJ 07663-6219
201-368-2208; Fax: 201-368-9770
Subjects: 21-31-43-45-76
Territory: US
Markets: SC-PL
Items: HC-PB-TA-TV

Reginald Fennell Subscription
Reginald Fennell, Owner
1002 W Michigan Ave
Jackson MI 49202
517-782-3132; Fax: 517-782-1109
Subjects: 99
Territory: 1 rep
Markets: CO-SC-PL-SL(hospitals)
Items: MG-NP
Memo: They are an agency & order from the publisher.

Renaissance Book Services
Harold & Barbara Levine, Owners
2490 Black Rock Turnpike #342
Fairfield CT 06430
203-372-0300; Fax: 203-374-4766
800-786-5427
Subjects: 21-76-79
Territory: US
Markets: SC-PL
Items: HC-PB
Memo: 20 publishers. Sells to school libraries.

Research Books Inc
Brad Purcell
38 Academy St
PO Box 1507
Madison CT 06443-1507
203-245-3279; Fax: 203-245-1830
Subjects: 19-23-59-65-67
Territory: E Coast-US intl publishers; 1 rep
Markets: SL(corporate only)
Items: HC-TX-PB-SW-TA

Research Periodicals & Book Service
James J Sullivan, Mgr
PO Box 720728
Houston TX 77272
713-779-2999; Fax: 713-779-2992
Subjects: 39-67
Territory: US
Markets: CO-PL
Items: PB-MG-NP
Memo: Specialize in scientific books & periodicals.

Richard Owen Roberts Wholesalers
Richard O Roberts, Co-Owner
Box 21
Wheaton IL 60189
708-584-8069; Fax: 708-653-8616
Subjects: 99
Territory: 3 reps
Markets: BK-SC-CO-PL-SL
Items: PB-TX-TV

Richardson's Books Inc
Angela Bonney, Book Buyer
2014 Lou Ellen Ln
Houston TX 77018-6118
713-688-2244; Fax: 713-688-8420
800-392-8562
Subjects: 21-61(TX)-76-99
Territory: US; 1 rep
Markets: BK-SC-PL-RO(specialty)
Items: HC-PB
Memo: Nancy Richardson, President. 30,000 titles, bestsellers, regional, travel.

Rider Circulation Services Inc
Stu Bienstock, Mktg Dir
550 N Brand Blvd #700
Glendale CA 91203
213-344-1200; Fax: 213-256-9999
Subjects: 99
Territory: US
Markets: BK
Items: MG-SW-NP
Memo: National distributor for wholesalers.

Rio Grande Book Co
Vinson McLeod, Mgr
1101 Upas Ave
Mc Allen TX 78501
210-682-7531; Fax: 210-686-6018
Subjects: 11-45-65-67
Territory: 4 reps
Markets: SC(K-12)
Items: TA-TX

Rittenhouse Book Dist Inc
511 Feheley Dr
King of Prussia PA 19406
800-345-6425; Fax: 800-223-7488
Subjects: 39M-59(medical jobber)
Territory: US; 10 reps
Markets: BK-RO(med/prof/govt)-CO-SC-SL
Items: TX
Memo: 5,000+ accounts; 34,000 titles carried, 300 publishers represented.

River Road Recipes Cookbook
Susanne Lockett
9523 Fenway Ave
Baton Rouge LA 70809
504-924-0300; Fax: 504-927-0257
Subjects: 27
Territory: US
Markets: BK
Items: PB

Rivers and Mountains
Beth Rundquist, Book Buyer
862 San Antonio Rd
Palo Alto CA 94303
415-424-1213
Subjects: 51-69R-71
Territory: US
Markets: RO(outdoor recreation retailers)
Items: HC-PB-CA

Riverside Book & Bible House
Steve Goodknight, Book Buyer
Clint Wrede, Music Buyer
Tim Williams, Purchasing Mgr
1500 Riverside Dr
PO Box 370
Iowa Falls IA 50126-0370
515-648-4271; Fax: 515-648-5106
800-247-5111; IA:800-362-2274
Fax: 800-822-4271
Subjects: 63-99
Territory: US
Markets: BK-RO(religious, churches)
Items: GA-GI-HC-PB-MM-RM-TA-TV-OT
Memo: 30,000+ titles

Rizzoli International Bookstore
Antonio Polita, Exec VP/Gen Mgr
300 Park Ave S
New York NY 10010
212-982-2300; Fax: 212-387-3434
Subjects: 11-12-14-41-47-75-83-90-95
Territory: US-IT-CN
Markets: BK-PL-SL-CO
Items: HC-PB-PO-CA-TV-TA

Robert Hale & Company
Robert Hale, Owner
Marine Book Distributors
1803 132nd Ave NE #4
Bellevue WA 98005
206-881-5212; Fax: 206-881-0731
Subjects: 15(marine)-51-70N(nautical)
Territory: US-IT
Markets: BK-CO-PL-SL-RO(marine stores)
Items: HC-PB-RM-CA-TA-TV

Rockbottom Books
Jill Abdo-Hansen, Owner
Pentagon Towers
PO Box 36036
Minneapolis MN 55435
612-831-2120; Fax: 612-831-1632
Subjects: 21-31-41-51B-69-84
Territory: US; 1 rep
Markets: SC(K-8)
Items: HC-TV

Roig Spanish Books
Vincent A Mahiques Sr, Mgr
29 West 19th St
New York NY 10011
212-675-1047; Fax: 212-229-0160
Subjects: 45(Spanish)-78-80
Territory: US
Markets: BK-CO
Items: HC-PO-MG

Roy Derstine Book Co
Roy Derstine, Owner
14 Birch Rd
Kinnelon NJ 07405
201-838-1109
Subjects: 10-11-23-27-29-41-67-69-86-90
Territory: Mid-Atlantic
Markets: SC-PL
Items: HC-RM

Royal Publications
Michael Van Meter, Book Buyer
790 W Tennessee Ave
PO Box 5793
Denver CO 80217-5793
303-778-8383; Fax: 303-744-9383
Subjects: 21-27-39H-53-57-69
Territory: US-IN(formerly Nutri-Books)
Markets: RO(health/gyms/drugs)-BK-CO
Items: HC-PB-RM-MM-MG-TA-TV
Memo: Distributes via catalog and at trade shows for the health food industry.

Russia Book & Art Shop Inc
Manager
799 Broadway
New York NY 10003
212-473-7480; Fax: 212-473-7480
Subjects: 21-45
Territory: US
Markets: BK
Items: HC-PB-TX-OP-RM-ML-PO

Ryukyu Martial Arts Co
Bill Wiswell, Pres
5005 Merriam Dr (66203)
PO Box 535
Olathe KS 66051
913-782-3920; Fax: 913-780-1750
800-383-4017
Subjects: 39H-53-69(martial arts)
Territory: US
Markets: BK-SC-PL-SL
Items: HC-PB
Memo: Wholesales and retails hundreds of books in 81 categories of martial arts.

S

S & L Sales Company
Rickey L Perritt, Mgr
2165 Industrial Blvd
PO Box 2067
Waycross GA 31502-2067
912-283-0210; Fax: 912-283-0261
Subjects: 99
Territory: US; 6 reps
Markets: BK-NS-SC-RO-MM
Items: PB-RM-HC

S & W Distributors Inc
William Sanders, Pres
1600H E Wendover Ave (27405)
PO Box 14689
Greensboro NC 27415
910-272-7394; Fax: 910-272-7394
Subjects: 21-59
Territory: 12 reps
Markets: SC-CO-PL
Items: HC-PB-TA
Memo: Marketing agent for publishers & jobbers.

Sagebrush Press
Dan & Janet Cronkhite, Owners
PO Box 87
Morongo Valley CA 92256
619-363-7398
Markets: BK
Items: HC-OP-US-PB-MA
Memo: Sagebrush Press Book Store, 55198A 29, Yucca Valley, CA 92284; 619-365-5671. Also publishes.

Salvation Army Supp/Purchasing
Lt Col Ronald Lyons, Mgr
440 W Nyack Rd
West Nyack NY 10994-0635
914-620-7200; Fax: 914-620-7275
Subjects: 99
Territory: 11 Eastern states, PR, VI
Markets: BK-CO-SC-SL
Items: HC-MM-PB

Sam Tuo Book Center
Donald Kim, Owner
3003 W Olympic Blvd #105
Los Angeles CA 90006
213-380-0212; Fax: 213-380-0264
Subjects: 99
Territory: US
Markets: BK
Items: HC-PB

Sam's Wholesale Club
Ken Hargis, Book Buyer
608 SW 8th St
Bentonville AR 72716
501-277-7000; Fax: 501-273-4053
Subjects: 99
Territory: US
Markets: Sam's Wholesale Club
Items: CA-CO-CR-HC-PB-PO-RM-ST-TA-TO-TV

San Diego Museum of Art Store
Chacho Herman
Balboa Park
PO Box 2107
San Diego CA 92112-2107
619-696-1971
Subjects: 11
Territory: US
Markets: MU-RO-mail order/phone
Items: HC-PB-PO-TV-ST

San Francisciana
Marilyn Blaisdell
PO Box 590955
San Francisco CA 94159
415-751-7222; Fax: 916-363-0317
Subjects: 99
Territory: US
Markets: BK
Items: MA-PO-photo books of SF

Saphograph Corp
K Pollak
4910-12 Fort Hamilton Pky
Brooklyn NY 11219-3344
718-331-1233
Subjects: 99
Markets: BK-CO-SC-PL-SL
Items: HC-PB-TX(foreign lang/dictionary)

Sathya Sai Book Center of Amer
Bob Bozzani
305 W First St
Tustin CA 92680-0278
714-669-0522; Fax: 714-669-9138
Subjects: 99
Territory: US
Markets: BK-CO-PL-SC
Items: PB-TV

Schmul Publishing Co Inc
H E Schmul, Pres
PO Box 716
Salem OH 44460-0716
216-222-2249; Fax: 216-222-2249
800-772-6657
Subjects: 63-75
Territory: US
Markets: BK-individuals
Items: HC-PB-TA

Schoenhof's Foreign Books Inc
David Leyenson, Book Buyer
76A Mount Auburn St Box 182
Cambridge MA 02138
617-547-8855; Fax: 617-547-8551
Subjects: 44-45(European)-59-80
Territory: US-IT
Markets: PL-SL-BK-SC-CO
Items: HC-PB-TX-TA
Memo: 270 language dictionaries.

The Scholar's Bookshelf
Ginny Goss, Mgr
110 Melrich Rd
Cranbury NJ 08512
609-395-6933; Fax: 609-395-0755
Subjects: 11-12-41-47-54-55-57-65-99
Territory: US
Markets: CO-BK-SL
Items: RM

Scholastic Book Fairs
PO Box 958411
Lake Mary FL 32795
407-829-7300; Fax: 407-829-2600
Subjects: 99
Territory: NC-SC-VA
Markets: SC-CO-PL-SL
Items: MM-PB

School Aid Company
Lisa Long, Mgr
911 Colfax
PO Box 123
Danville IL 61832-3395
217-442-6855
Subjects: 21-31-76
Territory: US; 2 reps
Markets: SC-PL-SL
Items: HC-PB-TX-SW-TV

School Book Fairs
Bobbie Wanamaker, Buyer, Elementary Books
801 94th Ave N
St Petersburg FL 33702
813-578-7600; Fax: 813-578-3113
Subjects: 21T-31-89-99
Territory: US
Markets: SC-PL
Items: HC-PB-MM-MG-PO-SB-SW-OT

School Book Service Inc
Kathleen Kuehne, Pres
3650 Coral Ridge Dr #112
Coral Springs FL 33065
305-341-7207; Fax: 305-341-7303
Subjects: 41-57
Territory: US; 4 reps
Markets: SC-CO
Items: MM-PB

School of Metaphysics Natl Hdqt
Daniel R Condron, Pres
HCR 1 Box 15
Windyville MO 65783
417-345-8411
Subjects: 21-39-53-54-57-69-75
Territory: US; 18 reps
Markets: BK(their own-14 centers Midwest)
Items: HC-MM-PB-TA-TV
Memo: Branches buy through headquarters. Sends books to Australia.

Schoolbell Books & Gifts Inc
Karyn Gregory Hutson, Mgr
10762 Wellerwoods Dr
Cincinnati OH 45242
513-530-9888
Subjects: 21
Territory: US
Markets: SC(K-8)
Items: HC-PB-SB(bookmarks)

Schroeder's Book Haven
Bert C Schroeder, Owner
104 Michigan Ave
League City TX 77573
713-332-5226; Fax: 713-332-1695
Subjects: 10-61(Texana)-83
Territory: TX; 1 rep
Markets: SC-CO-PL-SL(mostly libraries)
Items: HC-PB(college level)

Scientific & Medical Publication
Gerard G Juery, Pres
100 E 42nd St #1002
New York NY 10017
212-983-6278; Fax: 212-687-1407
Subjects: 39-45-65-67
Territory: US; 4 reps
Markets: BK-CO-SC-PL-SL
Items: HC-PB-TV
Memo: Full name: Scientific & Medical Publications of France.

Sea Challengers
Ann Gotshall, Owner/Pres
Four Sommerset Rise
Monterey CA 93940
408-373-6306; Fax: 408-373-6306
Subjects: 70(marine life)
Territory: US
Markets: BK-PL-RO
Items: HC-MM-PB

Selections Book Fairs Inc
Sally R Oddi, Pres/Mgr
890 Oakland Park Ave
Columbus OH 43224
614-262-0189; Fax: 614-268-3338
Subjects: 99
Territory: Sales area restricted-OH; 3 reps
Markets: SC
Items: HC-PB

Sewing Center Supply Company
Buyer
9631 NE Colfax St
Portland OR 97220-1232
503-252-1452; Fax: 503-252-7280
Subjects: 29(sewing)
Territory: US-IN
Markets: RO(sewing stores)
Items: Machines/needlework/crafts

Shen's Books & Supplies
Attn: Book Buyer
628 E Pamela Rd
Arcadia CA 91006
818-445-6958; Fax: 818-445-6940
Subjects: 44-45(Chinese)-80
Territory: US
Markets: BK-CO-SC-PL-SL
Items: HC-PB-MM-TA-TV

Sher Distributing
Krystyna Cook, Juvenile Buyer
Mary Ann Rosalia, Buyer
8 Vreeland Ave
Totowa NJ 07512
201-256-4050; Fax: 201-256-1314
Subjects: 21-31-76-79-89-99
Territory: US
Markets: RO
Item: RM
Memo: Sells to 2500 mass market and supermarket retailers.

Shuey Book Search
Claudia Shuey, Owner
8886 Sharkey Ave
Elkgrove CA 95624
916-685-3044
Subjects: 99
Territory: US-IT
Markets: Mail order only
Items: HC-OP

Silver Burdett & Ginn Co
Daniel C Wasp, Pres
250 James St
Morristown NJ 07960-6410
201-285-7700
Subjects: 21
Territory: 96 reps
Markets: BK-SC-PL-SL
Items: TX-SW-TV
Memo: Branches - Menlo Park, CA, Atlanta, GA, Deerfield, IL, Dallas, TX.

Small Changes
Shari Basom
316 Terry Ave N
Seattle WA 98109
206-382-1980; Fax: 206-382-1514
Subjects: 13-14-21-31-33-35-39-43-51-53-9
Territory: NW US
Markets: BK-CO-MM-NS-SC-PL-RO
Items: MG-CA
Memo: Barbara Wefferling, Publisher Contact. They distribute magazines and calendars, especially alternatives: environmental, health, women's issues, political issues, etc.

Small Press Distribution Inc
Steve Dickison, Book Buyer
1814 San Pablo Ave
Berkeley CA 94702-1624
510-549-3336; Fax: 510-549-2201
800-869-7553
Subjects: 47-75-83-90-95
Territory: US
Markets: BK-SC-CO-PL-SL
Items: HC-PB-MG-ML-TV
Memo: Specializes in poetry, broadsides, fiction, essays, and literary titles. 5,000 titles from 300+ publishers.

Sonshine Harbor Wholesale Books
John Osepchook, Owner
825 Glen Arden Way
Altamonte Springs FL 32701
407-339-0401; Fax: 407-331-0853
Subjects: 63
Territory: Christian schools only
Markets: SC
Items: HC-MM-PB-TA-TV-RM

South Carolina Bookstores Inc
Curtis Ridgeway/Dennis Fye, Mgrs
523 Jasper St
PO Box 4767
West Columbia SC 29171-4767
803-796-8200; Fax: 803-794-6927
Subjects: 99
Territory: US
Markets: BK-CO-SC
Items: MM-PB-TX

South Central Books
R B Lynam, Pres
17820 Kings Rd
Shawnee OK 74801
405-275-4522; Fax: 405-275-4533
Subjects: 99
Territory: South Central; 4 reps
Markets: SC-PL
Items: HC-RM

South Eastern Book Co Inc
Jim Sims, Pres
RR 2 Hwy 641 N
PO Box 309
Murray KY 42071
502-753-0732; Fax: 502-759-4742
800-633-9645
E-Mail:
    sebmurray@mursuky.campus.mci.net
Subjects: 59
Territory: US
Markets: CO
Items: TX

Southeast News
Connie Houston, Mgr
110 Central Junction Blvd #AD
Savannah GA 31405-1567
912-234-3429; Fax: 912-234-8021
800-929-8274
Subjects: 99
Territory: SC & GA; 20 reps
Markets: BK-CO-SC-PL-SL
Items: MM-PB-MG-NP

Southeastern Book Company
William Ewing, VP
2001 SW 31st Ave
Hallandale FL 33009
305-652-5393; Fax: 305-651-3861
Subjects: 99
Territory: US - 20 reps
Markets: PL-SL-CO-SC
Items: HC-PB-RM

Southeastern News Company
Bruce Sherbow, Gen Mgr
4070 Shirley Dr SW
Atlanta GA 30336
404-691-2800; Fax: 404-691-3502
800-929-8274
Subjects: 99
Territory: GA-CA-NC-SC-FL; 15 reps
Markets: NS-MM-RO
Items: GA-MG-MM-NS-OT

Southern Book Service Inc
Barbara Franzen, Buyer
Palmetto Lakes Industrial Park
5154 NW 165th St
Hialeah FL 33014-6335
305-624-4545; Fax: 305-621-0425
US: 800-828-6254; FL: 800-766-3254
Subjects: 61(FL-South)-99
Territory: US
Markets: BK-SC-CO-PL
Items: HC-PB-MM
Memo: 15,000 titles.

Southern Michigan News
Mike Puglie, Hard Cover Buyer
Richard Stoll, Owner
Shirley Grove, Soft Cover Buyer
2571 Saradan Rd
PO Box 908
Jackson MI 49201
517-784-7163; Fax: 517-784-0075
Subjects: 99
Territory: Southern MI
Markets: BK-CO-SC-RO
Items: HC-PB-MG

Southern Periodicals
Norman Davis, Mgr
211 Industrial Dr
PO Drawer 407
Rayne LA 70578-0417
318-334-9661; Fax: 318-334-9663
Subjects: 99
Territory: US; 28 reps
Markets: BK-RO-NS-MM
Items: HC-MM-MG-CA-CO-MA-SB-PO

Southern Publishers Group
Steve Parker, Acquisitions Dir
147 Corporate Way
PO Box 1360
Pelham AL 35124
205-664-6980; Fax: 205-664-6984
800-628-0903
Subjects: 21-61-41-27-69-99
Territory: US
Markets: BK
Items: HC-PB-MM
Memo: Services the Books-A-Million chain of superstores. Previously a regional wholesaler, now primarily an exclusive distributor.

Southern Wisconsin News Co
Robert Purnell III, Owner
4836 S John Paul Rd
Milton WI 53562
608-756-2376; Fax: 608-756-2357
Subjects: 99
Territory: 3 reps
Markets: BK-SC-CO-PL-SL-MM-NS
Items: MM-PB-RM-MG

Southwest Book Co
John Dorroh, Mgr
13003 H Murphy Rd
Stafford TX 77477
713-498-2603
Subjects: 21
Territory: US
Markets: BK(some)-SC-CO
Items: HC-PB-TX

Southwest Cookbook Distributors
Leigh Ann Sams, Buyer
1430 Texas Ave PO Box 707
Banham TX 75418
800-725-8898; Fax: 800-725-2522
Subjects: 27(Southwest cookbooks)
Territory: US
Markets: BK-RO(gift shops/Jr League)
Items: HC-PB
Memo: 500 cookbooks from US & Canada.

Southwest Natural/Cultural Herit
Stephen G Maurer, Buyer
6501 4th St NW #I
Albuquerque NM 87107
505-345-9498; Fax: 505-344-1543
Subjects: 99
Territory: US
Markets: BK-SL
Items: HC-PO-TV-GC-OT(pins, t-shirts)
Memo: Full name: Southwest Natural & Cultural Heritage Association.

Southwest School Book Depository
Gary Havner, Pres
1815 Monetary Ln
Carollton TX 75006
214-245-8588; Fax: 214-245-2077
Subjects: 21-31-76-79-89-99
Territory: TX
Markets: SC(K-12)
Items: HC-PB-TX

Spanish & European Bookstore
Dr Ephrem E Compte, Owner
3102 Wilshire Blvd
Los Angeles CA 90010
213-739-8899; Fax: 213-739-0087
Subjects: 45-47-59
Territory: US
Markets: SC-PL-RO
Items: TA-TX(all in Spanish)

Specialty Promotions Co Inc
Abdul Salaam, Owner
6841 S Cregier Ave
Chicago IL 60649-1405
312-493-6900; Fax: 312-721-9374
Subjects: 63(Islamic literature)
Territory: 1 rep
Markets: BK-CO-PL-SL
Items: PB(hard soft covers)

Spencer Museum Publications
Bernadette Traiger
Spencer Museum of Art
University Of Kansas
Lawrence KS 66045-2136
913-864-4710; Fax: 913-864-3112
Subjects: 11-41(art history books/chidren)
Territory: US
Markets: Mail order
Items: HC-PB

Square Deal Records Book Dept
R W Ferris, Owner
303 Higuera St
San Luis Obispo CA 93401-1002
805-543-3636; Fax: 805-543-3938
Subjects: 14M-33
Territory: US
Markets: BK
Items: RM(music overstock)-OP-SW-TA

SRI Aurobindo Association
Wayne Bloomquist
306 Fulton St #310
Berkeley CA 94704-1449
510-848-1841; Fax: 510-848-8531
Subjects: 53-54-63
Territory: US
Markets: PL-SL-BK-CO-SC
Items: HC-PB-TV(few)
Memo: SRI Aurobindo Information, Evanston, IL 60204, 708-869-6547; SRI Aurobindo Ctr of Progress, Los Angeles, CA 90025, 310-444-9818.

Standard Publishing Co
Robert Ditterch, Pres
8121 Hamilton Ave
Cincinnati OH 45231
513-931-4050; Fax: 513-931-0904
Subjects: 21
Territory: US
Markets: BK-CO-SL-PL-RO
Items: HC-PB

Star Book Sales
Tim and Carol Timmins, Owners
3804 Overton Park
Fort Worth TX 76109
817-927-0324
Subjects: 21-99
Territory: TX
Markets: SC-PL
Items: HC-PB-TV

Starkmann Book Service
Helda Biggs, VP
38 River St
Winchester MA 01890
617-721-1537; Fax: 617-721-2825
Subjects: 19E-31-39-41-55-57-65
Territory: US; 3 reps
Markets: CO-BK-SL
Items: TX(college textbooks only)
Memo: A wholesaler which orders college textbooks for their client colleges. They do not sell or stock books-they only take orders; they do not stock titles.

Starscript Distributing Company
3945 East Carey
Las Vegas NV 89115
702-453-2525
Subjects: 39-53-54-57
Territory: US
Markets: BK-RO-MM
Items: PB(health & nutrition)

Sterling Rock Falls News Agency
Wallace Feldman, Owner/Mgr/Buyer
224 E 3rd Stt
Sterling IL 61081-3612
815-625-0241
Subjects: 21
Territory: Sales area restricted; 2 reps
Markets: BK-CO-SC
Items: HC-MG-NP-MM-PB-GC-TO

Stoll Multi-Media Services
Doug Mote, Gen Mgr
3149 W Michigan Ave (49202)
PO Box 4051
Jackson MI 49204
517-796-9225
Subjects: 99
Territory: US
Markets: BK
Items: HC-MG

Stonebridge Publishers Inc
William A Goshorn, Pres
660 W 400 North
PO Box 877
Cedar City UT 84721-0877
801-586-7670; Fax: 801-586-8080
Subjects: 21-31-76 (childrens K-12)
Territory: US
Markets: SC-PL
Items: HC-PB-TV

Summit Beacon International
5751 Highway 89 S
Livingston MT 59047
406-222-9000
Subjects: 53
Territory: US
Markets: BK
Items: HC-PB

Sun/Day Distributors Corporation
Don Patterson, Owner
1300 El Camino Ave
Sacramento CA 95815
916-922-4370; Fax: 916-921-5504
CA: 800-235-1419
Subjects: 11-29
Territory: US-CA-IN
Markets: RO(craft stores)
Items: HC-PB-MG(craft supplies)

Sunbelt Publications
Terry Cochran, Backlist Buyer
Heather Stevenson, Buyer
Diana Lindsay, Manager and Calendar Buyer
1250 Fayette St
El Cajon CA 92020
619-258-4911; Fax: 619-258-4916
800-626-6579
E-Mail: rww514a@prodigy.com
Subjects: 27-51-61(West)-69-71
Territory: West US
Markets: BK-RO(bike shops/outdoor retail)
Items: HC-PB-CA
Memo: Sells to regional buyers at the chains, the Nature Company, REI, other outdoor retailers, bicycle shops. 4,000 titles from 700+ publishers, Specialities: regional travel and reference, natural history, outdoor adventure books, maps. Box 191126, San Diego, CA 92159.

Sundance Publishers & Dist
Anne Sterling, Buyer
234 Taylor St
Littleton MA 01460-4326
508-486-9201; Fax: 508-486-1053
Subjects: 21-31-39-47-51-67-76-99
Territory: US-CA; 45 reps
Markets: SC-PL-SL-CO
Items: PB-MM-SW-TV
Memo: Distributor of paperbacks to the school market.

Superior Books
Mr Jody Richards, Pres
PO Box 1371
Bowling Green KY 42102-1371
502-781-9946; Fax: 502-781-9963
Subjects: 21-21T-75-99
Territory: US-CA; 15 sales reps
Markets: SC-PL
Items: 1-TA-TV
Memo: 5,000 titles, Distributes to libraries nationally. Prefers to buy books from publishers with lines.

Supermart Book Distributors
Rochelle LaRosa, Buyer, Mass-Market Paperbacks
Karen Patterson, Hardcover Buyer
Bob Weitrak, Juvenile Buyer
40 Commerce Dr
Cranbury NJ 08512-3502
609-655-8335; Fax: 609-655-3524
Subjects: 75-81-82-84-85-86-87-88-99
Territory: East Coast; 15 reps
Markets: MM
Items: HC-PB-RM-MM-CA-MA-OT(imports)

Susan's Card Co
Susan Hoy, Owner
239 San Anselmo Ave
San Anselmo CA 94960
415-456-1333; Fax: 415-456-4935
Subjects: 99
Territory: 10 reps
Markets: BK-RO
Items: HC-PB-GC

Swedus Imports
Mats Ludwig
10331 Dellwood Rd N
Stillwater MN 55082
612-426-8492; Fax: 612-426-2022
Subjects: 71F-80(Scandinavian books)
Territory: US-CN
Markets: GI(Scandinavian gift shops)
Items: HC-PB-GI
Memo: Ethnic-oriented products.

T

T R Books
Elena Hovestadt, Mdse Dir
822 North Walnut
PO Box 310279
New Braunfels TX 78130
210-625-2665; Fax: 210-620-0470
Subjects: 31-45(Spanish)-78-80-99(Spanish
Territory: US; 2 reps
Markets: PL-SC-SL-CO
Items: HC-PB-MM-RM-OP-TX-SW-MG-MA-TV-OT
Memo: Spanish language books, CD-ROM products, videos, & music. 6,000 titles; 300+ publishers represented.

T-V Library Assoc Wholesalers
Donna Carden, Owners
1216 Henry Ruff
PO Box 190
Garden City MI 48135
313-427-9074
Subjects: 99
Territory: 3 reps
Markets: PL-SC-CO
Items: HC-PB-TX

Taj Book Service
Timothy A Jones, Owner/Mgr
737 Rock Creek Church Rd
Washington DC 20010-1616
202-722-0701
Subjects: 800-223-8250
Territory: 1 rep
Markets: SC-CO-individuals
Items: TX

Tatnuck Bookseller
Lawrence Abramoff, Owner/Pres
335 Chandler St
Worcester MA 01602
508-756-7644; Fax: 508-756-9425
Subjects: 99
Territory: US-IT; 8 reps out of the country
Markets: CO-SC-PL-SL
Items: HC-PB-MM

Taylor & Francis
Kevin Bradley, Exec VP
1900 Frost Rd #101
Bristol PA 19007-1598
215-785-5800; Fax: 215-785-5515
Subjects: 31-39-41-55-59-67
Territory: US-IT
Markets: BK-PL-OT(research inst)-SL(univ)
Items: HC-TX-PB(journals)

Texas Book Co
Brent Dyer, Pres
2601 King
PO Box 212
Greenville TX 75401
903-455-6937; Fax: 903-454-2442
Subjects: 99
Territory: 10 reps
Markets: BK-CO
Items: TX(college)

Texas Educational Paperbacks Inc
Paul Davidson, Owner
4433 Mint Way
Dallas TX 75236
214-339-8309; Fax: 214-330-8725
Subjects: 99
Territory: US
Markets: SC
Items: MM-PB

Texas Library Book Sales
Raymond A Williams, Owner
1408 W Koenig Ln
Austin TX 78756
512-452-4140
Subjects: 21-31-76
Territory: US
Markets: SC-PL
Items: HC

Thieme Med Publishers Inc
Brian Scanlan, Pres
381 Park Ave S
New York NY 10016
212-683-5088; Fax: 212-779-9020
Subjects: 39
Territory: US
Markets: BK-CO-PL
Items: HC-PB-TX-TV

Thomas Brothers Maps
Robert Foster
17731 Cowan
Irvine CA 92714
714-863-1984; Fax: 714-852-9189
Subjects: 99
Territory: 4 reps
Markets: BK-CO-SC-PL-SL
Items: MA-SW
Memo: Branch - San Francisco, CA.

Time Distribution Services
Cameron Cloeter, VP Natl Sls Mgr
Time & Life Bldg
New York NY 10020
212-522-8444; Fax: 212-522-0467
Subjects: 99
Territory: US
Markets: BK-NS-RO
Items: BK

Tis Wholesale
Ray Tichenor, Owner
5005 N State Rd
37 Business
Bloomington IN 47404-1626
812-332-3307; Fax: 812-331-7690
800-367-4002
Subjects: 99
Territory: 5 reps
Markets: CO-SC
Items: HC-PB-TX

Title Books Inc
Herman Moore, Pres
3013 Second Ave S
Birmingham AL 35233
205-324-2596; Fax: 205-324-2598
800-854-2889
Subjects: 99
Territory: AL; 2 reps
Markets: CO-SC
Items: HC-SW

Total Information
John Smith, Pres
844 Dewey Ave
Rochester NY 14613-1995
716-254-0621; Fax: 716-254-0153
Subjects: 23-24-67 (technical books, science, engineering)
Territory: US(import titles from UK/Japan)
Markets: PL-SL-corporate/special librarys
Items: HC-SW-TX-TV

Tout De Suite A La Microwave Inc
Jean K Durkee, Owner
119 Green Meadow Rd
Lafayette LA 70503-6103
318-984-2903
Subjects: 27
Territory: 3 reps
Markets: BK-PL
Items: PB-TV

TransAllegheny Books
Gordon Simmons, Buyer
118 Capitol St
Charleston WV 25301
304-346-0551; Fax: 304-345-0911
Subjects: 61(Appalachia)-71
Territory: US
Markets: BK-MM
Items: HC-PB
Memo: 2 reps. Distributes regional titles to libraries, Waldenbooks, B Dalton, department stores, state parks, specialty shops, and mass-market outlets.

Transbooks Inc
Stanley Salmen, Pres
130 Cedar St
New York NY 10006
212-566-1944; Fax: 212-566-1807
Subjects: 11-19-31-45
Territory: US
Markets: BK-JB-CO-SC-PL-SL-RO
Items: HC-PB-TA-TV

Traveler Restaurant Bookseller
Arthur Murdock, Owner
1257 Buckley Hwy
Rte 84 Exit 74
Union CT 06076
203-684-4920
Subjects: 99
Territory: US
Markets: BK-PL
Items: HC-MM-PB-US-CO

Treasure Hunt Publications
Dr H A Tony Hyman, Owner
PO Box 3028
Pismo Beach CA 93448
805-773-6777; Fax: 805-773-8436
Subjects: 28-29H
Territory: US
Markets: RO(direct mail order)
Items: HC-PB (trash or treasure)

Tree Frog Trucking Company
Bill Kloster, Buyer
Katie Radditz, Juvenile Buyer
318 SW Taylor St
Portland OR 97204-2412
503-227-4760; Fax: 503-227-0829
Subjects: 75-95-86-37-57-14M-33-54
Territory: US; 2 reps
Markets: BK-RO(natural foods)-NS
Items: MG

Tree of Life Inc
Julie Andrew, Book Buyer
1750 Tree Blvd
PO Box 410
Saint Augustine FL 32086
904-824-8181; Fax: 904-825-2012
Subjects: 27-39-53-69
Territory: East Coast(wholesale food chain)
Markets: BK-RO(natural food stores)
Items: HC-PB-MM-MG-NP

Tree of Life Midwest
Terry Landis, Book Buyer
225 Daniels Way
PO Box 2629
Bloomington IN 47402-2629
812-333-1511
Subjects: 27-39H-53-69
Territory: Midwest(wholesale food chain)
Markets: BK-RO(natural food stores)
Items: HC-PB-MM-MG-NP

Tri-fold Book Service
Douglas Cass, Owner
81 Lawton Blvd
PO Box 1093 Sta Q
Toronto ON Canada M4T 2P2
416-482-2279
Subjects: 99
Territory: CN
Markets: SC-PL
Items: HC-PB

Trolle Associates
100 Corporate Dr
Mahwah NJ 07430
201-529-4000
Subjects: 21-31-76
Territory: US
Markets: SC-PL
Items: HC-PB

Tunde Dada House of Africa
Temi Tayo, Buyer
356 Main St
Orange NJ 07050
201-673-4446; Fax: 201-673-4581
Subjects: 49B-78-80
Territory: US
Markets: BK-RO
Items: HC-PB-TA-CL

Turner Company
Vernon Cain, Pres
1005 W Pines Rd
Oregon IL 61061
212-254-4454; Fax: 815-732-4489
800-847-4201
Subjects: 56M-99(subscription services)
Territory: 1 rep
Markets: PL-SL
Items: MG-NP

U

Ultra Books Inc
Martin S Ruback, Pres
PO Box 945
Oakland NJ 07436
201-337-8787
Subjects: 39H-53-54
Territory: NE; 3 reps
Markets: RO(New Age/health food stores)
Items: PB-MA

Unarius Educational Foundation
Charles Spiegel, Mgr/Buyer
145 S Magnolia Ave
El Cajon CA 92020-4522
619-447-4170; Fax: 619-447-8465
Subjects: 39H-41-54-57-67
Territory: 10 reps
Markets: BK-SC(catalog)-PL
Items: HC-PB-TV

Unicorn Books & Crafts Inc
Lars Malmberg, Co-owner
1338 Ross St
Petaluma CA 94954-6502
707-762-3362; Fax: 707-762-0335
Subjects: 29
Territory: Sales area restricted
Markets: SL-RO
Items: HC-PB-MG(old)

United Society of Shakers
Leonard Brooks, Mgr/Buyer
707 Shaker Rd
New Gloucester ME 04260
207-926-4597
Subjects: 21-29-41-51
Territory: US
Markets: BK-SC-PL
Items: HC-PB-OP-RM

United Techbook Co
Gilbert T Lopez, Owner
249 Main
Box 1658
Longmont CO 80502
303-651-3184; Fax: 303-651-3405
800-247-4808
E-Mail: utc@utcbooks.com
Subjects: 99
Territory: 1 rep
Markets: Individuals only
Items: HC-PB

US Games Systems Inc
Stuart R Kaplan, Chm
179 Ludlow St
Stamford CT 06902
203-353-8400; Fax: 203-353-8431
800-544-2637
Subjects: 54
Territory: US-IT; 50 reps

Markets: BK-CO-PL-SC-SL-MU-RO(gift shops)
Items: PB

V

Val Publishing Co
16 S Terrace Ave
Mount Vernon NY 10551
914-664-7077
Subjects: 99
Territory: US
Markets: NS
Items: PB

Valley Distributors Inc
Hugh Olbrich, Owner
2947 Felton Rd
Norristown PA 19401-1345
610-279-7650; Fax: 610-279-9093
800-355-BOOK
Subjects: 21-76-99
Territory: Mid-Atlantic
Markets: BK-CO-SC-SL-PL
Items: HC-PB-MM-CA
Memo: 12,000 titles including childrens' books and calendars.

Van Khoa Bookstore
Do Dinh Tuan, Owner/Mgr
9200 Bolsa Ave #123
Westminster CA 92683
714-892-0801; Fax: 714-892-0801
Subjects: 45(Vietnamese)
Territory: CA
Markets: BK-PL
Items: PB(dictionaries)-CD

Vintage Book Distributors
Tom Pieper, Owner/Buyer
678 Cunard Dr
Napa CA 94558
707-226-8867; Fax: 707-224-5139
Subjects: 27(wine)-71
Territory: 1 rep
Markets: BK
Items: PB

Vision Works
Dick McLeester, Owner
14 Chapman St
PO Box 92
Greenfield MA 01301
413-772-6569; Fax: 413-772-6559
800-933-7326
E-Mail: visionw@aol.com
Subjects: 15-27-31-39H-43G-49A-51E
Territory: US-New England; 2 reps
Markets: BK-RO-CH-MM
Items: HC-PB-CA-GC-SB-TA

Vistabooks
Penny Kerr and William R Jones, Partners
0637 Blue Ridge Rd
Silverthorne CO 80498
970-468-7673; Fax: 970-468-7673
Subjects: 41-51(historical reprints)
Territory: US
Markets: MU(National Parks)
Items: PB

Vitality Distributors Inc
Donald Scarborough, Co-owner
1010 NW 51st Pl
Fort Lauderdale FL 33309
305-771-0445; Fax: 305-771-4749
800-226-8482
Subjects: 27-39
Territory: FL-GA-Caribbean; 1 rep
Markets: Health food/drug stores/mkts
Items: HC-PB

Voyles News Agency Inc
Harry A Voyles, Owner
310 N Eight Ave
PO Box 399
Richmond IN 47375
317-962-3718
Subjects: 99
Territory: US
Markets: NW
Items: NS-MG

W

W T Cox Subscriptions Inc
W T Cox, Owner
411 Marcia Dr
Goldsboro NC 27530
919-735-1001; Fax: 919-734-3332
800-553-8088
E-Mail: wtcox.com
Subjects: 45(med journals)
Territory: 8 reps
Markets: SC-PL-CO
Items: MG-SW

W W Wickel Co
R Anderson, Pres
8970 Hanslek Ct
Naperville IL 60564-5629
708-820-0044; Fax: 708-820-0057
Subjects: 21
Territory: 1 rep
Markets: SC(pre K-12)-PL-RO
Items: PB-MM-RM

W Warner Book Distributors
Wayne Warner, Owner
198-16 Linden Blvd
St Albans NY 11412
718-949-5910; Fax: 718-949-0115
800-465-4402
Subjects: 49(African-American literature)
Territory: US
Markets: BK-SC-CO
Items: HC-PB-TX
Memo: Over 100 titles.

Wa Book Service Inc
26 Ranick Rd
PO Box 1700
Hauppauge NY 11788
516-234-2255
Subjects: 99
Territory: US
Markets: BK-CO-SC-PL-SL
Items: HC-PB-MM

Warner Press Inc
Robert G Rist, Pres
PO Box 2499
Anderson IN 46018
317-644-7721; Fax: 317-649-3664
Subjects: 63
Territory: US-IT; 14 reps
Markets: BK
Items: HC-PB-GI-GC-ST

Wasatch Book Distribution
Bruce Roberts, Book Buyer
268 South 200 E
Salt Lake City UT 84111
801-575-6735; Fax: 801-575-6834
Subjects: 61-71
Territory: West Coast/Rocky Mtns
Markets: BK-SC-PL-MU
Items: HC-PB-CA-MA

Washington Toy Company
Theresa Silva, Book Buyer
220 9th St
San Francisco CA 94103-3891
415-863-5965; Fax: 415-863-2880
Subjects: 21-29-45(Spanish)-76
Territory: US
Markets: BK-RO(toy/pharmacies)
Items: HC-TX-PB-GI-TA-TO-GA

Waverly News Co Inc
Owner
Not Sure News
17 State St
Newburyport MA 01950
508-465-0581
Subjects: 99
Territory: Sales area restricted - MA
Markets: BK-CO-SC-PL
Items: PB-MG-NP

Wayne Finger Lakes Area
Barbara Schmidt, Dir
Teacher Resource Center
3501 County Road 20
Stanley NY 14561
315-331-1584;
Subjects: 21-23-31-99
Territory: NY regional
Markets: SC
Items: HC-PB-SW

Western Library Books
Marc Rogell, Pres
560 S San Vicente Blvd
Los Angeles CA 90048
213-653-8880
Subjects: 99
Territory: 2 reps
Markets: SC-PL
Items: HC-PB(children's books)

Western Michigan News Inc
Shirley Grove, Buyer
Seymore Square Sta
PO Box 7319
Grand Rapids MI 49510
616-241-4453
Subjects: 99
Territory: Western/Northern MI
Markets: BK-CO-SC-RO
Items: HC-PB-MG

Western Publishing
1220 Mound Ave
Racine WI 53404
414-633-2431
Subjects: 99
Territory: US
Markets: BK-MM
Items: HC-TX-MM-MA-RM-SW-TA-TV

Whiting News Co Inc
Jay Chrustowski
1417 119th St
Whiting IN 46394
219-659-0775
Subjects: 27-59
Territory: Whiting area - 1 rep
Markets: BK-SC-PL
Items: MG-NP-GC-OT(office supplies)

Wholesale Art Materials
Ariana Storm
PO Box 2632
Berkeley CA 94702
510-649-4780; Fax: 510-548-1774
800-994-ARTS
Subjects: 11
Territory: US
Markets: CO-SC-RO
Items: HC-PB-MG-ST-OT

Wilcor International Book Dept
William Corrigan, Owner
700 Broad St
Utica NY 13501
315-733-3542; Fax: 315-733-3215
Subjects: 21
Territory: Sales area restricted-all NE US
Markets: BK-RO
Items: HC-PB-TO-GI

William S Hein & Co Inc
Ken Roth
1285 Main St
Buffalo NY 14209-1987
716-882-2600; Fax: 716-883-8100
Subjects: 39-55
Territory: 2 reps
Markets: BK-CO-PL-SL-SC
Items: HC-PB-US

Wilshire Book Co
Melvin Powers, Owner
12015 Sherman Rd
North Hollywood CA 91605-3781
818-765-8579; Fax: 818-765-2922
Subjects: 99
Territory: 18 reps
Markets: BK-PL

Womontyme Distribution Company
Janet Liss, Book Buyer
PO Box 50145
Long Beach CA 90815-6145
310-429-4802; Fax: 310-425-6494
800-247-8903
Subjects: 37-39D-57-73
Territory: US
Markets: BK-RO
Items: HC-PB-TA-TV-GI-PC-GC
Memo: Orders only: 800-247-8903. They feature books on sexual assault, incest, domestic violence, dependency, and recovery from such abuse.

Woodcrafters Lumber Sales Inc
Stephen Penberthy, Pres
212 NE Sixth Ave
Portland OR 97232
503-231-0226; Fax: 503-232-0511
Subjects: 29(woodworking)
Territory: 2 reps
Markets: SC-CO-RO
Items: HC-PB-TV

The Word For Today Inc
Buyer
PO Box 8000
Costa Mesa CA 92628
714-979-0706; Fax: 714-549-8865
Subjects: 63
Territory: US
Markets: BK(affiliated church bookstore)
Items: HC-PB-MG-TV-TA
Memo: AE Wilder bks/Pastor Chuck Smith.

Word of Life Distributors
Paul Jun, Mgr
2717 W Olympic Blvd #103
Los Angeles CA 90006-3002
213-382-4538; Fax: 213-382-1154
Subjects: 63(Christian)
Territory: US
Markets: BK-CO-PL-SL
Items: HC-PB

World Book Marketing
Jeffrey Press, Pres
455 Somerset Ave #2A
PO Box 622
North Dighton MA 02764
508-880-5555; Fax: 508-880-0469
Subjects: 99
Territory: US-CN-IT; 6 reps
Markets: BK-JB-MM
Items: PB-RM-MM-BT-ST-TO-TV

World Life International USA
Reto Lingenhag, Pres
PO Box 11118
Fort Lauderdale FL 33339-1118
954-565-8888; Fax: 954-565-8775
Subjects: 39-69-70A-71
Territory: US
Markets: BK
Items: TV

World University Bookstore
Howard John Zitko
Mescal-Salcido Rd
PO Box 2470
Benson AZ 85602
520-586-2985; Fax: 520-586-4764
Subjects: 39-41-53-54-57-63
Territory: US
Markets: BK-RO(some)-individuals
Items: HC-PB

Y

Yankee Book Peddler
Helmut Schwarzer, Dir
999 Maple St
Contoocook NH 03229
603-746-3102; Fax: 603-746-5628
800-258-3774
E-Mail:hschwarz@office.ybp.com
Subjects: 19-21-23T-47-76-99
Territory: US; 7 reps
Markets: CO-SL(academic)
Items: HC-PB-SW

Yankee News Company
Marvin Brownstein, Buyer
Andrew Gioroano, Mdse Mgr
62 Harper Ave
Waterbury CT 06705
203-757-9606; Fax: 203-754-6217
800-992-0001
Subjects: 99
Territory: Central & Western CT; 2 reps
Markets: NS-MM-RO
Items: PB-MM-CA-MG-MA-OT(novelty items)
Memo: 115 accounts served; 200 titles; 30 publishers represented

Yarn Tree Designs
Beth Johnson, Book Buyer
PO Box 724
Ames IA 50010-0724
515-232-3121; Fax: 515-232-0789
800-247-3952
Subjects: 11-29(needlework)
Territory: US-IA
Markets: RO(craft stores)
Items: HC-PB(craft supplies)

Yosemite Association Bookstore
Pat Wright, Mgr
PO Box 230
El Portal CA 95318
209-379-2646; Fax: 209-379-2486
Subjects: 51
Territory: US
Markets: BK-CO-PL-SC-RO
Items: HC-PB-GA-GC-TV

CANADA

A

Ad Astra Books
Don McVicar, Owner
PO Box 53081
Dorval Sta PQ Canada H9S 5W4
514-636-6080
Internet: Adstra@hexonx.com
Subjects: 41-70A
Territory: 1 rep
Markets: BK-CO-PL
Items: HC-PB

Atlantic Book Learningland Ltd
Lloyd F Russell, Pres
35 Cobequid Dr
Truro NS Canada B2N 5R1
902-893-1057
Subjects: 21-31
Territory: 1 rep
Markets: PL-SL-CO-SC
Items: HC-PB-MM-TA-RC
Memo: Branch — Dartmouth, NS.

B

Bomber Joe's
R J Burke, Mgr
Unit 29 4440 Cowley Crescent
Richmond BC Canada V7B 1B8
604-278-8021; Fax: 604-278-4255
Subjects: 70A(aviation training)
Territory: 4 reps
Markets: CO
Items: SW-TV-CA-MG

BookExpress
Allan MacDougall, Pres
8680 Cambie St
Vancouver BC Canada V6P 6M9
604-323-7100 or 604-323-7115
Fax: 604-323-7109
Subjects: 71-99
Territory: CN: 14 reps
Markets: BK-PL-SL-RO
Items: HC-PB-CA-ST-TA
Memo: Wholesale div of Raincoast Books.

The Book Store
M & A Benko, Owners
7 Perron St
St Albert AB Canada T8N 1E3
403-459-2525; Fax: 403-460-2530
Subjects: 23(engineering)
Territory: CN
Markets: BK-SC-CO(individuals)
Items: Reed's Engineering Series(tech)

Brodart Industries Ltd
Mr Franck Chenet
109 Roy Blvd
Brantford ON Canada N3T 5N3
519-759-4350; Fax: 800-363-0483
800-265-8470
Subjects: 99
Territory: CN; 2 reps
Markets: SC-CO-PL-SL
Items: HC-PB-MM-TX-TV-SW

C

Canav Books
Larry Milberry, Publisher
51 Balsam Ave
Toronto ON Canada M4E 3B6
416-698-7559; Fax: 416-690-4344
Subjects: 70A(aviation & military history)
Territory: US-CN-IT; 1 rep
Markets: BK-JB-PL-SL-SC-CO-RO(hobby shops)
Items: HC-PB
Memo: 200+ accounts; 150 titles; 30 publishers represented.

Carann Distributors
Ann Herbert, Mgr
2668 Cavendish Ave
Victoria BC Canada V8R 2G6
604-592-3637
Subjects: 99
Territory: 2 reps
Markets: BK-CO-PL
Items: RM & their own books

Cariad Ltd
Rex Williams, Pres
1103-89 Isabella St
Toronto ON Canada M4Y 1N8
416-924-1918
Subjects: 99
Territory: 4 reps
Markets: BK-CO-SC-PL
Items: HC

Children's Bookstore
Judy Sarick, Pres
2532 Young St
Toronto ON Canada M4P 2H7
416-480-0233; Fax: 416-480-9345
Subjects: 21-99
Territory: US
Markets: BK-SC-CO-PL
Items: HC-PB-MM-TA-TV-CD

Children's BookStore Dist
Sandy Gardner, Mktg Dir
1400 Bayly St #7
Pickering ON Canada L1W 3R2
905-831-1995; Fax: 800-385-6612
800-668-0242
Subjects: 14M-21(children's music/audio)
Territory: US-CN
Markets: BK-SC-PL-RO
Items: CD-SW-TA

Choice Books
Miss Clausen
844-K McCloud Ave
Winnipeg MB Canada R2G 2T7
204-661-0157; Fax: 204-661-8530
Subjects: 99
Territory: Sales area restricted; 60 reps
Markets: SC-RO
Items: PB-MM-RM

Cooperative Etudiante
Denis Cauvier
2900 Edouard Mont Petit
PO Box 6079 Sta A
Montreal PQ Canada H3C 3A7
514-340-4851; Fax: 514-340-4543
Subjects: 45
Territory: CN
Markets: BK-CO-PL
Items: HC-PB-TX-MG-ST-SW

Cross Country Books
Douglas Fisher, Pres
354 Wellesley St E
PO Box 550 Sta P
Toronto ON Canada M4X 1H3
416-925-7807; Fax: 416-925-9946
Subjects: 99
Territory: 2 reps
Markets: SC-PL(some)
Items: HC-PB-MA-MM(Canadiana)
Memo: Branch - Great Northern Books, Lewiston, NY.

Crown Publications Inc
Carolyn Pettersen, Buyer
521 Fort St
Victoria BC Canada V8W 1E7
604-386-4636; Fax: 604-386-0221
Subjects: 55
Territory: CN
Markets: BK-CO-PL-SL
Items: MA(charts, documents, legislation)

D

David C Cook Dist
Harold Hamilton
55 Woodslee Ave
Paris ON Canada N3L 3E5
519-442-7853; Fax: 519-442-1303
Subjects: 99
Territory: 5 reps
Markets: BK-CO-PL-RO(Cole's)
Items: HC-PB-MM-TX-CA-GI-MG-TO-TA-TV-OT

Dawn Distributors
David Campbell, Gen Mgr
3400 Pharmacy Unit 12
Scarborough ON Canada M1W 3J8
416-491-9497; Fax: 416-491-7276
Subjects: 21
Territory: 26 reps
Markets: BK-RO(gift stores)
Items: HC(Penguin bks)-MM-GI-ST-TO

Diffusion Dimedia Inc
Pascal Assathiany, Pres
539 Blvd Lebeau
Montreal PQ Canada H4N 1S2
514-336-3941; Fax: 514-331-3916
Subjects: 21-45-47-65-75
Territory: CN; 3 reps
Markets: BK-JB-NS-SC-PL-RO
Items: HC-PB-TX-CA-MG-MA-PO-SE-TA-TV

Diffusion Soussan Edilivre Inc
David Soussan, Mgr
5740 Ferrier
Montreal PQ Canada H4P 1M7
514-738-0202; Fax: 514-738-5102
Subjects: 21-27
Territory: 24 reps
Markets: BK-RO
Items: HC-PB-MM-TO

Doormouse Distributing
Les Bowser, Owner
65 Metcalfe St #6
Toronto ON Canada M4X 1R9
416-968-6890
Subjects: 39H-53(magazines only)
Territory: US-CA
Markets: BK-NS-RO
Items: MG-CA

E

Encore Books
Trevor Clare, Pres
4188 Virginia Crescent
North Vancouver BC Canada V7R 3Z6
604-980-2598; Fax: 604-988-7021
Subjects: 99
Territory: BC; 1 rep
Markets: SC-PL
Items: HC-PB

F

Faxon-SMS Canada
John Ashby, VP
PO Box 2382
London ON Canada N6A 5A7
519-472-1005; Fax: 519-472-5987
Subjects: 99
Territory: 5 reps
Markets: CO-SC-PL-SL
Items: HC-MG-NP
Memo: Subscription serv for libraries. Street address: 10 Rutledge St, Hyde Park ON Canada N0M 1Z0.

G

Glenbow Shop
Carol Smith
130 Ninth Ave SE
Calgary AB Canada T2G 0P3
403-268-4228; Fax: 403-262-4045
Subjects: 11-21-49A
Territory: Western Canada
Markets: MU
Items: HC-PB-CA-GI-GC-MA-PO-TO-TV-OT(jewelry)

H

H A Kidd Company Ltd
Attn: Book Buyer
2 Mark St
Toronto ON Canada M5A 1T8
416-364-6451; Fax: 416-364-4860
Subjects: 29
Territory: CN
Markets: RO
Items: PB-CR-(notions/needlework)

Heritage House Publishing Co
Roger Touchie
17921 55th Ave Unit 8
Surrey BC Canada V3S 6C4
604-574-7067; Fax: 604-574-9942
Subjects: 99
Territory: CN
Markets: BK-CO-PL-SL
Items: PB

I

Inter - Livres
Carmen Ladouceur, Dir
1703 Rue Belleville
Lemoyne PQ Canada J4P 3M2
514-465-0037; Fax: 514-923-8966
Subjects: 99
Territory: CN-IT; 1 rep
Items: HC-PB-MG
Memo: Book buyers come to the center where there is a display of books that they can purchase.

ITMB Publishing Ltd
John G Joyce, Owner/Mgr
736A Granville St
Vancouver BC Canada V6Z 1G3
604-687-3320; Fax: 604-687-5925
Subjects: 71
Territory: US-CN-IT; 2 reps
Markets: BK-CO-SC-PL
Items: HC-PB-MA

J

JLH Law Books Ltd
Jack L Heath, Owner
166 Bullock Dr
Markham ON Canada L3P 1W2
905-472-0219
Subjects: 55L
Territory: IT; 1 rep
Markets: CO-PL-SL(law schools/firms)
Items: HC-PB(some)

John Markham & Associates
John Markham
11210 Elderberry Way
Sidney BC Canada V8L 5J6
604-655-1823; Fax: 604-655-1826
Subjects: 43G
Territory: US-CN-MX; 2 reps
Markets: BK-RO
Items: HC-PB-PO-OT(plant labels)
Memo: 9 titles; 1 publisher represented.

K

Koala Books of Canada Ltd
John J Carolan, Gen Mgr
14327-95A Ave
Edmonton AB Canada T5N 0B6
403-452-5149; Fax: 403-452-5149
Subjects: 21
Territory: 2 reps
Markets: BK-CO-SC-PL-SL
Items: HC-PB-TA-TV

L

Le Diffuseur G Vermette Inc
151A De Martagne Blvd
Boucherville PQ Canada J4B 6G4
514-641-1334; Fax: 514-641-2002
Subjects: 19-23-45-59
Territory: CN
Markets: BK-CO-PL
Items: HC-TX

Les Editions Heritage Inc
Jacques Payette, Pres
300 Arran
St Lambert PQ Canada J4R 1K5
514-672-6710; Fax: 514-672-1481
Subjects: 21-27
Territory: Restricted; 6 reps
Markets: BK-SC(K-12)
Items: PB(children)-MG

Les Editions Levesque Publ
Rodrigue Levesque, Owner
Dufresne 189
Gatineau PQ Canada G8R 3E1
819-663-6748
Subjects: 19-41
Territory: CN; 2 reps
Markets: BK-CO-SC-PL-SL
Items: HC-PB

Librairie Papeterie Le Bouquin
Denise Chiarore, Mgr
395 Blvd Cartier Quest
Laval-Des-Rapides PQ Canada H7N 2K8
514-688-6036; Fax: 514-688-8844
Subjects: 99
Territory: CN
Markets: BK-SC-PL-SL
Items: HC-PB-TX-US-OP

Lilmur Publishing
Murray Horowitz, Mgr
147 Brooke Ave #410
North York ON Canada M5M 2K3
416-486-0145; Fax: 416-486-5380
Subjects: 21-45-79
Territory: CN
Markets: BK-SC-PL
Items: TX-ST

M

Marcel Didier Inc
Herve Foulon, Pres/Gen Mgr
7360 Newman Rd
La Salle PQ Canada H8N 1X2
514-364-0323; Fax: 514-364-7435
Subjects: 45
Territory: 6 reps
Markets: BK-CO-SC-PL-SL
Items: HC-PB-TX

Marginal Distribution
Unit 102 277 George St N
Peterborough ON Canada K9J 3G9
705-745-2326; Fax: 705-745-2326
Subjects: 11-14-75-95
Territory: 2 reps
Markets: BK-CO
Items: PB-MG-NP-RC-TA

McBeth Corp
Don Flicker, Pres
110 Morton Ave E Unit 2
Brantford ON Canada N3R 7J7
519-753-1903; Fax: 519-753-4811
Subjects: 63
Territory: 2 reps
Markets: BK-CO-SC
Items: HC-PB(Christian books)
Memo: Formerly: **Evangel of Canada.**

Meakin & Associates
Donald Meakin, Owner
81 Auriga Dr Unit 17
Nepean ON Canada K2E 7Y5
613-226-4381; Fax: 613-226-1687
Subjects: 63P
Territory: CN
Markets: PL-SL
Items: HC-PB
Memo: 30,000 titles.

Messageries Dynamiques
900 St Martin W Blvd
Lavil PQ Canada H7S 2K9
514-663-9000
Subjects: 99
Territory: Sales area restricted; 87 reps
Markets: BK
Items: PB-MM-MG-NP

Monarch Books of Canada
R Gurfinkel, Mgr
5000 Dufferin St Unit K
Downsview ON Canada M3H 5T5
416-663-8231; Fax: 416-736-1702
Subjects: 99
Territory: CN
Markets: BK-CO-SC-PL-SL
Items: PB-MM

N

Nicholas Hoare Ltd
Nicholas Hoare, Owner
2165 Madison Ave
Montreal PQ Canada H4B 2T2
514-489-9341; Fax: 514-489-1784
Subjects: 99
Territory: CN; 2 reps
Markets: SC-PL
Items: HC-PB

Novalis
Lauretta Santarossa
6255 Hutchison St
Montreal PQ Canada H2V 4C7
514-278-3020; Fax: 514-278-3030
800-387-7164
Subjects: 21-63 (English)
Territory: CN
Markets: CO-mail order
Items: HC-PB-RC-PO-TA
Memo: Catholic publishers/Catholic resource.

O

Ontario Library Services Center
Michael Monahan
141 Dearborn Pl
Waterloo ON Canada N2J 4N5
519-746-4420; Fax: 519-746-4425
Subjects: 31-99
Territory: 2 reps
Markets: SC-PL-SL
Items: PB-MM-RM-TA-TV-SW

P

Pan Asian Publications Inc
Sheng D Chiu, Owner/Mgr
110 Silver Star Blvd Unit 109
PO Box 131 Agincourt Sta
Scarborough ON Canada M1S 3B4
416-292-4468; Fax: 416-292-2191
Subjects: 44A-45(Far East)-49O-75
Territory: 2 reps
Markets: PL-CO-SL-RO
Items: HC-PB-BT-SW-CD ROM-TA-TV
Memo: Branch: Union City, CA. Bi-lingual childrens' books.

Pannonia Books
Kate Karacsony, Owner
Postal Station B
PO Box 1017
Toronto ON Canada M5T 2T8
416-966-5156
Subjects: 44-45(Hungarian)-80
Territory: CN
Markets: RO-MO
Items: HC-PB,-TV-TA-CD-MA-GI

Prairie House Books
Wayne Magnuson
Box 84007 Sta G
Calgary AB Canada T3A 5C4
403-229-2040; Fax: 403-247-3675
Subjects: 31-59 (reference books)
Territory: CN
Markets: BK-SL
Items: PB

Promotional Book Co
R A C Dingman, Co-Owner
36 N Line Rd
Toronto ON Canada M4B 3E2
416-759-2226; Fax: 416-759-2150
Subjects: 99
Territory: 5 reps
Markets: BK
Items: RM(reprints)

R

Renouf Publishing Co Ltd
Gordon Grahame, Pres
1294 Algoma Rd
Ottawa ON Canada K1B 3W8
613-741-4333; Fax: 613-741-5439
Subjects: 19-55
Territory: US
Markets: CO-SL-PL
Items: HC-PB
Memo: Distribute to 200 publishers.

S

Saunders Book Co
Buyer
199 Campbell St
PO Box 308
Collingwood ON Canada L9Y 3Z7
705-445-4777; Fax: 705-445-9569
Subjects: 21-31-76-89
Territory: 12 reps
Markets: SC-PL
Items: HC-PB

Scholar's Choice Ltd
Scott Webster
2323 Trafalgar St
PO Box 4214
London ON Canada N5W 5W3
519-453-7470; Fax: 800-363-3398
Subjects: 21-31-65
Territory: CN
Markets: SC-public
Items: HC-TA-TV

Shirley Lewis Information Serv
Richard Jones
3081A Universal Dr
Mississauga ON Canada L4X 2E2
905-629-9119; Fax: 905-629-8001
Subjects: 21-31
Territory: Restricted-Canada only; 3 reps
Markets: PL-SL
Items: HC-PB-RM-TA-TV

Stanton & McDougall Ltd
Allan McDougall, Mgr
112 East Third Ave
Vancouver BC Canada V5T 1C8
604-874-1111
Subjects: 99
Territory: CN
Markets: BK
Items: HC-PB

T

Teacher's Book Depository
Charbel L Ahmar, Buyer
12245 131st St
Edmonton AB Canada T5L 1M8
403-453-7092; Fax: 403-451-3958
Subjects: 99
Territory: CN
Markets: CO-SC-PL-SL
Items: HC-PB-TX(few)-MA-TA

Terrific Titles for Young Reader
Barbara Jacob, Mgr
52 Hazelton Ave
Toronto ON Canada M5R 2E2
416-921-9557
Subjects: 21
Territory: CN
Markets: SC
Items: BK

Troyka Ltd
Lisa Kotonikolas, Mgr/Buyer
799 A College St
Toronto ON Canada M6G 1C7
416-535-6693; Fax: 416-535-3265
Subjects: 11-21-27-67
Territory: 4 reps
Markets: RO
Items: HC-PB-TX-GI-GC-MA-RC

True Remainders Ltd
43 Main St
PO Box 500
Jordan ON Canada L0R 1S0
416-562-5719; Fax: 416-562-7828
Subjects:99
Territory: 5 reps
Markets: BK
Items: RM

U

United Library Services Inc
Hal Whyte, Gen Mgr
7140 Fairmont Dr SE
Calgary AB Canada T2H 0X4
403-252-4426; Fax: 403-258-3426
Subjects: 75
Territory: Restricted Western Canada; 3 reps
Markets: SC-CO-PL-SL
Items: HC-PB

University Book Sales & Services
Louis Girard, Mgr
4823 rue Sherbrooke Quest
Bureau 110
Westmount PQ Canada H3Z 1G7
514-932-6308; Fax: 514-932-5929
Subjects: 11-39-45-47-67
Territory: CN
Markets: BK-CO-SC-PL-SL
Items: HC-PB

V

V & L Information Resources Corp
Lali Bhatia, Foreign Dist
7280 Victoria Park Ave Unit F
Markham ON Canada L3R 2M5
905-940-9809; Fax: 905-940-2329
Subjects: 99
Territory: 2 reps
Markets: PL-SL
Items: HC-PB
Items: PB

W

Windsor News
Evelyn Jeffery, Book Buyer
Jeff Mitchell
3350 N Talbot Rd
RR 1
Oldcastle ON Canada N0R 1L0
519-737-6921; Fax: 519-737-1612
Subjects: 99(Windsor & Essex counties)
Territory: 2 reps
Markets: CO-SC-PL-SL-NS-MM
Items: HC-PB-MM-RM-CA-MG-MA-RC-SB-TV-OT
Memo: 325 accounts served; 3500 titles; represents all publishers.

Abbreviations Used

Territory

CN	Canada
IT	International
MX	Mexico
OT	Other
US	United States with some state abbreviations for the different states

Markets

BK	Bookstores
CO	Colleges
JB	Jobbers
MM	Mass Markets
NS	Newsstands
OT	Other
PL	Public Libraries
RO	Retail Outlets
SC	Schools
SL	Special Libraries

Items

CA	Calendars
CO	Comics
CR	Craft Items
GA	Games
GC	Greeting Cards
GI	Gifts
HC	Hardcovers
MA	Maps and Atlases
MG	General / Special Magazines
ML	Literary Magazines
MM	Mass Market Books
NP	Newspapers
OP	Out of Print Books
OT	Other Items
PB	Trade Paperbacks
PO	Posters
RC	Records
RM	Remainders
SB	Stickers/Bookmarks
ST	Stationery
SW	Software
TA	Tapes, Audio
TO	Toys
TV	Tapes, Video
TX	Textbooks
US	Used books

Independent Distributors (Jobbers)

The following companies distribute magazines, mass-market paperbacks, and some trade books to local food stores, mini-marts, drug stores, newsstands, airport shops, and other retail outlets that feature magazines and mass-market paperbacks. Some of these companies are open to working with regional publishers to distribute cookbooks, travel guides, and other appropriate regional books (as well as some general books appropriate for their markets).

Alabama

Jefferson News Co Inc
Thomas Clark Jr, Owner
2316 First Ave S
Birmingham AL 35233
205-252-9265; Fax: 205-252-1291
Markets: BK-CO-NS-RO
Items: MM-MG-NP

Newsdealers Supply Company
Douglas Lurie/Ron Thomas/Owners
5822 W Main St
Dothan AL 36301-9304
334-792-5279; Fax: 334-792-3811
Territory: AL
Markets: RO
Items: MM-MG

Bookworld
Sammy & Gloria Nabors, Owners
PO Box 12236
Huntsville AL 35815
205-883-8555; Fax: 205-883-8555
Territory: AL
Markets: BK-RO(factory outlets)
Items: HC-PB-MG

Gulf Coast News
Book Buyer
3001 Mill St
Mobile AL 36607
334-479-1435
Territory: AL
Markets: BK-PL-SL-SC-CO-RO
Items: PB-CA-MA-MG-PO TA-TV-OT
Memo: Formerly the **Mobile News Co**.

Montgomery News Co Inc
Max Morton Jr, Gen Mgr
874 Martha St
PO Box 1149
Montgomery AL 36101-1149
334-262-6681; Fax: 334-269-9673
Territory: Sales area restricted; 12 reps
Markets: BK-CO-SC-PL-SL-RO
Items: MM-MG-PB-NP

Read News Agency
Martha Hallman
1110 14th St
PO Box 1339
Tuscaloosa AL 35403
205-752-3515
Territory: 12 reps
Markets: PL-SL-BK-CO-SC-RO
Items: HC-MM-MG-TX-NP-PB

Alaska

Alaska News Agency
Bob Johnson, Book Buyer
325 W Potter Dr
Anchorage AK 99518-1196
907-563-3251; Fax: 907-261-8523
Territory: AK; 10 reps
Markets: BK-CO-SC-PL-RO(supermarkets)-SL
Items: HC-PB-MM-RM-MG-BT

Fairbanks News Agency
Stan Lakefish, Owner
307 Ladd Ave
Fairbanks AK 99701-6617
907-452-4589; Fax: 907-452-4792
Territory: AK; 3 reps
Markets: BK-JB-NS-SC-CO-MM-PL
Items: PB-RM-MM-MG-CA-CO-MA-SB

Arkansas

Ozark News Agency Inc
T R Marshall, Gen Mgr
397 W Poplar
PO Box 1150
Fayetteville AR 72703
501-442-6441; Fax: 501-442-8137
Territory: Sales area restricted; 12 reps
Markets: BK-SC-CO-RO(groc stores)
Items: MM-MG

Lilly News
Todd Austin
4113 Service Rd
PO Box 2218
Jonesboro AR 72402-2218
501-932-9071
Territory: NE AR & SE MO; 6 reps
Markets: BK-RO(groc/drug stores)
Items: HC-MM-MG-PB-OT(ball cards)

Anderson News Company
Morris Hunter, Gen Mgr
10725 Ottee Creek E Blvd
PO Box 970
Mabelvale AR 72103-0970
501-455-5500; Fax: 501-455-5542
Territory: AR
Markets: RO-MM-BK
Items: HC-PB-MM-MG-TV

Arizona

Northern Arizona News Co
Beth Humphrey
1709 N East St
PO Box 1947
Flagstaff AZ 86004
602-774-6171; Fax: 602-779-1958
Territory: Sales area restricted; 3 reps
Markets: PL-SL-CO-SC-RO(supermarkets)
Items: HC-MM-MG-NP

Central Arizona Distributing
Book Buyer
4932 W Pasadena Ave
Glendale AZ 85301-7621
602-939-6511
Territory: AZ
Markets: BK-RO
Items: HC-PB-MM-MG-NP

Anderson News
Chuck Bullard, Book Buyer
1857 W Grant Rd (85745)
PO Box 5465
Tucson AZ 85703
520-622-2831; Fax: 520-623-2964
Territory: SW-US
Markets: BK-MM-RO-NS-CO-SC-PL-SL
Items: PB-MM-MG-NP
Memo: Headquarters - Knoxville, TN.

Desert News
Tara Cox, Mgr/Book Buyer
3242 S Richey Blvd
Tucson AZ 85713
602-747-0428
Territory: Restricted: Tucson & Phoenix Metro; 4 reps
Markets: BK
Items: MG-NP

Arizona Periodicals
Brian Weiner, Owner
2020 Factor Ave
Yuma AZ 85365
602-782-1822
Territory: Nevada/Arizona; 5 reps
Markets: CO-RO-MM
Items: PB-MM-MG-TX-NP
Memo: Books bought by Weiner News (Periodical Management Group).

California

United News Co
Pearl Lesler, Book Buyer
111 Lake St
PO Box 3426
Bakersfield CA 93385
805-323-7864; Fax: 805-323-0569
Territory: Sales area restricted; 6 reps
Markets: BK-PL-SL-CO-SC
Items: HC-MM-MG-PB

Aramark
Roger Rimball, Buyer
2970 N Ontario St
PO Box 3167
Burbank CA 91504
818-845-8347
Territory: CA
Markets: BK-NS-SC-CO-MM-PL-SL
Items: HC-MM-MG-PB

Red Rose Distributing
Dean Daniels, Sales Mgr or Pat Ogata, Mdse Dir
42 Adrian Ct
Burlingame CA 94010
800-451-5683; Fax: 415-692-9482
800-374-5505
Territory: CA; 5 reps
Markets: BK-MM-RO(gift shops)
Items: HC-PB-CA-GI-GC-PO-RC-TA-TV-OT
Memo: 1,500 accounts served; 30+ titles carried; 30+ publishers represented.

ART CONSULTING: SCANDINAVIA
Lena Torslow Hansen, Owner
25777 Punto de Vista
Calabasas CA 91302
818-222-1122; Fax: 818-222-2577
Territory: US-CN-ASIA
Markets: BK-PL-CO(library)-JB-MU
Items: HC-PB-PC-MG(special)
Memo: Books on Art & Architecture; also markets Individual persons; applied arts & photography books.

Chico News Agency Inc
Robert Sylvester, Owner
1205 W Seventh St (95928)
PO Box 690
Chico CA 95927
916-895-1000; Fax: 916-895-0158
Territory: CA & NV; 6 reps
Markets: BK-SL-PL-CO-SC-MM
Items: HC-MM-MG-PB-NP(tabloids)
Memo: Branch: Readmore Books, 704 Mangrove, Chico, CA 95928; 916-894-7323.

Armadillo & Company
Edward Ferrer, Buyer
5795 West Washington Blvd
Culver City CA 90232
213-937-7674
Territory: US-S California
Markets: BK-NS-RO
Items: HC-PB-MG

Van Dyke News Company
William R Van Dyke, Owner
5671 E Fountain Way
Fresno CA 93727-7894
209-291-7768

Territory: Sales area restricted; 4 reps
Markets: BK-CO-SC-NS
Items: HC-MM-MG-TX-PB

Santa Barbara News Agency
George Erhart, Owner
879 S Kellogg Ave
Goleta CA 93117
805-967-2367; Fax: 805-683-0877
Territory: Sales area restricted
Markets: BK-PL-SL-SC-CO-RO
Items: HC-MM-MG-PB-CO-MA

Desert News Company
Gordon Harrison, Owner
206 E Ave K-4 (93535)
PO Box 2197
Lancaster CA 93539-2197
805-945-4571; Fax: 805-945-9799
Territory: Southern CA; 3 reps
Markets: BK-NS-SC-CO-MM-RO(own) OT(USAF
Items: HC-PB-MM-MG-CA-CO-MA-SW-TA-TV-OT

Aramark
2340 S Fairfax Ave
PO Box 78003
Los Angeles CA 90016
213-936-6171; Fax: 213-936-5363
Territory: West Coast
Markets: CH-NS-RO
Items: PB-MM only

Merced News Co
Lee Carey, Book Buyer/Owner
1619 I St
PO Box 857
Merced CA 95340
209-722-5791; Fax: 209-722-1359
Territory: Merced County only - 4 reps
Markets: PL-SL-BK-CO-SC
Items: MM-MG-NP-PB

East Texas Distributing
George Klein/Chas Levy, Owners
1035 Reno Ave
PO Box 5038
Modesto CA 95352-5038
209-577-5551; Fax: 209-577-4194
Territory: Sales area restricted; 4 reps
Markets: BK-CO-SC-RO
Items: HC-MM-MG-TX-PB-NP
Memo: The company has been here 50 years & ETD has owned & operated it since 1990. Formerly known as **Modesto News Co**.

Bell Magazine Agency Inc
Richard Heiland, Owner
3 Justin Ct
Ryan Ranch
Monterey CA 93940
408-642-4668; Fax: 408-642-4672
Territory: CA
Markets: BK-CO-SC-PL-SL
Items: HC-MG-NP-PB-OT(postcards)

Cal-West Periodicals
Stewart Bennett, Book Buyer
2400 Filbert St
Oakland CA 94607
510-444-3570; Fax: 510-465-1982
Territory: CA; 10 reps
Markets: BK-RO(Safeway's, etc)
Items: HC-MM-MG

Pomona Valley News Agency Inc
Jack Gingold, Owner/Buyer; Hardcover and Trade Books
Shirley Inglehart, Buyer, Mass Market
10736 Fremont Ave
Ontario CA 91762-3909
909-591-3885; Fax: 909-627-1319
800-545-3396
Territory: Sales area restricted; West Coast
Markets: BK-PL-RO-SC
Items: HC-MM-MG-PB-NP-TV

NorCal News Co
Robert Erwin, Mgr
2040 Petaluma Blvd N
PO Box 2508
Petaluma CA 94953-2508
707-763-2606
Territory: Sales area restricted; 10 reps
Markets: CO-BK
Items: MM-MG-PB-RM

Aramark
Jerry Jacobs, Gen Mgr
6211 Power Inn Rd
PO Box 245230
Sacramento CA 95824-5230
916-381-3810
Territory: CA
Markets: BK-SC-CO-MM-RD
Items: HC-MM-MG-TA-SB-RM-CO-PB

Aramark
Wayne Allen, Gen Mgr
4645 Morena Blvd
PO Box 85408
San Diego CA 92186-5408
619-275-3090
Territory: CA; 24 reps
Markets: SC-RO
Items: HC-MM-MG-PB-RM-CO-TA-SB

Solana Periodicals
Sam & Joan Solana, Owners
7060 Convoy Ct
San Diego CA 92111
619-278-9050
800-333-9345
Territory: CA
Items: HC-MM-MG-RO

Iaconi Book Imports
Mariuccia Iaconi, Owner
970 Tennessee St
San Francisco CA 94107
415-821-1216; Fax: 415-821-1596
800-955-9577
E-Mail: mibibook@ix.netcom.com
Territory: US; 5 reps
Markets: SC-PL
Items: HC-PB-TA-TV-RC-SW-TX

Milligan News Company
Pat Milligan, Owner
150 N Autumn St
San Jose CA 95110-2388
408-298-3322; Fax: 408-286-7604
Territory: US-CA; 20 reps
Markets: BK-SC-CO-PL-SL
Items: HC-PB-RM-MM-MG-CA-CO-MA-TA-TV

Peninsula News Co
Sam Smith
1944 Leslie St
San Mateo CA 94403
415-349-7023; Fax: 415-349-7025
Territory: 6 reps
Markets: BK-CO-RO(retail & chain stores)
Items: HC-MM-PB-CA-CO-MA-SB

Serendipity Courier News
Sam Solana, Pres
470 Dubois St
San Rafael CA 94901
415-459-4000; Fax: 415-459-0833
Territory: 14 reps
Markets: BK-CO-SL
Items: HC-MM-MG-NP-TV

Tri-County News Co Inc
George W Marcum, Owner
1376 W Main St
Santa Maria CA 93454
805-925-6541; Fax: 805-925-6571
Territory: Sales area restricted; 7 reps
Markets: BK-SL-PL-CO-SC
Items: MM-MG-NP-PB

Schulze News Co Inc
David R Schulze
2907 Palma Dr
Ventura CA 93003
805-642-9759; Fax: 805-656-7045
Territory: Sales area restricted; 9 reps
Markets: CO-SC
Items: HC-MM-MG-PB-CA-CO-MA-TA-OT

Tulare County News Agency Inc
Mark Manning
637 S Lovers Ln
PO Box 831
Visalia CA 93279-0831
209-734-9206; Fax: 209-734-5732
Territory: Sales area restricted; 7 reps
Markets: BK-PL-SL-RO(chain stores)
Items: HC-MM-MG-CA-CO-MA-TA-OT

Drown News Agency
Jack A Drown, Owner
15172 Golden West Cir
Westminster CA 92683
714-892-7766; Fax: 714-894-6542
Territory: Sales area restricted; 42 reps
Markets: BK-PL-SL-CO-SC
Items: MM-MG-NP-PB

Kolb News Agency Inc
Ted or Craig Kolb, Owners
7044 Elmer Ave
Whittier CA 90602
310-693-1786; Fax: 310-945-3846
Territory: Sales area restricted; 6 reps
Markets: BK-PL-SL-CO-SC-RO
Items: HC-MM-MG-PB-RM-TV

Colorado

Anderson News Co
Rene Morgan, Office Mgr
1671 Valtec Ln
PO Box 9050
Boulder CO 80301-9050
303-449-1973; Fax: 303-449-3175
Territory: CO & surrounding areas; 18 reps
Markets: RO; Items: HC-MM-MG-PB-NP

Anderson News
Bill Laedie, Mgr, or Frank Timpano, Gen Mgr
Denver News Company
3601 E 46th Ave
Denver CO 80216-6595
303-321-1111
Territory: West US
Markets: MM-BK-SL-PL-SC-CO-SM
Items: HC-PB-MM-MG-TA
Memo: Anderson News Corporate Office is in Knoxville, TN.

Anderson News
Larry Flori, Buyer
208 Racquet Dr
PO Box 2105
Fort Collins CO 80522
303-221-2330; Fax: 303-221-1251
Territory: Northern CO & Southern WY
Markets: BK-CO-SC-MM-RO
Items: MM-MG-NP-HC-PB

Alpine News Distributors
Jay Rench, Gen Mgr
0105 Marand Rd
PO Box 1049
Glenwood Springs CO 81602
970-945-2269; Fax: 970-945-6441
Territory: CO; 7 reps
Markets: BK-CO-MM-RO
Items: HC-PB-MM-RM-MG

Colorado Periodical Distributors
Tim Osborne, Mgr
827 N First St (81501)
PO Box 2925
Grand Junction CO 81502
970-242-3865; Fax: 970-242-3760
Territory: 6 reps
Markets: BK-CO-SC-RO
Items: HC-PB-MM-TV

District of Columbia

Aramark
Robert Nashwinter, Gen Mgr
Box 1805
Washington DC 20013
301-277-4800; Fax: 301-779-5360
Territory:48 reps
Markets: BK-CO-SC-SL-PL-MM-RO
Items: HC-MM-MG-NP-PB-CO-RM-TA-SB
Memo: Physical location is in Brentwood, MD.

Florida

Anderson News
Maurice Agens, Mgr
1840 Mason Ave
PO Box 9850
Daytona Beach FL 32117
904-274-4526; Fax: 904-274-4752
Territory: Daytona beach & surrounding counties; 8 reps
Markets: BK-NS-RO-SC
Items: MM-MG-NP-PB-OT(trading cards)

Southeast Periodical & Book Sale
Arthur S Gelfand, Owner
10100 NW 25th St
PO Box 520155 Biscayne Annex
Miami FL 33152
305-592-8260; Fax: 305-477-0141
Territory: Sales area restricted; 56 reps
Markets: BK-CO-SC-NS-RO(airports)
Items: HC-MM-MG-PB-NP-CO-TA

News South Distributors
Jim Pattison Group, Owner
410 NW 27th Ave
PO Box 2198
Ocala FL 32678
904-732-3940; Fax: 904-351-1579
Territory: FL; 18 reps
Markets: BK-RO-MM-PL-SL-CO-SC
Items: HC-PB-MM-MG-ML-NP-TA

Anderson News
Book Buyer
3840 Vineland Rd
PO Box 681548
Orlando FL 32868-1548
407-841-8738; Fax: 407-872-0378
Territory: FL; 40 reps
Markets: BK-NS-SC-MM-CO
Items: HC-PB-RM-MM-MG-CO-GC-NP-TA-TV

Anderson News
Marty Thurber, Mgr
6355 N Palafox St
Pensacola FL 32503
904-477-0920; Fax: 904-484-9721
Territory: FL
Markets: SC-SL-RO-MM
Items: HC-MM-MG-PB-NP

Anderson News
Diane Hopkins, Buyer
3600 - 75th Terrace N
PO Box 5000
Pinellas Park FL 34664-5000
813-577-6808; Fax: 813-229-0248
Territory: South US - 26 reps
Markets: BK-MM-SC-PL-SL
Items: HC-MM-MG-TA-TV

Anderson News
Keith Rousseau, Mgr
395 Gus Hipp Blvd
PO Box 837
Rockledge FL 32955-0837
407-636-5909; Fax: 407-633-1418
Territory: 1 rep; Brevard Co SE US
Markets: BK-CO-SC-PL-SL-RO-MM
Items: HC-MM-MG-TX-TV-MG-PB

ETD Gulf Coast Dist Div
Charles Walker, Agency Mgr
2001 Limbus Ave
Sarasota FL 24243
800 755-4145; Fax: 914-758-1311
Territory: Sales area restricted; 12 reps
Markets: BK-RO-MM
Items: HC-MM-MG
Memo: Formerly: **Lakeland News Co**.

Anderson News
Raymond Chase, Mgr
3777 Hartsfield Rd
Tallahassee FL 32303
904-575-8070; Fax: 904-575-6541
Territory: FL
Markets: BK-SC-PL-SL-RO-MM
Items: HC-MM-MG-PB-MG-NP

Anderson News Co
Diane Hopkins, Book Buyer
7002 Parke East Blvd
PO Box 25738
Tampa FL 33622-5738
813-622-8087; Fax: 813-628-4145
Territory: US-IN
Markets: MM-RO
Items: HC-PB-MM-MG-NP

Georgia

Southeastern News
Bruce Sherbow
4070 Shirley Dr SW
Atlanta GA 30336
404-691-2800; Fax: 404-691-3147
Territory: SE-US; 200 reps
Markets: BK-NS-CO-SC-RO
Items: HC-PB-MM-MG-RM-CA-CO-GI-MA-SB-TA

Anderson News Co
5675 Transport Blvd
Columbus GA 31907
706-562-0004
Territory: GA
Markets: BK-CO-SC-PL-MM-RO
Items: HC-MM-MG-PB-RM-TA-TV

Service News Co
Spencer Reeves, Mgr
1745 Clinton Rd (31211)
PO Box 5027
Macon GA 31208-5027
912-743-6943; Fax: 912-743-8095
Territory: GA
Markets: RO
Items: HC-MM-MG

Rome News
Lindsay Preiss, Mgr
12 Redmond Ct
Rome GA 30165
706-232-1614; Fax: 706-232-1911
Territory: Sales area restricted
Markets: BK-RO
Items: MM-MG-PB-CO-MA
Memo: Arthur Preiss, Owner.

Idaho

Treasure Valley News
John Plaa
11420 W Executive Dr
Boise ID 83713
208-323-8480; Fax: 208-323-8499
Territory: ID
Markets: BK-RO
Items: HC-PB-MM-MG-CA-CO-MA-TA-SB-OT

Johnson News
Karl Johnson, Owner
2710 Julia St
Coeur D'Alene ID 83814
208-664-3444; Fax: 208-667-7253
Territory: Sales area restricted
Markets: PL-SL-BK-CO-SC
Items: HC-MG-PB
Memo: 80% mags - 20% books.

Johnson News Agency Inc
Karl Johnson, Owner
1320 Mountain View Rd
PO Box 9009
Moscow ID 83843
208-882-7088; Fax: 208-883-8380
Territory: Sales area restricted; 2 reps
Markets: BK-CO-SC-NS-RO
Items: MM-MG-PB-RM-CA-CO-MA-SW

Illinois

Central Illinois Periodicals
Craig Tharp, Book Buyer
304 S Mason
Bloomington IL 61701
309-829-9405; Fax: 309-828-6541
Territory: IL
Markets: BK-CO-SC-PL-SL
Items: HC-MM-MG-TX-MG-NP

Charles Levy Circulating Co
Shelly Ziech, Buyer
1200 Northbranch
Chicago IL 60622
312-440-4400; Fax: 312-440-7443
Territory: IL-IN
Markets: BK-RO-MM
Items: HC-MM-MG-trading cards

Cummins News
Mike Wilson, Mgr
815 E Voorhees St
PO Box 1695
Danville IL 61832-1695
217-446-4131
Territory: Restricted area IL; 6 reps
Markets: SL-PL-BK
Items: MM-MG-NP

Levy Home Entertainment
Diane Hund, Business Book Buyer
4201 Raymond Dr
Hillside IL 60162
708-547-4400; Fax: 708-547-4503
Territory: IL
Items: HC-PB-RM

Austin Periodical Services
Bob Austin, Owner
Highway 37 N
Johnston City IL 62951
618-983-6976
Territory: IL
Items: HC-PB-MM-MG-NP

Specialty Marketing Company
Ed Schondorf, Pres
PO Box 469
Oak Forest IL 60452
708-633-8670; Fax: 708-633-8672
Territory: IL
Markets: JB-wholesalers
Items: MG-catalogs
Memo: Located at 16555 S Oak Park Ave, Tenly Park, IL 60477.

Illinois News Service
George I Seidler, Owner
1301 SW Washington St
Peoria IL 61602-1795
309-673-4549; Fax: 309-673-8883
Territory: Sales area restricted; 1 reps
Markets: BK-CO-SC-PL
Items: MM-MG-PB

Austin Periodical Services
Garry Ratcliffe, Mgr
701 E Princeton
PO Box 31
Springfield IL 62705-0031
217-525-1417
Territory: Midwest
Markets: BK-CO-SC-PL-RO
Items: HC-PB-MM-MG-NP

North Shore Distributors Inc
James Levy, Owner/Pres
411 N Wolf Rd
Wheeling IL 60090
708-537-6900
Territory: 25 reps
Markets: BK
Items: MG-NP-PB

Indiana

Cummins News
Sue Chord, Book Buyer
524 N Fairview St
PO Box 1937
Bloomington IN 47402
812-332-4775; Fax: 812-332-7282
Territory: Southern IN; 7 reps
Markets: SL-PL-CO-SC-BK-RO
Items: HC-PB-MG-TX-NP

Anderson News Co
JoAnn Claridge, Book Buyer
9844 Heddon Rd
PO Box 1110
Evansville IN 47706-1110
812-867-7416; Fax: 812-867-7419
Territory: 14 reps
Markets: BK; Items: MM-MG-PB

Indiana Periodicals Distributors
Dennis Nuttall, Book Buyer
2120 S Meridian St
PO Box 966
Indianapolis IN 46206
317-786-1488; Fax: 317-782-4999
Territory: IN-restricted
Markets: BK-SC-PL-SL
Items: HC-PB-MG
Memo: Owned by the Stoll Company.

Twin City News Agency
Robert Feuer, Pres
316 N 3rd St
PO Box 466
Lafayette IN 47901
317-742-1051
Territory: Indiana area; 5 reps
Markets: BK-CO-SC-PL-NS-RO
Items: HC-MM-MG-NP-CO-MA

Beaver News
Charles Beaver Jr, Mgr
230 W Washington St
Rensselaer IN 47978
219-866-8114
Territory: IN
Markets: MM-MG-JB-RO-MM-OT
Items: PB

Vincennes News Agency
George Ragin, Mgr
1217 College Ave
PO Box 245
Vincennes IN 47591
812-882-2434
Territory: 4 reps
Markets: BK-CO-SC-PL-MM
Items: MM-MG-NP

Iowa

Ames News Agency
Gary Hurlbut, Mgr
2110 E 13th St
Ames IA 50010-5698
515-232-1788; Fax: 515-232-8020
Territory: IA; 2 reps
Markets: BK-PL-SL-SC-RO-CO
Items: HC-MM-MG

Husker News Company
Frank Leiferman, Mgr
1406 SW 7th St
Atlantic IA 50022
712-243-5557; Fax: 712-243-5559
Territory: Restricted to IA; 6 reps
Markets: PL-SL-BK-CO-SC-RO
Items: MG-NP-PB

Wholesale Distributors
Tina Wookey, Buyer
13035 Highway 61 N
PO Box 126
Burlington IA 52601-0126
319-753-1683
Territory: IA-IL-MO; 5 reps
Markets: BK-MM-SC-CO-PL-RO
Items: HC-MM-MG-NP-PB

Interstate Periodicals Dist Inc
Randy Duncan
8645 Northwest Blvd
PO Box 2470
Davenport IA 52809
319-391-3723; Fax: 319-391-3714
Territory: Midwest; 7 reps
Markets: BK-MM-NS-PL-SL-CO-SC-RO
Items: MM-PB-MG-TA-TV-NP-OT
Memo: Formerly: **Iowa & Illinios News.**

Iowa Periodicals Inc
Stanley Seidler, Owner
3301 McKinley Ave (50321)
PO Box 1297
Des Moines IA 50305
515-287-6655; Fax: 515-287-2747
Territory: Midwest; 12 reps
Markets: BK-MM-NS-CO(special)-SC
Items: HC-MM-PB-MG-CA-CO-MA-SB-SW(spec)

Norton News Agency Inc
Terry Norton, Mdse Dir
Peter Norton, Owner/Buyer
801 Cedar Cross Rd
Dubuque IA 52004-0569
319-556-8300; Fax: 319-556-8303
Territory: Midwest; 8 reps
Markets: BK-CO-SC-PL-SL-NS
Items: HC-MM-PB-TX-RM-SW-MG-TA-TV-OT
Memo: 600 accounts served, 5,000 titles; 65 publishers represented.

Nelson News Agency Inc
Christopher Nelson
728 First Ave N
Fort Dodge IA 50501-3820
515-573-7822; Fax: 515-573-8405
Territory: Midwest; 4 reps
Markets: BK-MM-NS-PL-SL-CO-SC
Items: MM-PB-MG-RM

Kansas

Kansas City Periodical Dist Co
Mikki Williams, Dir Mktg
9605 Dice Ln
PO Box 14948
Lenexa KS 66215
913-541-8600; Fax: 913-541-9413
Territory: Midwest-KS & MO; 36 reps
Markets: BK-MM-NS-RO
Items: MM-MG-PB-TV-TA-OT(trading cards)

Palmer News
Hank Lumkin, Book Mgr
1050 SE Republican St
PO Box 1400
Topeka KS 66607
913-234-6679; Fax: 913-234-6338
Territory: Midwest; 36 reps
Markets: BK-MM-NS-PL-SL-CO-RO
Items: MM-PB-MG

M S News Company, Inc
Robert L Hampton, Gen Mgr
3629 W 30th St S
Wichita KS 67217-1015
316-945-7108; Fax: 316-945-0662
Territory: KS
Markets: RO-MM
Items: PB-MM

Kentucky

Anderson News Co
Charlie Anderson, CEO
1236 Versailles Rd
Lexington KY 40508
606-254-2765; Fax: 606-254-3324
Territory: KY; 11 reps
Markets: SC-CO-PL-SL-BK
Items: HC-PB-RM-MM-MG-ML-CA-CO-MA-SB

Louisville News Company
Jane E Donaldson, Mgr
2106 Production Dr
PO Box 99008
Louisville KY 40299-0008
502-491-1950; Fax: 502-491-2028
Territory: 24 reps
Markets: BK-CO-SC-PL-RO-MM
Items: PB-TX-MG

East Kentucky News
Robin T Cooper, Owner
Kevin Wallen, Paperback/Children's Buyer
PO Box 510
Paintsville KY 41240-0510
606-789-8169; Fax: 606-789-1473
Territory: Eastern KY; 8 reps (approx)
Markets: BK-CO-SC-RO-MM
Items: HC-MM-MG-PB-NP-GC-TV-GA

Louisiana

Louisiana Periodicals
Brian Weiner, Owner
8201 Wyngate Blvd
PO Box 3723
Shreveport LA 71108
318-688-9560; Fax: 318-688-9561
Territory: 8 reps
Markets: BK-CO-RO-MM
Items: HC-MM-MG-PB-OT(trading cards)

Bayou Periodicals
John Kroger, Owner
180 James Dr E
St Rose LA 70087
504-467-5863; Fax: 504-464-6196
Territory: Restricted; 42 reps
Markets: BK-CO-SC-PL
Items: HC-MM-MG-PB-NP
Memo: Formerly: **Graham News Co.**

Maine

Augusta News
Howard Kunitz, Owner
569 Riverside Dr
PO Box 855
Augusta ME 04330
207-623-8493; Fax: 207-622-9759
Territory: US; 3 reps
Markets: BK
Items: MM-MG-NP

Magazines Inc
Jim McCree, Book Buyer
1135 Hammond St
Bangor ME 04401
207-942-8237; Fax: 207-942-9226
Territory: US
Markets: BK-NS-MM-SC-PL-SL
Items: HC-MM-MG-NP

Portland News Company
Ralph Bartholomew, Gen Mgr
10 Southgate Rd
PO Box 6970
Scarborough ME 04074
207-883-1300; Fax: 207-883-1321
Territory: New England
Markets: BK-SC-PL-SL-RO
Items: HC-PB-MM-MG-ML-NP-TX-TA-CA(specialty/seasonal)-(trading cards

Maryland

Maryland News Distributing Co
Wayne Mathias, Book Dept Mgr
4000 Coolidge Ave
PO Box 1777
Baltimore MD 21203
410-536-4545; Fax: 410-247-2950
Territory: 15 reps
Markets: BK-RO-PL-SL-NS
Items: HC-SW-TA

Mardelva News
Richard Mercer, Mgr
610 Beam St
PO Box 1758
Salisbury MD 21802
410-742-8613; Fax: 410-742-2616
Territory: 7 reps
Markets: BK-CO-SC-RO
Items: HC-MM-MG-NP-OT(baseball cards)

Massachusetts

Atlas News Agency
Robert Cohen, Owner
50 Shrewsbury St
Boylston MA 01505-1702
508-869-2195; Fax: 508-869-6969
Territory: New England; 2 reps
Markets: BK-CO-SC-PL-SL-RO
Items: PB-MM-MG-NP

Big Colony News
Kenneth A Martin, Owner
49 Potomska St
PO Box H-3051
New Bedford MA 02741
508-997-9346; Fax: 508-997-4153
Territory: New Bedford & surrounding area; 3 reps
Markets: BK-CO-SC-SL-MM
Items: HC-MM-MG-NP

Fall River News
David Boland, Owner
144 Robeson St
Box 1070
Fall River MA 02720-4925
508-679-5266
Territory: MA-RI
Markets: BK-NS-SC-CO-MM
Items: PB-MM-NP

Holyoke News Company
Jim Morten, Book Mgr
720 Main St
PO Box 990
Holyoke MA 01041-0090
413-534-4537; Fax: 413-538-7161
Territory: US(school accounts)
Markets: SC
Items: HC-PB-MM-MG

Interstate Distributors
Robert Cohen, Owner
199 Commander Shea Blvd
North Quincy MA 02171-1517
617-328-9500; Fax: 617-328-3026
Territory: US(Boston area)
Markets: BK-SC-PL-SL-CO-NS-MM
Items: HC-MM-MG-TA

Mullare News Agency Inc
David Mullare, Owner
35 Oak Hill Way
Box 578
Brockton MA 02401
508-580-1000; Fax: 508-586-0968
Territory: MA
Markets: BK-SC-CO-MM-RO
Items: MM-MG-PB-NP

North Shore News Company Inc
Thomas A Mulkern Sr and Thomas A Mulkern Jr, Owners
150 Blossom St
Lynn MA 01902
617-592-1300; Fax: 617-598-6510
Territory: 2 reps
Markets: BK-CO-SC
Items: HC-MM-MG-PB-NP

Pittsfield News
Steve Nichols, Book Buyer
6 Westview Rd
Pittsfield MA 01201
413-445-5682; Fax: 413-445-5683
Territory: MA
Markets: BK-CO-SC-PL-SL-NS
Items: PB-MG-NS-MM

Service News Co Inc
J Dwyer, VP
207 Popes Island
PO Box 5629
New Bedford MA 02742
508-997-3344; Fax: 508-990-8348
Territory: SE MA; 7 reps
Markets: BK-CO-SC-PL
Items: MM-MG-MA-NP-CA-CO(trading cards)

Michigan

Ludington News Co Inc
Chuck Przygachi
1600 E Grand Blvd
Detroit MI 48211-3195
313-925-7600; Fax: 313-922-3909
Territory: US
Markets: BK-CO-RO(drug/discount stores)
Items: HC-MM-MG-PB-OT(sports cards)
Memo: Buys for all subsidiaries. 313-925-7696.

Southern Michigan News Co
Glen Wagner, Supervisor
13470 Michigan Ave
Galesburg MI 49053
616-746-4811
Territory: MI
Items: HC-PB-MM

Michiana News Service Inc
Karen Rembold, Book Buyer
2232 S 11th St
Niles MI 49120-4410
616-684-3013; Fax: 616-684-8740
Territory: US; 20 reps
Markets: BK-SC-MM-PL-SL
Items: HC-PB-RM-MM-MG-CA-CO

Northern News Company
Ronald E Scherer, Book Buyer
3407M 119th
PO Box 543
Petoskey MI 49770
616-347-3936; Fax: 616-347-6475
Territory: Restricted; 8 reps
Markets: BK-CO-SC-PL-SL
Items: HC-MM-MG-PB

Minnesota

Aramark
Roger Walton, Gen Mgr
1006 Wright St
PO Box 448
Brainerd MN 56401
218-829-0362; Fax: 218-829-7981
Territory: Midwest; 23 reps
Markets: BK-MM-NS-CO-SC-PL-RO
Items: HC-MM-PB-MG-CO-TA-SB

Valley News Company
Carol Kunst, Buyer
1305 Stadium Rd
Mankato MN 56001-5397
507-345-4819; Fax: 507-345-6793
Territory: Central MN/N IA/Western SD; 10 reps
Markets: BK-CO-SC-PL-SL-RO-MM
Items: PB-RM-MM-TV

St Maries Gopher News
Bill Bevan, Mgr
9000 10th Ave N
Minneapolis MN 55427-4322
612-546-5300; Fax: 612-525-3100
Territory: MN; 4 reps
Markets: BK-RO(chain/groc/drug/discount)
Items: SW-TA-CA-CO-MA-SB(sports cards)
Memo: Branches in Duluth & Rochester MN.

Rochester News Co
Mike Berletic, Mgr
420 First Ave NW
Rochester MN 55901
507-282-8641; Fax: 507-282-8641
Territory: MN-IA; 2 reps
Markets: BK-CO-SC-PL-SL
Items: PB-MM-MG-NP-TV

Mississippi

Anderson News Co
Mike Bostic, Mgr
525 Belle Aire St
Greenville MS 38701
601-335-1712; Fax: 601-335-1712
Territory: Central MS/SE AR; 10 reps
Markets: RO
Items: MM-MG

Capital News
Don Pennington, Mgr
961 Palmyra St
PO Box 3169
Jackson MS 39207
601-355-8341; Fax: 601-352-1343
Territory: 14 reps
Markets: BK-RO
Items: HC-MM-MG

Missouri

Aramark
Ann Hoffmeister, Gen Mgr
12115 Prichard Farm Rd
PO Box 750
Bridgetown MO 63044
314-291-7775; Fax: 314-344-9438
Territory: Midwest; 12 reps
Markets: BK-MM-NS-SC-CO-PL-SL-MM-RO
Items: HC-MM-PB-MG-CO-RM-TA-SB
Memo: Located in Hazelwood, MO.

Cowley Distributing
Inez Killam, Book/Toy Mgr, or John Cowley II, Gen Mgr
732 Heisinger Rd
Jefferson City MO 65109-4700
314-636-6511; Fax: 314-636-6262
Territory: Regional; 10 reps
Markets: BK-NS-MM-RO
Items: HC-MM-MG-PB-TO

Ozark Periodicals Distrib Inc
Ken Giddens, Book Buyer
1630 N Eldon Ave
PO Box 6007
Springfield MO 65803
417-862-9224; Fax: 417-862-6642
Territory: Midwest
Markets: BK-MM-NS-RO
Items: HC-MM-PB-MG

Montana

Billings News
Donna Ginter, Book Buyer
711 Fourth Ave N
Billings MT 59101
406-245-5784; Fax: 406-245-0673
Territory: 5 reps
Markets: SL-PL-BK-CO-SC
Items: MM-MG-NP-PB-SW

CD Distributing Inc
Dan Barnhouse, Book Buyer
2609 E 17th St NE
PO Box 338
Black Eagle MT 59414
406-453-7867; Fax: 406-454-0415
Territory: MT
Markets: MM-RO-BK-RO
Items: HC-MM-MG-PB

Kalispell News Agency
Leigh Johnson, Owner
PO Box 1153
Kalispell MT 59903-1153
406-755-5430; Fax: 406-755-5522
Territory: 2 reps
Markets: BK-SL-RO(groc retail)
Items: HC-MM-MG-NP-CA-CO-SB-OT

Northwest News Company
Ken Grinsteiner, Mgr
1701 Rankin
PO Box 4965
Missoula MT 59802
406-721-7801; Fax: 406-721-7802
Territory: MT
Markets: BK-SL-CO-SC
Items: HC-MM-MG-PB-RM-TV

Nebraska

Lincoln News Agency
Lewis Britto
5130 S 16th St
PO Box 80267
Lincoln NE 68501
402-423-7134; Fax: 402-423-1859
Territory: Midwest
Markets: BK-MM-NS-RO(discount stores)
Items: HC-PB-MM-MG

Nelson News
Mike Odorisio
4657 G St
PO Box 27007
Omaha NE 68117
402-734-3333; Fax: 402-731-0516
Territory: Midwest
Markets: BK-MM-NS(groc/food chains)
Items: HC-PB-MM-MG

Kent News Agency Inc
Douglas H Kent, Owner
1402 Avenue B
PO Box 1828
Scottsbluff NE 69361-1828
308-635-2225; Fax: 308-635-2225
Territory: Restricted; 6 reps
Markets: BK-CO-SC-PL-SL-MM-RO
Items: MM-MG-PB

Nevada

Sierra News Company
Terry Riddle, Book Buyer
855 E Greg St #105
Sparks NV 89431

New Mexico

Aramark
Patrick Lundy, Gen Mgr
6815 Washington NE
PO Box 1340
Albuquerque NM 87199
505-345-5508
Territory: New Mexico
Markets: BK-SL-PL-CO-SC-MM-RO
Items: HC-MM-MG-PB-CO-TA-SB

Basin Distributing
Tom Fawcett, Owner
1900 Fawcett Ct
Farmington NM 87401
505-327-5324
Territory: Southwest US; 5 reps
Markets: BK-SL-PL-CO-SC
Items: MM-MG-PB

Gallup Distributing
Walter Tyler, Owner
205 Sunde Dr
Gallup NM 87301
505-863-4304; Fax: 505-863-4304
Territory: West NM and East AZ
Markets: RO
Items: MM-MG-NP

New York

Fulmont News Company
Gregory Simonson, Book Buyer
182 Division St
PO Box 389
Amsterdam NY 12010-0389
518-843-2421; Fax: 518-843-2845
Territory: 7 reps
Markets: BK-CO-SC-SL
Items: HC-MM-MG-PB-NP-RM-TA

William Schaeffer News Dist
Louis Rubin, Pres
23-25 Wall St
PO Box 596
Auburn NY 13021
315-252-0583
Territory: Restricted sales area
Markets: NS-RO-MM
Items: MM

Batavia Periodical Distributors
Robert Rubin, Owner
602-622 E main St
PO Box 821
Batavia NY 14021
716-343-3880; Fax: 716-343-6813
Territory: 4 reps
Markets: BK-SC-RO
Items: HC-MM-MG

Sepher-Hermon Press Co
Samuel Gross, Buyer
1265 46th St
Brooklyn NY 11219
718-972-9010; Fax: 718-972-9010
Territory: 1 rep
Markets: BK-SC-CO-PL-SL
Items: HC-PB

Empire State News
Dave Goeckel, Mdse Dir
2800 Walden Ave
Cheektowaga NY 14225
716-681-1100; Fax: 716-681-1120
Territory: New York area
Markets: BK-RO
Items: HC-PB-MG-NP
Memo: All book inquiries should be sent to: Empire State News, Buffalo, NY.

Southern Tier News Company
Jeff Rubin, Mgr
353 Upper Oakwood Ave
PO Box 2128
Elmira Heights NY 14903
607-734-7108; Fax: 607-734-6825
Territory: 3 reps
Markets: BK-CO-SC-PL-SL-RO
Items: MM-MG-PB-NP-CA-CO-MA-SB-TA

Seneca News Agency
Barry Budger, Pres
800 Pre-Emption Rd
PO Box 631
Geneva NY 14456
315-789-3551; Fax: 315-781-1015
Territory: Restricted-NY; 9 reps
Markets:
   BK-CO-SC-SL-RO(drug,disc/conv)
Items: MM-MG-NP(tabloids)

Burns News Agency
Michael O'Leary, Book Buyer
80-84 Glen St
PO Box 505
Glens Falls NY 12801
518-792-5138
Territory: NY; 4 reps
Markets: BK-CO-SC
Items: PB-MM-MG-NP

Columbia County News Agency
Mark Lando, Pres
135 Warren St
Hudson NY 12534
518-828-1017; Fax: 518-828-3393
Territory: Columbia; 3 reps
Markets: BK-CO-SC-PL-SL-NS-MM-RO
Items: MM-MG-NP

Empire News of Jamestown
Book Buyer
Station A
PO Box 2029
Jamestown NY 14701
716-487-1125; Fax: 716-484-7401
Territory: Restricted; 3 reps
Markets: BK-CO-SC-PL-SL
Items: HC-MM-MG-NP
Memo: Affiliate with Empire State News.
  All book inquiries should be sent to:
  Empire State News of Buffalo, NY.

Niagara County News
Robert Erb, Owner
70 Nicholls St
Lockport NY 14094
716-433-6466; Fax: 716-434-3667
Territory: 5 reps
Markets: SC(limited)-RO(retail stores)
Items: MM-MG-NP-CO-MA-TA-TV

Time Warner Publisher Serv Intl
Linda Greenblatt, Sales Dir
Time Life Bldg
1271 Ave of Americas 39th Fl
New York NY 10020
212-522-8900; Fax: 212-522-7158
Territory: US-IT; 10 reps
Markets: BK-JB-MM-RO
Items: HC-PB-MM

Cecchi News Agency
Albert Cecchi, Owner
234 Homer St
PO Box 564
Olean NY 14760-0564
716-372-8150; Fax: 716-373-5293
Territory: 5 reps
Markets: BK-SL-SC-MM-RO
Items: HC-PB-MM-MG-NP-RM

Manson News Distributors
Rick Rampone, Gen Mgr
634 South Ave
PO Box 1211
Rochester NY 14620
716-244-3880; Fax: 716-461-1388
Territory: NY; 6 reps
Markets: BK-CO-SC-PL-SL-RO
Items: PB-MG-NP-MA-TA-TV(some)

Morlock News
Lillian Hitchcock, Mgr
496 Duanesburg Rd
Schenectady NY 10306
518-355-9123; Fax: 518-463-3154
Territory: NY

Markets: BK-CO-SC-PL-SL-RO
Items: MM-MG-NP

Rockland-Catskill Inc
John Sisko, Co-Owner
26 Church St
PO Box 68
Spring Valley NY 10977
914-356-1222; Fax: 914-356-8415
Territory: 4 reps
Markets: BK-CO-SC-RO-MM
Items: HC-MM-MG-PB-TX-MA-CO
  (tradecards)

Onondaga News Agency
Jack Simiensyk, Mgr
474 E Brighton Ave
Syracuse NY 13210
315-475-3121; Fax: 315-475-3652
Territory: NY
Markets: BK-CO-SC-RO-MM
Items: HC-MM-NP-ML

Rubin Periodicals Group
John Rustin Sr, Gen Mgr
176 Third St
PO Box 388
Troy NY 12181
518-270-8400; Fax: 518-270-8410
Territory: NY
Markets: BK-CO-PL-SL-RO
Items: HC-MG-NP

Wolfe News Service
Cindy Boyer, Book Buyer
1125 Stark St
Utica NY 13502
315-733-2000; Fax: 315-724-0253
Territory: Restricted; 3 reps
Markets: BK-PL-SL-CO-SC
Items: HC-MM-MG-NP

North Carolina

Blue Ridge News Co
Carole Rector, Mgr
242 Broadway (28801)
PO Box 1110
Asheville NC 28802
704-258-2631
Territory: 6 reps
Markets: BK-CO-SC
Items: MM-MG-PB-NP

Dixie News Co
Jim Patterson, Owner
900 Atando Ave
PO Box 561129
Charlotte NC 28256
704-376-0140; Fax: 704-335-8604
Territory: 10 reps
Markets: BK-SL-PL-SC-NS-RO-MM
Items: HC-MM-MG-TX-PB

North Carolina News Inc
Bill Woodside, Gen Mgr
1207 Angier Ave
Durham NC 27701
919-682-5779; Fax: 919-682-3954
Territory: 3 reps
Markets: BK-CO-SC
Items: HC-MM-MG-PB-MG
Memo: Clay Evans Jr, Owner.

Elizabeth City News
George E McPherson, Book Buyer
504-508 E Elizabeth St
PO Box 767
Elizabeth City NC 27909
919-335-5930; Fax: 919-335-2044
Territory: 6 reps
Markets: BK-PL-SL-CO-SC
Items: MM-MG-NP-TV-PO

Carolina News Co
Greg Tyler, Book Buyer
245 Tillinghast St
Fayetteville NC 28301-4707
910-483-4135
Territory: 19 reps
Items: HC-MM-MG-TX-MA-PO

State News Company
Frank Taylor, Mgr
610 Industrial Ave
PO Box 16246
Greensboro NC 27406-4604
910-274-2459; Fax: 910-373-1473
Territory: 8 reps
Markets: BK-CO-SC(conv/drug/supermkts)
Items: HC-MG-TX-CA-CO-MA-TA

Raleigh News Agency Inc
Daniel Burger, Book Buyer
2420 Crabtree Blvd
PO Box 41128
Raleigh NC 27629-1128
919-833-2707; Fax: 919-833-1496
Territory: SE US; 18 reps
Markets: BK-CO-NS-MM-RO
Items: HC-PB-MM-MG-MA-SB

Rocky Mount News Agency
Calvert Batt, Mgr
Two Great State Ln
PO Box 4343
Rocky Mount NC 27803
919-443-3124; Fax: 919-443-0988
Territory: 8 reps
Markets: BK-CO-SC-NS-RO
Items: HC-MM-MG-PB-TX-CA-CO-MA-
  OT

Service News Co
Manager
1306 N 23rd St
PO Box 3788
Wilmington NC 28406
919-762-5542; Fax: 919-762-9539
Territory: 18 reps
Markets: BK-SL-PL-CO-SC-MM-RO
Items: HC-MM-MG-TX

Piedmont News
Ray McPherson, Pres
2750 Griffith Rd (27103)
PO Box 25367
Winston-Salem NC 27114
910-768-1165; Fax: 910-765-8842
Territory: NV
Markets: BK-CO-SC(retail/chain/drug/conv)
Items: MM-MG-PB-CA-CO-MA-OT

North Dakota

Saks News
Eric Sakariassen
2210 E Broadway
PO Box 58502
Bismark ND 58501-1857
701-223-0818; Fax: 701-223-8754
Territory: 9 reps
Markets: BK-CO-SC-PL-SL-RO
Items: HC-MM-MG-PB-NP-CA-CO-TA-TV-OT

Central News Agency
David Walter, Book Buyer
PO Box 750
Akron OH 44309-0750
330-535-6101; Fax: 330-376-8727
Territory: Restricted; 4 reps
Markets: BK
Items: MM-MG-PB-NP

Ohio

City News Agency
Gerald L Dentler, Mgr
220 Cherry Ave NE
Canton OH 44702
216-456-7179
Territory: Ohio; 6 reps
Markets: SL-PL-BK-SC
Items: MG-PB-NP-RM

Ohio Periodical Distributors
Ron Scherer, Owner
5109 Winton Rd
PO Box 145449
Cincinnati OH 45232
513-542-2216; Fax: 513-853-6245
Territory: OH
Markets: BK-CO-SC-PL-SL-RO
  (convenience stores)
Items: MG-PB

George R Klein News
Lucy Diaz, Book Buyer
1771 E 30th St
Cleveland OH 44114
216-623-0370; Fax: 216-623-0919
800-262-4433
Territory: OH-PA
Markets: BK-RO-MM
Items: HC-MM-MG

Ohio Periodical Distributors
James Brunner, Gen Mgr
777 W Goodale Blvd
PO Box 193
Columbus OH 43216
614-224-4901; Fax: 614-224-4118
Territory: OH
Markets: BK-CO-SC-PL-SL
Items: HC-PB-MM-MG-NP

Miami Valley News Agency Inc
David Persinger, Mgr
2127 Old Troy Pike
PO Box 315 N Dayton Sta
Dayton OH 45404
513-233-8650; Fax: 513-233-8544
Territory: OH-IN; 20 reps
Markets: BK-CO-SC-PL-SL
Items: PB-MG-NP-TV

Brunner News Agency
James J Brunner, Pres/Book Buyer
217 Flanders Ave
PO Box 598
Lima OH 45801-0598
419-225-5826; Fax: 419-225-5537
Territory: Ohio; 1 rep
Markets: BK-MM-SL-PL-CO-SC
Items: HC-PB-MM-MG-TV

Portsmouth News Agency
Wayne Cooper, Gen Mgr
3051 Walnut St
Portsmouth OH 45662
614-353-5760
Territory: OH
Markets: BK-CO-SC-PL-SL-RO
Items: MM-MG-CA-CO-MA-SB-TA-OT(cards)

Central News of Sandusky
Terry Hillery, Gen Mgr
2115 George St
Sandusky OH 44870
419-626-6962; Fax: 419-626-2880
Territory: Ohio area; 2 reps
Markets: BK-CO-SC
Items: MM-MG-NP-PB

La Belle News Agency
Tom Pentes
814 University Blvd
PO Box 1507
Steubenville OH 43952
614-282-9731; Fax: 614-282-2402
Territory: OH
Markets: BK-MM-NS-RO
Items: MM-MG-NP

Tiffin News Agency
Gary Thompson, Mgr
49 N Washington St
Tiffin OH 44883
419-447-3822
Territory: 3 reps
Markets: BK-CO-SC
Items: NP

Oklahoma

Aramark
Lee Podall, Mgr
7000 N Robinson
PO Box 25489
Oklahoma City OK 73125-0489
405-843-9383
Territory: OK; 45 reps
Markets: BK-CO-SL-PL-MM-RO
Items: HC-MM-MG-PB-CO-TA-SB

ARAMark
Wayne Clark, Gen Mgr
909 West 23rd St
PO Box 571060
Tulsa OK 74157
918-584-4754; Fax: 918-584-6190
Territory: 24 reps
Markets: BK-CO-SC-PL-SL-RO-MM
Items: HC-MM-MG-CO-TA-SB

Oregon

Aramark
Stan Ritari, Gen Mgr
3850 W First Ave
PO Box 15003
Eugene OR 97401
503-484-1300
Territory: OR; 36 reps
Markets: BK-SL-PL-SC-MM-RO
Items: HC-MM-MG-CO-TA-SB

Medford News
Paula Bodine, Mgr
550 Airport St
Medford OR 97504
541-779-5225
Territory: OR; 3 reps
Markets: BK-MM-RO
Items: MM-MG

Northwest News Co Inc
Stanley Lakefish, Owner
550 Airport Rd
Medford OR 97504
503-779-5225; Fax: 541-779-0587
Territory: Oregon South & Central; 18 reps
Markets: BK-CO-SC-SL-PL
Items: HC-MG-PB-CO-OT(sports cards)

Bay News Company
John Franznick, Gen Mgr
3155 NW Yeon Ave
Portland OR 97210
503-228-0251; Fax: 503-241-1877
Territory: NW US; 25 reps
Markets: CO-SC-PL-SL-BK
Items: HC-PB-MM-MG

INCORP Periodicals Inc
Dwane Friesen
32150 Hwy 34
Tangent OR 57389
541-926-8889; Fax: 541-926-9553
Territory: Mountain states; 4 reps
Markets: BK-CO-SC-RO
Items: HC-PB-MM-MG

Pennsylvania

Newborn Enterprises Inc
Barbara Rossi, Book Buyer, or John
  Kearns, Mkt Mgr
808-10 Green Ave
PO Box 1713
Altoona PA 16601
814-944-3593; Fax: 814-944-1881
Territory: Buys from a restricted list; 10 reps
Markets: PL-SL-BK-CO-SC
Items: HC-MG-PB-NP

Midstate Distributors
Frank Fogleman, Buyer
1201 Sheffler Dr
Chambersburg PA 17201
717-263-7742; Fax: 717-263-2413
Territory: US
Markets: BK-SC-CO-PL
Items: HC-PB-MG-TA-TV-NP

Easton News Co
Mrs Edward Tukeva, Mgr
2601 Dearborn St
Easton PA 18045
610-252-3151
Territory: Sales area restricted; PA & NJ; 3 reps
Markets: BK-CO-SC-RO
Items: MG-PB-NP

Lakeport Distributors Inc
John Mottillo, Book Buyer
PO Box 6195
Erie PA 16512
814-455-4461; Fax: 814-453-4479
Territory: US
Markets: SL-BK-CO-SC
Items: MM-MG-NP
Memo: William Landau and Steven Stroul Co-Owners; Meadville News Co Inc in Meadville, PA and Lakeport came together.

Harrisburg News Company
Dale Peters, Gen Mgr
980 Briarsdale Rd (17109)
PO Box 60307
Harrisburg PA 17106
717-561-8377; Fax: 717-561-1466
Territory: Sales area restricted; 4 reps
Markets: BK-CO-SC-SL-PL-RO
Items: HC-MM-MG-NP

Penn News Co
Gary Morton, Mgr
944 Franklin St
Johnstown PA 15905
814-536-7146; Fax: 814-539-7789
Territory: 2 reps
Markets: BK-SL-PL-CO-RO
Items: PB-NP-CA-CO-MA-SB

Lancaster County News Co
Dave & Steve Etter, Owners
221 N Queen St
Lancaster PA 17603-3599
717-393-3911
Territory: Sales area restricted PA; 5 reps
Markets: BK-SL-PL-CO-SC-RO
Items: MM-MG-NP

Triangle News Company
Marilyn Watson, Owner
3498 Grand Ave
Neville Island
Pittsburgh PA 15225
412-771-4433; Fax: 412-771-9812
Territory: 4 reps
Markets: BK-PL-SL-CO-SC-NS-RO
Items: MG-NP-CA-CO-MA-SB-TA-TV
Memo: 1,000 dealers.

Pottstown News Company
Andrew Lieb, Owner
557 W High St
Pottstown PA 19464-6639
610-326-2450; Fax: 610-326-3599
Territory: 3 reps
Markets: BK-SC-CO
Items: MG-PB-NP

Great Northern Distributors Co
Bob Kolinovsky, Buyer
935 N Washington Ave
PO Box 1123
Scranton PA 18501-1123
717-342-8159; Fax: 717-342-8139
Territory: PA-NJ
Markets: BK-SC-CO-RO
Items: HC-MM-MG-PB-NP-OT(trading cards)

Sharon News Agency
Toby Abrutz, Mgr
527 E Silver St
Sharon PA 16146-2255
412-342-7331
Territory: Sales area restricted; 4 reps
Markets: BK-CO-SC
Items: HC-MG-PB-TX-NP-RO

Mid-Penn Magazine Agency Inc
Jerri Demel, Book Buyer
100 Eck Cir
Williamsport PA 17701-3896
717-323-8471; Fax: 717-322-7029
Territory: Sales area restricted; 6 reps
Markets: BK-CO-SC-PL-SL
Items: HC-MM-MG-PB-NP-TV

South Carolina

E A Prince & Son
W T Prince, Pres
511 W Whitner
PO Box 436
Anderson SC 29622
803-224-0720; Fax: 803-224-4380
Territory: Anderson & surrounding counties; 10 reps
Markets: BK-PL-SL-RO
Items: MM-MG-PB-NP

Charleston News Company Inc
Robert MacInnes, Owner
2556 Oscar Johnson Dr
PO Drawer 29402
Charleston SC 29405
803-744-1611; Fax: 803-744-0806
Territory: Charleston & surrounding areas
Markets: BK-RO
Items: MM-MG-PB-NP

Central News
Marvin Gray, Book Buyer
920 Hemlock Dr
PO Box 1783
Columbia SC 29202
803-799-3414; Fax: 803-799-8858
Territory: Central South Carolina; 13 reps
Markets: BK-CO-SC
Items: HC-MM-MG-PB

Pee Dee News Co Inc
Hubert Gray, Mgr
2009 W Jody's Rd
PO Box 4569
Florence SC 29502
803-669-7563; Fax: 803-669-7563
Territory: Sales area restricted; 12 reps
Markets: CO-SC-BK-NS
Items: MG-PB(tabloids)

Anderson News Company
Chris Laundra
200 Sunbelt Ct
Greer SC 29650
803-848-0560; Fax: 803-848-0559
Territory: SC
Markets: BK-CO-NS
Items: HC-MM-MG-OT(sports cards)

Dixie News Co
Gary Pittman, Mgr
101 C SW Park
Spartanburg SC 29301
803-595-1966
Territory: SC
Markets: BK-PL-SL-RO-MM
Items: MG
Memo: Main office in Charlotte: 704-376-0140.

South Dakota

Rushmore News Inc
Michael Freese, Mgr
924 E St Andrew St
Rapid City SD 57701
605-342-2617; Fax: 605-342-9091
Territory: SD-WY; 8 reps
Markets: BK-CO-SL-PL-SC-RO
Items: PB-TA-CO-MA-SB

Dakota News Inc
Wayland Mitchell, Owner
221 Petro Ave
Sioux Falls SD 57107
605-336-3000; Fax: 605-336-7279
Territory: IA/SD/NE/MN
Markets: BK-CO-SC-PL-SL
Items: HC-MM-MG-PB-NP-SW-TV

Tennessee

Anderson News
Don Mize, Mgr
3945 Volunteer Dr
PO Box 22968
Chattanooga TN 37422
423-894-3945; Fax: 423-855-4901
Territory: 13 Field reps
Markets: BK-CO-SC-SL-PL-RO-MM
Items: HC-MM-MG-TX-PB-MB-NP

Austin Periodical Services
Bill Utley, Mgr
54 Lawrence Switch Rd
Jackson TN 38301
901-423-2955
Items: MM-MG

Tri-State News Agency
Dennis Painter, Book Buyer
604 Rolling Hills Dr
PO Box 778
Johnson City TN 37605
423-926-8159; Fax: 423-926-9791
Territory: Sales area restricted
Markets: BK-CO-SC
Items: MM-MG-NP

Anderson News
Calvin King, Mgr
125 Regional Park Dr
PO Box 1039
Kingsport TN 37662-1039
423-349-7145; Fax: 423-349-4688
Territory: TN
Markets: BK-SC-RO-MM
Items: HC-MM-MG-TV

Anderson News
Becky Rose, Sr Book Buyer
10612 Dutchtown Rd (37922)
PO Box 22998
Knoxville TN 37933-0998
615-966-7575; Fax: 615-671-0349
Territory: Eastern US
Markets: SC-CO-MM-RO
Items: HC-MM-PB
Memo: 29 agencies.

Austin Periodical Services
Suzanne Shaw, Book Buyer
499 Merritt Ave
Nashville TN 37203
615-256-3669
Territory: TN
Markets: NS
Items: HC-MM-MG

Texas

Amarillo Periodicals Distributor
Brian Weiner, Owner
2015 SE 27th
PO Box 31985
Amarillo TX 79120
806-372-5035
Territory: TX(panhandle)-KS-SW US
Markets: BK-RO
Items: HC-MM-MG
Memo: Buys locally, independently.

Austin News Agency
James L Robinson, Mgr
2830 Real St
PO Box 2133
Austin TX 78722
512-474-2311; Fax: 512-474-6921
Territory: Austin, TX only
Markets: BK-MM
Items: MM-MG
Memo: Buys primarily mass market books and magazines.

Golden Triangle Periodical Dist
David Thiele, Mgr
4785 Washington Blvd (77707)
PO Box 6526
Beaumont TX 77705
409-842-2262; Fax: 409-842-5166
Territory: SE Texas; 10 field reps
Markets: RO
Items: PB-TA-MG
Memo: Weekly catalog.

Brazos Periodical Distributors
Shawn Jackson, Book Buyer
1710 Groesbeck
PO Box 4131
Bryan TX 77805
409-775-2404
Territory: TX
Markets: BK-MM-RO
Items: HC-MM-MG-PB

Nueces News Agency
Cliff Chatham, Mgr
PO Box 2768 St
Corpus Christi TX 78403-5298
512-289-1441; Fax: 512-289-5813
Territory: South Texas
Markets: BK-CO-RO-MM
Items: MM-MG-PB

Memo: Address for freight & UPS only no mail: 209 N Padre Island Dr, Corpus Christi, TX 78406.

Nueces News Agency
Patsy Salazar, Book Buyer
209 N Padre Island Dr
PO Box 2768
Corpus Christi TX 78406
512-289-1441; Fax: 512-289-5213
Territory: TX
Markets: CO-NS-RO
Items: MM-MG

Martin News Agency Inc
Ben Martin, Owner
11325 Gemini Ln
Dallas TX 75229
214-241-8531; Fax: 214-243-6741
Territory: TX
Markets: BK-NS-RO(chain/food stores)
Items: HC-MM-MG-PB-TV-OT(t-shirts/cards

Pandora Distributors
Barger Giltmeyer, Buyer
7939 Heinen Dr
Dallas TX 75227
214-388-9620; Fax: 214-381-6462
Territory: TX
Markets: MM-RO
Items: HC-MM-MG-OT(t-shirts/sports mem)

West Texas News Co
Mike Billings, Book Buyer
1214 Barranca
PO Box 26488
El Paso TX 79926
915-594-7586; Fax: 915-594-7589
Territory: TX
Markets: BK-CO-SC-PL-SL
Items: HC-MG-NP

East Texas Distributing
Ron Eisenberg, Pres
7171 Grand Blvd
Houston TX 77054
713-748-8120; Fax: 713-748-2430
Territory: SW US; 12 field reps
Markets: BK-MM-RO(video/computer)
Items: HC-MM-MG-NP-TA-TV-PB

Texas Art Supply
John Gilbreath, VP
2001 Montrose Blvd
Houston TX 77006
713-526-5221; Fax: 713-524-7474
Territory: TX
Markets: BK-CO-art supply stores
Items: HB-PB-CR-RM-TA(craft supplies)

Lubbock News Co
Ron Ryan, Mgr
118 East 70th St
Lubbock TX 79404-5826
806-745-6000; Fax: 806-745-7028
Territory: TX & part of NM
Markets: BK-CO-SC
Items: HC-NP-PB

Angelina Periodicals
Sharlene Sowler, Mgr
1002 Ellis Ave
PO Box 1465
Lufkin TX 75901
409-634-8277
Territory: TX

Markets: NS
Items: HC-MM-MG

Basin News Agency
R Hollinsworth
5701 W Industrial
PO Box 3429
Midland TX 79706
915-694-2593
Territory: Restricted; 8 reps
Markets: BK-CO-SC
Items: HC-MM-MG-TX

Young's News Agency Inc
George Young, Mgr
124 W Cherry St
PO Box 837
Paris TX 75460
903-785-0713
Territory: TX; 7 reps
Markets: BK-CO-PL-SL-RO
Items: HC-MM-MG-PB

Texoma News Agency
Larry Zettler
2909 Fallon Dr
PO Box 1812
Sherman TX 75090
903-892-0631; Fax: 903-892-0631
Territory: 13 reps
Markets: BK-CO-NS-RO
Items: HC-MM-MG-PB-CA-CO-GC-MA-ST-TA-TV

ETD Kromar
Maria McKnight, Book Buyer or Rueben Lopez, Gen Mgr
3401 Lucious McCelzey Dr
PO Box 1090
Temple TX 76503
817-778-5261; Fax: 817-778-5267
Territory: TX
Markets: NS
Items: HC-MM-MG

C & S News Agency
Charles & Sam Cohen, Owners
101 Industrial Dr
Waxahachie TX 75165
214-937-2516; Fax: 214-938-1738
Territory: Restricted; 5 reps
Markets: BK-CO-SC-SL
Items: HC-MM-MG-NP

Cochran News Agency
Rodney Bertram, Mgr
1101 16th St
PO Box 1110
Wichita Falls TX 76307
817-766-1011; Fax: 817-766-1291
Territory: TX; 4 reps
Markets: BK-CO-SC-RO
Items: HC-MM-MG-TX-PB-NP

Utah

Newsstand Distributors Inc
John Childs, Gen Mgr
155 West 14th St
Ogden UT 84404
801-621-8361; Fax: 801-621-7336
Territory: Southern UT & WY; 5 reps
Markets: BK-CO-RO-SC
Items: MM-MG-PB

Bonneville News
Curt Butkovich, Book Buyer
965 Beardsley Pl
Salt Lake City UT 84119
801-972-5454; Fax: 801-972-1075
Territory: Restricted; 5 reps
Markets: PL-SL-CO-SC-MM-RO-AP
Items: HC-MM-MG-RM
Memo: Terry Watson, Gen Mgr.

Virginia

Alonso Book & Periodical Service
Al Alonso, Mgr
7670 Richmond Hwy
Alexandria VA 22306-2843
703-765-1211; Fax:
Territory: East Coast/Mid-Atlantic States
Markets: BK-NS-MM-RO(Computer)
Items: HC-PB-MM-MG-9C

Danville News Agency
J Lee Tyler, Owner
503 Hughes St
PO Box 2145
Danville VA 24541
804-792-1166; Fax: 804-792-6840
Territory: VA-NC; 6 reps
Markets: BK-CO-SC-SL
Items: HC-MM-MG-PB-NP

Books International Inc
Azad Ajamian, Owner
PO Box 605
Herndon VA 22070
703-689-0303; Fax: 703-689-0660
Territory: 2 reps
Markets: BK-CO-SC-PL-SL
Items: HC-PB-MM
Memo: Distributes for 30 publishers.

Hill-City News Agency
T Kenneth Fryman, Owner
3228 Oddfellows Rd
Lynchburg VA 24501
804-845-4231; Fax: 804-845-0864
Territory: Lynchburg & surrounding areas; 5 reps
Markets: BK-PL-SL-CO-SC
Items: MM-MG-PB-NP(tabloids)

Aramark
Dave Pearsall, Gen Mgr
1108 Tidewater Dr
PO Box 2240
Norfolk VA 23501
804-627-3631; Fax: 804-627-0052
Territory: 30 reps
Markets: BK-SL-PL-CO-SC-MM-RO
Items: HC-MM-MG-SB-CO-RM-PB

Capitol News Agency
Charles Messina, Gen Mgr
5203 Hatcher St
PO Box 7771
Richmond VA 23231
804-222-7252
Territory: Restricted
Markets: BK-SL-SP-RO
Items: MG-PB-NP-MA
Memo: Bobby Dooley, Booking, Clinton B Peters, Pres. Deals with national distribution only.

Washington

Aramark Magazine & Book Ser
Judi Hillis, Book Buyer
18825 67th Ave NE
Arlington WA 98223
360-435-2524; Fax: 360-435-6805
Territory: WA
Markets: BK-SC-CO-PL-SL-MM-RO
Items: HC-PB-RM-MM-MG-TA-TV-NP

Servatius News Agency Inc
Fred Servatius, Owner
601 Second St
Clarkston WA 99403-1995
509-758-7592; Fax: 509-758-6111
Territory: 4 reps
Markets: BK-CO-SC-RO(grocery/drug)
Items: HC-MM-MG-TV

Cascade News
Ken Galgher, Book Buyer
1055 Commerce Ave
Longview WA 98632
360-425-2450; Fax: 360-425-2451
Territory: Restricted; 4 reps
Markets: BK-CO-SC-SL-PL
Items: MM-MG-NP-PB

Adams News Company Inc
Bob Lofgren, Book Buyer
1555 W Galer St
Seattle WA 98119-3128
206-284-7617; Fax: 206-284-7599
Territory: NW US; 28 reps
Markets: BK-CO-SC-PL-SL
Items: PB-MM-MG-NP-OT(games/puzzles)

Aramark
Ladell Steed, Gen Mgr
15 Perry St
PO Box 4067
Spokane WA 99202
509-535-3059
Territory: WA
Markets: BK-SL-PL-CO-SC-RO-M
Items: HC-MM-MG-RM-CO-TA-SB

Lesnick News Co Inc
Anthony Lesnick, Owner
2442 Mottman Rd SW
Tumwater WA 98512
360-357-5341; Fax: 360-754-1595
Territory: Sales area restricted
Markets: BK-CO-SC-PL-SL-RO
Items: MM-MG-PB-OT(trading cards)

Wenatchee News Agency Inc
Jack L Davis, Pres/Owner
1501 N Miller Ave C
Wenatchee WA 98801
509-662-3511
Territory: WA; 4 reps
Markets: BK-NS-SC-CO-MM-PL-SL
Items: HC-PB-RM-MM-TA

Aramark
Paul Onkels, Gen Mgr
1419 Hathaway
PO Box 2399
Yakima WA 98907
509-248-7810
Territory: WA, 1 rep
Markets: BK-CO-SC-PL-SL-RO-MM
Items: HC-MM-MG-CO-TA-SB

West Virginia

Bluefield News Agency
James Granger, Book Buyer
Cumberland Park Lot 27
PO Box 947
Bluefield WV 24701
304-327-9198
Territory: 6 reps
Markets: BK
Items: MM-MG-NP

Crowley News
David Meadows, Book Buyer
1111 Nutter St
PO Box 2304
Clarksburg WV 26302-2304
304-623-6733; Fax: 304-623-6766
Territory: Clarksburg & 13 counties (1 county in Maryland; 9 reps
Markets: BK-CO-SC
Items: MM-MG-PB-NP

Semler News Agency
William Semler, Mgr
126 Moreland St
PO Box 526
Morgantown WV 26505
304-296-4325; Fax: 304-296-4325
Territory: WV
Markets: BK-CO-NS-RO (chain, disc, drug, convenience)
Items: HC-PB-MG

Valley News Service Inc
Dan S Stephan, Owner
1919 Garfield Ave
Parkersburg WV 26101-2595
304-428-1441; Fax: 304-428-2190
Territory: 8 reps
Markets: BK-CO-SC-PL-SL-RO-TV
Items: HC-MM-MG-PB-NP

West Virginia Periodicals
Vickie Church, Book Dept Mgr
121 Erskine Ln
PO Box 487
Scott Depot WV 25560-9752
304-757-8831; Fax: 304-757-8833
Territory: Sales area restricted; 12 reps
Markets: BK-CO-SC-PL-SL
Items: HC-MM-MG-NP-PB

Wisconsin

Badger Periodical
William Streur, Pres
2420 W Fourth St
Appleton WI 54914
414-731-9521; Fax: 414-731-3671
Territory: 38 reps
Markets: RO-MM-BK
Items: HC-MM-MG

Interstate Periodicals
Scott Heath, Mgr
2231 Heimstead Rd
Eau Claire WI 54701
715-835-5437; Fax: 715-835-7920
Territory: Northern WI; 4 reps
Markets: BK-SC-CO-PL-SL
Items: HC-MM-MG-PB

Interstate Periodical Dist
Frank Caruso, Gen Mgr
201 E Badger Rd
PO Box 2237
Madison WI 53701
608-271-3600; Fax: 608-271-5227
Territory: 15 reps
Markets: PL-SL-BK-CO-SC
Items: HC-MM-MG-TX-NP-PB

Interstate Periodical Distrib
Marty Fields
201 E Badger Rd
PO Box 1145
Madison WI 53713
608-271-3600; Fax: 608-271-5227
Territory: WI
Markets: PL-SL-BK-CO-SC
Items: HC-MM-MG-TX-NP-PB

Aramark
Walter Hardy, Gen Mgr
16150 W Lincoln Ave
New Berlin WI 53151
414-786-5650
Territory: 27 reps
Markets: BK-CO-PL-SL-SC-MM-RO
Items: HC-MM-MG-CO-TA-SB-PB

Wyoming

Wyoming Periodical Distributors
Gerald Benjamin, Owner
5734 W Old Yellowstone Hwy
PO Box 2340
Casper WY 82602-2340
307-266-5328
Territory: WY-SD
Markets: RO
Items: PB-MM-MG

CANADIAN Jobbers

ALBERTA

United News Wholesalers Ltd
Peggy Agnew, Book Buyer
5716 Burbank Rd SE
Calgary AB Canada T2H 1Z4
403-253-8856; Fax: 403-252-9743
Territory: Central/Southern AB & SE BC; 18 reps
Markets: BK-NS-MM
Items: HC-PB-MM-MG-CA-CO-MA-PO-SB-TA
Memo: Warehouse is located at: 2907 2nd Ave S, Lethbridge, AB T1J 4A9.

Provincial News Company
Robert Guenette, Pres
16504 - 121 A Ave (T5V 1J9)
PO Box 2378
Edmonton AB Canada T5J 2R8
403-454-0306; Fax: 403-453-3687
Territory: Sales area restricted
Markets: BK-RO
Items: MM-MG-NP-PB

British Columbia

Valley News Agency
Gary Morgan, Pres/Buyer
801 - 30th St
PO Box 3249
Courtenay BC Canada V9N 5N4
604-338-1366; Fax: 604-338-7387
E-Mail: gcmorgan@mars.ark.com
Territory: Sales area restricted
Markets: BK-CO-SC
Items: MM-MG-NP-PB-TX

Conacher News Ltd
Alec Conacher, Co-Owner
615 - 11th Ave
PO Box 390
Montrose BC Canada V0G 1P0
604-367-6565; Fax: 604-367-2213
Territory: Restricted - West Kootney
Markets: RO
Items: PB-MM-MG-NP

Northwest News
Helen Hladchuk, Book Buyer
1722 Ogilvie St #3
Prince George BC Canada V2N 1W9
604-564-5414; Fax: 604-564-4445
Territory: CN(Northern BC)
Markets: BK-NS-SC-CO-MM-PL-SL-RO
Items: HC-PB-RM-MM-MG-CA-CO-MA-TX
Memo: Manager: Russell Gurney.

Great Pacific News
John Seebach, Pres
2500 Vauxhall Pl
Richmond BC Canada V6V 1Y8
604-278-4841; Fax: 604-231-6195
Territory: Restricted; 4 reps
Markets: BK-SC-PL-SL-RO
Items: HC-MM-MG-PB

Monahan Agencies Ltd
Reg Shumay, Book Buyer
2506 41st St
Vernon BC Canada V1T 6J9
604-545-3235; Fax: 604-545-6695
Territory: 6 reps
Markets: BK-CO-SC-PL
Items: MM-MG-PB

Stan V Wright Ltd
Wayne Wright, Book Mgr
2120 Quadra St
PO Box 970
Victoria BC Canada V8W 2R9
604-384-0597; Fax: 604-384-0597
Territory: CN(British Columbia) - 10 reps
Markets: BK-NS-SC-CO-MM-PL-SL
Items: HC-PB-MM-MG-CA-CO-ML-MA-NW-TA-TV-TX-NP

Manitoba

Canadian News Company
E J Dickson, Owner
1530 Erin St
Winnipeg MB Canada R3E 3K5
204-786-3465; Fax: 204-772-1316
Territory: Restricted - Manitoba; 3 reps
Markets: BK-CO-SC-SL-PL
Items: MM-MG-PB

New Foundland

H H Marshall Ltd
Gordon Goobie, Mgr
66 Pippy Pl
PO Box 8628 Sta A
St Johns NF Canada A1B 3T1
709-754-3024; Fax: 709-754-3559
Territory: 5 reps
Markets: BK-CO-SC
Items: MG-PB-TX-NP

Nova Scotia

H H Marshall Ltd
John S Marshall, Pres
3731 Mackintosh St
PO Box 9301 Sta A
Halifax NS Canada B3K 5N5
902-454-8381; Fax: 902-455-3652
Territory: Sales area restricted; 22 reps
Markets: BK-CO-SC-PL-SL
Items: MM-PB

Ontario

Ottawa Valley News Agency Ltd
Steve Shepherd, Owner
44 MacDonald St N
PO Box 157
Arnprior ON Canada K7S 3H4
613-623-3197; Fax: 613-623-0193
Territory: Sales area restricted; 1 rep
Markets: BK-SC
Items: MM-MG-PB-NP-TV

General News & Novelty Co Ltd
Michael O'Brien, Owner
46 Alice St
PO Box 670
Brantford ON Canada N3T 5P9
519-756-1950; Fax: 519-756-6286
Territory: Sales area resticted; Ontario
Markets: BK
Items: HC-PB-MM-MG

Cornwall News Distributors
Andrew Davidson, Gen Mgr
840 Campbell St
Cornwall ON Canada K6H 6L7
613-932-2868; Fax: 613-932-7525
Territory: Ontario - NE; 2 reps
Markets: NS-BK-MM-CO-SC-PL-SL
Items: MG

Kingston News Service
E C Churchill, Pres
417 Bagot St
PO Box 1267
Kingston ON Canada K7L 4Y8
613-546-5051
Territory: ON
Items: HC-MM-MG

Teck News Agency Ltd
Cliff Connelly, Pres
5 Kirkland St PO Box 488
Kirkland Lake ON Canada P2N 3J6
705-567-3318; Fax: 705-567-6101
Territory: Sales area restricted
Markets: CO-SC-PL-SL
Items: MM-MG-NP-PB-TX

National News Co Ltd
Ron Hamson, Mgr
2655 Lancaster Rd
Ottawa ON Canada K1B 4L5
613-731-2840; Fax: 613-731-2320
Territory: 3 reps
Markets: PL-SL-RO
Items: HC-MM-MG-PB-TA-TV

Seaway News Co Ltd
Michael O'Brien, Mgr
217 Bunting Rd PO Box 1058
Saint Catharines ON Canada L2M 3Y2
905-684-7471; Fax: 905-684-3787
Territory: Sales area restricted; 6 reps
Markets: BK-SC-CO-RO
Items: MM-MG-NP-PB

Metro Toronto News Co
James B Neill, Owner
120 Sinnott Rd
Scarborough ON Canada M1L 4N1
416-752-8720; Fax: 416-285-2056
Territory: CN; 1 rep
Markets: BK-SC-CO-PL
Items: HC-TX-PB-MG-NP

Sudbury News Service Ltd
William Paden, Owner
309 Douglas St W
PO Box 1060
Sudbury ON Canada P3E 4S6
705-673-3643; Fax: 705-674-4771
Territory: ON
Markets: BK-CO-SC-PL-SL
Items: MG-NP-PB-TX

Central News Co Ltd
Marlene Lawrence, Mgr
626 Waterloo St
PO Box 753
Thunder Bay ON Canada P7E 2C5
807-623-9577; Fax: 807-622-7652
Territory: 3 reps
Markets: BK-SC-PL-SL
Items: MM-MG-NP

Kitchener News Co Ltd
Bob McKeag, Gen Mgr
455 Dutton Dr
PO Box 274
Waterloo ON Canada N2J 4A4
519-884-3710; Fax: 519-885-4640
Territory: CN; 4 reps
Markets: SC-CO-PL-SL-BK
Items: PB-MM-MG-NP-TA-TV

Quebec

Benjamin News
Paul Benjamin, Owner
9600 Jean Milot St
La Salle PQ Canada H8R 1X7
514-364-1780; Fax: 514-364-7245
Territory: Quebec only; 90 reps
Markets: BK-AP-MM-RO
Items: HC-MM-MG-TC-GI

Saskatoon

Mid-Western News Agency
Jack Shapiro, VP
344 Portage Ave
Saskatoon SK Canada S7J 4C6
306-934-4414; Fax: 306-934-3515
Territory: CN(Saskatchewan)
Markets: BK-SC-CO-PL-SL
Items: PB-MM-MG-NP-TX-TV

Regina News Ltd
Jack Shapiro, Owner
1201 Lorne St
Regina SK Canada S4R 2J9
306-525-3757; Fax: 306-569-9899
Territory: Sales area restricted; 4 reps
Markets: SL-BK-CO-SC-PL
Items: MG-NP-PB-TV-CA-CO-MA-SB-OT

Abbreviations Used

Territory

CN	Canada
IT	International
MX	Mexico
OT	Other
US	United States with some state abbreviations for the different states

Markets

BK	Bookstores
CO	Colleges
JB	Jobbers
MM	Mass Markets
NS	Newsstands
OT	Other
PL	Public Libraries
RO	Retail Outlets
SC	Schools
SL	Special Libraries

Items

CA	Calendars
CO	Comics
CR	Craft Items
GA	Games
GC	Greeting Cards
GI	Gifts
HC	Hardcovers
MA	Maps and Atlases
MG	General / Special Magazines
ML	Literary Magazines
MM	Mass Market Books
NP	Newspapers
OP	Out of Print Books
OT	Other Items
PB	Trade Paperbacks
PO	Posters
RC	Records
RM	Remainders
SB	Stickers/Bookmarks
ST	Stationery
SW	Software
TA	Tapes, Audio
TO	Toys
TV	Tapes, Video
TX	Textbooks
US	Used books

Sales Representatives

The following companies sell books and other items to retail stores. Most of these representatives cover a specific region of the country as well as specific markets (bookstores, gift stores, toy stores, school supply stores, or craft stores) as noted below.

A

Abraham Associates
Stuart Abraham
2402 University Ave W #701
St Paul MN 55114
612-927-0992; Fax: 612-927-9588
Territory: US(Midwest)
Markets: BK
Items: HC-PB-CA

Access Marketing
Gary Gustafson
8940 Lyndale Ave S
Fox Plz #110
Minneapolis MN 55420
612-884-9729; Fax: 612-884-9736
800-528-8546
Territory: Upper Midwest only
Markets: GI
Items: HC-PB(gift products)
Memo: He would prefer to pick up new titles through Independent Publishers Marketing.

Adcock-Dean Associates
Sandy Adcock, Principal
7256 World Trade Ctr
PO Box 580174
Dallas TX 75258
214-747-8697; Fax: 214-747-8698
Territory: TX-OK-AR-LA; 5 reps
Markets: RO(gifts & toy stores)
Items: GI-TO
Memo: SE TX — Sandy Adcock; S Central TX — Mimi Gorman; OK — Angela Bamburt; LA — Ann Arcemat; N & W TX — Judy Crawford; NW AR- Angela Bamburt.

Al Gilly Associates
Al Gilly
614 Trenton Ave
Point Pleasant Bch NJ 08742
908-295-4700; Fax: 908-899-5866
Territory: East Coast - VA to ME; 2 reps
Markets: MM-RO(toys, hobbies)
Items: TO-CR

Alaska Northwest Books
Sara Juday
733 W 4th Ave #300
Anchorage AK 99501 p73
907-278-8838; Fax: 907-278-8839
Territory: AK

All Art Products Inc
Shirley Longo, Pres
410 Leonhardt Dr
Saddle Brook NJ 07662-5026
201-791-6014; Fax: 201-791-4473
Territory: NE US; 3 reps
Markets: RO(school supply stores)
Items: Art supplies

Allan Davis & Associates
Allan Davis, Pres
6100 Fourth Ave S
6100 Bldg #133
Seattle WA 98108
206-762-6288; Fax: 206-767-4273
800-821-6384
Territory: WA-AK-ID-MT-OR; British Columbia & Alberta, CN; 7 sales reps
Markets: RO(gift)
Items: Gifts

Altwerger Associates Inc
Nick Altwerger, Pres
6346 Orchard Lake Rd #201
W Bloomfield MI 48322
810-626-5009; Fax: 810-626-1552
Territory: MI-OH-IN-IL-WI-IA-MN-MO-KS-NE-SD
Markets: BK-MM(anyone who resells books); 4 reps
Items: HC-PB-CA
Memo: Ian Booth, MN, Glen McHaney, MO, Van Hyatt, OH, & Greg Hamrin, Chicago. 300-500 titles per season.

Anderson-Crawford Associates
Ken Crawford, Owner
11285 Elkins Rd #D4
Roswell GA 30076
404-475-8801
Territory: SE US; 3 reps
Markets: MM-RO(toy stores, churches)
Items: TO-GM(toys, games)

Anne McGilvray & Company
Anne McGilvray, Buyer
2505 Dallas Trade Mart
2100 Stemmons Fwy
Dallas TX 75207
214-748-9400; Fax: 214-745-1731
Territory: US (SW & Midwest)
Markets: RO(gifts)
Items: HC-PB-GI-CA-PO-TA

Atrium Publishers Group
Paul Cohen (707-541-3324)
3356 Coffey Ln
Santa Rosa CA 95403
707-542-5400

Austin & Nelson
Rebecca Austin
104 S Union St #211
Travers City MI 49684
616-933-4649; Fax: 616-933-4659

B

Bang-Knudsen Inc
Peter Bang-Knudsen
PO Box 10568
Bainbridge Island WA 98110
206-767-6970; Fax: 206-763-6985
Territory: WA-OR-AK-ID; 4 reps
Markets: RO(gift, gourmet, mail-order, dept)
Items: HC-PB-GI
Memo: 500+ accounts; 8 publishers represented.

Barry Bloom, Representative
Barry Bloom
1260 Hopkins St #38
Berkeley CA 94702
510-528-1928
Territory: Bay area & Sacramento
Items: HC-PB

Beardsley & Associates
James Beardsley
13 Patroits Rd
Acton MA 01720
508-263-5530; Fax: 508-263-5166
Territory: NH-VT-ME-MA-RI-CT; 3 reps
Markets: BK
Items: HC-PB

Ben Schrager, Representative
Ben Schrager
735 Pelham Pky
Bronx NY 10467
718-654-1968
Territory: NY-DC(Mid-Atlantic)
Markets: BK-RO(chain stores)
Items: HC-PB

Betty Gaskill, Sales Rep
Betty Gaskill
18560 Vanowen St #21
Reseda CA 91335-5307
818-996-4038
Territory: CA-HI
Markets: BK-CO
Items: PB-CA-GC
Memo: Reps for: Wilshire Book Co & Visual Design Cards & Calendars.

Bob Harman & Associates
Bob Harman
512 W Lancaster Ave
Wayne PA 19087
215-688-7272
Territory: Mid-Atlantic
Markets: MM-RO(toy and hobby stores)
Items: TO-HO-GM-CR

Bob Simmons & Associates
Bob Simmons
PO Box 292
Sharon MA 02067
617-344-9004; Fax: 617-341-4199
Territory: New England; 2 reps
Markets: MM-TO
Items: TO-GM(toys and games)

Book Travellers West
Tom Fritzinger, John Gould
9551 Landfall Dr
Huntington Beach CA 92646
714-968-2301; Fax: 714-968-2301
Territory: Western States, 6 reps
Items: HC-PB
Memo: Craig McCroskey, John Majeska, Bob O'Connor, Scott Newcomb.

BookLink Inc
Sam Montgomery, Terry Hicks, Owner
PO Drawer 1439
506 Rutledge St
Camden SC 29020
803-432-5169; Fax: 803-424-8418
Territory: SE US
Markets: BK-MM-SC-CO-RO
Items: HC-PB-TA-TV

BookLink Inc
Steve Barringer
120 Lafoy Dr
Clayton NC 27520
919-553-1984; Fax: 919-553-1985
Territory: SE US
Markets: BK-MM-SC-CO-RO
Items: HC-PB-TA-TV

Botanical Interests
Judy Seaborn, Owner
5759 Slick Rock Ct
Boulder CO 80301
303-530-3300
Territory: CO-WY-NM-UT; 4 reps
Markets: GI(garden, gift, gourmet, hardware)
Items: HC-PB-GI
Memo: She prefers lines of books. Represents lines from Sterling, Bantam, Doubleday, Dell, and Simon & Schuster.

Bruck W J Walsh, Representative
Bruce W J Walsh
4377 Marquette
Montreal PQ Canada H2J 3X7
514-528-0679; Fax: 514-528-1298
Territory: Canadian rep for Routledge
Markets: BK
Items: HC-PB

Burdick Associates
Elwyn Burdick
PO Box 399
Dansville NY 14437-0399
716-335-6077; Fax: 716-335-8807
Territory: US

Markets: RO(school supply stores)
Items: HC-PB

C

Cambridge University Press
Joseph Bock, Sales Dir
40 W 20th St
New York NY 10011
800-221-4512; Fax: 212-691-3239
Territory: 8 reps
Markets: US-CN-Mexico

Carole Purkey, Representative
Carole Purkey
204 Cottage Place
Nashville TN 37214
615-885-2960; Fax: 615-885-2960
Territory: VA-NC-SC-WV-TN-GA-AL-FL

Carole Timkovich, Representative
Carole Timkovich
10727 S California Ave
Chicago IL 60655
312-239-4295
Territory: Midwest
Markets: BK
Items: HC-PB
Memo: Associated with Trim Associates.

Casey Group
Katie Casey, Partner
16801 SE Newport Way
Isaquah WA 98027
206-747-9400; Fax: 206-746-3330
Territory: Eastern WA-ID
Memo: Naomi Larsen, Sub-Rep.

Casey Group
Nikki Hoff, Partner
3939 NE Martin Luther King Blvd
Portland OR 97212
503-287-7443; Fax: 503-249-3614
Territory: OR-WA(along the Columbia River)

Chesapeake & Hudson
Bill Hoar and Ted Wedel
122 W Potomac St
Brunswick MD 31716
301-834-7170; Fax: 301-834-6497
800-231-4469
Territory: Mid-Atlantic: 5 reps
Markets: BK
Items: HC-PB

Christopher Ward & Co Inc
Christopher Ward
9 Partridge Trail
Sherman CT 06784-9617
860-355-8273; Fax: 860-350-8841
Territory: Mid-Atlantic: 800-289-8398
Markets: BK
Items: HC-PB

College Suppliers
Ned Walsh, Pres
642 Ridgewood Rd
Ridgeland MS 39157
601-856-4111; Fax: 601-856-4854
Territory: US; 2 reps
Markets: BK-CO
Items: TA-CD

Como Sales Company Inc
Henry Hirsch
799 Broadway
New York NY 10003-6845
212-677-1720; Fax: 212-533-9385
Territory: New England, Mid-Atlantic; 9 reps
Markets: BK-JB-CO-MM
Items: HC-PB-CA-MA-PO-ST-TA
Memo: 1,000 accounts served.

Consolino & Woodward
Thomas P Consolino
5 River Rd #302
Wilton CT 06897
203-762-0205; Fax: 203-762-0208
Markets: BK
Items: HC-PB-CA

Cookbook Resources USA Ltd
Kathy Reising, Pres
3914 N Stowell Ave
Milwaukee WI 53211
414-963-8801
Territory: Upscale gift books
Markets: RO(gourmet, gift, home furnishing)
Items: HC-PB
Memo: Custom publishing of cookbooks and premium sales important.

Craig E McCroskey Inc
Craig McCroskey
313 Marmona Dr
Menlo Park CA 94025
415-322-8962
Items: HC-PB

D

Dan Semi, Representative
Dan Semi
37 Salt Creek Rd
Roselle IL 60172
708-893-2146; Fax: 708-893-2146
Territory: Midwest rep for Routledge
Markets: BK
Items: HC-PB
Memo: Associated with Trim Associates.

Dave Hoff & Associates
Dave Hoff
PO Box 617015
Orlando FL 32861
407-295-2100
Territory: SE US 804-425-5150
Markets: MM-RO(toy stores)
Items: TO-GA(toys and games)

David Lantzer, Representative
David Lantzer
224 W State St
Pasadena CA 91105
818-799-0689
Territory: West Coast & Rocky Mtns

Diane Jackson, Representative
Diane Jackson
3923 SE Kelly
Portland OR 97202
503-233-2956; Fax: 503-233-8953
Territory: AK, OR, UT

Direct Micros
Don Myers, Owner
6405 Metcalf #310
Shawnee Mission KS 66202
913-722-1191
Territory: US(Midwest)
Markets: RO(computer stores)
Items: HC-PB-SW

Dryden Sales Company
Valerie or J R Dryden
10 Yarrow St
Lakewood CO 80226
Territory: Western US & El Paso, TX; 4 reps
Markets: BK-JB-MM-RO(crafts, mail order)
Items: HC-PB-TX-CR-PO-ST-OT(fabric, supp
Memo: 250 accounts served; 30 titles; 2 publishers represented.

Dusty Hawkins & Associates
Dustn Hawkins
4626 SW Beaverton-Hillsdale Hwy
Portland OR 97221
503-245-1435; Fax: 503-244-9914
Territory: OR, WA, AK; 4 reps
Markets: BK-MU-GI(card shops)
Items: CA-GI-GC-ST
Memo: 350 accounts served.

Dutton & Associates
Dory Dutton
PO Box 4865
North Hollywood CA 91617
818-762-7170; Fax: 818-508-5608
Territory: AZ-CO-NV-NM-UT-WY-Southern CA
Markets: BK
Items: HC-PB

E

Ed Hurt, Representative
Ed Hurt
2153 Washington Ave #5
Memphis TN 38104
901-276-0123; Fax: 901-276-2619
Territory: South, SE
Markets: BK
Items: HC-PB
Memo: Associated with George Scheer Associates.

Eerdmans Publishing
Theresa Peterlein
255 Jefferson Ave SE
Grand Rapids MI 49503
800-253-7521; Fax: 616-459-6540
Territory: 8 reps
Items: HC-PB
Memo: Rep their own books only!

Emory-Prosser-Seager
Joan Emory
PO Box 669
Bedford MA 01730
617-275-3354; Fax: 617-275-3369
Territory: New England & Upstate NY; 4 reps
Markets: BK-RO(gift shops)
Items: HC-PB-CA-CD
Memo: Number of titles carried depends on the season.

Erickson Marketing
Chuck Erickson, Rep
2804 Brookview Dr
Burnsville MN 55337
612-890-7639; Fax: 612-890-4512
Territory: Midwest

Errett Stuart Associates Inc
Terre Stuart, Pres
3118 Old Coach Dr
Camarillo CA 93010-1626
805-482-8755; Fax: 805-388-8199
800-635-0326
Territory: West US
Markets: BK
Items: HC-PB

F

Faherty & Associates Inc
Mark Wilson
5331 SW Macadam Ave #243
Portland OR 97213
503-232-7224; Fax: 503-224-3983
Territory: Northern ID, OR, WA, AK
Markets: BK-CO-WH
Items: HC-PB

Faherty & Associates Inc
Patrick Short
533 Airport Blvd #370
Burlingame CA 94010
415-548-1277; Fax: 415-348-0180
Territory: Northern-Southern CA, South NV
Markets: BK-CO-WH
Items: HC-PB

Faherty & Associates Inc
Thomas J Faherty Jr
533 Airport Blvd #370
Burlingame CA 94010-2018
415-548-1277; Fax: 415-348-0180
Territory: North CA, Hawaii, select Southern CA
Markets: BK-CO-WH
Items: HC-PB
Memo: In-house coordinators: Jennifer Loftis and Lucy Myers.

Faherty & Associates Inc
Trevin Matlock
9221 Mills Ave
Montclair CA 91763
909-624-1466; Fax: 909-624-2216
Territory: Southern CA
Markets: BK-CO-WH
Items: HC-PB

Faherty & Associates Inc
Molly Devine
2559 W 32nd Ave
Denver CO 80211
303-477-9754; Fax: 303-477-9755
Territory: AZ-CO-UT-MT-NM-WY
Markets: BK-CO-WH; Items: HC-PB

Faherty & Associates Inc
Ken Guerins
533 Airport Blvd #370
Burlingame CA 94010
415-548-1277; Fax: 415-348-0180
Territory: North-South CA, Southern NV
Markets: BK-CO-WH
Items: HC-PB

Fellow Travelers
Bob Richman, Mdse Dir
1325 Holly Ave
Columbus OH 43212
614-294-4659; Fax: 614-294-7077
Territory: Midwest; 16 reps
Markets: BK-CO-MU-RO(gift shops)
Items: GI-CA-GC-PO-SB-TA-OT
Memo: 2200 accounts served.

Flynn & Talley Associates
Lindsay Talley
42 Dennis Court
Highstown NJ 08520
609-443-0609; Fax: 609-443-0612
Territory: US; 7 reps
Markets: MM
Items: CA-OT(coloring, storybooks)
Memo: 200 accounts served; 2 publishers represented.

Frank Rizzo & Associates
Frank Rizzo
151 N Beacon St
Middletown NY 10940
914-343-6059

Franklin Marketeers
Frank Morton, Owner
6100 Fourth Ave South
6100 Bldg #236
Seattle WA 98108
206-763-2020; Fax: 206-767-9944
Territory: WA-OR-ID-AK
Markets: RO(gift, gourmet)
Items: HC-PB-GI
Memo: Sheila Lind, VP

Fujii Associates
Caesar Ward, Office Mgr
536 W Addison #174
Chicago IL 60613
312-549-0300; Fax: 312-549-0720
Territory: IA-IL-IN-KS-KY-MI-MN-MO-ND-NE-OH-SD-WI-OK-LA-AR; 8 reps
Markets: BK-CO
Items: HC-PB-CA-SW(CD-ROM
Memo: Territory includes: Bob Ahlers, Linda Ziegler, JerryStroud, Jeff Davidson, Mark Fleeman, Kevin King, Ken Rothman, Don Sturtz.

Fuller Associates
Alan Fuller, Pres
645 Manhattan Pl #310
Boulder CO 80303
303-494-0536; Fax: 303-494-1748
Territory: Rocky Mountain states
Markets: BK
Items: HC-PB-TA-CA

G

Gary and Riedel Co
200 Fifth Ave #514
New York NY 10010
212-675-4388
Territory: Mid-Atlantic-US
Markets: RO(toy stores)
Items: TO-GM(toys and games)

Gary Trim Associates
Gary Trim
2643 N Burling St
Chicago IL 60614-1513
312-871-1249
Territory: Midwest
Markets: BK
Items: HC-PB

Genesis Marketing Group
16 Wellington Ave
Greenville SC 29609-4902
803-233-2651
Territory: US
Markets: BK-RO(gift shops)
Items: HC-PB-GI-BC-TA-TV

George Scheer Associates
George F Scheer
918 Kings Mill Rd
Chapel Hill NC 27514-4418
910-967-1088; Fax: 910-854-6908
Territory: South, SE US; 5 reps
Markets: BK
Items: HC-PB

Gerry Sales Company
Ron Postema, Pres
8235 Amelia
Jenison MI 49428
616-669-3308; Fax: 616-669-3103
Territory: OH-MI-KY-IN-PA-VA-NY
Markets: MM-RO(toys, crafts, fairy tales)
Items: TO-GM-CR

Gordon Law & Associates
Gordon Law
12850 SW Chicory Ct
Tigard OR 97223
503-524-9314; Fax: 503-524-9314
Territory: OR-WA-ID-MT-AK; 3 reps
Markets: BK-MM
Items: HC-CA-MM-GI-ST-OT
Memo: 450 accounts served; 3 publishers represented.

Graphic Arts Center Pub
Ken Rowe, Dir of Trade Sales
PO Box 10306
3019 NW Yeon
Portland OR 97210
503-226-2402; Fax: 503-223-1410
Territory: OR-WA-ID-MT-UT-IT
Markets: BK-SC-CO
Items: HC-PB-CA
Memo: 4 house reps; 24 commission reps; also distributes for other publishers: Whitecaps Books, Vancouver, BC, Epicenter Press, Seattle, WA, & Harmsen Publishing, Phoenix, AZ.

Gregg Associates
Charles Gregg
1558 Tremont St
Duxbury MA 02332-3312
617-934-2701
Territory: New England states; 2 reps
Markets: BK-RO-MM-CH
Items: HC-PB-TA-TV

H

Hand Associates
Jock Hayward
16 Nelson Ave
Mill Valley CA 94941
415-383-3883; Fax: 415-383-1914
Territory: 11 Western states, AK & HI; 5 reps
Markets: BK
Items: HC-PB
Memo: Jock Hayward is main contact

Hand Associates
Linda Bigam
123 Bodega Ave
Petaluma CA 94952
708-776-4658
Territory: 5 reps
Markets: BK
Items: HC-PB

Hand Associates
Scott Bowers
3851 Daisy Cir
Seal Beach CA 90740
310-493-4145
Territory: 5 reps
Markets: BK
Items: HC-PB

Hand Associates
David Diehl
3608 E Denny Way
Seattle WA 98122
206-328-0295

Hand Associates
Richard Kolbert
2456 Carmel
Oakland CA 94602
510-482-0253; Fax: 510-482-1586
Territory: 5 reps
Markets: BK
Items: HC-PB

Harry Collins, Representative
Harry Collins
921 Springfield Dr
Campbell CA 95008
408-378-2367
Territory: N & Cent CA-OR-AK- N NV

Heinecken & Associates Ltd
Sandra Bartels
9069 Baker Ave
Northfield MN 55057
507-663-7174; Fax: 507-663-1045
Territory: IL/IA/IN/MN/WI
Memo: 800-398-0193

Heinecken & Associates Ltd
Charles Boswell
9629 Carriage Run Cir
Loveland OH 45140
513-677-3105; Fax: 513-677-3225
Territory: KY/WV/central-southern IN & OH

Heinecken & Associates Ltd
Wes Caliger
PO Box 1027
Iowa City IA 52244-1027
319-338-8988; Fax: 319-338-9075
800-397-2665.
Territory: IA/KS/MO/NE/some IL

Henry J Hubert
PO Box 1347
Arvada CO 80001
303-422-8640
Territory: CO-UT-WY-NM
Markets: BK-RO
Items: HC-PB-MM

Duke Hill, Martin Associates
Duke Hill
756 Collier Dr
San Leandro CA 94577
510-483-2939
Territory: West States
Markets: PL-CO-BK

Howard Ramer & Associates
Howard Ramer
41 Dunn St
Laguna Niguel CA 92677
714-249-2107; Fax: 714-582-7758
Territory: West US
Markets: SC-RO(toy, teacher stores)
Items: HC-PB-TO-GI

I

I-5 Associates
Henry Hubert
PO Box 1347
Arvada CO 80001
303-422-8640; Fax: 303-422-8640
Territory: S CA-AZ
Markets: BK-RO-WH
Items: HC-PB

I-5 Associates
George Carroll
PO Box 14628
Portland OR 97214
503-232-1023; Fax: 503-232-0851
Territory: AK-ID-MT-OR-WA
Markets: BK-RO-WH
Items: HC-PB

I-5 Associates
Wendy Werris
401 N Sycamore Ave #2
Los Angeles CA 90036
213-934-2653; Fax: 213-934-8068
Territory: S CA-AZ
Markets: BK-RO-WH
Items: HC-PB

I-5 Associates
Todd Hager
3871 Piedmont Ave #94
Oakland CA 94611
510-655-3166; Fax: 510-655-3166
Territory: N CA-NV-HI
Markets: BK-RO-WH
Items: HC-PB

J

J S Ide Associates Inc
Jay Ide
18-5 E Dundee Rd #201
Barrington IL 60010-3598
708-382-4500; Fax: 708-382-1361
Territory: Midwest
Markets: BK-CO-WH-SL-PL
Items: HC-PB-RM-CA-MA-TA

Jerry Levy Associates
Jerry Levy, Owner
6100 Fourth Ave S
6100 Bldg #437
Seattle WA 98108
206-762-6204
Markets: RO(gift)
Items: HC-PB-GI-TO-GC

John Daly, Representative
John Dally
7937 11th Ave Sw
Seattle WA 98106
206-767-8268; Fax: 206-763-6870
Territory: Western Regional Sales Mgr

John Kooistra, Representative
22 Olena St
Hilo HI 96720
808-935-5637; Fax: 808-935-5637
Items: HC-PB-MM
Memo: Prefers to rep lines, sells in HI only.

Johns Hopkins University Press
Michael Donatelli
2715 N Charles St
Baltimore MD 21218-4319
410-516-6936
Territory: New England & Mid-Atlantic
Items: HC-PB

Joseph Agnelli, Representative
Joseph Agnelli
2325 N Cleveland (Rear)
Little Rock AR 72207
501-666-5119; Fax: 501-666-5121
Territory: South, SE
Markets: BK
Items: HC-PB
Memo: Associated with George Scheer Associates

K

Kampmann, Kump & Bell
Eric Kampmann, Partner
27 W 20th St #1102
New York NY 10011
212-727-0190; Fax: 212-727-0195
Territory: US-Canada
Markets: BK-WH
Items: HC-PB-MM-CA

Keven Monahan & Associates
Kevin Monahan
9 Boothe Hill Rd
Chapel Hill NC 27514
919-933-7879; Fax: 919-929-0562
Territory: SE US(V-WV-NC-SC-GA-FL)
Markets: BK-RO-JB
Items: HC-PB

Kitchen Concepts
Leo Neeleman, VP Sales
1801 1, 2 N Orangethorpe Park
Anaheim CA 92801
714-879-3083; Fax: 714-879-3559
Territory: Southern CA-AZ-NV-HI; 5 reps
Markets: RO(gourmet, gift)
Items: HC-PB-OT

Krikorian-Miller Associates
Irwin Miller, Pres
11 Market Square #5
PO Box 271
Newburyport MA 01950
508-465-7377; Fax: 508-465-1101
Territory: New England
Markets: BK-RO(toy, gift trade)
Items: HC-PB-TO-GI-GC

Krotman & Berke
Allen Berke
1107 Broadway #1204
New York NY 10010
212-691-3030; Fax: 212-627-9736
Territory: NE US
Markets: RO(toy stores)
Items: TO-GM(toys and games)

Kurtzman Book Sales Inc
Susan Brody
17348 W 12 Mile Rd #101
Southfield MI 48076
810-335-7766; Fax: 810-557-7230
Territory: 2 reps
Markets: BK-CO-SC-PL-SL
Items: HC-PB

L

Lee Collins & Associates
Ted H Terry
19216 SE 46th Pl
Issaquah WA 98027
206-747-3411; Fax: 206-747-3411
Territory: AK-ID-UT-WA-OR
Items: HC-PB
Accounts: Aims Intnl, Baker Book House, Blake, Bilingual, Brookings Institute, Cornell U. Pr, Countryman, Childrens Pr, Crossroads, Continuum, Fordham U.Pr, Garborgs, Heinemann, Holiday House, Holt Text, IL U. Pr, IN U. Pr, John Hopkins Pr, L.S.U. Pr, Lyons & Burford, NC U. Pr, Northwestern U. Pr, Raintree, SteckVaughn, Revell, Springer, Verlag, Syracuse U. Pr, Trafalger Square, U. of AR Pr, U. of TX Pr, U. of WI Pr

Lee Collins &Associates
Brent Sill
814 E Homestead Dr
Highlands Ranch CO 80126
303-470-1325; Fax: 303-470-6065
Territory: MT

Lee R Collins Associates
Lee R Collins
4910 St Louis Ct
Culver City CA 90230-4318
310-838-4362; Fax: 310-838-5007
Territory: West US
Markets: BK
Items: HC-PB

Lolly and Company
Lolly Randall Middleton, Owner
6100 Fourth Ave S
6100 Building #355
Seattle WA 98108
206-762-6423; Fax: 206-762-2293
Territory: WA-OR-AK
Markets: RO(gift, toy)
Items: GI-TO

M

M J Daniel Company
Todd Pauletti, Buyer
1000 Beltline Rd
Carrollton TX 75006
214-245-3600; Fax: 214-245-1462
Territory: US-IT-(military PX's)
Markets: RO(military exchanges)
Items: TO-GM(toys and games)
Memo: Todd's ext: 305. Press release with book

Martin Beeman, Representative
Martin Beeman
2320 N Austin Ave
Georgetown TX 78626
512-863-0521; Fax: 512-869-2770
Territory: TX-LA-OK-AR
Markets: BK-WH
Items: HC-PB-TA-TV(CD's)

McCormick Associates
John Hopkins
9086 Hoyt St
Westminster CO 80021
303-423-1233; Fax: 303-940-8230
Territory: E WA-ID-MT-CO-UT-NM
Markets: BK
Items: HC-PB

McCormick Associates
Frank McCormick
2604-B El Camino Real #249
Carlsbad CA 92008
800-729-2512; Fax: 619-439-2512
Territory: W WA, AK
Markets: BK-RO
Items: HC-PB
Memo: Academy Chicago, Arte Publico, Astor, Chelsea Green, Country Roads, Dufour Eds, Fielding Ntn'l, Fisher Bks, Galison Bks, Graphique De France, H B J, Home Planners, Largely Literary Designs, Marketing Arm, McClanahan Bk Co, NBM, New Horizon, Pelican Pub, Pfeiffer & Co, Sound Prints.

McDonough & Associates
Dr John McDonough, Dir
540 North Ave
Pittsburgh PA 15209
412-821-4434; Fax: 412-821-8006
Territory: US-new American made products
Markets: RO-MM
Items: HC-PB-GI-TO-CR-GA-CL-FD(food)
Memo: Reps to military exchanges and federal government agencies. MUST be a NEW or well-established product

McQueen Associates
Horace McQueen
11419 Atwell
PO Box 35061
Houston TX 77035
713-723-9682; Fax: 713-723-8775
Territory: TX-AR-LA-OK
Markets: BK-MM(general trade)
Items: HC-PB-TA-TV

Melman-Moster Associates
Frank Moster
11 Lee Way
Oakland NJ 07436
201-337-0134; Fax: 201-337-0134
Territory: Mid-Atlantic states; 3 reps
Markets: BK-CO-JB-MU-RO
Items: HC-PB-RM-TX-CA-GC-TA-TV
Memo: 400+ accounts served; 20 publishers represented.

Metzger-Huset Associates
Gary Metzger, Bob Huset, Owners
5501 4th Ave S #202
Seattle WA 98108
206-762-4849; Fax: 206-762-4849
Territory: WA-OR-ID-AK
Markets: RO(gift, toy)
Items: GI-TO(party goods)

Meyer Religious Book Sales
Eileen Golinski, Sales Rep
24 Taylor St
Hampton NH 03842
603-929-0629
Territory: Sales rep, marketing, exhibits
Markets: BK-RO
Items: HC-PB

Michael Bills, Representative
Michael Bills
2016 Walnut St
Boulder CO 80302
303-449-3931; Fax: 303-449-3931
Territory: E WA-OR-ID-MT-WY-CO-NM-TX
Memo: Addison-Wesley, Benjamin, Cummings, Longman, Inc.

Michael Carley, Representative
Michael Carley
2705 32nd Ave S
Seattle WA 98144
206-723-7114; Fax: 206-723-7114
Territory: AK-ID-MT-OR-WA

Midpoint Trade Books
Eric Kampmann, Pres
27 W 20th St #1102
New York NY 10011
212-727-0190; Fax: 212-727-0195
Territory: National US accounts
Markets: BK-WH
Items: HC-PB-MM-CA

Miller Trade Book Marketing
Bruce Miller & Eric Miller
1801 W Byron #2K
Chicago IL 60613
312-404-1050; Fax: 312-404-1051
Territory: Midwest
Markets: BK-CO
Items: HC-PB
Memo: Bruce and Eric are Co-Owners.

N

Nanci McCrackin, Sales Rep
Nanci McCrackin, Sales Rep
138 Windy Row
Peterborough NH 03458
603-924-8766; Fax: 603-924-0096
E-Mail: mcbooks@aol.com
Territory: New England
Markets: BK-JB-MU
Items: HC-PB-CA-GC-ST-TA
Memo: 100+ accounts served; 8 publishers represented.

Nancy Suib & Associates
Nancy Suib
4500 Steele St
Oakland CA 94619
510-482-2303; Fax: 510-482-8573
Territory: West Coast
Markets: BK-WH-R0(specialty)
Items: PB-HC
Memo: Deals with publishers directly.

Nancy Suib Associates
Carl Schmidt
PO Box 158
Louisville CO 80027
303-666-7015; Fax: 303-661-0786
Territory: ID-MT
Markets: BK-RO
Items: HC-PB
Accounts: Cambridge Univ Press, Westview

National Book Network
Jeanine LaBorne
Proe & Proe Assoc
2000 Hamilton St #695
Philadelphia PA 19130
215-567-1654; Fax: 215-567-1513
Territory: NY & Mid-Atlantic rep
Markets: BK-JB-WH-CO
Items: HC-PB
Memo: Philadelphia, Cen & S NJ, East PA.

National Book Network
Elida Tamez
Sal McLemore & Assoc
505 Parkway
Denton TX 76201
817-382-5384
Territory: TX-LA-AR-OK
Markets: BK-JB-WH-CO
Items: HC-PB

National Book Network
Randall Spurgin
Spurgin & Sinclair Assoc
1465 Woodbury Ave #205
Portsmouth NH 03801 p73
603-742-1646; Fax: 603-431-3502
Territory: Boston area-VT-NH-ME
Markets: BK-JB-WH-CO
Items: HC-PB

National Book Network
David Roochvarg
Proe & Proe Assoc
Six Sealey Ave Apt 6B
Hempstead NY 11550
516-483-4492; Fax: 516-483-4492
Territory: Long Island, Hudson Valley, Westchester Co, Northern NJ
Markets: BK-JB-WH-CO; Items: HC-PB

National Book Network
Spencer Gale
67-38 108th St #A-14
Forest Hills NY 11375
718-575-4155; Fax: 718-575-4155
Territory: National accounts
Markets: BK-JB-WH-CO
Items: HC-PB

National Book Network
Terre Stuart
Stuart Associates
3118 Old Coach Dr
Camarillo CA 93010
805-482-8755; Fax: 805-388-8199
800-635-0326
Territory: Western rep - Southern CA
Markets: BK-JB-WH-CO
Items: HC-PB

National Book Network
Eric Hedin
Spurgin & Sinclair Assoc
PO Box 351 6 School Ln
Chester CT 06412
203-526-4483; Fax: 203-526-1609
Territory: CT-RI-Cape Cod
Markets: BK-JB-WH-CO
Items: HC-PB

National Book Network
Brian Stuart
Stuart Associates
6205 Glenhurst Way
Citrus Heights CA 95621
916-725-5276
Territory: No CA-NV-CO-UT-WY
Markets: BK-JB-WH-CO
Items: HC-PB
Memo: Stuart Associates: 800-635-0326.

National Book Network
Sal McLemore
Sal McLemore & Assoc
5330 Shady Gardens Dr
Kingwood TX 77339
713-360-5204; Fax: 713-360-5204
Territory: TX-LA-AR-OK
Markets: BK-JB-WH-CO
Items: HC-PB

National Book Network
Ray Wittrup
14485 Pine Lakes Dr
Strongsville OH 44136
216-572-1915; Fax: 216-572-0801
Territory: South MI-Chicago, IL-MO-KS-NE SD-IA-OH-IN-KY-ND-MN-WI
Markets: BK-JB-WH-CO
Items: HC-PB

National Book Network
Sara Sinclair
Spurgin & Sinclair Assoc
1465 Woodbury Ave #205
Portsmouth NH 03801
603-742-1646; Fax: 603-431-3502
Territory: Boston area-VT-NH-ME
Markets: BK-JB-WH-CO
Items: HC-PB

National Book Network
Anthony Proe
Proe & Proe Assoc
304 Farmer St
Syracuse NY 13203
315-471-8005; Fax: 315-475-5806
Territory: NYC-Upstate NY
Markets: BK-JB-WH-CO
Items: HC-PB

National Book Network
Michael Sullivan
265 Riverside Dr #11A
New York NY 10025
212-865-7790; Fax: 212-865-7790
Territory: National accounts
Markets: BK-JB-WH-CO
Items: HC-PB

National Book Network
Joyce Ruff Abdill
Stuart Associates
1113 SE Jackson
Roseburg OR 97470
503-672-4170
Territory: OR-WA-ID-MT
Markets: BK-JB-WH-CO
Items: HC-PB

National Book Network
Moira Megargee
Spurgin & Sinclair Assoc
20 Belmont Ave
Northampton MA 01060
413-584-5089; Fax: 413-584-5089
Territory: MA-VT-West NH
Markets: BK-JB-WH-CO
Items: HC-PB

National Book Network
Jason Stuart
Stuart Associates
13850 Mango Dr #27
Del Mar CA 92014
619-794-0491
Territory: AZ-NM-So CA
Markets: BK-JB-WH-CO
Items: HC-PB

National Book Network
Carole Purkey
204 Cottage Pl
Nashville TN 37214
615-885-2960; Fax: 615-885-2960
Territory: VA-NC-SC-WV-TN-GA-AL-FL-MS
Markets: BK-JB-WH-CO
Items: HC-PB

National Book Network
Jeff Stuart
Stuart Associates
824 Weaver Ln
Concord CA 94518
510-687-7878
Territory: North CA-AK-HI
Markets: BK-JB-WH-CO
Items: HC-PB

National Book Network
Cecelia Walthall
Proe & Proe Assoc
2027 Turtle Pond Dr
Reston VA 22091
703-642-9144; Fax: 703-716-3385
Territory: NY-DC-DE-MD-West PA
Markets: BK-JB-WH-CO; Items: HC-PB

National Book Network
Jane A Martin
Proe & Proe Assoc
304 Farmer St
Syracuse NY 13203
315-471-8005; Fax: 315-475-5806
Territory: NYC-Upstate NY
Markets: BK-JB-WH-CO
Items: HC-PB

New England Book Sales Co
Arnold A Nickelsberg
2 Wedgewood Rd
Westport CT 06880-2735
203-226-9262; Fax: 203-222-8006
Territory: New England

Nor'East Book Sales
Doug Paton, Sales Rep
440 Mendon Rd
North Attleboro MA 02760
508-761-5414; Fax: 508-761-6372
Territory: New England
Markets: BK-CO-PL-SL
Items: HC-PB

O

Oliver Gilliland, Representative
Oliver Gilliland
484 Lake Park Ave Box 14
Oakland CA 94610
510-834-7804
Territory: N CA-OR-WA

Oregon Historical Society
Virginia Linnman
1200 SW Park Ave
Portland OR 97205
503-222-1741; Fax: 503-221-2035
Territory: Northwest US

P

Palmer & Associates
Theron Palmer, Jr
1110 Indian Dr
Salado TX 76571
817-947-9560; Fax: 817-947-5680
Territory: SW US
Markets: BK-MU-CO
Items: HC-PB-TA-TV

Park Avenue Agents
Diana and John Park
6100 Fourth Ave S
6100 Building #575
Seattle WA 98108
206-762-4231; Fax: 206-762-7447
800-272-7275
Territory: WA-OR-ID-MT-AK
Markets: RO(gift, toy, art, kitchen stores)
Items: HC-PB-GI-TO

Patricia Alfonsi, Representative
Patricia Alfonsi
182 Carnelian
San Francisco CA 94131
415-647-5568; Fax: 415-647-5589
Territory: Northwest — 18 states
Memo: Random House Mdse(Juvenile).

Peter Clark, Representative
Peter Clark
PO Box 3563
Blaine WA 98231
604-531-5849
Territory: WA-OR-BC CN
Markets: BK(WA & OR only)-RO
Items: HC-PB
Memo: Non-traditional bookstores. No booksellers in BC & Alberta!

Print & Sound
Jim Walsh, Owner
PO Box 3616
Williamsburg VA 23187
804-565-2376; Fax: 804-565-3187
E-Mail: paspr@aol.com
Territory: AL-FL-GA-MS-NC-SC-TN-VA; 4 reps
Markets: RO-WH(booksellers)
Items: HC-PB-RM-CA-TA-TV-CD-SB-OT

Proe & Proe Associates
Cecilia Walthall
2027 Turtle Pond Dr
Reston VA 22091
703-716-3384; Fax: 703-716-3385
Territory: DC-DE-MD-W PA

Proe & Proe Associates
David Roochvag
Six Sealey Ave Apt 6B
Hempstead NY 11550
516-483-3392; Fax: 516-483-4492
Territory: Long Island, Hudson Valley

Proe & Proe Associates
Jayne Martin & Tony Proe
304 Farmer St
Syracuse NY 13203
315-471-8005; Fax: 315-475-5806
Territory: NYC-Ustate NY

Proe & Proe Associates
Jeanie LaBorne
2000 Hamilton St #695
Philadelphia PA 19130
215-567-1654; Fax: 215-567-1513
Territory: Phildaelphia-C & S NJ-E PA

R

Ray Wittrup, Representative
Ray Wittrup
14485 Pine Lakes Dr
Strongville OH 44136
216-572-1915; Fax: 216-572-0801
Territory: Midwest

Redwood Book Sales
Richard Fisher
6710 Wilton Dr
Oakland CA 94611
510-482-4355; Fax: 510-482-0161
Territory: OR-WA-ID-MT-AK

Richard DeRose, Representative
Richard DeRose
PO Box 1788
Martinez CA 94553
510-228-2875; Fax: 510-370-2276
Territory: AK-CA-HI-ID-MT-OR-WA-UT

Rick O'Shea Associates
Ann O'Shea
6100 Fourth Ave S
6100 Bldg #224
Seattle WA 98108
206-763-9167; Fax: 206-767-4718
Territory: WA-OR-Northern CA
Markets: RO(gift, toy)
Items: HC-PB-GI-TO-OT

Roghaar Associates
Linda Roghaar
2809 Azalea Pl
Nashville TN 37204
615-269-8977; Fax: 615-297-6630
Territory: SE US
Markets: BK-CO
Items: HC-PB

Ron Doussard & Associates
Ron Doussard
6 Castle Pine Ct
Lake of the Hills IL 60102
847-854-6090; Fax: 847-854-6092
Territory: Midwest
Markets: BK-JB-RO-CO-MM
Items: HC-PB-MM-CA-TA

Ronald Columbus, Representative
Ronald C Columbus
320 West 76th St p73
New York NY 10023-8058
212-873-0524; Fax:
Territory: New York & Washington DC
Markets: BK-CO
Items: HC-PB

Routledge
Paul C Williams, Dir of Sales
1 Penn Plz 41st Fl
New York NY 10119-4198
212-760-0098; Fax: 212-268-6736
800-797-3803
Markets: BK
Items: HC-PB
Memo: Paul's ext: 402.

Routledge
Kendrick Melish
805 Union St #1
Brooklyn NY 11215
718-399-9047; Fax: 718-399-9047
Territory: DE-MD-NJ-NY-PA-Washington, DC
Markets: BK
Items: HC-PB

Routledge
Judy Kucera
77 Cuvier St
San Francisco CA 94112
415-452-4221; Fax: 415-452-4221
Territory: ID-MT-OR-WA-AK-HI-Northern CA
Markets: BK
Items: HC-PB

Roy Perry Associates
Roy Perry, Pres
445 Rolling Hills Rd
Bridgewater NJ 08807
908-231-6609; Fax: 908-231-6610
Territory: North America
Markets: RO(art supply & craft stores)
Items: HC-PB-GI-supplies

Ryen Re Associates
Dick Ryen, Pres
585 Seminole St
Oradell NJ 07649
201-261-7450; Fax: 201-261-6294
Territory: NY-NJ-PA-MD-DE-DC; 4 reps
Markets: BK-RO-SC
Items: CA-HC-MA-PB-PO-SB-TA(book)

S

S & B Sales Associates
Stanley Goldman
27 Reservoir St
Brockton MA 02401 p73
508-559-9174; Fax: 508-559-9174
Territory: New England states
Markets: BK-SL
Items: HC-PB-CA-SB-TA(bookbags)

S & B Sales Associates
Bill Palizzolo
81 Indian Ridge Rd
Contoocook NH 03229
603-746-3547; Fax: 603-746-3547
Territory: New England states
Markets: BK-SL
Items: HC-PB-CA-SB-TA(bookbags)

Sal McLemore & Associates
Eida Tamez
505 Parkway
Denton TX 76201
817-382-5384
Territory: TX-LA-AR-OK

Sal McLemore & Associates
Sal McLemore
5330 Shady Gardens Dr
Kingwood TX 77339
713-360-5204; Fax: 713-360-5204
Territory: TX-LA-AR-OK

Sam Borofsky Associates
Sam Borofsky, Pres
PO Box 323
Roslyn NY 11576
516-484-2900; Fax: 516-484-5334
Territory: US
Markets: RO(toy, computer, electronics)
Items: HC-PB-SW

School Media Associates
Tom Kenworthy, Dir
2700 NE Express Way C-800
Atlanta GA 30345
404-728-8839; Fax: 404-728-9450
Territory: Southern US
Markets: SC-PL
Items: PB-MM-TA-TV

Scott Billyou, Representative
Scott Billyou
17 Scarsdale Rd
PO Box 555
West Hartford CT 06107
860-561-1234
Territory: New England-NY
Markets: BK
Items: HC-PB-RM

Scott LePine, Representative
Scott LePine
2360 Jeppesen Acres Rd
Eugene OR 97401
503-686-1364; Fax: 503-334-6229
Territory: Pacific Northwest
Items: HC-PB

Sea Mart Associates
Ken & Susan Atwell
6100 Fourth Ave S
6100 Bldg #381
Seattle WA 98108
206-762-4191
800-877-8017
Markets: RO(gift, art)
Items: HC-PB-GI-GC

Sewell Associates
Herb Sewell, Owner
4164 Coffman Ln
Minneapolis MN 55406
612-721-2662; Fax: 612-721-0072
Territory: MN-WI-SD-ND
Markets: BK-CO-GI
Items: HC-PB

Sheldon Wiener Sales Organization Inc
Sheldon Wiener, Pres
200 Fifth Ave #1225
New York NY 10010
212-645-5757; Fax: 212-627-3947
Territory: New England, Mid-Atlantic
Markets: MM-RO(toy stores)
Items: TO

Shirley Robins & Associates
Shirley Robins
5238 Beachside Dr
Minnetonka MN 55343
612-935-9083; Fax: 612-935-2233
Territory: MN-ND-SD
Markets: RO(gifts)-BK-CH
Items: HC-PB-GI-CA-PO-GC

Siddall Associates
Craig Siddall
1168 Hamilton St #200
Vancouver BC Canada V6B 2S2
604-662-3511; Fax: 604-683-7540
E-Mail: siddall@axionet.com
Territory: CN(Western Canada)
Markets: BK-JB-RO(computers)-MM-PL
Items: HC-TX-PB-CA-SW

Sirak & Sirak Associates
Jim or Lisa Sirak, Owners
Montville Chase Manhatten
20 Davenport Rd
Montville NJ 07045
201-299-0085
Territory: Mid-Atlantic
Markets: BK-RO-MU-WH
Items: HC-PB-RM-CA

Southern Territory Assoc Inc
Judy Stevenson, Business Mgr
2205 West Division #A4
Arlington TX 76012
Markets: BK-CO-RO(selected gift stores)-MU
Items: HC-PB-TA
Memo: Southern Territory Associates Inc, PO Box 13519, Arlington, TX 76094; Phone: 817-861-9644; 800-331-7016; FAX: 817-277-3199.

Southern Territory Associates
Geoff Rizzo
771 Northwest Placid Ave
Port St Lucie FL 34983
407-871-1222; Fax: 407-871-1222
Territory: FL(except panhandle)
Markets: BK-CO-RO(selected gift stores)MU
Items: HC-PB-TA

Southern Territory Associates
Deborah A Busch
1207 Oglethorpe Dr
Atlanta GA 30319
404-237-1013; Fax: 404-237-1013
Territory: GA
Markets: BK-CO-RO(selected gift stores)-MU
Items: HC-PB-TA
Memo: Selected accts in Charlotte NC, SC, Florida Panhandle, and Southern AL.

Southern Territory Associates
Corey D Godfrey
5816 Birchbrook Dr #218
Dallas TX 75206
214-265-0580; Fax: 214-265-0668
Territory: OK-AR-LA-selected accts N TX
Markets: BK-CO-RO(selected gift stores)-MU
Items: HC-PB-TA

Southern Territory Associates
Ed Springer, Publishers Rep
160 Westminster Dr NE
Atlanta GA 30309
404-892-6484; Fax: 404-873-3661
Territory: GA-TN-AL-major SE accounts
Markets: BK-CO-RO(selected gift stores)MU
Items: HC-PB-TA

Southern Territory Associates
Mike Donahue
10209 Venita Cove
Austin TX 78733
512-263-5211; Fax: 512-263-5211
Territory: Southern TX
Markets: BK-CO-RO(selected gift stores)MU
Items: HC-PB-TA
Memo: Walden & Dalton Regional Buyers

Southern Territory Associates
Edward Wood
Rt 2 Bennett Rd
PO Box 584
Siler City NC 27344
919-742-5855; Fax: 919-742-5044
Territory: NC-VA
Markets: BK-CO-RO(selected gift stores)MU
Items: HC-PB-TA

Southern Territory Associates
Janet H Fairchild
3102 Waterford Cir
Nashville TN 37221
615-662-0670; Fax: 615-662-0670
Territory: MS, Northern AL, TN
Markets: BK-CO-RO(selected gift stores)-MU
Items: HC-PB-TA

Southern Territory Associates
James C Shepherd
9849 Faircrest
Dallas TX 75238
214-343-9730; Fax: 214-343-9730
Territory: Major N & W TX; major SW account
Markets: BK-CO-RO(selected gift stores)MU
Items: HC-PB-TA

Spurgin & Sinclair Associates
Eric Hedin
PO Box 351
6 School Ln
Chester CT 06412
203-526-4483; Fax: 203-526-1609
Territory: CT-RI-CAPE COD
Markets: BK-SH-MU-RO
Items: HC-PB-TA

Spurgin & Sinclair Associates
Moira Megargee
20 Belmont Ave
Northampton MA 01060
413-584-5089; Fax: 413-584-5089
Territory: MA, VT, NH
Markets: BK-SH-MU-RO
Items: HC-PB-TA

Spurgin & Sinclair Associates
Randy Spurgin & Sara Sinclair
1465 Woodbury Ave #205
Portsmouth NH 03801
603-742-1646; Fax: 603-431-3502
Territory: VT, NH, ME, Boston Area
Markets: BK-SH-MU-RO
Items: HC-PB-TA

St Martin's Press
Christine Foye
1202 E Pike St #1239
Seattle WA 98122
206-632-3815; Fax: 206-632-4268
Territory: NW US & AK
Markets: Ind bookstores & whslers only
Items: HC-PB

Stack & Company
Ned Stack, Owner
6100 Fourth Ave S #281
Seattle WA 98108
206-762-7607; Fax: 206-762-8731
Territory: WA-OR-ID-MT-AK
Markets: RO(gift)-MM
Items: HC-PB-GI-GA-TA(New Age)

Stack and Co
Ned Stack, Owner
6100 Fourth Ave S #281
Seattle WA 98108
206-762-7607; Fax: 206-762-8731
Markets: MM-RO(toy)
Items: HC-PB-GI-TO

Stacy Kaye
Stacy Kaye
6001 Phinney Ave N #1
Seattle WA 98103
206-782-6226; Fax: 206-782-7206
Territory: WA(state)
Markets: NO BOOKS!
Items: CA-ST-GC(journals, blank books)

Stephen Berger-Sales Company
Stephen Berger, Pres
28 Michelle Ln
Randolph MA 02368
617-963-5433; Fax: 617-986-2620
Territory: New England
Markets: MM-RO(toy stores)
Items: TO-GM(toys and games)

Stephen James, Representative
Stephen James
200 Pine Valley Rd
Lake Oswego OR 97034
503-636-9703; Fax: 503-636-9703
Territory: ID-MT-OR-WA

Stephen Wilson, Representative
Stephen Wilson
168 Chestnut St
Cambridge MA 02139-4706
617-354-0785
Territory: New England
Markets: BK
Items: HC-PB

Stephen Young & Associates
Stephen Young, Pres
LA Mart #830
1933 S Broadway
Los Angeles CA 90007
213-748-8814; Fax: 213-748-5895
Territory: CA-AZ-Las Vegas
Markets: RO(gift)
Items: HC-PB-GI-GC

Strauss Consultants
Karen Strauss, Pres
475 Park Ave S
New York NY 10016
212-545-6913; Fax: 212-545-6915
Territory: Specialized in large accounts
Markets: CH-MM
Items: HC-PB
Memo: Specializes in selling books to the major chains and wholesale outlets.

Stuart Associates
Joyce Ruff Abdill
1113 SE Jackson St
Roseburg OR 97470
503-672-4170; Fax: 805-388-8199
Territory: 13 Western states; 5 reps
Markets: BK-JB-CO
Items: HC-PB-MM-CA
Memo: 1,000+ accounts; 25 publishers.

Stuart Associates
Terre Stuart
3118 Old Coach Dr
Camarillo CA 93010
805-482-8755; Fax: 805-388-8199
Territory: 13 Western states; 5 reps
Markets: BK-JB-CO
Items: HC-PB-MM-CA
Memo: 1,000+ accounts; 25 publishers.

Stuart Associates
Brian Stuart
6205 Glenhurst Way
Citrus Heights CA 95621
916-725-5276; Fax: 805-388-8199
Territory: 13 Western states; 5 reps
Markets: BK-JB-CO
Items: HC-PB-MM-CA
Memo: 1,000 accounts; 25 publishers.

Stuart Associates
Jason Stuart
13850 Mango Dr #27
Del Mar CA 92014
619-794-0491; Fax: 805-388-8199
Territory: 13 Western states; 5 reps
Markets: BK-JB-CO
Items: HC-PB-MM-CA
Memo: 1,000+ accounts; 25 publishers.

Stuart Associates
Jeff Stuart
824 Weaver Ln
Concord CA 94518
510-687-7878; Fax: 805-388-8199
Territory: 13 Western states; 5 reps
Markets: BK-JB-CO
Items: HC-PB-MM-CA
Memo: 1,000+ accounts; 25 publishers.

T

Talbot Associates
William Talbot or Neil Talbot
200 Fifth Ave #940
New York NY 10010
212-675-2650; Fax: 212-929-5158
Territory: NY(key chains, mail order accts)
Markets: MM-RO(toy stores)
Items: TO-GA
Memo: Sales reps to toy manufacturers.

Tom Stouras, Representative
Tom Stouras
Univ of California Press
2120 Berkeley Way
Berkeley CA 94720
510-642-9373; Fax: 510-642-1144
Territory: CA

Ted Weinstein & Associate
Ted Weinstein
6100 Fourth Ave S
6100 Bldg #282
Seattle WA 98108
206-763-9474;
Markets: RO(gift)
Items: HC-PB-GI-TO-GC

Theodore Lucia
Theodore Lucia
7244 NE 121st Pl
Kirkland WA 98034
206-821-5277; Fax: 206-820-7621
Territory: OR-WA-AK-ID-MT
Markets: RO
Items: PB-HC-RM

Thomas Allen & Son Ltd
James Allen
390 Steelcase Rd E
Markham ON Canada L3R 1G2
905-475-9126; Fax: 905-475-6747
Territory: CN

Thomas Murphy, Representative
Thomas Murphy
2103 N Decatur Rd #223
Decatur GA 30033
404-378-8527; Fax: 404-377-5097
Territory: South
Markets: BK
Items: HC-PB

Tom Shenk & Associates
Tom Shenk, Pres
8984 Home Guard Dr
Burke VA 22015
703-425-5321; Fax: 703-425-8605
Territory: Mid-Atlantic states
Markets: GI(gourmet shops)
Items: HC-PB

Trim Associates
Gary Trim
2643 N Burling St
Chicago IL 60614
312-871-1249; Fax: 312-871-1249
Markets: BK
Items: HC-PB

U

University Marketing Group
Horace Coward
801A Long Hill Rd
Middletown CT 06457
203-346-2476; Fax: 203-344-8307
Territory: New England
Items: HC-PB

University Marketing Group
David K Brown
1510 Croton Lake Rd
Yorktown Heights NY 10598
914-245-9364; Fax: 914-245-9364
Territory: New York City

University Marketing Group
Laura Waldron
285 Mt Airy-Harbourton Rd
Lambertville NJ 08530
609-397-9236
Territory: Mid-Atlantic States
Items: HC-PB

University of California Press
Steven C Ballinger
c/o Princeton Univ Press
41 William St
Princeton NJ 08540
609-258-5105
Territory: Mid-Atlantic & South

University of California Press
David Waag
749 S Lemay #A3-357
Ft Collins CO 80524
970-484-5372
Territory: Southwest

University of California Press
George Carroll
916 NE 65th St Box 622
Seattle WA 98115
206-524-8180; Fax: 206-524-7969
Territory: Northwest

University of California Press
Stanley Plona
2201 W 107th St
Chicago IL 60643
312-445-5344
Territory: Midwest

University of California Press
Sheldon Stolowich
1448 E 52nd St #108
Chicago IL 60615
312-363-7352
Territory: Midwest

University of California Press
Patrick Cullen
50 Follon St Apt 12
Cambridge MA 02138
617-661-1245
Territory: New England

University of New Mexico Press
Sheri Hozier
1780 Lomas Blvd NE
Albuquerque NM 87131-1591
505-277-7558;
Territory: New Mexico
Items: HC-PB

University of Oklahoma Press
Glenda Madden
1005 Asp Ave
Norman OK 73019
800-522-0772; Fax: 405-364-5798
Territory: Oklahoma
Items: HC-PB

University of Texas Press
Darrell Windham, Gretchen Webb
PO Box 7819
Austin TX 78713-7819
512-471-4032; Fax: 512-320-0668
Territory: TX-LA
Items: HC-PB

V

Van W Keck, Representative
Van W Keck
15820 SW Dusty Dr
McMinnville OR 97128
503-843-3688; Fax: 503-843-7179
Territory: OR-WA-N ID-HI

Vantage Sales & Marketing
William C Kohler, Pres
12 Village Ct
Hazlet NJ 07730
908-739-3313; Fax: 908-739-6404
Territory: US-Mid-Atlantic
Markets: BK-MM(major non-book chains)
Items: HC-PB-MM

W

Wayne Donnell, Representative
Wayne Donnell
3814 Walker Ave
Greensboro NC 27403
910-855-1374; Fax: 910-854-6908
Territory: South
Markets: BK
Items: HC-PB
Memo: Associated with George Scheer Associates

Wilcher Associates
John Little
1668 San Lorenzo Ave
Berkeley CA 94707-1848
510-525-7570
Territory: AK, S OR
Markets: BK
Items: HC-PB

Wilcher Associates
Richard Detrano
5131 Palatine Ave N
Seattle WA 98103
206-784-0772; Fax: 206-783-1848
Territory: N OR-W WA-HI

Wilcher Associates
Robert Arnold
1605 Zermat Dr
PO Drawer JJ
Pine Mountain Club CA 93222
805-242-2416; Fax: 805-242-2417
E-Mail: boblibris@aol.com

Wilcher Associates
Jeannie Dunham
3000 E Colfax Ave #263
Denver CO 80206
303-333-4396
Territory: E MT
Markets: BK
Items: HC-PB

William Hill, Representative
William Hill
PO Box 627
Seattle WA 98111
206-283-7612; Fax: 206-285-2762
Territory: AK-ID-MT-OR-WA-WY

William J Whitaker Associates
William J Whitaker Jr
9920 Maple Leaf Dr
Gaithersburg MD 20879-1134
301-258-0564; Fax: 301-258-9099
Territory: Mid-Atlantic, New York City
Markets: BK-JB-CO
Items: HC-PB-CA
Memo: Does not handle self-published, single books.

William Korr Sales Company
William Korr
3605 Woodhead Dr #109A
Northbrook IL 60062
708-205-9500; Fax: 708-205-9525
Territory: Midwest; 6 reps
Markets: RO(crafts)
Items: CR-GI
Memo: They would possibly take a "how-to" craft book on floral, etc; not big in publishing.

Worldwide Media Service Inc
Rebecca Nichols, Exp Sales Mgr
30 Montgomery St
Jersey City NJ 07302
201-332-7100; Fax: 201-332-1655
Territory: IT(foreign export reps);10 reps
Markets: BK-PL-SL-WH
Items: HC-PB-MM

Wybel Marketing Group
Terry Wybel
213 W Main St
Barrington IL 60010
708-382-0384; Fax: 708-382-0385
Territory: Midwest: 800-323-5297
Markets: BK-RO-CO
Items: HC-PB-TA-TV

Wybel Marketing Group
Rita Broderick
276 Geremma Dr
Ballwin MO 63011
847-382-0384; Fax: 314-394-8252
Territory: Midwest: 800-323-5297
Markets: BK-RO-CO
Items: HC-PB-TA-TV

International

Critiques Livres
56 rue Malmaison BP 93
93172 Bagnolet Cedex
France
(1)43644557; Fax: (1)48973706

HI Marketing
38 Carver Rd
London UK SE24 9LT
171-738-7751; Fax: 171-274-9160

Peribo
58 Beaumont Rd (NSW 2080)
Mt Kuring-gai Australia
02-457-0011; Fax: 02-457-0022

Propaganda Distributors Ltd
PO Box 582
Auckland New Zealand
9-309-5446; Fax: 9-309-5464

Abbreviations Used

Territory

CN	Canada
IT	International
MX	Mexico
OT	Other
US	United States with some state abbreviations for the different states

Markets

BK	Bookstores
CO	Colleges
JB	Jobbers
MM	Mass Markets
NS	Newsstands
OT	Other
PL	Public Libraries
RO	Retail Outlets
SC	Schools
SL	Special Libraries

Items

CA	Calendars
CO	Comics
CR	Craft Items
GA	Games
GC	Greeting Cards
GI	Gifts
HC	Hardcovers
MA	Maps and Atlases
MG	General / Special Magazines
ML	Literary Magazines
MM	Mass Market Books
NP	Newspapers
OP	Out of Print Books
OT	Other Items
PB	Trade Paperbacks
PO	Posters
RC	Records
RM	Remainders
SB	Stickers/Bookmarks
ST	Stationery
SW	Software
TA	Tapes, Audio
TO	Toys
TV	Tapes, Video
TX	Textbooks
US	Used books

Subject Category Codes

10 **General Non-Fiction**
11 **Fine Arts**
    11P   Photography
12 **Architecture / Construction**
    12A   Architecture
    12B   Building / Construction
13 **Alternative Social Issues**
14 **Performing Arts**
    14D   Dance
    14M   Music
    14T   Theatre / Drama
15 **Animals / Pets**
16 **Transportation**
    16A   Automobiles
    16R   Railroads
17 **Biographies / Celebrities**
    17B   Biographies
    17C   Celebrities
    17P   Real People
19 **Business / Economics**
    19A   Accounting
    19B   Banking
    19C   Careers / Labor
    19E   Economics
    19F   Fund-raising / Non-profits
    19G   Management
    19H   Real Estate / Home
    19I   Investment
    19L   Law
    19M   Marketing / Sales
    19O   Opportunity Seekers
    19P   Purchasing
    19R   Retail Sales
    19S   Small Business
    19X   Industrial / Production
21 **Children's Interests**
    21T   Teenagers
23 **Computers / Technology**
    23C   Computers
    23E   Home Electronics
    23T   Technology
24 **Engineering**
25 **Consumer Issues**
    25T   Consumer Taxes
27 **Cooking / Food / Nutrition**
28 **Collectibles / Antiques**
29 **Crafts / Hobbies / How-to**
    29C   Crafts
    29H   Hobbies and How-to
31 **Education / Child Development**
    31C   Child Development
    31E   Education / Teaching
    31P   Parenting
33 **Entertainment / Movies / Humor**
    33C   Comics / Comedy
    33H   Humor
    33M   Movies
    33T   Television / Radio

35 **Family / Marriage / Retirement**
    35A   Aging Issues / Retirement
    35F   Family
    35M   Marriage
    35R   Relationships / Romance
    35S   Sexual Issues
36 **Lifestyle/Feature**
37 **Gay / Lesbian**
39 **Health / Medicine / Exercise**
    39D   Disabilities
    39E   Exercise
    39H   Holistic Health
    39M   Medicine / Doctors
    39R   Recovery / Drug Abuse
40 **Beauty / Fashion**
    40B   Beauty
    40F   Fashion
41 **History**
    41A   American History
    41G   Genealogy / Family History
    41W   World History
43 **House / Garden**
    43D   Home Decorating
    43G   Gardening
    43H   House and Home
44 **International Issues and News**
    44A   Asia
    44E   Europe
    44F   Africa
    44S   South America
    44Z   Australia / New Zealand
45 **Languages**
    45X   Linquistics
    45W   Words
47 **Literature / Humanities**
48 **Military**
49 **Minority Issues and Studies**
    49A   Native American
    49B   Black
    49H   Hispanic / Chicano
    49O   Other
51 **Nature / Ecology / Conservation**
    51A   Agriculture / Farming
    51B   Biology / Botany
    51E   Environmental Issues
    51N   Nature
53 **New Age / Astrology**
54 **Philosophy / Metaphysics**
    54M   Metaphysics
    54P   Philosophy
55 **Politics / Government**
    55C   Crime / Police Work
    55G   Government
    55L   Law
    55P   Politics

56 **Publishing / PR / Writing**
    56M   Media / Publicity
    56P   Publishing
    56W   Writing
    56X   Printing
57 **Psychology / Self-Help**
    57B   Behavior
    57P   Psychology / Therapy
    57S   Self-Help / Advice
59 **Reference Books**
61 **Regional Issues and Interests**
63 **Religions**
    63C   Catholic
    63E   Eastern Religions
    63J   Jewish
    63M   Muslim
    63O   Other Religions
    63P   Protestant
65 **Sociology / Anthropology**
    65A   Anthropology
    65S   Social Issues
67 **Science / Mathematics**
    67A   Astronomy / Space
    67M   Mathematics
    67S   Science
69 **Sports / Games / Recreation**
    69G   Games
    69H   Hunting / Fishing
    69R   Recreation / Hiking
    69S   Spectator Sports
70 **Nautical / Aviation**
    70A   Aviation
    70N   Nautical / Sailing
71 **Travel / Geography**
    71D   Domestic Travel
    71F   Foreign Travel
    71G   Geography
73 **Women's Issues**

75 General Fiction

76 **Children's Stories**
77 **Contemporary Novels**
78 **Ethnic / Minority Literature**
79 **Folklore / Fairy Tales**
80 **Foreign Literature**
81 **Historical Novels**
82 **Horror Novels**
83 **Literary Novels**
84 **Mysteries / Detective Novels**
85 **Romances / Gothic Romances**
86 **Science Fiction / Fantasy**
87 **Suspense / Adventure Novels**
88 **Westerns**
89 **Young Adult Novels**
90 **Short Stories / Anthologies**
95 **Poetry**

97 News / Current Events

99 General Interest

Fulfillment Services

The following companies offer warehousing, order-processing, fulfillment, and/or distribution of books and other services.

Ad-Lib Publications
Marie Kiefer
51 W Adams
Fairfield IA 52556
515-472-6617; Fax: 515-472-3186
800-669-0773
Service: Order processing & fulfillment

Advanced Automation
Sean O'Regan
43 Manning Rd
Billerica MA 01821
508-262-9600; Fax: 508-262-9800
Service: Service bureau/subscription

Aim Marketing
Nancy Johnson, Sales
525 North D St
Fremont NE 68025
402-721-2077; Fax: 402-721-9171

American Book Center
Joe Savino, Pres
Brooklyn Naval Yard Bldg 3
Brooklyn NY 11205
718-834-0170; Fax: 718-935-9647
Service: Fulfillment/warehousing

American International Distrib
Peter Miller, Pres
2 Winter Sport Ln
Williston VT 05495
802-862-0095; Fax: 802-864-7626
800-488-2665

Associations Book Distributors
Michael Cheteyan, CEO
Buncher Commerce Park
Ave A Bldg 16
Leetsdale PA 15056
412-741-1142; Fax: 412-741-4161

Automated Fulfillment Corp
Alex Amoriello
75 Holly Hill Ln
Greenwich CT 06830
203-869-7070; Fax: 203-869-3380
Service: Service bureaus/subscriptions

Automated Resources Group
Hank Garcia, Exec VP
21 Philips Pky
Montvale NJ 07645
201-391-1500; Fax: 201-391-8357
Service: Product/subscription fulfillment

Book Pros
Ray Turner
the Distributors
702 S Michigan
South Bend IN 46601
219-232-8500; Fax: 219-288-4141

BookMasters Inc
Attn: Sales
2541 Ashland Rd
PO Box 2139
Mansfield OH 44905
419-589-5100; Fax: 419-589-4040
Service: Book storage & order fulfillment

BookWorld Services
Christine McFadden, Publ Serv Mg
Book Distribution & Fulfillment
1933 Whitfield Park Loop
Sarasota FL 34243
813-758-8094; Fax: 813-753-9396
800-444-2524

Brauch Publishing Systems Inc
Rolf Brauch
550 Alden Rd #105
Markham ON L3R 6A8
905-470-8550; Fax: 905-470-8561
Service: Book/product fulfillment

Burch Inc
Jenny Grimm, Client Sls Serv Mgr
300 Riverview Dr
Benton Harbor MI 49022
616-925-2121; Fax: 616-925-4825
800-336-5447
Service: Inquiry handling

Camby & West Inc
Diane Cuellar
120 North Route 9W
Congeres NY 10920
914-267-3490; Fax: 914-267-3503

Central Distribution Services
John Pollack, Supervisor
J J Keller & Assoc Inc
3003 W Breezwood Ln
Neenah WI 54957-0368
800-558-5011
Service: Book fulfillment

Communications Data Services
Dennis Luther
1901 Bell Ave
Des Moines IA 50315
515-246-6920; Fax: 515-246-6882

CompuPower Corporation
Steven Adler
One Harmon Plz
Secaucus NJ 07094
201-866-8600; Fax: 201-866-5902

Computer Action Inc
Pauline M Gramiak
1500 Market St
East Tower 12th Fl
Philadelphia PA 19102
215-265-3425; Fax: 215-246-3465

Corporate Fulfillment Systems
Timothy Slattery, Pres/Owner
1 Bert Dr
West Bridgewater MA 02379
508-583-5239; Fax: 508-583-9904
800-344-4501

CWC Software Inc
Andrew Conti
150 Grossman Dr
Braintree MA 02184
617-843-2010; Fax: 617-843-8365
Service: In-house systems

Datasystem Solutions Inc
Lorna Fenimore
4350 Shawnee Mission Pky #179
Shawnee Mission KS 06205
913-362-6969; Fax: 913-362-6383

The DirectLink Inc
Ronald Daggett
200 Kingston Dr
West Lafayette IN 47906
800-841-7881; Fax: 317-743-3545

EBSCO Industries
Angie Porter, Mktg Dir
Publisher Promo & Fulfillment
PO Box 1943
Birmingham AL 35201
205-991-1176; Fax: 205-995-1588
800-633-6088
Service: Fulfillment of mags & directories

EPI Fulfillment
Bill Knight, VP/Sales Mktg
4956 Wayne Rd
Battle Creek MI 49015
616-964-4600; Fax: 616-964-0626
800-562-9733

Epsilon Management Systems Inc
Louis Loglisci
75 Commercial St
Plainview NY 11803
516-349-1440; Fax: 516-349-0477

Express Book Freight
Scott Branson, Pres
Transaction Distribution
140 Ethel Rd W
Piscataway NJ 08854
908-777-0909; Fax: 908-777-0999
Service: Book and journal distribution

Fulco Inc
Bob Boyken
30 Broad St
Denville NJ 07834
201-6272427; Fax: 201-627-5872

Funaro Lufrano Associates
Barry Glaser
420 Lexington Ave
New York NY 10170
212-682-3810; Fax: 212-986-2846

Gage Distribution Co
Attn: Customer Service
164 Commander Blvd
Agincourt ON M1S 3C7
416-293-8141; Fax: 416-293-9009
Service: Book fulfillment center

Global Turnkey Systems Inc
Bill Donato
20 Waterview Blvd 3rd Fl
Parsippany NJ 07054
201-331-1010; Fax: 201-331-0042

Hallmark Data Systems
Raymond Miller
6201 W Howard St
Niles IL 60614
708-647-1200; Fax: 708-647-7055

Harrison Fulfillment Services
Carolyn Stringer, Adm Asst
2515 E 43rd St
Chattanooga TN 37407
615-867-9081; Fax: 615-867-5526
Service: Full service fulfillment

Headline Business Computer Syst
Jack Head
1582 S Parker Rd #300
Denver CO 80231
303-696-9480; Fax: 303-696-8018

The Hibbert Group
Lou Ferri
400 Pennington Ave
PO Box 8116
Trenton NJ 08650-0116
609-394-7500; Fax: 609-392-1237

Hutchins & Associates
Glen Giles
1865 East Valley Pky
Escondido CA 92027
818-567-2885; Fax: 619-745-7200

ICN
Bob Werner
200 Rittenhouse Cir #
West Bristol PA 19007
215-788-5500; Fax: 215-788-6887

IFS-Independent Fulfillment Serv
Hank Ferguson
500 Eastern Pky
Farmingdale NY 11735
516-756-2600; Fax: 516-756-2604

Integrated Distribution Services
Attn: Customer Service
Lower Mill Rd
North Stratford NH 03590
603-922-8316; Fax: 603-922-3348
Service: Fulfillment services

Intrepid Productions
Arthur Maranjian
6280 E Country Rd 60
Fort Collins CO 80524
303-493-3793; Fax: 303-493-8781
Service: Book and magazine fulfillment

IPP Shipping & Warehousing
Floyd Campbell, Mgr
211 E Harrison St
PO Box 50
Danville IL 61834-0050
217-442-1190; Fax: 217-442-9141

J V West
Paul Phillipson, Pres
PO Box 11950
Reno NV 89510-9959
702-359-9811; Fax: 702-359-9042
Service: Fulfills for 40 book publishers

JCI Data Processing Inc
Ray Liscik
200 South Rt 130
Cinnaminson NJ 08077
609-786-2600; Fax: 609-786-4415

Kable Fulfillment Serv of Ohio
Patty VanSickle, Client Rel Mgr
205 W Center St
Marion OH 43302
614-383-5231; Fax: 614-382-0409
Service: Order processing/fulfillment

Kable Fulfillment Services
Dick Bradfield
Kable Square
Mt Morris IL 61054
800-800-7451; Fax: 815-734-1227

KCMS
Jack Reed
3401 East West Hwy
Hyattsville MD 20782
301-853-6500; Fax: 301-559-5372

Llexell Fulfillment Services
Greg Lewellen
2821 W Euless Blvd
Euless TX 76039
817-685-2196

Login Fulfillment Services
Dean Manke, Mktg VP/LFS Dept
1436 W Randolph St
Chicago IL 60607
800-680-2889; Fax: 312-413-9905
Service: Book fulfillment

Lynx Media Inc
Len Latimer
12501 Chandler Blvd #202
North Hollywood CA 91607
800-451-LYNX; Fax: 818-761-7099

Mailways International
Robert Jacobs
PO Box 4926
Manchester NH 03108
603-669-5252; Fax: 603-669-2835

The Media Services Group Ltd
Terry Nathan
1010 Washington Blvd
Stamford CT 06901
800-234-4674; Fax: 203-921-1791

Mendon Associates Inc
Michael Miocevich
302-201 Dufferin ST
Toronto ON M6K 1Y9
800-361-1325; Fax: 416-537-4330

Mercedes Distribution Center
Joe Goldstein, Pres
62 Imlay St
Brooklyn NY 11231-1298
718-522-7111; Fax: 718-852-5341
Service: Book fulfillment center

Midpoint National
Nancy Fraser, Dir of Client Serv
2215 Harrison St
Kansas City MO 64108
816-842-8420; Fax: 816-842-0340
800-228-4321

National Business Services
701 Seneca St
Buffalo NY 14210
800-854-8233
Service: US & Canada

National Fulfillment Services
Bob Gagliardi, Controller
Holmes Corporate Ctr
100 Pine Ave
Holmes PA 19043-1484
610-532-4700; Fax: 610-586-3232
800-345-8112
Service: Books/magazines

Neodata Services Inc
833 W South Boulder Rd
Louisville CO 80027
800-NEODATA; Fax: 303-666-3999

New England Book Service Inc
Dee Morrow
RR 1 Prindle Rd
PO Box 1823
Charlotte VT 05445
802-425-3841; Fax: 802-425-3158
Service: New England

NexTech Systems Corp
Joel Cohn
3671 Old Yorktown Rd
Shrub Oak NY 10588
914-962-6000; Fax: 914-962-1338

NRL Direct
100 Union Ave
Cresskill NJ 07626
201-568-0707; Fax: 201-568-9893

Omeda Communications
Randy Renner
3005 MacArthur Blvd
Northbrook IL 60062
708-564-8900; Fax: 708-564-9154

The Order Fulfillment Group
8205 Zionsville RD
Indianapolis IN 46268
317-876-7755

Pacific Fulfillment Services
Douglas Denny
815 Arnold Dr #124
Martinez CA 94553
510-372-7045; Fax: 510-372-8582

Package Fulfillment Center
Jim Valenti, VP of Sales
1401 Lakeland Ave
Bohemia NY 11716
516-567-7000; Fax: 516-567-7801
Service: All fulfillment services

Palmer Publications
Ms Chris Doyle, Editor
PO Box 296
Amherst WI 54406
715-824-3214; Fax: 715-824-5806
Service: Single-copy mail order shipping

PBD Inc
James Dockter, Pres/CEO
Professional Book Distributors
1650 Bluegrass Lakes Pky
Alpharetta GA 30201
404-442-8633; Fax: 404-442-9742
Service: All fulfillment services

PCS Data Processing
Burt Rod, VP Sales
360 West 31st 11th Fl
New York NY 10001
212-564-3730; Fax: 212-971-7200
Service: Computer book fulfillment

Perfect Response Co
Christopher Michaels, Mkg
5441 Western Ave #A
Boulder CO 80301
303-541-9116; Fax: 303-938-1544

Publications Services Inc
Glen McComb
824 W 10th St #100
Austin TX 78701
512-795-5006; Fax: 512-478-9263
800-945-3132
Service: 800# order processing, fullfillment for small to medium publishers

Progressive Distribution Service
John McGovern, Pres
5505 36th
Grand Rapids MI 49512
616-957-5900; Fax: 616-957-2990

Publishers Creative Systems
Michael J Ciuffreda
508 W Mission Ave #200
Escondido CA 92025
619-738-4970; Fax: 619-738-4805

Publishers Resources Inc
Lynell Syler, Mgr
Client & Corp Development
1224 Heil Quaker Blvd
La Vergne TN 37086-7001
615-793-5090; Fax: 615-793-3915

Publishers Software System
Wayne Zafft
186 Lincoln St #305
Boston MA 02111
617-357-7301; Fax: 617-357-7317

Publishers Storage & Shipping
Daniel Quick, Mgr
215 Rutgers St
Maplewood NJ 07040
201-378-3908; Fax: 201-378-3909
Service: Book storage and fulfillment

Publishers Storage & Shipping
Peter Quick, VP
660 S Mansfield
Ypsilanti MI 48197
313-487-9720; Fax: 313-487-1890
Service: Book storage and fulfillment

Publishers Storage & Shipping
E B Quick, Pres
46 Development Rd
Fitchburg MA 01420
508-345-2121; Fax: 508-348-1233
Service: Book storage and fulfillment

Rayve Fulfillment
Norm Ray, Pres
7802 Bell Rd
PO Box 726
Windsor CA 95492
707-838-6200; Fax: 707-838-2220

Readme Agency
Gilda Winkelmeyer
5123 Ella Ln
Santa Barbara CA 93111
805-967-2310; Fax: 805-967-2310

RJV Computer Resources
Jim Lawson, VP
137 Wood Rd
Braintree MA 02184
617-843-9779; Fax: 617-356-8577
Service: Circulation fulfillment

RLS Associates
Robert L Smith Jr, Pres
250 Huron Ave
PO Box 5030
Port Huron MI 48961-5030
810-989-9500; Fax: 810-987-3562
800-842-8338

S&S Computer Services Inc
Doug Slavin
434 W Downer Pl
Aurora IL 60506
708-892-7222; Fax: 708-892-7466

Sapphire Systems
Daryl Popkes
671 Gunflint Trail
Grand Marais MN 55604
218-388-2200

Sisk Fulfillment Service
Wendy Young, VP
PO Box 463
Frederalsburg MD 21632
410-754-8141; Fax: 410-754-8223

Southwest School Book Depository
Jerry Baker, VP
1815 Monetary Ln
Carrollton TX 75006
214-245-8588; Fax: 214-245-2077
Service: Serves 40 publishers

Stark Bros
Jack Alexander
Hwy 54W
Louisiana MO 63353
314-754-5511; Fax: 314-754-5290

Stark Services
Carl David
12444 Victory Blvd
North Hollywood CA 91606
818-985-2003; Fax: 818-985-4513

Starr Fulfillment Corp
Joseph M Starr
100 Cooper Ctr
7905 Browing Rd
Pennsauken NJ 08109-4319
609-488-1881; Fax: 609-488-6188

STCS Inc
Chuck Eigen, Pres
PO Box 246
Glassboro NJ 08028
609-863-1030; Fax: 609-881-8042

Sunbelt Fulfillment Service
David Ely
307 Southgate Ct
Brentwood TN 37027
615-377-3322; Fax: 615-377-0525

Superior Fulfillment
Donald A Krueger
131 W First St
Duluth MN 55802
800-346-0085; Fax: 218-723-9377

Synergy Marketing Group Inc
Ray Del Monte
500 East Ave
Rochester NY 14607
716-461-8300; Fax: 716-461-0835
Service: Online/remote

Thomcomp Inc
Bob Brubaker
555 E North Ln
Conshohocken PA 19428
215-834-1120; Fax: 215-834-8890

Thompson Publishing Group
Frank Demelas
5201 W Kennedy Blvd #905
Tampa FL 33609-1823
813-282-8807; Fax: 813-282-4746

USA Fulfillment
Sheila Roy, Sales Mgr
201 Talbot Blvd #W
Chestertown MD 21620
410-758-0803; Fax: 410-810-0910
Service: Order processing/fulfillment

Watson-Guptill Distribution Ctr
Ted Misa, Gen Mgr
1695 Oak St
Lakewood NJ 08701
908-363-4511; Fax: 908-363-0338

WPL Associates Inc
Paul Levin
PO Box 1935
Bethesda MD 20827-1935
800-676-6407; Fax: 301-299-0206

Mailing Lists

Lists Available from Ad-Lib Publications

Ad-Lib Publications has more than 20,500 book marketing names in our database — everything from travel booksellers to radio talk shows, from mail order catalogs that feature books to newspaper food editors, and much more.

Lists are run in zip-code sequence on 2-up pressure-sensitive labels. (4 across Cheshire format is available) List counts are subject to change. Lists are restricted to one-time usage. If you want unlimited use of the mailing lists, they are available on disk (IBM-compatible or Macintosh). We can supply them to you on a 3.5" or 5.25" high or low density disk, in the mail-merge format of your choice (Dbase, ASCII, comma- or tab-delimited). Pricing will be double for disk. To order, call 800-669-0773. Or write to Ad-Lib Publications, PO Box 1102, Fairfield, IA 52556-1102. Special searches are available. Minimum List $10.00.

Booksellers

Here are just a **few** of the bookseller lists available. The number to the left is the total on the list.

- 464 — Art / Photography / Art History $ 45.00
- 107 — Animals / Pets $ 10.00
- 197 — Business / Careers / Economics $ 20.00
- 803 — Children's Books $ 80.00
- 142 — Computers / Technology $ 15.00
- 235 — Cooking / Nutrition $ 25.00
- 217 — Crafts / Hobbies $ 20.00
- 314 — Health / Medicine / Holistic Health $ 30.00
- 114 — Home / Garden $ 10.00
- 138 — Music / Dance / Drama $ 15.00
- 279 — Nature / Ecology / Environment $ 30.00
- 328 — New Age / Metaphysical $ 35.00
- 94 — Poetry $ 10.00
- 305 — Psychology / Self-Help $ 30.00
- 104 — Religion $ 10.00
- 187 — Science / Mathematics $ 15.00
- 115 — Sports / Games / Recreation $ 10.00
- 199 — Travel / Geography $ 20.00

Newspaper Editors

These lists can be selected from our newspaper file:

- 486 — Newspaper Book Reviewers $ 50.00
- 549 — Arts and Entertainment Editors $ 55.00
- 597 — Business Editors and Columnists $ 60.00
- 625 — Children's and Family Interests $ 60.00
- 187 — Computer Editors and Columnists $ 20.00
- 385 — Food / Cookbook Editors $ 40.00
- 313 — Health / Medical Editors $ 30.00
- 274 — Home Editors $ 20.00
- 480 — Lifestyle Editors $ 50.00
- 240 — Religion Editors $ 25.00
- 637 — Sports Editors and Columnists $ 65.00
- 317 — Travel Editors $ 30.00

Magazine Editors

Here are a few of the lists we can select from our magazine data file.

- 412 — Magazine Book Reviewers (all sorts) $ 40.00
- 77 — Magazines for Libraries/booksellers $ 10.00
- 633 — Serial Rights Buyers at Magazines $ 65.00
- 221 — Art Editors $ 20.00
- 1177 — Business Editors $115.00
- 249 — Children's Editors $ 25.00
- 550 — Computer Editors $ 55.00
- 241 — Crafts and Hobbies Editors $ 25.00
- 277 — Entertainment / Movie Editors $ 30.00
- 213 — Fashion Editors $ 20.00
- 315 — Food Editors $ 30.00
- 542 — Health / Medical Editors $ 55.00
- 295 — Home / Garden Editors $ 30.00
- 117 — New Age Magazine Editors $ 10.00
- 122 — Science Editors $ 10.00
- 325 — Sports Editors $ 35.00
- 317 — Travel Editors $ 30.00

Book Markets

Here are a **few** other marketing lists we offer for rent.

- 119 — Book Clubs (all sorts) $ 10.00
- 285 — Chain Store Buyers $ 35.00
- 823 — Mail Order Catalogs carrying books $ 75.00
- 45 — Book Remainder Dealers $ 10.00
- 483 — Independent Bookstores $ 50.00
- 788 — Bookstores doing Author Signings $ 75.00
- 127 — Book Distributors $ 15.00
- 191 — Publishers who also distribute books $ 20.00
- 710 — Book Wholesalers $ 70.00
- 252 — Wholesalers to other retail outlets $ 25.00 (toy, craft, computer, health stores, etc.)
- 294 — Paperback Book Jobbers (ID's) $ 40.00
- 240 — Sales Representatives (books/toys/...) $ 25.00

Other Specialized Lists

Here are a few other specialized lists that we offer from our various databases:

- 684 — Radio Shows with phone interviews $ 70.00
- 251 — Top TV Shows that do interviews $ 25.00
- 661 — Syndicated Columnists (all subjects) $ 65.00
- 877 — Mailing List Brokers and Managers $ 85.00
- 915 — Printers $ 85.00
- 212 — Foreign Printers $ 20.00

The Ad-Lib Customer List is also available for rent. Cost is $100.00 per thousand. There are more than 16,000 names on our list. You can select by geographical area.

Section II:

Book Marketing Channels

87 Bookstore Chains and Other Chain Stores

    87   Local Bookstore Chains
    89   Regional Bookstore Chains
    91   National Bookstore Chains
    92   Religious Bookstore Chains
    93   College Bookstore Chains
    94   Department Store Chains
    95   Other Chain Stores

97 Independent Booksellers

119 Book Clubs

125 Rights Buyers

    125   Audio Rights Buyers
    125   Entertainment Directories
    126   Large Print Rights Buyers
    126   Other Rights Buyers
    126   Paperback Rights Buyers
    126   Small Press Literary Agents
    127   Video Rights Buyers

129 Mail Order Catalogs that Feature Books

169 Remainder Dealers

    170   Books as Donations

Section II: Book Marketing Channels

Section II lists some of the major markets for books. Unlike the companies listed in Section I, these book marketing channels sell direct to the public. While many distributors and wholesalers will sell your books to the bookstore chains and top independent booksellers, they are not set up to sell to the other markets listed in this section. You will have to approach the book clubs, mail order catalogs, rights buyers, and remainer dealers on your own. You can, of course, also approach the chain stores and independent booksellers on your own. Many publishers successfully sell direct to these booksellers.

This section is broken down into six subsections as follows:

- **Bookstore chains** and other chain stores (including local, regional, and national bookstore chains; religious bookstore chains; college bookstore chains; department store chains that stock books; and other chain stores that feature books).
- **Independent booksellers** (a preliminary list of some of the largest, best known, or most influential independent bookstores in the country).
- **Book clubs**, both the major book clubs and all the smaller special-interest clubs.
- **Rights buyers** (a list of large print rights buyers, TV/movie rights buyers, and a few literary agents who specialize in representing smaller publishers when selling subsidiary rights).
- **Mail order catalogs** that sell books (a list of 834 catalogs).
- **Remainder dealers** — As a last resort, if you don't sell your books to any of the previous markets, you might want to remainder them to one of these dealers or, better yet, donate them to organizations that accept donations of books. A few of these organizations are listed on page 169. If you know of any other organizations that accept donations of books, please send us their name and address.

Bookstore Chains (and Others)

The following companies operate three or more stores that sell books. Most of the addresses listed here are for their central buying offices.

Local Bookstore Chains

Book Gallery
Anne McKenzie, Book Buyer
1352 Gaskins Rd
Richmond VA 23233
804-740-6723
Subjects: 10-11-12-14-21-27-35-43-51-99
Memo: 3 stores.

The Book Rack Ltd
Robert W Hugo, Owner
52 State St
Newburyport MA 01950
508-462-8615
Subjects: 99
Items: HC-PP-RM-GA-GC-PO-ST-TO-TA
Memo: Headquarters: Spirit of '76, Marblehead, MA.

Bookland of Maine
David Turitz, Owner
78 Atlantic Pl
South Portland ME 04106
207-874-2300; Fax: 207-874-9726
Subjects: 61(New England)-99
Items: HC-PB-MM
Memo: 13 stores. Buys independent or through Hdqtrs.

Books Connection
Patricia Franks, Book Buyer
52924 Van Dyke Ave
Shelby Township MI 48316-3545
810-731-6601
Subjects: 99
Items: PB-US-MM
Memo: 3 stores.

Books N Things
Tom Hines, Mgr
13035 Hwy 61
PO Box 126
Burlington IA 52601-0126
319-753-1683; Fax: 319-753-5988
Subjects: 99
Items: HC-PB-TV
Memo: 11 stores
Memo: Wholesale division: Wholesale Distributors.

Bookworld
Suzanne Shaw, Book Buyer
499 Merritt Ave
Nashville TN 37203
615-834-1862; Fax: 615-248-6386
Subjects: 99
Memo: 3 stores. Wholesale division: Austin Periodical Services.

Brunners News Agency
James Brunner, Book Buyer
Tom Brunner, Paperback Buyer
dba Readmore Bookstore
217 Flanders Ave
Lima OH 45801
419-225-5826; Fax: 419-225-5537
Subjects: 99
Memo: 9 stores.

Chapter 11
Katie Parker, Buyer
6305 Roswell Rd
Atlanta GA 30328
404-252-4478; Fax: 404-252-4357
Subjects: 99
Items: HC-PB-MG-CA-NS-CD-GC
Memo: 10 stores. Author signings.

Chicago Tribune Gift Stores
Ken Widelka, Mgr
Tribune Tower
435 N Michigan Ave
Chicago IL 60611-4022
312-222-3040
Subjects: 61(IL) by Tribune writers
Items: HC-PB-GI-CL
Memo: 3 stores. They sell books by Chicago Tribune writers, or books published by the Tribune. If you have a book of local interest(Chicago only) or general interest (and can be customized for them), you might want to contact them.

Community News Center
John O Stoll, Pres
3149 W Michigan Ave
Jackson MI 49202
517-783-2655; Fax: 517-349-7720
Subjects: 99
Items: HC-PB-TX-RM
Memo: 9 stores. Wholesale division: Southern Michigan News.

Computer Literacy Bookshops Inc
Sudha Parmer, Book Buyer
520 N Lawrence Expy
Sunnyvale CA 94086-4017
408-435-5015; Fax: 408-435-0689
Subjects: 23
Memo: 4 stores. Sudha's ext: 123.

Copperfield's Books
Paul Jaffe, New Book Buyer
138 N Main St
Sebastopol CA 95472
707-823-2618; Fax: 707-823-3271
Subjects: 21-31-35-39-53-54-57-99
Items: HC-PB-TA-GI-MG-GC-MA-ST
Memo: 7 stores. Headquarters.

Davis-Kidd Booksellers
Kay Ferree
869 N Pky
Jackson TN 38305
901-661-9757
Subjects: 21-75-76-99
Items: HC-PB-MM-RM
Memo: 4 stores. Buys through Ingram.

Davis-Kidd Booksellers
Steve Kerl, Mgr
397 Perkins Rd Extended
Memphis TN 38117
901-683-9801
Subjects: 21-45-75-76-99
Items: HC-PB-MM-RM
Memo: 4 stores. Buys through Ingram.

Davis-Kidd Booksellers
Mike Jaynes, Gen Mgr
113 N Peters Rd
Knoxville TN 37923
423-690-0136
Subjects: 21-23-75(new & backlist)-99
Items: HC-PB-MM-RM
Memo: 4 stores. Buys through Ingram.

Davis-Kidd Booksellers Inc
Tom Allen
624 Grassmere Park Dr #14
Nashville TN 37211
615-833-9192; Fax: 615-833-9019
Subjects: 21-75-76-99
Items: HC-PB-MM-RM
Memo: 4 stores. Buys mostly through Ingram. Corporate sales mainly business books.

Dickens Books Limited
John Eklund, Buyer
Harry W Schwartz Bookshops
409 E Silver Spring Dr
Milwaukee WI 53217
414-963-3100; Fax: 414-963-3105
Subjects: 75-99
Items: HC-PB-MM-RM
Memo: 6 stores: There are 4 Harry W Schwartz Bookshops & 2 Dickens Books Limited.

Godard Stationery Stores
Guillaune Godard, Owner
PO Box 124
Cornwall ON Canada K6H 5S7
613-347-1066; Fax: 613-347-1067
Subjects: 99
Items: PB-GC-LM
Memo: 6 stores. Buys most of their books from Cornwall News.

Gordon's Booksellers
Melvin Gordon
2113 N Charles St 2nd Fl
Baltimore MD 21218
410-576-1040; Fax: 410-576-1049
Subjects: 21-31-76-79
Items: HC-PB-RM
Memo: 3 stores.

Graham's Book & Stationery
Teri Graham, Co-Owner
460 Second St
PO Box 568
Lake Oswego OR 97034
503-636-5676
Subjects: 27(art)-(poetry)-69-71-99
Items: HC-PB-MM-BT-GI-ST-TA
Memo: 4 stores. Stationery/office supply stores.

Guzzardo's
George Guzzardo, Owner
111 N Main St
Kewanee IL 61443-2221
309-852-5621; Fax: 309-852-5622
Subjects: 99
Items: HC-RM-GI-GC(trade paperbacks)
Memo: 5 gift stores. Catalog.

Hatch's Inc
Katrina Agee
dba Hatch's Distributors
15677 East 17th Ave
Aurora CO 80011
303-341-7234; Fax: 303-341-0728
Subjects: 99
Items: HC-PB-RM-GA-GI-MA
Memo: 8 stores.

Honolulu Book Shops
Pat Banning, Buyer
287 Kalihi St
Honolulu HI 96819
808-847-5551; Fax: 808-841-4674
Subjects: 61(HI)-71-99
Items: HC-PB-MM
Memo: 4 stores.

Hudson News
Lisa Storelo, Buyer
Meadowlands Plz #902Rd
East Rutherford NJ 07073
201-939-5050; Fax: 201-939-6302
Subjects: 99
Items: HC-MM-MG-NP
Memo: 30 dealers. Mario DiDomizio, Pres.

Indiana Periodicals
Brenda Gilman, Mgr
2120 S Meridian
Indianapolis IN 46225
317-786-1488
Subjects: 99
Items: HC-PB-GC

Intimate Bookshop Inc
Wallace Kuralt, CEO; Services Group
Warren Bost, Paperback & Computer Book Buyer (910-218-7000)
Brenda Kuralt, Trade Book Buyer (919-929-0414)
PO Box 430
Chapel Hill NC 27514
919-968-6900; Fax: 919-968-8261
Subjects: 99
Items: HC-PB-CR-GA-RM-MA-MM-TA-TV-TO-OT
Memo: 9 stores.

Learningsmith
Cleo Coy, Book Buyer
10 Fawcett St 2nd Fl
Cambridge MA 02138
617-497-7000
Subjects: 11-14-27-31E-41-45
Items: HC-GA-SW-TA-TV-TO
Memo: 31 stores. David Mooney, CEO.

Librairie DeMarc
Andre Dandurand, Book Buyer
Headquarters
1691 est rue Fleury
Montreal PQ Canada H2C 1T1
514-384-8760; Fax: 514-384-4377
Subjects: 99-45(French)
Memo: 20 stores.

Libreria Giron
Juan Giron, Book Buyer
3547 West 26th St
Chicago IL 60623-3913
312-521-5651; Fax: 312-521-6870
Subjects: 23-27-39-41-45(Spanish)-80-99
Items: HC-PB-GC-MG-MA
Memo: 5 stores.

Majors Scientific Books Inc
Lynne Brotman, Mgr
2137 Butler St
Dallas TX 75235
214-631-4478; Fax: 214-630-0410
Subjects: 23-39-57-67
Items: HC-PB-TX
Memo: Catalog upon request. Buys independently.

Majors Scientific Books Inc
Rosemary Puckett
141 North Ave NE
Atlanta GA 30308
404-873-3229; Fax: 404-888-9427
Subjects: 23-24-39-57-67
Items: HC-PB-TX
Memo: Started in 1909. Buys independently.

Majors Scientific Books Inc
Kris Naylor, Retail Mgr
7205 Fannin
Houston TX 77030
713-799-9922; Fax: 713-799-1522
Subjects: 39-57-67
Items: HC-PB-TX
Memo: Buys independently.

Marjen Books
Marshall Miller, Owner
118 Maplewood Ave
Portsmouth NH 03801
603-430-8400; Fax: 603-433-4661
Subjects: 14-99
Items: HC-PB-MM-TA-CD
Memo: Three other store locations are: Kittery, ME 03862; North Hampton, NH 03904; and Stratham, NH 03885.

Mr Paperback Stores
Andy Lacher, Book Buyer
1135 Hammond St
Bangor ME 04401-5705
207-942-8237; Fax: 207-942-9226
Subjects: 99
Items: HC-PB-MM-MG-RM
Memo: 18 stores. Wholesale division: Magazines Inc. Author signings: Yes.

News 'N Novels
Chuck Carroll, Buyer
2222 Golden Gate Dr
Greensboro NC 27405
910-275-2220; Fax: 910-275-4921
Subjects: 75-99
Items: HC-PB-MM-BT-MG-CA-NP-CD-TA
Memo: 4 stores.

Newsboy Books & Video
983 W Foothill Blvd
Claremont CA 91711
909-626-0040
Subjects: 99(book/video stores)
Items: HC-PB-TV-MG
Memo: 5 locations. Buys only from Pomona Valley News Agency and Ingram.

Olsson's Books & Records
Alicia Greene
Leslie Clague, Children's Buyer
Deena Karas, Children's Buyer
1239 Wisconsin Ave NW
Washington DC 20007
202-338-9544; Fax: 202-342-2342
Subjects: 13-21-41-44-47-55-65-75-99
Items: HC-PB-MM-RC-TA-TV-MG-NP
Memo: 6 stores. Other phone: 202-298-6051. Other stores located: 1307 19th St, Washington, DC; 106 S Union St, Alexandria, VA; 1200 F St, Washington, DC; 418 7th St NW, Washington, DC; 7647 Old Georgetown Rd, Bethesda, MD.

Oxford Book Stores
360 Pharr Rd NE
Atlanta GA 30305
404-262-9975; Fax: 404-364-2729

Joe Goodman, Ad/Promotions Dir
Krishera Barrett, Asst/Distrib Buyer
Roni Pastore, Buyer (Maps & Calendars)
Carter Vineyard, Bus/Computer Buyer
Sonia Roy, Children's Book Buyer
Lange Thompson, Classics/Study Notes Buyer
Gloria Todd, Fine Arts Buyer
Chris Morris, Head Buyer
Debbie Hutchinson, Mass Mkt Buyer
Aaron Evans, New Age/Recreation/Sports Buyer
Rupert LeCraw, Owner
Dan Winn, Science/Tech Buyer

Subjects: 99
Items: HC-PB-PO-RC-SW-TV
Memo: 4 stores. One of the stores, Oxford Too, 2395 Peachtree Rd NE, Atlanta, is used books & specialty orders for out of print or hard to find books.

People's News and Book Mart
Mark Stephan
1919 Garfield Ave
Parkersburg WV 26101
304-428-1441
Subjects: 99
Items: PB-MM-MG-NP-GC-MA-TV
Memo: 6 stores. Wholesale division: Anderson-Stephan, 1919 Garfield Avenue, Parkersburg, WV 26101.

Powell's Book Store
David O'Halloran, Book Buyer
7 NW Ninth
Portland OR 97209
503-228-4651; Fax: 503-228-4631
Subjects: 43-43G
Items: HC-PB-MM-OP-US-MG-RM-MA-TA
Memo: 6 stores.

Powell's Books
Amy King, Mgr
8775 SW Cascade Ave
Beaverton OR 97008
503-643-3131; Fax: 503-641-1554
Subjects: 21-23T-31-76-77-89-99
Items: HC-PB-BT-GA-GI-RM-MM-CA-US-MG-SW
Memo: 7 stores.

Powell's Books at PDX
Judy Jewell, Mgr
7000 NE Airport Way
Portland OR 97218
503-249-1950; Fax: 503-249-1935
Subjects: 21-31-76-77-89-99
Items: HC-PB-TA-TV-GA-GI-RM-MM-CA
Memo: 7 stores. Hdqtrs at 1005 W Burnside, Portland, OR.

Readmor Bookstores
Jennifer Bennett
777 W Goodale Blvd
PO Box 193
Columbus OH 43216
614-889-7468; Fax: 614-889-7849
Subjects: 99
Items: HC-PB-MM-GA-PO-GC-MA-ST
Memo: 7 stores.

Readmore
Dave Scherer, Book Buyer
2127 Old Troy Pike
PO Box 315 N Dayton Sta
Dayton OH 45404
513-233-8650; Fax: 513-233-8544
Subjects: 99
Items: HC-PB-MM-MG
Memo: 12 stores. Owned by Miami Valley Dist. Readmore stores in Ohio and Indiana.

Readmore Magazines & Books
Pamela Branchini, Buying Mgr
2560 S Maryland Pky
Las Vegas NV 89109
702-732-4453
Subjects: 39-75-84-95-99
Items: HC-PB-MG
Memo: 5 stores.

S & S Bookstore
Sandra Fellman, Buyer
335-A Main St
Farmingdale NY 11735
516-249-9803; Fax: 516-249-0830
Subjects: 99
Items: HC-PB
Memo: 6 stores.

Shinder's Readmore Bookstores
Bob Parker, Book Buyer
912 Nicollet Mall
Minneapolis MN 55402
612-333-7002
Subjects: 75-82-84-85-86-87-88-99
Items: PB-MM-MG-NP-RM-US
Memo: 13 stores.

The Spirit of '76 Bookstore
Robert Hugo, Owner
Pleasant & School Sts
Marblehead MA 01945
617-631-7199
Subjects: 19-19G-23-70-75-99
Items: HC-PB-MM-RM-GC-TA
Memo: Hdqtrs for Book Rack & Water Street Bookstore.

St Paul Book & Stationery
Steve Holm, Purchaser
1233 W County Rd E
PO Box 64410
St Paul MN 55112-0410
612-636-2250; Fax: 612-638-8817
Subjects: 11(graphics arts)-21-31-76
Items: Art materials, teaching material
Memo: 10 stores.

Toys International
Gayle Hoepner, Owner
3333 Bristol St
Costa Mesa CA 92626
714-549-8919; Fax: 714-432-9130
Subjects: 21-76-79
Comments: Send to Attn: Buyer
Memo: 3 toy stores, 1 plush specialty store.

Trover Shop Books
Joseph Shuman, Owner/Buyer
221 Pennsylvania Ave SE
Washington DC 20003
202-547-2665; Fax: 202-547-5584
Subjects: 99
Items: HC-PB-MM-GC-BT
Memo: 3 stores.

Village Green Bookstores
John Borek, Book Buyer
Monroe Book Corp
766 Monroe Ave
Rochester NY 14607
716-442-1151; Fax: 716-442-9273
Subjects: 99
Items: MG-NP-GI-GC-ST-TV-HC-PB
Memo: 3 stores in PA, 1 in CT, and 4 in NY.

White Rabbit Books & Things
Keven Drewery, Buyer
1833 Spring Garden St
Greensboro NC 27403
919-272-7604
Subjects: 99
Items: HC-PB-CA-GC-RC
Memo: 3 stores. Stores in Greensboro, Raleigh, and Charlotte.

Wilkie News
Eric S Oda, Gen Mgr
101 S Ludlow St
Dayton OH 45402-1891
513-223-2541; Fax: 513-223-2869
Subjects: 23-49B-39-59-19-75
Items: HC-PB-GC-MA-ST
Memo: 3 stores. Newsstands.

Wills Book Stores
Ethel Allen, Book Buyer
103 Longale Rd
PO Box 19239
Greensboro NC 27419-9239
910-299-1411; Fax: 910-299-1414
Subjects: 21-99
Items: HC-PB-RM-GA-GI-GC-MA-PO
Memo: 9 stores. Catalog 6x a year.

Regional Bookstore Chains

Abranovic Associates
Mark Abranovic
161 S McKean St
Kittaning PA 16201
412-543-2005; Fax: 412-543-3477
Subjects: 27-99
Items: HC-PB-MM-MG(one kitchen store)
Memo: 6 stores.

Alaskan Natural History Assn
Book Buyer
605 West 4th Ave #85
Anchorage AK 99501
907-274-8440; Fax: 907-274-8343
Subjects: 11-29-41-51-61(AK)-71-99
Memo: Headquarters for 32 stores.

Bedford Books
Donald Alper, VP
18 Priscilla Ln
Auburn NH 03032
603-668-3496; Fax: 603-668-2156
Subjects: 99
Items: HC-PB MM
Memo: 5 stores.

Book & Game Company Inc
203 N Washington
Spokane WA 99201
509-838-6242; Fax: 509-838-4967
Shelley Dyer, Book Buyer; Children's Books
Julie Smith, Head Buyer
Ms Chris O'Harra, Owner
Subjects: 21-76-79
Items: HC-PB-MM-RM-OP-US-MG-NP-TA-GC-MA
Memo: 6 stores. Catalog 3x a year.

Book 'N Card Inc
Tom Bonday, Book Buyer
Warwick Village South Ctr
PO Box 1636
Newport News VA 23601
804-595-1141; Fax: 804-599-5918
Subjects: 99
Items: HC-PB
Memo: 5 stores.

Book Bag Stores
Harold Clark
The News Group
PO Drawer 40
Charleston SC 29402-0040
803-744-1611; Fax: 803-744-0806
Subjects: 99
Items: HC-MM-MG
Memo: 2556 Oscar Johnson Dr. Wholesale division: Charleston News. 10 stores.

The Book Emporium
Deb Rogers, Book Buyer
General Offices
1301 SW Washington St
Peoria IL 61602-1795
309-673-2327; Fax: 309-673-8883
Subjects: 99
Items: HC-PB-MM-MG-GA-GI-PO-ST

Book World Inc
Bill Streur, Book Buyer
Levy Badger News
2420 West 4th St
Appleton WI 54914-4621
414-731-9521; Fax: 414-731-3671
Subjects: 99
Items: HC-PB-MM-MG

Bookland Inc
Mark Lando
1135 S Edgar St
PO Box 202
York PA 17405
717-848-5358; Fax: 717-843-3129
Subjects: 99
Items: HC-PB-GC-GI
Memo: Wholesale divison: York News Agency.

Books Inc
Mike Grant, Pres
Corporate Office
160 Fulsom St
San Francisco CA 94105
415-442-0982; Fax: 415-442-1875
Subjects: 99
Items: HC-PB-RM-MA-SW-GC
Memo: 13 stores.

The Bookstore Inc
Barbara Rossi, Book Buyer
808 Green Ave
PO Box 1713
Altoona PA 16601-4724
814-944-3593; Fax: 814-944-1881
Subjects: 29-43-99-57-39-27-63-71-75
Items: HC-PB-MM-RM
Memo: Wholesale Division: Newborn Enterprises.

Canyonlands Natural History Assn
Nancy Gebhardt, Book Buyer
3031 S Hwy 191
Moab UT 84532
801-259-6003; Fax: 801-259-8263
Subjects: 11-29-41-51-61(UT)-71
Items: HC-PB-MA-PO-TV
Memo: 8 stores.

Civilized Traveller
Alan Vollweiler, Pres
54 W 21st St #505
New York NY 10010
212-229-0569
Subjects: 71(International)

Memo: 4,000 catalogs mailed annually. 5 stores. Other locations: 1072 3rd Ave, New York, NY 10021; 2003 Broadway, New York, NY 10023; 2 World Financial Ctr, New York, NY 10281. Also Roosevelt Field Shopping Ctr, Garden City, Long Island, and Phipps Plaza, Atlanta, GA.

Construction Bookstore
Jennifer Bickford, Buyer
PO Box 2959
Gainesville FL 32609-2959
800-253-0541; Fax: 888-237-2889
Subjects: 12
Items: HC-PB
Memo: Headquarters.

Deseret Book Company (Retail)
Susan Harris, Childrens Bks
Paul Hastings, Religious Books
James Asay, Trade Book Buyer
40 E South Temple
PO Box 30178
Salt Lake City UT 84130-0178
801-534-1515; Fax: 801-531-1621
Subjects: 21-31-35-63(Mormon)
Items: HC-PB-RM-GI-PO-SM-SW-TV
Memo: 25 stores. Branches buy through headquarters. Direct correspondence to headquarters.

Eastern National Park and Monument Assn
John Hornback, Purchasing Agent
446 North Ln
Conshohocken PA 19428
Subjects: 11-41-51-61(Eastern US)-71
Items: Several locations
Memo: Direct all correspondence to headquarters.

Eaton & Son Book Peddlers Inc
Goetz Eaton, Owner
196 Alps Rd
Athens GA 30606
706-546-7427
Subjects: 99
Items: HC-PB-MM-RM-GC-BT-PO-TA
Memo: 5 stores. Headquarters in Anderson, SC. Contact Margie, Office Manager at 864-231-9812 or FAX: 864-231-8353.

Golden Gate National Parks Association Bookstores
Clover Earl, Book Buyer
Fort Mason Bldg 201
San Francisco CA 94123
415-776-0693; Fax: 415-776-2205
Subjects: 11-41-51-61(Western US)-71-99
Memo: 15 stores.

Hall of Cards & Books Inc
Buyer
313 E Main St
Niles MI 49120
616-684-5115; Fax: 616-684-8428
Subjects: 99
Items: HC-PB-RM-GC-LM-ST
Memo: 24 stores. Wholesale division: Michiana News Service. Catalog - 4/yr.

Hawaii Natural History Assn
Buyer: Bookstores
PO Box 74
Hawaii Natl Park HI 96718-0074
808-967-7311; Fax: 808-967-8186
Subjects: 11-29-41-51-61(HI)-71-99
Items: HC-PB-PO-MA-TV
Memo: 5 stores.

J K Gill
Joe Whalen, Book Buyer
9767 SW Washington Sq Rd
Portland OR 97223
503-620-3777
Subjects: 10-11-19-59-99
Items: HC-PB-GI
Memo: 9 stores. Main offices in San Diego, but book buying offices in Portland.

Lauriat's and Royal Disc Bkstore
Christine Barnard, Book Buyer
Lorna Ruby, Juvenile Buyer
Sunil Sharma, Paperbacks
10 Pequot Way
Canton MA 02021
617-821-0071; Fax: 617-821-0167
Subjects: 99
Items: HC-PB-MM-TA(also audiotapes)
Memo: 120 stores.

Les Librairies Boyer
Marie Boyer Grefford, Book Buyer
10 Nicholson
Valleyfield PQ Canada J6T 4M2
514-373-6211; Fax: 514-856-7798
Subjects: 21-31-76-89
Items: HC-PB-GC-ST
Memo: 4 stores.

Parks & History Association Bookstores
Rose Fennell, Book Buyer
PO Box 40060
Washington DC 20016
202-472-3083; Fax: 202-755-0469
Subjects: 11-41-51-61(Eastern US)-71
Items: HC-PB-RM-GI-MA-PO-GC
Memo: 16 stores.

Pegasus Fantasy Books
John Richardson, Book Buyer
4133 NE Sandy Blvd
Portland OR 97214
503-284-4693; Fax: 503-284-4693
Subjects: 86
Items: HC-PB-GC-CO-GA-PO-TO
Memo: 4 stores.

Periodical Management Group
Mike Smith, Book Buyer
1011 N Frio
PO Box 7608
San Antonio TX 78207-0608
210-226-0772
Subjects: 99
Items: HC-PB-MM
Memo: 30+ stores. PMG buys books for many IDs including Weiner News (same address), Amarillo Periodicals, and Arizona Periodicals.

Readmore Books
Amy Gordy
5101 Hinkleville Rd #670
Paducah KY 42001
502-442-1372; Fax: 502-443-8432
Subjects: 99
Items: HC-PB-MM-MG
Memo: 10 stores. Wholesale division: Austin Periodicals.

Rocky Mountain Nature Assn
Bob Maitland, Exec Dir
Rocky Mountain National Park
Estes Park CO 80517
970-586-1258; Fax: 970-586-1310
Subjects: 11-41-51-61(CO)-71
Items: HC-PB-TV
Memo: 8 stores. When faxing, write: Attn: RockyMount.Nat Park Assoc.

Southwest Parks and Monuments
Assn Bookstores
Mitch Peterson, Buyer
221 N Court Ave
Tucson AZ 85701-1037
520-622-1999; Fax: 520-623-9519
Subjects: 11-41-51-61(SW US)-71
Memo: 50 stores.

Theodore Roosevelt Nature and History Association Bookstores
Jane Muggli Paulson, Book Buyer
PO Box 167
Medora ND 58645-0167
701-623-4884
Subjects: 11-41-51-61(ND/SD)-71
Memo: 6 stores.

Zany Brainy
Margaret Wroclawski, Buyer
270 E Lancaster Ave
Wynnewood PA 19096
610-896-1500
Subjects: 21-31-76-99
Items: Educational games/arts/crafts
Memo: 38 stores. Zany Brainy: A Zillion Neat Things For Kids, has stores the Eastern US.

Zion Natural Historical Association
Joanne Hinman, Book Buyer
Bookstore, Visitor Ctr
Zion National Park
Springdale UT 84767-1099
801-772-3264; Fax: 801-772-3908
Subjects: 41-51-61(AZ/UT)-71-45
Items: HC-PB-TV-PO-TA
Memo: 3 stores. Jamie Gentry, Exec Director.

National Bookstore Chains

American Opinion Bookstores
David Martin, Gen Mgr
770 Westhill Blvd
PO Box 8040
Appleton WI 54913
414-749-3780; Fax: 414-749-5062
Subjects: 19-29-31-41-55(conservative)

Memo: Catalog mailed 4x a year. Franchises buy independently & through headquarters; 26 stores.

The Armchair Sailor Bookstore
Susan Dye, Book Buyer
543 Thames St
Newport RI 02840
401-847-4252; Fax: 401-847-1219
Subjects: 70N
Memo: 8 stores buy independently.

B Dalton / Barnes & Noble
Karen Paterson, Buyer
Lee Stern, Buyer
George Greller, Buyer
Laura Zambrano, Buyer
David Garber, Buyer, Art/Performing Arts
Bill Costello, Buyer; Audio Buyer, Education/Games/Reference
Gail Doobinin, Buyer; Children's Books
Tom Dutcher, Calendar Buyer
Glen Timony, Buyer, History/Literature/True Crime
Rick Kenyon, Buyer, Magazines/Maps
Julie Arthur-Sherman, Regional Book Buyer
Marcella Smith, Small Press and University Press Buyer
David Garber, Travel Buyer
122 Fifth Ave
New York NY 10011-5605
212-633-3483; Fax: 212-675-0413
Subjects: 16-31E-59-69G
Items: HC-PB

Barbara's Bookstore
Isabella Reitzel, Book Buyer
3130 N Broadway
Chicago IL 60657
312-477-0411
Subjects: 11-13-27-53-54-75-84-86-95-99
Items: HC-PB-MM-MG-CA-GC-MA-CD-SW-NP-TA-TV-TO
Memo: Headquarters for 6 stores. Christmas catalog, author signings.

Black Bond Books
Cathy Jesson, Book Buyer
Headquarters
15562 24th Ave Unit #1
Surrey BC Canada V4A 2J5
604-536-4444; Fax: 604-536-3551
Subjects: 99
Items: HC-PB-RM
Memo: 8 stores.

Book Rack Management
Fred Darnell, Owner
2715 E Commercial Blvd
Fort Lauderdale FL 33308-4112
305-771-4310
Subjects: 75-77-81-82-84-85-86-87-88-99
Items: PB(new & used)
Memo: Franchises buy independently.

Borders
New Publisher Contact
5451 S State St
Ann Arbor MI 48108
313-913-1333; Fax: 313-995-5588
Subjects: 99
IMemo: Main #: 313-995-8282. Formerly **Book Inventory Systems.** They won't be adding any new publishers until Oct 1st. Don't send any materials.

Chapters
Janet Hawkins, Juvenile Buyer
Charlotte Chaplan, Mag Buyer
Debra Lewington, Mass Market
Ed Wilkinson, Rem Buyer
90 Ronson Dr
Etobicoke ON Canada M9W 1C1
416-243-3132; Fax: 416-243-8964
Subjects: 99
Items: MG
Memo: 230 stores. Coles Bookstores merged with Smith Books—now called Chapters.

Crown and Super Crown Books
Cynthia Holland, Softcover Buyer
Corporate Offices
3300 75th Ave
Landover MD 20785
301-731-1263; Fax: 301-773-2705
Subjects: 99(softcovers and small press)
Items: PB

Family Bookstores
Rick Forsythe, Buyer, Children's Books
Michael Hupp, Gift/Stationery Buyer
Bob Elder, Music Buyer
Don Kooima, Trade Bk/Church Supply
Zondervan Corp Hdqtrs
5300 Patterson Ave SE
Grand Rapids MI 49530
616-554-8700; Fax: 616-554-8694
Subjects: 21-63(Christian)-99
Memo: 170 stores.

Half Price Books
Charles Mitchell, Buyer
Texas Bookman
8650 Denton Dr
Dallas TX 75235
214-363-8374; Fax: 214-890-0850
Subjects: 99(used books and remainders)
Items: RM-US-MM-CD-SW-TA
Memo: 52 stores.

Hastings Books Music & Video
Larry Hollern, Book Buyer
Jeff Fulford, Sr Book Buyer
3601 Plains Blvd #1
Amarillo TX 79102
806-351-2300; Fax: 806-351-2728
Subjects: 14-17-33-99 (new titles)
Items: HC-PB-GA-GC-TS-PZ-PO-TV
Memo: 108 stores. John Marmaduke, President.They carry over 27,500 titles.

Hoover Brothers Inc
Pam Martin, Natl Retail Mgr
2050 Postal Way
PO Box 660420
Dallas TX 75266-0420
214-634-8474; Fax: 214-905-6034
Subjects: 21-31-99
Memo: 13 stores & catalog. Bought out by J L Hammett Co, but still going by the name: Hoover Bros.

J L Hammett's Learning World
Evie Kaatz, Book Buyer
100 Hammett Pl
PO Box 9057
Braintree MA 02184
617-848-1000; Fax: 617-843-4901
Subjects: 21-31-35-76-89
Memo: 14 stores. Hammett's Teachers Stores. Branches buy through headquarters.

Lemstone Book Branch
Rick Regenfuss, Book Buyer
1123 Wheaton Oaks Ct
Wheaton IL 60187
708-682-1400; Fax: 708-682-1828
Subjects: 63
Items: HC-PB-TA-TV-GI
Memo: 68 stores.

Little Professor Book Centers
John Glazer, Pres
130 S First St #300
Ann Arbor MI 48104
313-994-1212; Fax: 313-994-9009
Subjects: 99
Memo: 110 stores. All franchises buy independently

Rizzoli International Bookstores
Antonio Polito
300 Park Ave S
New York NY 10010-5399
212-387-3400; Fax: 212-387-3434
Subjects: 11-12-99
Items: HC-PB
Memo: 14 stores.

Smith & Hawken
Jan Lockie
117 E Strawberry Dr
Mill Valley Ca 94941
415-383-4415; Fax: 415-383-3465
Subjects: 43G
Items: HC-PB-OT
Memo: 22 stores. Catalog; this is the retail store information.

Smith Books
Nigel Berrisford, Purchasing
90 Ronson Dr
Etobicoke ON Canada M9W 1C1
416-243-3138
Subjects: 99
Items: GA-GI-GC-MA-HC-PB-MM-RM
Memo: 190 stores. Corp hdqtrs is Chapters. Another division is Coles.

Waldenbooks
S Biggs, Assistant Buyer: (Ext 1856): Travel, Regional
M Janus, Assistant Buyer (Ext 1860): Romance, Total Series Romance, Mystery/Adventure
C Lashinsky, Assistant Buyer (Ext 1855): Westerns, Regional
D Mayer, Assistant Buyer (Ext 1875): Fiction-Hardcover, Fiction-Trade, Large Print Books, Poetry
M McKenna, Assistant Buyer; (Ext 1857): Bargain
D Stymiest, Assistant Buyer (Ext 1859): Magazine, Graphic Novel, Home Repair
A Talberg, Assistant Buyer (Ext 1872): Games, Kid's Video, Audio, Art, Pets
M Thomas, Assistant Buyer (Ext 1876): Biography, History, True Crime
Stuart Carter, Buyer: Travel, Regional; (313-913-1863)
Joy Dallanegra-Sanger, Buyer: Fiction-HC/Trade Poetry; (313-913-1877)
Scott Ferguson, Buyer: Art, Performing Arts, Photography (313-913-1868)
Robert Fields, Buyer: Biography, History, True Crime (313-913-1878)
Christine Glynn, Buyer: Religion, Philosophy, New Age (313-913-1862)
Jennie Greeley, Buyer: Antiques, Cooking, Craft, Gardening (313-913-1861)
Susan Grimshaw, Buyer: Children's Books/Young Adult (313-913-1882)
John Hartley, Buyer: Keepsakes, Maps, Cards, Adult Video (313-913-1857)
Lucia Heinold, Buyer: Self-Help, Relationships (313-913-1870)
Joe Holtzman, Buyer: Bargain (313-913-1865)
Jay Hyde, Buyer: Business, Computer, Transportation (313-913-1866)
Helen Ibach, Buyer: Westerns, Regional (313-913-1854)
Beth Koehler, Buyer: Romance, Mystery, Adventure (313-913-1871)
Diane Mangen, Buyer: Children's Books (313-913-1881)
Michael Sgriccia, Buyer: Fiction(mass market)/Literature (313-913-1873)
Dan Shull, Buyer: Magazine, Graphic Novel (313-913-1850)
Kelly Small, Buyer: Fitness/Sports/Adult Video (313-913-1867)
Scott Snow, Buyer: Calendars (313-913-1852)
Chris Wang, Buyer: Science Fiction, Fantasy (313-913-1874)
Xavier Washington, Buyer: Games, Kid's Video, Audio, Art, Pets (313-913-1880)
100 Phoenix Dr
Ann Arbor MI 48106-2022
313-913-1800; Fax: 313-913-1918
Subjects: 75-95-99(large print)
Items: MA-GC-TV-ST-SB
Memo: 1000+ stores.

Waldenbooks
Beryl Needham, Dir
100 Phoenix Dr
Ann Arbor MI 48106-2022
313-913-1913; Fax: 313-913-1918
Subjects: 17-18-23-41-47-55C-65-75-95
Items: HC-PB-GA
Memo: Fiction, poetry, biography, history, true crime, social science, business, computer books, romance, mystery/adventure, literature, science fiction/fantasy, large print books.

Waldenbooks
Peter Thornton, Divisional Mdse Mgr
100 Phoenix Dr
Ann Arbor MI 48107-2022
313-913-1914; Fax: 313-913-1918
Subjects: 29H-35-39-43H-57S-59
Items: MG-CA

Waldenbooks
Mike Oprins, Divisional Mdse Mgr
100 Phoenix Dr
Ann Arbor MI 48106-2022
313-913-1849; Fax: 313-913-1918
Subjects: 11-14-27-33H-39E-69-73-88-99
Items: MA-GC-ST-SB-TV(adult)
Memo: Art, performing arts, humor, photography, drama, fitness/nutrition, sports, travel, westerns, keepsakes, maps, blank books, cards, stationery items, book marks/accessories, assorted non-book, adult video.

Waldenbooks
Beth Gorman, Divisional Mdse Mgr
100 Phoenix Dr
Ann Arbor MI 48107-2022
313-913-1848; Fax: 313-913-1918
Subjects: 15-21-27-28-31-53-54-55N-63-99
Memo: New Age, philosophy, religion, bibles, antiques, cooking, craft, gardening, bargain, children's books & games, nature/pets.

Waldenbooks
Karen Bell, Divisional Mdse Mgr
100 Phoenix Dr
Ann Arbor MI 48106-2022
313-913-1819; Fax: 313-913-1918
Subjects: 17-19-23-41-47-55-65-84-85-86-9
Memo: Fiction, large print books, poetry, biography, history, true crime, social science, business, computer books, transportation, romance, total series romance, mystery/adventure, literature, science fiction/fantasy, role playing.

Waterstone's Booksellers
Ed Anderson, Mgr
840 N Michigan
Chicago IL 60611
312-587-8080; Fax: 312-587-2700
Subjects: 99
Items: HC-PB-MM-RM-MG-CA-GC-MA-CD-SW-NP-SB-TA-TV-Music
Memo: Annual catalog in store(not mailed). Will special order British books. There are 2 other stores in Boston, and 5 airport stores throughout the USA. This is an England/British based bookseller.
Author signings: Yes

Religious Bookstore Chains

Agape Christian Bookstore
Ann Richman, Mgr
1066 Arlington Rd
Jacksonville FL 32211
904-724-9848
Subjects: 63(Christian)-99
Memo: Headquarters. 4 stores.

Augsburg Fortress Publishers
Roderick Olson, Book Buyer
426 South 5th St
PO Box 1209
Minneapolis MN 55440-1209
612-330-3319; Fax: 612-330-3455
Subjects: 14M-39-63(Lutheran)-99
Items: HC-MM-GC
Memo: 10 stores.

Baker Book House
Buyer
2768 E Paris Rd
PO Box 6287
Grand Rapids MI 49516-6287
616-957-3110; Fax: 616-957-0965
Subjects: 63P
Items: HC-PB-OP-RM-US
Memo: Branches buy independently. 5 stores.

Berean Bookstores
Daniel Miles, Gen Mgr
8121 Hamilton Ave
PO Box 31150
Cincinnati OH 45231
513-931-4050; Fax: 513-931-4045
Subjects: 63
Memo: Headquarters. Branches buy independently. 16 stores.

Bethany Fellowship Bookshop
Roxanne Swezey, Book Buyer
6820 Auto Club Rd
Minneapolis MN 55438-2898
612-829-2586
Subjects: 45-63P
Items: HC-PB-TX-TA
Memo: Headquarters. 3 stores.

Christian Armory
Betty Willke, Mgr
2250 Morse Rd
Columbus OH 43229
614-476-2600
Subjects: 63(Christian music)-99
Items: HC-PB-GI
Memo: 3 stores.

Christian Book & Gift Shop
John Snyder, Owner
107 N Jefferson St
Kittanning PA 16201-1535
412-548-4521
Subjects: 11-63(Christian)
Items: HC-PB-TA-GI
Memo: 3 stores.

Christian Supply Bookstore
Manager
10209 SE Division St
Portland OR 97266-1399
503-256-4520
Subjects: 63(Christian)-99
Items: HC-PB-GI-GC-TA-RC-TV-TX-OP-RM-US
Memo: 6 stores.

Cokesbury
Faye Lyons
201 Eighth Ave S
Nashville TN 37202
615-749-6352; Fax: 615-749-6079
Subjects: 11-14-19-23-39-49-63
Items: HC-PB-RM-GC-GI-ST-SW-TV
Memo: 38 stores. Each branch buy independently through headquarters.

Dickson's Bible Bookstores
Doug Stuwart, Book Buyer
1315 S Woodward Ave
Royal Oak MI 48067-3039
810-543-7444; Fax: 810-543-4683
Subjects: 63(Christian)-99
Memo: 6 stores.

Gospel Advocate Bookstores
Debbie Bumbalough, Book Buyer
Neil Anderson, Pres
1006 Elm Hill Pike
Nashville TN 37210
615-254-8781; Fax: 615-254-7411
Subjects: 63
IMemo: Other store is in Dallas, TX.

The Guild
Jim Weis, Book Buyer
400 Wyoming Ave
Scranton PA 18503-1226
717-342-8246; Fax: 717-342-5940
Subjects: 63C-99
Items: HC-PB-CD-TA-OT
Memo: 3 stores.

Joshua's Christian Stores
Jan McCarson, Buyer
1400 Everman Pky
Ft Worth TX 76410
817-568-7800; Fax: 817-293-0389
Subjects: 63(Protestant)
Items: HC-PB-TA-GC-GI
Memo: 75 stores. Catalog mailed periodically.

Kaufer Religious Supplies
Kevin Hurley, Book Buyer
55 Beverly St
San Francisco CA 94132
415-333-4494; Fax: 415-333-0402
Subjects: 63C
Items: HC-PB-GI-TA-TV
Memo: 3 stores. This store primarily services Catholic parishes, dioceses, and convents. They also distibute one catalog a year.

Moody Bookstores
Jackie Thomas, Mgr/Buyer
Chatham Ridge Mall
112 W 87th St
Chicago IL 60620
312-994-0633; Fax: 312-994-5886
Subjects: 63(Christian)
Items: HC-PB-SW-TA-TV
Memo: 5 stores.

Moody Bookstores
Kevin Howells, Mgr
Jay Jones, Buyer
150 W Chicago Ave
Chicago IL 60610
312-329-4352; Fax: 312-329-4363
Subjects: 63P
Items: HC-PB-GC-TV-TX-OT(bibles)

Northwestern Products
Bill Wright, Mgr
3255 Spring St NE
Minneapolis MN 55413-2993
612-331-9384; Fax: 612-331-6721
Subjects: 63(Protestant)
Items: HC-PB-MM-GI
Memo: 10 stores.

Pauline Books and Media
Sr Dorothy, Book Buyer
50 St Paul's Ave
Jamaica Plain MA 02130
617-522-8911; Fax: 617-541-9805
Subjects: 63C
Items: HC-PB-TV-GC
Memo: 23 stores.

Provident Bookstore
Mary Johnson, Mgr
165 Pittsburgh St
Scottdale PA 15683-1999
412-887-5020; Fax: 412-887-3110
Subjects: 14M-17-35-57-63(Mennonite)-99
Items: HC-PB-GI-GC-ST-RC
Memo: 15 stores. Each store does its own buying.

Rainbow West Christian Book
Joanna Adams, Book Buyer
1122 Lancaster Dr NE
Salem OR 97301
503-363-5155; Fax: 503-364-2391
Subjects: 63P
Items: HC-PB-GC-TA-TV
Memo: 6 stores. his is headquarters. Each store buys independently.

Salvation Army Supply Purchasing
Major William Simmons, Buyer
Book Dept
440 W Nyack Rd
West Nyack NY 10994-0635
914-620-7200; Fax: 914-620-7466
Subjects: 63(Christian)
Items: HC-PB-RM-GA-GC-ST

Western Christian Bookstores
Tom, Mgr
1618 Franklin St
Oakland CA 94612-2806
510-832-2040; Fax: 510-832-6505
Subjects: 63(Protestant)
Items: HC-PB-GI-GC
Memo: 7 stores.

College BookstoreChains

Beck's Book Store
Robert L Beck, Owner
4520 N Broadway
Chicago IL 60640
312-784-7963; Fax: 312-784-0066
Subjects: 55-99
Items: HC-PB-US-TX
Memo: 4 stores.

Campus Store Queens College
Deena Alstodt, Book Buyer
65-30 Kissena Blvd
Flushing NY 11367-1575
718-268-7252; Fax: 718-544-9003
Subjects: 99
Items: 12 college stores.

Follett College Stores
Bill Turk, VP/Text Buyer
Bill Scharnweber, Trade Books
400 W Grand Ave
PO Box 888
Elmhurst IL 60126
708-279-2330; Fax: 708-279-2569
Subjects: Textbooks & trade
Items: 59
Memo: 518 stores. Direct correspondence through headquarters. Do buy independently.

Harvard Coop
1400 Massachusetts Ave
Cambridge MA 02238-0001
617-499-2000; Fax: 617-868-7038
Francis Dibiscelia, Buyer
Bob Westoff, Textbook Buyer
Subjects: 99(textbooks)
Items: HC-PB-TX
Memo: Ext 2205 for bookstore. 5 stores.

Heald Business College Stores
James Clark, Bus Book Buyer
2665 N 1st St #110
San Jose CA 95130
408-370-2400
Subjects: 19
Items: HC-PB-TX

Heald Technical College Store
Kathy Harrington, Book Buyer
341-A Great Mall Pky
San Jose CA 95035
408-934-4900; Fax: 408-934-7777
Subjects: 23-24-39-67
Items: HC-PB-TX

Kent State Univ Bookstores
Jack Clemmons, Mgr
Kenneth Anderson, Textbook Buyer
Tom Parsons, Trade Buyer
Kent Student Ctr
Kent State Univ
Kent OH 44242
216-672-2762; Fax: 216-672-3758
Subjects: 31-99
Items: HC-PB-GI-CO-GC-BT-SW
Memo: 8 stores.

Nebraska Book Store
Jim Cornell, Gen Mgr
1300 Q St
Lincoln NE 68508-1500
402-476-0111; Fax: 402-476-7755
Subjects: 11-49-63-99
Items: HC-OP-PB-RM-US-GA-GI-GC-SW-TV

New Hampshire College Bookstore
John Rheault, Mgr
Campus Bookstores
2500 N River Rd
Manchester NH 03104-1394
603-645-9696; Fax: 603-645-9719
Subjects: 19A-19-19E-19B-99
Items: HC-PB-GC-ST
Memo: 5 stores. Headquarters: Follett College Service.

New York University Book Center
Jo Ann McGreevy, Dir
18 Washington Pl
New York NY 10003-6638
212-998-4650; Fax: 212-998-4118
Subjects: 11-19-23-31-39-41-47-55-57-65
Items: HC-PB-RM-US-SW-GI
memo: 4 stores.

Oakland Community College
Stephanie Reardon, Buyer (810-360-6210)
College Bookstore Box 812
7350 Cooley Lake Rd
Waterford MI 48327
810-360-3098; Fax: 810-360-3152
Subjects: 11-19-27-55L-39-99
Items: HC-PB

Memo: 5 stores.

OSU Bookstores
2009 Millikin Rd
Ohio State Univ
Columbus OH 43210
614-292-2991; Fax: 614-292-8983
Tom Hayward, Texbook Buyer
Louanne White, Trade Book Buyer
Subjects: 23-59-67-99
Items: HC-PB-OP-US-GI-GC-ST-SW-OT
Memo: 6 stores.

Univ of Cincinnati Bookstore
Mike Zimmerman, Mgr
Carol Sojka, Textbook Buyer
Lynne Pacella, Trade Buyer
Univ of Cincinnati
123 W University Ave
Cincinnati OH 45221
513-556-1700; Fax: 513-556-5555
Subjects: 99
Items: HC-PB-RM-US-SW-GC-GI-TA
Memo: 5 stores.

Univ of Connecticut Co-Operative
Jean Chaine, Mdse Mgr
Suzanna Staubach, Trade Mgr
81 Fairfield Rd
PO Box U-19
Storrs CT 06269-2019
203-486-3537; Fax: 203-486-4318
Subjects: 23-61-47-99
Items: PB-HC-TX-RM-US-SW-GC
Memo: 8 stores.

Univ of Minnesota Bookstores
Bill Breer, Gen Book Buyer
231 Pillsbury Dr SE
Minneapolis MN 55455-0001
612-625-6000; Fax: 612-624-4133
Subjects: 99
Items: Departments buy own textbooks
Memo: 4 stores.

Univ of Wisconsin Centers
Paul Koch, Library Book Buyer
Book Purchasing Office
Campus Drive
Fon du Lac WI 54935
608-263-7972
Subjects: 99
Memo: 13 stores. Headquarters located in Madison.

University of Hawaii Bookstore
Univ of Hawaii
2465 Campus Rd
Honolulu HI 96822
808-956-4326; Fax: 808-956-4338
Wayne Fugishige
Gladys Okuda, Textbook Buyer
Randy Tanaka, Trade Buyer
Subjects: 23-59-99
Items: HC-PB-TX-RM-PO-ST-SW
Memo: 7 stores. Catalog 2x per year.

University of Toronto Bookroom
Ron Johnson, Gen Mgr
Albert Sugarman, Medical Buyer
Nick Pashley, Trade Buyer
Koffler Student Services Ctr
214 College St
Toronto ON Canada M5T 3A1
416-978-7907; Fax: 416-978-7242
Subjects: 39-45-99
Items: HC-PB-RM-US-SW-LM
Memo: 6 stores. 50,000 titles. Catalog once a year.

University Supply Store
James Ussery, Trade Book Buyer
Ferguson Ctr
Box 870291
Tuscaloosa AL 35487
205-348-6126; Fax: 205-348-9239
Subjects: 99
Items: GM-CA-CO-CR-GI-MA-GC-PO-MG-NP-SW-SB-TA-TX-US

Wallace's Bookstores
928 Nandino Rd
PO Box 11039
Lexington KY 40512-1039
606-255-0886
Subjects: 99
Memo: 13 stores.

WVU Bookstores
West Virginia Univ
PO Box 6357
Morgantown WV 26506
304-293-7467
Subjects: 23-24-39-99
Items: HC-PB-US-SW-GC-ST
Memo: 13 college stores. They only buy through Barnes & Noble.

Department Store Chains

Abercrombie & Fitch
Book Buyer
4 Limited Pky
PO Box 182168
Reynoldsburg OH 43068
614-577-6500; Fax: 614-577-6565
Subjects: 99
Items: 12-27-28-51-69
Memo: 30 stores.

Ben Franklin Stores
Bernie Roser, Buyer, Activity and Juvenile Books
Linda Campbell, Buyer, Hard Crafts & Books
Janet O'Campo, Buyer, Mass-Market & Crosswords Books
Alice Handy, Buyer, Soft Crafts & Books
500 E North Ave
Carol Stream IL 60188
708-462-6100; Fax: 708-462-6395
Subjects: 29-43
Items: HC-PB-CR
Memo: 1700 stores.

Caldor's Department Stores
Karen Chur, Buyer
Book Dept
20 Glover Ave
Norwalk CT 06856-5620
203-846-1641; Fax: 203-849-2909
Subjects: 99
Items: HC-PB-MM
Memo: 124 discount department stores.

Castner-Knott Dept Stores
Buyer
1790 Galleria Blvd
Franklin TN 37067
615-771-2100; Fax: 615-771-7957
Subjects: 99
Memo: This is buying location for the stores. Hdqtrs in Nashville.

Dayton-Hudson Book Depts
Sharon Roth, Sr Book Buyer
Marshall Field, Book Dept
111 N State St
Chicago IL 60602-1658
312-781-5624; Fax: 312-787-3839
Subjects: 99
Memo: 9 stores. Department store. Also buys for stores in Minnesota & Michigan.

Eaton's Department Stores
Jo Anne Barresi, Buyer
Book Dept
250 Young StW 5th Fl
Toronto ON Canada M5B 1C8
416-343-4555
Subjects: 99
Items: Department stores
Memo: 86 stores. Buys through headquarters. Direct all correspondence to headquarters.

Shopko Stores
Claudine Starkey, Buyer
Book Dept
700 Pilgrim Way
Green Bay WI 54304
414-497-2211; Fax: 414-496-4133
Subjects: 99
Memo: Discount variety store. 129 stores.

Stone & Thomas Dept Stores
Debbie Fetty, Book Buyer
Book Dept
1030 Main St
Wheeling WV 26003-2710
304-232-3344
Subjects: 21-27-43-63-16A
Items: HC-PB
Memo: Department Store. 19 stores. Fax: Ext 360.

ZCMI Department Stores
Todd Floyd, Buyer
Book Dept
2200 South 900 W
Salt Lake City UT 84137-0001
801-579-6000; Fax: 801-579-6275
Subjects: 11-27-99
Memo: 14 stores.

Other Chains

Blockbuster Entertainment Corp
Book Buyer
1 Block Buster Plz
Fort Lauderdale FL 33301
954-832-3000; Fax: 954-832-3901
Subjects: 17-33
Items: TV-TA
Memo: Video store.

Bread & Circus
Tim Sperry, Head Buyer
17 Lincoln St
Newton Highlands MA 02161
617-332-2400; Fax: 617-332-2360
Subjects: 27-39H
Memo: Natural food stores. 7 stores. The northeast division of Whole Foods Supermarkets. Tim will see that the book gets to the right people.

Charrette
Craig Elliott
31 Olympia Ave
Woburn MA 01888
617-935-6000; Fax: 617-932-0985
Subjects: 11-12
Items: Design products catalog
Memo: 12 stores.

Clint's Books & Comics
Manager
3943 Main St
Kansas City MO 64111
816-561-2848
Subjects: 33-69(games)-86
Items: GA-CO-OT-RM-PB-OP
Memo: 3 stores.

Colborn School Supply Stores
Brad Larson, Book Buyer
999 S Jason (80223)
PO Box 9348
Denver CO 80209-0348
303-778-1220; Fax: 303-778-6151
Subjects: 21-31-76-89
Items: HC-PB-MA-SW-TV
Memo: 3 stores.

The Compleat Strategist Inc
Buyer
11 East 33rd St
New York NY 10016-5002
212-685-3880
Subjects: 48-86-87(military)
Items: HC-PB-MM-CA-SW-GA-TO
Memo: 10 outlets. 25,00 catalogs mailed annually.

Costco Wholesale
Penny Clark Ianniciello, Buyer, Book Dept
10809 120th Ave NE
Kirkland WA 98033
206-828-8100; Fax: 206-828-8101
Subjects: 99
Items: Warehouse chain (ext 524)
Memo: 56 stores.

Eastern Mountain Sports
Valerie Bentley, Book Buyer
Book Dept
1 Vose Farm Rd
Peterborough NH 03458-2128
603-924-9571; Fax: 603-924-9138
Subjects: 39-51-70-71
Items: HC-PB(hiking & climbing)
Memo: 60 stores. Hiking & climbing, cross country skiing, and travel guides.

Erehwon Mountain Outfitters
Stan Treadway, Book Buyer
65 E Palatine Rd #311
Prospect Heights IL 60070
708-215-5161; Fax: 708-215-5165
Subjects: 51-69-71
Items: HC-PB-MA(sporting goods/clothing
Memo: 4 stores.

F A O Schwarz Stores
Sr Buyer
Book Dept
767 Fifth Ave
New York NY 10153
212-644-9410; Fax: 212-753-1797
Subjects: 21-31-76-89
Items: HC-GA-PB-PO-SB-TA-TO-TV
Memo: 18 toy stores.

Farm Fresh Stores
Karen Webster, Buyer
Book and Video Operations
7530 Tidewater Dr
Norfolk VA 23505-3765
804-480-6700; Fax: 804-480-6399
Subjects: 99
Items: HC-PB-RM-GG-GI-GC-LM-MA

Fay's Drug Stores
Lyndon Johnson, Book Buyer
7245 Henry Clay Blvd
Liverpool NY 13088
315-451-8000; Fax: 315-451-2470
Subjects: 99
Memo: 277 stores.

Holcomb's Educational Materials
Debbie Cervelli, Buyer
3205 Harvard Ave
Cleveland OH 44105
216-341-3000; Fax: 216-341-5151
Subjects: 21-31-76
Memo: 10 stores. Also have a catalog.

House of Fabrics / So-Fro Fabric
Dwynn Helms, Book Buyer
13400 Riverside Dr
Sherman Oaks CA 91423-2598
818-995-7000; Fax: 818-385-2389
Subjects: 29C-40F-43D

Imaginarium Stores
Alison Kane, Book Buyer
Bill Obermeyer, Sr Toy Buyer
1600 Riveria Ave #280
Walnut Creek CA 94596
510-930-8666; Fax: 510-930-7134
Subjects: 21-31-76-79

J C Penney Stores
Robert Schuellein, Book Buyer
Children's Toy Dept
6501 Legacy Dr
Plano TX 75024
214-431-1000
Subjects: 21-76-79

Lone Star Comics/Science Fiction
Steve Schiavo, Buyer
511 E Abram St
Arlington TX 76010-1295
817-860-7827; Fax: 817-860-2769
Subjects: 33-69(games)-86
Items: CO-HC-PB-MM-US-GM-GI-GA
Memo: 8 stores.

Long's Drugs
John Russel, Mdse Mgr
141 N Civic Dr
Walnut Creek CA 94596
510-937-1170; Fax: 510-944-6657
Subjects: 99
Memo: Drug stores. 327 stores.

Majors Scientific Bookstore
Lynne Brotman, Gen Mgr
2137 Butler St
Dallas TX 75235
214-631-4478; Fax: 214-230-0410
Subjects: 39-57-67
Items: HC-PB-TX
Memo: 4 stores.

Mrs Gooch's Natural Foods
Buyer
15315 Magnolia Blvd #320
Sherman Oaks CA 91403
818-501-8484; Fax: 818-990-7089
Subjects: 27-39-53
Memo: 7 stores.

The Nature Company
Tracy Fortini, Buyer
Corporate Offices
750 Hearst Ave
Berkeley CA 94710-1927
510-644-1337; Fax: 510-649-5206
Subjects: 11-15-21-43-51-63-67-69-71
Items: HB-PB-TV-TA
Memo: Also has a catalog.

The Paper Cutter
Paula Olmstead, Book Buyer
Fay's Inc
4577 Buckley Rd
Liverpool NY 13088-2504
315-652-7000; Fax: 315-652-6798
Subjects: 19
Items: HC-PB-GC
Memo: 29 stores.

Pet Food Express
Mark Witriol, Mgr
421 23rd Ave
Oakland CA 94606
510-534-7777; Fax: 510-534-7787
Subjects: 15
Items: HC-PB-GI(pet food and products)
Memo: 8 stores.

Ratcliffe's Book & Office Supply
Richard Ratcliffe, Pres
724 N Custer
PO Box 588
Weatherford OK 73096-0588
405-772-3387; Fax: 405-772-3388
Subjects: 19-23-99
Memo: 7 office supply stores.

Sam Flax Inc
Jack Ptasiewicz, Buyer
12 W 20th St
New York NY 10001
212-620-3000; Fax: 212-633-1082
Subjects: 11-19M(advertising)-59
Items: Art supplies/commercial artists
Memo: Jack's ext: 254. 4 stores, 1 catalog mailed each year.

Service Merchandise
Jay Dworsky, Childrens Buyer
7100 Service Merchandise Dr
Brentwood TN 37027
615-660-6000; Fax: 615-660-7056
Subjects: 21-27
Items: HC-PB
Memo: Service Merchandise is a discount chain; only carries childrens and cook books. 355 stores.

Smithsonian Museum Shops
Norma Ryan, Book Buyer
600 Maryland Ave SW #295
Washington DC 20024
202-287-3563; Fax: 202-287-3080
Subjects: 11-17-29-41-49-51-55-67-80-99
Items: HC-PB-BT-RM-TV
Memo: 11 museum shops. Catalog mailed 3 times per year.

Sport Chalet
Todd Spivek, Book Buyer
920 Foothill Blvd
La Canada CA 91011
818-790-9800; Fax: 818-790-0087
Subjects: 51-69-71(hiking/camping/guides)
Items: HC-PB-GI-TO
Memo: 19 stores.

Studio Stores
Book Buyer
Warner Brothers Retail
3500 W Olive #450
Burbank CA 91505
818-954-5781; Fax: 818-954-4390
Subjects: 17C-33M-33T
Items: Hollywood nostalgia
Memo: 142 stores. First store opened in 1991 featuring Warner Brothers products.

Sun Wa Bookstore
19 Milliken Blvd
Scarborough ON Canada M1V 4A2
416-293-9438; Fax: 416-293-9438
Subjects: 45(Chinese)-80
Items: LM-ST-BR-HC-PB
Memo: 3 stores.

Target Stores
Therese Peterson, Sr Buyer
33 South 6th St
Minneapolis MN 55420
612-304-6365; Fax: 612-304-3788
Subjects: 99
Memo: 373 discount stores.

Thompson Book & Supply
Lowell Thompson, Owner
PO Box 11600
Oklahoma City OK 73136
405-478-3963; Fax: 405-478-4565
Subjects: 21-31-76
Items: HC-PB-SW-GI-GC
Memo: 5 stores.

Tower Records & Books
Jack Lamplough, Mktg Dir
Heidi Keller Cotler, VP Book Division
2601 Del Monte St
West Sacramento CA 95691
916-373-2500; Fax: 916-373-2583
Subjects: 14M-17
Items: CD-PB-HC-TA
Memo: 152 stores. All stores now have a small book division.

Toys-R-Us Stores
Leah Michaels, Book Buyer (Ext 6602)
Books R Us Dept
461 From Rd
Paramus NJ 07652
201-262-7800; Fax: 201-262-5950
Subjects: 21-76-89
Items: HC-PB-GA-GI-TO-TV-TA(toy stores)
Memo: 618 stores.

Walt's Hallmark
Rowena Hurlbut, Owner
2210 Main St
Ames IA 50010
515-232-1788; Fax: 515-232-8020
Subjects: 99
Items: HC-PB-GI-GC-ST(gift shop)
Memo: 6 stores. Division of Ames News Agency.

West Coast Video
Ed Humphreys, Video Buyer
9990 Global Rd
Philadelphia PA 19115
215-677-1000; Fax: 215-677-5804
Subjects: 17-33
Items: Video stores
Memo: 700 stores.

Whole Earth Access
Tony Garrett, Book Buyer (Ext 438)
Basic Living Products
1321 67th St
Emeryville CA 94608
510-428-1600; Fax: 510-652-4902
Subjects: 21-23-24-27-29-39-43-51-53-54
Items: HC-PB-MM-GI-MG-SW(how-to books)
Memo: 3 stores.

Williams-Sonoma Stores
Victoria Kalish, Book Buyer
3250 Van Ness Ave
San Francisco CA 94109
415-421-7900; Fax: 415-983-9887
Subjects: 27-43
Items: HC-PB-OT
Memo: 247 stores. Call their Products Submission Line. All products must go through the outlined procedures.

Woolco Department Stores
Peter Lavins, Mdse Mgr
Book Dept
50 Overlea Dr
Toronto ON Canada M4H 1B9
416-863-6400
Subjects: 21-99
Items: HC-PB
Memo: 70 variety stores.

Independent Booksellers

In 1990, we began to compile a list of the Independent General Booksellers (the biggest, best known, or most influential, ones that will go that extra mile for their customers). Please note that this list does not include the local and regional chains (large independents with three or more bookstores); these stores are listed in the previous section of chain stores.

If you know of any other independent booksellers who should be on this list, please send us the store name, book buyer, address, phone number, FAX number, subject specialties (if any), and number of book titles they stock (if known). Send your nominations to Ad-Lib Publications, Attn: Top 500 List, 51 ½ W Adams, Fairfield, IA 52556-3499. Thanks for your help.

Alabama

Auburn University Bookstore
Hank Bolton, Textbook Buyer
Margaret Hendricks, Trade Buyer
1360 Haley Ctr
Auburn AL 36849
334-844-4241; Fax: 334-844-1697
800-880-0392
Subjects: 99
Items: HC-PB-GC-ST-MA-MM
Memo: Mass mailings 1x a year or by request.
Author signings: Yes

Behind The Glass Cafe & Books
Eve Stalker and Rod Popwell, Managers
PO Box 1768
Auburn AL 36830
334-826-1106; Fax: 334-826-1106
Subjects: 27-47-54-55-73-76-77-83-95-97-9
Items: HC-PB-MM-GA-CA-GI-GC-ST-SB-TO
Other: 7,000 titles
Author Signings: Yes

Capitol Book and News
Cheryl Upchurch, Owner
1104 E Fairview
Montgomery AL 36106
334-265-1473; Fax: 334-834-2405
Subjects: 99
Items: HC-PB-MM-GC-MG-NP-BT
Author Signings: Yes; Catalog: Yes

Madison Books & Computers
Elizabeth Clark, Tech Book Manager
8006 Madison Pike
Madison AL 35758
205-772-9250; Fax: 205-461-8076
Subjects: 23-24-99
Items: HC-PB-MM-MG-CA-CL-CO-GI-GC-MA-PO-SW-ST-SB-TA
Author Signings: Yes

Verbatim Bookstore
Doug Barber, Owner
311 N McKenzie St
Foley AL 36535
334-943-2280; Fax: 334-943-2280
Subjects: 41-43-57-61-71-75-84-99
Items: HC-PB-MM-CA-GA-GC-MA-TA

Alaska

Baker & Baker Booksellers
Larry & Lynne Baker, Book Buyers
3627 Airport Way
Fairbanks AK 99709-4773
907-456-2278; Fax: 907-451-8208
Subjects: 99
Items: HC-PB-MM
Author Signings: Yes

The Bookstore
Sue Post or Jenny Stroyeck
436 Sterling Hwy 8
Homer AK 99603
907-235-7496; Fax: 907-235-5312
Subjects: 27-45-51-61-75-86-99
Items: HC-PB-RM-MM-CA-GA-MG-GC-MA-NP-ST-SB-TA
Author Signings: Yes

Cyrano's Bookstore & Cafe
Sandy & Jerry Harper, Buyers
413 D St
Anchorage AK 99501
907-274-2599; Fax: 907-277-4698
Subjects: 21-75-99
Items: HC-PB-CA-GI-MA-PO-SB-BT
Author Signings: Yes

Hearthside Books
Susan Hickey, Owner
Nugget Mall
8745 Glacier Hwy #260
Juneau AK 99801
907-789-2750; Fax: 907-789-7480
Subjects: 29-57-61-75-76-86-71
Items: HC-PB-MM-RM-CA-GA-PO-GC-MA-TV-TA-BT
Memo: Brochure available.
Author Signings: Yes

Kreig's Books
Ray Kreig, Owner
201 Barrow St #1
Anchorage AK 99501-2429
907-276-2025; Fax: 907-258-9614
Subjects: 24-67S(geology)
Items: HC-PB-US

Old Harbor Books
Don Muller, Manager
201 Lincoln St
Sitka AK 99835
907-747-8808; Fax: 907-747-8813
Subjects: 61(Alaska)-99
Items: HC-PB-TX-MG-MM-BT-SW
Author Signings: Yes

Parnassus
Lillian Ference, Owner
#5 Creek St
Ketchikan AK 99901
907-225-7690
Subjects: 11-13-14-17-21-27-29-35-37-39 (Native Am & NW Coast books)
Items: HC-PB-MM-RM-OP-US-TA-TV
Memo: Newsletter 3x a year.
Author Signings: Yes

UAF Bookstore
Sarah Triggs, General Book Buyer
College Bookstore
Constitution Hall
Fairbanks AK 99775
907-474-7348; Fax: 907-474-7739
Subjects: 19-23-27-31-37-39-53-61(AK)-99
Items: HC-PB-MM-TX-RM-US-MG-CA-CL-CO-CR-GA-GI-TA-TV
Author Signings: Yes

Arkansas

Campus Bookstore
John Griffiths, Buyer
624 W Dickson St
Fayetteville AR 72701
501-521-7048; Fax: 501-442-8264
Subjects: 99
Items: HC-TX-US-MG-GA-PB-RM-BT-MM-TA-OT
Author Signings: Yes

Curiosity Book Shop
Margaret Luffman, Owner
113 W Walnut
Rogers AR 72756
501-636-5326; Fax: 501-636-3685
Subjects: 99
Items: HC-PB-MG-BT-CA-CO-GA-MA-NP-TO

That Bookstore in Blytheville
Mary Gay Shipley, Owner
316 W Main
Blytheville AR 72315-3305
501-763-3333; Fax: 501-763-1125
Subjects: 99
Comments: Very large childrens section
Items: HC-PB-MM-RM-CA-CL-GI-GC-MA-SW-ST-TA-TO-BT
Memo: Monthly newsletter.
Author Signings: Yes

Arizona

Alcuin Books
Richard Murian and Patricia Gross, Owners
115 W Camelback
Phoenix AZ 85013
602-279-3031
800-449-3031
Subjects: 11-41-47-48-54-63(Theology)-70
Items: HC-RM-OP-US
Memo: 12-15 thousand titles; mailing lists with 50-100 books listed.

Atalanta's Music & Books
Joan Werner, Buyer
38 Main St
PO Box 317
Bisbee AZ 85603
520-432-9976
Subjects: 99
Comments: New & used
Items: HC-PB-MM-RM-MA-NP-CA-US-TA-CD
.Author Signings: Yes

The Book Island
Dexter Mapel, Buyer
1042 E Baseline Rd
Tempe AZ 85283
602-820-8405
Subjects: 99
Items: HC-PB-OP-US
Author Signings: Yes

Book Nook
Victoria Rovillard
1640 McCulloch Blvd
Lake Havasu City AZ 86403
602-855-8825
Subjects: 23-27-53-57-75-61-86-99
Items: HC-PB-MM-RM-US-GM-CA-CO-MA-NP-SW
Author Signings: Yes

Books Etc Inc
Joe McKersie, Manager
901 S Mill Ave
Tempe AZ 85281
602-967-1111; Fax: 602-967-1145
Subjects: 19-23-86-99
Items: HC-PB-CA-GA-GC-MG-NP-PO-TA
Author Signings: Yes

Changing Hands Bookstore
Clive Sommer, Buyer
414 S Mill St #109
Tempe AZ 85281
602-966-4019; Fax: 602-966-0881
Subjects: 21-47-51-53-54-57-61-99
Items: HC-PB-US-GC-CA-BT-MM-MG-TA-TV
Memo: Quarterly newsletter.
Author Signings: Yes

Eastside Records
Ben Wood
217 W University Dr
Tempe AZ 85281
602-968-2011; Fax: 602-804-1226
Subjects: 99
Items: HC-PB-BT-OP-TA
Author Signings: Yes

Fountain Hills Bookstore
Michele Stumpf, Owner
11819 N Saguaro Blvd
Fountain Hills AZ 85268-4621
602-837-0727
Subjects: 99
Items: HC-PB-US
Author Signings: Yes; Catalog: Yes

Haunted Bookshop
Jean H Wilson, Owner
7211 N Northern
Tucson AZ 85704
602-742-3627
Subjects: 99
Items: HC-PB-TA-MA-TO-BT
Memo: Newsletter 2x a year.
Author Signings: Yes

Tortuga Books
Allan D Haifley, Buyer
PO Box 4073
Tubac AZ 85646
520-398-2807
Subjects: 99
Items: HC-PB-CA-CR-MA(maps)-GC-TA-CD-TX-NP

Truepenny Books
William Laws
2509 N Campbell Ave #117
Tucson AZ 85719
602-881-4822; Fax: 602-884-5501
Subjects: 11A-76-99
Items: HC-GI-OP-US-BT-TV
Author Signings: Yes

California

1st Street Books
Mary Leary, Buyer
850 College Ave
Kentfield CA 94904
415-456-8770
Subjects: 21-99

9th Avenue Books
Lyle Stewart, Manager
1348 9th Ave
San Francisco CA 94122-2309
415-665-2938
Subjects: 99
Other: 5,000 titles

Aardvark Books
John Hadreas, Buyer
227 Church St
San Francisco CA 94114
415-552-6733
Subjects: 21-31-41-53-57-71-86-95-99
Other: 40,000 titles

Adams Avenue Bookstore
Brian Lucas, Owner
3502 Adams Ave
San Diego CA 92116
619-281-3330; Fax: 619-281-0683
Subjects: 47-54P-63(Theology)-99
Other: 100,000 titles

Agoura Book & Coffee Co
John Loesing, Buyer
5649 Kanan Rd
Agoura CA 91301
818-991-9256; Fax: 818-707-1508
Subjects: 99
Other: 10,000 titles
Author Signings: Occasionally

Aladdin Books
John Cannon, Owner
122 W Commonwealth Ave
Fullerton CA 92632
714-738-6115; Fax: 714-738-6288
Subjects: 14-86-99
Numbers: 15,000
Memo: Closed Mon & Tues.
Author Signings: Yes

Alexanders Book Co Inc
Bonnie Stuppin
50 2nd St
San Francisco CA 94105
415-495-2992; Fax: 415-495-3695
Subjects: 99
Numbers: 40,000 titles
Author signings: Yes
Catalog: Yes, mailed monthly.

Alhambra Book Store
Mike Smith, Buyer/Owner
225 E Main St
Alhambra CA 91801
818-289-4601
Subjects: 99
Catalog: Yes, mailed 2x a year: Christmas & New Years.

AS-UCLA Bookstore
308 Westwood Plz
Los Angeles CA 20024
310-206-4041; Fax: 310-206-7141
Richard MacBriar, Technical Bks
Doug Bowman, Textbook Buyer
Subjects: 23-99(also foreign languages)
Other: 75,000 titles
Memo: General info #: 310-206-0790.
Author Signings: Yes

Avenue Books Inc
Brian Rood, Owner
2904 College Ave
Berkeley CA 94705
510-549-3532; Fax: 510-549-3533
Subjects: 75-84-99(mostly fiction)
Other: 19,000 titles
Author Signings: Yes, occasionally
Catalog: Yes, newsletter 5x a year

Aztec Bookstore
Antonio Ayala, Owner/Manager
1429 W Adams Blvd
Los Angeles CA 90007
213-733-4040; Fax: 213-733-6496
Subjects: 45(Spanish)
Numbers: 1,600

Bay Books
Donna Davison, Owner
1669 Willowpass Rd
Concord CA 94520
510-671-2245; Fax: 510-671-0345
Subjects: 21-28-41A-70A-99
Other: 100,000 titles
Memo: New & used books. Also a store in San Ramon: 2415 San Ramon Valley Rd, 94583; 510-855-1524.

Beers Book Center
Jim Naify, Owner
1431 L St
Sacramento CA 95814
916-443-5165; Fax: 916-448-3916
Subjects: 53-54-61(West US/Americana)-99

The Book Center
Bill McDonald, Manager
321 Golf Club Rd
Pleasant Hill CA 94523
510-682-7363; Fax: 510-825-7419
Subjects: 99
Comments: TX-US-OT-SB-ST-TA

The Book Connection
Mrs Pat Walliser, Owner/Manager
Box 486
Mariposa CA 95338
209-966-2877
Subjects: 41-75-99
Author Signings: Yes

Book Loft
Joe Zangaro, Manager
9460 Mira Mesa Blvd #J
San Diego CA 92126
619-578-9760
Subjects: 21-57-75-76-73-19-86
Numbers: 20,000
Catalog: Yes

The Book Loft
Kathy Mullins, Owner
1680 Mission Dr
Solvang CA 93463
805-688-6010; Fax: 805-688-9930
Subjects: 99
Author Signings: Yes
Catalog; Yes; Newsletter mailed 2x a year.

Book Passage
Elaine Petrocelli, Owner
51 Tamal Vista Blvd
Corte Madera CA 94925
415-927-0960; Fax: 415-924-3838
800-999-7909
E-Mail: messages@bookpassage.com
Subjects: 44-45-71-99
Other HC-PB-MM
Numbers: 6,000 titles
Author Signings: Yes
Catalog; Yes, large travel catalog.

Book Soup
Glenn Goldman, Owner
8818 Sunset Blvd
West Hollywood CA 90069
310-659-3110; Fax: 310-659-3410
800-764-BOOK
Subjects: 11-12A-21-47-99
Numbers: 24,000
Author Signings: Yes
Catalog: Yes, monthly newsletter

Bookends Bookstore
Tom Pieper, Owner
1014 Coombs St
Napa CA 94559-2587
707-224-7455; Fax: 707-224-5139
Subjects: 99
Numbers: 15,000
Author Signings: Yes

Bookshop Benicia
Christine Mayall, Owner
856 Southampton Rd
Benicia CA 94510
707-747-5155
Subjects: 99
Author signings: Yes

Bookshop Santa Cruz
Neal Coonerty
1520 Pacific Ave
Santa Cruz CA 95060
408-423-0900; Fax: 408-423-8371
Subjects: 99
Author Signings: Yes
Catalog: Yes, Bimonthly

Booksmith
Gary Frank, Owner
1644 Haight St
San Francisco CA 94117
415-863-8688; Fax: 415-863-2540
Subjects: 99
Numbers: 35,000 titles
Author Signings: Yes

The Bookstore
Elizabeth Gage, Owner
217 Fifth St
Hollister CA 95023
408-637-3400
Subjects: 61-63-99
Author Signings: Yes; Catalog: Yes

Booktrader
Patricia A Lewis, Owner/Buyer
9219 Folsom Blvd
Sacramento CA 95826
916-363-9996; Fax: 916-363-6587
Subjects: 17-27-28-41-48-57-59-75-77-79-84-85-86-87-88-89
Numbers: 60,000 titles
Memo: Author signings.

Bookworks
Tracy Fishburn, Manager/Buyer
36 Rancho del Mar Ctr
Aptos CA 95003
408-688-4554; Fax: 408-688-0460
Subjects: 21-75-76-77-84-57-71-86-99
Author Signings: Yes
Catalog: Yes, monthly newsletter

The Bookworm
Mary Littell, Owner
2155 Ventura Blvd
Camarillo CA 93010
805-482-1384
Subjects: 21-99
Author Signings: Yes, local authors

Bountiful Books
Rhea Kuhlman, Owner
3834 5th Ave
San Diego CA 92103
619-491-0664
Subjects: 11-37-53-54-73-83-95
Numbers: 20,000 titles

Browser Books
Steven Damon, Owner
2195 Filmore St
San Francisco CA 94115
415-567-8027
Subjects: 99
Numbers: 30,000 titles
Author Signings: Yes

By The Book
John Menary and Allan Brinson, Owners
2501 E Broadway
Long Beach CA 90803
310-434-2220
Subjects: 37-53-73-99
Author Signings: Yes

Capitola Book Cafe
Kathy Kitsuse, Owner
1475 41st Ave
Capitola CA 95010
408-462-4415
Subjects: 99
Numbers: 27,000 titles

Chevalier's Books
Phyllis Winthrop, Owner
126 N Larchmont Blvd
Los Angeles CA 90004
213-465-1334; Fax: 213-465-6093
Subjects: 21-76-99
Author Signings: Yes

Christopher's Books
Tee Minot, Owner
1400 18th St
San Francisco CA 94107-2802
415-255-8802; Fax: 415-255-8642
Subjects: 99
Numbers: 10,000 titles
Author Signings: Yes

City Lights Booksellers & Publ
Nancy J Peters
261 Columbus Ave
San Francisco CA 94133
415-362-8193; Fax: 415-362-4921
Subjects: 14M-33-47-55-57-65A-75-95-99
Numbers: 19,000 titles
Author Signings: Yes; Catalog: Yes

A Clean Well-Lighted Place
Leona Weiss, Owner
601 Van Ness
San Francisco CA 94102
415-441-6670; Fax: 415-567-6885
Subjects: 19-21-23-54-75-99
Comments: Monthly newsletter
Author Signings: Yes; Catalog: Yes

A Clean Well-Lighted Place
2417 Larkspur Landing Cir
Larkspur CA 94939
415-461-0171

David Shavez, Buyer
Jude Sales, Buyer
Martha Jackson, Children's Buyer

Subjects: 21-31-76-99
Numbers: 60,000 titles
Memo: HQ: Cupertino (branch buys independently).
Author Signings: Yes; Catalog: Yes

Cody's Books Inc
Andy Ross
2454 Telegraph Ave
Berkeley CA 94704
510-845-9096; Fax: 510-841-6185
CA: 800-479-7744; US: 800-995-1180
E-Mail: codysbks@well.sf.ca.us
Subjects: 99
Numbers: 90,000 titles
Memo: They will ship anywhere.
Author Signings: Yes

Corric K's
Rick Burmester, Book Dept Manager
637 Fourth St
Santa Rosa CA 95404
707-546-2423; Fax: 707-546-8750
Subjects: 27-99
Items: GI
Author Signings: Yes; Catalog: Yes, monthly newsletter

Depot Bookstore & Cafe
Mary Turnbull, Owner
87 Throckmorton Ave
Mill Valley CA 94941-1915
415-383-2665; Fax: 415-383-1346
Subjects: 21-43G-51B-67-71-75
Author Signings: Yes; Catalog: Yes

Diesel: A Bookstore
Alison Reid and John Evans, Owners
5433 College Ave
Oakland CA 94608-1954
510-653-9965
Subjects: 21-27-75-83-95-99
Items: ST-NP-BT
Author Signings: Yes; Catalog: Yes

Dodds Book Shop
Kim Browning
4818 E Second St
Long Beach CA 90803
310-438-9948
Subjects: 99
Author Signings: Yes

Dutton's Books
Davis M Dutton
5146 Laurel Canyon Blvd
North Hollywood CA 91607-3199
818-769-3866; Fax: 818-769-6029
Subjects: 11-14M-21-33-41-47-75-83-95-99
Comments: New & used
Other: 3 stores
Memo: Brentwood store at: 11975 San Vicente Boulevard, Los Angeles, CA 90049-5003; 310-476-6263; Contact: Douglas Dutton.
Author Signings: Yes

Earth Song Bookstore
Ann Braciszewski, Owner
1440 Camino del Mar
Del Mar CA 92014
619-755-4254; Fax: 619-755-6787
Subjects: 35-39D-53-54-57-99
Author Signings: Yes; Catalog: Yes

Earthling Bookshop
Penny Davies, Owner
1137 State St
Santa Barbara CA 93101
805-965-0926; Fax:
Subjects: 11-21-27-36-41-51-54M-75-84-86
Memo: Cafe attached to bookstore.
Author Signings: Yes

East Bay Books
Barbara Keenen, Owner
1555 Washington Ave
San Leandro CA 94577
510-483-3990; Fax: 510-357-1337
Subjects: 21-45-53-75-99
Author Signings: Yes

Either/Or Bookstore
Roger Silly, Book Buyer
124 Pier Ave
Hermosa Beach CA 90254
310-374-2060
Subjects: 99
Items: TA-BT
Author Signings: Yes

Ex Libris
Jane Claire, Buyer
898 Main St C
Morro Bay CA 93442
805-772-2670
Subjects: 99
Items: Journals
Author Signings: Yes; Catalog: Yes, newsletter

Facts and Fictions
Linda Elsner, Owner
409 Walnut St
Red Bluff CA 96080
916-527-1449
Subjects: 29-53-57-84-43-61-76
Author Signings: Yes

Fig Garden Bookstore
Keith Shore, Co-Owner
5094 N Palm
Fresno CA 93704
209-226-1845; Fax: 209-226-3301
Subjects: 11-12-21-56-75-76-77
Author Signings: Yes

Forever After
Pat, Owner
1475 Haight St
San Francisco CA 94117
415-431-8299
Subjects: 39-57-63
Author Signings: Yes

Franciscan Shops, SFSU
Magie Crystal, Book Buyer
San Francisco State Univ
1650 Holloway Ave
San Francisco CA 94132
415-338-1475; Fax: 415-338-1450
Subjects: 11-37-41-47-49-73-75-99
Items: NP-ST-SB-TA
Numbers: 50,000 titles

Frazier Mountain Books
Yvonne Fyan, Owner
617 Monterey Tr #C Box 2350
Frazier Park CA 93225
805-245-0630
Subjects: 47-51-54-61-75-76-90
Items: Rubber stamps

Gallery Bookshop
Anthony Miksak, Owner
PO Box 270
Mendocino CA 95460
707-937-2665; Fax: 707-937-3737
Subjects: 11-21-27-31-39-51-71-75-76-84-9
Comments: 707-937-2215 # for publishers
Memo: **Bookwinkles Children's Bookstore** at same location.
Author Signings: Yes

Golden Apple Bookstores
Tony Edwards, Prod Manager
7711 Melrose Ave
Los Angeles CA 90046
213-658-6047; Fax: 213-852-9621
Subjects: 14M-33-33C-75-86
Items: PO-models
Numbers: 2 stores.

Green Apple Books
Richard Savoy, Owner
506 Clements St
San Francisco CA 94118
415-387-2272; Fax: 415-387-2377
Subjects: 99
Other: 150,000 titles

The Happy Booker
Ruth Petersen, Owner
4096 N Sierra Way
San Bernadino CA 92407
909-883-6110
Subjects: 15-17-27-33-57-69-75

Il Literature
Barry Fields, Owner
456 S La Brea Ave
Los Angeles CA 90036-3524
213-937-3505
Subjects: 99(fiction & art)
Author Signings: Yes, occasionally

Joanna's Bookworm of Upland
Joanna Hamilton, Owner
229 N 2nd Ave
Upland CA 91786
909-981-1134; Fax: 909-949-4694
Subjects: 21-31-45-76-79-80-99
Memo: Large section of childrens books.
Author Signings: Yes

John Cole's Bookshop
Barbara Cole, Owner
780 Prospect St
PO Box 1132
La Jolla CA 92037
619-454-4766; Fax: 619-454-8377
Subjects: 11-21-27-76-99
Author Signings: Yes, occasionally; Catalog: Yes, newsletter

Kalmin The Bookstore
Mina Lakhani, Owner
131 Avenida del Mar
San Clemente CA 92672-4017
714-492-9673
Subjects: 99
Other: 4,000
Catalog: Yes

Kelly's Books
Vi Kelly, Owner
2588 Olive Hwy #D
Oroville CA 95966
916-534-0911
Subjects: 39-57-76-86-85
Author Signings: Yes

Kipling Tyler Bookshop
Bruce Phillips
5738 Calle Real
Goleta CA 93117
805-967-8980; Fax: 805-967-3601
Subjects: 99
Author Signings: Yes; Catalog: Yes,
  monthly newsletter

Larry's Book Nook
Larry Sydes, Owner
730A Bancroft Rd
Walnut Creek CA 94598
510-933-2665; Fax: 510-934-6271
Subjects: 21-31-35-57-99
Author Signings: Yes

Malibu Books & Co
Barrie Gable, Owner
23410 Civic Ctr Way
Malibu CA 90265
310-456-1375
Subjects: 99

Margie's Book Nook
Margie Teeter, Owner
722 Main
Susanville CA 96130
916-257-2392
Subjects: 99
Numbers: 8,000
Author Signings: Yes

Modern Times Bookstore
Michael Rosenthal, Manager
888 Valencia St
San Francisco CA 94110-1739
415-282-9246; Fax: 415-282-4925
Subjects: 99
Numbers: 14,000 titles
Author Signings: Yes; Catalog: Yes,
  monthly newsletter

Moe's Books Inc
Laura Tibbals, Buyer
2476 Telegraph Ave
Berkeley CA 94704-2392
510-849-2087; Fax: 510-849-9938
Subjects: 11-12-21-47-54-75-95-99

Much Ado About Books
Donna Pohlman, Owner
208 E State St
Redlands CA 92373-5233
909-335-2011; Fax: 909-335-1681
Subjects: 99
Author Signings: Yes
Catalog: Yes, newsletter mailed monthly
  or every other month

North Town Books
Art Burton and Barbara Turner, Owners
957 H St
Arcata CA 95521
707-822-2834
Subjects: 99
Author Signings: Yes; Catalog: Yes,
  newsletter

Pendragon Books
Eve Sheehan, Book Buyer
5560 College Ave
Oakland CA 94618
510-652-6259; Fax: 510-652-5368
Subjects: 99
Other GC-CA-MG
Numbers: 20,000

Phoenix Books and Records
Kate Rosenberger, Book Buyer
3850 24th St
San Francisco CA 94114
415-821-3477; Fax: 415-282-0213
Subjects: 11-14-33-47-73-75-84-86-87-95-9
Other: 2 stores, one in San Francisco.
Numbers: 100,000 titles

The Phoenix Bookshop
Michael Goth, Owner
1514 5th St
Santa Monica CA 90401
310-395-9516; Fax: 310-393-2214
Subjects: 39H-48-53-54-57-99
Numbers: 20,000
Author Signings: Yes; Catalog: Yes,
  monthly calendar

The Phoenix
Karen Trotter, Book Buyer
Hwy 1
Big Sur CA 93920
408-667-2347; Fax: 408-667-2826
Subjects: 53-99
Other TV-CD-BT

Portrait of a Bookstore
Julie Von Zerneck
4355 Foreman Ave
Toluca Lake CA 91602-2515
818-769-3853
Subjects: 14-21-33-75-76-99
Numbers: 10,000 titles
Author Signings: Yes

Printers Inc Bookstore
Book Buyer
310 California Ave
Palo Alto CA 94306
415-327-6500; Fax: 415-327-7509
Subjects: 23-19-37-41-49-61-75
Items: MA-PO-SW-NP
Numbers: 50,000 titles
Memo: 2 stores.
Author Signings: Yes; Catalog: Yes

Recovery Shoppe
Tim Reiling, Owner
3483 S Bascom
Campbell CA 95008
408-377-0342; Fax: 408-377-0321
Subjects: 39-54-57
Items: TA-TV-BT
Author Signings: Yes

Riverside Book Center
Doris Stewart, Owner
3561 Riverside Plz
Riverside CA 92506
909-683-0520
Subjects: 99

Small World Books
Mary Goodfader, Owner
1407 Ocean Front Walk
Venice CA 90291
310-399-2360; Fax: 310-399-4512
Subjects: 17-21-71-75-76-83-84-95-99
Items: BT
Author Signings: Yes

Solar Light Books
David Hughes, Book Buyer
2068 Union St
San Francisco CA 94123
415-567-6082
Subjects: 99
Catalog: Yes, 4x a year

Stanford Bookstore
Patricia Michelin, Manager
515 Lasuen St
Stanford Univ
Stanford CA 94305-3079
415-329-1217; Fax: 415-322-1936
Subjects: 99
Comments: Monthly newsletter
Numbers: 125,000 titles
Author Signings: Yes; Catalog: Yes

Stover Landing Books
Susan Granzow, Owner
317 Main St
PO Box 646
Chester CA 96020
916-258-2318
Subjects: 27-51-57-61-75-76
Author Signings: Yes

Sundance Books
John Russell and Adrienne Harris, Owners
3450-9 Palmer Dr
Cameron Park CA 95682
916-677-4217
Subjects: 99

Sunshine Books
Ron Burns, Manager
8944 Knott Ave
Buena Park CA 90620
714-761-1552
Subjects: 75-99(fiction)

Tall Stories
Donna Rankin, Owner
2141 Mission St #301
San Francisco CA 94110
415-255-1915
Subjects: 84-86-83-78-75-82
Comments: Mainly antiquarian
Numbers: 4,000 titles

Thunderbird Bookshops Inc
John & May Waldroup, Owners
3600 The Barn Yard
PO Box 22830
Carmel CA 93923
408-624-1803; Fax: 408-624-9034
Subjects: 21-31-76-99
Items: TV
Author Signings: Yes; Catalog: Yes,
  newsletter

Tower Books
Ken Krieg, Manager
MTS Inc
2538 Watt Ave
Sacramento CA 95821-6392
916-481-6600; Fax: 916-481-6820
Subjects: 21-31-39-71-75-86-99
Memo: HQ: West Sacramento (branch
  buys independently).
Author Signings: Yes

Tower Books
Heidi Keller Cotler
2601 Del Monte Blvd
West Sacramento CA 95691
916-373-2500
Subjects: 21-39-71-75-99
Author Signings: Yes

Tustin Books
Wayne R Jewett, Owner
215 W First St #102
Tustin CA 92680-3136
714-731-6103
Subjects: 23-75-77-84-85-86
Numbers: 20,000+ titles
Author Signings: Yes

UCLA Bookstore
Alice Yamamoto, Book Buyer
Doug Bowman, Textbook Buyer
Richard McBriar, Trade Buyer
Univ of California at LA
221 Westwood Plz
Los Angeles CA 90024
310-206-0764; Fax: 310-825-0382
800-825-2724
Subjects: 11-12-19-33-39-41-51-55L-57-65-67-75- 99
Numbers: 75,000 titles
Memo: 3 stores: one general, one law, one medical.

Upchurch-Brown Booksellers
Nanette Heiser, Book Buyer
384 Forest Ave (92651)
PO Box 4919
Laguna Beach CA 92652
714-497-8373
Subjects: 11-14-21-31-47-71-76-79-99
Author Signings: Yes; Catalog: Yes, newsletter

Upstart Crow Bookstore
Ivor Sack
Seaport Village
835 W Harbor Dr
San Diego CA 92101-7704
619-232-4855; Fax: 619-232-4856
Subjects: 99
Memo: Also a coffee shop.

Uptown Book Co
Joseph Ross
68 N Washington St
Sonora CA 95370
209-533-0713
Subjects: 21(Western American)
Author Signings: Yes

Ventura Book Store
Ed Elrod, Buyer
522 E Main St
Ventura CA 93001-2629
805-643-4069; Fax: 805-643-0218
Subjects: 21-31-75-76-95-99
Author Signings: Yes

Vroman's Book & Stationery
Joel V Sheldon III
695 E Colorado Blvd
Pasadena CA 91101
818-449-5320; Fax: 818-792-7308
800-769-2665
Subjects: 21-76-99
Other 2 locations
Author Signings: Yes; Catalog: Yes, newsletter sent 2x a month

Wahrenbrock's Books
Charles Valverde, Manager
726 Broadway
San Diego CA 92101
619-232-0132; Fax: 619-232-3808
800-315-8643
Subjects: 99

Numbers: 200,000+ titles
Memo: Aaron Silverman and Jan Tonnesen, Buyers.

Warwick's Books
Barbara Christman, Manager
7812 Girard Ave
La Jolla CA 92037
619-454-0347; Fax: 619-454-9325
Subjects: 17-21-29-41-43G-71-84-99
Numbers: 30,000 titles
Author Signings: Yes; Catalog: Yes, newsletter monthly

Wessex Books And Records
Tom Haydon, Owner
558 Santa Cruz Ave
Menlo Park CA 94025
415-321-1333; Fax: 415-856-1984
E-Mail: www.essexatbest.com
Subjects: 99
Numbers: 50,000 titles
Author Signings: Yes

Williams' Book Store
Anne Gusha
443 W Sixth St
San Pedro CA 90731
310-832-3631
Subjects: 45-71-99
Author Signings: Yes

Colorado

Auroria Book Center
Eric Boss
955 Lawrence St (80204)
PO Box 173361 Campus Box T
Denver CO 80217-3361
303-556-3735; Fax: 303-556-8392
Subjects: 19-23-24-51-59-67
Other 30,000 titles
Author Signings: Yes

The Book Cellar
Terri Coffey, Owner
326 Elk Ave
Box 227
Crested Butte CO 81224
970-349-6245; Fax: 970-349-5610
Subjects: 21-49A-61-99
Numbers: 5,000 titles

Book Train
Rhonda Haff, Manager/Buyer
723 Grand Ave
Glenwood Springs CO 81601
970-945-7045; Fax: 970-945-7824
Subjects: 99
Comments: 300+ general magazines
Items: ST-SB-TA-TV

The Boulder Bookstore
David Bolduc, Owner
1107 Pearl St
Boulder CO 80302
303-447-2074; Fax: 303-447-3946
Subjects: 21-27-51-97-99
Numbers: 30,000 titles
Author Signings: Yes; Catalog: Yes

Capitol Hill Books
Valarie Abney, Owner
300 E Colfax Ave
Denver CO 80203-1816
303-837-0700; Fax: 303-860-7126
Subjects: 41-75-99
Numbers: 35,000 titles
Memo: Primarily a used book store.
Catalog: Yes, quarterly newsletter

Chinook Bookshop
Mark Burski, Book Buyer
210 N Tejon St
Colorado Springs CO 80903
719-635-1195; Fax: 719-635-0792
800-999-1195
Subjects: 99
Items: SW-ST
Numbers: 50,000 titles
Author Signings: Yes; Catalog: Yes, newsletter sent w/statements

McKinzey-White Booksellers
Karen Bauder, Owner
8005 N Academy
Colorado Springs CO 80920
719-590-1700
Subjects: 21-23-99
Numbers: 50,000
Author Signings: Yes

Narrow Gauge Newsstand
Colleen Collins, Manager
602 Main St
Alamosa CO 81101
719-589-6712; Fax: 719-589-1036
Subjects: 61(West)-99
Items: NP-SB-BT

Poor Richards
Ed Zasadny, Manager
320 N Tejon
Colorado Springs CO 80903
719-578-0012; Fax: 719-578-0323
Subjects: 99
Comments: Roy Jackson, Manager also
Items:: GC-BT
Numbers: 30,000 titles
Author Signings: Yes

Roundhouse Books
Peter Sullivan, Owner
526 Main St
Delta CO 81416-1826
970-874-5428
Subjects: 57-99
Author Signings: Yes

Snowmass Village Book Shoppe
Deborah Scanlon, Owner
PO Box 6997
Snowmass Village CO 81615
970-923-4896; Fax: 970-923-4896
Subjects: 99
Items: ST-SB-BT-OT
Author Signings: Yes

Stone Lion Bookstore
Donna Bathory, Buyer
Old Town Square
107 N College
Fort Collins CO 80524
970-493-0030; Fax: 970-482-8957
800-387-0030
Subjects: 21-27-39-41-49A-53-54-71-73-99
Numbers: 75,000 titles

Tattered Cover Book Store
Helen Downs, Audio Buyer
Karen Ellis, Children's Backlist Buyer
Judy Bulow, Buyer, Children's Books
Adel Thalos, Book Buyer, Computer & Science
Joyce Meskis, Owner
Derrick Lawrence, Book Buyer, Philosophy & Religion Titles
Carolyn Barndt, Buyer, Psychology Books
David Pepper, Travel Books
Louise Brueggemann, Buyer, Young Adults
1628 16th St St
Denver CO 80202
303-322-7727; Fax: 303-399-2279
Subjects: 99
Author Signings: Yes, Catalog: Yes, 2x a year

Connecticut

Clipper Ship Bookshop
Suzanne Coopersmith, Manager
12 N Main St
Essex CT 06426
203-767-1666
Subjects: 21-31-70-76-79-99
Author Signings: Yes

Just Books
Cheryl Barton, Manager
19 E Putnam Ave
Greenwich CT 06830
203-869-5023; Fax: 203-869-0633
Subjects: 99
Author Signings: Yes; on the street out front — inside is too small; Catalog: Yes, mailed monthly

Kleins of Westport
Stanley Klein
44 Main St
Westport CT 06880
203-226-4261; Fax: 203-226-9721
Subjects: 21-99
Numbers: 250,000
Author Signings: Yes

New Canaan Bookshop
John Netzer, Buyer
59 Elm St
New Canaan CT 06840-5499
203-966-1684
Subjects: 99
Other 2 stores
Memo: Also owns Hichory Stick Bookshop.
Author Signings: Yes; Catalog: Yes, Holiday catalog

R J Julia Booksellers
Roxanne Coady
768 Boston Post Rd
Madison CT 06443
203-245-3959; Fax: 203-245-8126
800-74-READS
Subjects: 21-99
Author Signings: Yes

The Village Bookshop
Denise Austin, Manager
945 Cromwell Ave
Rocky Hill CT 06067
203-529-2665
Subjects: 21-75-76-99
Author Signings: Yes

Yale Co-op
Don Straka, Manager/Trade Books
77 Broadway
New Haven CT 06520
203-772-2200; Fax: 203-772-3665
Subjects: 11-21-39-55L-67-99
Numbers: 95,000
Author Signings: Yes; Catalog: Yes, every 6 months

Delaware

McMahon Books Inc
Gordon McMahon
101 Christiana Mall
Newark DE 19702
302-366-7575
Subjects: 99
Numbers: 30,000
Author Signings: Yes

District of Columbia

Kramerbooks
David Tenney, Owner
1517 NW Connecticut Ave
Washington DC 20036
202-387-1400
Subjects: 99
Author Signings: Yes

Politics and Prose
Carla Cohen, Co-Owner
5015 Connecticut Ave NW
Washington DC 20008
202-364-1919; Fax: 202-966-7532
800-722-0790
Subjects: 13-41-47-55-57-75-99
Items: PO-SW
Numbers: 15,000 titles
Memo: Barbara Meade, Co-Owner. Seasonal newsletter.
Author Signings: Yes; Catalog: Yes

Reprint Book Shop
Michael Sullivan
455 L'Enfans Plz SW
Washington DC 20024
202-554-5070; Fax: 202-488-8931
Subjects: 19-23-49-67-71-78-97-99
Author Signings: Yes; Catalog: Yes, newsletter monthly

Sidney Kramer Books
Lansing Sexton, Buyer
1825 I St NW
Washington DC 20006
202-293-2685; Fax: 301-881-1930
Subjects: 19-23-44-55-65-67-71-99

Other: 2 stores
Numbers: 45,000 titles
Author Signings: Yes; Catalog: Yes, Spring/Summer/Fall catalog

Florida

Bargain Books
Book Buyer
1028 Truman Ave
Key West FL 33040
305-294-7446
Subjects: 37-47-61-70-75-77-82-83-84-85-8
Items: BT-MG(adult)-TV(adult)
Numbers: 200,000

Book Gallery West
Eric Vaness, Manager
4121 NW 16th Blvd
Gainesville FL 32605
904-371-1234
Subjects: 21-27-61-75-99
Memo: Bart and Sara Stein, Owners.

Books & Books Inc
Mitchell Kaplan, Owner
296 Aragon Ave
Coral Gables FL 33134
305-442-4408; Fax: 305-444-9751
Subjects: 11-12-21-54-63-76-90-95-99
Numbers: 50,000
Memo: Rare and used books.
Author Signings: Yes, Catalog: Yes, monthly newsletter

Books of Paige's
Michele, Manager/Buyer
420 NE 125th St
Miami FL 33161
305-893-2931
Subjects: 99
Author Signings: Yes

Bookworks
Manager
6766 Main St
Miami Lakes FL 33014
305-823-6886; Fax: 305-826-1076
Subjects: 61(FL)-99
Author Signings: Yes

Common Market Inc
Karen Willner, Manager
8400 SW 146th St
Miami FL 33158
305-238-9201; Fax: 305-232-0910
Subjects: 99

The Cummer Museum Shop
Phyllis Johnson, Manager
829 Riverside Ave
Jacksonville FL 32204
904-356-6857; Fax: 904-353-4101
Subjects: 11-43-99

Downtown Book Center Inc
Racquel Roque, Manager/Buyer
247 SE First St
Miami FL 33131-1998
305-377-9939; Fax: 305-371-5926
Subjects: 99
Comments: 2 stores
Author Signings: Yes; Catalog: Yes

Goerings' Book Center
Thomas D Rider, Owner
1310 W University Ave
Gainesville FL 32603
904-372-3975
Subjects: 41-53-54-57-71-75-95-98-99
Author Signings: Yes; Catalog: Yes

Haslam's Book Store Inc
Ray Hinst, Adult Book Buyer
2025 Central Ave
St Petersburg FL 33713
813-822-8616; Fax: 813-822-7416
Subjects: 21-23-53-54-76-79-99
Items: BT
Author Signings: Yes

Les Cousins Books & Records Shop
Viter & Henri Juste, Mgrs/Buyers
7858 NE Second Ave
Miami FL 33138
305-754-8445
Subjects: 99

Liberties Fine Books & Music
Eileen Becker, Buyer
Mizner Park
309 Plaza Real
Boca Raton FL 33432-3934
407-368-1300; Fax: 407-347-0872
Subjects: 21-31-76-79-99
Numbers: 100,000 titles
Author Signings: Yes; Catalog: Yes, Newsletter

Little Professor Book Center
Robert & Prudence Baldwin, Owner
Old St Augustine Plz
11250 St Augustine #15
Jacksonville FL 32257-1147
904-292-2665; Fax: 904-260-3880
Subjects: 99
Comments: All franchises buy independently

Park Books
Debby Gluckman, Owner
200 E Reading Way
Winter Park FL 32789-6048
407-628-1433
Subjects: 99
Numbers: 16,000 titles

Syl-la-bles Bookstore
Curt Atkin, Owner
1 Bridge Plz
12901 McGregor Blvd
Fort Myers FL 33919
813-433-1198
Subjects: 99
Comments: Small press books

Vero Beach Book Ctr
Thomas Leonard, Owner
2145 Indian River Blvd
Vero Beach FL 32960
407-569-2050; Fax: 407-569-5858
Subjects: 99
Author Signings: Yes

Georgia

Appalachian Bookstore
Larry Loyd, Owner
190 Old Orchard Square
East Ellijay GA 30539-1524
706-276-1992
Subjects: 61-99
Numbers: 10,000
Author Signings: Yes

Aspen Bookshop
Paul Blicksilver, Owner
5986 Memorial Dr
Stonewood Village Shopping Ctr
Stone Mountain GA 30083
404-296-5933
Subjects: 99
Other 60,000 titles
Memo: Used books a specialty.

The Book House
Sylvia Thurston, Owner
692 Puckett Dr
Mableton GA 30059-3312
770-944-3275
Subjects: 99
Items: PB-HC-US

Magnolia Bookshop
Diane Barret or Jim Anderson
2611 Central Ave
Augusta GA 30904
706-738-5184
Subjects: 99
Items: ST-TA-TV-OT
Memo: Owner: Diane Van Giesen.
Author Signings: Yes; Catalog: Yes, mailed every two months

The Science Store
Jean Hunter, Owner
395 Piedmont Ave NE
Atlanta GA 30308
404-522-5500; Fax: 404-525-6906
Subjects: 21-23T-67
Author Signings: Yes

Idaho

The Book Shop
Dan Wilson
906 Main St
Boise ID 83702
208-342-2659; Fax: 208-342-2025
Subjects: 21-31-41-61(ID)-76-79-99
Numbers: 50,000
Author Signings: Yes; Catalog: Yes, 400 newsletters mailed 2-3x a yr

BookPeople of Moscow Inc
Robert Greene, Buyer
512 S Main St
Moscow ID 83843
208-882-7957
Subjects: 21-61(Western)-73-76-95-99
Author Signings: Yes

The Bookshop
Dan Wilson, Owner
906 Main St
Boise ID 83702
208-342-2659; Fax: 208-342-2025
Subjects: 99
Numbers: 60,000 titles
Author Signings: Yes

University Bookstore ID State University
Jan Schritter, Book Dept Manager
Campus Box 8013
Pocatello ID 83209
208-236-3230; Fax: 208-236-4605
800-688-4781
Subjects: 99
Items: SW-SB
Numbers: 9,000
Author Signings: Yes; Catalog: Yes, Clothing & Xmas catalog yearly

Illinois

57th Street Books
Rodney Powell, Book Buyer
Franny Billingsly, Children's Buyer
1301 E 57th St
Chicago IL 60637
312-684-1300; Fax: 312-752-8507
Subjects: 21-31-76-89-99

57th Street Books
Helen Repp, Manager
1301 East 57th Street
Chicago IL 60637
312-684-1300
Subjects: 99
Numbers: 60,000 titles
Author Signings: Yes

Anderson's Bookshop
Robert Anderson, Manager
123 W Jefferson
Naperville IL 60540
708-355-2665; Fax: 708-355-2683
Subjects: 99
Items: BT
Memo: 2 stores: in Downer's Grove and Elmhurst.
Author Signings: Yes; Catalog: Yes, sends newsletters/3000 annually

Book Market
William Linzmeier, Owner
11138 W Grand Ave
Melrose Park IL 60164
708-455-4456
Subjects: 99
Items: PB-HC-US
Numbers: 70-80,000 titles

The Book Stall at Chestnut Court
Roberta Rubin, Owner
811 Elm St
Winnetka IL 60093
708-446-0882; Fax: 708-446-8891
Subjects: 99
Author Signings: Yes; Catalog: Yes

Bookmen's Alley
Roger Carlson, Owner
1712 (rear) Sherman Ave
Evanston IL 60201
708-869-6999
Subjects: 99
Numbers: 55,000 titles
Author signings: Sometimes

Books Off Berwyn
Philip La Palio Jr, Owner/Buyer
5220 N Clark St
Chicago IL 60640-2102
312-878-9800; Fax: 312-878-9800
Subjects: 11-14-75-99
Numbers: 5,000

BookZeller
Lee Mathers, Owner
202 S Main St
Naperville IL 60540
708-637-0200; Fax: 708-637-0200
Subjects: 99-21
Comments: Call ahead to FAX
Numbers: 30,000 titles
Author Signings: Yes; Catalog: Yes, newsletter mailed once every two months

Chapter One Bookstore
Patricia & Stuart Gresham/Owners
Fairhills Mall
1931 W Monroe
Springfield IL 62704
217-546-0305
Subjects: 99

Downtown News & Books
Cathy Twyman, Manager
229 S Sixth St
Springfield IL 62701
217-523-0016
Subjects: 19-41(Civil War)-59-75-85-99

Little Book Shop Inc
Robert T Silkett
13 W First St
Hinsdale IL 60521
708-323-1059
Subjects: 21-76-75-84-89-99
Numbers: 25,000
Author Signings: Yes; Catalog: Yes, sent monthly

Marshall Field's
Ann Canada, Manager
111 North State St
Chicago IL 60602
312-781-4282
Subjects: 21-27(cookbooks)-99
Comments: 312-781-4284: another # for store.
Numbers: 32,000 titles
Author Signings: Yes

Maurie's
Beth Smith
522 Court St
Pekin IL 61554-3301
309-347-2560
Subjects: 99

Northern Light Bookstore
John Mulopulos, Owner
221 W Lincoln Hwy
Dekalb IL 60115
815-756-6668
Subjects: 21-53-54-57-75-86-99
Author Signings: Yes

Pages For All Ages Bookstore Inc
Brandon Griffing, Owner
At Old Farm Shops
1749 W Kirby Ave
Champaign IL 61821-5500
217-351-7243; Fax: 217-351-1566
800-228-7243
Subjects: 21-99
Numbers: 25,000 titles
Author Signings: Yes; Catalog: Yes, monthly newsletter

Powell's Bookstore
Bradley Jonas
1501 E 57th St
Chicago IL 60637-2007
312-955-2967
Subjects: 99
Other 3 stores
Numbers: 200,000

Rizzoli Bookstore
Don Sechler, Store Manager
835 N Michigan Ave
Chicago IL 60611
312-642-3500; Fax: 312-642-6159
Subjects: 11-12A-99
Items: TA-TV-TO-NP(international)
Catalog: Yes, newsletter sent quarterly

Sandmeyer's Bookstore
Ellen Sandmeyer
714 S Dearborn St
Chicago IL 60605
312-922-2104; Fax: 312-922-2104
Subjects: 99
Author Signings: Yes

Seminary Cooperative Bookstore
John L Cella, Manager
5757 S University Ave
Chicago IL 60637-1597
312-752-4381
Subjects: 99
Author Signings: Yes; Catalog: Yes

Stuart Brent Books
Adam Brent, Manager
670 N Michigan Ave
Chicago IL 60611
312-337-6357; Fax: 312-337-2961
Subjects: 11-14-99 (literature)
Numbers: 60,000 titles
Author Signings: Some

Thrifty Scholar
Kenneth Corrigan, Buyer
142 N Yorke
Elmhurst IL 60616
708-834-7056
Subjects: 99
Comments: Buys out store remainders
Author Signings: Yes

Unabridged Bookstore
Ed Devereux, Owner
3251 N Broadway
Chicago IL 60657
312-883-9119; Fax: 312-885-9559
Subjects: 99-37
Author Signings: Yes

Indiana

Book Nation
Todd Nation, Manager
27 South 7th St
Terre Haute IN 47807
812-232-2595; Fax: 812-235-0129
Subjects: 99
Numbers: 10,000
Author Signings: Yes

The Book Shop
Richard H Green, Buyer
3325 N Everbrook Ln
Muncie IN 47304
317-288-7192
Subjects: 99
Author Signings: Yes

The Bookmark
Gary Hunt, Buyer
112 N Main St
Princeton IN 47670
812-385-5660; Fax: 812-385-5790
Subjects: 99

Chapters Bookshop
Doug & Pat Miller, Owner
8660 Purdue Rd
Indianapolis IN 46268
317-872-2665; Fax: 317-872-7616
Subjects: 99
Items: CD
Numbers: 45,000
Author Signings: Yes; Catalog: Yes, Christmas catalog; newsletter sent periodically

Danner's Book End
Susan Danner, Owner
309 S Walnut St
Muncie IN 47305-2457
317-288-1122
Subjects: 99
Author Signings: Yes; Catalog: Yes, newsletter mailed every other month

Howard's Bookstore
Howard Canada, Owner
116 Fountain Square
Bloomington IN 47404-6105
812-336-7662
Subjects: 11-14-21-27-39-43-57-65-71-75-9
Author Signings: Yes

Indiana University Bookstore
Anna Ensley, Trade Buyer
Indiana Memorial Union
Bloomington IN 47405-3201
812-855-8487; Fax: 812-855-4984
800-553-6471
Subjects: 11P-14-17-19-21-28-41-51-54-57-67-73-75-95-99
Author Signings: Yes; Catalog: Yes, gift catalogs

Ironwood Book Shop
Ellen C Leffler, Manager
20 W Pine St
Zionsville IN 46077
317-873-6353
Subjects: 21-31-76-79-99
Author Signings: Yes

Mijerek's News & Bookstore
Mike Mijerek, Owner
519 S Main St
Elkhart IN 46516
219-293-2521; Fax: 219-293-4398
Subjects: 99

Iowa

Big Table Books
Susan Bedell, Book Buyer
330 Main St
Ames IA 50010
515-232-8976; Fax: 515-230-8987
Subjects: 99
Other 12,000 titles
Author Signings: Yes

Book People Inc
Edith Greenstone, Owner
#22 Market Pl
2901 Hamilton Blvd
Sioux City IA 51104
712-258-1471
Subjects: 99
Author Signings: Yes; Catalog: Yes, mailed 1x a year.

Book Store
Megan Carson, Book Buyer
612 Locust St
Des Moines IA 50309
515-288-7267
E-Mail: books@citymac.com
Subjects: 99
Numbers: 10,000 titles
Memo: FYI: internet access & cafe.
Catalog: Yes, mailed 1x per year

Books & Things Newsland
Tom Hines, Manager
56 S Main
Fairfield IA 52556
515-472-3907
Subjects: 99
Comments: Owned by a wholesale distributor.

The Bookstore
Jim Stalker, Buyer
210 N Maple St
Creston IA 50801
515-782-8822; Fax: 515-782-8822
Subjects: 99
Items:: US-HC-PB-CD-TA-BT
Author Signings: Yes

Copperfield & Company
Katherine Marion, Owner
417 Main St
Keokuk IA 52632
319-524-1092
Subjects: 61(Iowa)-99
Memo: Holiday flyer at Xmas in store.
Author Signings: Yes

Good News Book & Gift
Tom Langel, Owner
201 Westgate Mall
Carroll IA 51401-2700
712-792-5207
Subjects: 63-99
Author Signings: Yes

Interstate Book Stores Inc
Rick Weinstein, Owner
1913 E Locust St
Davenport IA 52803
319-322-5552; Fax: 319-322-0544
Subjects: 99
Author Signings: Yes; Catalog: Yes

Iowa Book & Supply
Joe Ziegler, Buyer
8 S Clinton
PO Box 2030
Iowa City IA 52244
319-337-4188; Fax: 319-337-2045
Subjects: 99
Items BT-TA-sportswear
Memo: Mainly textbooks
Author Signings: Yes, occasionally

Prairie Lights Books
Paul Ingram, Book Buyer
15 S Dubuque St
Iowa City IA 52240
319-337-2681; Fax: 319-337-2605
800-295-BOOK
Subjects: 21-47-75-83-95-99
Comments: Jim Harris, Owne
Items: NP-PO-RM-SB
Numbers: 100,000 titles
Memo: Prairie Lights has a reading series in which they bring in authors during the school year. There is also a cafe included in the bookstore.
Author Signings: Yes

Word Play
Greg Johnson, Owner
801 4th Ave
Grinnell IA 50112
515-236-5288
Subjects: 63-99
Author Signings: Yes

Kansas

Adventure Bookstore
Suzan Rutledge
844 Massachusetts St
Lawrence KS 66044-2658
913-843-6424; Fax: 913-843-6121
Subjects: 21-31-71-76-79-80-86-99
Other 35,000 title
Memo: 25-30% are childrens' books. Mary Memofield, Owner.
Author Signings: Yes

Sandhill Books
John Dailey, Book Buyer
302 N Main
Garden City KS 67846
316-275-4998; Fax: 316-275-6876
Subjects: 21-31-76-79-99
Author Signings: Yes; Catalog: Yes, newsletter 2x a year

Town Crier Inc
John, Manager
1301 Gage
Topeka KS 66604
913-272-5060; Fax: 913-272-6099
Subjects: 99
Author Signings: Yes

Yellow Brick Road
June Butler, Buyer
206 S Main St
Ottawa KS 66067
913-242-4957
Subjects: 41-75-99(Kansas books)
Memo: Animated videos for children.
Author Signings: Yes

Kentucky

Joseph Beth Booksellers
Hap Houlihan, Inv Control Manager
3199 Nicholasville Rd
Lexington KY 40503
606-271-5330; Fax: 606-272-6948
Subjects: 11-15-19-21-28-43-63-71-75-77-8
Items: SW-NP-ST-SB--BY-TV-TA
Author Signings: Yes; Catalog: Yes, quarterly newsletter

The Tea Leaf
Jane Stevens, Buyer
230 W Broadway
Danville KY 40422
606-236-7456
Subjects: 21-27-76-79-99
Author Signings: Yes

Lousiana

Baton Rouge Book Warehouse
Gerald Phares, Owner
9596 Florida Blvd
Baton Rouge LA 70815-1125
504-925-9505; Fax: 504-925-9530
Subjects: 99
Numbers: 100,000 titles
Author Signings: Yes; Catalog: Yes, newsletter sent every 3 months

De Ville Books and Prints
Dave Bruewington, Gen Manager
344 Carondelet St
New Orleans LA 70130
504-525-1846
Subjects: 11-12-14-71-99
Numbers: 10,000 titles

Kumquat Bookstore
Book Buyer
228 N Lee Ln
Covington LA 70433
504-892-0686; Fax:
Subjects: 21-31-76-79-99
Author Signings: Yes

Old Town Book Merchant
Debra Ortego, Owner
124 Rue St Denis
Natchitoches LA 71457
318-357-8900; Fax: 318-357-8900
Subjects: 61(the South)-99
Numbers: 5,000 titles
Memo: Building a customer base at this time.
Author Signings: Yes; Catalog: Yes

Maine

Blue Hill Books
Nicholas Sichterman, Owner
2 Pleasant St
Blue Hill ME 04614
207-374-5632
Subjects: 99
Numbers: 17,000 titles
Author Signings: Yes; Catalog: Yes, 3x a year

Patricia Buck's Emporium
Patricia Buck, Owner
Main St
Kingfield ME 04947
207-265-2101
Subjects: 99
Memo: Branch: Sugarloaf USA, Carrasette Valley, ME 04907.

Thomaston Books & Prints
Georgia Hansen, Juvenile Buyer
Darrilyn Peters, Owner/Manager
105 Main St
Thomaston ME 04861-1211
207-354-0001
Subjects: 21-99
Author Signings: Yes; Catalog: Yes, yearly Xmas catalog

Maryland

Book Alcove
Carl Sickles, Owner
15976 Shady Grove Rd
Gaithersburg MD 20877
301-977-9166; Fax: 301-948-6476
Subjects: 99
Items: PB-HC-US

The Bookstall
Hugo Rizzoli, Owner
10144 River Rd
Potomac MD 20854-4903
301-469-7800
Subjects: 21-47-95-99
Author Signings: Yes

Chuck & Dave's
Charles Dukes, Owner
7001 Carroll Ave
Takoma Park MD 20912-4429
301-891-2665; Fax: 301-891-3426
Subjects: 99
Numbers: 15,000 titles
Author Signings: Yes

Cover to Cover
Marian Brown, Owner
7284 Cradlerock Way
Columbia MD 21045
410-381-9200; Fax: 410-381-9201
Subjects: 35-53-57-99
Author Signings: Yes; Catalog: Yes, newsletter

Main Street Books
Fred Powell, Manager
10 E Main St
Frostburg MD 21532-1332
301-689-5605
Subjects: 99
Author Signings: Yes

News Shop
Charles Weaver, Owner
13 S Main St
North East MD 21901
410-287-2211
Subjects: 21-99

Massachusetts

Baker Books
Ben Baker, Co-Owner
69 State Rd
North Dartmouth MA 02747
508-997-6700; Fax: 508-994-1785
Subjects: 21-70N-76-99

Birmingham Book Store Inc
Bonnie Weinstein, Owner
177 Commonwealth Ave #5
Boston MA 02116-2213
313-647-2665;
Subjects: 21-99
Numbers:: 35,000 titles

Bookport Hingham Square
Fran Aronivici, Buyer
21 Main St
Hingham MA 02043-2522
617-749-2670
Subjects: 99
Numbers: 20,000
Author Signings: Yes

Brookline Booksmith
Anne Wahlen, Buyer
279 Harvard St
Brookline MA 02146
617-566-6660; Fax: 617-734-9125
Subjects: 21-99
Numbers: 20,000
Author Signings: Yes

Bunch of Grapes Bookstore
Anne Nelson, Owner
68 Main St
PO Box 1608
Vineyard Haven MA 02568
508-693-2291; Fax: 508-693-2263
800-693-0221
Subjects: 99
Author Signings: Yes

Buttonwood Books & Toys
Betsey Detwiler, Buyer
Cushing Plz
Route 3A
Cohasset MA 02025
617-383-2665; Fax: 617-383-2903
Subjects: 21-31-76-79-99
Author Signings: Yes

Cabbages and Kings Bookstore
Elizabeth M Moye
628 Main St
Chatham MA 02633
508-945-1603
Subjects: 21-31-76-79-99
Comments: Large children's section.
Author Signings: Yes

Derby Square Bookstore
Frank A Monroe
215 Essex St
Salem MA 01970
508-745-8804
Subjects: 99
Numbers: 1000 titles

Evergreen Books
Kathy Hayes, Owner
Two Sudbury Crossing Rte 20
Sudbury MA 01776
508-443-7180
Subjects: 99
Numbers: 12,000
Author Signings: Yes; Catalog: Yes

Harvard Bookstores Inc
Carole Horne, Buyer
General Offices
1256 Massachusetts Ave
Cambridge MA 02138
617-661-0494; Fax: 617-661-1702
800-542-READ
Subjects: 19-39-47-54-55-57-65-75-95-99
Other: 2 stores
Numbers: 40,000 titles
Memo: Ed Olson, Manager.
Author Signings: Yes; Catalog: Yes, monthly newsletter

Harvard Cooperative Society
Peter Smyth, Trade Buyer
1400 Massachusetts Ave
Cambridge MA 02138
617-499-2000; Fax: 617-868-7038
Subjects: 21-23-27-59-71-73-76
Items: SB-TA-SW-CL-BY-TV-TA
Author Signings: Yes; Catalog: Yes

Schoolhouse Books Inc
Mark Brumberg, Owner
dba The Globe Bookshop
38 Pleasant St
Northampton MA 01060
413-586-5838
Subjects: 11-41-54-75-95-99
Author Signings: Yes; Catalog: Yes, newsletter 4x a year

Tatnuck Bookseller & Sons
Larry Abramoff
335 Chandler St
Worcester MA 01602
508-756-7644; Fax: 508-756-9425
Subjects: 57-73-75-99
Memo: Lawrence Abramoff, Owner.
Author Signings: Yes

Trident Booksellers
Bernard Flynn, Owner
338 Newbury St
Boston MA 02115
617-267-8688
Subjects: 21-53-54-99
Comments: Jim Barter, Manager

Wordsworth Bookstore
Donna Friedman, Book Buyer
30 Brattle St
Cambridge MA 02138
617-354-5201; Fax: 617-354-4674
Subjects: 47-65-75-77-83-90-95-99
Other: 3 stores
Numbers: 100,000
Author Signings: Yes; Catalog: Yes, 4x a year

World Eye Bookshop
Antha Smith
156 Main St
Greenfield MA 01301
413-772-2186
Subjects: 31-41-47-53-57-75-90-95-99
Numbers: 20,000
Author Signings: Yes

Michigan

Agape Bookseller
Bill Blakemore, Owner
22291 Eureka Rd
Taylor MI 48180
313-287-9120; Fax: 313-287-6827
Subjects: 63P
Numbers: 2 stores
Memo: Other store in Canton, MI.
Author Signings: Yes

Annie's Book Stop
Sharron Olds, Owner
33340 W 14 Mile Rd
West Bloomfield MI 48322-3572
810-851-3560
Subjects: 99
Items: US-PB-HC

The Book Tree
Fred Jensen, Owner
6431 28th St SE
Grand Rapids MI 49546
616-949-4220
Subjects: 99
Author Signings: Yes; Catalog: Yes, mailed at Thanksgiving & Christmas

Community Newscenter #1
Bookstore Manager
Frandor Shopping Ctr
418 Frandor Ave
Lansing MI 48912
517-351-7562; Fax: 517-351-7574
Subjects: 99
Memo: Small pamphlet mailed around the holidays.
Author Signings: Yes

Cuda's Book Store
Steve Wydendorf, Manager
14310 Michigan Ave
Dearborn MI 48126
313-581-5486;
Subjects: 75-99
Author Signings: Yes

Front Page Book & News
Chris Voynanoff, Manager
974 Joslyn Ave
Pontiac MI 48340
810-334-1150

Subjects: 99
Numbers: 2 stores

Horizon Books
Victor Herman, Owner
243 E Front St
Traverse City MI 49684-2525
616-946-7290; Fax: 616-946-2545
Subjects: 99
Other 3 stores
Memo: Branch: Petoskey, MI.
Author Signings: Yes

The Kids' Place
Ann La Pietra
106 N Jefferson
Marshall MI 49068-1548
616-781-3853
Subjects: 99
Comments: Newsletter
Author Signings: Yes; Catalog: Yes

Little Professor Book Ctr
Nicola Rooney
Westgate Shopping Ctr
2513 Jackson Rd
Ann Arbor MI 48103
313-662-4110; Fax: 313-662-0702
Subjects: 99
Author Signings: Yes; Catalog: Yes, bimonthly newsletter

Little Professor Book Ctr
Kevin Howell
130 S First St #300
Ann Arbor MI 48104
313-994-1212; Fax: 313-944-9009
Subjects: 99
Comments: All franchises buy independently
Author Signings: Yes; Catalog: Yes, weekly newsletter

New Horizons Book Shop Inc
Edward D'Angelo
20757 13 Mile Rd
Roseville MI 48066
810-296-1560
Subjects: 99

Oak Park Book Center
Book Buyer
23029 Coolidge Hwy
Oak Park MI 48237
810-399-2255
Subjects: 49B-99
Author Signings: Yes

Olson News Agency
Doreen Brown
113 Cleveland Ave
PO Box 129
Ishpeming MI 49849
906-486-4711
Subjects: 99

Reading Express Book Station
Venita Ciesla, Owner
23511 Sherman St
Oak Park MI 48237
313-477-7958
Subjects: 99

Schuler Books Inc
William Fehsenfeld
2660 28th St SE
Kentwood MI 49512

616-942-2561; Fax: 616-942-9238
800-331-1727
Subjects: 21-99
Author Signings: Yes

Singapore Bank Bookstore
Judy Hallisy, Owner
317 Butler St
PO Box 630
Sangatuck MI 49453-0630
616-857-3785
Subjects: 21-31-41-70-75-76-77-83-84-99
Numbers: 6,000 titles

Wise Owl Book Shoppe
Kenneth Klann
25873 Ford Rd
Dearborn Heights MI 48127
313-563-4555
Subjects: 99

Minnesota

Baxter's Books
Brian and Carol Baxter
North Star East #129
608 Second Ave S
Minneapolis MN 55402
612-339-4922; Fax: 612-339-6134
800-626-1049
Subjects: 19-21-23-31-67-76-79-99
Numbers: 35,000 titles
Author Signings: Yes; Catalog: Yes, newsletter mailed once every two months

The Bookcase at Wayzata
Peggy Burnet, Owner
607 E Lake St
Wayzata MN 55391
612-473-8341; Fax: 612-473-1407
Subjects: 99
Author Signings: Yes; Catalog: Yes, newsletter sent for special events

Carleton College Book Store
Dan Bergeson
Carleton College
One N College St
Northfield MN 55057
507-663-4149
Subjects: 41-47-55-57-65-75-99
Author Signings: Yes

Green Lion Books
Mark Goodman, Manager
2402 University Ave W #409
St Paul MN 55114
612-644-9070; Fax: 612-646-5591
Subjects: 33-47-37-84-86-87-88-82-83-90
Author Signings: Yes

Hungry Mind Bookstore
Tom Bielenberg, Psychology Buyer
1648 Grand Ave
St Paul MN 55105
612-699-0587; Fax: 612-699-0970
Subjects: 35-39-53-54-57
Numbers: 90,000 titles
Author Signings: Yes; Catalog: Yes

Lake Country Booksellers
Alta Johnson, Co-Owner
4766 Washington Square
White Bear Lake MN 55110
612-426-0918
Subjects: 21-31-76-99
Author Signings: Yes

Micawber's Bookstore
Annie Klessig, Manager/Buyer
2238 Carter Ave
St Paul MN 55108
612-646-5506
Subjects: 21-99
Numbers: 5,000 titles
Author Signings: Yes; Catalog: Yes,
    newsletter every 2 months

Orr Books
Charlie Orr, Owner
3043 Hennepin Ave S
Minneapolis MN 55408
612-823-2408
Subjects: 57-73-99
Author Signings: Yes; Catalog: Yes,
    newsletter 3x a year

SCS University Stores
R V Ward, Mdse Manager
Saint Cloud Univ
801 2nd Ave S
St Cloud MN 56301-4459
612-251-0061; Fax: 612-252-1672
Subjects: 99(mainly textbooks)

University of Minnesota Bookstores
Terry Labandz, Book Buyer
Bill Breer, Buyer, (612-626-1896)
231 Pillsbury Dr SE
Minneapolis MN 55455
612-626-0559
Subjects: 11-23-39-47-55-57-65-67-75-99
Memo: 5 stores: East Bank Store
    (612-625-6000), West Bank Store
    (612-625-3000), Saint Paul Store,
    (612-625-8600), and Computer Store
    (612-625-3854).
Author Signings: Yes

Missouri

A to Z Comics
Debbie Welch, Buyer
1400 West Hwy 40
Blue Springs MO 64015
816-224-0505; Fax: 816-229-7550
Subjects: 33C
Comments: Comic books only
Numbers: 30-40,000 titles

Anderson's Bookshops Inc
William/Jeannie Anderson, Owners
5429 Antioch Center Mall
Kansas City MO 64119
816-454-7677; Fax: 816-452-2045
Subjects: 21-99
Meom: Second store: 334 Blue Ridge
    Mall, Kansas City, MO 64133;
    816-358-5909.
Author Signings: Yes

Bennett Schneider Inc
Mary Kay Lott, Buyer
316 Ward Pky
Kansas City MO 64112
816-531-8484; Fax: 816-531-8401
Subjects: 99
Numbers: 25 titles
Author Signings: Yes

Book Shop at Brookside
Roy Beaty & Steve Paul, Owners
116 W 63rd St
Kansas City MO 64113
816-444-8187
E-Mail: spaul@tyrell.net
Subjects: 21-61-76-99
Numbers: 50,000
Author Signings: Yes; Catalog: Yes,
    newsletter mailed every 2 months

Hammond's Antiques
J Hammond, Owner
1939 Cherokee St
St Louis MO 63118
314-776-4737; Fax: 314-776-4737
800-776-4732
Subjects: 99

Left Bank Books
Barry Leibman
399 N Euclid
St Louis MO 63108
314-367-6731
Subjects: 11-21-37-49-53-54-65-95-99
Comments: Interested in minority writers.
Numbers: 25,000
Author Signings: Yes; Catalog: Yes

The Library Ltd
Allen & Terry Mittleman, Owners
7700 Forsyth
Clayton MO 63105
314-721-0378; Fax: 314-727-0478
Subjects: 21-75-99
Author Signings: Yes; Catalog: Yes,
    Holiday catalog.

Unity Bookstore
Carolyn Morris, Manager
1901 NW Blue Pkwy
Unity Village MO 64065
816-524-3550; Fax: 816-251-3550
Subjects: 21-27-31-33-35-37-39-53-54-57-5
Numbers: 4,200
Author Signings: Yes

Mississippi

Lemuria Bookstore
John Evans, Owner
202 Banner Hall
Jackson MS 39206
601-366-7619; Fax: 601-366-7784
Subjects: 11-12-27-47-54-76-80-83-84
Author Signings: Yes; Catalog: Yes,
    newsletter 2x a year

Square Books
Richard Howorth, Owner
On The Square
160 Ct House Sq
Oxford MS 38655
601-236-2262; Fax: 601-234-9630

Subjects: 99
Memo: They carry an extensive selection
    of books with authors from the South.
Author Signings: Yes; Catalog: Yes,
    bimonthly newsletter

Montana

Barjon's Books
Barbara E Shenkel, Owner
2718 Third Ave N
Billings MT 59101-1929
406-252-4398
Subjects: 37-53-54-57-99
Numbers: 7,000 titles
Author Signings: Yes

Big Sky Books
Kathryn Holt, Manager
525 Second Ave
Havre MT 59501
406-265-5750
MT only: 800-801-5750.
Subjects: 21-76-99
Items: US-PB-HC
Author Signings: Yes; Catalog: Yes

Book Hollow
Teri D Tuss
314 W Main
Lewistown MT 59457-2604
406-538-7209
Subjects: 21-99
Author Signings: Yes; Catalog: Yes

Books & Books
Joe Antonioli, Owner
206 W Park St
Butte MT 59701
406-782-9520
Subjects: 11-14-21-99
Numbers: 25,000 titles
Author Signings: Yes

The Bookworks
Susan Zahrobsky
110 Central Ave
Whitefish MT 59937
406-862-4980
Subjects: 21-29-31-51-61-76-79-99
Numbers: 2500

Country Bookshelf
Mary Jane DiSanti, Owner
28 W Main
Bozeman MT 59715
406-587-0166
Subjects: 99
Author Signings: Yes; Catalog: Yes,
    occasional newsletter

Fact & Fiction
Barbara Theroux, Buyer
216 W Main St
Missoula MT 59802-4310
406-721-2881; Fax: 406-721-2501
800-769-7323
Subjects: 41-61-76-83-95-77
Numbers: 10,000 titles
Author Signings: Yes; Catalog: Yes

Freddy's Feed & Read
Mark Watkins
1221 Helen Ave
Missoula MT 59801-4491
406-549-2127
Subjects: 13-49-51-53-54-55-57-65-73-99
Author Signings: Yes; Catalog: Yes

Nebraska

The Book End
Pam Svoboda and Jean Robinson, Owners
110 West C St
McCook NE 69001
308-345-7480
Subjects: 21-31-43-59-63-75-76
Memo: Educational materials and classroom resources also carried.
Author Signings: Yes

Cover to Cover Bookstore
Andy Zimmerman, Manager
1941 South 42nd #328
Omaha NE 68105
402-345-1225; Fax: 402-345-1215
Subjects: 99
Items: SB-TA
Numbers: 10,000 titles

Ketterson's Old Market Bookstore
Andy Ketterson, Co-Owner
1202 Howard St
Omaha NE 68102
402-341-9322; Fax: 402-341-9130
Subjects: 21-71-75-95-99
Author Signings: Yes; Catalog: Yes, newsletter 2x a year

Little Professor Book Center
Janet Grojean
Brentwood Square
8052 S 84th St
La Vista NE 68128
402-331-6628
Subjects: 99
Items: HC-PB-PO-SB

Village Book & Stationery
Sara Radil, Manager
8701 Country Side Plz
Omaha NE 68114
402-391-0100; Fax: 402-397-5151
Subjects: 21-75-27-(cookbooks)-71-47(lit)
Catalog: Yes, Bookpages sent twice a year to 5,000 customers

Nevada

Bookcellar
Janice Wakimoto, Owner
328 Fairview Dr
Carson City NV 89701
702-885-7772
Subjects: 21-99
Itemss: Coffee table books also
Numbers: 20,000 titles
Author Signings: Yes

Solomon Gundy's Book World
Sol and Elaine Levco, Owners
1442 E Charleston Blvd
Las Vegas NV 89104
702-385-6043
Subjects: 21-99

Sundance Bookstore
Daniel T Earl
1155 W 4th St #106
Reno NV 89503-5147
702-786-1188
Subjects: 99
Author Signings: Yes; Catalog: Yes, bimonthly newsletter

New Hampshire

Apple Tree Book Shop
Eric Griffel, Owner
24 Warren St
Concord NH 03301
603-228-8451
Subjects: 99
Numbers: 5,000 titles

BestSellers
Melissa MacKenzie, Manager
#22 Powerhouse
West Lebanon NH 03784
603-298-7980
Subjects: 99
Author Signings: Yes

Bye the Book Inc
Neil Moylan
Main St
PO Box 915
North Conway NH 03860-0915
603-356-2665
Subjects: 99
Numbers: 35,639 titles

The Dartmouth Bookstore Inc
David Cioffi
33 S Main St
Hanover NH 03755
603-643-3616; Fax: 603-643-5170
800-624-8800
E-Mail: bookstore.incatavalley.net
Subjects: 21-31-76-79
Comments: Large children's deptartment
Catalog: Yes

Little Professor Book Center
Patricia Weisbrot, Owners
Worth Plz
103 Congress St
Portsmouth NH 03801
603-436-1777; Fax: 603-436-3629
Subjects: 21-70-73-99
Numbers: 6,000 titles
Memo: Headquarters: Ann Arbor, Ml.
Author Signings: Yes

The Toadstool Bookshops
Willard P Williams
12 Depot Square
Peterborough NH 03458
603-924-3543; Fax: 603-924-7295
Subjects: 21-75-99
Other: 3 stores
Numbers: 40,000

The Toadstool Bookshops
Willard P Williams
Colony Mill Market Pl
Keen NH 03431
603-352-8815
Subjects: 21-75-99
Comments: Strong 21-75 section
Other: 3 stores
Numbers: 40,000 titles
Memo: Mike Wolf, Manager.

The Toadstool Bookshops
Willard P Williams
Lorden Plz
Milford NH 03055
603-673-1734;
Subjects: 21-75-99
Comments: Strong 21-75 section
Other: 3 stores
Numbers: 40,000 titles
Memo: Jeff Smull, Manager.

Village Book Store Inc
Ned Densmore, Owner
81 Main St
Littleton NH 03561
603-444-5263; Fax: 603-444-2513
800-640-9673.
Subjects: 99
Comments: Full-service book store
Author Signings: Yes; Catalog: Yes, Christmas catalog

Water Street Bookstore
Dan Chartrand, Co-Owner
125 Water St
Exeter NH 03883-2410
603-778-973
Subjects: 99

New Jersey

The Bay Bookstore
Karl & Ann Keffer, Owners
701 Lacey Rd
Forked River NJ 08731-1461
609-971-3044; Fax: 609-971-5973
800-734-6906
Subjects: 99
Comments: Full-service bookstore
Numbers: 1 store
Author Signings: Yes; monthly newsletter

Book World Inc
Stanley Sabin, Owner
895 Bloomfield Ave
West Caldwell NJ 07006
201-575-1818; Fax: 201-575-4818
Subjects: 99
Numbers: 35,000
Author Signings: Occasionally

Cranford Bookstore
Ms Meryl Layton, Owner
32 North Ave W
Cranford NJ 07016
908-276-0390; Fax: 908-276-6244
Subjects: 99
Other: 3 stores
Author Signings: Yes

Encore Books
Christine Wieland, Book Buyer
Princeton Shopping Ctr
301 N Harrison St
Princeton NJ 08540
609-252-0608
Subjects: 99-21(section)
Author Signings: Yes; Catalog, Yes, monthly

Little Professor Book Center
Mike & Susan Cullis, Owners
786 Rt 35 S
Middletown NJ 07748
908-615-0444; Fax: 908-615-0648
Subjects: 99
Comments: Buys independently
Numbers: 28,000 titles
Memo: Headquarters: Ann Arbor, MI.
Author Signings: Yes; Catalog: Yes

Watchung Booksellers
Trina Rogers/Margot Sage-El
33 Watchung Plz
Montclair NJ 07042
201-744-7177; Fax: 201-783-5899
800-299-3181
Subjects: 21-76-99
Comments: 1/3 children's books
Author Signings: Yes; Catalog: Yes, called **"Great Owl Book"**.

New Mexico

Bookworks
Nancy Rutland
4022 Rio Grande Blvd NW
Dietz Farm Plz
Albuquerque NM 87107
505-344-8139; Fax: 505-344-9948
Subjects: 99
Items: GI-TO-BT-CD
Numbers: 12,000 titles
Author Signings: Yes; Catalog: Yes

Bridge Street Books Ltd
Peter Dumont/Anne Stevenson
131 Bridge St
Las Vegas NM 87701-3426
505-454-8211
Subjects: 41-61-95
Numbers: 4,000 titles

Communications Media
Colleen C Olinger, Owner/Manager
DBA Otowi Sta
1350 Central Ave
Los Alamos NM 87544
505-662-9589; Fax: 505-662-3714
Subjects: 67-99
Numbers: 25,000 titles
Author Signings: Yes

Garcia Street Books
Ellen Stelling
376 Garcia St
Santa Fe NM 87501-2732
505-986-0151; Fax: 505-986-0129
Subjects: 99
Author Signings: Yes; Catalog: Yes, monthly newsletter

Living Batch Books
Gus Blaisdell
106 Cornell Dr SE
Albuquerque NM 87106
505-262-1619
Subjects: 11-12A-54-57-75-95-99
Numbers: 24,000 titles
Author Signings: Yes

Moby Dickens Bookshop
Arthur & Susan Bachrach, Buyers
#6 John Dunn House
124A Bent St
Taos NM 87571
505-758-3050; Fax: 505-758-8990
Subjects: 11-21-51-54-73-75-99
Numbers: 12,000 titles
Author Signings: Yes

Old Santa Fe Trail Books
Tonia Gould, Owner
613 Old Santa Fe Trail
Santa Fe NM 87501-4508
505-988-8878; Fax: 505-983-1398
Subjects: 61-99
Numbers: 17,000 titles
Author Signings: Yes

Read On!
Lisa Chavez, Manager
10131 Coors Rd NW
Albuquerque NM 87114
505-898-0000; Fax: 505-898-0110
Subjects: 99
Author Signings: Yes

New York

Bestseller
Patrick Payne, Owner/Manager
43 A Main St
Hempstead NY 11550
516-564-5103; Fax: 516-564-4607
Subjects: 49B-99
Author Signings: Yes

Book House of Stuyvesant Plaza
Susan Novotny, Owner
Stuyvesant Plz
Albany NY 12203-3586
518-489-4761; Fax: 518-489-4318
Subjects: 21-51-75-86-99
Numbers: 60,000 titles
Author Signings: Yes; Catalog: Yes, mailed randomly

Book Revue
Richard & Robert Klein, Owners
313 New York Ave
Huntington Village NY 11743
516-271-1442; Fax: 516-271-5890
Subjects: 99
Items: SB-CA
Numbers: 25,000 titles
Author Signings: Yes; Catalog: Yes, newsletter 1x a month

Bookberries
Tom Turvey
983 Lexington Ave
New York NY 10021-5103
212-794-9400; Fax: 212-794-7042
Subjects: 83(literary fiction)

Numbers: 25,000 titles

Bookmarks
Ted Marks, Prop
32 E Market St
Corning NY 14830
607-962-2665; Fax: 607-937-5777
Subjects: 99
Numbers: 12,000 titles
Catalog: Yes

Books 'n Things
Charles & Diane Newman, Owners
3 North Broadway
Tarrytown NY 10591
914-631-2966; Fax: 914-631-7287
Subjects: 21-76-99
Items: SW-ST-TA-TV

Burlington Bookshop
Jane Trichter, Owner
1082 Madison Ave
New York NY 10028
212-288-7420; Fax: 212-249-3502
Subjects: 11-27-75-84-99
Numbers: 4,000 titles
Author Signings: Yes

Coliseum Books Inc
George Liebson and Jay Grace, Book Buyers
1775 Broadway #507
New York NY 10019
212-581-5352; Fax: 212-586-5607
Subjects: 75-99
Numbers: 70,000 titles

Community Bookstore
Susan Scioli, Owner
143 Seventh Ave
Brooklyn NY 11215
718-783-3075; Fax: 718-783-7154
Subjects: 47-99
Numbers: 1 store
Author Signings: Yes; Catalog: Yes, newsletter mailed a few times a year

Corner Bookstore
Lenny Golay, Owner
1313 Madison Ave
New York NY 10128
212-831-3554; Fax: 212-831-2930
Subjects: 21-31-76-79-99
Comments: Does book searches
Author Signings: Yes; Catalog: Yes, in-house newsletter on occasion

Dolphin Bookshop
Patricia Vunk, Owner
941 Port Washington Blvd
Port Washington NY 11050-2910
516-767-2650; Fax: 516-767-0082
Subjects: 53-99
Author Signings: Yes; Catalog: Yes

Fox & Sutherland Stationery
Charles Edmonston, Book Buyer
15-17 S Moger Ave
Mt Kisco NY 10549
914-666-8088; Fax: 914-666-9421
Subjects: 11-23-29-39-59-61-63-71-75
Items: ST-TV-TO
Author Signings: Yes

Genesee Country Museum
Pat Baker, Dir of Admissions
Flint Hill Rd
Mumford NY 14511
716-538-6822; Fax: 716-538-2887
Subjects: 27-28-41-43-51-61-71
Items: TA-TO
Numbers: 2,000 titles

Madison Avenue Bookshop Inc
Perry Haberman
833 Madison Ave
New York NY 10021
212-535-6130; Fax: 212-794-5231
Subjects: 99
Author Signings: Yes; Catalog: Yes, newsletter

Putnam Book Center
Hank Jones, Buyer
Putnam Plz RR 6
Carmel NY 10512
914-228-1182; Fax: 914-228-0234
Subjects: 99
Numbers: 15,000 titles
Author Signings: Yes

Saint Mark's Bookshop
Robert Contant
31 3rd Ave
New York NY 10003
212-260-7853; Fax: 212-598-0987
Subjects: 54-55-73-83-95-99
Other 40,000 titles
Catalog: Yes, newsletter

Shakespeare & Co
William Kurland
2259 Broadway
New York NY 10024
212-580-7800; Fax: 212-580-8123
Subjects: 14-21-27-39R-57-71-86-99
Other: 2 stores
Memo: Mass Market Buyer: David Wetter.
Author Signings: Yes

Talking Leaves
Jonathan Welch, Manager
3158 Main St
Buffalo NY 14214-1311
716-837-8554; Fax: 716-837-3861
Subjects: 13-37-49A-49B-54-55-73-75-95-99
Author Signings: Yes; Catalog: Yes, newsletter 3x a year

Village Book Shop
Marianne & David Carlson, Owners
84 Purchase St
Rye NY 10580
914-967-0031; Fax: 914-967-0287
Subjects: 99
Author Signings: Yes

North Carolina

Bull's Head Bookshop
Erica Eisdorfer, Manager
UNC Student Stores
CB 1530 Daniels Bldg
Chapel Hill NC 27599-1530
919-962-5060; Fax: 919-962-7392
Subjects: 47-54-95-99
Author Signings: Yes

Davidson College Bookstore
Ruth Gardner, Trade Buyer
Main St
PO Box 1738
Davidson NC 28036
704-892-2349; Fax: 704-892-2513
Subjects: 99
Items: PO-CD-SW-TA
Numbers: TV-NP
Memo: Author signings on campus, not in bookstore.
Author Signings: Yes; Catalog: Yes, brochure mailed 1x year

The Island Ragpicker
Carmie Prete
Highway 12
PO Box 5
Ocracoke Island NC 27960-9999
919-928-7571
Subjects: 99
Numbers: 200 titles

The Muses
Shirley B Sprinkle, Pres
PO Box 1268
Morganton NC 28680
704-433-1314
Subjects: 21-31-51-61-76-99
Items: SB-TA-TO
Numbers: 25,000 titles
Author Signings: Yes

The Regulator Bookshop
Tom Campbell
720 Ninth St
Durham NC 27705
919-286-2700; Fax: 919-286-6063
Subjects: 21-53-57-73-75-99
Author Signings: Yes; Catalog: Yes, newsletter 4x a year

Ohio

ABC Center
Carlene Valencic, Owner
5122 Heatherdowns Blvd
Toledo OH 43614
419-381-1101
Subjects: 21-31E-76
Memo: 2 stores. Address for other store: 3606 W Sylvania Ave, Toledo, OH 43623.

Books & Co For Kids
Lou Lala
350 E Stroop Rd
Dayton OH 45429
513-298-6540; Fax: 513-298-7895
800-777-4881
Subjects: 21-99
Numbers: 90,000 titles
Author Signings: Yes; Catalog: Yes

Browse Awhile Books
William A Jones, Owner
118 E Main St
Tipp City OH 45371-1962
513-667-7200
Subjects: 99
Numbers: 50,000

Little Professor Book Center
Dennis or Linda Fennell, Buyers
1540 Spring Meadows Dr
Holland OH 43528
419-865-0013; Fax: 419-865-9397
Subjects: 99
Comments: 2,000 MG titles
Author Signings: Yes; Catalog: Yes, occasionally newsletters sent

Little Professor Book Company
Paul Burns, Book Buyer
155 Worthington Square
Columbus OH 43085
614-846-4319; Fax: 614-846-4929
Subjects: 99
Comments: John & Jennifer Gaylord, Owners
Numbers: 85,000 titles
Author Signings: Yes

Mac's Backs Paperbacks
Suzanne DeGaetano and James McSherry, Owners
1820 Conventry Rd
Cleveland Heights OH 44118
216-321-2665; Fax: 216-321-7323
Subjects: 99
Other: Postcards
Numbers: 75 titles
Memo: Author signings: Yes.

Miami Valley Gateway Books
Charles Thompson and Kathleen Thompson, Owners
Piqua East Mall
1216 E Ash St
Piqua OH 45356
513-773-5039
800-443-3029
Subjects: 99
Numbers: Small store
Author Signings: Yes, local

Mother O'Riley's Books
Elin Jones, Owner
232 Third St
Marietta OH 45750
614-373-8523; Fax: 614-373-8523
Subjects: 99
Author Signings: Yes

The News Depot Inc
Steve Todd and Sam Sliman, Owners
207 Market Ave N
Canton OH 44702-1492
216-454-4441
Subjects: 11-17-21-75-99
Author Signings: Yes

Newton's Book Store
Gary Newton, Owner/Manager
Country Square Shopping Ctr
320 W National Rd
Englewood OH 45322
513-836-8353
Subjects: 99
Items: SW-CA
Author Signings: Yes

Nickleby's Book Store Cafe
Palmer R Cook, Owner
1425 Grandview Ave
Columbus OH 43212-2853
614-841-2496
Subjects: 21-31-76-79
Author Signings: Yes

Turn of the Page
Victor & Maureen Pergola
14879 Detroit Rd
Lakewood OH 44107
216-521-9988; Fax: 216-521-9903
Subjects: 99
Comments: Special order textbooks
Items: BT-TA-CD
Numbers: 20,000 titles
Author Signings: Yes

Wilkie News
Eric Oda, Manager
1053 Centerville
Dayton OH 45358
513-434-8821
Subjects: 99
Items: SB
Memo: Office located at 101 S Ludlow St, Dayton, OH 45402. Phone #513-223-2869.
Author Signings: Yes

Oklahoma

Brace Books & More
Jean Brace, Manager
2205 N 14th St
Ponca City OK 74601
405-765-5173; Fax: 405-762-2313
800-256-5173
Subjects: 99
Items: HC-PB-US
Author Signings: Yes; Catalog: Yes, 4x a year.

Red Rock Entertainment
Bonnie Lee, Owner
105 W Harrison St
Guthrie OK 73044
405-282-8550; Fax: 405-282-5552
Subjects: 99
Numbers: 25,000 titles

Vic's Place
Sara Raupe, Owner
124 N Second St
Guthrie OK 73044-3163
405-282-7350; Fax: 405-282-6850
Subjects: 16-28-99
Author Signings: Yes

Oregon

The Book Vault
John Burger, Owner
3125 SW Cedar Hills Blvd
Beaverton OR 97005
503-646-8119; Fax: 503-646-4459
800-646-1919
Subjects: 21-86-99
Numbers: 35,000 titles
Author Signings: Yes; Catalog: Yes, newsletter sent on occasion

Books Etc
Richard Sept or Kathy O'Neil
1015 Commercial St
Astoria OR 97103
503-325-4225
Subjects: 99
Numbers: 25,000

The Bookshelf
Tracy Abernathy
Sunriver Mall #21A
PO Box 4428
Sunriver OR 97707
503-593-2166
Subjects: 99
Numbers: 10,000

Harvest Book Shoppe
Judith Lovell, Owner
307 Central Ave
Coos Bay OR 97420
503-267-5824
Subjects: 29-31-61-75-99
Author Signings: Yes

Looking Glass Bookstore
Bill Kloster, Buyer
Katie Radditz, Juvenile Buyer
318 SW Taylor St
Portland OR 97204
503-227-476
Subjects: 11-14-29-33-39-53-69-75-86-95-9
Author Signings: Yes

Marketplace Books
Karen Swank, Owner
Fifth St Public Market
296 E 5th Ave NBU 8-10
Eugene OR 97401
503-343-5614; Fax: 503-343-5614
Subjects: 51-75-99
Numbers: 25,000
Author Signings: Yes

Parnassus
Barbra Hansel
234 10th St
Astoria OR 97103
503-325-1363
Subjects: 21-61
Author Signings: Yes

Tree Frog Trucking Co
Bill Kloster, Buyer
318 SW Taylor St
Portland OR 97204-4760
503-227-476
Subjects: 14M-33-37-54-75-86
Comments: Also a wholesaler

Twenty-Third Avenue Books
Robert Maull, Owner
1015 NW 23rd Ave
Portland OR 97210
503-224-5097; Fax: 503-224-6203
Subjects: 37-73-99
Author Signings: Yes

Watertower Books
Doug Hawkins/Greg Rehn, Owners
John's Landing
Portland OR 97201
503-228-0290; Fax: 503-228-0168
Subjects: 99
Numbers: 12,000 titles
Author Signings: Yes

Pennsylvania

Bookworks Inc
Molly Montgomery
1139 Freeport Rd
Pittsburgh PA 15238
412-782-6661;
Subjects: 21-23-45-99-31-76-79
Numbers: 25,000 titles
Author Signings: Yes; Catalog: Yes, Holiday catalog

Das Book Haus
E Rhoads, Owner
Fairmont Village
7001 N Rte 309
Coopersburg PA 18036
215-536-6574; Fax: 215-536-6574
Subjects: 99
Author Signings: Yes

Farley's Bookshop
44 S Main St
New Hope PA 18938
215-862-2452; Fax: 215-862-5568
Rob Haley, Book Buyer
James H Farley, Onwer
Subjects: 99
Author Signings: Yes

Kenny's News Agency & Bookstore
Barbara Kenny Dommel, Owner
17 W State St
Doylestown PA 18901-4278
215-345-9030
Subjects: 99
Author Signings: Yes

Little Professor Book Center
Phil or Janet Semisch, Buyers
1758 Allentown Rd
Lansdale PA 19446
215-368-4551; Fax: 215-368-6247
Subjects: 99
Numbers: 45,000 titles
Author Signings: Yes; Catalog: Yes, newsletter sent once a month

Little Professor Book Ctr
Sheryl L Leckie, Owner
301 Oak Springs Rd
Washington PA 15301
412-228-2098
Subjects: 19-21-27-28-41-57-61-76-85-89
Items: SB-TA-BT
Author Signings: Yes

News Center West (Offices)
Lori Gouse, Book Buyer
224 West Shore Plz
Lemoyne PA 17043
717-761-2900
Subjects: 99
Author Signings: Yes

Puerto Rico

The Book Store
Richard Gilpin, Owner
255 San Jose St
Old San Juan PR 00901
809-724-1815; Fax: 809-724-8177
Subjects: 11-45(Spanish)-75-99
Numbers: 12,000 titles
Memo: 2/3rds English books.
Author Signings: Yes

South Carolina

Chapter Two Bookstore
Susan Davis, Owner
199 E Bay St
Charlestown SC 29401
803-722-4238; Fax: 803-577-7470
Subjects: 21-41
Comments: Newsletter sent
Numbers: 15,000 titles
Author Signings: Yes; Catalog: Yes

The Happy Bookseller
Rhett Jackson, Owner
4525 Forest Dr
Forest Village
Columbia SC 29206
803-787-3136
Subjects: 99
Numbers: 50,000 titles
Author Signings: Yes

Teachers Treasures
Harriette Duncan, Owner
320 Main St
Conway SC 29526
803-248-3340
Subjects: 21-31-99

South Dakota

Book & Company
Greg Theissen, Owner
2001 W Main
Rapid City SD 57702
605-348-2665; Fax: 605-348-5790
Subjects: 21-27-31-47-57-61-76
Numbers: 11,000
Author Signings: Yes; Catalog: Yes

Little Professor Book Center
Peggy Bieber, Manager
3315 6th SE Lakewood Mall
Aberdeen SD 57401
605-225-0632; Fax: 605-225-0645
Subjects: 99
Other SB-TO-GC-GI
Numbers: 15,000 titles
Memo: Marcie and Jeff Sveen, Owners.
Author Signings: Yes; Catalog: Yes, mailed quarterly, newsletter mailed monthly

Tennessee

21st Century Christian Bookstore
Barry Brewer, Book Buyer
2809 12th Ave S
Nashville TN 37204
615-383-3842
800-251-2477
Subjects: 63(Protestant)-99
Memo: Also a publisher.

Barrett & Co Booksellers
Peyton Hall, Owner
1101 Hixson Pike
Chattanooga TN 37405-3144
615-267-2665
Subjects: 19-21-71-75-76-99
Author Signings: Yes

The Book Place
Molly Thompson, Manager
420 W Walnut
Johnson City TN 37604-6766
615-929-2665
Subjects: 99-61
Items: CA
Author Signings: Yes; Catalog: Yes, newsletter every other month

Bookworld
Jim Austin, Owner
499 Merritt Ave
Nashville TN 37203
615-254-8247
Subjects: 21-35A-51B-75-86

Burke's Book Store Inc
Harriette M Beeson, Owner
1719 Poplar Ave
Memphis TN 38104-6416
901-278-7484; Fax: 901-272-2340
Subjects: 41(Civil War)-61(South)-99
Author Signings: Yes; Catalog: Yes, newsletter

Williams Booksellers
Libby Willis, Book Buyer
262 Heritage Park Dr
Murfreesboro TN 37129
615-890-5656; Fax: 615-890-5686
Subjects: 99
Comments: HC-PB-MM-MG-CA-CL-GC-MA-PO-CD-NP
Author Signings: Yes; Catalog: Yes, newsletter sent once every two months

Texas

Barber's Bookstore
Brian Perkins, Owner
215 W 8th St
Fort Worth TX 76102-6105
817-335-5469; Fax: 817-332-5319
800-327-5471
Subjects: 21-48-70-99
Numbers: 50,000 titles
Catalog: Yes, every 2 years

The Book Cottage
Mary Bracken, Owner
704 S Golid
Rockwall TX 75087
214-771-3638; Fax: 214-771-3638
Subjects: 21-27-31-61(TX)-76-99
Author Signings: Yes

Book People Inc
Doug Hymel, VP
603 N Lamar
Austin TX 78703
512-472-5050; Fax: 512-472-8291
800-853-9757
E-Mail: service@bookpeople.com
Subjects: 21-99
Items: GC-MA-PO-CD
Numbers: 250,000 titles

Books & More
Lawrence Whiddon
3418 Western
Amarillo TX 79109-4438
806-358-9348; Fax: 806-358-8107
Subjects: 21-76-99
Numbers: 15,000 titles
Author Signings: Yes

Brazos Bookstore Inc
Karl Kilian, Owner
2421 Bissonnet St
Houston TX 77005-1451
713-523-0701
Subjects: 11-12-14-47-71-75-83-95
Author Signings: Yes; Catalog: Yes, monthly newsletter/Xmas catalog

Colloquim Books
Kay Moore, Manager
320 University Dr
San Marcos TX 78666
512-392-6641; Fax: 512-392-1074
Subjects: 99(college)
Memo: Buys independently.

Congress Avenue Booksellers
Alice R Gaffney, Manager
716 Congress Ave
Austin TX 78701
512-478-1157
Subjects: 19-47-55-75-99
Numbers: 25,000 titles
Author Signings: Yes

River Oaks Bookstore
Jeanne Jard, Book Buyer
3270 Westheimer
Houston TX 77098
713-520-0061
Subjects: 99
Author Signings: Yes

Tattered Tales
Judy Hendricks, Owner
803 Frank
Lufkin TX 75904
409-632-7355
Subjects: 99

Whole Earth Provision Co
Jack Jones
2410 San Antonio St
Austin TX 78705
512-476-4811; Fax: 512-476-3301
Subjects: 11-13-14-21-27-29-43G-69-71
Other: 3 stores
Author Signings: Yes

Utah

The King's English
Elizabeth Burton, Owner
1511 S 1500 East
Salt Lake City UT 84105
801-484-9100; Fax: 801-484-1595
800-658-7928
Subjects: 21-83-84-95-99
Items: TV(children)
Memo: N Barbara Hoagland and Carolyn Ershler, Owners.
Author Signings: Yes; Catalog: Yes, newsletter 4x a year

Sam Weller's Zion Books
Jean McGean, Mdse Manager
254 S Main St
Salt Lake City UT 84101
801-328-2586; Fax: 801-363-0457
Subjects: 61-63(Mormon)-75-99
Numbers: 2 stores
Author Signings: Yes

Valley Book Center
Joan Walters, Owner
52 W Center St
Provo UT 84601
801-374-6260
Subjects: 99
Items; SB-BT

Waking Owl Books
Patrick De Freitas
208 South 13th E
Salt Lake City UT 84102
801-582-7323; Fax: 801-582-0839
Subjects: 11-12-14-27-29-51-69-71-75-95-9
Numbers: 8,000
Author Signings: Yes; Catalog: Yes, quarterly newsletter

Vermont

Abatis Books
Irving Bell, Owner
PO Box 451
Springfield VT 05156-0451
802-885-3151
Subjects: 41-99
Items: PB-HC-US

Bartleby's Books & Music
Peter Herrick, Owner
N Main St
PO Box 809
Wilmington VT 05363
802-464-5425
Subjects: 99
Numbers: 20,000 titles
Author Signings: Yes, Catalog: Yes, newsletter mailed 4x a year

The Book Cellar
Pierre Bonin, Owner
120 Main St
Brattleboro VT 05301
802-254-6026
Subjects: 71-95-99
Author Spignings: Yes

Chassman & Bem Booksellers
Stacy Visco, Author Signings
Stephen West, Book Buyer
Randy Chudnow, Owner
81 Church St
Burlington VT 05401
802-862-4332; Fax: 802-862-8714
Subjects: 11-12-21-47-76-99
Items: BT
Numbers: 100,000 titles
Author Signings: Yes; Catalog: Yes

Misty Valley Books
Dwight Currie/Michael Kohlmann
Main St
PO Box 700
Chester VT 05143
802-875-3400; Fax: 802-875-3411
Subjects: 27-29-51-61-71-75-99
Numbers: 9,000 titles
Author Signings: Yes; Catalog: Yes, newsletter 6x a year

Northshire Bookstore
Edward A Morrow Jr
Main St
PO Box 2200
Manchester Center VT 05255
802-362-2200; Fax: 802-362-1233
Subjects: 99
Numbers: 41,000
Author Signings: Yes; Catalog: Yes, newsletter

Norwich Bookstore Inc
Penny McConnel, Owner/Buyer
Main St
PO Box 307
Norwich VT 05055
802-649-1114
Subjects: 99
Catalog: Yes, give away newsletter in store

The Vermont Book Shop Inc
John & Laura Scott
38 Main St
Middlebury VT 05753-1416
802-388-2061; Fax: 802-388-9217
Subjects: 61-95(Robert Frost)-99
Numbers: 35,000
Author Signings: Yes

Virginia

The Best Seller
Beth Thompson, Owner
29 W Nelson St
Lexington VA 24450
703-463-4647; Fax: 703-463-3714
Subjects: 21-99
Items: US
Numbers: 12,000 titles
Catalog: Yes

The Book Cellar
Book Buyer
316 E Main St
Charlottesville VA 22902
804-979-7787; Fax: 804-979-7788
Subjects: 61(new)-all other books used/remainders

Horizon Books
Jamie King, Owner
504 Locust Ave
Waynesboro VA 22980-4415
703-943-7323
Subjects: 21-27-99

Main Street Books
Marie Frank
152 E Main #2W
Abingdon VA 24210
703-628-1232; Fax:
Subjects: 21-31-76-79-99
Author Signings: Yes; Catalog: Yes, newsletter

Prince Books
Sarah Pishko, Owner
109 E Main St
Norfolk VA 23510
804-622-9223; Fax: 804-622-9228
Subjects: 99
Author Signings: Yes; Catalog: Yes

Washington

Auntie's Bookstore
Julie Smith, Head Buyer
West 402 Main
Spokane WA 99201
509-838-0206; Fax: 509-838-4967
Subjects: 21-47-54-57-84-73-75-76-83-99
Other SW-TA-NP-SB
Numbers: 100,000 titles
Author Signings: Yes, weekly book signings
Catalog: Yes, 10,000 + newsletters sent 4-6x per year

Bailey-Coy Books
Barbara Bailey, Owner
414 Broadway E
Seattle WA 98102
206-323-8842; Fax: 206-323-0377
Subjects: 21-37-83-99
Numbers: 25,000 titles
Author Signings: Yes

Beks Bookstore
Marty Bucher, Manager
1201 3rd Ave
Seattle WA 98101
206-224-7028
Subjects: 61(NW)-71-99
Memo: 2 stores.
Author Signings: Yes

Book & Game Company Inc
Kristen Birchett, Adv Coord
North 203 Washington
Spokane WA 99201
509-838-6242; Fax: 509-838-4967
Subjects: 57S-73-77-83-84
Numbers: 100,000 + titles
Catalog: Yes, 6000 + mailed yearly

The Book Nook
Marion Kelly, Owner
722 Summitview
Yakima WA 98902
509-453-3762
Subjects: 31-37-35-53-54-57-73
Items: PB-HC-US

Earthlight Bookstore
David Cosby, Owner
321 E Main
Walla Walla WA 99362
509-525-4983
Subjects: 99
Author Signings: Yes

Elliott Bay Book Co
Walter T Carr
Children's Book Dept
101 S Main St
Seattle WA 98104
206-624-6600
Subjects: 47-54-75-77-83-95-99
Author Signings: Yes; Catalog: Yes

Encore Bookstore
Heather Spear, Manager
2516 W Nob Hill
Yakima WA 98902
509-457-4660;
Subjects: 99
Items: MA-ST-TA-TV
Numbers: 100,000
Catalog: Yes, newsletter

Fireside Bookstore
Jane Laclerque, Owner
116 E Legion Way
Olympia WA 98501
360-352-4006
Subjects: 99
Author Signings: Yes

Four Seasons Books/Carnegies
Dean & Carla Jones, Owners
302 E 7th
Olympia WA 98501
360-786-095
Subjects: 35-39-57-99
Author Signings: Yes

Globe Books
John Siscoe, Buyer
999 Third Ave
Seattle WA 98104
206-527-2480
Subjects: 47-49-75-99
Author Signings: Yes

M Coy Books Inc
Michael Coy, Owner
117 Pine St
Seattle WA 98101-1511
206-623-5354
Subjects: 21-27-75-77-84-99
Author Signings: Yes

Madison Park Books
Susanna Draper
4105 E Madison
Seattle WA 98112
206-328-7323
Subjects: 21-99
Catalog: Yes, newsletter 4x a year

Parkplace Book Co
Theodore Lucia
348 Park Place Ctr
Kirkland WA 98033-6229
206-828-6546
Subjects: 21-75-76-99
Numbers: 15,000 titles
Memo: Rental books-on-tape.
Author Signings: Yes; Catalog: Yes, bimonthly newsletter

Puss'N Books
Magda Hitzroth, Owner
15788 Redmond Way
Redmond WA 98052-3830
206-885-6828
Subjects: 21-76-75-98(Dr Who books)-99
Author Signings: Yes

Riverwalk Books Ltd
Libby Manthey, Owner
1113 S Emerson
PO Box 686
Chelan WA 98816
509-682-8901; Fax: 509-682-9103
Subjects: 99
Numbers: 7,000 titles
Catalog: Yes

University Book Store
Anne Robinson, Book Buyer
Megan McGinnis, Manager
990 102nd Ave NE
Bellevue WA 98004
206-632-9500; Fax: 206-646-3340
Subjects: 11-19-21-31-39-41-55-65-67-76-9
Numbers: 11,000 titles
Memo: 2 stores.
Author Signings: Yes

University Book Store
Robert H Cross, Gen Manager
4326 University Way NE
Seattle WA 98105-1005
206-634-3400; Fax: 206-634-0810
Subjects: 11-19-21-31-39-41-55-65-67-76-9
Comments: 2 stores
Other 110,000 titles
Author Signings: Yes; Catalog: Yes, monthly newsletter

Village Books
Krista Hunter
1210 11th St
Bellingham WA 98225
360-671-2626; Fax: 360-734-2573
800-392-2665
Subjects: 21-37-61-75-76-89
Items: CD-SW-NP-SB
Numbers: 55,000+ titles
Author Signings: Yes; Catalog: Yes, newsletter 4x a year

Wisconsin

Audubon Court Books Ltd
Jenny Ells, Buyer
383 W Brown Deer Rd
Milwaukee WI 53217
414-351-9140
Subjects: 99
Numbers 60,000 titles

The Bookworm
Book Buyer
PO Box 343
Boulder Junction WI 54512
715-385-2191
Subjects: 21-51-53-54-71-99

Conkey's Bookstore
Joe Goodfellow, Buyer
Mary Kay Smith, Children's Buyer
John Zimmerman, Owner/Buyer
226 E College Ave
Appleton WI 54911-5789
414-735-6223; Fax: 414-735-6227
Subjects: 21-76-99
Numbers: 100,000 titles

Rainbow Bookstore
Marsha Rummel, Manager
426 W Gilman St
Madison WI 53703
608-257-6050
Subjects: 41-55-57-73-99
Author Signings: Yes; Catalog: Yes, newsletter

Harry W Schwartz Bookshop
Nick Peters, Manager
209 E Wisconsin Ave
Milwaukee WI 53202
414-274-6400; Fax: 414-274-6408
800-236-7323
Subjects: 99
Numbers ST-SB-BT
Author Signings: Yes; Catalog: Yes, monthly newsletter

Wyoming

Cabin Fever Books
Judy Brannan
163 S Fifth St
Lander WY 82520-3001
307-332-9580
Subjects: 99
Author Signings: Yes

The Thistle Book Shop
Debra Reily, Buyer
1243 Rumsey Ave
Cody WY 82414
307-587-6635; Fax: 307-587-6635
Subjects: 99
Comments: Very small bookstore.

Tow Ocean Books
Anna Moscicki/Michael Kenny
128 E Ramshorn
PO Box 599
Dubois WY 82513
307-455-3554
Subjects: 61-99
Memo: Interested in basically anything interesting.
Author Signings: Yes

The Valley Bookstore Inc
Stephen W Ashley, Owner
125 N Cache
PO Box G
Jackson WY 83001
307-733-4533; Fax: 307-733-6498
Subjects: 99
Author Signings: Yes

Canada

British Columbia

Olivers Books
Mark Beugre, Owner
398 Baker St
Nelson BC V1L 4H5
604-352-7525; Fax: 604-352-7277
Subjects: 99
Numbers: 14,000 titles
Author Signings: Yes

People's Co-op Bookstore
Ray Viaud, Manager
1391 Commercial Dr
Vancouver BC V5L 3X5
604-253-6442
Subjects: 99

Abbreviations Used

Territory

CN	Canada
IT	International
MX	Mexico
OT	Other
US	United States with some state abbreviations for the different states

Markets

BK	Bookstores
CO	Colleges
JB	Jobbers
MM	Mass Markets
NS	Newsstands
OT	Other
PL	Public Libraries
RO	Retail Outlets
SC	Schools
SL	Special Libraries

Items

CA	Calendars
CO	Comics
CR	Craft Items
GA	Games
GC	Greeting Cards
GI	Gifts
HC	Hardcovers
MA	Maps and Atlases
MG	General / Special Magazines
ML	Literary Magazines
MM	Mass Market Books
NP	Newspapers
OP	Out of Print Books
OT	Other Items
PB	Trade Paperbacks
PO	Posters
RC	Records
RM	Remainders
SB	Stickers/Bookmarks
ST	Stationery
SW	Software
TA	Tapes, Audio
TO	Toys
TV	Tapes, Video
TX	Textbooks
US	Used books

Subject Category Codes

10 **General Non-Fiction**
11 **Fine Arts**
    11P   Photography
12 **Architecture / Construction**
    12A   Architecture
    12B   Building / Construction
13 **Alternative Social Issues**
14 **Performing Arts**
    14D   Dance
    14M   Music
    14T   Theatre / Drama
15 **Animals / Pets**
16 **Transportation**
    16A   Automobiles
    16R   Railroads
17 **Biographies / Celebrities**
    17B   Biographies
    17C   Celebrities
    17P   Real People
19 **Business / Economics**
    19A   Accounting
    19B   Banking
    19C   Careers / Labor
    19E   Economics
    19F   Fund-raising / Non-profits
    19G   Management
    19H   Real Estate / Home
    19I   Investment
    19L   Law
    19M   Marketing / Sales
    19O   Opportunity Seekers
    19P   Purchasing
    19R   Retail Sales
    19S   Small Business
    19X   Industrial / Production
21 **Children's Interests**
    21T   Teenagers
23 **Computers / Technology**
    23C   Computers
    23E   Home Electronics
    23T   Technology
24 **Engineering**
25 **Consumer Issues**
    25T   Consumer Taxes
27 **Cooking / Food / Nutrition**
28 **Collectibles / Antiques**
29 **Crafts / Hobbies / How-to**
    29C   Crafts
    29H   Hobbies and How-to
31 **Education / Child Development**
    31C   Child Development
    31E   Education / Teaching
    31P   Parenting
33 **Entertainment / Movies / Humor**
    33C   Comics / Comedy
    33H   Humor
    33M   Movies
    33T   Television / Radio

35 **Family / Marriage / Retirement**
    35A   Aging Issues / Retirement
    35F   Family
    35M   Marriage
    35R   Relationships / Romance
    35S   Sexual Issues
36 **Lifestyle/Feature**
37 **Gay / Lesbian**
39 **Health / Medicine / Exercise**
    39D   Disabilities
    39E   Exercise
    39H   Holistic Health
    39M   Medicine / Doctors
    39R   Recovery / Drug Abuse
40 **Beauty / Fashion**
    40B   Beauty
    40F   Fashion
41 **History**
    41A   American History
    41G   Genealogy / Family History
    41W   World History
43 **House / Garden**
    43D   Home Decorating
    43G   Gardening
    43H   House and Home
44 **International Issues and News**
    44A   Asia
    44E   Europe
    44F   Africa
    44S   South America
    44Z   Australia / New Zealand
45 **Languages**
    45X   Linquistics
    45W   Words
47 **Literature / Humanities**
48 **Military**
49 **Minority Issues and Studies**
    49A   Native American
    49B   Black
    49H   Hispanic / Chicano
    49O   Other
51 **Nature / Ecology / Conservation**
    51A   Agriculture / Farming
    51B   Biology / Botany
    51E   Environmental Issues
    51N   Nature
53 **New Age / Astrology**
54 **Philosophy / Metaphysics**
    54M   Metaphysics
    54P   Philosophy
55 **Politics / Government**
    55C   Crime / Police Work
    55G   Government
    55L   Law
    55P   Politics

56 **Publishing / PR / Writing**
    56M   Media / Publicity
    56P   Publishing
    56W   Writing
    56X   Printing
57 **Psychology / Self-Help**
    57B   Behavior
    57P   Psychology / Therapy
    57S   Self-Help / Advice
59 **Reference Books**
61 **Regional Issues and Interests**
63 **Religions**
    63C   Catholic
    63E   Eastern Religions
    63J   Jewish
    63M   Muslim
    63O   Other Religions
    63P   Protestant
65 **Sociology / Anthropology**
    65A   Anthropology
    65S   Social Issues
67 **Science / Mathematics**
    67A   Astronomy / Space
    67M   Mathematics
    67S   Science
69 **Sports / Games / Recreation**
    69G   Games
    69H   Hunting / Fishing
    69R   Recreation / Hiking
    69S   Spectator Sports
70 **Nautical / Aviation**
    70A   Aviation
    70N   Nautical / Sailing
71 **Travel / Geography**
    71D   Domestic Travel
    71F   Foreign Travel
    71G   Geography
73 **Women's Issues**

75 **General Fiction**

76 **Children's Stories**
77 **Contemporary Novels**
78 **Ethnic / Minority Literature**
79 **Folklore / Fairy Tales**
80 **Foreign Literature**
81 **Historical Novels**
82 **Horror Novels**
83 **Literary Novels**
84 **Mysteries / Detective Novels**
85 **Romances / Gothic Romances**
86 **Science Fiction / Fantasy**
87 **Suspense / Adventure Novels**
88 **Westerns**
89 **Young Adult Novels**
90 **Short Stories / Anthologies**
95 **Poetry**

97 **News / Current Events**

99 **General Interest**

Book Clubs

Here are the names and addresses of book clubs that might be interested in purchasing book club rights or actual copies of appropriate books. Send them information on your forthcoming books at least five to six months ahead of time (if at all possible). While some of the special-interest book clubs will buy books regardless of publication date, the large general interest book clubs require at least six months notice prior to publication date.

A

Arrow Book Club
Ms Pat Brigandi, Editor
Scholastic Inc
555 Broadway
New York NY 10012
212-343-6100; Fax: 212-343-6928
Subjects: 21-76
Numbers: 40 titles
Memo: Offers books, posters, and a few other items. Monthly — Sept thru June.

Audio Book Club
Marc Sinensky, Exec VP
2295 Corporate Blvd NW #222
Boca Raton FL 33442
407-241-1426; Fax: 407-241-9887
Subjects: 19-35R-53-57-75-99
Items: TA(spoken word audio only)

Audio-Tech Business Book Summaries
Bernard C Ebershaw, Editor
Suite A-461
117 W Harrison Bldg, 6th Fl
Chicago IL 60605
312-549-1910; Fax: 312-549-1913
800-776-1910
Subjects: 19-19G-19M
Comments: Audio summaries of books

Aviators' Guild
Chris Gemmel
McGraw-Hill/Tab Book Clubs
860 Taylor Station Rd
Black Lake OH 43004
614-759-3666; Fax: 614-759-3748
Subjects: 70A

Bob's Book Club
Bob Cox, Pres
6209 SW Third St
Des Moines IA 50315
515-285-7377
Subjects: 99
Comments: A very small book store
Memo: Catalog sent out to customers on request.

B

Book-of-the-Month Club
Tracy Brown, Editor-in-Chief
Time-Life Bldg
1271 Ave of the Americas
New York NY 10020-1368
212-522-4200; Fax: 212-522-0303
Subjects: 17-75-99
Memo: Victoria Skurnick & Andre Bernard, Exec Editors.

Book-of-the-Month Club
Phyllis Robinson, Calendar Ed
Time-Life Bldg
1271 Ave of the Americas
New York NY 10020-1368
212-522-4200; Fax: 212-522-0303
Subjects: 11-99(calendars)

Book-of-the-Month Club
Greg Tobin, Paperback Ed
Time-Life Bldg
1271 Ave of the Americas
New York NY 10020-1368
212-522-4200; Fax: 212-522-0303
Subjects: 99(trade paperbacks)

Books of Light
Leslie Swanson, Book Buyer
Ariel Press
14230 Phillips Cir
Alpharetta GA 30201
404-664-4886
800-336-7769
Subjects: 39-53-54-57-86

Books of My Very Own
David Allender, Dir
Book-of-the-Month Club/Time-Life
1271 Ave of the Americas
New York NY 10020-1368
212-522-4200; Fax: 212-522-0303
Subjects: 21-31-76
Numbers: 100 titles
Memo: Once every 5 weeks.

C

Carnival Book Club
Book Buyer
PO Box 6035
Columbia MO 65205
800-828-1696
Subjects: 21-76(simpler than arrow)
Comments: Some reprints, grades 3 to 5
Numbers: 33 titles

Cassette-of-the-Month Club
Jeffrey Norton
Audio Forum
96 Broad St
Guilford CT 06437
203-453-9794
800-243-1234
Subjects: 17-41-47-57-75-99
Comments: Audio tapes only.
Memo: Variety of catalogs sent 2x a year.

Catholic Book Club
Fr David Toolan, Editor
The America Press
106 West 56th St
New York NY 10019-3803
212-581-4640; Fax: 212-399-3596
Subjects: 63C
Numbers: 3,000

Catholic Digest Book Club
Patricia, Mgr
111 10th St
Des Moines IA 50709
515-284-6785
Subjects: 41-57-63C-75-84
Comments: For Catholic families.

Chemical Engineers Book Club
Chris Gemmel
McGraw-Hill Book Clubs
860 Taylor Station Rd
Black Lake OH 43004
614-759-3666; Fax: 614-759-3748
Subjects: 24(engineering)-67

Chemists' Book Club
Chris Gemmel
McGraw-Hill/Tab Book Clubs
860 Taylor Station Rd
Black Lake OH 43004
614-759-3666; Fax: 614-759-3748
Subjects: 67(chemistry)

Children Book-of-the-Month Club
Larry Shapiro, Dir
Time-Life Bldg
1271 Ave of the Americas
New York NY 10020-1368
212-522-4200
Subjects: 21-31-76

Cinema Book Society
D Richard Baer, Pres
Hollywood Film Archive
8344 Melrose Ave
Hollywood CA 90069
213-933-3345
Subjects: 33(movies/TV/video)
Comments: Movie reference books.

Civil Engineers' Book Club
Chris Gemmel, Mgr
McGraw-Hill/Tab Book Clubs
860 Taylor Station Rd
Black Lake OH 43004
614-759-3666; Fax: 614-759-3748
Subjects: 12-24(engineering)

Columbia House Audio Books
Gordon Henry
1221 Ave of the Americas
19th Fl
New York NY 10020
212-596-2680; Fax: 212-596-2213
Subjects: 99
Comments: Spoken word audio.

Columbia House Music Club
Doreen McCurley
Columbia House
1221 Ave of the Americas
New York NY 10020
212-445-7282; Fax: 212-596-2168
Subjects: 14M-17-33
Items: CD-RC-TA-OT(misc gift items)

Columbia House Video Club
Mktg Director
1221 Ave of the Americas
New York NY 10020
Fax: 212-596-2168
Subjects: 33M
Items: Videotapes/some misc gifts

The Computer Book Club
Chris Gemmel
McGraw-Hill/Tab Book Clubs
860 Taylor Station Rd
Black Lake OH 43004
614-759-3666; Fax: 614-759-3748
Subjects: 23C

Computer Professionals' Books Society
Chris Gemmel
McGraw-Hill/Tab Book Clubs
860 Taylor Station Rd
Black Lake OH 43004
614-759-3666; Fax: 614-759-3748
Subjects: 23C(mainframes/networks)

Conservative Book Club
Marian Kromberg, Editor
33 Oakland Ave
Harrison NY 10528-3709
914-835-0900; Fax: 914-835-2708
Subjects: 19-55-63
Comments: Conservative books.

Country Home & Garden Book Club
Jane Hamada, Editor
Meredith Book Clubs
150 East 52nd St 3rd Fl
New York NY 10022-6017
212-522-1212; Fax: 212-715-8781
Subjects: 27-28-29-35-39-43D-43G-43H-69

Crafter's Choice Book Club
B J Berti, Editor
BOMC / Time-Life Bldg
1271 Ave of the Americas
New York NY 10020-1368
212-522-4200; Fax: 212-522-0303
Subjects: 29-43D
Other: 15x a year
Numbers: 200-300 titles

Crossings Book Club
Michelle Rapkin, Editor-in-chief
Doubleday Book Clubs
1540 Broadway
New York NY 10036
212-782-7200; Fax: 212-782-7205
800-223-6834
Subjects: 35F-63-99(Christian book club)

D

Dance Book Club
Constance Woodford, Dir
Princeton Book Co
PO Box 57
Pennington NJ 08534
609-737-8178
Subjects: 14D

Deseret Book Club
Rex Carlisle
40 E South Temple
PO Box 30178
Salt Lake City UT 84130-0178
801-534-1515; Fax: 801-578-3392
Subjects: 31P-35F-63(Mormons)-99
Comments: HC-PB-MM
Other: Some trade
Numbers: 40M members

Detective Book Club
Herbert Cohen, Pres
Platinum Press
311 Crossways Park
Woodbury NY 11797
516-364-1800; Fax: 516-364-1899
Subjects: 84
Numbers: 30 catalogs per year

Doubleday Book Club
Barbara Hayes, Dir
6550 E 30th St
PO Box 6340
Indianapolis IN 46209-9463
Subjects: 99

Doubleday Book Club
Jean Glass, Dir
Music and Video
1540 Broadway
New York NY 10036
212-782-7200; Fax: 212-782-7205

Doubleday Childrens' Book Club
Margaret Milnes, Editor
Doubleday Book Clubs
1540 Broadway
New York NY 10036
212-782-7200; Fax: 212-782-7205
800-688-4442
Subjects: 21-76-79

E

Ecological Book Club
Roger Corbin
6 N Water St
Greenwich CT 06830-5817
203-531-7755
Subjects: 13-39-51E-51N-43G
Other: Catalog 6 x year
Memo: Mail order book club.

Electronics Book Club
Chris Gemmel
McGraw-Hill/Tab Book Clubs
860 Taylor Station Rd
Black Lake OH 43004
614-759-3666; Fax: 614-759-3748
Subjects: 23E-24(home hobbyists/electronics)

Electronics Engineers' Book Club
Chris Gemmel
McGraw-Hill/Tab Book Clubs
860 Taylor Station Rd
Black Lake OH 43004
614-759-3666; Fax: 614-759-3748
Subjects: 23-24(electronics)

Evangelical Book Club
Joyce Bohn, Gen Mgr
Mott Media
1000 E Huron St
Milford MI 48381
810-685-8773
Subjects: 63(Christian)
Comments: Evangelical pastors/students
Numbers: 11,000

F

Firefly Book Club
Steve Metzger, Editor
Scholastic Inc
555 Broadway
New York NY 10012
212-343-6100; Fax: 212-343-6928
Subjects: 21-76
Comments: Some reprints, preschool kids.
Numbers: 33 titles
Memo: This club is distributed through schools, monthly Sept thru June.

Fireside Theatre
Bess Whitingham, Editor
Doubleday Book Clubs
1540 Broadway
New York NY 11036
212-782-7200; Fax: 212-782-7205
Subjects: 11-14-33

G

The Good Cook
Pat Adrian, Editor
BOMC / Time-Life Bldg
1271 Ave of the Americas
New York NY 10020-1368
212-522-4200; Fax: 212-522-0303
Subjects: 27-29-39-43G
Catalogs 15x a year
Memo: BJ Berti, Craft Editor. Hundreds of titles.

Graphic Artist's Book Club
Ms Mert Ransdell, Dir
F & W Publishing
1507 Dana Ave
Cincinnati OH 45207
513-531-2222; Fax: 513-531-4744
Subjects: 11
Other 300 titles
Numbers: 20,000 members

Guild America Books
Barbara Greenman, Editor
Doubleday Book Clubs
1540 Broadway
New York NY 10036
212-782-7200; Fax: 212-782-7205
800-223-6834
Subjects: 99(publishes titles also)

H

History Book Club
Nancy Whitin, Dir
Kathleen McDermott, Editor
BOMC / Time-Life Bldg
1271 Ave of the Americas
New York NY 10020-1368
212-522-4200
Subjects: 17-41-55-65-97
Catalog 17x a year
Memo: Titles vary — 180+.

J

The Jewish Book Club
Pam Roth, Editor
Jason Aronson Inc
230 Livingston St PO Box 941
Northvale NJ 07647
201-767-4093; Fax: 201-767-4330
Subjects: 63J
Comments: Jamie Lochansky, Assoc Editor.

Judaica Book Club
Marvin Sekler
Jonathan David Publishers
68-22 Eliot Ave
Middle Village NY 11379-1131
718-456-8611; Fax: 718-894-2818
Subjects: 63J
Other: Catalog 6/yr
Numbers: 18,000 members

L

Laissez Faire Book Club
Andrea Millen Rich, Publ
Ctr For Independent Thought
73 Spring St #507
New York NY 10012-5802
212-925-8992; Fax: 212-219-1581
Subjects: 19E-25-31E-41-55-54
Comments: Book club is part of catalog.
Other: 200 titles
Memo: Center For Independent Thought, 942 Howard St, San Francisco, CA 94103; 415-541-9780; FAX: 415-541-0597; 800-326-0996. Anita Anderson, Editorial Director. David M Brown, Managing Editor. Books on liberty, libertarianism, objectivism, capitalism, philosophy, ethics, political theory, education, & economics.

Large Print Home Library
Ellen Asher, Co-Assoc Editor
Doubleday Book Clubs
1540 Broadway
New York NY 10036
212-782-7200; Fax: 212-782-7205
800-223-6834
Subjects: 99(large print books)
Memo: Andrew Wheeler, Co-Associate Editor.

Limited Editions Club
Sidney Shiff, Pres
980 Madison Ave
New York NY 10021
212-737-7600; Fax: 212-249-3939
Subjects: 11-75
Comments: Illustrated literature.
Memo: Original prints.

Literary Guild of America
Karen Daly, Editor-in-Chief
Doubleday Book Clubs
1540 Broadway
New York NY 10036
212-782-7253; Fax: 212-782-7205
800-223-6834
Subjects: 99
Memo: Sandra Sandler, Executive Editor.

Lucky Book Club
Eva Moore, Editor
Scholastic Inc
555 Broadway
New York NY 10012
212-343-6100; Fax: 212-343-6928
Subjects: 21-76
Comments: Some reprints, grades 2-3.
Numbers: 40 titles
Memo: This club is distributed through schools, monthly Sept thru June.

M

Mechanical Engineers' Book Club
Chris Gemmel, Mgr
McGraw-Hill/Tab Book Clubs
860 Taylor Station Rd
Black Lake OH 43004
614-759-3666; Fax: 614-759-3748
Subjects: 24(engineering)

Men's Health Book Club
Renee James, Assoc Aqs Mgr
Russ Wild, Editor
Bill Gottlieb, Editor-in-Chief
Rodale Press
400 S 10th St
Emmaus PA 18098-0099
610-967-5171; Fax: 610-967-8962
Subjects: 27-35-39-39H
Memo: Topics: holistic health, weight loss, nutrition, preventive medicine, stress control, etc.

Military Book Club
Michael Stephenson, Editor
Doubleday Book Clubs
1540 Broadway
New York NY 10036
212-782-7200; Fax: 212-782-7205
800-223-6834
Subjects: 41-48(military)-87

Money Book Club
Laurie Calkhoven, Editor
BOMC / Time-Life Bldg
1271 Ave of the Americas
New York NY 10020-1368
212-522-4200; Fax: 212-522-0303
Subjects: 19I
Other: 15x a year
Numbers: 300 titles

Movie Entertainment Book Club
Harry Crocker, Editor
Eagle Book Club
422 1st St SE
Washington DC 20003
202-546-5005
Subjects: 14-17-33

Music Book Society
Marc Comstock, Dir
Riverwalk Bldg 5
360 Merrimack St
Lawrence MA 01843-1999
508-689-7284; Fax: 508-689-3184
800-262-0065
Subjects: 14M-17-41

Mystery Guild
Mary Ann Eckels, Editor
Doubleday Book Clubs
1540 Broadway
New York NY 10036
212-782-7200; Fax: 212-782-7205
800-223-6834
Subjects: 84

N

Nature Book Society
Holly Lavieri, Asst Aqs Mgr
Rodale Press
400 S 10th St
Emmaus PA 18098-0099
610-967-5171; Fax: 610-967-8962
Subjects: 15-29-43-51-69-71

Nautical Book Club
Ms Mert Ransdell, Dir
F & W Publishing
1507 Dana Ave
Cincinnati OH 45207
513-531-2222; Fax: 513-531-4744
Subjects: 70N

North Light Book Club
Ms Mert Ransdell, Dir
F & W Publishing
1507 Dana Ave
Cincinnati OH 45207
513-531-2222; Fax: 513-531-4744
Subjects: 11(fine art)
Other: 300 titles
Numbers: 55,000

O

Organic Gardening Book Club
Holly Lavieri, Asst Aqs Mgr
Rodale Press
400 S 10th St
Emmaus PA 18098-0099
610-967-5171; Fax: 610-967-8962
Subjects: 27-43-51

P

Pathway Book Clubs
Marc Comstock, Editor
Riverwalk Bldg 5
360 Merrimack St
Lawrence Ma 01843
508-689-7284; Fax: 508-689-3184
800-262-0065
Subjects: 14M(classical & opera)

Prevention Book Club
Renee James, Assoc Aqs Mgr
Rodale Press
400 S 10th St
Emmaus PA 18098-0099
610-967-5171; Fax: 610-967-8962
Subjects: 27-35-39-39H
Comments: Primarily women, ages 45-65
Memo: Topics: holistic health, weight loss, nutrition, preventive medicine, stress control, etc.

Provident Book Store
Jack C Scott, Dir
616 Walnut Ave
Scottdale PA 15683-1945
412-887-8500; Fax: 412-887-3111
Subjects: 17-35-57-63(Mennonite)-99
Catalog: 6/yr
Numbers: 5500

Psychotherapy Book Club
Juliann Popp, Mg Editor
Jason Aronson Inc
230 Livingston St PO Box 941
Northvale NJ 07647
201-767-4093; Fax: 201-767-4330
Subjects: 57
Other: 1000 titles

Q

Quality Paperback Book Club
David Rosen, Sr Editor
BOMC / Time-Life Bldg
1271 Ave of the Americas
New York NY 10020-1368
212-522-6596; Fax: 212-522-0303
Subjects: 99
Comments: Greg Tobin, VP.
Memo: Judith Estrin, Sr Editor.

R

Reader's Digest Condensed Books
Barbara J Morgan, Editor
Reader's Digest Assn
Pleasantville NY 10570
914-238-1000; Fax: 914-238-4559
Subjects: 99
Comments: Condensed books

S

Science Fiction Book Club
Ellen Asher, Editor
Doubleday Book Clubs
1540 Broadway
New York NY 10036
212-782-7200; Fax: 212-782-7205
800-223-6834
Subjects: 86

See-Saw Book Club
Heidi Kilgraf, Editor
Scholastic Inc
555 Broadway
New York NY 10012
212-343-6100; Fax: 212-343-6928
Subjects: 21-76
Comments: Some reprints, grades K-1.
Numbers: 33 titles
Memo: This club is distributed through schools, monthly — Sept thru June.

Smart Practice Book Club
Joy Tevis, Buyer
3400 E McDowell (85038)
PO Box 29222
Phoenix AZ 85008
602-225-9090
800-528-1052
Subjects: 19-27(nutrition)39-57
Comments: For dental and medical offices.
Memo: Semantodonics. Karen Burk, Product Manager.

Spiritual Book Associates
Robert Hamma, Editor
Ave Maria Press Bldg
Notre Dame IN 46556
219-287-2838
Subjects: 63C
Catalog: 8x per yr
Numbers: 8,800 members

T

TAB Club
Greg Holch, Editor
Scholastic Inc
555 Broadway
New York NY 10012
212-343-6100; Fax: 212-343-6928
Subjects: 21T-89
Comments: Some reprints, grades 7-9.
Numbers: 40 titles
Memo: TAB stands for Teen Age Books. This club is distributed through schools, monthly — Sept thru June.

Theological Book Service
Denise Sedivy, Dir
7373 S Lovers Lane Rd
Franklin WI 53132-1800
414-529-6400; Fax: 414-529-6419
Subjects: 63(Christian)
Comments: Catholic/Protestant clergy.
Catalog: 14x per yr
Numbers: 22,000 members

Troll Book Club
Teacher's Specials
100 Corporate Dr
Mahwah NJ 07430
201-529-4000; Fax: 201-529-9347
800-526-5289
Subjects: 21-31E-76
Comments: Primarily for women and children.

Troll Book Club
Book Club Acquisitions
100 Corporate Dr
Mahwah NJ 07430
201-529-4000; Fax: 201-529-9347
800-526-5289
Subjects: 21-27-31-35-39-75-76-79-89-99
Comments: Primarily for women and children.

Troll Book Club
Children's Books
100 Corporate Dr
Mahwah NJ 07430
201-529-4000; Fax: 201-529-9347
800-526-5289
Subjects: 21-31-76-79-89
Comments: Primarily for women and children.

Troll Book Club
Editorial Dept
2 Lethbridge Plz
Mahwah NJ 07430-2139
800-541-1097; Fax: 201-529-8382
Subjects: 21-99
Comments: K thru 3rd grade. Primarily for women and children.

W

Woodworking Book Club
Mert Ransdell, Dir
F & W Publishing
1507 Dana Ave
Cincinnati OH 45207
513-531-2222; Fax: 513-531-4744
Subjects: 29H-43H
Other: 100 titles

Writer's Digest Book Club
Mert Ransdell, Dir
F & W Publishing
1507 Dana Ave
Cincinnati OH 45207
513-531-2222; Fax: 513-531-4744
Subjects: 47-56(writing)-59
Other: 150 titles

Y

Young Reader's Book Club
Barbara Gregory, Editor
Grolier Enterprises
Sherman Turnpike
Danbury CT 06816
203-797-3500; Fax: 203-797-3197
Subjects: 21-76-79
Comments: Ages 3-7
Memo: This company also publishes two other book clubs: The Disney Wonderful World of Reading Book Club (ages 3-10), and Dr. Seuss and Friends Beginning Reader's Program Book Club (ages 3-6).

Abbreviations Used

Territory

CN	Canada
IT	International
MX	Mexico
OT	Other
US	United States with some state abbreviations for the different states

Markets

BK	Bookstores
CO	Colleges
JB	Jobbers
MM	Mass Markets
NS	Newsstands
OT	Other
PL	Public Libraries
RO	Retail Outlets
SC	Schools
SL	Special Libraries

Items

CA	Calendars
CO	Comics
CR	Craft Items
GA	Games
GC	Greeting Cards
GI	Gifts
HC	Hardcovers
MA	Maps and Atlases
MG	General / Special Magazines
ML	Literary Magazines
MM	Mass Market Books
NP	Newspapers
OP	Out of Print Books
OT	Other Items
PB	Trade Paperbacks
PO	Posters
RC	Records
RM	Remainders
SB	Stickers/Bookmarks
ST	Stationery
SW	Software
TA	Tapes, Audio
TO	Toys
TV	Tapes, Video
TX	Textbooks
US	Used books

FOURTEEN PERMISSIONS CAVEATS, CURVEBALLS and NASTY LITTLE SECRETS

Copyright © by John B. McHugh, 1996

Seeking permissions is an activity with many interesting surprises. Maintain a healthy sense of skepticism when you seek permission so that you will not be unpleasantly surprised.

To help you navigate some of the more "tricky currents" inherent in permissions work, I offer the following fourteen suggestions.

- 1. Remember Copyright Attorney Lloyd Jassin's axiom: "There is no **free** speech, only **fee** speech."
- 2. Ask "Do I **really need** to request permission to use this material?"
- 3. Remember "more is less." Ask only for **those** rights you **need**.
- 4. Always get the permission **IN WRITING!**
- 5. Recognize that in some instances **both** author **and** publisher will need to grant permission.
- 6. Don't assume **out-of-print means** public domain.
- 7. Watch for "Third Party Content." The copyright holder of the major work **may not hold rights** to a portion of the material for which they received permissions from another copyright owner.
- 8. Alertness for possible "Third Party Content" will protect you from "embedded copyright," i.e., copyrighted material **not readily apparent** on the surface.
- 9. Beware of "Thin Copyright." "Thin Copyright" describes a situation when the apparent copyright holder may in fact **not be authorized** to grant permission. For example, a photographer may hold copyright to a transparency of a Picasso painting, but the ultimate copyright is vested in the Picasso estate.
- 10. Being alert for the "Thin Copyright" scenario may save you from the "False Positive" trap, i.e., when the grantor doesn't hold copyright and cannot grant you unencumbered permission.
- 11. Note, that some permissions are subject to professional standards, i.e., the content of client interviews by psychologists and psychiatrists may be **privileged** information and subject to a release from the client.
- 12. Never grant "on line" rights without requiring a **precise definition** of the meaning of "on line" rights. Grant only nonexclusive rights for a specific term, i.e., set a **time limit** on the license.
- 13. Remember courts assume that the rights belong to the creator or author in the absence of any evidence to the contrary.
- 14. "Good faith efforts" will not protect you from the consequences of copyright infringement if you have in fact infringed another's copyright.

Reprinted from *PERMISSIONS MANAGEMENT FOR REQUESTERS AND GRANTERS: DEALING WITH COPYRIGHT AND FAIR USE*, 1996, John B. McHugh, 5747 N. Ames, Glendale, WI 53209.

Rights Buyers

Here are the names and addresses of some of the major rights buyers for large print books, movie/TV rights, video and audio rights. At the end of this section are listed several literary agents who specialize in helping smaller publishers sell subsidiary rights to their books.

Besides large print and screenplay rights, you can also sell serial rights to magazines and newspapers, reprint rights to mass-market book publishers, book club rights (see previous section), and foreign rights.

Audio Rights Buyer

Audio Literature
John Hunt
370 W San Bruno Ave #F
San Bruno CA 94066
415-583-9700; Fax: 415-583-0235
Http://audioliterature.com
Subjects: 53-99

Audio Renaissance Tapes
Joe McNeely, Acquistion Mgr
5858 Wilshire Blvd #205
Los Angeles CA 90036
213-939-1840; Fax: 213-939-6436
Subjects: 19-39-53-57-71-84-86-88

Books on Tape
Barbara Singleton, Rights Buyer
PO Box 7900
Newport Beach CA 92658
714-548-5525; Fax: 714-548-6574
800-626-3333
Subjects: 10-17-87-99

Brilliance
Eileen Hutton, Editorial Dir
1810-B Industrial Park Dr
PO Box 114
Grand Haven MI 49417-0114
800-222-3225
616-846-5256
Subjects: 31E-75-84-99
Comments: Unabridge editions.

Dimension 5
Ester Nelson
Kingsbridge Sta
PO Box 403
Bronx NY 10463
718-548-6112
Subjects: 14M-14D-21
Comments: Children's songbooks.

Durkin Hayes Publishing
Willem Van Zon, Mg Ed
1 Colomba Dr
Niagara Falls NY 14305
716-298-5150; Fax: 716-298-5607
800-962-5200(orders/cust serv)
Subjects: 75-99

Harper Collins Audio
Cori Eckert, Assoc Editor
Ann Gaudinier, Editorial Dir
10 East 53rd St
New York NY 10022-5299
212-207-7000; Fax: 212-207-7759
Subjects: 99

Listen USA!
Diana White, Buyer
Greenwich Office Park
10 Valley Dr Bldg #9
Greenwich CT 06831
203-661-0101; Fax: 203-661-8472
Subjects: 99

Listening Library
Diana Pazizza, Purch Agent
One Park Ave
Old Greenwich CT 06870-1722
203-637-3616; Fax: 203-698-1998
Subjects: 21-76-99

Live Oak Media
Thelma Oakley
PO Box 652
Pine Plains NY 12567
518-398-1010; Fax: 518-398-1070
Subjects: 21-76

Metacom Inc
Tom Connelly, Bus Affairs Mgr
5353 Nathan Ln
Plymouth MN 55442
612-553-2000; Fax: 612-553-0424
800-328-4818
Subjects: 99
Memo: Phil Levin, Pres/CEO.

Random House Audiobooks
Harold Clarke
201 East 50th St 27th Fl
New York NY 10022-7703
212-751-2600
Subjects: 99

Recorded Books
Henry Trentman, Pres
270 Skipjack Rd
Prince Frederick MD 20678
800-638-1304; Fax: 410-535-5499
Subjects: 99
Comments: 600 titles.

Entertainment Directories

Film Directors Guide
Lone Eagle Publishing
2337 Roscomare Rd #9
Los Angeles CA 90077-1815
310-471-8066; Fax: 310-471-4969
Subjects: 33-99
Comments: 1-800-FILM-BKS
Other: $65.00

Film Producers Studios & Agents
Lone Eagle Publishing
2337 Roscomare Rd
Los Angeles CA 90077
310-471-8066
Subjects: 33-99
Comments: Movie rights possibilities.
Other: $55.00

Hollywood Creative Directory
3000 W Olympic Blvd #2525
Santa Monica CA 90404
310-315-4815; Fax: 310-315-4816
Subjects: 33M-33T(movie/TV rights buyers)
Comments: Published 3 times per year.
Other: $49.50

Who's Who in Entertainment
Marquis Who's Who
Reed Reference Publishing
121 Chanlon Rd
New Providence NJ 07974
908-464-6800; Fax: 908-665-6688
800-521-8110
Subjects: 11-14-17-33(entertainment)
Numbers: 18,000

Large Print Rights Buyers

ABC-CLIO
Mary Kay Opicka, Acquisitions
130 Cremenno Dr
PO Box 1911
Santa Barbara CA 93117
805-968-1911; Fax: 805-685-9685
800-422-2546
Subjects: 21-76(large print books)
Comments: Large print rights.

Other Rights Buyer

Allegro New Media
Barry Cinnamon, CEO
16 Passaic Bldg 6
Fairfield NJ 07004
201-808-1992; Fax: 201-808-2645
Subjects: 19-23C-71-86
Comments: Books on CD-ROM.

Paperback Rights Buyer

Ace Books
Sr Editor
Science Fiction & Fantasy
200 Madison Ave
New York NY 10016-3902
212-951-8800; Fax: 212-545-8917
Subjects: 86
Comments: MM publisher.

Avon Books
Linda Raglan Cunningham
Editorial Director
1350 Ave of the Americas
New York NY 10019
212-261-6800; Fax: 212-261-6895
Subjects: 99

Avon Books
Sr Editor
Avon Romance Line
1350 Ave of the Americas
New York NY 10019
212-261-6800; Fax: 212-261-6895
Subjects: 81-85

Baen Publishing Enterprises
PO Box 1403
Riverdale NY 10471
718-548-3100; Fax: 718-548-3102
Subjects: 86
Items: PB-MM

Ballantine Books
Buyer
201 East 50th St
New York NY 10022-7799
212-751-2600; Fax: 212-572-2676
Subjects: 75-81-85

Berkeley Publishing
Judity Palais, Editor
200 Madison Ave
New York NY 10016-3999
212-951-8800; Fax: 212-545-8917
Subjects: 99

Carroll & Graf Publishers
Kent Carroll, Exec Editor
260 Fifth Ave
New York NY 10001-6404
212-889-8772; Fax: 212-545-7909
Subjects: 17-75

DAW Books
Betsy Wollheim, Editor
375 Hudson 3rd Fl
New York NY 10014
212-366-2000
Subjects: 86

Del Rey Books
Buyer
Ballantine Books
201 East 50th St
New York NY 10022-7771
212-751-2600
Subjects: 86

Fawcett Books
Barbara Dicks, PB Rights Buyer
Random House
201 East 50th St
New York NY 10022-6502
212-751-2600; Fax: 212-572-4912
Subjects: 99

Gold Eagle Books
Randall Toye, Ed Dir
Harlequin Enterprises
225 Duncan Mill Rd
Don Mills ON M3B 3K9
416-445-5860; Fax: 416-445-8655
Subjects: 82-84-85-87

Harlequin Romances
Dominique Mondoulet-Wise, Editor
Randall Toye, Editorial Dir
Harlequin Enterprises
225 Duncan Mill Rd
Don Mills ON Canada M3B 3K9
416-445-5860
Subjects: 19-59-75-81-84-85

Kensington Books
Beth Lieberman, Editor
850 3rd Ave
New York NY 10022
212-407-1500
Subjects: 99

Leisure Books
Alicia Condon, Editor
276 Fifth Ave #1008
New York NY 10001
212-725-8811
Subjects: 75-81-85-88

New American Library
Hilary Ross, Editor
NAL/Signet
375 Hudson St
New York NY 10014
212-366-2000; Fax: 212-366-2666
Subjects: 75-77-81-85

Penguin Books
Patricia Mulcahy, Exec Editor
Viking Penguin
375 Hudson St 4th Fl
New York NY 10014
212-366-2000
Subjects: 99

Pocket Books
Linda Marrow, Editor
Simon & Schuster Bldg
1230 Ave of the Americas
New York NY 10020-1586
212-698-7000; Fax: 212-698-7007
Subjects: 73-75-77-82

Silhouette Books
Isabell Swift, Editor-in-Chief
Harlequin Enterprises
300 East 42nd St
New York NY 10017
212-682-6080; Fax: 212-682-4539
Subjects: 81-85

Tor Books
175 5th Ave 14th Fl
New York NY 10010-3297
212-388-0100; Fax: 212-388-0191
Subjects: 86

Warner Books
Editor
1271 Sixth Ave
New York NY 10020
212-522-7200
Subjects: 99

William B Eerdmans Publishing
Jon Pott, Editor-in-Chief
255 Jefferson Ave SE
Grand Rapids MI 49503
616-459-4591; Fax: 616-459-6540
Subjects: 63P

Small Press Literary Agents

B K Nelson
Bonita Nelson
84 Woodland Rd
Pleasantville NY 10570
212-889-0637
Subjects: 19-57-99
Comments: Non-fiction.

Jeff Herman Agency
Jeff Herman
500 Greenwich St #501C
New York NY 10013
212-941-0540
Subjects: 99(fiction & non-fiction)
Comments: Literary agent & sub rights.

Susan Herner Rights Agency
Susan Herner
PO Box 303
Scarsdale NY 10583
914-725-8967; Fax: 914-725-8969
Subjects: 99
Comments: Reps for authors.

Writers House Inc
Albert Zockerman
Subsidiary Rights Dept
21 W 26th St
New York NY 10010
212-685-2400; Fax: 212-685-1781
Subjects: 99
Comments: For 11 small publishers.

Joseph S Ajlouny, Attorney
JSA Publications
29205 Greening St
Farmington Hills MI 48334-2945
313-932-0090; Fax: 313-932-8763
Subjects: 99
Comments: Literary agent/sub rights/other.

Video Rights Buyer

MCA Home Video
100 Universal City Plz
Universal City CA 91608
818-777-1000
Subjects: 99

Random House Video
Harold Clarke
201 E 50th St 27th Fl
New York NY 10022-7703
212-751-2600
Subjects: 99

Abbreviations Used

Territory

CN	Canada
IT	International
MX	Mexico
OT	Other
US	United States with some state abbreviations for the different states

Markets

BK	Bookstores
CO	Colleges
JB	Jobbers
MM	Mass Markets
NS	Newsstands
OT	Other
PL	Public Libraries
RO	Retail Outlets
SC	Schools
SL	Special Libraries

Items

CA	Calendars
CO	Comics
CR	Craft Items
GA	Games
GC	Greeting Cards
GI	Gifts
HC	Hardcovers
MA	Maps and Atlases
MG	General / Special Magazines
ML	Literary Magazines
MM	Mass Market Books
NP	Newspapers
OP	Out of Print Books
OT	Other Items
PB	Trade Paperbacks
PO	Posters
RC	Records
RM	Remainders
SB	Stickers/Bookmarks
ST	Stationery
SW	Software
TA	Tapes, Audio
TO	Toys
TV	Tapes, Video
TX	Textbooks
US	Used books

Mailing Lists

Lists Available from Ad-Lib Publications

Ad-Lib Publications has more than 20,500 book marketing names in our database — everything from travel booksellers to radio talk shows, from mail order catalogs that feature books to newspaper food editors, and much more.

Lists are run in zip-code sequence on 2-up pressure-sensitive labels. (4 across Cheshire format is available) List counts are subject to change. Lists are restricted to one-time usage. If you want unlimited use of the mailing lists, they are available on disk (IBM-compatible or Macintosh). We can supply them to you on a 3.5" or 5.25" high or low density disk, in the mail-merge format of your choice (Dbase, ASCII, comma- or tab-delimited). Pricing will be double for disk. To order, call **800-669-0773**. Or write to **Ad-Lib Publications, PO Box 1102, Fairfield, IA 52556-1102**. Special searches are available. Minimum List $10.00.

Booksellers

Here are just a **few** of the bookseller lists available. The number to the left is the total on the list.

- 464 — Art / Photography / Art History — $ 45.00
- 107 — Animals / Pets — $ 10.00
- 197 — Business / Careers / Economics — $ 20.00
- 803 — Children's Books — $ 80.00
- 142 — Computers / Technology — $ 15.00
- 235 — Cooking / Nutrition — $ 25.00
- 217 — Crafts / Hobbies — $ 20.00
- 314 — Health / Medicine / Holistic Health — $ 30.00
- 114 — Home / Garden — $ 10.00
- 138 — Music / Dance / Drama — $ 15.00
- 279 — Nature / Ecology / Environment — $ 30.00
- 328 — New Age / Metaphysical — $ 35.00
- 94 — Poetry — $ 10.00
- 305 — Psychology / Self-Help — $ 30.00
- 104 — Religion — $ 10.00
- 187 — Science / Mathematics — $ 15.00
- 115 — Sports / Games / Recreation — $ 10.00
- 199 — Travel / Geography — $ 20.00

Newspaper Editors

These lists can be selected from our newspaper file:

- 486 — Newspaper Book Reviewers — $ 50.00
- 549 — Arts and Entertainment Editors — $ 55.00
- 597 — Business Editors and Columnists — $ 60.00
- 625 — Children's and Family Interests — $ 60.00
- 187 — Computer Editors and Columnists — $ 20.00
- 385 — Food / Cookbook Editors — $ 40.00
- 313 — Health / Medical Editors — $ 30.00
- 274 — Home Editors — $ 20.00
- 480 — Lifestyle Editors — $ 50.00
- 240 — Religion Editors — $ 25.00
- 637 — Sports Editors and Columnists — $ 65.00
- 317 — Travel Editors — $ 30.00

Magazine Editors

Here are a few of the lists we can select from our magazine data file.

- 412 — Magazine Book Reviewers (all sorts) — $ 40.00
- 77 — Magazines for Libraries/booksellers — $ 10.00
- 633 — Serial Rights Buyers at Magazines — $ 65.00
- 221 — Art Editors — $ 20.00
- 1177 — Business Editors — $115.00
- 249 — Children's Editors — $ 25.00
- 550 — Computer Editors — $ 55.00
- 241 — Crafts and Hobbies Editors — $ 25.00
- 277 — Entertainment / Movie Editors — $ 30.00
- 213 — Fashion Editors — $ 20.00
- 315 — Food Editors — $ 30.00
- 542 — Health / Medical Editors — $ 55.00
- 295 — Home / Garden Editors — $ 30.00
- 117 — New Age Magazine Editors — $ 10.00
- 122 — Science Editors — $ 10.00
- 325 — Sports Editors — $ 35.00
- 317 — Travel Editors — $ 30.00

Book Markets

Here are a **few** other marketing lists we offer for rent.

- 119 — Book Clubs (all sorts) — $ 10.00
- 285 — Chain Store Buyers — $ 35.00
- 823 — Mail Order Catalogs carrying books — $ 75.00
- 45 — Book Remainder Dealers — $ 10.00
- 483 — Independent Bookstores — $ 50.00
- 788 — Bookstores doing Author Signings — $ 75.00
- 127 — Book Distributors — $ 15.00
- 191 — Publishers who also distribute books — $ 20.00
- 710 — Book Wholesalers — $ 70.00
- 252 — Wholesalers to other retail outlets — $ 25.00 (toy, craft, computer, health stores, etc.)
- 294 — Paperback Book Jobbers (ID's) — $ 40.00
- 240 — Sales Representatives (books/toys/...) — $ 25.00

Other Specialized Lists

Here are a few other specialized lists that we offer from our various databases:

- 684 — Radio Shows with phone interviews — $ 70.00
- 251 — Top TV Shows that do interviews — $ 25.00
- 661 — Syndicated Columnists (all subjects) — $ 65.00
- 877 — Mailing List Brokers and Managers — $ 85.00
- 915 — Printers — $ 85.00
- 212 — Foreign Printers — $ 20.00

The Ad-Lib Customer List is also available for rent. Cost is $100.00 per thousand. There are more than 16,000 names on our list. You can select by geographical area.

Mail Order Catalogs that Feature Books

The following section lists mail order catalogs. These catalogs not only feature books, but other items such as videotapes, audiotapes and books-on-tape as well. We've listed their subject interest and other items they carry.

1996 Scripture Catalog
Lars Dunberg, Pres
International Bible Society
1820 Jet Stream Dr
Colorado Springs CO 80216-4998
719-488-9200; Fax: 719-488-0870
Subjects: 63P(scripture products)
Items: HC-PB-SW-OT(Bibles)
Other: 200+ titles

4-H Catalog
Richard Sauer, Pres
National 4-H Foundation
7100 Connecticut Ave
Chevy Chase MD 20815
301-961-2934; Fax: 301-961-2937
Subjects: 99

47th Street Photo
Abe Brown
Mail Order Dept
36 E 19th St
New York NY 10003
212-260-4410
Subjects: 23
Items: SW, hardware, supplies, and accessories
Catalog: 4x per year

800-Software
Ira Weise, Mktg Mgr
918 Parker St
Berkeley CA 94710
800-888-4880; FAX orders: 415-644-8226
Subjects: 23
Items: SW, hardware, and supplies
Catalog: 2x per year
Memo: Customer service: 415-644-1938; Technical info: 415-644-1388.

A

A Celebration Catalog
Patty Sachs
Celebration Creations
73729 Manzanita Ct
Palm Desert CA 92260
916-341-2066; Fax: 619-341-2066
Subjects: 33-43
Items: Parties & celebrations
Other: 100 titles

A.R.E. Press
Jon Robertson, Buyer
68th & Atlantic Ave
PO Box 595
Virginia Beach VA 23451
804-428-3588; Fax: 804-422-6921
Subjects: 27-53-54-63
Items: HC-PB-TA-TV-BT-SW
Catalog: Mailed 4x per year
Numbers: 150,000 mailed

Aardvark Adventures
Debbie Casteel, Owner
PO Box 2449
Livermore CA 94551
510-443-2687; Fax: 510-445-9998
Subjects: 11-28-29
Items: Fiber art supplies
Memo: This is no longer a retail store open to the public. It is a mailorder/supplies store.

Abracadata
Paul Berger, Mktg
PO Box 2440
Eugene OR 97402
800-451-4871; FAX orders: 503-683-1925
Subjects: 23(MAC & IBM)
Items: SW
Catalog mailed 1x per year
Numbers: 50,000 mailed
Memo: Customer service: 503-342-3030.

Abundant Life Seed Foundation
Jeanette Woodruff, Mgr
1029 Lawrence St
PO Box 772
Port Townsend WA 98368
360-385-5660; Fax: 360-385-7455
Subjects: 27-43G-51-59
Items: HC-PB
1 catalog mailed per year
Numbers: 40,000 mailed
Other: 60 titles

Access to Computer Supplies Inc
Tony Walker, Pres
20 B Pimental Ct #10
Novato CA 94949
415-382-0190; Fax: 415-382-1347
Subjects: 23
Items: Software & supplies
Catalog mailed 2x per year
Numbers: 50,000 mailed

Accoutrements
Mark Pahlow, Buyer
PO Box 30811
Seattle WA 98103
206-782-9450; Fax: 206-782-9413
Subjects: 33C-33H(weird gifts/toys)
Items: GI-TO-PB
Memo: Outfitters of popular culture. Store address: 3510 Stone Way N; 206-545-8344. Catalog address: PO Box 30852; 206-782-2344.

Acorn Naturalists
Jennifer Rigby, Buyer
17300 E 17 St #J236
Tustin CA 92680
714-838-4888; Fax: 714-838-5309
Subjects: 31-51-67
Items: HB-PB-TV-TA
Catalog mailed 1x or 2x per year, 1 large, 2 small
Numbers: 20,000 mailed

The ACP Computer Hotline
David Freeman
Advanced Computer Products Inc
1310 E Edinger
Santa Ana CA 92705
800-366-3227; FAX orders: 714-558-8849
Subjects: 23(Apple/IBM/Atari/CM-P)
Items: SW-HC-PB-hardware, and supplies
Catalog mailed 1x per year
Numbers: 100,000 mailed

ACP Inc
Drema Clemens, Book Buyer
PO Box 1426
Salisbury NC 28145-1426
704-636-3034; Fax: 704-633-8707
Subjects: 29
Items: CR-HC-PB(baskets)

ACS Software
Robert Marks, Pubns Dir
American Chemical Society
1155 16th St NW
Washington DC 20036-4899
800-227-5558; FAX orders: 202-872-6060
Subjects: 23(PC & MAC)
Catalog 1x per year

Action Computer Supplies
Joe La Berge, Pres
6100 Stewart Ave
Fremont CA 94538
800-822-3132
Subjects: 23
Items: SW-supplies
Catalog mailed 6x per year
Numbers: 50,000 mailed

Ad-Lib Recommended Books
Marie Kiefer, Buyer
51 1/2 W Adams
PO Box 1102
Fairfield IA 52556-1102
515-472-6617; Fax: 515-472-3186;
  800-669-0773
Subjects: 19M-56M-56P-56W-56X
Items: HC-PB-SW-mailing lists
Other: 75 titles

Adam and Eve
Charles Huff, Prod Coordinator
PHE Inc
302 Meadowlands Dr, PO Box 8200
Hillsboro NC 27278
919-644-8100; Fax: 919-644-8150
Subjects: 35S
Items: GA-GC-GI-TV-(bi-monthly)
Other: 15 titles

AdaptAbility
Winnie Lee, Mdse
76 Mill St
Colchester CT 06415
203-537-3451; Fax: 203-537-2866
Subjects: 99(large print titles only)
Items: CR
Other: 525 titles

Adobe Gallery
Alexander Anthony, Pres
413 Romero NW
Albuquerque NM 87104
505-243-8485
Subjects: 11-49A
Items: Native American art
Other: 500 titles

Adoption Book Catalog
Laurie Wallmark, Owner
Tapestry Books
PO Box 359
Ringoes NJ 08551-0359
908-806-6695; Fax: 908-788-2999
800-765-2367
Subjects: 31P-35F(adoption books)
Items: HC-PB
Other: 200 titles

Adoptive Families of America
Deb Harder, Mdse Buyer
3333 Hwy 100 N
Minneapolis MN 55422
612-535-4829; Fax: 612-535-7808
Subjects: 21-31C-31P-35F-49B-57-78
Items: TA-HC-GA-GC-TV-GI
Other: 450 titles
Memo: Parenting resource materials for
  adoptive families.

Advantage Computing
1803 Mission St #416
Santa Cruz CA 95060
800-356-4666
Subjects: 23(IBM/Apple/MAC/Commodore)
Items: Software

Adventures in Learning Catalog
John Deneen, Book Buyer
1560 Sherman Ave #1111
Evanstan IL 60201
708-570-8931; Fax: 708-570-8888
Subjects: 21-67-76
Items: Children's books with tapes
Other: 50 titles

Memo: They favor children's non-fiction
  books for ages 7 to 12 that are
  educational, especially those
  packaged with a tape or with an
  activity (such as the books published
  by Workman and Klutz Press).

After Loss Bookshelf
Marlene Christenson, Exec Dir
Harbor House West
216 E Victoria St
Santa Barbara CA 93101
805-965-0996; Fax: 805-965-0986;
  800-423-8811
Subjects: 35A-35-35R-57-65(death, grief)
Items: HC-PB
Other: 25 titles

After the Stork
Kathy Batson, Buyer
1501 12th St NW
Albuquerque NM 87104
505-243-7731; Fax: 505-764-9308
Subjects: 21-31
Items: HC-PB-TO-OT: 800-333-5437
Numbers: 8,500 mailed
Catalogs: 8 major plus 2 sale catalogs
  mailed a year

AgAccess
Jessica Brown
603 4th St (95616)
PO Box 2008
Davis CA 95617
916-756-7177; Fax: 916-756-7188
Subjects: 15-43-51A-67
Items: HC-PB-TA-GC-TV
Other: 200-300 titles
Numbers: 100,000 mailed

Air Craft Spruce & Specialty
Don Arrington, Gen Mgr
201 W Truslow Ave
PO Box 424
Fullerton CA 92632
714-870-7551; Fax: 714-871-7289
800-824-1930
Subjects: 70A

Air Land & Sea Catalog
Dimetrie Polistock, Owner
1215 King St
Alexandria VA 22314
703-684-5118
Subjects: 29(model aircrafts)-48-70A
Items: HC-PB-CR-PO-OP-US

Airliners Catalog
Pauline Drum, Book Buyer
World Transport Press
PO Box 521238
Miami FL 33152-1238
305-477-7163; Fax: 305-599-1995
Subjects: 70A(plane pictorials)
Items: HC-PB-TV-MG-PC-PO-(models)
Other: 200 items
Catalog mailed quarterly — affiliated with
  Airlines Magazine. Keith Armes,
  President.

AIS Inc
Tim Millar, Pres
421 E Palatine Rd
Palatine IL 60067
800-950-1100; FAX orders: 708-359-4019
Subjects: 23
Items: SW-supplies

Catalog mailed 4x per year
Memo: Customer service/tech support:
  708-359-2626.

Aldus Add-Ons Catalog
Paul Brainerd, Pres
Editor's Choice Software
4224 24th Ave W
Seattle WA 98199
800-641-1116; FAX orders: 206-282-8135
Subjects: 23
Items: Software/supplies/accessories
Catalog mailed 2x per year
Memo: Customer service: 800-333-2538 -
  Upgrade orders: 206-628-2320.

Allied Health & Nursing
Buyer
Opportunities for Learning
905 Hickory Ln
Mansfield OH 44905-2815
419-589-1700; Fax: 419-589-1522
800-243-7116
Subjects: 31E(safety)-39M
Items: HC-PB-SW-TV
Catalog mailed 1x per year
Memo: Other companies with this phone
  number: Pyramid Art Supply,
  Broadhead Garrett (technical items),
  Frey Scientific, & Elementary Speciality.

Alpha Products
Joseph Murphy, Pres
303 Linwood Ave
Fairfield CT 06430
203-259-7713
800-221-0916; FAX orders: 203-254-0169
Subjects: 23(IBM/Apple, Commodore,
  Tandy)
Catalog mailed 1x per year
Numbers: 70,000 mailed

Alpha Supply
Thomas Orme, Pres
1225 Hollis St
Bremerton WA 98310
360-377-5629; Fax: 360-377-9235
Subjects: 99
Items: HC-PB-OT

Alsto's Handy Helpers Catalog
Mike Voyles, Mgr
Alsto Handy Helper Co
RR 150 E PO Box 1267
Galesburg IL 61402-1267
309-343-6181; Fax: 800-522-5786;
  800-447-0048
Subjects: 29-43
Items: HC-PB-OT
Other: 2 titles
Numbers: 5,000 mailed
Memo: A division of Dick Blick.

Amazon Vinegar & Pickling Works
Janet Burgess, Mdse Dir
2218 E 11th St
Davenport IA 52803-3760
319-322-6800; Fax: 319-322-4003;
  800-798-7979
Subjects: 27-40F-41-43-99
Items: CR-GA-GM-GC-SB-TO-TV-HC-PB
Other: 1200+ titles

America's Hobby Center
146 W 22nd St
New York NY 10011-2466
212-675-8922; Fax: 212-633-2754
Subjects: 16-29-70A
Items: HC-PB-CR
Other: 300 titles

American Computer Supply
Joseph Salatino, Pres
Great North American
2828 Forest Ln #2071
Dallas TX 75234-7517
800-527-083; FAX orders: 214-243-2877
Subjects: 23
Items: SW-supplies
Catalog mailed 2x per year

American Family Publishers
Attn: Mdse Director
4 Gateway Ctr
Newark NJ 07102
201-645-1000
Subjects: 27-43-99
Items: Sweepstakes catalog
Memo: PO Box 62000, Tampa FL 33662-2000; 800-237-2400. Owned by McCalls, Time-Warner, and Meredith Corp.

American Indian Books
Robert K Moore, Pres
PO Box 16175
Huntsville AL 35802
205-881-6727
Subjects: 49A
Items: CR-OT
Other: 12,000 items
Catalog published bi-weekly

American Orchid Society Catalog
Bernardita Morgan, Book Dept Mgr
6000 S Olive Ave
West Palm Beach FL 33405
407-585-8666; Fax: 407-585-0654
Subjects: 43(orchids)
Items: HC-PB-CA-GC-PO-TV
Numbers: 54,000
Catalog mailed 2x per year

American Regional Cookbooks
William Neal, Mdse Dir
Lion House Distributors
PO Box 91283
Pittsburgh PA 15221-7283
412-243-6235; Fax: 412-243-0487
Subjects: 27
Items: HC-PB
Other: 320 titles

American Society for Mechanical Engineers
Dr David Belden, Pres
22 Law Dr
Fairfield NJ 07007
201-882-1167; Fax: 201-882-1717; 800-843-2763
Subjects: 24

American Society of Association Executives
Linda Munday, Buyer
1575 I St NW
Washington DC 20005
202-626-2783; Fax: 202-408-9634
E-Mail: Lmunday@asae.asaenet.org
Subjects: 19-23-44-55-56
Items: HC-PB-TA
Catalog mailed 2x per year
Other: 300 titles
Memo: To request a catalog or more info, use FAX number: 202-408-9634.

Amie's Books for Bakers
Amie & John Horgan, Buyers
440 Church St
Garberville CA 95442
800-923-4359;
Subjects: 27(desserts/baking/candy)
Items: HC-PB
Catalog mailed 2x maybe 3x this year
lOther: 15 titles

Ancestry
Jeff Sittner, Buyer
PO Box 476
Salt Lake City UT 84110
801-531-1790; Fax: 801-531-1798
Subjects: 41G
Items: HC-CA-SW-GC-MA-PO-ST-TV-OT
Catalog mailed 3x per year
Numbers: 750 mailed

Anglers Art-Books/Fly Fishermen
Barry Serviente, Pres
PO Box 148M
Plainfield PA 17081
717-243-9721; Fax: 717-243-8603
800-848-1020.
Subjects: 69H
Items: HC-PB-TV

Antheil Booksellers
N Rind, Mdse Dir
2177 Isabelle Ct
North Bellmore NY 11710
516-826-2094
Subjects: 48(military/naval)-70
Items: HC-PB
Catalog mailed 4x per year
Numbers: 2,000 mailed

Applause Theatre Book Catalog
David Cleaver, Buyer
211 W 71st St
New York NY 10023
212-496-7511; Fax: 212-721-2856
Subjects: 14T-33
Items: HC-TX-PB
Catalog mailed 2x per year
Numbers: 65,000 mailed

The Apple Catalog
PO Box 898
Lakewood NJ 08701-0898
FAX ordes: 302-678-9200
Subjects: 23(Apple)
Items: SW-hardware and supplies
Catalog mailed 2x per year

Aqua Quest Publications
Anthony Bliss Jr, Pres
PO Box 700
Locust Valley NY 11560-0700
516-759-0476; Fax: 516-759-4519
800-933-8989
Subjects: 11P-70N-71T
Items: HB-PB

Armchair Shopper
Buyer
PO Box 419464
Kansas City MO 64141
816-767-3200; Fax: 816-767-3330
800-729-1111
Subjects: 21-51E
Items: GI-OT(home decor)

Art Catalogues
Dagny Corcoran
43940 Battle Mountain Dr
Springville CA 93265
209-539-3160; Fax: 209-539-3162; 800-835-4404
Subjects: 11
Items: Catalogs to 10,000 annually

Art Network Catalog
Sarah Meyers
18757 Wildflower Dr
Penn Valley
Renaissance CA 95946
916-432-7630; Fax: 916-432-7633
Subjects: 11-19M
Catalog mailed once a year
Numbers: 2,000

Articles of War Ltd
Robert Ruman, Buyer
8806 Bronx Ave
Skokie Il 60077-1823
708-674-7445; Fax: 708-674-7449
Subjects: 41(historical novels)-48-70
Items: HC-PB

Artworx Software Co
Arthur Walsh, Pres
1844 Penfield Rd
Penfield NY 14526
800-828-6573; FAX orders: 716-385-1603
Subjects: 23(IBM compatibles)
Items: Entertainment/educational SW
Catalog mailed 3x per year
Memo: Tech support: 716-385-6120.

ASCD Products
Ron Miletta, Mktg Mgr
1250 N Pitt St
Alexandria VA 22314
703-549-9110; Fax: 703-549-3891
Subjects: 21-31E
Items: HC-PB

Asian World of Martial Arts
Book Buyer
917-21 Arch St
Philadelphia PA 19107
215-969-3500; Fax: 215-925-1194
Subjects: 69(martial arts)
Items: HC-PB-TV
Memo: Warehouse: 11601 Caroline Rd, Philadelphia, PA 19154.

ASM International Software
Sandy Dunigan, Software Mgr
Route 87
Materials Park OH 44073
216-338-5151; Fax: 216-338-4634
E-Mail: mem-ferv@po.asm-intl.org
Subjects: 23-24
Items: HC-PB-SW(engineering materials)
Catalog mailed 12x per year
Other: 100 titles
Memo: Customer service: 800-368-9800.

Atlantic Monthly Press
Attn: Book Buyer
841 Broadway
New York NY 10003
212-614-7850; Fax: 212-614-7915
Subjects: 41-27-57P-75-81
Items: HB-PB

Atlantic Software Catalog
PO Box 299
Wenham MA 01984-0699
800-659-4584
Subjects: 23-67
Items: Scientific/educational software
Catalog mailed 2x per year
Numbers: 10,000 mailed
Memo: Customer service: 508-922-4352.

Attachmate Corp
Joy Miller
13231 SE 36th St
Bellevue WA 98006-9930
206-644-4010; 800-426-6283; FAX orders: 206-747-9924
Subjects: 23(Windows/DOS/Graphics)
Items: SW-hardware

Attitudes Catalog
Buyer
Super Locomotion
1213 Elko Dr
Sunnyvale CA 94089
408-734-5279; Fax: 408-734-8004
Subjects: 27(fancy)
Items: CR-GA-ST-HB-PB-OT
Memo: Electronic products, upscale gifts, office supplies.

Audio Editions
Yvonne Strejcek, Buyer
Audio Partners
1133 High St PO Box 6930
Auburn CA 95604
916-888-7803; Fax: 916-888-7805; 800-231-4261
Subjects: 99
Items: TA-BT-TV(not many)
Other: Monthly
Numbers: 200,000 mailed
Memo: Linda Olsen, President.

Audio Forum
Sharon Eaton, Buyer
Jeffrey Norton Publishers
96 Broad St
Guilford CT 06437
203-453-9794; Fax: 203-453-9774
Subjects: 45-99
Items: TA

Audubon Workshop
Thomas Nelson, Mgr
1501 Paddock Dr
Northbrook IL 60062-6891
708-729-6660; Fax: 708-729-6682
800-325-9464
Subjects: 11(birds)
Items: TV-HC-PB
Memo: Identification books.

Aurora Book Companions
Michael Van Meter, Buyer
Royal Publications
PO Box 5793
Denver CO 80217
303-778-8383; Fax: 800-279-9196
Subjects: 27-39

Austad Company
Dave Austad, Pres
4500 E 10th St
PO Box 5428
Sioux Falls SD 57196-0001
605-336-3135; Fax: 605-339-0362
Subjects: 69(golf)
Items: GI-CL-TV(six videos)

Autom Wholesale
Alice Kavinsky, Buyer
2226 N 7th St
Phoenix AZ 85006
800-521-2914; Fax: 602-254-7141; AZ: 800-233-8073
Subjects: 63C

Aviation Book Company
Walter Winner, Pres
25133 Anza Dr Unit E
Santa Clarita CA 91355
805-294-0101; Fax: 805-294-0035
Subjects: 70A
Items: HC-PB-GI-PO-TA-TV
Other: 500+ titles
Memo: Also a store in Burbank.

B

B Klein
PO Box 8503
Coral Springs FL 33075
305-752-1708; Fax: 305-752-2547
Subjects: 59-99
Memo: Publishers of reference books and directories.

The Baggage Claim
Mdse Director
307 S Galena St
Aspen CO 81611
303-925-8777
Subjects: 71
Items: HC-GI-OT

Bakers Books
Nick Liacoupoulos, Buyer
Baker's Plays
100 Chauncy St
Boston MA 02111
617-482-1280; Fax: 617-482-7613
Subjects: 14M-14T-63-33
Items: PB-TA
Catalog mailed 1x per year
Other: 6,000 titles

Barnes & Noble Catalog
Donna Sepkowski, Buyer
1 Pond Rd
Rockleigh NJ 07647
201-767-8844; Fax: 201-767-6638
Subjects: 99

Baron Barclay Bridge Supplies
Randy Baron, Pres
3600 Chamberlain Ln #230
Louisville KY 40241
502-426-0410; Fax: 502-426-2044
800-274-222
Subjects: 69G(bridge)
Items: HC-PB-TA-TV
Catalog: 2x per year
Numbers: 70,000 mailed

Basic Crafts Co
William Klein, Buyer
1201 Broadway
New York NY 10001
212-679-3516; Fax: 212-679-3519
Subjects: 29
Items: HC-PB-CR-TV

Baudville Catalog
Debra Sikanas, Pres
5380 52nd St SE
Grand Rapids MI 49512-9765
800-728-0888; FAX orders: 616-698-0554
Subjects: 23
Items: Entertainment softwr/accessories
Catalog mailed 2x per year
Numbers: 1,000,000 mailed
Memo: Customer service: 616-698-0888.

BDL Homeware
Bette Laswell, Pres
2509 N Campbell Ave #328
Tucson AZ 85719
800-235-4235; FAX orders: 520-885-1606
Subjects: 23(home & small businesses)
Items: Pre-packaged software
Catalog mailed 2x per year
Numbers: 5,000 mailed
Memo: Customer service: 520-298-4212.

Beauty Ed Book Catalog
Martha Fernandez, Pres
PO Box 170070
Hialeah FL 33017-0070
305-362-6998
Subjects: 40B(hair-cutting/design)
Items: HC-PB-TV(cosmetology)
Other: 25 titles

Believers Book Distributor
Keel Germaine, Pres
764 Martin's Chapel Rd
Lawrenceville GA 30245
800-533-5471; Fax: 404-963-7700
Subjects: 63
Items: HC-PB(Bibles)
Numbers: 4,200 titles
Catalogs mailed 3x per year

Benjamin de Wit Bookseller
Benjamin de Wit, Owner
753 E Saginaw
East Lansing MI 48823-2827
517-351-2648
Subjects: 47-54-63
Numbers: HC-PB-RM

Bennett Marine Video
Nick Scherwin, Gen Mgr
Bennett Video Group
2321 Abbott Kinney Blvd
Venice CA 90291
310-821-3329; Fax: 310-306-3162
Subjects: 24-31E-70N-71
Items: HC-PB-TV
Catalog mailed 4x per year
Numbers: 1,000 mailed

Best Bits & Bytes
PO Box 8245
Van Nuys CA 91409
800-245-2983; FAX ordes: 818-764-4851
Subjects: 23(IBM/MAC)
Catalog mailed 6x per year
Numbers: 150M
Memo: Customer service: 818-764-4935.

The Best Software for Kids
Peter Kelman, Publ
Scholastic Inc
22931 E McCarty
Jefferson City MO 65102
800-541-5513; FAX orders: 314-635-5881
Subjects: 21-23
Items: SW for kids
Catalog mailed 1x per year
Numbers: 500,000 mailed

Bibliotherapy for Children
Denise Harrison-Ovaitt
Paperbacks For Educators
426 W Front St
Washington MO 63090
314-239-1999; Fax: 314-239-4515;
   800-227-2591
Subjects: 21-31-76
Items: HC-PB-MM
Other: 800 titles
One catalog issued per year
Numbers: 75,000 mailed

Bicycle Posters & Prints
Jerry Lambert, Mdse Dir
PO Box 7164
Hicksville NY 11802-7164
516-333-3545;
Subjects: 17-39-69(bicycling)
Items: HC-PB-GI-GC-PO-ST-TV-OT
Other: 15 titles
Catalog mailed 2x per year, Spring & Fall

Bicycle Tools & Small Parts
Book Buyer
The Third Hand
12225 Hwy 66
Ashland OR 97520
503-488-4800; Fax: 503-482-0080
Subjects: 69(bicycling)
Items: HC-PB-TV-OT(tools)
Catalog mailed 2x per year
Other: 30 titles

Big Blue Disk Software Catalog
Peter Bollinger, Mgr
Softdisk Publishing
606 Common St
Shreveport LA 71101
800-831-2694; FAX orders: 318-221-8710
Subjects: 23
Items: Personal productivity products
Catalog 4x per year
Numbers: 100,000 mailed
Memo: Customer service: 318-221-8718.

The Big Book of Software
Chuck Breazeale, Pres
People's Choice
235 Germantown Bend Cove
Cordova TN 38018
800-999-0471; FAX orders: 901-753-1429
Subjects: 23(IBM-PC & compatibles)
Catalog mailed 6x per year
Numbers: 50,000 mailed
Memo:Tech support: 901-753-2828

Big Books from Small Presses
Lisa Carlson, Mdse Dir
Upper Access Inc
PO Box 457 Upper Access Rd
Hinesburg VT 05461
802-482-2988; Fax: 802-482-3125
Orders only- 800-356-9315.
Subjects: 10-27-29-39-43-99
Items: HC-PB

Other: 100 titles
Catalog 1x per year

Biobottoms Inc
Mary Ann Nolan, Mdse Dir
617-C 2nd St
Petaluma CA 94952
707-778-7168; Fax: 707-778-0619
Subjects: 21-31-40F(children)-76
Memo: Seasonal catalogs; natural fiber
   childrens' clothing & cloth diapers.

Biosoft Catalog
Biosoft
PO Box 10938
Ferguson MO 63135-0938
314-524-8029; FAX orders: 314-524-8129
Subjects: 23-67
Items: Scientific software
Catalog mailed 1x per year
Numbers: 10,000 mailed

Bird Watcher's Digest
Elsa Thompson or Candice Heiss, Buyers
PO Box 110
Marietta OH 45750
614-373-5285; Fax: 614-373-8443
800-879-2473
Subjects: 15(birds)-51E-43-71
Items: HC-PB-PO-RC-CA-TA-TV
Other: 50 titles
Memo: Magazine mailed 6x per year,
   catalog by request.

Bits & Pieces Catalog
Debbie Bassler
Production Coordinator
575 Boylston St
Boston MA 02116
617-536-5088; 800-544-7297
Subjects: 69G
Items: HC-PB-GA-PZ
Other: 10 titles
Numbers: 7,000,000
Memo: Eli J Segal, President. Order
   address: 1 Puzzle Pl, Stevens Point,
   WI 54481-7199.

Black Box Corporation
President
1000 Park Dr, Lawrence PA 15055
PO Box 12800
Pittsburgh PA 15241
412-746-5500; Fax: 412-746-0746
Subjects: 23(data communication equip)
Items: Computer supplies

Blacklist Mail Order
Attn: Mdse Director
475 Velencia
San Francisco CA 94103
415-255-0388; Fax: 415-431-0425
Subjects: 13-55-65-73-75-83-90-95
Other: 100 titles

Blackship Computer Supply
Paul Gupta, Pres
2031 O'Toole Ave
San Jose CA 95131
408-432-7500; Fax: 408-432-1443
Subjects: 23
Items: HC-PB-SW

Blacksmith Corporation
Book Buyer
PO Box 1752
Chino Valley AZ 86323
602-636-4456; Fax: 602-636-4457
800-531-2665(for orders only)
Subjects: 69H
Items: HC-PB-TV

Blue Chip Gifts
Ed Fowler, Buyer
PO Box 6748
Lubbock TX 79493-6748
806-799-4289; Fax: 806-799-4249
800-289-4224
Subjects: 19-28-57-59-71
Items: HC-SW-PO-TA-TV-OT
Other: 300 titles
Memo: Catalog mailed as requested.

Blue Star
Kam Syal, Pres
Blue Star Computer Inc
2312 Cantral Ave NE
Minneapolis MN 55418
800-950-8884; FAX orders: 612-788-3442
Subjects: 23
Items: SW
Catalog mailed 1x per year
Memo: Customer serivce: 612-788-1098;
   International orders: 612-788-5000.

Boat/US Equipment Catalog
Jim Georgidis, Mdse Dir
Boat America Corp
880 S Pickett St
Alexandria VA 22304
703-370-4202; Fax: 703-461-2852
Subjects: 69-70N-71
Items: HC-PB-MA-OT-CA-TV
Other: 400 titles

Bolind Inc
Eileen Sharbonda, Mdse Mgr
5421 Western Ave
Boulder CO 80301
303-443-3142; Fax: 303-443-9899
Subjects: 28-29C-43
Items: CA-HC-PB-PO-ST-OT
Catalog mailed annuallly
Numbers: 2,000 mailed

Book Buyers Bargains
Clay Patino, Pres
PO Box 1760
Peoria IL 61656-1760
309-691-4610; Fax: 309-689-3818
Subjects: 99
Other: 150 titles

Book Publishing Company
Cynthia Holzapefal, Book Buyer
PO Box 188
Summertown TN 38483
615-964-3571; Fax: 615-964-3518
Subjects: 13-39H-51
Items: HC-PB

Book Tree
John & Anna Haines, Owners
12 Pine Hill Rd
Englishtown NJ 07726
908-446-3853; Fax: 908-446-5610
Subjects: 43G
Memo: Retails gardening books at
   nursery trade shows, flower shows,
   and mail order catalog.

Books About Cookbooks
Mary Barile, Mdse Dir
Heritage Publications
PO Box 335 Elliot Hills
Arkville NY 12406
914-586-3522; Fax: 914-586-2797
Subjects: 27-59
Items: HC-PB
Catalog mailed 2x/year
Numbers: 5,000 mailed

Books Bohemian
Robert J Manners
PO Box 17218
Los Angeles CA 90017
213-385-6761
Subjects: 37-47
Other: 400 titles

Books by Mail
Pat Wilson, Mdse Dir
1750 California Ave #114
Corona CA 91719
909-273-0900; Fax: 909-272-3979
Subjects: 69(clown/puppetry)
Items: HC-PB-MM-TO-OT(puppets)
Other: 300 items
Memo: Books for variety entertainers: clowns, puppeteers, etc. 75% of catalog is books.

Books for Animal Lovers
Jeremy Townsend, Buyer
J N Townsend Publishing
12 Greenleaf Dr
Exeter NH 03833
603-778-9883; Fax: 603-778-9883
800-333-9883(for orders only)
Subjects: 15
Items: HB-PB
Catalog mailed 2x/year
Numbers: 3,000 mailed

Books for Business Inc
Ralph W T Munroe, Owner
113 N Foushee St
PO Box 26923
Richmond VA 23261-6923
804-788-0807; Fax: 804-788-6820
Subjects: 14-19-23-25-59
Items: HC-TA-PB
Other: 300+ titles

Books for Your Business
Ray Lawrence, Book Buyer
Forum Publishing Co
383 E Main St
Centerport NY 11721
516-754-5000; Fax: 516-754-0630
Subjects: 19
Items: PB-TA-TV
Other: 150+ titles
Catalog mailed 4x per year
Numbers: 500,000 mailed

Books from Northwind Farms
David Oliver, Mgr
Northwind Farm Publications
RR 2 Box 246
Shevlin MN 56676-9535
218-657-2478
Subjects: 39H-43G
Other: 45 titles

Books in Motion
Gary Challender, Mgr
9212 E Montgomery #501
Spokane WA 99206-4270
509-922-1646; 800-752-3159(for ordering only)
Subjects: 19-33-75-99
Items: TA-TV(some, not very many)
Other: 600 titles
Catalog mailed 2x/year

Books of Wall Street Catalog
Carla Ferrelli, Mgr
309 S Willard St
PO Box 494
Burlington VT 05402
802-658-0322; Fax: 802-658-0260
Subjects: 19B-19E-19I
Items: HC-PB

Books for Financial Service Employees
Bill Ewings, Mdse Mgr
111 E Wacker Dr
Chicago IL 60601
312-946-8800; Fax: 312-946-8802
Subjects: 19-31E-35A
Items: HC-PB-TV
Other: 500 titles
Catalog mailed 6x per year

The Bookshelf
Sharon Brandt, Bookshelf Mgr
Teachers Magazine
4301 Connecticut Ave NW #432
Washington DC 20008
202-686-0800
800-346-1834
Subjects: 31E
Other: 30 titles

Borland International
1800 Green Hills Rd
Scotts Valley CA 95066-4928
408-438-3400
Subjects: 23
Items: SW for home & business
Catalog mailed 4x per year
Numbers: 2,500,000

Boston Museum of Fine Arts
Jim Adams, Book Buyer
465 Huntington Ave
Boston MA 02115
617-267-9300
Subjects: 11-43-76-(fine art)
Items: HC-PB-GC-CA-PO-GI

Boston Music Company
Charles A Constantine, Pres
172 Tremont St
Boston MA 02111
617-426-5100; Fax: 617-695-9142
Subjects: 14M
Items: Music books

Boston Rite Book &...
J A Kruza, Pres
Kruza Kaleidoscopix
PO Box 389
Franklin MA 02038
508-528-6211
Subjects: 21-11P-70N
Items: HC-PB-US
Memo: New & used children's books, photography, and nautical.

Brainstorms Catalog
Marshall Cordell, Pres
Anatomical Chart Co
8221 N Kimball Ave
Skokie IL 60076-2956
708-679-4700; Fax: 708-674-0211; 800-621-7500
Subjects: 21-27-31-35-39-39H-51-51E-57-67
Items: HC-PB-MA-TA-TV-PO-GI
Other: 400 titles
Numbers: 400,000 mailed

Bridge City Tool Works
Jill Palamountain, Mdse Dir
1104 NE 28th Ave
Portland OR 97232
503-282-6997; Fax: 503-287-1085
Subjects: 29-43
Items: HC-PB-GA-PO-OT
Hardware catalog mailed 1x per year
Numbers: 1,000 mailed

Bridge World
Attn: Mdse Director
39 W 94th St
New York NY 10025
212-866-5860
Subjects: 69(bridge)
Other: 60 titles

Broderbund Software Direct
Doug Carlston, Pres
17 Paul Dr
San Rafael CA 94903-2043
415-492-3200
Subjects: 23
Items: SW
Catalog mailed 2x per year

Brown Wrapper Bookstore
Len Buffinton
PO Box 647
Old Saybrook CT 06475
203-388-0362; Fax: 203-388-0381
Subjects: 35R-39-57S
Items: HC-PB-TV
Catalog mailed 3x per year
Other: 180 titles

Bueno Catalog
Eliza Reid, Buyer
In One Ear
29481 Manzanita Dr
Campo CA 91906
619-478-5619; Fax: 619-478-5363
Subjects: 21-31E-44-45-76-80
Items: HC-PB-CA-GC-MA-ST-OT-TA
Other: 40-50 titles
Catalog mailed 4x per year
Memo: 8 titles they publish themselves.

Builder's Booksource
George Kiskaddon, Buyer
1817 Fourth St
Berkeley CA 94710
510-845-6874; Fax: 510-845-7051
800-843-2028
E-Mail: builder@ix.netcom.com
Subjects: 12-19H-29-43H-43G
Items: HC-PB
Other: 6,000 titles
Catalog mailed 1x per year

Burpee Garden
Bob Volkhardt/Anne Wagner, Buyers
W Atlee Burpee & Co
300 Park Ave
Warminster PA 18974
215-674-4900; Fax: 215-674-3452
Subjects: 43G
Items: HC-PB-OT
Catalog mailed 3x per year
Numbers: 5,000 mailed

Business & Career Books
Ten Speed Press/Celestial Arts
PO Box 7123
Berkeley CA 94707
800-841-BOOK; Fax: 510-559-1629
Subjects: 19C
Memo: "1995-1996 Business/Career Bks" To receive info on future books, send your name to: TSP Business List Desk, PO Box 7123, Berkeley, CA 94707.

Business & Computer Bkstores Inc
Ken Taylor, Mdse Dir
213 N Easton Rd
Willow Grove PA 19090
215-657-8300; 800-223-0233
Subjects: 19-23
Items: HC-PB-MA-SW (800-223-0233)-TA
Other: 5,000 titles
Memo: Down-loadable catalog. Internet World Wide Web.

Business and Personal Success
James L Evers, Buyer
James L Evers Assoc
10 Rockland Ave
Nanuet NY 10954
914-623-7129
Subjects: 19-31(adult)-56-57
Items: HB-PB-TV-TA
Catalog mailed 3x/year
Numbers: 5,000 mailed

Business By Phone Catalog
Art Sobczak, Pres
Business By Phone Inc
13254 Stevens St
Omaha NE 68137
402-895-9399; Fax: 402-896-3353; 800-326-7721
E-Mail: 74051,1402@compuserve.com.
Subjects: 19M(telephone sales)
Items: HC-PB-TV-TA
Memo: Also sales training company.

Business By The Book
Tami Athens
PO Box 290284
Minneapolis MN 55429
612-536-5917
Subjects: 19-19S
Copy of cat available for $3
Memo: Publishers interested in getting books into their catalog may contact them at 612-924-2442. They require a review copy of the book(s)before making a decision on final selection. Review copies may be sent to their shipping address: 4215 Winnetka Ave North Suite 142, Minneapolis, MN 55428.

Business Reader
Theodore B Kinni, Pres
PO Box 41268
Brecksville OH 44141
216-838-8653; Fax: 216-838-8104
Subjects: 19G-19X-24(quality management)
Items: Titles reviewed in Quality Digest
Other: 500 titles
Catalogs mailed 6x per year
Memo: We mail print advertisements 4x per month in selected business magazine. Street address: 1355 Old Mill Path, Cleveland OH 44147.

Bytes and Pieces
Ruth Kahn/Barbara Gorman
6 Fox Rd
PO Box 525
East Setauket NY 11733
516-751-2535; 800-338-3475
Subjects: 23(Apple)
Items: SW & supplies
Catalog mailed 1x per year
Numbers: 10,000 mailed

C

C H I P S Catalog
Harry K Noe, Mktg Dir
1307 Golden Bear Ln
Kingwood TX 77339
713-359-2270; Fax: 713-359-2277
Subjects: 27-71
Items: HC-PB-TV
Catalog mailed 12x per year
Other: 1,600 titles
Memo: Books & video tapes about the culinary, hospitality, & travel industry.

Cabela's
812 13th Ave
Sidney NE 69160
308-254-5505; Fax: 308-254-7809
FAX: 800-496-6329
Subjects: 15-69H
Other: 10-20 titles

California Digital Inc
Terry Reiter, Pres
17700 Figueroa St
Gardena CA 90248
800-421-5041; FAX orders: 213-217-1951
Subjects: 23
Items: SW-hardware, and supplies
Catalog mailed 2x per year
Numbers: 250,000 mailed
Memo: Customer service: 213-217-0500 - Technical support: 213-217-1945.

California Kids History Catalog
Jim Silverman, Pres
PO Box 1521
Sonoma CA 95476
707-996-0121; Fax: 707-938-8718
Subjects: 21-41A-61(CA)
Items: HC-PB-MA-CA-TA-TV
Other: 100 titles

California Storytellers Catalog
Sandra MacLees
6695 Westside Rd
Healdsburg CA 95448
707-433-8728
Subjects: 41(US)-61(CA)-76-79
Items: HC-PB-TA-TV-CA-OT
Other: 100+ titles
Memo: Features books and tapes by California storytellers, especially folklore and folk tales. Storytelling dolls. 32 page catalogs.

Cambridge Parenting Catalog
Amy Pauley, Mg Editor
Cambridge Research Group
PO Box 2153
Charleston WV 25328-2153
800-468-4227; Fax: 304-744-9351
Subjects: 25-31P-35R-39H-57
Items: HC-PB-TV-TA-PO
Other: 200 titles
Memo: AKA Parenting and Family Life catalog. Shipping address: 90 MacCorkle Ave SW, South Charleston, WV 25303.

Canadian Academic Technology
Box 71
W Flamborough ON L0R 2K0
416-627-5361
Subjects: 23
Items: Software for education/business
Catalog mailed 1x per year

Cancer Fighters Bookshop
Helen Hecker
PO Box 129
Vancouver WA 98666
360-694-2462; Fax: 360-696-3210; 800-637-2256
Subjects: 39M-57
Items: HC-PB-TA-GA-TV

Caners Sourcebook
Jim Widess, Buyer
The Caning Shop
926 Gilman St
Berkeley CA 94710
510-527-5010
Subjects: 29(baskets)
Items: HC-PB-TV-CR
Catalog mailed 1x per year
Numbers: 12,000 mailed

Capability's Books for Gardeners
Kristen Gilbertson, Pres
Capability's Books Inc
2379 Highway 46
Deer Park WI 54007-7506
715-269-5346; Fax: 715-269-5531
Subjects: 43G-51E
Items: HC-PB-RM-TV
Other: 750 titles
One catalog & 4 updates mailed annually

Career Aids
Buyer
Opportunities for Learning
100 Paragon Pky
Mansfield OH 44903
419-589-1700; Fax: 419-589-1522; 800-243-7116
Subjects: 19C-25-27-31-39-55-67
Items: HC-PB-TA-TV-SW
Other: 200 titles
Numbers: 1,000 mailed
Catalog mailed 1x per year

Career Planning & Job Search
Sharon Griner, Buyer
JIST Works Inc
720 N Park Ave
Indianapolis IN 46202-3431
317-264-3720; Fax: 800-547-8329
800-648-JIST
Subjects: 31E-57(job search titles)
Other: 200 titles
Catalog mailed 2 or 3x per year

Career Planning/Adult Developmnt
Denise Harrison-Ovaitt, Cat Ed
Paperbacks For Educators
426 W Front St
Washington MO 63090
314-239-1999; Fax: 314-239-4515;
    800-227-2591
Subjects: 35-57
Items: HC-PB-MM
Other: 800 titles
Numbers: 60,000 mailed
Catalog mailed 1x per year
Memo: Careers & adult development.

Career Press
Buyer
3 Tice Rd
PO Box 687
Franklin Lakes NJ 07417
201-848-0310; Fax: 201-848-1727;
    800-CAREER-1
Subjects: 19-23-35M-39-59

Carol Wright Gifts
Roger Oxee, Book Buyer
Carol Wright Sales Inc
PO Box 10250
Stamford CT 06904
203-353-7325; Fax: 203-353-7380
Subjects: 99
Items: CR-GI-ST-HC-PB-CA-SW-PO-TO-TV
Other: 1-2 titles
Catalog mailed 10x per year
Memo: Bob King (203-353-7200) buys toys; Roger Oxee also buys housewares, gifts, & crafts; Allyson Vallerie buys apparel.

Carolan Craft Supplies
Mdse Manager
PO Box 9920
Cleveland OH 44142
216-252-5255
Subjects: 29
Items: PB-CR-OT
Catalog sent yearly

Carolina Biological Supply
Monica Jewell, Asst Dept Head
2700 York Rd
Burlington NC 27215
910-538-6297; Fax: 910-222-1926
Subjects: 23-31-39-51-59-67
Items: HC-PB-TX-GA-MA-PO-SW-TA-TV
Catalog mailed 1x/year
Numbers: 120,000 mailed
Memo: Catalog name: Carolina Science Materials.

Carousel Press
Carole T Meyers
PO Box 6061
Albany CA 94706-0061
510-527-5849
E-Mail: TFTraveLuv@aol.com
Subjects: 35F-71
Items: PB-RM-OP-GA-SB-TA-TV
Other: 100+ titles
Memo: 50+ publishers represented.

Carroll Reed Catalog
1001 Washington St
Conshohocken PA 19428
610-834-5454; Fax: 610-940-6745
Subjects: 99
Items: CL-GI
Catalog mailed 12x per year

Carson Enterprises Book Catalog
Mary or Glenn, Buyers
Carson Enterprises
Drawer 71
Deming NM 88031
505-546-3252
Subjects: 27-28-29
Items: HC-PB-MA-OT
Catalog mailed 6x per year
Numbers: 30,000 mailed
Memo: Topics are treasure-hunting, dowsing, cooking & Americana.

Casual Living USA
Book Buyer
5401 Hangar Ct
Tampa FL 33634
813-884-6955; Fax: 813-882-4605
Subjects: 33(trivia)-41-69
Items: HC-PB-GA-GI

Catalog on a Disk
Michael Ulick, Pres
Valley View Electronics
PO Box 128
St Peter MN 56082-0128
507-931-4578
Subjects: 23(IBM)
Items: IBM public domain software
Catalog mailed 5x per year

The Catalog Shop
6 Trowbridge Dr
PO Box 536
Bethel CT 06801-0536
203-743-0864; Fax: 203-743-0042
Subjects: 99
Catalog that offers catalogs

Catalogue from Golf House
Sue Scaglione
USGA
Liberty Corner Rd
Far Hills NJ 07931-0708
908-234-2300
Subjects: 69(golf)
Items: HC-PB-TA-TV-GI
Memo: Published for 450,000 members of the US Golf Association.

Catholic Answers Catalog
Karl Keating
PO Box 17490
San Diego CA 92177-9821
619-541-1131
Subjects: 63C(faith/doctrine/history)
Items: HC-PB

Cats Cats and More Cats
J Martin, Mdse Buyer
PO Box 270
Monroe NY 10950
914-782-4141; Fax: 914-782-7822
E-Mail: catscats@monroe.ny.frontiercomm.net
Web page :http:llny.frontiercomm.net/2catscats
Subjects: 15(cats & cat lovers)
Items: HC-PG-CR-GI-CA-GC-GA-PO-OT
Catalog mailed 7x per year

Celebration Creations Catalog
73-729 Manzanita Ct
Palm Desert CA 92260
Fax: 619-341-2066
Subjects: 21-23-29-33-35M-99

Center For Cuban Studies
Sandra Levinson, Mktg Mgr
124 West 23rd St
New York NY 10011
212-242-0559; Fax: 212-242-1937
Subjects: 44-45S
Items: HC-PB-TA-TV-MU
Catalog mailed 2x per year
Memo: Cuban studies.

Central Computer Products
Neal Singh, Pres
330 Central Ave
Fillmore CA 93015
800-456-4123; FAX orders: 805-524-4026
Subjects: 23(IBM)
Items: Software/hardware/supplies
Catalog mailed 4x per year
Numbers: 300,000 mailed
Memo: Customer service: 805-524-4700.

CFO Library
Susan Kron, Mg Editor
CFO Magazine
253 Summer St
Boston MA 02210
617-345-9700; Fax: 617-951-9306
Subjects: 19-19G-19
Items: Books for senior financial
Other: 25 titles

CFQ Bookshop
Lisa Coduto, Buyer
Cinefantastique Magazine
7240 W Roosevelt
Forest Park IL 60130
708-366-5566; Fax: 708-366-1441
800-798-6515
Subjects: 33-59-82-86
Items: HC-PB-TA-CA-TV
Other: 25-50 titles
Memo: SFF/occult films.

Chambers Catalog
Monelle Totah, Buyer
3250 Van Ness Ave
San Francisco CA 94109
415-421-7900; Fax: 415-616-9212
Subjects: 43H
Items: Bath/bed furnishings
Quarterly catalog
Memo: Parent company is Williams-Sonoma. Six to eight weeks for a review of new products.

Cheatsheet Products Inc
Margaret Pettis, Pres
PO Box 8369
Pittsburgh PA 15218-0369
412-243-1049; FAX orders: 412-731-2460
Subjects: 23(Apple/IBM/Commodore)
Items: SW-accessories
Catalog mailed 2x per year

Cherry Lane Catalog
Ted Piechocinski, Mdse Buyer
10 Midland Ave
Port Chester NY 10573
914-935-5224; Fax: 914-937-0614;
800-637-2852
Subjects: 14M
Items: HC-PB-RC
Other: 1x per year
Other: 25 titles
Memo: Also song sheets.

Chessler Books
Michael Chessler, Book Buyer
26030 Highway 74
PO Box 399
Kittredge CO 80457
303-670-0093; Fax: 303-670-9727;
800-654-8502
Subjects: 69(climbing/mountaineering)-71
Items: HC-PB-US-OP-CA
Other: 300+ titles

Chicken Boy Catalog
Amy Inouie
Future Studio
PO Box 292000
Los Angeles CA 90029
213-660-0620; Fax: 213-660-2571;
800-422-0505
Subjects: Pop culture/teens to baby boomers
Items: HC-PB-CD-TA-TV
Other: 12 titles
Memo: Catalogs are $1.00 on request.

Childcraft
Maria Young, Buyer
Childcraft Education Corp
250 Park Ave S
New York NY 10003
212-677-5530; Fax: 212-677-5653
Subjects: 21-31-76-89
Items: HC-PB-TO-GA
Other: 25-50 titles

Children's Books Catalog
Barbara Lopez, Book Buyer
2552 Sheridan Blvd (80214)
PO Box 19069
Denver CO 80219
303-237-4989; Fax: 303-433-6788
Subjects: 21-31-63-76-79
Items: HC-PB-TX
Other: 750 titles
Catalog mailed 2x per year

Childswork/Childsplay Catalog
Product Review Committee
Ctr for Applied Psychology
307 E Church Rd
King of Prussia PA 19406-2620
610-277-4020; Fax: 610-277-4556
Subjects: 21-31C-31P-39R-57
Items: HC-PB-GA-GI-TA-TV
Catalog mailed 4x per year
Other: 100 titles
Memo: A catalog addressing the mental health needs of children.

Chinaberry Book Service
Ann S Ruethling
2780 Via Orange Way #B
Spring Valley CA 91978
619-670-5200; Fax: 619-670-5203
800-776-2242
Subjects: 21-31-76-89

Items: HC-PB-TA-GA-TO-TV(few)-CR-GI
Catalog mailed 4x/year
Memo: Childrens books etc, from birth to age 13.

Christian Book Distributors
Book Buyer
137 Summit St (01960)
PO Box 7000
Peabody MA 01961-7000
508-977-5000; Fax: 508-977-5010
Subjects: 14M-21-31P-35-63-75-85
Items: HC-PB-MM-CA-TA-TV-CR-GI
Other: 500+ titles
Catalogs mailed 6 times per year

Chuck Wagon Outfitters
Jim Dutch Snowdy
250 Avila Beach Dr
San Luis Obispo CA 93405
805-595-2434; Fax: 805-595-7914
800-543-2359
Subjects: 27(dutch oven cookbooks)
Items: HC-PB-OT(ovens/cookware)
Catalog mailed 2x per year
Other: 50 titles

Churchill Livingstone
Jennifer Mitchell, VP of Profession & Reference Publish
650 Ave of the Americas
New York NY 10011
212-206-5000; Fax: 212-727-7808
Subjects: 39M
Items: HC-PB
Memo: The order fulfillment center is in Naperville IL.

Churchill Livingstone
Jennifer Mitchell, VP-Prof/Ref
650 Ave of the Americas
New York NY 10011
212-216-5000; Fax: 212-727-7805
Subjects: 39M
Items: HB-PB

Cinema Books
Stephanie F Ogle, Mgr
4753 Roosevelt Way NE
Seattle WA 98105
206-547-7667
Subjects: 33M
Items: HC-TX-PB-RM-MM-MG-CA-GC-PO-ST-TV
Other: 9,000 titles
Catalog mailed monthly

Cinema City
Mdse Director
PO Box 1012
Muskegon MI 49443
616-739-8303; Fax: 616-733-7234
Subjects: 33M
Items: PO(press kits)
Catalog 1mailed x per year
Memo: No books - just posters.

Circle Craft Supply
Dorothy Marie Berdit, VP
PO Box 3000
Dover FL 33527-3000
813-659-0992; Fax: 813-659-0017
Subjects: 29
Items: CR(leaf inst sheets)
Other: 3 titles

Circulator's Book Shelf
Bhanu Dhamija, Publ
Circulation Management Magazine
611 Broadway #510
New York NY 10012-2608
212-979-0730; Fax: 212-979-0961
E-Mail: cmedit@aol.com.
Subjects: 19M(direct marketing/circ)
Items: HC-PB
Other: 20 titles
Catalog mailed monthly

Classic Motorbooks
Mktg Manager
729 Prospect Ave
PO Box 1
Osceola WI 54020-0001
715-294-3345; Fax: 715-294-4448
Subjects: 16(all motorized vehicles)-70
Items: HC-PB
Other: 10,000 titles
Catalog mailed 2x per year
Memo: 8,000 aircraft titles. Also some nautical.

Clotilde Inc
Lee Ann Donathan, Book Buyer
4301 N Federal Hwy #200
Fort Lauderdale FL 33308-5209
305-491-2889; Fax: 305-493-8950
Subjects: 29(sewing)-29C(how-to)
Items: HC-PB(mainly)
Catalog mailed 2x per year

Club MAC
7 Hammond
Irvine CA 92718
800-258-2622; FAX orders: 714-768-9354
Subjects: 23(Apple/MAC)
Items: Software/supplies
Catalog mailed 4x per year
Memo: Tech support: 714-768-1490.

Clyde Robin Seed Catalog
Steve Atwood, Pres
3670 Enterprise Ave
Hayward CA 94545
510-785-0425; Fax: 510-785-6463
Subjects: 43G-51E
Items: HC-PB(wild flowers/seeds)
Memo: Catalog available anytime.

CMO Superstore & Catalog
Buyer
101 Reighard Ave
Williamsport PA 17701
717-327-9575; Fax: 717-327-1217;
800-233-8950
Subjects: 23(IBM compatible)
Items: HC-PB-SW(hardware)
Catalog mailed 4-5x per year

The Cockpit
Jeff Clyman, Owner
33-00 47th Ave
Long Island City NY 11101
718-482-1860; Fax: 718-472-9692
Subjects: 70A
Items: Bill Lukshides, New Prod Buyer
Catalog mailed 3x per year

Coldwater Creek
Dennis Pence
1 Coldwater Creek Dr
PO Box 2069
Sandpoint ID 83864-0907
208-263-2266; 800-262-0040;
    Fax: 800-262-0080
Subjects: 15-49A-51
Items: HC-PO-GI-CL-TV
Other: 6 titles
Memo: Produces 3 catalogs: Spirit of the
    West, 2x per year; North Country, 4x
    per year; Ecosong, 4x per year.

Cole Parmer Catalog
Product Mgr: Books
625 E Bunker Ct
Vernon Hills IL 60061
708-549-7600; Fax: 708-549-7676
Subjects: 23-24-67(engineering)
Items: HC-SW-TV
Catalog every 2 years
Memo: They deal with publishers. Kelly
    McCollum, ext 5854.

Colonial Garden Kitchens
Mary Lucich, Buyer
Hanover Direct Inc
1500 Harbor Blvd
Weehawken NJ 07087
201-863-7300; Fax: 201-319-3495
Subjects: 27-43(cookbooks)
Items: HC-PB-OT(kitchen/housewares)
Catalog mailed 6x per year

A Common Reader
James Mustich Jr, Pres
The Akadine Press Inc
141 Tompkins Ave
Pleasantville NY 10570
914-747-0777; Fax: 914-747-0778;
    800-832-7323
Subjects: 33-41-45W-47-59-75-83-84-95-99
Items: HC-PB-CD-TA-TV
Memo: Monthly catalog.

Comprehensive Health Education
ETR Associates
PO Box 1830
Santa Cruz CA 95061-1830
408-438-4060; Fax: 408-438-4284
Orders only number: 800-321-4407
    FAX: 800-435-8433
Subjects: 27-31E-35F-35S-39-39R-57
Items: HC-PB-MA-PO-TV-OT
Catalog mailed 7x per year
Numbers: 500 titles

Compuadd
Bill Hayden, CEO
Compuadd Corp
12303 Technology Blvd
Austin TX 78727
800-627-1967; FAX orders: 512-335-6236
Subjects: 23
Items: Over 100 superstores
Catalog mailed 12x per year
Numbers: 15,000,000 mailed
Memo: Customer service: 800-933-9002
    Tech support: 800-999-9901
    International sales: 512-258-5575.

CompuBooks Online Bookstore
Maria Munoz, Book Buyer
RR 1 Box 271D
Cedar Creek TX 78612-9733
512-321-9652; Fax: 512-321-4525;
    800-880-6818
Special orders on E-Mail:
    books@compubooks.com
Subjects: 23
Other: 6,000 titles
Memo: Electronic stores on Internet,
    CompuServe, & NIFTY-Serve in Japan.

Compuclassics Inc
Philip Cramer, Pres
PO Box 10958
Canoga Park CA 91309
800-733-3888; FAX orders: 818-347-9977
Subjects: 23(IBM compatible)
Items: SW-accessories, supplies
Semiannual catalog with monthly updates
Memo: Customer service: 818-347-9400
    International orders: 818-347-2444.

Compuser/Compudyne Direct
Steven Dukker, Pres
15167 Business Ave
Dallas TX 75244-2208
800-932-2667; FAX orders: 214-702-0300
Subjects: 23(IBM/MAC)
Items: SW-hardware
Catalog mailed 4x per year

Computability Consumer Electronics
Gary Rose, Editor/VP
PO Box 17882
Milwaukee WI 53217-0882
800-896-1334; FAX orders: 414-357-7814
Subjects: 23
Items: SW-accessories
Catalog mailed 12x per year
Memo: Customer service: 800-558-0003
    Tech info: 414-357-8181.

Computer Discount Warehouse
Gregg Zeman, Pres
1020 E Lake Cook Rd
Buffalo Grove IL 60089-1890
708-465-6000
800-781-4CDW; FAX orders: 414-357-7814
Subjects: 23
Items: Sw-hardware, accessories
Memo: FAX orders: 708-291-1737.

Computer Plus - Dealer Catalog
8182 Goldie St
Walled Lake MI 48390-4107
313-363-0100; FAX orders: 313-363-5150
Subjects: 23
Items: Wholesale SW-accessories
Catalog mailed 2x per year

Computer Software & Tutorials
Kathleen Howard, Pres
Noguska Industries
735-741 N Countyline St
Fostoria OH 44830-1004
419-435-0404
Subjects: 19-23
Items: SW
Catalog mailed 12x per year

Conceive Believe Achieve
Melinda Ball, Mdse Dir
Cambridge Educational
PO Box 2153
Charleston WV 25328-2153
304-744-9323; Fax: 304-329-6687;
    800-468-4227
Subjects: 57S
Items: HC-MA-PO-SW-TV
Catalog mailed 2x per year
Numbers: 250,000 mailed

Construction Bookstore
David J Buster, Buyer
1830 NE 2nd St
Gainsville FL 32609
904-378-9784; Fax: 904-378-2791;
    800-253-0541
Subjects: 12B
Items: HC-PB-SW
Catalog mailed 4x per year
Memo: Construction books, manuals,
    audio & video tapes; Two catalogs:
    Electrical Savvy (400 titles) &
    Construction Savvy (800 titles).

Constructive Playthings Catalog
Don Lynn, Book Buyer
U S Toy Co
1227 East 119th St
Grandview MO 64030
816-761-5900; Fax: 816-761-9295
Subjects: 21-31E-33(magic)-49-63J
Items: HC-PB-GA-TO
Catalog mailed
Numbers: 7 stores
Memo: U S Toy publishes 7 catalogs, but
    this is the only one that carries books.

Consumer Education Research Ctr
Book Buyer
1980 Springfield Ave
Maplewood NJ 07040
201-275-3955; Fax: 201-275-3980
800-872-0121
Subjects: 25-19C-19H-19M-19O-19S-43
Items: HC-PB
Catalog mailed every two years
Other: 200 titles
Memo: Consumer guides and aides.

Consumer Information Catalog
Book Buyer
Consumer Information Ctr
Pueblo CO 81009
719-948-3334; Fax: 719-948-9724
Subjects: 25
Items: PB
Catalog mailed 4x per year
Other: 200 titles
Memo: Consumer interest only.

Consumer Marketing Resources Inc
Harry Leifer/G Nelson
600 Huyler St
S Hackensack NJ 07606-1700
201-440-8900; FAX orders: 201-4402168
Subjects: 23
Items: SW-hardware
Catalog mailed
Numbers: 100,000

The Cook's Garden
Ellen Ogden, Buyer
Moffitts Bridge
PO Box 535
Londonderry VT 05148
802-824-3400; Fax: 802-824-3027
Subjects: 27-43G
Catalog mailed
Other: 35 titles
Memo: Now carrying cookbooks as well.

Coolware Inc
220 Stonehurst Blvd
Freehold NJ 07728
800-245-9399; FAX orders: 908-308-3955
Subjects: 23
Items: SW-spread sheets
Catalog mailed 4x per year
Memo: Info line: 908-294-0071.

Copper Electronics
Chester Massie III, Pres
3315 Gilmore Industrial Blvd
Louisville KY 40213
800-626-6343; FAX orders: 502-968-0449
Subjects: 23(IBM)
Items: Sw-accessories
Catalog mailed 12x per year
Numbers: 350,000 mailed
Memo: Customer service: 502-968-8500.

Cotton Patch
Carolie Hensley, Owner
1025 Brown Ave
Lafayette CA 94549
510-284-1177; Fax: 510-284-8470
Subjects: 29(quilting)
Items: CR-HC-PB
Catalog mailed 2x per year
Other: 300-350 titles

Covox Inc
Mark Stewart, Pres
675 Conger St
Eugene OR 97402
503-342-1271; FAX orders: 503-342-1283
Subjects: 23
Items: PC interactive systems
Catalog mailed 4x per year
Numbers: 250,000 mailed

Craft Business Books
James Dillehay, Publisher
Warm Snow Publishers
PO Box 75
Torreon NM 87061
505-384-1102; Fax: 505-384-1102
Subjects: 29
Items: HC-PB-SW
Catalog mailed 1x per year
Other: 30-40 titles
Numbers: 5,000 to 10,000 mailed

Craft King Inc
Susan Robins, Mktg Mgr
PO Box 90637
Lakeland FL 33804
813-648-2898; Fax: 813-648-2972
Subjects: 11-29
Items: CR-PB
Catalog mailed 1x/year
Numbers: 60-70 week

Crate & Barrel Catalog
Deborah Rethemeyer, Exec Dir
725 Landwehr Rd
Northbrook IL 60062
708-272-2888; Fax: 708-215-0482
Subjects: 27-43
Items: Home furnishings (no books)
Catalog mailed 4x per year

Crawford-Peters Aeronautica
James P Peters, Buyer
3702 Nassau Dr
PO Box 152528
San Diego CA 92195
619-287-3933
Subjects: 70A(space & aviation)
Catalog mailed
Memo: 10 different catalogs with aviation as the topic.

Crazy Bob's
ERM/Electronic Liquidators
50 New Salem St
Wakefield MA 01880-1979
800-776-5865; FAX orders: 617-246-6776
Internet: Cat 900@crazy bob.com
WWW: http://www.shore.net/~crazybob/
Subjects: 23-99
Items: All types multi-media software
Catalog mailed 1x per year
Memo: Customer service: 617-246-6767
Tech support: 617-246-6774.

Creative Machine
Robbie Fanning, Editor/Publ
Open Chain Publishing Inc
PO Box 2634
Menlo Park CA 94026
415-366-4440; Fax: 415-366-4455
Subjects: 29

Creative Needle
Marge Serck, Owner
6905 S Broadway #113
Littleton CO 80122
303-794-7312
Subjects: 29
Numbers: 2,000 mail
Memo: No catalog at the moment, but will have one in the future.

Crescent Books Catalog
Rowan Archer
735 Delaware Rd #195
Town of Tonawanda NY 14223
716-877-2416; Fax: 716-877-2416
Subjects: 10-75-82-83
E-Mail: CresBooks@aol.com
Memo: No poetry or chidrens books.

Critic's Choice Video
Nancy Hamlin, Buyer
800 W Thorndale Ave
Itasca IL 60143
708-775-3300; Fax: 708-775-3340
Subjects: 33M
Items: HC-TV-GI

Crutchfield Computer Catalog
William Crutchfield Jr, Pres
1 Crutchfield Park
Charlottesville VA 22906
800-521-4050; FAX orders: 804-973-1862
Subjects: 23
Items: Software/accessories/supplies
Catalog mailed 2x per year

Memo: Customer service: 800-446-7924
Tech support: 800-537-4050(hardware) or 800-538-4050(software).

CSI Direct
Mort Rosenthal, CEO
Corporate Software
PO Box 9125
Norwood MA 02062-9125
800-882-9506; FAX orders: 800-677-4008
Subjects: 23(business software)
Catalog mailed 2x per year

Culpepper Hughes & Head
Betty M Culpepper, Mktg VP
Black Studies & Books
9770 Basket Ring Rd
Columbia MD 21045
410-730-1484
Subjects: 49
Items: HC-PB-US
Catalog mailed 4x per year
Other: 2,000 titles

Cumberland General Store
John Ebert, Pres
#1 Hwy 68
Crossville TN 38555
615-484-8481; Fax: 615-456-1211
Subjects: 15-21-27-28-29-43-61
Items: HC-PB-GI-OT
Catalog mailed 1x per year
Numbers: 60,000
Other: 100+ titles;
Memo: Also have a store. New reproduction antiques catalogue $4.00 each.

Current Inc
Attn: Book Buyer
1025 East Woodman
Colorado Springs CO 80920
719-594-4100
Subjects: 99
Items: PB-GC-TO-OT
Catalog mailed approx 14x per year
Memo: Customer service: 800-525-7170.

CWI Products & Services
PO Box 4851
Anaheim CA 92803
800-777-5636; FAX orders: 714-879-1036
Subjects: 23(IBM)
Items: Low cost software
Catalog mailed 4x per year
Numbers: 7,500,000
Memo: Customer service: 714-879-7917.

The Cyclosource Catalog
Teri Maloughney
Adventure Cycling Assn
150 E Pine PO Box 8308
Missoula MT 59807
406-721-8719; Fax: 800-721-8719
E-Mail: acabike@aol.com
Subjects: 69(bicycling/safety)
Items: HC-PB-TV-MA-GI-OT(camping gear)
Catalog mailed 3x per year
Other: 80-100 titles
Memo: Priority members to get map discount, but do not have to be a member to order one.

D

Daily Planet
Doug Platt, Pres
180 Varick St 4th Fl
PO Box 1313
New York NY 10014
212-807-7200; Fax: 212-807-7252
Subjects: 44E(Russian)
Items: HC-PB-TV-GI

DAK
Drew Kaplan, Pres
DAK Industries Inc
8200 Remmet Ave
Canoga Park CA 91304-9955
800-325-0800; FAX orders: 818-888-2837
Subjects: 23
Items: SW-accessories
Catalog mailed 8x per year
Numbers: 500,000 mailed
Memo: Customer service: 818-888-8220.

The Dance Mart
A J Pischl, Pres
Dance Books
PO Box 994
Teaneck NJ 07666
201-833-4176
Subjects: 14D
Items: HC-PB
Catalog mailed 2x per year
Other: 2,000 titles

Dancing Dragon Catalog
Henry Collins, Buyer
5670 West End Rd #4
Arcata CA 95521
707-826-0189; Fax: 707-826-1370
E-Mail: dragon@northcoast.com
Subjects: 79-86(dragons only)
Items: HC-PB-CL-PO-GI-GA-OT(sculptures)
Catalog mailed 6-8x yearly
Other: 10 titles

Dangerous Visions
Lydia C Marano, Mdse Dir
13563 Ventura Blvd
Sherman Oaks CA 91423-3825
818-986-6963; Fax: 818-341-7354
E-Mail:specific@primenet.com
WWW: http://www.primenet.com/-specfic/
Subjects: 82-86
Items: HC-PB-CA
Catalog (more like a newsletter) mailed 6x per year
Other: 6,000 titles

Daniel Smith Catalog
Reid Jordan
4150 First Ave S
Seattle WA 98134
206-223-9599; Fax: 206-224-0404
800-426-6740
E-Mail: dsartmtrl@aol.com
Subjects: 11
Items: HC-PB-OT
Catalog mailed every 3 months.
Other: 10-15 titles

Dartek Computer Supply Catalog
Buyer
175 Ambassador Dr
Naperville IL 60540
708-355-3000; Fax: 708-355-3888; 800-832-7835
Subjects: 23
Catalog mailed 12x per year
Other: 50 titles

Data Command
PO Box 548
Kankakee IL 60901
800-528-7390
Subjects: 23-31E
Items: SW
Catalog mailed 1x per year

The Datamation Bookshelf
Susan Mael, Assoc Editor
Cahners Publishing Co
275 Washington St
Newton MA 02158
617-558-4438; Fax: 617-928-4438
E-Mail: smael@datamation.cahners.com
Subjects: 23C(information management)
Memo: She also selects books for review for the magazine.

Davidson School Catalog
John Patrick, Mktg Mgr
Davidson & Assoc Inc
19840 Pioneer Ave
Torrance CA 90503-1690
213-534-4070
Subjects: 23-31E
Items: SW
Catalog mailed 1x per year
Numbers: 300,000 mailed

Davka Hebrew/Judaic Software
7074 N Western Ave
Chicago IL 60645-3451
312-465-4070
Subjects: 23-49J
Items: Hebrew/Judaic SW-GI
Catalog mailed 1x per year

DEC Direct
Jay Atlas, Mktg VP
Digital Equipment Corp
PO Box 4076
Woburn MA 01888-4076
800-344-4825; Fax: 800-550-4743
FAX orders: 800-524-5694
Subjects: 23
Items: SW
Catalog mailed 2x per year

Decision Data Direct
Joe Kroger, Pres
410 Horsham Rd
Horsham PA 19044
800-356-3334; FAX orders: 215-675-8619
Subjects: 23(PC & MAC)
Items: SW-accessories, supplies
Numbers: 200,000 mailed

Dell Computer Corp
Michael Dell, CEO
PO Box 2385
Round Rock TX 78680-2385
800-963-3355; FAX orders: 800-727-8320.
Subjects: 23
Items: Computer systems built to order
Catalog mailed 12x per year

Design Originals
Linda Rocamentes, Pres
2425 Cullen St
Fort Worth TX 76107-1411
817-877-0067; Fax: 817-877-0861
Subjects: 29-29H
Items: HC-PB
Catalog mailed 3-4x per year
Other: 400 titles

Destiny Image Catalog
Keith Carroll, Publisher
Companion Press Books
167 Walnut Bottom Rd
Shippensburg PA 17257
717-532-3040; Fax: 717-532-9291; 800-722-6774
Http://www.reapernet.com
Subjects: 63
Catalog mailed 1x per year
Numbers: 120,000 mailed
Other: 50 titles

DG Direct
Ronald Albert/Tom Messier
Data General Corp
4400 Computer Dr
Westboro MA 01580
800-343-8842
FAX orders: 508-836-4209.
Subjects: 23
Items: SW-hardware, supplies
Catalog mailed 4x per year
Numbers: 250,000 mailed

Dick Blick Central
Jeff Woolsey, Buyer
PO Box 1267
Galesburg IL 61402-1267
309-343-6181; Fax: 800-621-8293; 800-447-0048
E-mail: info@dickblick.com
WWW: http://www.dickblick.com
Subjects: 11-29
Items: HC-PB-art supplies
One large yearly catalog & small one 4x per year
Memo: Art supply stores & catalog.

Dick Blick West
Book Buyer
1951 Ramrod
PO Box 521
Henderson NV 89105
702-451-7662; Fax: 702-451-8196
Subjects: 11
Items: HC-PB-OT
Catalog mailed 1x per year
Other: 100+ titles
Memo: Dick Blick Central, PO Box 1267, Galesburg, IL 61401. (309-343-6181).

The Dictionary Catalogue
Emanuel Molho, Buyer
Rockafeller Ctr Promenade
610 Fifth Ave
New York NY 10020
212-581-8810; Fax: 212-265-1094
Subjects: 45-59(dictionaries)-80
Items: HC-PB
Other: 50,000+ titles
Memo: French & European Publications Catalog carries many dictionaries in foreign languages.

A Different Light Review
Roz Parr/Dan Seitler
A Different Light
151 W 19th St
New York NY 10011
212-989-4850; Fax: 212-989-2158
Subjects: 13-37-73
Items: HB-PB-MM-RM-MG-CA-CO-GI-TA-TV-GC
Catalog mailed 2x per year
Numbers: 50,000 mailed
Other: 300 titles

Digital PC Catalog
Digital Equipment Corp
PO Box 9501
Merrimack NH 03054-9501
800-700-9890; FAX orders: 800-524-5694
Modem ordering: 800-234-1998
Subjects: 23
Items: SW-accessories, supplies
Catalog mailed 4x per year

Direct Marketing Library
Bjorn Hafgren, Buyer
Hoke Communications
224 Seventh St
Garden City NY 11530-5771
516-746-6700; Fax: 516-294-8141
E-Mail: 71410.2423@compuserve.com.
Subjects: 19M-19G(fundraising)
Items: HC-PB
Catalog mailed monthly
Other: 6 titles

Directory Marketplace
Todd Publications
PO Box 301
West Nyack NY 10994
800-747-1056; Fax: 914-358-6213
Subjects: 17C-19-23-31-44-49-56
Items: Lots of how-to

Disability Bookshop Catalog
Helen Hecker, Mdse Dir
Twin Peaks Press
PO Box 129
Vancouver WA 98666-0129
306-694-2462; Fax: 306-696-3210
Subjects: 12-14-19-21-23-25-27-31-35-39-9
Items: HC-TA-CA-GA-TV-GI(800-637-2256)
Catalog mailed 6x per year
Numbers: 250,000 mailed
Other: 500 titles

Discount Boating Supplies
F T Wichrowski, Mdse Dir
M & E Marine Supply Co Inc
PO Box 601
Camden NJ 08101
609-858-1010; Fax: 609-757-9175
Subjects: 70N
Items: HB-PB-OT
Catalog mailed 5x per year
Numbers: 1,000,000
Memo: 6 buyers

Discount Master Animal Care
Marc Glen, Mdse Dir
Humboldt Industries Inc
1 Maplewood Dr
Hazelton PA 18201-9798
717-384-5555; Fax: 717-384-2500
Subjects: 15
Catalog mailed 8x per year
Numbers: 5,000,000
Memo: 1 retail outlet.

Disk World Inc
Patricia Judge, Pres
4215 Main St
Skokie IL 60076-2046
800-255-5874; FAX orders: 708-492-5067
Subjects: 23
Items: SW-disks-supplies
Catalog mailed 4x per year
Numbers: 100,000 mailed

Diskette Gazette Catalog
D Daves, Editor
2278 Trade Zone Blvd
San Jose CA 95131-1801
800-222-6032
Subjects: 23(MAC)
FAX orders: 408-262-8906
Items: SW-disks-supplies
Catalog mailed 2x per year

Disks & Labels To Go Inc
Robert Peters, Pres
1702 Industrial Hwy #1
Cinnaminson NJ 08077-2567
800-426-3303; FAX orders: 609-265-0818
Customer service: 609-265-1500
Subjects: 23
Items: SW-supplies
Catalog mailed 2x per year

The Disney Catalog
Roseanne Mazzarella, Buyer
Disney Dir Marketing Service
250 Park Ave S
New York NY 10003
212-677-5530; Fax: 212-677-5653
Subjects: 21-76-43H-40F
Items: GI-TO-TV-OT(clothing/home items)
Catalog mailed 6x per year

DMA Publications Catalog
Betty Lawler, Catalog Mgr
Direct Marketing Assn
1120 Ave of the Americas
New York NY 10036-6700
212-768-7277; Fax: 212-391-1532
Subjects: 19M(direct marketing)
Items: HC-PB
Catalog mailed yearly catalog
Other: 50 titles

Doctors Foster & Smith Catalog
Book Buyer
2253 Air Park Rd
PO Box 100
Rhinelander WI 54501-0100
715-369-3305; Fax: 715-369-2821
Subjects: 15(cats and dogs)
Items: HC-PB-OT(supplies): 800-826-7206
Catalog mailed 4x per year
Other: 50 titles
Memo: Dr Race Foster and Dr Martin R Smith, Owners.

The Dog & Cat Book Catalog
Charlene Woodward, Mdse Dir
Direct Book Service
701-B Poplar
Wenatchee WA 98801
509-663-9115; Fax: 509-662-7233
E-Mail: dgctbook@cascade.com
Subjects: 15(dogs and cats)
Items: HC-PB-TA-TV-CA
Catalog mailed 3x per year
Numbers: 150,000 mailed

Dollspart Supply Co Inc
Marcy Buturla, Buyer
Dollspart Supply Co
8000 Cooper Ave
Ridgewood NY 11385
718-326-4500; Fax: 718-326-4971
Subjects: 28-29(dolls)
Items: HC-PB-OT(doll supplies)
Catalog mailed 4x per year
Other: 50 titles

Doolco
James P Doolin, Pres
11258 Goodnight Ln #105
Dallas TX 75229
214-241-2326; 800-886-2653)
Subjects: 19X(service work how-to books)
Items: HC-PB
Memo: Books on refrigeration, air conditioning & heating.

Dr MAC
Barry Light, Pres
11050 Randall St
Sun Valley Ca 91352
800-825-6227; FAX orders: 818-504-9380
Customer service: 818-504-1800
Subjects: 23(Macintosh)
Items: SW-hardware
Catalog mailed 4x per year
Numbers: 100,000 mailed

Dragich Auto Literature
John Dragich
1660 93rd Ln NE
Minneapolis MN 55449
612-786-3925; Fax: 612-786-8939
800-328-8484
Subjects: 16A
Items: HC-PB(owners/shop manuals)
Catalog mailed 1x per year
Other: 6,000 titles
Memo: Sales catalog mailed 2x per year.

Drawing Board Computer Supply
Attn: Mdse Director
Computer Supplies Division
PO Box 2995
New Hartford CT 06104-2995
800-527-9530; Fax: 800-253-1838
Subjects: 23
Items: GC-HC-PB-SW-ST
Catalog mailed 2x per year

Drawing Board Full Line Catalog
Dana Baldwin, Mktg Mgr
Greenwoods Industrial Park
PO Box 2995
New Hartford CT 06104-2995
800-527-9530; Fax: 800-253-1838
Subjects: 19(office supplies)
Items: GC-CA-OT-ST
Memo: Sell office supplies; labels, laser products.

DRB Motors Catalog
James Roseborough, Pres
168 Davenport Rd
Toronto ON Canada M5R 1J2
416-922-8860
Subjects: 16A
Items: HC-PB-TV
Catalog mailed 1x per year
Other: 2,500 titles

DreamHaven Books & Art
Greg Ketter, Owner
912 W Lake St
Minneapolis MN 55408
612-823-6070; Fax: 612-823-6062
E-Mail:dreamhavn@winternet.com
Subjects: 82-86
Items: HC-PB-MM-US
Catalog mailed every month
Other: 1,000 titles

DTP Direct
Desktop Publishing Catalog
5198 W 76th St
Edina MN 55439
800-890-9373; FAX orders: 612-832-0052
Subjects: 23
Items: SW-hardware, accessories
Catalog mailed 12x per year
Memo: Tech support: 800-759-2133.

Duncraft
Eileen Schlagenhaft, Buyer
102 Fisherville Rd
Penacook NH 03303-9020
603-224-0200; Fax: 603-226-3735
Subjects: 15(birds)-51
Items: PB-OT(bird seed/supplies)
Seasonal catalog mailed 4x per year
Other: 3-4 titles

Dunn's Supply
John Meador, Pres/Catalog Div
PO Box 449
Grand Junction TN 38039
901-764-6901; Fax: 901-764-6570
Subjects: 69H(shooting/training/etc)
Items: HC-PB-OT(supplies)
Catalog mailed every month except June

E

E & B Marine
Lynda Frink, Book Buyer
201 Meadow Rd
Edison NJ 08818
908-819-7400; Fax: 908-819-4794
Subjects: 70N
Items: HC-PB-GI-OT
Catalog mailed 1x per year

E F Schumacher Society
Bob Swann
RR 3 Box 76
Great Barrington MA 01230
413-528-1737; Fax: 413-528-4472
Subjects: 13-19-25-55-65

E/J Bloom Associates
Joy Bloom, VP
Educational Division
115 Duran Dr
San Rafael CA 94903
415-492-8443; Fax: 415-492-1239
E-Mail: 71147.3274@compuserve.com
Subjects: 24
Items: HC-PB-SW
Catalog mailed 1x per year
Other: 65 titles
Memo: Power electronics engineers;
  seminars.

Eagle Books
Peter Nash, Buyer
2446 NW 13th Pl
Gainesville FL 32605
904-372-4148
Subjects: 48-99
Catalog mailed 4x per year
Numbers: 10,000+ mailed

Eagle Books
Grace Adams, Buyer
The Grace Publishing Co
829 Langdon Ct
Rochester Hills MI 48307
810-650-9450; Fax: 810-650-9450
Subjects: 21-99(no fiction)
Items: HC-PB
Catalog mailed
Other: 35 titles
Memo: Catalog mailed 4x per year.

Early Childhood Catalog
Cindy Allen, Buyer
Gryphon House
PO Box 207
Beltsville MD 20704
301-595-9500; Fax: 301-595-0051
Subjects: 21
Items: HC-PB
Catalog mailed 1x per year
Other: 500 titles

Earth Guild Catalog
Michael Garner, Book Buyer
33 Haywood St
Asheville NC 28801
704-255-7818; Fax: 704-255-8593
Order line: 800-327-8448
Subjects: 29
Items: HC-PB-CR-OT(craft tools/supplies
Catalog mailed yearly with an update
  every two months.
Other: 445 titles

East West Market Exchange
Mdse Director
5533 N Broadway
Chicago IL 60640-1405
312-878-0686; Fax: 312-878-6874
Subjects: 69(martial arts)
Items: HC-PB-PO
Catalog mailed every 6 years
Other: 150 titles

The Eastwood Company
Jim Carlson, Purchaser
PO Box 296
Malvern PA 19355
610-640-1450; Fax: 610-644-0560
Subjects: 16A-28
Items: HC-PB-CA-GI-PO
Catalog mailed 10-12x per year
Other: 40 titles
Memo: Street address: 580 Lancaster
  Ave, Frazer, PA.

Eddie Bauer
Rick Fersch, Pres
PO Box 3700
Seattle WA 98124
800-426-8020; Fax: 206-649-7851
Subjects: 15-51-69
Items: CA-GI
Memo: Eddie Bauer Inc, 15010 NE 36th
  St, Redmond, WA 90852.

Editor's Choice Catalog
Hillary Heffernan, Publ
ON Technology Corp
1 Cambridge Ctr
Cambridge MA 02142-1604
800-381-5686; FAX orders: 617-374-9014
Subjects: 23
Items: SW-Novell networks

Edmund Scientific
Gwynne Edmund, Mktg VP
101 E Gloucester Pike
Barrington NJ 08007
609-573-6234; Fax: 609-573-6272
Subjects: 24-31E-39-51-67
Items: HC-PB-GA-MA-TO-OT
Catalog mailed 2x per year
Numbers: 3,500,000 mailed
Memo: Gwynne buys for their catalog.
  John Burgo, Store Manager, buys for
  their store.

Educalc
Brent Martin, Purchasing Agent
27953 Cabot Rd
Laguna Niguel CA 92677
714-582-2637; Fax: 714-582-1445
800-677-7001
Subjects: 12-19-23-24-31-67
Items: HC-PB-TX-RM-CA-SW
Catalog mailed 4x per year
Numbers: 250,000 mailed
Other: 50 titles

Educational Materials Catalog
Judy Koehly, Buyer
NL Associates Inc
PO Box 1199
Hightstown NJ 08520
609-448-8443
Subjects: 21-31E-67
Items: PB
Catalog mailed 2-3 times a year
Numbers: 30,000

Educational Resources
David Zasada, Mktg Mgr
1550 Executive Dr
Elgin IL 60123-9330
800-624-2926; FAX orders: 708-888-8499
Customer service: 708-888-8300
Subjects: 23(Hewlett Packard)
Items: SW
Catalog mailed 2x per year
Numbers: 500,000 mailed

Educational Spectrums Catalog
Jane Williams, Buyer
Bluestocking Press
Dept MOC PO Box 1014
Placerville CA 95667
916-621-1123; Fax: 916-642-9222
Subjects: 13-19-21-25-31E-55-71-76-81-89
Items: HC-PB-GA-MA-PO-TA-OT
Catalog mailed once a year
Other: 100+ titles

Educorp Software Catalog
Suzi Nawabi, Mktg VP
Educorp Computer Services
7434 Trade St
San Diego CA 92121-2410
800-843-9497; FAX orders: 619-536-2345
Internet: service@educorp.com
Subjects: 23
Catalog mailed 4x per year
Numbers: 2,000,000
Memo: Also Encyclopedia/CD-ROM Catalog. Customer service: 619-536-9999.

Egghead Software
Peter Grossman, Sr VP-Mktg/Mdse
22705 E Mission
Liberty Lake WA 99019
509-922-7031
Subjects: 23
Items: HC-PB-SW
Catalog mailed 12x per year
Monthly promotional sales catalog (50-70 pages)
Memo: Customer service: 800-EGG-HEAD.

Elderly Instruments
Book Buyer
1100 N Washington
PO Box 14210
Lansing MI 48901
517-372-7880; Fax: 517-372-5155
Orders only: 517-372-7890
E-Mail: web@elderly.com
Subjects: 14M
Items: HC-PB-CD-TV-TA
Catalog mailed 1x per year
Numbers: 35,000 mailed
Other: 50+ titles

Eldersong Publications
Beckie Karras, Pres
108 E Ridgeville Blvd #D
PO Box 74
Mount Airy MD 21771
301-829-0533; Fax: 301-829-5249
Subjects: 35A
Items: HC-PB-GA-TA-TV
Memo: Creative activity materials for older adults and recreation activity personnel.

Empire Books
Dennis Kroh, Pres
PO Box 2634
Ormond Beach FL 32175
904-677-7314; Fax: 904-677-7324
E-Mail: kroh@aol.com
Subjects: 41(Roman & Greek coins)
Items: HC-PB
Catalog mailed 2x a month
Other: 200 titles

The Enchanted Doll House
Carin Marsfelder, Pres
RR 1 Box 2535
Manchester Center VT 05255
802-362-1327; Fax: 802-362-4223
800-362-9001
Subjects: 28(collectibles only)
Items: HC-PB-GA-TO
Catalog mailed annually
Numbers: 35,000 mailed

English Literature & Reading
Buyer
Opportunities for Learning
100 Paragon Pky
Mansfield OH 44903
419-589-1700; Fax: 419-589-1522
800-243-7116
Subjects: 23-31E-47
Items: HB-PB-SW
Catalog mailed 1x per year

Entrepreneur's Bookshop Catalog
Victoria Nova, Mdse Dir
PO Box 129
Vancouver WA 98666-0129
360-694-2462; Fax: 360-696-3210
Subjects: 19-25-29-56-57-59
Items: HC-PB-SW-GI-TA-TV
Catalog mailed 4x per year
Numbers: 100,000 mailed

Environmental Media Corporation
Gwen Gerber, Mktg VP
PO Box 99
Beaufort SC 29901-0099
803-986-2333; Fax: 803-986-9093
Subjects: 51-56M-49(cultures)
Items: HC-PB-OP-TX-MG-TA-TV-MA-CD-ROMS
Catalog mailed once a year
Numbers: 78,000 mailed
Memo: Looking for an environmental atlas, and if they find one they will carry it. Catalog is sent once a year with special mailings throughout the year, and they are looking to get on the internet.

ET Valueline
Morton Goldman, Pres
Elek-Tek Inc
7550 N Linder Ave
Skokie IL 60077
800-395-1000
FAX orders: 708-677-7168
Subjects: 23
Items: SW-hardware, accessories
Catalog mailed 3x per year
Memo: IBM, Apple, Epson, Hewlett-Packard, Packard-Bell, Panasonic, Hayes, Okidata & over 4,000 products. Technical support: 708-677-7660.

EWA Miniature Cars USA
Carl Pflanzer, Mdse Dir
369 Springfield Ave
Berkeley Heights NJ 07922
908-665-7811; Fax: 908-665-7814
Subjects: 16A-28
Items: HC-PB-MG-TO-TV-OT
Catalog mailed 4x per year
Other: 2,500 titles

EXPO-LIT
Julie Maas, Editor
Lakewood Publications
50 South Ninth St
Minneapolis MN 55402
612-333-0471; 800-328-4329
Subjects: 29H-19-56-23
Items: Jerry C Noack, VP/Publisher
Catalog mailed once a year
Numbers: 30,000 mailed

Exposures Catalog
Susan Hope, Mdse VP
41 South Main St
South Norwalk CT 06854
203-854-1610; Fax: 203-854-5654
800-222-4947
Subjects: 11-28-29-35-43(displaying pix)
Items: HC-PB-CA-GC-PO-TV-TO-OT
Catalog mailed 12 times a year
Numbers: 13,00,000 mailed
Other: 10-12 titles

Express Direct
Glen Lombardi, Pres
2720 N Paulina Ave
Chicago IL 60614
800-925-6777; FAX orders: 312-244-3080
International FAX orders: 312-244-3081
Subjects: 23(MAC)
Items: SW-accessories, supplies
Catalog mailed 4x per year

F

Fairchild Books & Visuals
Marie Todor, Mdse Dir
7 West 34th St
New York NY 10001
212-630-3865; Fax: 212-630-3868
800-247-6622
Subjects: 56
Items: HC-PB
Catalog mailed 1x per year
Numbers: 40,000 mailed

The Faith Mountain Company
Kim Baader, Mdse Mgr
Main Street
PO Box 199
Sperryville VA 22740-0199
703-987-8824; Fax: 703-987-7288; 800-822-7238
Subjects: 40-43
Items: HC-PB-GI-OT(clothes)
Catalog mailed 4x per year

Family Software
Peter Kelman, Pres
Scholastic Inc
PO Box 7502
Jefferson City MO 65101
800-541-5513
FAX orders: 314-635-5881
Subjects: 23
Items: Sw-GA
Catalog mailed 1x per year
Numbers: 500,000 mailed

Family Travel Guides Catalogue
Carole T Meyers
Carousel Press
PO Box 6061
Albany CA 94706-0061
510-527-5849; Fax: 510-527-5849
Subjects: 21-35-45-71
Items: HC-PB-TA-GA-TV
Catalog mailed once a year
Numbers: 45,000 mailed
Other: 200 titles

Fantasy Etc
Buyer
808 Larkin St
San Francisco CA 94109-7119
415-441-7617
Subjects: 82-84-86-87
Items: HC-PB-CA
Numbers: 3,000 mailed

Fickes Crime Fiction
Patricia A Fickes, Owner
1471 Burkhardt Ave
Akron OH 44301-2305
216-784-1553
Subjects: 84
Items: HC-PB-MM-OP-US
500 catalogs mailed 4x per year
Other: 7000 titles

Find Catalog/SVP
Joanna Leefer, Mgr
The Information Co
625 Ave of the Americas
New York NY 10011
212-645-4500; Fax: 212-645-7681;
   800-346-3787
E-Mail: catalog@findsvp.com
Subjects: 19M
Items: PB
Catalog mailed every 2 months
Other: 200 titles

Firefighters Bookstore
Peggy Glenn, Owner
18281 Gothard St #105
Huntington Beach CA 92648
714-375-4888; Fax: 714-848-4566
Subjects: 19C
Items: HC-PB-TX-RM-CA-SW-OT
Catalog mailed 4x per year
Numbers: 800,000 mailed
Memo: The focus of our catalog is solely firefighters and medics. Please send information only on books, videos or computer software that are about firefighters or EMS providers or are directly related to firefighting or emergency medical services.

Flax Artists Materials
Philip Flax, Pres
1699 Market St
PO Box 7216
San Francisco CA 94120
415-468-7530; Fax: 800-352-9123
Orders: 800-547-7778
Subjects: 11
Items: HC-PB-GI-OT

Flower & Garden Book Service
Jeff Nightengale, Mgr
KC Publishing
700 W 47th St #310
Kansas City MO 64112
816-531-5730; Fax: 816-531-3873
Subjects: 43G
Items: HC-PB-PO
Numbers: 700,000 mailed

Font & Function Catalog
Adobe Systems Inc
1585 Charleston Rd #7900
Mountain View CA 94043-1225
415-961-4400
Subjects: 23
Catalog mailed 2x per year
Memo: Desktop publ & graphic design.

Food Products Press Catalog
Bill Cohen, Publisher
Food Products Press
10 Alice St
Binghamton NY 13904-1580
800-342-9678; Fax: 607-722-6362
Subjects: 27
Other: 200,000; 100 titles
Memo: Culinary arts/food science/agriculture.

Frank Mittermeier Catalog
Frank Mittermeier, Dir
3577 E Tremont Ave
PO Box 2W
Bronx NY 10465
718-828-3843; Fax: 718-518-7233
Subjects: 29
Items: HC-PB-CR-OT
Memo: Wood carving

Frey Scientific
Buyer
Frey Scientific Co
PO Box 8101
Mansfield OH 44905-8101
419-589-1900; Fax: 419-589-1522
Subjects: 67-67A-67S-67M-59
Items: HC-PB-SW-OT(scientific equip)
Memo: Biology, physiology, botany, chemistry, physics, lab equipment.

Frog Tool Company
Richard Watkins, Pres
2109 Illinios Rt 26
Dixon IL 61021
815-288-3811; Fax: 815-288-3919
Subjects: 29-43
Items: HC-PB-RM-OT
Memo: Fine hand woodworking, finishing materials, & book on woodworking.

Funny Side Up
Peggy Hunter, Buyer
425 Stump Rd
Montgomeryville PA 18936
215-361-5100; Fax: 215-368-8670
Subjects: 33-69
Items: GA-novelties
Other: 50 titles
Numbers: 7,000 mailed
Memo: Harriet Carter Gifts publishes this catalog.

Future Visions Books
Brad Frank, Mgr
10570 Northwest Fwy
Houston TX 77092
713-682-4212; Fax: 713-526-3515
Subjects: 86-87
Items: HC-PB-MM-PO-OP
Catalog mailed 3x per year
Other: 5,000 titles
Memo: Newsletter published every 6 weeks - sent to 35,000.

Future World Corporation
Dan Dimke, Company Dir
PO Box 153588
Irving TX 75015-3588
214-399-8400; Fax: 214-399-8300
E-Mail: future@onramp.net
http://www.future-world.com/central
Subjects: 19-34-53-57
Items: HB-PB-SW-TA
Catalog mailed 1x per year

Futurist Bookstore Catalog
Jeff Cornish, Book Buyer
World Future Society
7910 Woodmont Ave #450
Bethesda MD 20814-5089
301-656-8274; Fax: 301-951-0394
E-Mail: schley@tmn.com
Subjects: 23-39-67-99
Memo: Future trends/ideas/forecasts.

G

G C T Catalog
Fay Gold, Pres
PO Box 6448
Mobile AL 36660
334-478-4700; Fax: 334-478-4700
Subjects: 23-31
Items: HC-PB-SW
Memo: Educational materials for gifted students.

G Neil Companies Catalog
Kerri Winston, New Products
720 International Pky
PO Box 450939
Sunrise Fl 33345-0939
800-888-4040; Fax: 305-846-0777
Subjects: 19G-57(human resource products)
Items: PB(forms/awards/cards)
Other: 40 titles
Memo: Gary Neil Brown, President.

Gaan Computer Supplies
1745 Saratoga Ave #B
San Jose CA 95129-5206
408-255-4226; 800-523-1238; FAX orders: 408-255-0633
Subjects: 23
Catalog mailed 2x per year
Numbers: 100,000 mailed

Gale Research Catalog
Keith Lassner, Mktg Mgr
835 Penobscot Bldg
Detroit MI 48226
313-961-2242; Fax: 800-414-5093;
   800-223-GALE
Subjects: 59
Memo: Directories.

Gambler's Book Club
Howard Schwartz, Mktg Dir
630 S 11th St
Las Vegas NV 89101
702-382-7555; Fax: 702-382-7594;
   800-522-1777
Subjects: 69G(gambling)-17B-55C
Items: HB-PB-SW-TV-MM-RM-OP-US-MG-TA-NP
Other: 1,000 titles
Numbers: 40,000 mailed
Memo: The GBC catalog is sent free. Published once a year, 32 page tabloid is updated 3x per year. Has extensive section on organized crime, biographies, history, sociology, since the Mafia and gambling often parallel each other throughout this century.

Gamblers World Catalog
Addy Reiterman, Mdse Dir
1938 E University Dr
Tempe AZ 85281
602-968-2590
Subjects: 69G
Items: SW-TV-GA
Catalog mailed per request
Other: 600-800 titles
Memo: This lists different SW and videotapes (gambling games) for computers basically. Also a bookstore.

Gander Mountain
Ralph Freitag, Pres
PO Box 248
Wilmot WI 53192-0248
414-862-2331; Fax: 414-862-2741
800-558-9410
Subjects: 15-27-51-69H-71
Items: HC-PB-GI-CL-OT
Catalog mailed monthly
Other: 40 titles

The Garden of Beadin'
Charlotte
752 Redwood Dr
Garberville CA 95542
707-923-9120; Fax: 707-923-9160
800-232-3588
Subjects: 26C(beads)
Other: 35 titles
Memo: PO Box 1535, Redway, CA 95560.

Gardener's Eden
3250 Van Ness
San Francisco CA 94109
415-421-7900; Fax: 415-983-9887
Subjects: 43G
Items: HC-PB-OT(gardening supplies)

Gardener's Supply
Meg Smith, PR Mgr
128 Intervale Rd
Burlington VT 05401
802-660-3500; Fax: 802-660-3501
Subjects: 43G
Seasonal catalog 2-3 issues per season
Numbers: 7 million

Geary's Catalog
Bruce Meyer, Pres
351 N Beverly Dr
Beverly Hills CA 90210-4794
310-273-4741; Fax: 310-858-7555;
    800-243-2797
Subjects: 21-28-43G
Items: HC-GI
Other: 3 titles; 2 stores

Genium Publishing Corp
Mike Cinquanti, Pres
1 Genium Plz
Schenectady NY 12304-4690
518-377-8854; Fax: 518-377-1891
Subjects: 19-24-59
Items: HC-PB-TX-PO-SW-TV-OT(training bk
Other: 50 titles
Numbers: 180,000 mailed
Memo: The name of the catalog varies.

Gessler Educational Software
55 W 13th St
New York NY 10011
800-456-5825; FAX orders: 212-627-5948
Customer service: 212-627-0099
Subjects: 23
Items: SW (foreign language software)
Catalog mailed 1x per year

Gift Books Catalog
Denise Harrison-Ovaitt
Paperbacks for Educators
526 West Front St
Washington MO 63090
314-239-1999; Fax: 314-239-4515
Subjects: 99
Items: HC-PB-MM
Catalog mailed yearly
Other: 800 titles
Numbers: 20,000 mailed

Global Computer Supplies
Robert Leeds, Pres
11 Harbor Park Dr
Port Washington NY 11050-4622
800-845-6225; FAX orders: 516-625-6683
Customer service: 800-227-1246
Subjects: 23
Items: SW-hardware, accessories
Catalog mailed 12x per year
Numbers: 2MM

Global Trading Post
New Editions Intl Ltd
PO Box 2578
Sedona AZ 86336-2578
520-282-9574; Fax: 520-282-9730
E-Mail: newedit@sedona.net
Subjects: 39H-53-54-57

GMB Partnership
G R Brong, Partner
4530 Manatash Rd
Ellensburg WA 98926-9733
509-962-8238
Subjects: 19-31-55-56-57-70-97
Items: HB-PB-MM-SW
Other: 300+ titles

The Golden Harp of Joel Andrews
Joel Andrews, Mdse Dir
Golden Harp Enterprises
PO Box 335
Ben Lomond CA 95005
408-336-8888; Fax: 408-336-3379
Subjects: 14M
Items: PB-TA-CD
Catalog mailed 1x per year
Other: 2 titles
Memo: Well known for music.

GolfSmart Catalog
Guthrie Kraut, Buyer
PO Box 2373
Grass Valley CA 95945
916-272-1422; Fax: 916-272-2133
Orders: 800-637-3557(bks/videos)
Subjects: 69(golf)
Memo: Formerly GolfSmart Club.

Gooseberry Patch
27 N Union St
PO Box 190
Delaware OH 43015
800-854-6673; Fax: 614-363-7225
Subjects: 99

Gourmet Guides
Jean Bullock, Owner
Pier 12 Sandy Beach Rd
Vallejo CA 94590
707-644-6872; Fax: 707-554-1234
Subjects: 27-71
Items: HC-PB-RM-OP-TA-TV
Catalog mailed 12x per year
Other: 125 titles
Numbers: 10,000 mailed

Government Publications
H Baron, Mdse Mgr
601 Upland Ave
Upland PA 19015
610-499-7415; Fax: 610-499-7429
Subjects: 11-14-19-27-31-41-44-45-47-55-9
Items: HC-PB
Catalog mailed 6x per year
Numbers: 10,000 mailed

Great Christian Books
Paul Morris, Book Buyer
229 S Bridge St
Elkton MD 21922-8000
410-392-0800; Fax: 800-291-6341
www: http://www.greatchristianbooks.com
Subjects: 21-31-63P
Items: HB-PB(Bibles/home-schooling/theo
Catalog mailed 16x per year
Other: 14,000 titles

Great Games Products
Tom Troop
8804 Chalon Dr
Bethesda MD 20817
301-365-3297
Subjects: 23(Apple & MAC)
Items: Chess & Bridge SW
Catalog mailed 1x per year

The Great Kids Company
Micki Cabaaniss, Supv
Kaplan Corp
PO Box 609
Lewisville NC 27023-0609
910-766-7374; Fax: 910-766-5652;
    800-533-2166
Subjects: 21-31-76
Items: HC-PB-TO(educational)
Catalog mailed 2x per year

Greenhaven Press Library
Bruno Leone, Pres
Box 289009
San Diego CA 92129-9009
619-485-7424; Fax: 619-485-9549
800-231-5163
Subjects: 31E-41-99
Items: HB-PB
Catalog mailed 2x per year
Other: 300 titles

Grounds for Murder Newsletter
Phyllis Brown, Owner
3858 5th Ave
San Diego CA 92103
619-299-9500; Fax: 619-225-8580
Subjects: 84
Items: HC-RM-MM-MG-CA-GA-GI-TA
Catalog mailed 3x per year
Other: 10,000 titles
Memo: Newsletter sent sporadically — when there is a signing, new editions, etc.

Group Tech Catalog
Fred Scott, Pres
Group Tech Ltd
1 E Chase St #410
Baltimore MD 21202
410-625-2065; Fax: 410-625-2065
Subjects: 39-27N(African civilization)
Items: HC-PB-TV(health & nutrition)

Grower Talks Bookshelf
Sandy Smith, Buyer
335 N River St
Batavia IL 60510
708-208-9080; Fax: 708-208-9350
Subjects: 43G(greenhouse growers)
Items: HC-PB(professional books)

Guidance
Buyer
Opportunities for Learning
100 Paragon Pky
Mansfield OH 44903
419-589-1700; Fax: 419-589-1522;
    800-243-7116
Subjects: 19C-31E-57B
Items: HC-PB-SW
Catalog mailed 1x per year
Other: 4 titles

Guidance Associates
Book Buyer
100 S Bedford Rd
Mount Kisco NY 10549
914-666-4100; Fax: 914-666-5319
Subjects: 21T-31-35-39-57
Items: TV-SW

Guide Light
N Tyler, Buyer
PO Box 7838
New York NY 10150
212-688-8797
Subjects: 19M-59(directories)
Items: HC-TV-OT
Catalog mailed 2x per year
Other: 100 titles

Gurze Eating Disorders Bookshelf
Lindsey Cohn
Gurze Books
PO Box 2238
Carlsbad CA 92018
619-434-7533; Fax: 619-434-5476
800-756-7533
Subjects: 39H-39R
Items: HC-PB
Catalog mailed annually
Numbers: 115,000 mailed
Other: 120 titles

H

H Kauffman & Sons Book Dept
Charles Kauffman, Buyer
419 Park Ave S
New York NY 10016
212-684-6060; Fax: 212-213-0389;
    800-872-6687
Subjects: 15(horses)-29H
Items: HC-PB-OT(horse care supplies)
Memo: This company carries a wide
    variety of equipment to care for horses.

Hacker Art Books Inc
Pierre Colas
45 West 57th St
New York NY 10019-3909
212-688-7600; Fax: 212-754-2554
Subjects: 11-12A(decorative arts)-43D
Items: HC-PB
Catalog mailed 2x per year
Other: 800 titles

Hagstrom Map & Travel
Mahmudul-Azim, Buyer
Hagstrom Map & Travel Ctr
57 West 43rd St
New York NY 10036
212-398-1222; Fax: 212-398-9856
Subjects: 70-71
Items: HC-PB-MA
Catalog mailed every 3 years.
Other: 500 titles

Hammacher Schlemmer Catalog
Mary Kay Keyes, Buyer
303 W Erie
Chicago IL 60610
312-664-8170
Subjects: 69-43(personal care)-71
Items: TA-TV-TO(high tech gifts)
Catalog mailed monthly
Memo: Operations center: 9180 LeSaint
    Dr, Fairfield, OH 45014.

Hampton Books Catalog
Patrick Sullivan
Bace & Assoc
3818 DeSabla Rd
Cameron Park CA 95682
916-677-2254; Fax: 916-677-1030
Subjects: 19M-57(self-help/motivation)
Items: HC-PB-TA-TV
Catalog mailed 2x per year
Other: 200 titles

Hanover House Catalog
Madeline Krashinsky, Sr Buyer
Hanover Direct Inc
1500 Harbor Blvd
Weehawken NJ 07087
201-863-7300; Fax: 201-319-3495
Subjects: 99(low-priced gifts)
Items: HC-PB-GI
Catalog mailed 4x per year
Other: 5-10 titles
Memo: Madeline's direct line:
    201-330-3170.

Hard-to-Find Needlework Books
Bette S Feinstein, Pres
96 Roundwood Rd
Newton MA 02164
617-969-0942; Fax: 617-969-0942
Subjects: 29H-40F(needlework)
Items: HC-PB-RM-OP
Memo: Books only.

Harriet Carter Gifts
Catalog Mgr
425 Stump Rd
Montgomeryville PA 18936
215-361-5100; Fax: 215-368-8670
Subjects: 99
Items: HC-PB-GI(household/small items)
Catalog mailed 5x per year
Other: 75 titles
Memo: All items in the $10-$15 dollar
    range.

Haven Corp
Pamela Johnson, Dir of Sales
1227 Dodge Ave
Evanston IL 60202-1008
800-676-0098
Subjects: 23
Items: SW
Catalog mailed 1x per year
Memo: Mail Order Wizard & the Mail List
    Monarch.

Hazelden Educational Materials
Jerry Spicer, Pres
15251 Pleasant Valley Rd
PO Box 176
Center City MN 55012-0176
612-257-4010
Subjects: 39R-57B-57P-57S
Items: HC-PB-GI
Memo: Materials on AIDS — how to deal
    with it and how to cope.

Health Master
Conscious Living Foundation
PO Box 9
Drain OR 97435
503-836-2358; Fax: 503-836-2358
Subjects: 39H-53-57-27-31-69
Items: HC-TA-TV-PB-GA-SW
Catalog mailed 4x per year
Numbers: 80,000 mailed

Hearlihy & Co
Cecilia Backus, Buyer
714 W Columbia St Box 869
Springfield OH 45501
800-622-1000; FAX orders: 513-324-2260
Customer service: 513-324-5721
Subjects: 23
Items: Industrial tech/educ software
Catalog mailed 1x per year
Numbers: 50,000 mailed

Hearth Song Inc
6523 N Galena
Peoria IL 61656
309-689-3838; Fax: 309-689-3857; Orders:
    800-325-2502
Subjects: 21-29-31-35-63
Items: HC-PB
Catalog mailed
Other: 30 titles

Heathkit
Miles Hoffman, Mktg Mgr
The Heath Co
PO Box 1288
Benton Harbor MI 49022-8589
800-253-0570
FAX orders: 616-982-5577
Catalog orders: 800-444-3284.
Subjects: 23
Items: SW-accessories for kits
Catalog mailed 4x per year
Numbers: 3,000,000 mailed

Heizer Software
Ray Heizer, Pres
PO Box 232019
Pleasant Hill CA 94523
800-888-7667; FAX orders: 510-943-6882
Customer/tech service: 510-943-7667
Subjects: 23(IBM & MAC)
Items: SW-over 1,000 low-cost programs
Catalog mailed 4x per year

Hello Direct Catalog
Don Chiang, Product Mgr
5884 Eden Park Pl
San Jose CA 95138
408-972-1990; Fax: 408-972-8155
800-444-3556
E-Mail: xpressit@hihello.com
Tech support: hitech@hihello.com.
Subjects: 19M
8 catalogs per year with update in between
Memo: Telemarketing/supplies, headsets, answering systems, switches, office products, & cellular products.

Hemmings Motor News
Customer Service Dept
Hemmings Publishing
PO Box 76
Bennington VT 05201-0076
802-442-3101; Fax: 802-447-1561
Subjects: 16A
Items: HC-PB-OT(auto parts, cars)
Catalog mailed monthly
Numbers: 267,904 mailed
Memo: Terry Ehrich, President.

Heritage Books Inc
Leslie Towle, Buyer
1540-E Pointer Ridge Pl
Bowie MD 20716
301-390-7708; Fax: 301-390-7153
E-Mail: heritagebooks@usa.pipeline.com
Subjects: 41A-41G-41W
Items: HB-PB

Herrington
Lee Herrington, Pres
3 Symmes Dr
Londonderry NH 03053
603-437-4939
Subjects: 14-69
Items: TA-TV-GI
Memo: High-tech gifts - no books.

Hershey's Gift Catalog
Valerie Leonard, Buyer
Hershey's Mailorder
PO Box 800
Hershey PA 17033-0800
800-544-1347; Fax: 717-534-7947
Subjects: 27
Items: GI
Memo: Few books.

Highlander Company
Thomas Deighan, Pres
1072 N Jacoby Rd
Copley OH 44321
216-666-6748
Subjects: 69(golf)
Items: HC-PB-TV-PO

Highlights for Children
Elmer Mider, Pres
2300 W 5th Ave
Columbus OH 43215
614-486-0631; Fax: 614-487-2700;
800-848-8922
Subjects: 21-76
Items: HC-PB

Highsmith Microcomputer Catalog
Paul Moss, Mktg Mgr
Highsmith Co Inc
W5527 Hwy 106, PO Box 800
Ft Atkinson WI 53538-0800
800-558-2110; FAX orders: 800-835-2329
Customer service: 800-558-3899.
Subjects: 23
Items: SW-hardware
Catalog mailed 2x per year

Historic Aviation Catalog
James Horne, Book Buyer
1401 Kings Wood Rd
Eagan MN 55122-3811
612-454-2493; Fax: 612-454-8554
Subjects: 17-41-48-70A
Items: HC-PB-TV-PO(limited art prints)
Other: 300 titles
Memo: Also a wholesaler.

Hofcraft Catalog
Doug Freye, Book Buyer
PO Box 72
Grand Haven MI 49417
616-847-8822; Fax: 616-847-8989
Subjects: 11-29H(detail paintings)-OT
Items: HC-PB
Other: 150 titles
Numbers: 10,000 mailed
Memo: Painting supplies for the professional painter.

Hold Everything Catalog
Book Buyer
3250 Van Ness Ave
San Francisco CA 94109
415-421-7900; Fax: 415-616-9212
Subjects: 29-43
Items: Home organizers

Hoover's Educational Catalog
Ronnie Stefka, Buyer
Hoover Brothers Inc
2050 Postal Way
Dallas TX 75212
214-634-8474; Fax: 800-988-4279;
800-527-7766
Subjects: 14-21-31-59-67-69-71
Items: TA-TV-TX
Catalog mailed 1x per year
Memo: Educational materials/supplies.

The Horchow Collection
Book Buyer
111 Customer Way
Irving TX 75039
214-556-6000; 800-825-8255
Subjects: 71
Items: Home furnishings, gift books
Catalog mailed - 1 title
Memo: Upscale gifts

Horizons Catalog
Michael Mooers, Dir
Alpha Omega Publications
PO Box 3153
Tempe AZ 85281
602-438-2717; Fax: 602-438-2702;
800-821-4442
Subjects: 17-21-31-35-45-63-69-76
Numbers: 250,000 mailed
Other: 300 titles

House of 1776 Catalog
Maxine Miller, Owner
3110 S Jupiter
PO Box 472927
Garland TX 75047-2927
214-864-1776; Fax: 800-747-1779
Subjects: 27
Numbers: 200,000 mailed
Other: 5 titles

House of Tyrol
Bernhard Puck, Buyer
Tyrol International
66 E Kytle St
Cleveland GA 30528
706-865-5115; Fax: 706-865-7794;
800-241-5404
Subjects: 16-27-28-35-35R-44-45-70-71-79
Items: CA-GA-TA-TV
Catalog mailed 7x per year
Numbers: 10,000,000 mailed

How to Sell More/Today's Market
Henry Lavin, Mdse Mgr
Lavin Associates
12 Promontory Dr
Cheshire CT 06410-1497
203-272-9121; Fax: 203-250-1461
Subjects: 19-56
Items: Guide books only
Catalog mailed 1x per year
Numbers: 10,000 mailed
Other: 24 titles

HP Direct Computer Users Catalog
Gil Merme, Gen Mgr
Hewlett-Packard Co
1320 Kifer RD
Sunnyvale CA 94086
800-538-8787
Technical support: 800-858-8867
Subjects: 23
Items: Software/supplies/accessories
Catalog mailed 1x per year
Numbers: 1,000,000

HP Kopplemann Inc
140 Van Block Ave
PO Box 145
Hartford CT 06141-0145
203-549-6210; Fax: 203-293-0279
800-243-7724: for orders
CT: 800-842-2165
Subjects: 21-31-31E-76-79-84-89
Memo: This is a paperback book service with two separate catalogs-one for grades K-8, and another for grades 6-12.

HPK Language Arts Catalog 6-12
140 Van Block Ave
PO Box 145
Hartford CT 06141-0145
203-549-6210; Fax: 203-293-0279
Orders: 800-243-7724
CT: 800-842-2165.
Subjects: 21-31-31E-76-79-84-89
Memo: This is a paperback book service with two separate catalogs-one for grades K-8, and another for grades 6-12.

HPK Language Arts Catalog K-8
140 Van Block Ave
PO Box 145
Hartford CT 06141-0145
203-549-6210; Fax: 203-293-0279
Orders: 800-243-7724
CT: 800-842-2165.
Subjects: 21-31-31E-76-79-84-89
Memo: This is a paperback book service with two separate catalogs-one for grades K-8, and another for grades 6-12.

Hubert NDiaye Book Co
Hubert NDiaye
Times Square Sta
PO Box 2603
New York NY 10108
Fax: 212-382-0166
Subjects: 19-39R-53-57
Memo: NDiaye is correct spelling.

HUMOResources Bookstore Catalog
Anita Harris, Mgr
The Humor Project
110 Spring St
Saratoga Springs NY 12866
518-587-8770; Fax: 518-587-8771
E-Mail: DRJ3@aol.com
Subjects: 31-33-33C-33H-39-57
Items: HC-PB-TA-CA-GA-GC-PO-TV
Memo: Including humor and creativity, humor and wellness. Joel Goodman, President, The Humor Project.

I

ICS Books Inc
Thomas Todd/S Hilbrich, Buyers
1370 E 86th Pl
Merrillville IN 46410
800-541-7323; Fax: 800-336-833
Subjects: 27-33-39
Items: PB
Catalog mailed 2x per year
Numbers: 8,000 mailed
Other: 85 titles

Image Club Graphics Inc
Brad Zumwalt
c/o Publisher's Mail Service Inc
10545 W Donges Ct
Milwaukee WI 53224-9985
800-661-9410; FAX orders: 403-261-7013
Subjects: 12P-23
Items: Photos/clip art/bks/tapes/CD-ROM

Image Club Software Catalog
729 24th Ave SE
Calgary AB Canada T2G 1P5
800-661-9410; FAX orders: 403-261-7013
Customer service: 403-262-8008
Subjects: 23(MAC/PC Windows)
Items: Desktop publishing software
Catalog mailed 2x per year

Independent Press Catalog
Victoria Nova
Twin Peaks Press
PO Box 129
Vancouver WA 98666-0129
360-694-2462; Fax: 360-696-3210
Subjects: 99

Items: HC-PB-CA-TA-GA-MA-PO-TV-TO
Catalog mailed quarterly
Numbers: 100,000 mailed

Industrial Computer Master Srcbk
Martin Kleine, Editor
Industrial Computer Source
10180 Scripps Ranch Rd
San Diego CA 92131-1234
800-523-2320; FAX orders: 619-677-0898; FAX info: 800-677-7329
Subjects: 23(IBM compatible)
Items: Software/hardware/accessories
Catalog mailed 1x per year
Numbers: 1,000,000 mailed

Infosource Inc
Michael Werner, Pres
6947 University Blvd
Winter Park FL 32792-6707
407-677-0300
Subjects: 23
Items: SW
Catalog mailed 6x per year
Numbers: 1,000,000
Memo: Free catalog,

INMAC
Michael Wade, Mktg Mgr
PO Box 168065
Irving TX 75016-9901
800-547-5444; FAX orders: 800-972-3210
Subjects: 23
Items: SW, hardware, accessories
Catalog mailed 20x per yr
Computer ordering: 800-323-6905;
    Customer service: 800-972-9239;
    Technical support: 800-972-9233;
    Tech-support FAX: 800-972-3210

Intelletronics
Gregg Peters, Mktg Dir
Computer Stores Northwest
2305 NW Kings Blvd
Corvallis OR 97330
800-935-9993
FAX orders: 503-752-1791
Subjects: 23(Apple/Mac)
Items: SW-accessories, supplies
Catalog mailed 4x per year

Interact Direct
Dave Sparks, Pres
350 S Lake Ave #315
Pasadena CA 91101
800-479-1323; FAX orders: 818-578-0272
Internet: interacted@aol.com
Subjects: 23(PC & MAC)
Items: Wide variety of CD-ROM software
Catalog mailed 6x per year

International Marine Publishing
Paula Blanchard, Retail Cat Mgr
PO Box 220
Camden ME 04843
207-236-6039; Fax: 207-236-6314
Subjects: 70N-71
Other: 350 titles
Memo: Also has business and material relating to small boats.

International Wealth Success
Tyler Hicks, Pres
24 Canterbury Rd
Rockville Centre NY 11570
516-766-5850; Fax: 516-766-5919; 800-323-0548
Subjects: 19H
Items: HC-PB
Catalog mailed 1x per year
Memo: Books on real estate/import & export/small business. Also 2 newsletters 12x per year: Int Wealth Succes & Money Watch Bulletin.

Intertech Marketing Inc
John Segner, Pres
8820 Six Forks Rd
Raleigh NC 27615
800-762-7874; FAX orders: 919-870-8343
Customer service: 919-870-8404
Subjects: 23
Items: SW-accessories
Catalog mailed 1x per year

Invisible Ink: Books on Ghosts
Christie Woodyard, Editor
Kestrel Publications
1811 Stonewood Dr
Beavercreek OH 45432-4002
513-426-5110; Fax: 513-320-1832; 800-31G-HOST
Subjects: 53(ghosts and hauntings only)
Items: HC-PB-TA-TV
Catalog mailed 2x per year
Other: 400 titles

IPS Associates Catalog
Suzanne Crowell
Institute for Policy Studies
1601 Connecticut Ave NW 5th Fl
Washington DC 20009
202-234-9382; Fax: 202-387-7195
Subjects: 56M-13-19-55-51A
Items: HC-PB

IQRA Book Center
Mian Asif, Catalog Development
International Education Found
6410 N Campbell Ave
Chicago IL 60645
312-274-2665; Fax: 312-274-8733; 800-521-4272
Subjects: 63E(books on Islam and Muslims)
Items: HC-PB-TA
Other: 250 titles
Memo: Dr Abidullah Ghazi, Executive Director.

Irish Family
Michael O'Laughlin, Dir
Irish Family Journal
PO Box 7575
Kansas City MO 64116
816-454-2410; Fax: 816-454-2410
E-Mail: 71334.3034@compuserve.com
Subjects: 41W-44E-45(Irish)-80
Items: HC-MA(collectibles)
Catalog mailed 2x per year
Numbers: 100,000 mailed

Book Publishing Resource Guide Page 149

IWA Catalog
Robert Orenstein, Mdse Dir
International Wine Accessories
11020 Audelia Rd #B-113
Dallas TX 75243
214-349-6097; Fax: 214-349-8712;
  800-527-4072
Subjects: 27(wine)
Items: HC-PB-SW-GA-GC-PO-TV-OT
Catalog mailed 10x per year
Numbers: 3,000,000 mailed

J

Jameco Electronics Catalog
Ray Avanzino, Mktg Mgr
1355 Shoreway Rd
Belmont CA 94002
415-592-8097; Fax: 415-592-2503
E-Mail: info@Jameco.com
Sales only: 800-831-4242; FAX:
  800-237-6948
Subjects: 23-67
Items: HC-PB-OT(hardware)
Catalog yearly with supplements 4x per year

Jane's Catalog
Alfred Rolington
Jane's Information Group
1340 Braddock Pl #300
Alexandria VA 22314
703-683-3700; 800-243-3852;
  Fax: 703-836-0029; Sales: 800-824-0768
Subjects: 70A
Items: HC-CD-MG
Catalog mailed 1x per year
Other: 30 titles

Japan Catalog
H Baron, Mdse Dir
Diane Publishing Co
601 Upland Ave
Upland PA 19015
610-499-7415; Fax: 610-499-7429
Subjects: 44(Japan)
Items: PB
Catalog mailed 6x per year
Numbers: 10,000 mailed

Jax Photo Books & Videos
Jack Qualman, Pres
6834 Briarwood Dr
Carlsbad CA 92009
619-931-0797
Subjects: 11P
Items: HC-PB-TV
Catalog mailed 4x per year
Other: 200 titles; 125 videos

JDR Microdevices
Jeffrey Rose, Pres
2233 Samaritan Dr
San Jose CA 95124-4407
800-538-5000; FAX orders: 800-538-5005
Customer service: 800-538-5001
Tech support: 800-538-5002
International orders: 408-559-1200
Subjects: 23
Items: Windows software/accessories
Catalog mailed 6x per year

Jeffers Pet Catalog
Book Buyer
PO Box 948
West Plains MO 65775-0948
417-256-3196; Fax: 417-256-1550;
  800-533-3377
Subjects: 15(pets, horses)-51A
Items: HC-PB-TV-SW-GI
Catalog mailed
Other: 45 titles

Jensen Tools Inc
Andy Smiley, Tech Support
7815 S 46th St
Phoenix AZ 85044-5399
800-426-1194; Fax: 800-366-9662
Subjects: 23-59
Memo: Everything for PC and network test service.

Jerry Buchanan Bookstore
Jerry Buchanan
TOWERS Club USA
PO Box 2038
Vancouver WA 98668-2038
360-574-3084; Fax: 360-576-8969;
  800-524-4045
Subjects: 56
Items: HC-PB
Catalog mailed 2x per year
Other: 20 titles

Jerry's Catalog
Ira Alan, Dir
PO Box 1105 AL
New Hyde Park NY 11040
516-328-6633; Fax: 516-328-6752
800-221-2323
Subjects: 11A-29
Items: HC-TV-CR-OT
Catalog mailed 3x per year
Numbers: 700 mailed

Jessica's Biscuit Cookbooks
David Strymish, Pres
PO Box 301
Newtonville MA 02160
617-965-0530
00-878-4264
Subjects: 27
Numbers: 2,000 mailed

Jobs and Careers for the '90s
Ron Krannich, Pres
Impact Publications
9104-N Manassas Dr
Manassas Park VA 22111-5211
703-361-7300; Fax: 703-335-9486
Subjects: 19C-57-71
Items: HC-PB-TA-TV-SW-OT
Numbers: 200,000 mailed
Other: 2000 titles

Johnson-Smith Catalogs
New Products Division
4514 19th St Ct E
PO Box 25500
Bradenton FL 34206-5500
941-747-2356; Fax: 941-746-7896
Subjects: 11-14-15-21-25-33-53-69-86-99
Items: HC-PB-TA-CR-GA-PO-RC-TO-TV-GI
Catalog mailed 2x per month
Numbers: 1,000,000 mailed
Memo: Lighter Side; also Things You Never Knew Existed.

K

KC Publishing
Jeff Nightingale
700 W 47th St #310
Kansas City MO 64111-3015
816-531-5730; Fax: 816-531-3873
Subjects: 43G
Items: HC-PB
Catalog mailed bi-monthly
Numbers: 700,000 mailed

Keats Publishing Program
H Goldfind, Mdse Dir
27 Pine St
PO Box 876
New Canaan CT 06840
203-966-8721; Fax: 203-972-3991;
  800-858-7014
www.PMedia.com/Keats/kform.html
Subjects: 27-39-53-57-59
Items: HC-PB
Catalog mailed 2x per year
Other: 548 titles

Keepsake Quilting
Rosemary J Mack, Buyer
Route 25-B
PO Box 1618
Centre Harbor NH 03226-1618
603-253-8731; Fax: 603-253-8346
800-865-9458
Subjects: CR(quilting)-29C(quilting)
Items: HC-PB-CR-OT(quilting supplies)
4 catalogs & 3 newsletters per year
Other: 50 titles
Memo: Judy Sprague Sabanek, Owner.

Keithley-Data Acquis/Control
Ronald Bridgers, Pres
Keithley Metrabyte/Asyst/DAC
440 Myles Standish Blvd
Taunton MA 02780
800-348-0033
FAX orders: 508-880-0179
Customer service & Tech support:
  508-880-3000
Subjects: 23
Items: Acquisition, control system-SW
Catalog mailed 1x per year
Memo: Novice to expert.

KIDSRIGHT Catalog
Judith Foner
Acquisitions Dept
10100 Park Cedar Dr
Charlotte NC 28210
704-541-0100; Fax: 704-541-0113;
  800-892-5437
Subjects: 21-31-35S-57B-57P-57S-73-76
Items: HC-PB-GA-TA-TV-TO-OT
Catalog mailed 1x per year
Other: 1,000 titles

Kirchen Brothers Catalog
John Abens, Pres
6310 W Touhy Ave
Niles IL 60714-4624
708-647-6747; Orders only: 800-378-5024
Subjects: 29
Items: HC-PB
Catalog mailed 1x per year
Other: 100-150 titles

Klockit Catalog
Kristie Kramer, Buyer
PO Box 636
Lake Geneva WI 53147
414-248-7000; Fax: 414-248-9899
800-556-2548
Subjects: 29
Catalog mailed 2x per year
Other: 25-35 titles

Krell Software
Marcia Friedland, Pres
PO Box 1252
Lake Grove NY 11755-0552
800-245-7355
Information: 516-689-3500.
Subjects: 23
Items: Educational/test prep software
Catalog mailed 2x per year
Numbers: 250,000,000

KWN Systems Inc
Beverly Nelson, Pres
220 Stonehurst Blvd
Freehold NJ 07728
908-431-4244
FAX orders: 908-431-3089
Subjects: 23
Items: Low-cost comm/user-supp software
Catalog mailed 4x per year
Numbers: 100,000 mailed

L

L L Bean Catalog
Public Affairs Dept
Casco Street
Freeport ME 04033
800-221-4221; Fax: 207-797-8867
International number: 207-865-3161
Subjects: 15-51-69H-69R
Items: GI-CL-OT
Catalog mailed 20x per year

Lab Safety Supply Catalog
Geneve Harris, Product Mgr
PO Box 1368
Janesville WI 53547-1368
608-754-2345; Fax: 800-543-9910
Orders: 800-356-0783
Subjects: 24-67
Other: 25 titles
Memo: Lab safety managers. Physical address: 401 S Wright Rd, Janesville, WI 53546.

Lambda Rising News
Julie Bremer, Sr Book Buyer
Lambda Rising Bookstores
1625 Connecticut Ave NW
Washington DC 20009-1013
202-462-6969; Fax: 202-462-7257
Subjects: 13-37
Items: HC-PB-CA-GC-GI-PO-TA-MG-TV-CL-OP
Catalog mailed 4x per year
Numbers: 580,000
Other: 600 titles

Laserstar
Noreen Trudel, Owner
23 Garfield Ave
Woburn MA 01801
800-432-9989; FAX orders: 617-937-0564
Customer service: 617-932-8667
Subjects: 23
Items: Laser ink-jet supplies/software
Catalog mailed 2x per year
Numbers: 25,000

Laughter Works - The Warehouse
Jim Pelley, Owner
PO Box 1076
Fair Oaks CA 95628
916-863-1592; Fax: 916-863-5072;
  800-626-5233
E-Mail: laftrworks@aol.com
Subjects: 33H
Items: HC-PB(humor books only)
Catalog mailed 1x per year
Other: 40 titles

Law & Justice Catalog
H Baron, Mdse Dir
Diane Publishing Co
601 Upland Ave
Upland PA 19015
610-499-7415; Fax: 610-499-7429
Subjects: 19L
Items: PB
Catalog mailed 6x per year
Numbers: 10,000 mailed

Learn and Play Catalog
Jan Bitcon, Book Buyer
Troll Associates
100 Corporate Dr
Mahwah NJ 07430
201-529-8000; Fax: 201-529-9347
800-526-5289
Subjects: 21-31-76
Items: HC-PB-TO

The Learning Co Software Catalog
6493 Kaiser Dr
Fremont CA 94555
800-852-2255
Subjects: 23
Catalog mailed 4x per year
Memo: IBM-compatible & Apple/Macintosh computer software for the education of young people ages 3-12. Hard disk required.

Learning Tools Catalog
Jennifer Leigh, Product Dir
3060 Racetrack View Dr
Del Mar CA 92014
619-481-6360; Fax: 619-481-8441
Subjects: 57-57B-57P-57S
Items: HC-PB-TA-TV
Catalog mailed 1x per year
Other: 32 titles
Memo: Publish for their own authors.

Learning World Catalog
Sarah Thibaudeau, Book Buyer
Learning World
17500 West Valley Hwy
Tukwila WA 98188
206-656-2900; Fax: 206-656-2926
800-562-3214
Subjects: 21-31
Items: HC-PB-CR-CA-GA-MA-PO-ST-SB-TA-TO
Catalog mailed every 2 years
Memo: 11 retail outlets- US only.

Lefthanded Specialties
Lois Ruby, Owner
Left Hand Ctr
210 W Grant #215
Minneapolis MN 55403
612-375-0319
Subjects: 21-29(lefties)
Items: HC-PB-GC-PO-SB
Catalog mailed by request at $2.00 a copy
Other: 12 titles
Memo: Lefthanded specialty items only.

Lefthanders Magazine Catalog
Carol Riddle, Mdse Dir
Lefthanders International
PO Box 8249
Topeka KS 66608
913-234-2177; Fax: 913-232-3999;
  800-203-2177
Subjects: 99(for lefties)
Items: PB-GI-school supplies
Catalog mailed 6x per year
Other: 3 titles

Lessiter Publications
Frank D Lessiter, Pres
PO Box 624
Brookfield WI 53008-0624
414-782-4480; Fax: 414-782-1252
Subjects: 15-19-28-41-51A-51E-69-99
800-645-8455
E-Mail: lesspub@aol.com
Items: HC-PB
Catalog mailed 1x per year
Other: 80 titles

Let's Go Travel Publications
Keith Evans, Publ
14 Moore Dr
Sabattus ME 04280
207-375-8760
Subjects: 71

Letter Arts Book Club
John Neal, Bookseller
1833 Spring Garden St
Greensboro NC 27403
910-272-6139
Subjects: 11-29
Items: CR-HC-PB-CA-GC-TV
Memo: Calligraphy & related arts.

Libertyville Saddleshop Catalog
Mdse Director
306 Peterson Rd
PO Box M
Libertyville IL 60048
708-362-0570; Fax: 708-680-3200
800-872-3353
Subjects: 15-69R
Items: HC-PB-OT(horse supplies)

Librarian Friendly Comput Softwr
Right On Programs
755-A New York Ave
Huntington NY 11743
516-424-7777; FAX orders: 516-424-7207
Subjects: 23
Items: Software for librarians
Catalog mailed 1x per year

Lifestyle Fascination Inc
Scott Carpenter, Buyer
1935 Swarthmore Ave
Lakewood NJ 08701
908-364-5777; Fax: 908-364-1551;
   800-669-0987
Subjects: 99
Items: HC-PB-TO-OT(computers)
Catalog mailed 12x per year
Numbers: 2,000,000

Light Impressions Catalog
W Bird, Buyer
PO Box 940 Ave
Rochester NY 14603-0940
716-271-8960; Fax: 716-442-7318
Subjects: 11P
Items: HC-PB-GI
Catalog mailed 6x per year
Other: Many titles
Memo: Archival supplies: matt
   board/portfolio boxes/slide page.

The Lighter Side
Thomas Ronzi, Prod Mgr
Johnson-Smith Co
4514 19th St Ct E
Bradenton FL 34203-3799
941-747-2356; Fax: 941-746-7962
Subjects: 14M-21-28-33-33H-69G-71
Items: HC-PB-TA-CR-GA-PO-CD-TO-TV-GI
Catalog mailed 4-6x per year
Other: 50-100 titles

Lighthouse Books
Michael Slicker, Buyer
1735 First Ave N
St Petersburg FL 33713
813-822-3278
Subjects: 28-41-47
Items: HC-PB-MA
Catalog mailed 4x per year
Other: 100 titles
Memo: Books only.

Lillian Vernon Catalog
Buyer
Merchandising Dept
543 Main St
New Rochelle NY 10801
914-576-6400; Fax: 914-637-5740
Subjects: 99
Items: HC-PB-GI
Catalog mailed monthly
Other: 1 title
Memo: Some low-priced books/gifts.

Lilly's Kids Catalog
Thomas D'Ambrosio, Toy Buyer
543 Main St
New Rochelle NY 10801
914-576-6400; Fax: 914-637-5740
Subjects: 21-31-76-99
Items: HC-PB-GI-TO
Catalog mailed 4x per year
Other: 2 titles

Lindsay Electrical Books Catalog
Thomas Lindsay, Owner
PO Box 538
Bradley IL 60915
815-935-5353; Fax: 815-935-5477
Subjects: 23-24-29(h2w-to)-67-59
Items: HC-PB
Catalog mailed 5x per year
Other: 1,000 titles

The Literate Traveller
Nancy Heck, Owner
8306 Wilshire Blvd #591
Beverly Hills CA 90211
310-398-8781
800-850-BOOK
Subjects: 71
Items: HC-PB
Catalog mailed 1x/year
Other: 50 titles

A Little Bit Crafty
Mdse Director
13519 Duggan Rd
Central Point OR 97502
541-855-1318; Fax: 541-855-9300
Subjects: 29
Items: PB-CR(supplies)
Catalog mailed 1x per year
Other: 20 titles

The Living Source
Nancy Sommers, Owner
Lake Air Mall
5301 Bosque #241
Waco TX 76710
817-776-4878; Fax: 817-776-932; Orders
   only: 800-662-8787
Subjects: 27-39H-51E
Catalog mailed 1x per year plus
   supplements
Other: 50 titles

Lotus Selects
55 Cambridge Pky
Cambridge MA 02139-9946
800-635-6887; FAX orders: 617-693-3899
Customer service: 617-577-8500
Subjects: 23
Items: SW(IBM compatibles)
Catalog mailed 4x per year

Loyola Press Reader Catalog
Heidi Toboni, Mktg Coord
Loyola Univ Press
3441 N Ashland Ave
Chicago IL 60657
312-281-1818; Fax: 312-281-0555
Subjects: 61-63-76(religious)
Items: HC-PB - 800-621-1008
Catalog mailed 2x year
Numbers: 50-60,000 mailed
Memo: This reader catalog is sent to
   individuals.

Lyben Computer Systems
PO Box 130
Sterling Heights MI 48311-0130
313-649-4500
FAX orders: 313-649-2500
Subjects: 23
Items: SW-supplies by box or carton

Lynchburg Hardware/General Store
Clayton Knight, Buyer
Lynchburg TN 37352
615-759-4200; Fax: 615-759-6308
Subjects: 27-99
Items: HB-PB(cookbooks)-OT
Catalog mailed 1x per year

M

The MAC Zone
Sadru Kabani, Pres
Multiple Zones Intl
15815 SE 37th St
Bellevue WA 98006-1800
800-248-0800; FAX orders: 206-861-5771
Customer service: 206-883-1975
Subjects: 23(Apple/MAC)
Items: SW
Catalog mailed 6x per year
Numbers: 750,000
Memo: Accounting & personal finance,
   business & presentation software.

MAC's Place
Robert Wilkens, Pres
100 Financial Dr
Kalispel MT 59901-6000
406-758-8000; FAX orders: 406-758-8080.
Subjects: 23(Macintosh)
Items: SW-hardware
Catalog mailed 4x per year

MACAvenue
Ed Thomas, Pres
Compuadd Corp
12303 Technology Blvd
Austin TX 78727
800-888-6221; FAX orders: 512-250-2058
MacFax info: 800-933-9002
Customer service: 512-250-1489
Tech support: 800-766-6221
International FAX: 512-250-5760
Subjects: 23(Apple Macintosh)
Items: Software/accessories/supplies
Catalog mailed 4x per year
Numbers: 5,000,000

MACBeat
Jack Fishman, Pres
PO Box 428
Pecos NM 87552
800-MAC-BEAT; FAX orders: 505-473-4647
Customer support: 505-473-4929
Tech line: 505-473-5142.
Subjects: 23(MAC)
Items: Music software/hardware/peripher
Catalog mailed 1x per year

MACConnection
Patricia Gallup, Pres
14 Mill St
Marlow NH 03456
800-800-1111; FAX orders: 603-446-779
Tech support: 800-800-0015
Customer support: 603-446-1111
Subjects: 23(Macintosh)
Items: SW-accessories, supplies, hardware
Catalog mailed 4x per year

MACMall
Creative Computer
2645 Maricopa St
Torrance CA 90503-5144
800-222-2808; FAX orders: 310-222-5800
Corp/Education Sales: 800-552-8883
Corp FAX orders: 310-222-5805
Customer service: 800-560-6800
Tech support: 800-760-0300
Subjects: 23(Apple Macintosh)
Items: SW-hardware, over 2,500 products
Catalog mailed 12x per year

MACProducts
8303 Mopac #218
Austin TX 78759-8369
800-622-3475; FAX orders: 512-343-6141
Subjects: 23
Items: SW-hardware, accessories
Customer service: 512-343-9441

Macrobiotic Book Catalog
Carl Ferre, Buyer
George Ohsawa Macrobiotic Found
1991 Myers St
Oroville CA 95966-5340
916-533-7702; Fax: 916-533-7908
Subjects: 27(macrobiotic)-39H
Items: HC-PB
Catalog mailed 2-3x per year
Other: 200 titles

MACWarehouse
Div of MicroWarehouse Inc
1720 Oak St Box 3013
Lakewood NJ 08701
800-255-6227; FAX orders: 908-905-9279
Customer service: 800-445-9677
Subjects: 23(Apple & Macintosh)
Items: Software/supplies/accessories
Catalog mailed 12x per year

Mail Order Catalog
Cynthia Holzapfel
PO Box 180
Summertown TN 38483
615-964-3571; Fax: 615-964-3518;
  800-695-2241
Subjects: 13-15-21-27-35-39H-43G-49A-
  51-71
Items: HC-PB-OT
Catalog mailed 2x per year

Mailer's Software
Kahle Williams, Program Mgr
970 Calle Negocio
San Clemente CA 92673-6201
800-800-6245; FAX orders: 714-492-7086
Tech support: 714-492-7000
Subjects: 23
Items: SW for direct mail solutions
Catalog mailed 4x per year

Major Reference Works
Kim Cavellero, Mktg
660 White Plains Rd
Tarrytown NY 10591
914-524-9200; Fax: 914-333-2444
Subjects: 59
Items: HB-PB
Other: 1000 titles
Memo: Medical & scientific journals.

Manderley
Lucinda May, Pres
Soda Creek Press
13131 Hwy 253 PO Box 679
Boonville CA 95415-0679
707-895-3822; Fax: 707-895-3719
Subjects: 85-75
Items: HC-PB-GA-CA-TA-TV
Numbers: 800 mailed

Maplewood Crafts Catalog
Helene Rosenzweig, Mdse Dir
Humboldt Industries Inc
1 Maplewood Dr
Hazelton PA 18201-9798
717-384-1111; Fax: 717-384-2500
Subjects: 29
Items: HC-PB-CR-CA-SB-TA-TV
Catalog mailed 4x per year
Numbers: 1,000 mailed

Marine Supplies
William Chan Chee, Mdse Dir
Defender Industries
255 Main St PO Box 820
New Rochelle NY 10801
914-632-2414; Fax: 914-632-6544; Orders:
  800-628-8225
E-Mail: defender@sailnet.com
Subjects: 69-70N
Items: MA-TV-SW-OT
Other: 200 titles
Numbers: 350,000
Memo: John Wilson/Mr Williams, Buyers.

Mark Ziesing Bookseller
Mark Ziesing, Owner
PO Box 76
Shingletown CA 96088
916-474-1580; Fax: 916-474-1580
E-Mail: 103633.2555@compuserve.com
Subjects: 63-82-86-87
Items: HC-PB-MM-US-OP
Catalog mailed every 6 weeks

Marketers Bookshelf
Ken Erdman, Publisher
402 Bethlehem Pike
Erdenheim PA 19038
215-233-2234; Fax: 215-233-2203
Subjects: 19M-57S
Items: HC-GI
Catalog mailed 2x per year
Other: 5 titles

Marketing Power
Jim Madden, Buyer
American Demographics
127 W State St PO Box 68
Ithaca NY 14851
607-273-6343; Fax: 607-273-3196; Order:
  800-828-1133
E-Mail: demographics.com
Subjects: 19M(marketing research)
Items: HC-PB
Catalog mailed 6x per year
Other: 100 titles
Numbers: 35,000 mailed

Mary Maxim Catalog
Joyce Minnis, Buyer
2001 Holland Ave PO Box 5019
Port Huron MI 48061-5019
810-987-2000; Fax: 810-987-5056
Subjects: 29-29H
Items: PB-CR
Catalog mailed 4x per year

Master Animal Care Catalog
Judith Patterson, Mdse Dir
Humboldt Industries Inc
1 Maplewood Dr
Hazelton PA 18201
717-384-5555; Fax: 717-384-2500;
  800-346-0749
Subjects: 15(pet health care)
Items: HC-PB-GI-GC-PO-TA-TV-TO-CA
Catalog mailed 6x per year

Math Products Plus
Elvira Monroe, Partner
PO Box 64
San Carlos CA 94070
415-593-2839; Fax: 415-595-0802
Subjects: 67M-69G(puzzles/mazes)
Items: PB-CL-PZ-GA
Memo: Lots of books.

Maverick Mail Order Bookstore
Marilyn Ross, Buyer
Communication Creativity
Box 909-MOB
Buena Vista CO 81211
719-395-8659; Fax: 719-395-8374
Subjects: 19-56
Items: HC-PB
1 or 2 catalogs mailed annually
Numbers: 10,000 mailed

Maxis Software Toys Catalog
Maxis Inc
2 Theatre Square #230
Orinda Ca 94563-3346
800-336-2947; FAX orders: 510-253-3736
Technical service: 510-253-3755.
Subjects: 23
Items: Computer software games
Catalog mailed 1x per year

Maypop Books
Book Buyer
196 Westview Dr
Athens GA 30606
800-682-8637; Fax: 706-546-0914
E-Mail: dobarks@uga.cc.uga.edu
Subjects: 14D-14M-95
Items: HB-PB-TA-TV
Other: 20 titles

McQuerry Orchid Books
5700 West Salerno Rd
Jacksonville FL 32244-2354
904-387-5044; Fax: 904-387-5044
Subjects: 43G(orchid flowers only)
Items: HB-PB-MG-US
Catalog mailed 1x per year
Memo: Lots of books - 3 published titles.

Media Great
Mdse Director
Computers in Science & Art
PO Box 598
Nicasio CA 94946
415-662-2426
Subjects: 11-23-67
Items: HC-PB-SW-TV-OT-CA
Catalog mailed 1x per year
Other: 900 titles

Meeting Planners Computer Catalog
Nick Topitzes, Pres
Topitzes & Assoc Inc
6401 Odana RD
Madison WI 53719-1158
800-233-9767
Subjects: 23
Items: SW-supplies, accessories
Catalog mailed 2x per year
Numbers: 50,000 mailed

Mellinger's Garden Catalog
Jean or Phil Steiner, Book Buyers
Dept ADL
2310 W South Range Rd
North Lima OH 44452-9731
216-549-9861; Fax: 216-549-3716; Orders:
  800-321-7444
Subjects: 43G
Catalog mailed 1x per year
Numbers: 450,000 mailed

Metropolitan Museum of Art
Brittany Bowling, Children's Bks
Children's Catalog
PO Box 255 Gracie Sta
New York NY 10028
212-879-5500; Fax: 212-472-5049;
  800-468-7386
Subjects: 11-21-76
Memo: Carolina Morales is the manager
  of the children's retail shop.

Michael Wiese Productions
Michael Wiese
11288 Ventura Blvd #821
Studio City CA 91604
818-379-8799; Fax: 818-986-3408;
  800-379-8808
E-Mail: wiese@earthlink.net
Subjects: 33(videos)
Items: TV
Catalog mailed 1x per year
Other: 14 titles

Micro Electronics Inc
Jeffrey P Morris, Buyer
dba Micro Center
1555 W Lane Ave
Columbus OH 43221-3977
614-481-8041; Fax: 614-481-4439;
  800-634-3478
Subjects: 23
Items: HC-PB-SW-OT(computers)
Other: 300 titles
Memo: Catalog mailed quarterly or
  sometimes monthly if there are
  changes.

Micro Express
Art Afshar, Pres
1801 Carnegie Ave
Santa Ana CA 92705
800-642-7621; FAX orders: 714-852-1225
Customer service: 714-852-1400
Subjects: 23
Items: SW-desk top systems

Micromath Scientific Software
W Robin Kemker
PO Box 21550
Salt Lake City UT 84121-0550
800-942-6284; FAX orders: 801-943-0299
Customer service: 801-943-0290
Subjects: 23
Items: Scientific software
Catalog mailed 1x per year

Middle Earth Bookshop
Paul B Hudson, Owner
PO Box 81906
Rochester Hills MI 48308-1906
810-656-4989; Fax: 810-656-3063
Subjects: 39-53-54-57-79
Items: HC-OP
Catalog mailed every 4-6 weeks
Numbers: 2,000 mailed

Middle East & Islam Catalog
Dorothy J Perkins, Buyer
Diane Publishing Co
601 Upland Ave
Upland PA 19015
610-499-7415; Fax: 610-499-7429
Subjects: 63
Items: TA-HC-PB-MA-PO
Catalog mailed 4x per year
Numbers: 25,000 mailed

Midwest Computer Works
180 Lexington Dr
Buffalo Grove IL 60089
800-669-5208; FAX orders: 708-459-6933
Tech support: 708-459-6883
Subjects: 23
Items: SW-desk top computers, etc
Catalog mailed 1x per year

Miles Kimball
Book Buyer
41 West 8th Ave
Oshkosh WI 54906-0001
414-231-4886; Fax: 414-231-6942
Subjects: 14-15-21-27-33-43-99(trivia)
Items: HC-PB-CA-GA-GI-TO-OT-ST
Numbers: 3,500,000 mailed
Catalog mailed 6x per year

Military History Catalog
Michael Schnitter, Pres
Q M Dabney and Co
PO Box 42026
Washington DC 20015
301-881-1470; Fax: 301-881-0843
E-Mail: gmdabney@clark.net
Subjects: 41-48
Items: HC
Catalog mailed every 6-8 weeks
Other: Few titles

Mimi's Books & Patterns for the Serious Dollmaker
Gloria Winer, Buyer
300 Nancy Dr
Point Pleasant NJ 08742
908-899-0804; Fax: 908-714-3906
E-Mail: firebird@exit109.com
Subjects: 29(dollmaking)
Items: HB-PB(books & patterns)
Catalog mailed 2x/year
Other: 12 titles

Miners Inc
PO Box 1301
Riggins ID 83549-1301
208-628-3247; Fax: 208-628-3749
Subjects: 67(geology/mining)
Items: HC-PB(geological supplies)

Mirth-Aid Catalog
Pamela Stile
Steve Wilson & Co
344 S Merkle Rd #120
Bexley OH 43209-1820
614-268-1094; Fax: 614-237-4055
Subjects: 33H
Items: PB-TO-OT
Other: 3 titles

Misco Power Up
Howard Entin, Mktg Mgr
1 Misco Plz
Holmdel NJ 07733
800-851-2917; FAX orders: 908-888-9449
Customer service: 800-647-2699
Tech support: 908-264-8324
Subjects: 23
Items: SW-hardware, accessories
Catalog mailed 3x per year
Numbers: 500,000 mailed

The Mix Bookshelf Catalog
Ben Pittman
c/o White Hurst & Clark
100 Newfield Ave
Edison NJ 08837-3817
800-233-9604; Fax: 908-225-1562
Orders: 800-233-9604
Subjects: 14-23-24-59
Items: HB-PB-TA-OT
Catalog mailed 2x per year
Others: 200 titles
Memo: Professional information on audio
  recording, electronic music & the
  music business.

Moorshead Publications
1300 Don Mills Rd
Don Mills ON Canada M3B 3M8
416-445-5600
FAX orders: 416-445-8149
Subjects: 23(Apple/Macintosh)
Items: Mainly public domain software

Morrill's New Directions
Jane Morrill, Mgr
PO Box 30
Orient ME 04471
800-368-5057; Fax: 207-532-0895
Subjects: 15
Items: Natural pet care
Other: 35+ titles

Mother Jones
Book Buyer
Mother Jones Magazine
731 Market St #600
San Francisco CA 94103
415-357-0509; Fax: 415-665-6696
Subjects: 13-17-31-41-47-49-55-57-65-71-7
Items: HB-PB

Motherwear
Kerry Eckstrone, Inventory Buyer
320 Riverside Dr
PO Box 114
Northampton MA 01061
413-586-1978; Fax: 413-586-2712
Subjects: 13-27-31-35-39-51-73
Items: OT(brestfeeding)
2 catalogs mailed at least 3 times per year
Other: 14 titles
Numbers: 600,000 mailed

Mountain Ark Trader Catalog
Nick Massullo, Gen Mgr
Mountain Ark Trading Co
PO Box 3170
Fayetteville AR 72702-3170
800-643-8909
501-442-7191; Fax: 501-521-9100
Subjects: 27-39H
Items: HC-PB-GI-OT
Catalog mailed 3x per year
Other: 50 titles
Memo: Macrobiotic/natural foods.

Mountain Rose Herbs
Julie Bailey, Owner
PO Box 2000
Redway CA 95560
707-923-3941; Fax: 707-923-7867
800-879-3337
Subjects: 39H(herbal medicines/healing)
Items: HC-PB-BT-OT
Catalog mailed 2x per year
Other: 40 titles

Movies Unlimited
Ed Weiss, Gen Mgr
6736 Castor Ave
Philadelphia PA 19149
215-722-8298; Fax: 215-725-3683;
  800-4-MOVIES
E-Mail: movies@moviesunltd.com
Subjects: 99
Items: TV
Catalog mailed 1x per year

Murder Ink Ltd Catalog
Jay Pearsall, Owner
2486 Broadway
New York NY 10025
212-362-8905; Fax: 212-877-0112;
  800-488-8123
Subjects: 84
Items: HC-RM-MM-GA-GI-MG-TA
Catalog mailed 3-4 times per year
Other: 20,000 titles

Music for Little People
Duff Stokes, Buyer
PO Box 1720
Lawndale CA 90260
203-899-1200; 800-727-2233
Subjects: 13-14M-21-51-76
Items: TA-HC-PB-TA-TV-CD
Catalog mailed monthly

The Music Stand
Ted Peck, Buyer/New Prod Mgr
FanFare Enterprises
66 Benning St
Lebanon NH 03784
603-298-6116; Fax: 603-298-6633
Subjects: 11-14M-17-33
Items: HC-PB-CA-GA-PO-ST-TA-TV-OT
Catalog mailed 4x per year
Numbers: 20,000,000 mailed

Myron Kimnach Bookseller
Myron Kimnach, Owner
5508 N Astell Ave
Azusa CA 91702-5203
818-334-7349; Fax: 818-334-0658
E-Mail: mkimnach@aol.com
Subjects: 51B
Items: HC-PB-US-OP
Catalog mailed 1x per year
Other: 1500 titles

Mysteries By Mail
Lucinda May, Pres
Soda Creek Press
13131 Hwy 253 PO Box 679
Boonville CA 95415-0679
707-895-3822; Fax: 707-895-3719
Subjects: 17-33-56-59-75-84-85
Items: HC-PB-TA-GA-CA-TV (800 items)
Numbers: 1,400 mailed

The Mysterious Bookshop
Otto Penzler, Owner
129 W 56th St
New York NY 10019-3808
212-765-0900; Fax: 212-265-5478
Subjects: 84
Items: HC-PB-MM-US-OP
Catalog mailed 2x per year
Other: 1,100 titles

Mystic Moon Magic Catalog
Karne Riddle, Owner
8818 Troy St
Spring Valley CA 91977
619-697-9990
E-Mail: mmoon@intrepd.resun.com
Subjects: 54M
Items: HC-PB-GI-TA-TV-OT(t-shirts)
Catalog mailed monthly

Mystic Trader & Whole Life Products
Joseph Meyer, Buyer
Pacific Spirit Corp
1334 Pacific Ave
Forest Grove OR 97116
503-357-1566; Fax: 503-357-1669
Subjects: 28-39H-53-54-57-79
Items: HC-PB-CA-PO-TA-TV-CL-CR-GI-SW-ST
Catalog mailed monthly
Other: 200 titles

N

NAFE Bookshelf
Kati Milborn, Communications Dir
Natl Assn for Female Executives
30 Irvine Pl
New York NY 10003-2303
212-477-2200
Subjects: 19-73
Other: 20-50 titles
Numbers: 180,000 members
Memo: Executive Female Magazine.

Nashua Express
PO Box 775
Merrimack NH 03054-4811
800-835-9264; FAX orders: 603-598-2070
Subjects: 23
Items: SW-hardware, accessories
Catalog mailed 4x per year

National Fire Protection Assn
Steve Hickey, Project Mgr
1 Batterymarch Park
Quincy MA 02269
617-984-7524; Fax: 617-984-7130
Subjects: 43H(safety)
Items: HC-PB

National Instruments
Preston Johnson, Sales
6504 Bridge Point Pky
Austin TX 78730-5039
800-433-3488; FAX orders: 512-794-8411
Customer service: 512-794-0100.
Subjects: 23
Items: Measure application software
Catalog mailed 1x per year

National Plan Service
David Azam, Pres
222 James St
Bensonville IL 60106
708-833-0640; Fax: 708-238-8885;
  800-533-4350
Subjects: 29-43(planning/how-to)
Items: HC-PB
Catalog mailed 1x per year
Other: 125+ titles

National Storytelling Catalog
Sharon Jones, Dir/Membership Ser
NAPPS
PO Box 309
Jonesborough TN 37659
615-753-2171; Fax: 615-753-9331;
  800-525-4514
Subjects: 21-29-33-76-79-90-41
Items: HC-PB-TA-CL-GI
Other: 90 titles
Numbers: 60,000 mailed
Memo: National Association for the Preservation & Perpetuation of Storytelling.

National Training Center
Paul Franklin
123 NW Second Ave #405
Portland OR 97209
503-224-8834; Fax: 503-224-2104
E-Mail: pfconsults@aol.com
Subjects: 19-19M-19S
Items: HC-PB-SW-TA

National Wildlife Federation
Al Lamson, Buyer
8925 Leesburg Pike
Vienna VA 22184
703-790-4000; Fax: 703-442-7332
800-432-6564
Subjects: 15-51
Items: HC-PB-OT
Catalog mailed 4x per year
Numbers: 300 mailed
Other: 5-20 titles

Nationwide Computer Distrib Inc
PO Box 7AQ
Jersey City NJ 07307
800-777-1054
FAX orders: 201-659-3345
Tech support: 201-659-2977
Subjects: 23
Items: SW-hardware, supplies
Catalog mailed 4x per year

Natural Choice Catalog
Rudolf Reitz, Owner
Eco Design Co
1365 Rufina Cir
Santa Fe NM 87501
505-438-3448; Fax: 505-438-0199;
  800-621-2591
Subjects: 39H-51
Catalog mailed 4x per year
Other: 2-3 titles

The Natural Gardening Company
Karen Kramer and David Baldwin
217 San Anselmo Ave
San Anselmo CA 94960
415-456-5060; Fax: 707-766-9747
Subjects: 43G-51
Items: HC-PB(supplies)
Catalog mailed 3x per year
Other: Few titles

Natural Lifestyle Supplies
Tom & Deborah Athos, Buyers
16 Lookout Dr
Asheville NC 28804
704-254-9606; Fax: 704-252-3386;
 800-752-2775
Subjects: 13-27
Items: HC-PB-natural, organic food,
 healthy ecological products, cookware
Catalog mailed 3x/year
Other: 20+ titles

Natural Science & Biology Books
Patricia Ledlie, Mdse Dir
One Bean Rd PO Box 90
Buckfield ME 04220
207-336-2969; Fax: 207-336-2778
Subjects: 15-51
Items: HC-PB
Catalog mailed 5x per year
Numbers: 100,000 mailed

Nature's Jewelry/Pyramid Books
Diane Cormier, Buyer
Catalog Ventures Inc
222 Mill Rd
Chelmsford MA 01824
508-256-4100; Fax: 508-256-1961
Subjects: 11-15-21-27-28-29-39-40-56-57-7
Items: HC-PB-GI-CR-GC-PO-ST-TA-TV-OT
Memo: To be on mailing list or get
 catalog: 800-333-3235.

NCFE Money-Book Store Catalog
Paul Richard, VP
Natl Ctr for Financial Education
PO Box 34070
San Diego CA 92163-4070
619-232-8811
Subjects: 21-25(children's money books)
Items: HC-PB-GA-TV-TA-OT(board games)
Catalog mailed once per year-$2.00
Other: 150 titles
Memo: Catalog National Center for
 Financial Education, Loren Dunton,
 President, 2200 Sacramento #207,
 San Francisco CA 94115; 415-567-5290.

NCR Direct
Carol Barker, Computer Prod Cat
PO Box 251
Miamisburg OH 45342
800-543-8130
FAX orders: 513-439-8412
Customer service: 800-262-7782
Subjects: 23
Items: Software/supplies/accessories
Catalog mailed 2x per year
Numbers: 2.5M

Nebs Computer Forms & Software
Joe Dugan, Mktg Mgr
New England Business Service
500 Main St
Groton MA 01471-0001
800-225-9550; FAX orders: 800-234-4324
Canada FAX orders: 705-526-2764
Customer service: 800-225-9540
Subjects: 23
Items: Over 825 software packages
Catalog mailed 4x per year

NEC Select Solutions
NEC Technologies Inc
1414 Massachusetts Ave
Foxborough MA 01719
800-284-4484; FAX orders: 508-264-8831
Subjects: 23
Items: SW-hardware
Catalog mailed 4x per year
Numbers: 125,000 mailed

Ned Ludd Books
Dave Foreman, Buyer
PO Box 1399
Bernalillo NM 87004
505-867-0878
Subjects: 51E
Items: HC-PB-CD-TA-TV
Other: 300 titles
Memo: Wilderness/endangered species.

Neiman Marcus Catalog
Buyer
111 Customer Way
Irving TX 75039-3627
800-634-6267; Fax: 214-401-6306
Subjects: 99
Memo: Upscale clothing/gifts - several
 stores.

The Network Marketer's Toolbox
59 Crimson Ln
Elizabethtown PA 17022
717-361-9007; Fax: 717-361-0860
Subjects: 23
Memo: A Carson Services Inc/Cutting
 Edge Opportunities joint venture.

Networking Solutions
Brenda McGuire, Sales Rep
Innovative Technology Ltd
PO Box 726
Elk City OK 73648
800-253-4001; FAX orders: 405-243-2810
Subjects: 23
Items: Networking software/equipment
Catalog mailed 4x per year

New & Unique Videos
Mark Schulze, Pres
New & Unique Videos
2336 Sumac Dr
San Diego CA 92105
619-282-6126; Fax: 619-283-8264
Subjects: 29-69-71-31
Items: TV
Numbers: 15,000
Other: 12 videos

New Age Entrepreneur
Marc Sky, Buyer
PO Box 120
Marlboro NJ 07746
908-536-4847; Fax: 908-536-4847
Subjects: 19E-29-53-56
Items: HC-PB-GA-TA-TV-OT
Catalog mailed 1x per year
Numbers: 5,000

New Books of Interest to Gay Men
Skip Strickler/Charity Denlinger
Giovanni's Room
1145 Pine St
Philadelphia PA 19107
215-923-2960; Fax: 215-923-0813
E-Mail: giophilp@netaxs.com
Subjects: 37
Items: HC-PB-CA-CD-TV
Two catalogs mailed: one of interest to
 women, one to men, mailed every
 other month
Other: 40-60 titles

New Books of Interest to Women
Skip Strickler/Charity Denlinger
Giovanni's Room
1145 Pine St
Philadelphia PA 19107
215-923-2960; Fax: 215-923-0813
E-Mail: giophilp@netaxs.com
Subjects: 37-73
Items: HC-PB-CA-TV-OT
Two catalogs mailed: one of interest to
 women, one to men, mailed every
 other month
Other: 40-60 titles

New Directions Catalog
Peggy Hansa, Gen Mgr
Kaplan Corp
PO Box 609
Lewisville NC 27023-0609
910-766-7374; Fax: 910-766-5652
Subjects: 21-31
Memo: Classroom supplies also.

New Information Exchange
Randall Arena, Pres
27 Sylvan Way Box 370
Woodacre CA 94973
415-488-4760
Subjects: 23
Items: Software
Numbers: 25-30M

New Moon
Tom Alexander, Buyer
New Moon Publishing
215 SW 2nd St
Corvallis OR 97333
503-757-8477; Fax: 503-757-0028
Subjects: 43G
Items: PB-MG-TV
Catalog mailed 4x per year
Numbers: 80,000 mailed
Other: 20 titles
Memo: Part of **The Growing Edge Magazine.**

The Newman Group
Allan Newman, Pres
7400 Newman Blvd
Dexter MI 48130
313-426-3200
FAX orders: 313-426-0777
Internet: info@newman.com
Subjects: 23
Items: SW-hardware, supplies
Catalog mailed 12x per year

Next Decade Catalog
Buyer
39 Farmstead Rd
Chester NJ 07930-2732
908-879-6625; Fax: 908-879-6625
Subjects: 41-41G(immigration)
Memo: Publisher of immigration books.

Nichols Garden Nursery Catalog
Betty Walker, Mgr
1190 N Pacific Hwy
Albany OR 97321
541-928-9280; Fax: 541-967-8406
Subjects: 43G
Items: HC-PB-OT(gardening supplies)
Catalog mailed 1x per year

Nolo Press Bookstore
Sandy Coury
950 Parker St
Berkeley CA 94710-2589
510-549-1976; Fax: 510-548-5902
800-992-6656 or CA: 800-6400-6656.
www: http://gnn.com/gnn/bus/nolo
Subjects: 19-19L-55L
Items: PB-SW-TA-TV
Catalog mailed quarterly
Other: 100+ titles
Memo: Legal self-help books.

Nordic Track Fitness Catalog
Randy Guien, Catalog Mgr
Nordic Track
104 Peavey Rd
Chaska MN 55318
612-448-6987; Fax: 612-368-2777;
    800-445-2606
Subjects: 69
Items: HC-PB-OT(fitness items)
Catalog mailed 12x per year
Other: 2-3 titles

Northern Sun Merchandising
Scott Kramer, Owner
2916 E Lake St
Minneapolis MN 55406
612-729-2001; Fax: 612-729-0149
Subjects: 13-25-37-51-73
Items: CA-CL-CR-GA-GI-GC-MA-PO-TO
Other: 3 titles
Numbers: 400,000 mailed

NorthStyle Catalog
Alan Barch, Mktg VP
Northwood Press Inc
Box 1360
Minocqua WI 54548
715-356-9800; Fax: 715-356-1958
Subjects: 51(some nature books)
Items: HC-PB
Other: 100 titles
Memo: Trade catalog sells to retail stores 1-2x per year when there are new products.

NUFAX
Randall Arena, Pres
New Information Exchange
27 Sylvan Way Box 370
Woodacre CA 94973
415-488-4760
Subjects: 23
Items: 400+ software titles for rent
Catalog mailed 6x per year
Numbers: 5,000

The Old House Antiques & Gifts
Pearl Henshaw, Owner
294 Head of the Bay Rd
Buzzards Bay MA 02532
508-759-4942
Subjects: 28(wooden toys especially)
Items: GC-GI-TO
Memo: Gifts are the only items carried in the catalog.

Olde Methuen Book Shoppe
Aura Fluet, Book Buyer
250 Broadway
PO Box 545
Methuen MA 01844
508-682-9972
Subjects: 17-19-31-43-54-55-63-67-73-75-99
Items: MM-PB-US
Catalog mailed 12x per year
Other: 13,000 titles
Memo: Books only. **Book News** is the name of the catalog.

Omega Engineering
PO Box 4047
Stamford CT 06907-0047
203-359-1660; FAX orders: 203-359-7700
Subjects: 23(IBM compatible & MAC)
Items: Name-brand SW-discount
Catalog mailed 1x per year

On Three Inc
Robert Consorti, Pres
1802 Mitchell Rd
Lake Stevens WA 98258
206-334-8001
Subjects: 23(Apple III only)
Items: SW & drives
Catalog mailed 4x per year
Numbers: 2,000

The Opera Box Catalog
Tennessee Wild, Pres
PO Box 994
Teaneck NJ 07666
201-833-4176
Subjects: 14M(opera)
Items: HC-PB-OT(collectables)
Catalog mailed 2x per year
Other: 2-3,000 titles

The Orange Elephant
Jeanne Hopkins, Mdse Dir
90 MacCorkle Ave SW
South Charleston WV 25303
304-744-9323; Fax: 800-FAX-ONUS;
    800-467-5597
Subjects: 21(age 0-4 & parents)
Items: HC-GA-TO-TV
Catalog mailed 3x per year
Numbers: 500,000 mailed

Organic Agriculture Catalog
Phillip Unterschuetz, Owner
333 Ohme Gardens Rd
Wenatchee WA 98801
509-662-3179; Fax: 509-662-3179;
    800-332-3179
E-Mail: philu@televar.com
Subjects: 43G-51A(organic gardening)
Items: HC-PB(pest control)
Other: 30 titles

The Orvis Company Catalog
Paul Inbierowicz, Circ Planner
Historic Route 7A
Manchester VT 05254
802-362-3622; Fax: 802-362-3525
Subjects: 15-27-51-69H
Items: GI-CL
Memo: They have several catalogs. Subjects include fishing/hunting which each go out once a year, women's apparel 3 x's, clothing & gifts which is seasonal at 4 times a yr, and travel 3x.

Oxfam America Catalog
Laura Inouye
26 West St
Boston MA 02111
617-482-1211; Fax: 617-728-2594
800-565-8563
Subjects: 13-21-44-55
Items: HC-PB (Ext 580)

Pacific Spirit WholeLife Catalog
Joseph Meyer, Buyer
Pacific Spirit Corp
1334 Pacific Ave
Forest Grove OR 97116
503-357-1566; Fax: 503-357-1669
800-634-9057
Subjects: 13-14-39H-53-51E-57-63-73
Items: HC-PB-CA-GC-PO-TA-TV-OT
Catalog mailed 4x per year
Memo: The Mystic Trader catalog is also published.

Paladin Press
Janice Vierke, Mktg Dir
PO Box 1307
Boulder CO 80306-1307
303-443-7250; Fax: 303-442-8741;
    800-392-2400 orders only
E-Mail: pala@rmii.com.
Subjects: 29-33-48
Items: PB-HC-CR-OT(entertainment)
Catalog mailed every 2 months
Other: 500 titles
Memo: "How-to" action-oriented books (weapons, martial arts, and survival).

Pandora Book Peddlers Catalog
Pamela Sheldrick, Co-Owner
9 Waverly Pl
Madison NJ 07940
201-822-8388
Subjects: 37-73(gay/lesbian/feminist)
Items: HC-PB-MM-CA-GC-PO-RC-ST-TA
Catalog mailed 6x per year
Other: 10,000 titles
Memo: This bookstore with catalog does many author appearances.

Paperback Previews
Gypsy Kemp, Owner
PO Box 6781
Albuquerque NM 87197
505-345-5925
Subjects: 75-77-81-82-83-84-85-86-87-88-9
Items: HC-MM-PB-TA
Catalog mailed monthly
Numbers: 2,000 mailed
Other: 300 titles

The Paragon
Mary Jane Spooner, Catalog Mgr
89 Tom Harvey Rd
Westerly RI 02891-0511
401-596-0929; Fax: 401-596-6142
Subjects: 15-10-21-31-33-45-51-56-59-71
Items: HC-PB-CA-CL-GA-GI-ST-SB-TV-TA-TO
Other: 40 titles

Parenting Press Catalog
John Shoemaker, Acquisitions Ed
11065 Fifth Ave NE #F
PO Box 75267
Seattle WA 98155
206-364-2900; Fax: 206-364-0702
Subjects: 31-31P-35F
Items: PB
Catalog mailed 2x per year
Other: 75 titles
Numbers: 70,000
Memo: Published by Parenting Press.

Parenting Resources Catalog
Kim Cabaliero, Buyer
La Leche League Intl
1400 N Meacham
Schaumburg IL 60173
708-519-7730; Fax: 708-519-0035
800-525-3243
Subjects: 19S-31C-31P-35
Items: HC-PB-TV
Other: 50 titles
Memo: Also produces the La Leche League International Catalogue. Besides breast-feeding and parenting books, they are interested in ways to work at home.

Partner Village Store
Jennifer Hall, Book Buyer
999 Main Rd
PO Box 3051
Westport MA 02790
508-636-2572
Subjects: 21-76-27(wine and herbs)
Items: HC-PB-GI

PC America
60 N Harrison Ave
Congers NY 10920
800-722-6374; FAX orders: 914-267-3550
Customer service: 914-267-3500.
Subjects: 23
Items: Software/hardware/accessories
Catalog mailed 4x per year
Numbers: 250,000 mailed

PC Connection
Patricia Gallup, Pres
14 Mill St
Marlow NH 03456
800-334-4444; FAX orders: 603-446-7791
International orders: 603-446-1111
Tech support: 800-800-0015
Subjects: 23(IBM compatible)
Items: Software/hardware/supplies
Catalog mailed 6x per year

PC Zone
Deborah Sanders, Mktg Mgr
Multiple Zones Intl
15815 SE 37th St
Bellevue WA 98006-1800
800-258-2088; FAX orders: 206-603-2500
International orders: 206-603-2570
International FAX: 206-603-2550

Customer service: 800-248-9948
Subjects: 23(IBM compatible)
Items: SW-peripheral hardware
Catalog mailed 6x per year
Numbers: 750,000 mailed

PCs Compleat
34 St Martin Dr
Marlboro MA 01752
800-385-4622; FAX orders: 800-669-8329
Subjects: 23 (IBM/Toshiba/Compaq/NEC/TX In)
Items: Software/supplies
Catalog mailed 6x per year

Peaceful Valley Farm Supply
Mark or Kathleen Fenton
PO Box 2209
Grass Valley CA 95945
916-272-4769; Fax: 916-272-4794
Subjects: 43G-51A(organic gardening)
Items: HC-PB(seeds/supplies)
128 page catalog mailed once a year
Other: 30 titles

Pedigrees & R C Steele
Doug Case, Buyer
Sporting Dog Specialties
3001 Brockport Rd
Spencerport NY 14559
716-352-9160; Fax: 716-352-1272
Subjects: 15
Items: OT(pet supplies)
Catalog mailed every 3 months
Numbers: 14,000 mailed
Memo: Two separate catalogs-same info. 800-872-3773(RC Steele) & 800-548-4786 (Pedigrees). Jackie Sperandio, Mdse Dir. 5 stores.

Pendragon Software Library
PO Box 56
E Greenwich RI 02818-0056
800-828-3475; FAX orders: 401-884-6825
Subjects: 23
Items: 2,500 shareware, publ domain programs
Catalog mailed 2x per year

Personal & Financial Source Book
Harold Moe, Buyer
Harsand Financial Press
PO Box 515
Holmen WI 54636-0515
608-526-3848; Fax: 608-526-9563
Subjects: 19C-19I-19S-25-35R-57
Items: HC-PB-SW-TA-TV
Catalog mailed 2x per year
Numbers: 32,000
Memo: Personal/family/children/financial topics.

Personal Computing Tools
Chris Scozzari
The Programmer's Shop
90 Industrial Park Rd
Hingham MA 02043-4368
800-821-2492; FAX orders: 617-740-2728
Subjects: 23-24-67S
Items: 500 software/hardware products

A Photographer's Place
Harvey Zucker, Mdse Dir
133 Mercer St
New York NY 10012
212-431-9358; Fax: 212-941-7920
Subjects: 11P
Items: HC-PB-RM
Catalog mailed 6-7 times a year
Other: 1000+ titles
Numbers: 17,000 mailed

Pioneer Hi-Bred Intl
Willona Graham Goers, Prod Mgr
11153 Aurora Ave
Des Moines IA 50322
515-245-3500
Subjects: 23-51A
Items: SW
Catalog mailed 1x per year
Numbers: 50,000 mailed

Pipestone Indian Shrine Assn
Maddie Redwing, Bus Mgr
Pipestone National Monument
PO Box 727 W Reservation Ave
Pipestone MN 56164
507-825-5463; Fax: 507-825-2903
Subjects: 49A-78-79
Items: HC-PB-CR-OT
Catalog mailed 1x per year or as requested
Other: 2 titles

Planetary Publications Catalog
14700 West Park Ave
PO Box 66
Boulder Creek CA 95006
408-338-2161; Fax: 408-338-9861
800-372-3100
Subjects: 57-31C-39H
Items: PB-TA-CD
Catalog mailed 2x per year
Other: 12 titles

Planning For Excellence
Joy Rhodes, Mdse Dir
Leadership Education Development
1116 West 7th St #175
Columbia TN 38401
615-388-6135; Fax: 615-682-3801; 800-659-6138.
Subjects: 19G
Items: HB-PB
Catalog mailed 2-3x per year
Other: 20 titles

Play Fair Toys
Sue Lounsbury, Mdse Dir
1690 28th St
Boulder CO 80301
303-444-7502; Fax: 303-440-3393
Subjects: 14-21-31-69-76-79
Items: HC-PB-CR(childrens)-GA-TA-TO-TV
Catalog mailed 4x per year
Numbers: 1, 500,000

Players Library
Robert Mead, Pres
RCM Enterprises
PO Box 720
Wayzata MN 55391
612-473-5088; Fax: 612-473-7068; 800-451-9278
Subjects: 69(gambling)
Items: HC-PB-SW-TV
Catalog mailed 2x per month
Other: 30 titles

The Plow & Hearth
Norm Hensel, Mdse Mgr
State Rt 230 W
PO Box 500
Orange VA 22727
540-948-2272; Fax: 540-948-3544; FAX orders: 800-843-2509.
Subjects: 15-43G-51
Items: 800-866-6072
Catalog mailed 4x per year
Numbers: 11,000,000
Memo: Peter and Peggy Rice, Owners. Titles in recent catalog included 3 bird books and 1 book on butterflies.

Porter's Photographic & Equip
Dave Montz, Pres
Porter's Camera Store Inc
PO Box 628
Cedar Falls IA 50613
319-268-0104; Fax: 319-277-5254
Subjects: 11P
Items: HC-PB-MM-TX-CR-GI-SW-TA-TV
Catalog mailed 9 times yearly
Numbers: 1,000,000

Positive Bks/21st Century Kids
Constance Wilde, Mdse Dir
Aton International Inc
7654 Benassi Dr
Gilroy CA 95020
408-847-3531; Fax: 408-847-3531; Orders: 800-833-0835
E-Mail: aton@netcom.com
Subjects: 12-21-23-25-29-31-35-43-53-54-5
Items: HC-TA-GC-TV
Catalog mailed 1x per year with flyers
Numbers: 3,000+ growing

The Potters Shop
Steven Branfman, Pres
31 Thorpe Rd
Needham Heights MA 02194
617-449-7687; Fax: 617-449-9098
Subjects: Pottery/ceramics/related subj
Items: HC-TV-OT
Catalog mailed 5-6 times a year
Numbers: 5,000 sent each time; 450 titles

Pottery Barn
Laura Alber, Buyer
3250 Van Ness Ave
San Francisco CA 94109
415-421-7900; Fax: 415-983-9887
Subjects: 27-29-43
Items: HC-PB-GI-PC(pottery supplies)
Catalog mailed quarterly
Other: 2 titles
Memo: Parent company is WilliamsSonoma.

Power Up! Software
Linda Racine, Mktg Mgr
Power Up! Software Corp
2929 Campus Dr
San Mateo CA 94403
800-851-2917; FAX orders: 415-345-5575.
Subjects: 23
Items: Pers/bus software/accessories
Catalog mailed 4x per year
Numbers: 2,500,000

Prepress Direct!
Marc Daniels, VP Cat Operations
11 Mt Pleasant AVe
East Hanover NJ 07936
800-443-6600; FAX orders: 800-443-1102
Intl orders: 201-887-2300
Detailed prod info: 201-887-4919
Subjects: 23
Items: Software/hardware/accessories
Catalog mailed 4x per year

Presque Isle Wine Cellars
Mdse Director
9440 Buffalo Rd
North East PA 16428
814-725-1314; Fax: 814-725-2092; 800-488-7492
E-Mail: prwc@moose.erie.net
Subjects: 27(wine)
Items: HC-TX-PB-OT
Catalog mailed usually every other year
Other: 30 titles
Memo: Also sell wine-making supplies, equipment, grape juice, etc.

Print/Graphic Design Bookstore
Gloria Mason, Mgr
Print Magazine
3200 Tower Oak Blvd
Rockville MD 20852
301-770-2900; Fax: 301-984-3203
Subjects: 56X-(graphic designs)
Items: HC-PB
Other: 150 titles

The Printers Shopper
Dan Vaccaro, Pres/Mdse Dir
111 Press Ln
Chula Vista CA 91910
619-422-2200; Fax: 619-422-8563; 800-854-2911
Subjects: 56X
Items: HC-PB-OT
Catalog mailed every 2 months
Other: 60 titles

Productivity Programs
Chester Peterson, Pres
Sunshine Unlimited Inc
PO Box 471
Lindsborg KS 67456
913-227-3880
Subjects: 23(IBM/Apple II/MAC)
Items: Spreadsheet programs
Catalog mailed 2x per year
Numbers: 5,000

The Programmer's Shop
Bob Mielde, Buyer
90 Industrial Park Rd
Hingham MA 02043
617-740-2510; Fax: 617-740-1352
FAX orders: 617-749-2018
Customer service: 617-740-2510
Subjects: 23
Items: HC-SW
Catalog mailed 4x per year

Provantage
Michael Coralik, Pres
Provantage Corp
7249 Whipple Ave NW
North Canton OH 44720-7143
800-336-1166; FAX orders: 216-494-5260
Intl orders: 216-494-8715
Subjects: 23
Items: Discount SW-hardware, tools
Catalog mailed 4x per year
Numbers: 50,000 mailed

PsL Sourcebook
Nelson Ford, Pres
Public (software) Library
PO Box 35705
Houston TX 77235-5705
800-242-4775; FAX orders: 713-524-6398
Customer service: 713-524-6394
Subjects: 23
Items: Free & low-cost software
Catalog mailed 1x per year

Psychology Today Bookshelf/Tape
Lisa Liebman
Sussex Publishers Inc
49 E 21st 11th Fl
New York NY 10010
800-444-7792
Subjects: 57
Other: 34 titles
Memo: 2 pages in **Psychology Today Magazine.**

Public Brand Software
Terry Ramstetter, Pres
PO Box 51315
Indianapolis IN 46251-0315
800-426-3475; FAX orders: 317-856-2086
Tech support: 317-856-7535
Subjects: 23(IBM compatible)
Items: Shareware/public domain software
Catalog mailed 4x per year
Numbers: 150,000 mailed

Publications Catalog
Robert Persky, Pres
Photographic Arts Ctr
163 Amsterdam Ave
New York NY 10023
212-838-8640; Fax: 212-873-7065
Subjects: 11-11P
Items: HC-PB
Catalog mailed 1x per year
Other: 30 titles
Memo: Catalog published on only the fine arts and photography books they carry.

Publisher Inquiry Services
951 Broken Sound Pky NW Bldg 190
PO Box 3008
Boca Raton FL 33431-0908
407-998-9722; Fax: 800-555-4053
800-444-7366
Subjects: 99

Publisher's Clearinghouse
Jeannie Clarke, Exec Dir
382 Channel Dr
Port Washington NY 11050
516-883-5432; Fax: 516-767-3650
Customer serivce: 800-645-9242
Subjects: 21-25-27-29-43-57-76-99
Items: HC-PB
Other: 50 titles

Publisher's Overstock
Lucinda May, Pres
Soda Creek Press
13131 Hwy 253, PO Box 679
Boonville CA 95415-0679
707-895-3822; Fax: 707-895-3719
Subjects: 75
Items: HC-PB
Numbers: 700 mailed
Other: 750 items

Publisher's Toolbox
Kurt Chambers, Prod Mgr
PO Box 620036
Middleton WI 53562-0036
800-390-0461; Fax: 608-828-1112
www:http://www.pubtool.com/pubtool/
Subjects: 23-11
Items: SW-HC-PB
Catalog mailed bi-monthly
Numbers: 700,000 mailed
Memo: Miles Gerstein, President.

Publishing Perfection
PO Box 307
Menominee Falls WI 53051
800-782-5974; FAX orders: 414-255-9640
Customer service: 414-255-7600
Subjects: 23
Items: SW-hardware, accessories
Catalog mailed 1x per year

Pueblo To People Catalog
Dale Nichols, Book Buyer
PO Box 2545
Houston TX 77252-2545
713-956-1172; Fax: 713-956-8443;
 800-843-5257
Subjects: 21-44-55(all Latin American)-99
Items: HB-PB-CR-TA-CD
Catalog mailed 4x per year

The Pyramid Collection
Dawn Beausoleil, Buyer
Catalog Ventures Inc
222 Mill Rd
Chelmsford MA 01824
508-256-4100; Fax: 508-256-1961
Subjects: 11-15-21-27-28-29-39-40-56-57-7
Items: HC-PB-GI-CR-GC-PO-ST-TA-TV-OT
Memo: To be on mailing list or get
 catalog: 800-333-3235.

Quality Small Business Books
Bernard Kamoroff, Mdse Dir
Bell Springs Publishing
PO Box 640
Laytonville CA 95454
707-984-6746; Fax: 707-459-8614
Subjects: 19S
Items: PB
Other: 15 titles

Queblo
Tony Miller, Gen Mgr
1000 Florida Ave
Hagerstown MD 21741
800-523-9080; FAX orders: 800-554-8779
Customer service: 516-254-2000
Subjects: 23
Items: SW-accessories, supplies
Catalog mailed 12x per year
Numbers: 500,000 mailed

Queue Inc
Monica Kantrewitz, Pres
338 Commerce Dr
Fairfield CT 06430
800-232-2224; FAX orders: 203-336-2481
Subjects: 23
Items: Over 2,000 educational programs
Catalog mailed 2x per year

Quill Corporation Catalog
Jack Miller, Pres
100 Schelter Rd
Lincolnshire IL 60069-9585
708-634-4800; Fax: 708-789-8955;
 800-789-1331
Subjects: 19
Items: PB-OT
Monthly fliers with a semi-annual catalog
Other: 10-20 titles
Memo: Office supplies — few books.

Quinsept
S C Vorenburg, Pres
1465 Massachusetts
Arlington MA 02174
800-637-7668
Subjects: 23-41G
Items: Software for genealogy
Catalog mailed 1x per year
Numbers: 5,000
Memo: Customer service: 617-641-2930.

Quiz Control
Thomas Pitegoff, Pres
Quick Study Software Inc
170 Hamilton Ave
White Plains NY 10601
914-428-5727; FAX orders: 914-949-1094
Subjects: 23
Items: Software
Catalog mailed 2x per year
Numbers: 75,000

QVC Network
Paula Piercy, Book Buyer (ext 3970)
1365 Enterprise Dr
Westchester PA 19380
610-430-1000; Fax: 610-430-1356
Subjects: 27-43-99
Items: TV catalog sales network
Memo: Their audience is primarily
 female. Big book subjects are
 cookbooks and romance novels.

R B Walter Catalog
Jackie Kukowski, Prod Mgr
2405 S Calhoun Rd
PO Box 51710
New Berlin WI 53151
414-784-6880; Fax: 414-784-1176;
 800-558-6696
Internet: http://www.artsupplies.com
Subjects: 11-14D-29-31
Items: HC-PB
Catalog mailed 1x per year
Other: 60+ titles

Radio Shack Catalog
Bernard Appel, Pres
1800 One Tandy Ctr
Ft Worth TX 76102
817-390-3011
Subjects: 23
Items: Software/accessories
Catalog mailed 1x per year

The Rainbow Collection
Donna O'Toole, Book Buyer
477 Hannah Branch Rd
Burnsville NC 28714
704-675-5909; Fax: 704-675-9687

Subjects: 35(grief, dying)-57
Items: HC-PB-TV-TA-PO-OT
Catalog mailed 2x per year
Other: 400 titles

Ralin Wholesalers
Jim Ralin, Pres/CEO
PO Box 450
Orchard Park NY 14127
800-752-9512
FAX orders: 716-674-2108
Tech support: 716-674-6267
Customer service: 716-674-6267
Subjects: 23
Items: SW-hardware, accessories
Catalog mailed 4x per year

Reader's Catalog
Book Buyer
250 West 57th St #1330
New York NY 10107
212-262-7198; Fax: 212-307-1973
E-Mail: readcag@phantom.com
Subjects: 99
Items: Anything in print
Catalog mailed 2x per year
Other: 200-300 titles

Real Goods Catalog
John Schaeffer, Pres
555 Leslie Stt
Ukiah CA 95482
707-468-9292; Fax: 707-468-9394;
 800-762-7325
E-Mail: realgood@well.com
Subjects: 15-43G-43H-51-51E
Catalog mailed 1x per year
Memo: Recently bought the Earth Care
 Recycled Paper catalog.

Reasonable Solutions Software
Tom Knackstedt, Mktg Mgr
1221 Disk Dr
Medford OR 97501-9911
800-876-3475; FAX orders: 503-773-7803
Info: 503-776-5777
Tech support: 503-776-5777
Subjects: 23
Items: All types of software
Catalog mailed 6x per year
Numbers: 5,000,000

Recreational Equipment Inc
Mdse Director
REI Catalog
6750 South 228th St
Kent WA 98032
206-395-3780; Fax: 206-395-7759
Subjects: 51-69-71
Items: HC-PB
Memo: 44 stores; also a catalog.

Recreational Gaming & Lottery
Terry Archut, Dir
Intergalactic Publishing
321 New Albany Rd
Moorestown NJ 08057
609-778-8900; Fax: 609-273-6350;
 800-367-9681
Subjects: 69G
Items: HC-PB
Catalog mailed 2x per year

The Red Hot Company Catalog on Disk
Ed Durham
15 Brunswick Ln
Willingboro NJ 08046-1620
609-835-2347; Fax: 609-835-2324
Subjects: 19-23-70A
Items: HC-PB-TV-OT

Red Rose Collection Catalog
Shawna Brutoco, Owner
42 Adrian Ct
Burlingame CA 94010
415-692-4500; Fax: 415-692-1750
800-374-5505
Subjects: 39H-53-54-57
Items: HC-PB-TV-TA
Catalog mailed 3x per year
Memo: "Products for empowering people".

Reference Book Center Catalog
Book Buyer
175 Fifth Ave
New York NY 10010
212-677-2160; Fax: 212-533-0826
Subjects: 59
Items: HC
Catalog mailed 2 x per year at $2.00 per catalog
Other: 700 titles

Reference Books Catalog
Dorothy J Perkins, Buyer
Diane Publishing Co
601 Upland Ave
Upland PA 19015
610-499-7415; Fax: 610-499-7429
Subjects: 59
Items: HC-PB-MA(atlases)
Catalog mailed 4x per year
Other: 4,000 titles

Reliable Corporation Catalog
Buyer
1501 Woodfield Rd #300 W
Chicago IL 60173
312-666-1800; Fax: 708-413-8250
800-869-6000
Subjects: 19-23
Catalog mailed bi-annually

Remarkable Products
Jack Lahav, Pres
245 Pegasus Ave
Northvale NJ 07647
201-784-0900
FAX orders: 201-767-7463
Subjects: 23
Items: T-card system software/supplies
Catalog mailed 6x per year

ReSource: A Guide to Books/Audio
Keith Thompson, Catalog Ed
Institute of Noetic Sciences
475 Gate Five Rd #300
Sausalito CA 94965
415-331-5650; Fax: 415-331-5673
Subjects: 13-39H-53-54-57-65
Items: HC-PB-TA-TV
Other: 50 titles
Memo: Full name: ReSource: A Guide to Books, Audio Tapes, & Video Tapes.

Right On Programs
Barbara Feinstein, VP
Computeam Inc
755 New York Ave
Huntington NY 11743
516-424-7777; FAX orders: 516-424-7207
Internet: 74503.3556@compuserve.com
Subjects: 23
Items: Library management software
Catalog mailed 3x per year
Numbers: 150,000 mailed

Roberts Colonial House
570 W 167th St
PO Box 308
South Holland IL 60473-0308
708-331-6233; Fax: 708-331-0538
Subjects: 21-27-76
Items: HC-PB
Memo: Wholesale/retail.

Romantic Times Books by Mail
Kate Ryan, Books by Mail Director
Romantic Times
55 Bergen St
Brooklyn Heights NY 11211
718-237-1097; Fax: 718-624-6967
Subjects: 11-12-16-17-27-29-40-41-45-53-59-71-73
Items: HC-PB-TV-TA-GC-ST-GI-CR
Other: 350 titles
Numbers: 135,000 mailed

Rose Electronics
Peter Macourek, Mktg Mgr
10850 Wilcrest
Houston TX 77099
800-333-9343; FAX orders: 713-933-0044
Customer service: 713-933-7673
Subjects: 23
Items: SW-hardware and accessories
Catalog mailed 4x per year

The Rower's Bookshelf
Oakes Ames, Mdse Dir
PO Box 368
Eliot ME 03903
207-439-1507; Fax: 207-439-7062
Subjects: 69-70
Items: HB-PB-ST-PO-CA-GC-TV-OT
Catalog mailed 2x/year

S

S & P of New York Budo
Mdse Director
6049 Transit Rd
PO Box 2
Depew NY 14043
716-681-7911; Fax: 716-681-7912
Subjects: 69(martial arts)
Items: HC-PB-OT(supplies)

S & S Arts & Crafts
Martha France, Mdse
75 Mill St (06415)
PO Box 513
Colchester CT 06415-0513
203-537-2325; Fax: 203-537-2866; Orders: 800-243-9232
Fax: 800-566-6678
Subjects: 21-29-59-69G
Items: HC-PB-CR-GA
Other: 25 titles

S&MSS (Sales & Mktg Software Source
Dave Kopp, Pres
150 River Rd #N-1
Montville NJ 07045
800-437-0144
FAX orders: 201-335-1123
Subjects: 23
Items: SW-accessories and suppies
Catalog mailed 4x per year

Sailors Bookshelf
Henry Wagner, Pres
623 Ramsey Ave
PO Box 643
Hillside NJ 07205
908-964-4620; Fax: 908-964-8339
Subjects: 70N
Items: HC-PB-SW-TV

Saint Lawrence Nurseries Catalog
Bil MacKentley, Buyer
RR 5 Box 324
Potsdam NY 13676
315-265-6739
Subjects: 43G
Items: HC-PB-OT(tools)

Sales Automation Survival Guide
Rich Bohn, Pres
The Denaili Group Inc
2815 NW Pine Cone Dr
Issaquah WA 98027-8698
206-392-3514; Fax: 206-391-7982
Internet: rbohn@denali.com
Subjects: 19M-57S
Items: HC-PB-TV-TA
Numbers: 100,000 mailed; 40 titles
Memo: They are most interested in books/audio/videos on sales & marketing topics.

Saltspring Software
G102 Selby Bldg
700 Richmond St
London ON Canada N6A 5C7
519-661-1037
FAX orders: 519-661-1049
Subjects: 23
Items: Macintosh & DOC software

Samuel French Theatre/Film Bkshp
Gwen Feldman
7623 Sunset Blvd
Hollywood CA 90046-2795
213-876-0570; Fax: 213-876-6822
Subjects: 14M-33M
Items: HC-PB-PO
Memo: Musical plays in script form.

Sandpiper Gifts & Books
Amdrea Jenssen, Book Buyer
Sandpiper Publishing
1421 Alaskan Way
Seattle WA 98101
206-624-2835; Fax: 206-343-0196
Subjects: 27
Items: HB-PB-GI

Sandy Mush Herb Nursery Catalog
Kate Jayne
316 Surrett Cove Rd
Leicester NC 28748-9622
704-683-2014
Subjects: 27-43G(herbs)
Items: HC-PB-PC-GI
Other: 50 titles
Memo: Phone: Thurs/Fri/Sat 9am-5pm.

Save Energy Catalog
Michael Gorman, Pres
Save Energy Co
2410 Harrison St
San Francisco CA 94110
415-824-6010; Fax: 415-648-1891;
 800-326-2120
Subjects: 21-51E
Items: HC-PB-GI-TO(solar)

Sax Arts and Crafts Catalog
Gary Logan, Mktg Dir
2405 S Calhoun Rd
New Berlin WI 53151
414-784-6880; Fax: 414-784-1176
800-558-6696
Subjects: 11-14T-29-31
Numbers: 1,500+ mailed; 20 titles

Scholastic K-12 Educational Tech
Peter Kelman, Publ
Scholastic Inc
2931 E McCarty
Jefferson City MO 65101
800-541-5513; FAX orders: 314-635-5881
Subjects: 23-31E
Items: Education sftwre/teachers/school
Catalog mailed 1x per year
Numbers: 300,000 mailed

School Counselors Catalog 6-12
Denise Harrison-Ovaitt
Paperbacks for Educators
526 West Front St
Washington MO 63090
314-239-1999; Fax: 314-239-4515
Subjects: 21-31-57-76
Items: HC-PB-MM
Catalog mailed yearly
Numbers: 50,000 mailed
Other: 800 titles

School Counselors Catalog K-5
Denise Harrison-Oviatt, Cat Ed
Paperbacks For Educators
426 W Front St
Washington MO 63090
314-239-1999; Fax: 314-239-4515;
 800-227-2591
Subjects: 21-31-57-76
Items: HC-PB-MM
Catalog mailed yearly
Numbers: 50,000 mailed
Other: 800 titles

The Science Fiction Shop
Michael Franklin, Mdse Dir
168 Thompson St
New York NY 10012-2509
212-473-3010; Fax: 212-473-4384
Subjects: 76-79-82-86-89
Items: TA-HC-PB-CA
Catalog mailed 3x per year
Numbers: 3,000

Science News and Science News Books
Larry Sigler, Book Buyer
1719 N St NW
Washington DC 20036
202-785-2255; Fax: 202-785-1242;
 800-544-4565
Subjects: 12-21-23-24-31-39-51-67
Items: HC-PB-CA-GA-CL-PO-TA-TV-TO-GI-ST
Numbers: 250,000 mailed
Other: 560 titles
Memo: Weekly magazine with house ads in every issue and annual Fall holiday catalog.

SciTech Software for Science
Jennie Abrahamson
SciTech International Inc
2525 N Elston Ave
Chicago IL 60647-2003
800-622-3345; FAX orders: 312-486-9234
Customer service: 800-622-3307
Intl orders: 312-486-9191
Internet: info@scitechint.com
Subjects: 23(DOS/Windows/MAC/UNIX)
Items: Scientists/engineers/chemists
Catalog mailed 4x per year

Scott's Book Shop Catalog
Tom Grimes, Assoc Publisher
Scott's Bookshop
30595 Eight Mile Rd
Livonia MI 48152-1798
810-477-6650; Fax: 810-477-6795
Subjects: 11-19-28-29
Items: HC-PB-OP-CR-GC-PO-ST-SB
Other: 235 titles

Sea Challengers Catalog
Ann Gotshall, Pres
4 Sommerset Rise
Monterey CA 93940
408-373-6306; Fax: 408-373-4566
Subjects: 15A-70N
Items: HC-PB-PO-OT

Seasons Catalog
Linda Mielke, Book Buyer
Rivertown Trading Co
1000 Westgate Dr
St Paul MN 55114
612-659-4435; Fax: 612-659-0083
Subjects: 21-73-76-99
Items: HC-PB-PO-CA-GI
Other: 50 titles

Secondary Mathematics Catalog
Book Buyer
Dale Seymour Publications
1100 Hamilton Ct
Menlo Park CA 94025
800-872-1100; CA: 800-ABC-0766
Subjects: 21-67
Items: HC-PB-TX-CA

Seeds and Books Catalog
Alita Anderson, Mktg Mgr
1029 Lawrence St
PO Box 772
Port Townsend WA 98368
360-385-5660; Fax: 360-385-7455
Subjects: 13-27-43G-51-59
Items: HC
Catalog mailed 1x per year
Numbers: 40,000 mailed
Memo: Abundant Life Seed Foundation Catalog

Selected Booklist
Susan Aglietti, Mdse Dir
Vintage '45 Press
PO Box 266
Orinda CA 94563
510-254-7266
Subjects: 73-95
Items: HC-PB
Numbers: 15,000+ mailed
Memo: Catalog consists exclusively of books written by women directed toward the needs & interests of mid-life & older women.

Selective Books Inc
Lee Howard, Mdse Dir
PO Box 1140
Clearwater FL 34617
813-447-0100
Subjects: 19-19E-56
Items: HC-PB-TV(reference books)
Other: 100 titles
Memo: Catalog mailed 3x per year

Self-Help Warehouse
PO Box 683
Ashland OR 97520
818-587-6013; Fax: 503-488-7870
Subjects: 35A-35R-35S-39-53-57S

SelfCare Catalog
Joe Pickard, Pres
5850 Shellmound St #390
Emeryville CA 94608
510-658-0970; Fax: 510-658-1209
Subjects: 39
Items: HC-PB-OT

Seventh Generation Catalog
Amber Molholm, Buyer
Seventh Generation
49 Hercules Dr
Colchester VT 05446-1672
802-655-6777; Fax: 802-655-2700
Subjects: 51E
Catalog mailed 15 titles
Numbers: 100,000 per issue

Sewing & Craft Supplies
Mary Seng, Buyer
Newark Dressmaker Supply
6473 Ruch Rd
Bethlehem PA 18017
610-837-7500; Fax: 610-837-9115
Subjects: 29(sewing)
Items: HC-PB-CR-OT
Catalog mailed 2x per year
Numbers: 60,000 mailed

Sewing Bookshop
Helen Hecker, Mdse Dir
Twin Peaks Press
PO Box 129
Vancouver WA 98666
360-694-2462; Fax: 360-696-3210; Orders:
 800-637-2462
Subjects: 29-40
Items: TA-HC-PB-GI-TV
Catalog mailed 2x per year
Numbers: 20,000 mailed

Sewing Sampler
Kathy Sandman, Pres
12 East Central
Springfield MN 56087
507-723-5011
Subjects: 19C
Items: HC-PB-OT(notions)

Shareware Express
John Hatch, Pres
1908 Ashland St #D
Ashland OR 97520-2335
800-346-2842; FAX orders: 503-482-4230
Customer service: 503-482-5136
Subjects: 23IBM & compatible)
Items: Try-before-you-buy software
Catalog mailed 4-5x per year
Numbers: 500,000 mailed

Shareware Software for Apple/MAC
Alan Apel, Buyer
Budgetbytes Inc
1647 SW 41st St
Topeka KS 66609
913-266-2200
Subjects: 23(Apple Macintosh)
Catalog mailed 1x per year
Numbers: 25,000 mailed
Other: 10,000 titles

Shareware Spectacular
Star-Byte Inc
PO Box 220
Hatfield PA 19440-0220
800-243-1515; FAX orders: 215-997-2571
Subjects: 23
Items: SW
Catalog mailed 2x per year

Shop at Home Catalogs Directory
Belcaro Group
2080 S Holly St PO Box 221050
Denver CO 80222-9050
303-843-0302; Fax: 303-843-9906;
    800-315-1995
Subjects: 99
Memo: Each directory features over 600 catalogs.

Shop the World by Mail
Gail Baird, Pres
102 Common Wealth Ct
PO Box 5549
Cary NC 27512
919-481-4445; Fax: 919-481-9369
Subjects: 99
Items: HC-PB-GA-GI-PO-TO-TV
Memo: Great company that works with US companies and overseas companies to sell to different countries.

Signals Catalog
Judy Ryan, Book/Audio Buyer
Rivertown Trading Co
1000 Westgate Dr
St Paul MN 55164-0422
612-659-3700; Fax: 612-659-0083
Subjects: 11-14-33-47-75-79-99
Items: HC-PB-TA-RC-GI-TV
Other: 50 titles
Memo: The national public TV catalog. Judy Van Eeckhout buys videos. John Ollman buys general gifts.

Sizzleware Shareware Library
Charles Tekippe, Pres
PO Box 6429
Lake Charles LA 70606-6429
318-474-1548
Subjects: 23(IBM)
Items: Over 2,500 disks
Catalog mailed 6x per year
Numbers: 50,000 mailed

Ski World of Orlando
Terry Chadwick, Buyer
1425 N Orange Ave
Orlando FL 32804
407-894-5012
Subjects: 69
Items: HC-PB-OT(skiing equipment)
Memo: Snow & water skiing.

Skis & Snowboard Repair Tools
Tognar Toolworks
PO Box 212
Mount Shasta CA 96067
916-926-2600; Fax: 800-926-9904
Subjects: 69R(skiing/snowboarding)
Catalog mailed 1x per year in the Fall
Other: 20 titles

Sky Publications Catalogue
Susan Cummings, Dir/Book Div
Sky Publishing Corp
PO Box 9111
Belmont MA 02138
617-864-7360; Fax: 617-864-6117
Subjects: 67A-69
Items: HC-PB-TX-RM-OP-TV-TA-CA-GI-PO-SW
Numbers: 250,000 mailed
Other: 200 titles

Skydiving Book Service
Mike Truffer, Owner
1725 N Lexington Ave
PO Box 1520
De Land FL 32724
904-736-4793; Fax: 904-736-9786
Subjects: 69R-70A
Items: HC-PB-CD-TA-TV-OT-TX-RM-OP-SW-CL
Catalog mailed 6x per year
Numbers: 20,000 mailed
Other: 80 titles
Memo: Catalog mailed. Skydiving Book Service carries books, videos, and assorted items of interest to sport parachutists.

SME Catalog
Phil Roman
Society of Manufacturing Eng
One SME Dr PO Box 930
Dearborn MI 48121
313-271-1500; Fax: 313-271-2861
E-Mail: romaphi@sme.org
Subjects: 19X-24
Items: HC-PB-MG-TV
Catalog mailed 3-4x per year

Smith & Hawken Catalog
Book Buyer
117 E Strawberry Dr
Mill Valley CA 94941
415-383-4415; Fax: 415-383-9971
Subjects: 43G
Items: HC-PB-GI(supplies)
Other: 10-20 titles
Memo: Kathy Tierney, President.

Softcraft Font Catalog
Brian Olson, Mktg Mgr
16 N Carroll St #500
Madison WI 53703
800-351-0500; FAX orders: 608-257-6733
Customer service: 608-257-3300
Subjects: 23
Items: Computer font software
Catalog mailed 1x per year

Softdisk Publishing
Martee Gonsolin, Purchasing
PO Box 30008
Shreveport LA 71130
800-831-2694; FAX orders: 318-221-8870
Customer service: 318-221-8718
Subjects: 23(IBM PC/Apple II, MAC, Commodor)
Items: Consumer/small bus software
Catalog mailed 2x per year
Numbers: 100,000 mailed

Softshoppe Public Domain Shareware
Jay Park, Pres
Softshoppe Inc
PO Box 4437
Cerritos CA 90703-4437
310-802-1333
Subjects: 23(IBM compatibles/MAC)
Items: Public domain software/shareware
Catalog mailed 4x per year
Numbers: 500,000 mailed

Software Add-Ons
2 Greenwood Sq
3331 Street Rd #155
Bensalem PA 19020
800-822-8088; FAX orders: 215-639-7234
Customer service: 215-639-7110.
Subjects: 23
Items: Software specialists
Catalog mailed 1x per year

Software Excitement!
Michael Comish, Pres
6475 Crater Lake Hwy
Central Point OR 97502
800-444-5457; FAX orders: 503-826-8090
Customer service: 503-826-8086
Tech support: 503-826-6884.
Subjects: 23(IBM PC/MAC/Apple II/Comm/Ami
Items: Software/accessories
Catalog mailed 12x per year
Numbers: 700,000 mailed

Software Labs
3767 Overland Ave #112-115
Los Angeles CA 90034
800-359-9998
FAX orders: 213-559-3405
Customer service: 213-559-5456
Subjects: 23(IBM compatible)
Items: All types of software
Catalog mailed 2x per year

Software Source
Teri Cippolla, Mktg VP
2517 wy 35 Bldg N #201
Manasquan NJ 08736
908-528-0030; FAX orders: 908-528-9378
Subjects: 23
Items: Software for students/educators
Catalog mailed 2x per year

Software Spectrum
Rose Hultgren, Dir of Mktg
2140 Merritt Dr
Garland TX 75041
800-787-1166; FAX orders: 800-959-0066
Subjects: 23
Items: Software for home & office
Catalog mailed 4x per year

Solstice Catalog
Marvin Stiskin, Buyer
982 Stuyvesant Ave
Union NJ 07083-6906
908-810-0909; 800-765-7842
Subjects: 39H
Other: 20 titles
Memo: Chronic fatigue syndrome.

Solutions Catalog
Mdse Director
PO Box 6878
Portland OR 97228-6878
503-644-2666; Fax: 503-643-1973;
   800-342-9988
Subjects: 23-27-29-39-43
Memo: No books yet - gadgets &
   doodads.

Sounds True Catalog
Tami Simon, Owner
735 Walnut St
Boulder CO 80302
303-449-6229
Subjects: 53-54-57
Items: HC-PB-TV
Memo: All tapes & books.

Special Students
Buyer
Opportunities for Learning
941 Hickory Ln
Mansfield OH 44905-2815
419-589-1700; 800-243-7116
Subjects: 31C-31E-67-57B-41A
Items: HC-PB-SW-GA

Spiegel Catalog
Peter Piegore, Buyer
3500 Lacey Rd
Downers Grove IL 60515
708-986-8800; Fax: 708-769-3104
Subjects: 11P-19
Items: Office & camera supply

Spiegel Catalog
Buyer
Gourmet & Housewares Depts
3500 Lacey Rd
Downers Grove IL 60515
708-769-2947
Subjects: 21-27-43-76
Items: HC-PB-OT(cooking supplies)
Numbers: 708-986-8800
Memo: She buys cookbooks for the
   gourmet department as well as
   children's toys and books.

Spike & Friends Collection
Dawn Wrobel
Ain't No Creek Ranch
2553 W Offner Rd
Beecher IL 60401
708-534-3296; Fax: 708-534-3277
Subjects: 15(hedgehogs) and general pet
   books
Memo: Publishes the **Hedgehog Herald
   Newsletter.**

Sportsman's Guide Catalog
411 Farwell Ave
South St Paul MN 55075
612-451-3030; Fax: 612-450-6130
800-328-7222
Subjects: 27-33-48-51-69
Items: HC-PB-CA-GI
Numbers: 18,000 mailed

Staff Development Catalog
Denise Harrison-Ovaitt
Paperbacks for Educators
526 West Front St
Washington MO 63090
314-239-1999; Fax: 314-239-4515
Subjects: 21-31-57-76
Items: HC-PB-MM
Catalog mailed yearly
Numbers: 45,000 mailed
Other: 800 titles

Stage Step Catalog
Randolph Swartz
910 Cherry St
Philadelphia PA 19105
215-829-9800; Fax: 215-829-0508
Subjects: 14D
Items: HC-TX-PB-RM-MM-CA-GA-GI-PO-
   RC-TV-CD
Other: 2,000 titles

Staples Direct
PO Box 1020
Westboro MA 01581
800-333-3330; FAX orders: 800-333-3199
Customer service: 617-965-7030
Subjects: 23
Items: Software/supplies/accessories
Catalog mailed 2x per year

Stash Tea Catalog
Barbara Thomas
PO Box 610
Portland OR 97207
503-684-4482; Fax: 503-624-9744
Subjects: 27
Items: HC-PB-OT(Teas, accessories, and
   mixes)

Steamboats
Bill Mueller, Pres
RR 1 Box 262
Middlebourne WV 26149
304-386-4434
Subjects: 16(steamboats/steam
   engineering)
Items: HC-PB-MG-OT(photos)

Stories How to Books for Country
Allicia Clark, Mail Order Coord
Schoolhouse Rd
Pownal VT 05261
802-823-5811; Fax: 802-823-5818
Subjects: 43G-27(cooking)-29C(building)
Items: HC-PB-CR
Catalog mailed 1/yr
Numbers: 500,000
Memo: John Story: Owner. Proper name
   for catalog is: Stories' How to Books
   for Country Living. Another CA they
   publish is smaller and yearly featuring
   animals, bldgs, beer and wines,
   cooking, crafts, gardening, and kids &
   parents called "Stories Publishing
   Garden Way Publishing Trade Catalog".

Strategic Simulations Products Catalog
Joel Billings, Pres
Strategic Simulations Inc
675 Almanor Ave #201
Sunnyvale CA 94086-2930
408-737-6800; FAX orders: 408-737-6814
Subjects: 23(IBM/MAC/Atari/Comm
   64/Amiga)
Items: Entertainment software/games
Catalog mailed 1x per year

Success Spoken Here
Dan S Kennedy, Pres
Empire Communications Corp
5818 N 7th St #103
Phoenix AZ 85014
602-269-3111; Fax: 602-269-3113
Subjects: 19-54-55-56-57-71
Items: HC-PB-RM-TV-TA
Catalog mailed monthly
Numbers: 25,000 mailed

Sun Remarketing
Robin Colston
PO Box 4059
Logan UT 84321
800-821-3221; FAX orders: 801-755-3311;
   Support service: 900-786-7782
Subjects: 23(Apple Macintosh)
Items: Used/reconditioned hdwr/software
Catalog mailed 4x per year

Sunbooks Catalog
Skip Whitson, Mdse Dir
Sun Publishing
PO Box 5588
Santa Fe NM 87502-5588
505-471-5177; Fax: 505-473-4458
Subjects: 13-39H-41-53-54M-63
Items: HC-PB
Catalog mailed 3-4x per year
Numbers: 10,000 mailed

Sure-Fire Business Success Cat
Dr Jeffrey Lant, Pres
Jeffrey Lant Associates Inc
50 Follen St #507
Cambridge MA 02138
617-547-6372; Fax: 617-547-0061
Subjects: 19M-19O-19S-23-25-56-57
Items: HC-PB-TA-TV-OT-RM-OP-MG
Catalog mailed 4x per year
Numbers: 1,000,000 mailed

Surplus Software
489 N 8th St
Hood River OR 97031
800-753-7877
FAX orders: 503-386-4227
Subjects: 23
Items: Software clearinghouse
Catalog mailed 12x per year

Surveillant: Acq for Intell Prof
Elizabeth Bancroft, Buyer
Natl Intelligence Book Ctr
2020 Pennsylvania Ave NW #165
Washington DC 20006
202-797-1234; Fax: 202-331-7456
Subjects: 55-41-48-44-97-23-17-19-80
Items: HC-PB-MG-TA-TV-CA-CL-GI-MA-
   SW-NP
Catalog mailed 6x per year
Numbers: 6,800 mailed
Other: 250 titles

Swan Technologies
Tom Garrick/Chris Diprey
3075 Research Dr
State College PA 16801-2783
800-468-9044; FAX orders: 814-237-4450
Subjects: 23(Swan computers)
Items: Software/hardware/accessories
Catalog mailed 4x per year

Sweet Celebrations Catalog
Marge Bailey, Buyer
7009 Washington Ave S
Edina MN 55439
612-943-1661; Fax: 612-943-1688;
    800-328-6722
Subjects: 21-27-29
Items: HC-PB-GI-OT
Catalog mailed 2x per year

Sybervision Catalog
Thomas Judd, Whlse Acc Dir
SyberVision Systems Inc
One Sansome St #810
San Francisco CA 94104
415-677-8620; Fax: 612-433-3047
Subjects: 19-39-39E-69-35-57-45
Items: TV-TA
Numbers: 150,000 mailed
Other: 50 titles

The Sycamore Tree
Willam and Sandy Gogel, Owners
2179 Meyer Pl
Costa Mesa CA 92627
714-650-4466
Subjects: 21-31-35-63-76-79
Items: HC-PB-TS-GA-TO
Numbers: 10,000 mailed

T

T B Hagstoz and Son Catalog
Tom Hagstoz, Co-Owner
709 Sansom St
Philadelphia PA 19106-3205
215-922-1627; Fax: 215-922-7126
Subjects: 40(jewelry)
Items: HC-PB-OT(jewelry making supplies)

Talas Catalog
Marjorie Salik, Pres
Talas: Div Technical Libr Serv
568 Broadway
New York NY 10002
212-219-0770; Fax: 212-219-0735
Subjects: 29
Items: HC-PB-CR-OT
Numbers: 10,000 mailed

Taylor Gifts Catalog
Margo Firebaugh, Buyer
600 Cedar Hollow Rd
Wayne PA 19301
610-293-3609; Orders: 800-347-0201
Subjects: 99(low-priced gifts)
Items: HC-PB-GI
Other: 9 titles

Teacher-Parent Store
Brenda Zamary, Owner
93 Mill Plain Rd
Danbury CT 06811
203-794-0577; Fax: 203-798-9854;
    800-307-6278

Subjects: 21-31
Items: HC-PB-GA-OT(furniture)
Memo: Classroom supplies and teaching
    materials.

Technical Information Center
Obie de la Pena, Book Buyer
Lineal Publishing Co
2160 Stonington Ave
Hoffman Estates IL 60195
708-885-1995; Fax: 708-882-9168
Subjects: 12-19X-23-24-59-67
Items: HC-PB-SW-TV
Numbers: 100,000+
Other: 600 titles
Memo: Training books in English &
    Spanish.

Telecom Library Catalog of Books
Harry Newton, Pres
12 W 21st St
New York NY 10010
212-691-8215; Fax: 212-691-1191;
    800-999-0345
Subjects: 19M-23
Items: HC-PB-supplies
Other: 120 titles

Tenex Computer Express
Roger B Dooley, Pres
PO Box 6578
South Bend IN 46660
800-776-6781; FAX orders: 219-255-1778
Customer service: 219-259-7051
Subjects: 23(IBM compatible)
Items: Software/hardware/accessories
Catalog mailed 4x per year

That Patchwork Place Inc
PO Box 118
Bothell WA 98041-0118
800-426-3126; Fax: 206-486-7596
Subjects: 29(quilting)

The Book Lady
Michelle Harvath
8144 Brendwood Industrial Dr
PO Box 28809 (63123)
St Louis MO 63144
314-644-3252; Fax: 314-644-6238;
    800-766-7323
Subjects: 21-31E-31P
Items: HC-PB
Catalog mailed 1x per year
Other: 300 titles

Theos Resource Directory
Shelley Clark, Mktg Mgr
Theos Software Corp
1777 Bothelho Dr #110
Walnut Creek CA 94596
800-600-5660; FAX orders: 510-938-4367;
    Customer service: 510-935-1118
Subjects: 23
Items: Software/development languages
Catalog mailed 1x per year

Thinkercisers
Kathy Kolbe, Pres
Resources for the Gifted
3421 N 44th St
Phoenix AZ 85018
602-840-9770; Fax: 602-952-2706
Subjects: 21-31-76-79-89
Items: HB-PB
Catalog mailed 1x per year

Tigersoftware
Russ Strunk, Mktg Mgr
Tiger Direct Inc
9100 S Dadeland Blvd #1200
Miami FL 33156
800-666-2562; FAX orders: 305-529-2990
Subjects: 23(MAC/IBM PC)
Items: SW-accessories
Catalog mailed 6x per year

Timberdoodle Catalog
Dan & Deb Deffinbaugh, Buyers
E 1510 Spencer Lake Rd
Shelton WA 98584
360-426-0672; Fax: 360-427-5625
Subjects: 24-31-45-67
Items: TX-MA-SW-SB-TA-TV-GA
Catalog mailed 2-3 times per year
Other: 350 titles

TitleNet
Robin Humes, Mktg Dir
Inforonics Inc
550 Newtown Rd PO Box 458
Littleton MA 01460
508-486-8976
Internet: gopher.titlenet.com
Web: http://www.titlenet.com
Subjects: 56P(searching/ordering online)
Memo: 2 Catalogs: Gordon and Breach &
    John Benjamins.

Tools for Exploration Catalog
Attn: Teresa
4460 Redwood Hwy
San Rafael CA 94903
415-499-9050; Fax: 415-499-9047;
    800-456-9887
Subjects: 23E-23T
Items: HC-PB-TA-TV-SW
Catalog mailed 2x per year
Other: 30 titles

Total Solutions
Harold Cochran, Mktg
Corporate Software Inc
PO Box 9125
Norwood MA 02062-9125
800-275-1334; FAX orders: 800-677-4008
Subjects: 23
Items: Software/hardware/accessories
Catalog mailed 4x per year

Tower Hobbies Catalog
Buyer
1608 Interstate Dr
Champaign IL 61824
217-398-3630; Fax: 800-637-7303;
    800-637-6050
Compuserve: 72060,700
Subjects: 29(model airplanes)-70A
Items: Model kits/books
Catalog mailed 1x per year with
    salesfliers every other month
Other: 15 titles

Toys to Grow On Catalog
Michael Kaplan, Pres
2695 E Dominguez St
Parson CA 90749
310-603-8890; Fax: 310-587-5403;
    800-421-4354
Subjects: 21-31-76-79
Items: HC-PB-TA-TO
Catalog mailed 1x per year
Other: 50+ titles

Train of Thought
Christopher Nulph, Pres
DataPak Software Inc
9317 NE Hwy 99 #G
Vancouver WA 98665-8900
206-573-9155; FAX orders: 216-573-9269
Subjects: 23(MAC)
Items: Software developer
Catalog mailed 4x per year
Numbers: 100,000 mailed

Travel Tech
Mark Eppley, Pres
Traveling Software Inc
18702 N Creek Pky #116
Bothell WA 98011
800-343-8080; FAX orders: 206-485-6786
Subjects: 23
Items: Software/hardware/accessories
Catalog mailed 4x per year
Numbers: 75,000,000

Traveler's Checklist
Myron Silverman, Pres
335 Cornwall Bridge Rd
Sharon CT 06069
203-364-0144; Fax: 203-364-0369
Subjects: 71
Items: HC-PB(safety)-OT(travel items)
Catalog mailed by request only.

Traveller's Bookstore Catalog
Diana K Wells
22 West 52nd St
New York NY 10019
212-664-0995; Fax: 212-397-3084
800-755-8728.
Subjects: 71-75(travel)
Items: HC-PB
Catalog mailed 2x per year - May/Nov.
Other: Many titles

Treasure Book Catalogue
Book Buyer
Treasure Trove Archives
PO Box 448
Fremont NE 68025
402-721-8588
Subjects: 10-71G(Western America)
Items: HC-PB
Catalog mailed 1x per year
Other: 1,000 titles

Treasure House Catalog
Keith Carroll, Publisher
Companion Press Books
167 Walnut Bottom Rd
Shippensburg PA 17257
717-532-3040; Fax: 717-532-9291;
    800-722-6774
Http://www.reapernet.com
Subjects: 63
Catalog mailed 1x per year
Numbers: 120,000
Other: 50 titles

Trend-Lines Catalog
Paul Blacker, Mdse Buyer
135 American Legion Hwy
Revere MA 02151
617-853-0225; Fax: 617-853-0226;
    800-877-7899.
Subjects: 43H(woodworking)
Items: HC-PB-TV-OT(supplies)

Trumble Greetings
Tom Trumble, Pres
Leanin' Tree Inc
6055 Longbow Dr
Boulder CO 80301
303-530-7768; Fax: 303-530-7283
Subjects: 99
Items: GC-GI-PO-OT(mugs, t-shirts)
Catalog mailed 1x per year

Twin Peaks Speaks
Helen Hecker, Mdse Dir
Twin Peaks Press
PO Box 129
Vancouver WA 98666
360-694-2462; Fax: 360-696-3210; Orders:
    800-637-2256
Subjects: 33T(Twin Peaks)
Items: HC-TA-CA-GA-GI-RC-TV
Catalog mailed 6x/year
Numbers: 12,000

U

UARCO Computer Supplies Catalog
Mdse Director
UARCO Inc
121 N Ninth St
DeKalb IL 60115
815-756-9581; Fax: 800-435-6994;
    800-435-5555.
Subjects: 23
Items: HC-SW-OT
Catalog mailed 1x per year with periodic
    fliers
Numbers: 10,000

Undercover Book Services
Joel Turner, Owner
21899 Rye Rd
Shaker Heights OH 44122
216-295-1919
73323.3411@compuserve.com
Subjects: 99
Items: SL-SC-CO
Catalog mailed every 2 weeks
Other:Titles rotate - 25,000 total

Underground Books
Sebastion Orfali, Book Buyer
PO Box 522
Berkeley CA 94701
510-548-2124; Fax: 510-548-7326;
    800-858-2665
E-Mail: roninpub@aol.com
Subjects: 13-39R-51E-55-65 (Alternative
    politics & drugs)
Catalog mailed 1x per year
Other: 60 titles
Memo: Books on psychoactive drugs,
    cyberpunk, 60's, counter-cultural. Must
    have 50% discount. Prefers books not
    widely distributed in bookstores.

The Unicorn Textile Book Catalog
Lars Malmberg, Book Buyer
Unicorn Books & Crafts Inc
1338 Ross St
Petaluma CA 94954
707-762-3362; Fax: 707-762-0335;
    800-289-9276
Subjects: 40F-29

Items: HC-PB-TV-MG-OT(fabric,
    embroidery, weaving, spinning,
    lacemaking supplies)
Catalog mailed 1x per year with updates.
Other: 2,000 titles

Uniquity Catalog
Reuven E Epstein, Owner
215 4th St
PO Box 10
Galt CA 95632-0010
209-745-2111; Fax: 209-745-4430
Subjects: 13-21-31-33-35-37-39-57-59-69
    -99(child abuse/mental health)
Items: PB-GA-PO-TA-TV-TO-OT
Numbers: 1,000

UPCO Catalog for Birds Only
Frank, Walt & Ed Evans, Owners
3705 Pear St
PO Box 969
St Joseph MO 64502
816-233-8800; Fax: 816-233-9696;
    800-254-8726
Subjects: 15-29H
Items: HC-PB-OT(bird care supplies)
Memo: Complete bird care catalog.
    Several titles.

UPCO Complete Pet Store Catalog
Frank, Walt & Kim Evans, Owners
3705 Pear St
PO Box 969
St Joseph MO 64502
816-233-8800; Fax: 816-233-9696
Subjects: 15-29H
Items: HC-PB-OT(pet care supplies)
Memo: Medications, grooming aids: a
    very special catalog for special pets.
    40 years of business.

USA*Flex
471 Brighton Dr
Bloomingdale IL 60108
800-872-3539, FAX orders: 708-351-7204
Subjects: 23
Items: Software/hardware
Catalog mailed
Memo: International orders: 708-582-6202.

Useful Guide to Herbal Health
Book Buyer
Health Ctr for Better Living
1414 Rosemary Ln
Naples FL 33940
941-643-2477; Fax: 941-643-6335; Orders:
    800-544-4225.
Subjects: 39H
Catalog mailed quarterly
Other: 35 titles

USTA Tennis Publications
Joseph Roth
US Tennis Assn
70 W Red Oak Ln
White Plains NJ 10604
914-696-7000; Fax: 914-696-7167
Subjects: 31E-69
Items: HB-PB
Numbers: 50,000 mailed

Utrecht Art & Drafting Supplies
Harold Gulamerian, Pres
Utrecht Manufacturing Corp
33 35th St
Brooklyn NY 11232-2287
718-768-2525; Fax: 718-499-8815
Subjects: 29
Items: HC-PB-OT(art supplies, drafting)
Catalog mailed every 6 months
Other: 2-3 titles
Memo: Oil & acrylic paints, canvas, pads & other art & drafting supplies.

V

Valley of the Sun
Ms Jan Hale
Box 683
Ashland OR 97520
503-488-7880; Fax: 503-488-7870
Subjects: 53-54M-57S
Memo: There are 3 catalogs published quarterly, 1) Winners 2)Soaring Spirit 3)Self-Help Warehouse with a mailed of 250,000.

Vanguard International Cinema
Lisa Marie Lombardi, Mktg
5150 Wilshire Blvd #504
PO Box 36849
Los Angeles CA 90036
213-857-1272; Fax: 213-857-1274; 800-218-7888
Subjects: CD
Items: CD-ROM catalog

Vegetarian Resources
Debra Wasserman, Coord
Vegetarian Resource Group
PO Box 1463
Baltimore MD 21203
410-366-8343; Fax: 410-366-8804
E-Mail: thevrg@aol.com
Subjects: 27-39H
Items: Vegan-oriented
Catalog mailed 50 titles

The Ventura Companion
Affinity Publishing Inc
100 W Harrison St #225
Seattle WA 98119-4123
800-822-8221
Subjects: 23
Items: A guide to Ventura Publisher users

Verlinden Letterman & Stok
Bob Letterman, Owner
Lone Star Industrial Park
811 Lone Star Dr
O'Fallon MO 63366
314-281-5700; Fax: 314-281-5750
Subjects: 29H-59
Items: HC-PB-OT(hobby kits & paints)
Catalog mailed 1x per year
Other: 2+ titles
Memo: Publishes their own newsletter, but would review new items.

The Vermont Country Store
Bob Allen, Buyer
PO Box 1108
Manchester Center VT 05255
802-362-4667; Fax: 802-362-8288
Subjects: 61(VT)-99

Items: HC-PB-CA-GI-TO
Catalog mailed 10 titles
Numbers: 4,000 mailed

Vermont Life Catalog
Agency of Development
Vermont Life Magazine
6 Baldwin St
Montepelier VT 05602
802-828-3241; Fax: 802-828-3366
Subjects: 61(Vermont)
Items: HC-PB-OT(note cards)
Catalog mailed yearly
Memo: Also has magazine called "Vermont Life Magazine".

Vesper Publishing Catalog
Frederick Gould, Mdse Dir
Vesper Publishing
PO Box 150
Kenvil NJ 07847
201-927-9185; Fax: 201-927-9483
800-930-BOOK
Subjects: 99 (accepts all category codes except: 75-76-77-79-82-86-84-85-86-87-88-89-90-95-97)
Items: HC-PB-TA
Numbers: 1,000

Vet-Vax Catalog
Dennis Johnson, Mdse Dir
1203 Hwy 24-40
PO Box 400
Tonganoxie KS 66086
913-845-3760; Fax: 913-845-9472; 800-369-8297
Subjects: 15-39M-69H
Items: HC-PB-OT(animal health supplies)
Catalog mailed 2x per year
Other: 250 titles
Memo: Pet, hunting, training supplies.

Victorian Video Productions
Nancy Harvey, Owner
PO Box 1540
Colfax CA 95713
916-346-6184; Fax: 916-346-8887; 800-848-0284
Subjects: 11-29(textile)
Items: HC-PB-TV
Catalog mailed 2-3x per year
Other: Few titles

The Video Collection
Bob Bunshaft
Pacific Arts Publishing
11858 La Grange Ave
Los Angeles CA 90025
310-820-0991; Fax: 310-826-9351
E-Mail: bobpapai@primenet.com or nez@videoranch.com.
Subjects: 39-41-51-67-71-99
Items: Videos from books & TV
Memo: Michael Nesmith, President. You can also order videos online by calling 800-370-5361 with your modem.

Viking Discount Computer Supplies
Ted Gewanter, Gen Mgr
Viking Office Products
PO Box 61144
Los Angeles CA 90061-0144
800-421-1222; FAX orders: 800-762-7329
Subjects: 23
Items: Software/supplies/accessories
Catalog mailed 12x per year

Village Software
Debbie Pendleton, Mktg Mgr
186 Lincoln St
Boston MA 02111
800-724-9332; FAX orders: 617-695-1935
Customer service: 617-695-9332.
Subjects: 23(Lotus 1-2-3)
Items: Bus & personal software
Catalog mailed 4x per year
Numbers: 1,000,000

Virgin Mastertronic
Annette Childs, Mgr
Virgin Mastertronic Intl Inc
18061 Fitch
Irvine CA 92714-6018
714-833-8710; FAX orders: 714-833-8717
Subjects: 23
Items: Bus & entertainment software
Catalog mailed 4x per year
Numbers: 250,000 mailed

The Vitamin Shoppe Book Catalog
Helen Howard, Owner
4700 Westside Ave
North Bergen NJ 07047
800-852-7151; Fax: 800-852-7153; 201-866-7711 (local #)
Subjects: 27-39H
Catalog mailed 1x per month
Other: 200 titles

Volunteer Energy ResourceCatalog
Kristin Floyd, Publications Dir
Energize Inc
5450 Wissahickon Ave
Philadelphia PA 19144
215-438-8342; Fax: 215-438-0434; 800-395-9800
Subjects: 19G(volunteer management)
Items: PB-HC
Other: 30 titles

W

Ward's Natural Science Catalog
Daniel Weidel, Buyer
5100 W Henrietta Rd
PO Box 92912
Rochester NY 14692-9012
716-359-2502; Fax: 716-334-6174; 800-962-2660
Subjects: 39M-67
Items: HC-PB-GA-MA-SW-TA-TV
Catalog mailed 1x per year
Other: 50 titles

The Warm Store
Andy, President-Warm Inc
31 Mill Hill
Woodstock NY 12498
914-679-4242; Fax: 914-679-3082
800-889-WARM (9276)
Subjects: 13-15-51
Other: 30-40 titles
Memo: "Woodstock Animal Rights Movement."

Wayfarer Publications Catalog
Marvin Smalheiser, Mdse Dir
PO Box 26156
Los Angeles CA 90026-0156
213-665-7773; Fax: 213-665-1627;
　800-888-9119
Subjects: 39-54-69
Items: HC-PB-TA-PO-GI-TV-OT
Catalog mailed 2x per year
Numbers: 30,000
Other: 225 titles

Weaving Works Catalog
Buyer
4717 Brooklyn Ave NE
Seattle WA 98105
206-524-1221; Fax: 206-524-0250
Subjects: 29
Items: HC-PB-OT(supplies)
Catalog mailed every other year
Other: 500-1000 titles

White Flower Farm Catalog
Merchandiser
Route 63
Litchfield CT 06759
203-567-0801; Fax: 203-567-3507
Subjects: 43G
Items: HC-PB-OT(plants)
Catalog mailed 3 times a yr
Memo: Very few to no books in this
　catalog. To request a catalog call:
　203-496-9600.

The Whole Work Catalog
Tom Ellison, Buyer
The New Careers Ctr
1515 23rd St PO Box 339
Boulder CO 80306
303-447-1087; Fax: 303-447-8684
800-634-9024
Subjects: 19C-19M-19O-19S
Items: HC-PB-TA-TV
Catalog mailed 2x per year
Numbers: 175,000
Other: 1,200 titles

William Tricker Catalog
Cindy Ludrosky, Buyer
7125 Tanglewood Dr
Independence OH 44131
216-524-3491; Fax: 216-524-6688
Subjects: 43G
Items: HC-PG
Catalog mailed 1x per year
Other: 12 titles
Memo: Water gardening, plant, spools.

Williams-Sonoma Catalog
Tom O'Higgins, Mdse Dir
100 North Point
San Francisco CA 94133
415-421-7900; Fax: 415-983-9887
Subjects: 27-43
Items: HC-PB-GI
Catalog mailed 1x per month
Other: 5-10 titles
Memo: 125 stores. Customer service:
　800-541-1262.

Willmann-Bell Catalog
Book Buyer
PO Box 35025
Richmond VA 23235
804-320-7016; Fax: 804-272-5920;
　800-825-STAR
Subjects: 67A(astronomy)

Items: HC-PB-SW
Catalog mailed 1 or more times a year
Numbers: 1000 books

Wind in the Rigging Catalog
Jean Schanen, Buyer
PO Box 323
Port Washington WI 53074
414-284-3494; Fax: 414-284-0067
800-236-7444
Subjects: 70N-27
Items: HC-PB-GI-GA-PO-TV-OT
Catalog mailed 2x per year
Other: 10 titles

The Wine Enthusiast Company
Sybil Strum, Pres
8 Saw Mill River Rd
Hawthorne NY 10532
914-345-9463
Subjects: 27
Items: HC-PB-OT(racks, gifts)
Memo: This company carries any item to
　do with wine.

Wings Inc Catalog
Ken Okey
518A N Daleville Ave
Daleville AL 36322
334-598-2610; Fax: 800-229-4889
Subjects: 70A
Items: HC-PB-OT(supplies)
Catalog mailed 1x per year
Other: 300 titles

Winterthur Museum Bookstore
Marilyn Krussman, Book Buyer
Winterthur Museum & Gardens
Winterthur DE 19735
302-888-4781; Fax: 302-888-4858;
　800-448-3883
Subjects: 21-27-28C-29-43D
Other: 10 titles
Memo: Winterthur Gift Catalog, Book
　Buyer, Catalog Division, 100 Enterprise
　Place, Dover, DE 19901. Books on
　antique collecting, gardening, and
　children's books.

Wireless Catalog
Michele Willey, Book Buyer
Rivertown Trading Co
1000 Westgate Dr
St Paul MN 55114
612-659-3700; Fax: 612-659-0083; Orders:
　800-669-9999
Subjects: 11-15(cats)-35-41-51-59-71
Items: HC-PB-TA-TV-GI
Catalog mailed 2-3x per year
Other: 30 titles
Memo: Michele buys books, spoken word
　audio, and stationery.

Wisdom Publications
Donna Guerra, Book Buyer
361 Newbury St 4th Fl
Boston MA 02115-2710
617-536-3358; Fax: 617-536-1897
Subjects: 63E(Buddhist)
Items: HC-PB-PO-OT(post cards)
Other: 300 titles

Women's History Catalog
Molly Murphy MacGregor, Dir
Natl Women's History Project
7738 Bell Rd
Windsor CA 95492
707-838-6000; Fax: 707-838-0478
E-Mail: nwhp@aol.com
Subjects: 17-41A-73(women's history)
Items: HC-PB-PO-GI-CA-TV
Catalog mailed 2x per year
Other: 300 titles

Wooden Porch Books
Lois Mueller, Pres
RR 1 Box 262
Middlebourne WV 26149
304-386-4434; Fax: 304-386-4868
Subjects: 29(textiles)-40F
Items: HC-PB-RM-OP-MG-US
Catalog mailed 4x per year
Other: 10,000 titles

The WoodenBoat Store
Scot Bell, Mdse Dir
Naskette Rd
Brooklin ME 04616
207-359-4651; Fax: 207-359-8920
Subjects: 29-59-69
Items: CA-CL-CR-GI-MG-GC-PO-TV-TO
Catalog mailed 4 times yr
Other: 300 titles
Memo: Model kits and boatbuilding

Woodworker's Supply
1108 N Glenn Rd
Casper WY 82601-1698
307-237-5528; 800-645-9292;
　Fax: 307-577-5272
Subjects: 29-43H(woodworking)
Items: HC-PB-OT(tools/supplies)
Catalog mailed 4-6x per year
Other: 20 titles
Memo: 3 stores

The Woodworkers' Store
Steve Krohmer, Product Mgr
4365 Willow Dr
Medina MN 55340
612-478-8201; Fax: 612-478-8395;
　800-279-4441
Subjects: 29H-43H
Items: HC-PB-TV-SW
Catalog mailed 1x per year
Other: 20 titles

Woodworking Unlimited Catalog
John Folkerth, Pres
6930 Poe Ave
Dayton OH 45414
800-543-7586; Fax: 513-898-6070
Local #: 513-898-6070
E-Mail: shpsmith@aol.com
Subjects: 29H-43H
Items: HC-PB(woodworking)
Catalog mailed 2x per year

World Resources Institute
Brooks Clapp, Mktg Mgr
PO Box 4852
Hampden Sta
Baltimore MD 21121
410-516-6963; Fax: 410-516-6998;
　800-822-0504
E-Mail: ChrisD@wri.org
Subjects: 51-51E
Items: HC-PB-SW

World's Greatest Gaming Catalog
Dwight Davis, Pres
John Patrick Productions
150 Morris Ave
Springfield NJ 07081
201-467-4665; Fax: 201-467-8123
Subjects: 69G(gambling)-29
Items: HC-GA-TV-TA-CL-CR-GI
Catalog mailed 2x per year.
Numbers: 800,000 mailed

The Writewell Catalog
Karen Lett, Buyer
Rytex Co
5850 West 80th St
Indianapolis IN 46268
317-872-8553; Fax: 317-872-8535; 800-288-6824
Subjects: 15-33(humor/trivia)-56W
Items: HC-PB

X

Xerox Office Supplies Catalog
Delcina Pickens, Supplies Rep
Xerox Corp Mktg Ctr
300 N Route 303
Blauvelt NY 10913
800-822-2200; FAX orders: 800-338-7020
Customer service: 800-822-2502
Subjects: 23
Items: Software/supplies
Catalog mailed 4x per year

Y

Yang Sheng
John Du Cane, Publisher
Dragon Door Publications Inc
PO Box 4381
St Paul MN 55104
612-645-0517; Fax: 612-644-5676
Subjects: 39-53-63-69
Items: HC-PB-CA-CL-TA-TV-OT(herbs)
Numbers: 50,000 mailed; 35 titles

Yield House Catalog
Jan Brown, Buyer
Dept 6100
PO Box 5000
North Conway NH 03860-0500
603-356-5338; Fax: 603-356-3562; 800-258-4720
Subjects: 28-29-43(home furnishings)
Numbers: 18,000,000
Memo: Owned by Renovator's Supply. 75% of their customers are women. George Moore, President.

Yoga Journal Book & Tape Source
Linda Sparrowe, Mg Editor
California Yoga Teachers Assn
2054 University Ave #600
Berkeley CA 94704-1082
510-841-9200; Fax: 510-644-3101; 800-359-9642
Subjects: 39H-51E-53-54-57
Items: HC-PB-TA-TV
Other: 50 book/tape

Z

Zenith Books
Brad Siqueiros, Book Buyer
729 Prospect Ave
Osceola WI 54020
715-294-3345; Fax: 715-294-4448
800-826-6600
Subjects: 29
Items: HC-PB-CA-TV
Catalog mailed 2x per year

Zeos Quarterly
Wayne Wenzloff, Sales
Zeos International
1301 Industrial Blvd NE
Minneapolis MN 55413-3013
800-423-5891; FAX orders: 612-633-1325
Intl orders: 612-633-6131
Subjects: 23
Items: Software/hardware/accessories
Catalog mailed 4x per year

Zephyr Exclusive Software
James Paulsen, Pres
Zephyr Services
1900 Murray Ave
Pittsburgh PA 15217
412-422-6600; FAX orders: 412-422-9930
Subjects: 23(IMB compatibles)
Items: Over 140 software programs
Catalog mailed 2x per year
Numbers: 500,000 mailed

Zoo Review Catalog
Buyer
Zoo Book Sales
464 2nd St
Excelsior MN 55331
612-470-8733; Fax: 612-470-5013
E-Mail: zoobooks@mn.uswest.net
Subjects: 15-51E-48
Items: HC-PB
Catalog mailed 2x per year
Other: Many titles

Abbreviations Used

Territory

CN	Canada
IT	International
MX	Mexico
OT	Other
US	United States with some state abbreviations for the different states

Markets

BK	Bookstores
CO	Colleges
JB	Jobbers
MM	Mass Markets
NS	Newsstands
OT	Other
PL	Public Libraries
RO	Retail Outlets
SC	Schools
SL	Special Libraries

Items

CA	Calendars
CO	Comics
CR	Craft Items
GA	Games
GC	Greeting Cards
GI	Gifts
HC	Hardcovers
MA	Maps and Atlases
MG	General / Special Magazines
ML	Literary Magazines
MM	Mass Market Books
NP	Newspapers
OP	Out of Print Books
OT	Other Items
PB	Trade Paperbacks
PO	Posters
RC	Records
RM	Remainders
SB	Stickers/Bookmarks
ST	Stationery
SW	Software
TA	Tapes, Audio
TO	Toys
TV	Tapes, Video
TX	Textbooks
US	Used books

Remainder Dealers

The following companies will be happy to help you liquidate overstocks and remainders (remaining copies of a book that is going out of print). The most you can expect to receive from these dealers is your printing cost (and maybe a little more). If you'd rather donate your remaining books to a worthy cause, check the list of groups that accept such donations at the end of this section.

Abel Love Inc
Abraham Leiss, Rem Buyer
935 Lucas Creek Rd
Newport News VA 23608
804-877-2939; Fax: 804-877-2939
Subjects: 39
Comments: Medical books.

American Media Library Books
219 N Milwaukee St
Milwaukee WI 53202-5874
414-287-4600
Subjects: 21-76-89

Assorted Book Company
Donn Westervelt, Pres
230 Fifth Ave #1112
New York NY 10001
212-684-9000; Fax: 212-684-0590
Subjects: 99
Comments: Remainder books on tape.

Barnett Books
John or Pat Barnett, Buyers
20 N Plains Industrial Rd
Wallingford CT 06492
203-265-2013; Fax: 203-949-9472
Subjects: 99
Comments: PB-HC-MM(any books)

Book Margins Inc
Dave Hathaway, Gen Mgr
65 Richard Rd
Ivyland PA 18974
215-672-5150; Fax: 215-672-5460
Subjects: 75-85-99
Comments: Mass market paperbacks.

Bookland Stores
Tom Hudgeons, Buuyer
393 Rivers Edge Rd
Jupiter FL 33477
407-747-0912; Fax: 407-747-5497
Subjects: 99

The Bookmen Inc
Jim Henderson, Remainder Buyer
525 N Third St
Minneapolis MN 55401
612-341-3333; Fax: 612-341-3065;
   800-328-8411
Subjects: 99

Booksmith Promotional Co
Barry Hochberg, Rem Buyer
100 Paterson Plank Rd
Jersey City NJ 07307
201-659-2768; Fax: 201-659-3631
Subjects: 11-21-76-89-99
Comments: Art/juveniles their specialty.
Other phone: 718-782-0405

CAMEX Inc
Victor Benedetto, Rem Buyer
535 Fifth Ave
New York NY 10017
212-682-8400; Fax: 212-808-4669
Subjects: 11-21-27-76-99
Comments: Also buy reprint rights.

Corradetti Enterprises
1300 Taylors Ln
PO Box 2266
Cinnaminson NJ 08077
609-829-5353; Fax: 609-829-9203
Subjects: 99
Comments: Closeouts.

Daedalus Books
Mr Robin Moody, Buyer/Pres
4601 Decatur St
Hyattsville MD 20781
301-779-4102; Fax: 301-779-8112
800-333-5489: wholesale orders
Subjects: 99
Memo: Helaine Harris, Buyer/VP.

Edu-Tech Corporation
Robert Caston
65 Bailey Rd
Fairfield CT 06432
203-372-3353; Fax: 203-374-8050
Subjects: 10
Comments: Adult non-fiction books.
Items: PB-HC

Empire Publishing Service
David Cole, Rem Buyer
PO Box 1344
Studio City CA 91614
818-784-8918
Subjects: 14 ONLY

Faro House
Sandra Pulaski, Rem Buyer
404 Court St
Binghamton NY 13904
607-656-8778; Fax: 607-722-2659
Subjects: 99

Foxwood International Ltd
Michael Bailey, Rem Buyer
PO Box 523
Milton ON Canada L9T 4Z1
905-875-4410; Fax: 905-875-1668
Subjects: 11-12-27-28-29-31P-39-57-69-99
Comments: No computer books
Memo: Foxwood US: 2316 Delaware
   Avenue #609, Buffalo, NY 14216;
   800-361-2393;FAX: 800-353-2718.

Handleman Co
Joe Holtzman, Buyer
500 Kirts Blvd
Troy MI 48084
313-362-4400; Fax: 313-362-3615
Subjects: 29-75-76-99
Comments: Ext 292.

Infomax Trading Corp
Michael Goldstein
450 Broome St
New York NY 10013
212-431-4720; Fax: 212-966-9871
Subjects: 99

International Press Publications
Bali Sethi, Rem Buyer
90 Nolan Ct Unit 23
Markam ON Canada L3R 4L9
905-946-9588; Fax: 905-946-9590
Subjects: 59-45-76-80(almanacs/directory)
Comments: Yearbooks/serial book pubs.

J B Sales
Jack Bernstein
1616 Cavell
Highland Park IL 60035
708-831-9473
Subjects: 99(closeouts/remainders)

John K Sharpe Inc
Jack Sharpe, Book Buyer
PO Box 442
Wilmette IL 60091-0442
708-249-0513
Subjects: 99

Landmark Books international
Diana Shelley Priseman
131 Hicks St
Brooklyn Heights NY 11201
718-624-6419; Fax: 718-624-6419
Subjects: 11-41-47-55-56-57-59-63-65-80

Libra Wholesale
2228 Territorial Rd
St Paul MN 55114
612-645-2495; Fax: 612-645-1056
Subjects: 99
Comments: Manufacturer overstocks.

Louis Goldberg Library Books
Book Buyer
139 S Main
Nazareth PA 18064
215-759-9458
Subjects: 23-24-51-67

Magna Books
Vance Harvey, Pres
95 Madison Ave
New York NY 10016
212-686-8000; Fax: 212-686-7110;
  800-462-2665
Subjects: 11-17-21-27-29-33-41-49-75-76-9

Marboro Books
Fred Eisenhart, Rem Buyer
One Pond Rd
Rockleigh NJ 07647
201-784-4215; Fax: 201-784-4213
Subjects: 11-14-17-41-47-75-99
Comments: Barnes & Noble.

The Mazel Company
Bill Rinehart
31000 Aurora Rd
Solon OH 44139
216-248-5200; Fax: 216-349-1931;
  800-443-4789
Subjects: 99
Memo: Donn Westervelt, Book Buyer, Assorted Book Company, a division of Mazel.

National Library Service
Charles Doering, Sales Mgr
PO Box 352
Leonardtown MD 20650
301-475-5933; 800-638-1188
Subjects: 99

Ollis Book Corp
Kenneth Ollis, Book Buyer
28 E 35th St
Steger IL 60475-1712
708-755-5151
Subjects: 21-76

Outlet Book Co
Muriel Stewart, Rem Buyer
40 Engelhard Ave
Avenel NJ 07001
908-827-2700; Fax: 908-827-2641
Subjects: 99

Pen Notes
Book Buyer
134 Westside Ave
Freeport NY 11520-5499
516-868-5753
Subjects: 99

Pic 'n' Save
Chon Chomsky, Book Buyer
Corporate Hdqtrs
2430 E Del Amo Blvd
Dominguez CA 90220-6306
310-537-9220; Fax: 310-632-4295
Subjects: 21-76(children's remainders)
Comments: Discount stores.
Memo: MacFrugal's Bargains, Closeouts Inc.

Publishers Overstock Unlimited
Arthur Bartley, Pres/Buyer
149 Madison Ave #610
New York NY 10016-6713
212-481-0055; Fax: 212-213-6074;
  800-736-7336
Subjects: 99

Random House Value Publishing
Horace Whyte
34 Engelhard Ave
Avenel NJ 07001
908-827-2700; 800-726-0600
Subjects: 99

Riverside Book Co
Brian Eskenazi, Rem Buyer
250 W 57th St #1117
New York NY 10107
212-765-2680; Fax: 212-765-2682
Subjects: 11-12A-43D-43H
Comments: Send info by mail.

Rock Bottom Remainders Inc
2259 14th Ave
San Francisco CA 94116
415-664-3333; Fax: 415-664-0517

Rockport Publishers
Keith Gray
146 Granite St
Rockport ME 01966
508-546-9590; Fax: 508-546-7141
Subjects: 11(commercial)-12

S & L Sales Co
Ricky Perritt, Book Buyer
2165 Industrial Blvd (31503)
PO Box 2067
Waycross GA 31502
912-283-0210; Fax: 912-283-0261;
  800-243-3699 (orders only)
Subjects: 99
Memo: Spencer Perritt, Owner.

Smithmark Publishers
Harvey Markowitz, Rem Buyer (Ext 300)
16 E 32nd St 6th Fl
New York NY 10016
212-532-6600; Fax: 212-683-5768;
  800-645-9990
Subjects: 99
Memo: This is the showroom address.

The Texas Bookman
Charles Mitchell, Book Buyer
8650 Denton Dr
Dallas TX 75235
214-350-6648; Fax: 214-352-0726;
  800-566-2665
Subjects: 11-14-47-65-75-99(scholarly)

Universal International
Jerrey Lebowitz, Sr Buyer
5000 Winnetka Ave N
New Hope MN 55428
612-533-1169; Fax: 612-533-1158;
  800-634-8349
Subjects: 99
Memo: Electronics, housewares, hardware, sporting goods, foods, gifts, etc.

Universal Sales & Marketing
Stena Forsell, Rem Buyer
230 Fifth Ave #1212
New York NY 10001
212-481-3500; Fax: 212-481-3534
Subjects: 21-76-99
Comments: Sales and buying office

Victor Hotho & Co
Darryl Luttrell, Book Buyer
PO Box 9738
Fort Worth TX 76147-0738
817-335-1833;
Subjects: 99

Waldenbooks
Joe Holtzman, Buyer
Bargain
100 Phoenix Dr
Ann Arbor MI 48107-2022
313-913-1865; Fax: 313-913-1918
Subjects: 99(bargain)
Memo: M McKenna, Assistant Buyer (Ext 1857).

Zillman Enterprises
Book Buyer
911 Colfax Dr
Danville IL 61832-3395
217-442-6855
Subjects: 21-76-89-99
Comments: Athletic & record books.

Books as Donations

Books for Asia Program
Matthew King
The Asia Foundation
451 Sixth St
San Francisco CA 94103
415-982-4640; Fax: 415-543-8131
Subjects: 19-21-23-31-39-44-45-55-67-71-9
Comments: Sent to developing countries.

Books for Kids Foundation
Matthew Veno
515 East 88th St #4C
New York NY 10128-7747
212-439-7844
Subjects: 21-31-76-79-99

NAEIR - National Association for Exchange of Industrial Resources
Jack Zavada, Dir of Comm
560 McClure St
Galesburg IL 61401
309-343-0704; Fax: 309-343-0862;
  800-562-0955
E-mail: jackz.naeif@misslink.net or dpmpm.naeir@misslink.net
http://www.misslink.net/naeir/naeir.htm
Subjects: 99
Memo: Book donations to schools/non-profits.

Pre Release Center
Deo W Read, Ctr Coordinator
Green Haven Correction Facility
Rt 216
Stormville NY 12582
914-221-2711
Subjects: 99
Comments: Prison program donations.

Section III:

Magazines and Newspapers

173 Magazines

- 173 Magazines for Authors, Booksellers, Librarians, & Publishers
- 177 Magazine Book Reviewers and Editors
- 233 Business Trade Magazines
- 257 Professional Magazines
- 269 Marketing Magazines

273 Newspapers

- 273 Newspaper Editors and Book Reviewers
- 344 Canadian Newspaper Editors and Book Reviewers
- 349 Weekly Newspaper Editors and Book Reviewers

Section III: Magazines and Newspapers

Reviews and features in the print media are one of the most effective ways to promote your books and get word-of-mouth advertising working for you. This section lists more than 1,000 magazine and 3000 newspaper book reviewers and editors.

We did not include the broadcast media in this directory because they are covered in two special reports we update yearly: *Radio Phone Interview Shows: How to Do an Author Tour from Home* (which features 684 radio shows that conduct phone interviews) and *The Top 200 National TV News / Talk / Magazine Shows* (which, as the title suggests, features 200 of the top national TV shows which interview guests and/or report news in which they sometimes also discuss books or authors).

The magazines in this section have been divided into five subsections as follows:

- **Magazines for booksellers, librarians, and publishers** — These magazines feature pre-reviews or reviews of books to alert booksellers and librarians to the books they should be stocking. Some of the newsletters listed under this category publish book reviews for booksellers to give out to their customers.
- **Magazine book reviewers/editors** — This section features the book review editors or editors at more than 1,000 major and minor magazines. It does not list other editors. For names of these editors, consult the *PR ProfitCenter Data Files* or other media directories.
- **Business trade magazines** — This section lists 460 trade magazines which serve various retail businesses (such as *American Printer*, which serves the printing trade and *Playthings*, which serves the toy business).
- **Professional magazines** —This section lists 200 professional magazines which serve a particular profession. Many of the magazines published by The Haworth Press and Heldref Publications are professional magazines.
- **Marketing magazines** — This section lists magazines that feature news, reviews, and other items of interest to anyone involved in marketing products or services. These include advertising and marketing magazines, such as *Catalog Age* and *Adweek*.

Finally, Section III features the daily newspapers in the United States and Canada. Because many newspaper book reviewers tend to focus primarily on fiction, biographies, current events, and some general nonfiction, we also list the editors of the other major sections, such as business, arts and entertainment, sports, lifestyle, travel, and more.

While the magazine sections are all arranged alphabetically by the name of the magazine, the newspaper section is arranged by state. This arrangement should make it easier to target the major newspapers in your region.

Magazines for Authors, Booksellers, Librarians, Publishers and Writers

The following magazines publish news about the publishing industry and/or reviews of books for booksellers, librarians, and/or publishers. Some of these, such as *Booklist* and *Publishers Weekly*, provide previews of books before publications date for librarians and booksellers. Make sure to send review copies of your upcoming books to the appropriate magazines as far in advance of publication date as possible.

A

AB Bookman's Weekly
Jacob L Chernofsky, Publisher
PO Box AB
Clifton NJ 07015
201-772-0020; Fax: 201-772-9281
Focus: 99(reprints) For antiquarian booksellers
Frequency: Weekly; Circulation: 8,000

American Bookseller
Dan Cullen, Editor
American Booksellers Assn
828 S Broadway
Tarrytown NY 10591
914-591-2665; Fax: 914-591-2717
800-637-0037 ext 250
Focus: 99(for bookstores)
Frequency: 13; Circulation: 8,000

American Libraries
Kenneth K McNulty Sr, Editor/Publisher
50 E Huron St
Chicago IL 60611-2729
312-280-4216; Fax: 312-440-0901
Focus: 99
Frequency: Monthly; Circulation: 56,000

ARL Newsletter
Jaia Barrett, Editor
Assn of Research Librarians
21 Dupont Cir NW #800
Washington DC 20036
202-296-2296; Fax: 202-872-0884
Focus: 59-99
Frequency: 5x per year

Art Reference Services Quarterly
Edward H Teague, Editor
201 Fine Arts Bldg A
Univ of Florida
Gainesville FL 32611
904-392-0222; Fax: 904-392-7251
Focus: 11-12-59
Published by Haworth Press
Frequency: Quarterly

Association of Jewish Libraries Newsletter
Anna Olswanger, Column Editor
7117 Harps Mill Rd
Raleigh NC 27615
919-870-0555
Focus: 63J
Frequency: Quarterly; Circulation: 1,000

B

Behavioral & Social Sciences Lib
David Longergan, Editor
The Haworth Press Inc
10 Alice St
Binghamton NY 13904-1503
800-342-9678; Fax: 607-722-1424
Focus: 13-31-35-55-57-65-73(for librarians)
Frequency: 2x per year

Book Links
Barbara Elleman, Editor-in-Chief
American Library Assn
50 E Huron St
Chicago IL 60611-2729
312-280-5718; Fax: 312-337-6787
Focus: 21-59-76-79
Frequency: Bimonthly; Circulation: 40,000

Book Report
Carolyn Hamilton, Editor
Linworth Publishing Inc
480 E Wilson Bridge Rd #L
Worthington OH 43085-2372
614-436-7107; Fax: 614-436-9490
Focus: 21-31-76-89
For secondary school libraries
Frequency: 5x per yr; Circulation: 12,000

Booklist
American Library Assn
50 E Huron St
Chicago IL 60611-2729
312-944-6780; Fax: 312-337-6787
Sally Estes, Book Review Editor
Bonnie Smothers, Book Review Editor
Irene Wood, Editor
Stuart Whitwell, Managing Editor
Bill Ott, Publisher

Focus: 21T-89-99(books for public libraries)
Frequency: 2x per yr; Circulation: 30,000

BookPage
Anne Meador-Shayne, Editor
ProMotion Inc
2501 21st Ave S #5
Nashville TN 37212-5626
615-292-8926; Fax: 615-292-8249
Focus: 99
Newsletter for many SE bookstore
Frequency: Monthly; Circulation: 700,000

Bookstore Journal
Lynn Waalkes, Book Editor
2620 Venetucci Blvd #200
PO Box 200
Colorado Springs CO 80901-4003
719-576-7880; Fax: 719-576-0795
Focus: 63(Christian)-99
Christian bookstores
Frequency: Monthly; Circulation: 8,000

Business Information Alert
Donna Tuke Heroy, Editor-in-Chief
Alert Publications Inc
401 W Fullerton Pky
Chicago IL 60614-2805
312-525-7594; Fax: 312-525-7015
Focus: 19A-19I-19M(business publications and databases)-59
For business librarians
Frequency: 10x per yr

C

Cataloging & Classification Qly
Roger Brisson, Editor
The Haworth Press
10 Alice St
Binghamton NY 13904-1580
800-342-9678; Fax: 607-722-6362
Focus: 59(librarians)
Joining World Wide Web
Frequency: Quarterly

Catholic Library World
Allen Gruenke, Editor-in-Chief
6721 Wildwood
Houston TX 77023-4023
713-926-5035
Focus: 99
Frequency: Quarterly; Circulation: 3,000

Choice
Francine Graf, Managing Editor, Business and Economics
Helen MacLam, Subject Editor, History and Sociology
Judith Douville, Subject Editor, Math and Sciences
Ken McLintock, Subject Editor, Reference Books
Robert Balay, Subject Editor, Reference Books
100 Riverview Ctr
Middletown CT 06457
203-347-6933; Fax: 203-346-8586
Focus: 13-19-19C-19E-31E-55-65
Frequency: 11x per yr; Circulation: 5,000

Collection Management
Sul Lee, Editor
The Haworth Press Inc
10 Alice St
Binghamton NY 13904
Focus: 19G(libraries)
Frequency: Quarterly

College & Research Libraries
Glorianna St Clair, Editor
Pennsylvania State Univ
E506 Pattee Library
University Park PA 16802
814-865-1858; Fax: 814-863-7293
Focus: 99
College libraries
Frequency: 6x per yr; Circulation: 14,000

Community & Junior College Libs
Kathy Rutz, Editor
The Haworth Press Inc
10 Alice St
Binghamton NY 13904-1503
607-722-5857; Fax: 607-722-1424; 800-342-9678
Focus: 59
Frequency: 2x per yr

E

Emergency Librarian
Michele Farquharson, Assoc Editor
Ken Haycock, Editor-in-Chief
Box C34069 Dept 284
Seattle WA 98124-1069
604-925-0266; Fax: 604-925-0566
Focus: 21-76
Frequency: 5x per yr; Circulation: 26,000

F

Feminist Bookstore News
Carol Seajay, Managing Editor
2358 Market St (94114)
PO Box 882554
San Francisco CA 94188-2554
415-626-1556; Fax: 415-626-8970
Focus: 37-73-99(alternative issues)
Frequency: Bimonthly; Circulation: 800,000

H

Horn Book Guide
Anita Silvey, Editor-in-Chief
11 Beacon St #1000
Boston MA 02108-3002
617-227-1555; Fax: 617-523-0299; 800-325-1170
Focus: 21-76-79
Frequency: Bimonthly; Circulation: 24,000

Hungry Mind Review
Martha Davis-Beck, Childrens Editor, Children's Book Supplement
Margaret Maitland, Managing Editor, Children's Book Supplement
Bart Schneider, Editor
1648 Grand Ave
St Paul MN 55105-1896
612-699-2610; Fax: 612-699-0970
Focus: 11-21-3143-55-57-61(midwest)-75-95-99
Frequency: Quarterly; Circulation: 30,000

I

Information Technology & Library
Thomas W Leonhardt, Editor
American Library Assn
50 E Huron St
Chicago IL 60611-2729
312-280-4270; Fax: 312-280-3257
Focus: 23-99
Frequency: Quarterly; Circulation: 7,000

J

Journal of Academic Librarianship
Herbert Johnson, Publisher
JAI Press
PO Box 1678
Greenwich CT 06836
203-661-7602
Focus: 59-65
Frequency: Bimonthly; Circulation: 3,000

Journal of Business/Finance Librarians
Charles Popovich, Editor
The Haworth Press Inc
10 Alice St
Binghamton NY 13904-1503
800-342-9678; Fax: 607-722-1424
Focus: 19-59
Frequency: Quarterly

Journal of Interlibrary Loan/Document
Leslie R Morris, Editor
& Information Supply
10 Alice St
Binghamton NY 13904-1503
800-342-9678; Fax: 607-722-1424
Focus: 59
Published by The Haworth Press Inc
Frequency: Quarterly

Journal of Library Administration
Sul H Lee, Editor
The Haworth Press Inc
10 Alice St
Binghamton NY 13904-1503
800-342-9678; Fax: 607-722-1424
Focus: 59
Frequency: Quarterly; Circulation: 1,000

K

Kirkus Reviews
Anne Larson, Exec Editor
200 Park Ave S
New York NY 10003-1503
212-777-4554; Fax: 212-979-1352
Focus: 21-31-76-89
Frequency: Biweekly; Circulation: 4,000

Kliatt Paperback Book Guide
Claire Rosser, Editor
33 Bay State Rd
Wellesley MA 02181-3244
617-237-7577; Fax: 617-237-7577
Focus: 21T-89
Young adult books/audio books
Frequency: Bimonthly; Circulation: 2,000

L

Legal Reference Services Qtly
Robert C Berring JD MLS, Editor
The Haworth Press Inc
10 Alice St
Binghamton NY 13904-1503
800-342-9678; Fax: 607-722-1424
Focus: 55L-59
Frequency: Quarterly; Circulation: 1,000

Library & Archival Security
Bruce Shuman, Editor
The Haworth Press Inc
10 Alice St
Binghamton NY 13904-1503
813-388-3510
Focus: 59
Frequency: 2x per yr

Library Hi Tech News
Ken Wachsberger, Managing Editor
Pierian Press
5000 Washtenaw Ave
Ann Arbor MI 48108-1416
313-434-5530; Fax: 313-434-6409
Focus: 23-99
Libraries
Frequency: Quarterly; Circulation: 5

Library Journal
Mark Annichiarico, Assoc Editor, Audio
  Reviews and Books
Amy Bowaz Nugent, Assoc Editor, The
  Book Review Section
Wilda Williams, Assoc Editor, Professional
  Reading
Cheryl LaGuardia, CD-ROM Reviewer,
  Electronic Teaching Ctr
Eric Bryant, Magazine Editor,
  Magazine/Book Reviews
Bette-Lee Fox, Managing Editor, Video
  Reviews
249 West 17th St
New York NY 10011-5301
212-645-0067; Fax: 212-463-6734
E-Mail: berry-j@class.org
Focus: 27-37-39M-51-55-59-65-73

Library Talk
Carolyn Hamilton, Editor
Linworth Publishing Inc
480 E Wilson Bridge Rd #L
Worthington OH 43085-2372
614-436-7107; Fax: 614-436-9490
Focus: 76-79
For elementary school libraries
Frequency: 5x per yr; Circulation: 8,000

M

Magazine & Bookseller
Michelle Alumkal, Assoc Editor
Patricia McCarthy, Editor
North American Publishing
322 Eighth Ave 18th Fl
New York NY 10001-4808
212-620-7330; Fax: 213-620-7335
Focus: 19M-56P-75(news about
  paperbacks, magazines)
Frequency: 8x per yr; Circulation: 30,000

Medical Reference Services Qly
M Sandra Wood, Editor
The Haworth Press Inc
10 Alice St
Binghamton NY 13904-1503
607-722-5857; 800-342-9678;
  Fax: 607-722-1424
Focus: 39-59
Frequency: Quarterly; Circulation: 1,000

N

NAPRA ReVIEW
Matthew Gilbert, Managing Editor
6 Eastsound Square
PO Box 9
Eastsound WA 98245
360-376-2702; Fax: 360-376-2704
Focus: 39H-51E-53-54-56P-57-73
Frequency: Bimonthly; Circulation: 12,000

New York Review of Books
Robert Silvers and Barbara Epstein,,
  Editors
250 W 57th St
New York NY 10107-0001
212-757-8070; Fax: 212-333-5374
Focus: 10-41-55-65
Frequency: Biweekly; Circulation: 130,000

P

Primary Sources & Original Works
Lawrence J McCrank PhD, Editor
The Haworth Press Inc
10 Alice St
Binghamton NY 13904-1503
800-342-9678; Fax: 607-722-1424
Focus: 59
Frequency: Quarterly

Publishers Weekly
Trudi Rosenblum, Audio News Editor
  (E-Mail:TrudiRose@aol.com)
John Zinsser, Audio Reviewer
Shannon Maughan, Editor, Children's
  Books
Sybil Steinberg, Editor, Fiction Forecasts
Calvin Reid, News Editor
Genevieve Stuttaford, Editor, Non-Fiction
  Forecasts
John Mutter, Executive Editor,
  Bookselling (E-Mail:JMutter@aol.com)
Dulcy Brainard, Lifestyles, Mysteries,
  Poetry
Marie Simson, Paperback Editor
Diane Roback, Senior Editor, Children's
  Books
Paul Hilts, Technology Editor
249 West 17th St
New York NY 10011-5301
212-463-6782; Fax: 212-463-6631
Focus: 10
Frequency: Weekly; Circulation: 45,000

Publishers Weekly
Joseph Barbato, Reporter
Independent Publishing
1418 Juliana Pl
Alexandria VA 22304
703-370-0663 or Work phone:
  703-841-5300; Fax: 703-841-4283
Focus: 56P-83-90-95
Frequency: Monthly; Circulation: 45,000

Publishers Weekly
Phyllis Tickle, Religion Editor
3522 Lucy Rd S
Millington TN 38053-5301
901-357-5441
Focus: 63
Frequency: Weekly; Circulation: 45,000

Publishers Weekly
Bridget Kinsella, Midwest Correspondent
3527 N Broadway #109
Chicago IL 60657
312-975-0463; Fax: 312-975-0461
Focus: 56P-61(Midwest publishers)
Frequency: Weekly; Circulation: 45,000

Publishers Weekly
Bob Summer, Columnist, Southern
  Spotlight
PO Box 22392
Nashville TN 37202
615-352-4473; Fax: 615-256-4105
Focus: 61(Southern US publishers)-99
Frequency: Weekly; Circulation: 45,000

Publishers Weekly
Steve Sherman, New England
  Correspondent
PO Box 174
Hancock NH 03449
603-525-3581; Fax:
Focus: 56P-61(New England publishers)
Frequency: Weekly; Circulation: 45,000

Publishers Weekly
Lisa See, West Coast Correspondent
530 Tigertail Road
Los Angeles CA 90049
310-476-0608; Fax: 310-476-1513
Focus: 56P-61(West Coast)-99
Frequency: Monthly; Circulation: 45,000

R

The Reference Librarian
Bill Katz, Editor
The Haworth Press Inc
10 Alice St
Binghamton NY 13904-1503
800-342-9678; Fax: 607-722-1424
Focus: 59
Frequency: 2x per yr

Reference Services Review
Ken Wachsberger, Managing Editor
Pierian Press
5000 Washtenaw Ave
Ann Arbor MI 48108-1416
313-434-5530; Fax: 313-434-6409
Focus: 59
Frequency: Quarterly; Circulation: 2,000

Resource Sharing & Info Networks
Robert P Holley, Editor
The Haworth Press Inc
10 Alice St
Binghamton NY 13904-1503
607-722-5857; 800-342-9678;
  Fax: 607-722-1424
Focus: 59
Frequency: 2x per yr

S

School Library Journal
Luanne Toth, Assoc Editor, Books for Review
Phyllis Levy Mandell, Editor, Audiovisual Reviews
Lillian N Gerhardt, Editor-in-Chief, Children's Books for Review
249 West 17th St
New York NY 10011-5301
212-463-6759; Fax: 212-463-6689
Focus: 21-31-76-89-99
Send 2 copies/no textbooks
Audio & video tapes
Frequency: Monthly; Circulation: 45,000

School Library Media Quarterly
Mary K Biagini, Editor
American Library Assn
50 East Huron St
Chicago IL 60611-2729
312-280-4383; Fax: 312-664-7459
Focus: 11-23
Frequency: Quarterly; Circulation: 8,000

Science & Technology Libraries
Ruth Leidman, Editor
The Haworth Press Inc
10 Alice St
Binghamton NY 13904-1503
607-722-5857; Fax: 607-722-6362
Focus: 23-24-39-51-67
Frequency: Quarterly

Serials Review
Ken Wachsberger, Editor
Pierian Press
5000 Washtenaw Ave
Ann Arbor MI 48108-1416
313-434-5330; Fax: 313-434-6409
Focus: 99
Magazines and other periodicals
Frequency: Quarterly; Circulation: 2,000

Small Magazine Review
Len Fulton, Editor/Publisher
PO Box 100
Paradise CA 95967
916-877-6110; Fax: 916-877-0222
800-477-6110
Focus: 56M-95(focus on literary, alternative periodicals, magazines)
Frequency: Monthly; Circulation: 1,000

T

Technical Services Quarterly
Gary Pitkin, Editor
The Haworth Press Inc
10 Alice St
Binghamton NY 13904-1503
800-342-9678; Fax: 607-722-1424
Focus: 23-59
Frequency: Quarterly

U

Urban Academic Librarian
Mark Rosenzweig, Editor
Hunter College Library
695 Park Ave
New York NY 10021-5085
212-772-4168; Fax: 212-772-5113
Focus: 99
Frequency: 2x per yr

Abbreviations Used

Territory

CN	Canada
IT	International
MX	Mexico
OT	Other
US	United States with some state abbreviations for the different states

Markets

BK	Bookstores
CO	Colleges
JB	Jobbers
MM	Mass Markets
NS	Newsstands
OT	Other
PL	Public Libraries
RO	Retail Outlets
SC	Schools
SL	Special Libraries

Items

CA	Calendars
CO	Comics
CR	Craft Items
GA	Games
GC	Greeting Cards
GI	Gifts
HC	Hardcovers
MA	Maps and Atlases
MG	General / Special Magazines
ML	Literary Magazines
MM	Mass Market Books
NP	Newspapers
OP	Out of Print Books
OT	Other Items
PB	Trade Paperbacks
PO	Posters
RC	Records
RM	Remainders
SB	Stickers/Bookmarks
ST	Stationery
SW	Software
TA	Tapes, Audio
TO	Toys
TV	Tapes, Video
TX	Textbooks
US	Used books

Magazine Book Reviewers or Editors

Here are the names and addresses of book reviewers or editors at both large and small magazines. Many magazines do not have a book editor but they do do book reviews. These contacts were updated during the past year. Most will accept press releases.

3 & 4 Wheel Action
Steve Casper and Bill Lanphier, Editors
Hi-Torque Publications
25233 Anza Dr
Valencia CA 91355-1289
805-295-1910; Fax: 805-295-1278
Focus: 16
Frequency: Monthly; Circulation: 50,000

3-2-1 Contact Magazine
Curtis Slepian, Editor
Children's Television Workshop
1 Lincoln Plz 3rd Fl
New York NY 10023-7170
212-595-3456; Fax: 212-875-6105
Focus: 21-23-24-39-51-57-67
Science for children (ages 8-14)
Frequency: 10x per yr;
    Circulation: 400,000

4-Wheel & Off Road
David Freiburger, Editor
Petersen Publishing Co
6420 Wilshire Blvd
Los Angeles CA 90048
213-782-2000; Fax: 213-782-2223
Focus: 16
Frequency: Monthly; Circulation: 330,000

4-Wheel Drive
Phil Howell, Editor
McMullen & Yee Publishing Inc
774 S Placentia
Placentia CA 92670-6846
714-572-2255; Fax: 714-572-1864
Focus: 16-24
Frequency: Monthly; Circulation: N/A

A

A A U W Outlook
Elinor L Horwitz, Editor
1111 16th St NW
Washington DC 20036-4873
202-785-7728; Fax: 202-872-1425
Focus: 31-73
Frequency: Quarterly; Circulation: 135,000

A Better Life For You
Nancy Heinzel, Editor
200 N 4th
PO Box 1
Burlington IA 52601-0001
319-752-5415; Fax: 319-752-3421
Focus: 39-99
Frequency: Quarterly; Circulation: 2,000

A/E Monthly
Anne Rieschick, Editor
235 E 45th St
New York NY 10017
212-210-9750; Fax: 212-210-1326
Focus: 11-14-33
Frequency: Monthly; Circulation: 80,000

AAA Going Places
Phyllis Zeno, Editor-in-Chief
1515 N West Shore Blvd
Tampa FL 33607-4505
813-289-5923; Fax: 813-289-1318
Focus: 11-71
Florida/Georgia/W Tennessee
Frequency: 6x per yr; Circulation: 980,000

Abacus
Peter Ganick
181 Edgemont Ave
Elmwood CT 06110
203-233-2023
Focus: 56W(experimental & language poetry)
Usually features a single author per issue
Frequency: 8x per yr; Circulation: N/A

Abafazi
Della Scott, Co-Editor
African American Studies Program
Simmons College 300 The Fenway
Boston MA 02115
617-521-2258; Fax: 617-521-3199
Focus: 49B-73-95(issues and themes related to women of African descent)
Frequency: 2x per yr; Circulation: N/A

ABBWA Journal
Will Gibson, Editor-in-Chief
PO Box 10548
Marina del Rey CA 90295
310-822-5195; Fax: 310-398-0160
Focus: 44(African/Carribean)-49-78-80-99(books by Black authors)
ABBWA is the American Black Book Writers Association
Frequency: Quarterly; Circulation: 125,000

The Aboard Group
Gloria Shanahan, Managing Editor
100 Almeria Ave #220
Coral Gables FL 33134-6027
305-441-9738; Fax: 305-441-9739
Focus: 70A-71
Frequency: 6x per yr; Circulation: 130,000

Abraxas
Ingrid Swanberg
2518 Gregory St
Madison WI 53711
608-238-0175

Focus: 11-56W-95 (Poetry, essays, reviews, and critcisms)
Frequency: N/A; Circulation: N/A

Accent on Living
Betty Garee, Editor
PO Box 700
Bloomington IL 61702-0700
309-378-2961; Fax: 309-378-4420
Focus: 39D-57 (physical disabilities and consumer issues)
Frequency: Quarterly; Circulation: 20,000

Acoustic Guitar
Jeffrey Rodgers, Editor
String Letter Corp
PO Box 767
San Anselmo CA 94979-0767
415-485-6946; 800-827-6837;
    Fax: 415-485-0831
Focus: 14
Frequency: 6x per yr; Circulation: 45,000

Adoptive Families
Jolene Roehlkepartain, Editor
Adoptive Families of America
3333 Hwy 100 North
Minneapolis MN 55422
612-535-4829; Fax: 612-535-7808
Focus: 31P-35F
Frequency: 6x per yr; Circulation: 25,000

Adventure Cyclists
Daniel D'Ambrosio, Editor
Adventure Cycling Assn
150 E Pine
Missoula MT 59802-4515
406-721-1776; Fax: 406-721-8754
Focus: 69(bicycling)
Frequency: 9x per yr; Circulation: 40,000

Adventure Road
Michael Brudenell, Editor
Aegis Group Publishers
30400 Van Dyke Ave
Warren MI 48093-2316
810-558-7265; Fax: 810-558-5897
Focus: 71
Frequency: Quarterly; Circulation: 12,000

Adventure West
Marianne Mullins, Editor (916-587-3333)
Adventure Media Inc
PO Box 3210
Incline Village NV 89450-3210
702-832-3700; Fax: 702-832-3775
Focus: 61-71D(new things to do for the outdoor enthusiast)
Frequency: 6x per yr; Circulation: 150,000

The Advocate
Gerry Kroll, Editor
Liberation Publications
6922 Hollywood Blvd 10th Fl
Los Angeles CA 90028-6117
213-871-1225; Fax: 213-467-6805
Focus: 13-37-55-65-99
Frequency: 6x per yr; Circulation: 82,000

Aerial
Rod Smith,
PO Box 25642
Washington DC 20007
202-244-6258; Fax: 202-965-5200
Focus: 11-56W-75 (poetry, fiction, criticism, reviews)
Frequency: 1x per yr; Circulation: N/A

African American Review
Joe Weixlmann, Editor-in-Chief
  (812-237-2788)
Dept of English
Indiana State Univ
Terre Haute IN 47809-0001
812-237-2968; Fax: 812-237-4382
Focus: 47-49B-75-78-90-95
Frequency: Quarterly; Circulation: 4,000

African-American Heritage
Dennis W DeLoach, Editor
Dellco Publishing Co
8443 S Crenshaw Blvd #103
Inglewood CA 90305
213-752-3706
Focus: 49B
Frequency: Quarterly; Circulation: 25,000

The Afro-Hispanic Review
Marvin Lewis,
U of Missouri
143 Arts & Sciences Bldg
Columbia MO 65211
314-882-2030
Focus: 56W(Black)-49B-49H
Bi-lingual journal
Frequency: Once a year; Circulation: N/A

Afterimage
Lynn Love, Editor
31 Prince St
Rochester NY 14607-1405
716-442-8676
Focus: 11P
Frequency: 10 times per year; Circulation: 5,000

Agada
Reuven Goldfarb,
2020 Essex St
Berkeley CA 94703
510-848-0965
Focus: 56W(Jewish)-44-47-63J (Jewish themes/concerns)
Frequency: 20x per yr; Circulation: N/A

Agni
Jennifer Rose, Managing Editor
Dept WM Boston Univ
236 Bay State Rd
Boston MA 02215
617-353-5389
Focus: 95-75-99
Frequency: 2x per yr; Circulation: 2,000

Aim Magazine
Ruth Apilado, Editor
AIM Publishing Co
7308 S Eberhart Ave
Chicago IL 60619-1005
312-874-6184; Fax: 206-543-2746
Focus: 49
Frequency: Quarterly; Circulation: 7,000

Air & Space Smithsonian Magazine
George Larson, Editor
Ntl Air & Space Smithsonian Mag
370 L'Enfant Promenade SW 10 Fl
Washington DC 20024-2518
202-287-3733; Fax: 202-287-3163
Focus: 23-55-67-70A
Frequency: 6x per yr; Circulation: 310,000

Air Travel Journal
Colette Bachand Wood, Editor
120 Boylston St
Boston MA 02116-4611
617-561-4000; Fax: 617-423-1040
Focus: 70A-71
Frequency: 6x per yr; Circulation: 17,000

Akwe: Kon Press
Jose Barreiro, Editor
300 Caldwell Hall
Cornell University
Ithaca NY 14853
607-255-4308; Fax: 607-255-0185
Focus: 49A
Frequency: Quarterly; Circulation: 1,000

Akwesasne Notes
Salli Benedict, Editor
Mohawk Nation
Rooseveltown NY 13683-9999
518-358-9531; Fax: 613-575-2935
Focus: 49A
Frequency: Quarterly; Circulation: 6,000

Alabama Game & Fish
Jimmy Jacobs, Editor
Game & Fish Publications Inc
2250 Newmarket Pky #110
Marietta GA 30067-8749
770-953-9222; Fax: 770-933-9510
Focus: 15-51-61(AL)-69
Frequency: Monthly; Circulation: 509,000

Alaska Airlines
Paul Frichtl, Editor
Paradigm Press Inc
2701 First Ave #250
Seattle WA 98121-1123
206-441-5871; Fax: 206-448-6939
Focus: 61(West)-71-99
Frequency: Monthly; Circulation: 50,000

Alaska Magazine
Tobin Morrison, Editor
808 E St #200
Anchorage AK 99501-3532
907-272-6070; Fax: 907-272-2552
Focus: 61(AK)
Frequency: 10x per yr; Circulation: 235,000

Albatross
Richard Smyth
Box 7787
North Port FL 34287-0787
Focus: 56W-51E-51N (poetry, interviews, and artwork)
Frequency: 20x per yr; Circulation: N/A

Aldebaran Literary Magazine
Quantella Owens
Roger Williams Univ
1 Old Ferry Rd
Bristol RI 02809
401-253-1040
Focus: 56W-75-95
Frequency: N/A; Circulation: N/A

Aleene's Creative Living Magazine
Tiffany Windsor, Managing Editor
Aleene's Creative Living Prod
140 Industrial Way
Buellton CA 93427
805-686-8600; Fax: 805-686-8606
Focus: 29C
Frequency: Monthly; Circulation: N/A

Alfred Hitchcock Mystery Magazine
Cathleen Jordan, Editor
Dell Magazines
1540 Broadway
New York NY 10036-4039
212-782-8549; Fax: 212-782-8338
Focus: 84
Frequency: 13x per yr; Circulation: 249,000

All About Kids
Earladeen Badger PhD, Editor
1077 Celestal St
Cincinnati OH 45202-1629
513-684-0501; Fax: 513-684-0507
Focus: 21-31-35-76
Free magazine
Frequency: Monthly; Circulation: 55

All Chevy
Barry Kluczyk, Managing Editor
McMullen & Yee Publishing Inc
774 S Placentia Ave
Placentia CA 92670-6832
714-572-2255; Fax: 714-572-1864
Focus: 16-24
Frequency: Monthly; Circulation: 200,000

All Kids Considered
Jody Densmore, Editor
24567 Northwestern Hwy #150
Southfield MI 48075-2412
313-352-0990; Fax: 313-352-5066
Focus: 21-31-35-76
Frequency: Monthly; Circulation: 70,000

Allure
Lawrence Karol, Managing Editor
  212-880-2341
Conde Nast Publications Inc
350 Madison Ave
New York NY 10017-3704
212-880-8800; Fax: 212-880-8287;
  E-mail:alluremag@aol.com
Focus: 27-39-40-73
Frequency: Monthly; Circulation: 705,000

Alternative Medicine Digest
Richard Leviton, Editor
Future Medicine Publishing
10124 185th St Ct E
Puyallup WA 98371
800-320-0512
Focus: 39H-39
Frequency: Monthly; Circulation: N/A

America West Airlines Magazine
Michael Derr, Editor
4636 E Elwood St #5
Phoenix AZ 85040-1963
602-997-7200; Fax: 602-997-9875
Focus: 19-71-99(business and light humor book excerpts)
Frequency: Monthly; Circulation: 100,000

American Art Journal
Jayne A Kuchna, Editor-in-Chief
Kennedy Galleries
730 5th Ave 2nd Fl
New York NY 10019
212-541-9600; Fax: 212-977-3833
Focus: 11
Frequency: 2x per yr; Circulation: 2,000

American Artist
M Stephen Doherty, Editor-in-Chief or Karen Stanger, Managing Editor
Billboard Publications
1515 Broadway
New York NY 10036-8901
212-536-5165; Fax: 212-536-5351
Focus: 11-29
Reviews books and videos
Frequency: Monthly; Circulation: 160,000

American Atheist
Jon Garth Murray, Managing Editor
American Atheist Press
PO Box 140195
Austin TX 78714-0195
512-458-1244; Fax: 512-467-9525
Focus: 63
Frequency: Quarterly; Circulation: 50,000

American Baby
Anne Winthrop, Managing Editor
Cahners Publishing Co
475 Park Ave S
New York NY 10016-6901
212-645-0067; Fax: 212-463-6407
Focus: 21-31-35-76-79
Frequency: Monthly;
  Circulation: 1,400,000

American Bar Association Journal
Stefanie Goldburg, Books Editor
750 N Lakeshore Dr
Chicago IL 60611-4497
312-988-5000; Fax: 312-988-6014
Focus: 19L-55L
Frequency: Monthly; Circulation: 384,000

American Bicyclist
Ed McKinley, Editor
400 Skokie Blvd #395
Northbrook IL 60062-7903
708-291-1117; Fax: 708-559-4444
Focus: 69R(bicycling)
Frequency: Monthly; Circulation: 11,000

American Book Review
Romayne Rubinas, Managing Editor
Illinois State Univ
Box 4241
Normal IL 61790-4241
309-438-2127; Fax: 309-438-3523
Focus: 53-54-99-49-73
Frequency: 6x per yr; Circulation: 15,000

American Bungalow
George Murray, Editor
Brinkman Design Offices
123 S Baldwin Ave
Sierra Madre CA 91024-2556
818-355-3363; Fax: 818-355-1220
Focus: 12-28-29-43G-43H
Frequency: Quarterly; Circulation: 14,000

American Cheerleader
Julie Davis, Editor-in-Chief
350 W 50th St #2AA
New York NY 10019
212-861-8108
Focus: 21T(cheerleading-12-18 year olds)
Frequency: 6x per yr;
  Circulation: 125,000

American Civil War
Carl Von Wodtke, Managing Editor
Cowles Magazine Inc
741 Miller Dr SE #D2
Leesburg VA 22075
703-779-8302; Fax: 703-779-8345
Focus: 41-48-55G
Frequency: 6x per yr;
  Circulation: 125,000

American Civilization
Richard O'Donnell, Editor
Progress & Freedom Foundation
1250 H St NW #550
Washington DC 20005
202-484-2312; Fax: 202-484-9326;
  E-Mail: pff@aol.com
Focus: 55(a newspaper of progress and freedom)
Frequency: Monthly; Circulation: N/A

American Dane
Jerome Christensen, Admin Editor
The Danish Brotherhood in Amer
1905 Harney St #700
Omaha NE 68102
402-341-5049; Fax: 402-341-0830
Focus: 49(Danish heritage)
Frequency: Monthly; Circulation: 6,000

The American Enterprise
Karl Zinsmeister, Editor
1150 17th St NW
Washington DC 20036-4603
202-862-5829; Fax: 202-862-7178
Focus: 19-19I-19X-44-55-55L
Frequency: 6x per yr; Circulation: 11,000

American Forests
Michelle Robbins, Managing Editor
PO Box 2000
Washington DC 20013-2000
202-667-3300; Fax: 202-667-2407
Focus: 51-99
Frequency: 6x per yr; Circulation: 24,000

American Girl
Nancy Holyoke, Editor
Pleasant Company
8400 Fairway Pl
Middleton WI 53562-2548
608-836-4848; Fax: 608-831-7089
Focus: 21(8-12 yr old girls)
Frequency: 6x per yr; Circulation: 300,000

American Health
James Ellison, Book Editor
28 W 23rd St
New York NY 10010-5204
212-366-8900; 800-365-5005;
  Fax: 212-366-8760
Focus: 27-39-57
Frequency: 10x per yr;
  Circulation: 800,000

American Heritage
Jane Colihan, Book Editor
60 Fifth Ave
New York NY 10011
212-206-5500; Fax: 212-620-2332
Focus: 41-61
Frequency: 8x per yr; Circulation: 326,000

American Heritage of Invention
Frederic D Schwarz, Managing Editor
60 Fifth Ave
New York NY 10011
212-206-5588; Fax: 212-620-2332
Focus: 16A-23-24-41A-67
Frequency: Quarterly; Circulation: 100,000

American Historical Review
William Bishel, Book Editor
Indiana University
914 Atwater
Bloomington IN 47405
812-855-7609; Fax: 812-855-5827
Focus: 41
Frequency: 5x per yr; Circulation: 19,000

American History
Ed Holm, Editor
Cowles Magazine Inc
6405 Flank Dr
Harrisburg PA 17112
717-657-9555; Fax: 717-657-9526
Focus: 17B-48-49A-49B-55
Frequency: 6x per yr; Circulation: 150,000

American Hunter
John Zent, Managing Editor
NRA
470 Spring Park Pl #1000
Herndon VA 22070-5227
703-267-1316; Fax: 703-267-3971
Focus: 51-69H
Frequency: Monthly;
  Circulation: 1,457,000

American Indian Art Magazine
Roanne P Goldfein, Editor
American Indian Art Inc
1314 E Osborn Dr
Scottsdale AZ 85251
602-994-5445; Fax: 602-945-9533
Focus: 11-28(Indian)
Frequency: Quarterly; Circulation: 25,000

American Indian Quarterly
Robert A Black, Book Review Editor
Univ of Nebraska Press
312 N 14th St
Lincoln NE 68508-1623
402-472-5946; 800-755-1105;
    Fax: 402-472-6214
Focus: 49A
Frequency: Quarterly; Circulation: 800,000

American Industry
Jack S Panes, Editor
21 Russell Woods Rd
Great Neck NY 11021-4644
516-487-0990; Fax: 516-487-0809
Focus: 19(the field of industry, not production)
Frequency: 10x per yr; Circulation: 27,000

American Iron Magazine
Jonathan Gourley, Editor
TAM Communications Inc
6 Prowitt St
Norwalk CT 06855-1204
203-855-0008; Fax: 203-852-9980
Focus: 16(motorcycles)
Frequency: Monthly; Circulation: 85,000

American Journal of Nursing
Kathi Froio, Managing Editor
American Journal of Nursing Co
555 W 57th St
New York NY 10019-2968
212-582-8820; Fax: 212-586-5462
Focus: 35-39(nursing)
Frequency: Monthly; Circulation: 239,000

American Journalism Review
Carl Sessions Stepp, Sr Editor
Books Department
8701 Adelphi Rd
Adelphi MD 20783
301-431-4771; Fax: 301-431-0097
Focus: 56-56M(covers newspapers, radio, and TV)
Frequency: 10x per yr; Circulation: 28,000

American Legacy
Editor
60 Fifth Ave
New York NY 10011
212-206-5500; Fax: 212-620-2332
Focus: 49B
Frequency: Quarterly; Circulation: N/A

The American Legion
Miles Z Epstein, Managing Editor
700 N Pennsylvania St
Indianapolis IN 46206-1129
317-630-1200; Fax: 317-630-1280
Focus: 99
Frequency: Monthly;
    Circulation: 2,900,000

American Literature
Cathy N Davidson, Editor
PO Box 90660
Durham NC 27708-0660
919-687-3600; Fax: 919-688-4574
Focus: 47(American authors)
Frequency: Quarterly; Circulation: 5,500

American Motorcyclist
Bill Wood, Managing Editor
American Motorcyclist Assn
33 Collegeview
Westerville OH 43081-1463
614-891-2425; Fax: 614-891-5012
Focus: 16(motorcycles)
Frequency: Monthly; Circulation: 175,000

American Photo
David Schonauer, Editor
Hachette Filipacchi Magazines
1633 Broadway
New York NY 10019-6708
212-767-6273
Focus: 11P
Frequency: 6x per yr;
    Circulation: 250,000

American Poetry Review
David Bonanno, Book Editor
1721 Walnut St
Philadelphia PA 19103
215-496-0439; Fax: 215-569-0808
Focus: 47-95
Frequency: 6x per yr; Circulation: 18,000

American Rider
Buzz Buzzelli, Editor
TL Enterprises
3601 Calle Tecate
Camarillo CA 93012-5040
805-389-0300; Fax: 805-389-0378
Focus: 16-69 (motorcylce riding)
Frequency: 6x per yr; Circulation: 90,000

American Rifleman
E G Bell Jr, Editor
NRA
11250 Waples Mill Rd
Fairfax VA 22030-7400
703-267-1336; Fax: 703-267-3971
Focus: 51-69H
Frequency: Monthly;
    Circulation: 1,761,000

American Rodder
Joe Kress, Editor
Paisano Publications Inc
28210 Dorothy Dr
Agoura Hills CA 91301-2605
818-889-8740; 800-962-9857;
    Fax: 818-889-5214
Focus: 16-28-29
Frequency: Monthly; Circulation: N/A

American Scholar
Jean Stipicevic, Managing Editor
1811 Q St NW
Washington DC 20009-1613
202-265-3808; Fax:
Focus: 31-47-83-90-95
Frequency: Quarterly; Circulation: 26,000

American Survival Guide
Jim Benson, Editor
McMullen & Yee Publishing Inc
774 South Placentia
Placentia CA 92670-6846
714-572-2255; Fax: 714-572-1864
Focus: 69 (survival)
Frequency: Monthly; Circulation: 72,000

American Theater
Jim O'Quinn, Editor
355 Lexington Ave
New York NY 10017-6603
212-697-5230; Fax: 212-983-4847
Focus: 14T
Frequency: 10x per yr; Circulation: 23,000

American Times
Barbara Walsh, Editor
Grote Publishing
634 W Main St #207
Madison WI 53703
608-257-4640
Focus: 11-25-39-51-61(DC)-69-99
Frequency: Quarterly; Circulation: 117,000

American Visions
Joanne Harris, Editor
2101 S St NW
Washington DC 20008-4011
202-462-1779; 800-998-0864;
    Fax: 202-462-3997
Focus: 49B-65-78-80-99
Frequency: 6x per yr; Circulation: 125,000

American Voice Magazine
Frederick Smock, Editor
332 W Broadway
Louisville KY 40202
502-562-0045
Focus: 47-75-83-90-95
Frequency: 3x per yr; Circulation: 2,000

American Way Magazine
Bill Marvel, Book Reviews
American Airlines Publications
PO Box 619640
DFW Airport TX 75261-9640
817-967-1804; Fax: 817-967-1571;
    E-Mail:102131.711@compuserve.com
Focus: 19-71-99
Frequency: Biweekly; Circulation: 300,000

American Woman
Lynn Varacalli, Editor (Ext 275)
GCR Publishing Group
1700 Broadway 34th Fl
New York NY 10019-5905
212-541-7100; Fax: 212-245-1241
Focus: 19C-25-35R-35S-39E-57-73-99
Frequency: 6x per yr; Circulation: 175,000

American Woman Motorscene Magazine
Sue Elliott, Editor
2830 Santa Monica Blvd
Santa Monica CA 90404-2410
310-829-0012; Fax: 310-453-8850
Focus: 16
Frequency: 6x per yr; Circulation: 100,000

American Woodworker
Tim Snyder, Managing Editor
Rodale Press Inc
33 E Minor St
Emmaus PA 18049-4113
610-967-5171; Fax: 610-967-8956
Focus: 29H-43H(woodworking only)
Frequency: 6x per yr; Circulation: 300,000

American Writer
Editor
National Writers Union
873 Broadway #203
New York NY 10003
212-254-0279; Fax: 212-254-0673
Focus: 19C-56W
Frequency: Quarterly; Circulation: 8,000

American Writers Review
John Clausen, Editor
PO Box 1187
Skyland NC 28776
704-696-9708; Fax: 704-696-2379;
 E-Mail: WFMoney@aol.com
Focus: 56W
Frequency: 17x per yr; Circulation: N/A

The Americas Review
Lauro Flores, Editor
Art Publico Press
4800 Calhoun
Houston TX 77004-2610
713-743-2841; Fax: 713-743-2847
Focus: 44-45(Spanish)-47-78-80(Latino literature and arts)-95
Frequency: 3x per yr; Circulation: 3,000

Amicus Journal
Kathrin Lassila, Editor
Natural Res Defense Council
40 W 20th St
New York NY 10011-4211
212-727-2700; Fax: 212-727-1773
Focus: 44-51-55 (environmental affairs)
Frequency: Quarterly; Circulation: 120,000

AmigaWorld
Barbara Gefvert, Managing Editor
IDG Communications
80 Elm St
Peterborough NH 03458-1052
603-924-0100; Fax: 603-924-4066
Focus: 23(Amiga computers)
Frequency: Monthly; Circulation: 68,000

AMS Journal
Review Editor
American Musicological Society
Univ of PA 201 S 34th St
Philadelphia PA 19104-6313
215-898-8698
Focus: 14M
Frequency: 3x per yr; Circulation: 5,000

Amtrak Express
Melinda Stovall, Editor
Pace Communications Inc
1301 Carolina St #200
Greensboro NC 27401-1001
910-378-6065; Fax: 910-275-2864
Focus: 16R-71-99
22,000,000 passengers per year
Frequency: 6x per yr;
 Circulation: 253,000

AMWA Journal
Pamela P Powell, Editor
2701 N Blvd
Houston TX 77098
713-798-5483; Fax: 713-796-9438
Focus: 39-56W
Frequency: Quarterly; Circulation: 4,000

Analog Science Fiction & Fact
Tina Lee, Managing Editor
Dell Publishing
1540 Broadway 9th Fl
New York NY 10036-4039
212-782-8532; Fax: 212-782-7309
Focus: 86
Frequency: 13x per yr; Circulation: 81,000

Ancestry Magazine
Anne Lemmon, Managing Editor
Ancestry Inc
440 S 400 West
Salt Lake City UT 84101-2246
801-531-1790; 800-531-1790;
 Fax: 801-531-1798
Focus: 41G
Frequency: 6x per yr; Circulation: 10,000

Anemone
Nanette Morin, Editor
Box 369
Chester VT 05143
Focus: 11-56W(poetry)-99
Quarterly literary arts journal
Frequency: N/A; Circulation: N/A

The Angelus
Kenneth Novak, Editor
Angelus Press
2918 Tracy Ave
Kansas City MO 64109
816-753-3150; Fax: 816-753-3557
Focus: 63C(Catholic)
Frequency: Monthly; Circulation: N/A

Anglofile
William P King, Editor/Publisher
The Goody Press
PO Box 33515
Decatur GA 30033
404-633-5587; Fax: 404-321-3109
Focus: 33(British)
Frequency: Monthly; Circulation: 3,000

Animals Magazine
James Grisanzio, Book Review Editor
MSPCA
350 S Huntington Ave
Boston MA 02130-4803
617-522-7400; Fax: 617-522-4885
Focus: 15-51
Frequency: 6x per yr;
 Circulation: 100,000

The Animals' Voice
Laura Moretti, Editor
12190 1/2 Ventura Blvd #392
Studio City CA 91604
310-659-8801; Fax: 310-659-8806
Focus: 15
Frequency: 6x per yr; Circulation: 34,000

The Antioch Review
Melinda Kanner, Book Reviewer
Jon Saari, Book Reviewer
David St John, Poetry Editor
PO Box 148
Yellow Springs OH 45387
513-767-6389
Focus: 47-75-83-90-95
Frequency: Quarterly; Circulation: 6,000

Antipodes
Marian Arkin
190 Sixth Ave
Brooklyn NY 11217
718-482-5680
Focus: 56W-99 (focus is on Australian lit)
Frequency: N/A; Circulation: N/A

Antique Doll World
Donna Kaonis, Editor
IC Holdings Inc
225 Main St #300
Northport NY 11768-1744
516-261-8337; 800-828-1429;
 Fax: 516-261-8235
Focus: 28(antique dolls, teddy bears, and miniatures only)
Frequency: N/A; Circulation: 8,000

The Antique Trader Weekly
Carolyn Clark, and Carol Wood,
 Co-Editors
Landmark Specialty Publ Inc
100 Bryant St
Dubuque IA 52003-7405
319-588-2073; Fax: 319-588-0888
Focus: 28
Frequency: Weekly; Circulation: 55,000

Antiques & Auction News
Doris Ann Johnson, Editor
Route 230 West
PO Box 500
Mount Joy PA 17552
717-653-1833; 800-482-2886;
 Fax: 717-653-6165
Focus: 28
Frequency: Weekly; Circulation: 30,000

Antiques & Collectibles Magazine
Rich Branciforte, Editor/Publisher
PO Box 33
Westbury NY 11590-0033
516-334-9650; Fax: 516-334-5740
Focus: 28
Frequency: Monthly; Circulation: 10,000

Antiques & Collecting Hobbies
Frances L Graham, Editor-in-Chief
1006 S Michigan Ave
Chicago IL 60605-2209
312-939-4767; Fax: 312-939-0053
Focus: 28
Frequency: Monthly; Circulation: 18,000

Apalachee Quarterly
Barbara Hamby
PO Box 10469
Tallahassee FL 32302-2469
Focus: 56W-75-95-99 (poetry, fiction, reviews, photos)
Frequency: Quarterly; Circulation: N/A

Aperture
Michael Sand, Managing Editor
20 E 23rd St
New York NY 10010-4401
212-505-5555; Fax: 212-979-7759
Focus: 11P
Frequency: Quarterly; Circulation: 18,000

Appearances
Robert Witz,
165 West 26th St
New York NY 10001
212-675-3026
Focus: 11-56W-75-99 (poetry, fiction, reviews, photos, and interviews)
Frequency: N/A; Circulation: N/A

Applause Theatre Book Review
Glenn Young, Editor
211 W 71st St
New York NY 10023
212-595-4735; Fax: 212-721-2856
Focus: 14-17-33
Frequency: 2x per yr; Circulation: N/A

Application Technology
James C Sulecki, Editor
Meister Publishing Co
37733 Euclid Ave
Willoughby OH 44094
216-942-2000; Fax: 216-942-0662
Focus: 19M-51A-51E
Frequency: 6x per yr; Circulation: N/A

Aquarium Fish Magazine
Ed Bauman, Editor
Fancy Publications
3 Burroughs Dr
Irvine CA 92718-2804
714-855-8822; Fax: 714-855-3045
Focus: 15(fish)
Frequency: Monthly; Circulation: 81,000

Arabian Horse Times
Lynn Wright, Editor
1050 8th St NE
Waseca MN 56093
507-835-3204; Fax: 507-835-5138
Focus: 15(horses)
Frequency: Monthly; Circulation: 22,000

Arachne
Susan L Leach
162 Sturges St
Jamestown NY 14701
716-488-2601
Focus: 56W(poetry)-75-99
Frequency: Quarterly; Circulation: N/A

Architectural Digest
Paige Rense, Editor-in-Chief
Conde Nast Publications
6300 Wilshire Blvd 11th Fl
Los Angeles CA 90048-5202
213-965-3700; 800-637-0920;
   Fax: 213-933-4605
Focus: 12A-43
Frequency: Monthly; Circulation: 625,000

Architectural Record
Carolyn DeWitt, Managing Editor
1221 Ave of the Americas
New York NY 10020-1001
212-512-2000; Fax: 212-512-4256
Focus: 12
Frequency: 16x per yr; Circulation: 50,000

Architecture
Elizabeth Koby, Managing Editor
BPI Communications Inc
1130 Connecticut Ave NW #625
Washington DC 20036-3904
202-828-0993; Fax: 202-828-0825
Focus: 12-23T
Frequency: Monthly; Circulation: 67,000

Argonaut
Warren Hinckle, Editor
2250 Geary Blvd
San Francisco CA 94115
415-563-6033; Fax: 415-563-5934
Focus: 99 (literary journal)
Frequency: Quarterly; Circulation: 20,000

Arizona Highways
Bob Early, Editor
2039 W Lewis Ave
Phoenix AZ 85009
602-258-6641; Fax: 602-254-4505
Focus: 61(AZ)-71
Frequency: Monthly; Circulation: 350,000

Arkansas Business
Jeff Hankins, Editor
Journal Publishing Inc
201 E Markham #200
Little Rock AR 72201-1627
501-372-1443; Fax: 501-375-3623
Focus: 19L-39-55L-61(AR)
Frequency: Weekly; Circulation: 9,000

Arkansas Sportsman
Bob Borgwat, Editor
Game & Fish Publications Inc
2250 Newmarket Pky #110
Marietta GA 30067-8749
770-953-9222; Fax: 770-933-9510
Focus: 15-51-61(AR)-69
Frequency: Monthly; Circulation: 11,000

Armchair Detective
Kate Stine, Editor-in-Chief
129 W 56th St
New York NY 10019-3808
212-765-0902; Fax: 212-265-5478
Focus: 84
Frequency: Quarterly; Circulation: 4,000

Art & Antiques
John Wolfe, Managing Editor
3 East 54th St 11th Fl
New York NY 10022-3108
212-752-5557; Fax: 212-752-7147
Focus: 11-28(antiques)
Frequency: 10x per yr; Circulation: 150,000

Art & Auction
Ellen Brodsky, Managing Editor
440 Park Ave S 14th Fl
New York NY 10016-8012
212-447-9555; Fax: 212-447-5221
Focus: 11
Frequency: Monthly; Circulation: 40,000

Art Book Review Quarterly
Dawn Fulcher, Editor
1 Stewarts Ct
220 Stewarts Rd
London SW8 4UD England
Focus: 11-12-28-43
Frequency: Quarterly; Circulation: 15,000

Art in America
Nancy Marmer, Managing Editor
Brant Publications
575 Broadway
New York NY 10012
212-941-2800; Fax: 212-941-2885
Focus: 11
Frequency: Monthly; Circulation: 70,000

Art Times
Raymond J Steiner, Editor
PO Box 730
Mount Marion NY 12456-0730
914-246-6944; Fax: 914-246-6944
Focus: 11
Frequency: Monthly; Circulation: 15,000

Arthritis Today
Tracy Ballew, Managing Editor
Arthritis Foundation
1314 Spring St NW
Atlanta GA 30309-2810
404-872-7100; Fax: 404-872-9559
Focus: 39(arthritis)
Frequency: 6x per yr;
   Circulation: 500,000

The Artilleryman
C Peter Jorgensen, Publisher
RR 1 Box 36
Tunbridge VT 05077-9707
802-889-3500; Fax: 802-889-5627
Focus: 41
Frequency: Quarterly; Circulation: 3,000

Artist's Magazine
Mary Magnus, Editor
F & W Publications Inc
1507 Dana Ave
Cincinnati OH 45207-1056
513-531-2222; Fax: 513-531-2902
Focus: 11(fine and graphic art)
Frequency: Monthly; Circulation: 250,000

Artnews Magazine
Milton Esterow, Editor
ARTnews Assoc
48 W 38th St
New York NY 10018-6211
212-398-1690; Fax: 212-768-4002
Focus: 11(the art market)
Frequency: 10x per yr; Circulation: 73,000

Aspen Magazine
Janet O'Grady, Editor
413 E Cooper St Box G-3
Aspen CO 81611-1831
970-920-4040; Fax: 970-920-4044
Focus: 43-51-61(CO)-69-71
Frequency: 6x per yr; Circulation: 16,000

Aspire Magazine
Mary Hopkins Bailey, Editor-in-Chief
Thomas Nelson Inc Publ
404 BNA Dr #508 Bldg 200
Nashville TN 37217
800-889-0437; Fax: 615-889-0437;
   E-Mail: royalmaggp@aol.com
Focus: 35-39-57-63P
Frequency: 6x per yr; Circulation: 200,000

Atlanta Baby
Liz White, Editor
4330 Georgetown Square #506
Atlanta GA 30338-6217
770-454-7599; Fax: 770-454-7699
Focus: 21-31-35-76
Frequency: Quarterly; Circulation: 55,000

Atlanta Computer Currents
Michele Silvers, Managing Editor
3200 Professional Pky #245
Atlanta GA 30339-5927
770-984-9444; Fax: 770-933-9072
Focus: 23 (local companies and authors)
Frequency: Monthly; Circulation: 43,000

Atlanta Homes and Lifestyles
Barbara Tapp, Editor/Book Editor
5775 B Glenridge #580
Atlanta GA 30328
404-252-6670; Fax: 404-252-6673
Focus: 43-61(South)
Frequency: 8x per yr; Circulation: 38,000

Atlanta
Lee Walburn, Editor-in-Chief
Two Midtown Plz #1800
1360 Peachtree St
Atlanta GA 30309-3214
404-872-3100; Fax: 404-876-2748
Focus: 61(Atlanta GA)-99
Frequency: Monthly; Circulation: 68,000

Atlanta Parent
Peggy Middendorf, Editor
4330 Georgetown Square #506
Atlanta GA 30338
770-454-7599; Fax: 770-454-7699
Focus: 21-31-35-76
Frequency: Monthly; Circulation: 60,000

The Atlantic Monthly
Phoebe-Lou Adams, Books Editor
745 Boylston St
Boston MA 02116-2636
617-536-9500; Fax: 617-536-3975
Focus: 75-95-99
Frequency: Monthly; Circulation: 461,000

Audacity: Magazine of Business Experience
Cathryn Calhoun and Fredric Smoler, Co-Editors
Forbes
60 Fifth Ave
New York NY 10011-8890
212-206-5588; Fax: 212-620-2332
Focus: 19G-41A(history of business in America with application to today)
Frequency: Quarterly; Circulation: 100,000

Audio
Michael Riggs, Editor-in-Chief
Hachette Magazines
1633 Broadway 45th Fl
New York NY 10019
212-767-6940; Fax: 212-489-4536
Focus: 14M-99(audio tapes)
Frequency: Monthly; Circulation: 152,000

Audio Video Interiors
Maureen Jenson, Editor
21700 Oxnard St #1600
Woodland Hills CA 91367-3670
818-593-3900; Fax: 818-593-2274
Focus: 24(electronics)-33-43(design)
Frequency: N/A; Circulation: N/A

AudioFile
Robin Whitten, Editor
37 Silver St
PO Box 109
Portland ME 04112-0109
207-774-7563; 800-506-1212;
    Fax: 207-775-3744
Focus: 99(spoken word audiotapes)
Frequency: Monthly; Circulation: 12,000

Audubon Magazine
Mary-Powell Thomas, Managing Editor
700 Broadway
New York NY 10003-9501
212-979-3126; Fax: 212-422-9069

Focus: 51
Frequency: 6x per yr; Circulation: 600,000

Austin Child
Gwin Grogan, Editor
4125 Keller Springs Rd #146
Dallas TX 75244-2035
214-960-8474; Fax: 214-490-6748
Focus: 21-31-35-76
Frequency: Monthly; Circulation: 30,000

Auto Racing Digest
Ken Leiker, Sr Editor
Century Publishing Co
990 Grove St
Evanston IL 60201-4370
708-491-6440
Focus: 16A-69(auto racing)
Frequency: 6x per yr; Circulation: 48,000

Auto Sound & Security
Dan Leadbetter, Editor
McMullen & Yee Publishing Inc
774 S Placentia Ave
Placentia CA 92670-6848
714-572-2255; Fax: 714-572-1864
Focus: 16-24
Frequency: Monthly; Circulation: N/A

Autoweek
Larry Edsall, Managing Editor
1400 Woodbridge
Detroit MI 48207
313-446-0336; Fax: 313-446-0347
Focus: 19-16A
Frequency: Weekly; Circulation: 296,000

Avenue Magazine
Quinn Halford, Managing Editor
950 3rd Ave 5th Fl
New York NY 10022-2705
212-758-9516; Fax: 212-758-7395
Focus: 11-14-17-33-71(fine arts)
Frequency: Monthly; Circulation: 80,000

Aviation History
Art Sanselici, Editor
Cowles Magazine
741 Miller Dr SE
Leesburg VA 22075-8920
703-771-9400; Fax: 703-777-4627
Focus: 41-70A(history and aviation)
Frequency: 6x per yr; Circulation: 75,000

B

B'nai B'rith Intl Jewish Monthly
Jeff Rubin, Editor-in-Chief
1640 Rhode Island Ave NW
Washington DC 20036-3278
202-857-6645; Fax: 202-296-1092
Focus: 63J
Frequency: 8x per yr; Circulation: 150,000

Baby Connection News Journal
Gina Morris, Editor
PO Drawer 33550
San Antonio TX 78265-3550
Focus: 21-35
Frequency: N/A; Circulation: N/A

Baby Talk
Susan Strecker, Editor-in-Chief
Time Publishing Ventures
25 W 43rd St 20th Fl
New York NY 10036-7406
212-840-4200; Fax: 212-827-0019
Focus: 21-31-35-76-79
For expectant and new parents
Frequency: Monthly;
    Circulation: 1,300,000

Babybug
Marianne Carus, Editor-in-Chief
Cricket Magazine Group
315 Fifth St
Peru IL 61354-2859
815-223-2520; 800-827-0227;
    Fax: 815-224-6675
Focus: 21(6mo-2yrs)
Frequency: 9x per yr; Circulation: N/A

Back Home
Lorna Loveless, Editor
119 3rd Ave W
Hendersonville NC 28792-4313
704-696-3838; 800-992-2546;
    Fax: 704-696-0700
Focus: 13-19-29-43-51
Frequency: Quarterly; Circulation: 26,000

Backpacker Magazine
John Viehman, Editor
Rodale Press Inc
33 E Minor St
Emmaus PA 18049-4113
610-967-5171; Fax: 610-967-8181
Focus: 39-51-69-71(backpacking, canoeing, mountaineering, kayaking)
Frequency: 6x per yr;
    Circulation: 206,000

Backroads Bicycling
Randy Wyatt, Editor
PO Box 372
Clay Center KS 67432-0372
Focus: 69R(bicycling and touring)
Frequency: Quarterly; Circulation: N/A

Backwoods Home Magazine
Dave Duffy, Editor
1257 Siskiyou Blvd #213
Ashland OR 97520
916-459-3300
Focus: 29-43G-43H(self-sufficiency, growing your own food)
Frequency: 6x per yr; Circulation: 85,000

Balloon Life
Tom Hamilton, Editor/Publisher
Balloon Life Magazine Inc
2145 Dale Ave
Sacramento CA 95815-3632
916-922-9648; Fax: 916-922-4730
Focus: 16-70A
Frequency: Monthly; Circulation: 4,000

Baltimore Business Journal
Margie Freaney, Editor
American City Business Jrnls
117 Water St
Baltimore MD 21202-1044
410-576-1161; Fax: 410-752-3112
Focus: 19-61(Baltimore MD)
Frequency: Weekly; Circulation: 13,000

Baltimore Magazine
Ramsey Flynn, Editor
16 S Calvert St
Baltimore MD 21202-1305
410-752-7375; 800-935-0838;
 Fax: 410-625-0280
Focus: 61(Baltimore MD)
Frequency: Monthly; Circulation: 50,000

Baltimore's Child
Joanne Giza, Editor
11 Dutton Ct
Catonsville MD 21228-4922
410-367-5883; Fax: 410-719-9342
Focus: 21-31-35-76
Frequency: 11x per yr; Circulation: 70,000

Bam: The California Music Magazine
Bill Holdship, Editor
3470 Buskirk Ave
Pleasant Hill CA 94523-4316
510-934-3700; Fax: 510-934-3958
Focus: 14M
Frequency: Biweekly; Circulation: 123,000

Barron's National Business Financial Weekly
Edwin Finn Jr, Editor
Dow Jones & Co Inc
200 Liberty St
New York NY 10281-1003
212-416-2700; Fax: 212-416-2829
Focus: 19
Frequency: Weekly; Circulation: 287,000

Baseball Digest
John Kuenster, Editor
Century Publishing Co
990 Grove St
Evanston IL 60201-4370
708-491-6440; Fax: 708-491-6955
Focus: 69(baseball)
Frequency: Monthly; Circulation: 280,000

Basketball Digest
John Kuenster, Exec Editor
990 Grove St
Evanston IL 60201-4370
708-491-6440; Fax: 708-491-0459
Focus: 69(basketball)
Frequency: N/A; Circulation: 150,000

Bassin' Magazine
Gerald Pope, Publisher
15115 S 76th E Ave
Bixby OK 74008-4177
918-491-6100; Fax: 918-491-9424
Focus: 15(fish)-69H(fishing)
Frequency: 8x per yr; Circulation: 250,000

Bay Area Parent Newsmagazine
Mary Martin, Editor
401 Alberto Way #A
Los Gatos CA 95032-5404
408-358-1414; Fax: 408-356-4903
Focus: 21-31-35-76
Frequency: Monthly; Circulation: 60,000

Bay Area Reporter
Mike Salinas, News Editor
Benro Enterprises Inc
295 9th St
San Francisco CA 94103-3825
415-861-5019; Fax: 415-861-8144
Focus: 37-61(SF)
Frequency: Weekly; Circulation: 160,000

Beckett Baseball Card Monthly
Pepper Hastings, Managing Editor
4887 Alpha Rd #200
Dallas TX 75244-4632
214-991-6657; Fax: 214-233-6488
Focus: 28(baseball cards)-69
Frequency: Monthly; Circulation: 605,000

Beckett Focus on Future Stars
Jay Johnson, Managing Editor
15850 Dallas Pky
Dallas TX 75248-3308
214-991-6657; Fax: 214-233-6488
Focus: 28-69
Frequency: Monthly; Circulation: 81,000

Beckett Football Card Monthly
Jay Johnson, Managing Editor
15850 Dallas Pky
Dallas TX 75248-3308
214-991-6657; Fax: 214-233-6488
Focus: 28-69
Frequency: Monthly; Circulation: 206,000

Beckett Hockey Monthly
Jay Johnson, Managing Editor
15850 Dallas Pky
Dallas TX 75248-3308
214-991-6657; Fax: 214-233-6488
Focus: 28-69
Frequency: Monthly; Circulation: 163,000

Belles Lettres: A Review of Books by Women
Janet Palmer Mullaney, Editor
Phebe Davidson, Poetry Editor
11151 Captain's Walk Ct
North Potomac MD 20878-0441
301-294-0278; Fax: 301-294-0023
Focus: 17-47-73-75-83-90(books by & about women with reviews by women)
Frequency: 3x per yr; Circulation: 10,000

Bereavement
Andrea Gambill, Editor
Bereavement Publishing
8133 Telegraph Dr
Colorado Springs CO 80920-7169
719-282-1948; Fax: 719-282-1850
Focus: 35-39-65
Frequency: 6x per yr; Circulation: N/A

Best Recipes
Donna Driscoll, Book Review Editor
Morris Communications
1503 SW 42nd St
Topeka KS 66609-1265
800-678-5779; Fax: 913-274-4305
Focus: 27
Frequency: 6x per yr; Circulation: 227,000

Better Homes & Gardens
Lamont Olson, Managing Editor
1716 Locust St
Des Moines IA 50309-3038
515-284-3000; Fax: 515-284-3684
Focus: 43-99
Frequency: Monthly;
 Circulation: 7,400,000

Better Investing
D E Danko, Editor
711 W 13 Mile Rd
Madison Heights MI 48071-1806
810-583-6242; Fax: 810-583-4880
Focus: 19I
Frequency: Monthly; Circulation: 200,000

Better Nutrition for Today's Living
Frank Murray, Editor
Argus Business
6151 Powers Ferry Rd NW
Atlanta GA 30339-2959
770-955-2500; Fax: 770-618-0349
Focus: 19R-27-39H
Frequency: Monthly; Circulation: 500,000

A Better Tomorrow
Mary Hopkins, Editor
Thomas Nelson Publishers
404 BNA Dr #508 Bldg 200
Nashville TN 37217-2514
615-872-8080; 800-348-5080;
 Fax: 615-889-0437
Focus: 35A-63C-99(Christian lifestyles for people over age fifty)
Frequency: Monthly; Circulation: 80,000

Beverly Hills 213 Magazine
Brian Boye, Editor
9465 Wilshire Blvd #307
Beverly Hills CA 90212-2602
310-275-8850
Focus: 61(Beverly Hills CA)-99
Frequency: Weekly; Circulation: 50,000

Bicycling
Kathy Foster, Editor
Rodale Press
33 E Minor St
Emmaus PA 18098
215-967-5171; Fax: 215-967-8963
Focus: 39-69(bicycling)-71
Frequency: 10x per yr;
 Circulation: 394,000

Bikini
David Turin, Exec Editor
2110 Main St #100
Los Angeles CA 90405-2276
310-452-6222; Fax: 310-452-8076
Focus: 33-35-36-69-97-99
Frequency: 6x per yr; Circulation: 120,000

BioCycle
Jerome Goldstein, Editor/Publisher
JG Press
419 State Ave
Emmaus PA 18049-3025
610-967-4135
Focus: 51E-67 (recycling)
Frequency: Monthly; Circulation: 11,000

Bird Talk
Julie Ann Rach, Editor
Fancy Publications
3 Burroughs
Irvine CA 92718
714-855-8822; Fax: 714-855-0654
Focus: 15(birds)
Frequency: Monthly; Circulation: 150,000

Bird Watchers Digest
William Thompson III, Editor
149 Acme St
Marietta OH 45750-3402
614-373-5285; 800-879-2473;
 Fax: 614-373-8443
Focus: 15(birds)-69(bird watching)
Frequency: 6x per yr; Circulation: 95,000

Bird's-Eye reView
Sue Wells, Exec Dir
Natl Bird Feeding Society
2218 Crabtree Ln PO Box 23
Northbrook IL 60065-0023
708-272-0135
Focus: 15(birds)
Frequency: 6x per yr; Circulation: 15,000

Birds & Blooms
Tom Curl, Managing Editor
Reiman Publications
5400 S 60th St
Greendale WI 53129
414-423-0100; Fax: 414-423-3840
Focus: 43-51
Frequency: 6x per yr; Circulation: N/A

Biz Magazine
Mark Pawlosky, Editor-in-Chief
American City Business Journals
128 S Tryon St #2350
Charlotte NC 28202-5001
704-371-3254; 800-704-7440;
    Fax: 704-371-3253
Focus: 19
Frequency: Monthly; Circulation: 500,000

Black Beat
Rudy Meyer, Editor
Sterling-McFadden Partnership
233 Park Ave S 5th Fl
New York NY 10003-1606
212-780-3500; Fax: 212-780-3555
Focus: 14-17-21T-33-40-49B
Frequency: Monthly; Circulation: 175,000

Black Books Bulletin
Institute of Positive Education
7822 S Dobson Ave
Chicago IL 60619-3213
312-651-0700
Focus: 47-49B-99
Frequency: 6x per yr; Circulation: 5,000

The Black Collegian
Ruumba Kazi, Editor
1240 S Broad St
New Orleans LA 70125-2015
504-821-5694; Fax: 504-821-5713
Focus: 19C-31-49B-78 (minorities)
Frequency: Quarterly; Circulation: 107,000

Black Elegance
Sonia Alleyne, Editor
Starlog Communications Inc
475 Park Ave S
New York NY 10016-6901
212-689-2830; Fax: 212-889-7933
Focus: 49B-99
Frequency: 9x per yr; Circulation: 350,000

Black Enterprise Magazine
Mark Lowery, News Editor
130 Fifth Ave
New York NY 10011-4306
212-242-8000; Fax: 212-886-9610
Focus: 19I-23-25-49B
Frequency: Monthly; Circulation: 273,000

Black Health
Bonnie Maynard, Editor
59 Oakwood Dr
Madison CT 06443-1823
203-431-3454
Focus: 27-39-40-49B-57
Frequency: Quarterly; Circulation: 50,000

Black Moon Magazine
Armand Rosamilia
1385 Rt 35 #169
Middletown NJ 07748
908-787-2445
Focus: 79-82-84-87-95 (interviews/reviews)
Frequency: 9x per yr; Circulation: N/A

Blade Magazine
Steve Shackleford, Editor
700 E State St
Iola WI 54990-0001
715-445-2214; Fax: 715-445-4811
Focus: 28-69(knives)
Frequency: Monthly; Circulation: 150,000

The Bloomsbury Review
Katy Arndt, Childrens Book Editor
Tom Auer, Editor-in-Chief/Publ
Ray Gonzales, Poetry Editor
1762 Emerson St
Denver CO 80218
303-863-0406; Fax: 303-863-0408
Focus: 21-31-76-79
Frequency: 6x per yr; Circulation: N/A

Blue Ridge Country
Kurt Rheinheimer, Editor
3424 Brambleton Ave S
Roanoke VA 24018-6520
540-989-6138; 800-548-1672;
    Fax: 540-989-7603
Focus: 61(SE US)-71
Frequency: 6x per yr; Circulation: 75,000

Boating
John Owens, Editor-in-Chief
Hachette Filipacchi Magazines
1633 Broadway
New York NY 10019-6708
212-767-5585; Fax: 212-767-5618
Focus: 70N
Frequency: Monthly; Circulation: 208,000

Body Mind & Spirit Magazine
Nancy Burke, Editor
PO Box 701
Providence RI 02901
401-351-4320; Fax: 401-272-5767
Focus: 35-39-51-53-54-57
Frequency: 6x per yr; Circulation: 164,000

Boing-Boing
Carla Sinclair, Editor-in-Chief
11288 Ventura Blvd #818
Studio City CA 91604
310-854-5747; Fax: 310-289-4922
Focus: 33-75-86
Frequency: Quarterly; Circulation: 17,000

Bomb Magazine
Betsy Sussler, Editor-in-Chief
594 Broadway #1002-A
New York NY 10012-3289
212-431-3943; Fax: 212-431-5880
Focus: 11-12-14M-14T-33M-75-83-95
Frequency: 3x per yr; Circulation: 60,000

Bon Appetit
Catherine Gottlieb, Book Editor
6300 Wilshire Blvd 10th Fl
Los Angeles CA 90048
213-965-3600; Fax: 213-937-1206
Focus: 27
Frequency: Monthly; Circulation: 1,309,000

Book/Mark
Mindy Kronenberg, Editor
9 Garden Ave
Miller Place NY 11764
516-331-4118
Focus: 99(small press books)
Frequency: Quarterly; Circulation: 1,000

Books in Canada
130 Spadina Ave #603
Toronto ON Canada M5V 2L4
416-601-9880
Focus: 61(Canada)-99
Frequency: 9x per year; Circulation: 8,000

Bop Magazine
Rick Rodgers, Editor
Laufer Publishing
3500 W Olive Ave #850
Burbank CA 91505-4628
818-953-7999; Fax: 818-953-4107
Focus: 14-33-89 (teenage entertainment)
Frequency: Monthly; Circulation: 150,000

The Boston Book Review
Lucinda Jewell, Editor-in-Chief
30 Brattle St 4th Fl
Cambridge MA 02138-3727
617-497-0344; Fax: 617-497-0394;
    E-Mail: bbreview@shore.net
Focus: 99
Frequency: 10x per yr; Circulation: N/A

Boston Business Journal
Chuck Heschmeyer, Editor
MCP Inc
200 High St
Boston MA 02210-3036
617-330-1000; Fax: 617-330-1016
Focus: 19-61(MA)
Frequency: Weekly; Circulation: 15,000

Boston Magazine
Sarah Wright, Book Review Editor
300 Massachusetts Ave
Boston MA 02115-4544
617-262-9700; Fax: 617-262-4925
Focus: 19-61(Boston MA)
Frequency: Monthly; Circulation: 124,000

The Boston Parents' Paper
Bill Lindsay, Managing Editor
670 Centre St
Jamaica Plain MA 02130-2511
617-522-1515; Fax: 617-522-1694
Focus: 21-31-35-76
Frequency: Monthly; Circulation: 77,000

Boston Review
Kim Cooper, Managing Editor
33 Harrison Ave
Boston MA 02111-2008
617-350-5353
Focus: 11-14-33-47-75-95
Frequency: 6x per yr; Circulation: 20,000

Bostonia
Michael Shavelson, Managing Editor
10 Lenox St
Brookline MA 02146-4042
617-353-3081; Fax: 617-353-6488
Focus: 11-14-33-61(MA)-71-99
Frequency: Quarterly; Circulation: 189,000

Boulder County Business Report
Jerry W Lewis, Editor-in-Chief
4885 Riverbend Rd #D
Boulder CO 80301-2617
303-440-4950; Fax: 303-440-8954
Focus: 19
Frequency: Monthly; Circulation: 18,000

Boundary 2
Paul Bove, Editor
Duke Univ Press
PO Box 90660
Durham NC 27708-0660
919-687-3636; Fax: 919-688-4574
Focus: 47-75-83-95-99
Frequency: 3x per yr; Circulation: 875,000

Bow & Arrow Hunting
Roger Combs, Managing Editor
34249 Camino Capistrano
Capistrano Beach CA 92624-1156
714-493-2101; Fax: 714-240-8680
Focus: 69H(hunting)
Frequency: 6x per yr; Circulation: 98,000

Bowhunter
Richard Cochran, Managing Editor
Cowles Magazine Inc
6405 Flank Dr
Harrisburg PA 17112-2750
717-657-9555; Fax: 717-657-9552
Focus: 69H
Frequency: 6x per yr; Circulation: 200,000

Bowling Digest
Ken Leiker, Sr Editor
Century Publishing Co
990 Grove St
Evanston IL 60201-4370
708-491-6440
Focus: 69(bowling)
Frequency: 6x per yr; Circulation: 90,000

Boy's Life
Scott Stuckey, Editor
Boy Scouts of America
1325 Walnut Hill Ln
Irving TX 75038-3008
214-580-2000; Fax: 214-580-2079
Focus: 15-23-29-35-43-51-67-69
Frequency: Monthly;
    Circulation: 1,300,000

Bracket Racing U.S.A.
Dale Wilson, Editor
CSK Publishing Co Inc
299 Market St
Saddle Brook NJ 07663-5312
201-712-9300; Fax: 201-712-0990
Focus: 16A
Frequency: 8x per yr; Circulation: 37,000

Breakaway
Michael Ross, Editor
Focus on the Family
Colorado Springs CO 80995
719-531-5181
Focus: 33H-17C(profiles)-69-40F (for guys — teens 12 and up)
Frequency: Monthly; Circulation: 99,000

Bridal Guide
Stephanie Wood, Editor-in-Chief
Globe Communications Corp
441 Lexington Ave
New York NY 10017-3910
212-949-4040; 800-472-7744;
    Fax: 212-286-0072
Focus: 35-40-57
Frequency: 6x per yr; Circulation: 225,000

Bride's & Your New Home
Sally Kilbridge, Managing Editor
Conde Nast Corp
140 E 45th St 39th Fl
New York NY 10017-3144
212-880-8800; Fax: 212-880-8331
Focus: 43D-43H
Frequency: 6x per yr; Circulation: 400,000

Bride's Magazine
Sally Kelbridge, Managing Editor
Conde Nast Publications
140 E 45th St 39th Fl
New York NY 10017
212-880-8294; Fax: 212-880-8331
Focus: 35-40-43H-71
Frequency: 6x per yr; Circulation: N/A

Brio
Susie Shellenberger, Editor
Focus on the Family
Colorado Springs CO 80995
719-531-5181; Fax:
Focus: 33H-17C(profiles)-69-40F (for girls; teens 12 and up)
Frequency: Monthly; Circulation: 159,000

British Heritage
Gail Huganir, Editor
Cowles Media Co
6405 Flank Dr PO Box 8200
Harrisburg PA 17105-8200
717-657-9555; Fax: 717-657-9526
Focus: 41W-44E(Great Britain)
Frequency: 6x per yr; Circulation: 100,000

Brooklyn Bridge
Alison Tocci, Publisher
388 Atlantic Ave
Brooklyn NY 11217
718-596-7400; Fax: 718-852-1291
Focus: 61-99
Frequency: Monthly; Circulation: 80,000

Buffalo Spree
Ted Knight, Book Review Editor
4511 Harlem Rd
Buffalo NY 14226-3803
716-839-3405; Fax: 716-839-4384
Focus: 99
Frequency: Quarterly; Circulation: 21,000

Business Documents
John S Rosenberg, Editor (215-238-5478)
North American Publishing
401 N Broad St
Philadelphia PA 19108
215-238-5300; Fax: 215-238-5457
Focus: 19P-56X
Frequency: 10x per yr; Circulation: 7,000

Business News
Bob Howard, Managing Editor
2200 Old Germantown Rd
Del Ray Beach FL 33445-8223
407-265-4399; Fax: 407-279-3239
Focus: 19-19S
Frequency: Quarterly;
    Circulation: 1,500,000

The Business Owner
Tom Martin, Editor
383 S Broadway
Hicksville NY 11801-5000
516-681-2111
Focus: 19
Frequency: 6x per yr; Circulation: N/A

Business Start-Ups
Donna Clapp, Editor
Entrepreneur Media Inc
2392 Morse Ave
Irvine CA 92714
714-261-2083; Fax: 714-755-4211
Focus: 19
Frequency: Monthly; Circulation: 210,000

Business Today
Meridan Publishing Inc
1720 Washington Blvd
Ogden UT 84404-5753
801-394-9446
Focus: 19
Frequency: Monthly; Circulation: 40,000

Business Venture Magazine
Charles McDaniel, President
Miller Information Projects Co
7100 Spring Meadows West Dr #C
Holland OH 43528
419-868-7938; Fax: 419-868-7940
Focus: 19
Frequency: N/A; Circulation: N/A

Business Week
Hardy Green, Book Editor
McGraw-Hill Co Bldg
1221 Ave of the Americas
New York NY 10020
212-512-2000
Focus: 19-99
Frequency: Weekly; Circulation: 1,000,000

Buzz Magazine
Allan Mayer, Editor-in-Chief
11835 W Olympic Blvd #450
Los Angeles CA 90064-5005
310-473-2721; Fax: 310-473-2876;
    E-mail: buzzmag@aol.com
Focus: 11-14-17-33-40-43-61-99
Frequency: Monthly; Circulation: 70,000

BYTE
Rich Friedman, Book Reviewer
One Phoenix Mill Ln
Peterborough NH 03458
603-924-9281; Fax: 603-924-2550
Focus: 23 (news releases only)
Frequency: Monthly; Circulation: 512,000

C

CA Magazine
Nelson Luscombe, Editor-in-Chief
277 Wellington St W
Toronto ON Canada M5V 3H2
416-977-3222; Fax: 416-204-3409
Focus: 19-61(Canada)
Frequency: 10x per yr; Circulation: 67,000

California Game & Fish
Burt Carey, Editor
Game & Fish Publications Inc
2250 Newmarket Pky #110
Marietta GA 30067-8749
770-953-9222; Fax: 770-933-9510
Focus: 15-51-61(CA)-69
Frequency: Monthly; Circulation: N/A

California Senior Citizen
Carol Osmon, Editor
4805 Alta Canyada Rd
La Canada CA 91011-1732
818-790-0651
Focus: 35A-61-71
Frequency: Monthly; Circulation: 72,000

California Strategies
Bill King, Managing Editor
122 Tivoli Way
Sacramento CA 95819
800-326-2606; Fax: 916-322-3524
Focus: 19-19G-23-25-61
Frequency: Quarterly; Circulation: 30,000

Callaloo
Charles Rowell, Editor
Johns Hopkins Univ Press
2715 N Charles St
Baltimore MD 21218-4319
410-516-6982; Fax: 410-516-6968; E-mail: jlorder@jhunix.hcf.jhu.edu
Focus: 47-49B-75-78-90-95
Primarily black authors
Frequency: Quarterly;
    Circulation: 1,450,000

Callboard
Belinda Taylor, Editor
657 Mission #402
San Francisco CA 94105
415-957-1557; Fax: 415-957-1556
Focus: 14T (West Coast theater, jobs, shows)
Frequency: Monthly; Circulation: 5,000

Calliope: World History for Young People
Rosalie Baker, Editor
Cobblestone Publishing Inc
7 School St
Peterborough NH 03458-1441
603-924-7209; Fax: 603-924-7380
Focus: 41W-44(world history for young people ages 10-15)
Frequency: 5x per yr; Circulation: 9,000

Camping & RV Magazine
Debora Radtke, Editor
PO Box 337
Iola WI 54945-0337
715-373-5556; Fax: 715-373-5003
Focus: 51-69-70-71
Frequency: Monthly; Circulation: 7,000

Campus Life
Jim Long, Editor
465 Gundersen Dr
Carol Stream IL 60188-2415
708-260-6200; Fax: 708-260-0114
Focus: 31-63-89
Frequency: 10x per yr;
    Circulation: 120,000

Canadian Dimension
Michelle Torres, Operations Mgr
Dimension Publications Inc
228 Notre Dame Ave
Winnepeg MB Canada R3B 1N7
204-957-1519; Fax: 204-943-4617
Focus: 55-99
Frequency: 6x per yr; Circulation: 3,000

Canadian Living
Bonnie Baker Cowan, Editor-in-Chief
25 Sheppard Ave W #100
New York ON Canada M2N 6S7
416-733-7600; Fax: 416-733-3398
Focus: 61(CN)-99
Frequency: 13x per yr;
    Circulation: 2,400,000

Canadian Select Homes & Food
Barbara Dixon, Editor
25 Sheppard Ave W #100
North York ON Canada M2N 6S7
416-733-7600; Fax: 416-218-3632
Focus: 12B-43D-27
Frequency: 8x per yr; Circulation: 170,000

Canoe & Kayak Magazine
Dave Harrison, Editor-In-Chief
PO Box 3146
Kirkland WA 98083-3146
206-827-6363; Fax: 206-827-1893
Focus: 51-69-70(canoeing)-71
800-692-2663
Frequency: 6x per yr; Circulation: 72,000

Capper's
Nancy Peavler, Editor
Morris Communications Inc
1503 SW 42nd St
Topeka KS 66609-1214
913-274-4300; 800-678-5119; Fax: 913-274-4305
Focus: 25-35-39-67-71-99(focusing on central US)
Frequency: Biweekly; Circulation: 393

Car & Driver
Steve Spence, Managing Editor
Hachette Filipacchi Magazines
2002 Hogback Rd
Ann Arbor MI 48105-9736
313-971-3600; Fax: 313-971-9188
Focus: 16A
Frequency: Monthly;
    Circulation: 1,000,000

Car Craft
Chuck Schifsky, Editor
Petersen Publishing Co
6420 Wilshire Blvd
Los Angeles CA 90048-5502
213-782-2000; Fax: 213-782-2263
Focus: 16A
Frequency: Monthly; Circulation: 450,000

Car Stereo Review
William Wolfe, Editor-in-Chief
1633 Broadway 45th Fl
New York NY 10019-6708
212-767-6020; Fax: 212-767-5615
Focus: 16A-23-24(car stereos)
Frequency: 6x per yr;
    Circulation: 110,000

Careers & Colleges
Donald Rauf, Sr Editor
E M Guild Inc
989 Ave of the Americas
New York NY 10018-5410
212-563-4688; Fax: 212-967-2531
Focus: 19C-31E(financial aid, choosing colleges, job-hunting, etc)
Frequency: 2x per yr; Circulation: 500,000

Careers & the Disabled
James Schneider, Editor-in-Chief
Equal Opportunity Publications
150 Motor Pky #420
Hauppauge NY 11788-5108
516-273-0066; Fax: 516-273-8936
Focus: 39D
Frequency: Quarterly; Circulation: 10,000

Caribbean Travel & Life
Veronica Gould Stoddart, Editor-in-Chief
8403 Colesville Rd #830
Silver Spring MD 20910
301-588-2300
Focus: 61(Caribbean)-71
Frequency: 6x per yr; Circulation: 140,000

Carolina Parent
Gita Schonfeld, Editor
103 W Main St #210
Durham NC 27701-3638
919-956-2430; Fax: 919-956-2427
Focus: 21-31-35-76
Frequency: Monthly; Circulation: 40,000

Carolina Style
Anthony Policastro, Editor
3975-B Market St
Wilmington NC 28403-1403
910-341-3033; 800-500-9229;
    Fax: 910-341-3011
Focus: 61(NC/SC)-99(lifestyles)
Frequency: 6x per yr; Circulation: 100,000

Cars & Parts
Robert Stevens, Editor
Amos Press Inc
911 Vandemark Rd
Sidney OH 45367-0001
513-498-0803; 800-448-3611;
    Fax: 513-498-0808
Focus: 16A-28-29
Frequency: Monthly; Circulation: 110,000

Cat Fancy
Debbie Phillips-Donaldson, Editor
Fancy Publications
3 Burroughs
Irvine CA 92718-2804
714-855-8822; Fax: 714-855-3045
Focus: 15
Frequency: Monthly; Circulation: 300,000

Catalist
Cathy Richards, Editor-in-Chief
Red Rose Collection
42 Adrian Ct
Burlingame CA 94010
415-692-4500; Fax: 415-692-2394
Focus: 27-39H-51E-53-54
Frequency: 6x per yr; Circulation: 40,000

Catechist
Patricia Fischer, Editor
Peter Li Inc
330 Progress Rd
Dayton OH 45449-2322
513-847-5900; 800-543-4383;
    Fax: 513-847-5910
Focus: 63C
Frequency: 7x per yr; Circulation: 43,000

Catholic Parent
Greg Erlandson, Editor-in-Chief
200 Noll Plz
Huntington IN 46750
219-356-8400; 800-348-2440;
    Fax: 219-356-8472
Focus: 31P-35F-35M-63C
Frequency: 6x per yr; Circulation: 31,000

Cats Magazine
Tracey Copeland, Editor
2750A S Ridgewood Ave
Daytona Beach FL 32119-3540
904-788-2770; Fax: 904-788-2710
Focus: 15(cats)
Frequency: Monthly; Circulation: 148,000

CCD Astronomy
Tim Lyster, Managing Editor
Sky Publishing
49 Bay State Rd
Cambridge MA 02138
617-864-7360; Fax: 617-864-6117
Focus: 67A
Frequency: Quarterly; Circulation: 7,000

CD-ROM Today
Michael Brown, Reviews Editor
150 N Hill Dr
Brisbane CA 94005
415-468-4684; Fax: 415-468-4686
Focus: 23
Frequency: Monthly; Circulation: 114,544

Ceramic Arts & Crafts
Bill Thompson, Editor
30595 8 Mile Rd
Livonia MI 48152-1761
810-477-6650; 800-458-8237;
    Fax: 810-477-6795
Focus: 29(ceramics)
Frequency: Monthly; Circulation: 52,000

Ceramics Monthly
William C Hunt, Editor
1609 Northwest Blvd
Columbus OH 43212-2544
614-488-8236; Fax: 614-488-4561
Focus: 29(ceramics)
Frequency: Monthly; Circulation: 36,000

Cessna Owner Magazine
Frank Hamilton, Editor
Jones Publishing Inc
PO Box 337
Iola WI 54945-0337
715-445-5000; Fax: 715-445-4053
Focus: 70A
Frequency: Monthly; Circulation: 6,000

CFW: Competitor for Women
Camille Duvall, Editor
214 S Cedros Ave
Solana Beach CA 92075-1915
619-793-2711; Fax: 619-793-2710
Focus: 69(competitive sports)
Frequency: Quarterly; Circulation: 50,000

Challenge Magazine
Donna Borst, Editor
8 Melody Ter
Ft Madison IA 52627
319-372-2008; Fax: 319-372-2008
Focus: 21-31-76(activities that teachers
    can use for gifted students)
Frequency: 5x per yr; Circulation: 14,000

Changes Magazine
Jeffrey Laign, Managing Editor
Health Communications
3201 SW 15th St
Deerfield Beach FL 33442
305-360-0909; 800-851-9100;
    Fax: 305-360-0034
Focus: 35F-35R-39-57
Frequency: 6x per yr; Circulation: N/A

Changing Men
Michael Kimmel, Book Review Editor
Feminist Mens Publishing
PO Box 3121
Kansas City KS 53715-1002
816-374-5969
Focus: 12B-16A-19C-35-39-55-56-57-69-70-
    71 Mens issues
Frequency: 2x per yr; Circulation: 8,000

Charisma
Tessie Guell, Book Review Editor
Stang Communications Co
600 Rinehart Rd
Lake Mary FL 32746-4872
407-333-0600; Fax: 407-333-9753
Focus: 27-29-33-35-39-43-63-99
A Christian lifestyle magazine
Frequency: Monthly; Circulation: 220,000

Chatelaine
Diane Merlevede, Managing Editor
777 Bay St
Toronto ON Canada M5W 1A7
416-596-5425; 800-268-6811;
    Fax: 416-593-3197
Focus: 36-73-99
Frequency: Monthly; Circulation: 930,000

Chelsea
Richard Foerster, Editor
PO Box 773
Cooper Sta
New York NY 10276-0773
212-989-3083; Fax: 212-989-3083
Focus: 75-95
Frequency: 2x per yr; Circulation: 1,000

Chesapeake Bay Magazine
Jean Waller, Editor
1819 Bay Ridge Ave #158
Annapolis MD 21403-2835
410-263-2662; Fax: 410-267-6924
Focus: 61(mid-Atlantic)
Frequency: Monthly; Circulation: 33,000

Chess Life
Glenn Peterson, Editor
US Chess Federation
186 Route 9W
New Windsor NY 12553-7624
914-562-8350; 800-388-5444;
    Fax: 914-561-2437
Focus: 69G
Frequency: Monthly; Circulation: 68,000

Chicago Magazine
Richard Babcock, Editor
414 N Orleans #800
Chicago IL 60610-4418
312-222-8999; Fax: 312-222-0699
Focus: 11-12-19-55-61(IL)
Frequency: Monthly; Circulation: 165,000

Chicago Parent Newsmagazine
Mary Haley, Editor
141 S Oak Park Ave
Oak Park IL 60302-2972
708-386-5555; Fax: 708-524-0447
Focus: 21-31-35-76
Frequency: Monthly; Circulation: 82,000

Child & Youth Services
Jerome Beker, Editor
The Haworth Press Inc
10 Alice St
Binghamton NY 13904-1503
607-722-5857; 800-342-9678;
    Fax: 607-722-1424
Focus: 31-35-57-65
Frequency: 2x per yr; Circulation: N/A

Child Life
Stan Zukowski, Editor
1100 Waterway Blvd
Indianapolis IN 46202-2156
317-636-8881; Fax: 317-684-8094
Focus: 15-17-21-27-29-33-39-69-71-76-81-
    84-86
Children ages 9-11
Frequency: 8x per yr; Circulation: 80,000

Child
Jonathan Small, Book Review Editor
110 Fifth Ave
New York NY 10011-5601
212-463-1000; Fax: 212-463-1383
Focus: 21-35-39-76
Accepts kids books for review
Frequency: 10x per yr;
    Circulation: 700,000

Childbirth
Judy Nolte, Editor
Cahners Publishing
249 W 17th St
New York Ny 10011
212-645-0067; Fax: 212-463-6620
Focus: 35-39
Frequency: 1x per yr;
    Circulation: 2,000,000

Childbirth Instructor
Margaret Inman, Editor
Cradle Publishing Inc
52 Vanderbilt Ave #501
New York NY 10017-3808
212-986-1422; Fax: 212-986-0816
Focus: 31P (prenatal/childbirth education)
Frequency: Quarterly; Circulation: 15,000

Children's Book Insider
Laura Backes, Editor
The Backes Agency
PO Box 1030
Fairplay CO 80440-1030
719-836-0394
Focus: 21-56W-76-31(tips for children's
    book and magazine writers)
Frequency: Monthly; Circulation: N/A

Children's Book Review
Anita Sorenson, Exec Editor
Grove Communications
1204 New York Dr
Altadena CA 91001-3146
818-791-5595; Fax: 818-791-2905
Focus: 21-31P-76-79
Frequency: Quarterly; Circulation: N/A

Children's Digest
Elizabeth Rinck, Exec Editor
PO Box 567
Indianapolis IN 46206-0567
317-636-8881; Fax: 317-684-8094
Focus: 21(preteens)-27-29-33-39-76-79-81-84-86-89-95
Frequency: 8x per yr; Circulation: 100,000

Children's Ministry
Christine Yount, Editor-in-Chief
2890 N Monroe Ave
Loveland CO 80538-3274
970-669-3836; Fax: 970-669-1994
Focus: 21-31-63(Christian youth ministers)
Frequency: 6x per yr; Circulation: 50,000

Children's Playmate
Terry Harshman, Editor
1100 Waterway Blvd
Indianapolis IN 46202-2156
317-636-8881; Fax: 317-684-8094
Focus: 21(6-8yrs)-27-29-33-39
Frequency: 8x per yr; Circulation: 125,000

Childsplay
Barbara Cohen, Editor/Publisher
663 Dickinson St
Springfield MA 01108-3103
413-733-8055; Fax: 413-567-2492
Focus: 21-31-35-76
Frequency: 6x per yr; Circulation: 5,000

Chile Pepper Magazine
Dave DeWitt, Editor
PO Box 4278
Albuquerque NM 87196-4278
505-266-8322; Fax: 505-266-2127
Focus: 27(hot and spicy foods)
Frequency: 6x per yr; Circulation: 80,000

Chocolatier
Michael Schneider, Editor
Haymarket Group Ltd
45 West 34th St #600
New York NY 10001-3008
212-239-0855; Fax: 212-967-4184
Focus: 27(desserts)-28-29-43-71
Frequency: 6x per yr; Circulation: 150,000

The Christian Century
James M Wall, Editor
Christian Century Foundation
407 S Dearborn St
Chicago IL 60605-1111
312-427-5380; Fax: 312-427-1302
Focus: 63 (Ecumenical)
Frequency: 37x per year;
  Circulation: 35,000

Christian Parenting Today
Brad Lewis, Editor
7125 Disc Dr
Colorado Springs CO 80918-7101
719-531-7776; Fax: 719-535-0172
Focus: 31-35-63(Christian)
Frequency: 6x per yr;
  Circulation: 215,000

Christianity Today
John Wilson, Book Review Editor
465 Gundersen Dr
Carol Stream IL 60188-2415
708-260-6200; Fax: 708-260-0114
Focus: 63
Frequency: 14xper yr; Circulation: 193,000

The Chronicle of the Horse
John Strassburger, Editor
PO Box 46
Middleburg VA 22117-0046
540-687-6341; Fax: 540-687-3937
Focus: 69(horses)
Frequency: Weekly; Circulation: 23,000

Chronicles
Thomas Fleming, Editor
Rockford Institute
934 N Main St
Rockford IL 61103-7061
815-964-5054; Fax: 815-964-9403
Focus: 31E-44-55-63-65-75-90-95
Frequency: Monthly; Circulation: 15,000

Cineaste
Gary Crowdus, Editor-in-Chief
Cineaste Publishers Inc
200 Park Ave S
New York NY 10003-1503
212-982-1241
Focus: 33-86
Frequency: Quarterly; Circulation: 9,000

Cinefantastique
Frederick Clark, Publisher
PO Box 270
Oak Park IL 60303-0270
708-366-5566
Focus: 33-82-86
Frequency: 5x per yr; Circulation: 50,000

Cinescape
Doug Perry, Editor
Sendai Publishing Inc
1920 Highland Ave #222
Lombard IL 60148-6116
708-916-7222; Fax: 708-916-7227
Focus: 33-86-99
Frequency: Monthly; Circulation: N/A

Circle Track & Racing Technology
Glen Grissom, Editor
Peterson Publishing
8490 Sunset Blvd
Los Angeles CA 90069
310-854-2222
Focus: 16A
Frequency: Monthly; Circulation: 137,000

Circus Magazine
Gerald Rothberg, Editor/Publisher
6 W 18th St
New York NY 10011-4608
212-242-4902; Fax: 212-141-5734
Focus: 14M(rock music)
Frequency: Monthly; Circulation: 307,000

Citizen
Tom Hess, Editor
Focus on the Family
Colorado Springs CO 80995
719-531-5181
Focus: 55-31E-31P-35F-99
Frequency: Monthly; Circulation: 130,000

City Family
Ellen Finkel, Editor
PO Box 748 Ansonia Sta
New York NY 10023-0748
212-362-3052; Fax: 212-580-4833
Focus: 25-27-31P-35F-39-40F-43G-45S
  (lower income and immigrant families)
Frequency: Quarterly; Circulation: 200,000

City Parent
Barbara Greenwood, Book Review Editor
467 Speers Rd
Oakville ON Canada L6K 3S4
905-815-0017; 800-387-7682
Focus: 21-31-35-76
Frequency: Monthly; Circulation: N/A

Civil War Times Illustrated
James Kushlan, Editor-in-Chief
6405 Flank Dr
PO Box 8200
Harrisburg PA 17105-8200
717-657-9555; Fax: 717-657-9526
Focus: 41A-48
Frequency: 6x per yr; Circulation: 164,000

Class
Maier Deshell, Editor
American Jewish Congress
15 E 84th St
New York NY 10028-0458
212-360-1500
Focus: 49O(Jewish)
Frequency: Monthly; Circulation: 250,000

Classic Auto Restorer
Ted Kade, Managing Editor
Fancy Publications Inc
PO Box 57900
Los Angeles CA 90057-0900
714-855-8822; Fax: 714-855-3045
Focus: 16
Frequency: Monthly; Circulation: 70,000

Classic Toy Trains
Roger Carp, Editor
Kalmbach Publications Co
21027 Crossroads Cir
Waukesha WI 53186-4055
414-796-8776; 800-558-1544;
  Fax: 414-796-1383
Focus: 16R-29(models)
Frequency: 8x per yr; Circulation: 70,000

Cleveland Magazine
Liz Ludlow, Managing Editor
1422 Euclid Ave #730
Cleveland OH 44115-2001
216-771-2833; Fax: 216-781-6318
Focus: 61(Cleveland OH)-99
Frequency: Monthly; Circulation: 45,000

Climbing
Michael Kennedy, Editor
1101 Village Rd #11-L-B
Carbondale CO 81623-1571
970-963-9449; Fax: 970-963-9442
Focus: 69(almost any type of mountain climbing)
Frequency: 8x per yr; Circulation: 41,000

Clout
Tracy Baim, Mg Editor/Publisher
Lambda Publications
3059 N Southport
Chicago IL 60657
312-871-7610
Focus: 19(gay & lesbian business owners/professionals)
Frequency: N/A; Circulation: N/A

Clubhouse
Marianne Hering, Editor
Focus on the Family
Colorado Springs CO 80995
719-531-5181
Focus: 21-69G (children ages 8-12)
Frequency: Monthly; Circulation: 119,000

Clubhouse Jr
Lisa Brock, Editor
Focus on the Family
Colorado Springs CO 80995
719-531-5181
Focus: 29C-69G-21-79 (ages 4-8)
Frequency: Monthly; Circulation: 91,000

CM Magazine
Karlene Lukovitz, Editor
611 Broadway #510
New York NY 10012-2608
212-979-0730; Fax: 212-979-0961;
    E-Mail: cmedit@aol.com
Focus: 19G-19M-56
Frequency: Monthly; Circulation: N/A

Coast to Coast
Valerie Rogers, Managing Editor
Affinity Group
3601 Calle Tecate
Camarillo CA 93012
805-389-0300; Fax: 805-389-0484
Focus: 69R-71
Frequency: 8x per yr; Circulation: 300,000

Cobblestone
Meg Chorlian, Editor
Cobblestone Publishing Inc
7 School St
Peterborough NH 03458-1441
603-924-7209; Fax: 603-924-7380
Focus: 41A (history for young people 9-13)
Frequency: 10x per yr; Circulation: 38,000

Cobras
Jeff Holifield, Editor
McMullen & Yee Publishing Inc
774 South Placentia
Placentia CA 92670-6832
714-572-2255; Fax: 714-572-1864
Focus: 16-24
Frequency: Quarterly; Circulation: N/A

Coin
Alan Herbert, Editor
Krause Publications
700 E State St
Iola WI 54990-0001
715-445-2214; Fax: 715-445-4087
Focus: 28(coins)
Frequency: Monthly; Circulation: 15,000

Collecting Toys
Tom Hammel, Editor
Kalmbach Publishing Co
21027 Crossroads Cir
Waukesha WI 53186-4055
414-796-8776; 800-533-6644
Fax: 414-796-1383
Focus: 28-76(toys)
Frequency: 6x per yr; Circulation: 35,000

Collector Editions
Joan Muyskens Pursley, Editor
Collector Communications Corp
170 5th Ave 12th Fl
New York NY 10010-5911
212-989-8700; Fax: 212-645-8976
Focus: 28(plates, prints, figurines, steins, dolls, cottages)
Frequency: 7x per yr; Circulation: 93,000

Collector's SportsLook
Tucker Freeman Smith, Editor-in-Chief
Wizard Press
151 Wells Ave
Congers NY 10920-2036
914-268-2000; Fax: 914-268-0877
Focus: 28C-29H-69(sport cards/collectibles)
Frequency: Monthly; Circulation: 105,000

Collectors News
Linda Kruger, Editor
506 2nd St
Grundy Center IA 50638-1914
319-824-6981; 800-352-8039;
    Fax: 319-824-3414
Focus: 28
Frequency: Monthly; Circulation: 12,000

College Outlook
H Guyon Townsend III, Editor
7007 NE Parvin Rd
Kansas City MO 64117-1532
816-361-0616; 800-274-8867;
    Fax: 816-361-6164
Focus: 19C-31
Frequency: 2x per yr;
    Circulation: 1,340,000

College Teaching
Cherie Bottum, Editor
Heldref Publications
1319 18th St NW
Washington DC 20036-1802
202-296-6267; 800-365-9753;
    Fax: 202-296-5149
Focus: 31E-67
Frequency: Quarterly; Circulation: 2,000

Colonial Homes
Debra Muller, Managing Editor
Hearst Corp
1790 Broadway
New York NY 10019-1412
212-830-2900; Fax: 212-586-3455
Focus: 43
Frequency: 6x per yr; Circulation: 575,000

Color Publishing
Frank Romano, Editor
10 Tara Blvd 5th Fl
Nashua NH 03062-2800
603-891-0123; Fax: 603-891-0539
Focus: 23-56P
Frequency: 6x per yr; Circulation: 22

Colorado Homes & Lifestyles
Laurel Lund, Editor
7009 S Potomac
Englewood CO 80112-4029
303-397-7600; Fax: 303-397-7619
Focus: 12-27-31-33-43(CO)
Frequency: 6x per yr; Circulation: 25,000

Columbia Journalism Review
Suzanne Levine, Editor
700 Journalism Bldg
Columbia University
New York NY 10027-6937
212-854-1881; Fax: 212-854-8580;
    E-Mail: cjr@columbia.edu
Focus: 56(journalism/publishing)
Frequency: 6x per yr; Circulation: 31,000

Columbia Magazine
Richard McMunn, Editor
1 Columbus Plz
New Haven CT 06510-3325
203-772-2130; Fax: 203-777-0114
Focus: 35-63P(for Christian families)
Frequency: Monthly;
    Circulation: 1,500,000

The Comedy Magazine
David Jurek, Editor
Quality Services Co
5290 Overpass Rd
Santa Barbara CA 93111-2042
805-964-7841; 800-266-3888;
    Fax: 805-964-1073
Focus: 33H(cartoons/current humor/interviews with comedians/etc)
Frequency: 6x per yr;
    Circulation: 200,000

Comics Buyer's Guide
Maggie Thompson, Editor
Krause Publications
700 E State St
Iola WI 54990-0001
715-445-2214; 800-258-0929;
    Fax: 715-445-4087
Focus: 33C-86
Frequency: Weekly; Circulation: 25,000

Coming Attractions
Anne Sherber, Editor
550 Grand St
Jersey City NJ 07302-4115
201-333-4600; Fax: 201-333-1609
Focus: 33(videos)
Frequency: Monthly; Circulation: 429,000

Communications Daily
Daniel Warren, Managing Editor
Warren Publishing Inc
2115 Ward Ct NW
Washington DC 20037-1213
202-872-9200; Fax: 202-293-3435
Focus: 33T
Frequency: Daily; Circulation: N/A

Communications of the ACM
Diane Crawford, Exec Editor
Assn for Computing Machinery
1515 Broadway
New York NY 10036-8901
212-869-7440; Fax: 212-869-0481
Focus: 23-24
Frequency: Monthly; Circulation: 86,000

Complete Woman
Bonnie Krueger, Editor-in-Chief
Associated Publications Inc
875 N Michigan Ave #3434
Chicago IL 60611-1901
312-266-8680
Focus: 73-99
Frequency: 6x per yr; Circulation: 500,000

Computer Artist
Tom McMillan, Editor
10 Tara Blvd #500
Nashua NH 03062-2800
603-891-0123; Fax: 603-891-0539
Focus: 11-23(computer graphics)
Frequency: 6x per yr; Circulation: 31,000

Computer Design
Editor
10 Tara Blvd 5th Fl
Nashua NH 03062-2800
603-891-0123; Fax: 603-891-0514
Focus: 23(computer design)
Frequency: Monthly; Circulation: 103,000

Computer Gaming World
Terry Coleman, Review Editor
Ziff-Davis
135 Main St
San Francisco CA 94105
415-357-4900; Fax: 415-357-4977
Focus: 23-69G(computer games)
Frequency: Monthly; Circulation: 105,000

Computer Life
John Dickinson, Editor-in-Chief
Ziff-Davis
1 Park Ave
New York NY 10016-5802
415-357-5200; Fax: 415-357-5201
Focus: 23(computers/technology)
Frequency: Monthly; Circulation: 750,000

Computer Magazine
Marilyn Potes, Managing Editor
IEEE Computer Society
10662 Los Vaqueros Cir
Los Alamitos CA 90720-2513
714-821-8380; Fax: 714-821-4010
Focus: 23C-24
Frequency: Monthly; Circulation: 93,000

Computer Shopper
Barbara Krasnoff, Product Editor
Ziff-Davis Publishing
One Park Ave
New York NY 10016
212-503-3895; Fax: 212-503-3995
Focus: 23
Frequency: Monthly; Circulation: 500,000

Computer User
Editor
MSP Communications
220 S 6th St
Minneapolis MN 55402-4502
612-339-7571; Fax: 612-339-5806
Focus: 23C
Frequency: Monthly; Circulation: 55,000

Computers in Human Services
Dick Schoech PhD, Editor
The Haworth Press Inc
10 Alice St
Binghamton NY 13904-1503
607-722-5857; 800-342-9678;
    Fax: 607-722-6363
Focus: 23-31-35-57-65-73
Frequency: Quarterly; Circulation: 154,000

Computerworld
Bill Laberis, Editor-in-Chief
500 Old Connecticut Path
Framingham MA 01701-4649
508-879-0700; 800-343-6474;
    Fax: 508-875-8931

Focus: 23
Frequency: Weekly; Circulation: 140,000

Conde Nast Traveler
Cliff Hopkinson, News Editor
360 Madison Ave 10th Fl
New York NY 10017-3136
212-880-8800; Fax: 212-880-2190
Focus: 71
Frequency: Monthly; Circulation: 933,000

Confrontation
Martin Tucker, Editor/Publisher
English Dept
Long Island Univ/CW Post
Greenvale NY 11548
516-299-2391; Fax: 516-299-2735
Focus: 47-75-95
Frequency: 2x per yr; Circulation: 2,000

Confrontation
Lee Mhatre, Book Review Editor
English Dept
Long Island Univ/CW Post
Greenvale NY 11548
516-299-2391; Fax: 516-299-2735
Focus: 47-75-95
Frequency: 2x a year; Circulation: 2,000

Connecticut Magazine
Charles Monagan, Editor
Communications International
789 Reservoir Ave
Bridgeport CT 06606-3956
203-374-5488; Fax: 203-371-6561
Focus: 61(CT)-99
Frequency: Monthly; Circulation: 85,000

Consequences
John A White, Editor
Saginaw State Univ
7400 Bay Rd
University Center MI 48710
Fax: 517-652-8772
Focus: 51E-67(practical consequences of changes in global environment)
Frequency: N/A; Circulation: N/A

Consulting Specifying Engineer
Paul E Beck, Editor
Cahners Publishing
1350 E Touhy Ave PO Box 5080
Des Plaines IL 60017-5080
708-635-8800; Fax: 708-390-2200
Focus: 24(mechanical & electrical)
Frequency: 13x times per yr;
    Circulation: 48,000

Consumer Reports
Joel Gurin, Sr Editor
Consumers Union
101 Truman Ave
Yonkers NY 10703-1044
914-378-2000; Fax: 914-378-2900
Focus: 23E-23T-25-29-43
Very few book reviews; no samples
Frequency: Monthly; Circulation: 5000

Consumers Digest
Mary Butler, Editor and Elliott McCleary, Editor
5705 N Lincoln Ave
Chicago IL 60659-4707
312-275-3590; Fax: 312-275-7273
Focus: 25-43-99(also does books)
Frequency: 6x per yr;
    Circulation: 1,250,000

Consumers Research
Peter Spencer, Editor-in-Chief
800 Maryland Ave NE
Washington DC 20002-5306
202-546-1713; Fax: 202-546-1638
Focus: 25-27-39-43-69(how-to buy/consumer interest)
Frequency: Monthly; Circulation: 13,000

Continental Profiles
Anne Studabaker, Editor
Marblehead Communications
376 Boylston St
Boston MA 02116
617-424-7700; Fax: 617-437-7714
Focus: 19-71-99
Continental Airlines
Frequency: Monthly; Circulation: 350

Cooking Light
Nathalie Dearing Lowery, Managing Editor
2100 Lakeshore Dr
Birmingham AL 35209-6721
205-877-6000
Focus: 27-39-71(vacations for health)
Frequency: 10 x per yr; Circulation: 1200

Corel Magazine
D Scott Campbell, Editor
9801 Anderson Mill Rd #207
Austin TX 78750
512-219-3138; Fax: 512-219-3156
Focus: 23C(Corel art software and design)
800-856-0062: book reviews
Frequency: 10x per yr; Circulation: 40,000

Corporate Finance
Anthony Baldo, Editor
1328 Broadway
New York NY 10001-2121
212-594-5030; 800-829-5903;
    Fax: 212-629-0021
Focus: 19
Frequency: Quarterly; Circulation: 60,000

Corporate Report Minnesota
Terry Fiedler, Editor
City Media Inc
105 S 5th St #100
Minneapolis MN 55402-1207
612-338-4288; Fax: 612-373-0195
Focus: 19-61(Minneapolis MN)
Frequency: Monthly; Circulation: 20,000

Corvette Fever
Greg Pemula, Editor
Dobbs Publishing Group Inc
3816 Industry Blvd
Lakeland FL 33811-1340
941-644-0449; Fax: 941-644-1187
Focus: 16A
Frequency: Monthly; Circulation: 73,000

Corvette Quarterly
Jerry Burton, Exec Editor
Aegis Group
30400 Van Dyke Ave
Warren MI 48093-2316
810-574-9100; Fax: 810-558-5897
Focus: 16A-19
Geared to the Corvette owner
Frequency: Quarterly; Circulation: 250,000

Cosmopolitan
Guy Flatley, Managing Editor
224 West 57th St
New York NY 10019-3212
212-649-3570; Fax: 212-956-3268
Focus: 73-99
Frequency: Monthly;
 Circulation: 2,528,000

Cottage Life
David Zimmer, Managing Editor
111 Queen St E #408
Toronto ON Canada M5C 1S2
416-360-6880; Fax: 416-360-6814
Focus: 43
Frequency: 6x per yr; Circulation: 70,000

Countdown
Julie Mettenburg, Editor
Juvenile Diabetes Foundation
120 Wall St
New York NY 10005
212-785-9500; Fax: 212-785-9595
Focus: 39
Frequency: Quarterly; Circulation: 150,000

Country
Roy Reiman, Editor
Reiman Publications
5400 South 60th St
Greendale WI 53129-1404
414-423-0100; Fax: 414-423-1143
Focus: 27-28-29-33-43-51A-99
Frequency: 6x per yr; Circulation: 2,000

Country Accents
Donna Sapolin, Editor
GCR Publishing Group Inc
1700 Broadway 34th Fl
New York NY 10019-5905
212-541-7100; Fax: 212-245-1241
Focus: 27-28-29-43D-43H
Frequency: 6x per yr; Circulation: 350,000

Country Almanac
Anne Gutowitz, Managing Editor
Harris Publications
1115 Broadway
New York NY 10010-2803
212-807-7100; Fax: 212-627-4678
Focus: 29-43
Frequency: Quarterly; Circulation: 389,000

Country America
Bill Eftank, Managing Editor
Meredith Corp
1716 Locust St
Des Moines IA 50309-3038
515-284-3000; Fax: 212-551-6905
Focus: 14-17-27-29-31-35-39-43-51-71
Country music profiles/lifestyle
Frequency: 10x per yr;
 Circulation: 1,000,000

Country Business
Jeffrey Kehe, Editor
Sampler Productions
707 Kautz Rd
St Charles IL 60174-5302
708-377-8000; Fax: 708-377-8194
Focus: 19-29
Frequency: 6x per yr; Circulation: 30,000

Country Charm
Denise Friedel, Editor
Box 696
Palmerston ON Canada N0G 2P0
519-343-3059
Focus: 10-11-11P-33C-75-99
500-1000 words preferred
Frequency: Monthly; Circulation: N/A

Country Connections
Editor
PO Box 6748 Dept SM
Pine Mountain CA 93222-6748
805-242-1047; Fax: 805-242-5704;
 E-Mail: countryink@aol.com
Focus: 99
Frequency: 6x per yr; Circulation: N/A

Country Decorating Ideas
Anne Gutowitz, Managing Editor
Harris Publications
1115 Broadway
New York NY 10010-2803
212-807-7100; Fax: 212-627-4678
Focus: 29-43
Frequency: Quarterly; Circulation: 354,000

Country Folk Art Magazine
Rhonda Blakely, Editor-in-Chief
8393 E Holly Rd
Holly MI 48442-8819
810-634-9675; Fax: 810-634-3718
Focus: 11-29-71
Frequency: 6x per yr; Circulation: 240,000

Country Journal
Toni Apgar, Acting Editor
6405 Flank Dr
PO Box 8200
Harrisburg PA 17105-8200
717-657-9555; Fax: 717-657-9526
Focus: 27-29-43
Frequency: Monthly; Circulation: 367,000

Country Living
Mary Roby, Managing Editor
Hearst Corp
224 West 57th St
New York NY 10019-3212
212-649-3500; Fax: 212-956-3857
Focus: 27-28-29-35-43
Frequency: Monthly;
 Circulation: 1,800,000

Country Victorian
Donna Sapolin, Editor
GCR Publishing Group
1700 Broadway
New York NY 10019-5905
212-541-7100; Fax: 212-245-1241
Focus: 27-28-29-43D-43H-43G
Frequency: 6x per yr; Circulation: 65,000

Country Woman
Ann Kaiser, Editor
Reiman Publications
5400 South 60th St
Greendale WI 53129-1404
414-423-0100; Fax: 414-423-8463
Focus: 27-28-29-33-43-51A-73-99
For farm & country women
Frequency: 6x per yr; Circulation: N/A

Cowboy Magazine
Darrell Arnold, Editor
PO Box 126
La Veta CO 81055-0126
719-742-5250; 800-426-9269;
 Fax: 719-742-3034
Focus: 51-69
Frequency: Quarterly; Circulation: 12,000

CQ-Radio Amateur's Journal
Alan Dorhoffer, Editor
CQ Communications Inc
76 North Broadway
Hicksville NY 11801-2909
516-681-2922; Fax: 516-681-2926
Focus: 23-33T(radio)
Frequency: Monthly; Circulation: 91,000

Crafts 'N Things
Julie Stephani, Editor
Clapper Communications
2400 Devon #375
Des Plaines IL 60018-4618
708-635-5810; 800-272-3871;
 Fax: 708-635-6311
Focus: 29
Frequency: 10x per yr;
 Circulation: 350,000

Crain's Chicago Business
David Snyder, Editor
Crain Communications Inc
740 N Rush St
Chicago IL 60611-2525
312-649-5411; Fax: 312-649-5415
Focus: 19-61(Chicago IL)
Frequency: Weekly; Circulation: 50,000

Crain's Detroit Business
Mary Kramer, Editor
Crain Communications Inc
1400 Woodbridge
Detroit MI 48207-3187
313-446-6000; Fax: 313-393-0997
Focus: 19
Frequency: Weekly; Circulation: 33,000

Crain's New York Business
Steve Malanga, Exec Editor
 (212-210-0798)
Crain Communications Inc
220 East 42nd St
New York NY 10017-5806
212-210-0100; Fax: 212-210-0799
Focus: 19-61(New York City)
Frequency: Weekly; Circulation: 77,000

Crain's Small Business
Robert Reed, Editor
740 N Rush St
Chicago IL 60611-2525
312-649-5411; 800-278-2724;
 Fax: 312-280-3150
Focus: 19-19S(for businesses with fewer
 than one hundred employees)
Frequency: 10x per yr;
 Circulation: 50,000

Crappie Magazine
Mark Chesnut, Managing Editor
5300 CityPlex Tower
2448 E 81st St
Tulsa OK 74137-4248
918-491-6100; Fax: 918-491-9424
Focus: 15(fish)-69H(fishing)
Frequency: 6x per yr; Circulation: 100,000

Crayola Kids
Mary Heaton, Managing Editor
Meredith Corp
1912 Grand Ave
Des Moines IA 50309-3345
515-284-3000; 800-846-7968;
    Fax: 515-246-6924
Focus: 15-21-29-51-76
Frequency: 6x per yr; Circulation: 250,000

Creative Kids
Andrea Harrington, Editor
Prufrock Press
PO Box 8813
Waco TX 76714-8813
800-998-2208
Focus: 21(ages 8 to 14)
Frequency: Quarterly; Circulation: 60,000

Creative Loafing
Tony Paris, Managing Editor
Eason Publications
750 Willoughby Way
Atlanta GA 30312
404-688-5623; Fax: 404-420-1402
Focus: 99
Frequency: Weekly; Circulation: N/A

Creative New Jersey
Sally Gellert, Editor
PO Box 327
Ramsey NJ 07446-0327
201-670-8688; Fax: 201-670-4484
Focus: 11-33-56
Graphics/broadcast/advertising
Frequency: 6x per yr; Circulation: 19,000

Cricket
Debby Vetter, Editor
Carus Corp
315 Fifth St
Peru IL 61354-2859
815-223-2520; Fax: 815-224-6675
Focus: 21-76(stories, poems, games,
    puzzles, riddles) For children, ages 6
    to 9
Frequency: Monthly; Circulation: 100,000

**Critique:Studies in
    Contemporary Fiction**
Helen Strang, Editor
Heldref Publications
1319 18th St NW
Washington DC 20036-1802
202-296-6267; 800-365-9753;
    Fax: 202-296-5149
Focus: 53-17B-75
Frequency: Quarterly; Circulation: 1,000

Crochet Digest
Laura Scott, Editor
House of White Birches
306 East Parr Rd
Berne IN 46711
219-589-8741; Fax: 219-589-8093
Focus: 29(crocheting)
Frequency: 6x per yr; Circulation: 39,000

Crochet World
Susan Hankins, Editor
House of White Birches
306 East Parr Rd
Berne IN 46711
219-589-8741; Fax: 219-589-8093
Focus: 29
Frequency: 6x per yr; Circulation: 84,000

Crochet World Specials
Susan Hankins, Editor
House of White Birches
306 East Parr Rd
Berne IN 46711
219-589-8741; Fax: 219-589-8093
Focus: 29
Frequency: Quarterly; Circulation: 64,000

Crone Chronicles
Diane Vilas, Editor
Crone Corp
PO Box 81
Kelly WY 83011
307-733-5409
Focus: 53A-73(to celebrate aging women)
A journal of conscious aging
Frequency: Quarterly; Circulation: 2,000

Cross Country Skier
Jim Chase, Editor/Publisher
1823 Fremont Ave S
Minneapolis MN 55403-2931
612-377-0312; Fax: 612-377-0312
Focus: 25-27-29-39-69-71
All about cross-country skiing
Frequency: 6x per yr; Circulation: 75,000

Cross Stitcher
B J McDonald, Editor
Clapper Communications Co
2400 Dezon #375
Des Plaines IL 60018-4618
708-635-5810; 800-272-3871;
    Fax: 708-635-6311
Focus: 29
Frequency: 6x per yr; Circulation: 84,000

Cross-Stitch Plus
Lana Schurb, Editor
House of White Birches
306 East Parr Rd
Berne IN 46711
219-589-8741; Fax: 219-589-8093
Focus: 29
Frequency: 6x per yr; Circulation: 75,000

Cruise Travel
Charles Doherty, Managing Editor
World Publishing Co
990 Grove St
Evanston IL 60201-4370
708-491-6440
Focus: 70N-71(cruises)
Frequency: 6x per yr; Circulation: 200,000

Cruises & Tours
Mary Lu Abbott, Editor
Vacation Publications Inc
1502 Augusta Dr #415
Houston TX 77057-2484
713-974-6903; Fax: 713-914-0445
Focus: 71(cruises and tours)
Frequency: Quarterly; Circulation: 50,000

Cruising World
Bernadette Bernon, Editor
5 John Clarke Rd
Newport RI 02840
401-847-1588; Fax: 401-848-5048
Focus: 70N
Frequency: Monthly; Circulation: 151,000

Current Books Magazine
Edwin S Grosvenor, Editor
PO Box 34468
Bethesda MD 20827
301-530-8200; Fax: 301-530-8201
Focus: 99
Frequency: 6x per yr; Circulation: 30,000

Custom Rodder
Tom Vogele, Editor
McMullen & Yee Publishing Inc
774 South Placentia Ave
Placentia CA 92670-6832
714-572-2255; Fax: 714-572-1864
Focus: 16-24
Frequency: 6x per yr; Circulation: 100,000

Cutting Edge Opportunities
Kevin Mullen, Editor
National Biz-Opp Media
59 Crimson Ln
Elizabethtown PA 17022
Focus: 19M-19O(network mktg/bus
    opportunities)
Author columns & excerpts
Frequency: 6x per yr; Circulation: 17,000

Cycling USA
Jason Anderson, Managing Editor
United States Cycling Fed
1 Olympic Plz
Colorado Springs CO 80909-5746
719-578-4581; Fax: 719-578-4596
Focus: 69(bicycling)
Frequency: Monthly; Circulation: 36,000

D

D Magazine
Catherine Newton, Managing Editor
12200 Ford Rd #260
Dallas TX 75234-7264
214-243-3624; Fax: 214-243-3516
Focus: 11-14-61(Dallas City, TX)
Frequency: Monthly; Circulation: 120,000

Dallas Child
Betsy Robbins, Managing Editor
4125 Keller Springs Rd #146
Dallas TX 75244-2035
214-447-9188; Fax: 214-447-0633
Focus: 21-31-35-76
Frequency: Monthly; Circulation: 65,000

**Dallas Health & Fitness
    Magazine**
Diane Stafford, Editor
6320 LBJ Fwy #220
Dallas TX 75240
214-490-8880; Fax: 214-991-7258
Focus: 39-69
Frequency: Monthly; Circulation: 45,000

Datamation
Kevin Strehlo, Editor-in-Chief
Cahners Publishing
275 Washington St
Newton MA 02158
617-558-4281; Fax: 617-558-4506;
    E-Mail: kstrehlo@mcimail.com
Focus: 23C(large corporate computer
    users)
Frequency: Monthly; Circulation: 200,000

dBase Advisor
Dana Gardner, Managing Editor
Advisor Publications Inc
4010 Morena Blvd
San Diego CA 92117
619-483-6400; 800-336-6060;
   Fax: 619-483-9851
Focus: 19G-19M-19P-23C-23T
Frequency: 6x per yr; Circulation: N/A

DBMS
Editor
Miller Freeman Inc
411 Borel Ave
San Mateo CA 94402-3522
415-358-9500; Fax: 415-358-9855
Focus: 23(databases)
Frequency: Monthly; Circulation: 58,000

DECA Dimensions
Carol Lund, Editor
1908 Association Dr
Reston VA 22091-1503
703-860-5000; Fax: 703-860-4013
Focus: 31E-19-19M-19G-19C
Published during school year
Frequency: Quarterly; Circulation: 145,000

Decorative Artist's Workbook
Sandra Carpenter Forbes, Editor
F&W Publications Inc
1507 Dana Ave
Cincinnati OH 45207-1056
513-531-2222; 800-283-0963;
   Fax: 513-531-1843
Focus: 29
Frequency: 6x per yr; Circulation: 96,000

Decorative Arts Painting
Beth Browning, Editor
Clapper Communications
2400 Devon Ave #375
Des Plaines IL 60018-4618
708-297-7400; Fax: 708-297-8328
Focus: 29
Tole and decorative painting
Frequency: 6x per yr; Circulation: 85,000

Decoy Magazine
Joe Engers, Editor
PO Box 277
Burtonsville MD 20866
301-890-0262
Focus: 15-69H(decoys)
Frequency: 7x per yr; Circulation: N/A

Delicious
Laurel Kallenbach, Managing Editor
New Hope Communications
1301 Spruce St
Boulder CO 80302-4832
303-939-8440; Fax: 303-939-9559
Focus: 27-39H
Frequency: Monthly; Circulation: 300

Delicious
Sue Frederick, Editor
New Hope Communications
1301 Spruce St
Boulder CO 80302-4832
303-939-8440; Fax: 303-939-9559
Focus: 27-39H
Frequency: Monthly; Circulation: 300,000

Democratic Left
David Glenn, Managing Editor
Democratic Socialists of America
180 Varick St 12th Fl
New York NY 10014-4606
212-727-8610; Fax: 212-727-8616
Focus: 13-44-48-55-65
Frequency: 6x per yr; Circulation: 10,000

Deneuve
Rachel Pepper, Book Review Editor
Outspoken Enterprises
2336 Market St #15
San Francisco CA 94114
415-863-6538; Fax: 415-863-1609
Focus: 37-73(for lesbians)
Frequency: 6x per yr; Circulation: 40,000

Desert Skies
Editor
5045 E Speedway #B
Tucson AZ 85712
602-325-2570; Fax: 602-795-7350
Focus: 51-61(devoted to enjoyment and conservation of SW)
Semi-quarterly
Frequency: N/A; Circulation: N/A

Design Book Review
Richard Ingersoll, Editor
1418 Spring Way
Berkeley CA 94708
510-486-1956; Fax: 510-644-3938
Focus: 11-12-43H
Architecture/graphic design/etc
Frequency: Quarterly; Circulation: 7,000

Destination Discovery
Kathy Ely, Managing Editor
Discovery Publishing Inc
7700 Wisconsin Ave
Bethesda MD 20814-3578
301-986-0444; Fax: 301-986-4829
Focus: 99
Frequency: Monthly; Circulation: 200,000

Details Magazine
Lisa Murray, Managing Editor
632 Broadway 12th Fl
New York NY 10012-2614
212-598-3710; Fax: 212-598-0284
Focus: 11-14-17-33-40-99
Frequency: Monthly; Circulation: 477,000

Detroit Monthly
Megan Swoyer, Editor
1400 Woodbridge Ave
Detroit MI 48207-3110
313-446-0330; Fax: 313-446-1687
Focus: 39-43-61(MI)-99
Does book reviews
Frequency: Monthly; Circulation: 79,000

Diabetes Self-Management
James Hazlett, Editor-in-Chief
R A Rapaport Publishing
150 West 22nd St
New York NY 10011-2421
212-989-0200; Fax: 212-989-4786
Focus: 27-39(diabetes)
Frequency: Biweekly; Circulation: 320,000

The Diamond
Bill Gilbert, Editor
PO Box 8396
Scottsdale AZ 85252
602-949-0100; Fax: 602-949-9821
Focus: 41A-69(baseball history)
Frequency: Monthly; Circulation: 350,000

Dianne's Do's and Don'ts
Diane Johansson-Adams, Editor
George Mason Sta
PO Box 19107
Alexandria VA 22320
703-329-8206; Fax: 703-960-9618
Focus: 56-59
Fax on demand newsletter
Frequency: Monthly; Circulation: N/A

Digital Video Magazine
Heidi Carson, News/Products Editor
Brian Clark, Reviews Editor
ActiveMedia
600 Townsend St #170
San Francisco CA 94103
415-522-2400; 800-441-4403;
   Fax: 415-522-2409
Focus: 23E-33T
Frequency: Monthly; Circulation: N/A

Dinosaur Times
Ed Summer, Editor-in-Chief
CSK Publishing Inc
299 Market St
Saddle Brook NJ 07663-5312
201-712-9300; Fax: 201-712-9899
Focus: 15(dinosaurs) for kids age 9 and up
Frequency: Quarterly; Circulation: 70,000

Directions
Yvette Holland, Editor
PO Box 1845
Bloomfield NJ 07003
201-674-3344
Focus: 49B-35F
Frequency: 6x per yr; Circulation: N/A

Directory Strategies
Diane Johansson-Adams, Editor
Box 19107
Alexandria VA 22303
703-329-8206; Fax: 703-960-9618
Focus: 19-56-59(directories)
Frequency: 6x per yr; Circulation: 3,000

Discoveries
John Koenig, Editor
100 Bryant St
Dubuque IA 52003-7405
319-588-2073; Fax: 800-531-0880
Focus: 14M-75-99(books-on-tape, video, software)
Frequency: Monthly; Circulation: 25,000

Discovery - Allstate Motor Club
Steve Wilke, Editor
30400 VanDyke Ave
Warren MI 48093-2316
810-574-9100; Fax: 810-558-5897
Focus: 71
Allstate Motor Club members
Frequency: Quarterly;
   Circulation: 1,900,000

Disney Adventures
Suzanne Harper, Editor
114 Fifth Ave 13th Fl
New York NY 10011-5604
212-633-5953; Fax: 212-633-5936
Focus: 21-76
Frequency: Monthly; Circulation: 850,000

Diversion
Tom Passavant, Editor-in-Chief
Hearst Business Publishing
1790 Broadway 6th Fl
New York NY 10019
212-969-7500; Fax: 212-969-7557
Focus: 39
Frequency: Monthly; Circulation: 179,000

Dog Fancy
Kim Thornton, Editor
Fancy Publications
3 Burroughs
Irvine CA 92718-2804
714-855-8822; Fax: 714-855-3045
Focus: 15(dogs)
Frequency: Monthly; Circulation: 135,000

Dog World
Donna Marcel, Editort
MacLean Hunter Publishing
29 N Wacker Dr
Chicago IL 60606-3203
312-726-2802; Fax: 312-726-4103
Focus: 15(dogs)
Frequency: Monthly; Circulation: 55,000

Doll Collector Price Guide
Cary Raesner, Editor
House of White Birches
306 East Parr Rd
Berne IN 46711-1138
219-589-8741; Fax: 219-589-8093
Focus: 28-29
Frequency: Quarterly; Circulation: 63,000

Doll Reader
Carolyn Cook, Editor
Cowles Magazine Inc
6405 Flank Dr
Harrisburg PA 17112-2750
301-759-0212; Fax: 301-759-9108
Focus: 28-29H
Frequency: 9x times per yr;
  Circulation: 89,000

Doll World
Cary Raesner, Editor
House of White Birches
306 E Parr Rd
Berne IN 46711-1138
219-589-8741; Fax: 219-589-8093
Focus: 28(dolls, collectibles)
Frequency: 6x per yr; Circulation: 52,000

Dolls
Joan Muyskens Pusley, Editor
Collector Communications Corp
170 Fifth Ave
New York NY 10010-5911
212-989-8700; Fax: 212-645-8976
Focus: 28(antique & contemporary dolls)
Frequency: 10x times per yr;
  Circulation: 115,000

Dolphin Log
Elizabeth Foley, Editor
The Cousteau Society
870 Greenbriar Cir
Chesapeake VA 23320-2641
804-523-9335; Fax: 804-523-2747
Focus: 31-51
Non-fiction ages 7-15
Frequency: 6x per yr; Circulation: 80,000

DOS Resource World
Michael Comendul, Editor
80 Elm St
Peterborough NH 03458-1052
603-924-0100; Fax: 603-924-6972
Focus: 23C(DOS computers)
Frequency:N/A; Circulation: 75,000

Doubletake
Jay Woodruff, Managing Editor
1517 W Pettigrew St
Durham NC 27705
Focus: 11P-61(SE)-human stories with
  photographs
Frequency: Quarterly; Circulation: N/A

Down East Magazine
D W Kuhnert, Editor
PO Box 679
Camden ME 04843-0679
207-594-9544; Fax: 207-594-7215
Focus: 61(ME)-99
Frequency: Monthly; Circulation: 75,000

Down Syndrome Today
Debra Hoeft, Editor
PO Box 212
Holtsville NY 11742
516-654-3242; Fax: 516-654-3242
Focus: 39D
Frequency: Quarterly; Circulation: N/A

Dr Dobbs Journal of Software
John Erickson, Editor-in-Chief
411 Borel Ave
San Mateo CA 94402-3522
415-358-9500; Fax: 415-358-9749
Focus: 23
Frequency: Monthly; Circulation: 114,000

Dragon Magazine
Kim Mohan, Editor-in-Chief
201 Sheridan Springs Rd
Lake Geneva WI 53147-5104
414-248-3625; Fax: 414-248-0389
Focus: 69G (computer & video games)
Frequency: Monthly; Circulation: 90,000

Dream Merchant Magazine
Mike Foley, Editor
2309 Torrance Blvd #201
Torrance CA 90501
310-328-1925
Focus: 19M-19S(small business
  marketing info)
New ideas/products/services
Frequency: 6x per yr; Circulation: N/A

Dream Network
Julia Lane Widdop, Book Review Editor
175 Rainbow Dr
Grand Junction CO 81503
970-243-0388
Focus: 57-79
Dream & journal therapy
Frequency:N/A; Circulation: N/A

E

E Magazine
Jim Motavalli, Managing Editor
Earth Action Network Inc
28 Knight St PO Box 5098
Westport CT 06881-5098
203-854-5559; Fax: 203-866-0602;
  E-Mail: axgm65a@prodigy.com
Focus: 13-51E
Frequency: 6x yr; Circulation: 80,000

Early American Life
Mimi Handler, Editor
6405 Flank Dr
PO Box 8200
Harrisburg PA 17105-8200
717-657-9555; Fax: 717-657-9526
Focus: 27-28-29-41A-43-71
Frequency: 6x per yr;
  Circulation: 150,000

Earth Magazine
Tom Yulsman, Editor
Kalmbach Publications
21027 Crossroads Cir Box 1612
Waukesha WI 53187
414-796-8776; Fax: 414-796-0126
Focus: 51-67-71G
Frequency: 6x per yr; Circulation: N/A

Earthwatch Magazine
Peter Tyson, Managing Editor
680 Mount Auburn St
Watertown MA 02172-1500
617-926-8200; 800-776-0188;
  Fax: 617-926-8532
Focus: 51E
Frequency: 6x per yr; Circulation: 65,000

Eating Well
Jane Kirby, Editor
Telemedia Inc
Ferry Rd
Charlotte VT 05445-9984
802-425-3961; Fax: 802-425-3307
Focus: 27-39H
Frequency: 6x per yr; Circulation: 640,000

Ebony
Hans Massaquoi, Managing Editor
Johnson Publishing Co Inc
820 S Michigan Ave
Chicago IL 60605-2103
312-322-9200; Fax: 312-322-9375
Focus: 49-99
Frequency: Monthly;
  Circulation: 2,000,000

The Economist
Bill Emmont, Editor-in-Chief
111 West 57th St 9th Fl
New York NY 10019-2211
212-541-5730; Fax: 212-541-9378
Focus: 19
Frequency: N/A; Circulation: 180,000

Edge
Jonathon Hsu, Editor
Inside Edge Magazine
258 Harvard St #329
Brookline MA 02146-2904
617-497-5621
Focus: 21T-33-40-57-65S
For men ages 18-24
Frequency: 6x per yr; Circulation: 200,000

Edges: Journal of American Knife Collecting
Steve Shackleford, Editor
700 E State St
Iola WI 54990-0001
715-445-2214; 800-272-5233;
　　Fax: 715-445-4087
Focus: 28(knives)
Frequency: Quarterly; Circulation: 15,000

Editor's Digest
Bill Reinshagen, Editor
1613 Chelsea Rd #311
San Marino CA 91108
818-355-684
Focus: 56W
Frequency: 6x per yr; Circulation: 1,000

Educated Traveler
Ann Waigand, Editor
3262 White Barn Ct (22071)
PO Box 220822
Chantilly VA 22022
703-471-1063; Fax: 703-471-4807
Focus: 71--71F
International travel
Frequency: 6x per yr; Circulation: 1,000

Electric Consumer
Emily Born, Editor
720 North High School Rd
Indianapolis IN 46214-3756
317-487-2200; Fax: 317-247-5220
Focus: 25-39
Frequency: Monthly; Circulation: 271,000

Electronic Entertainment
Frederic Paul, Editor
Infotainment World
951 Mariners Island Blvd
San Mateo CA 94404-1558
415-349-4300; Fax: 415-349-7781
Focus: 23C-23E-23T-33(interactive
　　TV/home electronics/computer games)
Frequency: Monthly; Circulation: 100,000

Elegant Bride
Martie Hayworth Emory, Managing Editor
Pace Communications
1301 Carolina St 2nd Fl
Greensboro NC 27401
919-378-6065; Fax: 919-275-2864
Focus: 35M-40
Frequency: 6x per yr; Circulation: 123,000

Elks Magazine
Judith Keogh, Managing Editor
425 W Diversey Pky
Chicago IL 60614-6107
312-528-4500
Focus: 99
Frequency: 10x per yr;
　　Circulation: 1,500,000

Elle
Patricia Towers, Sr Features Editor
Hachette Magazines
1633 Broadway 44th Fl
New York NY 10019
212-767-5800; Fax: 212-489-4216
Focus: 99
Frequency: Monthly; Circulation: 950,000

Elle Decor
Marian McElvoy, Editor-in-Chief
Hachette Filipacchi Magazines
1633 Broadway
New York NY 10019-6708
212-767-5800; Fax: 212-489-4241
Focus: 14-17-29-33-40-43
Frequency: 6x per yr; Circulation: 450,000

Ellery Queen Mystery Magazine
Janet Hutchings, Editor
Dell Magazines
1540 Broadway 15th Fl
New York NY 10036-4039
212-782-8552; 800-223-6834;
　　Fax: 212-782-8309
Focus: 84
Frequency: Monthly; Circulation: 500,000

Emmy Magazine
Gail Polevoi, Managing Editor
5220 Lankshine Blvd
North Hollywood CA 91601
818-754-2800; Fax: 818-761-2827
Focus: 17-33T
Frequency: 6x per yr; Circulation: 14,000

Empire State Report
Jeff Plungis, Editor
State Report Network Inc
4 Central Ave 3rd Fl
New York NY 12210-1334
518-465-5502; Fax: 518-465-9822
Focus: 55-61(NY)
Public policy/politics in NY
Frequency: Monthly; Circulation: 12,000

The Energy Times
Joe Lamber, Editor
548 Broadhollow Rd
Melville NY 11747-3704
516-777-7773; Fax: 516-293-0349
Focus: 27-39H
Frequency: 6x per yr; Circulation: 575,000

Enterprise Communications
Laurie Watanabe, Managing Editor
Advanstar Communications
201 E Sandpointe Ave #600
Santa Ana CA 92707-5761
714-513-8400; Fax: 714-513-8482; E-Mail:
　　entercomm@aol.com
Focus: 23C(corporate and network
　　computing)
Frequency: Monthly; Circulation: 100,000

Entertainment Weekly
James Seymore Jr, Managing Editor
1675 Broadway 28th Fl
New York NY 10019-5820
212-522-5600; Fax: 212-522-0074
Focus: 11-14-17-33-75-99
Books/movies/TV/tapes
Frequency: Weekly; Circulation: 1,150,000

Entrepreneur
Rieva Lesonsky, Editor-in-Chief
Entrepreneur Media Group
2392 Morse Ave
Irvine CA 92714-6234
714-261-2325; Fax: 714-755-4211
Focus: 19S
Frequency: Monthly; Circulation: 385,000

Environment
Barbara Richman, Managing Editor
Heldref Publications
1319 18th St NW
Washington DC 20036-1802
202-296-6267; Fax: 202-296-5149
Focus: 51E
Frequency: 10x per yr; Circulation: 16,000

Environmental Action
Barbara Ruben, Editor
Environmental Action Foundation
6930 Carroll Ave #600
Takoma Park MD 20912
301-891-1100; Fax: 301-891-2218
Focus: 51E(environmental issues)
Frequency: Quarterly; Circulation: 16,000

Environmental Business Journal
Lynnette Thwaites and Vyvian Tenario,
　　Editors
4452 Park Blvd #306
San Diego CA 92116-4039
619-295-7685; Fax: 619-295-5743
Focus: 19M-51
Frequency: Monthly; Circulation: N/A

Equal Opportunity Publications
James Schneider, Editor
150 Motor Pky #420
Hauppauge NY 11788-5108
516-273-0066; Fax: 516-273-8936
Focus: 99
Frequency: 3x per yr; Circulation: 15,000

ESCAPE
Landis McIntire, Editor
3205 Ocean Park Blvd #160
Santa Monica CA 90405-3233
310-392-5235; Fax: 310-392-6416
Focus: 71 (global adventure/travel)
Frequency: Quarterly; Circulation: 75,000

Esquire
Will Blythe, Book Review Editor
250 W 55th St
New York NY 10019-5201
212-459-7500; Fax: 212-582-7067
Focus: 99
Frequency: Monthly; Circulation: 700,000

Essence
Charlotte Wiggers, Managing Editor
Essence Communications Inc
1500 Broadway 6th Fl
New York NY 10036-4071
212-642-0600; Fax: 212-921-5173
Focus: 99
Frequency: Monthly;
　　Circulation: 1,050,000

Eternelle
Valerie Foster, Publisher
PO Box 1646
Los Altos CA 94023-1646
415-917-1557; Fax: 415-917-1560
Focus: 73(ages 35-60+)
Frequency: Quarterly; Circulation: N/A

Euro Sport Car
Sherry Collins, Editor
McMullen & Yee Publishing Inc
774 South Placentia
Placentia CA 92670-6846
714-572-2255; Fax: 714-572-1864
Focus: 16-24
Frequency: 6x per yr; Circulation: 61,500

European Car
Stephanie Wolfe, Managing Editor
Argus Publishers
12100 Wilshire Blvd #250
Los Angeles CA 90025-7102
310-820-3601; Fax: 310-207-9388
Focus: 16
Frequency: Monthly; Circulation: 55,000

Everyday Men
Larry Riggles, Editor/Publisher
9301 View Ct
Frederick MD 21701-2242
301-898-3239
Focus: 29H-39-48-69
Frequency: Quarterly; Circulation: 10,000

Executive Denver Magazine
Jeff Rundles, Publisher
2601 Blake St #301
Denver CO 80205
303-292-6424; Fax: 303-296-8476
Focus: 19(Denver)
Frequency: Monthly; Circulation: 15,000

Executive Feedback
Connie Witt, Editor/Publisher
PO Box 18963
Huntsville AL 35804
205-536-1113; Fax: 205-534-7560
Focus: 19-51A(agribusiness)
Frequency: Monthly; Circulation: 22,000

Executive Female
Dorian Burden, Managing Editor
Natl Assn for Female Executives
30 Irving Pl 5th Fl
New York NY 10003-2303
212-477-2200; Fax: 212-477-8215
Focus: 19-73
Frequency: 6x per yr; Circulation: 250,000

Executive Summary/CA Education
Susan Holtzer, Managing Editor
Caddo Gap Press
3145 Geary Blvd #275
San Francisco CA 94118
415-750-9978; Fax: 415-668-5450
Focus: 31E-61(CA)
Frequency: Monthly; Circulation: N/A

Exercise for Men Only
John Bruel, Managing Editor
Chelo Publishing Inc
350 Fifth Ave #3323
New York NY 10118-0110
212-947-4322; Fax: 212-563-4774
Focus: 39E-69
Frequency: 6x per yr; Circulation: 145,000

Explorer
Anita Weber, Book Review Editor
Cleveland Mus of Natural History
University Cir
Cleveland OH 44106
216-231-4600; Fax: 216-231-5919

Focus: 41-51-65A-67S(sold to members and libraries)
Frequency: 3x per yr; Circulation: 10,000

Expressions
Editor
Potpourri
120 N Meadows Rd
Meadfield MA 02052
508-359-4649
Focus: 27-28-40F-43
Frequency: Biweekly; Circulation: 65,000

F

Faces: The Magazine About People
Carolyn Yoder, Editor-in-Chief
Cobblestone Publishing Inc
7 School St
Peterborough NH 03458-1441
603-924-7209; Fax: 603-924-7380
Focus: 21-44-65A(lifestyles and customs of other people)
Ages 9-13
Frequency: 9x per yr; Circulation: 14,000

Fairfield County Woman
Rita Papazian, Editor-in-Chief
15 Bank St
Stamford CT 06901-3008
203-323-3105; 800-690-6990;
    Fax: 203-323-4112
Focus: 19-61(CT)-73-99
Frequency: Monthly; Circulation: 90,000

FALCON Magazine
Kay Morton Ellenhoff, Exec Editor
PO Box 1718
Helena MT 59624
406-442-6597; Fax: 406-442-2995
Focus: 15-21-29-51
Magazine for kids
Frequency: 6x per yr; Circulation: 80,000

Family Circle
Kathy Sagan, Book Editor
110 Fifth Ave
New York NY 10011-5603
212-463-1799; Fax: 212-463-1808
Focus: 27-29-35-43-73-99
Frequency: 17x per yr;
    Circulation: 5,201,000

Family Fun Magazine
Sandy McDonald, Book Reviews
244 Main St
PO Box 929
Northampton MA 01060
413-585-0444; Fax: 413-586-5724
Focus: 21-76
Children's books
Frequency: 6x per yr; Circulation: 200,000

Family Handyman
Gary Havens, Editor
Home Service Publications
28 W 23rd St 8th Fl
New York NY 10010-5204
212-366-8686; Fax: 212-366-8618
Focus: 16A-29-43
Frequency: 10x per yr;
    Circulation: 1,076,000

Family Life
Wendy Israel, Managing Editor
1633 Broadway
New York NY 10019
212-767-4918
Focus: 21-27-29-35-67-76
Frequency: 6x per yr;
    Circulation: 400,000

Family Motor Coaching
Pamela Wisby Kay, Editor
8291 Clough Pike
Cincinatti OH 45244-2756
513-474-3622; Fax: 513-474-2332
Focus: 16-27-71
Frequency: Monthly; Circulation: 95,000

Family Times
Leigh Anne Perialas, Editor
Family Times Inc
1900 Superfine Ln
Wilmington DE 19802-4920
302-575-0935; 800-969-2666;
    Fax: 302-575-0933
Focus: 21-35
Frequency: Monthly; Circulation: 50,000

FamilyFun
Ann Hallock, Exec Editor
244 Main St
Northampton MA 01060
413-585-0444
Focus: 21-35F
Owned by Disney Magazine Publ
Frequency: 10x per yr;
    Circulation: 600,000

Fangoria Horror in Entertainment
Norman Jacobs, Publisher
Starlog Entertainment Inc
475 Park Ave S
New York NY 10016
212-689-2830; Fax: 212-889-7933
Focus: 33(horror)
Frequency: 10; Circulation: N/A

Fantasy & Science Fiction
Kristine Rusch, Editor
143 Crean Hill Rd
West Cornwall CT 06796-1205
203-672-6376; Fax: 203-672-2643
Focus: 86
Edward Ferman, Publisher
Frequency: Monthly; Circulation: 60,000

FASHE Magazine
Shi Kagy, Editor
Trans World
PO Box 4260
Malibu CA 90264-4260
310-456-0790; Fax: 310-456-3724
Focus: 40-43D-49O-73(for Asian-American women)
Frequency: 6x per yr; Circulation: 46,000

Fashion Reporter
Dahlia Dean, Editor
Model Properties
300 Park Ave S 3rd Fl
New York NY 10010
212-477-2343; Fax: 212-614-3018
Focus: 40
Frequency: Weekly; Circulation: 20,000

Fat Girl Magazine
Barbara McDonald, Editor
2215-R Market St #193
San Francisco CA 94114-1653
415-567-6757
Focus: 35S-37-73(a mag for fat dykes &
  the women who want them)
Frequency: Quarterly; Circulation: 5,000

FATE Magazine
Les Stern, Managing Editor
Llewellyn Worldwide Ltd
PO Box 64383
St Paul MN 55164-0383
612-291-1970; 800-THE-MOON; Fax:
  612-291-1908
Focus: 53-54
Frequency: Monthly; Circulation: 330,000

Fiberarts
Ann Batchelder, Editor
Altamont Press Inc
50 College St
Asheville NC 28801-2818
704-253-0467; Fax: 704-253-7952
Focus: 29
Frequency: 5x per yr; Circulation: 24,000

Field
Stuart Friebert, Editor
Rice Hall-Creative Arts Dept
Oberlin College
Oberlin OH 44074
216-775-8570
Focus: 47-95
Frequency: Biweekly; Circulation: 2,000

Field & Stream
David Petzal, Book Editor
Times Mirror Magazines
Two Park Ave
New York NY 10016-5601
212-779-5000; Fax: 212-725-3836
Focus: 15-51-69(hunting/fishing)
Frequency: Monthly; Circulation:
  2,007,000

Filipinas
Rene Ciria-Cruz, Managing Editor
655 Sutter St #333
San Francisco CA 94102
415-563-5878; Fax: 415-292-5993
Focus: 49-44A
Filipino Asian Americans
Frequency: Monthly; Circulation: 101,000

Film Comment
Gavin Smith, Book Review Editor
Film Society of Lincoln Ctr
70 Lincoln Center Plz
New York NY 10023-6548
212-875-5610; Fax: 212-875-5636
Focus: 33M-33T
Covers all aspects of film industry
Frequency: 6x per yr; Circulation: 40,000

Film Quarterly
Ann Martin, Editor
Univ of California Press
30 Schuyler Pl
Morristown NJ 07960-7802
201-285-6868; Fax: 201-285-6713
Focus: 33
Frequency: Quarterly; Circulation: 8,000

Financial World
Paul B Brown, Editor
1328 Broadway
New York NY 10001-2121
212-594-5030; Fax: 212-629-0026
Focus: 19
Geoffrey N Smith, also Editor
Frequency: Biweekly; Circulation: 500,000

Fine Cooking
Martha Holmberg, Editor
Taunton Press
63 S Main St
Newtown CT 06470-2355
203-426-8171; 800-926-8776; Fax:
  203-426-3434
Focus: 27(for professional & hobbiest)
Frequency: 6x per yr;
  Circulation: 120,000

Fine Gardening
Carole Turner, Managing Editor
Taunton Press
63 S Main St
Newtown CT 06470-2355
203-426-8171; Fax: 203-426-3434
Focus: 43G (focus on landscaping)
Frequency: 6x per yr;
  Circulation: 175,000

First For Women
Alan Petrucelli, Book Review Editor
270 Sylvan Ave
Englewood Cliffs NJ 07632-2513
201-569-6699; Fax: 201-569-6264
Focus: 73-99
Frequency: 18x per yr;
  Circulation: 1,500,000

First Visit
Deana Jamroz, Editor
EPI Corp
8003 Old York Rd
Elkins Park PA 19027-1410
215-635-1700; Fax: 215-635-6455
Focus: 31C-31P-39E-39M
New mothers
Frequency: Quarterly; Circulation: 2,000

First Year of Life
Judith Nolte, Editor
Cahners Publishing Co
249 W 17th St
New York Ny 10011
212-645-0067; Fax: 212-463-6620
Focus: 31-35-39
Frequency: Once per yr;
  Circulation: 3,200,000

Fitness
Consuela Golden, Managing Editor
110 Fifth Ave
New York NY 10011-5601
212-463-1181; Fax: 212-463-1170
Focus: 39E
Frequency: 6x per yr;
  Circulation: 600,000

The Five Owls
Susan Stan, Editor
HU MS-C1924
1536 Hewitt Ave
Saint Paul MN 55104
612-644-7377; Fax: 612-377-4814
Focus: 21-49-76-79-89
Multicultural children's books
Frequency: 6x per yr; Circulation: N/A

Florida Game & Fish
Jimmy Jacobs, Editor
Game & Fish Publications Inc
2250 Newmarket Pky #110
Marietta GA 30067-8749
770-953-9222; Fax: 770-933-9510
Focus: 15-51-61(FL)-69
Frequency: Monthly; Circulation: N/A

Florida Living
John Paul Jones Jr, Editor/Publisher
102 NE 10th Ave #6
Gainesville FL 32601-2322
904-372-8865; 800-881-6372;
  Fax: 904-372-3453
Focus: 17P-71-61(FL)
Frequency: Monthly; Circulation: 41,000

Florida Trend
John Berry, Editor
490 1st Ave S #800
St Petersburg FL 33701-4204
813-821-5800; 800-288-7363;
  Fax: 813-822-5083
Focus: 19-61(FL)
Frequency: Monthly; Circulation: 50,000

Flower & Garden
Kay M Olson, Editor
KC Publishing
700 West 47th St #310
Kansas City MO 64112
816-531-5730; Fax: 816-531-3873
Focus: 43G
Frequency: 6x per yr;
  Circulation: 600,000

Fly Fisherman
John Randolph, Editor
Cowles Media Inc
6405 Flank Dr
Harrisburg PA 17112-2750
717-657-9555; Fax: 717-657-9552
Focus: 69H
Frequency: 6x per yr;
  Circulation: 125,000

Focus on the Family
Mike Yorkey, Editor
8605 Explorer Dr
Colorado Springs CO 80920-1051
719-531-5181
Focus: 35-21-31E(teaching)-31P-57-63
Frequency: Monthly; Circulation: N/A

Food & Wine
Mary Ellen Ward, Managing Editor
1120 Ave of the Americas 9th Fl
New York NY 10036-6700
212-382-5618; Fax: 212-764-2177
Focus: 27
Frequency: Monthly; Circulation: 800,000

Football Digest
Larry Burke, Editor
Century Publishing Co
990 Grove St
Evanston IL 60201-4370
708-491-6440; Fax: 708-491-0459
Focus: 69(football)
Frequency: 10x per yr;
  Circulation: 180,000

Forbes
Lawrence Minard, Managing Editor
60 Fifth Ave
New York NY 10011-8802
212-620-2200; Fax: 212-243-1509
Focus: 19
Frequency: 6x per yr;
  Circulation: 765,000

Formula Magazine
C Demond, Publisher
14045-6 Yonge St #500
Aurora ON Canada L4G 6H8
905-727-8000; Fax: 905-727-8800
Focus: 16A
Frequency: 6x per yr; Circulation: N/A

Fort Worth Child Magazine
Joylyn Niebes Mortbert, Editor
4125 Keller Springs Rd
Dallas TX 75244-2011
214-447-9188; Fax: 214-447-0633
Focus: 21-31-35-76
Frequency: Monthly; Circulation: 30,000

Fortune
Walter Kiechel, Managing Editor
Time-Life Bldg, Rockefeller Ctr
New York NY 10020-1393
212-586-1212; Fax: 212-522-0096
Focus: 19
Frequency: Biweekly; Circulation: 870,000

Forum on Women in Higher Education
Marina Budhos, Editor
Women's Forum Publishers Inc
200 W 57th St
New York NY 10019
212-399-1087
Focus: 73
Frequency: Monthly; Circulation: 25,000

Four Wheel Drive & Sport Utility
Phil Howell, Editor
McMullen & Yee Publishing Inc
774 South Placentia
Placentia CA 92670-6832
714-572-2255; Fax: 714-572-1864
Focus: 16-24
Frequency: 6x per yr; Circulation: 93,000

Four Wheeler
John Stewart, Editor
3330 Ocean Park Blvd #115
Santa Monica CA 90405-3211
310-392-2998; Fax: 310-392-1171
Focus: 16A
Frequency: Monthly; Circulation: 325,000

FoxPro Advisor
John Hawkins, Editor
Advisor Publications Inc
4010 Morena Blvd #200
San Diego CA 92117-4547
619-483-6400; 800-336-6060;
  Fax: 619-483-9851
Focus: 19-23-25
Frequency: Monthly; Circulation: 25,000

Free Inquiry
Paul Kurtz, Editor-in-Chief
3965 Rensch Rd
Amherst NY 14228-2743
716-636-7571; Fax: 716-636-1733
Focus: 13-49-54-55-57-63-65
Frequency: Quarterly; Circulation: 25,000

Free Spirit Magazine
June Balish, Editor
107 Sterling Pl
Brooklyn NY 11217
718-638-3733; Fax: 718-230-3459
Focus: 53
Frequency: 6x per yr;
  Circulation: 200,000

Freebies
Linda Cook, Managing Editor
1135 Eugenia Pl
PO Box 5025
Carpenteria CA 93014-5025
805-566-1225
Focus: 11-15-21-27-29-31-35-39-43-69-71
Free offers
Frequency: 5x per yr Circulation: 400,000

Frequent Flyer
Laurie Berger, Editor-in-Chief
500 Plaza Dr
Secaucus NJ 07094-3619
212-902-2000; Fax: 212-902-1809
Focus: 19-71
Frequency: Monthly; Circulation: 350,000

Fresh Start
Cynthia MacGregor, Editor
566 Westchester Ave
Rye Brook NY 10573
914-939-2111; Fax: 914-939-5138
Focus: 35R-99
Divorced/separated men & women
Frequency: N/A; Circulation: N/A

Friendly Exchange
Adele Malott, Editor
PO Box 2120
Warren MI 48090-2120
810-558-7226
Focus: 71
Frequency: Quarterly; Circulation: 5700

The Friend
Vivian Paulsen, Editor
50 E North Temple
Salt Lake City UT 84150-0002
801-240-2210; Fax: 801-240-5997
Focus: 21-63
Ages 3-11
Frequency: Monthly; Circulation: 350,000

Funny Times
Raymond Lesser, Publisher
Funny Times Inc
2176 Lee Rd
Cleveland Heights OH 44118-2908
216-371-8600; Fax: 216-371-8696
Focus: 33H
Frequency: Monthly; Circulation: 45,000

G

Gallery
Barry Janoff, Editor-in-Chief
Montcalm Publishing Corp
401 Park Ave S
New York NY 10016-8808
212-779-8900; Fax: 212-725-7215
Focus: 99-37
Frequency: 13x per yr;
  Circulation: 425,000

Game Informer
Andrew McNamara, Editor
10120 West 76th St
Eden Prairie MN 55344-3728
612-946-7245; Fax: 612-946-7250
Focus: 69G (computer & video games)
Frequency: Monthly; Circulation: 200,000

Games Magazine
Mike Shenk, Editor
B & P Publishing Co Inc
575 Boylston St
Boston MA 02116-3607
617-536-5536; 800-886-6556;
Fax: 617-536-0558
Focus: 69G
Frequency: 6x per yr;
  Circulation: 250,000

Garden Design
Sean Callahan, Editor
Meigher Communications
100 Ave of the Americas 7th Fl
New York NY 10013-1689
212-334-1212; Fax: 212-334-1260
Focus: 12-43
Frequency: 6x per yr;
  Circulation: 100,000

Garden Gate Magazine
Todd Steadman, Editor
August Home Publishing Co
2200 Grand Ave
Des Moines IA 50312
800-978-9631; Fax: 515-282-6741
Focus: 43G
Books listed in Resources section
Frequency: 6x per yr; Circulation: N/A

Gateway Magazine
Julie Montagne, Editor
Gateway 2000 - 610 Gateway Dr
PO Box 2000 Mail Drop 23
North Sioux City SD 57049-2000
605-232-2000; 800-846-2000;
  Fax: 605-232-2023
Focus: 23
Frequency: Quarterly; Circulation: N/A

Gay Community News
Stephanie Poggi and Marla Erlienes,
  Co-Editors
25 West St Basement
Boston MA 02110
617-426-4469; Fax: 617-426-4469
Focus: 13-37-49-55-65-73
Frequency: Quarterly; Circulation: 3,000

Gaze
George Holdgrafer, Editor
2344 Nicollet Ave S #370
Minneapolis MN 55404-3354
612-871-7472; Fax: 612-871-0525
Focus: 11-14-17-33-37
Clark Bufkin, Publisher
Frequency: Biweekly; Circulation: 20,000

Genesis
Michael Banka, Editor
Jakel Corp
110 E 57th St #31
New York NY 10023-1304
212-644-8800; Fax: 212-644-9215
Focus: 35S-40-16A-37
Men's lifestyles
Frequency: 13x per yr; Circulation: 425,000

Genre Magazine
Ron Kraft, Editor-in-Chief
7080 Hollywood Blvd #1104
Hollywood CA 90028-6938
213-896-9778; Fax: 213-467-8365
Focus: 37(mens lifestyles)
Frequency: 10x per yr; Circulation: 45,000

Gent
Steve Dorfman, Editor
Dugent Publications Corp
14411 Commerce Rd #420
Miami Lakes FL 33016-1598
305-557-0071; Fax: 305-557-6005
Focus: 35S-16A-67-69-37
Frequency: 13x per yr; Circulation: 220,000

Gentlemen's Quarterly
Scott Omelianuk, Staff Writer/Bk Review
Conde Nast Publications
350 Madison Ave
New York NY 10017
212-880-8800; Fax: 212-880-8757;
    E-Mail: gqmag@aol.com
Focus: 99
Frequency: Monthly; Circulation: 685,000

The Georgia Review
Stanley W Lindberg, Editor
Univ of Georgia
Athens GA 30602-9009
404-542-3481; Fax: 404-542-0047
Focus: 11-47-75-90-95
Frequency: Quarterly; Circulation: 7,000

Georgia Sportsman
Jimmy Jacobs, Editor
Game & Fish Publications Inc
2250 Newmarket Pky #110
Marietta GA 30067-8749
770-953-9222; Fax: 770-933-9510
Focus: 15-51-61(GA)-69
Frequency: Monthly; Circulation: 51,000

Georgia Trend
Millard Grimes, Editor
Grimes Publications Inc
1770 Indian Trail Rd
Norcross GA 30093-2625
770-931-9410; Fax: 770-931-9505
Focus: 19-61(GA)
Frequency: Monthly; Circulation: 52,000

Gifted Child Today
Stephanie Stout, Editor
Prufrock Press
100 N 6th St #400
Waco TX 76701-2032
817-756-3337; 800-998-2208;
    Fax: 817-756-3339
Focus: 31
Frequency: 6x per yr; Circulation: 15,000

Girls' Life
Kim Childress, Book Editor
Monarch Avalon
4517 Harford Rd
Baltimore MD 21214
410-254-9200; Fax: 410-254-0991
Focus: 21T-40-99
Frequency: 6x per yr;
    Circulation: 100,000

Glamour
Laura Mathews, Book Review Editor
Conde Nast Publications
350 Madison Ave
New York NY 10017-3704
212-880-8800; Fax: 212-880-6922
Focus: 39-40-75-77-99(primarily
    contemporary fiction)
Frequency: Monthly;
    Circulation: 2,000,000

Gnosis: Journal of Western Inner Tradition
Richard Smoley, Editor
347 Dolores St #305
San Francisco CA 94110-1006
415-255-0400; Fax: 415-255-6329
Focus: 53-54-63(Western spiritualism)
Frequency: Quarterly; Circulation: 16,000

Goldmine
Jeff Tamarkin, Editor
Krause Publications Inc
700 State St
Iola WI 54990-0001
715-445-2214; 800-258-0929;
    Fax: 715-445-4087
Focus: 14M-17(rock stars)
Frequency: Biweekly; Circulation: 35,000

Golf Digest
Jerry Tarde, Editor
5520 Park Ave
Trumbull CT 06611-3426
203-371-7000; Fax: 203-373-7033
Focus: 39E-69(golf)-71
The Digest - short golf news bit
Frequency: Monthly;
    Circulation: 1,450,000

Golf Magazine
James Frank, Editor
Times Mirror Magazines
2 Park Ave
New York NY 10016-5603
212-779-5000; Fax: 212-779-5522
Focus: 39-69(golf)
Frequency: Monthly; Circulation:
    1,250,000

Golf Traveler
Valerie Law, Editor
2575 Vista Del Mar
Ventura CA 93001
805-389-0300
Focus: 69(golf)
Frequency: N/A; Circulation: 100,000

Golf World
Alan R Tays, Managing Editor
5520 Park Ave
Trumbull CT 06611
203-373-7000; Fax: 203-373-7062
Focus: 69(golf)
Frequency: Weekly; Circulation: 146,000

The Golfer
H K Pickens, Editor/Publisher
Briar & Wood
42 W 38th St
New York NY 10018-6210
212-768-8360; Fax: 212-768-8365
Focus: 69S
Frequency: 6x per yr;
    Circulation: 250,000

Good Apple Newspaper
Donna Borst, Editor
8 Melody Terr
Ft Madison IA 52627
319-372-2008; Fax: 319-372-2008
Focus: 21-31-76(for teachers)
Activity suggestions, grades 2-8
Frequency: 5x per yr; Circulation: 26,000

Good Housekeeping Magazine
Phyllis Levy, Books Editor
Hearst Corp
959 Eighth Ave
New York NY 10019-3737
212-649-2000; Fax: 212-265-3307
Focus: 17-27-29-35-43-73-99
Also Consumer Editor
Frequency: Monthly;
    Circulation: 5,137,000

Good Medicine
Doug Hall, Managing Editor
5100 Wisconsin Ave NW #404
Washington DC 20016
202-686-2210; Fax: 202-686-2216
Focus: 39-25-27
Frequency: Quarterly; Circulation: N/A

Good Old Days
Ken Tate, Editor
House of White Birches
306 East Parr Rd
Berne IN 46711
219-589-8741; Fax: 219-589-8093
Focus: 35
Frequency: Monthly; Circulation: 125,000

Good Old Days Special
Ken Tate, Editor
House of White Birches
306 East Parr Rd
Berne IN 46711
219-589-8741; Fax: 219-589-8093
Focus: 35
Frequency: 6x per yr;
    Circulation: 135,000

Good Times!
Kent Smith, Editor
Valley Media
1061 East 2100 S
Salt Lake City UT 84106
801-487-3221; Fax: 801-487-8926
Focus: 61-71-99(passengers of ValuJet
    Airlines)
Frequency: 6x per yr; Circulation: 20,000

Gourmet Magazine
Gail Zweigenthal, Editor-in-Chief
Conde Nast
560 Lexington Ave
New York NY 10022-6828
212-371-1330; Fax: 212-753-2596
Focus: 27-28-40-43
Frequency: Monthly; Circulation: 890,000

Grand Rapids Business Journal
Carole Valade, Editor
Gemini Publications
549 Ottawa Ave NW
Grand Rapids MI 49503-1424
616-459-4545; Fax: 616-459-4800
Focus: 11-33-61(MI)-99
Frequency: Weekly; Circulation: 6,000

Grand Rapids Parent
Carole Valade Smith, Editor
549 Ottawa Ave NW
Grand Rapids MI 49503-1424
616-459-4545; Fax: 616-459-4800
Focus: 21-31-35-76
Frequency: Monthly; Circulation: 10,000

Granta
Anne Kinard, Publisher
250 W 57th St #1316
New York NY 10107-0001
212-246-1313; Fax: 212-586-8003
Focus: 47-75-83-99
Frequency: Quarterly; Circulation: 50,000

Gray Areas
Netta Gilboa, Editor/Publisher
Gray Areas Inc
PO Box 808
Broomall PA 19008-0808
610-353-8238; Fax: 610-353-9693
Focus: 33-55
Frequency: Quarterly; Circulation: 10,000

Great Plains Game & Fish
Nick Gilmore, Editor
Game & Fish Publications Inc
2250 Newmarket Pky #110
Marietta GA 30067-8749
770-953-9222; Fax: 770-933-9510
Focus: 15-51-61(Great Plains Area)-69
Frequency: Monthly; Circulation: N/A

Greater Baton Rouge Business Rpt
Paulette Senior, Editor
5757 Corporate Blvd #402
Baton Rouge LA 70808-2560
504-928-1700; Fax: 504-923-3448
Focus: 19-61(Baton Rouge LA)
Frequency: 99; Circulation: 13,000

Greenhouse Grower
Robyn Dill, Managing Editor
Meister Publishing Co
37733 Euclid Ave
Willoughby OH 44094-5925
216-942-2000; Fax: 216-975-3447
Focus: 43G
Frequency: 14x per yr; Circulation: 22,000

Grit
Roberta Peterson, Editor
Morris Communications Inc
1503 SW 42nd St
Topeka KS 66609-1214
913-274-4330; Fax: 913-274-4305
Focus: 25-35-39-67-71-99
Small-town America
Frequency: N/A ; Circulation: 300,000

Guideposts Magazine
Harold Hostetler, Managing Editor
16 E 34th St
New York NY 10016-4328
212-251-8100; Fax: 212-684-0679
Focus: 57-63
Frequency: Monthly;
    Circulation: 3,900,000

Hadassah Magazine
Alan Tigay, Editor
50 West 58th St
New York NY 10019-2500
212-688-1408; Fax: 212-446-9521
Focus: 63J
Frequency: 10x per yr;
    Circulation: 287,000

Handcraft Illustrated
Carol Sterbenz, Editor
17 Station St
Brookline MA 02146-7371
617-232-1000; Fax: 617-232-1572
Focus: 29
Frequency: 6x per yr; Circulation: N/A

HandGunning
John Crowley, Editor
PJS Publications Inc
News Plaza
Peoria IL 61656
309-682-6626; 800-521-2885;
    Fax: 309-682-7394
Focus: 69H(guns)
Frequency: 6x per yr; Circulation: 100,000

Handwoven
Jean Scorgie, Editor
Interweave Press
201 E 4th St
Loveland CO 80537-5601
970-669-7672; Fax: 970-667-8317
Focus: 29
Frequency: 5x per yr; Circulation: 35,000

Happiness
Gilbert Wilks, Feature Editor
Wilks Publications
PO Box 388
Portland TN 37148
615-325-4196; Fax: 615-325-9809
Focus: 31-35-57
Frequency: Weekly; Circulation: 1,000,000

Harper's
Ellen Rosenbush, Managing Editor
666 Broadway 11th Fl
New York NY 10012-2317
212-614-6500; Fax: 212-228-5889
Focus: 11-14-47-75-99
Frequency: Monthly; Circulation: 221,000

Harper's Bazaar
Marguerite Kramer, Managing Editor
Hearst Corp
1700 Broadway
New York NY 10019-5905
212-903-5000
Focus: 99
Frequency: Monthly; Circulation: 728

Harvard Business Review
Joel Kurtzman, Editor
60 Harvard Way
Boston MA 02163
617-495-6800; Fax: 617-495-9933
Focus: 19G
Frequency: 6x per yr;
    Circulation: 204,000

Harvard Magazine
Christopher Reed, Managing Editor
7 Ware St
Cambridge MA 02138-4001
617-495-5746; Fax: 617-495-0324
Focus: 31-99
Frequency: 6x per yr;
    Circulation: 200,000

Health Magazine
Barbara Paulsen, Editor
301 Howard St 18th Fl
San Francisco CA 94105-2252
415-512-9100; Fax: 415-512-9600
Focus: 27-35-39-57
Frequency: 7x per yr; Circulation: 900,000

Health News & Review
Cheryl Hirsch, Editor
Keats Publishing Inc
27 Pine St
New Canaan CT 06840-5409
203-966-8721; 800-858-7014;
    Fax: 203-972-3991
Focus: 27-39H-53
Frequency: Quarterly; Circulation: 150,000

Health Pages
Martin Schneider, Publisher/Editor
135 Fifth Ave 7th Fl
New York NY 10010-7101
212-505-0103; Fax: 212-505-2546
Focus: 39
Frequency: 3x per yr; Circulation: 20,000

Health World Inc
Lyn Hikila, Managing Editor
1675 Rollins Rd #B3
Burlingame CA 94010-2320
415-697-4400; Fax: 415-697-7937
Focus: 27-39
Frequency: 6x per yr;
    Circulation: 100,000

Healthline
Laurie Marie Kurgas, Managing Editor
830 Menlo Ave #100
Menlo Park CA 94025
415-325-6457; Fax: 415-322-2436
Focus: 27-39-57 (Nutrition, fitness, and
    self-help)
Frequency: Monthly; Circulation: 14,000

Healthy Kids
Judith Nolte, Editor
Cahners Publications
249 W 17th St
New York NY 10016-6999
212-645-0067; Fax: 212-463-6620
Focus: 21-31-39
Frequency: 6x per yr;
    Circulation: 1,500,000

Heart & Soul
Teresa Ridley, Managing Editor
Rodale Press
733 Third Ave 15th Fl
New York NY 10017
212-697-2040; Fax: 212-338-9144
Focus: 39-40-49B(health/lifestyle guide for
    African-Americans)
Frequency: 6x per yr;
    Circulation: 260,000

Heartland USA
Brad Pearson, Editor
UST Publishing
100 W Putnam Ave
Greenwich CT 06830-5342
203-622-3456; Fax: 203-863-5258
Focus: 99 (blue-collar men's mag/small town)
Frequency: 5x per yr;
   Circulation: 1,100,000

Hemispheres Magazine
Sheryl Krieger Miller, Managing Editor
Pace Communications
1301 Carolina St
Greensboro NC 27401-1001
919-378-6065; Fax: 919-275-2864
Focus: 17-19-27-39-40-71-99
3-4 excerpts United Airlines
Frequency: Monthly; Circulation: 500,000

The Herb Companion
Dave Merrill, Editor
Interweave Press
201 E Fourth St
Loveland CO 80537-5601
970-669-7672; 800-272-2193;
   Fax: 970-667-8317
Focus: 43G(herbs)
Frequency: 6x per yr; Circulation: 37,000

Herb Quarterly
Linda Sparrowe, Editor
PO Box 689
San Anselmo CA 94979-0689
415-455-9540; Fax: 415-455-9541
Focus: 27-43G(herbs)
Frequency: Quarterly; Circulation: 40,000

High Country News
Betsy Marston, Editor
High Country Foundation
119 Grand Ave PO Box 1090
Paonia CO 81428
303-527-4898
Focus: 51N-51E
Frequency: 24; Circulation: 15,000

High Performance Mopar
Jeff Bauer, Book Editor
CSK Publishing Co Inc
299 Market St
Saddle Brook NJ 07663-5312
201-712-9300; Fax: 201-712-9899
Focus: 16A
Frequency: 8x per yr; Circulation: 49,000

High Performance Pontiac
Peter Easton, Managing Editor
CSK Publishing Co Inc
299 Market St
Saddle Brook NJ 07663-5312
201-712-9300; Fax: 201-712-9899
Focus: 16A
Frequency: 6x per yr; Circulation: 44,000

The Highlander
Angus J Ray Jr, Editor
202 S Cook St #214
Barrington IL 60010-4351
708-382-1035; Fax: 708-382-0322
Focus: 44E(Scottish heritage)
Frequency: 6x per yr; Circulation: 42,000

Highlights for Children
Kent L Brown Jr, Editor
803 Church St
Honesdale PA 18431-1824
717-253-1080; Fax: 717-253-0179
Focus: 17-21-29-51-67-76
Ages 2-12
Frequency: Monthly;
   Circulation: 3,000,000

Highways
Ron Epstein, Editor
TL Enterprises Inc
3601 Calle Tecate
Camarillo CA 93012-5040
805-389-0300; Fax: 805-389-0454
Focus: 16-71
Frequency: Monthly; Circulation: 910,000

Hinduism Today
Rev Palaniswami, Editor
107 Kaholalele Rd
Kapaa HI 96746-9304
808-822-7032; Fax: 808-822-4351
Focus: 44A-53-54-63E(Hinduism)
Frequency: Monthly; Circulation: 250,000

Hispanic
Melanie Cole, Managing Editor
98 San Jacinto #1150
Austin TX 78701-4039
512-476-5599; Fax: 512-320-1942
Focus: 49H
Frequency: Monthly; Circulation: 255,000

Hispanic Business
Hector Cantu, Managing Editor
360 S Hope Ave #300C
Santa Barbara CA 93105-4017
805-682-5843; Fax: 805-687-4546
Focus: 19-49H
Frequency: Monthly; Circulation: 170,000

Hispanic USA
Maggie Aguilar, Book Review Editor
51 W Erie St
Chicago IL 60610
312-943-1065; Fax: 312-977-0097
Focus: 19-49H-99
Frequency: Monthly; Circulation: 119,000

Historic Traveler
John Stanchak, Editor
6405 Flank Dr
PO Box 8200
Harrisburg PA 17105-8200
717-657-9555; Fax: 717-657-9526
Focus: 41A-71
Frequency: 6x per yr; Circulation: N/A

Hockey Illustrated
Stephen Ciacciarelli, Editor
Tilden Publications
233 Park Ave S
New York NY 10003
212-980-3500; Fax: 212-780-3555
Focus: 69(hockey)
Frequency: 8x per yr; Circulation: 125,000

Holistic Living
Meredith Gould Ruch, Editor
360 Nassau St
Princeton NJ 08540
609-924-8711; Fax: 609-924-3836
Focus: 53-54
Frequency: 6x per yr; Circulation: 22,000

Home & Away
Brian Nichol, Editor
910 N 96th St
PO Box 3535
Omaha NE 68103
402-390-1000; Fax: 402-390-0539
Focus: 71D-99 (for AAA members)
Frequency: 6x per yr;
   Circulation: 2,150,000

Home Cooking
Judi Merkel, Editor
House of White Birches
306 East Parr Rd
Berne IN 46711
219-589-8741; Fax: 219-589-8093
Focus: 27
Frequency: Monthly; Circulation: 60,000

Home Furniture
Tim Schreiner, Editor
Taunton Press
63 S Main St PO
Newton CT 06470-2355
203-426-8171; Fax: 203-426-3434
Focus: 43D-43H(home and furnishing)
Frequency: 6x per yr;
   Circulation: 225,000

Home Garden Magazine
Ann Maine, Managing Editor
Meredith Corp
1716 Locust St
Des Moines IA 50309-3038
515-284-3000; Fax: 515-284-2083
Focus: 29H-43G-51
Frequency: 6x per yr;
   Circulation: 400,000

Home Magazine
Gale Steves, Editor-in-Chief
(212-767-6810)
Hachette Filipacchi Magazines
1633 Broadway 44th Fl
New York NY 10019-6708
212-767-6000; Fax: 212-489-4576
Focus: 19H-43
Frequency: Monthly;
   Circulation: 1,000,000

Home Mechanix
Michael Chotiner, Editor-in-Chief
Times Mirror Magazines
2 Park Ave
New York NY 10016-5603
212-779-5000; Fax: 212-725-3281
Focus: 43-99
Frequency: 10x per yr;
   Circulation: 1,000,000

Home Office Computing
Dennis Eskow, Editor-in-Chief
411 Lafayette St
New York NY 10003
212-505-3580; 800-866-5821;
   Fax: 212-505-4256
Focus: 19M-23C-23E
Frequency: Monthly; Circulation: 450,000

Home PC
Amy Lipton, Exec Editor (516-562-5087)
CMP Publications
600 Community Dr
Manhasset NY 11030
516-532-7673; Fax: 516-562-7007
Focus: 23(computers for the home)
Frequency: Monthly; Circulation: 350,000

Homecoming Magazine
Cleve Dye III, Managing Editor
Tinsley-Metters Publ Co
100 Bridge St
Hampton VA 23669
804-722-1300; Fax: 804-723-8727
Focus: 19-19C-28-39-49B-69
Networking Black professionals
Frequency: 6x per yr; Circulation: 40,000

Homes Magazine
Rise Levy, Editor
178 Main St
Unionville ON Canada L3R 2G9
905-479-4663; 800-363-4663;
   Fax: 905-479-4482
Focus: 43H
Frequency: 8x per yr; Circulation: 100,000

Honolulu
John Heckathorn, Editor
36 Merchant St
Honolulu HI 96813-4311
808-524-7400; Fax: 808-531-2306
Focus: 11-14-19-33-61(Honolulu HI)-69
Frequency: Monthly; Circulation: 30,000

Hope Magazine
John Wilson, Editor
WoodenBoat Publications
PO Box 78
Brooklin ME 04616
207-359-4651; Fax: 207-359-8920
Focus: 99(inspirational without religious
   or political affiliations)
Frequency: 6x per yr; Circulation: 75,000

Horse & Horseman Magazine
Jack Lewis, Editor
34249 Camino Capistrano
Capistrano Beach CA 92624-1156
714-493-2101; Fax: 714-240-8680
Focus: 15-69R
Horses & horseback riding
Frequency: Monthly; Circulation: 90,000

Horse & Rider
Juli Thorson, Editor
6405 Flank Dr
PO Box 8200
Harrisburg PA 17105-8200
717-657-9555; Fax: 717-657-9526
Focus: 15-69R(horseback riding-western
   style)
Frequency: Monthly; Circulation: 165,000

Horse Illustrated
Audrey Pavia, Editor
Fancy Publications Inc
PO Box 6050
Mission Viejo CA 92690-6050
714-855-8822; Fax: 714-855-3045
Focus: 15(horses)-69R
Frequency: Monthly; Circulation: 120,000

HorsePlay
Cordelia Doucet, Editor
11 Park Ave
Gaithersburg MD 20877-2915
301-840-1866; Fax: 301-840-5722
Focus: 15
Frequency: Monthly; Circulation: 46,000

Horticulture
Thomas Cooper, Editor
98 N Washington St
Boston MA 02114-1913
617-742-5600; Fax: 617-367-6364
Focus: 43G
Frequency: 10x per yr;
   Circulation: 340,000

Hot Bike
John Morgan, Editor
McMullen & Yee Publishing Inc
774 South Placentia
Placentia CA 92670-6832
714-572-2255; Fax: 714-572-1864
Focus: 16-24
Frequency: Monthly; Circulation: 71,000

Hot Boat
Kevin Spaise, Editor
8484 Wilshire Blvd
Beverly Hills CA 90210-5515
213-651-5400; Fax: 310-274-7985
Focus: 70N
Frequency: Monthly; Circulation: N/A

Hot Rod Magazine
Drew Hardin, Editor
Petersen Publishing
6420 Wilshire Blvd
Los Angeles CA 90048-4901
213-782-2000; Fax: 213-782-2263
Focus: 16A
Frequency: Monthly; Circulation: 800,000

House Beautiful
Margaret Kennedy, Editor
Hearst Corp
1700 Broadway
New York NY 10019-5905
212-903-5000; Fax: 212-765-8292
Focus: 28-29-43-99
Frequency: Monthly; Circulation: 950,000

HousePlant Magazine
James Richards, Book Review Editor
RR 1 Box 271-2
Elkins WV 26241-9801
304-636-1212; 800-892-7594;
   Fax: 304-636-9723
Focus: 43G(house plants/indoor
   gardening)
Frequency: 6x per yr; Circulation: 50,000

Houston Business Journal
Bill Schadewald, Editor
1 West Loop S #650
Houston TX 77027-9009
713-688-8811; Fax: 713-963-0482
Focus: 19-61(Houston TX)
Frequency: Weekly; Circulation: 25,000

Houston Health & Fitness Sports
Diane Stafford, Editor
1900 Yorketown #670
Houston TX 77056-4115
713-552-9991; Fax: 713-552-9997
Focus: 27-39-69
Frequency: Monthly; Circulation: 85,000

Houston Metropolitan
Maria Moss, Managing Editor
5615 Kirby Dr #600
Houston TX 77005-2449
713-524-3000; Fax: 713-524-8213
Focus: 19-27-40-39-43-43-61(TX)-71
Frequency: Monthly; Circulation: 327,000

The Humanist
Fred Edwards, Editor
American Humanist Assn
7 Harwood Dr
Amherst NY 14226-4610
716-839-5080; 800-743-6646;
   Fax: 716-839-5079
Focus: 13-55-63-65-67
Frequency: 6x per yr; Circulation: 16,000

Humpty Dumpty's Magazine
Christine French Clark, Editor
1100 Waterway Blvd
Indianapolis IN 46202-2156
317-636-8881; Fax: 317-637-0126
Focus: 21(4-6yrs)-27-29-33-39-76-95
Frequency: 8x per yr; Circulation: 264,000

I Love Cats
Lisa Sheets, Editor
Grass Roots Publishing Co Inc
950 3rd Ave
New York NY 10022-2705
212-888-1855; Fax: 212-838-8420
Focus: 15(cats)
Frequency: 6x per yr; Circulation: 164,000

Illinois Game & Fish
Bill Hartlage, Editor
2250 Newmarket Pky #110
Marietta GA 30067-8749
770-953-9222; Fax: 770-933-9510
Focus: 15-51-61(IL)-69
Frequency: Monthly; Circulation: N/A

In Business
Nora and Jerome Goldstein, Editors
JG Press
419 State Ave
Emmaus PA 18049-3025
610-967-4135; Fax: 610-967-3015
Focus: 19-51E(environmental
   entrepreneuring)
Frequency: 6x per yr; Circulation: 7,000

In Fashion
Brandon Holly, Editor
29 W 38th St 15th Fl
New York NY 10018-5504
212-768-8450; Fax: 212-768-8472
Focus: 11-14-17-33-40
Frequency: Quarterly; Circulation: 200,000

In These Times
James Weinstein, Editor/Publisher
Institute for Public Affairs
2040 N Milwaukee Ave 2nd Fl
Chicago IL 60647-4002
312-772-0100; 800-827-0270;
   Fax: 312-772-4180
Focus: 31E(liberal, alternative perspective)
Frequency: Biweekly; Circulation: 60,000

In-Fisherman
Steve Quinn, Editor
PO Box 999
Brainerd MN 56401-0999
218-829-1648; 800-441-1740;
   Fax: 218-829-3091
Focus: 15(fish)-51-69(fishing)
Frequency: N/A; Circulation: 320,000

In-Line
Natalie Kurylko, Managing Editor
Sports & Fitness Publishing
2025 Pearl St
Boulder CO 80302
303-440-5111; Fax: 303-440-331
Focus: 69(skating)
Frequency: 9x per yr; Circulation: 60,000

Inc Magazine
John Case, Sr Writer
38 Commercial Wharf
Boston MA 02110
617-248-8000
Focus: 19
Frequency: Monthly; Circulation: 786,000

Income Plus
Donna Clapp, Editor
Opportunity Associates
73 Spring St #303
New York NY 10012
212-925-3180; Fax: 212-925-3612
Focus: 19M-19O-19S
Frequency: Monthly; Circulation: 200,000

Independent Business
Daniel Kehrer, Editor
Group 4 Communications
125 Auburn Ct #100
Thousand Oaks CA 91362-3617
805-496-6156; Fax: 805-496-5469
Focus: 19M-19S
Frequency: 6x per yr; Circulation: 613,000

Independent Living
Anne Kelly, Editor
150 Motor Pky #420
Hauppauge NY 11788-5108
516-273-0066; Fax: 516-273-8936
Focus: 39D
Frequency: 6x per yr; Circulation: 23,000

Indiana Business
Steve Kaeble, Editor
1200 Waterway Blvd
Indianapolis IN 46202-2157
317-692-1200; Fax: 317-692-4250
Focus: 19-61(IN)
Frequency: Monthly; Circulation: 35,000

Indiana Game & Fish
Ken Freel, Editor
2250 Newmarket Pky #110
Marietta GA 30067-8749
770-953-9222; Fax: 770-933-9510
Focus: 15-51-61(IN)-69
Frequency: Monthly; Circulation: N/A

Indiana Review
Gretchen Knapp, Editor
Indiana University
316 N Jordan
Bloomington IN 47405
818-855-3439
Focus: 47-75-95-99
Frequency: 2x per yr; Circulation: 1,000

The Indigo Sun
Carol Money, Co-Owner/Editor
Aquarian Publications
1200 Post Oak Blvd #341
Houston TX 77056
713-622-2108; 800-640-5191;
    Fax: 713-622-2060
Focus: 99
Frequency: Monthly; Circulation: 20,000

Individual Investor
Jonathan Steinberg, Editor-in-Chief
333 7th Ave 5th Fl
New York NY 10001-5004
212-843-2777; Fax: 212-843-2789
Focus: 19I
Frequency: Monthly; Circulation: 160,000

Indy's Child
Mary Winne-Cox, Editor
8900 Keystone Crossing #538
Indianapolis IN 46240-2130
317-843-1494; Fax: 317-574-3233
Focus: 21-31-35-76
Frequency: Monthly; Circulation: 70,000

Inside Sports
Ken Leiker, Editor
Century Publishing Co
990 Grove St
Evanston IL 60201-4370
708-491-6440; Fax: 708-491-6955
Focus: 69
Frequency: Monthly; Circulation: 692,000

Inside Triathlon
Chris Newbound, Editor
1830 N 55th St
Boulder CO 80301
303-440-0601; Fax: 303-444-6788
Focus: 69
Frequency: Monthly; Circulation: 24,000

Insight Magazine
Kirk Oberfeld, Managing Editor
3600 New York Ave NE
Washington DC 20002-1947
202-636-8800; Fax: 202-529-2484
Focus: 19-97-99
Frequency: 52; Circulation: 200,000

InSights
John Robbins, Editor
National Rifle Assn
11250 Waples Mill Rd
Fairfax VA 22030-7400
703-267-1586; Fax: 703-267-3994
Focus: 69H(for juniors)
Frequency: Monthly; Circulation: 60,000

InStyle
Martha Nelson, Managing Editor
Time-Life Bldg
1271 Ave of the Americas
New York NY 10020-1303
212-522-1212; Fax: 212-522-0051
Focus: 14-17-33-40F-99(celeb lifestyle
    mag for younger audiences)
Frequency: Monthly; Circulation: N/A

Internet World
David Dean, Book Review Editor
Mecklermedia Corp
20 Ketcham St
Westport CT 06880
203-226-6967; Fax: 203-454-5840;
    E-Mail: info@mecklermedia.com
Focus: 23C
Frequency: Monthly; Circulation: 280,000

Inventors' Digest
Joanne Hayes, Editor
4850 Galley Rd #209
Colorado Springs CO 80915
719-573-4540; Fax: 719-573-4679
Focus: 29
Frequency: 6x per yr; Circulation: 10,000

Investor's Business Daily
Wesley F Mann, Editor (310-448-6816)
1941 Armacost Ave
Los Angeles CA 90025-5210
310-448-6000; Fax: 310-577-7350
Focus: 19
Frequency: 99; Circulation: 180,000

Iowa Game & Fish
Bill Hartlage, Editor
Game & Fish Publications
2250 Newmarket Pky #110
Marietta GA 30067-8749
770-953-9222; Fax: 770-933-9510
Focus: 15-51-61(IA)-69
Frequency: Monthly; Circulation: N/A

Irish America Magazine
Patricia Harty, Editor-in-Chief
432 Park Ave S #1503
New York NY 10016-8013
212-725-2993; Fax: 212-779-1198
Focus: 49(Irish American)-99
Frequency: 6x per yr; Circulation: 85,000

Isaac Asimov Science Fiction
Gardner Dozois, Editor
Dell Magazines
1540 Broadway 9th Fl
New York NY 10036-4039
212-782-8532; Fax: 212-782-8338
Focus: 86
Frequency: 13x per yr; Circulation: 77,000

Island Parent Magazine
Selinde Krayenhoff, Editor
941 Kings Rd
Victoria BC Canada V8T 1W7
604-388-6905; Fax: 604-388-4391
Focus: 21-31-35-76
Frequency: Monthly; Circulation: 30,000

Islands Magazine
Joan Tappen, Editor-in-Chief
Islands Publishing
3886 State St
Santa Barbara CA 93105
805-682-7177; Fax: 805-569-0349
Focus: 71
Frequency: 6x per yr;
    Circulation: 180,000

J

Jack & Jill
Danny Lee, Editor-in-Chief
1100 Waterway Blvd
Indianapolis IN 46202-2156
317-636-8881; Fax: 317-637-0126
Focus: 21(7-10yrs)-27-29-33-39
Frequency: 8x per yr; Circulation: 343,000

JAM!!! (Junior America Magazine)
Evelyn Gay, Publisher
Children's Education Project
250 West 57th St #1527-130
New York NY 10107
212-332-9675;
Focus: 21-31E-49(hip-hop education mag
    for kids)
Frequency: N/A; Circulation: N/A

The James White Review
Bayne Holley, Editor
Butler Corner Sta
PO Box 3356
Minneapolis MN 55403
612-339-8317
Focus: 13-37-83-95
Frequency: Quarterly; Circulation: 5,000

Jaycees Magazine
Shelley Spong, Editor
4 West 21st St
Tulsa OK 74114-1114
918-584-2481; 800-331-3248;
  Fax: 918-584-4422
Focus: 23-67-99(future)
Frequency: Quarterly; Circulation: 234,000

Jazz Times Magazine
Mike Joyce, Managing Editor
7961 Eastern Ave #303
Silver Springs MD 20910-4833
301-588-4114; Fax: 301-588-5531
Focus: 14M
Frequency: 10x per yr; Circulation: 75,000

Jet Magazine
Malcolm West, Managing Editor
Johnson Publishing Co Inc
820 S Michigan Ave
Chicago IL 60605-2103
312-322-9200; Fax: 312-322-0951
Focus: 49-99
Frequency: Weekly; Circulation: 806,000

Jewish Action
Charlotte Friedland, Editor-in-Chief
333 7th Ave 18th Fl
New York NY 10001-5004
212-563-4000; Fax: 212-564-9058
Focus: 49O(Jewish)
Frequency: Quarterly; Circulation: 80,000

Jewish Journal
Gene Lichtenstein, Editor
3660 Wilshire Blvd #204
Los Angeles CA 90010
213-738-7778; Fax: 213-386-9501
Focus: 63J
Frequency: Weekly; Circulation: 77,000

Jive
Tonia Shakespeare, Editor
Sterling-McFadden Partnership
233 Park Ave S
New York NY 10003-1606
212-780-3500; Fax: 212-780-3555
Focus: 35R-39-40-49B-85
Frequency: Monthly; Circulation: 35,000

Journal of Italian Food & Wine
Robert DiLallo, Editor
609 W 114th St #77
New York NY 10025-7912
212-316-3026
Focus: 27
Frequency: 6x per yr; Circulation: 42,000

Journal of Popular Film & TV
Lisa Culp-Neikirk, Managing Editor
Heldref Publications
1319 18th St NW
Washington DC 20036-1802
202-296-6267; 800-365-9753;
  Fax: 202-296-5149
Focus: 33M-33T-57
Frequency: Quarterly; Circulation: 800

Journalism Quarterly
Dominic Lasorsa, Book Review Editor
Univ of South Carolina
1621 College St
Columbia SC 29208-0251
803-777-2005; Fax: 803-777-4728
Focus: 56(journalism)
Frequency: Quarterly; Circulation: 5,000

Junior Scholastic
Lee Baier, Editor
Scholastic Inc
555 Broadway
New York NY 10012-3919
212-343-6295; Fax: 212-343-6333
Focus: 31-65S-71G-97(grades 6-8)
Frequency: 18x per yr;
  Circulation: 585,000

Just CrossStitch Magazine
Lorna Reeves, Managing Editor
Symbol of Excellence Publ
405 Riverhills Business Park
Birmingham AL 35242
205-995-8860; Fax: 205-995-8428
Focus: 29C(cross stitch)
Frequency: 6x per yr; Circulation: 200,000

Kentucky Game & Fish
Bill Hartlage, Editor
2250 Newmarket Pky #110
Marietta GA 30067-8749
770-953-9222; Fax: 770-933-9510
Focus: 15-51-61(KY)-69
Frequency: Monthly; Circulation: N/A

KGB Magazine
Lukas Barr and Sean Gullette, Co-Editors
KGB Media Inc
133 Bowery
New York NY 10002-4906
212-343-1512; Fax: 212-343-1315
Focus: 14M-35-40F-99
Frequency: 6x per yr; Circulation: 25,000

Kid City
Maureen Hunter-Bone, Editor-in-Chief
Children's Television Workshop
1 Lincoln Plz
New York NY 10023-7129
212-875-6505; Fax: 212-875-6113
Focus: 21-99
Frequency: 10x per yr;
  Circulation: 285,000

Kid's World
Morgan Kopaska-Merkel, Editor
1300 Kicker Rd
Tuscaloosa AL 35404
Focus: 21(ages 2 70 17)
Frequency: N/A; Circulation: 225,000

Kiplinger's Personal Finance
Mark Solheim, Managing Editor
1729 H St NW
Washington DC 20006-3904
202-887-6400; 800-544-0155;
  Fax: 202-331-1206
Focus: 19-25-31-39-55(taxes)-69
Frequency: Monthly;
  Circulation: 1,000,000

Kit Car Illustrated
Jeff Holifield, Editor
McMullen & Yee Publishing Inc
774 South Placentia Ave
Placentia CA 92670-6832
714-572-2255; Fax: 714-572-1864
Focus: 16-24
Frequency: 6x per yr; Circulation: 72,700

Kitplanes
David Martin, Editor
Fancy Publications Inc
PO Box 6050
Mission Viejo CA 92690-6050
714-855-8822; Fax: 714-855-3045
Focus: 29H-70A
Frequency: Monthly; Circulation: 65,000

Kiwanis Magazine
Chuck Jonak, Managing Editor
Kiwanis International
3636 Woodview Ter
Indianapolis IN 46268-1168
317-875-8755; 800-549-2647;
  Fax: 317-879-0204
Focus: 99
Frequency: 10x per yr;
  Circulation: 280,000

LA Parent
David Jamieson, Managing Editor
PO Box 3204
Burbank CA 91504-3204
818-846-0400; Fax: 818-841-4380
Focus: 21-31-35-76
Frequency: Monthly; Circulation: 200,000

Ladies' Home Journal
Carolyn Noyes, Managing Editor
100 Park Ave
New York NY 10017-5516
212-557-6600; Fax: 212-455-1333
Focus: 21-31-35-57-76
Frequency: Monthly;
  Circulation: 5,000,000

Lady's Circle
Anne DiSimone, Cookbook Editor
Mary Bemis, Editor
Lopez Publications
105 E 35th St
New York NY 10016-3877
212-689-3933
Focus: 27
Frequency: 6x per yr; Circulation: 100,000

Ladybug
Marianne Carus, Editor-in-Chief
315 Fifth St
Peru IL 61354-2859
815-223-2520; Fax: 815-224-6675
Focus: 21-31(like Cricket, but for ages 2-6)
Frequency: Monthly; Circulation: 140,00

Lake Superior Magazine
Hugh Bishop, Managing Editor
325 Lake Ave S #600
Duluth MN 55802-2323
218-722-5002; Fax: 218-722-4096
Focus: 61(MN/WI)-70-71
Frequency: 6x per yr; Circulation: 20,000

Lambda Book Report
Jim Marks, Sr Editor
Lambda Rising Inc
1625 Connecticut Ave NW
Washington DC 20009-1013
202-462-7924; 800-621-6969;
　Fax: 202-462-7257
Focus: 37-73
Frequency: 6x per yr; Circulation: 11,000

LAN Times
Leonard Heymann, Editor-in-Chief
McGraw-Hill Inc
1900 O'Farrell St #200
San Mateo CA 94403-1311
415-513-6800; Fax: 415-513-6819
Focus: 23C(local area networks)
Frequency: 25x per yr; Circulation: 180,000

Latina Magazine
Patricia Duarte, Editor
1500 Broadway 6th Fl
New York NY 10036
212-642-0201
Focus: 49H-73
Ages 20-44 (Hispanic women)
Frequency: 6x per yr; Circulation: N/A

Latina Style
Anna Maria Arias, Editor
955 L'Enfant Plz North SW #4000
Washington DC 20024
800-651-8083
Focus: 49H-73
Written in English
Frequency: 6x per yr; Circulation: N/A

The Law Works
Douglas Dean, Editor
Omega Communications
1935 S Plum Grove Rd #158
Palatine IL 60067
708-705-7194; Fax: 708-705-7112
Focus: 19L-55L(attorneys/patent agents/others in the legal field)
Frequency: Monthly; Circulation: 16,000

Lawn & Garden
Carla Waldemar, Editor-in-Chief
Publication Partners
4151 Knob Dr
St Paul MN 55122-1876
612-452-0571; 800-728-3213;
　Fax: 612-454-5791
Focus: 43G
Frequency: 2x per yr; Circulation: 140,000

Lefthanded Magazine
Kim Kipers, Managing Editor
PO Box 8249
Topeka KS 66608-0249
913-234-2177
Focus: 99(left-hander information)
Frequency: 6x per yr; Circulation: 30,000

Let's Live
Patty Padilla-Gallagher, Editor
444 n Larchmont Blvd
Los Angeles CA 90004-3030
213-469-3901; Fax: 213-469-9597
Focus: 39-53
Frequency: Monthly; Circulation: 950,000

Let's Talk About Doll Making
Jim Winer, Managing Editor
300 Nancy Dr
Point Pleasant NJ 08742
908-899-0804; Fax: 908-714-3906;
　E-Mail: firebird@exit109.com
Focus: 29(doll making)
Frequency: Quarterly; Circulation: 2,000

Libido
Marianna Beck, Editor/Publisher
5318 N Paulina St
Chicago IL 60640-2020
312-275-0842; 800-495-1988;
　Fax: 312-275-0752
Focus: 35S-37-39-40-57(sex, romance, relationships, and pleasures)
Frequency: Quarterly; Circulation: N/A

Library Journal
Barbara Hoffert, Managing Editor
The Book Review Section
249 West 17th St
New York NY 10011-5301
212-645-0067; Fax: 212-463-6734
Focus: 11-47-54-75-76-83-90-95-99
Frequency: 20x per yr; Circulation: 24,000

Life Magazine
Daniel Okrent, Managing Editor
Time Inc Time-Life Bldg
Rockefeller Ctr
New York NY 10020
212-484-8000; Fax: 212-522-0304
Focus: 17-99
Frequency: Monthly; Circulation: 1,500,00

The Light Connection
Steve Hays, Editor/Publisher
914 S Santa Fe Ave L
Vista CA 92084-6202
619-631-1177; Fax: 619-631-1155
Focus: 13-39-51-53-54
Frequency: Monthly; Circulation: 50,000

Lilith Magazine
Susan Weidman Schneider, Editor-in-Chief
250 West 57th St #2432
New York NY 10107-0001
212-757-0818; Fax: 212-757-5705
Focus: 63J-73
Frequency: Quarterly; Circulation: 10

Link Magazine
Charles Laughlin, Editor (312-527-6080)
Merchandise Mart #2000
200 World Trade Ctr
Chicago IL 60654-1003
312-527-7426; Fax: 312-527-6240
Focus: 19M
Frequency: Monthly; Circulation: N/A

Link-Up
Lauree Padgett, Book Review Editor
Information Today Inc
143 Old Marlton Pike
Medford Lakes NJ 08055-8750
609-654-6266; Fax: 609-654-4309
Focus: 23C(online services for business/personal/education)
Also BBSs and CD-ROMs
Frequency: 6x per yr; Circulation: 10,000

Links
George Fuller, Managing Editor
PO Box 7628
Hilton Head Island SC 29938-7628
803-842-6200; Fax: 803-842-6233
Focus: 69(golf)
Frequency: 7x per yr; Circulation: 250,000

Linn's Stamp News
Michael Laurence, Editor/Publisher
Amos Press Inc
911 Vandemark Rd
Sidney OH 45365
513-498-0801; Fax: 513-498-0814
Focus: 29H(stamps)
Frequency: Weekly; Circulation: 71,000

The Lion
Patrick F Cannon, Managing Editor
Lions Clubs Intl
300 22nd St
Oak Brook IL 60521-8815
708-571-5466; Fax: 708-571-8890
Focus: 99
Frequency: Monthly; Circulation: 600,000

Literary Cavalcade
Cynthia Sosland, Editor
Scholastic Inc
555 Broadway
New York NY 10012
212-343-6100
Focus: 21T-31-77-81-95(grades 9-12)
Frequency: Monthly; Circulation: 270,000

Live Steam
Joe D Rice, Editor-in-Chief
2779 Aero Park Dr
Traverse City MI 49686-9101
616-946-3712; 800-773-7798;
　Fax: 616-946-3289
Focus: 29(steam engines)
Frequency: 6x per yr; Circulation: 12,000

Live!
Annie Gilbar, Editor
Ticketmaster Corp
3701 Wilshire Blvd #9
Los Angeles CA 90010
213-382-8111
Focus: 14-33(all lively arts except TV)
Frequency: Monthly; Circulation: N/A

Living Life!
Elaine Bragg, Contact
Ogilvy & Mather Direct
676 St Clair St 9th Fl
Chicago IL 60611
Fax: 312-988-2913
Focus: 39-57 (health challenges, not handicaps)
Frequency: N/A; Circulation: N/A

Llewellyn New Worlds
Krista Trempe, Editor
PO Box 64383
St Paul MN 55164-0383
612-291-1970; 800-843-6666;
　Fax: 612-291-1908
Focus: 53-54
Frequency: 6x per yr; Circulation: 135,000

Locations
Sue Khodarahmi, Managing Editor
Cadmus Custom Publishing
376 Boylston St
Boston MA 02116-3812
617-424-7700; Fax: 617-424-8905
Focus: 33M-71(location info for film/video production)
Frequency: Quarterly; Circulation: N/A

Log Home Living
Roland Sweet, Editor
4451 Brookfield Corp Dr #101
Chantilly VA 22021-1693
703-222-9411; 800-826-3893;
    Fax: 703-222-3209
Focus: 43H
Frequency: 6x per yr; Circulation: 200,000

Logos
Gordon Graham, Editor
5 Beechwood Dr
Marlow
Bucks SL7 2DH England
01628-477577; Fax: 01628-477577
Focus: 56P
Frequency: Monthly; Circulation: N/A

Long Island Business News
Paul Townsend, Editor-in-Chief
2150 Smithtown Ave
Ronkonkoma NY 11779-7348
516-737-1700; Fax: 516-737-1890
Focus: 19-61(NY)
Frequency: Weekly; Circulation: 12,000

Long Island Parenting News
Andrew Elias, Managing Editor
2-12 W Park Ave
Long Beach NY 11561-2025
516-889-5510; Fax: 516-889-5513
Focus: 21-31-35-76
Frequency: Monthly; Circulation: 50,000

Look Japan
Kunio Nishimura, Exec Editor-in-Chief
Look Japan Ltd
2-2 Kanda-Ogawamachi
Chiyoda-Ku, Tokyo Japan
03-3291-8951; Fax: 03-5280-8201;
    E-Mail: look@gol.com
Focus: 19-44
Frequency: Monthly; Circulation: N/A

Loose Change
Daniel R Mead, Editor/Publisher
1515 S Commerce St
Las Vegas NV 89102-2703
702-387-8750
Focus: 29(coin operated machines)
Frequency: 10x per yr; Circulation: N/A

Los Angeles Magazine
Lew Harris, Editor
1888 Century Park E #920
Los Angeles CA 90067-1713
310-557-7569; Fax: 310-557-7517
Focus: 11-14-33-61(Los Angeles CA)
Frequency: Monthly; Circulation: 175,000

Lost Treasure
Grace Michael, Managing Editor
PO Box 1589
Grove OK 74344-1589
918-786-2182; Fax: 918-786-2192
Focus: 29(lost treasures)
Frequency: Monthly; Circulation: 45,000

LottoWorld
Rich Holman, Editor
2150 Goodlette Rd #200
Naples FL 33940-4811
941-643-1677; Fax: 941-263-0809
Focus: 69G(lottery)
Frequency: Monthly; Circulation: 75,000

Lotus Notes Advisor
David Kodama, Managing Editor
Advisor Publications
4010 Morena Blvd
San Diego CA 92117
619-483-6400; 800-336-6060;
    Fax: 619-483-9851
Focus: 19-23
Frequency: 6x per yr; Circulation: N/A

Louis L'Amour Western Magazine
Elana Lore, Editor
Bantam Doubleday Dell Magazine
1540 Broadway
New York NY 10036-4039
212-782-8532; Fax: 212-782-8338
Focus: 17-41A-61(west)-88(profiles of heroes and events of the Old West)
Frequency: 6x per yr; Circulation: 200,000

Louisiana Game & Fish
Bob Borgwat, Editor
Game & Fish Publications
2250 Newmarket Pky #110
Marietta GA 30067-8749
770-953-9222; Fax: 770-933-9510
Focus: 15-51-61(LA)-69
Frequency: Monthly; Circulation: 19,000

Loving More Magazine
Ryam Nearing, Editor
Abundant Love Institute
PO Box 6306
Ocean View HI 96737
808-929-9691
Focus: 35F-35M-35R-35S(advocates polyamory)
Frequency: N/A; Circulation: N/A

The Lutheran
Edgar Trexler, Editor
ELCA
8765 W Higgins Rd
Chicago IL 60631-4101
312-380-2540; Fax: 312-330-1465
Focus: 63(Lutheran)
Frequency: Monthly; Circulation: 900,000

M

MAC Line
Brian Pomeroy, Editor
PO Box 845
Lansdowne PA 19050-0845
610-352-3622; Fax: 610-352-1047
Focus: 23C(Macintosh-how to use it in innovative ways)
Frequency: 6x per yr; Circulation: 12,000

MacHome Journal
Sandra Anderson, Editor
612 Howard St 6th Fl
San Francisco CA 94105-3905
415-957-1911; Fax: 415-882-9502
Focus: 23(MacIntosh consumers)
Frequency: Monthly; Circulation: N/A

MacUser
Cheryl England, Book Review Editor
Ziff-Davis
950 Tower Ln 18th Fl
Foster City CA 94404
415-378-5600; Fax: 415-378-5616
Focus: 23(Macintosh)
Frequency: Monthly; Circulation: 444,000

MacWeek
Brenda Benner, Managing Editor
Ziff-Davis Publishing
301 Howard St 15th Fl
San Francisco CA 94105
415-243-3500; Fax: 415-243-3651;
    E-Mail: macweek@macweek.ziff.com
Focus: 23(Macintosh)
Frequency: 48x per yr;
    Circulation: 951,000

MacWorld
Charles Barrett, Managing Editor
501 2nd St #600
San Francisco CA 94107-1431
415-243-0505; 800-888-8622;
    Fax: 415-442-0766
Focus: 23(MacIntosh)
Frequency: Monthly; Circulation: 525,000

Mademoiselle
Elizabeth Crow, Editor-in-Chief
Conde Nast Publications
350 Madison Ave
New York NY 10017-3704
212-880-8800; Fax: 212-880-8289
Focus: 99
Frequency: Monthly;
    Circulation: 1,178,000

Magical Blend
Michael Peter Langevin, Editor
PO Box 600
Chico CA 95927-0600
916-893-9037; E-Mail: magical@crl.com
Focus: 53-54
Frequency: Quarterly; Circulation: 50,000

Mailing & Shipping Technology
Ronald Brent, Editor
RB Publishing Co
2701 East Washington Ave
Madison WI 53704-5002
608-241-8777; Fax: 608-241-8666
Focus: 19-23T
Frequency: 6x per yr; Circulation: 40,000

Mainstream
Cyndi Jones, Publisher
Exploding Myths Inc
2973 Beech St
San Diego CA 92102-1529
619-234-3138
Focus: 19C-39D-55(disabled activism)
Frequency: 10x per yr; Circulation: 19,000

Manage Magazine
Douglas Shaw, Editor
National Management Assn
2210 Arbor Blvd
Dayton OH 45439-1506
513-294-0421; Fax: 513-294-2374
Focus: 19G
Frequency: Quarterly; Circulation: 65,000

Management Accounting
Kathy Williams, Editor
10 Paragon Dr
Montvale NJ 07645-1718
201-573-9000; Fax: 201-573-0639
Focus: 19A-19G-19I-23C
Frequency: Monthly; Circulation: 95,000

Manhattan Magazine
Rick Bard, Editor/Publisher
Bard Communications Inc
330 West 56th St #3G
New York NY 10019-4248
212-265-7970; Fax: 212-265-8052
Focus: 11-14-33-51-61(New York NY)-99
Frequency: Quarterly; Circulation: 50,000

Many Hands
Polly Baumer, Editor/Publisher
129 Main St
Northampton MA 01060
413-586-5037; Fax: 413-585-9036
Focus: 53-54
Frequency: Quarterly; Circulation: 30,000

Markair Magazine
Kathy Bachman, Sr Editor
Summit Publishing
9123 SE St Helens St #280
Clackamus OR 97015
503-655-4373; Fax: 503-557-3809
Focus: 19-61-71-99
Frequency: 6x per yr; Circulation: 27,000

Marriage Partnership
Ron Lee, Editor
465 Gundersen Dr
Carol Stream IL 60188-2415
708-260-6200; Fax: 708-260-0114
Focus: 35-63
Frequency: Quarterly; Circulation: 60,000

Martha Stewart Living
Martha Stewart, Editor-in-Chief
20 West 43rd St 24th Fl
New York NY 10036
212-522-1212; Fax: 212-522-7815
Focus: 43-71-33
Frequency: 6x per yr;
    Circulation: 1,200,000

Massachusetts Review
Mary Heath, Co-Editor
Memorial Hall
Univ of Massachusetts
Amherst MA 01003
413-545-2689
Focus: 11-47-55-75-90-95
Frequency: Quarterly; Circulation: 2,000

Mast
Ronald Brent, Editor
RB Publishing Co
2701 E Washington Ave
Madison WI 53704
608-241-8777; Fax: 608-241-8666
Focus: 19M(mailing and fulfillment)
Frequency: 6x per yr; Circulation: N/A

McCall's
Jane Farrell, Deputy/Book Editor
110 Fifth Ave
New York NY 10011
212-463-1000; Fax: 212-463-1403
Focus: 27-29-35-39-73-75-99
Frequency: Monthly;
    Circulation: 4,844,000

The McGuffey Writer
Janet Kretschmer, Children's Editor
5128 Westgate Dr
Oxford OH 45056
Focus: 21(ages 5 to 18)
Frequency: N/A; Circulation: N/A

Memphis Flyer
Leonard Gill, Book Review Editor
460 Tennessee St
Memphis TN 38103-4418
901-521-9000; Fax: 901-521-0129
Focus: 61(South)-99
Frequency: Weekly; Circulation: 50,000

Men's Fitness
Jeff Ducia, Managing Editor
21100 Erwin St
Woodland Hills CA 91367-3712
818-884-6800; Fax: 818-704-5734
Focus: 69(health and exercise)
Frequency: Monthly; Circulation: 250,000

Men's Journal
John Rasmus, Editor
Wenner Media
1290 Ave of the Americas
New York NY 10104-0101
212-484-1616; Fax: 212-767-8205
Focus: 11-14-17-40-55-99-71
Frequency: 10x per yr;
    Circulation: 310,000

Men's Perspectives
Trevor Miller, Editor
Metropolis Publishing
5670 Wilshire Blvd #1240
Los Angeles CA 90036
213-954-9100; Fax: 213-954-9520
Focus: 99
Frequency: Monthly; Circulation: 150,000

Men's Style
Marvin Bevans, Editor
Baio & Company Publishing
55 Fifth Ave 17th Fl
New York NY 10003-4301
212-924-3000; Fax: 212-924-3194
Focus: 11-14M-14T-33M-35-37-39-40F-
    43D-99 (lifestyle mag for gay men)
Frequency: Biweekly; Circulation: 104,000

Mentor: The Resource for Men
Alan Winter, Publisher
PO Box 11381
Portland OR 97211-0381
Focus: 75-86-84-85-men's issues
Submissions: 1200 words or less
Frequency: Quarterly; Circulation: N/A

Merlyn's Pen
James R Stahl, Editor
PO Box 1058
East Greenwich RI 02818
401-885-5175; 800-247-2027;
    Fax: 401-885-5222
Focus: 75(student writing only)
Frequency: Quarterly; Circulation: 24,000

Mervyn's California View
Katie Tamony, Editor
Sunset Publications Corp
80 Willow Rd
Menlo Park CA 94025
415-321-3600
Focus: 40F-43H
Frequency: Quarterly; Circulation: N/A

Messing About In Boats
Bob Hicks, Editor
29 Burley St
Wenham MA 01984
Focus: 70N(boating, especially small
    boats)
Frequency: 6x per yr; Circulation: N/A

Metlfax
Paul Miller, Editor
Huebeor Publications
29100 Aurora Rd #200
Solon OH 44139
216-248-1125; Fax: 216-248-0187
Focus: 19X-24
Frequency: Monthly; Circulation: 105

MetroKids Magazine
Nancy Lisagor, Editor-in-Chief
Kidstuff Publications Inc
1080 N Delaware Ave #702
Philadelphia PA 19125-4330
215-551-3200; Fax: 215-551-3203
Focus: 21-31-35-76
Frequency: Monthly; Circulation: 70,000

MetroParent Magazine
Jody Densmore, Editor
24567 Northwestern Hwy #150
Southfield MI 48075
810-352-0990; Fax: 810-352-5066
Focus: 21-31P-35-39-99
Frequency: N/A; Circulation: 45,000

Metropolitan Home
Lisa Higgins, Managing Editor
Hachette Filipacchi Inc
1633 Broadway
New York NY 10019-6708
212-767-6000; Fax: 212-767-5636
Focus: 12-27-28-43
Frequency: Monthly; Circulation: 600,000

Mexico Events / Mexico Update
Gabriela Flores, Editor-in-Chief
Travel Mexico Magazine Group
5838 Edison Pl
Carlsbad CA 92008-6519
619-929-0707; Fax: 619-929-0714
Focus: 44S-71F(Mexico)
Frequency: Quarterly; Circulation: 120,000

Michigan Florist
Sue Ann Stuever, Editor
5815 Executive Dr #B
Lansing MI 48911
517-394-2900; Fax: 517-394-3011
Focus: 19R-43G
Frequency: 6x per yr; Circulation: 12,000

Michigan Living
Larry Keller, Managing Editor
1 Auto Club Dr
Dearborn MI 48126
313-336-1211; Fax: 313-336-1344
Focus: 61(MI)-71
Frequency: Monthly;
    Circulation: 1,000,000

Michigan Sportsman
Dennis Schmidt, Editor
Game & Fish Publications
2250 Newmarket Pky #110
Marietta GA 30067-8749
770-953-9222; Fax: 770-933-9510
Focus: 15-51-61(MI)-69
Frequency: Monthly; Circulation: 30,000

Micro Computer Journal
Alexander Burawa, Managing Editor
CQ Communications
76 North Broadway
Hicksville NY 11801-2909
516-681-2922; Fax: 516-681-2926
Focus: 23
Frequency: 6x per yr; Circulation: 50,000

Microsoft Magazine
Jon Ganio, Editor-in-Chief
1 Microsoft Way
Redmond WA 98052-6399
206-936-8080; Fax: 206-936-7329
Focus: 23
Frequency: 6x per yr; Circulation: N/A

MicroTimes
Mary Eisenhart, Editor
3470 Buskirk Ave
Pleasant Hill CA 94523-4316
510-934-7351
Focus: 23
Frequency: Monthly; Circulation: 190,000

Microwaves & R F
Jack Browne, Editor
Penton Publishing
611 Rt 46 West
Hasbrouck Hts NJ 07604-3120
201-393-6293; Fax: 201-393-6297
Focus: 19G-19X-23T-24-44A(Japan)
Microwave/RF engineer(Jap)
Frequency: Monthly; Circulation: 61,000

Mid-Atlantic Game & Fish
Ken Freel, Editor
2250 Newmarket Pky #110
Marietta GA 30067-8749
770-953-9222; Fax: 770-933-9510
Focus: 15-51-61(Mid-Atlantic area)-69
Frequency: Monthly; Circulation: 50,000

Midwest Express Magazine
Eric Lucas, Editor
2701 First Ave #250
Seattle WA 98121-1123
206-441-5871; Fax: 206-448-6939
Focus: 19-71
Frequency: 6x per yr; Circulation: 30,000

Midwest Living
Dan Kaercher, Managing Editor
1912 Grand Ave
Des Moines IA 50309-3379
515-284-3062; Fax: 515-284-2832
Focus: 99
Frequency: 6x per yr; Circulation: 816,000

Might
David Moodie, Editor
544 2nd St
San Francisco CA 94107-1427
415-896-1528; Fax: 415-974-1216
Focus: 13-65S-99
For 20's; cultural commentary
Frequency: 6x per yr; Circulation: 30,000

Military History
C Brian Kelly, Editor
Cowles History Group
741 Miller Dr SE #D2
Leesburg VA 22075-8920
703-779-8222; Fax: 703-779-8345
Focus: 41A-48
Frequency: 6x per yr; Circulation: 231,000

Military Lifestyle
Hope M Daniels, Editor
Downey Communications Inc
4800 Montgomery Ln #710
Bethesda MD 20814-3432
301-718-7600; Fax: 301-718-7652
Focus: 48-55-70
Frequency: Monthly; Circulation: 100,000

Military Review
Patricia Dunn, Book Review Editor
US Army Command/Gen Staff Coll
290 Grant Ave
Ft Leavenworth KS 66027-1231
913-684-9327; Fax: 913-684-9328
Focus: 48-55-70
Frequency: 6x per yr; Circulation: 19,000

Milwaukee Magazine
John Fenell, Editor
312 E Buffalo St
Milwaukee WI 53202-5820
414-273-1101; Fax: 414-273-0016
Focus: 61(Milwaukee WI)-99
Frequency: Monthly; Circulation: 32,000

Mini Trucking
Steve Stillwell, Editor
McMullen & Yee Publishing Inc
774 South Placentia
Placentia CA 92670-6846
714-572-2255; Fax: 714-572-1864
Focus: 16-24
Frequency: Monthly; Circulation: N/A

Miniature Quilts
Christiane Meunier, Editor
Chitra Publications
2 Public Ave
Montrose PA 18801-1220
717-278-1984; 800-628-8244;
    Fax: 717-278-2223
Focus: 28
Frequency: Quarterly; Circulation: 110,000

Minnesota Monthly
Laurie Hertzel, Book Editor
Lumber Exchange Bldg
10 S Fifth St #1000
Minneapolis MN 55402
612-371-5800; Fax: 612-371-5801
Focus: 12-43-61(MN)-71-99
Frequency: Monthly; Circulation: 100,000

Minnesota Parent
Gail Rosenblum, Editor
Padres Publishing Inc
401 N 3rd St
Minneapolis MN 55401-1300
612-375-1203; Fax: 612-372-3782
Focus: 21-31-35-76
Frequency: Monthly; Circulation: 57,000

Minnesota Sports
Elizabeth Child, Editor
Skyway Publications
15 S 5th St #800
Minneapolis MN 55402-1013
612-375-9045; Fax: 612-375-9208
Focus: 61(MN)-69
Frequency: 11x per yr; Circulation: 43,000

Minnesota Sportsman
Dennis Schmidt, Editor
2250 Newmarket Pky #110
Marietta GA 30067-8749
770-953-9222; Fax: 770-933-9510
Focus: 15-51-61(MN)-69
Frequency: Monthly; Circulation: 40,000

Mirabella Magazine
Carolyn White, Book Review Editor
1633 Broadway
New York NY 10019
212-767-5800; Fax: 212-447-4708
Focus: 14-17-19-33-39-40-73-99
Frequency: 6x per yr; Circulation: 600,000

Mississippi Game & Fish
Bob Borgwat, Editor
Game & Fish Publications
2250 Newmarket Pky #110
Marietta GA 30067-8749
770-953-9222; Fax: 770-933-9510
Focus: 15-51-61(MS)-69
Frequency: Monthly; Circulation: 18,000

Missouri Game & Fish
Bill Hartlage, Editor
Game & Fish Publications
2250 Newmarket Pky #110
Marietta GA 30067-8749
770-953-9222; Fax: 770-933-9510
Focus: 15-51-61(MO)-69
Frequency: Monthly; Circulation: N/A

Model Builder
Richard Dowdy, Editor
34249 Camino Capistrano
Capistrano Beach CA 92624-1156
714-496-5411; Fax: 714-496-5427
Focus: 28-29H-70A(airplane model
    building)
Frequency: Monthly; Circulation: 96,000

Model Railroader
Andy Sperandeo, Editor
21027 Crossroads Cir
Waukeshaw WI 53186-4055
414-796-8776; Fax: 414-796-1142
Focus: 16R-29(models)
Frequency: Monthly; Circulation: 225,000

Modern Bride
Mary Ann Cavlin, Managing Editor
Cahners Publishing
249 W 17th St
New York NY 10011
212-645-0067; Fax: 212-337-7049
Focus: 25-35-39-57
Frequency: 6x per yr; Circulation: 353,000

Modern Drummer
Rick Van Horn, Managing Editor
870 Pompton Ave
Cedar Grove NJ 07009-1252
201-239-4140; Fax: 201-239-7139
Focus: 14M(professional drumming)
Frequency: Monthly; Circulation: 100,000

Modern Maturity
Henry Fenwick, Editor
Amer Assn of Retired People
3200 E Carson St
Lakewood CA 90712
310-496-2277; Fax: 310-496-4124
Focus: 99
Frequency: 36x per yr;
    Circulation: 22,453,000

Moderna
Christine Granados, Editor
98 San Jacinto Blvd #1150
Austin TX 78701-4039
512-476-5599; Fax: 512-320-1942
Focus: 40-49H
Targets women 18-34
Frequency: Quarterly; Circulation: N/A

Money Magazine
Dan Green, Book Review Editor
Time-Life Bldg
1271 Ave of the Americas
New York NY 10020-1393
212-522-1212; Fax: 212-522-0189
Focus: 19
Frequency: 13x per yr;
    Circulation: 1,900,000

Monitoring Times
Rachel Baughn, Editor
140 Dog Branch Rd
Brasstown NC 28902-9724
704-837-9200; 800-438-8155;
    Fax: 704-837-2216
Focus: 29(radio)
Frequency: Monthly; Circulation: 39,000

Monk Magazine
Michael Lane, Editor/Publisher
175 5th Ave #2322
New York NY 10010-7703
212-465-3231
Focus: 33-53-54-71-61
Frequency: Quarterly; Circulation: 40,000

Montana Magazine
Beverly Magley, Editor
3020 Bozeman Ave
Helena MT 59601-6454
406-443-2842; 800-654-1105;
    Fax: 406-443-5480
Focus: 61(MT)-71-99
Frequency: 6x per yr; Circulation: 45,000

Moody Magazine
Andrew Scheer, Editor
Moody Bible Institute
820 N LaSalle Blvd
Chicago IL 60610-3214
312-329-2164; Fax: 312-329-2149
Focus: 63P(Christian magazine)
Frequency: 11x per yr;
    Circulation: 135,000

Moose Magazine
Kurt Wehrmeister, Managing Editor
Moose International Inc
Supreme Lodge Bldg
Mooseheart IL 60539-1174
708-859-2000; Fax: 708-859-6620
Focus: 99
Clubs, fraternal organizations
Frequency: 6x per yr;
    Circulation: 1,300,000

Mopar Muscle
Mary Jean Wefche, Managing Editor
Dobbs Publishing Group
3816 Industry Blvd
Lakeland FL 33811-1340
941-644-0449; Fax: 941-648-1187
Focus: 16A
Frequency: 6x per yr; Circulation: 70,000

Mother Earth News
Matt Scanlon, Managing Editor
Susser Publishers
49 E 21st St 11th Fl
New York NY 10010
212-260-7210; Fax: 212-260-7445
Focus: 51A
Frequency: 6x per yr; Circulation: 550,000

Mother Jones
Jeffrey Klein, Editor-in-Chief
731 Market St #600
San Francisco CA 94103-2449
415-665-6637; Fax: 415-665-6696
Focus: 11-13-51-55-71-99
Frequency: 6x per yr; Circulation: 120,000

Mothering
Peggy O'Mara, Editor/Publisher
PO Box 1690
Santa Fe NM 87504-1690
505-984-8116; Fax: 505-986-8335
Focus: 21-31-35-73-76
Frequency: Quarterly; Circulation: 75,000

Motor Boating & Sailing
Peter A Janssen, Editor/Publisher
Hearst Corp
250 West 55th St
New York NY 10019-5201
212-649-4099; Fax: 212-489-9258
Focus: 70N
Frequency: Monthly; Circulation: 140,000

Motor Trend
Leonard Emanuelson, Editor
Petersen Publishing
6420 Wilshire Blvd
Los Angeles CA 90048-5502
213-782-2000; Fax: 213-782-2263
Focus: 16A
Frequency: Monthly; Circulation: 900,000

Motorcycle Consumer News
Fred Rau, Editor
Fancy Publications
PO Box 6050
Mission Viejo CA 92690-6050
714-855-8822; 800-241-6100;
    Fax: 714-855-0654
Focus: 16A(motorcycles)
Frequency: Monthly; Circulation: N/A

Motorhome
Jim Brightly, Managing Editor
TL Enterprises
3601 Calle Tecate
Camarillo CA 93012-5040
805-389-0300; Fax: 805-389-0484
Focus: 16-71
Frequency: Monthly; Circulation: 130,000

Motorland
Linn Ferrin, Editor
150 Van Ness Ave
San Francisco CA 94109
415-565-2451
Focus: 16-71
Frequency: 6x per yr;
    Circulation: 2,200,000

Mountain Bike
Nelson Pena, Editor
Rodale Press Inc
33 E Minor St
Emmaus PA 18049-4113
610-967-5171; Fax: 610-967-8960

Focus: 27-35F-39-57-73
Frequency: 11x per yr;
    Circulation: 110,000

Mountain Living
Karen Coe, Editor
7009 S Potomac St #200
Englewood CO 80112
Fax: 303-397-7619
Focus: 43H-61
Mtn homes/legends/resorts
Frequency: Quarterly; Circulation: N/A

Movie Marketplace
Robert Meyers, Editor-in-Chief
World Publishing Co
990 Grove St
Evanston IL 60201-4370
708-491-6440; Fax: 708-491-0459
Focus: 17-33
Frequency: 6x per yr; Circulation: 150,000

Movieline
Virginia Campbell, Co-Editor
Movieline Inc
1141 S Beverly Dr
Los Angeles CA 90035-1164
310-282-0711; Fax: 310-282-0859
Focus: 17-33(movies, stars, Hollywood)
Frequency: Monthly; Circulation: 143,000

Mpls-St Paul Magazine
Brian E Anderson, Editor
MSP Communications
220 South 6th St #500
Minneapolis MN 55402-4501
612-339-7571; Fax: 612-339-5806
Focus: 61(Minneapolis, St Paul MN)-99
Frequency: Monthly; Circulation: 65,000

Ms Magazine
Marsha Gillespie, Editor
Lang Communications
230 Park Ave
New York NY 10169-0004
212-551-9500; Fax: 212-551-9384
Focus: 17-31-39-55-57-65-73-75-99
Frequency: 6x per yr; Circulation: 200,000

MultiCultural Review
Sean Maloney, Book Review Editor
88 Post Rd
PO Box 5007
Westport CT 06881
203-226-3571; Fax: 203-226-6009
Focus: 45-49-78-80-99
Frequency: Quarterly; Circulation: 5,000

Multimedia Producer
Kandy Arnold, Editor
Knowledge Industry Publications
701 Westchester Ave
White Plains NY 10604
914-328-9157; 800-800-5474;
    Fax: 914-328-9093
Focus: 23C-56P(producers of interactive
    media for entertainment, education,
    business)
Frequency: Monthly; Circulation: 40,000

Muscle and Fitness
Tom Deters, Editor-in-Chief
21100 Erwin St
Woodland Hills CA 91367
818-884-6800; Fax: 818-704-5734
Focus: 39-69
Frequency: Monthly; Circulation: 600,000

Muscle Car Review
Tom Shaw, Editor-in-Chief
Dobbs Publishing Group
3816 Industry Blvd
Lakeland FL 33811-1340
941-644-0449; Fax: 941-648-1187
Focus: 16A
Frequency: 24x per yr; Circulation: 74,000

Muscle Mustangs & Fast Fords
Jim Campisano, Editor
CSK Publishing Co Inc
299 Market St
Saddle Brook NJ 07663-5312
201-712-9300; Fax: 201-712-9899
Focus: 16A
Frequency: 11x per yr; Circulation: 65,000

Museums New York
Missy Sullivan, Editor-in-Chief
Art Knowledge Corp
401 Broadway #1111
New York NY 10013-3005
212-581-9570; Fax: 212-586-4643
Focus: 11-41-51-61(NY)-67(museums in New York)
Frequency: 6x per yr; Circulation: 100,000

Mustang Illustrated
Bob McClurg, Managing Editor
McMullen & Yee Publishing Inc
774 South Placentia
Placentia CA 92670-6832
714-572-2255; Fax: 714-572-1864
Focus: 16-24
Frequency: 6x per yr; Circulation: 125,000

Mustang Monthly
Jerry Pitt, Editor
Dobbs Publishing Group
3816 Industry Blvd
Lakeland FL 33811-1340
941-644-0449; Fax: 941-648-1187
Focus: 16A
Frequency: Monthly; Circulation: 80,000

Mystery Readers Journal
Janet Rudolph, Editor
Mystery Readers Intl
PO Box 8116
Berkeley CA 94707-8116
510-339-2800
Focus: 84
Frequency: Quarterly; Circulation: 2,000

N

Na'amat Woman
Judith A Sokoloff, Editor
Na'amat USA
200 Madison Ave
New York NY 10016-3903
212-725-8010
Focus: 49O(Jewish)-73
Frequency: 5x per yr; Circulation: 25,000

Napa Valley Appellation
Antonio Allegia, Editor
PO Box 663
St Helena CA 94574-0663
707-963-3393; Fax: 707-963-2250
Focus: 27-61(CA)
Frequency: 6x per yr; Circulation: 72,000

Nascar Super Truck Racing
Steve Stillwell, Editor
McMullen & Yee Publishing Inc
774 South Placentia
Placentia CA 92670-6846
714-572-2255; Fax: 714-572-1864
Focus: 16-24
Frequency: 6x per yr; Circulation: N/A

National Business Woman
Marcia Eldredge, Sr Editor
2012 Massachusetts Ave NW
Washington DC 20036-1070
202-293-1100
Focus: 19-73
Frequency: Quarterly; Circulation: 75,000

National Dragster
Phil Burgess, Editor
NHRA
2035 Financial Way
Glendora CA 91741-4602
818-963-7695; Fax: 818-335-4307
Focus: 16A
Frequency: Quarterly; Circulation: 80,000

National Gardening
Vicky Congdon, Managing Editor
National Gardening Assn
180 Flynn Ave
Burlington VT 05401-5482
802-863-1308; Fax: 802-863-5962
Focus: 43G
Frequency: 6x per yr; Circulation: 247,000

National Geographic
William Allen, Editor
National Geographic Society
1145 17th St NW
Washington DC 20036-4701
202-857-7000; Fax: 202-775-6141
Focus: 44-51-61-67-71
Frequency: Monthly;
    Circulation: 9,700,000

National Geographic Traveller
Richard Busch, Editor
National Geographic Society
1145 17th St NW
Washington DC 20036-4701
202-828-5485; Fax: 202-828-6640
Focus: 44-61-71
Frequency: 6x per yr; Circulation: 700,000

National Geographic World
Susan Tejada, Editor
National Geographic Society
1145 17th St NW
Washington DC 20036-4701
202-857-7000; 800-638-4077;
    Fax: 202-429-5712
Focus: 14-21-51-67-69-71
Frequency: Monthly;
    Circulation: 1,300,000

National Journal
Richard Frank and Michael Wright,
    Co-Editors
1501 M St NW
Washington DC 20005
202-739-8400; Fax: 202-833-8069
Focus: 55P
Frequency: Weekly; Circulation: 63,000

National Lampoon
Gene Grey, Editor
J2 Communications
10850 Willshire Blvd #1000
Los Angles CA 90024-4322
310-474-5252; Fax: 310-474-1219
Focus: 33
Frequency: 6x per yr; Circulation: 200,000

National Parks Magazine
Linda Rancourt, Book Review Editor
Natl Parks and Conservation
1776 Massachusetts Ave NW
Washington DC 20036-1904
202-223-6722; Fax: 202-659-0650
Focus: 51-69-71
Frequency: 6x per yr; Circulation: 450,000

National Review
John O'Sullivan, Editor
150 East 35th St
New York NY 10016-4178
212-679-7330; Fax: 212-696-0309
Focus: 41-55
Frequency: 2x per yr; Circulation: 260,000

National Wildlife
Mark Wexler, Editor
National Wildlife Federation
8925 Leesburg Pike
Vienna VA 22184-0001
703-790-4524; 800-432-6564;
    Fax: 703-442-7332
Focus: 15-51-67-69R
Frequency: 6x per yr; Circulation: 670,000

The Nation
Victor Navasky, Editorial Dir/Publ
John and Sue Leonard, Literary Editors
Katrina Vanden Heuvel, Managing Editor
72 Fifth Ave
New York NY 10011-8046
212-242-8400; Fax: 212-463-9712
Focus: 47-75-83-90-95-99
Frequency: 48x per yr;
    Circulation: 100,000

Native Peoples
Gary Avey, Editor
5333 North 7th #C-224
Phoenix AZ 85014-2803
602-252-2236; Fax: 602-265-3113
Focus: 17-49-55-65
Frequency: Quarterly; Circulation: 125,000

Natural Foods Merchandiser
Frank Lampe, Editor
New Hope Communications
1301 Spruce St
Boulder CO 80302
303-939-8440; Fax: 303-939-9559
Focus: 19R-27-39H (retail sales/holistic health)
Frequency: Monthly; Circulation: 11,010

Natural Health
Bill Thompson, Book Editor
17 Station St
Brookline MA 02146-7371
617-232-1000; Fax: 617-232-1572
Focus: 13-27-31-35-39H-40-43-51-53-54-57-63E
Frequency: 6x per yr; Circulation: 200,000

Natural History
Bruce Stutz, Editor
Amer Museum of Natural History
Central Park West at 79th St
New York NY 10024
212-769-5500; Fax: 212-769-5511
Focus: 15-51-67
Frequency: Monthly; Circulation: 518,000

Naturally Magazine
Bernard Loibl, Editor-in-Chief
PO Box 317
Newfoundland NJ 07435-0317
201-697-8313; Fax: 201-697-8313
Focus: 35S-40F(naturalist)
Frequency: Quarterly; Circulation: 25,000

NEA Retired
Diane Dismuke, Editor
National Education Assn
1201 16th St NW
Washington DC 20036-3207
202-822-7207; Fax: 202-822-7206
Focus: 31
Publ during school year
Frequency: 6x per yr; Circulation: 124,000

Netguide
Dan Rosenbaum, Editor-in-Chief
CMP Publications
600 Community Dr
Manhasset NY 11030
516-562-5000; Fax: 516-562-7406
Focus: 23C(online services, the Internet, BBSs)
Frequency: Monthly; Circulation: 200,000

Network Magazine
Lynne Tempest, Editor
155 East 4905 S
Salt Lake City UT 84107-4862
801-262-8091; Fax: 801-262-5623
Focus: 19-61(UT)-73-99
Frequency: Monthly; Circulation: 18,000

Network Administrator
Joe Casad, Managing Editor
R & D Publications Inc
1601 W 23rd St #200
Lawrence KS 66046
913-841-1631; Fax: 913-841-2624
Focus: 19-23
Frequency: 6x per yr; Circulation: 15,000

Network Computing Magazine
Joe Caponi, Managing Editor
CMP Publications
600 Community Dr
Manhasset NY 11030-3847
516-562-5000; Fax: 516-562-7293
Focus: 23C (networks)
Frequency: Monthly; Circulation: 175,000

Network World
John Dix, Editor
161 Worcester Rd
Framingham MA 01701-5300
508-875-6400; 800-622-1108;
    Fax: 508-820-3467
Focus: 23(networking)
Frequency: Weekly; Circulation: 150,000

Nevada Magazine
David Moore, Editor
State of Nevada
1800 East Hwy 50
Carson City NV 89701-3209
702-687-5416; Fax: 702-687-6159
Focus: 11-14-33-35-61(NV)-69-71(books of interest to Nevadans)
Frequency: 6x per yr; Circulation: 101,000

New Age Magazine
Peggy Taylor, Editor
New Age Publishing Inc
42 Pleasant St
Watertown MA 02172
617-926-0200; Fax: 617-926-5021
Focus: 13-23-39-43-51-53-54-57-67-71
Frequency: 6x per yr; Circulation: 98,000

New Age Retailer
Dwight Lucky, Editor
Continuity Publishing
1300 N State St #105
Bellingham WA 98225
360-676-0789; Fax: 360-676-0932
Focus: 39H-53-54-57
Frequency: 7x per yr; Circulation: 6,000

New Beginnings
Judy Torgus, Exec Editor
La Leche League Intl
1400 N Meacham
Schaumburg IL 60173
708-519-7730; Fax: 708-519-0035
Focus: 31C-31P-35F-39
Frequency: 6x per yr; Circulation: N/A

New Electric Railway Journal
Richard Kunz, Director
717 Second St NE
Washington DC 20002
202-546-3000; Fax: 202-544-2819
Focus: 16R(electric railway systems)
Frequency: Quarterly; Circulation: 5,000

New England Bride
Lisa Amore, Editor
215 Newbury Dr
Peabody MA 01960-2400
508-535-4186; Fax: 508-535-3090
Focus: 35-43
Frequency: Monthly; Circulation: 15,000

New England Game & Fish
Steve Carpenteri, Editor
Game & Fish Publications
2250 Newmarket Pky #110
Marietta GA 30067-8749
770-953-9222; Fax: 770-933-9510
Focus: 15-51-61(New England Area)-69
Frequency: Monthly; Circulation: N/A

New Frontier Magazine
Swami Virato, Exec Editor/Founder
New Frontier Education Society
PO Box 17397
Asheville NC 28816-7397
704-251-0109; Fax: 704-251-0727;
    E-Mail: swamiv@aol.com
Focus: 53-54
Frequency: Monthly; Circulation: 60,000

New Living
Christine Harvey, Editor/Publisher
PO Box 1519
Stony Brook NY 11790-0909
516-981-7232; Fax: 516-585-4606;
    E-Mail: newlivin@ios.com
Focus: 39-69
Frequency: Monthly; Circulation: 50,000

New Mexico Business Journal
Jack Hartsfield, Editor-in-Chief
PO Box 30550
Albuquerque NM 87190-0550
505-889-2911; Fax: 505-889-0822
Focus: 19-61(NM)
Frequency: Monthly; Circulation: 19,000

New Mexico Living
Helen Hopkins, Managing Editor
7200 Montgomery NE #329
Albuquerque NM 87109
505-875-0055; Fax: 505-875-0033
Focus: 61-71
Frequency: 6x per yr; Circulation: 75,000

New Mexico Magazine
Emily Drabanski, Editor-in-Chief
Lew Wallace Bldg
495 Old Santa Fe Trail
Santa Fe NM 87501-2750
505-827-7447; 800-898-6639;
    Fax: 505-827-6496
Focus: 61(NM)-99
Frequency: Monthly; Circulation: 130,000

New Moon Parenting
Joe Kelly, Managing Editor
2127 Columbus Ave
Duluth MN 55803-2222
218-728-5507; Fax: 218-728-0314
Focus: 21-31P-99 (for girls 8-14)
Frequency: 6x per yr; Circulation: 3,000

New Orleans Magazine
Erol LaBorde, Editor
111 Veterans Blvd #1810
Metairie LA 70005
504-831-3731; Fax: 501-837-2258
Focus: 19-61(New Orleans LA)
Frequency: Monthly; Circulation: 31,000

The New Republic
Leon Wieseltier, Literary Editor
1220 19th St NW #600
Washington DC 20036-2474
202-331-7494; Fax: 202-331-0275
Focus: 75-99
Frequency: 48x per yr;
    Circulation: 110,000

New Texas Magazine
Steven Dodds, Editor
1512 1/2 S Congress Ave
Austin TX 78704-2437
512-462-1990; Fax: 512-448-3927
Focus: 61(TX)-99
Frequency: Monthly; Circulation: 60,000

New Woman
Debra Birnbaum, Book Review Editor
215 Lexington Ave
New York NY 10016-6023
212-251-1500; Fax: 212-251-1590
Focus: 99
Frequency: Monthly;
    Circulation: 1,393,000

New Writer's Magazine
George Haborak, Editor
Sarasota Bay Publishing
PO Box 5976
Sarasota FL 34277
941-953-7903
Focus: 56W
Frequency: 6x per yr; Circulation: 6,000

New York Family
Susan Ross-Benamram and Felice
   Shapiro, Co-Publishers
141 Halstead Ave #D
Mamaroneck NY 10543-2652
914-381-7474; Fax: 914-381-7672
Focus: 21-31-35-76
Frequency: 11; Circulation: 60,000

New York Game & Fish
Steve Carpenteri, Editor
Game & Fish Publications
2250 Newmarket Pky #110
Marietta GA 30067-8749
770-953-9222; Fax: 770-933-9510
Focus: 15-51-61(NY)-69
Frequency: Monthly; Circulation: N/A

New York Magazine
Judith Shulevitz, Literary Editor
755 Second Ave
New York NY 10017-5906
212-880-0700; Fax:
Focus: 11-14-33-39-61(New York
   NY)-56M-56P-99(also covers magazine
   and book publishing)
Frequency: Weekly; Circulation: 450,000

New York Native
C Ortleb, Editor
PO Box 1475
New York NY 10008-1475
212-627-2120; Fax: 212-727-9321
Focus: 13-37-49-55-65-73
Frequency: Weekly; Circulation: 12,000

New Yorker
Tina Brown, Editor
20 West 43rd St
New York NY 10036-7406
212-536-5400; Fax: 212-536-5735
Focus: 17
Frequency: Weekly; Circulation: 830,000

NewMedia Magazine
Gillian Newson, Products Editor
HyperMedia Communications
901 Mariners Island Blvd #365
San Mateo CA 94404
415-573-5170; Fax: 415-573-5131
Focus: 23C-56M
Frequency: 13x per yr;
   Circulation: 250,000

Newsweek
Ray Sawhill, Asst Book Editor
Jeff Giles, General Editor, Popular Music
   & Books
David Gates, Sr Writer/Books
251 W 57th St
New York NY 10019-1894
212-445-4000; Fax: 212-445-5068;
   E-Mail: Letters@newsweek.com
Focus: 99
Frequency: Weekly; Circulation: 3,200,000

Nob Hill Gazette
Marsha Monroe, Editor
53rd St #222
San Francisco CA 94103-3203
415-227-0190; Fax: 415-974-5103
Focus: 61(San Francisco CA)
Frequency: Monthly; Circulation: 65,000

Nolo News
Mary Randolph, Editor
Nolo Press
950 Parker St
Berkeley CA 94710-2589
510-549-1976; Fax: 510-548-5902
Focus: 19A-19L-55L
Frequency: Quarterly; Circulation: 150,000

Nonprofit World Journal
Jill Muehrcke, Editor
6314 Odana Rd #1
Madison WI 53719-1129
608-274-9777; 800-424-7367;
   Fax: 608-274-9978
Focus: 19(fundraising)-56
Frequency: 6x per yr; Circulation: 15,000

North American Fisherman
Steve Pennaz, Editor
North American Fishing Club
PO Box 3401
Minnetonka MN 55343-2101
612-936-9333; Fax: 612-936-9755
Focus: 69H
Frequency: 6x per yr; Circulation: 450,000

North American Hunter
Bill Miller, Editor
North American Hunting Club
12301 Whitewater Dr #260
Minnetonka MN 55343-4108
612-936-9333; Fax: 612-936-9755
Focus: 69H
Frequency: 7x per yr; Circulation: 260,000

North American Whitetail
Gordon Whittington, Editor
2250 Newmarket Pky #110
Marietta GA 30067-8749
770-953-9222; Fax: 770-933-9510
Focus: 15-51-69
Frequency: 8x per yr; Circulation: N/A

North Carolina Game & Fish
Jeff Samsel, Editor
Game & Fish Publications
2250 Newmarket Pky #110
Marietta GA 30067-8749
770-953-9222; Fax: 770-933-9510
Focus: 15-51-61(NC)-69
Frequency: Monthly; Circulation: N/A

North Jersey Traveler
Editor
North Jersey AAA
418 Hamburg Tpke
Wayne NJ 07470
Focus: 16A-71
Frequency: N/A; Circulation: N/A

North Shore Magazine
Asher Bimbaum, Editor
PB Communications
874 Green Bay Rd
Winnetka IL 60093-1805
708-441-7892
Focus: 61(IL)-99
Frequency: Monthly; Circulation: 55,000

Northwest Travel
Judy Fleagle, Editor
1525 W 12th St #C
Florence OR 97439-9412
503-997-8401; Fax: 503-997-1124
Focus: 61(OR/WA)-71
Frequency: 6x per yr; Circulation: 20,000

Nugget
Christopher James, Editor-in-Chief
Dugent Publishing Corp
14411 Commerce Rd #420
Miami Lakes FL 33016-1598
305-557-0071; Fax: 305-557-6005
Focus: 35S-37-99
Frequency: 9x per yr; Circulation: 120,000

Nutshell News
Sybil Harp, Editor
Kalmbach Publishing Co
21027 Crossroads Cir
Waukesha WI 53186-4055
414-796-8776; Fax: 414-796-1383
Focus: 28(collectibles)-29C(miniatures)
Frequency: Monthly; Circulation: 40,000

Oasis
Donna Borst, Editor
8 Melody Terr
Ft Madison IA 52627
319-372-2008; Fax: 319-372-2008
Focus: 21-31-76(teachers: time-saving,
   skill-building activities)
Actvity suggestions, grades 5-9
Frequency: 5x per yr; Circulation: 16,000

Odyssey Magazine
Beth Lindstrom, Editor
Cobblestone Publishing Inc
7 School St
Peterborough NH 03458-1441
603-924-7209; Fax: 603-924-7380
Focus: 21-51-67A(for children 8-14 years
   old)
Frequency: 10x per yr; Circulation: 32,000

Off Duty
Jo Molnar, Book Review Editor
3303 Harbor Blvd #C-2
Costa Mesa CA 92626-1530
714-549-7172; Fax: 714-549-4222
Focus: 19-27-35-39-71
Frequency: 6x per yr;
   Circulation: 500,000

Off Our Backs
Editor
2337 B 18th St NW
Washington DC 20009-2003
202-234-8072; Fax: 202-234-8092
Focus: 13-55-65-73
Feminist news journal
Frequency: Monthly; Circulation: 22,000

Ohio Game & Fish
Ken Freel, Editor
2250 Newmarket Pky #110
Marietta GA 30067-8749
770-953-9222; Fax: 770-933-9510
Focus: 15-51-61(OH)-69
Frequency: Monthly; Circulation: N/A

Oklahoma Game & Fish
Nick Gilmore, Editor
2250 Newmarket Pky #110
Marietta GA 30067-8749
770-953-9222; Fax: 770-933-9510
Focus: 15-51-61(OK)-69
Frequency: Monthly; Circulation: N/A

Oklahoma Living
Mary Logan, Editor
PO Box 54309
Oklahoma City OK 73154-1309
405-478-1455; Fax: 405-478-0246
Focus: 61(OK)
Frequency: Monthly; Circulation: 240,000

Oklahoma Today
Jeanne Devlin, Editor-in-Chief
401 Will Rogers Bldg
23rd & Lincoln Blvd
Oklahoma City OK 73105
405-521-2496; Fax: 405-521-3992
Focus: 61-71
Also Book Review Editor
Frequency: 6x per yr; Circulation: 43,000

Old Cars Price Guide
James Lenzke, Sr Editor
Krause Publications
700 E State St
Iola WI 54990 -000
715-445-2214; Fax: 715-445-4087
Focus: 16A (pricing guide for vintage autos)
Frequency: 6x per yr; Circulation: 104,000

Old Time Crochet
Anne Morgan Jefferson and Marion Kelly, Editors
House of White Birches
306 East Parr Rd
Berne IN 46711
219-589-8741; Fax: 219-589-8093
Focus: 29
Frequency: Quarterly; Circulation: 88,000

On the Issues
Ronnie Sandroff, Managing Editor
97-77 Queens Blvd
Flushing NY 11374-3317
718-275-6020; Fax: 718-997-1206
Focus: 99
Frequency: 6x per yr; Circulation: 25,000

On-Demand
Matt Stump, Editor
Cowles Business Media
1905 Sherman St #1000
Denver CO 80203
303-837-0900; Fax: 303-837-0915
Focus: 19X
Frequency: Monthly; Circulation: 10,000

Online Access
Kathryn McCabe, Editor-in-Chief
Chicago Fine Print Inc
900 N Franklin #310
Chicago IL 60610-3124
312-573-1700; Fax: 312-573-0520
Focus: 23C
Frequency: Monthly; Circulation: 150,000

Online Time
Debra A velsmid, Editor/Publ
Write Way Communications
PO Box 186
Glen Oaks NY 11004
718-225-8374
Focus: 23-35F (families using online services)
Frequency: 9x per yr; Circulation: N/A

Online User
Nancy Garman, Editor
462 Danbury Rd
Wilton CT 06897-2126
203-761-1466
Focus: 19-23T
Frequency: 6x per yr; Circulation: 50,000

Ontario Craft
Anne McPhearson, Editor
Ontario Crafts Council
35 McCaul St
Toronto ON Canada M5T 1V7
416-977-3551; Fax: 416-977-3552
Focus: 29
Frequency: Quarterly; Circulation: N/A

Open Wheel Magazine
Dick Berggren, Editor
47 South Main St
PO Box 715
Ipswich MA 01938-2321
508-356-7030; Fax: 508-356-2492
Focus: 16A
Frequency: Monthly; Circulation: 60,000

Opera News
Patrick Smith, Editor
Metropolitan Opera Guild
70 Lincoln Center Plz
New York NY 10023-6548
212-769-7080; Fax: 212-769-7007
Focus: 14M(opera)
Frequency: 17x per yr; Circulation: 133,000

Opportunity Magazine
Donna Clapp, Editor
Opportunity Assoc
73 Spring St #303
New York NY 10012
212-925-3180; Fax: 212-925-3612
Focus: 19M-19O-19S
Frequency: Monthly; Circulation: 200,000

Orange Coast Magazine
Allison Joyce, Managing Editor
245-D Fischer Ave #8
Costa Mesa CA 92626
714-545-1900; Fax: 714-545-1932
Focus: 17-19-39-40-61(CA)-71-99
Upscale lifestyle
Frequency: Monthly; Circulation: 38,000

Orbit
Katie McInery, Editor
Big Fun Inc
919 S Main St #2001
Royal Oak MI 48067-3203
810-541-3900
Focus: 14M-36-61-99
Frequency: Monthly; Circulation: 50,000

Oregon Business
Kathy Dimond, Editor
Media America Inc
921 SW Morrison #407
Portland OR 97205-2734
503-223-0304; Fax: 503-221-6544
Focus: 19
Frequency: Monthly; Circulation: 20,000

Oregon Coast Magazine
Dave Peden, Editor
1525 W 12th #C
Florence OR 97439-9412
503-997-8401; Fax: 503-997-1124

Focus: 61(OR)-71
Frequency: 6x per yr; Circulation: 70,000

Oregon Cycling
Tracy Miller, Editor
455 W 1st Ave
Eugene OR 97401-2276
503-686-9885; Fax: 503-686-1015
Focus: 69(cycling)
Frequency: 10x per yr; Circulation: 15,000

Organic Gardening
Mike McGrath, Editor
Rodale Press
33 E Minor St
Emmaus PA 18098-0001
610-967-5171; Fax: 610-967-8956
Focus: 27-39H-43G
Frequency: 9x per yr; Circulation: 800,000

Organica
Susan Hussey, Editor-in-Chief
Aubrey Organics
4419 N Manhattan Ave
Tampa FL 33614-7650
813-876-4879; Fax: 813-876-8166
Focus: 13-39H-51-53-54-57-86
Frequency: Quarterly; Circulation: 300,000

Orion Magazine
H Emerson Blake, Managing Editor
The Myrin Institute
136 East 64th St
New York NY 10021
212-758-6475; Fax: 212-758-6784
Focus: 39H-51-51E
Frequency: Quarterly; Circulation: 12,000

Orlando Magazine
Fred Abel, Editor
PO Box 2207
Orlando FL 32802-2207
407-539-3939; Fax: 407-539-0533
Focus: 19-61(Central FL)
Frequency: Monthly; Circulation: 30,000

Our Children
Editor
Natl Congress of Parent/Teachers
330 N Wabash Ave
Chicago IL 60611
312-670-6782
Focus: 31E-31P-35F
Frequency: N/A; Circulation: N/A

Our Kids & Teens Magazine
Elaine Heitman, Editor
1100 South Mint St
Charlotte NC 28203
704-344-1980; Fax: 704-344-1983
Focus: 21-31-35-76
Frequency: Monthly; Circulation: 40,000

Our Kids Houston
Gail Goodwin, Editor
Branford Publishing Inc
2500 Tanglewilde #106
Houston TX 77063-2123
713-781-7535; Fax: 713-781-5620
Focus: 21-31-35-76
Frequency: Monthly; Circulation: 65,000

Book Publishing Resource Guide

Our Kids San Antonio
Nancy Diehl, Editor-in-Chief
Branford Publishing Inc
8400 Blanco Rd #201
San Antonio TX 78216-3055
210-349-6667; Fax: 210-349-5618
Focus: 21-31-35-76
Frequency: Monthly; Circulation: 35,000

Our Sunday Visitor
Mitch Finley, Book Review Editor
200 Noll Plz
Huntington IN 46750-4310
219-356-8400; 800-348-2440;
    Fax: 219-356-8472
Focus: 63C
Frequency: Weekly; Circulation: 96

Out
David Doorley, Book Review Editor
747 South Ave
Pittsburgh PA 15221-2939
412-243-3350; Fax: 412-243-4067
Focus: 37
Frequency: Monthly; Circulation: 30,000

Out Magazine
Bruce Steele, Managing Editor
110 Greene St #800
New York NY 10012-3836
212-334-9119; Fax: 212-334-9227
Focus: 37
Frequency: 10x per yr;
    Circulation: 175,000

Out West
Chuck Woodbury, Editor
408 Broad St #11
Nevada City CA 95959
800-274-9378
Focus: 61(West)-71(ghost towns,
    out-of-way places)
Frequency: Quarterly; Circulation: 12,000

Outbound Traveler
Carmi Zona-Paris, Editor
Travel Review Publ
14 Watson St
Marblehead MA 01945
617-631-1690; Fax: 617-631-0203
Focus: 19-71F(travel agents/planners of
    international travelers)
Frequency: 6x per yr; Circulation: 25,000

Outcry Magazine
Barbara Kremer, Editor
Lara Publications
PO Box 52176
St Louis MO 63136
314-653-0467; Fax: 314-653-6543
Focus: 35R-49B-55-57-63-65
Frequency: Monthly; Circulation: N/A

Outdoor Action
Dan Sanchez, Editor
McMullen & Yee Publishing Inc
774 South Placentia
Placentia CA 92670-6846
714-572-2255; Fax: 714-572-1864
Focus: 69-69R
Frequency: 9x per yr; Circulation: N/A

Outdoor America
Denny Johnson, Editor
Izaak Walton League
707 Conservation Ln Level B
Gaithersburg MD 20878-2982
301-548-0150; Fax: 301-548-0146
Focus: 15-51-69-71
Frequency: Quarterly; Circulation: 45,000

Outdoor Life
Vin Sparano, Editor-in-Chief
2 Park Ave
New York NY 10016-5603
212-779-5000; Fax: 212-686-6877
Focus: 15-29-39-51-69-71
Frequency: Monthly;
    Circulation: 1,500,000

Outside Kids
Lisa Twyman Bessone, Editor
Outside Plz
400 Market St
Santa Fe NM 87501-7300
505-989-7100; Fax: 505-989-4700
Focus: 21-51-69-71
Frequency: Quarterly; Circulation: 150,000

Outside Magazine
Mike Pateniti, Book Review Editor
Mariah Media, Outside Plz
400 Market St
Santa Fe NM 85701
505-989-7100; Fax: 505-989-4700
Focus: 51-69-71
Frequency: Monthly; Circulation: 385,000

The Oxford American
Marc Smirnoff, Editor
114A South Lamar Blvd
Oxford MS 38655-4008
601-236-1836; Fax: 601-236-3141
Focus: 61-99(Southern)
Frequency: 6x per yr; Circulation: 65,000

Pack-O-Fun
Bill Stephani, Editor
Clapper Communications
2400 Devon #375
Des Plaines IL 60018-4618
708-635-5810; 800-272-3871;
    Fax: 708-635-6311
Focus: 29
Frequency: 6x per yr; Circulation: 159,000

Paint Horse Journal
Dan Streeter, Book Review Editor
APHA
10405 I-35 NW
Fort Worth TX 76131
817-439-3400; Fax: 817-439-3484
Focus: 15(horses)
Frequency: Monthly; Circulation: 18,000

Palm Springs Life
Stewart Weiner, Editor
303 N Indian Ave
Palm Springs CA 92262-6015
619-325-2333; Fax: 619-325-7008
Focus: 61(CA)-99
Frequency: Monthly; Circulation: 25,000

Palmer Video Magazine
Susan Baar, Editor
1767 Morris Ave
Union NJ 07083-3511
908-686-3030; Fax: 908-686-2151
Focus: 33M
Goes to Palmer Video Members
Frequency: Monthly; Circulation: 60,000

Paper Boat Magazine
Maura Alia Bramkamp, Editor
Paper Boat Press
PO Box 2615
Poulsbo WA 98370
Focus: 11-75-95
Frequency: Quarterly; Circulation: N/A

Paper Collectors Marketplace
Doug Watson, Publisher
Watson Graphic Designs
PO Box 128
Scandinavia WI 54977-0128
715-467-2379; Fax: 715-467-2243
Focus: 28
Frequency: Monthly; Circulation: 4,000

Parabola Magazine
Virginia Baron, Editor
656 Broadway 6th Fl
New York NY 10012-2301
212-505-6200; 800-560-6984;
    Fax: 212-979-7325
Focus: 53-54(essays on myth & tradition)
Frequency: Quarterly; Circulation: 41,000

Paraplegia News
Cliff Crase, Sr Editor
Paralyzed Veterans of America
2111 E Highland Ave #180
Phoenix AZ 85016-4732
602-224-0500; Fax: 602-224-0507
Focus: 39D
Frequency: Monthly; Circulation: 28,000

Parentguide News
Leslie Elgort, Editor
419 Park Ave S 13th Fl
New York NY 10016-8410
212-213-8840; Fax: 212-447-7734
Focus: 21-31-35-76
Frequency: Monthly; Circulation: 210,000

Parenting Magazine
Bruce Raskin, Managing Editor
301 Howard St 17th Fl
San Francisco CA 94105-2252
415-546-7575; Fax: 415-546-0578
Focus: 21-31P-35F-76-79
Frequency: 10x per yr;
    Circulation: 925,000

Parents & Teenagers
Cindy Parolini, Managing Editor
2890 N Monroe
PO Box 481
Loveland CO 80539
970-669-3836; Fax: 970-669-3269
Focus: 31-35-63(Christian)-89
Frequency: 6x per yr; Circulation: 20,000

Parents Magazine
Pat Abrams, Editor, Parents Bookshelf
685 Third Ave
New York NY 10017-4024
212-878-8700; Fax: 212-867-4583
Focus: 31P-35F
Frequency: Monthly;
    Circulation: 1,825,000

Parents of Teenagers
Gloria Chisholm, Editor
7125 Disc Dr
Colorado Springs CO 80918-7101
719-531-7776; Fax: 719-535-0172
Focus: 31-35-63(Christian)-89
Frequency: 6x per yr; Circulation: 50,000

Parents' Choice
Diana H Green, Editor-in-Chief
Parents' Choice Foundation
1191 Chestnut St
Newton Upper Falls MA 02164-1351
617-965-5913; Fax: 617-965-4516
Focus: 21-31-76-89
Frequency: Quarterly; Circulation: 90,000

Parents' Press
Lynne Verbeek, Managing Editor
1454 Sixth St
Berkeley CA 94710-1431
510-524-1602; Fax: 510-524-0912
Focus: 21-31-35-76
Frequency: Monthly; Circulation: 75,000

ParentSource
John Kendrick, Editor
Targeted Marketing Solutions Inc
470 Totten Pond Rd 3rd Fl
Watham MA 02154-1905
617-487-2222; Fax: 617-487-2233;
    E-Mail: JBKendrick@aol.com
Focus: 19C-21-25-31C-31E-31P-35F-35M-35R
Frequency: 6x per yr; Circulation: N/A

Paris Review
George A Plimpton, Editor
45-39 171 Pl
Flushing NY 11358
Focus: 75-90-95-99
Frequency: Quarterly; Circulation: 9,000

Parnassus: Poetry in Review
Herbert Leibowitz, Editor
41 Union Square W #804
New York NY 10003-3208
212-463-0889
Focus: 47-95
Frequency: 2x per yr; Circulation: 5,000

Partisan Review
William Phillips and Edith Kurzweil, Co-Editors
236 Bay State Rd
Boston MA 02215-1403
617-353-4260; Fax: 617-353-7444
Focus: 11-14-47-55-75-90-95-99
Frequency: Quarterly; Circulation: 8,000

PC Computing
Wendy Taylor, Exec Editor
Ziff-Davis Publishing
950 Tower Ln 19th Fl
Foster City CA 94404
415-578-7000; Fax: 415-578-7059;
    E-Mail: 76000.21@compuserve.com
Focus: 23(IBM-PC)
Frequency: Monthly; Circulation: 895,000

PC Gamer
Matthew Firme, Editor
1350 Old Bayshore Hwy #210
Burlingame CA 27407-1614
415-696-1688; Fax: 415-696-1678
Focus: 23C-69G(computer games)
Frequency: Monthly; Circulation: 145,000

PC Laptop
Cassandra Cavannah, Exec Editor
9171 Wilshire Blvd #300
Beverly Hills CA 90210-5515
310-858-7155; Fax: 310-274-7985
Focus: 23(PC)
Frequency: Monthly; Circulation: N/A

PC Magazine
Paul B Ross, Managing Editor
Ziff Communications Co
1 Park Ave 4th Fl
New York NY 10016-5802
212-503-5255; Fax: 212-503-5519
Focus: 19-23(IBM)
Frequency: 22x per yr;
    Circulation: 140,000

PC Novice
Ron Kobler, Editor
120 W Harvest Dr
Lincoln NE 68521-4408
402-477-8900; 800-424-7900; Fax:
    402-477-9252
Focus: 23(for beginners)
Frequency: Monthly; Circulation: 300,000

PC Presentations Productions
Don Johnson, Editor/Publisher
Pisces Publishing Group
417 Bridgeport Ave
Milford CT 06460-4105
203-877-1927
Focus: 23C-23T-33T
Frequency: 6x per yr; Circulation: N/A

PC Techniques
Jeff Duntemann, Editor-in-Chief
Coriolis Group Publishing
7721 E Gray RD #204
Scottsdale AZ 85260-6912
602-483-0192; 800-410-0192;
    Fax: 602-483-0193
Focus: 23C
Frequency: 6x per yr; Circulation: 28,000

PC Today
Ronald Kobler, Editor/Publisher
PO Box 85380
Lincoln NE 68501-5380
402-477-8900; 800-544-1264;
    Fax: 402-477-9252
Focus: 23
Frequency: Monthly; Circulation: 250,000

PC World
Luis Camus, Managing Editor
501 Second St
San Francisco CA 94107-1431
415-243-0500; Fax: 415-442-1891
Focus: 23
Frequency: Monthly; Circulation: 929,000

PC World Lotus Edition
Eric Bender, Exec Editor
77 Franklin St #300
Boston MA 02110
617-482-8470; Fax: 617-426-0235
Focus: 23(Lotus software related)
Frequency: Monthly; Circulation: N/A

Peachtree Magazine
Daniel F DeLong, Editor-In-Chief
C S Publishers Inc
120 Interstate N Pky E #445
Atlanta GA 30339-2158
770-956-1207; Fax: 770-988-8976
Focus: 11-12-14-17-27-28-33-39-40-41-43-61-69-71
Frequency: Monthly; Circulation: 51,000

Pennsylvania Game & Fish
Steve Carpenteri, Editor
Game & Fish Publications
2250 Newmarket Pky #110
Marietta GA 30067-8749
770-953-9222; Fax: 770-933-9510
Focus: 15-51-61(PA)-69
Frequency: Monthly; Circulation: N/A

Pennsylvania Magazine
Matt Holliday, Editor
PO Box 576
Camp Hill PA 17001-0576
717-761-6620
Focus: 61(PA)
Frequency: 6x per yr; Circulation: 40,000

Penthouse
Susan Shapiro, Book Reviewer
277 Park Ave 4th Fl
New York NY 10173-0003
212-702-6000; Fax: 212-702-6262;
    E-Mail: PentEdit@aol.com;
    Http://www.penthousemag.com
Focus: 99
Frequency: Monthly;
    Circulation: 1,250,000

People Weekly
Ralph Novak, Book Editor
Time-Life Bldg
Rockefeller Ctr
New York NY 10020
212-522-4461; Fax: 212-522-0031
Focus: 14M-33M-75-99
Frequency: Weekly; Circulation: 3,158,000

Perspectives on Political Science
Lisa Culp-Neikirk, Managing Editor
Heldref Publications
1319 18th St NW
Washington DC 20036-1802
202-296-6267; Fax: 202-296-5149
Focus: 44-48-49-55-65
Frequency: Quarterly; Circulation: N/A

Pets Magazine
Halvor Moorshead, Publisher
10 Gateway Blvd #490
North York ON M3C 3T4
416-696-5488; Fax: 416-696-7395
Focus: 15
Frequency: 6x per yr; Circulation: N/A

Philadelphia
Eliot Kaplan, Editor
1818 Market St 36th Fl
Philadelphia PA 19103-3602
215-564-7700; Fax: 215-656-3502
Focus: 61(Philadelphia PA)-99
Frequency: Monthly; Circulation: 149,000

Philadelphia Gay News
Al Patrick, Editor
254 South 11th St
Philadelphia PA 19107-6735
215-625-8501; Fax: 215-925-6437
Focus: 13-37
Frequency: Weekly; Circulation: 15,000

Phoenix Home & Garden
Mary Chesterfield, Editor
4041 N Central Ave #A-100
Phoenix AZ 85012-3330
602-234-0840; Fax: 602-277-7857
Focus: 27-43-61(AZ)
Frequency: Monthly; Circulation: 38,000

Phoenix Magazine
Dick Vonier, Editor
5555 N 7th Ave #B-200
Phoenix AZ 85013-1755
602-207-3750; Fax: 602-207-3777
Focus: 27-40-43-61(Phoenix AZ)-71
Frequency: Monthly; Circulation: 52,000

The Phoenix
Roseanne Bane, Editor
3307 14th Ave S
Minneapolis MN 55407-2206
612-722-1149; Fax: 612-722-4139
Focus: 39R-57
Frequency: Monthly; Circulation: 41,000

Photo Techniques
Mike Johnson, Editor
7800 Merrimac Ave
Niles IL 60714
708-965-0566; Fax: 708-965-7639
Focus: 11P
Frequency: N/A; Circulation: N/A

PieceWork: All This By Hand
Veronica Patterson, Editor
Interweave Press
201 E Fourth St
Loveland CO 80537-5601
970-669-7672; 800-272-2193;
    Fax: 970-667-8317;
E-mail: pw@iwp.ccmail.compuserve.com
Focus: 29C
Frequency: 6x per yr; Circulation: 66,000

Piper's Magazine
Frank Hamilton, Editor
PO Box 337
Iola WI 54945-0337
715-445-5000; Fax: 715-445-4053
Focus: 70A
Frequency: Monthly; Circulation: 3,000

Pittsburgh Business Times
Paul Furiga, Editor
2313 E Carson
Pittsburgh PA 15203-2161
412-481-6397; Fax: 412-481-9956
Focus: 19-61(Pittsburgh PA)
Frequency: Weekly; Circulation: 18,000

Pittsburgh Magazine
Christopher Fletcher, Editor
QED Communications
4802 Fifth Ave
Pittsburgh PA 15213-2957
412-622-1360; 800-495-7323;
    Fax: 412-622-7066
Focus: 11-14-17-61(Pittsburgh PA)
Frequency: Monthly; Circulation: 65,000

Pittsburgh's Child
Pat Poshard, Editor
PO Box 418
Gibsonia PA 15044-0418
412-443-1891; Fax: 412-443-1877
Focus: 14-21-31-35-76
Frequency: Monthly; Circulation: 63,000

Plane & Pilot
Steve Werner, Editor-in-Chief
Werner Publishing Corp
12121 Wilshire Blvd #1220
Los Angeles CA 90025-1175
310-820-1500; Fax: 310-826-5008
Focus: 70
Frequency: Monthly; Circulation: 127,000

Plastic Canvas Crafts
Laura Scott, Editor
306 East Parr Rd
Berne IN 46711-1138
219-589-8741; Fax: 219-589-8093
Focus: 29
Frequency: 6x per yr; Circulation: N/A

Plastic Canvas World
Marjorie Pearl, Editor
306 East Parr Rd
Berne IN 46711
219-589-8741; Fax: 219-589-8093
Focus: 29
Frequency: 6x per yr; Circulation: 68,000

Play
Michael Fagien, Editor-in-Chief
3620 NW 43rd St #D
Gainesville FL 32606-8100
904-375-3705; 800-247-2160;
    Fax: 904-375-1268
Focus: 21-23C-33-71-76
Frequency: Quarterly; Circulation: 100,000

Playbill
Judy Samelson, Editor
52 Vanderbilt Ave 11th Fl
New York NY 10017-3808
212-557-5757; Fax: 212-682-2932
Focus: 14D
Frequency: Monthly;
    Circulation: 1,069,000

Playboy
Alice Turner, Fiction Editor (Short stories)
747 Third Ave
New York NY 10017
212-688-3030; Fax: 212-957-2900
Focus: 75-99
Frequency: Monthly;
    Circulation: 3,671,000

Playboy
Barbara Nellis, Book/Music Editor
680 N Lake Shore Dr
Chicago IL 60611-1695
312-751-8000; Fax: 312-751-2818
Focus: 75-99
Frequency: Monthly;
    Circulation: 3,671,000

Playgirl
Charlene Keel, Managing Editor
801 Second Ave
New York NY 10017-4706
212-661-7878; Fax: 212-697-6343
Focus: 14-17-33-35-39-40-73-99
Frequency: Monthly; Circulation: 500,000

Poetry Flash
Joyce Jenkins, Book Reviewer
1450 Fourth St #4 (94710)
PO Box 4172
Berkeley CA 94704-0172
510-525-5476; Fax: 510-540-1057
Focus: 47-95-61(San Francisco Bay area)
Frequency: Monthly; Circulation: N/A

Polish-American Journal
Mark Kohan, Editor
Panagraphics Corp
1275 Harlem Rd
Buffalo NY 14206-1960
716-893-5771; Fax: 716-893-5783
Focus: 49O
Frequency: Monthly; Circulation: 18,000

Popular Ceramics
Barbara Case, Editor
Jones Publishing Inc
N7450 Aanstad Rd
Iola WI 54945-0331
715-445-5000; 800-331-0038;
    Fax: 715-445-4053
Focus: 29(ceramics)
Frequency: Monthly; Circulation: 24,000

Popular Electronics
Carl Laron, Editor
Gernsback Publications
500-B Bi-Country Blvd
Farmingdale NY 11735-3931
516-293-3000; Fax: 516-293-3115
Focus: 23-29(electronic hobbyists)
Frequency: Monthly; Circulation: 86,000

Popular Hot Rodding
Doug Marion, Editor
Argus Publishers Corp
12100 Wilshire Blvd #250
Los Angeles CA 90025-7102
310-820-3601; Fax: 310-207-9388
Focus: 16A
Frequency: Monthly; Circulation: 210,000

Popular Mechanics
Joseph Oldham, Editor-in-Chief
Hearst Corp
224 West 57th St
New York NY 10019-3212
212-649-2000; Fax: 212-586-5562
Focus: 19-23T-24-29H(men)-43H-51-69
Frequency: Monthly;
    Circulation: 1,635,000

Popular Science
Richard Stepler, Editor
2 Park Ave
New York NY 10016-5603
212-779-5000; Fax: 212-779-5468
Focus: 99
Frequency: Monthly;
    Circulation: 1,800,000

A Positive Approach Inc
Patricia Johnson, Editor
PO Box 910
Millville NJ 08332
609-451-4777; Fax: 609-451-6678
Focus: 39D
Frequency: Quarterly; Circulation: N/A

Potpourri
Kathryn Taylor, Book Editor
PO Box 8278
Prairie Village KS 66208
913-642-1503; Fax: 913-642-3128
Focus: 56W-75-95-97-99(literary arts)
Frequency: Quarterly; Circulation: 3,000

PR Watch
John Stauber, Editor
Ctr for Media and Democracy Inc
3318 Gregory St
Madison WI 53711-1725
608-233-3346; Fax: 608-238-2236;
    E-Mail: 74250.735@compuserve.com
Focus: 56M
Frequency: Quarterly; Circulation: 4,000

Prairie Fire
Andre Taskans, Editor
Prairie Fire Press Inc
100 Arthur St #423
Winnepeg MB R3B 1H3
204-943-9066; Fax: 204-942-1555
Focus: 47-95-75-99
Frequency: Quarterly; Circulation: 1,000

Pre
Anne Russell, Editor-in-Chief
Cowles Business Media
470 Park Ave S 7th Fl N Tower
New York NY 10016
212-683-3540; Fax: 212-683-4572;
    CowlesNews@aol.com
Focus: 56P
Frequency: 6x per yr; Circulation: N/A

Premiere Magazine
Susan Lyne, Editor
2 Park Ave
New York NY 10016-5303
212-545-3500; Fax: 212-481-6428
Focus: 14-17-33M
Frequency: Monthly; Circulation: 600,000

Prevention
Lewis Vaughn, Managing Editor
Rodale Press
33 E Minor St
Emmaus PA 18098
610-967-5171
Focus: 27-39
Frequency: Monthly;
    Circulation: 3,416,000

Prime
Bridget Miller
7116 Helen C White Hall
Madison WI 53706
Focus: 49B (For college students of color)
Frequency: N/A; Circulation: N/A

Private Pilot
J Patrick O'Leary, Editor
Fancy Publications Inc
PO Box 6050
Mission Viejo CA 92690-6050
714-855-8822; Fax: 714-855-3045
Focus: 70A
Frequency: Monthly; Circulation: N/A

The Professional Communicator
Leslie Sanson, Editor
Women in Communications Inc
3717 Columbia Pike #310
Arlington VA 22204-4255

703-920-5555; Fax: 703-920-5556;
    E-mail: smith@igc.org
Focus: 19C-56M-73
Frequency: 5x per yr; Circulation: 11,000

The Progressive Review
Sam Smith, Editor/Publisher
1739 Connecticut Ave NW
Washington DC 20009-1126
202-232-5544; Fax: 202-234-6222;
    E-mail: smith@igc.org
Focus: 13-25T-48-49-55-65-73-97
Frequency: 10x per yr; Circulation: 2,000

The Progressive
Matthew Rothschild, Book Review Editor
409 E Main St
Madison WI 53703-2863
608-257-4626; Fax: 608-257-3373
Focus: 11-13-19E-55
Frequency: Monthly; Circulation: 30,000

The Prolific Freelancer
Brian S Konradt, Editor-in-Chief
PO Box 554
Oradell NJ 07649
201-262-3277
Focus: 56W(freelancing)
Frequency: 6x per yr; Circulation: N/A

Providence Business News
Frank Prosnitz, Editor
300 Richmond St
Providence RI 02903-4244
401-273-2201; Fax: 401-274-0670
Focus: 11-19-55-61(RI)
Frequency: Weekly; Circulation: 11,000

Psychology Today
Lisa Liebman, Sr Editor
Sussex Publishers Inc
49 E 21st Eleventh Fl
New York NY 10010
212-260-7210; Fax: 212-260-7445
Focus: 39-57
Frequency: 6x per yr; Circulation: 400,000

Public Citizen
Peter Nye, Editor
2000 P St NW
Washington DC 20036-5915
202-833-3000; Fax: 202-296-1727
Focus: 13-25-39-51-55-65
Frequency: 6x per yr; Circulation: 130,000

Publishing Entrepreneur
Tom Bodus, Editor
The Jenkins Group
121 E Front St #401
Traverse City MI 49685-6126
616-933-0445; Fax: 616-933-0448
E-mail: info.entrepreneur@smallpress.com
Focus: 19M-23-56P
Frequency: Monthly; Circulation: N/A

Pulse!
Suzanne Mikesell, Managing Editor
Tower Records
2500 Del Monte St Bldg C
West Sacramento CA 95691-3820
916-373-2450; Fax: 916-373-2480
Focus: 14M-33
Frequency: 11x per yr;
    Circulation: 300,000

Pure
Amy Flamming, Editor/Publisher
1608 N Milwaukee #404
Chicago IL 60647-5464
312-772-5570; Fax: 312-772-5570
Focus: 13-14M-65S-99
Music & cultural magazine
Frequency: 6x per yr; Circulation: 10,000

Pure-Bred Dogs/American Kennel Gazette
Beth Adelman, Editor
American Kennel Club
51 Madison Ave 19th Fl
New York NY 10010-1603
212-696-8333; Fax: 212-696-8299
Focus: 15(dogs)
Frequency: Monthly; Circulation: 56,000

Q

QST
Mark J Wilson, Editor
American Radio Relay League
225 Main St
Newington CT 06111-1400
203-666-1541; Fax: 203-665-7531
Focus: 29(radio)
Frequency: Monthly; Circulation: 165,000

The Quarter Horse Journal
Jim Jennings, Editor-in-Chief
PO Box 32470
Amarillo TX 79120-2470
806-376-4888; Fax: 806-376-8364
Focus: 15(horses)
Frequency: Monthly; Circulation: 75,000

Quick & Easy Crafts
Beth Schwartz Wheeler, Editor
House of White Birches
306 East Parr Rd
Berne IN 46711-1138
219-589-8741; Fax: 219-589-8093
Focus: 29
Frequency: 6x per yr; Circulation: 310,000

Quick & Easy Quilting
Sandra Hatch, Editor
House of White Birches
306 East Parr Rd
Berne IN 46711-1138
219-589-8741; Fax: 219-589-8093
Focus: 29
Frequency: 6x per yr; Circulation: 66,000

Quilt World
Sandra Hatch, Editor
House of White Birches
306 East Parr Rd
Berne IN 46711-1138
219-589-8741; Fax: 219-589-8093
Focus: 29
Frequency: 6x per yr; Circulation: 68,000

Quilting International
Marion Buccieri, Editor
All American Crafts Inc
243 Newton-Sparta Rd
Newton NJ 07860-2748
201-383-8080; Fax: 201-383-8133
Focus: 29
Frequency: 6x per yr; Circulation: 85,000

Quilting Today
Christiane Meunier, Editor
Chitra Publications
2 Public Ave
Montrose PA 18801-1220
717-278-1984; 800-628-8244;
　　Fax: 717-278-2223
Focus: 29
Frequency: 6x per yr; Circulation: 50,000

R

Racquet Magazine
Matthew Tolan, Managing Editor
42 W 38th St
New York NY 10018-8210
212-768-8360; Fax: 212-768-8365
Focus: 39-57-69(tennis)-71
Frequency: 6x per yr; Circulation: 155,000

Radiance Magazine
Alice Ansfield, Editor
PO Box 30246
Oakland CA 94604-6346
510-482-0680; Fax: 510-482-0680
Focus: 39-40-73
Frequency: Quarterly; Circulation: 8,000

Railroad Model Craftsman
William C Schaumberg, Editor-in-Chief
Freedon-Springdale Rd
Newton NJ 07860
201-383-3355; Fax: 201-383-4064
Focus: 29
Frequency: Monthly; Circulation: 77,000

Rain
Greg Bryant, Editor/Book Review Editor
PO Box 30097
Eugene OR 97403-1097
503-683-1504
Focus: 13-51-65
Frequency: Quarterly; Circulation: 4,000

Ranger Rick
Gerald Bishop, Editor
National Wildlife Federation
8925 Leesburg Pike
Vienna VA 22184-0001
703-790-4274; Fax: 703-442-7332
Focus: 15-21-29-67 (ages 6-12)
Frequency: Monthly; Circulation: 850,000

Rapport
David Dreis, Editor/Publisher
Rapport Publishing Co Inc
5265 Fountain Ave #6
Los Angeles CA 90029-1300
213-660-0433; 800-397-1266;
　　Fax: 213-660-0434
Focus: 99
Frequency: 6x per yr; Circulation: 60,000

Ray Gun
Randy Bookasta, Editor
Ray Gun Publishing
2110 Main St #100
Santa Monica CA 90405-2276
310-452-6222; Fax: 310-452-8076
Focus: 14M
Frequency: 10x per yr;
　　Circulation: 120,000

Reader's Digest
William Schulz, Managing Editor
Reader's Digest Rd
Pleasantville NY 10570
914-238-1000;800-431-1246;
　　Fax: 914-238-4559
Focus: 39-99
Frequency: Monthly;
　　Circulation: 16,262,000

The Reading Teacher
Nancy Padek, Editor
International Reading Assn
800 Barksdale Rd
Newark DE 19711-3204
302-731-1600; 800-336-7323;
　　Fax: 302-731-1057
Focus: 21-31-76
Frequency: 8x per yr; Circulation: 61,000

The Real Estate Finance Journal
Steven Errick, Editor-In-Chief
Warren Gorham Lamont
1 Penn Plz
New York NY 10119-0002
212-971-5000; 800-950-1205;
　　Fax: 212-971-5025
Focus: 19B-19H-44-51E-55G
Frequency: Quarterly; Circulation: 3,000

Reason
Virginia Postrel, Editor
Reason Foundation
3415 S Sepulveda Blvd #400
Los Angeles CA 90034-6060
310-391-2245; Fax: 310-391-4395
Focus: 41-44-54-55-65(conservative
　　viewpoint)
Frequency: 11x per yr; Circulation: 50,000

Recipe Digest
Shelly Vaughan, Editor
House of White Birches
306 East Parr Rd
Berne IN 46711-1138
219-589-8741; Fax: 219-589-8093
Focus: 27
Frequency: 6x per yr; Circulation: N/A

Reckon: Magazine of Southern Culture
Lynn McKnight, Managing Editor
Hill Hall Rm 301
Univ of Mississippi
University MS 38677
Fax: 601-232-7842
Focus: 61(South)
Frequency: N/A; Circulation: N/A

Recreation News
M M Ghannam, Editor
Icarus Publishers Inc
PO Box 32335
Washington DC 20007-0635
202-965-6960
Focus: 69
Frequency: Monthly; Circulation: 104

The Red Herring Mystery Magazine
Polly W Swafford, Consulting Editor
PO Box 8278
Prairie Village KS 66208
913-642-1503; Fax: 913-642-3128
Focus: 84(mysteries)-90(short stories)
Frequency: Quarterly; Circulation: 1,500

Redbook
Dawn Raffel, Book/Fiction Editor
224 West 57th St 6th Fl
New York NY 10019-3299
212-649-3450; Fax: 212-581-8114;
　　Http://www.homearts.com
Focus: 75-76-81-83
Frequency: Monthly;
　　Circulation: 3,500,000

Reference Desk
George Kurian, Editor
The Encyclopediasts
PO Box 519
Baldwin Place NY 10505-0519
914-962-3287
Focus: 59
Frequency: Quarterly; Circulation: N/A
Review copies to 3689 Campbell Ct,
　　Yorktown Heights, NY 10398

Reform Judaism
Steven Schnur, Book Editor
Union of Am Hebrew Congregations
838 Fifth Ave
New York NY 10021-7012
212-249-0100; Fax: 212-734-1560
Focus: 63J-97-99
Frequency: Quarterly; Circulation: 295,000

Relix Magazine
Toni A Brown, Editor-in-Chief
PO Box 94
Brooklyn NY 11229-0094
718-258-0009; Fax: 718-692-4345
Focus: 14M(rock music)
Frequency: 6x per yr; Circulation: 60,000

Remember Magazine
Craig Peters, Publisher
Family Digest Inc
7002 W Butler Pike
Ambler PA 19002
215-643-6385; Fax: 215-540-0146
Focus: 41-99(nostalgia and cultural
　　history)
Frequency: 6x per yr; Circulation: N/A

Reminisce
Mike Beno, Editor
Reiman Publications
5400 S 60th St
Greendale WI 53129-1404
414-423-0100; Fax: 414-423-1143
Focus: 41A(reader reminiscenses about
　　the good old days)
Frequency: 6x per yr;
　　Circulation: 2,100,000

Reptiles
Phillip Samuelson, Editor
Fancy Publications
3 Burroughs
Irvine CA 92718-2804
714-855-8822; Fax: 714-855-3045
Focus: 15(reptiles)
Frequency: Monthly; Circulation: 90,000

Reunions Magazine
Carol Burns, Editor
PO Box 11727
Milwaukee WI 53211-0727
414-263-4567; Fax: 414-263-6331
Focus: 29H-33-35F-41G
Frequency: Quarterly; Circulation: 5,000

Rhode Island Monthly
Dan Kaplan, Editor
18 Imperial Pl
Providence RI 02903-4641
401-421-2552; Fax: 401-831-5624
Focus: 11-17-27-33-43-61(RI)-99
Frequency: Monthly; Circulation: 32,000

The Rhode Island Parents' Paper
Kim Stowell, Editor (401-294-1238)
PO Box 148
North Kingstown RI 02852-0148
401-295-7208; Fax: 401-295-7208
Focus: 21-31-35-76
Frequency: Monthly; Circulation: 30,000

Rider
Joe McNeill, Managing Editor
TL Enterprises
3601 Calle Tecate
Camarillo CA 93012
805-389-0300; Fax: 805-389-0484
Focus: 16-69 (motorcylce riding)
Frequency: Monthly; Circulation: N/A

Right On!
Cynthia Horner, Editor/Book Editor
Sterling-McFadden Partnership
233 Park Ave S
New York NY 10003
212-780-3500; Fax: 212-780-3555
Focus: 11-14-17-21T-33-40-49-89
Frequency: Monthly; Circulation: 200,000

Road & Track
Ellida Maki, Managing Editor
 (714-720-5382)
Hachette Filipacchi Magazines
1499 Monrovia Ave
Newport Beach CA 92663-2752
714-720-5300; Fax: 714-631-2757
Focus: 16A
Frequency: Monthly; Circulation: 725,000

The Robb Report
Robert Feeman, Editor
1 Acton Pl
Acton MA 01720-3945
508-263-7749; 800-229-7622;
 Fax: 508-263-0722
Focus: 17-19H-19I-99(upscale lifestyle)
Frequency: Monthly; Circulation: 85,000

Rocky Mountain Rider
Natalie Riehl, Editor/Publisher
PO Box 1011
Hamilton MT 59840
406-363-4085
Focus: 15(horses)-17P-41(Western)-
 61(Rocky Mtns)
Frequency: Monthly; Circulation: N/A

Rocky Mountain Sports Magazines
Don Silver, Editor
Sports & Fitness Publications
2025 Pearl St
Boulder CO 80302
303-440-5111; Fax: 303-440-3313;
 E-mail: 73201.411@compuserve.com
Focus: 69-73
Frequency: Monthly; Circulation: 42,000

Rocky Mountain Game & Fish
Burt Carey, Editor
Game & Fish Publications
2250 Newmarket Pky #110
Marietta GA 30067-8749
770-953-9222; Fax: 770-933-9510
Focus: 15-51-61(Rocky Mtn Area)-69
Frequency: Monthly; Circulation: N/A

Rod & Custom Magazine
DeEtte Crow, Publisher
Petersen Publishing
6420 Wilshire Blvd
Los Angeles CA 90048-5502
213-782-2000; Fax: 213-782-2263
Focus: 16A
Frequency: Monthly; Circulation: 100,000

Rolling Stone
Sid Holt, Managing Editor
Straight Arrow Publishers
1290 Ave of the Americas
New York NY 10104
212-484-1616; Fax: 212-767-8203
Focus: 14M-75-99
Frequency: 24; Circulation: 1,249,000

Romantic Times
Kathe Robin, Book Review Editor
 (historical romances)
Melinda Helfer, Book Review Editor
 (series romances)
55 Bergen St
Brooklyn NY 11201-6336
718-237-1097; Fax: 718-624-4231
Focus: 85
Frequency: Monthly; Circulation: 135,000

The Rotarian
Willmon L White, Editor
Rotary International
1560 Sherman Ave
Evanston IL 60201-4818
708-866-3000; Fax: 708-328-8554
Focus: 99
Frequency: Monthly; Circulation: 520,000

Rubber Ducky Magazine
Jon Accarrino, Editor
PO Box 799
Upper Montclair NJ 07043
201-783-0029
Focus: 10-11P-14M-14T-33H-97-99
Frequency: Quarterly; Circulation: N/A

Rug Hooking
MacDonald Kennedy, Editor
500 Vaughn St
Harrisburg PA 17110-2220
717-234-5091; 800-233-9055;
 Fax: 717-234-1359
Focus: 29C
Frequency: 5x per yr; Circulation: 12,000

Runner's World
Amby Burfoot, Book Review Editor
Rodale Press
33 E Minor St
Emmaus PA 18049-4113
610-967-5171; Fax: 610-967-7726
Focus: 39-69
Frequency: Monthly; Circulation: 447,000

Running Times
Scott Douglas, Editor
98 N Washington St
Boston MA 02114-1913
617-367-2228; Fax: 617-367-2350
Focus: 69(running)
Frequency: 10x per yr; Circulation: 59,000

S

SafeSteps
Lynda Shulman, Editor
100 Grandview Rd #310
Braintree MA 02184
617-843-5100
Focus: 21(child safety)
Frequency: 4x; Circulation: 1,000,000

SAIL Magazine
Patience Wales, Editor
275 Washington St
Newton MA 02158-1630
617-964-3030; Fax: 617-558-4677
Focus: 99
Frequency: Monthly; Circulation: 180,000

Sailing World
John Burnham, Editor-in-Chief
5 John Clarke Rd
Middletown RI 02842-5641
401-847-1588; Fax: 401-848-5048
Focus: 70N
Frequency: Monthly; Circulation: 65,000

Salon
Dwight Garner, Book Editor
221 Main St #940
San Francisco CA 94105
415-247-1195
Focus: 99
Frequency: N/A; Circulation: N/A

The Sample Case
Megan S Woitovich, Editor-in-Chief
632 N Park St
Columbus OH 43215-1627
614-228-3276; Fax: 614-228-1898
Focus: 71
Frequency: 6x per yr; Circulation: 140,000

San Diego Family Press
Sharon Bay, Editor/Publisher
PO Box 23960
San Diego CA 92193-3960
619-541-1162
Focus: 21-31-35-76
Frequency: Monthly; Circulation: 70,000

San Diego Parent Magazine
Jack Bierman, Editor
3160 Camino Del Rio S #313
San Diego CA 92108-3813
619-624-2770; Fax: 619-624-2777
Focus: 35F
Frequency: Monthly; Circulation: 70,000

San Francisco Focus
Amy Rennert, Editor-in-Chief
2601 Mariposa St
San Francisco CA 94110-1400
415-553-2800; Fax: 415-533-2470
Focus: 11-14-33-61(San Francisco CA)-99
Frequency: Monthly; Circulation: 180,000

San Francisco Peninsula Parent
Lisa Rosenthal, Editor-in-Chief
PO Box 1280
Millbrae CA 94030-5280
415-342-9203; Fax: 415-342-9276
Focus: 21-31-35-76
Frequency: Monthly; Circulation: 60,000

San Francisco Review of Books
Donald Paul, Editor
126 S Park
San Francisco CA 94107
415-543-7372; Fax: 415-243-8514
Focus: 11-17-31-41-47-55-57-63-65-75-99
Frequency: 6x per yr; Circulation: 10,000

Santa Barbara Magazine
Daniel Denton, Editor
226 E Canon Perdido St #H
Santa Barbara CA 93101-2234
805-965-5999; Fax: 805-965-7627
Focus: 61(CA)-99
Frequency: Quarterly; Circulation: 14,000

Sassy
Catherine Ettlinger, Editor
437 Madison Ave
New York NY 10022-7001
212-935-9150; Fax: 212-593-5447
Focus: 14-17-33-35-39-40-57-89 (for girls age 15-19)
Frequency: Monthly; Circulation: 750,000

Satellite Orbit
Linda Casey, Managing Editor
8330 Boone Blvd #600
Vienna VA 22182-2624
703-827-0511; Fax: 703-356-6179
Focus: 33T
Frequency: Monthly; Circulation: 415,000

Satellite TV Week
James Scott, Editor
140 S Fortuna Blvd
Fortuna CA 95540-2705
707-725-6951; 800-345-8876;
    Fax: 707-725-9639
Focus: 33T
Frequency: Weekly; Circulation: 440,000

Saturday Evening Post
Cory Ser Vaas, Editor
1100 Waterway Blvd
Indianapolis IN 46202-2156
317-636-8881; 800-289-7678;
    Fax: 317-637-0126
Focus: 75
Frequency: 6x per yr; Circulation: 500,000

Saveur
Christy Hobart, Editor
100 Ave of the Americas 7th Fl
New York NY 10013-1689
212-334-1212; Fax: 212-334-1260
Focus: 27-71
Frequency: 6x per yr; Circulation: 100,000

Scenario
Tod Lippi, Editor
104 Fifth Ave
New York NY 10011
Focus: 33M-56W
Screenplays/interviews
Frequency: Quarterly; Circulation: N/A

SCENTSITIVITY
Sara Hindman, Editor
Ntl Assn / Holistic Aromatherapy
PO Box 17622
Boulder CO 80309
800-566-6735; Fax: 415-564-6799
Focus: 13-15(care)-25-31
Frequency: Quarterly; Circulation: 2,000

Scholastic DynaMath
Joe D'Agnese, Editor
Scholastic Inc
730 Broadway
New York NY 10003-9511
212-343-6432; Fax: 212-343-6334
Focus: 31-67M (grades 5-6)
Frequency: 8x per yr; Circulation: 254,000

Scholastic Math Power
Carolyn Brunetto, Editor
Scholastic Inc
555 Broadway
New York NY 10012-3919
212-343-6458; 800-631-1586;
    Fax: 212-343-6334
Focus: 25-67M (grades 7-9)
Frequency: 8; Circulation: 202,000

Scholastic News
Patrick Daley, Editor
Scholastic Inc
555 Broadway
New York NY 10012-3919
212-343-6442; 800-325-6149;
    Fax: 212-343-6484
Focus: 21-31-97-99(separate issue for each grade 1-6)
Frequency: Biweekly; Circulation: 4,000

Scholastic Scope
John Rearick, Editor
Scholastic Inc
555 Broadway
New York NY 10012
212-343-6100; Fax: 212-343-6333
Focus: 21-31-75-77-81-97 (grades 6-8)
Frequency: 20x per yr;
    Circulation: 800,000

Scholastic Update
Steven Manning, Editor
Scholastic Inc
730 Broadway
New York NY 10003-9511
212-343-6271; Fax: 212-343-6333
Focus: 19-44-55-65S-71-97 (grades 8-12)
Frequency: Monthly; Circulation: 225,000

School Mates
Brian Bugbee, Editor
US Chess Federation
186 Route 9W
New Windsor NY 12553-7624
914-562-8350; Fax: 914-561-2437
Focus: 69G (for classes 4 to 6)
Frequency: 6x per yr; Circulation: 24,000

Science Fiction Age
Scott Edelman, Editor-in-Chief
457 Carlisle Dr
Herndon VA 22070-4819
703-471-1556; Fax: 703-471-1559
Focus: 86
Frequency: 6x per yr; Circulation: 65,000

Science Fiction Chronicle
Don D'Ammassa, Book Review Editor
PO Box 022730
Brooklyn NY 11202-2730
718-643-9011; Fax: 718-643-9011;
    E-Mail: ddammassa@genie.geis.com
Focus: 86
Frequency: Monthly; Circulation: 6,000

Science of Mind
Sandra Sarr, Editor
3251 W 6th St
Los Angeles CA 90020-5023
213-388-2181; 800-247-6463;
    Fax: 213-388-1926
Focus: 53-54
Frequency: Monthly; Circulation: 82,000

Science Spectra
Heather Wagner, Managing Editor
Gordon & Breacy Science Publ SA
820 Town Centre Dr
Langhorne PA 19047
215-750-2642
Focus: 67S
Frequency: N/A; Circulation: N/A

The Sciences
Peter Brown, Editor
2 East 63rd St
New York NY 10021-7210
212-838-0230; Fax: 212-888-2894
Focus: 23-67
Frequency: 6x per yr; Circulation: 60,000

Scientific American
Michelle Press, Managing Editor
415 Madison Ave
New York NY 10017-1179
212-754-0550; Fax: 212-755-1976
Focus: 99
Frequency: Monthly; Circulation: 657,000

Scientific Computing/Automation
Aimee Kalnoskas, Editor
Gordon Publications Inc
301 Gibraltar Dr PO Box 650
Morris Plains NJ 07950-0650
201-292-5100; Fax: 201-898-9281
Focus: 23(computers/technology)
Frequency: Monthly; Circulation: 70,000

Scouting
John Halter, Editor
1325 W Walnut Hill Ln
PO Box 75015
Irving TX 75015-2079
214-580-2368; Fax: 214-580-2079
Focus: 99 (adult leaders of scouting)
Frequency: 6x; Circulation: 1,000,000

Sea Magazine
Duncan McIntosh Jr, Publisher
17782 Cowan #C
Irvine CA 92714-6012
714-660-6150; Fax: 714-660-6172
Focus: 70N-71
Frequency: Monthly; Circulation: 53,000

Season's Greetings
Christopher Byrne, Editor
150 Fifth Ave 8th Fl
New York NY 10011
212-691-1100; Fax: 212-691-6185
Focus: 99(seasonal mdse & holiday gifts)
Frequency: 6x per yr; Circulation: 37,000

Seattle Magazine
Giselle Smith, Editor
701 Dexter Ave N #101
Seattle WA 98109-4339
206-284-1750; 800-858-0628;
　　Fax: 206-284-2550
Focus: 61(WA)-71-99
Frequency: 8x per yr; Circulation: 34,000

Seattle's Child
Ann Bergman, Editor/Publisher
2107 Elliot Ave #303
Seattle WA 98121-2159
206-441-0191; Fax: 206-441-4919
Focus: 21-31-35-76
Frequency: Monthly; Circulation: 27,000

Self
Rochelle Udell, Editor-in-Chief
Conde Nast Publications
350 Madison Ave
New York NY 10017-3704
212-880-8050; Fax: 212-880-8110
Focus: 99
Frequency: 12x; Circulation: 1,257,000

Senior World of Los Angeles
Laura Impastato, Editor-in-Chief
11835 W Olympic Blvd #135
Los Angeles CA 90064-5002
310-820-1125
Focus: 35A-99 (target audience—older Americans)
Frequency: Monthly; Circulation: 155,000

Ser Padres (Being Parents)
Joceline Frank, Exec Editor
685 Third Ave
New York NY 10017-4024
212-878-8700; Fax: 212-878-4648
Focus: 31-35-49H
Frequency: 6x per yr; Circulation: 425,000

Sesame Street Magazine
Ira Wolfman, Editor-in-Chief
Children's Television Workshop
1 Lincoln Plz
New York NY 10023-7129
212-595-3456; Fax: 212-875-6105
Focus: 21-31-39-76
Frequency: 10x; Circulation: 1,100,000

Seventeen Magazine
Joe Bargmann, Features Editor
850 Third Ave 9th Fl
New York NY 10022-6222
212-759-8100;
　　E-Mail: seventeenm@aol.com
Focus: 99(buys rights)
Frequency: 12x; Circulation: 1,960,000

Sewanee Review
George Core, Editor
735 University Ave
Sewanee TN 37383-0001
615-598-1246; Fax: 615-598-1145
Focus: 47-75-83-90-95
Frequency: Quarterly; Circulation: 3,000

Sewing Decor
Susan Voigt-Reising, Editor
PJS Publications, News Plz
PO Box 1790
Peoria IL 61656-1790
309-682-6626; Fax: 309-682-7394
Focus: 29C(sewing)
Frequency: 6x per yr; Circulation: 100,000

Shape Magazine
Nancy Gottesman, Features/Book Editor
21100 Erwin St
Woodland Hills CA 91367
818-596-0476; Fax: 818-716-5626
Focus: 99
Frequency: Monthly; Circulation: 800,000

Sharing Ideas Newsmagazine
Dottie Walters CSP, Editor-in-Chief/Publ
PO Box 1120
Glendora CA 91740
818-335-8069; Fax: 818-335-6127;
　　E-mail: call4spk@aol.com
Focus: 19M-56(speaking)
Frequency: 6x per yr; Circulation: 3,000

Shofar Magazine
Jeff Hoffman, Editor
1640 Rhode Island Ave NW
Washington DC 20036-3278
202-857-6633; Fax: 202-857-6568
Focus: 21-63J
Frequency: 3x per yr; Circulation: 30,000

Shooting Times
Jim Bequette, Editor
PJS Publications
News Plaza
Peoria IL 61614
309-682-6626; Fax: 309-682-7394
Focus: 69H
Frequency: Monthly; Circulation: 215,000

Shutterbug
Bonnie Paulk, Managing Editor
PO Box 1209
Titusville FL 32781-1209
407-268-5010; Fax: 407-267-7216
Focus: 11P
Frequency: Monthly; Circulation: 150,000

Sierra Magazine
Mark Mardon, Book Editor
Sierra Club
730 Polk St
San Francisco CA 94109
415-776-2211; Fax: 415-776-4868
Focus: 51-71
Frequency: 6x per yr; Circulation: 51,000

Silver Circle Magazine
Jay A Binkly, Editor
Home Savings of America
4900 Rivergrade Rd
Irwindale CA 91706-1404
818-814-7282
Focus: 19-99
Frequency: Quarterly; Circulation: 500,000

Sing Out! Magazine
Mark Moss, Editor-in-Chief
PO Box 5253
Bethlehem PA 18015-0253
610-865-5366; Fax: 610-865-5129
Focus: 14M
Frequency: Quarterly; Circulation: 10,000

The Single Family Home Plans
Richard Compen, Publisher
Archway Press
19 West 44th St
New York NY 10036
212-757-5580; Fax: 212-869-5215
Focus: 12-43
Frequency: 2x per yr; Circulation: 50,000

The Single Parent
Mercy Vance-Ehrler, Editor-in-Chief
Parents Without Partners Inc
401 N Michigan Ave
Chicago IL 60611-4212
312-644-6610; Fax: 312-245-1003
Focus: 21-31-35
Frequency: Quarterly; Circulation: 70,000

Single-Parent Family
Lynda Hunter, Editor
Focus on the Family
Colorado Springs CO 80995
719-531-5181
Focus: 31P-35F
Frequency: Monthly; Circulation: N/A

Ski Magazine
Dick Needham and Lisa Gosselin, Co-Editors
Times Mirror Magazines
2 Park Ave
New York NY 10016-5603
212-779-5000; Fax: 212-481-9261
Focus: 69(skiing)
Frequency: 8x per yr; Circulation: 450,000

Skipping Stones
Arun N Toke, Editor/Publisher
PO Box 3939
Eugene OR 67403-0939
503-342-4956
Focus: 49-51-65S-99
Frequency: 5x per yr; Circulation: 3,000

Sky and Telescope
Tim Lister, Managing Editor
Sky Publishing
49 Bay State Rd
Cambridge MA 02138
617-864-7360; Fax: 617-864-6117
Focus: 67A
Frequency: Monthly; Circulation: 95,000

Skywriters
Tara Allen, Editor
245 Spring St SW
Concord NC 28025
Focus: 10-95-99 (primarily for disabled people)
Frequency: Quarterly; Circulation: N/A

Slow Lane Journal
J Thomas McClelland, Editor
PO Box 361
Rocklin CA 95677
Focus: 16A-61-71(travel guide to the backroads of America)
Frequency: Quarterly; Circulation: N/A

Small Business Journal
Aaron Horton, Editor
632 Vine St
Provident Bank #828
Cincinnati OH 45202-2425
513-579-8725; Fax: 513-345-4192
Focus: 19
Frequency: Monthly; Circulation: 10,000

Smart Electronics
Bill Roche, Editor
774 South Placentia
Placentia CA 92670-6832
714-572-2255; Fax: 714-572-1864
Focus: 23-24
Frequency: 6x per yr; Circulation: 175,000

SmartKid
J P Faber, Editor-in-Chief
1 Biscayne Tower
2 S Biscayne Blvd #3710
Miami FL 33131
305-789-9940; Fax: 305-789-9941
Focus: 21-23-31E
Frequency: Monthly; Circulation: 50,000

Smithsonian
Don Moser, Editor
900 Jefferson Dr SW
Washington DC 20560-0001
202-786-2900; Fax: 202-786-2564
Focus: 23-41-51-55-67-71
Frequency: Monthly;
    Circulation: 2,169,000

Snow Country
Roger Toll, Editor
5520 Park Ave
Trumbull CT 06611-3426
203-373-7000; Fax: 203-373-7111
Focus: 61-69(skiing)-71-99(lifestyle info for mountain living)
Frequency: 8x per yr; Circulation: 460,000

Snow Goer
Dan Hauser, Editor
601 Lakeshore Pky #600
Minnetonka MN 55305-5215
612-476-2200; Fax: 612-476-8065
Focus: 69-71(snowmobiling)
Frequency: Quarterly; Circulation: 100,000

Snow Week
Dan Hauser, Editor
601 Lakeshore Pky #600
Minnetonka MN 55305-5215
612-476-2200; Fax: 612-476-8065
Focus: 69(snowmobile racing)
Frequency: 17x per yr; Circulation: 23,000

Snowboarding
Jamie Meiselman, Managing Editor
Transworld Publications
353 Airport Rd
Oceanside CA 92054
619-722-7777; Fax: 619-722-0653
Focus: 69-19
Frequency: 8x per yr; Circulation: N/A

Snowmobile Magazine
Dan Hauser, Editor
601 Lakeshore Pky #600
Minnetonka MN 55305-5215
612-476-2200; 800-848-6247;
    Fax: 612-476-8065
Focus: 69(snowmobiles)
Frequency: Quarterly; Circulation: 500,000

Soap Opera Digest
Lynn Leahey, Editor-in-Chief
45 West 25th St 8th Fl
New York NY 10010-2003
212-645-2100; Fax: 212-645-0683
Focus: 33T
Frequency: Biweekly;
    Circulation: 1,300,000

Sober Times
J D Miller, Publisher
PO Box 31967
Seattle WA 98103-0067
206-523-8005; Fax: 360-533-8085
Focus: 39R
Frequency: 6x per yr; Circulation: 50,000

Soccer Digest
Ken Leiker, Sr Editor
Century Publishing Co
990 Grove St
Evanston IL 60201-4370
708-491-6440
Focus: 69(soccer)
Frequency: 6x per yr; Circulation: 45,000

Software Development
Larry O'Brien, Editor
Miller Freeman
600 Harrison St
San Francisco CA 94107-1370
415-905-2200; Fax: 415-905-2234
Focus: 23C(software development, languages, multiple platforms, programs)
Frequency: Monthly; Circulation: 72,000

Soldier of Fortune
Tom Slizewski, Managing Editor
PO Box 693
Boulder CO 80306-0693
303-449-3750; Fax: 303-444-5617
Focus: 48-55-70
Frequency: Monthly; Circulation: 125,000

Sound & Image
Mike Mettler, Managing Editor
1633 Broadway 45th Fl
New York NY 10019-6708
212-767-6020; Fax: 212-767-5615
Focus: 14(audio)
Frequency: 6x per yr; Circulation: 60,000

South Carolina Game & Fish
Jeff Samsel, Editor
Game & Fish Publications
2250 Newmarket Pky #110
Marietta GA 30067-8749
770-953-9222; Fax: 770-933-9510
Focus: 15-51-61(SC)-69
Frequency: Monthly; Circulation: 24,000

South Florida Bride
Kip Bradshaw, Editor
800 Douglas Rd #500
Coral Gables FL 33134-3186
305-445-4500; Fax: 305-445-4600
Focus: 35-43-61(FL)
Frequency: 2x per yr; Circulation: 20,000

South Florida Magazine
Jerry Renninger, Editor
800 Douglas Rd #500
Coral Gables FL 33134-3186
305-445-4500; Fax: 305-445-4600
Focus: 61(FL)-43-69-71
Frequency: Monthly; Circulation: 52,000

Southern Accents
Lynn Carter, Managing Editor
2100 Lakeshore Dr
Birmingham AL 35209-6721
205-877-6000; Fax: 205-877-6422
Focus: 11-29-43D-43H-61(Southern)
Frequency: 6x per yr; Circulation: 275,000

Southern Boating
Skip Allen Sr, Editor/Publisher
1766 Bay Rd
Miami Beach FL 33139-1414
305-538-0700; Fax: 305-532-8657
Focus: 70-71
Frequency: Monthly; Circulation: 30,000

Southern Exposure
Pat Arnow, Editor
2009 Chapel Hill Rd
Durham NC 27707-1109
919-419-8311; Fax: 919-419-8315
Focus: 51E-55-61(South)-65(social and cultural change in the south)
Frequency: Quarterly; Circulation: 6,000

Southern Living
Melissa Bigner, Book Review Editor
2100 Lakeshore Dr
Birmingham AL 35209-6721
205-877-6000
Focus: 27-43-61(Southern)71
Frequency: Monthly;
    Circulation: 2,275,000

Southern Living Vacations
Karen Lingo, Editor
2100 Lakeshore Dr
Birmingham AL 35209-6721
205-877-6000; 800-366-4712;
    Fax: 205-877-6700
Focus: 61(South)-71
Frequency: Quarterly; Circulation: 200,000

Southwest Art
Susan H McGarry, Editor-in-Chief
5444 Westheimer #1440
Houston TX 77056-5306
713-850-0990; Fax: 713-850-1314
Focus: 11
Frequency: Monthly; Circulation: 63,000

Speak Magazine
Neil Feineman, Editor
5150 El Camino Real #B24
Los Altos CA 94022-1527
415-428-0150
Focus: 99(18- to 29-year-olds)
Frequency: Quarterly; Circulation: 40,000

Spider
Marianne Carus, Editor-in-Chief
315 Fifth St
Peru IL 61354-2859
815-223-2520; 800-435-6850;
    Fax: 815-224-6675
Focus: 15-21-35-67-76(children 6 & up)
Frequency: Monthly; Circulation: N/A

Spin
Madison Bell, Printed Matter
6 West 18th St
New York NY 10011
212-633-8200; Fax: 212-633-9041; E-mail: Spinonline@aol.com
Focus: 14M-99
Frequency: Monthly; Circulation: N/A

Spin-Off
Deborah Robson, Editor
201 E 4th St
Loveland CO 80537-5601
303-669-7672; 800-272-2193;
    Fax: 303-667-8317
Focus: 29(weaving)
Frequency: Quarterly; Circulation: 15,000

Splash
Jeff Ames, Editor
774 South Placentia
Placentia CA 92670-6846
714-572-2255; Fax: 714-572-1864
Focus: 70N (personal water craft)
Frequency: 6x per yr; Circulation: N/A

Sport Compact Car
Larry Saavedra, Editor
McMullen & Yee Publishing Inc
774 South Placentia
Placentia CA 92670-6846
714-572-2255; Fax: 714-572-1864
Focus: 16
Frequency: Monthly; Circulation: N/A

Sport Magazine
Cameron Benty, Editor
437 Madison Ave
New York NY 10022-7001
212-935-9150; Fax: 212-593-5447
Focus: 69
Frequency: Monthly; Circulation: 909,000

Sport Truck Magazine
Peter MacGillivray, Editor
6420 Wilshire Blvd
Los Angeles CA 90048-5502
213-782-2013; Fax: 213-782-2867
Focus: 16A(trucks)
Frequency: Monthly; Circulation: 196,000

Sporting Classics Magazine
Chuck Wechsler, Editor
1111 Broad St
Camden SC 29020-3611
803-736-2424; 800-849-1004;
    Fax: 803-736-3404
Focus: 69
Frequency: 6x per yr; Circulation: 30,000

Sporting News
Steve Gietschier, Book Reviewer
PO Box 56
St Louis MO 63166
314-993-7787; Fax: 314-993-7723
Focus: 17(sports heros)-69(reference and history)
Frequency: 6x per yr; Circulation: 684,000

Sports 'N Spokes
Cliff Crase, Publisher
Paralyzed Veterans of America
2111 E Highland Ave #180
Phoenix AZ 85016-4732
602-224-0500; Fax: 602-224-0507
Focus: 39D
Frequency: 6x per yr; Circulation: 14,000

Sports Afield
Frank Golad, Sr Assoc Editor
250 West 55th St
New York NY 10019
212-649-4000; Fax: 212-581-3923
Focus: 70N-69H-69R
Frequency: 10x per yr;
    Circulation: 527,000

Sports Collectors Digest
Tom Mortenson, Editor-in-Chief
700 E State St
Iola WI 54990-0001
715-445-2214; Fax: 715-445-4087
Focus: 28-69
Frequency: Weekly; Circulation: 50,000

Sports Focus Magazine
Manny Rosenberg, Co-Editor
124 E Diamond Ave #6
Gaithersburg MD 20877-3072
301-670-6717; Fax: 301-670-9043
Focus: 39-69
Frequency: Monthly; Circulation: 145,000

Sports Illustrated
Bill Colson, Editor
Time-Life Bldg
1271 Ave of the Americas 4th Fl
New York NY 10020-1393
212-522-1212; Fax: 212-522-4543;
    E-mail: LettersSI@is.compuserve.com
Focus: 51-69
Frequency: Weekly; Circulation: 3,150,000

Sports Illustrated for Kids
Craig Neff, Managing Editor
Time-Life Bldg
1271 Ave of the Americas 4th Fl
New York NY 10020-1393
212-522-5437; Fax: 212-522-0120;
    E-Mail: cneff@aol.com
Focus: 21-69
Frequency: Monthly; Circulation: 350,000

SportStyle
Larry Carlat, Editor
7 West 34th St
New York NY 10001-8100
212-630-3750
Focus: 19R-40F-69
Frequency: Monthly; Circulation: 25,000

Spotlight
Jena Hofstedt, Assoc Editor
126 Library Ln
Mamaroneck NY 10543
914-381-4740
Focus: 11-39-40-55-61-99
Frequency: Monthly; Circulation: N/A

St Anthony Messenger
Barbara Beckwith, Book Review Editor
1615 Republic St
Cincinnati OH 45210-1219
513-241-5615; Fax: 513-241-0399
Focus: 63C
Frequency: Monthly; Circulation: 325,000

St Louis Small Business Monthly
Judith Meador, Editor/Publisher
1173 N Price Rd
St Louis MO 63132-2301
314-569-0076
Focus: 19S
Frequency: Monthly; Circulation: 30,000

Stamp Collector
Ken Palke, Editor
PO Box 10
Albany OR 97321-0006
503-928-3569; Fax: 503-967-7262
Focus: 28
Frequency: Weekly; Circulation: 19,000

Star Magazine
Reed Sparling, Book Editor
660 White Plains Rd
Tarrytown NY 10591-5182
914-332-5000; Fax: 914-332-5043
Focus: 17-39E-40B-40F-75-77
Frequency: Monthly;
    Circulation: 1,000,000

Starlog
David McDonnell, Editor
475 Park Ave S
New York NY 10016-6901
212-689-2830; Fax: 212-889-7933
Focus: 86
Frequency: Monthly; Circulation: 250,000

Staten Island Parent
Roselle Farina, Editor
2110 Clove Rd #D
Staten Island NY 10305-1502
718-273-5700; Fax: 718-273-2539
Focus: 11-14-17-33-43-61(NY)-99
Frequency: Monthly; Circulation: 50,000

Stereo Review
Louise Boundas, Managing Editor
Hachette Filipacchi Magazines
1633 Broadway 45th Fl
New York NY 10019-6708
212-767-6000; Fax: 212-767-5615
Focus: 14M-23E(electronics)
Frequency: Monthly; Circulation: 503,000

The Stitchery
Editor
Potpourri
120 N Meadows Rd
Meadfield MA 02052
508-359-4649
Focus: 29(stitchery kits)-43
Frequency: Monthly; Circulation: 230,000

Stitches Magazine
Melissa Maher, Editor
Intertec Publishing Corp
9800 Metcalf
Overland Park KS 66212-2216
913-341-1300; Fax: 913-967-1905
Focus: 29C(embroidery, monogramming and sewing)
Frequency: Monthly; Circulation: 15,000

Stone Soup
Gerry Mandel, Articles/Fiction Editor
Children's Art Foundation
PO Box 83
Santa Cruz CA 95063
408-426-5557; Fax: 408-426-1161
Focus: 21-76
Stories/art/reviews by ages 6-13
Frequency: 6x per yr; Circulation: 9

Storytelling Magazine
Mary Weaver, Editor
Natl Storytelling Assn
PO Box 309
Jonesborough TN 37659-0309
423-753-2171; 800-525-4514;
    Fax: 423-753-9331
Focus: 75-76-90(storytelling)
Frequency: 6x per yr; Circulation: 10,000

Storytime Monthly
Phyllis Heller, Publisher
NPR Services, PO Box 71403
4013 Coyte Ct
Marietta GA 30007-1403
404-971-5200; Fax: 404-977-7810
Focus: 21-76-95(children's stories gender neutral/politically correct)
No excessive violence, ethical
Frequency: Monthly; Circulation: N/A

Street & Smith's Sports Books
Jerry Kavanagh, Editor
Conde Nast Publications
140 East 45th St
New York NY 10017
212-880-8098; Fax: 212-880-4347
Focus: 69
Frequency: 1x per yr; Circulation: N/A

Street Rod Action
Jon Gobetti, Editor
Challenge Publications
7950 Deering Ave
Canoga Park CA 91304-5007
818-887-0550; Fax: 818-884-1343
Focus: 16-28
Frequency: Monthly; Circulation: 80,000

Street Rodder
Tom Vogele, Editor
McMullen & Yee Publishing Inc
774 South Placentia
Placentia CA 92670-6832
714-572-2255; Fax: 714-572-1864
Focus: 16-24
Frequency: Monthly; Circulation: 116,000

Studio Photography
Faye Guercio, Editor
PTN Publishing Co
445 Broad Hollow Rd
Melville NY 11747
516-845-2700; Fax: 516-845-2797
Focus: 11P
Frequency: Monthly; Circulation: N/A

Style Weekly
Beth Barmettler, Editor
1118 W Main St
Richmond VA 23220
804-358-0825; Fax: 804-355-9089
Focus: 61(VA)-99
Books by local authors/regionals
Frequency: Weekly; Circulation: 38,000

Success!
Scott DeGarmo, Editor-in-Chief
Lang Communications
230 Park Ave 7th Fl
New York NY 10169-0005
212-551-9500; Fax: 212-599-0783
Focus: 19-57
Frequency: 10x per yr;
    Circulation: 440,000

Successful Black Parenting
Marta Sanchez-Speer, Editor
KLS Communications Inc
PO Box 6359
Philadelphia PA 19139
215-476-7660
Focus: 31P-35F
Frequency: Quarterly; Circulation: 35,000

Successful Farming
Loren Kruse, Editor
Meredith Corp
1716 Locust St
Des Moines IA 50309-3023
515-284-3000; Fax: 515-284-3127
Focus: 51A
Frequency: 15x per yr;
    Circulation: 500,000

Successful Farming @griculture
John Walter, Contact Person
Meredith Corp
1716 Locust St
Des Moines IA 50309-3023
515-284-3000; Fax: 515-284-3127;
    http://www.agricultur.com
Focus: 51-67
Frequency: Monthly; Circulation: N/A

Summit
John Harlin, Editor
1221 May St
Hood River OR 97031-1549
503-387-2200; Fax: 503-387-2223
Focus: 11-15-39-51-69
Mountains/ecology/hiking/etc
Frequency: 6x per yr; Circulation: 35,000

Sunset Magazine
William Marken, Editor
Sunset Publishing Corp
80 Willow Rd
Menlo Park CA 94025-3661
415-321-3600; Fax: 415-321-0551
Focus: 27-29-35-43-61(Western)
Frequency: Monthly;
    Circulation: 1,500,000

The Sun
Sy Safransky, Managing Editor
107 N Roberson St
Chapel Hill NC 27516-9908
919-942-5282; Fax: 919-932-3101
Focus: 99
Literary magazine
Frequency: Monthly; Circulation: 28,000

Super Chevy
Terry Cole, Editor
12100 Wilshire Blvd #250
Los Angeles CA 90025-7102
310-820-3601; Fax: 310-207-9388
Focus: 16A
Frequency: Monthly; Circulation: 163,000

Super Ford
Tom Wilson, Editor-in-Chief
Dobbs Publishing Group Inc
3816 Industry Blvd
Lakeland FL 33811-1340
941-644-0449; Fax: 941-648-1187
Focus: 16A
Frequency: Monthly; Circulation: 70,000

Super Stock & Drag Illustrated
Steve Collison, Editor, General Media
6728 Eton Ave
Canoga Park CA 91303-2813
818-992-4777; Fax: 818-992-4979
Focus: 16A
Frequency: Monthly; Circulation: 55,000

Symphony Magazine
Sandra Hyslop, Editor
777 14th St NW
Washington DC 20005-3201
202-628-0099; Fax: 202-783-7228
Focus: 14M (for people working
    w/orchestras)
Frequency: 6x per yr; Circulation: 17,000

Talking Leaves
Carolyn Moran, Editor
Deep Ecology Education Project
1430 Willamette St #367
Eugene OR 97401
503-342-2974; 800-309-2974
Focus: 51E-53
Frequency: Monthly; Circulation: 100,000

Taste of Home
Ann Kaiser, Managing Editor
5400 S 60th St
Greendale WI 53129-1404
414-423-0100; 800-344-6913;
    Fax: 414-423-8463
Focus: 27
Frequency: 6x per yr;
    Circulation: 2,000,000

Tea
Tom Kagy, Publisher
PO Box 4260
Malibu CA 90264-4260
310-456-0790; Fax: 310-457-0535
Focus: 49(Asian/American)
Frequency: Quarterly; Circulation: N/A

Teachers in Focus
Chuck Johnson, Editor
Focus on the Family
Colorado Springs CO 80995
719-531-5181
Focus: 31D-31E
Frequency: Monthly; Circulation: 28,000

Teddy Bear and Friends
Deborah Thompson, Managing Editor
Cowles Magazine Inc
6405 Flank Dr
Harrisburg PA 17112-2750
717-657-9555; Fax: 717-657-9552
Focus: 29-28
Frequency: 6x per yr; Circulation: 41,000

Teen Magazine
Roxanne Camron, Editor
6420 Wilshire Blvd
Los Angeles CA 90048-5502
213-782-2000; 800-800-8336;
    Fax: 213-782-2660
Focus: 21T-99
Frequency: Monthly;
    Circulation: 1,200,000

Tennessee Sportsman
Jeff Samsel, Editor
2250 Newmarket Pky #110
Marietta GA 30067-8749
770-953-9222; Fax: 770-933-9510
Focus: 15-51-61(TN)-69
Frequency: Monthly; Circulation: 16,000

Tennis Magazine
Donna Doherty, Editor
5520 Park Ave
Turnbull CT 06611-3426
203-373-7000; Fax: 203-371-2127
Focus: 39-69-71(tennis)
Frequency: Monthly; Circulation: 800,000

Tennis Match
Norman Zeitchick, Editor-in-Chief
24 Post Road E
Westport CT 06880-3404
203-221-0343; Fax: 203-454-2438
Focus: 69(tennis)
Frequency: 6x per yr; Circulation: 75,000

Texas Highways
Jack Lowry, Managing Editor
1101 E Anderson Ln
Austin TX 78752-1745
512-483-3675; 800-839-4997;
    Fax: 512-483-3672
Focus: 16A-61(TX)-71
Frequency: Monthly; Circulation: 400,000

Texas Monthly
Gregory Curtis, Editor
PO Box 1569
Austin TX 78767-1569
512-320-6900; Fax: 512-476-9007
Focus: 61(TX)
Frequency: Monthly; Circulation: 300,000

Texas People & Places
Billy Huckaby, Editor/Publisher
PO Box 810
Joshua TX 76058-0810
817-556-3605; Fax: 817-645-3497
Focus: 17-61-71(Texas)
Recommended books list & reviews
Frequency: Monthly; Circulation: 30,000

Texas Sportsman
Nick Gilmore, Editor
2250 Newmarket Pky #110
Marietta GA 30067-8749
770-953-9222; Fax: 770-933-9510
Focus: 15-51-61(TX)-69
Frequency: Monthly; Circulation: N/A

This Magazine
Naomi Klein, Editor
16 Skey Ln
Toronto ON Canada M6J 3S4
416-588-6580; Fax: 416-588-6638
Focus: 13-55-61(CN)-65
Frequency: 8x per yr; Circulation: N/A

Time Magazine
Paul Gray, Sr Writer/Book Reviews
R Z Sheppard, Contributor/Book Review
Time-Life Bldg
1271 Ave of the Americas
New York NY 10020-1393
212-522-1212; Fax: 212-522-0323
Focus: 17-99
E-Mail: TimeLetter@aol.com
Frequency: Weekly; Circulation: 4,250,000

Time Out New York
Cyndi Stivers, Editor
627 Broadway 7th Fl
New York NY 10012
212-539-4444; Fax: 212-460-8744
Focus: 11-14-61
Frequency: Weekly; Circulation: N/A

The Toastmaster
Suzanne Frey, Editor
23182 Arroyo Vista
R Santa Margarita CA 92688-2620
714-858-8255; Fax: 714-858-1207
Focus: 99
Frequency: Monthly; Circulation: 180,000

Today's Collector
Steve Ellingboe, Editor
700 E State St
Iola WI 54990-0001
715-445-2214; Fax: 715-445-4087
Focus: 28C-29H
Frequency: Monthly; Circulation: 40,000

Today's Old West Traveler
Sandra Guggenmos, Editor
2796 Harbor Blvd (92626)
PO Box 2928 #148
Costa Mesa CA 92628
714-540-5200
Focus: 61-71-88(anything about the West & cowboys)
Frequency: 6x per yr; Circulation: N/A

Total Health
Boo Kennedy, Health Editor
6001 Topanga Canyon #300
Woodland Hills CA 91367-3643
818-887-6484; Fax: 818-887-7960
Focus: 39-53
Frequency: 6x per yr; Circulation: 100,000

Town & Country
Susan Bleecher, Managing Editor
1700 Broadway
New York NY 10019-5905
212-903-5000; Fax: 212-765-8308
Focus: 43-99(upscale lifestyle)
Frequency: Monthly; Circulation: 500,000

Traditional Quilter
Phyllis Barbieri, Editor
243 Newton-Sparta Rd
Newton NJ 07860-2748
201-383-8080; Fax: 201-383-8133
Focus: 29
Frequency: 6x per yr; Circulation: N/A

Traditional Quiltworks
Christiane Meunier, Editor
2 Public Ave
Montrose PA 18801-1220
717-278-1984; 800-628-8244;
    Fax: 717-278-2223
Focus: 29
Frequency: 6x per yr; Circulation: 95,000

Trailer Life
Barbara Leonard, Editorial Dir
3601 Calle Tecate
Camarillo CA 93012-5040
805-389-0300; Fax: 805-389-0484
Focus: 16-71
Frequency: Monthly; Circulation: 300,000

Training
Chris Lee, Managing Editor
50 South Ninth St
Minneapolis MN 55402-3118
612-333-0471; Fax: 612-333-6526
Focus: 19(personnel)
800-328-4329
Frequency: Monthly; Circulation: 55,000

Trains
Kevin Keefe, Editor
21027 Crossroads Cir
Waukesha WI 53186-4055
414-796-8776; Fax: 414-796-1142
Focus: 16R-29(models)
Frequency: Monthly; Circulation: 111,000

Trans Pacific
Tom Kagy, Publisher
PO Box 4260
Malibu CA 90264-4260
310-456-0790; Fax: 310-457-0535 or
    310-457-0567
Focus: 49(Asian/American)
Frequency: 6x per yr; Circulation: N/A

Travel & Leisure
Mark Orwoll, Senior Editor
American Express Publishing
1120 Ave of the Americas
New York NY 10036-6708
212-386-5719; Fax: 212-926-1748
Focus: 39-69-71
Frequency: Monthly;
    Circulation: 1,296,000

Travel 50 & Beyond
Mary Lu Abbott, Managing Editor
1502 August Dr #415
Houston TX 77057-2484
713-974-6903; Fax: 713-914-0445
Focus: 35A-71(for people ages 50+)
Frequency: Quarterly; Circulation: 200,000

Travel America
Randy Mink, Managing Editor
World Publishing Co
990 Grove St
Evanston IL 60201-4370
708-491-6440; Fax: 708-491-0459
Focus: 71
Frequency: 6x per yr; Circulation: 417,000

Travel Holiday
Jack Bettridge, Features Editor
28 West 23rd St #9
New York NY 10010
212-366-8700; Fax: 212-366-8798
Focus: 44-61
Frequency: 10x per yr;
    Circulation: 582,000

Travelhost
Jill Kahan, Editor
7600 E Arapahoe Rd #120
Englewood CO 80112
303-796-0078; Fax: 303-796-0091
Focus: 71(CO)
Frequency: Monthly; Circulation: N/A

Travelin' Magazine
Russ Heggen, Editor
860 W 6th Ave
PO Box 23005
Eugene OR 97402-0424
541-485-8533; Fax: 541-485-8528;
    E-mail: travelin@teleport.com
Focus: 61(West)-71
Frequency: 6x per yr; Circulation: 10,000

Traverse Magazine
Ellyn Tarrant, Managing Editor
121 S Union St
Traverse City MI 49684
616-941-8174; Fax: 616-941-8391
Focus: 61(MI)-99
Frequency: Monthly; Circulation: 20,000

Tropical Fish Hobbyist
Jerry Walls, Book Review Editor
211 W Sylvania Ave
Neptune City NJ 07753-6233
908-988-8400; Fax: 908-988-9635
Focus: 15(fish)
Frequency: Monthly; Circulation: 60,000

True Detective
Rose Mandelsberg, Editor-in-Chief
460 W 34th St
New York NY 10001-2320
212-947-6500; Fax: 212-947-6727
Focus: 55C-84
Frequency: 7x per yr; Circulation: 35,000

True Love
Kristina Kracht, Editor
Sterling Macfadden Ptnship
233 Park Ave S
New York NY 10003-1606
212-979-4800; Fax: 212-979-7342
Focus: 35M-35R-35S
Frequency: Monthly; Circulation: 250,000

Tucson Lifestyle
Sue Giles, Managing Editor
7000 E Tanque Verde
Tucson AZ 85715-5325
520-721-2929; Fax: 520-721-8665
Focus: 11-14-19-33-39-43-61(AZ)-71-99
Frequency: Monthly; Circulation: 27,000

Turtle Magazine/ Preschool Kids
Nancy Axelrod and Sandra Grieshop,
    Co-Editors
1100 Waterway Blvd
Indianapolis IN 46202-2156
317-636-8881; Fax: 317-684-8094
Focus: 11-21(preschool 2-5
    years)-27-29-33-39
Frequency: 8x per yr; Circulation: 469,000

TV Guide
Jack Curry, Managing Editor
1211 Ave of the Americas
New York NY 10036-8701
212-852-7500; Fax: 212-852-7470
Focus: 17-33T
Frequency: Weekly;
    Circulation: 15,000,000

TWA Ambassador
Joseph Manghise, Managing Editor
Niles Howard & Assoc
PO Box 1326
New Canaan CT 06840
203-866-8485
Focus: 71-99
Frequency: Monthly; Circulation: 265,000

Twins Magazine
Barbara Unell, Editor-in-Chief
6740 Antioch #155
Shawnee Mission KS 66204-1261
913-722-1090; Fax: 913-722-1767
Focus: 31C-31P-35(twins)
Frequency: 6x per yr; Circulation: 50,000

U

U S Kids
Steve Charles, Editor-in-Chief
1100 Waterway Blvd
Indianapolis IN 46202-2156
317-636-8881; Fax: 317-684-8094
Focus: 21-31-51-67-69-76-79
Health/fitness/news for children
Frequency: 8x per yr; Circulation: 260,000

UCLA Magazine
Jeffrey Hirsch, Editor
Univ of Calif at Los Angeles
405 Hilgard Ave
Los Angeles CA 90024-1420
310-206-0686; Fax: 310-206-5673
Focus: 99(UCLA alumni news)
Frequency: Quarterly; Circulation: 140,000

UFO Magazine
Vicki Cooper, Editor
PO Box 1053
Sunland CA 91041-1053
818-951-1250; Fax: 818-951-3102
Focus: 53
Frequency: 6x per yr; Circulation: 24,000

Union Plus
Robert Benchley, Editor
Cadmus Communications
376 Boylston St
Boston MA 02116-3812
617-424-7700; Fax: 617-437-7714
Focus: 19C-25-39-43(lifestyle magazine
    for union members)
Focus on union products/interest
Frequency: Quarterly;
    Circulation: 1,700,000

Unique Hair & Beauty
Anne Alfond, Editor
HG Publications
315 E 65th St #3H
New York NY 10021-6862
212-744-8981; Fax: 212-744-8478
Focus: 40-49B
Frequency: 6x per yr; Circulation: 125,000

Unique Homes
Richard Goodwin, Editor
801 2nd Ave
New York NY 10017-4706
212-599-3377; 800-443-7373;
    Fax: 212-599-8297
Focus: 43
Frequency: 6x per yr; Circulation: 70,000

Unity Magazine
Philip White, Editor
Unity School of Christianity
1901 NW Blue Pky
Unity Village MO 64065-0001
816-524-3550;
Focus: 53-54-63
Frequency: Monthly; Circulation: N/A

Upscale Magazine
Sheila Bronner, Editor-in-Chief
PO Box 10798
Atlanta GA 30310-0798
404-758-7467; 800-877-2253;
    Fax: 404-758-2314
Focus: 11-14-17-33-39-40-43-49B-65-71
Lifestyle mag for Blacks
Frequency: 9; Circulation: 250,000

Urban Family Magazine
Spencer Perkins, Editor-in-Chief
PO Box 40125 Ave
Pasadena CA 91114-7125
818-791-7439; Fax: 818-791-7451
Focus: 17R-35-49-55-65
Frequency: 6x per yr; Circulation: 35,000

US Boat & Ship Modeler
Cal Stewart, Editor
34249 Camino Capistrano
Capistrano Beach CA 92624-1156
714-496-5411; Fax: 714-496-5427
Focus: 28-29H-70N(boat/ship model
    building)
Frequency: Quarterly; Circulation: 50,000

US Magazine
Juliann Garey, Sr Writer, Essentials
1290 Ave of the Americas 2nd Fl
New York NY 10104-0298
212-484-1616; Fax: 212-767-8214
Focus: 11-14-17-33-40-55-99
Reviews: 212-484-1769
Frequency: N/A; Circulation: 950,000

US News and World Report
Christopher Ma, Deputy Editor/Books
2400 N St NW
Washington DC 20037-1196
202-955-2000; Fax: 202-955-2685
Focus: 99
Frequency: Weekly; Circulation: 2,400,000

USA Gymnastics
Luan Peszek, Editor
201 S Capitol Ave #300
Indianapolis IN 46225-1058
317-237-5050; Fax: 317-237-5069
Focus: 39-69(gymnastics)
Frequency: 6x per yr; Circulation: 60,000

USA Weekend
Marcia Bullard, Editor
Gannett Company
1000 Wilson Blvd
Arlington VA 22229-0012
703-276-4526; Fax: 703-276-5518
Focus: 27-39-40-99
Frequency: Weekly;
    Circulation: 15,805,000

Utne Reader
Joshua Glenn, Book Review Editor
1624 Harmon Pl
Minneapolis MN 55403-1900
612-338-5040
Focus: 99
Frequency: 6x per yr; Circulation: 300,000

V

Vacations
Mary Lu Abbott, Managing Editor
Vacation Publications Inc
1502 Augusta Dr #415
Houston TX 77057-2484
713-974-6903; Fax: 713-974-0445
Focus: 71
Frequency: Quarterly; Circulation: 350,000

Valley Magazine
Jane Boeckmann, Editor
16800 Debonshire St #275
Granada Hills CA 91344-7403
818-365-0414; Fax: 818-837-1286
Focus: 61(CA)-99
Frequency: Quarterly; Circulation: 31,000

Vanity Fair
Aimee Bell, Sr Editor/Book Ed
350 Madison Ave
New York NY 10017-3704
212-880-8800; Fax: 212-880-6707;
    E-Mail: vfmail@vf.com
Focus: 11-14-17-33
Frequency: Monthly;
    Circulation: 1,131,000

Vantage Magazine
Ann Cade, Editor-in-Chief
200 N Martingale Rd
Schaumburg IL 60173-2040
708-605-7418; Fax: 708-605-4528
Focus: 15-21-27-29-35-43-99 (for mature
    market)
Frequency: 6x per yr; Circulation: 380,000

Vegetarian Gourmet
Jessica Dubey, Editor
2 Public Ave
Montrose PA 18801-1220
717-278-1984; 800-628-8244;
    Fax: 717-278-2223
Focus: 27
Frequency: 5x per yr; Circulation: 127,000

Vegetarian Journal
Debra Wasserman, Editor
PO Box 1463
Baltimore MD 21203-1463
410-366-8343
Focus: 27-39H-43G-51E-53
Frequency: 6x per yr; Circulation: 18,000

Vegetarian Times
Catherine Shemo, Managing Editor
1140 Lake St #500
Oak Park IL 60301-1053
708-848-8100; Fax: 708-848-8175
Focus: 27-39
Frequency: Monthly; Circulation: 50,000

Veggie Life
Marge Lemas, Editor
1041 Shary Cir
Concord CA 94518-2407
510-671-9852; Fax: 510-671-0692
Focus: 27-39H-43G(vegetarian lifestyle)
Frequency: 6x per yr; Circulation: 200,000

VeloNews
John Wilcockson, Editor
1830 N 55th St
Boulder CO 80301
303-440-0601; Fax: 303-444-6788
Focus: 69(cycling)
Frequency: 20x per yr; Circulation: 48,000

Vermont Life Magazine
Thomas Slayton, Editor-in-Chief
6 Baldwin St
Montepelier VT 05602-2109
802-828-3241; 800-455-3399;
    Fax: 802-828-3366
Focus: 61(VT)
Frequency: Quarterly; Circulation: 120,000

Vette
Peter Easton, Managing Editor
CSK Publishing Co Inc
299 Market St
Saddle Brook NJ 07663-5312
201-712-9300; Fax: 201-712-9899
Focus: 16A
Frequency: Monthly; Circulation: 59,000

VFW Magazine
Richard Kolb, Editor
406 W 34th St
Kansas City MO 64111-2721
816-756-3390; Fax: 816-968-1169
Focus: 41A-48-99
Frequency: 11x per yr;
    Circulation: 2,100,000

Vibe Magazine
Joe Angio, Managing Editor
Time Inc Ventures
205 Lexington Ave 2nd Fl
New York NY 10016
212-522-7092; Fax: 212-522-4578
Focus: 14M
Frequency: 10; Circulation: N/A

Vibrant Life
Barbara Jackson-Hall, Editor-in-Chief
55 W Oak Ridge Dr
Hagerstown MD 21740-7301
301-791-7000; Fax: 301-791-7012
Focus: 39
Frequency: 6x per yr; Circulation: 50,000

Video Magazine
Bill Wolfe, Editor (212-767-6018)
1633 Broadway
New York NY 10019-6708
212-767-6273; Fax: 212-489-4536
Focus: 33M
Frequency: Monthly; Circulation: 300,000

Video Store Magazine
Thomas K Arnold, Editor
201 E Sandpointe Ave #600
Santa Ana CA 92707-8700
714-513-8400; 800-854-3112;
    Fax: 714-513-8402
Focus: 19-99(video)
Frequency: N/A; Circulation: 44,000

VideoGames
Chris Bieniek, Editor
LFP Inc
8484 Wilshire Blvd
Beverly Hills CA 90210-5515
213-651-5400; Fax: 310-274-7985
Focus: 23-33
Frequency: Monthly; Circulation: 120,000

The Village Voice
Doug Simmons, Managing Editor
36 Cooper Square
New York NY 10003
212-475-3300; Fax: 212-475-8944
Focus: 99
Frequency: Weekly; Circulation: 154,000

Vintage Rails
John Gruber, Editor
PO Box 379
Waukesa WI 53187
414-542-4900
Focus: 10-16R
Frequency: Quarterly; Circulation: 30,000

Virginia Game & Fish
Jeff Samsel, Editor
2250 Newmarket Pky #110
Marietta GA 30067-8749
770-953-9222; Fax: 770-933-9510
Focus: 15-51-61(VA)-69
Frequency: Monthly; Circulation: N/A

Virtue Magazine
Jeanette Thomason, Editor
7125 Disc Dr(80918)PO Box 36630
Colorado Springs CO 80936-3663
719-531-7776; Fax: 719-535-0172
Focus: 17-29-35-43-63(Christian)
Frequency: 6x per yr; Circulation: 120,000

Vogue
Michael Boodro, Arts/Book Editor
Conde Nast Publications
350 Madison Ave
New York NY 10017
212-880-8800; Fax: 212-880-8260;
E-Mail: voguemail@aol.com
Focus: 99
Frequency: Monthly;
    Circulation: 1,352,000

Vogue Knitting
Nancy Thomas, Editor-in-Chief
Butterick Co Inc
161 Ave of the Americas
New York NY 10013-1205
212-620-2500; Fax: 212-620-2746
Focus: 29
Frequency: Quarterly; Circulation: 200,000

VQ Magazine
Dick Teresi, Editor
Paisano Publications Inc
28210 Dorothy Dr
Agoura Hills CA 91301-2605
818-889-8740; 800-962-9857;
    Fax: 818-889-5214
Focus: 16A(for Harley-Davidson
    enthusiasts)
Frequency: Quarterly; Circulation: N/A

VW Trends
Jason Wroth, Managing Editor
774 South Placentia
Placentia CA 92670-6832
714-572-2255; Fax: 714-572-1864
Focus: 16-24
Frequency: Monthly; Circulation: 113,000

W Magazine
Thomas Moran, Managing Editor
Fairchild Publications
7 West 34th St
New York NY 10001-8100
212-630-4000; Fax: 212-630-4919
Focus: 43D-43H
Frequency: Monthly; Circulation: 331,000

Wake Boarding
Tom James, Editor
330 W Canton Ave
Winter Park FL 32789-3150
407-628-4802; Fax: 407-628-7061
Focus: 69(skiboarding and knee boarding)
Frequency: 6x per yr; Circulation: 40,000

Walking Magazine
Seth Bauer, Editor
9-11 Harcourt St
Boston MA 02116
617-266-3322; Fax: 617-266-7373
Focus: 27-39-69-71
Frequency: 6x per yr; Circulation: 513,000

Warp Magazine
Mark Woodlief, Book Review Editor
353 Airport Rd
Oceanside CA 92054-1203
619-722-7777; 800-334-8152;
    Fax: 619-722-0653
Focus: 36-99(young men)
Frequency: 6x per yr; Circulation: N/A

Washington Business Journal
David Yochum, Editor
American City Business Jrnls
2000 14th St N 500
Arlington VA 22201-2573
703-875-2200; Fax: 703-875-2231
Focus: 19
Frequency: Weekly; Circulation: 20,000

The Washington Monthly
Charles Peters, Editor-in-Chief
1611 Connecticut Ave NW
Washington DC 20009-1033
202-462-0128; Fax: 202-332-8413
Focus: 19E-44-55-56
Frequency: Monthly; Circulation: 35,000

Washington Post Weekly
Lawrence Meyer, Managing Editor
1150 15th St NW
Washington DC 20071-9100
202-334-4256; Fax: 202-496-3809
Focus: 99
Frequency: Weekly; Circulation: 110,000

Washington Technology
Beau Brendler, Editor
8500 Leesburg Pike #7500
Vienna VA 22182-2409
703-848-2800; Fax: 703-848-2353
Focus: 23
Frequency: 24x per yr; Circulation: 30,000

Washingtonian
John Limpert, Editor
1828 L St NW #200
Washington DC 20036-5104
202-296-3600
Focus: 61(Washington DC)-99
Frequency: Monthly; Circulation: 165,000

Water Ski
Rob May, Editor
330 W Canton Ave
Winter Park FL 32789-3150
407-628-4802; Fax: 407-628-7061
Focus: 69(water skiing)
Frequency: 10 per yr; Circulation: 109,000

Wearable Crafts
Beth Schwartz Wheeler, Editor
House of White Birches
306 East Parr Rd
Berne IN 46711
219-589-8741; Fax: 219-589-8093
Focus: 29-40
Frequency: 6x per yr; Circulation: 96,000

Weatherwise
Jeff Rosenfeld, Managing Editor
Heldref Publications
1319 18th St NW
Washington DC 20036-1802
202-296-6267; Fax: 202-296-5149
Focus: 51-67
Frequency: 6x per yr; Circulation: 14,000

Weekend Woodcrafts
Ben Green, Editor
1041 Shary Cir
Concord CA 94518-2407
510-671-9852; Fax: 510-671-0692
Focus: 29
Frequency: 6x per yr; Circulation: 200,000

Weight Watchers Magazine
Nancy Gardgagliardi, Editor
360 Lexington Ave
New York NY 10017-6547
212-370-0644; Fax: 212-687-4398
Focus: 27-39-40-69
Frequency: Monthly;
    Circulation: 1,114,000

West Coast Woman
Louise Bruderle, Editor
PO Box 819
Sarasota FL 34230-0819
941-954-3300; Fax: 941-954-3300
Focus: 35F-40-61(FL)-73(women of
    Sarasota and Manatee counties)
Frequency: Monthly; Circulation: 27,000

West Virginia Game & Fish
Ken Freel, Editor
Game & Fish Publications
2250 Newmarket Pky #110
Marietta GA 30067-8749
770-953-9222; Fax: 770-933-9510
Focus: 15-51-61(WV)-69
Frequency: Monthly; Circulation: N/A

Westchester Family
Susan Ross Benamram and Felice
    Shapiro, Co-Publishers
141 Halstead Ave #3D
Mamaroneck NY 10543-2652
914-381-7474; Fax: 914-381-7672
Focus: 21-31-35-76
Frequency: 11x per yr; Circulation: 60,000

The Western Horseman
Pat Close, Editor
Western Horseman Inc
3850 N Nevada Ave
Colorado Springs CO 80907-5339
719-633-5524; Fax: 719-633-1392
Focus: 15(horses)
Frequency: Monthly; Circulation: 227,000

Western Outdoor News
Pat McDonell, Editor
PO Box 2027
Newport Beach CA 92659-1027
714-546-4370; Fax: 714-662-3486
Focus: 51-61(west)-69
Frequency: Weekly; Circulation: 70,000

Western Outdoors
Jack Brown, Editor
PO Box 2027
Newport Beach CA 92659-1027
714-546-4370; Fax: 714-662-3486
Focus: 61-69(West)
Frequency: 9x per yr; Circulation: 138,000

Western Photographer
S T Bear, Editor/Publisher
2021 Unit A Via Burton
Anaheim CA 92806-1200
619-535-1166; Fax: 714-535-7546
Focus: 11P-40(modeling)
Frequency: Monthly; Circulation: 10,000

Western Styles
Sue Copeland, Editor
Cowles Magazine Inc
12265 W Bayaud #300
Lakewood CO 80228-2116
303-914-3000; Fax: 303-914-3099
Focus: 61-14D-14M-11P
Frequency: 6x per yr; Circulation: 195,000

Westways
Susan LaTempa, Editor-in-Chief
PO Box 2890
Los Angeles CA 90051-0890
213-741-4760; Fax: 213-741-3033
Focus: 71(Southern CA)
Frequency: Monthly; Circulation: 440,000

White's Guide: Collecting Figurines
Zach Reid, Editor
Collecting Concepts
PO Box K-46
Richmond VA 23288
804-285-0994
Focus: 28(collecting figurines)
Frequency: Monthly; Circulation: 15,000

Whole Earth Review
Ruth Kissane, Editor
Point Foundation
27 Gate Five Rd
Sausalito CA 94965-1401
415-332-1716; Fax: 415-332-3110
Focus: 19S-23-23T-39H-51E-53-57-71-99
Frequency: Quarterly; Circulation: 45,000

Wild Earth Magazine
John Davis, Editor
Bridge St
Richmond VT 05477-0455
802-434-4077
Focus: 51E
Frequency: Quarterly; Circulation: 5,000

Wild West Magazine
Greg Lalire, Editor
Cowles History Group
741 Miller Dr SE #D2
Leesburg VA 22075-3907
703-771-9400; Fax: 703-779-8345
Focus: 41A-49A-61(west)(gunfighter bios)
Frequency: 6x per yr; Circulation: 97,000

Wildlife Art News
Rebecca Hakala Rowland, Editor
4725 Hwy 7
St Louis Park MN 55416-2203
612-927-9056; 800-626-0934;
    Fax: 612-927-9353
Focus: 11-15
Frequency: 6x per yr; Circulation: N/A

The Wilson Quarterly
Jim Carman, Managing Editor
370 L'Enfant Promenade #704
Washington DC 20024
202-287-3000; Fax: 202-287-3772
Focus: 99
Frequency: Quarterly; Circulation: 70,000

Windsurfing
Debby Snow, Editor
330 West Canton Ave
Winter Park FL 32789-3150
407-628-4802; Fax: 407-628-7061
Focus: 69(windsurfing)
Frequency: 8; Circulation: 70,000

Windy City Woman
Julie LaGuardia, Editor
1450 W Randolph
Chicago IL 60607
312-421-1551
Focus: 19-73 (working women 25-45)
Frequency: Monthly; Circulation: 50,000

Wine Enthusiast
W R Tish, Editor-in-Chief
8 Saw Mill River Rd
Hawthorne NY 10532-1504
914-345-8463; 800-356-8466;
    Fax: 914-345-3028
Focus: 27-71
Frequency: 6x per yr; Circulation: 75,000

Wine Spectator
Harvey Steiman, Book Review Editor
387 Park Ave S
New York NY 10016-8810
212-684-4224; Fax: 212-684-5424
Focus: 27(wine)
Frequency: 20x per yr;
   Circulation: 151,000

Wired
John Battelle, Managing Editor
520 3rd St
San Francisco CA 94107-1815
415-222-6200; 800-769-4733;
   Fax: 415-222-6209
Focus: 23C-23E-23T
Frequency: Monthly; Circulation: 170,000

The Wisconsin Light
Terry Boughner, Editor
Novo Graphics Ltd
1843 N Palmer St
Milwaukee WI 53212-3718
414-372-2773; Fax: 414-372-1840
Focus: 37-73
Frequency: 25x per yr; Circulation: 13,000

Wisconsin Sportsman
Dennis Schmidt, Editor
Game & Fish Publications
2250 Newmarket Pky #110
Marietta GA 30067-8749
770-953-9222; Fax: 770-933-9510
Focus: 15-51-61(WI)-69
Frequency: Monthly; Circulation: 40,000

Wisconsin Trails
Howard Mead, Editor
6225 University Ave
Madison WI 53705-1088
608-231-2444; 800-236-8088;
   Fax: 608-231-1557
Focus: 61(WI)-71
Frequency: 6x per yr; Circulation: 47,000

The Woman Rebel
Diane Glass,
McCormack PO Box 2474
Boston MA 02208
617-623-4141
Focus: 11-11P-73-75-99
Frequency: Quarterly; Circulation: N/A

Woman's Day
Jane Chesnutt, Editor-in-Chief
Hachette Magazines
1633 Broadway 42nd Fl
New York NY 10019
212-767-6000; Fax: 212-767-5610;
   E-Mail: WOMANSDAY@aol.com
Focus: 39-40
Frequency: 17x per yr;
   Circulation: 4,583,000

Woman's Day Special Interest Publications
Carolyn Gatto, Specials Editor
Hachette Magazines Inc
1633 Broadway 42nd Fl
New York NY 10019
212-767-6000; Fax: 212-767-5610
Focus: 99
18 single subject magazines
Frequency: N/A; Circulation: N/A

Woman's World
Stephanie Saible, Book Review Editor
Bauer Publishing
270 Sylvan Ave
Englewood Cliffs NJ 07632-2513
201-569-6699; Fax: 201-569-3584
Focus: 99
Frequency: Weekly; Circulation: 1,461,000

Women Circle
Marjorie Pearl, Editor
House of White Birches
306 East Parr Rd
Berne IN 46711
219-589-8741; Fax: 219-589-8093
Focus: 27-35-73
Frequency: 6x per yr; Circulation: 46,000

Women In Business
Wendy Myers, Editor
9100 Ward Pky
Kansas City MO 64114-3306
816-361-6621; Fax: 816-361-4991
Focus: 19-73
Frequency: 6x per yr; Circulation: 90,000

Women Today
Anne Alfond, Editor
Michael Morse Inc
315 E 65th St #3H
New York NY 10021-6848
212-744-8981; Fax: 212-744-8478
Focus: 11-19C-25-27-29-31-35-39-40-57-71-73
Frequency: 6x per yr; Circulation: 150,000

Women's Forum
Susan Crain Bakos, Editor
277 Park Ave
New York NY 10172
212-496-6100
Focus: 99-37-39-55
Frequency: Monthly; Circulation: 300,000

Women's Household Crochet
Susan Hankins, Editor
House of White Birches
306 East Parr Rd
Berne IN 46711
219-589-8741; Fax: 219-589-8093
Focus: 29
Frequency: Quarterly; Circulation: 38,000

Women's News
Joan Steinauer, Editor-in-Chief
33 Halstead Ave
Harrison NY 10528-4117
914-835-5400; Fax: 914-835-5718
Focus: 19-61(NY)-73-99
Frequency: Monthly; Circulation: 60,000

Women's Sports and Fitness
Mary Duffy, Managing Editor
2025 Pearl St
Boulder CO 80302
303-440-5111; Fax: 303-440-3313
Focus: 39-40-69-73
Frequency: 8x per yr; Circulation: 250,000

Women's Sports Traveler
Karen Walden, Editor-in-Chief
167 Madison Ave #405
New York NY 10016
212-686-6480
Focus: 69-71 (ages 30-50)
Frequency: N/A; Circulation: N/A

Wood Digest
Steve Ehle, Editor
PTN Publishing Co
445 Broad Hollow Rd
Melville NY 11747
516-845-2700; Fax: 516-845-2797
Focus: 29
Frequency: Monthly; Circulation: N/A

WoodenBoat Magazine
Matthew Murphy, Editor
Naskeag Rd
Brooklin ME 04616
207-359-4651; Fax: 207-359-8920
Focus: 29H-70N(wooden boat building
   and using)
Frequency: 2x per yr; Circulation: 105,000

Woodmen Magazine
Scott J Darling, Editor
1700 Farnam St
Omaha NE 68102-2002
402-342-1890; Fax: 402-271-7269
Focus: 99
Frequency: 6x per yr; Circulation: 500,000

WordPerfect Magazine
Lisa Bearnson, Managing Ed - DOS
Scott Larson, Managing Ed - Windows
Ivy International Inc
270 West Center St
Orem UT 84057
800-228-9626; Fax: 801-227-3478
Focus: 23
Frequency: Monthly; Circulation: N/A

Workbasket
Kay Olson, Editor
KC Publishing
700 West 47th St #310
Kansas City MO 64112
816-531-5730; Fax: 816-531-3873
Focus: 29C
Frequency: 6x per yr; Circulation: 850,000

Workbench
A Robert Gould, Editor
KC Publishing
700 West 47th St #310
Kansas City MO 64112
816-531-5730; Fax: 816-531-3873
Focus: 29H-43H
Frequency: 6x per yr; Circulation: 900,000

Working Mother
Andrea Burtman, Managing Editor
   (212-551-9531)
Lang Communications
230 Park Ave
New York NY 10169-0005
212-551-9406; Fax: 212-599-4763
Focus: 99
Frequency: Monthly; Circulation: 951,000

Working Woman
Lynn Povich, Editor-in-Chief
Lang Communications
230 Park Ave 7th Fl
New York NY 10169-0005
212-551-9500; Fax: 212-599-4763
Focus: 19-73-99
Frequency: Monthly; Circulation: 750,000

The World & I
Michael Marshall, Exec Editor
5400 New York Ave NE
Washington DC 20002-1949
202-636-4000; 800-822-2822;
 Fax: 202-526-3497
Focus: 99
Frequency: Monthly; Circulation: 30,000

World Art
Sarah Bayless, Editor
Gordon & Breach Publishing Group
2 Gateway Ctr 11th Fl
Newark NJ 07102-5003
201-643-7500; Fax: 201-643-7676
Focus: 11(gallery and museum)
Frequency: Quarterly; Circulation: 28,000

World Press Review
Larry Martz, Editor-in-Chief
The Stanley Foundation
200 Madison Ave
New York NY 10016-3903
212-889-5155; Fax: 212-889-5634
Focus: 44-55-65
Frequency: Monthly; Circulation: 60,000

World War II Magazine
Michael Haskew, Editor
Cowles History Group
741 Miller Dr SE #D-2
Leesburg VA 22075-8920
703-771-9400; Fax: 703-777-4627
Focus: 41A-41W-48
Frequency: 6x per yr; Circulation: 186,000

World Watch
Ed Ayres, Editor
World Watch Institute
1776 Massachusetts Ave NW
Washington DC 20036-1904
202-452-1999; Fax: 202-296-7365
Focus: 51-51E
Frequency: 6x per yr; Circulation: 30,000

Worship Leader Magazine
Chuck Fromm, Editor
107 Kenner Ave
Nashville TN 37205-2207
615-386-3011; Fax: 615-386-3380
Focus: 63P(for pastors and worship
 leaders)
Frequency: 6x per yr; Circulation: 45,000

Writer's Workshop Review
Rhia R Drouillard,
511 W 24th St
Vancouver WA 98660
360-693-6509
Focus: 10-11-33H-90-95-97
Frequency: Monthly; Circulation: N/A

Y

Yachting
Charles Barthold, Editor
Times Mirror Magazines
2 Park Ave
New York NY 10016-5603
212-779-5300; Fax: 212-725-1035
Focus: 70N-75(nautical)
Frequency: Monthly; Circulation: 133,000

Yankee Magazine
Judson Hale Sr, Editor-in-Chief
Main St
PO Box 520
Dublin NH 03444
603-563-8111; Fax: 603-563-8252
Focus: 29-43-61(New England)-99
Frequency: Monthly; Circulation: 756,000

Yard & Garden
Dan Kirkpatrick, Editor
1233 Janesville Ave
Fort Atkinson WI 53538-2738
414-563-6388; Fax: 414-563-1702
Focus: 19M-19R-43G
Frequency: 10x per yr; Circulation: 35,000

YM Magazine
Sally Lee, Editor
Gruner & Jahr USA Publishing
685 Third Ave 28th Fl
New York NY 10017-4024
212-878-8700; Fax: 212-286-0935
Focus: 14-17-33-40-57-73-89-99
Frequency: 10x per yr;
 Circulation: 1,930,000

Yo! Youth Outlook
Nell Bernstein, Editor
450 Mission St #506
San Francisco CA 94105-2526
415-243-4364; Fax: 415-243-0815
Focus: 21T-99(written by teenagers)
Frequency: Quarterly; Circulation: 325,000

Yoga International
Deborah Willoughby, Editor-in-Chief
Himalayan Intl Institute
RR 1 Box 407
Honesdale PA 18431-9718
717-253-4929; 800-821-9642;
 Fax: 717-253-6360
Focus: 39H-53-54(yoga)
Frequency: 6x per yr; Circulation: 40,000

Yoga Journal
Anne Cushman, Sr Editor
2054 University Ave #302
Berkeley CA 94704
510-548-1680; Fax:
Focus: 39H-51E-53(yoga)-54-57
Frequency: 6x per yr; Circulation: 85,000

Young Horizons Indigo
Terry Williams, Editor
2897 Bradmoor Ct
Decatur GA 30034-2832
404-241-5003; Fax:
Focus: 31E-31P-35F-49B(parents/teachers
 of African-American kids)
Frequency: Monthly; Circulation: 15,000

Young Voices
Char Simons, Editor
PO Box 2321
Olympia WA 98507
Focus: 21(grades K-12)
Frequency: N/A; Circulation: N/A

Your Health
Susan Gregg, Editor
Globe Communications Corp
5401 NW Broken Sound Blvd
Boca Raton FL 33487-3512
407-997-7733; Fax: 407-997-7733
Focus: 39
Frequency: Biweekly; Circulation: 43,000

Your Home/Indoors & Out
Editor
Meridian Publishing Inc
1720 Washington Blvd
Ogden UT 84404-5753
801-394-9446; Fax: 801-627-1453
Focus: 43
Frequency: Monthly; Circulation: 65,000

Your Money
Dennis Fertig, Sr Editor
Consumers Digest Inc
5705 N Lincoln Ave
Chicago IL 60659-4707
312-275-3590; Fax: 312-275-7273
Focus: 19
Frequency: 6x per yr; Circulation: 460,000

Your Pet
Dominique Davis, Editor
Your Pet Magazine Inc
30 Lincoln Plz #6-D
New York NY 10023-7109
212-489-1416; Fax: 212-974-3254
Focus: 15
Frequency: Quarterly; Circulation: 550,000

Youthwalk
Millicent Manning, Editor
Walk Thru the Bible(publishers)
4201 N Peachtree Rd
Atlanta GA 30341
800-868-9882; Fax: 404-454-9313
Focus: 63
Frequency: Monthly; Circulation: 27,000

Z

Zillions
Moye Thompson, Managing Editor
Consumers Union of the US
101 Truman Ave
Yonkers NY 10703-1044
914-378-2551; Fax: 914-378-2904
Focus: 21-23-25-29-43-69
Frequency: 6x per yr; Circulation: 300,000

Zone Magazine
Michele Savoy, Editor
Zone Publishing
119 E 7th St #2
Tempe AZ 85281-3710
602-966-6352; 800-949-5271;
 Fax: 602-967-0168
Focus: 11-14-23T
Frequency: Quarterly; Circulation: 27,000

Subject Category Codes

10 **General Non-Fiction**
11 **Fine Arts**
    11P   Photography
12 **Architecture / Construction**
    12A   Architecture
    12B   Building / Construction
13 **Alternative Social Issues**
14 **Performing Arts**
    14D   Dance
    14M   Music
    14T   Theatre / Drama
15 **Animals / Pets**
16 **Transportation**
    16A   Automobiles
    16R   Railroads
17 **Biographies / Celebrities**
    17B   Biographies
    17C   Celebrities
    17P   Real People
19 **Business / Economics**
    19A   Accounting
    19B   Banking
    19C   Careers / Labor
    19E   Economics
    19F   Fund-raising / Non-profits
    19G   Management
    19H   Real Estate / Home
    19I   Investment
    19L   Law
    19M   Marketing / Sales
    19O   Opportunity Seekers
    19P   Purchasing
    19R   Retail Sales
    19S   Small Business
    19X   Industrial / Production
21 **Children's Interests**
    21T   Teenagers
23 **Computers / Technology**
    23C   Computers
    23E   Home Electronics
    23T   Technology
24 **Engineering**
25 **Consumer Issues**
    25T   Consumer Taxes
27 **Cooking / Food / Nutrition**
28 **Collectibles / Antiques**
29 **Crafts / Hobbies / How-to**
    29C   Crafts
    29H   Hobbies and How-to
31 **Education / Child Development**
    31C   Child Development
    31E   Education / Teaching
    31P   Parenting
33 **Entertainment / Movies / Humor**
    33C   Comics / Comedy
    33H   Humor
    33M   Movies
    33T   Television / Radio

35 **Family / Marriage / Retirement**
    35A   Aging Issues / Retirement
    35F   Family
    35M   Marriage
    35R   Relationships / Romance
    35S   Sexual Issues
36 **Lifestyle/Feature**
37 **Gay / Lesbian**
39 **Health / Medicine / Exercise**
    39D   Disabilities
    39E   Exercise
    39H   Holistic Health
    39M   Medicine / Doctors
    39R   Recovery / Drug Abuse
40 **Beauty / Fashion**
    40B   Beauty
    40F   Fashion
41 **History**
    41A   American History
    41G   Genealogy / Family History
    41W   World History
43 **House / Garden**
    43D   Home Decorating
    43G   Gardening
    43H   House and Home
44 **International Issues and News**
    44A   Asia
    44E   Europe
    44F   Africa
    44S   South America
    44Z   Australia / New Zealand
45 **Languages**
    45X   Linquistics
    45W   Words
47 **Literature / Humanities**
48 **Military**
49 **Minority Issues and Studies**
    49A   Native American
    49B   Black
    49H   Hispanic / Chicano
    49O   Other
51 **Nature / Ecology / Conservation**
    51A   Agriculture / Farming
    51B   Biology / Botany
    51E   Environmental Issues
    51N   Nature
53 **New Age / Astrology**
54 **Philosophy / Metaphysics**
    54M   Metaphysics
    54P   Philosophy
55 **Politics / Government**
    55C   Crime / Police Work
    55G   Government
    55L   Law
    55P   Politics

56 **Publishing / PR / Writing**
    56M   Media / Publicity
    56P   Publishing
    56W   Writing
    56X   Printing
57 **Psychology / Self-Help**
    57B   Behavior
    57P   Psychology / Therapy
    57S   Self-Help / Advice
59 **Reference Books**
61 **Regional Issues and Interests**
63 **Religions**
    63C   Catholic
    63E   Eastern Religions
    63J   Jewish
    63M   Muslim
    63O   Other Religions
    63P   Protestant
65 **Sociology / Anthropology**
    65A   Anthropology
    65S   Social Issues
67 **Science / Mathematics**
    67A   Astronomy / Space
    67M   Mathematics
    67S   Science
69 **Sports / Games / Recreation**
    69G   Games
    69H   Hunting / Fishing
    69R   Recreation / Hiking
    69S   Spectator Sports
70 **Nautical / Aviation**
    70A   Aviation
    70N   Nautical / Sailing
71 **Travel / Geography**
    71D   Domestic Travel
    71F   Foreign Travel
    71G   Geography
73 **Women's Issues**

75 General Fiction

76 **Children's Stories**
77 **Contemporary Novels**
78 **Ethnic / Minority Literature**
79 **Folklore / Fairy Tales**
80 **Foreign Literature**
81 **Historical Novels**
82 **Horror Novels**
83 **Literary Novels**
84 **Mysteries / Detective Novels**
85 **Romances / Gothic Romances**
86 **Science Fiction / Fantasy**
87 **Suspense / Adventure Novels**
88 **Westerns**
89 **Young Adult Novels**
90 **Short Stories / Anthologies**
95 **Poetry**

97 News / Current Events

99 General Interest

Business Trade Magazines

The following magazines feature news, reviews, and other items of interest to a particular retail or wholesale business, trade, industry, or profession. Write for a sample copy of any trade magazine that publishes in a retail field you want to target (whether toy stores, gift stores, office supply stores, or whatever).

A

33 Metalproducing
Robert Brooks, Managing Editor
Penton Publishing
1100 Superior Ave
Cleveland OH 44114
216-696-7000; Fax: 216-696-7658
Focus: 19X-23T-24-97)
Market: Metal-prod Industry
Frequency: Monthly; Circulation: 18,000

AAII Journal
Jean Henrich, Assoc Editor
625 N Michigan Ave #1900
Chicago IL 60611-3109
312-280-0170; Fax: 312-280-1625
Focus: 19I(theory)
Frequency: Monthly; Circulation: 170,000

Accessory Merchandising
Cori Dunn, Editor
400 Kingsbridge Pky
Lincolnshire IL 60069-3613
708-634-2600; Fax: 708-634-4379
Focus: 19R-40F
Frequency: 9x per yr; Circulation: 20,000

Accounting Today
Rick Telberg, Editor
Faulkner & Grey
11 Penn Plz
New York NY 10001-2006
212-967-7000; Fax: 212-564-9896
Focus: 19A
Frequency: Biweekly; Circulation: 30,000

Advanced Imaging
Barry Mazor, Editor-in-Chief
PTN Publishing Co
445 Broad Hollow Rd
Melville NY 11747
516-845-2700; Fax: 516-845-2797
Focus: 23(audio-video technology)
Frequency: Monthly; Circulation: N/A

AG Consultant
Judy Ferguson, Editor
Meister Publishing Co
37733 Euclid Ave
Willoughby OH 44094-5925
216-942-2000; Fax: 216-942-0662
Focus: 51A-51E-19M
Frequency: 6x per yr; Circulation: 25,000

Agent & Manager Magazine
Michael Caffin, Managing Editor
Bedrock Communications
650 First Ave
New York NY 10016-3240
212-532-4150; Fax: 212-213-6382
Focus: 14M-33-69S ("bible" for entertainment, sports, facilities, exposition)
Frequency: Monthly; Circulation: 29,000

Aging Today
Paul Kleyman, Editor
American Society on Aging
833 Market St #511
San Francisco CA 94103-1824
415-974-9619; 800-537-9728;
    Fax: 415-974-0300
Focus: 35A-39-55-57
Frequency: 6x per yr; Circulation: 15,000

Agri Marketing
Debby Hartke, Editor
11701 Borman Dr #100
St Louis MO 63146-4193
314-569-2700; Fax: 314-569-1083
Focus: 19M-51A
Frequency: 11x per yr; Circulation: 10,000

Air Force Magazine
Frances McKenney, Book Editor
Air Force Assn
1501 Lee Hwy
Arlington VA 22209-1198
703-247-5800; Fax: 703-247-5855
Focus: 48-55-70
Frequency: Monthly; Circulation: 250,000

Air Line Pilot
Esperison Martinez Jr, Editor
535 Herndon Pky
Herndon VA 22070-5226
703-689-4176; Fax: 703-689-4370
Focus: 70A
Frequency: Monthly; Circulation: 62,000

Air Transport World
James A Donohue, Editor
421 Aviation Way
Frederick MD 21701-4756
301-695-2350; Fax: 301-695-2180
Focus: 16-19G-19X-23T-24-55G-70A
Market: Airline industries
Frequency: Monthly; Circulation: 310,000

Airbrush Action
Joseph LaSala, Editor
Airbrush Action Inc
PO Box 2052
Lakewood NJ 08701-8052
908-364-2111; 800-232-8998;
    Fax: 908-367-5908
Focus: 11
Frequency: 6x per yr; Circulation: 55,000

Airport Business
John Infanger, Editor-in-Chief
Johnson Hill Press
1233 Janesville Ave
Fort Atkinson WI 53538-2794
414-563-6388; Fax: 414-563-1702
Focus: 19G-70A(airport maintenance, security, management, operations)
Frequency: 9x per yr; Circulation: 19,000

Amer Jnl of Occupational Therapy
Elaine Viseltear, Editor-in-Chief
4720 Montgomery Ln
Bethesda MD 20814-5320
301-652-2682; 800-877-1383;
    Fax: 301-652-7711
Focus: 39
Frequency: 10x per yr; Circulation: 50,000

America's Network
Robert E Stoffels, Editor-in-Chief
233 N Michigan Ave #2423
Chicago IL 60601-5702
312-938-2378; Fax: 312-938-4854
Focus: 23T(telephone engineering)
Frequency: Biweekly; Circulation: 48,000

American Agent & Broker
George Williams, Editor
330 N 4th St
St Louis MO 63102-2036
314-421-5445; Fax: 314-421-1070
Focus: 19(insurance)
Frequency: Monthly; Circulation: 39,000

American City & County
Janet Ward, Editor
Argus Business Inc
6151 Powers Ferry Rd NW
Atlanta GA 30339-2959
770-955-2500; Fax: 770-955-0400
Focus: 55(city government)
Frequency: Monthly; Circulation: 70,000

American Craft
Lois Moran, Editor & Publisher
American Craft Council
72 Spring St
New York NY 10012
212-274-0630; Fax: 212-274-0650
Focus: 29C-12A (for professional craftsmen)
Frequency: 6x per yr; Circulation: 40,000

American Demographics
Nancy TenKate, Managing Editor
127 W State St (14850)
PO Box 68
Ithaca NY 14851
607-273-6343; Fax: 607-273-3196
Focus: 19M(consumer trends and statistics)-99
Books affecting demographics
Frequency: Monthly; Circulation: 35,000

American Druggist
Veronika Ullmer, Managing Editor
Hearst Business Publishing
1790 Broadway 6th Fl
New York NY 10019-1412
212-969-7500; Fax: 212-969-7557
Focus: 39M(retail pharmacy practice)
Frequency: Monthly; Circulation: N/A

American Farrier
Frank Lessiter, Editor
PO Box 624
Brookfield WI 53008-0624
414-782-4480; 800-645-8455;
    Fax: 414-782-1252
Focus: 15(horses)
Frequency: 7x per yr; Circulation: 6,000

American Fruit Grower
Gary Acuff, Managing Editor
Meister Publishing Co
37733 Euclid Ave
Willoughby OH 44094-5925
216-942-2000; Fax: 216-942-0662
Focus: 43G-(fruit growing)
Commercial fruit growing
Frequency: Monthly; Circulation: 56,000

American Machinist
Diane Hallum, Exec Editor
Penton Publishing
1100 Superior Ave
Cleveland OH 44114-2518
216-696-7000; Fax: 216-696-0177
Focus: 19G-19X-23C-23T-24-67S
Market: Metalworking industries
Frequency: Monthly; Circulation: 80,000

American Nurseryman
Sally Benson, Editor
77 W Washington St #2100
Chicago IL 60602-2801
312-782-5505; 800-621-5727;
    Fax: 312-782-3232
Focus: 43G
Frequency: Biweekly; Circulation: 14,000

American Police Beat
Cynthia Brown, Editor
On The Beat
57 Reservoir St
Cambridge MA 02138
617-491-8878; Fax: 617-354-6515
Focus: 55C(police pay, benefits, liability, media problems)
Frequency: 6x per yr; Circulation: 60,000

American Printer
Jill Roth, Editor-in-Chief
Mark Smith, Managing Editor
MacLean Hunter Publishing Co
29 N Wacker Dr
Chicago IL 60606-3203
312-726-2802; Fax: 312-726-3091
Focus: 56X
Frequency: Monthly; Circulation: 96,000

American Vegetable Grower
Jim Sulecki, Editor
Meister Publishing Co
37733 Euclid Ave
Willoughby OH 44094-5925
216-942-2000; Fax: 216-975-3447
Focus: 43G
Commercial vegetable growing
Frequency: Monthly; Circulation: 37,000

Amusement Business
Lisa Zhito, Managing Editor
49 Music Square W
Nashville TN 37203-3213
615-321-4250; 800-999-3322;
    Fax: 615-327-1575
Focus: 14(performing arts)-19-33-69(fairs, amusement parks, carnivals)
Frequency: Weekly; Circulation: 12,000

Animation Magazine
Barbara Wexler, Managing Editor
28024 Dorothy Dr
Agoura Hills CA 91301-2635
818-991-2884; Fax: 818-991-3773
Focus: 11(cartoon animation)-33M
Frequency: 6x per yr; Circulation: 25,000

Antiques & Collectibles Magazine
Rich Branciforte, Editor/Publisher
PO Box 33
Westbury NY 11590-0033
516-334-9650; Fax: 516-334-5740
Focus: 28
Frequency: Monthly; Circulation: 10,000

Apparel Merchandising
Jeffrey Arlen, Editor
Lebhar-Friedman
425 Park Ave 6th Fl
New York NY 10022
212-756-5130; Fax: 212-756-5270
Focus: 19R-19M
Frequency: 8x per yr; Circulation: 35,000

Appliance
Scot Stevens, Editor
Dana Chase Publications
1110 Jorie Blvd CS 9019
Oak Brook IL 60521-2223
708-990-3484; Fax: 708-990-0078
Focus: 19X-43
Frequency: Monthly; Circulation: 30,000

Architectural Specifier
Greg Ettling, Editor
Century Publishing Co
6201 Howard St
Niles IL 60714-3435
708-647-1200; Fax: 708-647-7055
Focus: 12A-12B-43H(roofing, glazing, insulation, exterior walls)
Residential & commercial
Frequency: 6x per yr; Circulation: 29,000

Army Magazine
Mary Blake French, Editor
2425 Wilson Blvd
Arlington VA 22201-3326
703-841-4300; Fax: 703-525-9039
Focus: 48-55-70
Frequency: Monthly; Circulation: 125,000

Art Business News
Sarah Seamark, Editor
Advanstar Communications
19 Old King Hwy S
Darien CT 06820-4526
203-656-3402; Fax: 203-656-1976
Focus: 11-19 (art galleries/framers)
Frequency: 13x per yr; Circulation: 32,000

ASHA Magazine
Russell L Malone, Managing Editor
10801 Rockville Pike
Rockville MD 20852-3226
301-897-5700; Fax: 301-571-0457
Focus: 39
Frequency: 11; Circulation: 89,000

The Association Executive
Rosalyn Gist Porter, Editor
765 Douglas Ave
Altamonte Springs FL 32714-2566
407-862-7737; Fax: 407-862-8102
Focus: 19(trade)
Frequency: Monthly; Circulation: 5,000

Association Management
Ann Mahoney, Editor
Keith Skillman, Managing Editor
Amer Society of Assn Executives
1575 Eye St NW
Washington DC 20005
202-626-2708; Fax: 202-408-9635
Focus: 19(associations)
Goes to members of association
Frequency: Monthly; Circulation: 21,000

ASTA Agency Management
Michael Driscoll, Editor
1301 Carolina St
Greensboro NC 27401-1001
910-378-6065; Fax: 910-378-6828
Focus: 19G-71(American Society of Travel Agents)
Frequency: Monthly; Circulation: 30,000

Atlanta Business Chronicle
David Black, Editor
1801 Peachtree St #150
Atlanta GA 30309-1859
404-249-1000; Fax: 404-249-1048
Focus: 19-61(GA)
Frequency: Weekly; Circulation: 35,000

Atlanta Small Business Monthly
Mitzi Crall, Editor
6129 Oakbrook Pkwy
Norcross GA 30093
770-446-5434; Fax: 770-446-3970
Focus: 19-61(GA)
Frequency: Monthly; Circulation: 28,000

B

Balloons and Parties Today
April Anderson, Managing Editor
Festivities Publications
1205 W Forsyth St
Jacksonville FL 32204-1423
904-634-1902; Fax: 904-633-8764
Focus: 19R-33-43(party decorating ideas)
Frequency: Monthly; Circulation: 10,000

Bank Security Report
Ken Feinleib, Editor
Warren Gorham Lamont
1 Penn Plz
New York NY 10119-0002
212-971-5582; Fax: 212-971-5024
Focus: 19B-55G
Frequency: Monthly; Circulation: 2,000

Bank Systems & Technology
Holly Sraeel, Editor (212-626-2515)
Miller Freeman Inc
1 Penn Plz
New York NY 10119-1198
212-714-1300; Fax: 212-714-1313
Focus: 19B-23
Frequency: Monthly; Circulation: 26,000

Bankers Letter of the Law
Steve Errick, Editor
Warren Gorham Lamont
One Penn Plz 42nd Fl
New York NY 10119-0002
212-971-5000; Fax: 212-971-5588
Focus: 19B-19L-55G
Frequency: Monthly; Circulation: 4,000

The Bankers Magazine
Kathleen McEwan, Editor
Warren Gorham Lamont
One Penn Plz
New York NY 10119-0002
212-971-5000; Fax: 212-971-5588
Focus: 19B-55G
Frequency: 6x per yr; Circulation: 4,000

Banking Law Journal
Gerald Dunne, Editor-in-Chief
Warren Gorham Lamont
1 Penn Plz
New York NY 10119-0002
212-971-5218; Fax: 212-971-5215
Focus: 19B-19L-55G
Frequency: 10x per yr; Circulation: 5,000

Beauty Inc
Denise Rucci, Editor
Beauty & Barber Supply Inst
271 US Hwy 46 #F209
Fairfield NJ 07004-2415
201-808-7444; Fax: 201-808-9099
Focus: 19R-40B(wholesalers, manufacturers, and sales reps for supplies)
Frequency: Monthly; Circulation: 10,000

Before & After
Gaye McWade, Editor-in-Chief
1830 Sierra Gardens Dr #30
Roseville CA 95661-2942
916-784-3880; Fax: 916-784-3995
Focus: 11-23C(features design & page layout for desktop publishers)
How to design cool stuff
Frequency: 6x per yr; Circulation: N/A

Bicycle Business Journal
Rex Quinn, Editor
Quinn Publications Inc
1904 Wenneca
Fort Worth TX 76102-4321
817-870-0341; Fax: 817-332-1619
Focus: 19R-69R(bicycling)
Frequency: Monthly; Circulation: 10,000

Bicycle Dealer Showcase
Walt Jarvis, Editor-in-Chief
9560 SW Nimbus Ave
Beaverton OR 97008-7163
503-520-1955; Fax: 503-520-1275
Focus: 19R-69R(bicycling)
Frequency: Monthly; Circulation: 11,000

Bicycle Retailer & Industry News
Marc Sani, Editor-in-Chief
1444-C S St Francis Dr
Santa Fe NM 87505-4038
505-988-5099; Fax: 505-988-7224
Focus: 19R-69
Frequency: 18x per yr; Circulation: 14,000

Billboard
Eric Boehlert, Features Editor
BPI Communications
1515 Broadway 15th Fl
New York NY 10036-5701
212-764-7300; Fax: 212-536-5358
Focus: 14-33
Frequency: Weekly; Circulation: 49,000

BioCycle
Jerome Goldstein, Editor/Publisher
JG Press
419 State Ave
Emmaus PA 18049-3025
610-967-4135
Focus: 51E-67 (recycling)
Frequency: Monthly; Circulation: 11,000

Biopeople
Cynthia Robbins-Roth, Editor-in-Chief
BioVenture Publishing Inc
32 W 25th Ave #203
San Mateo CA 94403-2237
415-574-7128; Fax: 415-574-8319
Focus: 17-19G-39-67
Frequency: Quarterly; Circulation: 4,000

Bird Breeder
Kathleen Etchepare, Editor
Fancy Publications
PO Box 6050
Los Angeles CA 92690
714-755-3045
Focus: 15(birds)
Frequency: Monthly; Circulation: 30,000

Bobbin Magazine
Susan Black, Editor-in-Chief
Blenheim Publishing Inc
1110 Shop Rd
Columbia SC 29201-4743
803-771-7500; Fax: 803-799-1461
Focus: 40F (apparel & other sewn products)
Frequency: Monthly; Circulation: 9,000

Book Dealers World
Al Galasso, Editor-in-Chief
N American Bookdealers Exchange
PO Box 606
Cottage Grove OR 97424-0026
503-942-7455
Focus: 99(small press)
Primarily reviews of member pubs
Frequency: Quarterly; Circulation: 20,000

Bovine Veterinarian
Geni Wren, Editor-in-Chief
Vance Publishing Corp
10901 W 84th Ter
Lenexa KS 66214-1649
913-438-8700; 800-255-5113;
    Fax: 913-438-0695
Focus: 15-51A
Frequency: 7x per yr; Circulation: 9,000

Broadcast Engineering
Brad Dick, Editor
Intertec Publishing Corp
9800 Metcalf
Overland Park KS 66212-2216
913-341-1300; Fax: 913-967-1898
Focus: 24E-33T
Frequency: Monthly; Circulation: 36,000

Broadcasting & Cable
Donald V West, Editor
Cahners Publishing Co
1705 DeSales St NW
Washington DC 20036-4405
202-659-2340; Fax: 202-429-0651
Focus: 33T(broadcasting equipment and technology)
Frequency: Weekly; Circulation: 34,000

Broker World
Sharon Chace, Editor
10709 Barkley #3
Overland Park KS 66211-1100
913-383-9191; 800-762-3387;
    Fax: 913-383-1247
Focus: 19(insurance)
Frequency: Monthly; Circulation: 27,000

Builder Magazine
Noreen S Welle, Editor
Hanley-Wood Inc
655 15th St NW #475
Washington DC 20005-5701
202-452-0800; Fax: 202-785-1974
Focus: 12-43(home building)
National Assn of Home Builders
Frequency: Monthly; Circulation: 212,000

Building Renovation
Tom Fisher, Editor-in-Chief
Penton Publishing
600 Summer St
Stamford CT 06901-1403
203-348-7531; Fax: 203-348-4023
Focus: 12-19H-23T
Non-residential renovations
Frequency: Quarterly; Circulation: 40,000

Bus World
Julian Wolinsky, Managing Editor
24125 Albers St (91367)
PO Box 39
Woodland Hills CA 91365
818-710-0208
Focus: 16A(buses)
Frequency: Quarterly; Circulation: N/A

Business & Health
Joseph Burns, Editor
Medical Economics Publishing
5 Paragon Dr
Montvale NJ 07645-1725
201-358-7200; Fax: 201-573-8979
Focus: 19-39
Frequency: Monthly; Circulation: 45,000

Business Communications Review
Fred Knight, Editor
950 York Rd
Hinsdale IL 60521-2950
708-986-1432
Focus: 19(communications)-56
Frequency: Monthly; Circulation: 12,000

Business Ethics
Craig Cox, Editor
52 S 10th St #110
Minneapolis MN 55403-2001
612-962-4700;800-769-9852
Focus: 19G-54(ethics management)
Frequency: 6x per yr; Circulation: 15,000

Business Insurance
Tim Stanton, Managing Editor
740 N Rush St
Chicago IL 60611-2525
312-649-5398; 800-678-2724;
    Fax: 312-280-3174
Focus: 19(insurance)
Frequency: Weekly; Circulation: 52,000

The Business of Herbs
David Oliver, Editor
RR 2 Box 246
Shevlin MN 56676-9535
218-657-2478; Fax: 218-657-2447
Focus: 43G
Frequency: 6x per yr; Circulation: 2,000

C

CabinetMaker
Bruce Plantz, Editor
1350 E Touhy Ave
PO Box 5080
Des Plaines IL 60017-5080
708-635-8800; Fax: 708-390-2200
Focus: 12A-12B-43
Frequency: 8x per yr; Circulation: 30,000

Cable Avails
Peggy Conger, Editor
Cowles Business Media
1905 Sherman St #800
Denver CO 80203-1147
303-837-1215; Fax: 303-837-0915
Focus: 19X
Frequency: Monthly; Circulation: 8,000

Cable World
Bob Diddlebock, Editor
Cowles Business Media
1905 Sherman St #1000
Denver CO 80203-1149
303-837-0900
Focus: 19X
Frequency: Weekly; Circulation: 16,000

Cablevision
Craig Leddy, Editor
Capitol Cities/ABC Inc
825 7th Ave 6th Fl
New York NY 10019-6014
212-887-8400; Fax: 212-887-8585
Focus: 23-24(goes to cable TV operators, owners, installers, etc)
Frequency: Biweekly; Circulation: 15,000

California Horse Review
Jennifer Meyer, Editor/Publisher
3569 Recycle Rd #14
Rancho Cordova CA 95742-7329
916-638-1519; Fax: 916-638-1784
Focus: 15(horses)-69(horse riding)
Frequency: Monthly; Circulation: 10,000

Call Center
Keith Dawson, Editor
Telecom Library Inc
12 West 21st St
New York NY 10010-6902
212-691-8215; Fax: 212-677-3435
Focus: 19M-23(telephones marketing and call center management)
Frequency: Monthly; Circulation: 45,000

Can Technology International
Fred Church, Editor
Trend Publishing Inc
625 N Michigan Ave #2500
Chicago IL 60611-3109
312-654-2300; Fax: 312-654-2323
Focus: 19X
Frequency: 6x per yr; Circulation: 6,000

Canadian Banker
Simon Hally, Editor
Commerce Ct Postal Sta
Toronto ON Canada M5L 1G2
416-362-6092; Fax: 416-362-5658
Focus: 19B-61(CN)
Frequency: 6x per yr; Circulation: 33,000

Career Pilot
David A Jones, Editor
4959 Massachusetts Blvd
Atlanta GA 30337-6607
770-997-8097; 800-538-5627;
    Fax: 770-997-8111
Focus: 70A
Frequency: Monthly; Circulation: 14,000

Catalogue & Mail Order Business
Jane Revell-Higgins, Editor/Publ
101 Upton Rd, Slough
Berks UK SL1 2AE
01753-516526; Fax: 01753-516517
Focus: 19
Intl code: +44-1753
Frequency: 9x per yr; Circulation: N/A

CD-ROM Professional
David Guenette, Editor
649 Massachusetts Ave #10
Cambridge MA 02139
617-492-0268; 800-222-3766;
    Fax: 617-492-3159
Focus: 23-56P
Frequency: Monthly; Circulation: 10,000

CEE News
Michael Harrington, Managing Editor
Intertec Publishing Corp
9800 Metcalf
Overland Park KS 66212-2216
913-341-1300; Fax: 913-967-1905
Focus: 19X-23T-24 (electrical system design)
Frequency: Monthly; Circulation: 106,000

Chain Store Age Executive
John Rapuzzi, Publisher
Lebhar-Friedman Inc
425 Park Ave
New York NY 10022-3506
212-756-5252; Fax: 212-756-5270
Focus: 19R
Frequency: Monthly; Circulation: 35,000

Change
Nanette Wiese, Editor
Heldref Publications
1319 Eighteenth St NW
Washington DC 20036-1802
202-296-6267; Fax: 202-296-5149
Focus: 39H (holistic health)
Frequency: N/A; Circulation: N/A

Chef Magazine
Paul Clarke, Editor
Talcott Communications
20 N Wacker Dr #3220
Chicago IL 60606
312-849-2220; Fax: 312-670-0830
Focus: 27 (for professional chefs)
Frequency: Monthly; Circulation: 32,000

Chemical Week
David Hunter,
    Editor-in-Chief(212-621-4964)
Chemical Week Associates
888 7th Ave 26th Fl
New York NY 10106-0001
212-621-4900; Fax: 212-621-4949
Focus: 19G-19X-24-67
Frequency: 50x per yr; Circulation: 45,000

Chevy High Performance
Mike Magda, Editor
Petersen Publishing Co
6420 Wilshire Blvd
Los Angeles CA 90048-5502
213-782-2000; Fax: 213-782-2263
Focus: 16A
Frequency: Monthly; Circulation: N/A

Chicago Advertising & Media
Joe Brar, Editor
JB Communications
2240 West 23rd Pl
Chicago IL 60608-3904
312-847-4444; Fax: 312-847-4044
Focus: 19M-56M
Frequency: Biweekly; Circulation: 6,000

Chicago Books in Review
Nellie Goddard, Editorial Asst
5840 N Kenmore Ave
Chicago IL 60660-3721
312-561-6280
Focus: 61(Chicago)
Reviews of Chicago authors/books
Frequency: N/A; Circulation: N/A

Chicago Lawyer
Donna Gill, Managing Editor
415 N State St
Chicago IL 60610-4607
312-644-7800; Fax: 312-644-4255
Focus: 19L-55L-61(IL)
Frequency: Monthly; Circulation: 12,000

Children's Business
Monique Greenwood, Editor-in-Chief
Fairchild Publications
7 West 34th St
New York NY 10001-8100
212-630-4500; Fax: 212-630-4511
Focus: 40F(children), (primarily clothing)
Frequency: Monthly; Circulation: 22,000

Chip Chats
Edward F Gallenstein, Editor
National Wood Carvers Assn
7424 Miami Ave
Cincinnati OH 45243-2109
513-561-0627
Focus: 29(woodcarving)
Frequency: 6x per yr; Circulation: 54,000

The Chronicle of Philanthropy
Marty Michaels, Book Review Editor
1255 23rd St NW #775
Washington DC 20037-1125
202-466-1200; Fax: 202-466-2078
Focus: 19(fundraising)
Frequency: 26x per yr; Circulation: 29,000

Circulation Management
Karlene Lukovitz, Editor
Ganesa Corp
611 Broadway #510
New York NY 10012-2608
212-979-0730; Fax: 212-979-0961
Focus: 19M-56M(circulation)
Frequency: Monthly; Circulation: 11,000

Clavier
Elizabeth Hintch, Editor
200 Northfield Rd
Northfield IL 60093-3312
708-446-5000
Focus: 14M (for piano, organ players, teachers)
Frequency: 10x per yr; Circulation: 18,000)

Cleaner Times
Charlene Yarbrough, Editor
17319 Crystal Valley Rd
Little Rock AR 72210-3608
501-455-1441; Fax: 501-455-2479
Focus: 19X (pressure cleaning)
Frequency: Monthly; Circulation: 14,000

Clergy Journal
Clyde Steckel, Editor
6160 Carmen Ave E
Inner Grove Height MN 55076-4420
612-451-9945; 800-328-0200;
    Fax: 612-457-4617
Focus: 63
Frequency: 10; Circulation: 10,000

Closing the Gap
Paul M Malchow, Managing Editor
PO Box 068
Henderson MN 56044-0068
612-248-3294; Fax: 612-248-3810
Focus: 39D
Frequency: 6x per yr; Circulation: 10,000

CoffeeTalk
Kate LaPoint, Editor
1306 Western Ave #406
Seattle WA 98101-2957
206-382-2112; Fax: 206-623-0446;
    E-Mail: ctmag@halcyon.com
Focus: 19G-27(for coffee-house owners and managers)
Frequency: Monthly; Circulation: 10,000

College Store Journal
Ron Stevens, Editor
500 E Lorain St
Oberlin OH 44074-1267
216-775-7777; Fax: 216-775-4769
Focus: 19R (bookstores/retail sales)
Frequency: 6x per yr; Circulation: 7,000

Collision Magazine
J A Kruza, Editor
Kruza Kaleidoscopix Inc
PO Box M
Franklin MA 02038-0822
508-528-6211
Focus: 16A(auto repair shops/body shops)
Frequency: 9x per yr; Circulation: 14,000

Color Publishing
Pat Mills, Book Review Editor
Frank Romano, Editor
10 Tara Blvd 5th Fl
Nashua NH 03062-2800
603-891-0123; Fax: 603-891-0539
Focus: 23-56P
Frequency: 6x per yr; Circulation: 22,000

Communication Arts
Patrick & Jean Coyne, Editors
410 Sherman Ave
Palo Alto CA 94306-1826
415-326-6040; 800-258-9111;
    Fax: 415-326-1648
Focus: 11-11P(graphics and photography)
Frequency: 8x per yr; Circulation: 63,000

Communication World
Gloria Gordon, Editor
Intl Assn of Bus Communicators
1 Hallidie Plz #600
San Francisco CA 94102-2818
415-433-3400; Fax: 415-362-8762
Focus: 56(PR/communication)
Frequency: 10x per yr; Circulation: 13,000

Computer Reseller News
Robert Faletra, Editor-in-Chief
CMP Publications
1 Jericho Plz Wing A
Jericho NY 11753
516-733-6700; Fax: 516-733-8636
Focus: 23(Macintosh)
Frequency: Weekly; Circulation: 71,000

Computer-Aided Engineering
Bob Mills, Editor-in-Chief
Penton Publishing
1100 Superior Ave
Cleveland OH 44114-2518
216-696-7000; Fax: 216-361-1309
Focus: 12-19X-23C-23T-24-55G
Computer design/analy/mfg
Frequency: Monthly; Circulation: 60,000

Contemporary Long-Term Care
Elise Nakhnikian, Editor
Bill Communications Inc
355 Park Ave S
New York NY 10010
212-592-6200; Fax: 212-592-6489
Focus: 19G-35A-39M
Frequency: Monthly; Circulation: 35,000

Contemporary Urology
James Swan, Editor
Medical Economics Inc
5 Paragon Dr
Montvalle NJ 07645-1725
201-358-7606; 800-223-0581;
    Fax: 201-358-7260
Focus: 39M(urology)
Frequency: Monthly; Circulation: 9,000

Contracting Business
Dominick Guarino, Editor-in-Chief
Penton Publishing Co
1100 Superior Ave
Cleveland OH 44114-2518
216-696-7000; Fax: 216-696-7932
Focus: 12B-19G-19H-19O-23T-51E
Environmental control
Frequency: Monthly; Circulation: 53,000

Controller Magazine
Greg Northrup, Publisher
Duke Communications Int Inc
221 E 29th St
Loveland CO 80538
970-663-4700
Focus: 19G(financial managers)
Frequency: Monthly; Circulation: 100,000

Convene
Amy Cates Lyle, Managing Editor
Prof Convention Management Assn
100 Vestavia Office Park #220
Birmingham AL 35216-9970
205-823-7262; Fax: 205-822-3891
Focus: 19G-39M-71
Frequency: 10x per yr; Circulation: N/A

Convenience Store News
Maureen Azzato, Editor
BMT Communications Inc
7 Penn Plz
New York NY 10001-3900
212-594-4120; 800-223-9638;
    Fax: 212-714-0514
Focus: 19R
Frequency: 16x per yr; Circulation: 118,000

Converting Magazine
Yolanda Simonsis, Managing Editor
Cahners Publishing
1350 E Touhy Ave PO Box 5080
Des Plaines IL 60017-5080
708-635-8800; Fax: 708-390-2200
Focus: 19X
Frequency: Monthly; Circulation: 44,000

Copy Imaging & Reproduction
Karen Lowery, Editor
1680 SW Bayshore Blvd
Port St Lucie FL 34984-3568
407-879-6666; Fax: 407-879-7388
Focus: 56X
Frequency: 6x per yr; Circulation: 65,000

Corporate & Incentive Travel
Ed Defort, Managing Editor
Costal Communications Corp
488 Madison Ave
New York NY 10022-5702
212-888-1500; Fax: 212-888-8008
Focus: 19-71
Frequency: Monthly; Circulation: 60,000

Corporate Cleveland Magazine
Robert Rosenbaum, Managing Editor
Playhouse Square Bldg
1720 Euclid Ave #300
Cleveland OH 44115-2106
216-621-1644; Fax: 216-621-5918
Focus: 19-61(OH)
Frequency: Monthly; Circulation: 31,000

Corporate Meetings & Incentives
Connie Goldstein, Editor/Assoc Publisher
Adams Laux Co
420 Lexington Ave #1650
New York NY 10170-1699
212-338-9124; Fax: 212-338-9259;
    E-mail: 74117.250@compuserve.com
Focus: 19G-71
Frequency: Monthly; Circulation: 36,000

Corporate Travel
Loren Ginsberg, Editor
Miller Freeman Inc
1 Penn Plz 10th Fl
New York NY 10119-1191
212-714-1300; Fax: 212-714-1313
Focus: 19-71
Frequency: Monthly; Circulation: 47,000

Cotton Grower
William Spencer, Editor
Meister Publishing Co
8001 Centerview Pky #212
Cordova TN 38018-4242
901-756-8822; Fax: 901-756-8879
Focus: 19M-51A-51E
Frequency: Biweekly; Circulation: 55,000

Country Handcrafts
Kathleen Zimmer, Editor
Reiman Publications
5400 South 60th St
Greendale WI 53129-1404
414-423-0100; 800-344-6913;
    Fax: 414-423-1143
Focus: 29C
Frequency: 6x per yr; Circulation: N/A

Country Inns/Bed & Breakfast
Gail Rudder-Kent, Editor-in-Chief
15 S Orange Ave
South Orange NJ 07079-1716
201-762-7090; Fax: 201-762-1491
Focus: 61-71
Frequency: 6x per yr; Circulation: 180,000

Crafts Magazine
Judith Brossart, Editor
PJS Publications Inc
News Plz
Peoria IL 61656
309-682-6626; 800-521-2885;
    Fax: 309-682-7394
Focus: 29
Frequency: Monthly; Circulation: 400,000

Creative Classroom
Jamie Kyle McGillian, Sr Editor
Children's Television Workshop
1 Lincoln Plz
New York NY 10023-7170
212-595-3456
Focus: 21-31-76 (for teachers grades K-6)
Frequency: 6x per yr; Circulation: 175,000

Creative Exhibiting Techniques
Paula Marlow, Editor
745 Marquette Bank Bldg
Rochester MN 55904
507-289-6556; Fax: 507-289-5253
Focus: 19M(trade show exhibiting)
Frequency: Monthly; Circulation: 3,000

Creative Retirement
R Alan Fox, Publisher
Vacation Publications Inc
1502 Augusta Dr #415
Houston TX 77057-2484
713-974-6903; Fax: 713-914-0445
Focus: 35A-69-99(lifestyle news for
    wealthy, intellectual sr citizens)
Frequency: Quarterly; Circulation: 35,000

Creativity Magazine
Anthony Vagnoni, Editor
Crain Communications
220 East 42nd St
New York NY 10017-5806
212-210-0100; 800-283-2724;
    Fax: 212-210-0215
Focus: 11-19M(creative side of the
    advertising business)
Frequency: 10; Circulation: 30,000

Credit Card Management
John Stewart, Publisher
Faulkner & Gray Publishing Inc
11 Penn Plz 17th Fl
New York NY 10001-2006
212-967-7000; 800-535-8403;
    Fax: 212-967-7162
Focus: 19A-19B
Frequency: Biweekly; Circulation: 17,000

Credit Union Magazine
Steve Rodgers, Editor
5710 Mineral Point Rd
Madison WI 53705-4454
608-231-4000; Fax: 608-231-4370
Focus: 19B
Frequency: Monthly; Circulation: 44,000

Current
Joyce Horn, Editor
Heldref Publications
1319 Eighteenth St NW
Washington DC 20036-1802
202-296-6267; Fax: 202-296-5149
Focus: 31-54-55-65S
Frequency: 10x per yr; Circulation: 3,000

Custom Home
Leslie Ensor, Editor
Hanley-Wood Inc
1 Thomas Cir NW #600
Washington DC 20005
202-452-0800; Fax: 202-785-1974
Focus: 43H
Frequency: 6x per yr; Circulation: 40,000

Cycle World
David Edwards, Editor-in-Chief
Hachette Filipacchi Magazines
1499 Monrovia Ave
Newport Beach CA 92663-2752
714-720-5300; Fax: 714-631-0651
Focus: 16(motorcycles)
Frequency: Monthly; Circulation: 353,000

D

Dance Magazine
Richard Philip, Editor-in-Chief
33 W 60th St
New York NY 10023-7905
212-245-9050; Fax: 212-956-6487
Focus: 14D
Frequency: Monthly; Circulation: 53,000

Dance Magazine
Robert Johnson, News Editor
33 W 60th St
New York NY 10023-7905
212-245-9050; Fax: 212-956-6487
Focus: 14D
Frequency: Monthly; Circulation: 53,000

Dance Magazine
Marian Horosko, Lifestyle Editor
33 W 60th St
New York NY 10023-7905
212-245-9050; Fax: 212-956-6487
Focus: 14D-36
Frequency: Monthly; Circulation: 53,000

Data Based Advisor
John Hawkins, Editor
AnnMarie Garcia, Managing Editor
Advisor Publications Inc
4010 Morena Blvd
San Diego CA 92119
619-483-6400; Fax: 619-483-9851
Focus: 19M-19P-19R-23(database
    software)
800-336-6060
Frequency: Monthly; Circulation: 38,000

DBMS
Editor
Miller Freeman Inc
411 Borel Ave
San Mateo CA 94402-3522
415-358-9500; Fax: 415-358-9855
Focus: 23(databases)
Frequency: Monthly; Circulation: 58,000

Dealernews
Robin Hartfield, Editor-in-Chief
Advanstar Communications
201 E Sandpointe Ave #600
Santa Ana CA 92707-8700
714-513-8400; 800-854-3112;
   Fax: 714-513-8414
Focus: 16(water craft sports)
Frequency: Monthly; Circulation: 13,000

Dealerscope Merchandising
Judy Bocklage, Editor
North American Publishing
401 N Broad St
Philadelphia PA 19108-1001
215-238-5300; Fax: 215-238-5457
Focus: 23E-43H (consumer electronics and appliances)
Frequency: 2x per yr; Circulation: 50,000

Decor Magazine
Gary Goldman, Editor
330 North 4th St
St Louis MO 63102-2036
314-421-5445; Fax: 314-421-1070
Focus: 11-43(interior design) (for art galleries and buyers)
Frequency: 13x per yr; Circulation: 26,000

Descant
Tracy Jenkins, Managing Editor
PO Box 314 Sta P
Toronto ON Canada M5S 2S8
416-603-0223
Focus: 47
Frequency: Quarterly; Circulation: 1,000

Design Fax
Terry Persun, Editor
Hubcore Communications
29100 Aurora Rd #200
Solon OH 44139
216-248-1125; Fax: 216-248-0187
Focus: 19-24
Frequency: Monthly; Circulation: 110,000

Design News
Lawrence D Maloney, Editorial Director
Cahners Publishing
275 Washington St
Newton MA 02158-1630
617-964-3030; Fax: 617-558-4677
Focus: 19-23(design)
Frequency: Biweekly; Circulation: 175,000

Direct Magazine
Ray Schultz, Editor
911 Hope St
Six River Bend
Stamford CT 06907-2318
203-358-9900; Fax: 203-357-9014
Focus: 19M
Frequency: Monthly; Circulation: 43,000

Directory World
Carl Mercurio, Editor
SIMBA Information Inc
213 Danbury Rd
Wilton CT 06897-4006
203-834-0033; Fax: 203-834-1771;
   E-Mail: simba@aol.com
Focus: 56P-59(directories and yellow pages)
Frequency: 8x per yr; Circulation: N/A

Discount Store News
Tony Lisanti, Editor
Lebhar-Friedman Inc
425 Park Ave
New York NY 10022-3506
212-756-5100; Fax: 212-756-5125
Focus: 19R
Frequency: Biweekly; Circulation: 33,000

Distribution
Thomas Foster, Editor-in-Chief
1 Chilton Way
Radnor PA 19087-0001
610-964-4386; Fax: 215-964-4381
Focus: 16-19X(transportation, logistics, and warehouse managenent)
Frequency: Monthly; Circulation: 70,000

DO-IT-YOURSELF-RETAILING
Christopher A Jensen, Managing Editor
National Retail Hardware Assn
5822 W 74th St
Indianapolis IN 46278-1756
317-297-1190; Fax: 317-328-4354
Focus: 19G-19M-19R-12
Frequency: Monthly; Circulation: 71,000

Document Processing Technology
Marll Thiede, Editor
R B Publishing
2701 E Washington Ave
Madison WI 53704
608-241-8777; Fax: 608-241-8666
Focus: 19-23-25
Frequency: 5x per yr; Circulation: N/A

Drug Store News
Marie Griffin, Editor
425 Park Ave 6th Fl
New York NY 10022-3506
212-756-5244; 800-453-2427;
   Fax: 212-756-5250
Focus: 19R-39
Frequency: 26x per yr; Circulation: 43,000

Drum Business
Kevin Kearns, Managing Editor
Modern Drummer Publications
12 Old Bridge Rd
Cedar Grove NJ 07009
201-239-4140; Fax: 201-239-7139
Focus: 14M(drums)-19R(drum retailers)
Frequency: 6x per yr; Circulation: 5,000

E

EDI World
Michael McGarr, Editor
2021 Coolidge St
Hollywood FL 33020-2400
305-925-5900; 800-336-4887;
   Fax: 305-925-7533
Focus: 23C(electronic data interchange)
Frequency: Monthly; Circulation: N/A

Editor & Publisher
John Consoli, Executive Editor
11 West 19th St
New York NY 10011-4209
212-691-7287; Fax: 212-691-6939
Focus: 56P
Frequency: Weekly; Circulation: 28,000

Education Week
Ronald Wolk, Editor
4301 Connecticut Ave NW #250
Washington DC 20008-2304
202-364-4114; Fax: 202-364-1039
Focus: 31 (elementary and high school)
Frequency: 41x per yr; Circulation: 60,000

Educational Dealer
J Kevin Fahy, Editor
Fahy-Williams Publishing
118 Genesee St
Geneva NY 14456-1746
315-789-0458
Focus: 31
Frequency: 5x per yr; Circulation: 14,000

Educational Marketer
Patrick Quinn, Editor
SIMBA Information
213 Danbury Rd PO Box 7430
Wilton CT 06897
203-834-0033; Fax: 203-834-1771
Focus: 19M-31
Frequency: 36x per yr; Circulation: 1,000

EE Product News
Joseph Del Gatto, Editor
707 West Chester Ave
White Plains NY 10604-3102
914-949-8500; Fax: 914-682-0922
Focus: 19X-24(engineering)
Frequency: Monthly; Circulation: 102,000

Electric Light & Power
Robert Smock, Editor
1421 S Sheridan
Tulsa OK 74112-6619
918-835-3161; Fax: 918-831-9834
Focus: 19-19X
Frequency: Monthly; Circulation: 46,000

Electrical Wholesaling
Jim Lucy, Editor
Intertec Publishing Co
9800 Metcalf
Overland Park KS 66212-2216
913-341-1300; Fax: 913-967-1905
Focus: 19M-19G
Frequency: Monthly; Circulation: 23,000

Electronic Business Buyer
Rob Lineback, Editor-in-Chief
275 Washington St
Newton MA 02158-1646
617-964-3030; Fax: 617-558-4705
Focus: 19-23
Frequency: Monthly; Circulation: 73,000

Electronic Buyers News
Jeremy Young, Editor-in-Chief
600 Community Dr
Manhasset NY 11030-3847
516-562-5000; Fax: 516-562-5016
Focus: 19X-23(electronics)
Frequency: Weekly; Circulation: 61,000

Electronic Design
Roger Allen, Editor
Penton Publishing
611 Rt 46 W
Hasbrouck Heights NJ 07604-3120
201-393-6060; Fax: 201-393-0204
Focus: 19G-19X-23C-23T-24 (elec orig equip manufacturers)
Frequency: 26; Circulation: 165,000

Electronic Distribution Today
Edward J Walter, Editor-in-Chief
Custom Media Inc
7912 Country Ln
Chagrin Falls OH 44023-6330
216-543-9451; Fax: 216-543-9764
Focus: 19M-23
Frequency: 6x per yr; Circulation: 7,000

Electronic Entertainment
Frederic Paul, Editor
Infotainment World
951 Mariners Island Blvd
San Mateo CA 94404-1558
415-349-4300; Fax: 415-349-7781
Focus: 23C-23E-23T-33(interactive TV/home electronics/computer games)
Frequency: Monthly; Circulation: 100,000

Electronic Information Report
Paulette Donnelly, Editor
SIMBA Information
213 Danbury PO Box 7430
Wilton CT 06897-7430
203-834-0033; Fax: 203-834-0729
Focus: 19M-23C-56(trends and developments in information services)
Electronic publ info/distrib
Frequency: Weekly; Circulation: 3,000

Electronic Media
P J Bednarski, Editor
Crain Communications Inc
740 N Rush St
Chicago IL 60611-2525
312-649-5293; Fax: 312-649-5465
Focus: 33T
Frequency: Weekly; Circulation: 28,000

Electronic News
Frank Barbetta, Editor-in-Chief
302 5th Ave
New York NY 10001-3604
212-736-3900; Fax: 212-736-5125
Focus: 23-23T
Frequency: Weekly; Circulation: 24,000

Electronic Retailing
Brett Bush, Editor
Creative Age Publications
7628 Densmore Ave
Van Nuys CA 91406-2042
818-782-7328; Fax: 818-782-7450;
    E-mail: Eretaining@aol.com.
Focus: 19M(selling via electronics)
Frequency: 7x per yr; Circulation: 22,000

Electronic Servicing and Technology
Conrad Persson, Editor
CQ Communications
76 North Broadway
Hicksville NY 11801-2909
516-681-2922; 800-853-9797;
    Fax: 516-681-2926
Focus: 23
Frequency: Monthly; Circulation: 30,000

Electronics
Jonah McLeod, Editor
Penton Publishing Inc
1100 Superior Ave
Cleveland OH 44114-2518
216-696-7000; Fax: 216-696-7668
Focus: 19G-19X-23T-44(US/Europe/Asia)-97(electronics, engineering management)
Frequency: Biweekly; Circulation: 10,000

Empire State Report
Jeff Plungis, Editor
State Report Network Inc
4 Central Ave 3rd Fl
New York NY 12210-1334
518-465-5502; Fax: 518-465-9822
Focus: 55-61(NY) (public policy, politics in NY)
Frequency: Monthly; Circulation: 12,000

The English Journal
Leila Christenbury, Editor
1111 W Kenyon Rd
Urbana IL 61801-1010
217-328-3870; 800-369-6283;
    Fax: 217-328-0977
Focus: 31E-45L(whole language for middle/high school teachers)
Frequency: 8x per yr; Circulation: 50,000

Environment Today
Paul Harris, Editor
1483 Chain Bridge Rd #202
McLean VA 22101
703-448-0322; Fax: 703-448-0270
Focus: 51E
Frequency: 6x per yr; Circulation: N/A

Environmental Protection
Tom Barron, Editor
Stevens Publishing Corp
225 North New Rd
Waco TX 76710-6931
817-776-9000; Fax: 817-662-7075
Focus: 51E
Frequency: Monthly; Circulation: 91,000

Event World
Sharon Gorup, Editor
Intl Special Events Society
9202 N Meridian St #200
Indianpolis IN 46260
317-571-5601; 800-688-ISES;
    Fax: 317-571-5603
Focus: 19M(for event planners)
Frequency: Quarterly; Circulation: 20,000

Expansion Management
Jack Wimer, Editor
New Hope Communications
9500 Nall #400
Shawnee Mission KS 66207-2967
913-381-4800; Fax: 913-381-8858
Focus: 19X-44 (global manufacturing expansion)
Frequency: 6x per yr; Circulation: 41,000

Eyecare Business
Stephanie Walter, Editor
50 Washington St
Norwalk CT 06854-2710
203-838-9100; Fax: 203-838-2550
Focus: 39(eyes)
Frequency: Monthly; Circulation: 40,000

F

Facilities Design & Management
Eileen McMorrow, Editor-In-Chief
1 Penn Plz 10th Fl
New York NY 10019-1198
212-714-1300; Fax: 212-714-1313
Focus: 12-19G
Frequency: Monthly; Circulation: 35,000

Facilities Planning News
Lee Ingalls, Editor
115 Orinda Way
Orinda CA 94563-2333
510-254-6386; Fax: 510-254-2744
Focus: 12A-12B-24(commercial buildings)
Frequency: Monthly; Circulation: 1,000

Fancy Food Magazine
Lisa White, Exec Editor
Talcott Communications Corp
20 N Wacker Dr #3230
Chicago IL 60606
312-849-2220; Fax: 312-849-2174
Focus: 19R-27
Frequency: Monthly; Circulation: 24,000

Farm Industry News
Joe Degnan, Editor
Intertec Publishing
7900 International Dr 3rd Fl
Minneapolis MN 55425-1510
612-851-9329; Fax: 612-851-4601
Focus: 19-51A
Frequency: Monthly; Circulation: 255,000

Farm Journal
Earl Ainsworth, Editor
230 W Washington Square
Philadelphia PA 19106-3522
215-829-4700; Fax: 215-829-4873
Focus: 51A
Frequency: Monthly; Circulation: 800,000

Farmer's Digest
Frank Lessiter, Editor
Lessiter Publications
PO Box 624
Brookfield WI 53008-0624
414-782-4480; 800-645-8455
    Fax: 414-782-1252
Focus: 51A
Frequency: Monthly; Circulation: 14,000

FDA Consumer
Judith Levine Willis, Editor
5600 Fishers Ln
Rockville MD 20857-0001
301-443-3220
Focus: 27-39
Frequency: 10x per yr; Circulation: 25,000

Feedstuffs
Jon Scheid, Editor
12400 Whitewater Dr
Minnetonka MN 55343-9466
612-931-0211; Fax: 612-938-1832
Focus: 15(feed)
Frequency: Weekly; Circulation: 19,000

Fine Homebuilding
Kevin Ireton, Exec Editor
Taunton Press Inc
63 S Main St
Newtown CT 06470-2355
203-426-8171; Fax: 203-426-3434
Focus: 12-43(for prof & do-it-yourself)
Frequency: 7x per yr; Circulation: 236,000

Fine Woodworking
Scott Gibson, Editor
Taunton Press
63 S Main St
Newtown CT 06470-2355
203-426-8171; Fax: 203-426-3434
Focus: 29(woodworking, for professional & hobbiest)
Frequency: 6x per yr; Circulation: 285,000

Fisheries Product News
Susan Jones, Editor
PO Box 37
Stonington ME 04681-0037
207-367-2396; 800-989-5253;
 Fax: 207-367-2490
Focus: 15(fish)-19X
Frequency: 6x per yr; Circulation: 23,000

Flash Magazine
Walter Vose Jeffries, Editor/Publisher
Black Lightning Publishing Inc
Riddle Pond Rd
West Topsham VT 05086
802-439-6462; Fax: 802-439-6463
Focus: 56X (desktop printing)
Frequency: 6x per yr; Circulation: 54,000

FloraCulture International
Debbie Hamrick, Editor
PO Box 9
Batavia IL 60510-0009
708-208-9080; Fax: 708-208-9350
Focus: 43G (cut flowers/producers/sellers)
Frequency: Monthly; Circulation: 11,000

Floral Management
Kate Penn, Publisher
1601 Duke St
Alexandria VA 22314-3406
703-836-8700; 800-336-4743;
 Fax: 703-836-8705
Focus: 19R-43G(flowers)
Frequency: Monthly; Circulation: 15,000

Floral Mass Marketing
Rosemary Baldwin, Editor
120 S Riverside Plz #464
Chicago IL 60606-3908
312-258-8500; 800-732-4581;
 Fax: 312-258-8558
Focus: 19M-43G
Frequency: 6x per yr; Circulation: 18,000

Flower News
Editor
Cenflo Inc
PO Box 1067
Placitas NM 87043
800-426-6356; Fax: 505-867-4241
Focus: 19R-43G(flowers)
Frequency: Weekly; Circulation: N/A

Fluid Power Service Center
Tobi Goldoftas, Editor
Penton Publishing Co
1100 Superior Ave
Cleveland OH 44114-2518
216-696-7000; Fax: 216-696-1819
Focus: 19X-23T (fluid power service ctrs)
Frequency: Quarterly; Circulation: 15,000

Folio:
Anne Russell, Editor
Six River Bend Ctr
911 Hope St PO Box 4949
Stamford CT 06907-0949
203-358-9900; Fax: 203-357-9014
Focus: 19M-56P(magazines)
Frequency: Biweekly; Circulation: 14,000

Food & Beverage Marketing
Dave Wellman, Editor
PTN Publishing Co
445 Broad Hollow Rd
Melville NY 11747
516-845-2700; Fax: 516-845-2797
Focus: 19R-27
Frequency: N/A; Circulation: N/A

Food Arts
Beverly Stephen, Sr Editor
387 Park Ave S 8th Fl
New York NY 10016
212-684-4224; Fax: 212-684-5424
Focus: 27 (upscale restaurants)
Frequency: 10x per yr; Circulation: 50,000

Food Merchandising/Non-Food Retailing
Rick Van Warner, Editor
Lebhar-Friedman
425 Park Ave
New York NY 10022-3506
212-756-5186; 800-453-2427;
 Fax: 212-756-5215
Focus: 19M-27
Frequency: Weekly; Circulation: 180,000

FoodService Director
Walter Schruntek, Editor
Bill Communications
355 Park Ave S
New York NY 10010-1706
212-592-6200; Fax: 212-592-6539
Focus: 27
Frequency: Monthly; Circulation: 45,000

Foreign Trade Magazine
Russell Goodman, Editor-in-Chief
FT Inc
6849 Old Dominion Dr #200
McLean VA 22101-3705
703-448-1338
Focus: 44
Frequency: 10x per yr; Circulation: 13,000

Forests and People
Janet Tompkins, Editor
Louisiana Forestry Assn
2316 S MacArthur Dr
Alexandria LA 71301-3037
318-443-2558
Focus: 51(forest management)-61(LA)
Forest managers and researchers
Frequency: Quarterly; Circulation: 7,000

Foundry Management & Technology
Dean Peters, Editor
Penton Publishing Co
1100 Superior Ave
Cleveland OH 44114-2518
216-696-7000; Fax: 216-696-7658
Focus: 19G-19X-23T-24 (foundry industry)
Frequency: Monthly; Circulation: 20,000

Fund Raising Management
William Olcott, Editor-in-Chief
Hoke Communications
224 7th St
Garden City NY 11530-5747
516-746-6700; 800-229-6700;
 Fax: 516-294-8141
Focus: 19C-19F-55-97
Frequency: Monthly; Circulation: 10,000

Furniture/Today
Lester Craft, Editor
Cahners Publishing
7025 S Albert Pick Rd
Greensboro NC 27409
910-605-0121; Fax: 910-605-1143
Focus: 43(furniture)
Frequency: Weekly; Circulation: 28,000

Futures Magazine
Ginger Szala, Editor
Oster Communications
250 S Wacker Dr #1150
Chicago IL 60606-5834
312-977-0999; Fax: 312-977-1042
Focus: 19
Frequency: 14; Circulation: 60,000

Futurific Magazine
Charlotte Kellar, Editor
150 Haven Ave Ter 3
New York NY 10032-1135
212-297-0502; 800-696-2836
Focus: 23-67-86
Frequency: Monthly; Circulation: 10,000

G

General Aviation News & Flyer
Kirk Gormley, Managing Editor
NW Flyer Inc
PO Box 39099
Tacoma WA 98439-0099
206-471-9888; 800-426-8538;
 Fax: 206-471-9911
Focus: 16
Frequency: Biweekly; Circulation: 38,000

Gift & Stationery Business
Katherine Krassner, Editor
1 Penn Plz 10th Fl
New York NY 10119-1198
212-714-1300; Fax: 212-302-6273
Focus: 19R(gifts)
Frequency: Monthly; Circulation: 32,000

Gift Basket Review
Elizabeth Skelton, Editor
Festivities Publications Inc
1205 W Forsyth St
Jacksonville FL 32204-1423
904-634-1902; Fax: 904-633-8764
Focus: 19R-29(gift baskets)
Frequency: Monthly; Circulation: 15,000

Gifts & Decorative Accessories
Phyllis Sweed, Editor
51 Madison Ave
New York NY 10010-1603
212-689-4411; Fax: 212-683-7929
Focus: 19R-27-33
Frequency: Monthly; Circulation: 34,000

Giftware News
Anthony DeMasi, Editor-in-Chief
112 Adrossan Ct
Deptford NJ 08096-4201
609-227-0798; 800-229-1967;
   Fax: 609-227-6511
Focus: 19R-99(gifts)
Frequency: Monthly; Circulation: 41,000

Golf Pro
Ken Cohen, Editor
7 West 34th St
New York NY 10001-8100
212-630-4870; Fax: 212-630-4879
Focus: 19R-40F-69(golf)
Frequency: Monthly; Circulation: 14,000

Golf Shop Operations
W Tim Murphy, Editor
5520 Park Ave
Trumbull CT 06611
203-373-7000; Fax: 203-371-2172
Focus: 19R-69(golf)
Frequency: 10; Circulation: 16,000

Good Times!
Kent Smith, Editor
Valley Media
1061 East 2100 S
Salt Lake City UT 84106
801-487-3221; Fax: 801-487-8926
Focus: 61-71-99(passengers of ValuJet Airlines)
Frequency: 6x per yr; Circulation: 20,000

Government Computer News
Tom Temin, Editor
8601 Georgia Ave #300
Silver Spring MD 20910-3438
301-650-2000; Fax: 301-650-2111
Focus: 23-55
Frequency: 26x per yr; Circulation: 80,000

Government Executive
Timothy Clark, Editor/Publisher
National Journal Inc
1501 M St NW #300
Washington DC 20005
202-739-8400; Fax: 202-793-8511
Focus: 19G-55G (for government officials)
Frequency: Monthly; Circulation: 60,000

Government Products News
Leslie Drahos, Editor
Penton Publishing Co
1100 Superior Ave
Cleveland OH 44114-2518
216-696-7000; Fax: 216-696-7658
Focus: 19-55 (all levels of government)
Frequency: Monthly; Circulation: 85,000

Grand Street
Jean Stein, Editor
New York Foundation for the Arts
131 Varick St #906
New York NY 10013-1410
212-807-6548; Fax: 212-807-6544
Focus: 47-75-95
Frequency: Quarterly; Circulation: 7,000

Graphic Arts Monthly
Roger Ynostroza, Editor
Cahners Publishing Co
249 West 17th St
New York NY 10011
212-645-0067; Fax: 212-463-6620
Focus: 11(graphics)-56X
Frequency: Monthly; Circulation: 89,000

Graphic Design USA
Milton Kaye, Editor
1556 3rd Ave
New York NY 10128-3106
212-534-5500; Fax: 212-534-4415
Focus: 11-19M
Frequency: Monthly; Circulation: 30,000

Greenhouse Business
Editor
McCormick Communications Group
PO Box 698
Park Ridge IL 60068
708-823-5650; Fax: 708-696-3445
Focus: 19G-43G (commercial greenhouse growers)
Frequency: Monthly; Circulation: 20,000

Greenhouse Grower
Robyn Dill, Managing Editor
Meister Publishing Co
37733 Euclid Ave
Willoughby OH 44094-5925
216-942-2000; Fax: 216-975-3447
Focus: 43G
Frequency: 14; Circulation: 22,000

Greetings Magazine
Milton Kristt, Editor
Mackay Publishing Corp
307 Fifth Ave
New York NY 10016-6517
212-679-6677;800-886-6677;
   Fax: 212-679-6374
Focus: 33(greeting cards)
Frequency: Monthly; Circulation: 9,000

The Greyhound Review
Gary Guccione, Editor
PO Box 543
Abilene KS 67410-0543
913-263-4660; Fax: 913-263-4689;
   E-Mail: mga@access_1.com
Focus: 15(greyhounds)
Frequency: 16x per yr; Circulation: 6,000

Grocery Marketing
Ryan Mathews, Editor
625 N Michigan AVE #2500
Chicago IL 60611-3109
312-654-2300; Fax: 312-654-2323
Focus: 19M-19R-27
Frequency: Monthly; Circulation: 63,000

Groom and Board
Karen Long MacLeod, Editor
H H Backer Assoc Inc
20 E Jackson Blvd #200
Chicago IL 60604-2205
312-663-4040; Fax: 312-663-5676
Focus: 15 (for pet care facilities)
Frequency: 9x per yr; Circulation: 16,000

Grounds Maintenance
Mark Welterlen, Editor
Intertec Publishing Corp
9800 Metcalf
Overland Park KS 66212-2216
913-341-1300; Fax: 913-967-1905
Focus: 43G
Frequency: Monthly; Circulation: 48,000

Group Practice Journal
Laura Johnson, Editor
1422 Duke St
Alexandria VA 22314-3403
703-838-0033; Fax: 703-548-1890
Focus: 19-39
Frequency: 6x per yr; Circulation: 47,000

The Group Travel Leader
Herb Sparrow, Editor
130 N Broadway #101
Lexington KY 40507-1227
606-253-0455; Fax: 606-253-0499
Focus: 35A-71 (group travel leaders)
Frequency: Monthly; Circulation: 36,000

GrowerTalks
Chris Beytes, Managing Editor
335 N River St
Batavia IL 60510-2357
708-208-9080; Fax: 708-208-9350
Focus: 43G (professional greenhouse growers)
Frequency: Monthly; Circulation: 11,000

Growing Edge
Trisha Coene, Editor-in-Chief
New Moon Publishing Inc
215 SW 2nd
Corvallis OR 97333-4633
503-757-8477; Fax:
Focus: 43G(hi-tech)
Frequency: Quarterly; Circulation: 24,000

H

Hardware Age
Richard Carter, Managing Editor
Chilton Publications
1 Chilton Way
Radnor PA 19089-0001
610-964-4274; 800-695-1214;
   Fax: 610-964-4273
Focus: 19R-43H
No book reviews
Frequency: Monthly; Circulation: 71,000

Hay & Forage Grower
Neil Tietz, Editor
Intertec Publishing Corp
7900 International Dr
Minneapolis MN 55425-1510
612-851-9329; Fax: 612-851-4601
Focus: 51A
Frequency: 3x per yr; Circulation: 82,000

Health Foods Business
Gina Geslewitz, Editor
PTN Publishing
567 Morris Ave
Elizabeth NJ 07208-1985
201-487-7800; Fax: 201-487-1061
Focus: 19R-27-39 (health food stores)
Frequency: Monthly; Circulation: 12,000

The Hearing Review
Pauline Davies, Editor
Fladmark Publishing Co
101 W Second St #209
Duluth MN 55802
218-722-8352; Fax: 218-722-8587
Focus: 39 (for hearing professionals)
Frequency: Monthly; Circulation: 22,000

Hearth & Home
Richard Wright, Editor
Village West
Gilford NH 03246
603-528-4285; 800-258-3772;
    Fax: 603-524-0643
Focus: 19R-43(retail sales)
Frequency: Monthly; Circulation: 18,000

Heating/Piping/Air Conditioning
Bob Korte, Editor
180 North Stetson
Chicago IL 60601-6710
312-861-1287; Fax: 312-861-0874
Focus: 12B-19X-23T-24 (mechanical systems engineering)
Frequency: Monthly; Circulation: 55,000

HerbalGram
Mark Blumenthal, Editor/Publisher
PO Box 201660
Austin TX 78720-1660
512-331-8868; Fax: 512-331-1924
Focus: 27-39H (herbal plants & medicines)
Frequency: Quarterly; Circulation: 20,000

High Times
Alison Jones, Managing Editor
Trans-High Corp
235 Park Ave S #5 FL
New York NY 10003-1405
212-387-0500; Fax: 212-475-7604
Focus: 39-51(drugs)
Frequency: Monthly; Circulation: 250,000

High Volume Printing
Steve Austin, Publisher
425 Huehl Rd #11
Northbrook IL 60062-2319
708-564-5940; 800-247-3306;
    Fax: 708-564-8361
Focus: 56X
Frequency: 6x per yr; Circulation: 42,000

Hobby Merchandiser
Andy Hecht, Editor
225 Gordons Corner rd
Manalapan NJ 07726-3342
908-446-4900; Fax: 908-446-5488
Focus: 19R-29
Frequency: Monthly; Circulation: 9,000

Hockey Digest
Norman Jacobs, Publisher
Century Publishing Co
990 Grove St
Evanston IL 60201-4370
708-491-6440; Fax: 708-491-0459
Focus: 69(hockey)
Frequency: 8x per yr; Circulation: 102,000

Holistic Living
Meredith Gould Ruch, Editor
360 Nassau St
Princeton NJ 08540
609-924-8711; Fax: 609-924-3836
Focus: 53-54
Frequency: 6x per yr; Circulation: N/A

Home Gym & Fitness
James O'Connor, Managing Editor
Century Publishing
990 Grove St
Evanston IL 60201-4370
708-491-6440
Focus: 39-69
Frequency: 6x per yr; Circulation: 175,000

Horsemen's Yankee Pedlar Newspaper
Jane Sullivan, Managing Editor
785 South Bridge St
Auburn MA 01501
508-832-9638; Fax: 508-832-6744
Focus: 15(horses)
Frequency: Monthly; Circulation: 15,000

Horses All
Mickey Dumont, Editor
4000 19th St NE
Calgary AB Canada T2E 6P8
403-250-6633
Focus: 15
Frequency: Monthly; Circulation: 8,000

Hospital Topics
Walter Beach, Publisher
Heldref Publications
1319 18th St NW
Washington DC 20036-1802
202-296-6267; Fax: 202-296-5149
Focus: 39-19G-19M
Frequency: Quarterly; Circulation: 2,000

Hospitality Design
John Radulski, Editor
Bill Communications
355 Park Ave S
New York NY 10010-1706
212-592-6355; Fax: 212-592-6359
Focus: 19G-43D
Frequency: 6x per yr; Circulation: 30,000

Hotels
Jeff Weinstein, Editor-in-Chief
249 W 17th St
New York NY 10011
212-463-6477; Fax: 708-390-2200
Focus: 19G-27
Frequency: Monthly; Circulation: 60,000

HOW Magazine
Kathleen Reinmann, Editor
1507 Dana Ave
Cincinnati OH 45207-1056
513-531-2690; Fax: 513-531-2902
Focus: 11(graphics)-56P
Frequency: 6x per yr; Circulation: 38,000

HRMagazine
Phaedra Brotherton, Book Review Editor
Society for Human Resource Mgmt
606 N Washington St
Alexandria VA 22314-1914
703-548-3440; Fax: 703-836-0367
Focus: 19
Frequency: Monthly; Circulation: 75,000

HRNews
Phaedra Brotherton, Book Review Editor
Leon Rubis, Managing Editor
Society for Human Resource Mgmt
606 N Washington St
Alexandria VA 22314-1914
703-548-3440; Fax: 703-836-0367
Focus: 19
Frequency: 13x per yr; Circulation: 65,000

Hydraulics & Pneumatics
Dick Schneider, Editor
Penton Publishing
1100 Superior Ave
Cleveland OH 44114-2518
216-696-7000; Fax: 216-696-1819
Focus: 19X-23T-24 (fluid/motion systems)
Frequency: Monthly; Circulation: 50,000

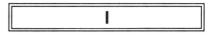

IEEE MultiMedia
Ramesh Jain, Editor-in-Chief
IEEE Computer Society
10662 Los Vaqueros Cir
Los Alamitos CA 90720-2513
714-821-8380; Fax: 714-821-4010
Focus: 23C(multimedia)
Frequency: Quarterly; Circulation: 14,000

In Motion
Katie Schuerholz, Managing Editor
7811 Montrose Rd
Potomac MD 20854-3363
301-340-1520; 800-777-5006;
    Fax: 301-340-0542
Focus: 33(production)
Frequency: Monthly; Circulation: 15,000

In-Plant Printer
Mary Ellin Innes, Publisher
425 Huehl Rd #11
Northbrook IL 60062-2319
708-564-5940; Fax: 708-564-8361
Focus: 56X
Frequency: 6x per yr; Circulation: 41,000

Incentive Magazine
Jennifer Juergens, Editor-in-Chief
Bill Communications Inc
355 Park Ave S
New York NY 10010-1706
212-592-6453; Fax: 212-592-6459
Focus: 19M
Frequency: Monthly; Circulation: 42,000

Income Opportunities
Stephen Wagner, Editor
1500 Broadway
New York NY 10036-4015
212-642-0600; Fax: 212-302-8269
Focus: 19M-19O
Frequency: Monthly; Circulation: 350,000

Independent Agent
Maureen Wall, Editor
127 S Peyton St
Alexandria VA 22314-2803
703-683-4422; Fax: 703-683-7556
Focus: 19(insurance)
Frequency: Monthly; Circulation: 43,000

Independent Energy Magazine
John Anderson, Managing Editor
620 Central Ave N
Milaca MN 56353-1744
612-983-6892; Fax: 612-983-6893
Focus: 24-51-67
Frequency: 10x per yr; Circulation: 11,000

Industrial Computing
Ed Bassett, Editor
67 Alexander Dr
Res Triangle Park NC 27709
919-549-8411; Fax: 919-549-8288
Focus: 19X-23-24(design/engineering)
Frequency: Monthly; Circulation: 45,000

Industrial Purchasing Agents
Pearl Shaine, Editor
21 Russell Woods Rd
Great Neck NY 11021-4644
516-487-0990; Fax: 516-487-0809
Focus: 19X
Frequency: 10x per yr; Circulation: 27,000

Industry Week
Chuck Day, Editor-in-Chief
Penton Publishing
1100 Superior Ave
Cleveland OH 44114-2518
216-696-7000; Fax: 216-696-7670
Focus: 19C-19G-19X-23T
Frequency: 2x per yr; Circulation: 288,000

Inside Media
Steve Ellwanger, Contact
911 Hope St Bldg 6
PO Box 4949
Stamford CT 06907
203-358-9900; Fax: 203-348-5792
Focus: 19M
Frequency: Biweekly; Circulation: N/A

Inside PR
Paul A Holmes, Editor/Publisher
Editorial Media Marketing Intl
235 West 48th St
New York NY 10036-1404
212-245-8680; Fax: 212-245-8699
Focus: 56M
Frequency: 6x per yr; Circulation: 12,000

Instant/Small Commercial Printer
Anna Marie Mohan, Editorial Dir
425 Huehl Rd #11
Northbrook IL 60062-2319
708-564-5940; Fax: 708-564-8361
Focus: 56X
Frequency: 10x per yr; Circulation: 62,000

Institutional Distribution
Caroline Perkins, Editor
Bill Communications Inc
355 Park Ave S 3rd Fl
New York NY 10017-1706
212-592-6550; Fax: 212-592-6559
Focus: 19G
Frequency: Monthly; Circulation: 47,000

International Railway Journal
Michael Knutton, Editor
Simmons-Boardman Publ Corp
345 Hudson St
New York NY 10014-4502
212-620-7200; Fax: 212-633-1165
Focus: 16R
Frequency: Monthly; Circulation: 10,000

ITS World
Editor
Advanstar Communications
7500 Old Oak Blvd
Cleveland OH 44130
216-243-8100; Fax:
Focus: 71(transportation)
Frequency: 6x per yr; Circulation: 20,000

J

Jack O'Dwyer's Newsletter
Jack O'Dwyer, Editor/Publisher
271 Madison Ave
New York NY 10016-1001
212-679-2471; Fax: 212-683-2750
Focus: 19M-56M
Frequency: Weekly; Circulation: 30,000

Java Monthly
Michelle Savoy, Editor
119 E 7th St #2
Tempe AZ 85281-3710
602-966-6352; 800-949-5271;
    Fax: 602-967-0168
Focus: 27(coffee)
Frequency: Monthly; Circulation: 16,000

Journal of Aging & Social Policy
Scott A Bass PhD, Editor
The Haworth Press Inc
10 Alice St
Binghamton NY 13904-1503
607-722-5857; Fax: 607-722-1424
Focus: 35A-55-65
Frequency: Quarterly; Circulation: N/A

Journal of College & University Foodservice
Mahmood Khan, Editor
The Haworth Press Inc
10 Alice St
Binghamton NY 13904-1503
703-231-5515; Fax: 703-231-8313
Focus: 27(for food service professionals)
Frequency: N/A; Circulation: N/A

Journal of Cost Management
Barry J Brinker, Mamging Editor
Warren Gorham Lamont
1 Penn Plz
New York NY 10119-0002
212-971-5228; Fax: 212-971-5588
Focus: 19
Frequency: Quarterly; Circulation: 6,000

Journal of East-West Business
Stan Paliwoda, Editor
The Haworth Press Inc
10 Alice St
Binghamton NY 13904-1503
607-722-1424
Focus: 19-44
Frequency: Quarterly; Circulation: N/A

Journal of Experimental Education
Paige Jackson, Editor
Heldref Publications
1319 Eighteenth St NW
Washington DC 20036-1802
202-296-6267; Fax: 202-296-5149
Focus: 31E
Frequency: N/A; Circulation: N/A

Journal of Health Care Benefits
Joseph Duva, Co-Editor
Warren Gorham Lamont
One Penn Plz
New York NY 10119-4098
212-971-5000; Fax: 212-971-5588
Focus: 19C-39-55G
Jeffrey Mamorsky, Co-Editor
Frequency: 6x per yr; Circulation: N/A

Journal of Hospital Marketing
William J Winston, Editor
The Haworth Press Inc
10 Alice St
Binghamton NY 13904-1503
510-524-6144; Fax: 607-722-1424
Focus: 19M-39
Frequency: 2; Circulation: N/A

Journal of Hospitality & Leisure Marketing
Bonnie Knutson, Editor
The Haworth Press Inc
10 Alice St
Binghamton NY 13904-1503
800-342-9678; Fax: 607-722-1424
Focus: 19M-71
Frequency: Quarterly; Circulation: N/A

Journal of International Financial Markets/Inst
Ike Mathur PhD, Editor
Haworth Press Inc
10 Alice St
Binghamton NY 13904-1503
800-342-9678; Fax: 607-722-1424
Focus: 19-44
Frequency: Quarterly; Circulation: N/A

Journal of Marketing Channels
Bert Rosenbloom PhD, Editor
The Haworth Press Inc
10 Alice St
Binghamton NY 13904-1503
800-342-9678; Fax: 607-722-1424
Focus: 19M
Frequency: Quarterly; Circulation: N/A

Journal of Marketing for Higher Education
James A Burns, Editor
The Haworth Press Inc
10 Alice St
Binghamton NY 13904-1503
800-342-9678; Fax: 607-722-1424
Focus: 19-31
Frequency: 2x per yr; Circulation: N/A

Journal of Multicultural Social Work
Paul Keys PhD, Editor
The Haworth Press Inc
10 Alice St
Binghamton NY 13904-1503
607-722-5857; Fax: 607-722-6362
Focus: 49-65
Frequency: Quarterly; Circulation: N/A

Journal of Offender Rehabilitation
Nathaniel J Pallone PhD, Editor
10 Alice St
Binghamton NY 13904-1503
607-722-5857; Fax: 607-722-1424
Focus: 39R
Frequency: Quarterly; Circulation: N/A

Journal of Organizational Behavior Management
Thomas Mawhinney PhD, Editor
10 Alice St
Binghamton NY 13904-1503
800-342-9678; Fax: 607-722-1424
Focus: 19G-57
Frequency: 2x per yr; Circulation: N/A

Journal of Partnership Taxation
Charles Emley, Editor-In-Chief
Warren Gorham Lamont
One Penn Plz
New York NY 10119-4098
212-971-5000; Fax: 212-971-5588
Focus: 19-55G
Frequency: Quarterly; Circulation: N/A

Journal of Pharmaceutical Marketing & Management
Mickey C Smith PhD, Editor
The Haworth Press Inc
10 Alice St
Binghamton NY 13904-1503
800-342-9678; Fax: 607-722-1424
Focus: 19G-19M-39D
Frequency: Quarterly; Circulation: N/A

Journal of Professional Services Marketing
William J Winston, Editor
The Haworth Press Inc
10 Alice St
Binghamton NY 13904-1503
800-342-9678; Fax: 607-722-1424
Focus: 19M
Frequency: Quarterly; Circulation: N/A

Journal of Promotion Management
Fred G Crane PhD, Editor
The Haworth Press Inc
10 Alice St
Binghamton NY 13904-1503
800-342-9678; Fax: 607-722-1424
Focus: 19M
Frequency: Quarterly; Circulation: N/A

Journal of Taxation of Employee Benefits
Cathryn Graf, Editor-In-Chief
Warren Gorham Lamont
One Penn Plz 42nd Fl
New York NY 10119-4098
212-971-5000; Fax: 212-950-5588
Focus: 19L-55G-55L
Frequency: 6x per yr; Circulation: N/A

Journal of Taxation of Exempt Organization
Robert Murdich, Editor-In-Chief
Warren Gorham Lamont
One Penn Plz 42nd Fl
New York NY 10119-4098
212-971-5000; Fax: 212-950-5588
Focus: 19A-55G
Frequency: 6x per yr; Circulation: N/A

Juvenile Merchandising
Claudia DeSimone-Lucey, Editor/Publisher
E W Williams Publications
2125 Center Ave #305
Fort Lee NJ 07024
201-592-7007; Fax: 201-592-7171
Focus: 21-76
Frequency: Monthly; Circulation: 11,000

K

Kart Marketing International
Robert Cycon, Publisher
PO Box 101
Wheaton IL 60189-0101
708-653-7368; Fax: 708-653-2637
Focus: 16A(go-kart products, track management, no driving tips or repair info)
Frequency: Monthly; Circulation: 5,000

Kitchen & Bath Business
Ed Pell, Editor
Miller Freeman Inc
1 Penn Plz 10th Fl
New York NY 10119-1198
212-714-1300; Fax: 212-714-1313
Focus: 43
Frequency: Monthly; Circulation: 50,000

Kitchenware News
Eric Schwartz, Editor
United Publications Inc
38 LaFayette St
Yarmouth ME 04096-1600
207-846-0600; Fax: 207-846-0657
Focus: 27-43(kitchenware)
Frequency: Monthly; Circulation: 12,000

Knives Illustrated
Bud Lang, Editor
McMullen & Yee Publishing Inc
774 South Placentia
Placentia CA 92670-6832
714-572-2255; Fax: 714-572-1864
Focus: 16-24
Frequency: 6x per yr; Circulation: 100,000

L

Lapidary Journal
Merle White, Editor-in-Chief
60 Chestnut Ave #201
Devon PA 19333-1328
610-293-1112; 800-676-4336;
    Fax: 610-293-1717
Focus: 29(rocks/gems)
Frequency: Monthly; Circulation: 45,000

Lingua Franca
Alexander Star, Editor
22 W 38th St 4th Fl
New York NY 10018
212-302-0336; Fax: 212-302-0847
Focus: 31E
Frequency: 6x per yr; Circulation: 20,000

Lodging
Philip Hayward, Editor-in-Editor
American Hotel Assn Dir Corp
1201 New York Ave NW
Washington DC 20005-3917
202-289-3100; Fax: 202-289-3199
Focus: 19G-23
Frequency: Monthly; Circulation: 41,000

Lodging Hospitality
Ed Watkins, Editor
Penton Publishing Inc
1100 Superior Ave
Cleveland OH 44114-2518
216-696-7000; Fax: 216-696-7658
Focus: 12-19C-19F(financing)-19G-19H-19M-19P-23C-27-43-71D
Frequency: Monthly; Circulation: 50,000

Lottery Players Magazine
Sam Valenza Jr, Editor/Publisher
321 New Albany Rd
Morristown NJ 08057-1120
609-778-8900; 800-367-9681;
    Fax: 609-273-6350
Focus: 69(gambling)
Frequency: Monthly; Circulation: 130,000

M

Machine Design
Ron Khol, Editor
Penton Publishing
1100 Superior Ave
Cleveland OH 44114-2518
216-696-7000; Fax: 216-696-0177
Focus: 19X-23T-24 (design engineering)
Frequency N/A; Circulation: 180,000

Mailer's Review
Michelle Touhy, Editor
8933 NE Marx Dr #C
Portland OR 97220-1368
503-257-0764; Fax: 503-257-7935
Focus: 19M
Frequency: Monthly; Circulation: 40,000

Managed Healthcare
Joseph McKenna, Editor
859 Williamette St
Eugene OR 97401-2918
503-343-1200; Fax: 503-683-8841
Focus: 39(specialized health care) (books on management only)
Frequency: Monthly; Circulation: 36,000

Managing Office Technology
Lura K Romei, Editor
1100 Superior Ave
Cleveland OH 44114-2518
216-696-7000; Fax: 216-696-7648
Focus: 19-23C-23T
Frequency: Monthly; Circulation: N/A

Marine Corps Gazette
Lt Col Steven M Crittendon, Managing Editor
Marine Corps Assn
Bldg 715
Quantico VA 22134
703-640-6161; 800-336-0291;
    Fax: 703-640-0823
Focus: 48-55-70
Frequency: Monthly; Circulation: 35,000

Marine Log
Nick Blenkey, Editor
Simmons-Boardman Publ Corp
345 Hudson St
New York NY 10014-4502
212-620-7200; Fax: 212-633-1165
Focus: 70N
Frequency: Monthly; Circulation: 22,000

Market: Asia Pacific
Doris Walsh, Editor/Publisher
W-TWO Publications
202 The Commons #401
Ithaca NY 14850-5578
607-277-0934; Fax: 607-277-0935
Focus: 19M-44A
Frequency: Monthly; Circulation: N/A

Market: Europe
Margaret Nichols, Managing Editor
W-TWO Publications
202 The Commons #401
Ithaca NY 14850-5578
607-277-0934; Fax: 607-277-0935
Focus: 19M-44E
Frequency: Monthly; Circulation: N/A

Market: Latin America
Margaret Nichols, Managing Editor
W-TWO Publications
202 The Commons #401
Ithaca NY 14850-5578
607-277-0934; Fax: 607-277-0935
Focus: 19M-44S
Frequency: Monthly; Circulation: N/A

Marketing Tools
Claudia Montague, Managing Editor
127 W State St
Ithaca NY 14850-5427
607-273-6343; Fax: 607-273-3196
Focus: 19M(marketing strategies, clusters, mapping, DM campaigns)
Frequency: 8x per yr; Circulation: 20,000

Masthead
Editor
North Island Publishing
1606 Sedlescomb Dr Unit 8
Mississauga ON Canada L4X 1M6
905-625-7070; 800-331-7408;
    Fax: 905-625-4856
Focus: 56P(magazines)
Frequency: 10x per yr; Circulation: 4,000

Material Handling Engineering
Bernie Knill, Editor
Penton Publishing
1100 Superior Ave
Cleveland OH 44114-2518
216-696-7000; Fax: 216-696-7658
Focus: 19G-19X-23T-24
Frequency: Monthly; Circulation: 113,000

Media & Methods
Diane Falten, Managing Editor
Amer Society of Educators
1429 Walnut St
Philadelphia PA 19102-3218
215-563-3501; 800-523-4540
    Fax: 215-587-9706
Focus: 99
Frequency: 6x per yr; Circulation: 42,000

Media Week
Cheryl Heuton, Editor
1515 Broadway
New York NY 10036-8901
212-536-5336; Fax: 212-536-6594
Focus: 56M
Frequency: Weekly; Circulation: 20,000

Medical Equipment Designer
Terry Persun, Editor
Huebeor Publications
29100 Aurora Rd #200
Solon OH 44139
216-248-1125; Fax: 216-248-0187
Focus: 24-39
Frequency: 6x per yr; Circulation: 15,000

Meetings & Conventions
Gregg Lieberman, Managing Editor
Technology Newsletter
500 Plaza Dr
Secaucus NJ 07094-3626
201-902-1700; Fax: 201-319-1796
Focus: 23C-23E-23T
Frequency: Monthly; Circulation: 81,000

Merchant Magazine
David Koenig, Sr Editor
Cutler Publishing Inc
4500 Campus Dr #480
Newport Beach CA 92660-1828
714-852-1990; Fax: 714-852-0231
Focus: 19R
Frequency: Monthly; Circulation: 4,000

Microwaves & R F
Jack Browne, Editor
Penton Publishing
611 Rt 46 West
Hasbrouck Hts NJ 07604-3120
201-393-6293; Fax: 201-393-6297
Focus: 19G-19X-23T-24-44A(Japan) Microwave/RF engineer(Japan)
Frequency: Monthly; Circulation: 61,000

Mid-America Commerce & Industry
Ray Lippe, Editor/Publisher
1824 Cheyenne
Topeka KS 66604-3704
913-272-5280
Focus: 19X-23-24
Frequency: Monthly; Circulation: 9,000

Millimeter
Bruce Stockler, Editor
Penton Publishing Inc
826 Broadway
New York NY 10003-4826
212-477-4700; Fax: 212-228-5859
Focus: 19-23T-33M-33T (film/video production)
Frequency: Monthly; Circulation: 29,000

Minority Markets Alert
Ira Mayer, Editor/Publisher
EPM Communications Inc
488 E 18th St
Brooklyn NY 11226-6702
718-469-9330; Fax: 718-469-7124
Focus: 19M-49(minority markets)
Frequency: Monthly; Circulation: N/A

Mobile Office
Rich Malloy, Editor
911 Hope St
PO Box 4949
Stamford CT 06907
219-358-9900
Focus: 24-19-16(car phones)
Frequency: Monthly; Circulation: N/A

Model Retailer
Carl Smith, Book Editor
Kalmbach Miniatures Inc
14121 Parke-Long Ct #112
Chantilly VA 22021-1647
703-263-0900; 800-486-9200;
    Fax: 703-263-0905
Focus: 16R-28-29(models)
Frequency: Monthly; Circulation: 6,000

Modern Grocer
Robert Reis, Managing Editor
15 Emerald St
Hackensack NJ 07601-6102
201-488-1800
Focus: 27
Frequency: Biweekly; Circulation: 19,000

Modern Office Technology
Lura K Romei, Editor
1100 Superior Ave
Cleveland OH 44114-2518
216-696-7000; Fax: 216-696-7648
Focus: 19G-19P-23C-23T
Frequency: Monthly; Circulation: 130,000

Modern Tire Dealer
Lloyd Stoyer, Editor
Bill Communications
PO Box 3599
Akron OH 44309-3599
216-867-4401; Fax: 216-867-0019
Focus: 16A(tires)
Frequency: 13x per yr; Circulation: 34,000

Money Maker's Monthly
Eric Anderson and Ed Bauer, Editors
6827 W 171st ST
Tinley Park IL 60477
708-633-8888; Fax: 708-633-8889
Focus: 19-19G-19I-19M-19O
Frequency: Monthly; Circulation: N/A

Multimedia Merchandising
Jim McCullaugh, Editorial Director
Eastman Media
1632 Fifth St #220
Santa Monica CA 90401-3316
310-458-3102; Fax: 310-458-3192
Focus: 19R-23
Frequency: Monthly; Circulation: 32,000

Multimedia World
Don Wenn, Editor-in-Chief
501 2nd St #110
San Francisco CA 94107-1431
415-281-8650; Fax: 415-978-3191
Focus: 23C-23T(news & reviews about multimedia technology)
Frequency: Monthly; Circulation: 120,000

Music Connection
Kenny Kerner, Editor
6640 Sunset Blvd #120
Los Angeles CA 90028-7100
213-462-5772; Fax: 213-462-3123
Focus: 14M-53
Frequency: 25x per yr; Circulation: 75,000

Musical Success Letter
Bob Baker, Editor
7350 Manchester #200
St Louis MO 63143
314-781-0400; Fax: 314-781-0287
Focus: 14M(tips on making money w/ music)
Frequency: 6x per yr; Circulation: N/A

Musician
Bob Doerschuk, Editor
Billboard Publications Inc
1515 Broadway 11th Fl
New York NY 10036-8901
212-536-5208; Fax: 212-536-6616
Focus: 14M (rock/jazz/pop for grownups)
Frequency: Monthly; Circulation: 122,000

Mustang & Ford Magazine
Jim Smart, Editor
Petersen Publishing
6420 Wilshire Blvd
Los Angeles CA 90048-5502
213-782-2000; Fax: 213-782-2494
Focus: 16A
Frequency: 6x per yr; Circulation: 112,000

N

Nation's Business
Robert Gray, Editor-in-Chief
US Chamber of Commerce
1615 H St NW
Washington DC 20062-0001
202-463-5650; Fax: 202-887-3437
Focus: 11-14-27-29-31-33-35-39-43-57-71-73
Frequency: Monthly; Circulation: 850,000

Nation's Restaurant News
Rick Van Warner, Editor
Lebhar-Friedman Inc
425 Park Ave
New York NY 10022-3506
212-756-5000; Fax: 212-756-5215
Focus: 19S-27(restaurants)
Frequency: Weekly; Circulation: 95,000

National Dipper
Editor
1850 Oak St
Northfield IL 60093
708-446-8434
Focus: 27
Frequency: N/A; Circulation: N/A

National Hog Farmer
Dale Miller, Editor
Intertec Publishing Corp
7900 International Dr 3rd Fl
Minneapolis MN 55425-1510
612-851-9329; Fax: 612-851-4601
Focus: 51A
Frequency: 14x per yr; Circulation: 95,000

National Home Center News
John Caulfield, Editor
Lebhar-Friedman Inc
425 Park Ave
New York NY 10022-3506
212-756-5151; 800-453-2427;
 Fax: 212-756-5176
Focus: 19R-19M-43
Frequency: 26x per yr; Circulation: 52,000

National Jeweler
S Lynn Diamond, Editor-in-Chief
1 Penn Plz
New York NY 10119-1198
212-714-1300; 800-950-1314;
 Fax: 212-944-7164
Focus: 40(jewelry)
Frequency: 2x per yr; Circulation: 36,000

National Public Accountant
Mary Beth Loutinsky, Editor
1010 N Fairfax St
Alexandria VA 22314-1504
703-549-6400; Fax: 703-549-2984
Focus: 19A
Frequency: Monthly; Circulation: 21,000

National Real Estate Investor
Paula Stephens, Editor
Argus Business Inc
6151 Powers Ferry Rd NW
Atlanta GA 30339-2959
770-618-0215; Fax: 770-618-0348
Focus: 19H
Frequency: Monthly; Circulation: 34,000

Natural Foods Merchandiser
Frank Lampe, Editor
New Hope Communications
1301 Spruce St
Boulder CO 80302
303-939-8440; Fax: 303-939-9559
Focus: 19R-27-39H
Frequency: Monthly; Circulation: N/A

Naval Affairs
Pat Williamson, Editor
125 North West St
Alexandria VA 22314-2709
703-683-1400; 800-372-1924;
 Fax: 703-549-6610
Focus: 16-25-27-33-39-40-43-48-51-67-69-71-73-99
Frequency: Monthly; Circulation: 180,000

Nest Egg
Peter Maloney, Editor
Investment Dealers' Diegest
2 World Trade Ctr 18th Fl
New York NY 10048-0203
212-432-2584; Fax: 212-432-2781
Focus: 19I(investment strategies of
 upper-income readers)
Frequency: 10x per yr;
 Circulation: 2,000,000

New Age Retailer
Dwight Lucky, Editor
Continuity Publishing
1300 N State St #105
Bellingham WA 98225
360-676-0789; Fax: 360-676-0932
Focus: 39H-53-54-57
Frequency: 7x per yr; Circulation: 6,000

New Equipment Digest
Robert King, Editor
Penton Publishing
1100 Superior Ave
Cleveland OH 44114-2518
216-696-7000; Fax: 216-696-8208
Focus: 19G-19P-19X-24
Frequency: Monthly; Circulation: 211,000

The New Farm
Greg Bowman, Managing Editor
Rodale Institute
222 Main St
Emmaus PA 18049-2749
610-967-8405; Fax: 610-967-8959
Focus: 43G-51A-51E (aimed at large-scale
 growers)
Frequency: 7x per yr; Circulation: 50,000

News From the Home Office
Brian Cassidy, Editor
Natl Home Office Assn
1828 L St NW
Washington DC 20036
800-664-6462; Fax: 800-665-6462
Focus: 19(home offices)
Frequency: Monthly; Circulation: N/A

Non-Foods Merchandising
Al Heller, Editor
Cardinal Business Media
298 Fifth Ave
New York NY 10001-4522
212-563-5301; Fax: 212-967-4662
Focus: 19R
Supermarket management magazine
Frequency: Monthly; Circulation: 20,000

Nursery Management & Production
David Morgan, Editor
120 St Louis Ave
Fort Worth TX 76104-1228
817-332-8236; Fax: 817-877-1862
Focus: 19-43G
Frequency: Monthly; Circulation: 15,000

Nursing
Jane Benner, Managing Editor
1111 Bethlehem Pike
PO Box 908
Spring House PA 19477-1114
215-646-8700; Fax: 215-646-4399
Focus: 39(nursing)
Frequency: Monthly; Circulation: 424,000

O

Object Magazine
Marie Lenzi, Editor
588 Broadway #604
New York NY 10012-5408
212-274-0640; Fax: 212-274-0646
Focus: 23C-23T
Frequency: 6x per yr; Circulation: 20,000

Office Dealer Magazine
Scott Cullen, Editor
1111 Bethlehem Pike
Spring House PA 19477-1114
215-628-7716; Fax: 215-540-8041
Focus: 19P-23
Frequency: 7x per yr; Circulation: 20,000

OS/2 Professional
Bradley Kliewer, Editor
172 Rollins Ave
Rockville MD 20852-4010
301-770-3333; Fax: 301-770-7062
Focus: 23C (IBM-PC)
All about OS/2 operating system
Frequency: Monthly; Circulation: N/A

Outdoor Retailer
Wendy Geister, Managing Editor
31652 2nd Ave
South Laguna CA 92677-3180
714-499-4591; Fax: 714-499-5554
Focus: 11P-51N-69(water sports, CC,
 camping, mtn biking)-71
Frequency: Monthly; Circulation: 14,000

P

P-O-P & Sign Design
William Schober, Editor
7400 Skokie Blvd
Skokie IL 60077-3339
708-675-7400; Fax: 708-675-7494
Focus: 11-19X-24(for point-of-purchase display designers)
Frequency: 5x per yr; Circulation: 17,000

P-O-P Times
Rex Davenport, Editor
Hoyt Publishing Co
7400 Skokie Blvd
Skokie IL 60077-3339
708-675-7400; Fax: 708-675-7494
Focus: 19M(point-of-purchase display ideas/resources for retailers)
Frequency: 10; Circulation: 19,000

Pacific Fishing
Steve Shapiro, Managing Editor
Salmon Bay Communications
1515 NW 51st St
Seattle WA 98107
206-789-5333; Fax: 206-784-5545
Focus: 15(fish)-70N (commercial fishing)
Frequency: Monthly; Circulation: 10,000

Panel World
David Knight, Co-Publisher
Hatton-Brown Publishers Inc
225 Hanrick St
Montgomery AL 36104-3317
334-834-1170; Fax: 334-834-4525
Focus: 12-19-51-55
Frequency: 6x per yr; Circulation: 10,000

Paper Industry
Peter N Williamson, Editor-in-Chief
Trinity Communications Group
804 S Perry St #101
Montgomery AL 36104-5059
334-265-4337; Fax: 334-265-4310
Focus: 12-19-24-51
Frequency: 6x per yr; Circulation: 15,000

Parameters: US Army War College
John J Madigan III, Editor
Quarterly
US Army War College
Carlisle Barricks PA 17013
717-245-4943
Focus: 48-55-70
Frequency: Quarterly; Circulation: 13,000

Parnassus: Poetry in Review
Herbert Leibowitz, Editor
41 Union Square W #804
New York NY 10003-3208
212-463-0889
Focus: 47-95
Frequency: 2x per yr; Circulation: 5,000

Partisan Review
William Phillips ane Edith Kurzweil, Co-Editors
236 Bay State Rd
Boston MA 02215-1403
617-353-4260; Fax: 617-353-7444
Focus: 11-14-47-55-75-90-95-99
Frequency: Quarterly; Circulation: 8,000

Party Source
Maria Sagurton, Editor
Miller Freeman Publications
1515 Broadway 32nd Fl
New York NY 10036-8901
212-869-1300; Fax: 212-302-6273
Focus: 19R (party supplies)
Frequency: 6x per yr; Circulation: 12,000

PC Gamer
Matthew Firme, Editor
1350 Old Bayshore Hwy #210
Burlingame CA 27407-1614
415-696-1688; Fax: 415-696-1678
Focus: 23C-69G(computer games)
Frequency: Monthly; Circulation: 145,000

PC Magazine
Paul B Ross, Managing Editor
1 Park Ave 4th Fl
New York NY 10016-5802
212-503-5255; Fax: 212-503-5519
Focus: 19-23(IBM)
Frequency: 22; Circulation: 140,000

PC Techniques
Jeff Duntemann, Editor-in-Chief
Coriolis Group Publishing
7721 E Gray RD #204
Scottsdale AZ 85260-6912
602-483-0192; 800-410-0192;
 Fax: 602-483-0193
Focus: 23C
Frequency: 6x per yr; Circulation: 28,000

PC Today
Ronald Kobler, Editor/Publisher
PO Box 85380
Lincoln NE 68501-5380
402-477-8900; 800-544-1264;
 Fax: 402-477-9252
Focus: 23
Frequency: Monthly; Circulation: 250,000

Pension Management
Laurie Heavey, Editor
Argus Business Inc
6151 Powers Ferry Rd NW
Atlanta GA 30339-2959
770-618-0199; Fax: 770-618-0348
Focus: 19I
Frequency: Monthly; Circulation: 29,000

Personal Selling Power
Malcolm Fleschner, Book Review Editor
1127 International Pky
Fredericksburg VA 22406-1142
540-752-7000; Fax: 540-752-7001
Focus: 19M
Frequency: 8x per yr; Circulation: 186,000

Perspective
Mary Rose Mazza, Managing Editor
341 Merchandise Mart
Chicago IL 60654-1104
312-467-1950; Fax: 312-467-0779
Focus: 12A
Frequency: Quarterly; Circulation: 9,000

Pet Age
Karen Long MacLeod, Editor
H H Backer Assoc Inc
20 E Jackson Blvd #200
Chicago IL 60604-2205
312-663-4040; Fax: 312-663-5676
Focus: 15(pets, retail pet stores)
Frequency: Monthly; Circulation: 21,000

The Pet Dealer
Mark Hawver, Managing Editor
PTN Publishing Co
445 Broad Hollow Rd
Melville NY 11747
516-845-2700; Fax: 516-845-2797
Focus: 15 (retail pet stores)
Frequency: Monthly; Circulation: N/A

Pet Product News
Jack Sweet, Managing Editor
Fancy Publications
3 Burroughs Dr
Irivne CA 92718-2804
714-855-8822; 800-426-2516;
 Fax: 714-855-4517
Focus: 15(pets)-19R
Frequency: Monthly; Circulation: 20,000

Pharmacy Today
Marie Rosenthal, Editor
Slack Inc
6900 Grove Rd
Thorofare NJ 08086-9447
609-848-1000; Fax: 609-853-5991
Focus: 39(for pharmacists)
Frequency: 23x per yr; Circulation: 95,000

Photo District News
Nancy Madlin, Editor
1515 Broadway
New York NY 10036-8901
212-536-5222; Fax: 212-536-5224
Focus: 11P
Frequency: Monthly; Circulation: 25,000

Photographer's Forum
Glen Serbin, Editor
511 Olive St
Santa Barbara CA 93101-1609
805-963-0439; Fax: 805-965-0496
Focus: 11P
Frequency: Quarterly; Circulation: 10,000

The Pilot Log
Editor
Pilot International
PO Box 4844
Macon GA 31213-0599
912-743-7403; Fax: 912-743-2173
Focus: 99
Frequency: 6x per yr; Circulation: 20,000

Pizza and Pasta
Editor
304 S 2nd Ave PO Box 100
Holland IN 47541
812-536-4762
Focus: 27(pizza operators)
Frequency: Monthly; Circulation: N/A

Pizza Today
Gerald Dumell, Editor
137 E Market St
New Albany IN 47150-3432
812-949-0909; Fax: 812-941-9711
Focus: 27(pizza)
Frequency: Monthly; Circulation: 50,000

Plastic News
Bob Grace, Exec Editor
Crain Communications
1725 Merriman Rd
Akron OH 44313
330-836-9180; Fax: 330-836-2322
Focus: 19X(plastics)
Frequency: Weekly; Circulation: 60,000

Plastics Engineering
Roger Ferris, Editor
Soc of Plastics Engineers
14 Fairfield Dr
Brookfield CT 06804-3911
203-775-0471; Fax: 203-775-8490
Focus: 19X-24
Frequency: Monthly; Circulation: 35,000

Plastics Technology
Matthew Naitove, Editor
355 Park Ave S 3rd Fl
New York NY 10010-1706
212-592-6570; Fax: 212-592-6579
Focus: 19X(plastics)
Frequency: 13x per yr; Circulation: 49,000

Plastics World
Jim Callari, Editor
PTN Publishing Co
445 Broad Hollow Rd
Melville NY 11747
516-845-2700; Fax: 516-845-2797
Focus: 69X(plastics)
Frequency: Monthly; Circulation: 64,000

Playthings
Frank Reysen Jr, Editor
Geyer-McAllister Publications
51 Madison Ave
New York NY 10010-1603
212-689-4411; Fax: 212-683-7929
Focus: 19R-69(games)
Frequency: Monthly; Circulation: 15,000

Ploughshares: Journal of New Writing
Don Lee, Editor
100 Beacon St
Emerson College
Boston MA 02116-1596
617-578-8753; Fax: 617-578-8509
Focus: 47-75-83-95-99
Frequency: 3x per yr; Circulation: 6,000

Police Magazine
Gerald Mortimer, Publisher
6300 Yarrow Dr
Carlsbad CA 92009-1542
619-438-2511; Fax: 619-931-5809
Focus: 55C
Frequency: Monthly; Circulation: 58,000

Pollution Engineering
Diane Pirocanac, Editor
Cahners Publishing Co
1350 E Touhy Ave PO Box 5080
Des Plaines IL 60017-5080
708-635-8800; Fax: 708-390-2636
Focus: 19X-24-51E
Frequency: 13; Circulation: 59,000

Popular Photography
Jason Schneider, Editor-in-Chief
1633 Broadway
New York NY 10019-6708
212-767-6162; Fax: 212-489-4217
Focus: 11P
Frequency: Monthly; Circulation: 450,000

Popular Woodworking
Robert Cook, Editor
1507 Dana Ave
Cincinnati OH 45207-1056
513-531-2222; Fax: 510-671-0692
Focus: 29
Frequency: 6x per yr; Circulation: 200,000

Power Equipment Trade
Dan Shell, Managing Editor
225 Hanrick St
Montgomery AL 36104-3317
334-834-1170; Fax: 334-834-4525
Focus: 19R
Frequency: Monthly; Circulation: 23,000

Power Transmission Design
Phil Kingsley, Editor
1100 Superior Ave
Cleveland OH 44114-2518
216-696-7000; Fax: 216-696-7648
Focus: 16A-19P-19X-23T-24
Frequency: Monthly; Circulation: 53,000

Practical Horseman
Miranda Lorraine, Editor
Cowles Media Inc
PO Box 589
Unionville PA 19375-0589
610-380-8977; Fax: 610-380-8304
Focus: 15-69R (English-style horseback riding)
Frequency: Monthly; Circulation: 82,000

Printed Circuit Design
Pete Waddell, Editor
2000 Powers Ferry Ctr #450
Marietta GA 30067-9442
770-952-1303; Fax: 770-952-6461
Focus: 19-23-67
Frequency: Monthly; Circulation: 25,000

Printed Circuit Fabrication
Elizabeth Clark, Editor
600 Harrison St
San Francisco CA 94107-1370
415-905-2200
Focus: 23E
Frequency: Monthly; Circulation: 22,000

Printing Impressions
Mark Michelson, Editor
401 N Broad St
Philadelphia PA 19108-1001
215-238-5300; Fax: 215-238-5484
Focus: 56X
Frequency: Monthly; Circulation: 95,000

Printing News Midwest
Bill Esler, Editor
PTN Publishing Co
445 Broad Hollow Rd
Melville NY 11747
516-845-2700; Fax: 516-845-2797
Focus: 56X
Frequency: Monthly; Circulation: N/A

Printing News/East
Patrick Henry, Editor
PTN Publishing Co
445 Broad Hollow Rd
Melville NY 11747
516-845-2700; Fax: 516-845-2797
Focus: 56X
Frequency: N/A; Circulation: N/A

Produce Business
Editor
7161 N Cicero Ave
Lincolnwood IL 60646
708-679-1100
Focus: 19R-27-43G
Produce & floral industries
Frequency: Monthly; Circulation: N/A

Produce Merchandising
Elaine Symanski, Editor-in-Chief
7950 College Blvd
Overland Park KS 66210-1821
913-451-2200; 800-255-5113;
    Fax: 913-451-6681
Focus: 19R-43G
Frequency: Monthly; Circulation: 13,000

Professional Boatbuilder
Paul Lazarus, Editor
Naskeag Rd
Brooklin ME 04616
207-359-4651; Fax: 207-359-8920
Focus: 29H-70N (boat building)
Frequency: 6x per yr; Circulation: 20,000

Professional Counselor
Richard Fields, Editor
3201 SW 15th St
Deerfield FL 33442-8157
305-360-0909; Fax: 305-360-0034
Focus: 57-31E-39R-13-65S
Frequency: 6x per yr; Circulation: 40,000

Professional Tool & Equip News
Tom Carruthers, Editor-in-Chief
23030 Lake Forest Dr #201
Laguna Hills CA 92653-1331
714-830-7520; Fax: 714-830-7523
Focus: 16A (auto shop owners)
Frequency: 7x per yr; Circulation: 106,000

Profit: Info Tech for Entrepreneur
Timothy Nolan, Editor-In-Chief
590 Madison Ave 8th Fl
New York NY 10022-2521
212-745-6387; Fax: 212-745-6058
Focus: 19S-23(information technology for businesses)
Frequency: 6x per yr; Circulation: 201,000

Progressive Architecture
John Morris Dixon, Editor-in-Chief
Penton Publishing
600 Summer St
Stamford CT 06901-1403
203-348-7531; Fax: 203-348-4023
Focus: 12-19C-23T (architectural design)
Frequency: Monthly; Circulation: 56,000

Progressive Grocer
Priscilla Donegan, Managing Editor
4 Stamford Forum
Stamford CT 06901-3238
203-325-3500; Fax: 203-325-4377
Focus: 19R-27
Frequency: Monthly; Circulation: 71,000

The PT Distirbutor
Phil Kingsley, Editor
Penton Publishing Inc
1100 Superior Ave
Cleveland OH 44114-2518
216-696-7000; Fax: 216-696-7648
Focus: 16A-19C-19M-19P-19X-23T-24
Frequency: Quarterly; Circulation: 10,000

Public Relations News
Donna Engelgau, Editor
7811 Montrose Rd
Potomac MD 20854-3363
301-340-1520; Fax: 301-424-2231
Focus: 56M
Frequency: Weekly; Circulation: N/A

Public Relations Tactics
Adam Shell, Editor
Public Relations Society
33 Irving Pl
New York NY 10003-2376
212-460-1428; Fax: 212-995-0757;
  E-Mail:74224.1456@compuserve.com
Focus: 19M-56M
Frequency: Monthly; Circulation: 15,000

Pulp & Paper
Ken Patrick and Jim Young,, Co-Editors
Miller Freeman Inc
600 Harrison St
San Francisco CA 94107-1370
415-905-2200; Fax: 415-905-2240
Focus: 29H(paper mills)
Frequency: Monthly; Circulation: 40,000

Purchasing Magazine
James P Morgan, Editor
Cahners Publishing Co
275 Washington St
Newton MA 02158-1646
617-964-3030; Fax: 617-558-4327
Focus: 19P
Frequency: Biweekly; Circulation: N/A

PW Religion BookLine
Editor
Publishers Weekly
249 W 17th St
New York NY 10011-5301
212-463-6758; Fax: 212-463-6631
Focus: 63
Frequency: 26x per yr; Circulation: 1,000

Q

Qualified Remodeler
Mary Burkhart, Editor
PTN Publishing Co
445 Broad Hollow Rd
Melville NY 11747
516-845-2700; Fax: 516-845-2797
Focus: 19-43
Frequency: N/A ; Circulation: N/A

Quality Digest
Marion Harmon, Managing Editor
1350 Vista Way
Red Bluff CA 96080-4510
916-527-8875; Fax: 916-527-6983
Focus: 19G-19X-24(quality
  management/engineering)
Frequency: Monthly; Circulation: 25,000

Quality in Manufacturing
Jim Destesani, Editor
Huebcor Communications
29100 Aurora Rd #200
Solon OH 44139
216-248-1125
Focus: 19X
Frequency: 7x per yr; Circulation: 65,000

Quick Printing
Tara Marini, Managing Editor
Coast Grafix Inc
1680 SW Bayshore Blvd
Port Saint Lucie FL 34984-3568
407-879-6666; Fax: 407-879-7388
Focus: 56X
Frequency: Monthly; Circulation: 68,000

Quill & Quire
Stephen Smith, Book Review Editor
Ted Mumford, Editor
70 The Esplande 2nd Fl
Toronto ON Canada M5E 1R2
416-360-0044; Fax: 416-955-0794;
  E-Mail: quill@hookup.net
Focus: 56P
Frequency: Monthly; Circulation: N/A

Quirks Marketing Research Review
Joseph Rydholm, Editor-in-Chief
8030 Cedar Ave S
Minneapolis MN 55425-1213
612-854-5101; Fax: 612-854-8191
Focus: 19M (surveys/marketing res/trends)
Frequency: 10x per yr; Circulation: 16,000

R

Railway Age
Luther Miller, Editor
Simmons-Boardman Publishing Corp
345 Hudson St
New York NY 10014-4502
212-620-7200; Fax: 212-633-1165
Focus: 16R
Frequency: Monthly; Circulation: 24,000

Railway Track & Structures
Robert Tuzik, Editor
345 Hudson St
New York NY 10014-4502
212-620-7200; Fax: 212-633-1165
Focus: 16R
Frequency: Monthly; Circulation: 8,000

The Real Estate Finance Journal
Steven Errick, Editor-In-Chief
Warren Gorham Lamont
1 Penn Plz
New York NY 10119-0002
212-971-5000; 800-950-1205;
  Fax: 212-971-5025
Focus: 19B-19H-44-51E-55G
Frequency: Quarterly; Circulation: 3,000

Real Estate Review
Norman Weinberg, Editor
24 Oak St
Woodmere NY 11598-2646
516-295-2179; Fax: 516-569-2448
Focus: 19H-55G
Frequency: Quarterly; Circulation: 9,000

Realtor News
Marjorie Green, Editor
National Assn of Realtors
777 14th St NW
Washington DC 20005-3201
202-383-1193; Fax: 202-383-7563
Focus: 19H
Frequency: Biweekly; Circulation: 700,000

Recreation Resources
Galynn Nordstrom, Editorial Dir
Adams Publishing Corp
527 Marquette AVe #1300
Minneapolis MN 55402-1315
612-342-2121; 800-923-2326;
  Fax: 612-342-2480
Focus: 33-69
Frequency: 9x per yr; Circulation: 51,000

Remodeling Magazine
Wendy Jordan, Editor-in-Chief
Hanley-Wood Inc
655 15th St NW #475
Washington DC 20005-5701
202-452-0800; Fax: 202-785-1974
Focus: 43(remodeling)
Frequency: Monthly; Circulation: 93,000

Research Alert Newsletter
Ira Mayer, Editor/Publisher
EPM Communications Inc
488 E 18th St
Brooklyn NY 11226-6702
718-469-9330; Fax: 718-469-7124
Focus: 19M-56 (media marketing/market
  research)
Frequency: Biweekly; Circulation: N/A

Reseller Management
John R Russell, Editor-in-Chief
Cahners Publishing Co
275 Washington St
Newton MA 02158-1646
617-558-4723; Fax: 617-558-4757
Focus: 19R-23(to computer resellers)
Frequency: Monthly; Circulation: 85,000

Residential Lighting
Cori Dunn, Editor/Publisher
Vance Publishing Corp
400 Knightsbridge Pky
Lincolnshire IL 60069-3613
708-634-2600; Fax: 708-634-4379
Focus: 12-19 (targeted to showrooms and
  retail)
Frequency: Monthly; Circulation: 12,000

Resource Recycling
Meg Lynch, Editor
PO Box 10540
Portland OR 97210-0540
503-227-1319; Fax: 503-227-6135
Focus: 51E(recycling)-67
Frequency: Monthly; Circulation: 16,000

Restaurant Business
Joan Oleck, Assoc Editor
355 Park Ave S
New York NY 10010
212-592-6500; Fax: 212-592-6409
Focus: 19S-27(restaurants)
Frequency: 18x per yr; Circulation:
  130,000

Restaurant Hospitality
David Farkas, Features Editor
Penton Publishing
1100 Superior Ave
Cleveland OH 44114
216-696-7000; Fax:
Focus: 19-27-97(foodservice) (commercial
  foodservice industry)
Frequency: Monthly; Circulation: 123,000

Restaurant Publicity News
Alisa Gordon, Editor
Gordon-Bay Group
770 N Halsted St #205
Chicago IL 60622-5972
312-421-2900; Fax: 312-733-7838
Focus: 19M-56M
Frequency: Monthly; Circulation: 5,000

Restaurants & Institutions
Michael Bartlett, VP/Editor
Cahners Publishing
249 W 17th St
New York NY 10011
212-463-6480
Focus: 27(management, operations, equipment)
Frequency: Biweekly; Circulation: 162,000

Retail Store Image
Katherine Field, Editor
Argus Inc
6151 Powers Ferry Rd NW
Atlanta GA 30339-2959
770-955-2500; Fax: 770-618-0349
Focus: 12-19R-43(store design)
Frequency: 9x per yr; Circulation: 23,000

Retailing News
Martin Barsky, Managing Editor
14962 Bear Valley Rd #288
Victorville CA 92392-9236
619-241-2454
Focus: 19R(appliance/electronics)
Frequency: Monthly; Circulation: 12,000

The Retired Officer
Kris Hegle, Book Review Editor
Julia Leigh, Managing Editor
Retired Officers Assn
201 N Washington St
Alexandria VA 22314-2529
703-549-2311; 800-245-8762;
  Fax: 703-838-8179
Focus: 35A-55-99
Frequency: Monthly; Circulation: 398,000

Retirement Life
Kathleen Delaney, Editor
1531 New Hampshire Ave NW
Washington DC 20036-1203
202-234-0832; Fax: 202-797-9698
Focus: 35A-39-55-71 (for federal employees 40+)
Frequency: Monthly; Circulation: 495,000

RN Magazine
Marianne Mattera, Editor
Medical Economics Publishing
5 Paragon Dr
Montvale NJ 07645
201-358-7300
Focus: 39(nursing, books by nurses for nurses)
Frequency: Monthly; Circulation: 286,000

RV Business
Steve Boilon, Editor
3601 Calle Tecate
Camarillo CA 93012-5040
805-389-0300; Fax: 805-389-0484
Focus: 16A-71
Frequency: Monthly; Circulation: 18,000

S

Sailing Magazine
Micca Hutchins, Editor
125 E Main St
Port Washington WI 53074-1915
414-284-3494; Fax: 414-284-7764
Focus: 70N
Frequency: Monthly; Circulation: 35,000

Sales and Mktg Strategies & News
Bill Hughes, Editor-in-Chief
211 W State St PO Box 197
Rockford IL 61105
815-963-4000; 800-435-2937;
  Fax: 815-963-7773
Focus: 19M
Frequency: 8x per yr; Circulation: N/A

Sales Manager's Bulletin
Paulette Kitchens, Editor
Bureau of Business Practice
24 Rope Ferry Rd
Waterford CT 06386-0001
203-442-4365; 800-243-0876;
  Fax: 203-434-3078
Focus: 19G
Frequency: Biweekly; Circulation: 5,000

Salon News
Melissa Bedulis, Editor
Fairchild Publications
7 West 34th St
New York NY 10001-8100
212-630-4607; Fax: 212-630-4837
Focus: 19M-19R-40B-40F(how to use styler as a marketing tool)
Controlled circulation to beauty salons
Frequency: Monthly; Circulation: 80,000

Science Books and Films
Tracy Gath, Editor
AAAS
1333 H St NW
Washington DC 20005-4707
202-326-6454; Fax: 202-371-9849
Focus: 23-24-31-39-51-59-67(for use in science education)
Frequency: 9x per yr; Circulation: 5,000

Science News
Patrick Young, Editor
1719 N St NW
Washington DC 20036-2890
202-785-2255
Focus: 39-67(chemistry)
Frequency: Weekly; Circulation: 237,000

Scott Stamp Monthly
Stuart Morrissey, Publisher
PO Box 828
Sidney OH 45365-0828
513-498-0802; Fax: 513-498-0808
Focus: 28
Frequency: Monthly; Circulation: N/A

Seafood Business
Linda Skinner, Editor
120 Tillson Ave
Rockland ME 04841-3424
207-594-6222; Fax: 207-594-8978
Focus: 19 (seafood)
Frequency: 7x per yr; Circulation: 16,000

The Secretary
Tracy Fellin Savidge, Managing Editor
2800 Shirlington Rd #706
Arlington VA 22206-3601
703-998-2534; Fax: 703-379-4561
Focus: 19C-19P-23(office products)
Frequency: 9x per yr; Circulation: 44,000

Semiconductor International
Pete Singer, Editor
1350 E Touhy Ave
Des Plaines IL 60018-3303
708-635-8800; Fax: 708-390-2770
Focus: 24(semiconductor processing)
Frequency: Monthly; Circulation: 45,000

Sew News
Linda Griepentrog, Editor
News Plz
PO Box 1790
Peoria IL 61656-1790
309-682-6626; Fax: 309-682-7394
Focus: 29C(sewing)
Frequency: Monthly; Circulation: 260,000

Seybold Report on Public Systems
Peter Dyson, Book Review Editor
PO Box 644
Media PA 19063-0644
610-565-2480; 800-325-3830; Fax:
  610-565-4659
Focus: 23-56P
Frequency: 22x per yr; Circulation: N/A

Shelby Report of the Southeast
Gary Shelby, Editor/Publisher
517 Green St
Gainsville GA 30501-3313
770-534-8380; Fax: 770-535-0110
Focus: 27
Frequency: Monthly; Circulation: 18,000

Shopping Center World
Teresa DeFranks, Editor
Argus Inc
6151 Powers Ferry Rd NW
Atlanta GA 30339-2959
770-955-2500; Fax: 770-955-0400
Focus: 19R
Frequency: Monthly; Circulation: 36,000

Signal
Clarence Robinson Jr, Editor-in-Chief
AFCEA
4400 Fair Lakes Ct
Fairfax VA 22033-3811
703-631-6181; 800-336-4583;
  Fax: 703-222-8762
Focus: 19-67-99
Frequency: Monthly; Circulation: 39,000

SignCraft
Tom McIltrot, Editor-in-Chief
PO Box 06031
Fort Meyers Beach FL 33932-6031
941-939-4644; Fax: 941-939-0607
Focus: 11(signs)
Frequency: 6x per yr; Circulation: 20,000

Signs of the Times
Mervin Moore, Editor
Pacific Press
PO Box 7000
Boise ID 83707-1000
208-465-2579; Fax: 208-465-2531
Focus: 13-39H-63P(Seventh-day Adventist Church)
Frequency: Monthly; Circulation: 245,000

The Skeptical Inquirer
Barry Karr, Exec Director
CSICP
PO Box 703
Buffalo NY 14226-0703
716-636-1425; Fax: 716-636-1733
Focus: 53-54-57-63(trys to disprove paranormal experiences)
Frequency: Quarterly; Circulation: 37,000

Skin Diver
Bill Gleason, Editor/Publisher
Jim Walker, Features Editor
6420 Wilshire Blvd
Los Angeles CA 90048-5502
213-782-2960; Fax: 213-782-2121
Focus: 69(skin diving)
Frequency: Monthly; Circulation: 216,000

Small Business Controller
Stephen Collins, Managing Editor
Warren Gorham Lamont
1 Penn Plz
New York NY 10119
212-971-5201; Fax: 212-971-5588
Focus: 19S
Frequency: Quarterly; Circulation: 10,000

Small Farm Today
Ronald Macher, Editor
3903 W Ridge Trail Rd
Clark MO 65243-9525
314-687-3525; 800-683-2535;
    Fax: 314-687-3148
Focus: 15-43-51A
Frequency: 6x per yr; Circulation: 12,000

SMART Computer & Software Retail
Lester Craft Jr, Editor (910-605-1121)
7025 Albert Pick Rd #200
PO Box 2754
High Point NC 27261
910-605-0121; Fax: 910-605-1143
Focus: 19R-23C
Frequency: 21x per yr; Circulation: 35,000

Snack Food
Paul Rogers, Managing Editor
1935 Shermer Rd #100
Northbrook IL 60062-5354
708-205-5660; 800-337-8989;
    Fax: 708-205-5680
Focus: 27
Frequency: Monthly; Circulation: 13,000

Software Engineering Strategies
Nancy Heller, Sr Editor
1 Penn Plz
New York NY 10119-0002
212-971-5089
Focus: 23-24
Frequency: 6x per yr; Circulation: N/A

Software Magazine
Mike Bucken, Editor
1 Research Dr #400 B
Westborough MA 01581-3922
508-366-2031; Fax: 508-366-8104
Focus: 23 (reviews business software)
Frequency: Monthly; Circulation: 100,000

Software Solutions
Steven Bobker, Editor-in-Chief
Chilton Publications
One Chilton Way
Radnor PA 19089
610-964-4000
Focus: 23C-24(engineers relying on PC systems)
Frequency: 6x per yr; Circulation: 60,000

SOHO America Newsletter
Editor
SOHO America
2626 E 82nd St #325
Minneapolis MN 55425
800-495-SOHO
Focus: 19(home offices)
Frequency: Monthly; Circulation: N/A

Solar Today
Maureen McIntyre, Editor
Amer Solar Energy Society
2400 Central Ave #G-1
Boulder CO 80301-2843
303-443-3130; Fax: 303-443-3212
Focus: 51E
Frequency: 6x per yr; Circulation: 6,000

Sound & Video Contractor
Ted Uzzle, Editor
Intertec Publishing Corp
9800 Metcalf
Overland Park KS 66212-2216
913-341-1300; Fax: 913-967-1905
Focus: 23T
Frequency: Monthly; Circulation: 21,000

Sound Track Magazine
Don Kulak, Editor
317 Skyline Lake Dr
PO Box 609
Ringwood NJ 07456
201-831-1317; Fax: 201-831-1317
Focus: 14M-33
Frequency: 6x per yr; Circulation: N/A

Southern Boating
Skip Allen Sr, Editor/Publisher
1766 Bay Rd
Miami Beach FL 33139-1414
305-538-0700; Fax: 305-532-8657
Focus: 70-71
Frequency: Monthly; Circulation: 30,000

Southern Graphics
Cathy Donohue, Editor
1680 SW Bayshore Blvd
Port Saint Lucie FL 34984-3568
407-879-6666; Fax: 407-879-7388
Focus: 11(graphics)
Frequency: Monthly; Circulation: 23,000

Southwest Spirit
John Clark, Editor
PO Box 619640
DFW Airport TX 75261-9640
817-967-1804; Fax: 817-967-1571
Focus: 11-14-19-33-39-71-99
Southwest Airlines
Frequency: Monthly; Circulation: 197,000

Souvenirs & Novelties
Sandford Meschkow, Editor
Kane Communications Inc
7000 Terminal Square #210
Upper Darby PA 19082-2310
610-734-2420; Fax: 610-734-2423
Focus: 33(novelties)-71(souvenirs)
Frequency: 7x per yr; Circulation: 29,000

Specialty Food Merchandising
Dara Chadwick, Exec Editor
406 Water St
Warren RI 02885-3330
401-245-4500; Fax: 401-245-4699
Focus: 19R-27(specialty foods)
Frequency: 6x per yr; Circulation: 20,000

Sporting Goods Business
Andrew Gaffney, Editor
Miller Freeman Inc
1 Penn Plz
New York NY 10119-1198
212-714-1300; Fax: 212-714-1313
Focus: 69
Frequency: Monthly; Circulation: 27,000

Sporting Goods Dealer
Tom Sosnowski, Editor
PTN Publishing Co
445 Broad Hollow Rd
Melville NY 11747
516-845-2700; Fax: 516-845-2797
Focus: 19R-69
Frequency: Monthly; Circulation: N/A

Sports Trend
Brad Wolverton, Managing Editor
Shore Communications Inc
6255 Barfield Rd #200
Atlanta GA 30328-4318
404-252-8831; 800-241-9034;
    Fax: 414-252-4436
Focus: 19-69
Frequency: Monthly; Circulation: 28,000

Stacks: The Network Journal
Dave Brambert, Editor
Miller Freeman Inc
600 Harrison St
San Francisco CA 94107-1370
415-905-2200; Fax: 415-905-2232
Focus: 23C(network integration for VARs and integrators)
Frequency: Monthly; Circulation: 30,000

Step-by-Step Graphics
Catherine Fishel, Managing Editor
Dynamic Graphics Inc
6000 N Forest Park Dr
Peoria IL 61614-3556
309-688-2300; 800-255-8800;
    Fax: 309-688-8515
Focus: 11(graphics)
Frequency: 6x per yr; Circulation: 48,000

Stock Car Racing Magazine
Dick Berggren, Editor
General Media Intl Inc
47 S Main St
Ipswich MA 01938-2321
508-356-7030; Fax: 508-356-2492
Focus: 16A
Frequency: Monthly; Circulation: 193,000

Successful Meetings
Andrea Welch, Editor-in-Chief
Bill Communications Inc
355 Park Ave S 3rd Fl
New York NY 10010-1706
212-592-6200; Fax: 212-592-6402
Focus: 19
Frequency: Monthly; Circulation: 75,000

Supermarket Business
Editor
342 Madison Ave
New York NY 10173
212-867-2350
Focus: 27
Frequency: N/A; Circulation: N/A

Supermarket News
David Merrefield, Editor
7 West 34th St
New York NY 10001-8100
212-630-3770; Fax: 212-630-3768
Focus: 19A-19R
Frequency: Weekly; Circulation: 52,000

Sys Admin
Martha Masinton, Managing Editor
R & D Publications Inc
1601 W 23rd St #200
Lawrence KS 66046-2703
913-841-1631; Fax: 913-841-2624
Focus: 19-23 (For UNIX Systems administrators)
Frequency: 6x per yr; Circulation: 18,000

T

T H E Journal
Sylvia Charp, Editor-in-Chief
150 El Camino Real #112
Tustin CA 92680-3615
714-730-4011; Fax: 714-730-3739
Focus: 23-31 (tech horizons in education)
Frequency: 11x per yr;
    Circulation: 145,000

Tack & Togs
Daniel DeWeese, Editor
Miller Publishing
12400 Whitewater Dr #160
Minnetonka MN 55343-9466
612-930-4390; Fax: 612-938-1832
Focus: 15(horses)
Frequency: 13x per yr; Circulation: 20,000

Talkers Magazine
Michael Harrison, Editor
Goodphone Communications Inc
PO Box 60781
Longmeadow MA 01116-0781
413-567-3189; Fax: 413-567-3168
Focus: 33(radio news/talk shows)
Frequency: 10x per yr; Circulation: 15,000

Technology in Government
Jerry Fiedenberg, Editor
Plesman Publications Ltd
2005 Sheppard Ave E 4th Fl
Willowdale ON M2J 5B1
416-497-9562; Fax: 416-497-9427;
    E-Mail: plesman@globalx.net
Focus: 23-55G
Frequency: Monthly; Circulation: N/A

Telecommunications Reports Int
Victoria Mason, Editor-in-Chief
1333 H St NW
West Tower 11th Fl
Washington DC 20005-4707
202-842-3006; Fax: 202-842-3047
Focus: 19
Frequency: Biweekly; Circulation: N/A

Telephony
Karen Egoff, Editor
55 E Jackson Blvd
Chicago IL 60604-4103
312-922-2435; Fax: 312-922-1408
Focus: 19M-23T
Frequency: 51x per yr; Circulation: 49,000

Tennis Buyer's Guide
Sandra Dolbow, Editor
5520 Park Ave
Turnbull CT 06611-3426
203-373-7000; Fax: 203-373-7033
Focus: 39-69-71(tennis)
Frequency: 6x per yr; Circulation: 10,000

Threads Magazine
Chris Timmons, Editor
Taunton Press Inc
63 S Main St
Newtown CT 06470
203-426-8171; Fax: 203-426-3434
Focus: 29(needlework)-40F
Frequency: 6x per yr; Circulation: 150,000

Today's Catholic Teacher
Mary Noschang, Editor
Peter Li Inc
330 Progress Rd
Dayton OH 45449-2322
513-847-5900; Fax: 513-847-5910
Focus: 31E-63C
Frequency: Monthly; Circulation: 65,000

Tole World
Judy Swager, Editor
1041 Shary Cir
Concord CA 94518-2407
510-671-9852; Fax: 510-671-0692
Focus: 11-29(tole painting)
Frequency: 6x per yr; Circulation: 110,000

Tooling & Production
Jim Lorincz, Editor
Huebeor Publications
29100 Aurora Rd #200
Solon OH 44139
216-248-1125; Fax: 216-248-0187
Focus: 19X-24
Frequency: Monthly; Circulation: 100,000

Tour & Travel News
Mary Pat Sullivan, Editor
1 Penn Plz 10th Fl
New York NY 10119-1198
212-714-1300; Fax: 212-714-1313
Focus: 71
Frequency: Weekly; Circulation: 54,000

TR Wireless News
Jennifer Walsh, Editor
1333 H St NW 11th Fl W Tower
Washington DC 20005-4707
202-842-3006; Fax: 202-842-3047
Focus: 16-24
Frequency: 26x per yr; Circulation: N/A

Tradeshow Week
Darlene Gudea, Editor-in-Chief
12233 W Olympic #236
Los Angeles CA 90064-1039
310-826-5696; Fax: 310-826-2039
Focus: 19M
Frequency: Weekly; Circulation: 3,000

Traditional Building
Judith Lief, Managing Editor
Historical Trends Corp
69A 7th Ave
Brooklyn NY 11217
718-636-0788; Fax: 718-636-0750
Focus: 12-19H-43
Frequency: 6x per yr; Circulation: 15,000

Traffic World
Bob Rost, Managing Editor
741 National Press Bldg
Washington DC 20045-1701
202-383-6140; Fax: 202-737-3349
Focus: 16-55G-97
Frequency: Weekly; Circulation: 10,000

Trains
Kevin Keefe, Editor
Kalmbach Publishing Co
21027 Crossroads Cir
Waukesha WI 53186-4055
414-796-8776; Fax: 414-796-1142
Focus: 16R-29(models)
Frequency: Monthly; Circulation: 111,000

Transmission & Distribution
Rick Bush, Editorial Dir
Intertec Publishing Corp
9800 Metcalf
Overland Park KS 66212-2216
913-341-1300; Fax: 913-967-1898
Focus: 23T
Frequency: Monthly; Circulation: 36,000

Transportation & Distribution
Perry Trunick, Editor-in-Chief
Penton Publishing Inc
1100 Superior Ave
Cleveland OH 44114-2518
216-696-7000; Fax: 216-696-4135
Focus: 19C-19G-19P-19X-23T
Frequency: Monthly; Circulation: 72,000

Travel Agent Magazine
James Ruggia, Editor
801 2nd Ave
New York NY 10017
212-370-5050; Fax: 212-370-4491
Focus: 71
Frequency: Weekly; Circulation: 53,000

Travel Weekly
Alan Frederick, Editor-in-Chief
Reed Travel Group
500 Plaza Dr
Secaucus NJ 07094
201-902-1700; Fax: 201-319-1947
Focus: 71
Frequency: 2x per wk; Circulation: 51,000

Travel World News
Sara Southworth, Editor
Travel Industry Network
50 Washington St
Norwalk CT 06854
203-853-4955; Fax: 203-866-1153
Focus: 19-71
Frequency: Monthly; Circulation: 35,000

TravelAge
John Whitmarsh, Editor
Reed Travel Group
500 Plaza Dr
Secaucus NJ 07094-3619
201-902-2000; Fax: 201-902-1967
Focus: 71
Frequency: Weekly; Circulation: 81,000

Treasure Chest
Howard Fischer, Editor
Venture Publishing Co
2112 Broadway #414
New York NY 10023-2142
212-469-2234
Focus: 28(collectibles)
Frequency: Monthly; Circulation: 50,000

Truck/Sport Utility High Performance
Kipp E Kington, Editor/Publisher
Mag-Tec Productions Inc
9952 Hamilton Ave
Huntington Beach CA 92646-8016
714-962-7795; Fax: 714-965-2268
Focus: 16A
Frequency: 6x per yr; Circulation: 61,000

Truckin Classic Trucks
Bill Turner, Editor
McMullen & Yee Publishing Inc
774 South Placentia
Placentia CA 92670-6846
714-572-2255; Fax: 714-572-1864
Focus: 16-24
Frequency: 6x per yr; Circulation: N/A

Truckin'
Steve Stillwell, Editor
McMullen & Yee Publishing Inc
774 South Placentia
Placentia CA 92670-6846
714-572-2255; Fax: 714-572-1864
Focus: 16-24
Frequency: Monthly; Circulation: N/A

The Trumpeter
Eck Spahich, Editor
1512 Lancelot
Borger TX 79007-6341
806-273-7225
Focus: 28-29
Frequency: Quarterly; Circulation: 1,000

TWICE
Stephen Smith, Editor
Cahners Publishing Co
249 West 17th St
New York NY 10011-5300
212-337-6980; Fax: 212-337-7066
Focus: 19R-23-24(consumer electronics)
Smith: 212-337-6987
Frequency: 26; Circulation: 30,000

Twin Cities Business Monthly
Jay Novak, Editor
MSP Communications
220 S 6th St #500
Minneapolis MN 55402-4501
612-339-7571; Fax: 612-339-5806
Focus: 19-61(MN)
Frequency: Monthly; Circulation: 30,000

U

U S Art Magazine
Frank Sisser, Editor
220 S 6th St
Minneapolis MN 55402-4501
612-339-7571; Fax: 612-339-5806
Focus: 11-28
Frequency: Monthly; Circulation: 55,000

UnixWorld
Walter Zintz, Book Review Editor
McGraw-Hill Inc
1900 O'Farrell St
San Mateo CA 94403-1311
415-513-6800; Fax: 415-513-6985
Focus: 23C(Unix)
Frequency: Monthly; Circulation: 67,000

Upside Magazine
Eric Nee, Editor-in-Chief
Upside Publishing Co
2015 Pioneer Ct
San Mateo CA 94403-1736
415-377-0950; Fax: 415-377-1961
Focus: 19-23-24(the business magazine for the technology elite)
Frequency: Monthly; Circulation: 58,000

V

VAR Business
Richard March, Editor
CMP Publications
1 Jericho Plz
Jericho NY 11753-1635
516-733-6967; 800-842-0780;
  Fax: 516-733-6964
Focus: 23C(value-added resellers)
Frequency: Monthly; Circulation: 92,000

Variety
Elizabeth Guider, Managing Editor
249 W 17th St
New York NY 10011-5300
212-337-6925; Fax: 212-337-6977
Focus: 14(performing arts)-17-33
Frequency: Weekly; Circulation: 30,000

Video Business
Bruce Apar, Editor
Capitol Cities/ABC Inc
825 7th Ave
New York NY 10019-6014
212-887-8448; Fax: 212-887-8484
Focus: 19-99(video)
Frequency: Weekly; Circulation: 44,000

Video Systems
Jerry Whitaker, Editor
Intertec Publishing Corp
9800 Metcalf
Overland Park KS 66212-2216
913-341-1300; Fax: 913-967-1905
Focus: 23T-33 (professional video production)
Frequency: Monthly; Circulation: 45,000

Vietnam Magazine
Harry Summers Jr, Editor
Cowles History Group
741 Miller Dr SE #D2
Leesburg VA 22075
703-771-9400; Fax: 703-779-8345
Focus: 41A-41W-44A-48
Frequency: 6x per yr; Circulation: 60,000

Vim & Vigor
Fred Petrovsky, Editor
8805 N 23rd Ave #11
Phoenix AZ 85021-4171
602-395-5850; Fax: 602-395-5853
Focus: 39
Frequency: Quarterly; Circulation: 950,000

Vineyard & Winery Management
J William Moffett, Editor
103 Third St
PO Box 231
Watkins Glen NY 14891
607-535-7133; Fax: 607-535-2998
Focus: 43G (vineyard mgmt/wine-making)
Frequency: 6x per yr; Circulation: 37,000

Virtual Reality Special Report
Kay Keppler, Editor
Miller Freeman Inc
600 Harrison St
San Francisco CA 94107-1370
415-905-2200; Fax: 415-905-2234
Focus: 23C(virtual reality)
Frequency: 6x per yr; Circulation: N/A

Virtual Reality World
Sandra Helsel, Editor
11 Ferry Ln W
Westport CT 06880-5808
203-226-6967; Fax: 203-454-5840
Focus: 23C(virtual reality)
Frequency: 6x per yr; Circulation: 47,000

W

Ward's Auto World
David Smith, Editor
Intertec Publishing Corp
3000 Town Ctr #2750
Southfield MI 48075-1102
810-357-0800; Fax: 810-357-0810
Focus: 16A-23T
Frequency: Monthly; Circulation: 100,000

Ward's Automotive International
David Zoia, Editor
Intertec Publishing Corp
3000 Town Ctr #2750
Southfield MI 48075-1102
810-357-0800; Fax: 810-357-0810
Focus: 16A (trends and statistics)
Frequency: Biweekly; Circulation: N/A

Ward's Automotive Reports
David Zoia, Editor
Intertec Publishing Corp
3000 Town Ctr #2750
Southfield MI 48075-1102
810-357-0800; Fax: 810-357-0810
Focus: 16A (trends and statistics)
Frequency: Weekly; Circulation: 97,000

Ward's Engine/Vehicle Tech Update
David Zoia, Editor
3000 Town Ctr #2750
Southfield MI 48075-1102
810-357-0800; Fax: 810-357-0810
Focus: 16A-24(engine/drive train technology)
Frequency: 26x per yr; Circulation: N/A

Washington Flyer Magazine
Laurie McLaughlin, Editor
11 Canal Ctr Plz #111
Alexandria VA 22314-1595
703-739-9292; Fax: 703-683-2848
Focus: 19-70A-71-99
Frequency: 6x per yr; Circulation: 160,000

Watercraft Business
Glenn Hansen, Managing Editor
601 Lakeshore Pky #600
Minnetoka MN 55305-5215
612-476-2200; Fax: 612-476-8065
Focus: 69-70
Frequency: 6x per yr; Circulation: 500,000

Waters Magazine
David Longobardi, Editor
270 Lafayette St #700
New York NY 10012-3327
212-925-6990; Fax: 212-925-7585
Focus: 19I-23T(financial technoloy professionals)
Frequency: Quarterly; Circulation: 5,000

Welding Design & Fabrication
Rosalie Brosilow, Editor
Penton Publishing
1100 Superior Ave
Cleveland OH 44114-2518
216-696-7000; Fax: 216-696-7658
Focus: 19G-19X-23T-24
Frequency: Monthly; Circulation: 43,000

Western English World
Kathryn Martin, Editor
451 E 58th St #4781
Denver CO 80216-1404
303-293-0222; Fax: 303-293-0227
Focus: 19-19M-69
Frequency: 6x per yr; Circulation: 11,000

Whole Foods
Donna Ohlson, Book Review Editor
3000 Hadley Rd
South Plainfield NJ 07080-1117
908-769-1160; Fax: 908-769-1171
Focus: 19R-27(natural foods)
Frequency: Monthly; Circulation: 13,000

Wildfowl Carving & Collecting
Cathy Hart, Editor
500 Vaughn St
Harrisburg PA 17110-2220
717-234-5091; 800-233-9015;
    Fax: 717-234-1359
Focus: 28-29H
Frequency: Quarterly; Circulation: 15,000

Window Fashions Magazine
Linnea Addison, Editor
4225 White Bear Pky #450
St Paul MN 55110-3349
612-293-1544; Fax: 612-653-4308
Focus: 40F-43D(independent interior designers)
Frequency: Monthly; Circulation: 25,000

Window Sources
Diane D'Angelo, Managing Editor
Ziff-Davis Publishing
One Park Ave
New York NY 10016
212-503-3500; Fax: 212-503-4199
Focus: 23
Frequency: Monthly; Circulation: 400,000

Windows/Dos Developers Journal
Martha Masington, Managing Editor
R & D Publications Inc
1601 W 23rd St #200
Lawrence KS 66046-2700
205-534-1170; Fax: 205-834-4525
Focus: 19-23 (for experienced programmers)
Frequency: Monthly; Circulation: N/A

Wines & Vines
Editor
1800 Lincoln Ave
San Rafael CA 94901-1221
516-671-2502
Focus: 27(wine making)
Frequency: 13x per yr; Circulation: 6,000

Women's Wear Daily
Mort Sheinman, Managing Editor
David Moin, Retail Editor
Fairchild Publications
7 West 34th St
New York NY 10001-8100
212-630-4000; Fax: 212-630-4580
Focus: 40F(clothing)
Frequency: Daily; Circulation: 55,000

Wood & Wood Products
Jerry Metz, Contributing Editor
Consult Jerry Metz
2203 Southridge Dr
Palm Springs CA 92264
708-634-4347; Fax: 708-634-4379
Focus: 12B-19M-43H(marketing/selecting wood products)
Q&A column
Frequency: Monthly; Circulation: N/A

Woodshop News
Tom Clark, Book Review Editor
Ian C Bowen, Editor
Soundings Publications Inc
35 Pratt St
Essex CT 06426-1152
203-767-8227; Fax: 203-767-1048
Focus: 29(woodworking)-43(home how-to)
Frequency: Monthly; Circulation: 90,000

Woodsmith
Donald B Peschke, Editor
2200 Grand Ave
Des Moines IA 50312-5306
515-282-7000; 800-444-7002;
    Fax: 515-282-6741
Focus: 29(woodworking)
Frequency: 6x per yr; Circulation: 400,000

Woodwork
John McDonald, Editor
Ross Periodicals
PO Box 1529
Ross CA 94957-1529
415-382-0580; Fax: 415-382-0587
Focus: 29
Frequency: 6x per yr; Circulation: 70,000

Workbench
Larry Okrend, New Products Editor
KC Publishing
700 West 47th St #310
Kansas City MO 64112
816-531-5730; Fax: 816-531-3873
Focus: 29H-43H
Frequency: 6x per yr; Circulation: 900,000

World Broadcast News
Gerald Walker, Editor-in-Chief
Intertec Publishing Corp
9800 Metcalf
Overland Park KS 66212-2216
913-341-1300; Fax: 913-967-1905
Focus: 23T-33T
Frequency: 10x per yr; Circulation: 13,000

Writer's Digest
Thomas Clark, Editor
1507 Dana Ave
Cincinnati OH 45207-1056
513-531-2222; Fax: 513-531-1843
Focus: 56W
Frequency: Monthly; Circulation: 215,000

The Writer
Elizabeth Preston, Managing Editor
120 Boylston St
Boston MA 02116-4611
617-423-3157
Focus: 56W
Frequency: Monthly; Circulation: 54,000

Y

Yale Review
Susan Bianconi, Managing Editor
Yale Univ
PO Box 208243
New Haven CT 06520-8243
203-432-0499; Fax: 203-432-0510
Focus: 47-75-99
Frequency: Quarterly; Circulation: 5,000

Your Company
Robert Casey, Editor
1120 Ave of the Americas
New York NY 10036-6700
212-382-5741; Fax: 212-382-5812
Focus: 19-19C-19G-19H-19L-19S
Frequency: Quarterly; Circulation: 1500,000

Youth Markets Alert
Ira Mayer, Publisher
EPM Communications Inc
488 E 18th St
Brooklyn NY 11226-6702
718-469-9330; Fax: 718-469-7124
Focus: 19M-21(youth markets)
Frequency: Monthly; Circulation: N/A

Subject Category Codes

10 **General Non-Fiction**
11 **Fine Arts**
   11P   Photography
12 **Architecture / Construction**
   12A   Architecture
   12B   Building / Construction
13 **Alternative Social Issues**
14 **Performing Arts**
   14D   Dance
   14M   Music
   14T   Theatre / Drama
15 **Animals / Pets**
16 **Transportation**
   16A   Automobiles
   16R   Railroads
17 **Biographies / Celebrities**
   17B   Biographies
   17C   Celebrities
   17P   Real People
19 **Business / Economics**
   19A   Accounting
   19B   Banking
   19C   Careers / Labor
   19E   Economics
   19F   Fund-raising / Non-profits
   19G   Management
   19H   Real Estate / Home
   19I   Investment
   19L   Law
   19M   Marketing / Sales
   19O   Opportunity Seekers
   19P   Purchasing
   19R   Retail Sales
   19S   Small Business
   19X   Industrial / Production
21 **Children's Interests**
   21T   Teenagers
23 **Computers / Technology**
   23C   Computers
   23E   Home Electronics
   23T   Technology
24 **Engineering**
25 **Consumer Issues**
   25T   Consumer Taxes
27 **Cooking / Food / Nutrition**
28 **Collectibles / Antiques**
29 **Crafts / Hobbies / How-to**
   29C   Crafts
   29H   Hobbies and How-to
31 **Education / Child Development**
   31C   Child Development
   31E   Education / Teaching
   31P   Parenting
33 **Entertainment / Movies / Humor**
   33C   Comics / Comedy
   33H   Humor
   33M   Movies
   33T   Television / Radio

35 **Family / Marriage / Retirement**
   35A   Aging Issues / Retirement
   35F   Family
   35M   Marriage
   35R   Relationships / Romance
   35S   Sexual Issues
36 **Lifestyle/Feature**
37 **Gay / Lesbian**
39 **Health / Medicine / Exercise**
   39D   Disabilities
   39E   Exercise
   39H   Holistic Health
   39M   Medicine / Doctors
   39R   Recovery / Drug Abuse
40 **Beauty / Fashion**
   40B   Beauty
   40F   Fashion
41 **History**
   41A   American History
   41G   Genealogy / Family History
   41W   World History
43 **House / Garden**
   43D   Home Decorating
   43G   Gardening
   43H   House and Home
44 **International Issues and News**
   44A   Asia
   44E   Europe
   44F   Africa
   44S   South America
   44Z   Australia / New Zealand
45 **Languages**
   45X   Linquistics
   45W   Words
47 **Literature / Humanities**
48 **Military**
49 **Minority Issues and Studies**
   49A   Native American
   49B   Black
   49H   Hispanic / Chicano
   49O   Other
51 **Nature / Ecology / Conservation**
   51A   Agriculture / Farming
   51B   Biology / Botany
   51E   Environmental Issues
   51N   Nature
53 **New Age / Astrology**
54 **Philosophy / Metaphysics**
   54M   Metaphysics
   54P   Philosophy
55 **Politics / Government**
   55C   Crime / Police Work
   55G   Government
   55L   Law
   55P   Politics

56 **Publishing / PR / Writing**
   56M   Media / Publicity
   56P   Publishing
   56W   Writing
   56X   Printing
57 **Psychology / Self-Help**
   57B   Behavior
   57P   Psychology / Therapy
   57S   Self-Help / Advice
59 **Reference Books**
61 **Regional Issues and Interests**
63 **Religions**
   63C   Catholic
   63E   Eastern Religions
   63J   Jewish
   63M   Muslim
   63O   Other Religions
   63P   Protestant
65 **Sociology / Anthropology**
   65A   Anthropology
   65S   Social Issues
67 **Science / Mathematics**
   67A   Astronomy / Space
   67M   Mathematics
   67S   Science
69 **Sports / Games / Recreation**
   69G   Games
   69H   Hunting / Fishing
   69R   Recreation / Hiking
   69S   Spectator Sports
70 **Nautical / Aviation**
   70A   Aviation
   70N   Nautical / Sailing
71 **Travel / Geography**
   71D   Domestic Travel
   71F   Foreign Travel
   71G   Geography
73 **Women's Issues**

75 General Fiction

76 **Children's Stories**
77 **Contemporary Novels**
78 **Ethnic / Minority Literature**
79 **Folklore / Fairy Tales**
80 **Foreign Literature**
81 **Historical Novels**
82 **Horror Novels**
83 **Literary Novels**
84 **Mysteries / Detective Novels**
85 **Romances / Gothic Romances**
86 **Science Fiction / Fantasy**
87 **Suspense / Adventure Novels**
88 **Westerns**
89 **Young Adult Novels**
90 **Short Stories / Anthologies**
95 **Poetry**

97 News / Current Events

99 General Interest

Professional Magazines

The following magazines feature news, reviews, and other items of interest to a particular profession. Write for a sample copy of any magazine that publishes in a field you want to target.

A

Academe
Jonathan Knight, Book Review Editor
1012 14th St NW
Washington DC 20005-3406
202-737-5900; Fax: 202-737-5526
Focus: 31 (articles/reports on higher education)
Frequency: 6x per yr; Circulation: 44,000

Across the Board
A J Vogl, Editor
The Conference Board
845 Third Ave
New York NY 10022-6601
212-759-0900; Fax: 212-980-7014
Focus: 19-23-67-99
AJ's #: 212-339-0450
Frequency: Monthly; Circulation: 30,000

Activities Adaptation & Aging
Phyllis Foster, Editor
10 Alice St
Binghamton NY 13904-1503
607-722-5857; Fax: 607-722-6362
Focus: 35A-39-57-69
Published by Haworth Press
Frequency: Quarterly; Circulation: 985,000

Administration in Social Work
Rino J Patti, Editor
Univ of Southern California
School of Social Work
Los Angeles CA 90089-0001
213-740-8311; Fax: 213-740-0879
Focus: 19G-57-65
Published by Haworth Press
Frequency: Quarterly;
    Circulation: 1065,000

Affilia: Journal of Social Work
Carol H Meyer, Editor
School of Social Work
Columbia Univ 622 W 113th St
New York NY 10025
212-854-5183; Fax: 212-854-2975
Focus: 31-55-57-73
Frequency: Quarterly; Circulation: N/A

Alcoholism Treatment Quarterly
Thomas McGovern, Editor
The Haworth Press
10 Alice St
Binghamton NY 13904-1503
800-342-9678; Fax: 607-722-1424
Focus: 39R
Frequency: Quarterly; Circulation: 628,000

American Medical News
Barbara Bolsen, Editor
American Medical Assn
515 N State St
Chicago IL 60610-4320
312-464-4429; Fax: 312-464-4184
Focus: 39M
Frequency: Weekly; Circulation: 220,000

American Music Teacher
Michael Oxley, Editor
Music Teachers National Assn
441 Vine St #505
Cincinnati OH 45202-2814
513-421-1420; Fax: 513-421-2503
Focus: 14-31
Frequency: 6x per yr; Circulation: 25,000

American Scientist
Hannah Andrews, Book Editor
PO Box 13975
Durham NC 27709-3975
919-549-0097; Fax: 919-549-0090
Focus: 23-24-39-51-57-67(general science bks as well as research)
Frequency: 6x per yr;
    Circulation: 105,000

ANQ
Arthur Wrobel, Managing Editor
1319 Eighteenth St NW
Washington DC 20036-1802
202-296-6267; Fax: 202-296-5149
Focus: 17-31E
Frequency: Quarterly; Circulation: 1,000

Apothecary
Susan Keller, Managing Editor
PO Box AP
Los Altos CA 94023-4042
415-941-3955; Fax: 415-941-2303
Focus: 19
Frequency: Quarterly; Circulation: 60,000

Applied Mechanics Reviews
Alexander Majewski, Editor
Amer Soc of Mechanical Engineers
345 E 47th St
New York NY 10017-2392
212-705-7722; Fax: 212-705-7671
Focus: 24
Frequency: Monthly; Circulation: 1,000

Archives of Environmental Health
Pat McCready, Managing Editor
1319 18th St NW
Washington DC 20036-1802
202-296-6267; Fax: 202-296-5149
Focus: 39-51E
Frequency: 6x per yr; Circulation: 2,000

Arizona Business Magazine
Jessica McCann, Editor-in-Chief
3111 North Central #230
Phoenix AZ 85012-2650
602-277-6045; Fax: 602-277-6046
Focus: 19-61(AZ)
Frequency: Quarterly; Circulation: 18,000

Arts Education Policy Review
Sheila Barrows, Editor
Heldref Publications
1319 Eighteenth St NW
Washington DC 20036-1802
202-296-6267; Fax: 202-296-5149
Focus: 11-31-14-21T
Frequency: 6x per yr; Circulation: 1,000

Asian Affairs: An American Review
John Neikirk, Editor
Heldref Publications
1319 18th St NW
Washington DC 20036-1802
202-296-6267; Fax: 202-296-5149
Focus: 44A-31E-55P
Frequency: Quarterly; Circulation: N/A

Association Trends
Lak Vohra, Editor
Martineau Corp
7910 Woodmont Ave #1150
Bethesda MD 20814-3015
301-652-8666; Fax: 301-656-8654
Focus: 19(associations)
Frequency: 50x per yr; Circulation: 7,000

Aviation Week & Space Technology
Donald Fink, Editor-in-Chief
1221 Ave of the Americas 42nd Fl
New York NY 10020-1001
212-512-4117; Fax: 212-512-6068
Focus: 23-67(airplanes)
New York Bureau
Frequency: Weekly; Circulation: 152,000

B

Behavioral Health Management
Richard Peck, Managing Editor
629 Euclid Ave #500
Cleveland OH 44114
216-522-9700; Fax: 216-522-9707
Focus: 39
Frequency: 6x per yr;
    Circulation: N/A

Behavioral Medicine
Martha Wedeman, Managing Editor
Heldref Publications
1319 18th St NW
Washington DC 20036-1802
202-296-6267; Fax: 202-296-5149
Focus: 39M-57
Frequency: Quarterly; Circulation: N/A

Bioscience
Julie Ann Miller, Editor-in-Chief
730 11th St NW
Washington DC 20001-4510
202-628-1500; Fax: 202-628-1509;
 E-Mail: aibs@gwuvm.gwu.edu
Focus: 67
Frequency: Monthly; Circulation: 12,000

Black Careers
Jerusa C Wilson, Book Review Editor
PO Box 8214
Philadelphia PA 19101-8214
215-387-1600
Focus: 19C-49B
Minority issues
Frequency: 6x per yr;
 Circulation: 300,000

The Black Scholar
Robert Allen, Sr Editor
485 65th St
Oakland CA 94609-1101
510-547-6633; Fax: 510-547-6679
Focus: 13-49B-65-78
Frequency: Quarterly; Circulation: 10,000

Bulletin of Bibliography
Willard Fox, Book Review Editor
88 Post Road W
Westport CT 06880-4208
203-226-3571; 800-225-5800;
 Fax: 203-226-6009
Focus: 11-14-33-41-47-56(books)-57-
 59(bibliographies)-65
Frequency: Quarterly; Circulation: N/A

Business Education Forum
Regina McDowell, Editor
National Business Educ Assn
1914 Association Dr
Reston VA 22091-1538
703-860-8300; Fax: 703-620-4483
Focus: 19-31
Frequency: Quarterly; Circulation: 18,000

Business New Hampshire
Holly Babin, Editor
404 Chestnut St #201
Manchester NH 03101-1803
603-626-6354; Fax: 603-626-6359
Focus: 19
Frequency: Monthly; Circulation: 14,000

Business North Carolina
David Kinney, Editor
5435 77 Center Dr #50
Charlotte NC 28217-0711
704-523-6987; Fax: 704-523-4211
Focus: 19-61(NC)
Frequency: Monthly; Circulation: 28,000

C

C/C++ Users Journal
P J Plauger, Editor
R & D Publications Inc
1601 W 23rd St #200
Lawrence KS 66046-2700
913-841-1631; Fax: 913-841-2624
Focus: 19-23 (for experienced
 programmers)
Frequency: Monthly; Circulation: 43,000

Campaigns & Elections
Ron Faucheux, Editor
1511 K St NW #1020
Washington DC 20005-1403
202-638-7788; 800-888-5737;
 Fax: 202-638-4668
Focus: 55P(political campaigns)
Frequency: 10x per yr; Circulation: 64,000

Camping Magazine
Karen Pavlicin, Managing Editor
American Camping Assn
5000 SR 67 N
Martinsville IN 46151-7903
317-342-8456; Fax: 317-342-2065
Focus: 29-69R(for owners of
 campgrounds and children's camps)
Camping-related products
Frequency: 6x per yr; Circulation: 7,000

Canadian Author
Weleyn W Katz, Editor
1225 Wonderland Rd N
London ON Canada N6G 4X1
519-641-6768; Fax: 519-473-4450
Focus: 99
Frequency: Quarterly; Circulation: N/A

Canadian Business
Arthur Johnson, Editor
777 Bay St 5th Fl
Toronto ON Canada M5W 1A4
416-596-5100; Fax: 416-596-5155
Focus: 19-61(CN)
Frequency: Monthly; Circulation: 85,000

Capital District Business Review
Marlene Kennedy, Editor-in-Chief
American City Business Jrnls
PO Box 15081
Albany NY 12212-5081
518-437-9855; Fax: 518-437-0764
Focus: 19-61(NY)
Frequency: Weekly; Circulation: 11,000

CFO
Susan Kron, Managing Editor
253 Summer St
Boston MA 02210-1114
617-345-9700; Fax: 617-951-4090
Focus: 19A-19l
Frequency: Monthly; Circulation: 350,000

Child & Family Behavior Therapy
Cyril M Franks PhD, Editor
The Haworth Press Inc
10 Alice St
Binghamton NY 13904-1503
607-722-5857; 800-342-9678;
 Fax: 607-722-6362
Focus: 31-35-57-73
Frequency: Quarterly; Circulation: N/A

Child Care Info Exchange
Bonnie Nengebauer, Managing Editor
PO Box 2890
Redmond WA 98073-2890
206-883-9394; 800-221-2864;
 Fax: 206-867-5217
Focus: 21-31-35
Frequency: 6x per yr; Circulation: 25,000

CIO Magazine
Lew McCreary, Editor
492 Old Connecticut Path
Framingham MA 01701-4584
508-872-8200; Fax: 508-879-7784
Focus: 19G-23C-23T (for chief information
 executives)
Frequency: 21x per yr; Circulation: 80,000

Civil Engineering
Virginia Fairweather, Editor-in-Chief
345 East 47th St
New York NY 10017-2330
212-705-7463; 800-548-2723;
Fax: 212-705-7486
Focus: 24
Frequency: Monthly; Circulation: 112,000

The Clearing House
Judy Cusick, Editor
Heldref Publications
1319 18th St NW
Washington DC 20036-1802
202-296-6267; 800-365-9753;
 Fax: 202-296-5149
Focus: 13-55-65-31E
Frequency: 6x per yr; Circulation: 3,000

CMA Magazine
Dan Hicks, Editor/Publisher
PO Box 176
Hamilton ON Canada L8N 3C3
905-525-4100; Fax: 905-525-4533
Focus: 19A-19l
Frequency: 10x per yr; Circulation: 75,000

Consulting Specifying Engineer
Paul E Beck, Editor
Cahners Publishing
1350 E Touhy Ave PO Box 5080
Des Plaines IL 60017-5080
708-635-8800; Fax: 708-390-2200
Focus: 24(mechanical & electrical)
Frequency: 13x per yr; Circulation: 48,000

Contemporary Pediatrics
Kathryn Caldwell-Brown, Editor
Medical Economics Co
5 Paragon Dr
Montvale NJ 07645-1725
201-358-7200; Fax: 201-358-7260
Focus: 21-39M
Frequency: Monthly; Circulation: 42,000

Corporate Cashflow
Richard Gamble, Editor
Argus Inc
6151 Powers Ferry Rd NW
Atlanta GA 30339-2959
770-955-2500
Focus: 19A-19l
Frequency: Monthly; Circulation: 40,000

Corporate Detroit Magazine
Claire Hinsberg, Editor
3031 W Grand Blvd #624
Detroit MI 48202-3019
313-872-6000; Fax: 313-872-6009
Focus: 19-61(MI)
Frequency: 13x per yr; Circulation: 32,000

Corporate Legal Times
Zan Hale, Managing Editor
3 E Huron St
Chicago IL 60611-2705
312-654-3500
Focus: 19L (gen counselors/in-house lawyers)
Frequency: Monthly; Circulation: 40,000

Creative New Jersey
Sally Gellert, Editor
PO Box 327
Ramsey NJ 07446-0327
201-670-8688; Fax: 201-670-4484
Focus: 11-33-56 (graphics, broadcast, advertising)
Frequency: 6x per yr; Circulation: 19,000

Criminal Law Bulletin
Fred Cohen, Editor-in-Chief
Warren Gorham Lamont
1 Penn Plz
New York NY 10119-0002
212-971-5216; Fax: 212-971-5025
Focus: 55C-55L
Frequency: 6x per yr; Circulation: 3,000

Critique:Studies in Contemporary Fiction
Helen Strang, Editor
Heldref Publications
1319 18th St NW
Washington DC 20036-1802
202-296-6267; 800-365-9753;
    Fax: 202-296-5149
Focus: 53-17B-75
Frequency: Quarterly; Circulation: 1,000

D

Database Programming & Design
Annalisa Chamberlain, Managing Editor
600 Harrison St
San Francisco CA 94107-1370
415-905-2200; Fax: 415-905-2234
Focus: 23 (software for mainframes)
Frequency: Monthly; Circulation: 29,000

Dental Economics & Proofs
Editor
Penwell Publishing
1421 S Sheridan
Tulsa OK 74112
800-331-4463
Focus: 39(dental)
Frequency: N/A; Circulation: N/A

E

Editorial Eye
Linda Jorgensen, Editor
Editorial Experts
66 Canal Center Plz #200
Alexandria VA 22314
703-683-0683; Fax: 703-683-4915
Focus: 56P-56W
Frequency: Monthly; Circulation: 3,000

EDPACS: EDP Audit/Control/Security
Belden Menkus, Editor
Auerbach Publications
1 Penn Plz
New York NY 10119-0002
212-971-5000; 800-950-1205;
    Fax: 212-971-5024
Focus: 23
Frequency: Monthly; Circulation: 3,000

Education Digest
Ken Schroeder, Managing Editor
275 Metty Dr #1
Ann Arbor MI 48103-9444
313-769-1211; 800-530-9673;
    Fax: 313-769-8383
Focus: 31
Frequency: Monthly; Circulation: 25,000

Educational Leadership
Ronald Brandt, Editor
1250 N Pitt St
Alexandria VA 22314-1457
703-549-9110; Fax: 703-549-3891
Focus: 31E(education trends/practical ideas/classroom stories)
Frequency: 8x per yr; Circulation: 210,000

Electronic Engineering Times
Richard Wallace, Editor (516-562-5623)
CMP Publications Inc
600 Community Dr
Manhasset NY 11030-3847
516-562-5840; Fax: 516-562-5995
Focus: 23-24
Frequency: Weekly; Circulation: 130,000

Electronic Products
Frank Egan, Editor/Publisher
Hearst Corp
645 Stewart Ave
Garden City NY 11530-4709
516-227-1300; Fax: 516-227-1444
Focus: 19X-23E-23T-24
Frequency: Monthly; Circulation: 124,000

Employee Assistance Quarterly
Keith McClellan, Editor
14100 Balfour
Oak Park MI 48237-4106
810-398-3429; 800-342-9678;
    Fax: 607-722-1424
Focus: 19-57S
Frequency: Quarterly; Circulation: 3,000

Engineering Times
Stefan Jaeger, Editor
1420 King St
Alexandria VA 22314-2750
703-684-2875; Fax: 703-836-4875
Focus: 24(engineering)
Frequency: Monthly; Circulation: 70,000

Entertainment Marketing Letter
Michael Schau, Editor
EPM Communications Inc
488 East 18th St
Brooklyn NY 11226-6702
718-469-9330; Fax: 718-469-7124
Focus: 14-19M-33-56M
Frequency: Monthly; Circulation: N/A

Estate Planning
Nancy Shurtz, Book Review Editor
Warren Gorham Lamont
1 Penn Plz
New York NY 10119-0002
212-971-5000; Fax: 212-971-5113
Focus: 19-25-35A-55G
Frequency: 2x per yr; Circulation: 12,000

Executive Excellence
Ken Shelton, Editor
1344 E 1120 S
Provo UT 84606
801-375-4014; 800-304-9782;
    Fax: 801-377-5960
Focus: 19G-57(for top executives)
Frequency: Monthly; Circulation: 10,000

The Explicator
George Arms, Editor
Heldref Publications
1319 18th St NW
Washington DC 20036-1802
202-296-6267; 800-365-9753;
    Fax: 202-296-5149
Focus: 47-95-14
Frequency: Quarterly; Circulation: 2,000

F

Family Practice Management
Robert Edsall, Editor-in-Chief
Amer Academy of Family Physician
8880 Ward Pky
Kansas City MO 64114-2756
816-333-9700; 800-274-2237;
    Fax: 816-333-0303
Focus: 19G-39M(family physicians management)
Frequency: 16x per yr; Circulation: 91,000

Farm Chemicals
Dale L Little, Editor
Meister Publishing Co
37733 Euclid Ave
Willoughby OH 44094-5925
216-942-2000; Fax: 216-975-3447
Focus: 19M-51A-51E
Frequency: Monthly; Circulation: 33,000

Federal Computer Week
Paul McCloskey, Editor
Anne Armstrong, Editor-in-Chief
3110 Fairview Park Dr #1040
Falls Church VA 22042-4503
703-876-5100; Fax: 703-876-5126
Focus: 23
Frequency: Weekly; Circulation: 60,000

Flying
J Mac McClellan, Editor-in-Chief
Hachette Filipacchi Magazines
500 West Putnam Ave 2nd Fl
Greenwich CT 06830-6086
203-622-2700; Fax: 203-622-2725
Focus: 70A
Frequency: Monthly; Circulation: 330,000

Focus on Autistic Behavior
Richard L Simpson, Editor
Pro Ed Journals
8700 Shoal Creek Blvd
Austin TX 78758-6816
512-451-3246; Fax: 512-451-8542
Focus: 31-35F
Frequency: 6x per yr; Circulation: 2,000

G

Genetic/Soc/Gen Psych Monographs
Doris Chalfin, Editor
Heldref Publications
1319 18th St NW
Washington DC 20036-1802
202-296-6267; 800-365-9753;
 Fax: 202-296-5149
Focus: 39-57
Frequency: Quarterly; Circulation: N/A

Germanic Review
Heidi Whitesell, Editor
Heldref Publications
1319 18th St NW
Washington DC 20036-1802
202-296-6267; 800-365-9753;
 Fax: 202-296-5149
Focus: 45(German)-47
Frequency: Quarterly; Circulation: N/A

H

Healthcare Forum Journal
Susan Anthony, Editor
425 Market St 16th Fl
San Francisco CA 94105-2406
415-356-4300; Fax: 415-356-9300
Focus: 39M
Frequency: 6x per yr; Circulation: 26,000

Hippocrates
Tio Furdado, Managing Editor
301 Howard St 18th Fl
San Francisco CA 94105-2252
415-512-9100; Fax: 415-512-9600
Focus: 39
Frequency: 10x per yr; Circulation: 125,000

Historical Methods
Barbara Kahn, Editor
Heldref Publications
1319 18th St NW
Washington DC 20036-1802
202-296-6267; 800-365-9753;
 Fax: 202-296-5149
Focus: 39-23-31
Frequency: Quarterly; Circulation: N/A

History of Political Economy
S Todd Lowry, Book Review Editor
PO Box 90660
Durham NC 27708-0660
919-687-3636; Fax: 919-688-4574
Focus: 19-41-55-65
Frequency: Quarterly; Circulation: 2,000

History: Reviews of New Books
John Neikirk, Editor
Heldref Publications
1319 18th St NW
Washington DC 20036-1802
202-296-6267; Fax: 202-296-5149
Focus: 41-65
Frequency: Quarterly; Circulation: 1,000

Home Furnishings Executive
Patricia Bowling, Editor
Pace Publications Inc
1301 Carolina St
Greensboro NC 27401-1001
910-378-6065; Fax: 910-275-2864
Focus: 19R-28-43H
Frequency: Monthly; Circulation: 13,000

Home Health Care Services Quarterly
Brahna Trager, Editor
The Haworth Press Inc
10 Alice St
Binghamton NY 13904-1503
800-342-9678; Fax: 607-722-1424
Focus: 39
Frequency: Quarterly; Circulation: N/A

The Hospice Journal
Madalon O'Rawe Amenta DPH RN, Editor
The Haworth Press Inc
10 Alice St
Binghamton NY 13904-1503
800-342-9678; Fax: 607-722-1424
Focus: 39
Frequency: Quarterly; Circulation: 3,000

I

IEEE Computer Graphics & Apps
Nancy Hays, Managing Editor
IEEE Computer Society
10662 Los Vaqueros Cir
Los Alamitos CA 90720-2513
714-821-8380; Fax: 714-821-4010
Focus: 11-23(computer graphics, animation, CAD/CAM)
Frequency: 6x per yr; Circulation: 15,000

IEEE Design & Test of Computers
Marie English, Managing Editor
IEEE Computer Society
10662 Los Vaqueros Cir
Los Alamitos CA 90720-2513
714-821-8380; Fax: 714-821-4010
Focus: 23C-24(automation design and testing)
Frequency: 6x per yr; Circulation: 12,000

IEEE Expert
Dick Price, Managing Editor
IEEE Computer Society
10662 Los Vaqueros Cir
Los Alamitos CA 90720-2513
714-821-8380; Fax: 714-821-4010
Focus: 23C-24(engineering, neural networks, natural language processing)
Frequency: 6x per yr; Circulation: 9,000

IEEE Micro
Marie English, Managing Editor
IEEE Computer Society
10662 Los Vaqueros Cir
Los Alamitos CA 90720-2513
714-821-8380; Fax: 714-821-4010
Focus: 23C-24(systems integration, RISC, multiprocessing, communications)
Frequency: 6x per yr; Circulation: 17,000

IEEE Software
Angela Burgess, Managing Editor
IEEE Computer Society
10662 Los Vaqueros Cir
Los Alamitos CA 90720-2513
714-821-8380; Fax: 714-821-4010
Focus: 23C-24(programming, environments, interfaces, security, and techniques)
Frequency: 6x per yr; Circulation: 22,000

Information Systems Management
Paul Gray, Book Review Editor
Auerbach Publications
1 Penn Plz
New York NY 10119-0002
212-971-5000; 800-950-1205;
 Fax: 212-971-5024
Focus: 19G-23
Frequency: Quarterly; Circulation: 5,000

Information Today
David Hoffman, Editor
Information Today Inc
143 Old Marlton Pike
Medford Lakes NJ 08055-8750
609-654-6266; Fax: 609-654-4309
Focus: 19-23-56M(information, communications)
Frequency: Monthly; Circulation: 10,000

InformationWeek
Peter Krass, Features Editor
Mitch Irsfeld, Editor
CMP Publication
600 Community Dr
Manhasset NY 11030
516-562-5898; Fax: 516-562-5036
Focus: 19-23
Main number: 516-562-5000
Frequency: 51x per yr;
 Circulation: 181,000

INTECH
Jim Strothman, Editor
PO Box 12277
Res Triangle Park NC 27709-2277
919-549-8411; Fax: 919-549-8288
Focus: 19X-24(design, engineering)
Frequency: Monthly; Circulation: 53,000

InterActivity
Dominic Milano, Editor
Miller Freeman Inc
411 Borel Ave #100
San Mateo CA 94402-3516
415-358-9500; Fax: 415-358-8728;
     E-Mail: thogan@mf1.com
Focus: 23C
Frequency: 6x per yr; Circulation: 60,000

Interior Design Magazine
Stanley Abercrombie, Editor
Cahners Publishing Co
249 West 17th St
New York NY 10011-5300
212-463-6676; Fax: 212-463-6667
Focus: 12(interior design)-28-29-43D
Frequency: Monthly; Circulation: 55,000

Internal Auditing Alert
Stephen Collins, Editor
Warren Gorham Lamont
One Penn Plz
New York NY 10119-0002
212-971-5201; Fax: 212-971-5588
Focus: 19A(auditing)
Frequency: Monthly; Circulation: 3,000

International Musician
Jessica Roe, Managing Editor
Amer Fed of Musicians
1501 Broadway #600
New York NY 10036-5501
212-869-1330; Fax: 212-302-4374
Focus: 14M
Frequency: Monthly; Circulation: 120,000

IPM Practitioner
William Olkowski, Book Review Editor
Bio-Integral Resource Ctr
PO Box 7414
Berkeley CA 94707-0414
510-524-2567; Fax: 510-524-1758
Focus: 43G-51A-51E(natural pest control
     for commercial growers)
Frequency: 10x per yr; Circulation: 5,000

Issues in Science and Technology
Bill Hendrickson, Editor
Univ of Texas at Dallas
PO Box 830688 MS AD 13
Richardson TX 75083-0688
214-883-6325; Fax: 214-883-6327
Focus: 23-24-39-51-55-67
Policy issues
Frequency: Quarterly; Circulation: 18,000

J

Journal of Accountancy
Colleen Katz, Editor
Harborside Financial Ctr
201 Plaza 3
Jersey City NJ 07311
201-938-3292

Focus: 19A
Frequency: Monthly; Circulation: 339,000

Journal of Addictive Diseases
Barry Stimmel, Editor
The Haworth Press Inc
10 Alice St
Binghamton NY 13904-1503
800-342-9678; Fax: 607-722-1424
Focus: 39R
Frequency: Quarterly; Circulation: N/A

Journal of Agromedicine
Stanley Schuman MD, Editor
The Haworth Press Inc
10 Alice St
Binghamton NY 13904-1503
803-792-2281; Fax: 803-792-4702
Focus: 39
Frequency: Quarterly; Circulation: N/A

Journal of Analytic Social Work
Jerrold R Brandell PhD, Editor
The Haworth Press Inc
10 Alice St
Binghamton NY 13904-1503
607-722-5857; 800-342-9678;
     Fax: 607-722-1424
Focus: 65
Frequency: Quarterly; Circulation: N/A

Journal of Ambulatory Care Management
Seth Goldsmith, Co-Editor
200 Orchard Ridge Rd #200
Gaithersburg MD 20878-1978
301-417-7500; 800-638-8437;
     Fax: 301-417-7550
Focus: 19M-39
Frequency: Quarterly; Circulation: 2,000

Journal of Applied Aquaculture
Carl Webster, Editor
The Haworth Press Inc
10 Alice St
Binghamton NY 13904-1503
800-722-1424; Fax: 607-722-1424
Focus: 43G-51A
Frequency: Quarterly; Circulation: N/A

Journal of Applied Biomechanics
Robert Gregor, Editor
PO Box 5076
Champaign IL 618-25-507
217-351-5076; Fax: 217-351-2674
Focus: 69
Frequency: Quarterly; Circulation: 1,000

Journal of Arts Management & Law
Zell Rosenfelt, Editor
Heldref Publications
1319 18th St NW
Washington DC 20036-1802
202-296-6267; 800-365-9753;
     Fax: 202-296-5149
Focus: 14-19G-19L-55L-31E
Frequency: Quarterly; Circulation: N/A

The Journal of Bank Taxation
John W Alexander, Editor-In-Chief
Warren Gorham Lamont
1 Penn Plz 40th Fl
New York NY 10119-0002
212-971-5000; 800-950-1252;
     Fax: 212-971-5113

Focus: 19-55G(taxation of banks)
Frequency: Quarterly; Circulation:
     1500,000

Journal of Blacks in Higher Education
Theodore L Cross, Editor
200 W 57th St 15th Fl
New York NY 10019-3211
212-399-1084; Fax: 212-245-1973
Focus: 49
Frequency: Quarterly; Circulation: 5,000

Journal of Cell Biology
Norton Gilula, Editor
Rockefeller Univ Press
222 E 70th St
New York NY 10021-5405
212-327-7938; Fax: 212-327-7944
Focus: 51-67
Frequency: 2x per yr; Circulation: 6,000

Journal of Chemical Dependency Treatment
Dana Finnegan PhD, Editor
The Haworth Press Inc
10 Alice St
Binghamton NY 13904-1503
607-656-7981; 800-342-9678;
     Fax: 607-656-7876
Focus: 39R
Frequency: 2x per yr; Circulation: N/A

Journal of Child Sexual Abuse
Robert A Geffner PhD, Editor
The Haworth Press Inc
10 Alice St
Binghamton NY 13904-1503
607-722-5857; 800-342-9678;
     Fax: 607-722-6362
Focus: 31-35F-31S
Frequency: Quarterly; Circulation: 2,000

Journal of Couples Therapy
Barbara Brothers, Editor
Haworth Press
10 Alice St
Binghamton NY 13904-1503
800-342-9678; Fax: 607-722-1424
Focus: 35-57-73
Frequency: Quarterly; Circulation: N/A

Journal of Divorce & Remarriage
Craig A Everett PhD, Editor
1050 E River Rd #202
Tucson AZ 85718-5736
520-888-3896; Fax: 520-888-3301
Focus: 35-57-73
Frequency: Quarterly; Circulation: N/A

Journal of Economic Education
Rosalind Springsteen, Managing Editor
Heldref Publications
1319 18th St NW
Washington DC 20036-1802
202-296-6267; 800-365-9753;
     Fax: 202-296-5149
Focus: 19E-31E
Frequency: Quarterly; Circulation: 1,000

Journal of Education for Business
Isabella Owen, Editor
Heldref Publications
1319 18th St NW
Washington DC 20036-1802
202-296-6267; Fax: 202-296-5149
Focus: 19-19G-31E
Frequency: 6x per yr; Circulation: 2,000

Journal of Educational Research
Jeanne Bebo, Editor
Heldref Publications
1319 18th St NW
Washington DC 20036-1802
202-296-6267; Fax: 202-296-5149
Focus: 31E
Frequency: 6x per yr; Circulation: 4,000

Journal of Elder Abuse & Neglect
Rosalie S Wolf PhD, Co-Editor
The Haworth Press Inc
10 Alice St
Binghamton NY 13904-1503
508-793-6166; 800-342-9678;
   Fax: 607-722-1424
Focus: 35A-39-57
Frequency: Quarterly; Circulation: N/A

Journal of Emotional/Behavioral
Michael Epstein Ed.D and Douglas Cullinan Ed.D., Co-Editors
Pro-Ed Inc
8700 Shoal Creek Blvd
Austin TX 78757-6816
512-451-3246; Fax: 512-451-8542
Focus: 57
Frequency: Quarterly; Circulation: 2,000

Journal of Environmental Education
Marla Fogelman, Editor
Heldref Publications
1319 Eighteenth St NW
Washington DC 20036-1802
202-296-6267; Fax: 202-296-5149
Focus: 31E-51E
Frequency: Quarterly; Circulation: N/A

Journal of Euromarketing
Erdener Kaynak PhD, Editor
The Haworth Press Inc
10 Alice St
Binghamton NY 13904-1503
717-566-3054; 800-342-9678;
   Fax: 717-566-8589
Focus: 19M-44
Frequency: Quarterly; Circulation: N/A

Journal of Experimental Medicine
Ralph Steinman, Editor
Rockefeller Univ Press
222 E 70th St
New York NY 10021-5405
212-327-7938; Fax: 212-327-9944
Focus: 39-67
Frequency: Monthly; Circulation: 4,000

Journal of Family Psychotherapy
Joe Wetchler, Book Review Editor
The Haworth Press Inc
10 Alice St
Binghamton NY 13904-1503
800-342-9678; Fax: 219-989-2777
Focus: 35-57-73
Frequency: Quarterly; Circulation: N/A

Journal of Family Social Work
Thomas Edward Smith PhD, Editor
The Haworth Press Inc
10 Alice St
Binghamton NY 13904-1503
607-722-5857; 800-342-9678;
   Fax: 607-722-1424
Focus: 35F-57-65
Frequency: Quarterly; Circulation: N/A

Journal of Feminist Family Therapy
Janine Roberts, Editor
10 Alice St
Binghamton NY 13904-1503
607-656-7981; 800-342-9678;
   Fax: 607-722-6362
Focus: 31-35-57-73
Frequency: Quarterly; Circulation: N/A

Journal of Food Products Marketing
John Stanton, Editor
The Haworth Press Inc
5600 City Ave
Philadelphia PA 19131-1308
610-660-1607; 800-342-9678;
   Fax: 610-660-1604
Focus: 19M-27
Frequency: Quarterly; Circulation: N/A

Journal of Gay & Lesbian Psychotherapy
David Scasta, Editor-in-Chief
The Haworth Press Inc
10 Alice St
Binghamton NY 13904-1503
607-722-5857; 800-342-9678;
   Fax: 607-722-6362
Focus: 37-57
Frequency: Quarterly; Circulation: 1,000

Journal of General Psychology
Nancy Geltman, Managing Editor
Heldref Publications
1319 18th St NW
Washington DC 20036-1802
202-296-6267; 800-365-9753;
   Fax: 202-296-5149
Focus: 57
Frequency: Quarterly; Circulation: 1,000

Journal of Genetic Psychology
Judith Diggs, Editor
Heldref Publications
1319 18th St NW
Washington DC 20036-1802
202-296-6267; Fax: 202-296-5149
Focus: 39-57-65-67
Frequency: Quarterly; Circulation: 1,000

Journal of Geriatric Drug Therapy
James Cooper Phd FCP, Editor
The Haworth Press Inc
10 Alice St
Binghamton NY 13904-1503
800-342-9678; Fax: 607-722-1424
Focus: 35A-39R
Frequency: Quarterly; Circulation: N/A

Journal of Gerontological Social Work
Rose Dobrof, Editor
10 Alice St
Binghamton NY 13904-1503
607-722-5857; 800-342-9678;
   Fax: 607-722-1424
Focus: 35A-65
Frequency: Quarterly; Circulation: N/A

Journal of Global Marketing
Erdener Kaynak PhD, Editor
The Haworth Press Inc
10 Alice St
Binghamton NY 13904-1503
717-566-3054; Fax: 717-566-8589
Focus: 19M-44
Frequency: Quarterly; Circulation: N/A

Journal of Group Psychotherapy
Helen Kress, Managing Editor
Heldref Publications
1319 18th St NW
Washington DC 20036-1802
202-296-6267; 800-365-9753;
   Fax: 202-296-5149
Focus: 57-31E-57P
Frequency: Quarterly; Circulation: 1,000

Journal of Health/Social Policy
Marvin D Feit PhD, Co-Editor
The Haworth Press Inc
10 Alice St
Binghamton NY 13904-1503
607-722-5857; 800-342-9678;
   Fax: 607-722-1424
Focus: 13-39-55-57-65-73
Frequency: Quarterly; Circulation: N/A

Journal of Homosexuality
John P De Cecco PhD, Editor
The Haworth Press Inc
10 Alice St
Binghamton NY 13904-1503
607-722-5857; 800-342-9678;
   Fax: 607-722-6362
Focus: 37
Frequency: Quarterly; Circulation: 1,000

Journal of International Consumer Marketing
Erdener Kaynak PhD, Editor
10 Alice St
Binghamton NY 13904-1503
717-566-3054; 800-342-9678;
   Fax: 717-566-8589
Focus: 19-44
Frequency: Quarterly; Circulation: N/A

Journal of International Food/Agribusiness Marketing
Erdener Kaynak PhD, Editor
10 Alice St
Binghamton NY 13904-1503
717-566-3054; 800-342-9678;
   Fax: 717-566-8589
Focus: 19-44-51A
Frequency: Quarterly; Circulation: N/A

Journal of Light Construction
Sal Alfano, Editor
RR 2 Box 146
Richmond VT 05477-9607
802-434-4747;800-375-5981 ;
   Fax: 802-434-4467
Focus: 12B-19-29-43H
Frequency: Monthly; Circulation: 44,000

Journal of Marketing Research
Francesca Van Gorp, Editor
250 S Wacker Dr #200
Chicago IL 60606-5834
312-648-0536; Fax: 312-993-7542
Focus: 19M
Frequency: Quarterly; Circulation: 7,000

Journal of Motor Behavior
Betty Adelman, Editor
Heldref Publications
1319 18th St NW
Washington DC 20036-1802
202-296-6267; Fax: 202-296-5149
Focus: 39-57
Frequency: Quarterly; Circulation: 1,000

Journal of Ministry in Addiction/Recovery
Robert E Stevens, Editor
The Haworth Press Inc
10 Alice St
Binghamton NY 13904-1503
800-342-9678; Fax: 607-722-1424
Focus: 39R-63
Frequency: Quarterly; Circulation: N/A

Journal of Multinational Financial Management
Ike Mathur, Editor
Haworth Press
10 Alice St
Binghamton NY 13904-1503
618-453-2459; Fax: 618-453-7961
Focus: 19A-19E-44
Frequency: Quarterly; Circulation: N/A

Journal of Musculoskeletal Pain
I Jon Russell MD PhD, Editor
The Haworth Press Inc
10 Alice St
Binghamton NY 13904-1503
800-342-9678; Fax: 607-722-1424
Focus: 39
Frequency: Quarterly; Circulation: N/A

Journal of Negro History
Marcellus Barksdale, Book Review Editor
Assn for Study of Afro-American
Morehouse College PO Box 20
Atlanta GA 30301-0020
404-215-2620; Fax: 404-215-2715
Focus: 41-49B
Frequency: Quarterly; Circulation: 4,000

Journal of Nonprofit/Public Sector Mkt
Donald R Self, Editor
The Haworth Press Inc
10 Alice St
Binghamton NY 13904-1503
607-722-5857; 800-342-9678;
    Fax: 607-722-6362
Focus: 19M
Frequency: Quarterly; Circulation: N/A

Journal of Nutritional Immunology
Julian E Spallholz PhD, Editor
The Haworth Press Inc
10 Alice St
Binghamton NY 13904-1503
800-342-9678; Fax: 607-722-1424
Focus: 27-39
Frequency: Quarterly; Circulation: N/A

Journal of Petroleum Technology
Holly Hargadine, Editor
Society of Petroleum Engineers
222 Palisades Creek Dr
Richardson TX 75080-2040
214-952-9393; Fax: 214-952-9435
Focus: 23
Frequency: Monthly; Circulation: 52,000

Journal of Pharmaceutical Care in Pain
Arthur Lipman, Editor
10 Alice St
Binghamton NY 13904-1503
800-342-9678; Fax: 607-722-1424
Focus: 39-39D
Frequency: Quarterly; Circulation: N/A

Journal of Pharmaceutical Care/HIV....
Roberta J Wong, Editor
10 Alice St
Binghamton NY 13904-1503
800-342-9678; Fax: 607-722-1424
Focus: 39
Frequency: Quarterly; Circulation: N/A

Journal of Pharmacoepidemiology
Jack E Fincham PhD, Editor
The Haworth Press Inc
10 Alice St
Binghamton NY 13904-1503
913-864-3591; 800-342-9678;
    Fax: 607-722-1424
Focus: 39
Frequency: Quarterly; Circulation: N/A

Journal of Pharmacy Teaching
Mickey Smith PhD, Editor
The Haworth Press Inc
10 Alice St
Binghamton NY 13904-1503
800-342-9678; Fax: 607-722-1424
Focus: 31-39
Frequency: Quarterly; Circulation: N/A

Journal of Psychology/Human Sexuality
Eli Coleman PhD, Editor
The Haworth Press Inc
10 Alice St
Binghamton NY 13904-1503
612-625-1500; 800-342-9678;
    Fax: 612-626-8311
Focus: 35-57-73
Frequency: Quarterly; Circulation: N/A

Journal of Psychosocial Oncology
Grace H Christ ACSW, Editor
The Haworth Press Inc
10 Alice St
Binghamton NY 13904-1503
800-342-9678; Fax: 607-722-1424
Focus: 57-65
Frequency: Quarterly; Circulation: N/A

Journal of Rehabilitation
Ron Acquavita, Managing Editor
633 S Washington St
Alexandria VA 22314-4109
703-836-0850; Fax: 703-836-0848
Focus: 39R
Frequency: Quarterly; Circulation: 15,000

Journal of Research on Computing in Education
Dennis Spuck, Co-Editor
Univ of Oregon
1787 Agate St
Eugene OR 97403-1923
503-346-4414; 800-342-9678;
    Fax: 503-346-5890
Focus: 23-31
Frequency: Quarterly; Circulation: 4,000

Journal of Social Psychology
Marcie Kanakis and Leonard W Doob,
    Co-Editors
Heldref Publications
1319 18th St NW
Washington DC 20036-1802
202-296-6267; Fax: 202-296-5149
Focus: 57-65
Frequency: 6x per yr; Circulation: 2,000

The Journal of Special Education
Douglas Fuchs, PhD and Lynn Fuchs,,
    Co-Editors
Pro Ed Journals
8700 Shoal Creek Blvd
Austin TX 78757-6816
512-451-3246; Fax: 512-451-8542
Focus: 31
Frequency: Quarterly; Circulation: 3,000

The Journal of Taxation
Joseph Graf, Editor
Warren Gorham Lamont
1 Penn Plz
New York NY 10119-0002
212-971-5000; 800-950-1252;
    Fax: 212-971-5113
Focus: 19-25T-44-55G
Frequency: Monthly; Circulation: 18,000

Journal of Teaching in Social Work
Florence Vigilante DSW, Editor
The Haworth Press Inc
10 Alice St
Binghamton NY 13904-1503
607-722-5857; 800-336-5191;
    Fax: 607-722-1424
Focus: 31-65
Frequency: 2x per yr; Circulation: N/A

Journal of Vegetable Crop Production
M Leron Robbins PhD, Editor
10 Alice St
Binghamton NY 13904-1503
607-722-5857; 800-342-9678;
    Fax: 607-722-6362
Focus: 43-51A
Frequency: Quarterly; Circulation: N/A

Journal of Women & Aging
J Dianne Garner DSW, Editor
The Haworth Press Inc
10 Alice St
Binghamton NY 13904-1503
607-722-5857; 800-342-9678;
    Fax: 607-722-6362
Focus: 39-73-35A
Frequency: Quarterly; Circulation: N/A

K

Kaleidoscope
Darshan Perusek, Editor-in-Chief
Kaleidoscope Press
326 Locust St
Akron OH 44302-1876
330-762-9755; Fax: 330-762-0912
Focus: 39D
Frequency: 2x per yr; Circulation: 2,000

L

Leaders Magazine
Darrell Brown, Editor
59 East 54th St
New York NY 10022-4211
212-758-0740; Fax: 212-593-5194
Focus: 17-19-55-71
Frequency: Quarterly; Circulation: 35,000

Learning Magazine
Charlotte Perkins, Managing Editor
The Education Ctr
1607 Battleground Ave POB 9753
Greensboro NC 27429
910-273-9409; Fax: 910-272-8020
Focus: 21-31-76(elementary education)
Frequency: 8x per yr; Circulation: N/A

M

Marketing Computers
David Evans, Editor
BPI Communications
1515 Broadway 12th Fl
New York NY 10036-5701
212-536-5336; Fax: 212-536-6551
Focus: 19M-23C(marketing computers)
Frequency: Monthly; Circulation: 15,000

Marketing Management
Carolyn Neal, Editor
American Marketing Assn
250 S Wacker Dr #200
Chicago IL 60606-5834
312-648-0536; Fax: 312-993-7540
Focus: 19M
Frequency: Quarterly; Circulation: 3,000

Marriage & Family Review
Marvin Sussman, Editor
The Haworth Press Inc
10 Alice St
Binghamton NY 13904-1503
800-342-9678; Fax: 607-722-1424
Focus: 35-57
Frequency: Quarterly; Circulation: N/A

Mathematics Teacher
Harry Tunis, Managing Editor
Natl Council of Teachers of Math
1906 Association Dr
Reston VA 22091-1502
703-620-9840; Fax: 703-476-2970
Focus: 31E-67M(secondary/college teachers)
Grades 7-14
Frequency: 9x per yr; Circulation: 61,000

Medical Economics
Stephen K Murata, Editor
Medical Economics
5 Paragon Dr
Montvale NJ 07645-1725
201-358-7200; 800-526-4870;
    Fax: 201-573-0867
Focus: 19-39
Frequency: 24x per yr; Circulation: 155,000

Medical Tribune for Family Phys
Sandra Thompson, Editor
100 Ave of the Americas 9th Fl
New York NY 10013-1689
212-274-7000; Fax: 212-431-0500
Focus: 39
Frequency: 24x per yr; Circulation: 70,000

Meeting News
Todd Englander, Editor-in-Chief
Miller Freeman Inc
1 Penn Plz
New York NY 10119-1198
212-714-1300; Fax: 212-714-1313
Focus: 19M-71
Frequency: 18x per yr; Circulation: 61,000

Midnight Engineering
Bill Gates, Editor
1700 Washington Ave
Rocky Ford CO 81067-2246
719-254-4558; Fax: 719-254-4517
Focus: 19S-24(engineering product development at home)
Frequency: 6x per yr; Circulation: 33,000

Military Review
Patricia Dunn, Book Review Editor
US Army Command/Gen Staff Coll
290 Grant Ave
Ft Leavenworth KS 66027-1231
913-684-9327; Fax: 913-684-9328
Focus: 48-55-70
Frequency: 6x per yr; Circulation: 19,000

Mobile Radio Technology
Don Bishop, Editor
Intertec Publishing Corp
9800 Metcalf
Overland Park KS 66212-2216
913-341-1300; Fax: 913-967-1905
Focus: 23T
Frequency: Monthly; Circulation: 25,000

Modern Healthcare
Clark Bell, Editor
740 N Rush St
Chicago IL 60611-2525
312-649-5342; Fax: 312-280-3189
Focus: 39(health industry)
Frequency: Weekly; Circulation: 90,000

Mortgage & Real Est Exec Report
Alvin Arnold, Editor
Warren Gorham Lamont
1 Penn Plz 42nd Fl
New York NY 10119-0002
212-971-5591; 800-950-1205;
    Fax: 212-971-5025
Focus: 19B(mortgage)-19H
Frequency: 24x per yr; Circulation: N/A

MRS Bulletin
Carl J McHargue, Book Review Editor
Materials Research Society
9800 McKnight Rd
Pittsburgh PA 15237-6004
412-367-3003; Fax: 412-367-4373
Focus: 24-67
Frequency: Monthly; Circulation: 13,000

MultiCultural Review
Sean Maloney, Book Review Editor
88 Post Rd
PO Box 5007
Westport CT 06881
203-226-3571; Fax: 203-226-6009
Focus: 45-49-78-80-99
Frequency: Quarterly; Circulation: 5,000

MultiMedia Schools
Jean Reese, Reference Shelf Editor
Education Libr Box 325 Peabody
Vanderbilt Univ
Nashville TN 37203-5601
615-322-8248
Focus: 23-31E(books, software, mags, videos, and electronic media)
Frequency: 5x per yr; Circulation: N/A

N

National Law Journal
Ben Gerson, Editor-in-Chief
545 Park Ave S
New York NY 10021-8108
212-779-9200; 800-888-8300;
    Fax: 212-696-1875
Focus: 19L-55L
Frequency: Weekly; Circulation: 41,000

New England Journal of Medicine
Jerome Kassirer, MD, Editor
10 Shattuck St
Boston MA 02115-6011
617-893-3800; Fax: 617-893-8103
Focus: 39
Frequency: Weekly; Circulation: 236,000

New England Review
Stephen Donadio, Editor
Middlebury College
Middlebury VT 05753
802-388-3711
Focus: 47-75-83-90-95-99
Frequency: Quarterly; Circulation: 2,000

New Thought
Blaine C Mays, Editor
5003 E Broadway Rd
Mesa AZ 85206-1301
602-830-2461
Focus: 53-54
Frequency: Quarterly; Circulation: 5,000

NJEA Review
Martha DeBlieu, Editor
New Jersey Education Assn
180 W State St
Trenton NJ 08608-1104
609-599-4561; Fax: 609-392-6321
Focus: 31
Frequency: 9x per yr; Circulation: 147,000

O

Occupational Hazards
Steve Minter, Editor
Penton Publishing Inc
1100 Superior Ave
Cleveland OH 44114-2518
216-696-7000; Fax: 216-696-7658
Focus: 19C-19G-19X-23T-31E-39-51E
Frequency: Monthly; Circulation: 60,000

Occupational Health & Safety News
Ceel Pasternak, Editor
Stevens Publishing Corp
3630 Interstate Hwy 34
Waco TX 76706
817-776-9000; Fax: 817-776-7075
Focus: 39
Frequency: Monthly; Circulation: 85,000

Occupational Therapy in Health Care
Susan Cook Merrill, Editor
The Haworth Press Inc
10 Alice St
New York NY 13904-1503
800-342-9678; Fax: 607-722-1424
Focus: 57
Frequency: Quarterly; Circulation: N/A

Office Systems 95
Scott Cullen, Editor
Springhouse Corp
1111 Bethleham Pike PO Box 908
Springhouse PA 19477-0908
215-628-7716
Focus: 19P-23
Frequency: Monthly; Circulation: N/A

The Officer
Norman Burzynski, Editor
1 Constitution Ave NE
Washington DC 20002-5618
202-479-2200
Focus: 48
Frequency: Monthly; Circulation: 100,000

P

Pharmaceutical & Medical Packaging
James Wagner, Editor
15 Paoli Plz #6
Paoli PA 19301-1368
610-647-8585; Fax: 610-647-8565
Focus: 19M-39
Frequency: Monthly; Circulation: 20,000

Physical & Occupational Therapy
Ellen D Taira, Editor
The Haworth Press Inc
10 Alice St
Binghamton NY 13904-1503
800-342-9678; Fax: 607-722-1424
Focus: 39-35A
Frequency: Quarterly; Circulation: N/A

Physician
Keith Wall, Editor
Focus on the Family
Colorado Springs CO 80995
719-531-5181
Focus: 39H-39M
Frequency: 6x per yr; Circulation: 53,000

Physics Today
Stephan Benda, Editor
500 Sunnyside Blvd
Woodbury NY 11797-2924
516-576-2478; Fax: 516-576-2481
Focus: 67(physics)
Frequency: Monthly; Circulation: 114,000

PI Magazine
Bob Mackowiak, Editor/Publisher
755 Bronx St
Toledo OH 43609-1723
419-382-0967
Focus: 17P-55C(true stories)
Private investigation
Frequency: Quarterly; Circulation: 3,000

Preaching Magazine
Michael Duduit, Editor
409 Godfrey Ave
Louisville KY 40206-2605
502-899-3119; 800-288-9673;
    Fax: 502-893-5069
Focus: 63P(for Christian preachers)
Frequency: 6x per yr; Circulation: 10,000

Prepared Foods
Bob Swientek, Editor
455 N Cityfront Plz Dr 23rd Fl
Chicago IL 60611-5506
312-222-2000; Fax: 312-222-2026
Focus: 27
Frequency: 13x per yr; Circulation: 72,000

Prevention in Human Services
Robert Hess PhD, Editor
The Haworth Press Inc
10 Alice St
Binghamton NY 13904-1503
800-342-9678; Fax: 607-722-1424
Focus: 39-65
Frequency: 2x per yr; Circulation: N/A

Print
Martin Fox, Editor
RC Publications
104 Fifth Ave 19th Fl
New York NY 10011-6901
212-463-0600; Fax: 212-989-9891
Focus: 11(graphics)-19M
Frequency: 6x per yr; Circulation: 52,000

Professional Pilot
Kirby Harrison, Managing Editor
Queensmith Communications
3014 Colvin St
Alexandria VA 22314-4555
703-370-0606; Fax: 703-370-7082
Focus: 16
Frequency: Monthly; Circulation: 32,000

Psychodrama & Sociometry
Helen Kress, Editor
Heldref Publications
1319 18th St NW
Washington DC 20036-1802
202-296-2267; Fax: 202-296-5149
Focus: 57
Frequency: N/A; Circulation: N/A

Publish
Jake Widman, Editor
501 Second St #310
San Francisco CA 94107-1431
415-243-0600; Fax: 415-975-2613
Focus: 11(graphics)-23C-56P-56X
Desktop publishing
Frequency: Monthly; Circulation: 125,000

Q

Quest
Amelia Lee, Editor
PO Box 5076
Champaign IL 61825-5076
217-351-5076; Fax: 217-351-2674
Focus: 31E (physical education/higher grades)
Frequency: Quarterly; Circulation: 2,000

Quest
Bob Mackle, Managing Editor
MDA National Hdqtrs
3300 E Sunrise Dr
Tucson AZ 85718-3208
520-529-2000; Fax: 520-529-5300
Focus: 39M
Frequency: Quarterly; Circulation: 85,000

Quest Magazine
Shawn Turney, Editorher
432 S Broadway
Denver CO 80209-1518
303-722-5965; Fax: 303-698-1187
Focus: 13-37
Frequency: Monthly; Circulation: 10,000

R

RE:view
Helen Strang, Managing Editor
Heldref Publications
1319 18th St NW
Washington DC 20036-1802
202-296-6267; 800-365-9753;
    Fax: 202-296-5149
Focus: 31E-39D
Frequency: N/A; Circulation: 5,000

Red Herring
Christopher Alden, Editor
Flipside Communications
1550 Bryant St #950
San Francisco CA 94103-4832
415-865-2277; Fax: 415-865-2280;
    E-Mail: theherring@aol.com
Focus: 19I-23C-23T(technology and venture capital investments)
Frequency: Monthly; Circulation: 10,000

Religion Teacher's Journal
Deborah McCann, Book Review Editor
Gwen Costello, Editor
Twenty-Third Publications
PO Box 180
Mystic CT 06355-0180
203-536-2611; 800-321-0411;
    Fax: 203-572-0788
Focus: 31-63C
Frequency: 7x per yr; Circulation: 40,000

Remedial and Special Education
Lorna Idol, Editor-in-Chief
Pro Ed Journals
8700 Shoal Creek Blvd
Austin TX 78757-6816
512-451-3246; Fax: 512-451-8542
Focus: 31
Frequency: 6x per yr; Circulation: 3,000

Residential Treatment/Children..
Gordon Northrup, Editor
10 Alice St
Binghamton NY 13904-1503
800-342-9678; Fax: 607-722-1424
Focus: 31-35-39-57
Frequency: Quarterly; Circulation: N/A

Rethinking Schools
Phyllis Sides, Editorial Asst
1001 E Keefe Ave
Milwaukee WI 53212
414-964-9646; Fax: 414-964-7220
Focus: 31E(urban education)
Frequency: Quarterly; Circulation: N/A

ReVISION Journal
Adele Mujal, Editor
Heldref Publications
1319 18th St NW
Washington DC 20036-1802
202-296-6267; Fax: 202-296-5149
Focus: 57-67-65-51-54
Frequency: Quarterly; Circulation: 2,000

Rocks & Minerals
Marie Huizing, Editor
Heldref Publications
1319 18th St NW
Washington DC 20036-1802
202-296-6267; 800-365-9753l;
    Fax: 202-296-5149
Focus: 51-67(geology)
Frequency: 6x per yr; Circulation: 6,000

S

Savings & Community Banker
Brian Nixon, Editor (202-857-3142)
Savings/Comm Bankers of America
900 19th St NW
Washington DC 20006-2105
202-857-3100; Fax: 202-296-8716
Focus: 19B
Frequency: Monthly; Circulation: 13,000

Scholastic Coach & Athletic Director
Herman Masin, Editor
555 Broadway
New York NY 10012-3919
212-505-4970; Fax: 212-260-8587
Focus: 31-69(athletic directors, coaches, and trainers)
Frequency: 10x per yr; Circulation: 44,000

Science & Children
Joan Braunagel McShane, Editor
National Science Teachers Assn
1840 Wilson Blvd
Arlington VA 22201-1171
703-243-7100; Fax: 703-243-7177
Focus: 21-23-67(elementary to junior high)
Frequency: 8x per yr; Circulation: 22,000

Science Activities
Claire Wilson, Managing Editor
Heldref Publications
1319 18th St NW
Washington DC 20036-1802
202-296-6267; 800-365-9753;
    Fax: 202-296-5149
Focus: 23-39-51-67-31
Frequency: Quarterly; Circulation: 1,000

Science Magazine
Monica Bradford, Managing Editor
AAAS
1333 H St NW
Washington DC 20005-4707
202-326-6500; Fax: 202-371-9227
Focus: 23-24-39-51-59-67
Frequency: Weekly; Circulation: 150,000

Science Teacher
Janet Gerking, Editor-in-Chief
National Science Teachers Assn
1840 Wilson Blvd
Arlington VA 22201-3000
703-243-7100; Fax: 202-243-7177
Focus: 23-24-31E-39-51-67
Frequency: 9x per yr; Circulation: 27,000

Scientific American
Corey Powell, Review Editor
415 Madison Ave
New York NY 10017-1179
212-754-0550; Fax: 212-755-1976
Focus: 99
Frequency: Monthly; Circulation: 657,000

Searcher
Barbara Quint, Editor
Information Today Inc
143 Old Marlton Pike
Medford Lakes NJ 08055-8750
609-654-6266; Fax: 609-654-4309
Focus: 23C(database search professionals)
Frequency: 10; Circulation: 4,000

Securities Regulation Law Journal
Marc Steinberg, Editor-In-Chief
Warren Gorham Lamont
1 Penn Plz
New York NY 10119-0002
212-971-5000; 800-950-1205;
    Fax: 212-971-5025
Focus: 19-55G(SEC regulations)
Frequency: Quarterly; Circulation: 1,000

Security Management
Sherry Harwoitz, Sr Editor
Amer Soc for Industrial Security
1655 N Fort Myer Dr #1200
Arlington VA 22209-3108
703-522-5800; Fax: 703-522-5226
Focus: 19G-23T-55C(industrial security and crises management)
Frequency: Monthly; Circulation: 25,000

Selling Magazine
Geoffrey Precourt, Editor
Capital Cities/ABC Inc
488 Madison Ave
New York NY 10022-5702
212-303-3450; Fax: 212-303-3433
Focus: 19M
Frequency: 10x per yr; Circulation: 150,000

Selling to Seniors
Mark Binker, Editor
CD Publications
8204 Fenton St
Silver Springs MD 20910
301-588-6380; 800-666-6380;
    Fax: 301-588-6385
Focus: 19M(selling to senior citizens)-35A
Frequency: Monthly; Circulation: N/A

Social Education
Editor
Natl Council for Social Studies
3501 Newark St
Washington DC 20016-3100
202-966-7840; Fax: 202-966-2061
Focus: 21-31-55-65
Frequency: 7x per yr; Circulation: 22,000

Social Science History Magazine
Russell Menard, Co-Editor
PO Box 90660
Durham SC 27708-0660
919-687-3636; Fax: 919-688-4574
Focus: 55-65
Frequency: Quarterly; Circulation: 2,000

The Social Studies
Helen Kress, Editor
Heldref Publications
1319 18th St NW
Washington DC 20036-1802
202-296-6267; 800-365-9753;
    Fax: 202-296-5149
Focus: 41-55-57-65-31E
Frequency: 6x per yr; Circulation: 2,000

Social Work in Health Care
Gary Rosenberg PhD, Editor
The Haworth Press Inc
10 Alice St
Binghamton NY 13904-1503
607-722-5857; 800-342-9678;
    Fax: 607-722-1424
Focus: 39-65
Frequency: Quarterly; Circulation: 2,000

Social Work with Groups
Roselle Kurland PhD, Editor
The Haworth Press Inc
10 Alice St
Binghamton NY 13904-1503
607-722-5857; 800-342-9678;
    Fax: 607-722-1424
Focus: 65
Frequency: Quarterly; Circulation: N/A

Sociology of Sport Journal
Jay Coakley, Editor
Dept of Sociology PO 7150
Univ of Colorado
Colorado Springs CO 80933-7150
719-593-3144; Fax: 719-593-3362
Focus: 65-69
Frequency: Quarterly; Circulation: N/A

Southern Loggin' Times
Rich Donnell, Editorial Dir
Hatton-Brown Publishers Inc
225 Hanrick St
Montgomery AL 36104-3317
334-834-1170; Fax: 334-834-4525
Focus: 12-19-51-55
Frequency: Monthly; Circulation: 11,000

Special Services in the Schools
Charles A Maher, Editor
The Haworth Press Inc
10 Alice St
Binghamton NY 13904-1503
800-342-9678; Fax: 607-722-1424
Focus: 31-57
Frequency: 2x per yr; Circulation: N/A

Symposium
Jeanne Bebo, Managing Editor
1319 18th St NW
Washington DC 20036-1802
202-296-6267; 800-365-9753;
    Fax: 202-296-5149
Focus: 31-47
Frequency: Quarterly; Circulation: N/A

T

Taxation for Accountants
Sandra K Lewis, Editor
Warren Gorham Lamont
1 Penn Plz 4th Fl
New York NY 10119-0002
212-971-5000; 800-950-1252;
    Fax: 212-971-5113
Focus: 19A-55G(taxes)
Frequency: Monthly; Circulation: 13,000

Teacher Magazine
Blake Hume Rodman, Editor
4301 Connecticut Ave NW
Washington DC 20008-2304
202-686-0800; Fax: 202-686-0797
Focus: 31E
Frequency: Monthly; Circulation: 95,000

Teaching Children Mathmetics
Harry Tunis, Editor
Natl Council of Teachers of Math
1906 Association Dr
Reston VA 22091-1502
703-620-9840; Fax: 703-476-2970
Focus: 21-31-67(math)(elementary school
    teachers 1-6)
Frequency: 9x per yr; Circulation: 60,000

Teaching Pre K-8
Allen Raymond, Editor
Highlights for Children
40 Richards Ave
Norwalk CT 06854-2319
203-855-2650; Fax: 203-855-2656
Focus: 31E-47-56W-76
Frequency: 8x per yr; Circulation: 142,000

Teaching Tolerance
Sara Bullard, Editor
Southern Poverty Law Ctr
400 Washington Ave
Montgomery AL 36104-4344
334-264-0286; Fax: 334-264-3121
Focus: 49B-55-65
Frequency: N/A; Circulation: 200,000

Tech Directions
Victoria Vandenberg, Book Review Editor
Prakken Publications Inc
275 Metty Dr #1
Ann Arbor MI 48103-9444
313-769-1211; 800-530-9673;
    Fax: 313-769-8383
Focus: 19-31-67
Frequency: 10x per yr; Circulation: 45,000

Technical Communication
Roger Grice, Editor
901 N Stuart St #904
Arlington VA 22203-1854
703-522-4114; Fax: 703-522-2075
Focus: 19(communication)-23
Frequency: Quarterly; Circulation: 18,000

Technology and Learning
Judy Salpeter, Managing Editor
Peter Li Inc
2169 Francisco Blvd #A-4
San Rafael CA 94901-5520
415-457-4333; Fax: 415-457-4379
Focus: 23C-31E
Frequency: 8x per yr; Circulation: 80,000

Technology Teacher
Judy Miller, Editor
1914 Association Dr
Reston VA 22091-1538
703-860-2100; E-Mail: hea@tmn.com
Focus: 23-31-67
Frequency: 8; Circulation: 8,000

Telemarketing
Linda Driscoll, Editor
Technology Marketing Corp
1 Technology Plz
Norwalk CT 06854-1924
203-852-6800; 800-243-6002;
    Fax: 203-853-2845
Focus: 19M-23
Frequency: Monthly; Circulation: 30,000

Timber Harvesting
David Knight, Co-Publisher
Hatton-Brown Publishers Inc
225 Hanrick St
Montgomery AL 36104-3317
334-834-1170; Fax: 334-834-4525
Focus: 12-19-51-55
Frequency: 10x per yr; Circulation: 16,000

Today's CPA
Kellye Norris, Editor
Texas Society of CPAs
1421 W Mockingbird Ln #100
Dallas TX 75247-4978
214-689-6000; Fax: 214-689-6046
Focus: 19A-19F
Frequency: 6x per yr; Circulation: 31,000

Today's Parish
Dan Connors, Editor
Twenty-Third Publications
PO Box 180
Mystic CT 06355-0180
203-536-2611; 800-321-0411;
    Fax: 203-572-0788
Focus: 31-63C
Frequency: 7x per yr; Circulation: 13,000

Trial Magazine
Elizabeth Yeary, Editor
Assn of Trial Lawyers of America
1050 31st St NW
Washington DC 20007-4409
202-965-3500; Fax: 202-965-0030
Focus: 19L-25-55L
Frequency: Monthly; Circulation: 60,000

U

Urban Forests
Michelle Robbins, Editor
PO Box 2000
Washington DC 20013-2000
202-667-3300; Fax: 202-667-2407
Focus: 51-61
Frequency: 6x per yr; Circulation: 37,000

V

Virginia Review
Alyson Taylor-White, Editor-in-Chief
PO Box 860
Chester VA 23831-0860
800-827-3843; Fax: 804-796-6931
Focus: 47-75-83-90-95
Frequency: 6x per yr; Circulation: 5,000

W

Windows NT
Jane Morrill, Editor
Duke Communications Intl
221 E 29th St
Loveland CO 80538
303-663-4700
Focus: 23(NT professionals)
Frequency: Monthly; Circulation: 50,000

Women & Criminal Justice
Clarice Feinman PhD, Editor
The Haworth Press Inc
10 Alice St
Binghamton NY 13904-1503
800-342-9678; Fax: 607-722-1424
Focus: 55-65-73
Frequency: 2x per yr; Circulation: N/A

Women & Health
Jeanne Stellman PhD, Editor
The Haworth Press Inc
10 Alice St
Binghamton NY 13904-1503
718-230-8822; Fax: 212-305-3405
Focus: 39-73
Frequency: Quarterly; Circulation: N/A

Women & Politics
Janet M Clark, Editor
The Haworth Press Inc
10 Alice St
Binghamton NY 13904-1503
607-722-2493; 800-342-9678;
    Fax: 607-722-1424
Focus: 13-55-73
Frequency: Quarterly; Circulation: N/A

Women & Therapy
Marcia Hill, Editor
The Haworth Press Inc
10 Alice St
Binghamton NY 13904-1503
607-722-2493; Fax: 607-722-1424
Focus: 57-73
800-342-9678
Frequency: Quarterly; Circulation: 2,000

World Affairs
Joyce Horn, Editor
Heldref Publications
1319 18th St NW
Washington DC 20036-1802
202-296-6267; Fax: 202-296-5149
Focus: 44-55-65-45
Frequency: Quarterly; Circulation: N/A

World Literature Today
Djelal Kadir, Editor-in-Chief
Univ of Oklahoma
110 Monnet Hall
Norman OK 73019-0375
405-325-4531; Fax: 405-325-7495
Focus: 44-45-75-90-95(all foreign)
Frequency: Quarterly; Circulation: 2,000

World's Fair
Alfred Heller, Editor
300 Tamal Plz #120
Corte Madera CA 94925-1131
415-924-6035; Fax: 415-924-8245
Focus: 99
Frequency: Quarterly; Circulation: 5,000

Writer's Guidelines
Susan Salaki, Editor/Publisher
PO Box 608
Pittsburg MO 65724
417-993-5544; Fax: 417-993-5544
Focus: 56W
Frequency: 6x per yr; Circulation: 13,000

Writers' Journal
Valerie Hockert, Editor/Publisher
3585 N Lexington Ave #328
St Paul MN 55126-8056
612-486-7818
Focus: 56W
Frequency: 6x per yr; Circulation: 51,000

Abbreviations Used

Territory

CN	Canada
IT	International
MX	Mexico
OT	Other
US	United States with some state abbreviations for the different states

Markets

BK	Bookstores
CO	Colleges
JB	Jobbers
MM	Mass Markets
NS	Newsstands
OT	Other
PL	Public Libraries
RO	Retail Outlets
SC	Schools
SL	Special Libraries

Items

CA	Calendars
CO	Comics
CR	Craft Items
GA	Games
GC	Greeting Cards
GI	Gifts
HC	Hardcovers
MA	Maps and Atlases
MG	General / Special Magazines
ML	Literary Magazines
MM	Mass Market Books
NP	Newspapers
OP	Out of Print Books
OT	Other Items
PB	Trade Paperbacks
PO	Posters
RC	Records
RM	Remainders
SB	Stickers/Bookmarks
ST	Stationery
SW	Software
TA	Tapes, Audio
TO	Toys
TV	Tapes, Video
TX	Textbooks
US	Used books

Marketing Magazines

The following magazines feature news, reviews, and other items of interest to anyone involved in marketing products and services. Write away for a sample copy of any magazine that addresses a marketing niche you are interested in pursuing.

A

Ad Age's Business Marketing
Chuck Paustian, Editor
Crain Communications
740 N Rush St
Chicago IL 60611-2590
312-649-5260; Fax: 312-649-5462
Focus: 19M(business-to-business marketing)
Frequency: Monthly; Circulation: 30,000

AdcomNet
Karen Sullivan, Editor
PO Box 840
Sherborn MA 01770-0840
508-651-3932; Fax: 508-653-7214
Focus: 19
Frequency: Monthly; Circulation: 5,000

Advertising Age
Steve Yahn, Editor
Crain Communications
740 N Rush St
Chicago IL 60611-2590
312-649-5200; Fax: 312-649-5331
Focus: 19M
Frequency: 52x per yr; Circulation: 85,000

Adweek
Craig Reiss, Editor-in-Chief
BPI Communications
1515 Broadway
New York NY 10036-8901
212-536-5336; Fax: 212-536-5353
Focus: 19(advertising)
Frequency: 52x per yr; Circulation: 48,000

American Marketplace
Dave Speights, Editor
Business Publishers Inc
951 Pershing Dr
Silver Spring MD 20910-4432
301-587-6300; 800-274-6737;
    Fax: 301-589-8493
Focus: 19M-19R(market statistics)
Frequency: 26x per yr; Circulation: N/A

B

Book Marketing Update Newsletter
John Kremer, Editor
209 S Main St #200
PO Box 205
Fairfield IA 52556-0205
515-472-6130; Fax: 515-472-1560;
    E-mail: JohnKremer@aol.com
Focus: 19M-56M-56P-56W-56X
Frequency: Monthly; Circulation: 3,000

Book Promotion Hotline
Marie Kiefer, Editor
Ad-Lib Publications
51 W Adams
PO Box 1102
Fairfield IA 52556-1102
515-472-6617; 800-669-0773;
    Fax: 515-472-3186;
    E-mail: Adlib100@aol.com
Focus: 56M-56P
Frequency: 26x per yr; Circulation: 100

Book Publishing Report
Linda Kopp, Managing Editor
SIMBA Information
213 Danbury Rd PO Box 7430
Wilton CT 06897
203-834-0033; Fax: 203-834-1771;
    E-mail: SIMBA99@aol.com
Focus: 56P(books and audio)
Frequency: 52x per yr; Circulation: N/A

Bookviews
Theological Book Service
7373 S Lovers Ln Rd
Franklin WI 53132
414-529-6400; Fax: 414-529-6419
Focus: 63C
Frequency: N/A; Circulation: N/A

Bulldog Reporter Central Edition
Aimee Grove, Editor
InfoCom Group
1250 45th St #200
Emeryville CA 94608
510-596-9300; Fax: 510-596-9331
Focus: 56M
Frequency: 24x per yr; Circulation: N/A

Bulldog Reporter Eastern Edition
Erin Strathamann, Editor
InfoCom Group
1250 45th St #200
Oakland CA 94601-4712
510-596-9300; Fax: 510-596-9331
Focus: 56M
Frequency: 24x per yr; Circulation: N/A

Bulldog Reporter Western Edition
Carolyn Huffman, Editor
InfoCom Group
1250 45th St #200
Emeryville CA 94608
510-596-9300; Fax: 510-596-9331
Focus: 56M
Frequency: 24x per yr; Circulation: N/A

Business Marketing
Char Kosek, Managing Editor
740 N Rush St
Chicago IL 60611-2525
312-649-5200; Fax: 312-649-5462
Focus: 19M(business-to-business marketing)
Frequency: Monthly; Circulation: 30,000

C

Catalog Age
Laura Christiana, Editorial Dir
6 River Bend
Stamford CT 06907-1426
203-358-9900; Fax: 203-357-9014
Focus: 19M
Frequency: Monthly; Circulation: 14,000

Cellular Business
Rhonda Wickham, Editor
Intertec Publishing
9800 Metcalf
Overland Park KS 66212-2216
913-341-1300; Fax: 913-967-1905
Focus: 19M-23T
Frequency: Monthly; Circulation: 20,000

Club Management
Thomas Finan, Editor
Finan Publishing
8730 Big Bend Blvd
St Louis MO 63119-3730
314-961-6644; Fax: 314-961-4809
Focus: 99
Frequency: 6x per yr; Circulation: 15,000

Computer Publishing/Advertising
Linda Kopp, Editor
SIMBA Information
PO Box 7430
Wilton CT 06897
203-834-0033; Fax: 203-834-1771
Focus: 19M-23C(info about computer advertisers & publishers)
Frequency: 24x per yr; Circulation: N/A

Consultants News
David Lord, Editor-in-Chief
Kennedy & Kennedy Inc
Templeton Rd
Fitzwilliam NH 03447
603-585-6544; 800-531-0007; Fax: 603-585-9555
Focus: 19(consulting)-19M
Frequency: Monthly; Circulation: N/A

Creative Selling
Bob Langdon, Editor
Bentley-Hall Inc
120 Walton St #201
Syracuse NY 13202
315-422-4488; 800-724-9700; Fax: 315-422-3837
Focus: 19S-57S(monthly newsletter of current sales strategies)
Frequency: Monthly; Circulation: N/A

Cyberspace PR Newsletter
Editor
Public Relations Society
33 Irving Pl
New York NY 10003-2376
212-460-1428; Fax: 212-995-0757; E-Mail: 74224.1456@compuservr.com
Focus: 19M-23C-56M
Frequency: 22x per yr; Circulation: N/A\

D

Direct Marketing
Ray Schultz, Editor
Six River Bend Ctr
911 Hope St PO Box 4949
Stamford CT 06907-0949
203-358-9900; Fax: 203-357-9014; E-Mail: directmag@aol.com
Focus: 19M
Frequency: Monthly; Circulation: 43,000

Direct Marketing Success Letter
Ted Nicholas, Editor
Nicholas Direct Inc
PO Box 877
Indian Rocks Beach FL 34635
813-596-4966; Fax: 813-596-6900
Focus: 19M
Frequency: 10x per yr; Circulation: N/A

Direct Media News
Max Bartko, Editor
Direct Media
200 Pemberwick Rd PO Box 4565
Greenwich CT 06830
203-532-1000; Fax: 203-531-1452
Focus: 19M (lists)
Frequency: 6x per yr; Circulation: 1,000

Direct Response Communication
Dean Rieck, Editor
2102 Brookhurst Ave
Columbus OH 43229-1545
614-882-8823; Fax: 614-882-8823
Focus: 19M-56W(direct mail copywriting tips)
Frequency: Quarterly; Circulation: 1,000

DM News
Nuna Alberts, Managing Editor
Mill Hollow Corp
100 Ave of the Americas
New York NY 10013
212-925-7300; Fax: 212-925-8758
Focus: 19M
Frequency: 48x per yr; Circulation: 35,000

E

EDK Forecast
Susan Jessop, Managing Editor
EDK Association
235 West 48th St
New York NY 10036
212-582-4504; 800-335-7655; Fax: 212-265-9348
Focus: 73-99(what motivates women to buy)
Frequency: 10x per yr; Circulation: N/A

The Exhibit Review
Editor
Phoenix Communications
PO Box 5808
Beaverton OR 97006-0808
503-643-2783; 800-235-3324; Fax: 503-644-7107
Focus: 19M(trade show exhibiting)
Frequency: Quarterly; Circulation: N/A

Exhibitor Magazine
Lee Knight, Editor
206 S Broadway #745
PO Box 368
Rochester MN 55903
507-289-6556; Fax: 507-289-5253; E-Mail: ExhMag@aol.com
Focus: 19M(trade show exhibiting)
Frequency: Monthly; Circulation: 15,000

H

Healthcare Financial Management
Ted Berland, Managing Editor
2 Westbrook Ctr #700
Westchester IL 60154-5723
708-531-9600; Fax: 708-531-0032
Focus: 19A-19I-39M
Frequency: Monthly; Circulation: 32,000

Hotline Newsletter
Rebecca Evans, Editor
Newsletter Publishers Assn
1401 Wilson Blvd #207
Arlington VA 22209-2306
703-527-2333; Fax: 703-841-0629
Focus: 56P
Frequency: 24; Circulation: N/A

I

Info Marketing Report
Jerry Buchanan, Editor
PO Box 2038
Vancouver WA 98668-2038
360-574-3084; Fax: 360-576-8969
Focus: 19M-19O-19S-56P
Frequency: Monthly; Circulation: 1,000

Lifestyle Media-Relations Report
John Papageorge, Editor
InfoComm Group
1250 45th St #200
Emeryville CA 94608
510-596-9300; Fax: 510-596-9331
Focus: 25-27-29-33-36-40-43-56M-71-99(lifestyle editors)
Frequency: 24x per yr; Circulation: N/A

M

Marketing Technology Newsletter
Kristin Zhivago, Editor
Zhivago Marketing Partners
70 Princeton Rd
Menlo Park CA 94025-5327
415-328-8600; Fax: 415-322-9149; E-Mail: kristin@zhivago.com
Focus: 19M-23C-23T(marketing technical products)
Frequency: Monthly; Circulation: N/A

Marketing To Women
Cindy Tripp, Managing Editor
Janice Leeming, Publisher
33 Broad St
Boston MA 02109-4216
617-723-4337; Fax: 617-723-7107
Focus: 19-39-73
Book reviews & book lists
Frequency: Monthly; Circulation: N/A

Multimedia Business Report
Tom O'Reilly, Editor
SIMBA Information
213 Danbury Rd PO Box 7430
Wilton CT 06897-7430
203-834-0033; Fax: 203-834-1771
Focus: 23-31-33(new media products)
Frequency: 46x per yr; Circulation: N/A

N

New Age Marketing Opportunities
Sophia Tarila, Editor
2855 Southwest Dr #1 (86636)
PO Box 2578
Sedona AZ 86639
520-282-9574; Fax: 520-282-9730
Focus: 19M-53
Frequency: 6x per yr; Circulation: N/A

News Future
Sandra Stencel, Editor
Congressional Quarterly
1414 22nd St NW
Washington DC 20037
202-887-8595
Focus: 99
Frequency: Weekly; Circulation: N/A

O

The Online Marketing Letter
Jonathan Mizel, Editor
564 Mission St #638
San Francisco CA 94105
415-337-7405; 800-934-8731
Focus: 19M-23C(marketing via computer online services)
Frequency: Monthly; Circulation: 1,000

P

Potentials in Marketing
Catherine Eberlein, Editor
Lakewood Publications
50 S Ninth St
Minneapolis MN 55402-3118
612-333-0471; Fax: 612-333-6526
Focus: 19M
Frequency: 10x per yr; Circulation: 62,000

PR Reporter
Patrick Jackson, Editor
Dudley House
PO Box 600
Exeter NH 03833-0600
603-778-0514; Fax: 603-778-1741
Focus: 56M(publicity)
Frequency: Weekly; Circulation: 10,000

Promo
Kerry J Smith, Managing Editor
Smith Communications Inc
47 Old Ridgefield Rd
Wilton CT 06897-3034
203-761-1510; Fax: 203-761-1522
Focus: 19M(promotional marketing)
Frequency: Monthly; Circulation: 20,000

R

Response TV Magazine
David Nagel, Editor
Advanstar Communications
201 E Sandpointe Ave #600
Santa Ana CA 92707
714-513-8453; Fax: 714-513-8482;
   E-Mail: rtvdave@aol.com
Focus: 19M-33T-56M(direct response television-long and short term)
Frequency: Monthly; Circulation: N/A

S

School Marketing Newsletter
Lynn Vosburgh, Editor
School Market Research Institute
1721 Saybrook Rd PO Box 10
Haddam CT 06438
203-345-8183; 800-838-3444
Focus: 19M-31
Frequency: Monthly; Circulation: N/A

The Selling Advantage
Editor
Progressive Business Publication
370 Technology Dr
Malvern PA 19355
800-220-5000; Fax: 610-647-8089
Focus: 19M(features excerpts from books as well as notes, interviews with authors)
Frequency: 22x per yr; Circulation: N/A

T

Target Market News
Ken Smikle, Editor
228 S Wabash Ave #408
Chicago IL 60604
312-408-1881; Fax: 312-408-1867
Focus: 19M-49B (Black consumer marketing)
Frequency: Monthly; Circulation: N/A

Target Marketing
Alicia Orr, Managing Editor
North American Publishing
401 N Broad St
Philadelphia PA 19108
215-238-5300; Fax: 215-238-5270
Focus: 19M
Frequency: Monthly; Circulation: 38,000

Today's Collector
Steve Ellingboe, Editor
Krause Publications
700 E State St
Iola WI 54990-0001
715-445-2214; Fax: 715-445-4087
Focus: 28C-29H
Frequency: Monthly; Circulation: 40,000

Travelwriter Marketletter
Robert Scott Milne, Editor
301 Park Ave #1850
New York NY 10022-6806
212-759-6744; Fax: 212-758-9209
Focus: 56W-71
Frequency: Monthly; Circulation: 1,000

V

Vietnam Opportunities
N K Andersen, Editor
VINA USA Business Liaison Corp
10 E 22nd St #200
New York NY 10010
212-673-5041; Fax: 212-673-1955
Focus: 19M-19O
Frequency: 26x per yr; Circulation: N/A

W

What's Working in Sales Mgmt
Richard Kern, Editor-in-Chief
Progressive Business Publication
370 Technology Dr
Malvern PA 19355
800-220-5000; Fax: 610-647-8089
Focus: 19G-19M(inside info on what top sales executive are doing)
Frequency: 22x per yr; Circulation: N/A

Y

Young Adult/Teen Market Report
C Dalley Oliver, Editor
210 Willimantic Dr
Marston Mills MA 02648
508-428-7287
Focus: 19M-31-89(marketing to teens)
Frequency: Quarterly; Circulation: 1,000

Subject Category Codes

10 **General Non-Fiction**
11 **Fine Arts**
    11P   Photography
12 **Architecture / Construction**
    12A   Architecture
    12B   Building / Construction
13 **Alternative Social Issues**
14 **Performing Arts**
    14D   Dance
    14M   Music
    14T   Theatre / Drama
15 **Animals / Pets**
16 **Transportation**
    16A   Automobiles
    16R   Railroads
17 **Biographies / Celebrities**
    17B   Biographies
    17C   Celebrities
    17P   Real People
19 **Business / Economics**
    19A   Accounting
    19B   Banking
    19C   Careers / Labor
    19E   Economics
    19F   Fund-raising / Non-profits
    19G   Management
    19H   Real Estate / Home
    19I   Investment
    19L   Law
    19M   Marketing / Sales
    19O   Opportunity Seekers
    19P   Purchasing
    19R   Retail Sales
    19S   Small Business
    19X   Industrial / Production
21 **Children's Interests**
    21T   Teenagers
23 **Computers / Technology**
    23C   Computers
    23E   Home Electronics
    23T   Technology
24 **Engineering**
25 **Consumer Issues**
    25T   Consumer Taxes
27 **Cooking / Food / Nutrition**
28 **Collectibles / Antiques**
29 **Crafts / Hobbies / How-to**
    29C   Crafts
    29H   Hobbies and How-to
31 **Education / Child Development**
    31C   Child Development
    31E   Education / Teaching
    31P   Parenting
33 **Entertainment / Movies / Humor**
    33C   Comics / Comedy
    33H   Humor
    33M   Movies
    33T   Television / Radio

35 **Family / Marriage / Retirement**
    35A   Aging Issues / Retirement
    35F   Family
    35M   Marriage
    35R   Relationships / Romance
    35S   Sexual Issues
36 **Lifestyle/Feature**
37 **Gay / Lesbian**
39 **Health / Medicine / Exercise**
    39D   Disabilities
    39E   Exercise
    39H   Holistic Health
    39M   Medicine / Doctors
    39R   Recovery / Drug Abuse
40 **Beauty / Fashion**
    40B   Beauty
    40F   Fashion
41 **History**
    41A   American History
    41G   Genealogy / Family History
    41W   World History
43 **House / Garden**
    43D   Home Decorating
    43G   Gardening
    43H   House and Home
44 **International Issues and News**
    44A   Asia
    44E   Europe
    44F   Africa
    44S   South America
    44Z   Australia / New Zealand
45 **Languages**
    45X   Linquistics
    45W   Words
47 **Literature / Humanities**
48 **Military**
49 **Minority Issues and Studies**
    49A   Native American
    49B   Black
    49H   Hispanic / Chicano
    49O   Other
51 **Nature / Ecology / Conservation**
    51A   Agriculture / Farming
    51B   Biology / Botany
    51E   Environmental Issues
    51N   Nature
53 **New Age / Astrology**
54 **Philosophy / Metaphysics**
    54M   Metaphysics
    54P   Philosophy
55 **Politics / Government**
    55C   Crime / Police Work
    55G   Government
    55L   Law
    55P   Politics

56 **Publishing / PR / Writing**
    56M   Media / Publicity
    56P   Publishing
    56W   Writing
    56X   Printing
57 **Psychology / Self-Help**
    57B   Behavior
    57P   Psychology / Therapy
    57S   Self-Help / Advice
59 **Reference Books**
61 **Regional Issues and Interests**
63 **Religions**
    63C   Catholic
    63E   Eastern Religions
    63J   Jewish
    63M   Muslim
    63O   Other Religions
    63P   Protestant
65 **Sociology / Anthropology**
    65A   Anthropology
    65S   Social Issues
67 **Science / Mathematics**
    67A   Astronomy / Space
    67M   Mathematics
    67S   Science
69 **Sports / Games / Recreation**
    69G   Games
    69H   Hunting / Fishing
    69R   Recreation / Hiking
    69S   Spectator Sports
70 **Nautical / Aviation**
    70A   Aviation
    70N   Nautical / Sailing
71 **Travel / Geography**
    71D   Domestic Travel
    71F   Foreign Travel
    71G   Geography
73 **Women's Issues**

75 General Fiction

76 **Children's Stories**
77 **Contemporary Novels**
78 **Ethnic / Minority Literature**
79 **Folklore / Fairy Tales**
80 **Foreign Literature**
81 **Historical Novels**
82 **Horror Novels**
83 **Literary Novels**
84 **Mysteries / Detective Novels**
85 **Romances / Gothic Romances**
86 **Science Fiction / Fantasy**
87 **Suspense / Adventure Novels**
88 **Westerns**
89 **Young Adult Novels**
90 **Short Stories / Anthologies**
95 **Poetry**

97 News / Current Events

99 General Interest

Newspaper Editors and Book Reviewers

Here are the addresses and phone numbers of the daily newspapers (and a few others) in the United States and Canada. You will find the listing alphabetical by state, city, and paper name.

Alabama

Alexander City Outlook
548 Cherokee Rd
Alexander City AL 35010-2503
205-234-4281; Fax: 205-234-6550
Circulation: 6,000

Andalusia Star News
209 Dunson St
Andalusia AL 36420-3705
205-222-2402; Fax: 205-222-6597
Circulation: 4,000

Anniston Star
216 W 10th St
Anniston AL 36201-5616
205-236-1551; Fax: 205-231-0027
Circulation: 35,000; Sun: 32,000

Cody Hall, Book Editor
Randolf Murray, Managing Editor

Athens News Courier
410 W Green St
Athens AL 35611-2518
205-232-2720; Fax: 205-233-7753
Circulation: 8,000; Sun: 10,000

Birmingham News
2200 4th Ave N
PO Box 2553
Birmingham AL 35202-2553
205-325-2466; Fax: 205-325-3345
Circulation: 180,000; Sun: 215,000

Joey Kennedy, Book Review Editor
Dean Barber, Business Editor
Chuck Dean, Education Editor
Scottie Vickery, Family Editor
Jo Ellen O'Hara, Food Editor
Charles McCauley, Health Editor
Terri Troncale, Lifestyle Editor
Carol Nunnelly, Managing Editor
John Clark, News Editor
Mike Bolton, Outdoors/Recreation Editor
Glenn Stevens, Political Editor
Greg Garrison, Religion Editor
Jeff Hansen, Science Editor
Tom Arenberg, Sports Editor

Birmingham Post Herald
2200 4th Ave N (35203)
PO Box 2553
Birmingham AL 35202-2553
205-325-2222; Fax: 205-325-2410

Circulation: 65,000 (Combines with **Birmingham News** on Saturday)
Daril Powell, Arts/Entertainment Editor
Mitchel Diggs, Book Editor
Michaelle Chapman, Education Reporter
John Staed, Health/Medical Reporter
Cabica Sparks, Lifestyle Editor
Jim Willis, Managing Editor
Steve Bell, Metro Editor
Ted Bryant, Political Editor
William Singleton, Religion Editor
John Staed, Science Editor
Don Kausler, Sports Editor

Cullman Times
300 4th Ave SE
Cullman AL 35055-3611
205-734-2131; Fax: 205-734-7310
Circulation: 9,000; Sun: 11,000

Decatur Daily
201 1st Ave SE
Decatur AL 35601-2333
205-353-4612; Fax: 205-340-2366
Circulation: 31,000; Sun: 32,000

Dothan Eagle
227 N Oates St
Dothan AL 36303-4555
334-792-3141; Fax: 334-792-7975
Circulation: 35,000; Sun: 37,000

Enterprise Ledger
106 N Edwards St
Enterprise AL 36330-2524
334-347-9533; Fax: 334-347-0825
Circulation: 10,000; Sun: 11,000

Times Daily
219 W Tennessee St
Florence AL 35630-5440
205-766-3434; Fax: 205-740-4700
Circulation: 34,000; Sun: 37,000

Times Journal
PO Box 349
Ft Payne AL 35967-0349
205-845-2550; Fax: 205-845-7459
Circulation: 8,000

Gadsden Times
401 Locust St
Gadsden AL 35901-3737
205-549-2000; Fax: 205-549-2105
Circulation: 29,000; Sun: 33,000

Huntsville News
2111 W Clinton Ave
Huntsville AL 35805-3007
205-532-4500; Fax: 205-532-4530
Circulation: 17,000

Huntsville Times
2317 Memorial Pky S
PO Box 1487
Huntsville AL 35807-1487
205-532-4000; Fax: 205-532-4420
Circulation: 74,000; Sun: 84,000

Howard Miller, Arts/Entertainment Editor
Rhonda Miskelley, Book Editor/Reviewer
Ray Garner, Business Editor
Phil Taylor, Education Editor
Mickey Ellis, Food Editor
Marion Accardi, Home Editor
Marion Accardi, Lifestyle/Feature Editor
Joe Duncan, News Editor
David Stephens, Science Editor
Martin Burkey, Science Writer
John Pruett, Sports Editor
Debra Storey, Travel Editor

Daily Mountain Eagle
1301 E 19th St
Jasper AL 35502-4970
205-221-2840; Fax: 205-221-2421
Circulation: 15,000; Sun: 15,000

Valley-Times News
220 N 12th St
Lanett AL 36863-1204
334-644-1101; Fax: 334-644-5587
Circulation: 11,000

Mobile Press-Register
304 Government St
PO Box 2488
Mobile AL 36630-0002
334-433-1551; Fax: 334-434-8662
Circulation: 117,000; Sun: 127,000

Carol Cain, Arts/Entertainment Editor
Shana Crabtree, Book Review Editor
David Tortortano, Business Editor
Gerald Hyche, City Editor
Brett Blackledge, Education Editor
Jennifer Zoghby, Health/Medical Editor
Kathy Jumper, Lifestyle Editor
Ronni Patriquin, Political Editor
Parker Holmes, Religion Editor
John Cameron, Sports Editor

Montgomery Advertiser-Journal
200 Washington Ave
PO Box 1000
Montgomery AL 36101-1000
334-262-1611; Fax: 334-261-1505
Circulation: 52,000; Sun: 86,000

Jim Earnhardt, Book Editor
David Rountree, Business Editor
Rick Harman, Entertainment Editor
Ginney Smith, Features Editor
M P Wilkerson, Fine Arts & Travel

Elizabeth Via-Brown, Home Editor
Jim Tharpe, Managing Editor
Reagan Ingram, Sports Editor

Opelika-Auburn News
3505 Pepperell Pky
Opelika AL 36801-6020
334-749-6271; Fax: 334-749-1228
Circulation: 14,000; Sun: 14,000

Daily Sentinel
701 Veterans Dr
Scottsboro AL 35768-2132
205-259-1020; Fax: 205-259-2709
Circulation: 7,000; Sun: 8,300

Selma-Times Journal
1018 Water Ave
Selma AL 36701-4617
334-875-2110; Fax: 334-872-4588
Circulation: 10,000; Sun: 10,000

Daily Home
Carol Pappas, Managing Editor
PO Box 977
Taladega AL 35161
205-362-1000; Fax: 205-249-4315
Circulation: 10,000

Troy Messenger
918 S Brundidge St
Troy AL 36081-3222
334-566-4270; Fax: 334-566-4281
Circulation: 3,400; Sun: 4,000

Crimson White
Univ of Alabama
923 University Blvd
Tuscaloosa AL 35401-7134
205-348-7839; Fax: 205-348-8036
Circulation: 15,000

Tuscaloosa News
2001 6th St
Tuscaloosa AL 35401-1724
205-345-0505; Fax: 205-349-0802
Circulation: 40,000; Sun: 41,000

Alaska

Anchorage Daily News
1001 Northway Dr (99508-2030)
PO Box 149001
Anchorage AK 99514-9001
907-257-4200; Fax: 907-258-2157
Circulation: 76,000; Sun: 100,000

Mike Dunham, Arts Editor
Bill White, Business Editor
Howard Weaver, Editor-in-Chief
Kin Severson, Entertainment Editor
Linda Sievers, Food Editor
Kathleen McCoy, Lifestyle Editor
Patrick Dougherty, Managing Editor
Rich Mauer, News Editor
Lew Freedman, Sports Editor
Leon Unruh, Travel Editor

Fairbanks Daily News-Miner
PO Box 710
Fairbanks AK 99707-0710
907-456-6661; Fax: 907-452-7917
Circulation: 19,000; Sun: 24,000

Juneau Empire
3100 Channel Dr
Juneau AK 99801-7814
907-586-3740; Fax: 907-586-9097
Circulation: 7,000; Sun: 8,000

Margaret Thomas, Arts/Entertainment Editor
Margaret Thomas, Book Editor/Reviewer
Suzanne Downing, Managing Editor
Richard Schmitz, Sports Editor

Peninsula Clarion
150 Trading Bay Dr
Kenai AK 99611-7716
907-283-7551; Fax: 907-283-3299
Circulation: 6,000

Ketchikan Daily News
501 Dock St
Ketchikan AK 99901-6411
907-225-3157; Fax: 907-225-1096
Circulation: 5,000; Sun: 6,000

Kodiak Daily Mirror
1419 Selig St
Kodiak AK 99615-6450
907-486-3227; Fax: 907-486-3088
Circulation: 4,000

Daily Sitka Sentinel
PO Box 7998
Sitka AK 99835-0799
907-747-3219; Fax: 907-747-8898
Circulation: 3,000

Arizona

Bisbee Daily Review
12 Main St
Bisbee AZ 85603
520-432-2231; Fax: 602-432-2356
Circulation: 3,000; Sat: 6,000

Mohave Valley Daily News
2435 Miracle Mile
Bullhead City AZ 86442-7311
520-763-2505; Fax: 520-763-7820
Circulation: 10,000; Sun: 10,000

Casa Grande Dispatch
200 W 2nd St
Casa Grande AZ 85222-4409
520-836-7461
Circulation: 9,000

Chandler Arizonan Tribune
25 S Arizona Pl #565
Chandler AZ 85225-5561
602-821-7474; Fax: 602-821-7480
Circulation: 8,700; Sun: 8,700

Daily Dispatch
530 11th St
Douglas AZ 85607-2014
520-364-3424; Fax: 520-364-6750
Circulation: 3,100; Sun: 3,100

Arizona Daily Sun
417 W Sante Fe
Flagstaff AZ 86001-5318)
520-774-4545; Fax: 520-773-1934
Circulation: 15,000; Sun: 17,000

Becky Blakenship, Book Editor
Randy Wilson, Business Editor

Mary Tolan, Education Editor
Leon Keith, Environmental Editor
Jan Stevens, Family Editor
Jan Stevens, Food/Garden Editor
Leon Keith, Health/Medical Editor
Jan Stevens, Lifestyle/Feature Editor
Mike Patrick, Managing Editor
Leon Keith, Science Editor

Kingman Daily Miner
3015 Stockton Hill Rd
Kingman AZ 86401-4162
520-753-6397; Fax: 520-753-6944
Circulation: 8,200; Sun: 8,500

Lake Havasu City Herald
2225 W Acoma Blvd
Lake Havasu City AZ 86403-2907
520-855-2197; Fax: 520-855-2637
Circulation: 7,500

Today's News Herald
1890 W Acoma Blvd
Lake Havasu City AZ 86403-2959
520-453-4237; Fax: 520-855-2637
Circulation: 8,400; Sun: 8,600

Gilbert Tribune
120 W 1st Ave
Mesa AZ 85210-1312
602-898-6500; Fax: 602-898-6362
Circulation: 4,000; Sun: 4,000

Mesa Tribune
120 W First Ave
PO Box 1547
Mesa AZ 85211-1547
602-898-6532; Fax: 602-898-6362
Circulation: 51,000; Sun: 52,000

Martha Reinke, Business Editor
Phil Boas, City Editor
Sheilah Wagner, Columnist, By Request (Food)
Liz Merritt, Features Editor
Dave Lumia, Sports Editor
Bruce Christian, TV Writer

Arizona Republic/Phoenix Gazette
120 E Van Buren (85004)
PO Box 1950
Phoenix AZ 85001
602-271-8000; Fax: 602-271-8933
Circulation: 385,000; Sun: 585 to 600,000

Linda Vachata, Arizona Home Editor
Tami Thornton, Asst Features Editor
Phil Hennessey, Asst Features Editor
Marian Frank, Business Editor
David Hoye, Computer Writer
Doug Carroll, Deputy Feature Editor
James Hill, Editorial Page Editor
Steve Yozwiak, Environmental Writer
Anne Spitza, Fashion Writer
Judy Walker, Food Writer
Thomas Ropp, Garden/Gen Assignment
Jodie Snyder, Health/Medical Writer
Pam Johnson, Managing Editor
Dave Wagner, Political Editor
Ben Winton, Religion Writer
Kathy Tulumello, Sports Editor
Jeff Dozbaba, Sunday Projects/Mg Editor

Prescott Courier
James I Garner, Editor
147 N Cortez (83601)
PO Box 312
Prescott AZ 86302-0312
602-445-3333; Fax: 602-445-4218
Circulation: 17,000; Sun: 19,000

Scottsdale Progress
7525 E Camelback Rd #100
Scottsdale AZ 85251-7206
602-941-2300; Fax: 602-970-2360
Circulation: 18,000; Sun: 18,500

Sierra Vista Herald
102 Fab Ave
Sierra Vista AZ 85635-1741
520-458-9440; Fax: 520-459-0120
Circulation: 11,000; Sun: 11,000

Daily News Sun
10102 Sante Fe Dr
Sun City AZ 85351-3106
602-977-8351; Fax: 602-876-3689
Circulation: 23,000

State Press
Arizona State Univ
PO Box 871502
Tempe AZ 85287-1502
602-965-7572; Fax: 602-965-8484
Circulation: 21,000

Tempe Daily News Tribune
51 W 3rd St #106
Tempe AZ 85281-2833
602-898-5680; Fax: 602-968-8030
Circulation: 11,000; Sun: 12,000

Arizona Daily Star
4850 S Park Ave
PO Box 26807
Tucson AZ 85726-6807
602-573-4220; Fax: 602-573-4144
Circulation: 90,000; Sun: 180,000

Debbie Kornmiller, Accent/Family Editor
Colette Bancroft, Arts/Entertainment Editor
Julia Portillo, Assistant Editor
B J Bartlett, Asst Accent Editor
Maria Parham, Book Editor
J C Martin, Book Reviewer
John Bolton, Business Editor
John McDermott, Chief News Editor
John Silva, City Editor
James Reel, Classical/Jazz Writer
Gene Armstrong, Dance & Pop Writer
Scot Skinner, Drama Writer
Steve Auslander, Editor
Jacquie Villa, Food Editor
Debbie Kornmiller, Lifestyle/Feature Editor
Bobbie Jo Buel, Managing Editor
Scot Skinner, Movie Editor
Tom Foust, Outdoors Editor
Tom Turner, Religion Writer
Jim Erickson, Science Writer
Mark Stewart, Sports Editor
Jacquie Villa, Travel Editor
Frank Cermak, TV Listings Coordinator

Arizona Daily Wildcat
University of Arizona
Student Union, Room 5
Tucson AZ 85721-0001
E-mail: wcnews@ccit.arizona.edu
Circulation: 20,000

Daily Territorial
Cheri Cross, Editor
1 W Orange Grove
Tucson AZ 85704
602-297-1107; Fax: 602-297-6253
Circulation: 1,000

Tucson Citizen
4850 S Park Ave
PO Box 26767
Tucson AZ 85726-6767
602-573-4613; Fax: 602-573-4632
Circulation: 52,000

Julie Szekeley, Book Editor/Reviewer
Jennifer Boice, Business Editor
James Wyckoff, City Editor
Julie Szekeley, Features Editor
Angela Hagen, Food Editor
Cara McClain, Health Editor
Julie Szekeley, Lifestyle Editor
Richardo Pimenetel, Managing Editor
Bill Quimby, Outdoors Editor
Dave Pittman, Political Editor
Larry Copenhaver, Schools Editor
Dan Sorenson, Science Editor
Peter Madrid, Sports Editor

Yuma Daily Sun
2055 Arizona Ave
Yuma AZ 85364-6549
520-783-3333; Fax: 520-343-1009
Circulation: 30,000; Sun: 32,000

Arkansas

Daily Siftings Herald
205 S 26th St
Arkadelphia AR 71923-5423
501-246-5525; Fax: 501-246-6556
Circulation: 4,000

Batesville Guard
258 W Main
Batesville AR 72501-6711
501-793-2383; Fax: 501-793-9268
Circulation: 9,000

Benton County Daily Record
904 NW A St
Bentonville AR 72712-4735
501-271-3700; Fax: 501-273-7777
Circulation: 8,000

Benton Courier
1 Courier Pl
Bentonville AR 72015
501-778-8228; Fax: 501-776-1230
Circulation: 9,000

Blytheville Courier News
PO Box 1108
Blytheville AR 72315-1108
501-763-4461; Fax: 501-763-6874
Circulation: 6,000

Camden News
113 Madison Ave
Camden AR 71701
501-836-8192; Fax: 501-837-1414
Circulation: 5,000

Log Cabin Democrat
1058 Front St
Conway AR 72032-4356
501-327-6621; Fax: 501-327-6787
Circulation: 9,000

De Queen Daily Citizen
PO Box 1000
De Queen AR 71832-1000
501-642-2111; Fax: 501-642-3138
Circulation: 2,000

El Dorado News-Times
111 N Madison
El Dorado AR 71730-6124
501-862-6611; Fax: 501-862-2421
Circulation: 11,000

Northwest Arkansas Times
PO Drawer D
Fayetteville AR 72702-1758
501-442-1777; Fax: 501-442-1714
Circulation: 17,000

Gwen Rule, Business Editor
Amanda Fincher, Education Editor
Melissa Blouin, Family/Food/Garden
Melissa Blouin, Lifestyle/Feature Editor
Mike Masterson, Main Editor
Ritta Martin, Managing Editor
Dudley Dawson, Sports Editor

Times-Herald
222 N Izard St
Forrest City AR 72335-3324
501-633-3130; Fax: 501-633-0599
Circulation: 4,000

Southwest Times Record
920 Rogers Ave (72901)
PO Box 1359
Fort Smith AR 72902-1359
501-785-7757; Fax: 501-784-0413
Circulation: 41,000; Sun: 45,689

Jack Mosely, Editor
Nancy Steel, Lifestyle/Feature Editor
Grant Tolley, Sports Editor

Harrison Daily Times
111 W Rush St
Harrison AR 72601-4218
501-741-2325; Fax: 501-741-5632
Circulation: 12,000

Daily World
417 York St
Helena AR 72342-3232
501-338-9181; Fax: 501-338-9184
Circulation: 5,000

Hope Star
W 3rd & Grady Sts
Hope AR 71801
501-777-8841; Fax: 501-777-3311
Circulation: 4,000

Sentinel Record
300 Spring St
Ht Spr Nat'l Park AR 71901-4148
501-623-7711; Fax: 501-623-2984
Circulation: 18,000

Jacksonville Patriot
1108-B W Main
Jacksonville AR 72076-4304
501-982-6506; Fax: 502-985-2054
Circulation: 2,000

Jonesboro Sun
518 Carson St
Jonesboro AR 72401-3128
501-935-5525; Fax: 501-935-5823
Circulation: 28,000

Arkansas Democrat-Gazette
Capitol Ave and Scott St
PO Box 2221
Little Rock AR 72203-2221
501-378-3400; Fax: 501-372-3908
Circulation: 150,000

Ed Gray, Book Editor
Christi Phelps, Business Editor
Ellis Widner, Entertainment Editor
Frank Fellone, Features Editor
Irene Wassell, Food Editor
Bob Lutgen, Managing Editor
Karen McAllister, Medical Editor
Rex Nelson, Political Editor
Gaynell Terrell, Science Editor
Libby Smith, Travel Editor

Daily Record
PO Box 1106
Little Rock AR 72203-1106
501-374-5103; Fax: 501-868-4844
Circulation: 2,000

Banner-News
134 S Washington
Magnolia AR 71753-3523
501-234-5130; Fax: 501-234-2551
Circulation: 5,000

Malvern Daily Record
219 Locust St
Malvern AR 72104-3721
501-337-7523; Fax: 501-337-1226
Circulation: 6,000

Mena Star
501-507 Mena St
Mena AR 71953-3337
501-394-1900; Fax: 501-394-1908
Circulation: 3,000

Baxter Bulletin
16 W 6th St
Mountain Home AR 72653-3508
501-425-3133; Fax: 501-425-5091
Circulation: 9,000

Daily News
PO Box 1087
Mountain Home AR 72653-1087
501-425-6301; Fax: 501-424-4488
Circulation: 2,000

Newport Daily Independent
2408 Hwy 67 N
Newport AR 72112-2324
501-523-5855; Fax: 501-523-6540
Circulation: 3,000

Paragould Daily Press
Hwy 49 at Hunt St
Paragould AR 72451
501-239-8562; Fax: 501-239-8565
Circulation: 5,000

Pine Bluff Commercial
300 Beach St
Pine Bluff AR 71601-4039
501-534-3400; Fax: 501-543-1455
Circulation: 22,000

Courier-Democrat
201 E 2nd St
Russellville AR 72801-5102
501-968-5252; Fax: 501-968-4037
Circulation: 11,000

Daily Citizen
3000 E Race Ave
Searcy AR 72143-4808
501-268-8621; Fax: 501-268-6277
Circulation: 6,000

Morning News Northwest Arkansas
2560 N Lowell Rd
Springdale AR 72764-1818
501-751-6200; Fax: 501-751-6209
Circulation: 32,000

Stuttgart Daily Leader
111 W 6th St
Stuttgart AR 72160-4243
501-673-8533; Fax: 501-673-3671
Circulation: 5,000

Evening Times
111 E Bond St
West Memphis AR 72301-3107
501-735-1010; Fax: 501-735-1020
Circulation: 9,000

California

Alameda Times Star
Thomas Tuttle, Editor
1516 Oak St
Alameda CA 94501-2947
510-293-2370; Fax: 510-293-2381
Circulation: 10,000; Sun: 10,000

Ledger/Dispatch
1650 Cavallo Rd (94509)
PO Box 2299
Antioch CA 94531-2299
510-757-2525; Fax: 510-706-2305
Circulation: 26,000; Sun: 26,000

Mark Cohen, Business Editor
Ken Maryanski, City Editor
Holly Hacker, Education Editor
Judy Prieve, Lifestyle/Book/Food Editor
Bob Goll, Managing Editor
Frank Reichert, News Editor
Kerry Young, Sports Editor

Auburn Journal
1030 High St
Auburn CA 95603-4707
916-885-5656; Fax: 916-885-4902
Circulation: 15,000

Bakersfield Californian
1707 I St
PO Bin 440
Bakersfield CA 93302-0440
805-395-7500; Fax: 805-395-7519
Circulation: 83,000; Sun: 91,000

Mike Stepanovich, Business Editor
Denise Zapata, Higher Education Editor
Joan Swenson, Home Editor
Pat Nolan, Lifestyle/Feature Editor
Roberta Westerfield, Lower Education Editor
Mike Jenner, Managing Editor
Tamara Welch, Medical/Science Editor

Alex Edillor, News Editor
Scott Forter, Political Editor
Ed King, Religion Editor
John Millman, Sports Editor

Record Gazette
218 N Murray
Banning CA 92220-5512
909-849-4586; Fax: 909-849-2437
Circulation: 17,000

Desert Dispatch
130 Coolwater Ln
Barstow CA 92311-3222
619-256-2257; Fax: 619-256-0685
Circulation: 7,000

Benicia Herald
820 1st St
Benicia CA 94510-3216
707-745-0733; Fax: 707-557-6380
Circulation: 10,000

Beverly Hills Today
421 S Beverly Dr 5th Fl
Beverly Hills CA 90212-4400
310-553-2111; Fax: 310-772-0082
Circulation: 25,000

Camarillo Star
1000 Avenida Acaso
Camarillo CA 93012-8712
805-987-5001; Fax: 805-987-5655
Circulation: 12,000

Chico Enterprise-Record
400 East Park Ave
PO Box 9
Chico CA 95927
916-891-1234; Fax: 916-342-3617
Circulation: 30,000; Sun: 32,0-00

Gary Kupp, Book Editor
Ray Kirk, City Editor
Steve Sconover, Home/Garden Editor
Sandra Ashworth, Lifestyle/Feature Editor
Jack Winning, Managing Editor
Skip Reager, Sports Editor

Daily Pilot
330 W Bay St
PO Box 1560
Costa Mesa CA 92627
714-642-4321; Fax: 714-631-5902
Circulation: 40,000

Bill Lobdell, Editor-in-Chief
Matt Coker, Entertainment Editor
Joyce Sherer, Food Editor
Matt Coker, Lifestyle/Feature Editor
Steve Marble, Managing Editor
Roger Carlson, Sports Editor

Los Angeles Times-Orange County
Marty Baron, Editor
1375 Sunflower Ave
Costa Mesa CA 92626
714-966-5824; Fax: 714-966-5663
Circulation: 200,000

San Gabriel Valley Daily Tribune
PO Box 1259
Covina CA 91722-0259
818-962-8811; Fax: 818-962-8849
Circulation: 122,000; Sun: 122,000

Cathy Porrelli, Arts/Entertainment Editor
Susan Gill, Book Editor

Tania Soussan, Business Editor
Robert Frank, Co-City Editor
Julie Look, Family/Food, Lifestyle/Feature Editor
Robert Frank, Political Editor
Sam Pollak, Sports Editor

Triplicate
312 H St
Crescent City CA 95531-4018
707-464-2141; Fax: 707-464-5102
Circulation: 6,000

California Aggie
Univ of California-Davis
25 Lower Freeborn
Davis CA 95616
916-752-0208; Fax: 916-752-0355
E-mail: aggia@ucdavis.edu
Circulation: 13,000

Davis Enterprise
315 G St
PO Box 1470
Davis CA 95617
916-756-0800; Fax: 916-756-1668
Circulation: 11,000

Elisabeth Sherwin, Book Reviewer
Gene Fynes, Lifestyle/Feature Editor
Debbie Davis, Managing Editor
Marek Warszawski, Sports Editor

El Cajon Daily Californian
PO Box 1565
El Cajon CA 92022-1565
619-442-4404; Fax: 619-447-6165
Circulation: 25,000

Karen Pearlman, Business Editor
Della Elliott, City Editor
Lori Arnold, Lifestyle/Feature Editor
Della Elliott, Managing Editor
Bill Dickens, Sports Editor

Imperial Valley Press
205 N 8th St
PO Box 2770
El Centro CA 92244
619-352-2211; Fax: 619-353-3003
Circulation: 19,000

Alec Rosenberg, Business Editor
Peggy Dale, Lifesytle/Feature Editor
Murray Anderson, Sports Editor

North County Times
207 E Pennsylvania Ave
Escondido CA 92025
619-745-6611; Fax: 619-745-3769
Circulation: 90,000; Sun: 150,000

Laura Groch, Book Editor
Kathy Day, Business Editor
Ann Zivolsky, Entertainment Editor
Laura Groch, Food Editor
Deniene Husted, Higher Education Editor
Laura Groch, Lifestyle/Feature Editor
Wayne Halberg, Local News Editor
Andrea Moss, Lower Education Editor
Rusty Harris, Managing Editor
Chris Moran, Political Editor
Debbie Rosen, Religion Editor
Gary Hyvonen, Sports Editor
Tom Spain, Sunday Editor
Debbie Rosen, Travel Editor

Times-Standard
PO Box 3580
Eureka CA 95502
707-441-0500; Fax: 707-441-0501
Circulation: 23,000; Sun: 25,000

Peter Allard, City Editor
Kathy Dillon, Lifestyle/Feature Editor
Rex Wilson, Managing Editor
Ted Silliampaa, Sports Editor

Fairfield Daily Republic
1250 Texas St
PO Box 47
Fairfield CA 94533
707-425-4646; Fax: 707-425-5924
Circulation: 20,000; Sun: 22,000

Matt Peiken, Arts/Entertainment Editor
Ian Thompson, Book Reviewer
Doug Robson, Business Editor
Kathy Lecluse, City Editor
Judith Faught, Education Editor
Amy Maginnis, Family Editor
Patty Amador, Garden Editor
Kathy Lecluse, Lifestyle/Feature Editor
Bill Buchanan, Managing Editor
Patty Amador, Religion Editor
Brad Stanhope, Sports Editor
Matt Peiken, Travel Editor

Fremont Argus
Jack Lyness, Managing Editor
39737 Paseo Padre
Fremont CA 94538
510-661-2600; Fax: 510-353-7029
Circulation: 33,000

Daily Collegian
California State Univ-Fresno
Keats Campus Bldg
Fresno CA 93701
209-278-2486; Fax: 209-278-2679
Circulation: 3,000

Fresno Bee
1626 E St
Fresno CA 93786-0001
209-441-6111; Fax: 209-441-6436
Circulation: 152,000; Sun: 190,912

Tom Becker, Arts/Entertainment Editor
Cathy Clarey, Book Editor/Reviewer
Irwin Spizer, Business Editor
Cindy Fontana, Education Editor
Gail Marshall, Food Editor
Jerry Bier, Health/Medical Editor
Gail Marshall, Lifestyle/Feature Editor
George Baker, Managing Editor
Jolene Krawczak, Metro Editor
Jim Boren, Political Editor
John Taylor, Religion Editor
Rick Vacek, Sports Editor

Daily Titan
California State Univ-Fullerton
800 North State College Blvd
Fullerton CA 92631-3547
714-773-3373; Fax: 714-773-2707
Circulation: 6,000

Dispatch
6400 Monterey St
Gilroy CA 95020-6628
408-842-6400; Fax: 408-842-7105
Circulation: 6,000

Asbarez Armenian Daily Newspaper
419 W Colorado St
Glendale CA 91204-1548
818-500-9363; Fax: 818-956-0503
Circulation: 8,000

Glendale News-Press Leader
425 W Broadway #300
Glendale CA 91204-1269
818-241-4141; Fax: 818-241-1975
Circulation: 35,000

Stacy Turner, Business Editor
David Heitz, City News Editor
Bill Lobdell, Exec/Managing Editor
Joyce Rudolph, Features/Travel Editor
David Sweet, Sports Editor

Grass Valley Union
11464 Sutton Way
Grass Valley CA 95945
916-273-9561; Fax: 916-273-1854
Circulation: 16,000

Paul Harrar, Arts/Entertainment Editor
Paul Harrar, Book Editor
Mike Marois, Business Editor
Shawn Neidorf, Education Editor
Heather McDonald, Food Editor
Paul Shigley, Health/Medical Editor
Heather McDonald, Lifestyle/Feature Editor
John Seelmeyer, Managing Editor
Janet Lee, Religion Editor
Chuck Smock, Sports Editor

Hanford Sentinel
300 W 6th St
Hanford CA 93230-4518
209-582-0471; Fax: 209-582-8631
Circulation: 14,000

Hayward Daily Review
Mario Dianda, Managing Editor
116 W Winton Ave
PO Box 5050
Hayward CA 94544
510-783-6111; Fax: 510-293-2490
Circulation: 45,000; Sun: 50,000

Free Lance
350 6th St
Hollister CA 95023-3835
408-637-5566; Fax: 408-637-4104
Circulation: 4,000

Lake County Record-Bee
2150 S Main
Lakeport CA 95453-5620
707-263-5636; Fax: 707-263-0600
Circulation: 9,000

Lodi News-Sentinel
125 N Church St
Lodi CA 95240-2102
209-369-2761; Fax: 209-369-1084
Circulation: 18,000

Lompoc Record
115 North H St
Lompoc CA 93436-6818
805-736-2313; Fax: 805-736-5654
Circulation: 9,000

Daily Forty-Niner
Calif State Univ-Long Beach
1250 Bellflower Blvd
Long Beach CA 90840-0006
310-985-8001; Fax: 310-985-1740
E-mail: gsparks@csulb.edu
Circulation: 10,000

Press-Telegram
604 Pine Ave
Long Beach CA 90844-0003
310-435-1161; Fax: 310-437-7892
Circulation: 123,000; Sun: 139,852

Stephanie Goodman, Arts/Entertainment
    Editor
Tim Grobty, Book Editor
Jim Robertson, Business Editor
Andy Alderett, Business Editor
Dan DeVise, Education Editor
Jim Robertson, Enterprise Editor
Neil Strassman, Environmental Editor
Debbie Arrington, Food Editor
Susan Jacobs, Health/Medical Editor
Susan Jacobs, Lifestyle/Feature Editor
Rich Archbold, Managing Editor
Andy Rows, News Editor
Joy Thompson, Religion Editor
Jim McCormick, Sports Editor
Susan Jacobs, Travel Editor

Central Daily
Mid-American Publishing Corp
690 Wilshire Pl
Los Angeles CA 90005-3980
213-368-2500; Fax: 213-384-9223
Circulation: 50,000

Daily Bruin
University of California-Los Angeles
225 Kerckhoff
308 Westwood Plaza
Los Angeles Ca 90024-8311
310-825-2787; Fax: 310-206-0528
Circulation: 22,000

Daily Commerce
915 E 1st St
Los Angeles CA 90012-4050
213-229-5300; Fax: 213-625-0945
Circulation: 6,000

Daily Trojan
University of Southern California
STU 404
Los Angeles CA 90089-0001
213-740-2707; Fax: 213-740-5701
Circulation: 12,000

Daily Variety
5700 Wilshire Blvd #120
Los Angeles CA 90036-3659
213-857-6600; Fax: 213-857-0494
Circulation: 25,000

Tim Grey, Book Reviewer
Dan Cox, Business Editor
Todd White, Co-Asst Managing Editor
Tim Grey, Co-Asst Managing Editor
Steve West, Executive Editor
Jonathon Taylor, Managing Editor
Kinsey Lowe, News Editor
Brian Lowry, Sports/TV Editor
Tim Grey, Travel Editor

Hollywood Reporter
5055 Wilshire 6th Fl
Los Angeles CA 90036-6100
213-525-2000; Fax: 213-525-2777
Circulation: 25,000

Jeff Daniels, Business Editor
Howard Burns, Managing Editor

Investor's Business Daily
The New America
12655 Beatrice St
Los Angeles CA 90066
310-448-6000; Fax: 310-577-7350
Circulation: 180,000

Susan Warfel, Senior Editor
Anne Rackham, Business Editor
Tim Deady, Computer/Science Editor
Benjamin Cole, Finance
Ron Shinkman, Health Editor
Marty Ahern, Managing Editor
Doug Young, News Editor

La Opinion
411 W 5th St
Los Angeles CA 90013-1000
213-622-8332; Fax: 213-896-2177
Circulation: 85,000

Los Angeles Daily Journal
915 E 1st St
Los Angeles CA 90012
213-229-5300; Fax: 213-625-0945
Circulation: 40,000

Ken Rutman, Book Editor
Steve Trousdale, Managing Editor

Los Angeles Times
Times Mirror Square
Los Angeles CA 90053
213-237-5000; Fax: 213-237-7190
Circulation: 1,058,000; Sun circ: 1,457,853

Robert Magnuson, Business Editor
Mark Saylor, CA Political Editor
Tim Reiterman, Deputy Metro Editor
Thomas Plate, Editorial Page Editor
Elaine Woo, Educational Editor
John Lindsay, Executive Editor; Calendar
    Section
Mary Rourke, Fashion Editor
Claudia Luther, Feature Projects Editor
Lauri Ochoa, Food Editor
Alice Short, Lifestyles/View Editor
George Coltliar, Managing Editor
Kelly Scott, Mg Entertainment Editor
Claudia Eller, Movie Editor
Norman C Miller, National Editor
Bob Chamberlin, Photo Editor
Richard Barnes, Real Estate Editor
Elaine Woo, Religion Editor
Joel Greenberg, Science/Medical Editor
Janice Mall, Society News Editor
Bill Dwyre, Sports Editor
Lee Margulies, Television Editor
Leslie Ward, Travel Editor
Barbara Saltzman, TV Times Editor

Metropolitan News-Enterprise
210 S Spring St
Los Angeles CA 90012-3710
213-628-4384; Fax: 213-687-3886
Circulation: 3,000

Nihon Keizai Shimbun
American Satellite Edition
725 S Figueroa St
Los Angeles CA 90017-5524
213-955-7470; Fax: 213-955-7479
Circulation: 16,000

Rafu Shimpo
259 S Los Angeles St
Los Angeles CA 90012-3704
213-629-2231; Fax: 213-687-0737
Circulation: 24,000

Madera Tribune
100 E 7th St
Madera CA 93638-3742
209-674-2424; Fax: 209-673-6526
Circulation: 9,000

Manteca Bulletin
531 E Yosemite
Manteca CA 95336-5806
209-239-3531; Fax: 209-239-1801
Circulation: 7,000

Appeal-Democrat
1530 Ellis Lake Dr
Marysville CA 95901-4258
916-741-2345; Fax: 916-741-0140
Circulation: 24,000; Sun: 25,000

Wendy Weitzel, Arts/Entertainment/Food
Laura Nicholson, Health/Medical Editor
Laura Nicholson, Lifestyle/Feature Editor
Julie Shirley, Managing Editor
Brad Hall, Sports Editor
Wendy Weitzel, Travel Editor

Merced Sun Star
3033 North G St
PO Box 739
Merced CA 95341-0739
209-722-1511; Fax: 209-384-2226
Circulation: 23,000

Deborah Salonen, Arts/Entertainment
    Editor
Pat Mc Nally, Business Editor
Barbara Hale, Family, Food,
    Health/Medical. Lifestyle/Feature,
    Religion, Travel Editor
Mike Conway, Garden Editor
Norman Martin, Managing Editor
Pat Mc Nally, Political Editor
Vern Williams, Sports Editor

Modesto Bee
1325 H St
PO Box 3928
Modesto CA 95352-3928
209-578-2000; Fax: 209-578-2207
Circulation: 80,000; Sun: 92,000

Judy Sly, Book Editor
Becky Bisbee, Business Editor
Alvie Lindsay, City Desk
Joanne Sbranti, Education Editor
Jan Bannerman, Food Editor
Donna Berch, Health/Medical Editor
Judy Sly, Lifestyle/Feature Editor
Mark Vasche, Managing Editor
Dave Hill, Political Editor
Dennis Roberts, Religion Editor
Dave Hill, Science Editor
Dave Lyghtle, Sports Editor
Walt Williams, Travel Editor
Larry McSwain, Viewpoint Editor

Dodge Construction News Green Sheet
1333 S Mayflower Ave 3rd Fl
Monrovia CA 91016-4066
818-932-6161; Fax: 818-932-6163
Circulation: 3,000

Monterey County Herald
PO Box 271
Monterey CA 93942
408-372-3311; Fax: 408-372-8401
Circulation: 35,000; Sun: 40,000

Fred Hernandez, Book Editor
Alex Hulanicki, Business Editor
Deborah Petit, City Editor
Eve Britton, Education Editor
Roslyn White, Feature Editor
Barbara Taylor, Food Editor
Walter Dawson, Managing Editor
Donald Degn, Religion Editor
Tom Tebbs, Sports Editor

Moorpark Star
530 Moorpark Ave
Moorpark CA 93021-1861
805-523-7440; Fax: 805-523-7816
Circulation: 6,000

Napa Valley Register
1615 Second St
PO Box 150
Napa CA 94559
707-226-3711; Fax: 707-224-3963
Circulation: 22,000

Bruce Baird, Arts/Entertainment Editor
Kevin Courtney, Business Editor
Marilee Talley, City Editor
Doug Wilks, Computer Editor
Bruce Baird, Food Editor
Kevin Courtney, Health/Medical Editor
Bruce Baird, Lifestyle/Feature Editor
Frank Gordon, News Editor
Marilee Talley, Political Editor
Marty James, Sports Editor
Kim Beltran, Travel Editor

Daily Sundial
California State Univ
18111 Nordhoff St
Northridge CA 91330-8258
818-885-2998; Fax: 818-885-3638
Circulation: 8,000

Marin Independent Journal
150 Alameda del Prado
PO Box 6150
Novato CA 94948-6150
415-883-8600; Fax: 415-883-5458
Circulation: 40,000; Sun: 45,000

Rebecca Larsen, Book, Family, Food, Garden Editor
Sheryl Jean, Business Editor
Janet Korenblum, Computer/Technology Editor
Pamela Moreland, Lifestyle Editor
Nells Johnson, Local News Editor
Brad Breithaupp, Political Editor
Ken Sain, Sports Editor
Doug Wilks, Topics Editor

Inner-City Express
Tom Barkley, Editor
171 12th St #203
Oakland CA 94607
510-465-3121; Fax: 510-465-1576
Circulation: 2,000

Oakland Tribune
66 Jack London Sq
PO Box 28884
Oakland CA 94604
510-208-6300; Fax: 510-208-6477
Circulation: 90,000; Sun circ 120,000

Sharyn Betz, Arts Editor
Robert Taylor, Book Review Editor
David Tong, Business Editor
Matt Richtel, Computer Editor
Sharyn Betz, Consumer Interests Editor
Tim Graham, Editor
Sharyn Betz, Entertainment Editor
Dennis Oliver, Environmental Editor
Sharyn Betz, Family Editor
Sharyn Betz, Fashion Editor
Sharyn Betz, Features Editor
Matt Richtel, Financial Editor
Paula Hamilton, Food Editor
Bari Brenner, Health Editor
Bari Brenner, Home/Garden Editor
Sharyn Betz, Lifestyle Editor
Brian Aronstam, Managing Editor
Rachelle Kanigel, Medical Editor
Cathy Schutz, Metro Editor
Sharyn Betz, Movie Editor
Bill Friar, Music Editor
Brian Aranstam, National Editor
Cathy Schutz, News Editor
Sharyn Betz, Outdoor Editor
Ron Reisterer, Photo Editor
Diana Williams, Political Editor
David Tong, Real Estate Editor
Kathryn Pfrommer, Religion Editor
Cecily Burt, Science Editor
Don Coulter, Sports Editor
Bari Brenner, Travel Editor
Sharyn Betz, Women's Editor

Inland Valley Daily Bulletin
PO Box 4000
Ontario CA 91761
909-987-6397
Circulation: 100,000; Sunday 80,000

Bryan Soergel, Arts/Entertainment Editor
Rob Wagner, Book Editor
Randy Drummer, Business Editor
Rob Wagner, Education Editor
Rob Wagner, Food Editor
Rob Wagner, Lifestyle/Feature Editor
Rob Wagner, Managing Editor/News
David Wert, Political Editor
Louis Brewster, Sports Editor
Rob Wagner, Travel Editor

Oroville Mercury Register
2081 2nd St
Oroville CA 95965-3413
916-533-3131; Fax: 916-533-3127
Circulation: 9,000

Oxnard Star
804 N Ventura Rd
Oxnard CA 93030-4400
805-981-9004; Fax: 805-981-9905
Circulation: 19,000

Palm Springs Desert Sun
750 N Gene Autry Trail (92262)
PO Box 2734
Palm Springs CA 92263
619-322-8889; Fax: 619-778-4654
Circulation: 59,000

Brian Bean, City Desk Editor
Jan Fraser, Business Editor
Bruce Fessier, Entertainment Editor

Paul Profeta, Food Editor
Holly Rizzo, Lifestyle/Feature Editor
Ray Griffiths, Managing Editor
John Husar, Real Estate Editor
Tom Elliott, Sports Editor

Antelope Valley Press
PO Box 880
Palmdale CA 93590
805-273-2700; Fax: 805-947-4870
Circulation: 62,000

Steve Hendrickson, Arts Editor
Todd Weiss, Book Editor
Anne Aldrich, Business Editor
Mike Pottage, City Editor
Larry Grooms, Editor-in-Chief
Rich Breault, Features Editor
Darren Leon, Food Editor
Sarah Shanklin, Health/Medical Editor
Darlene Phillips, Lifestyle Editor
Vern Lawson, Managing Editor
Darren Jones, Sports Editor
Linda Lee, Travel Editor

Pasadena Star-News
525 E Colorado Blvd
Pasadena CA 91109
818-578-6300; Fax: 818-856-2758
Circulation: 115,000; Sun: 93,000

Cathie Lou Porrelli, Arts/Entertainment Editor
Susan Gill, Book Editor
Ali Sar, Business Editor
Tania Soussan, Computers
Naomi Bradley, Education Editor
Steve Scauzillo, Environmental Editor
Catherine Gaugh, Family Editor
Richard Swearinger, Food Editor
Dorothy Reinhold, Garden Editor
Tania Soussan, Health/Medical Editor
Lisa Cooke, Lifestyle/Feature Editor
Lawrence Wilson, Managing Editor
Danny Pollock, News and City Editor
Patt Diroll, People/Society Editor
Ludi Reid, Religion Editor
Tania Soussan, Science Editor
Sam Pollak, Sports Editor
Richard Irwin, Travel Editor

Daily Press
1050 Park St
Paso Robles CA 93446-2519
805-238-0330; Fax: 805-238-6504
Circulation: 5,000

Mountain Democrat
PO Box 1088
Placerville CA 95667
916-622-1255; Fax: 916-622-7894
Circulation: 14,000; Published Mon, Wed, Thur, and Fri

Diana Lambert, Arts/Entertainment Editor
Diana Lambert, Book Editor
Michele Dawson, Business Editor
Diana Lambert, Lifestyle/Feature Editor
Mike Raffety, Main Editor
Leslie Vandever, Religion Editor
Pete Webster, Sports Editor

Tri-Valley Herald
Tim Hunt, Managing Editor
4770 Willow Rd
Pleasanton CA 94588-2762
510-734-8600; Fax: 510-416-4850
Circulation: 36,000

Valley Times
127 Spring St
PO Box 607
Pleasanton CA 94566-6623
510-462-4160; Fax: 510-847-2189
Circulation: 40,000; Sun: 45,000

Linda Davis, Book Editor
Mara DerHovanesian, Business Editor
Paul Hefner, City Editor
John Van Landinghan, Education Editor
Karen Magnuson, Managing Editor
David Goll, Religion Editor
Peter Weiss, Science Editor
Dan Wood, Sports Editor

Recorder
115 E Oak Ave
Porterville CA 93257-3807
209-784-5000; Fax: 209-784-1689
Circulation: 12,000

Daily News
545 Diamond Ave
Red Bluff CA 96080-4302
916-527-2153; Fax: 916-527-3719
Circulation: 9,000

Record-Searchlight
PO Box 492397
Redding CA 96049-2397
916-243-2424; Fax: 916-225-8236
Circulation: 40,000; Sun: 42,000

John Crow, Arts/Entertainment Editor
Laura Christman, Book Editor
George Winchip, Business Editor
Betty Lease, Lifestyle/Feature Editor
Tom King, Managing Editor
Jim Schultz, Political Editor
David Little, Sports Editor

Redlands Daily Facts
700 Brookside Ave
Redlands CA 92373-5102
909-793-3221; Fax: 909-793-9588
Circulation: 9,000

Daily Construction Service
2625 Manhatten Beach Blvd #110
Redondo Beach CA 90278-1604
310-643-1263; Fax: 310-643-1270
Circulation: 1,000

West County Times
4301 Lakeside Dr
Richmond CA 94606-5281
510-758-8400; Fax: 510-262-2776
Circulation: 34,000; Sun: 35,000

Daily Independent
224 E Ridgecrest Blvd
Ridgecrest CA 93555-3975
619-375-4481; Fax: 619-375-4880
Circulation: 9,000

Riverside Press Enterprise
3512 14th St
PO Box 792
Riverside CA 92502
909-684-1200; Fax: 909-782-7572
Circulation: 161,000; Sun: 171,000

Rich Deatley, Arts Editor
Joel Blain, Book Editor
Andy McCue, Business Editor
Norman Bell, City Editor
Mike Quinn, Computer Editor
Elaine Regus, Education Editor
Gary Polakovic, Environmental Editor
Judith Graffam, Lifestyle/Feature Editor
Mel Opotowsky, Managing Editor
Jack Holley, News Editor
Dave Rush, Political Editor
Cindy Friday, Religion Editor
Mike Schwartz, Science Editor
John Garret, Sports Editor
Bob Hirt, Travel Editor

Daily Recorder
1115 H St
Sacramento CA 95814-2811
916-444-2355; Fax: 916-444-0636
Circulation: 2,000

Sacramento Bee
2100 Q St
PO Box 15779
Sacramento CA 95852
916-321-1000; Fax: 916-321-1109
Circulation: 281,000; Sunday 353,953

Bruce Dancis, Arts/Entertainment Editor
Bruce Dancis, Book Editor
Terry Dvorak, California Life Editor
Jack Sirard, Exec Business Editor
Mike Dunne, Food Editor
Patricia Beach Smith, Home Furnishing Editor
Scott Lebar, Lifestyle Editor
Carlos Alcia, Lower Education Editor
Rick Rodriguez, Managing Editor
Marjorie Lunstrom, Metro Editor
John Jacobs, Political Editor
Paul Clegg, Religion Editor
Scott Lebar, Scene Editor
Steve Blust, Sports Editor
Janet Fullwood, Travel Editor

The Californian
123 W Alisal St
PO Box 81091
Salinas CA 93912
408-424-2221; Fax: 408-754-4293
Circulation: 25,000

Sylvia Ulloa, Arts/Lifestyle Editor
Brandy Tuzon, Business Editor
Larry Parsons, City/Book Editor
Brad Wong, Education Editor
Tom Leyde, Health/Medical Editor
Cindy McCurry-Ross, Managing Editor
Jim Albanese, Religion Editor
Richard Martin, Sports Editor

San Bernardino Sun
399 N D St
San Bernardino CA 92401
909-889-9666; Fax: 909-885-8741
Circulation: 94,000; Sun: 100,000

Mark Muckensuss, Arts Editor
Marie DeVarenne, Book Editor
Jim Steinberg, Business Editor
Beth Szymkowski, Education Editor
Marie Vasari, Food Editor
Owen Sherran, Garden Editor
Gigi Hanna, Health/Medical Editor
Catherine Hamm, Managing Editor
Carla Wheeler, Religion Editor
Paul Oberjuege, Sports Editor
John Weeks, Travel Editor

Daily Sun Post News
95 Avenida Del Mar
San Clemente CA 92672-4961
714-492-5121; Fax: 714-492-0401
Circulation: 7,000

Daily Aztec
San Diego State Univ
Prof Studies/Arts Bldg Rm 361
San Diego CA 92182-0763
619-594-6975; Fax: 619-594-7277
Circulation: 19,000

San Diego Daily Transcript
PO Box 85469
San Diego CA 92186
619-232-4381; Fax: 619-236-8126
Circulation: 10,000

John Willet, Arts/Education Editor
Gary Shaw, Editor
Martin Krurming, Editor-in-Chief
Andrew Kleske, Environmental Editor
Lynn Carrier, Family/Food/Garden Editor
Susan Dembrowski, Health/Medical Editor

San Diego Union-Tribune
350 Camino de la Reina (92108)
PO Box 191
San Diego CA 92112-4106
619-293-1896
Circulation: 385,000

Marilyn Salisbury, Abilities Columnist
Robert Pincus, Art Critic
Ann Jarmusch, Art/Architecture Editor
Lee Grant, Arts/Entertainment Editor
Mary Hellman, Asst Homes Editor
Craig Rose, Bio-Tech Writer
Arthur Salm, Books Editor
Bruce Bigelow, Bus News/Computer Tech
Don Freeman, Columnist
Dennis Mammana, Columnist, Stargazers / Fleet Space Theater
Jack Williams, Columnist, Keeping Fit Column
Robert Wade, Columnist, Spadework Column
Jay Hansen, Condominiums Columnist
Suzanne Choney, Currents Editor
Valerie Scher, Drama/Dance Critic
Anne Marie Welsh, Drama/Dance Critic
Steve Schmidt, Education Writer
Steve LaRue, Environmental Writer
Donald Bauder, Financial Editor
Margaret King, Food Editor
Karen Wilson, Garden Editor
Michele Molnar, Home Work Columnist
Roger Showley, Homes Dept
Carl Larsen, Homes Editor
Susan Duerksen, Medical Writer
Rex Dalton, Medical Writer
James Crawley, Military Writer
David Elliott, Movie Critic
George Varga, Music Critic/Pop Beat
Pam Dixon, Music Writer/Classical
T Michael Crowell, Night & Day Editor
Rolla Williams, Outdoors Columnist
Ed Zieralski, Outdoors Columnist
Michael Smolens, Political Editor
Gerry Braun, Political Reporter, Inside Politics
Leigh Fenly, Quest Editor, Just For Kids Column
Sandra Dolbee, Religion Writer
Robin Klever, Restaurant Critic
Scott LaFee, Science Writer
Karen Clark, Solutions Editor
Tom Cushman, Sports Columnist
Todd Merriman, Sr News Editor
Kathryn Balint, Staff Writer
R J Ignelzi, Staff Writer
Michael Phillips, Theater Critic
Alison Da Rosa, Travel Editor
John Freeman, TV/Radio News Writer

Chinese Times
686 Sacramento St
San Francisco CA 94111
415-982-0136; Fax: 415-982-3387
Circulation: 15,000

Chong Kai Lee, Assistant Editor
M K Lee, Chief Editor

Daily Construction Service
589 Howard St
San Francisco CA 94105-3001
415-781-8088; Fax: 415-495-4797
Circulation: 2,000

Daily Pacific Builder
221 Main St 8th Fl
San Francisco CA 94105-1906
415-495-4200; Fax: 415-543-4902
Circulation: 5,000

Hokubel Mainichi
1746 Post St
San Francisco CA 94115-3606
415-567-7323; Fax: 415-567-3926
Circulation: 10,000

Nichi Bei Times
2211 Bush St
San Francisco CA 94115-3121
415-921-6820; Fax: 415-921-0770
Circulation: 8,000

Recorder
625 Polk St #500
San Francisco CA 94102-3327
415-749-5400; Fax: 415-749-5449
Circulation: 6,000

Russian Life
2458 Sutter St
San Francisco CA 94115-3016
415-921-5380; Fax: 415-921-8726
Circulation: 2,000

San Francisco Chronicle
901 Mission St
San Francisco CA 94103-2988
415-777-1111; Fax: 415-512-8196
Circulation: 518,000; **Sun: 684,134

Pat Holt, Book Editor
Pimm Fox, Business Editor
Michael Yamamoto, City Editor
David Einstein and Michelle Quinn, Computer Editors
Liz Lufkin, Datebook Editor
Nanette Asimov, Education Editor
Liz Lufkin, Entertainment Editor
Michael Bauer, Food Editor
Sabin Russell, Health/Medical Editor
Connie Ballard, Home and Garden Editor
Liz Lufkin, Lifestyles/Feature Editor
Paul McHugh, Outdoors/Recreation Editor
Liz Lufkin, People/Society Editor
Susan Yoachum, Political Writer
Don Lattin, Religion Editor
David Perlman, Science Editor
Rosalie M Wright, Special Sections Editor, Features Section
John Curley, Sports Editor
Rosalie M Wright, Travel Editor

San Francisco Chronicle and **San Francisco Examiner** combine for the Sunday issue

San Francisco Daily Journal
1390 Market St #1210
San Francisco CA 94102-5306
415-252-0500; Fax: 415-252-0288
Circulation: 8,000

San Francisco Examiner
110 Fifth St
PO Box 7260
San Francisco CA 94120
415-777-2424; Fax: 415-777-8933
Circulation: 155,000; **Sun: 684,134

David Talbot, Arts/Features Editor
Joan Smith, Book Review Editor
K T Rabin, Business Editor
Jo Mancuso, Epicure Editor
Jay Johnson, Exec News Editor
Heidi Benson, Features Editor
Jim Wood, Food/Wine Editor
Lisa Krieger, Health Editor
Zahid Sardar, Home Design Editor
Pamela Scott, Managing Editor
Corrie Anders, Real Estate Editor
Glenn Schwarz, Sports Editor
Cynthia Robins, Style Editor
John Slinn, Travel Editor

San Francisco Chronicle and **San Francisco Examiner** combine for the Sunday issue

Hemet News
474 W Esplanade Ave
San Jacinto CA 92583-5006
909-487-2200; Fax: 909-487-2250
Circulation: 15,000

Post-Record
90 N 1st St #100
San Jose CA 95113-1223
408-287-4866; Fax: 408-287-2544
Circulation: 1,000

San Jose Mercury News
750 Ridder Park Dr
San Jose CA 95190
408-920-5000; Fax: 408-288-8060
Circulation: 284,000; Sun: 345,432

Holly Hayes, Arts/Entertainment Editor
Carol Muller, Book Editor
Peter Hillan, Business Editor
Dan Gilmor, Computer Editor
Aleta Watson, Education Editor
Paul Rogers, Environmental Writer
Joan Jackson, Garden Editor
Broderick Perkins, Home Real Estate Ed
Holly Hayes, Living Editor
David Yarnold, Managing Editor
Phil Trounstine, Political Editor
David Pollak, Science/Medical Editor
Dave Tepps, Sports Editor
Zeke Wigglesworth, Travel Editor
Fran Smith, West Magazine Editor

Spartan Daily
San Jose State Univ
1 Washington Square
San Jose CA 95112-3613
408-924-3270; Fax: 408-924-3282
Circulation: 7,000

Mustang Daily
California Polytechnic State Un
Graphic Arts 226
San Luis Obispo CA 93407
805-756-1143; Fax: 805-756-6784
Circulation: 6,000

Telegram-Tribune
3825 S Higuera
PO Box 112
San Luis Obispo CA 93406-0112
805-781-7800; Fax: 805-781-7905
Circulation: 33,000

Monica Fiscalini, Arts/Entertainment Editor
Mike Stover, City Editor
Monica Fiscalini, Family/Food/Garden Ed
Kate Stark, Graphics Editor
Monica Fiscalini, Lifestyle/Feature Editor
John Moore, Managing Editor
Mike Stover, Political Editor
Mike Stover, Religion Editor
Mike Stover, Science Editor
Eric Burdick, Sports Editor
Monica Fiscalini, Travel Editor

San Mateo Times
1080 S Amphlett Blvd
PO Box 5400
San Mateo CA 94402-0400
415-348-4321; Fax: 415-348-4446
E-mail: smtimes@crl.com
Circulation: 49,000

Judy Richter, Arts/Entertainment Editor
Rick Eymer, Book Editor
Dave Madden, Business Editor
Bob Rudy, City Editor
Dale Martin, Education Editor
Miriam Morgan, Food Editor
Judy Richter, Garden Editor
Sandra Burnett, Health/Medical Editor
Mary Jane Clinton, Lifestyle/Feature Editor
Terry Greenberg, Managing Editor
Terry Robertson, Political Editor
Tom Krogstad, Religion Editor
Sandra Burnett, Science Editor
John Horgan, Sports Editor
Christine Delsol, Travel Editor

News-Pilot
362 7th St
San Pedro CA 90731-3324
310-832-0221; Fax: 310-833-1540
Circulation: 15,000; Sun: 15,000

Orange County Register
625 N Grand Ave (92701)
PO Box 11626
Santa Ana CA 92711
714-835-1234; Fax: 714-542-5037
Circulation: 358,000; Sun: 420,783

Mike Hewitt, Book Editor/Show Editor
Jeff Rowe, Business Book Reviews
Russ Stanton, Business Editor
Ken Niedziela, Education Editor
Theresa Walker, Family Editor
Lisa Lytle, Fashion Editor
Steve Plesa, Feature/Accent Editor
Steve Plesa, Food Editor
Nick Harder, Home Editor
Cathy Artstrong, Lifestyle Editor
Ken Brusic, Managing Editor
Larry Burroughs, Metro/News Editor
Russ Stanton, Money Editor
Dennis Foley, Political Editor
Carol McGraw, Religion Editor
John Doussard, Science/Environment Editor
Jan Norman, Small Business Column
Mark Tomascewski, Sports Editor
Chris Smith, Topic Editor
Kitty Morgan, Travel Editor

Daily Nexus
Univ of California-Santa Barbara
PO Box 13402
Santa Barbara CA 93107-3402
805-893-3828; Fax: 805-893-2795
E-mail: 2033kirt@ucsb.edu
Circulation: 11,000

Santa Barbara News-Press
PO Box 1359
Santa Barbara CA 93102-1359
805-564-5200; Fax: 805-966-6258
E-mail: sbnp@aol.com
Circulation: 52,000; Sun: 56,000

Linda Bowen, Assistant Managing Editor
Joan Crowder, Book Reviewer
Linda Bowen, Business Editor
R B Brenner, City Editor
Melinda Johnson, Entertainment Editor
Allen Parsons, Exec Editor
Melinda Johnson, Food Editor
Tom Bolton, Managing Editor
Patty Smith, Religion Editor
Mark Patton, Sports Editor

The Signal
PO Box 801870
Santa Clarita CA 91380-1870
805-259-1234; Fax: 805-254-8068
Circulation: 44,000; Sun: 46,000

Cheri Jensen, Business Editor
David Foy, City Editor
Jill Dolan, City Issues
Tim Whyte, Editor
Sylvia Olinde, Education Writer
John Boston, Entertainment Editor
Carol Rock, Lifestyle Editor
Chris Rustom, News Editor
Kevin Smith, Political Editor
David Shefter, Sports Editor

Santa Cruz County Sentinal
207 Church St
PO Box 638
Santa Cruz CA 95061-0638
408-423-4242; Fax: 408-429-9620
Circulation: 32,000

Tom Long, Arts/Entertainment Editor
Christine Watson, Book Editor
Jon DiGumz, Education Editor
Michael Blaesser, Lifestyle/Feature Editor
Tom Honig, Managing Editor
Bill Condy, News Editor
Ed Vyeda, Sports Editor

Santa Maria Times
PO Box 400
Santa Maria CA 93456
805-925-2691; Fax: 805-928-5657
E-mail: casmt01@plink.geis.com
Circulation: 22,000; Sun: 24,100

Michele Morris, Book/Entertainment Editor
Tim Epperson, Business Editor
Christine Bedell, Co-Political Editor
Ken Miller, Co-Political Editor
Monica Prinzing, Education Editor
Michele Morris, Lifestyle/Assignment Editor
Michael Todd, Managing Editor
Michele Morris, Religion Editor
Rich Guiremand, Sports Editor
Wayne Agner, Travel Editor

The Outlook
1920 Colorado Ave (90404)
PO Box 590
Santa Monica CA 90406-0590
310-829-6811; Fax: 310-453-3085
Circulation: 26,000

Saul Rubin, Book Editor
Ed Moosbrugger, Business Editor
Lisa Mascaro, Education Editor
Terri Moore, Family/Food/Garden Editor
Lou Braucaccio, Managing Editor
Joge Casuso, Political Editor
Eric Stephens, Sports Editor

Santa Rosa Press Democrat
Rich Nelson, Book Editor
427 Mendocino Ave
Santa Rosa CA 95402
707-546-2020; Fax: 707-546-7538
Circulation: 100,000; Sun: 101,000

Brad Bollinger, Business Editor
Catherine Barnett, City Editor
Brian Moe, Copy Desk Editor
Tina Anima, Education Editor
Susan Leathers, Lifestyle/Feature Editor
Bob Swofford, Managing Editor
Suzanne Boynton, Religion Editor
Jim Jenks, Sports Editor

Sonoma Co Daily Herald-Recorder
1818 4th St
Santa Rosa CA 95404-3203
707-545-1166; Fax: 707-545-6310
Circulation: 1,000

Simi Valley Star
888 Easy St (93065)
PO Box 869
Simi Valley CA 93062-0869
805-526-6211; Fax: 805-526-0479
Circulation: 16,000; Sun: 17,000

Michael Huffman, City Editor
Sheila Schmitz, Lifestyle/Feature Editor
Loren Ledin, Sports Reporter

Union Democrat
84 S Washington
Sonora CA 95370-4711
209-532-7151; Fax: 209-532-5139
Circulation: 14,000

Lenore Rutherford, Arts/Entertainment Editor
Gary Linehan, Book Editor
Amy Nilson, Business Editor
Kerry McCray, Education Editor
Lenore Rutherford, Food Editor
Gary Linehan, Health/Medical Editor
Lenore Rutherford, Lifestyle/Feature Editor
Buzz Eggleston, Managing Editor
Larry Hashman, News Editor
Lenore Rutherford, Religion Editor
Kevin Sauls, Sports Editor

Tahoe Daily Tribune
PO Box 1358
South Lake Tahoe CA 96156-1358
916-541-3880; Fax: 916-541-8238
Circulation: 10,000

The Record
530 E Market St
PO Box 900
Stockton CA 95201-0900
209-943-6397; Fax: 209-546-8288
Circulation: 55,000; Sun: 65,000

Eric Grunder, Business Editor
Dana Nichols, College Education Editor
Dana Nichols, Education Editor
Betty Liddick, Executive Editor
Jim Gold, Managing Editor
Paul Feist, Metro News Editor
Joe Pasley, Sports Editor
Sheri Spence, Travel Editor

Daily Midway Driller
PO Bin Z
Taft CA 93268
805-763-3171; Fax: 805-763-5638
Circulation: 5,000

Tim Neher, Business Editor
Dave Hook, Environmental Editor
Sunny Johnson, Food Editor
Sunny Johnson, Health/Medical Editor
Sunny Johnson, Home/Garden Editor
Sunny Johnson, Lifestyle/Feature Editor
Tim Neher, News Editor
Dave Hook, Outdoors/Recreation Editor
Sunny Johnson, People/Society Editor
Tim Neher, Political Editor
Dave Hook, Science Editor
Dave Hook, Sports Editor
Sunny Johnson, Travel Editor

Californian
27450 Ynez Rd #300
Temecula CA 92591-4681
909-676-4315; Fax: 909-694-1215
Circulation: 12,000

Thousand Oaks Star
2595 E Thousand Oaks Blvd
Thousand Oaks CA 91362-3259
805-496-3211; Fax: 805-494-4523
Circulation: 20,000

Daily Breeze
5215 Torrance Blvd
Torrance CA 90509-4009
310-540-5511; Fax: 310-540-6272
Circulation: 131,000

Charles Britton, Arts/Entertainment Editor
Don Lechman, Book Reviewer
Cyndia Zwahlen, Business Editor
Frank Suraci, City Editor
Lisa Messinger, Food Editor
Meredith Grenier, Garden/Society Editor
Terry Moore, Lifestyle/Feature Editor
Marie Montgomery, Lower Education
Jean Adelsman, Managing Editor
Kathleen Dougherty, Political Editor
Thom Mead, Religion Editor
Lee Peterson, Science/Health Editor
Robert Whitley, Sports Editor
Don Chapman, Travel Editor

Tracy Press
145 W 10th St
Tracy CA 95376-3903
209-835-3030; Fax: 209-835-0655
Circulation: 10,000

Tulare Advance-Register
388 E Cross Ave
Tulare CA 93274-2854
209-688-0521; Fax: 209-688-7503
Circulation: 9,000

Turlock Journal
138 S Center
Turlock CA 95380-4508
209-634-9141; Fax: 209-632-8813
Circulation: 10,000

Ukiah Daily Journal
590 S School St
PO Box 749
Ukiah CA 95482-5438
707-468-0123; Fax: 707-468-5780
Circulation: 9,000

Lois O'Rourke, Arts/Entertainment Editor
K C Meadows, Business Editor
Lois O'Rourke, Education Editor
Lois O'Rourke, Lifestyle/Feature Editor
Randy Foster, Managing Editor
Jody Martinez, News Editor
Steve Guertin, Sports Editor

Vacaville Reporter
916 Cotting Ln
Vacaville CA 95688-9338
707-448-2200; Fax: 707-447-8411
Circulation: 20,000; Sun: 23,000

Dan Reichl, City Editor
Diane Barney, Managing Editor

Vallejo Times Herald
440 Curtola Pky
PO Box 3188
Vallejo CA 94590-6923
707-644-1141; Fax: 707-643-0128
Circulation: 26,000; Sunday: 29,000

Mark Mazzaferro, City Desk Editor
Joe Lowell, Managing Editor

Ventura County Star
5250 Ralston St (93003)
PO Box 6711
Ventura CA 93003
805-650-2900; Fax: 805-650-2950
Circulation: 50,000; Sun: 56,000

Colleen Cason, Arts Editor
Sheila Schmitz, Book Editor
Frank Moraga, Business Editor
Burton Swope, City Editor
Charles Flora, Education Editor
Sheila Schmitz, Family/Food/Garden Editor
Jim McLain, Health/Medical Editor
John Cressy, Outdoors/Recreation Editor
Sheila Schmitz, Religion Editor
Burton Swope, Science Editor
Mike Blackwell, Sports Editor
John Garcia, Travel Editor

Daily Press
13891 Park Ave (92392)
PO Box 1389
Victorville CA 92393-0964
619-241-7744; Fax: 619-241-1860
Circulation: 30,000; Sun: 34,000

Veronica Hill, Arts/Entertainment Editor
Veronica Hill, Book Editor
Jerry Siegel, Business Editor
Steve Williams, Chief Editor
Judith Pfeffer, City Editor
Joanne Bartholomew, Community Editor
Mary Lou Thomas, Family Editor
John Iddings, Managing Editor
Lena Houston, Religion Editor
Veronica Hill, Science Editor
Russ Lemmon, Sports Editor

Visalia Times-Delta
330 N West St
Visalia CA 93291
209-734-5821; Fax: 209-734-5843
Circulation: 25,000

Erik Olvera, Arts/Entertainment Editor

Tom Bray, Book Editor
Ron Trujillo, Business Editor
Michelle Martin, Education Editor
Gay Taguchi, Lifestyle/Feature Editor
Tom Bray, Managing Editor
Paul Hurley, Political Editor
Steve Griffits, Science Editor
Jon Matsune, Sports Editor
Erik Olvera, Travel Editor

Contra Costa Times
2640 Shadelands Dr (94598)
PO Box 5088
Walnut Creek CA 94596-0088
510-935-2525; Fax: 510-943-8362
Lisa Wrenn, Book Editor/Reviewer
Marcia Parker, Business Editor
Doug Kim, Entertainment Editor
Deborah Byrd, Food Editor
Elizabeth Hayes, Health/Medical Editor
Deborah Byrd, Home Editor
Bev Britton, Lifestyle/Feature Editor
Clayton Haswell, Managing Editor
Catherine Snapp, News Editor, Metro
Danny DeFreitas, Sports Editor
Carol Fowler, Travel Editor
Deborah Carvallaho, TV Editor

Watsonville Register-Pajaronian
1000 Main St
PO Box 50077
Watsonville CA 95076-3732
408-761-7300; Fax: 408-722-8386
Circulation: 13,000

Steve Palopoli, Arts/Entertainment Editor
Steve Palopoli, Book Review Editor
Bob Smith, Co-Editor
Debra Brinson, Education Editor
Becky Kimball, Health/Medical Editor
Steve Palopoli, Lifestyle/Feature Editor
Steve Palopoli, Religion Editor
Dave Burge, Sports Editor
Diane Noland, Travel Editor

Whittier Daily News
PO Box 581
Whittier CA 90608
310-698-0955; Fax: 310-698-0450
Circulation: 19,000; Sun: 65,000

Cathy Porrelli, Arts/Entertainment Editor
Susan Gill, Book Review Editor
Brett Sporich, Business Editor
Nick Owchar, Education Editor
Brett Sporich, Health/Medical Editor
Valerie Marrs, Lifestyle/Feature Editor
Bill Bell, Managing Editor
Mike Sprague, Political Editor
Mike Sprague, Science Editor
Robert Morales, Sports Editor
Rich Irwin, Travel Editor

Daily Democrat
711 Main St
Woodland CA 95695-3406
916-662-5421; Fax: 916-662-1288
Circulation: 11,000

Los Angeles Daily News
PO Box 4200
Woodland Hills CA 91365
818-713-3131; Fax: 818-713-3545
Circulation: 202,000

Daryl Miller, Arts Editor
Mark Lacter, Assoc Editor Opinion Page
Kate Seago, Book Editor
Jane Robison, Business Editor

Kim Candy, Education Editor
Tony Knight, Environmental Writer
Barbara DeWitt, Fashion Editor
Barbara Jones, Features Editor
Natalie Haughton, Food Editor
Susan Love, Lifestyle Editor
Ron Kaye, Managing Editor
John Corrigan, News/Metro Editor
Steve Getzug, Religion Editor
Todd Leonard, Sports Editor
Susanne Hopkins, Travel Editor

Siskiyou Daily News
PO Box 129
Yreka CA 96097
916-842-5777; Fax: 916-842-6787
Circulation: 6,000

David Kennard, Arts/Entertainment Editor
David Kennard, Book Review Editor
David Kennard, Business Editor
Lori Sellstrom, Education Editor
David Kennard, Lifestyle/Feature Editor
David Kennard, Managing Editor
David Kennard, News Editor
Dan Murphy, Sports Editor

Colorado

Valley Courier-Alamosa
401-407 State Ave
Alamosa CO 81101-2645
719-589-2553; Fax: 719-589-6573
Circulation: 5,000

Aspen Times Daily
310 E Main
Aspen CO 81611-1930
970-925-3414; Fax: 970-925-6240
Circulation: 12,000

Daily Camera
1048 Pearl St
PO Box 591
Boulder CO 80306
303-442-1462; Fax: 303-449-9358
Circulation: 35,000

Vicki Gitts, Business Editor
Juliet Wittman, Discovery Editor
Gary Burns, Managing Editor
Doug Bell, News Editor
Dan Creedon, Sports Editor

Canon City Daily Record
PO Box 2020
Canon City CO 81215-2020
719-275-7565; Fax: 719-274-1353
Circulation: 9,000

Daily Transcript
22 N Sierra Madre
Colorado Springs CO 80903-3311
719-634-1593; Fax: 719-632-0762
Circulation: 1,000

Gazette Telegraph
30 S Prospect St (80903)
PO Box 1779
Colorado Springs CO 80901-1779
719-632-5511; Fax: 719-636-0202
Circulation: 105,000; Sun: 117,000

Gil Asakawa, Arts/Entertainment Editor
Leslie Weddell, Book Editor
Russ Small, Business Editor
Trudy Welsh, Education Writer

Jan Spiegel, Food Editor
Leslie Weddell, Garden/Travel Editor
Rick Ansorge, Health/Medical Editor
Leslie Weddell, Home Editor
Todd Hegert, Lifestyle/Feature Editor
Wayne Stewart, Managing Editor
Scott Smith, Sports Editor

Northwest Colorado Daily Press
466 Yampa Ave
Craig CO 81625-2610
970-824-7031; Fax: 970-824-6810
Circulation: 3,000

Daily Journal
2000 S Colorado Blvd #2000
Denver CO 80222-7910
303-756-9995; Fax: 303-756-4465
Circulation: 6,000

Denver Post
1560 Broadway
PO Box 1709
Denver CO 80201
303-820-1010; Fax: 303-820-1369
Circulation: 262,000; Sun: 428,391

Glenn Giffin, Book Editor
Jeff Copeland, Business/News Editor
Vince Bzdek, Deputy Mg Editor/Sun
Edward P Smith, Editor, Empire Magazine
Diane Carmen, Entertainment Editor
Mark Obmascik, Environment Editor
Jim Bates, Exec News Editor
Neil Westerguard, Executive Editor
Francine Parnes, Fashion Editor
Cynthia Pasquele, Feature Editor
John Kessler, Food Editor
Isabel Spencer, Managing Editor
Howie Morshovitz, Movie Critic
Todd Engdahl, New Media Editor
Charlie Meyers, Outdoor Editor
Steve Larson, Photography Editor
Fred Brown, Political Editor
Virginia Culver, Religion Editor
Joanne Davidson, Society Editor
Mike Conneley, Sports Editor
Mark Harden, State Editor
Bob Sheue, Travel Editor
Joanne Ostrow, TV-Radio Critic

Rocky Mountain News
400 W Colfax Ave (80204)
PO Box 719
Denver CO 80201
303-892-5000; Fax: 303-892-2841
Circulation: 356,000

Mike Pearson, Arts/Entertainment Editor
Margie Carlin, Book Editor
Don Knox, Business Editor
Chris Broderick, Education Editor
Mary Winter, Lifestyle/Feature Editor
John Temple, Managing Editor
Barry Forbis, Sports Editor

Durango Herald
1275 Main Ave
Durango CO 81301-5137
970-247-3504; Fax: 970-259-5011
Circulation: 9,000

Collegian
Colorado State Univ
Lory Student Ctr PO Box 13
Fort Collins CO 80523-0001
970-491-7941; Fax: 970-491-0620
Circulation: 11,000

Coloradoan
PO Box 1577
Fort Collins CO 80522-1577
970-224-7730; Fax: 970-224-7899
Circulation: 29,000; Sun: 37,000

Summit Daily News
275 Main St
Frisco CO 80443-9999
970-668-3998; Fax: 970-668-3859
Circulation: 8,000; Sun: 8,000

Fort Morgan Times
329 Main St
Ft Morgan CO 80701-2108
970-867-5651; Fax: 970-867-7448
Circulation: 5,000

Glenwood Post
2014 Grand Ave
Glenwood Springs CO 81601-4116
303-945-8515; Fax: 303-945-8518
Circulation: 6,000

Grand Junction Daily Sentinel
734 S Seventh St
PO Box 668
Grand Junction CO 81502
970-242-5050; Fax: 970-244-8578
Circulation: 35,000; Sun: 38,000

Michelle Willits, Arts/Entertainment Editor
Kathy Jordan, Book Editor
Ginger Rice, Business Editor
Gary Harmon, City Editor
Pat Cleary, Education Editor
Michelle Willits, Lifestyle Editor
Dennis Herzog, Managing Editor
Rick Jussel, Sports Editor

Greeley Tribune
501 8th Ave
Greeley CO 80631-3913
970-352-0211; Fax: 970-356-5780
Circulation: 24,000

Gunnison County Times
218 N Wisconsin
Gunnison CO 81230-2626
970-641-1414; Fax: 970-641-6515
Circulation: 3,000

La Junta Tribune-Democrat
422 Colorado Ave
La Junta CO 81050-2336
719-384-4475; Fax: 719-384-4478
Circulation: 3,000

The Daily Times On Line
Ben Miller, News Editor
1224 Wadsworth Blvd
Lakewood CO 80215
303-239-9890; Fax: 303-239-9808
On line # 303-235-8910
Circulation: 0,000

Lamar Daily News
310 S 5th St
Lamar CO 81052-2712
719-336-2266; Fax: 719-336-2526
Circulation: 3,000

Longmont Daily Times-Call
350 Terry St
Longmont CO 80501-5440
303-776-2244; Fax: 303-678-8615
Circulation: 20,000

Loveland Daily Reporter-Herald
201 E 5th St
Loveland CO 80537-5605
970-669-5050; Fax: 970-667-1111
Circulation: 17,000

Montrose Daily Press
535 S 1st St
Montrose CO 81401-3910
970-249-3444; Fax: 970-249-3331
Circulation: 7,000

Pueblo Chieftain
825 W 6th St
PO Box 4040
Pueblo CO 81003
719-544-3520; Fax: 719-544-5897
Focus: 28-29-43-75-95-99
Circulation: 50,000; Sun: 54,000

Pete Strescino, Book Editor
John Norton, Business Editor
Steve Henson, City Editor
Peter Roper, Education Editor
Pete Strescino, Food Editor
Ada Brownell, Health Editor
Margie Wood, Lifestyle Editor
Len Gregory, Managing Editor
Ada Brownell, Science Editor
Judy Hildner, Sports Editor

Rocky Ford Daily Gazette
912 Elm Ave
Rocky Ford CO 81067-1249
719-254-3351
Circulation: 3,000

Mountain Mail
125 E 2nd St
Salida CO 81201-2114
719-539-6691; Fax: 719-539-6630
Circulation: 3,000

Steamboat Today
1041 Lincoln Ave
Steamboat Springs CO 80477
970-879-1505; Fax: 970-879-2888
Circulation: 6,000

Journal-Advocate
504 N 3rd St
Sterling CO 80751-3203
970-522-1990; Fax: 970-522-2320
Circulation: 6,000

Chronicle News
200 Church St
Trinidad CO 81082-2607
719-846-3311; Fax: 719-846-3612
Circulation: 4,000

Vail Daily
143 E Meadow Dr
Vail CO 81657-5331
970-476-0555; Fax: 970-476-5268
Circulation: 12,000

Connecticut

Connecticut Post
410 State St
Bridgeport CT 06604-4568
203-333-0161; Fax: 203-367-8158
Circulation: 90,000; Sun: 70,000

Patrick Quinn, Arts Editor
Joe Meyers, Book Editor
Tom Caruso, Business Editor
Kathy Katello, Lifestyle Editor
Rick Sayers, News Managing Editor
Jean Santopatre, Photo Editor
Mark Faller, Sports Editor

Bristol Press
99 Main St
Bristol CT 06010-6528
203-584-0501; Fax: 203-584-2192
Circulation: 20,000

News Times
333 Main St
Danbury CT 06810-5818
203-744-5100; Fax: 203-792-4211
Circulation: 38,000; Sun: 45,000

Greenwich Time
20 E Elm St
Greenwich CT 06830-6529
203-625-4400; Fax: 203-625-4419
Circulation: 14,000

Hartford Courant
285 Broad St
Hartford CT 06115
203-241-6549; Fax: 203-241-3865
Focus: 11-14-17-33
Circulation: 228,000; Sun: 325,000

Garret Condon, Arts Editor
Jocelyn McClurg, Book Editor
Robert Weisman, Business Editor
Patricia McNerney, City Editor
Claude Albert, Deputy Managing Editor
Dave Barrett, Editor
Robert Frahm, Education Editor
Linda Giuca, Food Editor
Nancy LaRoche, Lifestyle Editor
Clifford L Teutsch, Managing Editor
Jeff Otterbein, Sports Editor
Steve Silk, Travel Editor

Journal Inquirer
306 Progress Dr
Manchester CT 06040-9002
203-646-0500; Fax: 203-646-9867
Circulation: 45,000

Meriden Record-Journal
11 Crown St, PO Box 915
Meriden CT 06450-0915
203-235-1661; Fax: 203-639-0210
Circulation: 31,000; Sun: 31,000

Phyllis Donavan, Arts/Entertainment Editor
Marjorie Fay, Book Editor
Jim Zebora, Business Editor
Jim Smith, Exec News Editor
Phyllis Donavan, Food Editor
Phyllis Donavan, Home Editor
Phyllis Donavan, Lifestyle/Feature Editor
Don Schiller, Managing Editor
Marjorie Fay, Religion Editor
Bob Morrissette, Sports Editor
Phyllis Donavan, Travel Editor

Middletown Press
2 Main St
Middletown CT 06457-3407
203-347-3331; Fax: 203-347-3380
Circulation: 18,000

Kathy O'Connell, Arts Editor
Carolyn Caprioliglioo, Lifestyle Editor
Bill O'Brien, Managing Editor
Charlie Standard, News Editor
Chris Cosenza and Adam Minichino, Sports Editors

New Haven Register-Milford Edition
349 New Haven Ave
Milford CT 06460-6647
203-876-6800; Fax: 203-877-4772
Circulation: 7,000

Herald
1 Herald Square
New Britain CT 06051-5006
203-225-4601; Fax: 203-225-4601
Circulation: 33,000

New Haven Register
40 Sargent Dr
New Haven CT 06511-5918
203-789-5200; Fax: 203-865-7894
Circulation: 142,000; Sun: 155,000

Mary Colurso, Arts
Mary Colruso, Book Editor
Paul Jackson, Business Editor
Joe Brady, City Editor
Patrick Dilger, Education Editor
Fran Fried, Entertainment Editor
Rick Sandella, Food Editor
Abe Katz, Health/Medical Editor
Rick Sandella, Lifestyle Editor
Dave Funkhouser, Managing Editor
Abe Katz, Science Editor
Doug Jacobs, Sports Editor

Yale Daily News
Yale University
202 York St
New Haven CT 06511-4804
203-432-2424; Fax: 203-432-7425
Circulation: 5,000

Day
47 Eugene O'Neill Dr
New London CT 06320-6306
203-442-2200; Fax: 203-442-5599
Circulation: 40,000; Sun: 47,000

The Hour
John Reilly, News Editor
PO Box 790
Norwalk CT 06852
203-846-3281; Fax: 203-846-9897
Circulation: 22,000

Norwich Bulletin
66 Franklin St
Norwich CT 06360
203-887-9211; Fax: 203-887-9666
Circulation: 34,000; Sun: 38,000

John Hopkins, Book Editor
Ian Gertzen, Business Editor
Molly Palmer, Lifestyle/Feature Editor
Keith Fontaine, Managing Editor
Gary Samek, Sports Editor

Advocate
75 Tresser Blvd
Stamford CT 06904-3304
203-964-2200; Fax: 203-964-2345
Circulation: 35,000; Sunday 50,000

Beth Cox, Business Editor
Robin Foster, City News Editor
Stacy Shelton, Education Editor
Valerie Foster, Food Editor
Daniel Berman, Health/Medical Editor
Daniel Berman, Home Editor
Daniel Berman, Lifestyle/Feature Editor
Barry Hoffman, Managing Editor
Daniel Berman, Science Editor
Bob Kennedy, Sports Editor

Daily Campus
Univ of Connecticut
11 Dog Ln
Storrs Mansfield CT 06268-2206
203-486-3407; Fax: 203-486-4388
Circulation: 10,000

Register Citizen
190 Water St
Torrington CT 06790-5336
203-489-3121; Fax: 203-489-6790
Circulation: 16,000

Waterbury Republican American
389 Meadow St
PO Box 2090
Waterbury CT 06722-1808
203-574-3636; Fax: 203-596-9277
Circulation: 63,000; Sun: 79,000

Claire Lefleur, Arts/Entertainment
Jack Dailey, Book Editor
Howard Fielding, Business Editor
Bob Fredericks, City Editor
Jeanne Kennedy, Education Editor
Jennifer Gangloff, Health/Medical Editor
Claire Lefleur, Lifestyle/Feature Editor
Bob Viellete, Managing Editor
Greg Hanisek, News Editor
Connie Lepore, Political Editor
John Gillespie, Religion Editor
Leroy Lewis, Sports Editor
Claire Lefluer, Travel Editor

Chronicle
1 Chronicle Rd
Willimantic CT 06226-1932
203-423-8466; Fax: 203-423-7641
Circulation: 12,000

Delaware

Delaware State News
Webbs Ln & New Burton Rd
PO Box 737
Dover DE 19903-0737
302-674-3600; Fax: 302-674-4752
Circulation: 32,000; Sun: 38,000

Gwen Guerke, Book Editor
Gwen Guerke, Lifestyle/Feature Editor
Mike Pelrine, Managing Editor
Andy Walter, Sports Editor

Daily Whale
PO Box 37
Lewes DE 19958-0037
302-645-2265; Fax: 302-645-2267
Circulation: 6,000

The News Journal Company
PO Box 15505
Wilmington DE 19850-5505
302-324-2500; Fax: 302-324-5509
Circulation: 124,000; Sun: 144,000

Gary Mullinax, Arts Editor
Gary Mullinax, Book Editor
Peter Frank, Business Editor
Sandy Dennison, Education Reporter
Merritt Wallick, Environmental Editor
Gretchen Day-Bryant, Features Editor
Stephanie Whyche, Food Editor
Jane Harriman, Health/Medical Editor
Gretchen Day-Bryant, Home Editor
Mark Wert, News Editor
Cecilia Cohen, Political Editor
Rhonda Graham, Religion Editor
Phil Milford, Science Editor
Chris Adams, Sports Editor
Gretchen Day-Bryant, Travel Editor

District of Columbia

Aerospace Daily
1200 G St NW #200
Washington DC 20005-1704
202-383-2350; Fax: 202-383-2438
Circulation: 22,000

Aviation Daily
1200 G St NW #200
Washington DC 20005-1704
203-383-2350; Fax: 203-383-2438
Circulation: 0,000

Communications Daily
2115 Ward Ct NW
Washington DC 20037-1213
203-872-9200; Fax: 203-293-3435
Circulation: N/A

Congress Daily
,501 M St NW #300
Washington DC 20005-1700
202-739-8400; Fax: 202-296-6110
Circulation: 4,000

Congressional Monitor
1414 22nd St NW
Washington DC 20037-1003
202-822-1440; Fax: 202-728-1863
Circulation: 3,000

Energy Daily
627 National Press Bldg
Washington DC 20045-1601
202-622-9720; Fax: 202-662-9744
Circulation: N/A

Journal of Commerce
Washington Bureau
740 National Press Bldg
Washington DC 20045
202-383-6100; Fax: 202-383-6121
Circulation: 23,000

Aviva Freudmann, Asst Editoral Dir--DC
Tom Connors, Editor--Washington DC
Leo Abruzzese, Editorial Director-DC

Oil Daily
1401 New York Ave NW #500
Washington DC 20005-2102
202-662-0700; Fax: 202-783-8230
Circulation: 3,000

Travel Management Daily
1155 15th St NW #510
Washington DC 20005-2706
202-467-8087; Fax: 202-872-0966
Circulation: N/A

Washington Post
1150 15th St NW
Washington DC 20071-0001
202-334-6000; Fax: 202-334-4344
Circulation: 812,000; Sun: 1,150,000

Mary Hader, Arts/Entertainment Editor
Larry Thompson, Asst Health Editor, Health Supplement
Nina King, Book Editor
David Ignatius, Business Editor
Ken Bredemeier, Editor, Real Estate Section
Lawrence Meyer, Editor, National Weekly Edition
Leonard Downie, Exec News Editor
Janet Duckworth, Fashion Editor
Debra Simmons, Food Editor
Abigail Trafford, Health/Medical Editor
Linda Hales, Home Editor
Frank Swoboda, Labor Editor
Karen DeYoung, National Editor
Allison Howard, Religion Editor
Boyce Rensberger, Science Editor
George Solomon, Sports Editor
Linda Halsey, Travel Editor

Washington Post Magazine
Linton Weeks, Managing Editor
1150 15th St NW
Washington DC 20071-0001
202-334-6000; Fax: 202-334-4344
Circulation: 814,000

Washington Times
3600 New York Ave NE
Washington DC 20002
202-636-3000; Fax: 202-269-3419
Circulation: 104,000

Fran Coombs, Asst Managing Editor
Colin Walters, Book Editor
Anne Veigle, Business Editor
Kenneth McIntyre, City Editor
Weslie Pruden, Editor-in-Chief
Dan Simmons, Feature Editor
Debra Simmons, Food Editor
Jennifer Harper, Home Editor
Kevin Chaffee, People Editor, About Town Column
Don Lambro, Political Editor
Richard Slusser, Travel Editor, The Times Traveller

Florida

De Soto Sun Herald
105 W Oak St
Aracadia FL 33821-3913
941-494-7600; Fax: 941-494-9596
Circulation: 4,000

Auburndale Star
213 E Lake Ave
Auburndale FL 33823-3438
941-967-4134; Fax: 941-967-2707
Circulation: 24,000

Boca Raton News
33 SE Third St (33432)
PO Box 580
Boca Raton FL 33429
407-338-4910; Fax: 407-338-4944
Circulation: 28,000; Sun: 26,000

Skip Sheffield, Arts Editor
Mary Lou Simms, Book Editor/Reviewer
Terence Shepard, Business Editor
Joci Sampson, Education Editor
Kristine Hussey, Environmental Editor
Mary Lou Simms, Family Editor
Mary Lou Simms, Food Editor
Mary Lou Simms, Health/Medical Editor
Mary Lou Simms, Home Editor
Phyllis Gilchrist, News Managing Editor
Taylor Scott, Outdoors/Recreation Editor
Tracy Allerton, Religion Editor
Taylor Scott, Sports Editor

Bradenton Herald
102 Manatee Ave W
PO Box 921
Bradenton FL 34206
813-748-0411; Fax: 813-745-7097
Circulation: 49,000; Sunday: 55,000

Laura Cianci, Business Editor
Gary Brown, City News Editor
Teri Grimes, Lifestyle/Feature Editor
Bruce Lind, Managing Editor
Mike Mersch, Sports Editor

Daily Breeze
2510 Del Prado Blvd
Cape Coral FL 33904-5750
941-574-1110; Fax: 941-574-3403
Circulation: 6,000

Citrus County Chronicle
Ken Melton, Managing Editor
1624 N Meadowcrest Blvd
Crystal River FL 32629
904-563-6363; Fax: 904-563-3280
Circulation: 26,000; Sunday: 32,000

The News Journal
901 Sixth St (32117)
PO Box 2831
Daytona Beach FL 32120-2831
904-252-1511; Fax: 904-258-8465
Circulation: 100,000; Sun: 125,000

Gerry Bauer, Book Editor/Reviewer
Tom Brown, Business Editor
Mike Czeczot, City Editor
Linda Trimble, Education Writer
Cathy Klasne, Food Editor
Suzanne Kridner, Lifestyle Editor
Don Lindley, Managing Editor
Carol Fuquay, Religion Writer
Lydia Hinshaw, Sports Editor
Suzanne Kridner, Travel Editor

New Volusian
111 S Alabama Ave
Deland FL 32724-5513
904-734-3661; Fax: 904-736-8972
Circulation: 22,000; Sun: 25,000

Sun Herald
167 W Dearborn St
Englewood FL 34223-3260
941-474-5521; Fax: 941-426-3576
Circulation: 31,000; Sun: 35,000

Sun-Sentinel
200 E Las Olas Blvd
Ft Lauderdale FL 33301-2293
305-356-4000; Fax: 305-356-4676
Circulation: 240,000; Sun: 300,000

Chauncey Mabe, Book Editor
Kevin Gale, Business Editor
John Dolen, Entertainment Editor, Showtime Section
Debbie Hartz, Food Editor
Charlyne Varkonyi, Home/Garden Editor
Mark Gauert, Lifestyle Editor
Ellen Soeteber, Managing Editor
Tom Davidson, Metro Editor
Jim Davis, Religion Editor
Kirk Saville, Science Editor
Fred Turner, Sports Editor
Tom Swick, Travel Editor

Fort Myers News-Press
2442 Martin Luther King Jr Blvd
PO Box 10
Fort Myers FL 33902
813-335-0200; Fax: 813-334-0708
Circulation: 100,000; Sun: 100,000

Jill Friedel, Arts Editor
Harriet Simpson, Business Editor
Paulette Walker, Education Writer
Jill Fredel, Food Editor
Lisa Bryant, Health/Medical Editor
Jill Fredel, Lifestyle/Feature Editor
Vickie Kilgore, Managing Editor
Mike Clocke, Sports Editor
Karen Feldman Smith, Travel Editor

News Tribune
600 Edwards Rd
Fort Pierce FL 34982-6230
407-461-2050; Fax: 407-461-4447
Circulation: 26,000; Sun: 26,000

Northwest Florida Daily News
200 Racetrack Rd NW
Fort Walton Beach FL 32547-1645
904-863-1111; Fax: 904-863-7834
Circulation: 40,000; Sun: 50,000

Gainesville Sun
2700 SW 13th St
Gainesville FL 32608-2015
904-374-5000; Fax: 904-338-3125
Circulation: 56,000; 63,000

Independent Florida Alligator
Univ of Florida
1105 W University Ave
Gainesville FL 32601-5111
904-378-4446; Fax: 904-376-4556
Circulation: 32,000

Florida Times Union
1 Riverside Ave (32202)
PO Box 1949
Jacksonville FL 32231
904-359-4111; Fax: 904-359-4478
Circulation: 200,000; Sun: 258,000

Mike Richey, Assistant Managing Editor
Robin Clark, Business Editor
Steve Spears, Computer Editor
Lloyd Brown, Editorial Page Editor
Jim Saunders, Education Editor
Sara Wildberger, Features Editor
Belinda Hulin-Salkin, Food Editor
Michael Stobbe, Health Editor
Susan Respess, Home Editor
Mary Kress, Managing Editor

John Burr, Metro Editor
Nick Bournias, Nightime Editor
Lilla Ross, Religion Editor
Steve Patterson, Science Editor
Joe DeSalvo, Sports Editor
Allison Lucian, Travel Editor

Key West Citizen
3420 Northside Dr
Key West FL 33040-4254
305-294-6641; Fax: 305-294-0768
Circulation: 12,000; Sun: 12,500

Lake City Register
126 E Duval St
Lake City FL 32055-4025
904-752-1293; Fax: 904-752-9400
Circulation: 10,000

Lakeland Ledger
Lime & Missouri Sts
PO Box 408
Lakeland FL 33802-0408
813-687-7000; Fax: 813-687-7090
Circulation: 80,000; Sun: 100,000

Lynne Cook, Arts/Entertainment Editor
Jeff Kline, Business Editor
Hunter George, City Desk Editor
Lynne Duke, Education Reporter
Skip Perez, Executive Editor
Trent Rowe, Food Editor
Barry Friedman, Garden Editor
Robin Adams, Health/Medical Reporter
Lynne Cook, Home Editor
Barry Friedman, Lifestyle/Feature Editor
Bruce Giles, Managing Editor
Barry Friedman, News Editor
Lynne Cook, People/Society Editor
Bill Rusty, Political Editor
Maryalice Quinn, Religion Editor
John Valerino, Sports Editor

Daily Commercial
212 E Main St
Leesburg FL 34748-5227
904-365-8200; Fax: 904-365-1951
Circulation: 34,000; Sun: 34,000

Jackson County Floridan
4403 Constitution Ln
Marianna FL 32448-4472
904-526-3614; Fax: 904-482-4478
Circulation: 6,000

Florida Today
1 Gannett Plz (32940)
PO Box 419000
Melbourne FL 32941-9000
407-242-3898; Fax: 407-242-6620
Circulation: 87,000; Sun: 113,600

Hanna Krause, Book Editor/Reviewer
Anne Straub, Business Editor
Tom Kehoe, Computer Editor
Bennie Ivory, Executive Editor
Marilyn Myer, Health Reporter
Robbyn Footlick, Lifestyle Editor
Melinda Meers, Managing Editor
Bob Stover, Metro Editor
Bill Sargent, Outdoors/Recreation Editor
Todd Halvorson, Science Editor
Tom Squires, Sports Editor

Daily Business Review
1 SE 3rd Ave #900
Miami FL 33131-1704
305-377-3721; Fax: 305-374-8474
Circulation: 11,000

Diario Las Americas
2900 NW 39th St
Miami FL 33142
305-633-3341; Fax: 305-635-7668
Circulation: 68,000; Sunday: 71,000

Vivian Crucet, Arts/Entertainment Editor
Roman Campa, Book Editor
Enrique Llaca, Business Editor
Jorge Consuegra, Computer Editor
Helen Ferre, Education Editor
Virginia Flores, Food Editor
Helen Ferre, Health/Medical Editor
Magda Gonzalez, Lifestyle/Feature Editor
Victor Vega, Managing Editor
Yolanda Gonzalez, News Editor
Ariel Remos, Political Editor
Luis Lima, Sports Editor
Irene Puig, Travel Editor

El Nuevo Herald
1 Herald Pl
Miami FL 33132-1609
305-376-3535; Fax: 305-376-2207
Circulation: 101,000; Sun: 127,000

Miami Herald
One Herald Plz
Miami FL 33132-1609
305-350-2111; Fax: 305-376-8950
Circulation: 433,000; Sun: 523,000

Margaria Fichtner, Book Editor
David Satterfield, Business Editor
Bill Grueskin, City Editor
Steve Sonsky, Entertainment Editor
Doug Clifton, Executive Editor, Tropic Magazine
James Russell, Financial Editor
Kathy Martin, Food Editor
Ileina Oroza, Foreign Editor
Georgia Tasker, Garden Editor
Sandy Jacobs, Health Editor
Mark Washburn, Health Editor, Health Beat Supplement
Lynn Medford, Living Today Editor
Rick Hirsch, Metro Editor
Susan Miller-Degnan, Outdoors Editor
Peggy Landers, Religion Editor
Steve Doig, Science Editor
Paul Anger, Sports Editor
Jay Clarke, Travel Editor

Naples Daily News
1075 Central Ave
Naples FL 33940
941-262-3161; Fax: 941-263-4708
Circulation: 53,000; Sun: 67,468

John Lockhart, Business Editor
Phil Lewis, Managing Editor
Tom Rife, Sports Editor

Observer
823 S Dixie Fwy
New Smyrna Beach FL 32168-7461
904-427-1000; Fax: 904-428-1265
Circulation: 5,000

Ocala Star-Banner
2121 SW 19th Rd
Ocala FL 34474
904-867-4010; Fax: 904-867-4018
Circulation: 53,000

Okeechobee News
107 SW 17th St #D
Okeechobee FL 34974-6110
941-763-3134; Fax: 941-763-5901
Circulation: 4,000

Clay Today
1564 Kingsley Ave
Orange Park FL 32073-4511
904-264-3200; Fax: 904-269-6958
Circulation: 10,000

Orlando Sentinel
633 N Orange Ave
Orlando FL 32801
407-420-5000; Fax: 900-288-NEWS
Circulation: 273,000; Sun: 400,000

Nancy Pate, Book Editor
John Babinchak II, Central Fl Business
   Editor, Central Florida Business Section
Mike Lafferty, Education Editor
Barry Glenn, Entertainment Editor
Dana Eagles, Features Editor
Mick Lochridge, Features Editor, Glitter
   Column
Heather McPherson, Food Editor
Terri Winefordner, Garden Editor
Delthia Ricks, Health Editor
Terri Winefordner, Home Section Editor
Jane Healy, Managing Editor
Jim Toner, Metro Editor
Mike Lafferty, Religion Editor
Ned Popkins, Science Editor
Steve Doyle, Sports Editor
Micky Lochridge, Style Editor
Richard Burnett, Technology Editor
Lisa Carden, Travel Editor

Palatka Daily News
1825 St Johns Ave
Palatka FL 32177-4442
904-328-7250; Fax: 904-325-0663
Circulation: 14,000

Palm Beach Daily News
265 Royal Poinciana Way
Palm Beach FL 33480-4007
407-820-3800; Fax: 407-655-4594
Circulation: 9,000; Sun: 9,000

News Herald
501 W 11th St
Panama City FL 32401-2330
904-763-7621; Fax: 904-763-4636
Circulation: 38,000

Pensacola News Journal
PO Box 12710
Pensacola FL 32574-2710
904-435-8500; Fax: 904-435-8633
Circulation: 61,000; Sun: 87,000

Susan Catron, Arts/Entertainment Editor
Cindy Hall, Food Editor
Michael Ryan, Managing Editor
David McFarland, Metro Editor
Gordon Paulus, Sports Editor

Sun Herald
23170 Harborview Rd
Port Charlotte FL 33980-2100
941-629-2855; Fax: 941-629-2085
Circulation: 97,000

Sanford Herald
300 N French Ave
Sanford FL 32771-1118
407-322-2611; Fax: 407-323-9408
Circulation: 8,000

Sarasota Herald Tribune
PO Box 1719
Sarasota FL 34230
813-953-7755; Fax: 813-957-5276
Circulation: 125,000

Joel Welim, Arts/Entertainment Editor
Laura Sperling, Book Editor
Tom Buckingham, Business Editor
Rod Thomson, Education Editor
Linda Brandt, Food/Fashion Editor
Bill Steiden, Health/Medical Editor
Diane Tennant, Lifestyle Editor
Mark Howard, Main City Editor
Bruce Jiles, Managing Editor
Waldo Proffitt, Political Editor
Scott Peterson, Sports Editor
Diane Tennant, Travel Editor

St Augustine Record
158 Cordova St
St Augustine FL 32084-5020
904-829-6562; Fax: 904-829-6664
Circulation: 17,000; Sun: 17,000

St Petersburg Times
490 First Ave S (33701)
PO Box 1121
St Petersburg FL 33731-1121
813-893-8111; Fax: 813-893-8675
Circulation: 352,000; Sun: 450,000

Margo Hammond, Book Editor
Andrew Barnes, Editor
Ann Lindberg, Education Editor
Chris Sherman, Food Editor
Bette Smith, Garden Editor
Susan Landry, Health/Medical Editor
Judy Stark, Home Editor
Nancy Waclaweck, Lifestyle/Feature Editor
Neil Brown, Managing Editor
Jack Sheppard, Sports Editor
Bob Jenkins, Travel Editor

Stuart News
1939 S Federal Hwy (34994)
PO Box 9009
Stuart FL 34995-9009
407-287-1550; Fax: 407-221-4246
Circulation: 40,000; Sun: 51,000

Mary Dodge, Business Editor
Laura Kelly, Entertainment Editor
Martha Wilson, Feature Editor
Kim Hurt, Food Editor
Nancy Smith, Managing Editor
Kevin Conway, Sports Editor

Florida Flambeau
Florida State Univ
505 S Woodward St
Tallahassee FL 32304-4337
904-681-6692; Fax: 904-681-3577
Circulation: 21,000

Tallahassee Democrat
277 N Magnolia Dr (32301)
PO Box 990
Tallahassee FL 32302-0990
904-599-2100
Circulation: 60,000; Sun: 78,000

Judy Doyle, Business Editor
Gary Fineout, Education Editor
Zilpha Underwood, Feature Editor
Lorrie Guttman, Food Editor
Bob Shaw, Managing Editor
Byron Dobson, News Editor
Bill Cotterell, Political Editor
Zannah Lyle, Science Editor
Pete Reinwald, Sports Editor
Chuck Beard, Travel Editor

Tampa Tribune
202 S Parker St
PO Box 191
Tampa FL 33601
813-259-7711; Fax: 813-259-7676
Circulation: 286,000; Sun: 300,000

Joe Guidry, Book Editor
Steve Matthews, Business Editor
Frank Ruiz, Computer Editor
Robert Bowden, Food Editor
Beth Dolan, Home Editor
Lawrence McConnell, Managing Editor
Dave Hardin, News Editor
William March, Political Editor
Larry Fletcher, Regional Editor
Michelle Bearden, Religion Editor
Kurt Lost, Science Editor
Paul Smith, Sports Editor
Karen Long, Travel Editor

USF Oracle
Univ of South Florida
4202 E Fowler Ave CPR-472
Tampa FL 33620-9951
813-974-2617; Fax: 813-974-4887
Circulation: 15,000

Vero Beach Press-Journal
1801 US Hwy 1
Vero Beach FL 32960-5415
407-562-2315; Fax: 407-978-2364
Circulation: 33,000; Sun: 34,000

Palm Beach Post
2751 S Dixie Hwy
West Palm Beach FL 33405
407-820-4100; Fax: 407-820-4407
Circulation: 182,000; Sun: 227,000

Larry Aydlette, Arts/Entertainment Editor
Tom Peeling, Assignment Editor
Scott Eyman, Book Editor
Kevin Miller, Business Editor
Viola Gienger, Education Editor
Jan Norris, Food Editor
Stephanie Artero, Health/Medical Editor
Melissa Segrest, Lifestyle Editor
Tom O'Hara, Managing Editor
Fred Zipp, Metro Editor
Price Patton, Political Editor
Stephanie Artero, Science Editor
Tim Burke, Sports Editor
Cheryl Blackerby, Travel Editor

News Chief
650 6th St
Winter Haven FL 33882
813-294-7731; Fax: 813-294-2008
Circulation: 11,000; Sun: 12,000

Georgia

Albany Herald
126 N Washington St
Albany GA 31701-2552
912-888-9300; Fax: 912-888-9357
Circulation: 33,000; Sun: 41,000

Americus Times-Recorder
1612 Vienna Rd
Americus GA 31709
912-924-2751; Fax: 912-928-6344
Circulation: 8,000

Athens Banner-Herald
1 Press Pl
Athens GA 30601-2605
706-549-0123; Fax: 706-208-2246
Circulation: 12,000

Athens Daily News
1 Press Place
Athens GA 30601-2605
706-549-0123; Fax: 706-208-2246
Circulation: 14,000; Sun: 36,000

Red & Black
Univ of Georgia
123 N Jackson St
Athens GA 30601-2735
706-543-1791; Fax: 706-548-7251
Circulation: 16,000

Atlanta Journal & Constitution
72 Marietta St NW
PO Box 4689
Atlanta GA 30302
404-526-5100; Fax: 404-526-5766
Circulation: 282,000

Howard Sabulis, Arts/Entertainment Editor
Michael Skube, Book Editor
Susan Wells, Business Editor
Cindy Gorley, Education Editor
Ann Morris, Features Editor
Susan Puckett, Food Editor
Nick Tate, Health Editor
Connie Green, Home Editor
John Walter, Managing Editor
Mike King, Metro News
Gail White, Religion Editor
Nick Tate, Science Editor
Furman Bisher, Sports Editor
Scott Thurston, Travel Editor

Daily Report
190 Pryor St SW
Atlanta GA 30303-3607
404-521-1227; Fax: 404-523-5924
Circulation: 5,000

Augusta Chronicle
725 Broad St
PO Box 1928
Augusta GA 30903-1928
706-724-0851; Fax: 706-823-3345
Circulation: 83,000; Sun: 102,000

Les Simpson, Arts/Entertainment Editor
Donna Rogers, Business Editor
Les Simpson, Family Editor
Ben Palmer, Health/Medical Editor
Les Simpson, Home Editor
Les Simpson, Lifestyle/Feature Editor
John Fish, Managing Editor
Tom Dardenne, News Editor
Alison Kennedy, Religion Editor

Ben Palmer, Science Editor
Les Simpson, Society Editor
Ward Clayton, Sports Editor

Brunswick News
3011 Altama Ave
Brunswick GA 31520-4608
912-265-8320; Fax: 912-264-4973
Circulation: 16,000

Times Georgian
901 Hays Mill Rd
Carrollton GA 30117-9576
770-834-6631; Fax: 770-834-9991
Circulation: 11,000

Daily Tribune News
251 S Tennessee St
Cartersville GA 30120-3605
770-382-4545; Fax: 770-382-2711
Circulation: 10,000

Columbus Ledger-Enquirer
17 W 12th St (31901)
PO Box 711
Columbus GA 31902-0711
706-324-5526; Fax: 706-576-6290
Circulation: 68,000; Sun: 54,000

Dusty Nix, Book Editor
Carol Hazard, Business Editor
Jeff Davison, City News Editor
Chuck Crouch, Computer Editor
Liza Benham, Education Editor
Judith Bethel, Food Editor
Mandy Williams, Health/Medical Editor
Kassie Sledge, Lifestyle Editor
Sam Jones, Managing Editor
Harry Franklin, Outdoor Editor
Chuck Williams, Sports Editor

Rockdale Citizen
969 S Main St
Conyers GA 30207-4501
770-483-7108; Fax: 770-483-5797
Circulation: 11,000

Cordele Dispatch
306 13th Ave W
Cordele GA 31015-2348
912-273-2277; Fax: 912-273-7239
Circulation: 6,000

Daily Citizen-News
308 S Thornton Ave
Dalton GA 30720-8268
706-278-1011; Fax: 706-275-6641
Circulation: 15,000

Douglas County Sentinel
6405 Fairburn Rd
Douglasville GA 30134-6911
770-942-6571; Fax: 770-949-7556
Circulation: 11,000

Courier Herald
115 S Jefferson St
Dublin GA 31021-5146
912-272-5522; Fax: 912-272-2189
Circulation: 13,000

Gainesville Times
345 Green St NW
PO Box 838
Gainesville GA 30503
770-532-1234; Fax: 770-532-0457
Circulation: 23,000; Sun: 28,000

Jeff Gill, City Editor

Ron Sirmans, Lifestyle/Feature Editor
John Drucken Miller, Managing Editor
Keith Abertson, Sports Editor

Times
345 Green St NW
Gainesville GA 30501-3388
770-532-1234; Fax: 770-532-0457
Circulation: 23,000

Griffin Daily News
323 E Solomon
Griffin GA 30223-3315
770-227-3276; Fax: 770-412-1678
Circulation: 13,000

Clayton News/Daily
138 Church St
Jonesboro GA 30236-3514
770-478-5753; Fax: 770-473-9032
Circulation: 8,000

La Grange Daily News
105 Ashton St
La Grange GA 30240-3111
706-884-7311; Fax: 706-884-8712
Circulation: 16,000

Macon Telegraph
120 Broadway (31201)
PO Box 4167
Macon GA 31213-4199
912-744-4200; Fax: 912-744-4385
Circulation: 75,000; Sun: 100,000

Paul Alexander, Book Editor
Steve Bills, Business Editor
Bill Weaver, City Editor
Sharese Shields, Education Editor
Jane Self, Food Editor
Jodi White, Health/Medical Editor
James Palmer, Lifestyle Editor
Barbara Stinson, Managing Editor
Ron Woodegard, Managing News Editor
Jane Self, Religion Editor
Jodi White, Science Editor
Kevin Proctor, Sports Editor

Marietta Daily Journal
580 Fairground St
Marietta GA 30060-2797
404-428-9411; Fax: 404-422-9533
Circulation: 29,000

Suzzane Van Atten, Arts/Entertainment Editor
Melissa Gurrido, Business Editor
Jay Dillon, City Editor
Jamie Cart, Education Editor
Martha Collins, Lifestyle/Feature Editor
Rodney Shumake, Managing Editor
Billie Mitchell, Sports Editor
Suzzane Van Atten, Travel Editor

Union-Recorder
PO Box 520
Milledgeville GA 31061-0520
912-452-0567; Fax: 912-452-9539
Circulation: 8,000

Moultrie Observer
25 N Main St
Moultrie GA 31768-3861
912-985-4545; Fax: 912-985-3569
Circulation: 8,000

Rome News-Tribune
305 E 6th Ave
Rome GA 30161-6007
706-291-6397; Fax: 706-234-6478
Circulation: 21,000

Savannah News-Press
111 W Bay St
Savannah GA 31401-1191
912-236-9511; Fax: 912-234-6522
Circulation: 80,000; Sun: 82,000

Doug Wyatt, Book Editor
Bob Mathews, Community News Editor
Anne Muller, Education Reporter
Steve Thomas, Govt/Business Editor
Gene Downs, Health/Medical Writer
Dan Suwyn, Managing Editor
David Donal, Projects Editor
Anthony Stastany, Sports Editor

Statesboro Herald
1 Herald Square
Statesboro GA 30458-4500
912-764-9031; Fax: 912-489-8181
Circulation: 8,000

Thomasville Times-Enterprise
106 South St
Thomasville GA 31792-6061
912-226-2400; Fax: 912-228-5863
Circulation: 11,000

Tifton Gazette
211 N Tift Ave
Tifton GA 31794-4463
912-382-4321; Fax: 912-387-7322
Circulation: 9,000

Valdosta Daily Times
201 N Troup St
Valdosta GA 31601-5737
912-244-1880; Fax: 912-244-2560
Circulation: 21,000

Daily Sun
1553 Watson Blvd
Warner Robins GA 31093-3449
912-923-6432; Fax: 912-328-7682
Circulation: 8,000

Waycross Journal-Herald
400 Isabella St
Waycross GA 31501-3637
912-283-2244; Fax: 912-285-5255
Circulation: 13,000

Hawaii

Hawaii Tribune Herald
355 Kinoole St
PO Box 767
Hilo HI 96721
808-935-6621; Fax: 808-961-3680
Circulation: 20,000; Sun: 24,000

Eugene Tao, Managing Editor
D Hunter Bishop, News Editor
Bill O'Rear, Sports Editor

Hawaii Hochi
917 Kokea St
Honolulu HI 96817-4528
808-845-2255; Fax: 808-847-7215
Circulation: 8,000

Honolulu Advertiser
605 Kapiolani Blvd
PO Box 3110
Honolulu HI 96802
808-525-8090; Fax: 808-525-8037
Circulation: 103,000

Wayne Harada, Arts/Entertainment Editor
Ilene Aleshire, Business Editor
Joanne Clark, Food Editor
Wanda Adams, Island Life Editor
Wanda Adams, Lifestyle/Feature Editor
Beverly Creamer, Medical Editor
John Strobel, News Editor
Jamie Turner, Sports Editor
Editor Kennedy, Travel Editor

Honolulu Star-Bulletin
605 Kapiolani Blvd
PO Box 3080
Honolulu HI 96802
808-525-8640; Fax: 808-523-8509
Circulation: 100,000

Burl Burlingame, Book Editor
Editor Lynch, Business Editor
Cynthia Oi, Lifestyle Editor
Dave Shapiro, Managing Editor
Helen Altonn, Science Editor
Paul Carvalho, Sports Editor
Frank Bridgewater, Travel Editor

Ka Leo O Hawaii
Univ of Hawaii at Manoa
1755 Pope Rd Ka Leo Bldg
Honolulu HI 96822-2337
808-956-7043; Fax: 808-956-9962
Circulation: 18,000

United Chinese Press
100 N Beretania St Rm 204
Honolulu HI 96817-4709
808-536-6883; Fax: 808-536-6883
Circulation: 2,000

West Hawaii Today
Reed Flickinger, Managing Editor
75-5580R Kuakini Hwy (96740)
PO Box 789
Kailua Kona HI 96745
808-329-9311; Fax: 808-329-4860
Circulation: 13,000

The Garden Island
Rita DeSilva, Editor
3137 Kuhio Hwy
PO Box 231
Lihue HI 96766
808-245-3681; Fax: 808-245-5286
Circulation: 8,000; Sun: 8,420

Idaho

Morning News
34 N Ash
Blackfoot ID 83221-2101
208-785-1100; Fax: 208-785-4239
Circulation: 5,000

Idaho Statesman
1200 N Curtis Rd
PO Box 40
Boise ID 83707-0040
208-377-6400; Fax: 208-377-6449
Circulation: 68,000; Sun: 84,000

Paul Beebe, Business Editor
Fredreka Schouten, City Editor
Ralph Poore, Editorial Editor
Jonathon Brinkman, Environmental Editor
Michael Deeds, Feature Editor
Michelle Cole, Higher Education Editor
David Woolsey, Lower Classroom Editor
Karen Baker, Managing Editor
Art Lawler, Sports Editor

South Idaho Press
230 E Main St
Burley ID 83318-1830
208-678-2201; Fax: 208-678-0412
Circulation: 7,000

Coeur d'Alene Press
201 2nd Ave
Coeur d'Alene ID 83814-2803
208-664-8176; Fax: 208-664-0212
Circulation: 16,000

Post Register
333 Northgate Mile (83401)
PO Box 1800
Idaho Falls ID 83403
208-522-1800; Fax: 208-529-9683
E-mail: prnews@srv.net
Circulation: 30,000; Sun: 30,000

Paul Menser, Arts\Entertainment
Paul Menser, Book Editor
Jon Jensen, Business Editor
Dean Miller, City/Metro Editor
Dan Egan, Environmental Editor
Paul Menser, Lifestyle\Feature Editor
Mei-Mei Chan, Managing Editor
Cindy Dodson, Medical Editor
Jeff Pinkham, Sports Editor

Shoshone News-Press
401 Main St
Kellogg ID 83837-2630
208-783-1107; Fax: 208-784-6791
Circulation: 5,000

Lewistown Morning Tribune
505 C St
PO Box 957
Lewiston ID 83501-1843
208-743-9411; Fax: 208-746-1185
Circulation: 26,000

Rebecca Huntington, Arts/Entertainment Editor
Rebecca Huntington, Book Editor
Lorraine Nelson, Business Editor
Sandy Lee, Education Editor
Bill Loftus, Environmental Editor
Jeannie DePaul, Food Editor
Joan Abrams, Health/Medical Editor
Jeannie DePaul, Home & Garden Editor
Jeannie DePaul, Lifestyle/Feature Editor
Paul Emerson, Managing Editor
Bill Furstenau, News Editor
Mike Wickline, Political Editor
Jeannie DePaul, Religion Editor
Bert Sahlberg, Sports Editor
Rebecca Huntington, Travel Editor

Moscow-Pullman Daily News
409 S Jackson
Moscow ID 83843-2251
208-882-5561; Fax: 208-883-8205
Circulation: 10,000

Idaho Press-Tribune
1618 N Midland Blvd
Nampa ID 83651-1751
208-467-9251; Fax: 208-467-9562
Circulation: 21,000

Idaho State Journal
305 S Arthur St
PO Box 431
Pocatello ID 83204-3306
208-232-4161; Fax: 208-233-8007
Circulation: 21,000

Mark Mendiola, Business Editor
Tim Jackson, Environment/Science Editor
Juanita Rodriguez, Health Editor
Joy Morrison, Life Editor
Don Black, Managing Editor
Bob Brundage, Sports Editor
Dianna Troyer, Travel Editor

Bonner County Daily Bee
310 Church St
Sandpoint ID 83864-1345
208-263-9534; Fax: 208-263-9091
Circulation: 6,000

Times-News
132 3rd St W
Twin Falls ID 83301-5842
208-733-0931; Fax: 208-734-5538
Circulation: 23,000

Illinois

Telegraph
111 E Broadway
Alton IL 62002-6218
618-463-2500; Fax: 618-463-9829
Circulation: 35,000

Daily Herald
PO Box 280
Arlington Heights IL 60006-1411
708-870-3600; Fax: 708-398-0172
Circulation: 126,000

Cheryl terHorst, Book Editor
Renee Trappe, City Editor
Anna Madrzyk, Fashion Editor
Jean Rudolph, Feature Editor
Jackie Dulen, Food Editor
Dan Rozek, Health/Science Editor
Pat Gerlach, Home/Garden Editor, Seeds for Thought
John Lampinen, Managing Editor
Tom Quinlan, Metro Editor
Jim Cook, Sports Editor
Eileen Brown, Travel Editor

The Beacon News
101 South River St
Aurora IL 60506
708-844-5844; Fax: 708-844-1043
Circulation: 40,000

Dan Waitt, Book/Lifestyles Editor
Jim Peters, Business Editor
John Russell, City Editor
Mike Chapin, Managing Editor
Joe Gillette, Political Editor
Mike Bambach, Sports Editor

Belleville News-Democrat
120 S Illinois St
Belleville IL 62220-2130
618-234-1000; Fax: 618-235-0556
Circulation: 51,000

Belvidere Daily Republican
401 Whitney Blvd
Belvidere IL 61008-3710
815-544-9811; Fax: 815-544-6334
Circulation: 5,000

Benton Evening News
111-113 E Church St
Benton IL 62812-2238
618-439-9550; Fax: 618-435-2413
Circulation: 5,000

Pantagraph
301 W Washington St
PO Box 2907
Bloomington IL 61702-2907
309-829-9411; Fax: 309-829-7000
Circulation: 55,000; Sun: 65,000

Mark Lewis, Art/Entertainment Editor
Jane Pickering, Business Editor
Fred Kardon, Exec Editor
Steve Gleason, Focus/Book Editor
Jan Dennis, Managing Editor
Mark Pickering, News Editor
Brian Bloodworth, Sports Editor

Daily Egyptian
Southern Illinois Univ
Communications Bldg Rm 1259
Carbondale IL 62901
618-536-3311; Fax: 618-453-1992
Circulation: 27,000

Southern Illinoisan
710 N Illinois Ave
Carbondale IL 62901-1283
618-529-5454; Fax: 618-457-2935
Circulation: 32,000

Carmi Times
Barry Cleveland, Managing Editor
323 E Main St
Carmi IL 62821
618-382-4176; Fax: 618-384-2163
Circulation: 3,000

Centralia Sentinel
232 E Broadway
Centralia IL 62801-3251
618-532-5601; Fax: 618-532-1212
Circulation: 15,000; Sun: 17,000

Luanne Droege, Arts/Entertainment Editor
Marcia Mercer, Education Editor
Luanne Droege, Family/Food Editor
Randy Snyder, Managing Editor
Mark Hodapp, Political Editor
Luanne Droege, Religion
Randy List, Sports Editor
Judith Joy, Travel Editor

News Gazette
15 Main St (61820)
PO Box 677
Champaign IL 61824-0677
217-351-5252; Fax: 217-351-5374
Circulation: 50,000

Tom Kacich, Arts/Entertainment Editor
Tom Kacich, Book Editor/Reviewer
Julie Wurth, Education Editor
Linda Zimmer, Elem Education Editor
Tom Kacich, Food Editor
Tom Kacich, Lifestyle/Feature Editor
John Beck, Managing Editor
Dan Corkery, News Editor
Jean McDonald, Sports Editor

Daily Eastern News
Eastern Illinois Univ
Student Publ 600 Lincoln Ave
Charleston IL 61920
217-581-2812; Fax: 217-581-2823
Circulation: 8,000

Times-Courier
307 6th St
Charleston IL 61920-1558
217-345-7085; Fax: 217-345-7090
Circulation: 7,000

Chicago Daily Law Bulletin
415 N State St
Chicago IL 60610-4607
312-644-7800; Fax: 312-644-4255
Circulation: 7,000

Chicago Defender
2400 S Michigan Ave
Chicago IL 60616-2329
312-225-2400; Fax: 312-225-9231
Circulation: 33,000

Chicago Sun-Times
401 N Wabash
Chicago IL 60611-3593
312-321-3000; Fax: 312-321-3679
Circulation: 531,000; Sun: 520,000

Dan Jedlicka, Auto Writer
Henry Kisor, Book Editor
Steve Duke, Business Editor
Maudlyne Iherjirka, Charities/Soc Services
Irv Kupcinet, Columnist, Kup's Column
Michael Sneed, Columnist, Michael Sneed Column
Judy Moore, Columnist, Decorating Column
Dorsey Connors, Columnist, Dorsey Connors Column
Jeffrey Zaslow, Columnist
Richard Roeper, Columnist
Bill Cunniff, Columnist, Homelife
Cindy Richards, Columnist, Editorial Pages
Bill Zwecker, Columnist, Bill Zwecker's People
Dolores & Roger Flaherty, Columnists, Paperbacks Column
Michelle Stevens, Editorial Page Editor
Bill Adee, Exec Sports Editor
Maureen Jenkins, Fashion Writer
Kristi Kempf, Features Editor, Arts & Show/WeekendPlus
Barbara Sadek, Food Editor
Della deLafuente, Health Care/Computers
Roger Ebert, Movie Critc
Jorge Oclander, Multicultural Affairs
Adrienne Drell, Museum/Cultural Editor
Lisa Holton, Pers Finance/Banking
Steve Neal, Political Columnist
Tom McNamee, Publ Health/Medical Editor
Rob Feder, Radio/TV Columnist
Steve Rynkiedicz, Real Estate Editor, Real Estate News
William Smith, Real Estate/Markets Editor
Andrew Hermann, Religion Writer
Brenda Rotzoll, Reporter, City Desk
Mary Ellen Podmolik, Retail/Transportation

Jim Ritter, Science Writer
John Barron, Showcase Editor
Francine Knowles, Small Bus/Women Editor
Rick Telander, Sports Columnist
Jay Mariotti, Sports Columnist
Len Ziehm, Sports Writer
Hedy Weiss, Theatre Critic
Mi-Ai Ahern, Travel Editor
Lon Grahnke, TV Critic
Mary Skilton, Writer, TV Prevue
Bill Rumbler, Writer, Personal Finance Column
Janet Stewart, Writer, Consumer Trends

Chicago Tribune
435 N Michigan Ave
Chicago IL 60611-4041
312-222-3232; Fax: 312-222-3143
Circulation: 700,000; Sun: 1,700,000

Blair Kamin, Architecture Critic, The Arts Section
Doug Balz, Assoc Sunday Managing Editor, Sunday Arts Section
Jim Mateja, Auto Editor
Larry Kart, Book Editor, Tribune Books
William Gruber, Business Columnist, On Business
Patrick Reardon, Urban Affairs Writer
Andrew Leckey, Business & Financial Column, On Personal Finance Column
Richard Christiansen, Chief Critic, The Arts Section
Mary Elson, City Editor
Bill Rice, Columnist, Food and Wine Columns
Mike Conklin, Columnist, Inc Column
Judy Hevrdejs, Columnist, Inc Column
Carol Kleiman, Columnist, The Gardener, Home Section
George Lazarus, Columnist, On Marketing
Denis Gosselin, Editor, Sunday Magazine
Steve Cvengros, Editor of Kid News, Kidnews
Jacqueline Heard, Education Writer, City Education News & Features
Steve Swanson, Environmental Reporter
Teresa Wiltz, Fashion Editor
Lisa Skolnik, Features Columnist, Street Smarts, Home Section
Mary Stevens, Features Columnist, New on Video Column
Kathy O'Malley, Features Columnist, O'Malley & Collin Inc
Cheryl Lavin, Features Columnist, Fast Track Column
Owen Youngman, Features Editor
Carol Haddix, Food Editor, Good Eating
Pamela Sherrod, Garden Writer, The Gardener, Home Section
William Aldrich, Garden Writer, Your Place Section
Cindy Shrueder, Health/Science Writer
Elaine Matsushita, Home Editor
Sallie Gaines, Home Editor, Transportation News & Features
Joseph Coates, Literary Critic, Tribune Books
Ronald Kotulak, Medical/Science Editor
John Wade, Mg Editor of Business
Fred Mitchell, Odds & Ins
John Husar, Outdoors Columnist, On the Outdoors
Clarence Petersen, Paperbacks Reviewer, Tribune Books
Tom Hardy, Political Reporter
Steve Kerch, Real Estate Editor

Paul Galloway, Religion Editor
Peter Gorner, Science Writer
Tim Franklin, Sports Editor
Jon Van, Tech & Science Reporter, Computer & High Technology
Rick Kogan, Tempo Editor
Randy Curwin, Travel Editor
Marla Krause, Women's News Editor

Daily Southtown
5959 S Harlem
Chicago IL 60638-3187
312-586-8800; Fax: 312-229-2555
Circulation: 40,000

George Haas, Book Editor
John Obrecht, Business Editor
Bill Padjen, Community News Editor
George Haas, Feature Editor
Eloise Valadez, Food Editor
Doug Williams, Metro Editor
Mike Waters, Sports Editor

Dodge Construction News
180 N Stetson Ave #910
Chicago IL 60601-6710
312-616-3261; Fax: 312-616-3276
Circulation: 1,000

Draugas
4545 W 63rd St
Chicago IL 60629-5532
312-585-9500; Fax: 312-585-8284
Circulation: 6,000

El Manana Daily
2700 S Harding Ave
Chicago IL 60623-4407
312-521-9137; Fax: 312-521-5351
Circulation: 20,000

Journal of Commerce & Commercial
Paul Conley, Editor--Chicago Bureau
Chicago Mercantile Exchange Bldg
30 S Wacker Dr #1810
Chicago IL 60606
312-466-4480; Fax: 312-930-1515
Circulation: 23,000

Clinton Daily Journal
Rt 54 West
Clinton IL 61727
217-935-3171; Fax: 217-935-6086
Circulation: 9,000

Northwest Herald
1 Herald Square
Crystal Lake IL 60014-8196
815-459-4040; Fax: 815-477-4960
Circulation: 30,000

Commercial News
17 West North
Danville IL 61832-5728
217-446-1000; Fax: 217-446-9825
Circulation: 21,000

Daily Chronicle
1586 Barber Greene Rd
De Kalb IL 60115-8487
815-756-4841; Fax: 815-756-2079
Circulation: 12,000

Northern Star
Northern Illinois Univ
615 Lincoln Ter
De Kalb IL 60115-3052
815-753-0101; Fax: 815-753-0708
Circulation: 17,000

Decatur Herald & Review
PO Box 311
Decatur IL 62525-1802
217-429-5151; Fax: 217-421-7965
Circulation: 43,000; Sun: 54,692

Bill Runinski, Business Editor
Jan Touney, City Editor
George Althoff, Editor
Kristi Ruggles, Education Reporter
Dave Moore, Environmental Editor
Theresa Churchill, Features Editor
Jan Touney, News Editor
Bob Fallstrom, People Editor
Mark Tupper, Sports Editor

Dixon Telegraph
113-115 Peoria Ave
Dixon IL 61021
815-284-2222; Fax: 815-284-2870
Circulation: 11,000

Du Quoin Evening Call
9 N Division St
Du Quoin IL 62832-1405
618-542-2133; Fax: 618-542-2726
Circulation: 4,000

Edwardsville Intelligencer
117 N 2nd St
Edwardsville IL 62025-1938
618-656-4700; Fax: 618-656-7618
Circulation: 7,000

Effingham Daily News
201 N Banker St
Effingham IL 62401-0370
217-347-7151; Fax: 217-342-9315
Circulation: 13,000

Eldorado Daily Journal
1200 Locust St
Eldorado IL 62930-1723
618-273-3379; Fax: 618-273-3738
Circulation: 2,000

The Courier News
300 Lake St
Elgin IL 60120
708-888-7800; Fax: 708-888-7836
Circulation: 32,000

Marge Holbrook, Arts/Entertainment Editor
Dave Gathman, Book Editor
Nick Petersen, Business Editor
Nick Petersen, Food Editor
Michael Bailey, Managing Editor
Paul Harth, Science Editor
Don Wojciechowski, Sports Editor

Daily Northwestern
Northwestern University
1999 Sheridan Rd
Evanston IL 60208-0825
708-491-7206; Fax: 708-491-9905
Circulation: 8,000

Daily Clay County Advocate-Press
105 W North Ave
Flora IL 62839-1613
618-662-2108
Circulation: 3,000

Freeport Journal-Standard
27 S State Ave
Freeport IL 61032-4210
815-232-1171; Fax: 815-232-3601
Circulation: 18,000

Galesburg Register-Mail
140 S Prairie St
Galesburg IL 61401-4605
309-343-7181; Fax: 309-342-5171
Circulation: 19,000

Mike Pulliam, City Editor
Robert Harrison, Editor
Janet Saunders, Lifestyle/Feature Editor
Mike Homco, News Editor
Mike Trueblood, Sports Editor

Kane County Chronicle
1000 Randall Rd
Geneva IL 60134-2567
708-232-9222; Fax: 708-232-4976
Circulation: 17,000

Cindy DiDonna, Arts/Entertainment, Food/Travel, Health/Medical, Lifestyle/Feature, Religion Editor
Roald Haase, Lower Education Editor
Ann Davis, Business Editor
Lee Husfeldt, Managing Editor
Judy Reinert, People/Society Editor
Mark Foster, Political Editor
Daryel Mellema, Sports Editor

Daily Register
35 S Vine
Harrisburg IL 62946-1725
618-253-7147; Fax: 618-252-0863
Circulation: 6,000

Jacksonville Journal Courier
235 W State St
Jacksonville IL 62650-2001
217-245-6121; Fax: 217-245-1226
Circulation: 15,000

Joliet Herald-News
300 Caterpillar Dr
Joliet IL 60436-1047
815-729-6161; Fax: 815-729-6059
Circulation: 51,000

Daily Journal
8 Dearborn Square
Kankakee IL 60901-3909
815-937-3300; Fax: 815-937-3301
Circulation: 33,000; Sun: 35,000

John Stewart, Book Reviewer
Roy Bernard, Business Editor
Phil Angelo, Editor
Martha Purdy, Family/Food Editor
Mary Lu Laffey, Lifestyle/Feature Editor
Ray Bachar, News Editor
Tim Yonke, Sports Editor

Star-Courier
105 E Central Blvd
Kewanee IL 61443-2245
309-852-2181; Fax: 309-852-0010
Circulation: 7,000

Daily News-Tribune
426 Second St
La Salle IL 61301
815-223-3200; Fax: 815-223-2543
Circulation: 21,000

Beverly Sons, Art/Entertainment Editor
Kim Anderson, Business Editor
Linda Kleczewski, Managing Editor
Dave Elsesser, Sports Editor

Times-Illinois
2 River Pl
Lansing IL 60438-6028
708-418-2913; Fax: 708-474-2897
Circulation: 15,000

Lawrence Daily Record
1209 State St
Lawrenceville IL 62439-2332
618-943-2331; Fax: 618-943-3976
Circulation: 4,000

Lincoln Courier
601 Pulaski St
Lincoln IL 62656-2825
217-732-2101; Fax: 217-732-7039
Circulation: 7,000

News-Herald
112 E Ryder
Litchfield IL 62056-2031
217-324-2121; Fax: 217-324-2122
Circulation: 6,000

Macomb Journal
128 N Lafayette St
Macomb IL 61455-2226
309-833-2114; Fax: 309-833-2346
Circulation: 7,000

Marion Daily Republican
502 W Jackson St
Marion IL 62959-2355
618-993-2626; Fax: 618-993-8326
Circulation: 4,000; Sun: 4,300

Mattoon Journal-Gazette
100 Broadway
Mattoon IL 61938-4512
217-235-5656; Fax: 217-235-1925
Circulation: 20,000

Dispatch
1720 5th Ave
Moline IL 61265-7907
309-764-4344; Fax: 309-797-0311
Circulation: 28,000

Daily Review Atlas
400 S Main
Monmouth IL 61462-2164
309-734-3176; Fax: 309-734-7649
Circulation: 4,000

Morris Daily Herald
1804 Division St
Morris IL 60450-1127
815-942-3221; Fax: 815-942-0988
Circulation: 8,000

Register-News
118 N 9th St
Mount Vernon IL 62864-4002
618-242-0117; Fax: 618-242-8286
Circulation: 12,000

Daily Republican Register
115 E 4th St
Mt Carmel IL 62863-2110
618-262-5144; Fax: 618-263-4437
Circulation: 4,000

Daily Vidette
Illinois State Univ, Locust and University
Normal IL 61761
309-438-7685; Fax: 309-438-5211
Circulation: 14,000

Olney Daily Mail
206 Whittle Ave
Olney IL 62450-2251
618-393-2931; Fax: 618-392-2953
Circulation: 5,000

Daily Times
110 W Jefferson St
Ottawa IL 61350-5010
815-433-2000; Fax: 815-433-1626
Circulation: 14,000

Paris Daily Beacon News
218 N Main St
Paris IL 61944-1738
217-465-6424; Fax: 217-463-1232
Circulation: 7,000

Paxton Daily Record
218 N Market St
Paxton IL 60957-1124
217-379-2356; Fax: 217-379-3104
Circulation: 2,000

Pekin Daily Times
20 S 4th St
Pekin IL 61554-4203
309-346-1111; Fax: 309-346-9815
Circulation: 16,000

Peoria Journal Star
1 News Plz
Peoria IL 61643-0001
309-686-3000; Fax: 309-686-3296
Circulation: 82,000; Sun: 102,000

Paul Gordon, Business Editor
Jerry McDowell, City Editor
Dayna Brown, Education Editor
Nancy Trueblood, Feature Editor
Dave Moll, Food Editor
Sally McKee, Health Editor
Jack Brimeyer, Managing Editor
Mike Miller, Religion Editor
Kirk Wessler, Sports Editor
Nancy Trueblood, Travel Editor

Daily Leader
318 N Main St
Pontiac IL 61764-1930
815-842-1153; Fax: 815-842-4388
Circulation: 8,000

Quincy Herald-Whig
130 S 5th
Quincy IL 62301-3916
217-223-5100; Fax: 217-223-9757
Circulation: 26,000

Daily News
302 S Cross St
Robinson IL 62454-2137
618-544-2101; Fax: 618-544-9533
Circulation: 7,000

Rock Island Argus
1724 4th Ave
Rock Island IL 61201-8713
309-786-6441; Fax: 309-786-7639
Circulation: 14,000

Rockford Register Star
99 E State St
Rockford IL 61104
815-987-1200; Fax: 815-987-1365
Circulation: 73,000; Sun: 90,000

Belinda Stewart, City Editor
Jeri Nikolai, Education Editor
Linda Cunningham, Exec Editor
Richard Ramhoff, Features Editor
C W Johnson, Managing Editor
Wally Haas, News Editor
Mark Fraser, Photo Editor
Chuck Sweeny, Political Editor
Randy Ruef, Sports Editor

Shelbyville Daily Union
110 W Main St
Shelbyville IL 62565-1652
217-774-2161; Fax: 217-774-5732
Circulation: 5,000

State Journal-Register
1 Copley Plz
PO Box 219
Springfield IL 62705
217-788-1303; Fax: 217-788-1551
Circulation: 70,000; Sun: 78,000

Margaret Boswell, Arts Editor
Mike Kienzler, Book Editor
Chris Dettro, Business Editor
Steve Fagan, Editor
Doug Tokorski, Education Editor
Charlyn Fargo, Food Editor
Tony Cappaso, Health/Medical Editor
Paul Povse, Lifestyle Editor
Patrick Coburn, Managing Editor
Mike Kienzler, Science Editor
Lynda Schmitz, Travel Editor

Daily Gazette
312 2nd Ave
Sterling IL 61081-3607
815-625-3600; Fax: 815-625-9390
Circulation: 15,000

Times-Press
115 Oak St
Streator IL 61364-2805
815-673-3771; Fax: 815-672-9332
Circulation: 10,000

Breeze Courier
212 S Main St
Taylorville IL 62568-2219
217-824-2233; Fax: 217-824-2026
Circulation: 7,000

Daily Illini
Univ of Illinois
Champaign-Urbana Campus
Urbana IL 61801
217-333-3733; Fax: 217-244-6616
Circulation: 10,000

Times-Republic
1492 E Walnut St
Watseka IL 60970-1806
815-432-5227; Fax: 815-432-5159
Circulation: 4,000

News-Sun
100 W Madison St
Waukegan IL 60085-4312
708-336-7000; Fax: 708-249-7202
Circulation: 40,000

Daily American
111 S Emma St
West Frankfort IL 62896-2729
618-932-2146; Fax: 618-937-6006
Circulation: 4,000

Indiana

Anderson Herald-Bulletin
1133 Jackson St
Anderson IN 46016-1433
317-622-1212; Fax: 317-649-3271
Circulation: 33,000

Evening Star
118 W 9th St
Auburn IN 46706-2225
219-925-2611; Fax: 219-925-2625
Circulation: 8,000

Times-Mail
813 16th St
Bedford IN 47421-3822
812-275-3355; Fax: 812-275-4191
Circulation: 15,000

Knox County Daily News
310 N Main St
Bicknell IN 47512-1720
812-735-2222; Fax: 812-735-2244
Circulation: 3,000

Evening World
29 W Main St
Bloomfield IN 47424-1423
812-384-3501; Fax: 812-384-3741
Circulation: 4,000

The Herald-Times
1900 S Walnut St
PO Box 909
Bloomington IN 47402-0909
812-332-4401; Fax: 812-331-4383
Circulation: 30,000; Sun: 48,000

Kathleen Mills, Book Editor
Brian Werth, Business Editor
Bill Strother, City Editor
Scott Schurez, Editor-in-Chief
Steve Hinnefeld, Education Editor
Bill Strother, Environmental Writer
Kay Long, Lifestyle/Feature Editor
Robert Zaltsberg, Main Editor
Bill Strother, News Editor
Bill Strother, Science Editor
Bob Hammel, Sports Editor

Indiana Daily Student
Indiana University
Ernie Pyle Hall Rm 120
Bloomington IN 47405
812-855-0763; Fax: 812-855-8009
Circulation: 11,000

News-Banner
125 N Johnson St
Bluffton IN 46714-1907
219-824-0224; Fax: 219-824-0700
Circulation: 5,000

Brazil Times
100 Times Square
Brazil IN 47834-2172
812-446-2216; Fax: 812-446-0938
Circulation: 5,000

Chesterton Tribune
,193 S Calumet Rd
Chesterton IN 46304-2433
219-926-1131; Fax: 219-926-6389
Circulation: 5,000

Daily Clintonian
422 S Main St
Clinton IN 47842-2414
317-832-2443
Circulation: 6,000

Post & Mail
116 N Chauncey
Columbia City IN 46725-2002
219-244-5153; Fax: 219-244-7598
Circulation: 5,000

Columbus Republic
333 Second St
Columbus IN 47201
812-372-7811; Fax: 812-379-5711
Circulation: 26,000; Sun: 30,000

Doug Showalter, Book/Life/Features Editor
Mike Martoccia, Business Editor
J K Murphy, Managing Editor
John Harmon, News Editor
Steve Jenson, Sports Editor

Connersville News-Examiner
406 Central Ave
Connersville IN 47331-1926
317-825-0588; Fax: 317-825-4599
Circulation: 9,000

Journal-Review
119 N Green
Crawfordsville IN 47933-1708
317-362-1200; Fax: 317-364-5424
Circulation: 11,000

Decatur Daily Democrat
141 S 2nd St
Decatur IN 46733-1664
219-724-2121; Fax: 219-724-7981
Circulation: 6,000

Elkhart Truth
421 S 2nd St
Elkhart IN 46516-3238
219-294-1661; Fax: 219-294-3895
Circulation: 30,000

Call-Leader
317 S Anderson St
Elwood IN 46036-2018
317-552-3355; Fax: 317-552-3358
Circulation: 4,000

Evansville Courier
300 E Walnut St
Evansville IN 47713-1938
812-424-7711; Fax: 812-422-8196
Circulation: 62,000; Sun: 117,980

Tim Barker, Business Editor
Paul McAuliff, Executive Editor
John Reiter, Features/Food Editor
Mary Lou Berry, Lifestyle Editor
David Johnson, Sports Editor

Evansville Press
300 E Walnut St
Evansville IN 47713-1938
812-424-7711; Fax: 812-464-7641
Circulation: 33,000

Mel Runge, Business Editor
Rick Mark, Feature Editor
Bob Gustin, Managing Editor
Tim Ethridge, Sports Editor

Times
251 E Clinton St
Frankfort IN 46041-1906
317-659-4622; Fax: 317-654-7031
Circulation: 7,000

Daily Journal
PO Box 699
Franklin IN 46131-0699
317-736-7101; Fax: 317-736-2713
Circulation: 17,000

Fort Wayne Journal-Gazette
600 W Main St
PO Box 88
Ft Wayne IN 46801-0088
219-461-8364; Fax: 219-461-8893
Circulation: 63,000; Sun: 139,000

Tom Pellegrene, Business/Science Editor
Sandy Thorn Clark, Features Editor
Sherry Skufca, Managing Editor
Tracy Warner, Metro Editor
Keith Elchert, News Editor
Phil Bloom, Outdoor Editor
Pam Heinecke, People/Book Editor
Justice B Hill, Sports Editor
Harriet Heithaus, Travel/Arts Editor
Tim Sosbe, TV Editor

The News-Sentinel
600 W Main St (46802)
PO Box 102
Ft Wayne IN 46801-0102
219-461-8222; Fax: 219-461-8817
Circulation: 54,000

Marcia Werts, Arts/Entertainment Editor
Marilyn Karst, Business Editor
Lisa Kim Bach, Education Editor
Marcia Werts, Family Editor
Carol Tannehill, Food Editor
Marcia Werts, Garden Editor
Marcia Werts, Health/Medical Editor
Richard Battin, Managing Editor
Mike Johnson, Metro Editor
Mike Dooley, Political Editor
Marcia Werts, Religion Editor
Marcia Werts, Science Editor
Kerry Hubartt, Sports Editor

Gary Post-Tribune
1065 Broadway
Gary IN 46402-2998
219-881-3000; Fax: 219-881-3232
Circulation: 98,000; Sun: 128,000

Linda Williams, Business Editor
Peter L Blum, Editorial Page Editor
William Sutton Jr, Executive Editor
Sharon Wilmore, Lifestyle Editor
Kay Manning, Managing Editor
Kay Manning, News Editor
Don Ward, Sports Editor
Betty Sacek, Travel Editor

Goshen News
114 S Main St
Goshen IN 46526-3702
219-533-2151; Fax: 219-553-0839
Circulation: 16,000

Banner-Graphic
100 N Jackson St
Greencastle IN 46135-1240
317-653-5151; Fax: 317-653-2063
Circulation: 6,000

Daily Reporter
22 W New Road
Greenfield IN 46140-1090
317-462-5528; Fax: 317-467-6009
Circulation: 8,000

Greensburg Daily News
135 S Franklin St
Greensburg IN 47240-2023
812-663-3111; Fax: 812-663-2985
Circulation: 6,000

News-Times
123 S Jefferson St
Hartford City IN 47348-2270
317-348-0110; Fax: 317-348-0112
Circulation: 3,000

Huntington Herald-Press
7 N Jefferson
Huntington IN 46750-2839
219-356-6700; Fax: 219-356-9026
Circulation: 8,000

Court and Commercial Record
431 N Pennsylvania St
Indianapolis IN 46204-1806
317-636-0200; Fax: 317-263-5259
Circulation: 1,000

Indianapolis News
307 N Pennsylvania St (46204)
PO Box 145
Indianapolis IN 46206
317-633-1240; Fax: 317-630-9565
Circulation: 135,000

Zach Dunkin, Arts Editor
George Moore, Auto Editor
David Mannweiler, Book Editor
Pam Klein, Business Editor
Ellen Miller, Daily Features Editor
Frank Caperton, Executive Editor
Patti Denton, Food Editor
Eric Schoch, Health/Medical Editor
Ruth Holiday, Lifestyle/Feature Editor
Ted Daniels, Managing Editor
Nancy Comiskey, Managing Editor
Greg Weaver, Political Editor
Eric Schoch, Science Editor
David Mannweiler, Travel Editor
Steve Hall, TV Editor

Indianapolis Star
307 N Pennsylvania St (46204)
PO Box 145
Indianapolis IN 46206
317-633-1240; Fax: 317-630-9565
Circulation: 229,000; Sun: 400,000

Zach Dunkin, Arts Editor
George Moore, Auto Editor
David Mannweiler, Book Editor
Pam Klein, Business Editor
Ellen Miller, Daily Features Editor
Frank Caperton, Executive Editor
Patti Denton, Food Editor
Eric Schoch, Health/Medical Editor
Ruth Holiday, Lifestyle/Feature Editor
Ted Daniels, Managing Editor
Nancy Comiskey, Managing Editor
Greg Weaver, Political Editor
Eric Schoch, Science Editor
David Mannweiler, Travel Editor

The Herald
216 E 4th St
Jasper IN 47546-3102
812-482-2424; Fax: 812-482-4104
Circulation: 13,000

The Evening News
221 Spring St
Jeffersonville IN 47130-3353
812-283-6636; Fax: 812-284-7080
Circulation: 14,000

The News-Sun
102 N Main St
Kendalville IN 46755-1714
219-347-0400; Fax: 219-347-2693
Circulation: 8,000

Kokomo Tribune
300 N Union St
Kokomo IN 46901-4612
317-459-3121; Fax: 317-456-3815
Circulation: 29,000; Sun: 32,000

Tom Carey, Health/Medical Editor
Tom Carey, Lifestyle/Feature Editor
John Wiles, Managing Editor
David Kitchell, Outdoors/Recreation Editor
Steve Jackson, Political Editor
Julie McClure, Religion Editor
Julie McClure, Science Editor
David Kitchell, Sports Editor
Sydne Brewer, Travel Editor

La Porte Herald-Argus
701 State St
La Porte IN 46350-3328
219-362-2161; Fax: 219-362-2166
Circulation: 13,000

Lafayette Journal & Courier
217 N Sixth St
Lafayette IN 47901-1420
317-423-5511; Fax: 317-420-5246
Circulation: 40,000; Sun: 46,000

Dave Bangert, Arts/Entertainment Editor
Greg Hall, Business Editor
Phil Fiorini, City Editor
David Smith, Computer Editor
Matt Showalter, Education Writer
Greg Hall, Health/Medical Editor
Dave Bangert, Home Editor
Dave Bangert, Lifestyle/Feature Editor
Byron Parvis, Religion Editor
Byron Parvis, Science Editor
Jim Lefko, Sports Editor
Kathy Matter, Travel Editor

Reporter
PO Box 1100
Lebanon IN 46052-3004
317-482-5400; Fax: 317-482-4652
Circulation: 7,000

Linton Daily Citizen
79 S Main St
Linton IN 47441-1818
812-847-4487; Fax: 812-847-9513
Circulation: 9,000

Pharos-Tribune
517 E Broadway
Logansport IN 46947-3154
219-722-5000; Fax: 219-722-5238
Circulation: 13,000

Madison Courier
310 Courier Square
Madison IN 47250
812-265-3641
Circulation: 9,000

Chronicle-Tribune
610 S Adams
Marion IN 46953-2041
317-664-5111; Fax: 317-664-6292
Circulation: 21,000

Daily Reporter
60 S Jefferson St
Martinsville IN 46151-1968
317-342-3311; Fax: 317-342-1446
Circulation: 8,000

News-Dispatch
121 W Michigan St
Michigan City IN 46360-3274
219-874-7211; Fax: 219-872-8511
Circulation: 14,000

Herald Journal
114 S Main St
Monticello IN 47960-2328
219-583-5121; Fax: 219-583-4241
Circulation: 5,000

Ball State Daily News
Ball State Univ
West Quadrangle Rm 212
Muncie IN 47306-0001
317-285-8218; Fax: 317-285-8248
Circulation: 14,000

Muncie Evening Press
125 S High St
PO Box 2408
Muncie IN 47302-0408
317-747-5700; Fax: 317-747-5727
Circulation: 14,000

Ellen Ball, Book, Feature, and Travel Ed
David Penticuff, Business Editor
Brian Walker, Editor
Robin Gibson, Education Editor
Diane Baer, Food Editor
Douglas Walker, Political Editor
Renee Jennings, Religion Editor
Tim Cleland, Sports Editor

Muncie Star
125 S High St
PO Box 2408
Muncie IN 47305
317-747-5700; Fax: 317-747-5748
Circulation: 35,000; Sun: 38,000

Rodney Ritchey, Arts/Entertainment Editor
Kerry Arter, Asst Managing Editor
Rodney Ritchey, Book Editor/Reviewer
Mandy Cheesman, Business Editor
Larry Shores, Editor
Donna Penticuff, Health/Medical and
    Lifestyle/Feature Editor
Larry Lough, Managing Editor
G K Hawes, Metro News Editor
Randy Benson, Sports Editor
Donna Penticuff, Travel Editor

The Times
601 45th Ave
Munster IN 46321
219-933-3200; Fax: 219-933-3249
Circulation: 70,000; Sun: 78,000

Matt Mansfield, Arts/Entertainment, Book
    Family, Food, and Garden Editor
Doug Ross, Business Editor
Tracy Hayhurst, Education Editor
Michelle Gerry, Health/Medical Editor
Tim Harmon, Managing Editor
Melinda Mitchell, People/Society Editor
Bob Brown, Political Editor
Alisson Skertic, Religion Editor
Mitch Krugel, Sports Editor

Tribune
303 Scribner Dr
New Albany IN 47150-3549
812-944-6481; Fax: 812-949-6585
Circulation: 11,000

Courier-Times
201 S 14th St
New Castle IN 47362-3328
317-529-1111; Fax: 317-529-1731
Circulation: 12,000

Noblesville Daily Ledger
957 Logan St
Noblesville IN 46060-2226
317-773-1210; Fax: 317-773-3872
Circulation: 11,000

Observer
Notre Dame Univ
314 La Fortune Student Ctr
Notre Dame IN 46556
219-631-7471; Fax: 219-631-6927
Circulation: 13,000

Peru Daily Tribune
26 W 3rd St
Peru IN 46970-2155
317-473-6641; Fax: 317-472-4438
Circulation: 8,000

Pilot-News
217-223 N Center St
Plymouth IN 46563-2103
219-936-3101; Fax: 219-936-3844
Circulation: 8,000

Commercial Review
309 W Main St
Portland IN 47371-1803
219-726-8141; Fax: 219-726-8143
Circulation: 6,000

Princeton Daily Clarion
100 N Gibson
Princeton IN 47670-1855
812-385-2525; Fax: 812-386-6199
Circulation: 7,000

Rensselaer Republican
117 N Van Rensselaer St
Rensselaer IN 47978-2651
219-866-5111; Fax: 219-866-3775
Circulation: 3,000

Palladium-Item
1175 North A St
Richmond IN 47374-3226
317-962-1575; Fax: 317-973-4570
Circulation: 21,000

Rochester Sentinel
118 E 8th St
Rochester IN 46975-1508
219-223-2111; Fax: 219-223-5782
Circulation: 5,000

Rushville Republican
219 N Perkins St
Rushville IN 46173-1851
317-932-2222; Fax: 317-932-4358
Circulation: 4,000

Seymour Daily Tribune
1215 E Tipton
Seymour IN 47274-3531
812-522-4871; Fax: 812-522-7691
Circulation: 10,000

Shelbyville News
123 E Washington St
Shelbyville IN 46176-1463
317-398-6631; Fax: 317-398-0194
Circulation: 12,000

South Bend Tribune
225 W Colfax Ave
South Bend IN 46626-0001
219-235-6161; Fax: 219-236-1765
Circulation: 88,000; Sun: 126,000

Andy Hughes, Book Editor
Ray Leliaert, Business Editor
Greg Swiercz, City Editor
Howard Dukes, Education Editor
Becky Tull, Fashion Editor
Charlotte Smith, Food Editor
Tyna Landgrebe, Home Editor
Virginia Black, Living Today Editor
Tim Harmon, Managing Editor
Nancy Soulk, Metro Editor
Jack Colwell, Political Editor
Sharon Brown, Science Editor
Bill Bilinski, Sports Editor
Kathleen McKernen, Travel Editor

Spencer Evening World
114 E Franklin
Spencer IN 47460-1818
812-829-2255; Fax: 812-829-4666
Circulation: 4,000

Sullivan Daily Times
115 W Jackson Ave
Sullivan IN 47882-1505
812-268-6356; Fax: 812-268-3110
Circulation: 5,000

Tribune-Star
721 Wabash Ave
Terre Haute IN 47807-3220
812-231-4200; Fax: 812-231-4234
Circulation: 35,000; Sun: 45,000

Tipton County Tribune
110 W Madison St
Tipton IN 46072-1832
317-675-2115; Fax: 317-674-4147
Circulation: 4,000

Vidette Times
1111 Glendale Blvd
Valparaiso IN 46383-3724
219-462-5151; Fax: 219-465-7298
Circulation: 16,000

Vincennes Sun-Commercial
702 Main St
Vincennes IN 47591-2910
812-886-9955; Fax: 812-885-2235
Circulation: 14,000

Wabash Plain Dealer
123 W Canal St
Wabash IN 46992-3042
219-563-2131; Fax: 219-563-0816
Circulation: 8,000

Times-Union
Times Bldg
Warsaw IN 46580
219-267-3111
Circulation: 14,000

Washington Times-Herald
102 E Vantress St
Washington IN 47501-2943
812-254-0480; Fax: 812-254-7517
Circulation: 10,000

Purdue Exponent
Purdue University
460 Northwestern Ave
West Lafayette IN 47906-2966
317-743-1111; Fax: 317-743-6087
Circulation: 21,000

News-Gazette
224 W Franklin St
Winchester IN 47394-1808
317-584-4501; Fax: 317-584-3066
Circulation: 5,000

Iowa

Ames Daily Tribune
317 5th St
Ames IA 50010-6101
515-232-2160; Fax: 515-232-2364
Circulation: 10,000

Iowa State Daily
Iowa State Univ of Science/Tech
Ames IA 50011
515-294-4120; Fax: 515-294-4119
Circulation: 16,000

Atlantic News-Telegraph
410 Walnut St
Atlantic IA 50022-1365
712-243-2624; Fax: 712-243-4988
Circulation: 6,000

The Hawk Eye
PO Box 10
Burlington IA 52601
319-754-8461; Fax: 319-754-6824
Circulation: 20,000

Dena Bennett, Arts/Entertainment Editor
Steve Delaney, Business Editor
Kathy Oberle, Education Editor
Criss Wilson, Environmental Editor
Dena Bennett, Lifestyle/Feature Editor
Dale Alison, Managing Editor
Jeff Lehr, Political Editor
Craig Fesker, Sports Editor

Carroll Daily Times-Herald
508 N Court St
Carroll IA 51401-2747
712-792-3573; Fax: 712-792-5218
Circulation: 6,000

The Gazette
500 Third Ave SE (52401)
PO Box 511
Cedar Rapids IA 52406
319-398-8211; Fax: 319-398-5846
Circulation: 71,000; Sun: 80,000

Cindy Chapman, Arts/Entertainment Editor
Lynn Feurback, Assoc Financial Editor
Bridget Janus, Book Editor
Lyle Muller, Bureau Chief
George C Ford, Business Editor
Jerry Elsea, Editorial Page Editor
Becky Stover, Education Editor
Dave Morris, Features Editor
Anne Rutter, Food Editor
Dave Morris, Lifestyle Editor
Mark Bowden, Managing Editor
Mary Sharpe, Metro-Iowa/News Editor
Bev Duffy, Religion Editor
Ken Sullivan, Senior Editor
Kathy Phelps Hogan, Special Sections Editor
Mark Dukes, Sports Editor

Daily Iowegian
105 N Main St
Centerville IA 52544-1732
515-856-6336; Fax: 515-856-8118
Circulation: 3,000

Charles City Press
801 Riverside
Charles City IA 50616-2248
515-228-3211; Fax: 515-228-2641
Circulation: 3,000

Cherokee Daily Times
111 S 2nd St
Cherokee IA 51012-1839
712-225-5111; Fax: 712-225-2910
Circulation: 3,000

Clinton Herald
221 6th Ave S
PO Box 2961
Clinton IA 52733-2961
319-242-7101; Fax: 319-242-3854
Circulation: 25,000

Dave Overby, Book Editor
Lynn Darr, Business Editor
Penny Smith, Food Editor
Penny Smith, Lifestyle/Feature Editor
Bill Baker, Managing Editor
George Kampling, Sports Editor

Council Bluffs Nonpareil
117 Pearl St
Council Bluffs IA 51501-4264
712-328-1811; Fax: 712-328-1597
Circulation: 21,000; Sun: 24,000

Jim Lovely, Arts/Entertainment Editor
Jim Lovely, Book Editor/Reviewer
Katherine Stoltzfus, Business Editor
Ruth Hall, City Editor
Carla Chance, Lifestyle Editor
Charles Gates, Managing Editor
Steve Sigafoose, Sports Editor

Creston News-Advertiser
503 W Adams St
Creston IA 50801-3112
515-782-2141; Fax: 515-782-6628
Circulation: 5,000

Quad City Times
500 E Third St (52801)
PO Box 3828
Davenport IA 52808-3828
319-383-2334; Fax: 319-383-2370
Circulation: 60,000; Sun: 84,000

Julia LaBua, Book Reviewer
Bill Jacobs, Business Editor
Daniel K Hayes, Editor
Alma Gaul, Family/Food/Garden Editor
Linda Barr-Barlow, Health Editor
Jim Renkes, Lifestyle/Feature Editor
Chris Juzwik, Sports Editor
Shirley Davis, Travel Editor

Bulletin & Review
Denison Newspapers Inc
Box 550
Denison IA 51442-0550
712-263-2123
Circulation: 5,000

Dale Wegner, Education Editor
Lisa Akers, Lifestyle Editor
Richard Knowles, Managing Editor
Chuck Signs, News Editor
Todd Danner, Sports Editor

Des Moines Register
715 Locust St (50309)
PO Box 957
Des Moines IA 50304
515-284-8535; Fax: 515-286-2504
Circulation: 199,000; Sun: 324,000

Joan Bunke, Arts/Book Editor
Rick Jost, Business Editor
Richard Doak, Editorial Page Editor
Randy Evans, Education Editor
David Witke, Exec Sports Editor
Jerry Perkins, Farm Editor
Jeanne Abbott, Feature Editor
Randy Evans, Iowa News Editor
Christine Riccelli, Lifestlye Editor
Diane Graham, Managing Editor
Robert Borsellino, Metro Editor
David Yepson, Political Editor

Telegraph Herald
80 Bluff St
PO Box 688
Dubuque IA 52004-0688
319-588-5611; Fax: 319-588-5745
Circulation: 35,000; Sun: 40,000

Jim Swenson, Arts/Entertainment Editor
Kathy Berg Strom, Business Editor
Jim Swenson, Computer Editor
Mike Krapfe, Education Editor
Mike Krapfe, Environmental Editor
Jim Swenson, Family/Food Editor
Jim Swenson, Health/Medical Editor
Soren Nielsen, Managing Editor
Lyn Jerde, Religion Editor
Renny Zeutz, Sports Editor

Estherville Daily News
Ron Menendez, Publ/Editor
10 North 7th St
Estherville IA 51334-2232
712-362-2622; Fax: 712-362-2624
Circulation: 2,000

The Fairfield Ledger
112-114 East Broadway
PO Box 171
Fairfield IA 52556-3202
515-472-4129; Fax: 515-472-1916
Circulation: 8,000

Desi Avaux, Book Reviewer
Martha Jacobs, Lifestyle Editor
Beth Dalbey, News Editor
Bobby Lowenberg, Religion Editor
Matt Brindley, Sports Editor
Marni Mellen, Staff Reporter

The Messenger
713 Central Ave
Fort Dodge IA 50501-3813
515-573-2141; Fax: 515-573-2141
Circulation: 22,000

Larry Johnson, Arts/Entertainment Editor
Larry Johnson, Book Editor/Reviewer
B W Hughes, Business Editor
Russ Roberts, Computer Editor
Molly Bates, Education Editor
Larry Johnson, Environmental Editor
Kara Hildreth, Family/Food/Garden Editor
Kara Hildreth, Lifestyle/Feature Editor
Larry Johnson, Managing Editor
Russ Roberts, Science/News Editor
Bill McIntyre, Sports Editor

Daily Democrat
1226 Ave H
Fort Madison IA 52627-4544
319-372-6421; Fax: 319-372-3867
Circulation: 7,000

Harlan Tribune
Tribune Newspapers Inc
1114 7th Box 721
Harlan IA 51537
712-755-3111; Fax: 712-755-3324
Circulation: 5,000 (Mon and Thurs)

Alan Mores, Computer Editor
Steve Mores, Managing Editor

Daily Iowan
Univ of Iowa
201 Communication Ctr
Iowa City IA 52242-1528
319-335-6063; Fax: 319-335-6184
Circulation: 20,000

Iowa City Press-Citizen
Press Citizen Co
1725 N Dodge
Iowa City IA 52245-2606
319-337-3181; Fax: 319-339-7342
Circulation: 18,000

Laurie Miles, Book Editor/Reviewer
Steve Smith, Education Editor
Jan Nierling, Lifestyle/Feature Editor
Dan Hogan, Managing Editor
Susan Gage, News Editor
Steve Riley, Sports Editor

Daily Gate City
1016 Main St
Keokuk IA 52632-4656
319-524-8300; Fax: 319-524-4363
Circulation: 6,000

Le Mars Daily Sentinel
41 1st Ave NE
Le Mars IA 51031-3535
712-546-7031; Fax: 712-546-7035
Circulation: 4,000

Times-Republican
135 W Main St
Marshalltown IA 50158-5843
515-753-6611; Fax: 515-753-7221
Circulation: 12,000

Globe-Gazette
300 N Washington
Mason City IA 50401-3222
515-421-0500; Fax: 515-421-0516
Circulation: 21,000

Mount Pleasant News
215 W Monroe St
Mount Pleasant IA 52641-2110
319-385-3131
Circulation: 4,000

Muscatine Journal
301 E 3rd St
Muscatine IA 52761-4116
319-263-2331; Fax: 319-262-8042
Circulation: 9,000

Newton Daily News
,200 1st Ave E
Newton IA 50208-3716
515-792-3121; Fax: 515-792-5505
Circulation: 8,000

Daily Register
25 1st St SE
Oelwein IA 50662-2306
319-283-2144; Fax: 319-283-3268
Circulation: 6,000

Oskaloosa Herald
Donrey Media Group
Box 530
Oskaloosa IA 52557-0530
515-672-2581; Fax: 515-672-2294
Circulation: 4,000

Kimberly Walker, Managing Editor

Ottumwa Courier
213 E Second St
Ottumwa IA 52501-2902
515-684-4611; Fax: 515-684-7834
Circulation: 19,000

Judy Krieger, Arts/Entertainment Editor
Tricia Kenyon, Business Editor
Tricia DeWall, Health Editor
Rusty Cunningham, Managing Editor
Sally Finder-Koziol, News Editor
Tricia DeWall, Political Editor
Bob Fenske, Sports Editor

Valley News Today
702 W Sheridan
Shenandoah IA 51601-1742
712-246-3097; Fax: 712-246-3099
Circulation: 3,500

Sioux City Journal
Sixth & Pavonia Sts
Sioux City IA 51102
712-279-5075; Fax: 712-279-5059
Circulation: 60,000

Bruce Miller, Arts/Entertainment Editor
Bruce Miller, Book Editor/Reviewer
Mark Reinders, Business Editor
Julie Schoenherr, Education Editor
Marcia Poole, Food Editor
Lynn Zerschling, Health/Medical Editor
Bruce Miller, Lifestyle/Feature Editor
Glenn Olson, News Editor

Glenn Olson, Political Editor
Glenn Olson, Religion Editor
Terry Hersom, Sports Editor
Bruce Miller, Travel Editor

Daily Reporter
416 1st Ave W
Spencer IA 51301-4006
712-262-6610; Fax: 712-262-3044
Circulation: 4,000

Pilot-Tribune
111 West 7th
Storm Lake IA 50588-1824
712-732-3130; Fax: 712-732-3152
Circulation: 6,000

Cedar Valley Daily Times
Mid-American Publishing Corp
108 E 5th St Box 468
Vinton IA 52349-1759
319-472-2311
Circulation: 3,000

Doug Linder, Business Editor
Mary Stephens, Family Editor
Dan Adix, Managing/Lifestyle Editor
Jeff Holmes, Sports Editor

Washington Evening Journal
PO Box 471
Washington IA 52353-0471
319-653-2191; Fax: 319-653-7524
Circulation: 4,000

Waterloo-Cedar Falls Daily Courier
501 Commercial St (50701)
PO Box 540
Waterloo IA 50704
319-291-1400; Fax: 319-291-2069
Circulation: 50,000; Sun: 60,000

Carolyn Cole, Arts/Entertainment Editor
Melody Parker, Book Review Editor
Pat Kinney, Business Editor
Saul Shapiro, Editor
Eric Woolson, Editorial Page Editor
Curtis Glenn, Family/Food/Garden Editor
Carolyn Cole, Lifestyle/Feature Editor
Nancy Raffensperger, Managing Editor
Kevin Evans, Sports Editor

Daily Freeman-Journal
720 2nd St
Webster City IA 50595-1437
515-832-4350; Fax: 515-832-2314
Circulation: 4,000

Kansas

Abliene Reflector-Chronicle
303 Broadway
Abilene KS 67410-2616
913-263-1000; Fax: 913-263-1645
Circulation: 4,700

Arkansas City Traveler
200 E 5th Ave
Arkansas City KS 67005-2606
316-442-4200; Fax: 316-442-7483
Circulation: 6,000

Atchison Daily Globe
1015-25 Main St
Atchison KS 66002-2711
913-367-0583; Fax: 913-367-7531
Circulation: 5,000

Augusta Daily Gazette
204 E 5th St
Augusta KS 67010-1012
316-775-2218; Fax: 316-775-3220
Circulation: 7,000

Beloit Daily Call & Post
122 E Court St
Beloit KS 67420-2311
913-738-3537; Fax: 913-738-6442
Circulation: 2,000

Chanute Tribune
15 N Evergreen
Chanute KS 66720-1831
316-431-4100; Fax: 316-431-2635
Circulation: 4,000

Clay Center Dispatch
805 5th St
Clay Center KS 67432-2502
913-632-2127
Circulation: 3,000

Coffeyville Journal
8th & Elm Sts
Coffeyville KS 67337
316-251-3300; Fax: 316-251-1905
Circulation: 7,000

Colby Free Press
155 W 5th St
Colby KS 67701-2312
913-462-3963; Fax: 913-462-7749
Circulation: 3,000

Columbus Daily Advocate
215 S Kansas
Columbus KS 66725-1718
316-429-2773; Fax: 316-429-3223
Circulation: 3,000

Blade-Empire
510 Washington St
Concordia KS 66901-2117
913-243-2424; Fax: 913-243-4407
Circulation: 3,000

Council Grove Republican
208 W Main St
Council Grove KS 66846-1705
316-767-5123
Circulation: 2,000

Daily Reporter
201 S Baltimore
Derby KS 67037-1405
316-788-2835; Fax: 316-788-0854
Circulation: 2,000

Dodge City Daily Globe
705 2nd
Dodge City KS 67801
316-225-4151; Fax: 316-225-4154
Circulation: 8,000

El Dorado Times
114 North Vine
El Dorado KS 67042-2028
316-321-1120; Fax: 316-321-7722
Circulation: 4,000

Emporia Gazette
517 Merchant St
Emporia KS 66801-4060
316-342-4800; Fax: 316-342-8108
Circulation: 11,000
Peggy Mooney, Business Editor
Susan Heff, City Editor
Barbara White Walker, Editor
Ray Call, Executive Editor
Gwen Larson, Lifestyle/Feature Editor
Pat Kelley, Managing Editor
Brent Maycock, Sports Editor

Fort Scott Tribune
6 E Wall St
Fort Scott KS 66701-1423
316-223-1460; Fax: 316-223-1469
Circulation: 4,000

Garden City Telegram
310 N 7th St
Garden City KS 67846-5521
316-275-8500; Fax: 316-275-5165
Circulation: 12,000

Great Bend Tribune
2012 Forest St
Great Bend KS 67530-4014
316-792-1211; Fax: 316-792-3441
Circulation: 8,000

Daily News
507 Main St
Hays KS 67601-4228
913-628-1081; Fax: 913-628-8186
Circulation: 13,000

Hiawatha Daily World
607 Utah St
Hiawatha KS 66434-2319
913-742-2111; Fax: 913-742-2276
Circulation: 3,000

Hutchinson News
PO Box 190
Hutchinson KS 67504-0190
316-662-3311; Fax: 316-694-5767
Circulation: 42,000
Joyce Hall, Book Editor/Reviewer
Sara Peterson, Business Editor
Jim Beasley, Computer Editor
Chris Koger, Education Editor
Karen Martinez, Food Editor
Joyce Hall, Lifestyle Editor
Steve Whitmore, Managing News Editor
Stephanie Prince, Religion Editor
Bob Davidson, Sports Editor
Pat Holland, Travel Editor

Independence Daily Reporter
320 N 6th
Independence KS 67301-3129
316-331-3550; Fax: 316-331-3550
Circulation: 9,000

Iola Register
302 S Washington St
Iola KS 66749-3225
316-365-2111; Fax: 316-365-6289
Circulation: 4,000

Daily Union
222 W 6th
Junction City KS 66441-3047
913-762-5000; Fax: 913-762-4584
Circulation: 7,000

Kansas City Kansan
901 N 8th St
Kansas City KS 66101-2706
913-371-4300; Fax: 913-342-8620
Circulation: 14,000

Tiller and Toiler
115 W 5th St
Larned KS 67550-3016
316-285-3111; Fax: 316-285-6062
Circulation: 3,000

Journal-World
609 New Hampshire
Lawrence KS 66044-2243
913-843-1000; Fax: 913-843-4512
Circulation: 20,000

University Daily Kansan
Univ of Kansas
119 Stauffer-Flint Hall
Lawrence KS 66045-0001
913-864-4358; Fax: 913-864-5261
Circulation: 13,000

Southwest Daily Times
16 S Kansas Ave
Liberal KS 67901-3732
316-624-2541; Fax: 316-624-0735
Circulation: 7,000

Lyons Daily News
210 W Commercial
Lyons KS 67554-2716
316-257-2368; Fax: 316-257-2369
Circulation: 2,000

Kansas State Collegian
Kansas State University
Kedzie 103
Manhattan KS 66506
913-532-6555; Fax: 913-532-7309
Circulation: 14,000

Manhattan Mercury
318 N 5th St
Manhattan KS 66502-5910
913-776-2200; Fax: 913-776-8807
Circulation: 15,000

McPherson Sentinel
301 S Main
McPherson KS 67460-4831
316-244-2422; Fax: 316-241-2425
Circulation: 6,000

Newton Kansan
121 W 6th St
Newton KS 67114-2117
316-283-1500; Fax: 316-283-2471
Circulation: 8,000

Telegram
PO Box 320
Norton KS 67654-0320
913-877-3361
Circulation: 2,000

Olathe News
514 S Kansas
Olathe KS 66061-4548
913-764-2211; Fax: 913-764-3672
Circulation: 9,000

Herald
104 S Cedar St
Ottawa KS 66067-2318
913-242-4700; Fax: 913-242-9420
Circulation: 6,000

Parsons Sun
220 S 18th St
Parsons KS 67357-4218
316-421-2000; Fax: 316-421-2217
Circulation: 7,000

Morning Sun
701 N Locust St
Pittsburg KS 66762-4038
316-231-2600; Fax: 316-231-0645
Circulation: 12,000

Pratt Tribune
320 S Main St
Pratt KS 67124-2706
316-672-5511; Fax: 316-672-5514
Circulation: 3,000

Russell Daily News
802 N Maple St
Russell KS 67665-1937
913-483-2116; Fax: 913-483-4012
Circulation: 4,000

Salina Journal
333 S 4th St
Salina KS 67401-3903
913-823-6363; Fax: 913-823-3207
Circulation: 31,000

Topeka Capital-Journal
616 SE Jefferson
Topeka KS 66607-1120
913-295-1111; Fax: 913-295-1230
Circulation: 70,000; Sun: 80,00

Mark Sommer, Arts/Entertainment Editor
Joe Taschler, Business Editor
Kristen Hays, Education Editor
Karen Sipes, Feature Editor
Lisa Sodders, Food Editor
Mark Sommer, Health Editor
Mark Sommer, Living Editor
Anita Miller, Managing Editor
Jim Ramberg, Outdoor Writer
Roger Myers, Political Editor
Mark Sommer, Religion Editor
Pete Goehring, Sports Editor
Karen Sipes, Travel Editor

Wellington Daily News
113 W Harvey
Wellington KS 67152-3840
316-326-3326; Fax: 316-326-3290
Circulation: 4,000

Wichita Eagle
825 E Douglas
PO Box 820
Wichita KS 67201
316-268-6000; Fax: 316-268-6627
Circulation: 112,000; Sun: 188,828

Susan Rife, Arts/Entertainment Editor
Chuck Potter, Book Editor
Anita Schrodt, Business Editor
Davis Merritt, Editor
Suzanne Perez Tobias, Education Editor
Jean Hays, Environmental Editor
Tom Koetting, Family Editor
Bonnie Bing, Fashion/Society Editor
Lori Linenberger, Food Editor

Frank Good, Garden Editor
Karen Shideler, Health/Medical Editor
Tom Schaefer, Lifestyle/Feature Editor
Pete Ellis, Metro Editor
Steve Harper, Outdoors Editor
Bill Bartel, Political Editor
Tom Schaefer, Religion Editor
Tom Shine, Sports Editor
Jane Bernhart, Travel Editor

Winfield Daily Courier
201 E 9th St
Winfield KS 67156-2817
316-221-1050; Fax: 316-221-1101
Circulation: 6,000

Kentucky

Daily Independent
224 17th St
Ashland KY 41101-7606
606-329-1717; Fax: 606-324-8434
Circulation: 25,000

Daily News
813 College St
Bowling Green KY 42101-2132
502-781-1700; Fax: 502-781-0726
Circulation: 21,000

Times-Tribune
201 N Kentucky St
Corbin KY 40701-1529
606-528-2464; Fax: 606-528-9850
Circulation: 8,000

Kentucky Post
421 Madison Ave
Covington KY 41011-1519
606-292-2642; Fax: 606-291-2525
Circulation: 50,000

Tom Williams, Business Editor
Debra Vance, Education Editor
Rosemary Weathers, Health/Medical Editor
Becky Whitlock, Lifestyle/Feature Editor
Mike Farrell, Managing Editor
Sacha Deveroomen, Religion Editor
Tom Gamble, Sports Editor

Advocate-Messenger
330 S 4th St
Danville KY 40422-2033
606-236-2551; Fax: 606-236-9566
Circulation: 12,000

News-Enterprise
408 W Dixie Ave
Elizabethtown KY 42701-2433
502-769-2312; Fax: 502-765-7318
Circulation: 16,000

State Journal
Carl West, Editor
321 W Main St
Frankfort KY 40601
502-227-4556; Fax: 502-227-2831
Circulation: 12,000

Glasgow Daily Times
100 Commerce Dr
Glasgow KY 42141-1153
502-678-5171; Fax: 502-678-5052
Circulation: 10,000

Harlan Daily Enterprise
1548 Hwy 421 S
Harlan KY 40831-2501
606-573-4510; Fax: 606-573-0042
Circulation: 7,000

Gleaner
455 Klutey Park Plz
Henderson KY 42420-5213
502-827-2000; Fax: 502-827-2765
Circulation: 11,000

Kentucky New Era
PO Box 729
Hopkinsville KY 42240-4430
502-886-4444; Fax: 502-887-3222
Circulation: 16,000

David Jennings, Arts/Entertainment Editor
David Riley, Assistant Editor
David Jennings, Book Editor/Reviewer
Mary D Ferguson, Business Editor
Lamar Bryan, City Editor
Tanya Smith, Education Editor
Laura Field, Lifestyle/Feature Editor
Mike Herndon, Managing Editor
Ray Duckworth, Outdoors/Recreation Editor
Tanya Smith, Religion Editor
Ray Duckworth, Sports Editor
Mary D Ferguson, Travel Editor

Kentucky Kernel
Univ of Kentucky
026 Journalism Bldg
Lexington KY 40506-0001
606-257-2872; Fax: 606-323-1906
Circulation: 30,000

Lexington Herald-Leader
100 Midland Ave
Lexington KY 40508-1712
606-231-3100; Fax: 606-254-9738
Circulation: 125,000; Sun: 165,000

Sheila Reed, Arts/Entertainment Editor
Art Jester, Book Editor
Cheryl Truman, Business Editor
Todd Pack, Computer Editor
Tim Kelley, Executive Editor
Paula Anderson, Feature Editor
Angie Muhs, Higher Education Editor
Betty Lee-Mastin, Home Editor
Lucy May, Lower Education Editor
Jim Warren, Medical/Health Editor
Jamie Lucke, Political Editor
Paul Prather, Religion Editor
Gene Abell, Sports Editor

Daily Record
436 S 7th St 3rd Fl
Louisville KY 40203-1966
502-583-4471; Fax: 502-585-5453
Circulation: 300

Louisville Courier-Journal
525 W Broadway
PO Box 740031
Louisville KY 40201-7431
502-582-4011; Fax: 502-582-4200
Circulation: 240,000; Sun: 321,692

Maureen McNerney, Arts & Entertainment Editor
Larry Pellegrino, Book Editor
Linda Raymond, Business Editor
Hunt Helm, City Editor
Greg Johnson, Feature Editor
Sarah Fritschner, Food Editor

Diane Heilenman, Home Editor
Stephen Ford, Managing Editor
Al Cross, Political Editor
Harry Bryan, Sports Editor

Messenger
221 S Main St
Madisonville KY 42431-2557
502-821-6833; Fax: 502-821-6855
Circulation: 10,000

Mayfield Messenger
201 N 8th St
Mayfield KY 42066-1825
502-247-5223; Fax: 502-247-6336
Circulation: 7,000

Ledger Independent
41-43 W 2nd St
Maysville KY 41056-1101
606-564-9091; Fax: 606-564-6893
Circulation: 9,000

Middlesboro Daily News
120 N 11th St
Middlesboro KY 40965-1024
606-248-1010; Fax: 606-248-7614
Circulation: 7,000

Murray Ledger and Times
PO Box 1040
Murray KY 42071-1040
502-753-1916; Fax: 502-759-1927
Circulation: 8,000

Messenger-Inquirer
1401 Frederica St
Owensboro KY 42301-4804
502-926-0123; Fax: 502-685-3446
Circulation: 32,000

Paducah Sun
408 Kentucky Ave
Paducah KY 42003-1550
502-443-1771; Fax: 502-442-7859
Circulation: 30,000

Richmond Register
380 Big Hill Ave
Richmond KY 40475-2012
606-623-1669; Fax: 606-623-2337
Circulation: 10,000

Commonwealth-Journal
110 E Mt Vernon St
Somerset KY 42501-1411
606-678-8191; Fax: 606-679-9225
Circulation: 8,000

Winchester Sun
Wall & Cleveland
Winchester KY 40391
606-744-3123; Fax: 606-745-0638
Circulation: 7,000

Louisana

Abbeville Meridional
318 N Main St
Abbeville LA 70510-4608
318-893-4223; Fax: 318-898-9022
Circulation: 5,200; Sun: 6,000

Alexandria Daily Town Talk
1201 3rd St
Alexandria LA 71301-8246
318-487-6397; Fax: 318-484-6315
Circulation: 41,000

Bastrop Daily Enterprise
119 E Hickory
Bastrop LA 71220
318-281-4421; Fax: 318-283-1699
Circulation: 6,000

The Advocate
525 Lafayette St
PO Box 588
Baton Rouge LA 70821-0588
504-383-1111; Fax: 504-388-0371
Circulation: 100,000

Sarah Sue Goldsmith, Book Editor
Bobby Lamb, Business Editor
Katherine Flournoy, City Editor
Linda Lightfoot, Exec Editor
Butch Muir, Executive Sports Editor
Madeline Lamb, Fashion Editor
Tommy Simmons, Food Editor
Jim Whittum, Managing Editor
Douglas Manship Jr, National Political Editor
Tom Herline, News Editor
Freda Dunne, News Feature Editor
Pat Tessier, People Editor
Carl Redman, Political Editor
Ed Pratt, Religion Editor
Ed Pratt, Saturday Editor
Elizabeth Spence, Spec Sections Editor
James Minton, Suburban Editor
Art Adams, Sunday Editor
Cynthia Campbell, Travel Editor

Baton Rouge Daily News
8252 W El Cajon Dr
Baton Rouge LA 70815-8036
504-926-8882; Fax: 504-927-2742
Circulation: 300

Daily Reveille
Louisiana State Univ
39 Hodges LSU
Baton Rouge LA 70803-0001
504-388-1697; Fax: 504-388-1698
Circulation: 19,000

Daily News
525 Ave V
Bogalusa LA 70427-4413
504-732-2565; Fax: 504-732-4006
Circulation: 8,000

Crowley Post-Signal
602 N Parkerson Ave
Crowley LA 70526-4354
318-783-3450; Fax: 318-788-0949
Circulation: 6,000

Beauregard Daily News
903 W 1st St
De Ridder LA 70634-3701
318-462-0616; Fax: 318-463-5347
Circulation: 8,000

Franklin Banner-Tribune
115 Wilson St
Franklin LA 70538-6150
318-828-3706; Fax: 318-828-2874
Circulation: 3,000

Daily Journal of Commerce
118 Terry Pky
Gretna LA 70056-2523
504-368-8900; Fax: 504-368-8999
Circulation: 3,000

Daily Star
725 S Morrison Blvd
Hammond LA 70403-5401
504-345-2333; Fax: 504-542-0242
Circulation: 11,000

Houma Daily Courier
3030 Barrow St
Houma LA 70360-7641
504-879-1557; Fax: 504-857-2233
Circulation: 20,000

Jennings Daily News
238 Market St
Jennings LA 70546
318-824-3011; Fax: 318-824-3019
Circulation: 6,000

Daily Advertiser
PO Box 3268
Lafayette LA 70502-3268
318-289-6300; Fax: 318-237-8940
Circulation: 39,000

Lake Charles American Press
4900 Hwy 90 East (70601)
PO Box 2893
Lake Charles LA 70602-2893
318-433-3000; Fax: 318-494-4070
Circulation: 42,000

Mike Jones, Book Editor
Jim Beam, Managing Editor
Brett Downer, Metro Editor
Ed Alderman, Metro Editor
Linda Young, Political Editor
Scooter Hobbs, Sports Editor

Leesville Daily Leader
206 E Texas
Leesville LA 71446-4056
318-239-3444; Fax: 318-238-1152
Circulation: 14,000

Minden Press-Herald
203 Gleason
Minden LA 71055-3455
318-377-1866; Fax: 318-377-1895
Circulation: 5,000

The News-Star
411 N Fourth St
PO Box 1502
Monroe LA 71210
318-322-5161; Fax: 318-362-0273
Circulation: 34,000; Sun: 40,000

Lori Tucker, Arts/Entertainment Editor
,Cecil Brumley, Business Editor
Kathy Spurlock, Editor
Kelly Magee, Education Editor
Lori Tucker, Family/Food/Garden Editor
Lori Tucker, Lifestyle/Feature Editor
Marilyn Mitchell, Managing Editor
Lori Tucker, Religion Editor
Jeff Duncan, Sports Editor

Daily Review
1014 Front St
Morgan City LA 70380-3226
504-384-8370; Fax: 504-384-4255
Circulation: 6,000

Daily Iberian
926 E Main St
New Iberia LA 70560-3828
318-365-6773; Fax: 318-367-9460
Circulation: 14,000

The Times-Picayune
3800 Howard Ave
New Orleans LA 70140-1097
504-826-3300; Fax: 504-826-3007
Circulation: 279,000; Sun: 400,000

Mary Lou Atkinson, Asst Living Editor
Susan Larson, Book Editor
Charley Blaine, Business Editor
Leslie Williams, Education Editor
Karen Taylor, Entertainment Editor
Dale Curry, Food Editor
Bettye Andinge, Lifestyle/Feature Editor
Bettye Anding, Living Editor
Jim Amoss, Managing Editor
Peter Kovacs, Metro Editor
Paul Bartelf, National Political Editor
Bruce Nolann, Religion Editor
John Pope, Science Editor
Tim Ellerby, Sports Editor
Paul Bartelf, State Political Editor
Millie Ball, Travel Editor

Daily World
2781 I-49 S Service Rd
Opelousas LA 70570
318-942-4971; Fax: 318-948-6572
Circulation: 14,000

Ruston Daily Ledger
208 W Park Ave
Ruston LA 71270-4314
318-255-4353; Fax: 318-255-4006
Circulation: 6,000

Daily Legal News
501 Texas St Rm M-103
Shreveport LA 71101-5401
318-222-0213
Circulation: 500

Shreveport Times
222 Lake St
Shreveport LA 71101
318-459-3200; Fax: 318-459-3301
Circulation: 82,000; Sun: 103,000

Lane Crockett, Arts/Entertainment Editor
Lane Crockett, Book Editor
Tom Haywood, Business Editor
Kathie Rowell, Food Editor
Tom Haywood, Health/Medical Editor
Kathie Rowell, Lifestyle/Feature Editor
Bob Bryan, Managing Editor
Mike Whitehead, News Editor
David Westerfield, Religion Editor
Michael Lafort, Sports Editor

Slidell Sentry-News
3648 Pontchartrain Dr
Slidell LA 70458-4849
504-643-4918; Fax: 504-643-4966
Circulation: 5,000

Southwest Daily News
716 E Napoleon St
Sulphur LA 70663-3402
318-527-7075; Fax: 318-528-3044
Circulation: 16,000

Daily Comet
705 W 5th St
Thibodaux LA 70301-3148
504-448-7600; Fax: 504-448-7606
Circulation: 12,000

Maine

Kennebec-Journal
274 Western Ave
Augusta ME 04332
207-623-3811; Fax: 207-623-2220
Circulation: 19,000; Sun: 20,000

Maryann Brooke, Book Editor
Stan Eames, Business Editor
Patty Ammons, City, Education, and Environmental Editor
Alan Buncher, Executive Editor
Terri Sanborn, Food Editor
Maryann Brooke, Health/Medical, Science and Travel Editor
Terri Sanborn, Lifestyle/Feature Editor
Douglas Rooks, Political Editor
Tedda Henry, Religion Editor
Jerry Lauzon, Sports Editor

Bangor Daily News
491 Main St
PO Box 1329
Bangor ME 04401-6243
207-990-8000; Fax: 207-941-9476
Circulation: 80,000; Sat: 100,000

Andrew Kekacs, Health/Education Editor
Jeanne Curran, Lifestyle/Feature Editor
Robert Kelleter, Managing Editor
Jeanne Curran, Religion Editor
Robert Haskell, Sports Editor
Dale McGarrigle, TV Editor

Journal Tribune
Alfred Rd
Biddeford ME 04005
207-282-1535; Fax: 207-282-3138
Circulation: 15,000

Times Record
6 Industry Rd
PO Box 10
Brunswick ME 04011
207-729-3311; Fax: 207-729-5728
Circulation: 13,000

Hilary Nangle, Book Editor
Jim McCarthy, Business Editor
Bernie Monegain, City Editor
Barbara Bartels, Feature Editor
Hilary Nangle, Food Editor
Martin McKenna, Managing Editor
William Cutlip, People/Society Editor
William Cutlip, Religion Editor
Dave Borke, Sports Editor

Sun Journal
104 Park St
PO Box 4400
Lewiston ME 04243-4400
207-784-5411; Fax: 207-777-3436
Circulation: 43,000

Lisa Giguere, Business Editor
Wendy Watkins, City Editor
Mary Lou Wendell, Education Writer
Carol Coultas, Managing Editor
Sue Dillingham, Special Sections Editor
Doug Clawson, Sports Editor

Portland Press Herald
390 Congress St
PO Box 1460
Portland ME 04104
207-780-9000; Fax: 207-791-6920
Circulation: 78,000; Sun: 143,000

Jane Lord, Book/Feature/Style Editor
John Gormley, Business Reporter
Eric Conrad, Day City Editor
Deiter Bradbury, Environmental Writer
Curt Hazlett, Exec Editor
Meredith Goad, Health/Science Editor
Lloyd Ferris, Home Editor
Louis Ureneck, Managing Editor
Steve Greenlee, Night City Editor
Nancy Perry, Political Editor
David McNabb, Sports Editor
Tom Atwell, Travel Editor

Central Maine Morning Sentinel
25 Silver St
Waterville ME 04901-6648
207-873-3341; Fax: 207-873-6145
Circulation: 26,000

Maryland

The Capital
Capital-Gazette Newspapers
2000 Capitol Dr
Annapolis MD 21401
410-268-5000; Fax: 410-280-5953
Circulation: 50,000; Sunday: 55,000

Rick Hutzell, Business Editor
Edward Casey, Exec Editor
Kathy Edwards, Family/Food/Garden
Kathy Edwards, Health/Medicine
Tom Marquardt, Managing Editor
Joe Gross, Sports Editor

Baltimore Sun
501 N Calvert St
Baltimore MD 21278-0001
410-332-6000; Fax: 410-752-6049
Circulation: 238,000; Evening 167,154; Sun: 494,091

Michael Pakenham, Book Editor
Jerry Merrill, Business Editor
Jim Asher, City Editor
William Salganik, Education Editor
Tom Clifford, Entertainment Editor
Tim Wheeler, Environmental Writer
Kim Marcum, Feature Editor
Catherine Cook, Food/Fashion/Home Editor
John Bor, Health Editor
Frank Somerville, Religion Reporter
Doug Birch, Science Editor
Jack Gibbons, Sports Editor
Lorena Blas, Travel Editor

Daily Record
11-15 E Saratoga St
Baltimore MD 21202-2109
410-752-3849; Fax: 410-752-5469
Circulation: 5,000

Daily Banner
1000 Goodwill Rd
Cambridge MD 21613-2972
410-228-3131; Fax: 410-228-6547
Circulation: 8,000

Health News Daily
5550 Friendship Blvd #1
Chevy Chase MD 20815-7201
301-657-9830; Fax: 301-656-3094
Circulation: N/A

Diamondback
Univ of Maryland
3150 S Campus Dining Hall
College Park MD 20742-0001
301-314-8200; Fax: 301-314-8358
Circulation: 21,000

Cumberland Times-News
19 Baltimore St
Cumberland MD 21502-3023
301-722-4600; Fax: 301-722-4870
Circulation: 33,000

Easton Star Democrat
29088 Airpark Dr
PO Box 600
Easton MD 21601
410-822-1500; Fax: 410-820-6519
Circulation: 17,000

Dave Williams, Book Editor
Eric Fisher, Business Editor
Len Foxwell, Education Editor
Denise Reiley, Executive Editor
Barbara Sauers, Food Editor
Sally Peters, Health/Medical Editor
Janice Colvin, Lifestyle/Feature Editor
Barbara Sauers, Managing Editor
Janice Colvin, People/Society Editor
Marcie Alvarado, Political Reporter
William Haufe, Sports Editor
Denise Riley, Travel Editor

Cecil Whig
601 Bridge St
Elkton MD 21921-5307
410-398-3311; Fax: 410-398-4044
Circulation: 18,000

Frederick News
200 E Patrick St
Frederick MD 21701-5666
301-662-1177; Fax: 301-662-8299
Circulation: 51,000

Frederick Post
200 E Patrick St
Frederick MD 21701-5666
301-662-1177; Fax: 301-662-8299
Circulation: 27,000

Daily Mail
100 Summit Ave
Hagerstown MD 21740-5509
301-733-5131; Fax: 301-733-7264
Circulation: 18,000

Morning Herald
100 Summit Ave
Hagerstown MD 21740-5509
301-733-5131
Circulation: 21,000

Prince George's Journal
9410 Annapolis Rd
Lanham MD 20706-3026
301-459-3131; Fax: 301-731-8363
Circulation: 45,000

Montogomery Journal
2 Reasearch Court
Rockville M 20850-3221
301-670-1400; Fax: 301-670-1421
Circulation: 30,000

Daily Times
E Carroll St
Salisbury MD 21802
410-749-7171; Fax: 410-543-8736
Circulation: 30,000

Carroll County Times
201 Railroad Ave
Westminster MD 21157-4823
410-848-4400; Fax: 410-857-1176
Circulation: 24,000

MASSACHUSETTS

Massachusetts Daily Collegian
Univ of Massachusetts
113 Campus Ctr
Amherst MA 01003
413-545-3500; Fax: 413-545-1592
Circulation: 17,000

Athol Daily News
225 Exchange St
Athol MA 01331-1867
508-249-3535; Fax: 508-249-9630
Circulation: 6,000

Sun Chronicle
34 S Main St
PO Box 600
Attleboro MA 02703-2920
508-222-7000; Fax: 508-226-5851
Circulation: 25,000

Betsy Johnson, Family/Garden Editor
Betsy Johnson, Lifestyle/Feature/Food
Rusty D'Orconte, Managing Editor
Ned Bristol, News Editor
Hank Reilly, News Editor
Linda Hill, Religion Editor
Bill Stedman, Sports Editor

Salem Evening News
32 Dunham Rd
Beverly MA 01915-1844
508-744-0600; Fax: 508-744-1010
Circulation: 40,000

Boston Globe
PO Box 2378
Boston MA 02107-2378
617-929-2000; Fax: 617-929-3192
Circulation: 500,000; Sun: 800,000

Mary Jane Wilkinson, Arts Editor
Gail Caldwell, Book Editor/Reviewer
Larry Edelman, Business Editor
Teresa Hanafin, City Editor
Wendy Fox, Education Editor
Donald Skwar, Executive Sports Editor
Fiona Luis, Food Editor
Peter Hotton, Garden Editor
Peter Hotton, Handyman Home Editor
Nick King, Lifestyle Editor
Gregory Moore, Managing Editor
Christine Chimlund, National Editor
Jim Franklin, News Editor
Jerry Morris, Travel Editor

Boston Herald
One Herald Square
PO Box 2096
Boston MA 02106-2096
617-426-3000; Fax: 617-695-9949
Circulation: 356,000; Sun: 283,000

Bill Weber, Arts/Entertainment Editor
Mark Chapman, Book/Travel Editor
Mary Helen Gillespie, Business Editor
Jules Crittenden, Environmental Editor
Andy Costello, Executive Editor
Jane Dornbusch, Food Editor
Sonia Turek, Lifestyle/Feature Editor
Andrew Gully, Managing Editor
Dana Bisbee, People/Society Editor
Joe Sciacca, Political Editor
Robert Sales, Sports Editor

Christian Science Monitor
1 Norway St
Boston MA 02115-2122
617-450-2000; Fax: 617-450-2317
Circulation: 88,000

April Austin, Arts Editor
Jim Bencivenga, Book Editor
David Francis, Economy Page Editor
David Cook, Editor
Earl Foell, Editorial Page Editor
Elizabeth Lund, Home Forum Editor
Marilyn Gardener, Lifestyle Editor
John Dillin, Managing Editor
Scott Armstrong, National Editor
Owen Thomas, Sports Editor
Elizabeth Ross, Travel Editor

Daily Free Press
Boston University
842 Commonwealth Ave
Boston MA 02215-1205
617-232-6841; Fax: 617-232-0592
E-mail: dfpress@aol.com
Circulation: 12,000

Brockton Enterprise
60 Main St
PO Box 1450
Brockton MA 02403
508-586-6200; Fax: 508-586-6506
Circulation: 63,000

Fred Nobles, Book Editor
Terrance Downing, Business Editor
Bruce Smith, Managing Editor
George Dyroff, News Editor
William Abramson, Sports Editor

Harvard Crimson
Harvard University
14 Plympton St
Cambridge MA 02138-6606
617-576-6600; Fax: 617-576-7860
Circulation: 3,500

Daily Item
PO Box 710
Clinton MA 01510
508-368-0176; Fax: 508-368-1151
Circulation: 6,000

Jan Gottesman, Business Editor
Paulette Zelent, Food Editor
Jan Gottesman, Managing Editor
Sue Wessling, Sports Editor

Fall River Herald-News
207 Pocasset St
Fall River MA 02722
508-676-8211; Fax: 508-676-2566
Circulation: 39,000

Tom Ward, Arts/Entertainment Editor
Tom Ward, Book Editor/Reviewer
Paul Palange, Editor
Mike Silva, Exec Sports Editor
Art Jones, Food Editor

Sentinel and Enterprise
808 Main St
Fitchburg MA 01420-3153
508-343-6911; Fax: 508-342-1158
Circulation: 22,000

Middlesex Daily News
33 New York Ave
Framingham MA 01701
508-626-3800; Fax: 508-626-4400
Circulation: 50,000

Pat Hyde, Arts/Entertainment Editor
Pat Hyde, Book Editor
Maureen McLellan, Business Editor
Carol Beggy, Food Editor
Andrea Hayes, Managing Editor
Paul McNamara, News Editor
Virginia Lucier, People/Society Editor
Mark Murphy, Sports Editor
Karen Buckley, Trend Editor

Gardner News
309 Central St
Gardner MA 01440-3839
508-632-8000; Fax: 508-630-5410
Circulation: 8,000

Gloucester Daily Times
Whittemore St
Glouceser MA 01930
508-283-7000; Fax: 508-281-5748
Circulation: 12,000

Recorder
14 Hope St
Greenfield MA 01301-3308
413-772-0261; Fax: 413-774-5511
Circulation: 16,000

Haverhill Gazette
447 W Lowell Ave
Haverhill MA 01832-3507
508-374-0321; Fax: 508-521-6790
Circulation: 15,000

Cape Cod Times
319 Main St
Hyannis MA 02601-4004
508-775-1200; Fax: 508-771-3292
Circulation: 50,000; Sun: 60,000

Tim Miller, Arts/Entertainment Editor
North Cairn, Book Editor/Reviewer
James Kinsella, Business Editor
Bill Breisky, Editor-in-Chief
Alicia Blaisdall-Bannon, Lifestyle Editor
Tim White, Managing Editor
Mark Sullivan, News Editor
Bill Higgins, Sports Editor
Jim Kirshner, Travel/Sunday Editor

Eagle-Tribune
100 Turnpike
North Andover MA 01845-5033
508-685-1000; Fax: 508-687-6045
E-mail: news@eagletribune.com
Circulation: 57,000; Sun: 62,000

Ken Johnson, Business Editor
Alan White, City Editor
Chris Young, Education Editor
Daniel Warner, Exec Editor
Mary Fitzgerald, Food Editor
Marge Sherman, Health/Medical Editor
Mary Fitzgerald, Home Editor
Mary Fitzgerald, Lifestyle Editor
Russ Conway, Sports Editor
Tom Witkoski, Travel Editor

Lowell Sun
15 Kearney Sq (01852)
PO Box 1477
Lowell MA 01853-1477
508-458-7100; Fax: 508-970-4600
Circulation: 57,000

Carol McQuaid, Arts/Entertainment Editor
Gail Ross, Business Editor
Richard Cook, Education Editor
Christopher Scott, Environmental Writer
Carol McQuaid, Feature Editor
David McArdle, Local Editor
Dennis Whitton, Sports Editor
Phil Nussel, Suburban Editor

Daily Evening Item
38 Exchange St (01901)
PO Box 951
Lynn MA 01903
617-593-7700; Fax: 617-581-3178
Circulation: 30,000

William Brotherton, Business Editor
Bonnie Phillips, Lifestyle Editor
Ralph Nelson, News Editor
Paul Halloran, Sports Editor
Frederick Goodard, Travel Editor

The Daily News Mercury
Stephon Freker, Managing Editor
Malden Publications
277 Commercial St
Malden MA 02148-6767
617-321-8000; Fax: 617-321-8008
Circulation: 16,000

Enterprise Sun
John Towne, Managing Editor
230 Maple St
Marlboro MA 01752
508-485-5200; Fax: 508-485-2133
Circulation: 7,000

Tufts Daily
Tufts University
Curtis Hall Basement
Medford MA 02155
617-627-3090; Fax: 617-627-3910
Circulation: 5,000

Milford Daily News
159 S Main St
Milford MA 01757-3255
508-473-1111; Fax: 508-478-8769
Circulation: 14,000

Boston Tab
David Trueblood, Managing Editor
25 2nd Ave
Nedham MA 02194
617-964-2400; Fax: 617-433-8202
Circulation: 17,000

New Bedford Standard Times
25 Elm St
New Bedford MA 02740-6228
508-997-7411; Fax: 508-997-7491
Circulation: 47,000; Sun: 53,000

John Ackerman, Book Editor
Mike Conery, City Editor
Carlos Cunha, Editor
Steve DeCosta, Feature Editor
Ann Radigian, Lifestyle Editor
Walter Thomas, Sports Editor

Daily News of Newburyport
23 Liberty St
Newburyport MA 01950
508-462-6666; Fax: 508-465-8505
Circulation: 14,000

Tom Salemi, Business Editor
Victor Tine, City Editor
Carol Conroy, Education Editor
Ellen Small Davis, Feature Editor
Calhoun Killeen, Managing Editor
Kevin Doyle, Sports Editor
Tal Muench, Suburban Editor

Transcript
124 American Legion Dr
North Adams MA 01247-3942
413-663-3741; Fax: 413-662-2792
Circulation: 10,000

Daily Hampshire Gazette
115 Conz St
PO Box 299
Northampton MA 01060-3891
413-584-5000; Fax: 413-585-5222
Circulation: 23,000

Elise Gibson, Book/Feature Editor
Kay Moran, Business Editor
Larry Parness, City Editor
Jim Foudy, Managing Editor
Deb Oakley, Sports Editor

Berkshire Eagle
75 S Church St
Pittsfield MA 01201
413-447-7311; Fax: 413-499-3419
E-mail: eaglelinks@aol.com
Circulation: 34,000; Sun: 35,000

Jeff Borak, Arts/Entertainment Editor
Ruth Bass, Book Editor
Lew Cuyler, Business Editor
Lynne Daley, Education Editor
Holly Taylor, Health/Medical Editor
Ruth Bass, Lifestyle/Feature Editor
David Scribner, Managing Editor
Donna Mattoon, Political Editor
Randall Howe, Religion Editor
Bob McDonough, Sports Editor
Ruth Bass, Travel Editor

The Patriot Ledger
400 Crown Colony Dr
Quincy MA 02169
617-786-7000; Fax: 617-786-7025
Circulation: 100,000

Jon Lehman, Arts/Book Editor
Colin Stewart, Business Editor
Randy Keith, City Editor
Paul Williams, Computer Editor
Vicki Fitzgerald, Food Editor
Jeremy Crockford, Political Writer
Earl La Chance, Sports Editor
Vera Vida, Travel/Fashion Editor

Salem Evening News
155 Washington St
Salem MA 01970
508-744-0600; Fax: 508-744-1010
Circulation: 34,000

Eileen Garver, Arts/Entertainment Editor
Eileen Garver, Business Editor
Karen Andreas, Lifestyle/Food Editor
David Marcus, Main Editor
Karen Andreas, Political Editor
Paul Parcellin, Science Editor
Paul Leighton, Sports Editor

News
25 Elm St
Southbridge MA 01550-2605
508-764-4325; Fax: 508-764-6743
Circulation: 5,000

Springfield Union News
The Republican Company
1860 Main St
Springfield MA 01101
413-788-1264; Fax: 413-788-1301
Circulation: 115,000; Sun: 160,000

Doris Schmidt, Arts/Entertainment Editor
Carolyn Robbins, Business Editor
Larry Ravias, City Editor
Mary Ellen O'Shea, Education Editor
Stan Freeman, Environmental Editor
Larry McDermott, Exec Editor
Mimi Rigali, Lifestyle/Feature Editor
Wayne Phaneus, Managing Editor
John O'Connell, Political Editor
Stan Freeman, Science Editor
Richard Lord, Sports Editor

Taunton Daily Gazette
5 Cohannet St
Taunton MA 02780-3903
508-880-9000; Fax: 508-880-9049
Circulation: 15,000

Wakefield Daily Item
26 Albion St
Wakefield MA 01880-2803
617-245-0080; Fax: 617-246-0061
Circulation: 5,000

Daily Transcript
580 Winter St
Waltham MA 02154-1225
617-487-7200; Fax: 617-487-7377
Circulation: 12,000

News-Tribune
580 Winter St
Waltham MA 02154-1225
617-487-7200; Fax: 617-487-7377
Circulation: 10,000

Westfield Evening News
62-64 School St
Westfield MA 01085-2835
413-562-4181; Fax: 413-562-4185
Circulation: 6,000

Daily Times Chronicle
One Arrow Dr
Woburn MA 01801-2090
617-933-3700; Fax: 617-932-3321
Circulation: 16,000

James Hagerty III, Book Editor
James Hagerty III, Business/Travel Editor
John White, Editor/Burlington Edition
Christopher Connelley, Editor/Winchester Edition
James Hagerty III, Editor-in-Chief
Ken McGuire, Editor/Wakefield/Readin
Pamela Mieth, Education Editor
William Sullivan, Feature Editor
Nancy Halliday, Food/Lifestyle Editor
Charles Ryan, Health/Medical Editor
Charles Ryan, Managing Editor
Rick Pearl, Sports Editor

Worcester Telegram & Gazette
20 Franklin St (01613)
PO Box 15012
Worcester MA 01615-0012
508-793-9100; Fax: 508-793-9281
Circulation: 118,000; Sun: 147,000

David Mawson, Arts Editor
David Mawson, Book Editor
Andi Esposito, Business Editor
Clive McFarlane, Education Editor
Harry T Whitin, Exec Editor-in-Chief
Geraldine Collier, Health Editor
David Mawson, Lifestyle Editor
Jim Sacks, News Editor
Bud Barth, Sports Editor
Diana Scott, Travel Editor

MICHIGAN

Daily Telegram
135 N Winter St
Adrian MI 49221-2042
517-265-5111; Fax: 517-263-4152
Circulation: 17,000

Albion Recorder
111 W Center St
Albion MI 49224-1755
517-629-3984; Fax: 517-629-5790
Circulation: 3,000

Alpena News
130 Park Pl
Alpena MI 49707
517-354-3111; Fax: 517-354-2096
Circulation: 14,000

Diane Speer, Arts/Entertainment Editor
Rich Crofton, Business Editor
Cathy Mason, Education Editor
Diane Speer, Food Editor
Diane Speer, Health/Medical Editor
Diane Speer, Lifestyle/Feature/Travel Editor
Rich Crofton, Managing Editor
Rich Crofton, Outdoors/Recreation Editor
Rich Crofton, Political Editor
Susan Bowen, Religion Editor
Rich Crofton, Science Editor
Rodney Hart, Sports Editor

Ann Arbor News
340 E Huron St
Ann Arbor MI 48104-1909
313-994-6989; Fax: 313-994-6879
Circulation: 50,000; Sun: 70,000

Anne Martino, Book Editor
Mike Kersmarki, Business Editor
Jan Cook-Webb, Copy Editor
Pat Widsor, Education Editor
Bruce Martin, Entertainment Editor
Julie Weinik, Family Editor
Steve Cagle, Food Editor
Roy Sleep, Garden Editor
Julie Wienik, Health/Medical Editor
Editor Petykiewicz, Managing Editor
Andy Chapelle, News Editor
Rick Fitzgerald, Political Editor
Don Faber, Religion Editor
Carl Bates, Science Editor
Geoff Larcom, Sports Editor
Steve Cagle, Travel Editor

Michigan Daily
Univ of Michigan
420 Maynard
Ann Arbor MI 48109-1314
313-764-0554; Fax: 313-764-4275
Circulation: 16,000

Huron Daily Tribune
211 N Heisterman
Bad Axe MI 48413-1239
517-269-6461; Fax: 517-269-9893
Circulation: 10,000

Battle Creek Enquirer
155 W Van Buren
Battle Creek MI 49017-3002
616-964-7161; Fax: 616-964-0299
Circulation: 38,000

Mark Schwerin, Arts/Entertainment Editor
Amy Wilson, Business Editor
Marilynn Fryer, City Desk Editor
Nan Seelman, Executive Editor
Nancy Kaley, Food Editor
Leslie Rardin, Lifestyle/Feature Editor
Bill Church, Managing Editor
Nancy Kaley, Religion Editor
Kim Kaufman, Sports Editor

Bay City Times
311 Fifth St
Bay City MI 48708-5853
517-895-8551; Fax: 517-893-0649
Circulation: 42,000; Sat-Sun AM circ 52,000

Elizabeth Gunther, Arts/Entertainment Editor
Greg Helmling, Book Editor
Steve Sirianni, Business Editor
Jenny Laidman, Environmental Editor
Elizabeth Gunther, Family Editor
Jenny Laidman, Health/Medical Editor
Elizabeth Gunther, Home Editor
Elizabeth Gunther, Lifestyle/Feature Editor
Irene Portnoy, Political Editor
Bob Carrier, Religion Editor
Jenny Laidman, Science Editor
Dick Hardy, Senior News Editor
Jim DeLand, Sports Editor
Georgia Taylor, TV Editor

Pioneer
502 N State St
Big Rapids MI 49307-1469
616-796-4831; Fax: 616-796-1152
Circulation: 6,000

Cadillac Evening News
130 N Mitchell St
Cadillac MI 49601-1856
616-775-6565
Circulation: 11,000

Cheboygan Daily Tribune
308 N Main St
Cheboygan MI 49721-1545
616-627-7144; Fax: 616-627-5331
Circulation: 6,000

Daily Reporter
15 W Pearl St
Coldwater MI 49036-1912
517-278-2318; Fax: 517-278-6041
Circulation: 8,000

Detroit Free Press
321 W Lafayette Blvd
Detroit MI 48231
313-222-6400; Fax: 313-223-4726
Combines w/Detroit News on Sun
Circulation: 575,000

Linnea Lannon, Book Editor
Tom Walsh, Business Editor
Joe H Stroud, Editorial Mg Editor
Dale Parry, Feature Editor
Patty Stearns, Food Editor
Joan Richardson, Higher Education Editor
Judy Rose, Home Editor
Kathy O'Gorman, K-12 Education Editor
Thom Fladung, Lifestyle Editor
Bob McGruder, Managing Editor
Pat Anstett, Medical Editor
Dale Parry, Mg Editor/Features/Bus
Chuck Mitchell, National Political Editor
Bob McGruder, News Editor
Nancy Ross-Flanigan, Science Editor
Gene Myers, Sports Editor
Gerry Volgenau, Travel Editor

Detroit Legal News
2001 W Lafayette
Detroit MI 48216-1852
313-961-3949; Fax: 313-961-7817
Circulation: 3,000

Detroit News
615 W Lafayette Blvd
Detroit MI 48226
313-222-2300; Fax: 313-222-2335
Circulation: 434,000

Alan Fisk, Book Editor
Nolan Finley, Business Editor
Judy Diebolt, City Editor
Frank Lovinski, Deputy Mg Editor
Marty Fischhoff, Feature Editor
Pam Schermeyer, Feature/News Editor
Lynda Page, Food Editor
Shanna Flower, Health Editor
Christina Bradford, Managing Editor
Jim Tobin, Medical Editor
Jim Higgons, National Desk Editor
Jeremy Pearce, Outdoor Editor
Tarek Hamada, Religion Editor
Karl Bates, Science Editor
Phil Laciura, Sports Editor
Tim Kiska, TV Editor, Radio/TV Section

Dowagiac Daily News
205 Spaulding St
Dowagiac MI 49047-1451
616-782-2101; Fax: 616-782-5290
Circulation: 32,000

State News
Michigan State Univ
346 Student Services Bldg
East Lansing MI 48824-1113
517-355-3447; Fax: 517-353-2599
Circulation: 32,000

Daily Press
600-602 Ludington St
Escanaba MI 49829-3830
906-786-2021; Fax: 906-786-9006
Circulation: 12,000

Flint Journal
200 E First St
Flint MI 48502-1925
810-767-0660; Fax: 810-767-7518
Circulation: 120,000

Cookie Wascha, Arts/Lifestyle Editor
Brooke Rausch, Associate Editor
Gene Mierzejewski, Book Editor
Carl Stoddard, Business Editor
Dan Shriner, Computer Editor
Tom Lindley, Editor
Dave Murray, Education Editor
Ron Krueger, Food Editor
Marcia Mattson, Health Editor
Cookie Wascha, Home Editor
Roger Van Nord, Managing Editor
Mike Riha, News Editor
Betty Brenner, Religion Editor
Marcia Mattson, Science Editor
Dave Poniers, Sports Editor
Julie Murray, Travel Editor

Grand Haven Tribune
101 N 3rd St
Grand Haven MI 49417-1209
616-842-6400; Fax: 616-842-9584
Circulation: 12,000

Grand Rapids Press
155 Michigan Ave NW
Grand Rapids MI 49503-2563
616-459-1400; Fax: 616-459-1409
Circulation: 150,000; Sun: 196,000

Sue Wallace, Arts/Entertainment Editor
Susan Thoms, Book Editor/Reviewer
Jim Harger, Business Editor
Roland Wilkerson, Education Editor
Ann Wells, Food Editor
Sue Schroeder, Lifestyle Editor
Andrew Angelo, Metro News Editor
Jim O'Neill, News Editor
Ed Golder, Political Editor
John Sinkevics, Science Editor
Bob Becker, Sports Editor
Hank Bornheimer, Travel Editor

Daily News
109 N Lafayette St
Greenville MI 48838-1853
616-754-9301; Fax: 616-754-8559
Circulation: 8,000

Hillsdale Daily News
33 McCollum
Hillsdale MI 49242-1630
517-437-7351; Fax: 517-437-3963
Circulation: 8,000

Holland Sentinel
54 W 8th St
Holland MI 49423-3104
616-392-2311; Fax: 616-392-3526
Circulation: 20,000

Daily Mining Gazette
206 Shelden Ave
Houghton MI 49931-2134
906-482-1500; Fax: 906-482-2726
Circulation: 13,000

Sentinel-Standard
114 N Depot
Ionia MI 48846-1602
616-527-2100; Fax: 616-527-6860
Circulation: 5,000

Daily News
215 E Ludington
Iron Mountain MI 49801-2917
906-774-2772; Fax: 906-774-7660
Circulation: 10,000

Ironwood Daily Globe
118 E McLeod Ave
Ironwood MI 49938-2120
906-932-2211; Fax: 906-932-5358
Circulation: 9,000

Jackson Citizen Patriot
214 S Jackson St
Jackson MI 49201-2213
517-787-2300; Fax: 517-787-9711
Circulation: 38,000

Kalamazoo Gazette
401 S Burdick St (49007)
PO Box 2007
Kalamazoo MI 49003
616-345-3511; Fax: 616-388-8447
Circulation: 70,000; Sun: 80,000

Kathy Doud, Book Editor
Paul Cox, Business Editor
Linda Mah, College Editor Writer
Rosemary Burch, Computer Writer
James Mosby, Editor
Larry Trent, Food Editor
Bill Christine, Health/Medical Editor
Erlene Mc Michael, K-12 Writer
Joyce Pines, Lifestyle/Feature Editor
Becky Pierce, Metro Editor
Lane Wick, News Editor
Charlotte Channing, Political Editor
Bill Krasean, Science Editor
Jack Moss, Sports Editor
Shirley Bumgardner, Travel Editor

Lansing State Journal
120 E Lenawee St
Lansing MI 48919-0001
517-377-1000; Fasx: 517-377-1298
Circulation: 72,000; Sun: 91,000

Mike Hughes, Arts/Entertainment Editor
Kathleen Lavey, Book and
    Lifestyle/Feature Editor
Les Smith, Business Editor
Mike Andrejevic, Education Editor
Roni Rucker-Water, Managing Editor
Stephanie McKinnon, Science Editor
Steve Klein, Sports Editor
Norris Ingells, Travel Editor

Ludington Daily News
202 N Rath Ave
Ludington MI 49431-1663
616-845-5181; Fax: 616-843-4011
Circulation: 8,000

Manistee News-Advocate
75 Maple St
Manistee MI 49660-1554
616-723-3592; Fax: 616-723-4733
Circulation: 5,000

Mining Journal
249 W Washington St
Marquette MI 49855-4321
906-228-2500; Fax: 906-228-5556
Circulation: 19,000

Marshall Chronicle
15 S Grand St
Marshall MI 49068-1513
616-781-3943; Fax: 616-781-4012
Circulation: 7,000

Midland Daily News
124 S McDonald St
Midland MI 48640-5161
517-835-7171; Fax: 517-835-6991
Circulation: 17,000

Monroe Evening News
20-22 West 1st
Monroe MI 48161-2333
313-241-6300; Fax: 313-242-0937
Circulation: 24,000

Morning Sun
215 N Main St
Mount Pleasant MI 48858-2306
517-772-2971; Fax: 517-773-0382
Circulation: 10,000

Macomb Daily
100 Macomb Dr
Mt Clemens MI 48043-2347
810-469-4510; Fax: 810-469-2892
Circulation: 50,000

Mitch Hotts, Arts/Entertainment Editor
Mitch Kehetian, Book Editor
Bill Fleming, Business/Religion Editor
Mitch Kehetian, Editorial Page Editor
Bill Driskell, Education Editor
Ken Kish, Environmental Editor
Debbie Komar, Food Editor
Debbie Komar, Lifestyle/Feature Editor
Ken Kish, Managing Editor
Chad Selweski, Political Editor
George Pohly, Sports Editor
Debbie Komar, Travel Editor

Muskegon Chronicle
981 3rd St
Muskegon MI 49440-1236
616-722-0320; Fax: 616-722-2552
Circulation: 48,000

Niles Daily Star
217 N 4th St
Niles MI 49120-2301
616-683-2100; Fax: 616-683-2175
Circulation: 4,000

Argus-Press
201 E Exchange St
Owosso MI 48867-3009
517-725-5136; Fax: 517-725-6376
Circulation: 12,000

Petoskey News-Review
319 State St
PO Box 528
Petoskey MI 49770-0528
616-347-2544; Fax: 616-347-6833
Also publishes the Graphic Plus
Circulation: 8,000

Ken Winter, Editor
Kendall Stanley, Managing Editor

Oakland Press
48 W Huron (48342)
PO Box 436009
Pontiac MI 48343
810-332-8181; Fax: 810-332-8885
Circulation: 180,000

Ginny Stolicker, Book Editor
Steve Spalding, Business Editor
Diana Dillaber-Murray, Education Editor
Dan Grantham, Feature Editor
Jody Headly, Food and Home/Garden Ed
Gary Gilbert, Managing Editor
Kenn Jones, News Editor
Keith Langlois, Sports Editor

Times Herald
911 Military St
PO Box 5009
Port Huron MI 48061-5009
810-985-7171; Fax: 810-989-6294
Circulation: 31,000; Sun: 39,000

Judith McLean, Book Editor
Rick Barett, Business Editor
Judith McLean, City Editor
Michael Connell, Exec Editor
Tracy Wilson, Health/Medical Editor
Jill Carlson, Lifestyle/Feature Editor
Jim Ketchum, Religion Editor
Jim Whymer, Sports Editor

Daily Tribune
210 E 3rd St
Royal Oak MI 48067-2603
810-541-3000; Fax: 810-541-7903
Circulation: 42,000

Curt Jordet, Book Editor
Victoria Mielke, Business Editor
Bob Ball, Computer Editor
Mike Beeson, Editor
Curt Jordet, Entertainment Editor
Jeff Kuen, Sports Editor

Saginaw News
203 S Washington Ave
Saginaw MI 48607-1283
517-776-9710; Fax: 517-752-3115
Circulation: 57,000; Sun: 67,261

Janet Martineau, Arts/Entertainment Editor
Penny Nickel, Book Editor
Jennifer Pruden, Business Editor
Rob Handeside, City Editor
Paul Rau, Education Editor
Mary Foreman, Food Editor
Curt Leece, Photography Editor
Denise Mitchell, Religion Editor
Geri Rudolf, Science Editor
Jim Buckley, Sports Editor
Ken Tabacsko, Travel Editor

Evening News
109 Arlington St
Sault Sainte Marie MI 49783-1901
906-632-2235; Fax: 906-632-1222
Circulation: 8,000

South Haven Daily Tribune
950 Bailey Ave #4
South Haven MI 49090-9701
616-637-1104; Fax: 616-637-8415
Circulation: 3,000

Herald-Palladium
3450 Hollywood Rd
St Joseph MI 49085-9581
616-429-2400; Fax: 616-429-7661
Circulation: 33,000

Sturgis Journal
209 John St
Sturgis MI 49091-1459
616-651-5407; Fax: 616-651-2296
Circulation: 10,000

Traverse City Record Eagle
120 W Front St
PO Box 632
Traverse City MI 49685-0632
616-946-2000; Fax: 616-946-8273
Circulation: 25,000; Sun: 35,000

Bill Echlin, Business Editor
Loraine Anderson, City Editor
Teresa Fowler, Community Editor
John Tune, Editor-in-Chief
Michael Ready, Editorial Page Editor
Kathy Gibbons, Lifestyle/Feature Editor
Deb Fleming, Managing Editor
Gordon Charles, Outdoor Editor
Kathy Gibbons, Section Editor
Nick Edson, Sports Editor
David Miller, Sunday Editor

MINNESOTA

Albert Lea Tribune
PO Box 60
Albert Lea MN 56007
507-373-1411; Fax: 507-373-0333
Circulation: 9,000

Jeri McShane, Business Editor
Marlene Behle, Lifestyle/Feature Editor
Floyd Jenigan, Managing Editor
Jim Lutgens, Sports Editor

Austin Daily Herald
310 NE 2nd St
Austin MN 55912-3436
507-433-8851; Fax: 507-437-8644
Circulation: 9,000

Pioneer/Advertiser
1320 Neilson Ave SE
Bemidji MN 56601-5406
218-751-3740; Fax: 218-751-6914
Circulation: 8,000

Brainerd Daily Dispatch
506 James St
Brainerd MN 56401-2942
218-829-4705; Fax: 218-829-7735
Circulation: 15,000

Crookston Daily Times
124 S Broadway
Crookston MN 56716-1955
218-281-2730; Fax: 218-281-7234
Circulation: 5,000

Duluth News-Tribune
424 W 1st St
PO Box 169000
Duluth MN 55816-9000
218-723-5281; Fax: 218-720-4120
Circulation: 64,000; Sun: 92,000

Linda Hanson, Book Editor
Sheri Vazzano, Co-Business Editor
Anne Bretts, Education Editor
John Myers, Environmental Editor
Marilyn Walters, Food Editor
Mark Stodgill, Health Editor
Linda Hanson, Home/Garden Editor
Craig Gemoules, Managing Editor
Vicki Gowler, News Editor
Sam Cook, Outdoor/Recreation Editor
Sam Cook, Outdoors Writer
Linda Hanson, People/Society Editor
John Welbes, Political Editor

Susan Hogan-Albach, Religion Editor
Joe Bissen, Sports Editor
Dorriane Earnest, Travel Editor

Sentinel
64 Downstown Plz
Fairmont MN 56031-1732
507-235-3303; Fax: 507-235-3718
Circulation: 11,000

Faribault Daily News
514 Central Ave
Faribault MN 55021-4304
507-334-1853; Fax: 507-334-8569
Circulation: 8,000

Fergus Falls Daily Journal
914 E Channing Ave
PO Box 506
Fergus Falls MN 56538
218-736-7513; Fax: 218-736-5919
Circulation: 11,000

Colleen Speer, Education, Food, Lifestyles, Feature Editor
John Bryan, Managing Editor
Joel Myhre, Sports Editor

Hibbing Daily Tribune
2142 1st Ave
Hibbing MN 55746-1805
218-262-1011; Fax: 218-262-4318
Circulation: 10,000

Daily Journal
North Star Publishing Co Inc
500 3rd St
International Falls MN 56649-2311
218-285-7411; Fax: 218-285-7206
Circulation: 5,000

Free Press
418 S 2nd St
Mankato MN 56001-3727
507-625-4451; Fax: 507-388-4355
Circulation: 27,000

Marshall Independent
Jim Tate, Editor
508 W Main St
Marshall MN 56258
507-537-1551; Fax: 507-537-1557
Circulation: 9,000

Finance & Commerce
615 S 7th St
Minneapolis MN 55415-1601
612-333-4244; Fax: 612-333-3243
Circulation: 1,000

Minneapolis Star Tribune
425 Portland Ave S
Minneapolis MN 55488-0002
612-673-4000; Fax: 612-673-7122
Circulation: 400,000; Sun: 700,000

Dave Wood, Book Editor
Larry Werner, Business Editor
Steve Alexander, Computer Editor
Marie McCarthy, Education Editor
Tom Meersman, Environmental Editor
Lee Dean, Family/Food/Garden Editor
Kriston Tillotson, Fashion Editor
Gordon Slovut, Health/Medical Editor
Ingrid Sundstrom, Home Editor
Delma Francis, Lifestyle Editor
Sherrie Marshall, Metro Editor
Martha Allen, Religion Editor
Julie Engebrecht, Sports Editor

Cathy Watson, Travel Editor
Noel Holston, TV Editor

Minnesota Daily
Univ of Minnesota
2301 University Ave SE
Minneapolis MN 55414-3030
612-627-4080; Fax: 612-627-4159
Circulation: 30,000

Journal
303 N Minnesota St
New Ulm MN 56073-1733
507-359-2911; Fax: 507-359-7362
Circulation: 10,000

Owatonna People's Press
135 W Pearl St
Owatonna MN 55060-2316
507-451-2840; Fax: 507-451-6020
Circulation: 8,000

Republican-Eagle
2760 N Service Dr
Red Wing MN 55066-1985
612-388-8235; Fax: 612-388-8912
Circulation: 8,000

Post-Bulletin
18 1st Ave SE
Rochester MN 55904-3722
507-285-7600; Fax: 507-285-7666
Circulation: 42,000

St Cloud Times
3000 North 7th St
PO Box 768
St Cloud MN 56302
612-255-8700; Fax: 612-255-8775
Circulation: 29,000; Sun: 36,216

Mike Nistler, Book Review Editor
Becky Beyers, Business Editor
Mike Nistler, Family/Food/Garden Editor
Mike Nistler, Lifestyle/Feature Editor
John Bodette, Managing Editor
Dave Deland, Sports Editor

St Paul Legal Ledger
46 E 4th St
Minnesota Bldg Rm 640
St Paul MN 55101-1163
612-222-0059
Circulation: 1,000

St Paul Pioneer Press Dispatch
345 Cedar St
St Paul MN 55101-1014
612-222-5011; Fax: 612-228-5500
Circulation: 195,000; Sun: 211,000

Mary Ann Grossman, Book Editor
Judith Willis, Business Editor
Sam Elrod, Food Writer
Pat McMorrow, Health/Medical Editor
Dave Peters, Higher Education Editor
Sue Campbell, Lifestyle Editor
Ken Doctor, Managing Editor
Martha Malan, National/World Editor
Chris Niskanen, Outdoor Editor
Kate Perry, Political Editor
Clark Morphew, Religion Writer
Dick Pufall, Sports Editor
Dave Fryxell, Technical Editor
Sam Elrod, Travel Editor

Stillwater Gazette
102 S 2nd St
Stillwater MN 55082-5132
612-439-3130; Fax: 612-439-4713
Circulation: 4,000

Mesabi Daily News
704 7th Ave S
Virginia MN 55792-3086
218-741-5544; Fax: 218-741-1005
Circulation: 12,000

West Central Tribune
2208 W Trott Ave
Willmar MN 56201-2723
612-235-1150; Fax: 612-235-6769
Circulation: 16,000

Winona Daily News
601 Franklin St
Winona MN 55987-3822
507-454-6500; Fax: 507-454-1440
Circulation: 15,000

Worthington Daily Globe
300 11th St
Worthington MN 56187-2451
507-376-9711; Fax: 507-376-5202
Circulation: 15,000

MISSISSIPPI

Sun Herald
PO Box 4567
Biloxi MS 39535-4567
601-896-2100; Fax: 601-896-2362
Circulation: 48,000

Daily Leader
North Railroad Ave
Brookhaven MS 39601
601-833-6961; Fax: 601-833-6714
Circulation: 8,000

Clarksdale Press Register
123 2nd St
Clarksdale MS 38614
601-627-2201; Fax: 601-624-5125
Circulation: 8,000

Bolivar Commercial
821 N Chrisman
Cleveland MS 38732-2110
601-843-4241; Fax: 601-843-1830
Circulation: 8,000

Commercial Dispatch
516 Main St
Columbus MS 39701-5734
601-328-2424; Fax: 601-329-8937
Circulation: 16,000

Daily Corinthian
1607 S Harper Rd
Corinth MS 38834-6742
601-287-6111; Fax: 601-287-3525
Circulation: 9,000

Delta Democrat-Times
988 N Broadway
PO Box 1618
Greenville MS 38702
601-335-1155; Fax: 601-335-2860
Circulation: 17,000; Sun: 21,000

Woodrow Wilkins, Business Editor
Lynn Lafoe, Lifestyle/Feature Editor
Sally Gresham, Managing Editor
Mitch Ariff, Sports Editor

Greenwood Commonwealth
329 Hwy 82 W
Greenwood MS 38930-6538
601-453-5312; Fax: 601-453-2908
Circulation: 9,000

Daily Sentinel Star
158 Green St
Grenada MS 38901-2619
601-226-4321; Fax: 601-226-8310
Circulation: 8,000

Hattiesburg American
825 N Main St
Hattiesburg MS 39401-3433
601-582-4321; Fax: 601-583-8244
Circulation: 26,000

Clarion Ledger
311 E Pearl St
PO Box 40
Jackson MS 39205-0040
601-961-7000; Fax: 601-961-7211
Circulation: 115,000; Sun: 130,000

Kim Willis, Arts/Entertainment Editor
Jana John, Book Editor/Reviewer
Joe Dove, Business Editor
Ruth Ingram, Education Editor
Lisa Hitt, Food Editor
Felder Rushing, Garden Editor
Debbie Skipper, Health/Medical, Political
Margaret Downing, Managing Editor
Dan Davis, Metro Editor
John Hemmack, News Editor
Donald Dodd, Sports Editor

Laurel Leader-Call
130 Beacon St
Laurel MS 39440-4428
601-428-0551; Fax: 601-426-3550
Circulation: 10,000

Enterprise-Journal
112 Oliver Emmerich Dr
PO Box 910
McComb MS 39648-3903
601-684-2421; Fax: 601-684-0836
Circulation: 13,000; Sun: 12,800

Jack Ryan, Managing Editor

Meridian Star
814 2nd Ave
Meridian MS 39301-5023
601-693-1551; Fax: 601-485-1275
Circulation: 23,000

Natchez Democrat
503 N Canal St
PO Box 1447
Natchez MS 39120
601-442-9101; Fax: 601-442-9101
Circulation: 13,000

Kelly Beasley, Feature/Food Editor
Jimmy Sexton, Managing and News Ed
Mike Grubb, Sports Editor

Oxford Eagle
916 Jackson Ave
Oxford MS 38655-3636
601-234-4331; Fax: 601-234-4351
Circulation: 6,000

Mississippi Press
405 Delmas Ave
Pascagoula MS 39567-4136
601-762-1111; Fax: 601-934-1454
Circulation: 21,000; Sun: 23,000

Picayune Item
214 Curran Ave
Picayune MS 39466
601-798-4766; Fax: 601-798-8602
Circulation: 6,000

Starkville Daily News
316 University Dr
Starkville MS 39759-2968
601-323-1642; Fax: 601-323-6586
Circulation: 6,000

NE Mississippi Daily Journal
1655 S Green
Tupelo MS 38801-6557
601-842-2611; Fax: 601-842-2233
Circulation: 38,000

Daily Mississippian
Univ of Mississippi
Main Campus
University MS 38677-9999
601-232-5503; Fax: 601-232-5703
Circulation: 11,000

Vicksburg Evening Post
920 South St
Vicksburg MS 39180-3256
601-636-4545; Fax: 601-634-0897
Circulation: 16,000

Daily Times Leader
227 Court St
West Point MS 39773-2926
601-494-1422; Fax: 601-494-1414
Circulation: 3,000

MISSOURI

Blue Springs Examiner
500 West RD Mize Rd
Blue Springs MO 64014-2421
816-229-9161; Fax: 816-224-7245
Circulation: 6,000

Boonville Daily News & Record
412 E High
Boonville MO 65233-1242
816-882-5335; Fax: 816-882-2256
Circulation: 4,000

Branson Tri-Lakes Daily News
114 N Commercial St
Branson MO 65616-2404
417-334-3161; Fax: 417-334-4299
Circulation: 56,000

News-Bulletin
107-109 N Main
Brookfield MO 64628-1627
816-258-7237; Fax: 816-258-7238
Circulation: 4,000

Lake Sun Leader
114 N Hwy 5
Camdenton MO 65020-9781
314-346-2132; Fax: 314-346-4508
Circulation: 6,000

Southeast Missourian
301 Broadway
Cape Girardeau MO 63701-7330
314-335-6611; Fax: 314-334-7288
Circulation: 20,000

Carthage Press
527 S Main
Carthage MO 64836-1648
417-358-2191; Fax: 417-358-7428
Circulation: 5,000

Chillicothe Constitution-Tribune
818 Washington St
Chillicothe MO 64601-2232
816-646-2411; Fax: 816-646-2028
Circulation: 5,000

St Charles Watchman
200 S Bemiston Ave #201
Clayton MO 63105-1915
314-725-1515; Fax: 314-725-1716
Circulation: 10,000

St Louis Watchman Advocate
200 S Bemiston Ave #201
Clayton MO 63105-1915
314-725-1515; Fax: 314-725-1716
Circulation: 10,000

Clinton Daily Democrat
212 S Washington
Clinton MO 64735-2073
816-885-2281; Fax: 816-885-2265
Circulation: 5,000

Columbia Daily Tribune
4th & Walnut St
Columbia MO 65205
314-449-3811; Fax: 314-874-6413
Circulation: 18,000

Columbia Missourian
PO Box 917
Columbia MO 65205
314-882-5700; Fax: 314-882-5702
Circulation: 5,000; Sun: 6,000

George Kennedy, Managing Editor

Daily Statesman
33 S Walnut St
Dexter MO 63841-2151
314-624-4545; Fax: 314-624-7449
Circulation: 14,000

Standard
417 Thompson St
Excelsior Springs MO 64024
816-637-6155; Fax: 816-637-8411
Circulation: 3,000

Fulton Sun
115 E 5th St
Fulton MO 65251-1714
314-642-7272; Fax: 314-642-0656
Circulation: 6,000

Hannibal Courier-Post
200 N 3rd
Hannibal MO 63401-3504
314-221-2800; Fax: 314-221-1568
Circulation: 12,000

Independence Examiner
410 S Liberty St
Independence MO 64050-3850
816-254-8600; Fax: 816-836-3805
Circulation: 34,000

Jeff Fox, Arts/Entertainment Editor
Audrey Stubbart, Book Editor/Reviewer
Frank Haight, Business Editor
Tim Todd, Education Editor
Jill Ritchie, Health Editor
Joe Ritchie, Lifestyle/Feature Editor
Kate Lee, Managing Editor
Coral Beach, Religion Editor
Dale Brendel, Sports Editor
Forest Martin, Travel Editor

Daily Capital News
210 Monroe St
Jefferson City MO 65101-3210
314-636-3131; Fax: 314-636-7035
Circulation: 3,000

Jefferson City News & Tribune
210 Monroe St
Jefferson City MO 65101-3210
314-636-3131; Fax: 314-636-7035
Circulation: 22,000; Sun: 24,000

Dwight Warren, Arts/Entertainment Editor
Dwight Warren, Book Editor
Don Norfleet, Business Editor
Rick Brown, Education Editor
Doug Waggoner, Executive Editor
John Egan, Health/Political Editor
Jane Verry, Lifestyle/Feature Editor
Richard McGonegal, Managing Editor
Tom Rackers, Sports Editor

Post-Tribune
210 Monroe St
Jefferson City MO 65101-3210
314-636-3131; Fax: 314-636-7035
Circulation: 18,000

Joplin Globe
117 E Fourth St
Joplin MO 64801
417-623-3480; Fax: 417-623-8450
Circulation: 36,000; Sun: 45,000

Brian Hutton, Arts Editor
Rich Polen, Business Editor
Willa Younger, Food Editor
Gloria Turner, Lifestyle Editor
Tom Murray, Managing Editor
Michael Stair, News Editor
Wendell Redden, Sports Editor

Daily Record
3611 Troost Ave
Kansas City MO 64109-2668
816-931-2002; Fax: 816-561-6675
Circulation: 1,000

Kansas City Star
1729 Grand Ave
Kansas City MO 64108-1413
816-234-4141; Fax: 816-234-4926
Circulation: 282,000

Steve Paul, Book Editor
Doug Weaver, Business Editor
Ellen Foley, Feature Editor
Melanie Gray, Feature Editor
Jill Silva, Food Editor
Mike Hendricks, Higher Education Editor
Marjen Busby, Home Editor
Tim O'Connor, Lower Education Editor
Art Brisbane, Managing Editor
Bill Dalton, Metro Editor
Robert Butler, Movie Editor, About Town Column
Steve Kraske, Political Editor
Jeanne Meyers, Preview Editor, Arts & Entertainment Section
Helen Gray, Religion Editor
Dale Bye, Sports Editor
Marylou Nolan, Travel Editor
Barry Garron, TV Editor

Daily Democrat
203 1st St
Kennett MO 63857-2052
314-888-4505; Fax: 314-888-5114
Circulation: 15,000

Kirksville Daily Express & News
110 E McPherson St
Kirksville MO 63501-3506
816-665-2808; Fax: 816-665-2608
Circulation: 7,000

Lebanon Daily Record
290 S Madison
PO Box 192
Lebanon MO 65536-0192
417-532-9131; Fax: 417-532-8140
Circulation: 7,000

Steve Hilton, Managing Editor
Jim Adair, Sports Editor
Ed Sisson, Sunday Editor

Macon Chronicle-Herald
217 W Bourke St
Macon MO 63552-1503
816-385-3121; Fax: 816-385-3082
Circulation: 4,000

Democrat-News
121 N Lafayette
Marshall MO 65340-1747
816-886-2233
Circulation: 4,000

Maryville Daily Forum
111 E Jenkins St
Maryville MO 64468-2318
816-562-2424; Fax: 816-562-2823
Circulation: 4,000

Mexico Ledger
300 N Washington
Mexico MO 65265-2756
314-581-1111; Fax: 314-581-2029
Circulation: 10,000

Moberly Monitor-Index/Democrat
218 N Williams
Moberly MO 65270-1534
816-263-4123; Fax: 816-263-3626
Circulation: 8,000

Monett Times
505 Broadway
Monett MO 65708-2333
417-235-3135; Fax: 417-235-8852
Circulation: 5,000

Neosho Daily News
1006 W Harmony St
Neosho MO 64850-1631
417-451-1520; Fax: 417-451-6408
Circulation: 6,000

Nevada Daily Mail/Sunday Herald
131 S Cedar St
Nevada MO 64772-3309
417-667-3344; Fax: 417-667-8121
Circulation: 4,000

Daily Journal
1513 St Joe Dr
Park Hills MO 63601-2402
314-431-2010; Fax: 314-431-7640
Circulation: 10,000

Daily American Republic
208 Poplar St
Poplar Bluff MO 63901
314-785-1414; Fax: 314-785-2706
Circulation: 22,000; Sun: 24,000

John Willey, Business Editor
Linda Redeffer, Education Editor
Barbara Horton, Food Editor
John Willey, Health/Medical Editor
Barbara Horton, Lifestyle/Feature Editor
John Willey, Managing Editor
Barbara Horton, Religion Editor
Ron Smith, Sports Editor
John Willey, Travel Editor

Daily News
204 W North Main
Richmond MO 64085-1610
816-776-5454; Fax: 816-637-1639
Circulation: 3,000

Rolla Daily News
101 W 7th St
Rolla MO 65401-3243
314-364-2468; Fax: 314-341-5847
Circulation: 6,000

Sedalia Democrat
7th St & Massachusetts Ave
Sedalia MO 65301
816-826-1000; Fax: 816-826-2413
Circulation: 14,000

Standard Democrat
205 S New Madrid
Sikeston MO 63801-2953
314-471-1137; Fax: 314-471-6277
Circulation: 9,000

Daily Events
PO Box 1
Springfield MO 65801-0001
417-866-1401; Fax: 417-866-1491
Circulation: 350

Springfield News-Leader
651 Boonville Ave
Springfield MO 65806-1005
417-836-1100; Fax: 417-837-1381
Circulation: 67,000; Sun: 104,000

Bill Tatum, Assignment Editor
Kelley Bass, Assistant Managing Editor
Louise Whall, Business Editor
Everett Kennell, Copy Editor
Diane Robinson, Feature Editor
Kate Marymont, Managing Editor
Bob Edwards, Political Reporter
James Walker, Sports Editor

Courier Post
PO Box 1077
St Charles MO 63302-1077
314-278-4450; Fax: 314-949-6973
Circulation: 1,000

St Joseph Daily Courier
1014 S 10th St
St Joseph MO 64503-2407
816-279-3441; Fax: 816-279-3441
Circulation: 250

St Joseph News Press
PO Box 29
St Joseph MO 64502-0029
816-271-8500; Fax: 816-271-8692
Circulation: 40,000; Sun: 52,000

Terry Raffensperger, Business Editor
Mark Sheehan, Editorial Editor
Suzanne Jones, Education Reporter
Robert Unger, Exec Editor
Linda Wiedmaier, Food Editor
Cheryl Whittenauer, Health Editor
Denise Kerns, Home/Garden Editor
Preston Filbert, Lifestyle Editor
Pat Spencer, People/Society Editor
Julie Buzbee, Religion Editor
Paul Suellentrop, Sports Editor
Cathy Woolridge, Travel Editor

St Louis Countian
7777 Bonhomme #1208
St Louis MO 63105-1911
314-421-1880; Fax: 314-727-7407
Circulation: 1,000

St Louis Daily Record
612 N 2nd St 4th Fl
St Louis MO 63102-2553
314-421-1880; Fax: 314-421-0436
Circulation: 1,000

St Louis Post-Dispatch
900 N Tucker Blvd
St Louis MO 63101-1099
314-340-8000; Fax: 314-340-8000
Circulation: 340,000; Sun: 500,000

Jabari Asim, Book Editor
Phil Gaitens, Business Editor
Robert Duffy, Cultural News Editor
William F Woo, Editor
Tom Uhlembrock, Environmental Editor
Becky Homan, Fashion/Home Furn Editor
Dick Weiss, Feature Editor
Judy Evans, Food Editor
Roge Signor, Health/Medical Editor
Phyllis Librach, Higher Education
Ellen Gardner, Lifestyle Editor
Joan Little, Lower Education
Foster Davis, Managing Editor
Carolyn Kingcade, News Editor
Phil Dine, Political Editor

Gary Clark, Real Estate Editor
Pat Rice, Religion Editor
Bob Pastin, Sports Editor
Kathleen Nelson, Travel Editor

Republican-Times
122 E 8th St
Trenton MO 64683-2183
816-359-2212; Fax: 816-359-4414
Circulation: 4,000

Star-Journal
135 E Market St
Warrensburg MO 64093-1817
816-747-8123; Fax: 816-747-8110
Circulation: 5,000

Daily Guide
108 Holly Dr
Waynesville MO 65583-9546
314-336-3711; Fax: 314-336-4640
Circulation: 17,000

Daily Quill
125 N Jefferson
West Plains MO 65775-2774
417-256-9191; Fax: 417-256-9196
Circulation: 9,000

Chris White, Asst City Editor
Carol Bruce, City Editor
Frank Martin III, Editor-in-Chief
Chris White, Lifestyle Editor
Jerry Womack, Managing Editor
Dennis Crider, Sports Editor

MONTANA

Billings Gazette
401 N Broadway (59101)
PO Box 36300
Billings MT 59107-6300
406-657-1200; Fax: 406-657-1208
Circulation: 54,000; Sun: 61,000

Christine Meyers, Arts/Book Reviewer
Nancy Nottingham, Business Editor
Tom Howard, Education Editor
Chris Rubich, Feature Editor
Richard Wesnick, Managing Editor
Mike Gast, News Editor
Jim Gransbery, Political Editor
Sue Olp, Religion Editor
Warren Rogers, Sports Editor

Bozeman Daily Chronicle
32 S Rouse St (59717)
PO Box 1188
Bozeman MT 59771
406-587-4491; Fax: 406-587-7995
Circulation: 14,000

Louanne Rod, Business Editor
Gail Schontzler, City Editor
Rob Chaney, Education Reporter
Parker Heinlein, Feature Editor
Parker Heinlein, Lifestyle Editor
Bill Wilke, Managing Editor
Mike Yawitz, Sports Editor

Montana Standard
25 W Granite St
Butte MT 59701-9213
406-496-5500; Fax: 406-496-5551
Circulation: 16,000

Great Falls Tribune
205 River Dr S
Great Falls MT 59405-1854
406-791-1444; Fax: 406-791-1431
Circulation: 36,000

Ravalli Republic
232 Main St
Hamilton MT 59840-2552
406-363-3300; Fax: 406-363-1767
Circulation: 52,000

Havre Daily News
119 2nd St
Havre MT 59501-3507
406-265-6795; Fax: 406-265-6798
Circulation: 5,000

Independent Record
317 Cruse St
PO Box 4249
Helena MT 59604
406-447-4000; Fax: 406-447-4052
Circulation: 14,000; Sun: 15,000

David Shors, City Editor
Charles Wood, News Editor
Roy Pace, Sports Editor

Daily Inter Lake
727 E Idaho
Kalispell MT 59901-3202
406-755-7000; Fax: 406-752-6114
Circulation: 16,000

Livingston Enterprise
401 S Main
Livingston MT 59047-3418
406-222-2000; Fax: 406-222-8580
Circulation: 4,000

Miles City Star
13 N 6th St
Miles City MT 59301-3101
406-232-0450; Fax: 406-232-6687
Circulation: 4,000

The Missoulian
PO Box 8029
Missoula MT 59807
406-523-5240; Fax: 406-523-5294
Circulation: 31,000; Sun: 40,000

John Engen, Arts/Entertainment Editor
Jim Ludwick, Business Editor
David Rutter, Editor
Theresa Johnson, Family/Food/Garden Editor
Theresa Johnson, Lifestyle/Feature Editor
Mike McInnally, News Editor
John Taylor, Religion Editor
Bob Meserrol, Sports Editor

Montana Kaimin
Univ of Montana
Journalism 206
Missoula MT 59812-0001
406-243-6541; Fax: 406-243-5475
Circulation: 6,000

NEBRASKA

Alliance Times-Herald
114 E 4th
Alliance NE 69301-3402
308-762-3060
Circulation: 3,000

Beatrice Daily Sun
200 N 7th St
Beatrice NE 68310-3916
402-223-6233; Fax: 402-228-3571
Circulation: 11,000

Columbus Telegram
1254 27th Ave
Columbus NE 68601-5656
402-564-2741; Fax: 402-563-4127
Circulation: 11,000

Fremont Tribune
135 N Main St
Fremont NE 68025-5673
402-721-5000; Fax: 402-721-8047
Circulation: 10,000

Independent
1st & Cedar Sts
Grand Island NE 68802
308-382-1000; Fax: 308-382-8129
Circulation: 24,000

Hastings Tribune
908 W 2nd St
Hastings NE 68901-5063
402-462-2131; Fax: 402-461-4657
Circulation: 14,000

Holdrege Daily Citizen
418 Garfield St
Holdrege NE 68949-2219
308-995-4441; Fax: 308-995-5992
Circulation: 3,000

Kearney Hub
13 E 22nd St
Kearney NE 68847-5404
308-237-2152; Fax: 308-234-5736
Circulation: 13,000

Daily Nebraskan
Univ of Nebraska
1400 R St 34 Nebraska Union
Lincoln NE 68588
402-472-2588; Fax: 402-472-1761
Circulation: 16,000

Daily Reporter
2145 N Cotner
Lincoln NE 68505-2921
402-466-8521; Fax: 402-466-6272
Circulation: 1,000

Lincoln Journal-Star
926 P St
PO Box 81609
Lincoln NE 68501
402-475-4200
Circulation: 40,000

   Kent Wolgamott, Arts/Entertainment Editor
   George Wright, Book Editor
   John Barrette, Business Editor
   Linda Olig, City Editor
   Jack Kennedy, Education Editor
   Mark Krassnowski, Food Editor
   Martha Stoddard, Health Editor
   Linda Olig, Lifestyle Editor
   Tom White, Managing Editor
   Brian Hill, Sports Editor
   Connie Walter, Travel Editor

McCook Daily Gazette
West 1st & E Sts
McCook NE 69001
308-345-4500; Fax: 308-345-7881
Circulation: 8,000

Nebraska City News-Press
123 S 8th St
Nebraska City NE 68410-2445
402-873-3334; Fax: 402-873-5436
Circulation: 3,000

Norfolk Daily News
525 Norfolk Ave
Norfolk NE 68701-5236
402-371-1020; Fax: 402-371-5802
Circulation: 21,000

Telegraph
621 N Chestnut
North Platte NE 69101-4131
308-532-6000; Fax: 308-532-9268
Circulation: 15,000

Daily Record
3323 Leavenworth
Omaha NE 68105-1623
402-345-1303; Fax: 402-345-2351
Circulation: 1,000

Omaha World Herald
1334 Dodge St
Omaha NE 68102-1122
402-444-1000; Fax: 402-345-0183
Circulation: 231,000; Sun: 301,000

   Kyle McMillian, Arts/Music Editor
   Steve Jordon, Business Editor
   Rick Ruggles, College Education
   Jeff Gauger, Computers/Technical Editor
   Deb Shanahan, Education Editor K-12
   Pat Waters, Feature Editor
   Jane Palmer, Food Editor
   Mary McGrath, Health/Medical Editor
   Chris Olson, Home Editor
   Deanna Sands, Managing Editor
   Larry King, Metro Editor
   Dave Kotok, Political Editor
   Joanne Stewart, Regional Editor
   Julia McCord, Religion Editor
   Steve Sinclair, Sports Editor
   Marilee Megiera, Travel Editor

Star-Herald
1405 Broadway
Scottsbluff NE 69361-3151
308-632-0670; Fax: 308-635-1258
Circulation: 16,000

Sidney Telegraph
809 Illinois
Sidney NE 69162-1641
308-254-5555; Fax: 308-254-5607
Circulation: 3,000

York News-Times
Kelly Harre, Managing Editor
327 Platte Ave
PO Box 279
York NE 68467
402-362-4478; Fax: 402-362-6748
Circulation: 6,000

NEVADA

Nevada Appeal
200 Bath St
PO Box 2288
Carson City NV 89702
702-882-2111; Fax: 702-887-2420
Circulation: 11,000; Sun: 11,000

   Sandi Wright, Business Editor
   Sue Morrow, City Editor
   Don Ham, Editor
   Rhonda Costa, Lifestyle Editor
   Lou Thomas, Sports Editor

Elko Daily Free Press
3720 Idaho St
Elko NV 89801-4611
702-738-3118; Fax: 702-738-2215
Circulation: 7,000

Ely Daily Times
700 Aultman Ave
Ely NV 89301-1556
702-289-4491; Fax: 702-289-4566
Circulation: 3,000

Fallon Eagle Standard
PO Box 1297
Fallon NV 89407-1297
702-423-6041; Fax: 702-423-0474
Circulation: 5,000

Lahontan Valley News
PO Box 1297
Fallon NV 89407-1297
702-423-6041; Fax: 702-423-0474
Circulation: 5,000

Las Vegas Review-Journal
1111 W Bonanza Rd
PO Box 70
Las Vegas NV 89125-0070
702-385-4241; Fax: 702-383-0302
Circulation: 142,000; Sun: 208,000

   Mike Weatherford, Arts/Entertainment Editor
   Mike Paskevich, Arts/Entertainment Editor
   Rafael Tarmariello, Business Editor
   Laura Wingard, City Editor
   Natalie Patton, Education Editor
   Keith Rogers, Environmental Editor
   Pat Morgan, Food Editor
   Jan Greene, Health/Medical Editor
   Linn Mills, Home/Garden Editor
   Frank Fertado, Lifestyle/Feature Editor
   Charlie Zobell, Managing Editor
   Jim Fossum, Outdoors Editor
   John Przybys, Religion Editor
   Jim Fossum, Sports Editor
   Ken White, Travel Editor

Las Vegas Sun
800 S Valley View
PO Box 4275
Las Vegas NV 89127
702-385-3111; Fax: 702-383-7264
Circulation: 48,000

   Phil Hagen, Arts/Entertainment Editor
   Rick Velotta, Business Editor
   Jeff Schuemacher, City News Editor
   Muriel Stevens, Food Editor
   Mary Manning, Health/Medical Editor
   Phil Hagen, Lifestyle/Feature Editor
   Sandra Thompson, Managing Editor

Phil Hagen, People Editor
Muriel Stevens, Travel Editor

Nevada Daily Legal News
516 S 4th St
Las Vegas NV 89101-6513
702-382-2747; Fax: 702-598-0641
Circulation: 1,000

Reno Gazette Journal
955 Kuenzli
PO Box 22000
Reno NV 89520-2000
702-788-6397; Fax: 702-788-6458
Circulation: 85,000

Jim Sloan, Arts Editor
Sandra Macias, Food Editor
Jim Sloan, Lifestyle Editor
Tonia Cunning, Managing Editor
Sharon Genung, Religion Editor
Ray Hagar, Sports/Outdoor Editor
Peggy Santoro, Travel Editor

Daily Sparks Tribune
1002 C St
Sparks NV 89431-4929
702-358-8061; Fax: 702-359-3837
Circulation: 6,000

NEW HAMPSHIRE

Berlin Daily Sun
55 Main St
Berlin NH 03570-2416
603-752-5858; Fax: 603-752-4160
Circulation: 7,000

Berlin Reporter
151 Main St
Berlin NH 03570-2417
603-752-1200; Fax: 603-752-2339
Circulation: 7,000

Eagle Times
RR 2 Box 301
Claremont NH 03743-2504
603-542-5121; Fax: 603-542-9705
Circulation: 10,000

Dan O'Brien, Business Editor
Todd Driscoll, Editor
Todd Driscoll, News Editor
Lawrence Walsh, Sports Editor

Concord Monitor
1 Monitor Dr
PO Box 1177
Concord NH 03302
603-224-5301
Circulation: 23,000

Brenda Charpentir, Arts/Entertainment Editor
Hans Schulz, Book Editor/Reviewer
Scott Calvert, Business Editor
Brenda Charpentir, Food Editor
Brenda Charpentir, Lifestyle/Feature Editor
Sandra Smith, Sports Editor
Hans Schulz, Sunday Editor

Foster's Daily Democrat
333 Central Ave
Dover NH 03820-4127
603-742-4455; Fax: 603-749-7079
Circulation: 30,000

Dartmouth
Dartmouth College
6175 Robinson Hall
Hanover NH 03755-3507
603-646-2600
Circulation: 2,000

Telegraph
17 Executive Dr
Hudson NH 03051-4903
603-882-2741; Fax: 603-882-5138
Circulation: 30,000

Keene Sentinel
60 West St
Keene NH 03431-3373
603-352-1234; Fax: 603-352-0437
Circulation: 16,000

Citizen
171 Fair St
Laconia NH 03246-3323
603-524-3800; Fax: 603-524-6702
Circulation: 12,000

The Union Leader
100 William Loeb Dr
PO Box 9555
Manchester NH 03108-9555
603-668-4321; Fax: 603-668-0382
Circulation: 72,000; Sun: 100,000

Barry Palmer, Book Editor/Reviewer
Bill Regan, Business Editor
Patrick Sheeran, City Editor
Patrick Sheeran, Education Editor
Barry Palmer, Entertainment Editor
Charles Perkins, Exec Editor
Ellie Ferriter, Lifestyle/Feature Editor
Jim Linehan, Managing Editor
Greg Ardruskevich, Religion Editor
Maureen Milliken, Sports Editor
Jim Adams, Travel Editor

Conway Daily Sun
64 Seavey St
North Conway NH 03860-5355
603-356-2999; Fax: 603-356-8774
Circulation: 14,000

Portsmouth Herald
111 Maplewood Ave
Portsmouth NH 03801-3715
603-436-1800; Fax: 603-427-0550
Circulation: 17,000

Valley News
7 Interchange Dr
West Lebanon NH 03784-2002
603-298-8711; Fax: 603-298-0212
Circulation: 18,000

NEW JERSEY

Urner Barry's Price-Current
182 Queens Blvd
Bayville NJ 08721-2741
908-240-5330; Fax: 908-341-0891
Circulation: 1,000

Bridgeton Evening News
100 E Commerce St
Bridgeton NJ 08302-2602
609-451-1000; Fax: 609-451-7214
Circulation: 13,000

Millville News
100 E Commerce St
Bridgeton NJ 08302-2602
609-327-1100; Fax: 609-451-7214
Circulation: 3,000

Courier-News
1201 Route 22
PO Box 6600
Bridgewater NJ 08807-0600
908-722-8800; Fax: 908-707-3252
Circulation: 55,000; Sun: 58,000

Paul Grazella, Arts/Entertainment Editor
Marilyn Ostermiller, Business Editor
Paul Grazella, Lifestyle/Feature Editor
Laura Harrigan, Managing Editor

Camden Courier-Post
301 Cuthbert Blvd
Cherry Hill NJ 08002-2905
609-663-6000; Fax: 609-663-2831
E-mail: couriemj@aol.com
Circulation: 87,000

Bill Reinhardt, Arts/Entertainment Editor
Dave Hoh, Education Editor
Bill Reinhardt, Family Editor
Pam Lyons, Food Editor
Jim Koncos, Health/Medical Editor
Deidre Comegys, Lifestyle/Feature Editor
Glen Holdcraft, Managing Editor
Carl Winter, Political Editor
Karen Morgan, Religion Editor
Chuck Bausman, Sports Editor

Home News & Tribune
35 Kennedy Blvd
East Brunswick NJ 08816
908-246-5500; Fax: 908-246-6046
Circulation: 54,000; Sun: 61,795

Kathy Dzielak, Arts/Entertainment Editor
Phil Hartman, Business Editor
Tia Swanson, Education Editor
Teresa Klink, Feature Editor
Jess Milgram, Food Editor
Cinda Becker, Health/Medical Editor
Theresa Klink, Lifestyle/Feature Editor
Andrea Glick, Lower Education Editor
Anthony Bersani, Managing Editor
Suzanne Pavkovic, News Editor
Teresa Klink, Religion Editor
Jack Genung, Sports Editor
Mary Price, Television Editor

The Record
Bergen Record Co
150 River St
Hackensack NJ 07601-7110
201-646-4000; Fax: 201-646-4135
Circulation: 160,000; Sun: 225,000

Kathleen Sullivan, Business Editor
Anna Fragetta, Computer Editor
Glenn Ritt, Editor-in-Chief
Caroline Hendrie, Education Editor
Lois Ditommaso, Feature Editor
Patricia Mack, Food Editor
Lindy Washburn, Health/Medical Editor
Vivian Waixel, Managing Editor
Tim Nostrand, News Editor
David Gibson, Religion Editor
Gabe Buonauro, Sports Editor
Jill Schensul, Travel Editor

Daily Racing Form
10 Lake Dr
Hightstown NJ 08520-5321
609-448-9100; Fax: 609-448-3684
Circulation: 16,000

Jersey Journal
30 Journal Square
Jersey City NJ 07306-4199
201-653-1000; Fax: 201-653-1414
Circulation: 70,000

Marty Murphy, Arts/Entertainment Editor
Greg Wilson, Business Editor
Ron Leir, Education Editor
Robert Larkins, Health/Medical Editor
Margaret Schmidt, Lifestyle/Feature Editor
George Latanzio, Managing Editor
John Watson, News Editor
Ron Leir, Religion Editor
Harvey Zucker, Sports Editor

Svoboda
30 Montgomery St
Jersey City NJ 07302-3821
201-434-0237; Fax: 201-451-5486
Circulation: 12,000

Asbury Park Press
3601 Hwy 66
PO Box 1550
Neptune NJ 07754
908-922-6000; Fax: 908-922-4818
Circulation: 170,000; Sun: 237,000

Isaiah Pole, Arts/Entertainment Editor
Wally Stroby, Book Editor
Bob Hordt, Business Editor
Rona Sutow, Family/Home Editor
Andrea Clurfeld, Food Editor
Bob Cullinane, Health/Medical Editor
Harry Ziegler, Lifestyle/Feature Editor
Fred Kerr, Managing Editor-News
Sherry Conohan, Political Editor
Joe Adelizzi, Recreation Editor
Rona Sutow, Religion Editor
John Quinn, Sports Editor
Victor Zak, Travel Editor

Daily Targum
Rutgers University
126 College Ave #431
New Brunswick NJ 08901-1166
908-932-7051; Fax: 908-246-7299
Circulation: 17,000

Star-Ledger
Star Ledger Plz
Newark NJ 07102
201-877-4141; Fax: 201-643-4945
Circulation: 476,000

Roger Harris, Book Editor
Dave Allen, Business Editor
Nick Chiles, Education Editor
Art Martinez, Feature Editor
Karla Cook, Food Editor
John Van de Water, Garden Editor
Shirley Friedman, Home Editor
Charles Harrison, Managing Editor
Gale Scott, Medical Editor
David Wald, Political Editor
Jerry Krupnick, Radio/TV Editor
Steve Chambers, Religion Editor
Kitta McPherson, Science Editor
Kevin Whitmore, Sports Editor
Mike Shoup, Travel Editor

New Jersey Herald
2 Spring St
Newton NJ 07860-2077
201-383-1500; Fax: 201-383-9284
Circulation: 20,000

Daily Record
629 Parsippany Rd
Parsippany NJ 07054
201-428-6200; Fax: 201-428-6666
Circulation: 60,000

Lorrain Ash, Arts/Entertainment Editor
Chriss Swaney, Business Editor
Lorrain Ash, Feature/Book Editor
Ruth Eames, Food Editor
Jim McGarvey, Health Editor
Jack Bowie, Managing Editor
Jim McGarvey, Metro Editor
Lou Hansen, Sports Editor

North Jersey Herald & News
988 Main Ave
Passaic NJ 07055
201-365-3100; Fax: 201-614-0906
Circulation: 80,000; Sun: 80,000

Michael Starr, Arts/Entertainment Editor
Ken Pringle, Asst Managing Editor
Michael Starr, Book Editor/Reviewer
Wes Pollard, Business Editor
Richard Zmijewski, City Editor
Wes Pollard, Food Editor
Merry Firschein, Lifestyle/Feature Editor
Jim Brennan, Sports Editor

Atlantic City Press
22 Devins Ln
Pleasantville NJ 08232
609-272-1100; Fax: 609-272-7224
Circulation: 90,000; Sun: 100,000

Kevin Post, Business Editor
Paul Merkoski, Editor
Alice Cranston, Feature/Book Editor
Cindy Nevitt, Lifestyle Editor
Maryjane Briant, Managing Editor
Mike Sheperd, Sports Editor

Daily Princetonian
Princeton University
48 University Pl
Princeton NJ 08544-0001
609-924-7570; Fax: 609-924-4039
Circulation: 3,000

Today's Sunbeam
93 5th St
Salem NJ 08079-1041
609-935-1500; Fax: 609-845-3139
Circulation: 12,000

Ocean County Observer
8 Robbins St
Toms River NJ 08753-7629
908-349-3000; Fax: 908-349-8636
Circulation: 18,000

The Trenton Times
500 Perry St
PO Box 847
Trenton NJ 08605-0847
609-396-3232; Fax: 609-394-2819
Circulation: 84,000; Sun: 95,000

Tim Quinn, Arts/Entertainment Editor
Hilary Winter, Book Editor
David Newhouse, Business Editor
Brian Mallone, Exec Editor
Kris Jesson, Feature Editor

Kris Jesson, Food Editor
Kate McCartin, Health/Medical Editor
Peter Callas, Metro Editor
Jim Davis, Political Editor
Rich Miller, Religion Editor
Kate McCartin, Science Editor
Jim Gauger, Sports Editor

The Trentonian
600 Perry St
Trenton NJ 08602-3996
609-989-7800; Fax: 609-393-6072
Circulation: 75,000; Sun: 67,000

Jim Fitzsimmons, Business Editor
Barbara Lempert, City Editor
Mark A Waligore, Editor
Jeff Price, Feature Editor
Jeff Price, Food Editor
Barbara Lempert, Political Editor
Jeff Price, Science Editor
John Buonara, Sports Editor

Daily Journal
891 E Oak Rd
Vineland NJ 08360-2394
609-691-5000; Fax: 609-691-2031
Circulation: 24,000

America Oggi
55 Bergenline Ave
Westwood NJ 07675-3104
201-358-6692; Fax: 212-268-0379
Circulation: 60,000

Burlington County Times
4284 Route 130
Willingboro NJ 08046
609-871-8000; Fax: 609-871-0490
Circulation: 44,000; Sun: 46,000

Joe Dipolo, Arts/Entertainment Editor
Ron Martin, Book Editor
Elsbeth DiFurio, Business Editor
Irma Getz, Education Editor
Martha Esposito, Food Editor
Penny Sundstrom, Lifestyle/Feature Editor
Gary Lindenmuth, Managing Editor
Wayne Richarson, Sports Editor
Ron Martin, Sunday Editor

Gloucester County Times
309 Broad St
Woodbury NJ 08096
609-845-3300; Fax: 609-845-5480
Circulation: 30,000

Jennifer Watson, Arts/Entertainment Editor
Jim Six, Book Editor
Tom Durso, Business Editor
Jennifer Watson, City Editor
William Long, Editor
Jan Watson, Food Editor
Jan Watson, Lifestyle/Feature Editor
Jim Childs, Religion Editor
Tom Murray, Sports Editor
Jim Six, Travel Editor

NEW MEXICO

Alamogordo Daily News
518 24th St
PO Box 870
Alamogordo NM 88310
505-437-7120; Fax: 505-437-7795
Circulation: 10,000

Heather Border, City Editor
Richard Coltharp, Managing Editor
Michael Shinaberg, Sports Editor

Albuquerque Journal
7777 Jefferson St NE (87109)
PO Drawer J
Albuquerque NM 87103
505-823-3912; Fax: 505-823-3994
Circulation: 121,000; Sun: 158,000

Maria Elena Alverez, Arts/Entertainment Editor
David Steinberg, Book Editor
Steve McMillan, Business Editor
Valerie Santillanes, Education Editor
Nancy Baca, Food Editor
Rex Graham, Health/Medical Editor
Tom Harmon, Lifestyle/Feature Editor
Rod Deckert, Managing Editor
Ken Walston, News Editor
John Robertson, Political Editor
Martin Frentzel, Recreation Editor
Bruce Daniels, Religion Editor
John Fleck, Science Editor
Mike Hall, Sports Editor

New Mexico Daily Lobo
Univ of New Mexico
Marron Hall Rm 131
Albuquerque NM 87131-0001
505-277-5656; Fax: 505-277-6228
Circulation: 15,000

Artesia Daily Press
503 W Main
PO Drawer 190
Artesia NM 88211
505-746-3524
Circulation: 4,000

Darrel Pehr, Editor

Carlsbad Current-Argus
620 S Main St
PO Box 1629
Carlsbad NM 88221
505-887-5501; Fax: 505-885-1066
Circulation: 9,000

Valerie Lemon, Lifestyle Editor
Hal Miller, Managing Editor
Bill Riggs, Sports Editor
Darin Fenger, Business Editor

Clovis News Journal
521 Pile
PO Box 1689
Clovis NM 88102-1689
505-763-3431; Fax: 505-762-3879
Circulation: 13,000; Sun: 13,000

Mike Wheeler, Managing Editor

Deming Headlight
219 E Maple
Deming NM 88030-4267
505-546-2611; Fax: 505-546-8116
Circulation: 4,000

Daily Times
201 N Allen (87401)
PO Box 450
Farmington NM 87499
505-325-4545; Fax: 505-327-6651
Circulation: 19,000

Wayne Leopold, City Editor
Jack Swickard, Executive Editor
Dorothy Nobis, Lifestyle Editor
Ralph Damiani, Managing Editor
Mark Esper, News Editor
Ed Thompson, Sports Editor

Gallup Independent
500 North 9th
PO Box 1210
Gallup NM 87305
505-863-6811; Fax: 505-722-5750
Circulation: 19,000

Ted Rushton, Managing Editor

Hobbs Daily News-Sun
201 N Thorp
PO Box 860
Hobbs NM 88240
505-393-2123; Fax: 505-393-5724
Circulation: 15,000

Mani Marquez, Managing Editor

Las Cruces Sun-News
256 W Las Cruces Ave (88005)
PO Box 1749
Las Cruces NM 88004
505-523-6464; Fax: 505-523-7913
Circulation: 22,000

Harold Cousland, Editor

Las Vegas Daily Optic
614 Lincoln
PO Box 2607
Las Vegas NM 87701
505-425-6796; Fax: 505-425-1005
Circulation: 5,000

Andrea Buchanan, Editor

Los Alamos Monitor
256 DP Rd
Los Alamos NM 87544-3233
505-662-4185; Fax: 505-662-4334
Circulation: 5,000

Lovington Daily Leader
14 W Ave B
Lovington NM 88260-4404
505-396-2844; Fax: 505-396-5775
Circulation: 3,000

Portales News-Tribune
101 E First
PO Box 848
Portales NM 88130
505-356-4481; Fax: 505-356-3630
Circulation: 4,000; Sun: 4,500

Daren Watkins, Managing Editor

Roswell Daily Record
2301 N Main St
PO Box 1897
Roswell NM 88201
505-622-7710; Fax: 505-625-0421
Circulation: 14,000; Sun: 15,500

Richard Olmstead, Bus/Science/Travel Ed
Greg Peretti, Education/Managing Editor
Marifrank DaHarb, Lifestyle/Feature Editor
Harry Readel, Sports Editor

Santa Fe New Mexican
202 E Marcy St (87501-2021)
PO Box 2048
Santa Fe NM 87504-2048
505-983-3303; Fax: 505-986-9147
Circulation: 26,000; Sun: 25,000

Bob Quick, Business Editor
Aaron Baca, Education Editor
Keith Easthouse, Health/Medical Editor
Nancy Plevens, Lifestyle/Feature Editor
Rob Dean, Managing Editor
David Royball, Political Editor
Keith Easthouse, Science Editor
Pancho Morris, Sports Editor

Silver City Daily Press/Indep
300 W Market
Silver City NM 88061-4956
505-388-1576; Fax: 505-388-1196
Circulation: 7,000

NEW YORK

Albany Times-Union
PO Box 15000
Albany NY 12212-5000
518-454-5420; Fax: 518-456-5628
Circulation: 115,000

Michelle Sullivan, Arts and Lifestyle Editor
Alan Abbey, Business Editor
Colleen Fitzpatrick, City Editor
Chris Ringwald, Education Editor
Yancy Roy, Environmental Editor
Joann Crupi, Feature/Book Editor
Rex Smith, Managing Editor
Harvey Lipman, Political Editor
Joe Layden, Sports Editor
Mike Virtanen, Travel Editor

Recorder
1 Venner Rd
Amsterdam NY 12010-5617
518-843-1100; Fax: 518-843-1338
Circulation: 14,000

Citizen
25 Dill St
Auburn NY 13021-3605
315-253-5311; Fax: 315-253-6031
Circulation: 16,000

Daily News
2 Apollo Dr
Batavia NY 14020-3002
716-343-8000; Fax: 716-343-2623
Circulation: 17,000

Press & Sun Bulletin
Vestal Pky E
PO Box 1270
Binghamton NY 13902-1270
607-798-1234; Fax: 607-798-1113
Circulation: 87,000; Sun: 100,000

Gene Grey, Arts/Entertainment Edit
Bruce Estes, Asst Managing Editor
Barbara Van Atta, Asst Travel Editor
Gene Grey, Book Editor
Jeff Platsky, Business Editor
Barry Rothfeld, Exec Editor
Joy Crocker, Feature, Health, Lifestyle Ed
Leslie Spalding, News Editor
Don Sbarra, Political Editor
Charlie Jaworksi, Sports Editor

Daily Bulletin
125 Montague St
Brookly NY11201-3402
718-624-0536; Fax: 718-624-2716
Circulation: 5,000

New York Daily Challenge
Dawad Phillip, Managing Editor
1360 Fulton St
Brooklyn NY 11216-2600
718-636-9500; Fax: 718-857-9115
Circulation: 80,000

Buffalo News
1 News Plz
PO Box 100
Buffalo NY 14240-0100
716-849-4444; Fax: 716-856-5150
Circulation: 305,000; Sun: 382,054

Terry Doran, Arts Editor
Jeff Simon, Book Editor
Murray B Light, Exec Editor
Susan LoTempio, Feature/Lifestyle Editor
William Flynn, Financial News Editor
Janis Okun, Food Editor
Henry Davis, Health Writer
Foster Spencer, Managing Editor
Michael Vogel, Science/Environment Edi
Howard Smith, Sports Editor
Joyce Ware, Travel Editor

Daily Messenger
73 Buffalo St
Canandaigua NY 14424-1001
716-394-0770; Fax: 716-394-1675
Circulation: 15,000

Daily Mail
30 Church St
Catskill NY 12414-1609
518-943-2100; Fax: 518-943-2063
Circulation: 6,000

Daily Editor
59 E Main St
Cobleskill NY 12043-1607
518-234-4368; Fax: 58-234-8849
Circulation: 6,000; Sun: 6,000

The Leader
34 W Pulteney St
Corning NY 14830-2211
607-936-4651; Fax: 607-936-9939
Circulation: 16,500; Sun: 16,500

Cortland Standard
110 Main St
Cortland NY 13045
607-756-5665; Fax: 607-756-5665
Circulation: 13,000

Toni Patrillo, Arts/Entertainment Editor
Paul LaDolce, Business Editor
Laura Jones, Family/Food/Health Editor
Laura Jones, Home/Garden/People Editor
Kevin Howe, Managing Editor
Skip Chapman, News/Religion Editor
Connie Nogas, Political Editor
Jere Dexter, Sports Editor

Evening Observer
Keith Sheldon, Managing Editor
8-10 E Second St
Dunkirk NY 14048
716-366-3000; Fax: 716-366-3005
Circulation: 15,000

Star-Gazette
201 Baldwin St
Elmira NY 14901-3002
607-734-5151; Fax: 607-733-4408
Circulation: 35,000; Fax: 50,000

Neo-Asian American Times
135-19 Roosevelt Ave
Flushing NY 11354-5305
718-461-2555; Fax: 718-460-3533
Circulation: 10,000; Sun: 10,000

Finger Lake Times
218 Genessee St
Geneva NY 14456-2323
315-789-3333; 315-789-4077
Circulation: 20,000; Sun: 20,000

The Post-Star
Lawrence & Cooper St
Glen Falls NY 12801
518-792-3131; Fax: 518-761-1255
Circulation: 34,000; Sun: 37,000

Leader-Herald
8-10 E Fulton St
Gloversville NY 12078
518-725-8616; Fax: 518-725-7407
Circulation: 13,000

Jessica Smrtic, City Editor
Thomas Nevich, Managing Editor

Evening Telegram
111 Green St
Herkimer NY 13350-1914
315-866-2220; Fax: 315-866-5913
Circulation: 7,000

Evening Tribune
85 Canisteo St
Hornell NY 14843-1544
607-324-1425; Fax: 607-324-1753
Circulation: 9,000

Register-Star
364 Warren St
Hudson NY 12534-2419
518-828-1616; Fax: 518-828-9437
Circulation: 12,000

Cornell Daily Sun
Cornell University
119 S Cayuga St
Ithaca NY 14850-5507
607-273-3606; Fax: 607-273-0746
E-mail: sun-mailbox@cornell.edu
Circulation: 5,200

Ithaca Journal
123 W State St
Ithaca NY 14850-5427
607-274-9233; Fax: 607-272-4335
Circulation: 18,000; Sat: 23,421

David Hill, Agriculture Editor
Matt Palm, Book Reviewer Editor
John Yaukey, Computer Editor
Stephen Landesman, Feature/Lifestyle Ed
Ted Haider, Managing Editor
Kathryn Holvis, Metro Editor
Eric Hegedus, Photo Editor
Brian Kohn, Political Editor
Tom Fleischman, Sports Editor

Post-Journal
15 W 2nd St
Jamestown NY 14701-5215
716-487-1111; Fax: 716-664-3119
Circulation: 24,000

Kingston Daily Freeman
79-97 Hurley Ave
Kingston NY 12401
914-331-5000; Fax: 914-338-0672
Circulation: 25,000; Sun: 30,000

Edwina Henderson, Lifestyle Dept
Sam Daleo, Managing Editor

Evening Times
347 S 2nd St
Little Falls NY 13365-1411
315-823-3680; Fax: 315-823-4086
Circulation: 7,000

Union-Sun & Journal
459 S Transit St
Lockport NY 14094-5506
716-439-9222; Fax: 716-439-9239
Circulation: 18,000

Korea Times
42-22 27th St
Long Island NY 11101-4107
718-482-1111; Fax: 718-784-9131
Circulation: 50,000

National Herald
41-17 Crescent St
Long Island City NY 11101-3805
718-784-5255; 718-472-0510
E-mail: kyrikav@aol.com
Circulation: 40,000

Proini
25-50 Crescent St
Long Island City NY 11102-2938
718-626-7676; Fax: 718-626-7830
Circulation: 50,000

Malone Telegram
387 E Main St
Malone NY 12953-9701
518-483-2000; Fax: 518-483-8579
Circulation: 7,000

Journal-Register
409-13 Main St
Medina NY 14103-1416
716-798-1400; Fax: 716-798-0290
Circulation: 5,000

Newsday
235 Pinelawn Rd
Melville NY 11747-4250
516-843-2020; Fax: 516-843-2953
Circulation: 700,000; Sun: 800,000

Tom Incantalupo, Automotive Reporter
Paul Schreiber, Business Columnist
Henry Gilgoff, Consumer Writer
Warren Beery, Editor Special Sections
John Hildebrand, Education Writer
Jennifer Krauss, Entertainment Editor
Dan Fagin, Environmental Writer
Rosemary Skapley, Kidsday Editor
Barbara Schuler, Lifestyle Editor
Steve Sink, Long Island Bus Editor
Tony Marro, Managing Editor
Michael Unger, Pharm/Biotech Editor
Stephen Williams, Pop Music Editor
Steve Ruinsky, Sports Editor

Marjorie Robbins, Travel Editor
Stephen Williams, Travel Reporter
Joe Gelmis, Video Editor, TV Plus Magazine
Noel Rubinton, Viewpoint Editor

Times Herald-Record
40 Mulberry St
Middletown NY 10940-6302
914-343-2181; Fax: 914-343-2170
Circulation: 90,000; Sun: 105,000

Emily Morrison, Arts/Entertainment Editor
Moe Mitterling, Book Editor
Judith Rife, Business Editor
Mark Pittman, City Desk Editor
Deborah MacConnell, Family Editor
Beth Mullally, Health/Medical Reporter
Debbie Botti, Lifestyle/Feature Editor
Jeff Storey, Managing Editor
Allan Gaul, News Editor
Bill Burr, Sports Editor
Moe Mitterling, Travel Editor

American Banker
1 State St Plz
New York NY 10004-1505
212-803-8200; Fax: 212-843-9600
Circulation: 18,000

American Metal Market
825 7th Ave
New York NY 10019-6014
212-887-8580; Fax: 212-887-8522
Circulation: 12,000

Bond Buyer
1 State St Plz
New York NY 10004-1505
212-803-8200; Fax: 212-843-9617
Circulation: 4,000

China Daily
1 World Trade Ctr #3369
New York NY 10048-3399
212-488-9677; Fax: 212-488-9493
Circulation: 5,000

China Tribune
396 Broadway 10th Fl
New York NY 10013-3500
212-925-6790
Circulation: 8,000

Chinese United Journal
83 White St
New York NY 10013-6026
212-513-1440; Fax: 212-693-1392
Circulation: 35,000

Columbia Daily Spectator
Columbia University
1125 Amsterdam Ave 2nd Fl
New York NY 10025-1717
212-280-3634; Fax: 212-280-4763
Circulation: 10,000

Daily News Bulletin
330 7th Ave 11th Fl
New York NY 10001-5007
212-643-1890; Fax: 212-643-8498
Circulation: N/A

Daily News Record
7 W 34th St
New York NY 10001-8100
212-630-3600; Fax: 212-630-3602
Circulation: 26,000

Daily Yomiuri
666 5th Ave
New York NY 10103-0001
212-765-1111; Fax: 212-765-1618
Circulation: 19,000

El Diario la Prensa
143-155 Varick St
New York NY 10013-1106
212-807-4600; Fax: 212-807-4705
Circulation: 70,000

Hurriyet
500 5th Ave #1024
New York NY 10110-0002
212-921-8880; Fax: 212-391-4017
Circulation: 6,000

Journal of Commerce & Commercial
Two World Trade Ctr 27th Fl
New York NY 10048-0203
212-837-7000; Fax: 212-837-7130
Circulation: 23,000

Donald D Holt, Editor
Rosalind McLymont, Trade Editor
Mark Getzfred, Transportation Editor

Korea Herald
150 W 51st St
New York NY 10019-6836
212-582-5205
Circulation: 20,000

New York Daily News
220 East 42nd St
New York NY 10017-5858
212-210-2100; Fax: 212-210-2203
Circulation: 800,000; Sun: 1,000,000

John Sullivan, Arts Editor
Sherryl Connelly, Book Editor
James Hairston, Business Editor
Pat Mangan, Education Editor
Rosemary Black, Food Editor, Food Finds
Annette Fuentes, Health Editor
Liz Forgang, Home Editor, Home Furnishings Section
Margaret Farley, Lifestyle Editor
Richard Esposito, Metro Editor
George Salas, Real Estate Editor
Jerry Kenney, Recreation Editor
Bill Bell, Religion Editor
Kathy Larkin, Society Editor
Kevin Whitmer, Sports Editor
Jeff Weingrad, Television Editor
Gunna Dickson, Travel Editor

New York Law Journal
345 Park Ave S
New York NY 10010-1707
212-779-9200; Fax: 212-696-4514
Circulation: 16,000

New York Post
1211 6th Ave 10th Fl
New York NY 10036
212-930-8000; Fax: 212-930-8540
Circulation: 552,000

Dave Yelland, Business Editor
Lawrence Goodman, Education Editor
Vincent Musetto, Entertainment Editor, Entertainment Section
Steve Cuozzo, Executive Editor
Larry Hackett, Feature Editor
Marc Kalech, Managing Editor
Debra Orin, National Political Editor

Roger Field, Science Editor
Joe Nicholson, Science Editor
Greg Gallo, Sports Editor
Pucci Meyer, Travel Editor
Adam Buckman, TV Editor

New York Times
229 W 43rd St
New York NY 10036
212-556-1234; Fax: 212-556-7126
Circulation: 1,115,000

Connie Rosenblum, Arts/Leisure Editor
Tom Bodkin, Asst Managing Editor
Dulcie Leimbach, Children's Book Editor, New York Times Book Review
Paul Goldberger, Culture Editor, Domestic Correspondent
William Stockton, Daily Business Editor
Charles McGrath, Editor, New York Times Book Review
Nancy Sharkey, Education Editor
Joseph Lelyveld, Executive Editor
Claudia Payne, Fashion Editor
Eric Asimov, Food Editor
William Keller, Foreign Editor
Nicholas Wade, Health/Science Editor, Science Times
Barbara Graustark, Home Editor, Home Section
Trish Hall, Living Section Editor
John Montorio, Living Style Editor
Gene Roberts, Managing Editor
Martin Arnold, Media Editor
Donna Laurie, National Edition Editor
Michael Leahy, Real Estate Editor
William Borders, Senior Editor
Neil Amdur, Sports Editor
Bernie Gwertzman, Sr Editor
Glenn Kramon, Sunday Business Editor
Judith Wilner, Technology Editor
Nancy Newhouse, Travel Editor

Noticias del Mundo
401 5th Ave
New York NY 10016-3317
212-684-5656; Fax: 212-889-0024
Circulation: 32,000

Novoye Russkoye Slovo
111 5th Ave
New York NY 10003-1005
212-387-0299; Fax: 212-387-9050
Circulation: 62,000

Nowy Dziennik Polish Daily
333 W 38th St 42nd Fl
New York NY 10018-2914
212-594-2266; Fax: 212-594-2383
Circulation: 39,000

Platts' Oilgram News
1221 Ave of the Americas 42nd Fl
New York NY 10020-1001
212-512-2563; Fax: 212-512-4008
Circulation: N/A

Redemption Digest & Securities
99 Hudson St
New York NY 10013-2815
212-219-1551; Fax: 212-966-2637
Circulation: 10,000

Sing Tao Daily
185 Canal St
New York NY 10013-4682
212-431-9030; Fax: 212-431-1816
Circulation: 55,000

Standard & Poor's Daily News
25 Broadway
New York NY 10004-1010
212-208-8377; Fax: 212-509-8997
Circulation: 3,000

Standard & Poor's Dividend Record
25 Broadway 19th Fl
New York NY 10004-1010
212-208-8369; Fax: 212-412-0514
Circulation: 2,000

Wall Street Journal
200 Liberty St
New York NY 10281-0001
212-416-2500; Fax: 212-416-3299
Circulation: 2,000,000

Raymond Sokolov, Arts/Ent/Leisure Editor
Eric Eichman, Book Editor
Leon E Wynter, Business & Race Editor
Glen Meeks, Editor, Money and Investing Section
Robert Bartley, Editor-in-Chief
Steven Stecklow, Education Editor
Roger Ricklefs, Enterprise Editor
Fred Bleakley, Finance Editor
Neil Ulman, Health/Medical Editor
Francine Schwadel, Law Editor
David Crook, News Editor
Al Hunt, Political Editor
Neil Ulman, Science Editor
Mark Robichax, Sports Editor
Ann Podd, Spot News Editor
Jonathan Dahl, Travel Editor

Washington Square News
New York Univ Loeb Student Ctr
566 LaGuardia Pl 9th Fl
New York NY 10012-1097
212-998-4300; Fax: 212-995-3790
Circulation: 26,000

Women's Wear Daily
Ron Cohen, City Editor
7 W 34th St
New York NY 10001
212-630-4000; Fax: 212-630-3566
Circulation: 56,000

Niagara Gazette
310 Niagara St
Niagara Falls NY 14303-1141
716-282-2311; Fax: 716-286-3895
Circulation: 25,000

Tonawanda News
435 River Rd
North Tonawanda NY 14120-6809
716-693-1000; Fax: 716-693-8573
Circulation: 13,000

Evening Sun
45-47 Hale St
Norwich NY 13815-2038
607-334-3276; Fax: 607-334-8273
Circulation: 6,000

Journal
308 Isabella St
Ogdensburg NY 13669-1407
315-393-1000; Fax: 315-393-5108
Circulation: 6,000

Olean Times Herald
639 Norton Dr
Olean NY 14760-1402
716-372-3121; Fax: 716-372-0740
Circulation: 23,000

Oneida Daily Dispatch
130 Broad St
Oneida NY 13421-1648
315-363-5100; Fax: 315-363-9832
Circulation: 9,000

Daily Star
102 Chestnut St
Oneonta NY 13820-2409
607-432-1000; Fax: 607-432-5847
Circulation: 19,000

Palladium-Times
140 W 1st St
Oswego NY 13126-1514
315-343-3800; Fax: 315-343-0273
Circulation: 11,000

Press Republican
170 Margaret St
Plattsburgh NY 12901-1838
518-561-2300; Fax: 518-561-3362
Circulation: 23,000

Sports Eye
18 Industrial Park Dr
Port Washington NY 11050-4621
516-484-3300; Fax: 516-484-6104
Circulation: N/A

Courier-Observer
71 Market St
Potsdam NY 13676-1746
315-265-6000; Fax: 315-265-6001
Circulation: 9,000

Poughkeepsie Journal
85 Civic Center Plz
PO Box 1231
Poughkeepsie NY 12602-1231
914-454-2000; Fax: 914-437-4921
Circulation: 45,000; Sun: 60,000

Florence Schetzel, Arts/Entertainment Editor
Paul Lander, Book Editor
Michelle Leder, Business Editor
Claudie Rowe, Education Editor
Derek Osenenko, Exec Editor
Dennis Kipp, Health/Medical Editor
Gerry McNulty, Political Editor
Curtis Leone-Schmidt, Sports Editor

Daily Record
PO Box 6
Rochester NY 14601-0006
716-232-6920; Fax: 716-232-2740
Circulation: 3,000

Democrat and Chronicle
55 Exchange Blvd
Rochester NY 14614-2001
716-232-7100; Fax: 716-258-2487
Circulation: 137,000

Times-Union
55 Exchange Blvd
Rochester NY 14614-2001
716-232-7100; Fax: 716-258-2487
Circulation: 52,000

Daily Sentinel
333 W Dominick St
Rome NY 13440-5701
315-337-4000; Fax: 315-337-4704
Circulation: 19,000

Salamanca Press
36-42 River St
Salamanca NY 14779-1474
716-945-1644; Fax: 716-945-4285
Circulation: 3,000

Adirondack Daily Enterprise
61 Broadway
Saranac Lake NY 12983-1703
518-891-2600; 518-891-2756
Circulation: 6,000

Saratogian
20 Lake Ave
Saratoga Springs NY 12866-2314
518-584-4242; Fax: 518-587-7750
Circulation: 12,000

The Daily Gazette
2345 Maxon Rd
Schenectady NY 12308-1090
518-374-4141; Fax: 518-395-3089
Circulation: 61,000; Sun: 62,000

Peg Wright, Arts/Entertainment Editor
Sherryl McGill, Book Editor
Eric Anderson, Business Editor
Nick Cantiello, City News Editor
Shirin Parsavand, Education Editor
Dick Bennett, Food Editor
Dick Bennett, Lifestyle/Feature Editor
Tom Woodman, Managing Editor
Butch Walker, Sports Editor

Staten Island Advance
950 Fingerboard Rd
Staten Island NY 10305-1495
718-981-1234; Fax: 718-981-5679
Circulation: 85,000; Sun: 95,000

Richard Ryan, Arts/Entertainment Editor
Mark Hanley, Book Editor
Jeff O'Heir, Business Editor
Tom Checchi, City News Editor
Diane Rory, Education Reporter
Caroline Rushessky, Environmental Editor
Jane Milza, Food Editor
Ken Paulsen, Lifestyle/Feature Editor
Julia Martin, Religion Editor
Lou Bergonzi, Sports Editor
Sharon Silke, Travel Editor

Daily Orange
Syracuse University
744 Ostrom Ave
Syracuse NY 13210-2942
315-443-2314; Fax: 315-443-3689
Circulation: 9,000

Herald-Journal
Clinton Square
PO Box 4915
Syracuse NY 13221-4915
315-470-2265; Fax: 315-470-3019
Circulation: 89,000; Sun: 220,550/Evening

Ken Peters, Automotive Editor
Dan Padovano, Business Editor
Janis Barth, City Editor
Al Fasoldt, Computer Editor
J B McCampbell, Entertainment Editor
Mark Weiner, Environmental Reporter
Mary Beth Mulder, Food Editor

Amber Smith, Health/Medical Editor
Kathy Schneider, Lifestyle/Feature Editor
Marie Morelli, News Editor
Marie Morelli, Political Editor
James Riley, Religion Reporter
Mark Weiner, Science Editor
Steve Carlic, Sports Editor
Bob Long, Travel Editor

Syracuse Post Standard
1 Clinton Square (13202)
PO Box 4818
Syracuse NY 13221-4818
315-470-0011; Fax: 315-470-3081
Circulation: 90,000; Sun: 250,000

Charles Jackson, Book Review Editor
Dave Berman, Business Editor
John Lammers, City News Editor
Paul Riede, Education Editor
Kathy Schneider, Family/Food Editor
Rosemary Robinson, Managing Editor
Luther Boliven, Political Editor
Tom Boll, Religion Reporter
John Lammers, Sports Editor

Record
501 Broadway
Troy NY 12180-3324
518-270-1200; Fax: 518-270-1202
Circulation: 32,000

Observer-Dispatch
221 Oriskany Plz
Utica NY 13501-1201
315-792-5000; Fax: 315-792-5033
Circulation: 51,000

Watertown Daily Times
260 Washington St
Watertown NY 13601-3364
315-782-1000; Fax: 315-782-1040
Circulation: 41,000; Sun: 46,500

Mary Kaskan, Arts/Entertainment Editor
Keith Button, Business Editor
Tracy Valentine, Education Editor
Chris Taylor, Environmental Editor
Judy Jacobs, Food Editor
Roger Smith, Health/Medical Editor
Mary Kaskan, Lifestyle/Feature Editor
John B Johnson Jr, Managing Editor
Mary Kaskan, People/Society Editor
Gene Warnick, Sports Editor
Mary Kaskan, Travel Editor

Wellsville Daily Reporter
159 N Main St
Wellsville NY 14895-1149
716-593-5300; Fax: 716-593-5303
Circulation: 4,000

Rockland Journal-News
200 N Route 303
West Nyack NY 10994-1619
914-358-2200; Fax: 914-578-2342
Circulation: 40,000

Gannette Suburban Newspapers
1 Gannett Dr
White Plains NY 10604-3406
914-694-9300; Fax: 914-694-5018
Circulation: 166,000; Sunday: 205,254

Georgette Gouveia, Arts/Entertainment Editor
Jean Lucasey, Book Editor
Mark Land, Business Editor
Karen Jenkins Holt, Education Editor

Debra Porterfield, Food Editor
Tad Clark, Lifestyle Editor
Dave Georget, Sports Editor
Janet McMillan, Sr Managing Editor
Kathy McClusky, Travel Editor

The following papers make up **Gannett Suburban Newspapers**. Use the Gannet address and phone for any one of them.

Citizen Register
Circulation: 7,000; Sun 8,000

Daily Item
Circulation: 9,000; Sun: 10,000

Daily News
Circulation: 4,000; Sun: 5,000

Daily Times
Circulation: 6,000; Sun: 6,000

Herald Statesman
Circulation: 25,000; Sun: 37,00

Mount Vernon Argus
Circulation: 8,000; Sun: 10,000

Putnam Reporter Dispatch
Circulation: 9,000; Sun: 14,000

Reporter Dispatch-Metro Edition
Circulation: 30,000; Sun: 31,000

Reporter Dispatch-Northern Edition
Circulation: 12,000; Sun: 16,000

Standard-Star
Circulation: 11,000; Sun: 13,000

Star
Circulation: 6,000; Sun: 10,000

World Journal
141-07 20th Ave
Whitestone NY 11357-3097
718-746-9006; Fax: 718-746-6445
Circulation: 215,000

NORTH CAROLINA

Moore County Citizen News-Record
202 N Sandhills Blvd
Aberdeen NC 28315-2412
910-944-2356; Fax: 910-944-3586
Circulation: 8,000

Courier-Tribune
500 Sunset Ave
Asheboro NC 27203-5330
910-625-2101; Fax: 910-626-7074
Circulation: 17,000

Asheville Citizen-Times
14 O'Henry Ave
PO Box 2090 (28802)
Asheville NC 28801-8794
704-252-5611; Fax: 704-251-0585
Circulation: 65,000; Sun: 80,000

Tony Kiss, Arts Editor
Dale Neal, Book Editor
Paul Johnson, Business Editor

Susan Dryman, Education Editor
Clarke Morrison, Environmental Editor
Larry Pope, Exec Editor
Nancy Marlowe, Features Editor
Clarke Morrison, Health Editor
Clyde Osborne, Home/Garden Editor
Carole Currie, Lifestyle Editor
Ed Dawson, Managing Editor
Robert Satterwhite, Outdoor Editor
Doug Mead, Sports Editor
Dale Neal, Travel Editor

Daily Times-News
707 S Main
Burlington NC 27215-5844
910-227-0131; Fax: 910-229-2463
Circulation: 29,000; Sun: 31,000

Daily Tar Heel
Univ of North Carolina
PO Box 3257
Chapel Hill NC 27515-3257
919-962-1163; Fax: 919-962-1609
Circulation: 20,000

Charlotte Observer
600 S Tryon St (28202)
PO Box 30308
Charlotte NC 28230-0308
704-358-5000; Fax: 704-358-5036
Circulation: 230,000; Sun: 310,000

Michael Maschal, Arts Editor
Polly Paddock, Book Editor
Brian Melton, Business Editor
Jennie Buckner, Editor
Kathy Purvis, Food Editor
Dave Enna, Home Editor
Mary Curtis, Lifestyle Editor
Frank Barrows, Managing Editor
Anne Spenner, News Editor
Gary Schwab, Sports Editor
John Bordsen, Travel Editor

Sampson Independent
303 Elizabeth St
Clinton NC 28328-4426
910-592-8137; Fax: 910-592-8756
Circulation: 9,000

Concord Tribune
125 Union St S
Concord NC 28025-5011
704-782-3155; Fax: 704-786-0645
Circulation: 13,000

Daily Record
Lucknow Square
Dunn NC 28334
910-891-1234; Fax: 910-891-4445
Circulation: 11,000

The Chronicle
Duke University 101 W Union
PO Box 90858
Durham NC 27708-0858
919-684-2463; 919-684-4696
Circulation: 15,000

Durham Herald Sun
2828 Picket Rd (27705)
PO Box 2092
Durham NC 27702-2092
919-419-6500; Fax: 919-419-6889
Circulation: 54,000; Sun: 68,000

Ed Hodges, Book Editor
Ward Best, Business Editor
Betsy Hall, Education Editor
Jo Craven, Feature/Ent Editor
Jeff Zimmer, Food/Health Editor
Tom Beavers, Home Town Editor
Kim Weaver Spurr, Lifestyle Editor
Bill Stagg, News Editor
Jimmy Dupree, Sports Editor
Jim Wise, Travel Editor

Eden Daily News
804 Washington St
Eden NC 27288-6031
910-623-2155; Fax: 910-623-2228
Circulation: 8,000

Daily Advance
216 S Poindexter
Elizabeth City NC 27909-4835
919-335-0841; Fax: 919-335-4415
Circulation: 14,000

Bladen Journal
PO Box 67
Elizabethtown NC 28337-0067
910-862-4163; Fax: 910-862-6602
Circulation: 4,000

Fayetteville Observer & Times
458 Whitfield St (28306)
PO Box 849
Fayetteville NC 28302
910-323-4848; Fax: 910-486-3545
Circulation: 71,000; Sun: 82,000

Cathryn Pritchard, Business Editor
Roy Parker Jr, Contributing Editor
Frances Hasty, Food/Travel Editor
Elanor Yates, Home Editor
Michael Futch, Lifestyle/Feature Editor
Michael Arnholt, Managing Editor
Howard Ward, Sports Editor

Daily Courier
1111 Oak St
Forest City NC 28043-2805
704-245-6431; Fax: 704-248-2790
Circulation: 11,000

Gaston Gazette
2500 E Franklin Blvd
Gastonia NC 28056-9297
704-864-3291; Fax: 704-867-6988
Circulation: 41,000

News-Argus
PO Box 10629
Goldsboro NC 27532
919-778-2211; Fax: 919-778-9891
Circulation: 22,000; Sun circ: 25,000

Jim Meachen, Business Editor
Bob Johnson, City Editor
Becky Barcley, Family/Food/Garden Editor
Mike Rouse, Managing Editor
David Williams, Sports Editor

News & Record
200 E Market St (27401)
PO Box 20848
Greensboro NC 27420
910-373-7001; Fax: 910-373-7382
Circulation: 128,000; Sun: 130,000

Ron Miller, Book Editor/Reviewer
Mark Sutter, Business Editor
Pat Yack, Editor
Carla Bagley, Food Editor
Ann Alexander, Lifestyle/Feature Editor
Terressa Prout, Political Editor
Allen Johnson, Sports Editor

Daily Reflector
209 Cotanche St
Greenville NC 27858-1125
919-752-6166; Fax: 919-752-9583
Circulation: 18,000

Henderson Daily Dispatch
304 S Chestnut St
Henderson NC 27536-4225
919-492-4001; Fax: 919-430-0125
Circulation: 10,000

Times-News
1717 Four Seasons Blvd
Hendersonville NC 28792-2859
704-692-0505; Fax: 704-692-2319
Circulation: 22,000

Hickory Daily Record
1100 Park Pl
Hickory NC 28602
704-322-4510; Fax: 704-328-9378
Circulation: 26,000

High Point Enterprise
210 Church Ave (27262)
PO Box 1009
High Point NC 27261
910-888-3500; Fax: 910-841-5582
Circulation: 40,000; Sun: 44,000

Vicki Tucker-Knopfler, Arts/Entertainment Editor
Tommye Morrison, City Editor
Kathleen Keener, Education Editor
Judy Phillips, Lifestyle/Feature Editor
Ken Irons, Managing Editor
Craig Miller, Political Editor
Nick Mahers, Religion Editor
Benny Phillips, Sports Editor
Vince Wheeler, Travel Editor

Daily News
724 Bell Fork Rd
PO Drawer 196
Jacksonville NC 28540
910-353-1171; Fax: 910-353-7316
Circulation: 24,000; Sun: 25,000

Jeri Smith, Arts/Entertainment Editor
Eileen Brady, Business Editor
Elliott Potter, Editor
Carol Childers, Food Editor
Carol Childers, Lifestyle/Feature Editor
Madison Taylor, Managing Editor
Carol Childers, Religion Editor
Robert Holland, Sports Editor
J T Oliver, Sunday/Book Editor

Daily Independent
123 N Main
Kannapolis NC 28081-3427
704-932-3131; Fax: 704-933-4444
Circulation: 10,000

Kinston Free Press
2103 North Queen St
Kinston NC 28501
919-527-3191; Fax: 919-527-1813
Circulation: 14,000; Sun circ: 15,000

Robin Rodes, Business Editor
Mary Ellison Turner, Family/Food/Garden and Lifestyle/Feature Editor
Rick Thomason, Managing Editor
David Howell, Sports Editor

Lenoir News-Topic
123 Penton Ave
Lenoir NC 28645
704-758-7381; Fax: 704-754-0110
Circulation: 12,000

Dispatch
30 E 1st Ave
Lexington NC 27292-3302
704-249-3981; Fax: 704-249-0712
Circulation: 13,000

Robesonian
121 W 5th St
Lumberton NC 28358-5538
910-739-4322; Fax: 910-739-6553
Circulation: 15,000; Sun: 18,000

McDowell News
26 N Logan St
Marion NC 28752-3944
704-652-3313; Fax: 704-652-4769
Circulation: 7,000

Enquirer-Journal
500 W Jefferson St
Monroe NC 28112-4657
704-289-1541; Fax: 704-289-2929
Circulation: 13,000

News Herald
301 Collett St
Morganton NC 28655-3322
704-437-2161; Fax: 704-437-5372
Circulation: 11,000

Mount Airy News
319 N Renfro St
Mount Airy NC 27030-3838
910-786-4141; Fax: 910-789-2816
Circulation: 9,000

Sun Journal
226 Pollock St
New Bern NC 28560-4943
919-638-8101; Fax: 919-638-4664
Circulation: 17,000

Observer-News-Enterprise
309 N College Ave
Newton NC 28658-3255
704-464-0221; Fax: 704-464-1267
Circulation: 4,000

The News & Observer
215 S McDowell St
Raleigh NC 27602
919-829-4500; Fax: 919-829-4529
Circulation: 150,000; Sat circ: 175,000; Sun: 200,000

Susan Brown, Arts Editor
David Perkins, Book Editor
Dan Gerarino, Business Editor
Mike Yopp, Daily Editor
David Pickle, Editor for Presentation

Anders Gyllenhaal, Enterprise Editor
Laurie Evans, Family/Food/Garden Editor
Debbie Moose, Lifestyle/Feature Editor
Ned Barnett, News Editor
Michael Carmean, News Media
Steve Riely, Political Editor
Tinker Ready, Science/Health/Educ Editor
George Lawrence, Sports Editor
Judy Bolch, Staff Editor
Charles Fishman, Strategy Editor
Debbie Moose, Travel Editor

Reidsville Review
225 Turner Dr
Reidsville NC 27320-5736
910-349-4331; Fax: 910-342-2513
Circulation: 23,000

Daily Herald
916 Roanoke Ave
Roanoke Rapids NC 27870-2720
919-537-2505; Fax: 919-537-2314
Circulation: 12,000

Richmond County Daily Journal
105 Washington St
Rockingham NC 28379
910-997-3111; Fax: 910-997-4321
Circulation: 9,000

Rocky Mount Evening Telegram
150 Howard St
PO Box 1080
Rocky Mount NC 27802
919-446-5161; Fax: 919-446-4057
Circulation: 19,000; Sun: 21,000

Shawn Lewis, Book Editor
Tom Murphy, Business Editor
Julie Gollobin, Education Editor
Leona Mason, Family/Food/Garden Editor
Shawn Lewis, Lifestyle/Feature Editor
Jeff Herrin, Managing Editor
Charlie Hall, News Editor
Mark Aumann, Sports Editor

Salisbury Post
PO Box 4639
Salisbury NC 28145-4639
704-633-8950; Fax: 704-639-0003
Circulation: 26,000; Sun: 26,000

Paris Goodnight, Business Editor
Elizabeth Cook, Editor
Sylvia Wiseman, Lifestyle Editor
Frank DeLoache, Managing Editor

Sanford Herald
208 St Clair Ct
Sanford NC 27330-3916
919-708-9000; Fax: 919-708-9001
Circulation: 14,000

Shelby Star
315 E Graham St
Shelby NC 28150-5452
704-484-7000; Fax: 704-484-0805
Circulation: 19,000

Statesville Record & Landmark
220 E Broad ST
Statesville NC 28677-5325
704-873-1451; Fax: 704-872-3150

Daily Southerner
504 W Wilson St
Tarboro NC 27886-4239
919-823-3106; Fax: 919-823-4599
Circulation: 6,000

College Connection
Montgomery Technical College
PO Box 787
Troy NC 27371-0787
910-572-3691; Fax: 910-576-2176
Circulation: 500

Tryon Daily Bulletin
106 N Trade St
Tryon NC 28782-3012
704-859-9151; Fax: 704-859-5575
Circulation: 5,000

Washington Daily News
217 N Market St
Washington NC 27889-4949
919-946-2144; Fax: 919-946-9797
Circulation: 10,000

Wilmington Morning Star
1003 S 17th St
Wilmington NC 28401-8023
910-343-2000; Fax: 910-343-2227
Circulation: 55,000

Wilson Daily Times
2001 Downing St
Wilson NC 27893-4611
919-243-5151; Fax: 919-243-2999
Circulation: 18,000

Winston-Salem Journal
418 N Marshall St (27101)
PO Box 3159
Winston-Salem NC 27102-2815
910-727-7211; Fax: 910-727-7315
Circulation: 105,000; Sun: 240,000

Sara Fox, Arts Editor
Linda C Brinson, Book Editor
Frank Brill, Business Editor
Ken Otterbourg, City Editor
Susan Abramson, Education Editor
Sara Fox, Feature Editor
Michael Hastings, Food Editor
Julie Hulcher-Harris, Health/Medical Editor
Julie Hulcher-Harris, Home Editor
Carl Crothers, Managing Editor
Frank Tursi, Science Editor
Terry Oberle, Sports Editor
Guy Lucas, State Editor
Michael Hastings, Travel Editor

NORTH DAKOTA

Bismarck Tribune
707 E Front Ave
PO Box 1498
Bismarck ND 58502-1498
701-223-2500; Fax: 701-223-2063
Circulation: 33,000; Sun: 33,000

John Peterson, City Editor
Rebecca Lentz, Education Editor
Vicki Voskuil, Entertainment Editor
Kevin Giles, Managing Editor
Jeff Olson, Outdoor Editor
Fredrick Smith, Political Editor(Local)
Don Davis, Political Editor(State)
Karen Hergoz, Religion Editor
Abe Winter, Sports Editor

Devils Lake Daily Journal
516 4th St
Devils Lake ND 58301-2502
701-662-2127; Fax: 701-662-3115
Circulation: 5,000

Dickinson Press
127 1st St W
Dickinson ND 58601-5109
701-225-8111; Fax: 701-225-4205
Circulation: 7,000

Fargo Forum
101 N Fifth St
PO Box 2020
Fargo ND 58107-2020
701-235-7311; Fax: 701-241-5487
Circulation: 55,000; Sun: 70,500

John Lohman, Associate & Outdoor Editor
Dave Jurgens, Business Editor
Joseph Dill, Editor
Ross Raihala, Entertainment Editor
Tammy Swift, Food Editor
Catherine Zaiser, Lifestyle Editor
Terry Devine, Managing Editor
Kevin Schnepf, Sports Editor
Janna Anderson, Travel Editor

Grand Forks Herald
303 2nd Ave N (58202)
PO Box 6008
Grand Forks ND 58206
701-780-1114; Fax: 701-780-1123
Circulation: 39,000; Sun: 41,000

Julie Copland, Agri-Business Editor
Carrisea Green, Book Editor
Mike Jacobs, Editor
Liz Fedor, Editorial Page Editor
Sally Johnson, Feature Editor
Jeff Tiedeman, Food Editor
Sue Ellyn Scaletta, Home/Environmental
Greg Turosak, Managing Editor
Kevin Grinde, News Editor
Ben Harris, Photo Editor
Ryan Bakken, Sports Editor
Jim Durkin, Sr Managing Editor

Jamestown Sun
122 2nd St NW
Jamestown ND 58401-3117
701-252-3120; Fax: 701-251-2873
Circulation: 7,000

Minot Daily News
301 4th St SE
Minot ND 58701-4066
701-857-1900; Fax: 701-857-1961
Circulation: 26,000

Valley City Times-Record
146 3rd St NE
Valley City ND 58072-3047
701-845-0463; Fax: 701-845-0175
Circulation: 4,000

Daily News
601 Dakota Ave
Wahpeton ND 58075-4325
701-642-8585; Fax: 701-642-1501
Circulation: 5,000

Williston Daily Herald
14 W 4th St
Williston ND 58801-5308
701-572-2165; Fax: 701-572-1965
Circulation: 6,000

OHIO

Akron Beacon Journal
44 E Exchange St
PO Box 640
Akron OH 44309
216-996-3000; Fax: 216-376-9235
Circulation: 159,000; Sun: 226,000

Joan Rice, Book Review Editor
Geoff Gevalt, Business Editor
Dale Allen, Editor-in-Chief
Bill Eichenberger, Exec Sports Editor
Margaret Corvini, Feature Editor
Glenn Guzzo, Managing Editor
Steve Hoffman, Political Editor
Bill O'Connor, Religion Editor
Betsy Lammerding, Travel Editor
John Olesky, TV Editor

Akron Legal News
60 S Summit Ave
Akron OH 44308-1719
216-376-0917; Fax: 216-376-7001
Circulation: 1,000

Alliance Review
40 S Linden Ave
Alliance OH 44601-2447
216-821-1200; Fax: 216-821-8258
Circulation: 12,000

Ashland Times-Gazette
40 East 2nd St
Ashland OH 44805-2304
419-281-0581; Fax: 419-281-5591
Circulation: 12,000

Star-Beacon
4626 Park Ave
Ashtabula OH 44004-6933
216-998-2323; Fax: 216-992-9655
Circulation: 23,000

Athens Messenger
Rt 33 N & Johnson Rd
Athens OH 45701
614-592-6612; Fax: 614-592-4647
Circulation: 14,000

Post
Ohio University
20 E Union St
Athens OH 45701-2911
614-593-4010; Fax: 614-593-0567
Circulation: 14,000

Beavercreek News Current
1350 N Fairfield Rd
Beavercreek OH 45432-2644
513-426-5263; Fax: 513-426-4548
Circulation: 4,000

Bellefontaine Examiner
127 E Chillicothe Ave
Bellefontaine OH 43311-1957
513-592-3060; Fax: 513-592-4463
Circulation: 11,000

Bellevue Gazette
107 N Sandusky St
Bellevue OH 44811-1425
419-483-4190; Fax: 419-483-3737
Circulation: 3,000

The BG News
Bolwing Green State Univ
214 W Hall
Bowling Green OH 43403-000
419-372-2601; 419-372-0202
Circulation: 11,200

Daily Sentinel-Tribune
300 E Poe Rd
Bowling Green OH 43402-1329
419-352-4611; Fax: 419-354-0314
Circulation: 14,000

Bryan Times
127 S Walnut St
Bryan OH 43506-1718
419-636-1111; Fax: 419-636-8937
Circulation: 11,000

Telegraph-Forum
119 W Rensselaer St
Bucyrus OH 44820-2215
419-562-3333; Fax: 419-562-9162
Circulation: 7,000

Daily Jeffersonian
831 Wheeling Ave
Cambridge OH 43725-2316
614-439-3531; Fax: 614-432-6219
Circulation: 13,000

Repository
500 Market Ave S
Canton OH 44702-2195
216-454-5611; Fax: 216-454-5745
Circulation: 65,000; Sun: 84,000

Gary Brown, Book Review Editor
Ed Semmler, Business Editor
Rick Senften, City Editor
Dan Kane, Entertainment Editor
Jim Weber, Exec Editor
Gayle Beck, Feature/Living Editor
Charita Goshay, Religion Editor
Bob Stewart, Sports Editor

Daily Standard
123 E Market St
Celina OH 45822-1730
419-586-2371; Fax: 419-586-6271
Circulation: 10,000

Chillicothe Gazette
50 W Main St
Chillicothe OH 45601-3103
614-773-2111; Fax: 614-773-2160
Circulation: 14,000

Cincinnati Court Index
119 W Central Pky
Cincinnati OH 45202-2122
513-241-1450; Fax: 513-684-7821
Circulation: 1,000

Cincinnati Enquirer
312 Elm St
Cincinnati OH 45202
513-768-8495; Fax: 513-768-8330
Circulation: 317,000; Sun: 400,000

Sara Pearce, Book Editor, Feature Editor, Tempo and Arts & Leisure Section
Jon Talton, Business Editor
Chuck Martin, Food Editor
Tim Morehouse, Gardening Editor
Ann Johnston Haas, Home Editor
Janet Leach, Managing Editor
Jenny Barker, News Editor
Greg Noble, Sports Editor
Alan Vonderhaar, Wheels Editor

Cincinnati Post
125 E Court St
Cincinnati OH 45202
513-352-2785; Fax: 513-621-3962
Circulation: 130,000

Maureen Conlan, Book Editor
Joyce Rosencrans, Food Editor
Carole Philipps, Lifestyle/Feature Editor
Bob Kraft, Managing Editor
David Holthaus, Medical/Science Editor
Mike Philipps, News Editor
Carmen Carter, Religion Editor
Mark Tomasik, Sports Editor

Circleville Herald
210 N Court St
Circleville OH 43113-1608
614-474-3131; Fax: 614-474-9525
Circulation: 9,000

Daily Legal News
2935 Prospect Ave
Cleveland OH 44115-2607
216-696-3322; Fax: 216-696-6329
Circulation: 1,000

The Plain Dealer
1801 Superior Ave NE
Cleveland OH 44114-2107
216-999-5000; Fax: 216-999-6354
Circulation: 440,000; Sun: 550,000

Janice Harayda, Book Editor
Tom Coscarelli, Business Editor
David Squiers, City Editor
Cheryl Kushner, Entertainment Editor
Janet McCue, Fashion Editor
Christine Jindra, Features Editor
Toni Tipton-Martin, Food Editor
Mike Bennett, Living Section Editor
Gary Clark, Managing Editor
D'Arcy Egan, Outdoor Editor
Darryl Holland, Religion
Roy Hewitt, Sports Editor
David Molyneaux, Travel Editor

Columbus Dispatch
34 S Third St
Columbus OH 43215-4241
614-461-5000; Fax: 614-461-7580
Circulation: 263,000; Sun: 410,000

Michele Toney, Arts Editor
George Myers Jr, Book Critic
Gerald Tebben, Business Editor
Sue Dawson, Food Editor
Pam Kaufman, Home Editor
T R Fitchko, Lifestyle Editor
Mike Curtin, Managing Editor
Dennis Mahoney, News Editor
George Strode, Sports Editor
Lisa Reuter, Travel Editor

Daily Reporter
329 S Front St
Columbus OH 43215-5005
614-224-4835; Fax: 614-224-8649
Circulation: 26,000

Lantern
Ohio State University
242 W 18th Ave
Columbus OH 43210-1107
614-292-2031; Fax: 614-292-3722
Circulation: 30,000

Coshochton Tribune
550 Main St
Coshochton OH 43812-1612
614-622-1122; Fax: 614-622-7341
Circulation: 8,000

Daily Court Reporter
120 W 2nd
Dayton OH 45402-1604
513-222-6000; Fax: 513-341-5020
Circulation: 1,000

Dayton Daily News
45 S Ludlow St
Dayton OH 45402
513-225-2335; Fax: 513-225-2489
Circulation: 180,000; Sun: 231,949

Laura Dempsey, Book Editor
Gregg Stricharchuk, Business Editor
Jim Dillon, Computer Editor
Chris Ledbetter, Feature Editor
Ann Heller, Food Editor
Mark Fisher, Higher Education Editor
Max Jennings, Managing Editor
Kevin Riley, News Editor
Jim Robey, Outdoor Editor
Dave Mendell, Political Editor
Jillian Gaynair, Religion Editor
Jim Dillon, Science Editor
Ray Marcano, Sports Editor

Crescent-News
Perry & 2nd Sts
Defiance OH 43512
419-784-5441; Fax: 419-784-1492
Circulation: 17,000

Delaware Gazette
18 E William St
Delaware OH 43015-2332
614-363-1161; Fax: 614-363-6262
Circulation: 8,000

Delphos Daily Herald
405-409 N Main
Delphos OH 45833-1577
419-695-0015; Fax: 419-692-7704
Circulation: 4,000

Evening Review
210 E 4th St
East Liverpool OH 43920-3144
216-385-4545; Fax: 216-385-7114
Circulation: 13,000

Elyria Chronicle
PO Box 4010
Elyria OH 44036
216-329-7000; Fax: 216-329-7282
Circulation: 44,000; Sun: 44,000

Steve Brown, Arts/Entertainment Editor
Bob Jacobs, Book Review Editor
Rudy Dicks, Sports Editor
Joe Klinec, Sunday Editor

Fairborn Daily Herald
1 Herald Square
Fairborn OH 45324-7817
513-878-3993; Fax: 513-878-8314
Circulation: 17,000

Courier
701 W Sandusky
Findlay OH 45840-2325
419-422-5151; Fax: 419-422-2937
Circulation: 25,000

Review Times
113 E Center St
Fostoria OH 44830-2905
419-435-6641; Fax: 419-435-9073
Circulation: 8,000

News-Messenger
1700 Cedar St
Fremont OH 43420-1114
419-332-5511; Fax: 419-332-9750
Circulation: 14,000

Galion Inquirer
378 N Market St
Galion OH 44833-1924
419-468-1117; Fax: 419-468-7255
Circulation: 5,000

Gallipolis Daily Tribune
825 3rd Ave
Gallipolis OH 45631-1624
614-446-2342; Fax: 614-446-3008
Circulation: 6,000

Greenfield Daily Times
345 W Jefferson St
Greenfield OH 45123-1352
513-981-2141; Fax: 513-981-2880
Circulation: 4,000

Daily Advocate
W Main & Sycamore
Greenville OH 45331
513-548-3151; Fax: 513-548-3913
Circulation: 8,000

Journal-News
228 Court St
Hamilton OH 45011-2820
513-863-8200; Fax: 513-863-7988
Circulation: 28,000

Ironton Tribune
2803 S 5th St
Ironton OH 45638-2866
614-532-1441; Fax: 614-532-1506
Circulation: 9,000

Daily Kent Stater
Kent State Univ
Taylor Hall Rm 101
Kent OH 44242-0001
216-672-2586; Fax: 216-672-4880
Circulation: 14,000

Kenton Times
201 E Columbus St
Kenton OH 43326-1544
419-674-4066; Fax: 419-673-1125
Circulation: 7,000

Eagle-Gazette
138 W Chestnut St
Lancaster OH 43130-4308
614-654-1321; Fax: 614-654-8271
Circulation: 18,000

Lima News
121 E High St
Lima OH 45801-4417
419-223-1010; Fax: 419-229-2926
Circulation: 42,000

Morning Journal
308 Maple St
Lisbon OH 44432-1226
216-424-9541; Fax: 216-424-0048
Circulation: 13,000

Logan Daily News
72 E Main St
Logan OH 43138-1221
614-385-2107; Fax: 614-385-4514
Circulation: 6,000

Madison Press
30 S Oak St
London OH 43140-1066
614-852-1616; Fax: 614-852-1620
Circulation: 6,000

Morning Journal
1657 Broadway
Lorian OH 44052-3439
216-245-6901; Fax: 216-245-5637
Circulation: 44,000

News Journal
70 W 4th St
Mansfield OH 44903-1676
419-522-3311; Fax: 419-522-6177
Circulation: 41,000

Marietta Times
700 Channel Ln
Marietta OH 45750-2342
614-373-2121; Fax: 614-373-6251
Circulation: 13,000

Marion Star
150 Court St
Marion OH 43302-3026
614-387-0400; Fax: 614-382-2210
Circulation: 17,000

Times-Leader
200 S 4th St
Martins Ferry OH 43935-1312
614-633-1131; Fax: 614-633-1122
Circulation: 20,000

Marysville Journal-Tribune
207 N Main St
Marysville OH 43040-1174
513-644-9111; Fax: 513-644-9211
Circulation: 6,000

The Evening Independent
50 North Ave NW
Massillon OH 44647-5444
216-833-2631; Fax: 216-833-2635
Circulation: 16,000

Medina County Gazette
885 W Liberty St
Medina OH 44256-1312
216-725-4166; Fax: 216-725-4299
Circulation: 17,000

Middletown Journal
52 S Broad St
Middletown OH 45044-4031
513-422-3611; Fax: 513-422-8698
Circulation: 23,000; Sun: 24,000

Mount Vernon News
18 E Vine St
Mount Vernon OH 43050-3226
614-397-5333; Fax: 614-397-1321
Circulation: 11,000

Northwest-Signal
PO Box 567
Napoleon OH 43545-0567
419-592-5055; Fax: 419-592-9778
Circulation: 6,000

Times-Reporter
629 Wabash Ave NW
New Philadelphia OH 44663-4145
216-364-5577; Fax: 216-364-8449
Circulation: 28,000; Sun: 30,500

The Advocate
22 N 1st St
Newark OH 43055-5608
614-345-4053; Fax: 614-345-1634
Circulation: 23,000; Sun: 23,000

Norwalk Reflector
61 E Monroe St
Norwalk OH 44857-1532
419-668-3771; Fax: 419-668-2424
Circulation: 9,000

Piqua Daily Call
310 Spring St
Piqua OH 45356-2334
513-773-2721; Fax: 513-773-2782
Circulation: 10,000

The Daily Sentinel
111 Court St
Pomeroy OH 45769-1016
614-992-2156; Fax: 614-992-2157
Circulation: 6,000; Sun: 12,500

News-Herald
115 W 2nd St
Port Clinton OH 43452-1012
419-734-3141; Fax: 419-734-3141
Circulation: 6,000

Portsmouth Daily Times
637 6th St
Portsmouth OH 45662-3924
614-353-3101; Fax: 614-353-7280
Circulation: 17,000; Sun: 17,000

Record-Courier
126 N Chestnut St
Ravenna OH 44266-2254
216-296-9657; Fax: 216-296-2698
Circulation: 22,000; Sun: 23,000

The Salem News
161 N Lincoln Ave
Salem OH 44460-2903
216-332-4601; Fax: 216-332-1441
Circulation: 10,000

Sandusky Register
314 W Market St
Sandusky OH 44870-2410
419-625-5500; Fax: 419-625-3007
Circulation: 24,000; Sat & Sun: 26,683

The Daily Globe
37 W Main St
Shelby OH 44875-1238
419-342-4276
Circulation: 4,000

The Sidney Daily News
911 S Vandemark Rd
Sidney OH 45365-8974
513-498-2111; Fax: 513-498-0806
Circulation: 14,000

Springfield News-Sun
202 N Limestone St
Springfield OH 45501
513-328-0300; Fax: 513-328-0328
Circulation: 35,000; Sun: 42,000
Lawrene Calder, Arts/Entertainment Editor
Carl Hunnel, Book Editor
Mike Wagner, Education Editor
Rod Lockwood, Environmental Editor
Tom Stafford, Lifestyle Editor
Jack Bianchi, Managing Editor
Dick Minnig, News Editor
Steve Cooper, Specialty Page Editor
Dave Shedloski, Sports Editor

The Evening Leader
102 E Spring St
St Marys OH 45885-2310
419-394-7414; Fax: 419-394-7202
Circulation: 6,000

Herald Star
401 Herald Square
Steubenville OH 43952-2059
614-283-4711; Fax: 614-282-4261
Circulation: 29,000; Sun: 28,639

Advertiser-Tribune
320 Nelson St
Tiffin OH 44883-9359
419-448-3200; Fax: 419-447-3274
Circulation: 12,000; Sun: 12,000

The Blade
The Toledo Blade Co
541 N Superior St
Toledo OH 43660-0001
419-245-6000; Fax: 419-245-6439
Circulation: 154,000; Sun: 220,000
Tom Gearhart, Arts/Entertainment Editor
Greg Braknis, Business Editor
Dave Murray, City News Editor
Tom Troy, Education Editor
Tom Gearhart, Family Editor
Joe Crea, Food Editor
Ron Royhab, Managing Editor
Dave Murray, Political Editor
Rebekah Scott, Religion Editor
Michael Woods, Science Editor
Bob Kinney, Sports Editor

Legal News
520 Madison Ave #218
Toledo OH 43604-1300
419-241-3333; Fax: 419-244-2222
Circulation: 1,000

Troy Daily News
224 S Market St
Troy OH 45373-3327
513-335-5634; Fax: 513-335-3552
Circulation: 12,000; Sun: 13,200

Daily Chief-Union
111 W Wyandot Ave
Upper Sandusky OH 43351-1348
419-294-2332; Fax: 419-294-5608
Circulation: 4,000

Urbana Daily Citizen
220 E Court St
Urbana OH 43078-1805
513-652-1331; Fax: 513-652-1336
Circulation: 7,000

Times-Bulletin
700 Fox Rd
Van Wert OH 45891-2441
419-238-2285; Fax: 419-238-0447
Circulation: 7,000

Wapakoneta Daily News
8 Willipie St
Wapakoneta OH 45895-1969
419-738-2128; Fax: 419-738-5352
Circulation: 5,000

Tribune Chronicle
240 Franklin St SE
Warren OH 44483-5711
216-841-1600; Fax: 216-841-1717
Circulation: 45,000; Sun: 47,000

Record-Herald
138 S Fayette St
Wash Court House OH 43160-2232
614-335-3611; Fax: 614-335-5728
Circulation: 6,000

News Herald
7805 Mentor Ave
Willoughby OH 44094
216-951-0000; Fax: 216-975-2293
Circulation: 46,000; Sun: 54,000
Patricia Ambrose, Book Editor/Reviewer
Greg Connel, Business Editor
Jim Collins, Editor
Randy Lavuzinski, Entertainment Editor
Tal Campbell, Exec Managing Editor
Patricia Ambrose, Feature/Food Editor
Patricia Ambrose, Home Editor
Glen Gilbert, Managing Editor
Dave Jones, Political Editor
Rob Whitehouse, Religion Editor
Jim Murphy, Sports Editor
Janet Podolack, Travel Editor

Wilmington News Journal
47 South St
Wilmington OH 45177
513-382-2574; Fax: 513-382-4392
Circulation: 7,000

Daily Record
212 E Liberty St
Wooster OH 44691-4348
216-264-1125; Fax: 216-264-3756
Circulation: 25,000; Sun: 26,000

The Xenia Daily Gazette
37 S Detroit St
Xenia OH 45385-3581
513-372-4444; Fax: 513-372-3385
Circulation: 11,000

Daily Legal News
112 W Commerce St #1
Youngstown OH 44503-1127
216-747-7777
Circulation: 1,000

Vindicator
Vindicator Square
PO Box 780
Youngstown OH 44501-0780
330-747-1471; Fax: 330-747-6712
Circulation: 110,000; Sun: 150,000

Don Shilling, Business Editor
Rea Taiclet, City News Editor
Ron Cole, Education Editor
Deb Shaulis, Entertainment Editor
Mark Niquette, Environmental Writer
Linda Johnson, Health/Medical Editor
Mike McCowan, Lifestyle Editor
Rick Logan, News Editor
Mark Nikquette, Political Editor
Marie Shellack, Religion Editor
Linda Johnson, Science Editor
Matt Arnold, Sports Editor
Tony Paglia, Sr Regional Editor
Mike Braun, Sunday Feature Editor
Mike Braun, Travel Editor

The Times Recorder
34 S 4th St
Zanesville OH 43701-3417
614-452-4561; Fax: 614-453-9417
Circulation: 25,000; Sun: 25,000

OKLAHOMA

Ada Evening News
116 N Broadway
Ada OK 74820-5004
405-332-4433; Fax: 405-332-8734
Circulation: 10,000

Brenda Tollett, Lifestyle/Sections Editor
Steve Boggs, Managing Editor
Mike Wingo, Sports Editor

The Altus Times
218-20 W Commerce St
Altus OK 73521-3810
405-482-1221; Fax: 405-482-5709
Circulation: 6,000; Sun: 6,600

Alva Review-Courier
620 Choctaw
Alva OK 73717-1626
405-327-2200; Fax: 405-327-2454
Circulation: 2,000; Sun: 2,000

The Anadarko Daily News
117-119 E Broadway
Anadarko OK 73005-2823
405-247-3331; Fax: 405-247-5571
Circulation: 5,000

The Daily Ardmorette
117 W Broadway
Ardmore OK 73401-6238
405-223-2200; Fax: 405-226-2363
Circulation: 11,000; Sun: 14,090

Examiner-Enterprise
4125 Nowata Rd
Bartlesville OK 74006-5120
918-335-8200; Fax: 918-335-3111
Circulation: 13,000; Sun: 16,000

Blackwell Journal-Tribune
113 E Blackwell Ave
Blackwell OK 74631-2907
405-363-3370; Fax: 405-363-4415
Circulation: 3,000; Sun: 3,000

Chickasha Daily Express
302 N 3rd
Chickasha OK 73018
405-224-2600; Fax: 405-224-7087
Circulation: 7,000

Kent Bush, Editor
Paula Huffines, Lifestyle/Feature Editor

Chickasha Star
117 S 4th St
Chickasha OK 73018-3455
405-224-5123; Fax: 405-224-2711
Circulation: 9,000

The Clinton Daily News
522 Avant Ave
Clinton OK 73601-3436
405-323-5151; Fax: 405-323-5154
Circulation: 5,000; Sun: 5,400

Cushing Daily Citizen
115 S Cleveland
Cushing OK 74023-3719
918-225-3333; Fax: 918-225-1050
Circulation: 3,000

The Duncan Banner
10th & Elm Sts
Duncan OK 73534
405-255-5354; Fax: 405-255-8889
Circulation: 9,000; Sun: 11,000

Durant Daily Democrat
,200 W Beech St
Durant OK 74701-4316
405-924-4388; Fax: 405-924-6026
Circulation: 7,000; Sun: 8,000

Edmond Evening Sun
123 S Broadway
Edmond OK 73034-3843
405-341-2121; Fax: 405-340-7363
circulation: 10,000; Sun: 10,500

Elk City Daily News
200-206 W Broadway
Elk City OK 73644-4742
405-225-3000; Fax: 405-243-2414
Circulation: 5,000; Sun: 10,000

Enid News and Eagle
227 W Broadway
Enid OK 73701-4017
405-233-6600; Fax: 405-233-7645
Circulation: 23,000; Sun: 25,010

Frederick Leader
304 W Grand
Frederick OK 73542-5232
405-335-2188; Fax: 405-335-2047
Circulation: 2,000; Sun: 2,300

Guthrie Daily Leader
107 W Harrison
Guthrie OK 73044-4728
405-282-2222; Fax: 405-282-7378
Circulation: 3,000; Sun: 3,200

Henryetta Daily Free-Lance
812-16 W Main St
Henryetta OK 74437-4250
918-652-3311; Fax: 918-652-7347
Circulation: 2,000

Holdenville Daily News
112 S Creek St
Holdenville OK 74848-3226
405-379-5411; Fax: 405-379-5413
Circulation: 3,000; Sun: 3,350

Hugo Daily News
128 E Jackson St
Hugo OK 74743-4035
405-326-3311; Fax: 405-326-6397
Circulation: 3,000

McCurtain Daily Gazette
107 S Central St
Idabel OK 74745-4847
405-286-3321; Fax: 405-286-2208
Circulation: 7,000; Sun: 8,200

The Lawton Constitution
102 SW 3rd St
Lawton OK 73501-4031
405-353-0620; Fax: 405-585-5140
Circulation: 26,000; Sun: 30,000

McAlester News-Capital/Democrat
500 S 2nd
McAlester OK 74501-5812
918-423-1700; Fax: 918-426-3081
Circulation: 12,000; Sun: 12,800

Miami News-Record
14 1st Ave
Miami OK 74354
918-542-5533; Fax: 918-542-1903
Circulation: 8,000; Sun: 8,300

Muskogee Daily Phoenix/Times-Dem
214 Wall St
Muskogee OK 74401-6644
918-684-2900; Fax: 918-684-2865
Circulation: 20,000; Sun: 21,000

The Norman Transcript
215 E Comanche St
Norman OK 73069-6007
405-321-1800; Fax: 405-366-3520
Circulation: 16,000; Sun: 17,000

The Oklahoma Daily
Univ of Oklahoma
860 Ven Vleet Oval
Norman OK 73019-2050
405-325-2521; Fax: 405-325-7517
Circulation: 14,000

Oklahoma Journal Record
621 N Robinson
Oklahoma City OK 73102-6217
405-235-3100; Fax: 405-278-6918
Circulation: 3,000

Oklahoma Legislative Reporter
605 NW 13th St #C
Oklahoma City OK 73103-2213
405-521-1405; Fax: 405-521-0457
Circulation: 1,000

Oklahoma Oil Reporter
605 NW 13th St #C
Oklahoma City OK 73103-2213
405-521-1405; Fax: 405-521-0457
Circulation: 1,000

Oklahoman
9000 N Broadway (73114)
PO Box 25125
Oklahoma City OK 73125-0125
405-475-3311; Fax: 405-475-3183
Circulation: 335,000; Sun: 350,000

Kelly Hochenauer, Arts/Entertainment Editor
Ann De Frange, Book Editor
Dan Bush, Business Editor
Sue Hale, Computer Editor
Sharon Dowell, Food Editor
Karen Klinka, Health/Medical Reporter
Sharon Dowell, Home/Family Editor
Kelly Hochenauer, Lifestyle/Feature Editor
Ed Kelly, Managing Editor
Mike Shannon, News Editor
David Zizzo, Political Reporter
Pat Gilliland, Religion Editor
Bob Colon, Sports Editor

Okmulgee Daily Times
114 E 7th St
Okmulgee OK 74447-4606
918-756-3600; Fax: 918-756-8197
Circulation: 6,000; Sun: 6,000

Pauls Valley Daily Democrat
PO Box 790
Pauls Valley OK 73075-0790
405-238-6464; Fax: 405-238-3042
Circulation: 3,000; Sat & Sun: 4,300

Perry Daily Journal
714 Delaware
Perry OK 73077-6425
405-336-2222; Fax: 405-336-3222
Circulation: 3,000

The Ponca City News
300 N 3rd
Ponca City OK 74601-4336
405-765-3311; Fax: 405-762-6397
Circulation: 12,000; Sun: 14,000

The Poteau Daily News & Sun
804 N Broadway
Poteau OK 74953-3535
918-647-3188; Fax: 918-647-8198
Circulation: 5,000

The Daily Times
105 S Adair
Pryor OK 74361-3625
918-825-3292; Fax: 918-825-1965
Circulation: 6,000; Sun: 7,300

Sapulpa Daily Herald
16 S Park
Sapulpa OK 74067-1370
918-224-5185; Fax: 918-224-5196
Circulation: 7,000; Sun: 7,300

The Seminole Producer
121 N Main St
Seminole OK 74868-4627
405-382-1100; Fax: 405-382-1104
Circulation: 5,000; Sun: 5,600

Shawnee News-Star
215 N Bell
Shawnee OK 74801-6913
405-273-4200; Fax: 405-273-4207
Circulation: 12,000; Sun: 13,000

The Daily O'Collegian
Oklahoma State Univ
Paul Miller Bldg Rm 109
Stillwater OK 74078-0001
405-744-8372; Fax: 405-744-7936
Circulation: 10,000

News-Press
PO Box 2288
Stillwater OK 74076-2288
405-372-5000; Fax: 405-372-3112
Circulation: 12,000; Sun: 12,500

Tahlequah Daily Pictorial Press
106 W 2nd St
Tahlequah OK 74464-4724
918-456-8833; Fax: 918-456-2019
Circulation: 7,000; Sun: 7,000

Tahlequah Daily Times Journal
PO Box 1839
Tahlequah OK 74465-1839
918-458-0816; Fax: 918-458-0450
Circulation: 3,000

Tulsa Daily Commerce and Legal News
8545 E 41st St
Tulsa OK 74145-3305
918-663-1414
Circulation: 8,000

Tulsa World
318 S Main Mall (74103)
PO Box 1770
Tulsa OK 74102-1770
918-581-8300; Fax: 918-581-8353
Circulation: 175,000; Sun: 250,000

Cathy Logan, Arts/Entertainment Editor
Judy Randel, Book Editor
Gene Seabolt, Business Editor
Scott Cherry, Food Editor
Russell Studebaker, Garden Editor
Laurie Winslow, Health/Medical Editor
Heather Saucier, Home Editor
Rusty Lang, Lifestyle/Feature Editor
Susan Ellerbach, Managing Editor
Wayne Greene, News Editor
Rob Martindale, Political Editor
Carolyn Jenkins, Religion Editor
Bill Connors, Sr Sports Editor
Cathy Logan, Travel Editor

Vinita Daily Journal
140 S Wilson
Vinita OK 74301-3730
918-256-6422; Fax: 918-256-7100
Circulation: 4,000

Weatherford Daily News
118 S Broadway
Weatherford OK 73096-4924
405-772-3301; Fax: 405-772-7329
Circulation: 5,000; Sun: 5,200

Wewoka Daily Times
210 S Wewoka Ave
Wewoka OK 74884-2640
405-257-3341; Fax: 405-257-3342
Circulation: 1,000; Sun: 1,300

Woodward News
904 Oklahoma Ave
Woodward OK 73801-4660
405-256-2200; Fax: 405-254-2159
Circulation: 6,000; Sun: 6,400

OREGON

Albany Democrat-Herald
660 Lyon St
Albany OR 97321-2919
503-926-2211; Fax: 503-926-5298
Circulation: 22,000; Sun: 22,000

The Daily Tidings
1661 Siskiyou Blvd
Ashland OR 97520-2400
503-482-3456; Fax: 503-482-3688
Circulation: 6,000

The Daily Astorian
949 Exchange
Astoria OR 97103-4605
503-325-3211; Fax: 503-325-6573
Circulation: 9,000

Baker City Herald
1915 1st St
Baker City OR 97814-3338
503-523-3673; Fax: 503-523-6426
Circulation: 3,000

The Bulletin
1526 Hill St
Bend OR 97701-1958
503-382-1811; Fax: 503-385-5802
Circulation: 26,000; Sun: 27,000

The World
350 Commercial St
Coos Bay OR 97420-2269
503-269-1222; Fax: 503-267-0294
Circulation: 17,000

Corvallis Gazette-Times
600 SW Jefferson Ave
Corvallis OR 97333-4510
503-753-2641; Fax: 503-758-9505
Circulation: 13,000; Sun: 15,000

Daily Barometer
Oregon State University
118 Mu East
Corvallis OR 97331-1617
503-737-2231; Fax: 503-737-4999
Circulation: 11,000

Oregon Daily Emerald
University of Oregon
300 EMU
Eugene OR 97403-1226
503-346-5511; Fax: 503-346-5821
Circulation: 13,000

The Register Guard
975 High St (97401)
PO Box 10188
Eugene OR 97440-2188
503-485-1234; Fax: 503-683-7631
Circulation: 73,000; Sun: 81,000

Dave Baker, Asst Mg Editor
Christian Wihtol, Business Editor
Lance Robertson, Environmental Writer
Bob Welch, Life/Feature Editor
Jim Godbold, Managing Editor
John Conrad, Sports Editor

Grants Pass Daily Courier
409 SE 7th
Grants Pass OR 97526-3003
503-474-3700; Fax: 503-474-3814
Circulation: 18,000

Herald and News
1301 Esplanade
Klamath Falls OR 97601-5902
503-885-4410; Fax: 503-885-4456
Circulation: 18,000; Sun: 19,000

The Observer
1406 5th St
La Grande OR 97850-2402
503-963-3161; Fax: 503-963-7804
Circulation: 8,000

Mail Tribune
111 N 1st St
PO Box 1108
Medford OR 97501
503-776-4411; Fax: 503-776-4376
Circulation: 35,000; Sun: 35,000

Al Reiff, Arts/Entertainment Editor
Bill Varble, Book Editor/Reviewer
Paul Macomber, Business Editor
Tom Hill, Education Editor
JoNel Aleccia, Food Editor
Cleve Twitchell, Lifestyle Editor
Robert Hunter, Managing Editor
Jim Peak, News Editor
Peter Wong, Political Editor
Gary Nelson, Religion Editor
Bill Varble, Science Editor
Randy Hammerickson, Sports Editor
Cleve Twitchell, Travel Editor

Argus Observer
PO Box 130
Ontario OR 97914-0130
503-889-5387; Fax: 503-889-3347
Circulation: 8,000; Sun: 8,700

East Oregonian
211 SE Byers St
Pendleton OR 97801-2346
503-276-2211; Fax: 503-276-8314
Circulation: 13,000

Daily Journal of Commerce
2840 NW 35th Ave
Portland OR 97210-2345
503-226-1311; Fax: 503-224-7140
Circulation: 5,000

Daily Shipping News
7831 SE Stark St #200
Portland OR 97215-2357
503-255-2142; Fax: 503-255-2735
Circulation: 1,000

The Oregonian
1320 SW Broadway
Portland OR 97201-3469
503-221-8327; Fax: 503-227-5306
Circulation: 337,000; Sun: 450,000

Karen Brooks, Arts/Entertainment Editor
Bob Hill, Automotive Editor
Ellen Heltzel, Book Editor
Paul Pintarich, Book Reviewer
Judy Rooks, Business Editor
Jacqui Banaszynski, Environmental Editor
Ginger Johnston, Food Editor
Peter Bhatia, Managing Editor
Michele Mclellan, Political Editor

Therese Bottomly, Science Editor
Dennis Peck, Sports Editor
Sue Hobart, Travel Editor
Stan Horton, TV Editor, TV Click Magazine

The Vanguard
Portland State University
PO Box 751
Portland OR 97207-0751
503-725-4531; Fax: 503-725-5860
Circulation: 10,000

The News-Review
345 NE Winchester St
Roseburg OR 97470-3328
503-672-3321; Fax: 503-673-5994
Circulation: 21,000; Sun: 21,000

Salem Statesman-Journal
280 Church St NE (97301)
PO Box 13009
Salem OR 97309-1015
503-399-6611; Fax: 503-399-6808
Circulation: 67,000, Sun: 70,877

Ron Cowan, Arts Editor
Grant Butler, Book Editor
Joan Drake, Business Editor
Dan Davies, City News Editor
Jillyn McCullough, Education Editor
Theressa Novak, Environmental Editor
Grant Butler, Feature Editor
Thomas Forstrom, Food Editor
Kristin Gilger, Managing Editor
Roy Gault, Sports Editor
Grant Butler, Travel Editor

The Dalles Chronicle
414 Federal Sts
The Dalles OR 97058-2521
503-296-2141; Fax: 503-298-1365
Circulation: 6,000; Sun: 8,600

PENNSYLVANIA

The Morning Call
PO Box 1260
Allentown PA 18105-1260
610-820-6500; Fax: 610-820-6693
Circulation: 136,000; Sun: 190,000

Len Righi, Arts/Entertainment Editor
Paul Willistein, Book Editor
Eloise DeHann, Business/Real Estate Editor
David Erdman, City Editor
Martin Psleiger, Environmental Writer
Diane Stoneback, Food Editor
Paul Willistein, Lifestyle/Feature Editor
Raymond Holton, Managing Editor
David Dawson, Natl Political Editor
Rosa Salter, Science Writer
Paul Reinhard, Sports Editor
Randy Kraft, Travel Writer
Polly Rayner, Womens Editor

Altoona Mirror
301 Cayufa Ave
Altoona PA 16602-4323
814-946-7411; Fax: 814-946-7540
Circulation: 37,000; Sun: 42,000

Beaver County Times
PO Box 400
Beaver PA 15009-0400
412-775-3200; Fax: 412-775-4180

Circulation: 53,000; Sun: 58,000
Marsha Keefer, Book Editor
Stephonie Waite, Business Editor
Dennis Dible, Executive Editor
Marsha Keefer, Lifestyle/Feature Editor
Rick Wasko, Managing Editor
Greg Brown, Political Editor
Ed Rose, Sports Editor

Bedford Daily Gazette
424 W Penn St
Bedford PA 15522-1230
814-623-1151; Fax: 814-623-5055
Circulation: 11,000; Sun: 19,300

Press-Enterprise
3185 Lackawanna Ave
Bloomsburg PA 17815-3329
717-784-2121; Fax: 717-784-9226
Circulation: 23,000

Bradford Era
43 Main St
Bradford PA 16701-2019
814-368-3173; Fax: 814-362-6510
Circulation: 13,000

Butler Eagle
114 W Diamond St
Butler PA 16001-5747
412-282-8000; Fax: 412-282-1280
Circulation: 31,000; Sun: 31,000

Sentinel
457 E North St
Carlisle PA 17013
717-243-2611; Fax: 717-243-3121
Circulation: 18,000

Jerry Peterson, Arts/Entertainment Editor
Sue Erb, Book Editor
Cynthia Jacobson, Business Editor
Sue Erb, Education Editor
Sue Erb, Food Editor
Jerry Peterson, Health/Medical Editor
Sue Erb, Lifestyle/Feature Editor
Kurt Wanfried, Managing Editor
Cynthia Jacobsen, People/Society Editor
Fred Burgess, Political Editor
Larry Kerr, Religion Editor
Jerry Peterson, Science Editor
Shelly Stallsmith, Sports Editor
Cynthia Jacobsen, Travel Editor

Public Opinion
77 N 3rd St
Chambersburg PA 17201-1812
717-264-6161; Fax: 717-264-2009
Circulation: 22,000; Sat: 24,000

Progress
206 E Locust St
Clearfield PA 16830-2423
814-765-5581; Fax: 814-765-5165
Circulation: 17,000

Delaware County Daily Times
500 Mildred Ave
Clifton Heights PA 19018-2914
610-622-8810; Fax: 610-622-8887
Circulation: 60,000

Trisha Cofiell, Arts/Entertainment Editor
Don Scott, Business Editor
Linda DeMeglio, Managing Editor
Bob Tennant, Sports Editor

Daily Courier
127 W Apple St
Connellsville PA 15425-3132
412-628-2000; Fax: 412-628-4496
Circulation: 12,000

Corry Journal
28 W South St
Corry PA 16407-1810
814-665-8291; Fax: 814-664-2288
Circulation: 4,000; Sat:7,500

Danville News
14 E Mahoning St
Danville PA 17821-1934
717-275-3235; Fax: 717-275-7624
Circulation: 4,000

Intelligencer-Record
333 N Broad St
Doylestown PA 18901-3407
215-345-3000; Fax: 215-345-3150
Circulation: 46,000; Sat: 52,700

Courier-Express
500 Jeffers St
Du Bois PA 15801-2430
814-371-4200; Fax: 814-371-3241
Circulation: 12,000; Sun: 14,000

The Express-Times
PO Box 391
Easton PA 18044-0391
610-258-7171; Fax: 610-258-7130
Circulation: 60,000; Sun: 53,000

Robert K Hays, Arts/Lifestyle Editor
Daniel Sheehan, Education Editor
Jill Owens, Managing Editor
Editor Laubach, Sports Editor

Ellwood City Ledger
835 Lawrence Ave
Ellwood City PA 16117-5908
412-758-5573; Fax: 412-758-2410
Circulation: 7,000

Erie Times-News
205 W 12th St
Erie PA 16534-0001
814-870-1600; Fax: 814-870-1808
Circulation: 79,000; Sun: 110,000

Doug Rieder, Arts/Ent/Showcase Editor
Pat Howard, Book Editor
Pat Cuneo, City Editor
Jerry Trambley, Co-Business Editor
Marnie Mead Oberle, Co-Business Editor
Dana Massing, Education Editor
Tony Pasquale, Managing Editor
Phyllis Stewart, Mg Lifestyle/Feature Editor
Jack Grazier, Science Editor
Kevin Cuneo, Sports Editor

Morning News
Times Square
W 12th & Sassafras Sts
Erie PA 16534-0001
814-870-1600; Fax: 814-870-1808
Circulation: 33,000; Sun: 105,000

News-Herald
631 12th St
Franklin PA 16323-1440
814-432-3141; Fax: 814-432-3144
Circulation: 8,000

Gettysburg Times
18 Carlisle St
Gettysburg PA 17325-1800
717-334-1131; Fax: 717-334-4243
Circulation: 10,000

Standard Observer
RD 1 Rte 136
Greensburg PA 15601-9801
412-863-3601; Fax: 412-523-6805
Circulation: 13,000

Tribune-Review
Cabin Hill Dr
Greensburg PA 15601
412-834-1151; Fax: 412-838-5171
Circulation: 77,000; Sun: 130,000

Bob Karlovitz, Art/Entertainment Editor
Jack Markowitz, Business Editor
Frank Myers, City Editor
Sue McFarland/Dave Miller, News Editors
Connie Gore, Education Editor
George Beidler, Exec/Managing Editor
Robin Stahl, Feature Editor
Lynn Kuhn, Food Editor
Valerie Glenz, Lifestyle Editor
Paul Koloski, Political Editor
Dave Ailes, Sports Editor

Record-Argus
10 Penn Ave
Greenville PA 16125
412-588-5000; Fax: 412-588-4691
Circulation: 6,000

Evening Sun
135 Baltimore St
Hanover PA 17331-3111
717-637-3736; Fax: 717-637-7730
Circulation: 21,000; Sun: 21,000

Patriot-News
812 Market St (17101)
PO Box 2265
Harrisburg PA 17105-2265
717-255-8100; Fax: 717-255-8456(news only)
Circulation: 175,000; Sun: 177,000

John McGinley, Arts Editor
Nance Woodward, Book/Living Editor
Allen Mayers, Business Editor
Bob Heisse, City Editor
John Troutman, City Editor
Garry Lenton, Environmental Writer
Tom Baden, Managing Editor
Bob Vucic, National Editor
Tony Perry, Religion Editor
Nick Horvath, Sports Editor

Standard-Speaker
21 N Wyoming St
Hazelton PA 18201-6068
717-455-3636; Fax: 717-455-4244
Circulation: 24,000

The Wayne Independent
220 8th St
Honesdale PA 18431-1854
717-253-3055; Fax: 717-253-5387
Circulation: 8,000

Montgomery County Record
145 Easton Rd
Horsham PA 19044-3101
215-957-8100; Fax: 215-957-8165
Circulation: 45,000; Sun: 51,000

Daily News
325 Penn St
Huntingdon PA 16652-1455
814-643-4040; Fax: 814-643-0376
Circulation: 11,000

The Indiana Gazette
899 Water St
PO Box 10
Indiana PA 15701
412-465-5555; Fax: 412-349-4550
Circulation: 22,000

Carl Kologie, City Editor
Rebecca Cochran, Education Editor
Lynn Scott, Feature Editor
Sam Bechtel, Managing Editor
Tony Coccagna, Sports Editor

Johnstown Tribune Democrat
425 Locust St
PO Box 340
Johnstown PA 15907-0340
814-532-5199; Fax: 814-539-1409
Circulation: 53,000; Sun: 50,000

Art Heinz, Arts/Entertainment, Food, Home, and Lifestyle/Feature Editor
Marcia Lewis, Asst News Editor
Steve Liebman, Book Editor/Reviewer
Jeff McCready, Business Editor
Steve Liebman, Education Editor
Steve Liebman, Health/Medical Editor
Larry Hudson, Managing Editor
Chip Minemyer, Sports Editor

The Kane Republican
200 N Fraley St
Kane PA 16735-1177
814-837-6000; Fax: 814-837-2227
Circulation: 2,000

Leader-Times
115-121 N Grant Ave
Kittanning PA 16201-1401
412-543-1303; Fax: 412-545-6768
Circulation: 12,000

Lancaster Intelligencer Journal
8 W King St
Lancaster PA 17603
717-291-8622; Fax: 717 399-6507
Circulation: 50,000; Sun: 100,000

Bill Bert, Arts/Entertainment Editor
Jim Loose, Business Editor
Joe Vulopos, Education Editor
Jean Korten, Food Editor
Lynn Schmidt, Lifestyle/Feature Editor
Robert Kozak, Managing Editor
Donna Wardsmith, Religion Editor
Dennis Fisher, Sports Editor

Lancaster New Era
8 W King St (17603-3809)
PO Box 1328
Lancaster PA 17608-1328
717-291-8811; Fax: 717-399-6506
Circulation: 54,000; Sun: 107,000

John Gates, Arts/Entertainment Editor
Jim Loose, Business Editor
Sara Barton, Education Editor
Jean Korten, Family/Food/Garden Editor
Cindy Staffer, Health/Medical Editor
Robert Kozak, Managing Editor
Donna Ward-Smith, Religion Editor
Ernie Schreiber, Science Editor
Dennis Fisher, Sports Editor
David Hennigan, Sunday Editor

The Reporter
307 Derstine Ave
Lansdale PA 19446-3532
215-855-8440; Fax: 215-855-3432
Circulation: 20,000

Latrobe Bulletin
1211 Ligonier St
Latrobe PA 15650-1921
412-537-3351; Fax: 412-537-0489
Circulation: 9,000

Daily News
718 Poplar St
Lebanon PA 17042-6755
717-272-5611; Fax: 717-274-1608
Circulation: 25,000; Sun: 25,000

Times News
1st & Iron Sts
Lehighton PA 18235
610-377-2051; Fax: 610-377-5800
Circulation: 17,000

Bucks County Courier Times
8400 Route 13
Levittown PA 19057
215-949-4000; Fax: 215-949-4177
Circulation: 70,000; Sun: 75,000

Carl Lavo, Arts/Entertainment, Book
    Reviewer, Computer, Health, Medical,
    Lifestyle, Feature Editor
Patricia Wandling, Business Editor
Bill Steinauer, Exec Managing Editor
Betty Cichy, Food Editor
Milt Krugman, Garden Editor
Mary Ellen Bornek, News Editor
Guy Petroziello, News Editor
John Fisher, Religion Editor

Sentinel
375 6th St
Lewistown PA 17044-1214
717-248-6741; Fax: 717-248-3481
Circulation: 15,000

Express
9-11 W Main St
Lock Haven PA 17745-1217
717-748-6791; Fax: 717-748-1544
Circulation: 12,000

Daily News
409 Walnut St
PO Box 128
McKeesport PA 15132
412-664-9161; Fax: 412-664-3974
Circulation: 29,000

Donald Dulac, Assoc Editor
Pam Cotter, Business Editor
Bonniejean Adams, City Editor
John Cindrich, Education Editor
David Sallinger, Entertainment Editor
Carol Waterloo, Food Editor
Carol Waterloo, Health/Medical Editor
Carol Waterloo, Lifestyle/Feature Editor
Norm Vargo, Sports Editor
Carol Waterloo, Travel Editor

Meadville Tribune
947 Federal Court
Meadville PA 16335-3234
814-724-6370; Fax: 814-724-8755
Circulation: 17,000; Sun: 17,000

Lewisburg Daily Journal
19 Arch St
Milton PA 17847-0259
717-742-9671; Fax: 717-742-9876
Circulation: 1,000; Sat: 10,000

Milton Daily Standard
19 Arch St
Milton PA 17847-0259
717-742-9671; Fax: 717-742-9876
Circulation: 3,000; Sat: 10,000

Valley Independent
Eastgate 19
Monessen PA 15062
412-684-5200; Fax: 412-684-8104
Circulation: 19,000

New Castle News
27 N Mercer St
New Castle PA 16105-1728
412-654-6651; Fax: 412-654-9593
Circulation: 20,000

Times Herald
410 Markley St
Norristown PA 19401-4617
610-272-2500; Fax: 610-272-4003
Circulation: 30,000; Sun: 30,000

Derrick
1510 W 1st
Oil City PA 16301-3211
814-676-7444; Fax: 814-677-8347
Circulation: 19,000

The Daily Pennsylvanian
Univ of Pennsylvania
4015 Walnut St
Philadelphia PA 19104-3513
215-898-6581; Fax: 215-898-2050
Circulation: 14,000

Legal Intelligencer
1617 John F Kennedy Blvd #960
Philadelphia PA 19103-1823
215-557-2300; Fax: 215-557-2301
Circulation: 5,000

Philadelphia Daily News
400 N Broad St
Box 7788
Philadelphia PA 19101
215-854-5900; Fax: 215-854-5910
Circulation: 225,000

Todd Beamon, Business Editor
Jackie Jones, City Editor
Frank Heick, Computer Editor
Ramona Smith, Enviromental Editor
Debi Licklider, Feature Editor
Debi Licklider, Lifestyle Editor
Brian Toolan, Managing Editor
Gar Joseph, Political Editor
Mike Rathet, Sports Editor

Philadelphia Inquirer
400 N Broad St
PO Box 8263
Philadelphia PA 19101
215-854-2000; Fax: 215-854-4794
Circulation: 500,000

Fred Mann, Arts Editor
Mike Schaffer, Book Editor, Book/View
    Section
Paul Schweizer, Business Editor
Dale Mezzocapa, Education Editor

Julie Busby, Features Editor
Gerald Etter, Food Editor
Sue Caba, Home Editor
Art Carey, Medical Editor
Outdoors Writer
Real Estate Editor
Bob Macklin, Religion Editor
Reviewer, Audio Books
Dorothy Brown, Science Editor
Nancy Cloney, Sports Editor
Mike Shoup, Travel Editor

Temple News
Temple Univ - Activities Ctr
13th & Montgomery
Philadelphia PA 19122
215-204-6098; Fax: 215-204-7978
Circulation: 10,000

Phoenix
225 Bridge St
Phoenixville PA 19460-3449
610-933-8926; Fax: 610-933-1187
Circulation: 7,000

The Pitt News
Univ of Pittsburgh
434 William Pitt Union
Pittsburgh PA 15260-5999
412-648-7980; Fax: 412-648-8491
Circulation: 16,000

Pittsburgh Legal Journal
400 Koppers Bldg 4th Fl
Pittsburgh PA 15219
412-261-6255; Fax: 412-261-3622
Circulation: 2,000

Pittsburgh Post Gazette
Bob Hoover, Book Editor
34 Boulevard of the Allies
PO Box 566
Pittsburgh PA 15233
412-263-1601; Fax: 412-391-8452
Circulation: 250,000; Sun: 500,000

Tom O'Boyle, Business Editor
Carl Remensky, City Editor
Tim Dunham, Computer Editor
Carmen Lee, Education Editor
Susan Puskar, Entertainment Editor
Tom O'Boyle, Finance Editor
Suzanne Mortanson, Food Editor
Susan Puskar, Food/Lifestyle/Magazine
Byron Spice, Health/Science
Madeline Ross, Managing Editor
Barbrah Griffen, News Editor
Jim O'Toole, Political Editor
Fritz Heysman, Sports Editor
Susan Puskar, Travel Editor

The Mercury
24 N Hanover St
Pottstown PA 19464-5410
610-323-3000; Fax: 610-327-3308
Circulation: 33,000; Sun: 32,000

Pottsville Republican
111-13 Mahantongo St
Pottsville PA 17901-3008
717-622-3456; Fax: 717-628-6092
Circulation: 28,000; Sat circ 30,000

Spirit
510 Pine St
Punxsutawney PA 15767-1404
814-938-8740; Fax: 814-938-3794
Circulation: 6,000

Reading Eagle Times
PO Box 582
Reading PA 19603-0582
610-371-5000; Fax: 610-371-5098
Circulation: 78,000; Sun: 116,000

George Hatza, Arts/ Entertainment Editor
Jonathon Weaver, Book Editor
Greg Kreitz, Business Editor
Mark Leukens, Computer Editor
Christine Burger, Feature Editor
Dawn Drago, Food Editor
Christine Burger, Lifestyle Editor
Debbie Marton, Local News Editor
Frank Mazurkiewicz, National News Editor
Mike Miorellii, Sports Editor
Charles Adams, Travel Editor

Ridgeway Record
20 Main St
Ridgeway PA 15853-1718
814-773-3161; Fax: 814-776-1086
Circulation: 3,000

Evening Times
201 N Lehigh Ave
Sayre PA 18840-2220
717-888-9643; Fax: 717-888-6463
Circulation: 7,000

The Scranton Times-Tribune
PO Box 3311
Scranton PA 18505
717-348-9100; Fax: 717-348-9145
Circulation: 80,000; Sun: 83,000

Michelle Solomon, Arts/Entertainment Editor
Michelle Solomon, Book Editor/Reviewer
Vince Coveleskie, Business Editor
Karen Mears, Lifestyle Editor
Robert Burke, Managing Editor
Terri Bonifonti, News/City Editor
Tom Robinson, Sports Editor

News-Item
707 N Rock
Shamokin PA 17872-4930
717-648-4641; 717-644-0892
Circulation: 15,000

The Herald
South Dock & E State Sts
Sharon PA 16146
412-981-6100; Fax: 412-981-5116
Circulation: 25,000; Sun: 24,000

Evening Herald
19 N Main St
Shenandoah PA 17976-1776
717-462-2777; Fax: 717-462-4730
Circulation: 11,000

Daily American
334 W Main St
Somerset PA 15501-1508
814-445-9621; Fax: 814-445-2935
Circulation: 14,000

Daily Press
245 Brussels St
St Marys PA 15857-1501
814-781-1596; Fax: 814-834-7473
Circulation: 5,000

Centre Daily Times
Penn State Univ, 3400 E College Ave
State College PA 16801-7528
814-238-5000; Fax: 814-237-5966
Circulation: 27,000; Sun: 35,000

The Daily Collegian
123 S Burrowes St
State College PA 16801-3867
814-865-1828; Fax: 814-865-1126
Circulation: 19,000

Pocono Record
511 Lenox St
Stroudsburg PA 18360-1516
717-421-3000; Fax: 717-424-2625
Circulation: 22,000; Sun: 6,000

Daily Item
200 Market St
Sunbury PA 17801-3402
717-286-5671; Fax: 717-988-5348
Circulation: 25,000; Sun: 29,000

Valley News Dispatch
4th Ave & Wood St
Tarentum PA 15084
412-226-1006; Fax: 412-226-4677
Circulation: 38,000; Sun: 40,000

The Titusville Herald
209 W Spring St
Titusville PA 16354-1654
814-827-3634; Fax: 814-827-2512
Circulation: 5,000

Daily Review
116 Main St
Towanda PA 18848-1832
717-265-2151; Fax: 717-265-4200
Circulation: 9,000; Sun: 9,300

Tyrone Daily Herald
1018 Pennsylvania Ave
Tyrone PA 16686-1514
814-684-4000; Fax: 814-684-4238
Circulation: 3,000; Sat circ 6,100

Herald-Standard
8-18 E Church St
Uniontown PA 15401-3563
412-439-7500; Fax: 412-439-7559
Circulation: 33,000; Sun: 33,300

Warren Times-Observer
205 Pennsylvania Ave W
Warren PA 16365-2412
814-723-8200; Fax: 814-723-6922
Circulation: 13,000

North Hills News Record
137 Commonwealth Dr
Warrendale PA 15086-7503
412-772-3900; Fax: 412-772-3915
Circulation: 24,000; Sun: 24,000

Observer-Reporter
122 S Main St
Washington PA 15301-4904
412-222-2200; Fax: 412-222-3982
Circulation: 39,000; Sun: 40,000

Record-Herald
30 Walnut St
Waynesboro PA 17266-1644
717-762-2151; Fax: 717-762-3824
Circulation: 10,000

Daily Local News
250 N Bradford Ave
West Chester PA 19382
610-696-1775; Fax: 610-430-1180
Circulation: 34,000; Sun: 34,000

John Chambless, Arts Editor
Bill Lowe, Business Editor
Caroline Burns, Education Editor
Bill Caufield, Exec Editor
Elene Brown, Food Editor
Bruce Mowday, Managing Editor
John DeSanto, Sports Editor

Citizens' Voice
75 N Washington St
Wilkes-Barre PA 18711-0540
717-821-2000; Fax: 717-825-2882
Circulation: 42,000; Sun: 32,500

Times Leader
15 N Main St
Wilkes-Barre PA 18711
717-829-7100; Fax: 717-829-5537
Circulation: 48,000; Sun: 78,000

Paul Gallagher, Arts/Entertainment Editor
Jim Mullay, Business Editor
Renita Fennick, Education Reporter
Cliff Schechtman, Exec Editor
Ann Woelfel, Health/Medical Editor
Chris Ritchie, Lifestyle/Feature Editor
Rick Stouch, Sports Editor

Williamsport Sun-Gazette
252 W 4th St
Williamsport PA 17701-6102
717-326-1551; Fax: 717-323-0948
Circulation: 33,000; Sun: 43,000

York Daily Record
1750 Industrial Highway
York PA 17401-2229
717-840-4000; Fax: 717-840-2009
Circulation: 42,000; Sat: 72,000

York Dispatch/York Sunday News
205 N George
York PA 17401-1124
717-854-1575; Fax: 717-843-2958
Circulation: 51,000; Sun: 75,000

Dara Dixon, Arts/Entertainment Editor
Dara Dixon, Book Editor
Judy Strausbaugh, Business Editor
Scott Miller, Computer Editor
Carolyn Luzzatto, Education Editor
Stan Hough, Health/Medical Editor
Dara Dixon, Lifestyle/Feature Editor
Stan Hough, News Director Editor
Stan Hough, Political Editor
Lori Goodlin, Religion Editor
Greg Bowers, Sports Editor
Pam Saylor, Sunday News Editor
Lori Goodlin, Travel Editor

RHODE ISLAND

Good 5 Cent Cigar
Univ of Rhode Island
Memorial Union Bldg
Kingston RI 02881
401-792-2914; Fax: 401-792-5607
Circulation: 7,000

The Newport Daily News
101 Malbone Rd
Newport RI 02840-1340
401-849-3300; Fax: 401-849-3306
Circulation: 15,000; Sat: 16,000

The Times
23 Exchange St
Pawtucket RI 02860-2026
401-722-4000; Fax: 401-727-9252
Circulation: 22,000

Brown Daily Herald
Brown University
195 Angell St
Providence RI 02906-1207
401-351-3260; Fax: 401-351-9297
Circulation: 5,000

Providence Journal-Bulletin
75 Fountain St
Providence RI 02902-0050
401-277-7000; Fax: 401-277-7346
Circulation: 202,000; Sun: 265,000

Donita Naylor, Arts/Entertainment Editor
Doug Riggs, Book Editor
Andrew Burkhardt, City News Editor
Morgan McVicar, Education Editor
Peter Phipps, Financial Editor
Donna Lee, Food Editor
Alan Rosenberg, Lifestyle/Feature Editor
James Rosenthal, Managing Editor
David Bloss, Sports Editor
Alan Kerr, Travel Editor

The Kent County Daily Times
1353 Main St
West Warwick RI 02893-3859
401-821-7400; Fax: 401-828-0810
Circulation: 10,000

The Westerly Sun
56 Main St
Westerly RI 02891
401-596-7791; Fax: 401-348-5080
Circulation: 12,000; Sun: 12,300

The Call
75 Main St
Woonsocket RI 02895-4312
401-762-3000; Fax: 401-765-2834
Circulation: 26,000; Sun: 26,000

SOUTH CAROLINA

Aiken Standard
124 Rutland Dr
Aiken SC 29801-4006
803-648-2311; Fax: 803-648-6052
Circulation: 15,000; Sun: 15,000

Anderson Independent-Mail
PO Box 2507
Anderson SC 29622
803-224-4321; Fax: 803-260-1276
Circulation: 47,000; Sun: 49,000

Linda Grinburg, Arts/Entertainment, Book Editor/Reviewer, Family, Food, Home Editor, Lifestyle/Feature and Outdoors/Recreation Editor
Sandy Baker, Business Editor
Jenna Russell, Education, Health/Medical Editor
John Gouch, Managing Editor

Willette Wooten, People/Society Editor
Lisa Ross, Political Editor
Dale Emch, Religion Editor
Randy Beard, Sports Editor
Lisa Ross, Travel Editor

The Beauford Gazette
1556 Salem Rd
Beauford SC 29902-5236
803-524-3183; Fax: 803-524-8728
Circulation: 10,000; Sun: 10,000

Charleston Post & Courier
134 Columbus St
Charleston SC 29403-4809
803-577-7111; Fax: 803-937-5579
Circulation: 125,000

John Burbage, Assignment Editor
Bill Thompson, Book Editor
Teresa Taylor, Business Editor
Betsy Cantler, Feature Editor
Grace Kutkus, Managing Editor
John Burbage, Metro Editor
Lynne Langley, Science Editor
Ken Burger, Sports Editor

The State
1401 Shop Rd
PO Box 1333
Columbia SC 29202
803-771-6161; Fax: 803-771-8430
Circulation: 135,000

Jeffrey Day, Arts/Entertainment Editor
William W Starr, Book Editor
Claudia Raby, Business Editor
Steve Brook, Day News Editor
Gil Thelan, Executive News Editor
Pat McGovern, Food Editor
Scott Farrund, Graphics Editor
Pat McGovern, Lifestyle/Feature Editor
Paula Ellis, Managing Editor
Chuck Crumbo, Metro News Editor
Lee Bauknight, Night News Editor
Carolyn Click, Political Editor
Richard Bush, Sports Editor

Florence Morning News
141 S Irby
Florence SC 29501-4409
803-669-1771; Fax: 803-661-6558
Circulation: 33,000; Sun: 34,000

The Greenville News
305 S Main St
PO Box 1688
Greenville SC 29602
803-298-4110; Fax: 803-298-4395
Circulation: 95,000; Sun: 145,000

Robert Scott, Business Editor
Steve Belli, Education Editor
Francis Evans, Food Editor
Jan Phillips, Lifestyle/Feature Editor
Tom Hutchison, Managing News Editor
Chris Weston, Mg Editor/Local News
Tom Inman, News Editor
Shiela Carnett, Science Editor
Editor McGranahan, Sports Editor

The Index-Journal
Phoenix and Fair
Greenwood SC 29646
803-223-1811; Fax: 803-223-7331
Circulation: 17,000; Sun: 17,500

The Island Packet
Executive Park
1 Pope Ave
Hilton Head Island SC 29928-4701
803-785-4293; Fax: 803-686-3407
Circulation: 11,000; Sun: 14,500

Sun News
914 Frontage Rd E (29577)
PO Box 406
Myrtle Beach SC 29578
803-626-8555; Fax: 803-626-0356
Circulation: 40,000; Sun: 42,000

Andy Shain, Business Editor
Gwen Fowler, Deputy Mg Editor
Jerry Ausband, Editorial Editor
Mona Prufer, Lifestyle/Feature Editor
John Miller, Managing Editor
John Stevenson, News Editor
Mike Soraghan, Political Editor
John Brasier, Sports Editor

The Times and Democrat
211 Broughton St SE
Orangeburg SC 29115-5904
803-534-3352; Fax: 803-533-5595
Circulation: 19,000; Sun: 18,000

The Herald
132 W Main
Rock Hill SC 29730-4430
803-329-4000; Fax: 803-329-4021
Circulation: 31,000; Sun: 32,000

Spartanburg Herald-Journal
Scott Kearns, Managing Editor
189 W Main St
Spartanburg SC 29306-2334
803-582-4511; Fax: 803-594-6349
Circulation: 62,000; Sun: 68,000

The Item
20 N Magnolia St
Sumter SC 29150-4940
803-775-6331; Fax: 803-775-1024
Circulation: 21,000; Sun: 22,000

Union Daily Times
100 Times Blvd
Union SC 29379-7705
803-427-1234; Fax: 803-427-1237
Circulation: 7,000

SOUTH DAKOTA

Aberdeen American News
124 S 2nd St
Aberdeen SD 57401-4010
605-225-4100; Fax: 605-229-3954
Circulation: 19,000; Sun: 20,000

Brookings Register
312 5th St
PO Box 177
Brookings SD 57006
605-692-6271; Fax: 605-692-2979
Circulation: 6,000

Doug Kott, Business Editor
Linda Berkland, Community Editor
Molly Miron, Education and Food Editor
Amy Dunkle, Managing Editor
Bill Macken, Outdoor Editor
Linda Berkland, Religion Editor
Bill Macken, Sports Editor

The Plainsman
49 3rd SW
Huron SD 57350-1907
605-352-6401; Fax: 605-352-7754
Circulation: 11,000; Sun: 11,000

The Black Hills Pioneer
7 S Main St
Lead SD 57754-1542
605-584-2303; Fax: 605-584-2735
Circulation: 4,000

Madison Daily Leader
214 S Egan Ave
Madison SD 57042-2911
605-256-4555; Fax: 605-256-6190
Circulation: 3,000

The Daily Republic
120 S Lawler St
Mitchell SD 57301-3443
605-996-5514; Fax: 605-996-7793
Circulation: 13,000

Pierre Capitol Journal
333 W Dakota
PO Box 878
Pierre SD 57501
605-224-7301; Fax: 605-224-9210
Circulation: 6,000

Leta Nolan, Arts/Entertainment Editor
Dorinda Daniel, Book Editor/Reviewer
Mike Smith, Health/Medical Editor
Parker Knox, Lifestyle/Feature Editor
Mike Hipple, Managing Editor
Mike Smith, Sports Editor

Rapid City Journal
507 Main St
PO Box 450
Rapid City SD 57709
605-394-8300; Fax: 605-342-4610
Circulation: 34,000; Sun: 37,000

Lynn Taylor Rick, Book Reviewer
Dan Daly, Business Writer
Robin McMacken, Feature Editor
Mark Anderson, Health/Medical Writer
Heidi Bell, Higher Education Writer
Steve Miller, Managing Editor
Mary Duffy, Religion Writer
Don Linder, Sports Editor
Erin Anderson, Youth/Education Reporter

Argus Leader
200 S Minnesota
PO Box 5034
Sioux Falls SD 57117
605-331-2200; Fax: 605-331-2294
Circulation: 49,000; Sun: 73,000

Ann Grauvogl, Book Editor/Reviewer
Brenda Wade-Schmidt, Business Editor
Corrine Olson, Education Editor
Jack Marsh, Exec Editor
Joyce Terveen, Food Editor
Ann Grauvogl, Garden Editor
Joyce Terveen, Health/Medical Editor
Jon Walker, Lifestyle/Feature Editor
Pete Ellis, Managing Editor
Jim Cheesman, Recreation Editor
Jim Cheesman, Sports Editor

Watertown Public Opinion
120 3rd Ave NW
Watertown SD 57201-2311
605-886-6901; Fax: 605-886-4280
Circulation: 17,000

Daily Press & Dakotan
319 Walnut St
Yankton SD 57078-4344
605-665-7811; Fax: 605-665-1721
Circulation: 10,000

TENNESSEE

The Daily Post-Athenian
320 S Jackson St
Athens TN 37303-4715
423-745-5664; Fax: 423-745-8295
Circulation: 12,000

Chattanooga Free Press
400 E 11th St
PO Box 1447
Chattanooga TN 37401-1447
423-756-6900; Fax: 423-757-6383
Circulation: 48,000; Sun: 115,000

Karen Glendenning, Book Editor
John Vass, Business Editor
Kenny Sloan, City Editor
Ken Speer, Education Editor
June Hatcher, Entertainment Editor
Roy Exum, Exec Sports Editor
Ann Braly, Food Editor
Judy Lowe, Garden Editor
Irby Park, Home/Real Estate Editor
Susan Pierce, Lifestyle Editor
Lee Anderson, Managing Editor
Chris Vass, Medical Editor
David Cooper, News Editor
Victor Miller, Political Editor
Jim Ashley, Religion Editor
Tom Turner, State Editor
Diane Siskin, Travel Editor

Chattanooga Times
100 E 10th St (37402)
PO Box 951
Chattanooga TN 37401
615-756-1234; Fax: 615-752-3388
Circulation: 43,000

Randy Arnold, Arts/Entertainment Editor
Wes Hasden, Book Editor
Michael Davis, Business Editor
Mike Loftin, Education Editor
Suzanne Hall, Food Editor
Ron Smith, Managing Editor
Dave Flessner, News Editor
Michelle Dulabaum, Religion Editor
Andy Daffron, Sports Editor

The Leaf-Chronicle
200 Commerce St
Clarksville TN 37040-5101
615-552-1808; Fax: 615-648-8001
Circulation: 23,000;. Sun: 25,000

Cleveland Daily Banner
PO Box 3600
Cleveland TN 37320-3600
423-472-5041; Fax: 423-476-1046
Circulation: 40,000

Bettie Marlowe, Arts/Entertainment, Book,
   Lifestyle/Feature and Travel Editor
George Starr, Business Editor
Byron Clark, City Editor
Allen Mincey, Education Editor
George Starr, Exec Editor
George Starr, Health/Medical Editor
Chuck Thurman, Sports Editor

The Daily Herald
1115 S Main St
Columbia TN 38401-3733
615-388-6464; Fax: 615-388-1003
Circulation: 14,000; Sun: 16,000

Herald-Citizen
124 S Dixie Ave
Cookeville TN 38501-3402
615-526-9715; Fax: 615-526-1209
Circulation: 11,000; Sun: 13,000

State Gazette
Hwy 51 Bypass
Dyersburg TN 38025
901-285-4091; Fax: 901-285-9747
Circulation: 9,000

Elizabethon Star
300 Sycamore St
Elizabethon TN 37643
423-542-4151; Fax: 423-542-2004
Circulation: 10,000; Sun: 10,500

The Greeneville Sun
121 W Summer
Greeneville TN 37743-4923
423-638-4181; Fax: 423-638-3645
Circulation: 15,000; Sat: 15,700

Jackson Sun
PO Box 1059
Jackson TN 38302-1059
901-427-3333; Fax: 901-425-9639
Circulation: 38,000; Sun: 43,000

Lisa Meals, Arts/Entertainment Editor
Beth Todd, Book Editor
Scott Porch, Business Editor
Chris Poynter, Education Editor
Jacque Hillman, Food Editor
Beth Todd, Health/Medical Editor
Jacque Hillman, Lifestyle/Feature Editor
Patrick Rice, Managing News Editor
Chris Rook, Metro Editor
Tom Corwin, Political Editor
Donna Miller-Hicks, Region Editor
Tonya Smith, Religion Editor
Steve Locklin, Sports Editor

Johnson City Press
204 W Main St (37601)
PO Box 1717
Johnson City TN 37605-1717
615-929-3111; Fax: 615-929-7484
Circulation: 35,000; Sun: 40,000

Lesia Paine-Brooks, Book Editor/Reviewer
Brad Jolly, City News Editor
Mark Stevens, Lifestyle/Feature Editor
Henry Samples, Managing Editor
Robert Pierce, Religion Editor
Kelly Hodge, Sports Editor

Daily News
310 E Sullivan St
Kingsport TN 37660-4404
423-246-4800; Fax: 423-247-2502
Circulation: 2,000

Kingsport Times-News
701 Lynn Garden Dr
PO Box 479
Kingsport TN 37662-5607
423-246-8121; Fax: 423-392-1385
Circulation: 46,000; Sun: 47,000

Sharon Hayes, Business Editor
Lisa Eldreth, Education Editor

Becky Whitlock, Family/Food/Garden Editor
Becky Whitlock, Lifestyle/Feature Editor
Ted Como, Managing Editor
Ron Bliss, Sports Editor
Becky Whitlock, Travel Editor

The Daily Beacon
Univ of Tennessee
5 Communications Bldg
Knoxville TN 37996-0001
423-974-3231
Circulation: 16,000

Knoxville News-Sentinel
PO Box 59038
Knoxville TN 37950-9038
615-523-3131; Fax: 615-521-8186
Circulation: 200,000; Sun: 245,000

Jan Avent, Book Editor
Lois Thomas, Business Editor
Harry Moskos, Editor
Mike Wilkinson, Education Reporter
Barbara Asbury, Entertainment Editor
Frank Cagle, Exec Metro Editor
Edwina Ralston, Food Editor
Barbara Aston-Wash, Home Editor
Edwina Ralston, Lifestyle Editor
Betsy Pickle, Movie Critic
Bob Barrett, Religion Editor
Wynne Brown, Science Editor
Steve Ahillen, Sports Editor
Edwina Ralston, Travel Editor

Lebanon Democrat
402 N Cumberland St
Lebanon TN 37087-2306
615-444-3952; Fax: 615-444-1358
Circulation: 10,000

Maryville Daily Times
Frank Trexler, Managing Editor
PO Box 9740
Maryville TN 37802-9740
423-981-1100; Fax: 423-981-1175
Circulation: 30,000

The Commercial Appeal
495 Union Ave
Memphis TN 38103-3242
901-529-2211; Fax: 901-529-2522
Circulation: 193,000; Sun: 284,151

Jon Sparks, Arts/Entertainment Editor
Fred Koeppel, Book Editor
Bob Hetherington, Business Editor
Karanja Ajanaku, Education Editor
Chris Arpe Gang, Family/Food/Garden Editor
Mary Powers, Health Editor
Henry Stokes, Managing Editor
David Waters, Religion Editor
John Stamm, Sports Editor
Charlotte Durham, Travel Editor

The Daily Helmsman
Memphis State Univ
Campus Box 528194
Memphis TN 38152-0001
901-678-2191; Fax: 901-678-4792
Circulation: 10,000

Daily News
193 Jefferson Ave
Memphis TN 38103-2322
901-523-1561; Fax: 901-526-5813
Circulation: 50,000

Citizen Tribune
1609 W 1st North St
Morristown TN 37814-3724
423-581-5630; Fax: 423-581-3061
Circulation: 22,000; Sun: 25,800

The Daily News Journal
224 N Walnut St
Murfreesboro TN 37130-3622
615-893-5860; Fax: 615-896-8702
Circulation: 18,000; Sun: 21,000

Nashville Banner
1100 Broadway
Nashville TN 37203-3116
615-259-8800; Fax: 615-259-8890
Circulation: 67,000

Sue McClure, Book Editor
Tim Tanton, Business Editor
Tim Ghianni, Feature Editor
Pat Embry, Managing Editor
Ed Cromer, Political Editor
Bill Snyder, Science Editor
Lance McKerley, Sports Editor

The Tennessean
1100 Broadway
Nashville TN 37203-3116
615-259-8095; Fax: 615-259-8093
Circulation: 130,000; Sun: 227,000

Patrick Connolly, Arts Editor
Linda Quigley, Book Editor
Candy McCampbell, Business Editor
Kathy Straight, Entertainment Editor
Anne Paine, Environmental Editor
Thayer Wine, Food Editor
Tammie Smith, Health Editor
Patrick Connolly, Home Editor
Tommy Goldsmith, News Editor
Larry Daugherty, Political Editor
Ray Waddle, Religion Editor
Neil Scarbrough, Sports Editor
Thom Storey, Travel Editor

The Oak Ridger
785 Oak Ridge Tpk
Oak Ridge TN 37830-7076
423-482-1021; Fax: 423-482-7824
Circulation: 12,000

The Paris Post-Intelligencer
208 E Wood
Paris TN 38242-4139
901-642-1162; Fax: 901-642-1165
Circulation: 8,000

The Mountain Press
119 Riverbend Dr
Sevierville TN 37862-3557
423-428-0746; Fax: 423-453-4913
Circulation: 10,000; Sun: 11,000

Shelbyville Times-Gazette
323 E Depot St
Shelbyville TN 37160-4027
615-684-1200; Fax: 615-684-3228
Circulation: 10,000

Union City Daily Messenger
613 Jackson St
Union City TN 38261-5239
901-885-0744; Fax: 901-885-0782
Circulation: 9,000

TEXAS

Abilene Reporter-News
101 Cypress St
PO Box 30
Abilene TX 79604-0030
915-673-4271; Fax: 915-673-1901
Circulation: 43,000; Sun: 54,500

Bob Lapham, Arts/Entertainment Editor
Larry Lawrence, Book Editor
Doug Williamson, Business Editor
Glenn Drumgoole, Editor
Pam Percival, Family Editor
Jaryl Young, Food Editor
Carol Lackey, Garden Editor
Pam Percival, Health Editor
Jerry Reed, Higher Education Editor
Kathleen Wittmire, Home Editor
Pamela Percival, Lifestyle Editor
Leslie Carleton, Lower Education Editor
Danny Reigan, Managing Editor
Jerry Reed, Medical Editor
Bob Bruce, Oil Editor
Richard Horn, Political Editor
Roy Jones, Religion Editor
Pam Percival, Society Editor
Al Pickett, Sports Editor
Bob Bruce, Travel Editor

Alice Echo News
405 E Main St
Alice TX 78332-4968
512-664-6588; Fax: 512-668-1030
Circulation: 6,000; Sun: 6,400

Amarillo Globe-News
900 S Harrison
PO Box 2091
Amarillo TX 79166
806-376-4488; Fax: 806-373-0810
Circulation: 65,000

Jeff Rhoads, Arts/Travel Editor
Mary Kate Tripp, Book Editor
Mike Rupe, Business Editor
Matt Curry, City Editor
John Kanelis, Editorial Editor
Melanie Yeager, Education Writer
Kathy Martindale, Exec Managing Editor
Mike Hughes, Health/Medical Writer
Beth Duke, Lifestyle/Family Editor
Dennis Spies, Managing Editor
Jon Mark Beilue, Sports Editor

The Shorthorn
Univ of Texas - 520 S West St
204 Ransom Hall
Arlington TX 76019-0001
817-273-3188; Fax: 817-794-5009
Circulation: 14,000

Athens Daily Review
201 S Prairieville St
Athens TX 75751-2541
903-675-5626; Fax: 903-675-9450
Circulation: 7,000; Sun: 7,800

Austin American-Statesman
305 S Congress
PO Box 670
Austin TX 78767
512-445-3500; Fax: 512-445-3679
Circulation: 180,000; Sun: 240,000

Ed Crowell, Arts/Entertainment Editor
Anne Morris, Book Editor

Jerry Mahoney, Business/Computer Editor
Diane Porter, Education Editor
Dale Rice, Family Editor
Kitty Crider, Food Editor
Dick Stanley, Health/Medical Editor
Linda Wienandt, Lifestyle Editor
Laylan Copelan, Political Editor
Mark Levin, Recreation Editor
Lee Kelly, Society Editor
Tracy Dodds, Sports Editor
Janet Wilson, Travel Editor

The Daily Texan
Univ of Texas
Texas Student Publ PO Box D
Austin TX 78713-8904
512-471-4591; Fax: 512-471-1576
Circulation: 30,000

Daily Tribune-Matagorda County
2901 Carey Smith Blvd
Bay City TX 77414-3768
409-245-5555; Fax: 409-244-5908
Circulation: 6,000; Sun: 6,700

Baytown Sun
Kurt Gaston, Managing Editor
1301 Memorial Dr
Baytown TX 77520
713-422-8302; Fax: 713-427-6283
Circulation: 16,000

Beaumont Enterprise
380 Main St (77701)
PO Box 3071
Beaumont TX 77704
409-838-2876; Fax: 409-838-2857
Circulation: 70,000; Sun: 85,000

David Galloway, Business Editor
Dave Long, City Editor
Elaine Wikstrom, Food Editor
Sheila Friedrick, Lifestyle/Feature Editor
William Mock, Managing Editor
Jennifer Bagwell, Religion Editor
Dave Long, Science Editor
Joe Heiling, Sports Editor

Big Spring Herald
710 Scurry St
Big Spring TX 79720-2723
915-263-7331; Fax: 915-264-7205
Circulation: 8,000; Sun: 9,000

Bonham Daily Favorite
314 N Center
Bonham TX 75418-4332
903-583-2124; Fax: 903-583-8321
Circulation: 3,000

Borger News-Herald
207-209 N Main
Borger TX 79007-4711
806-273-5611; Fax: 806-273-2552
Circulation: 7,000; Sun: 7,300

Brenham Banner-Press
2000 Stringer
Brenham TX 77833-5703
409-836-7956; Fax: 409-830-8577
Circulation: 7,000

The Brownsville Herald
1135 E Van Buren
Brownsville TX 78520-7055
210-542-4301; Fax: 210-542-0840
Circulation: 18,000; Sun: 20,000

El Heraldo de Brownsville
1135 E Van Buren
Brownsville TX 78520-7055
210-542-4301; Fax: 210-542-0840
Circulation: 6,000; Sun: 7,000

Brownwood Bulletin
700 Carnegie
Brownwood TX 76801-7040
915-646-2541; Fax: 915-646-6835
Circulation: 8,000; Sun: 11,000

Bryan-College Station Eagle
1729 Briarcrest Dr
Bryan TX 77802-2712
409-776-4444; Fax: 409-776-0496
Circulation: 28,000; Sun: 30,000

Cleburne Times-Review
108 S Anglin
Cleburne TX 76031-5602
817-645-2441; Fax: 817-645-4020
Circulation: 8,000; Sun: 9,500

Brazosport Facts
720 S Main
PO Box 549
Clute TX 77531
409-265-7411; Fax: 409-265-9052
Circulation: 23,000; Sun: 28,000

Leslie Burleson, Arts/Entertainment
Susan Roth, Business Editor
Julie Myers, Education Editor
Rob Ludwig, Family Editor
Leslie Burleson, Food Editor
Susan Roth, Health/Medical Editor
Rob Ludwig, News Editor
Mike Sullivan, Political Editor
Susan Roth, Religion Editor
Jim Carley, Sports Editor

The Battalion
Texas A & M Univ
Reed McDonald Bldg Rm 230
College Station TX 77843-1111
409-845-2611; Fax: 409-845-5408
Circulation: 24,000

The Conroe Courier
100 Ave A
Conroe TX 77301-2946
409-756-6671; Fax: 409-756-6676
Circulation: 14,000

Corpus Christi Caller-Times
820 Lower Broadway
PO Box 9136
Corpus Christi TX 78469-9136
512-884-2011; Fax: 512-886-3732
Circulation: 67,000; Sun: 91,000

Jim Steinberg, Business Editor
Vaughn Haggerty, Education Editor
Vaughn Haggerty, Health/Medical Editor
Vaughn Haggerty, Lifestyle Editor
Warren Weber, News Editor
Richard Oliver, Sports Editor

Corsicana Daily Sun
405 E Collin St
Corsicana TX 75110
903-812-3931; Fax: 903-872-6878
Circulation: 8,000; Sun: 9,000

Judy Green, Book Editor
Kris DeCanio, Business Editor
Jim Goodson, Editor
Wendell Edwards, Education Editor
Judy Green, Environmental Editor
Judy Green, Food/Family Editor
Judy Green, Health/Medical Editor
Judy Green, Lifestyle/Feature Editor
Kris DeCanio, Religion Editor
Todd Wills, Sports/Outdoors Editor

Dalhart Daily Texan
410 Denrock St
Dalhart TX 79022-2628
806-249-4511; Fax: 806-249-2395
Circulation: 3,000; Sun: 3,000

The Daily Campus
Southern Methodist Univ
3140 Dyer St Hughes-Trigg Ctr
Dallas TX 75275-0456
214-768-4555; Fax: 214-768-4573
Circulation: 5,000

Daily Commercial Record
706 Main St
Dallas TX 75202-3610
214-741-6366
Circulation: 3,000

Dallas Morning News
PO Box 655237
Dallas TX 75265-5237
214-977-8222; Fax: 214-977-8319
Circulation: 500,000; Sun: 800,000

Tom Kessler, Arts/Entertainment Editor
Robert Compton, Book Editor
Mindy Fetterman, Business Editor
Bob Bersano, Dallas Life Editor
Leslie Snyder, Education Editor
Tracy Hayes, Fashion Editor
Cathy Barber, Food Editor
Lennox Samuels, Foreign Editor
Jen Okamoto, Health/Medical Editor
Ira Hadnot, Lifestyle Editor
Ed Stuart Wilk, Managing Editor
Ray Sasser, Outdoors/Recreation Editor
Ed Dufner, Political Editor
Janie Palleschic, Religion Editor
Tom Seigfried, Science Editor
Dave Smith, Sports Editor
Karen Jordan, Travel Editor
Nor Cavzos, TV Editor
Ira Hadnot, Women's Editor

Del Rio News-Herald
321 S Main St
Del Rio TX 78840-5566
210-775-1551; Fax: 210-774-2610
Circulation: 7,000; Sun: 7,200

The Denison Herald
331 W Woodward
Denison TX 75020-3136
903-465-7171; Fax: 903-465-7188
Circulation: 11,000; Sun: 12,000

Denton Record-Chronicle
314 E Hickory
Denton TX 76201-4272
817-387-3811; Fax: 817-434-2400
Circulation: 17,000; Sun: 20,000

North Texas Daily
Univ of North Texas State
Denton TX 76203-5278
817-565-2353; Fax: 817-565-4659
Circulation: 11,000

Edinburg Daily Review
215 E University
Edinburg TX 78539-3547
210-383-2705; Fax: 210-383-3172
Circulation: 5,000; Sun: 5,400

El Paso Herald-Post
300 N Campbell (79901)
PO Box 20
El Paso TX 79999
915-546-6100; Fax: 915-546-6349
Circulation: 34,000

Deborah Martin, Arts Editor
Charles Edgren, Book Editor
Ken Baake, Business Editor
Judy Wiley, City Editor
Tom Kink, Editor
Sunny Lopez, Education Editor
Karen Brehm, Feature Editor
Joe Muench, Sports Editor

El Paso Times
300 N Campbell (79901)
PO Box 20
El Paso TX 79999
915-546-6100; Fax: 915-546-6415
Circulation: 60,000; Sun: 105,000

Melissa Schapiro, Arts/Entertainment Editor
Melissa Schapiro, Book Editor
Laurie Patternoster, Business Editor
Ramon Barcamontes, City Editor
Leticia Zamarripa, Feature Editor
Paula Moore, Managing Editor
Lee Williams, Sports Editor
Melissa Schapiro, Travel Editor

The Ennis Daily News
,213 N Dallas St
Ennis TX 75119-4011
214-875-3801; Fax: 214-875-9747
Circulation: 5,000

Fort Worth Commercial Recorder
3032 S Jones
Ft Worth TX 76104-6747
817-926-5351; Fax: 817-926-5377
Circulation: 1,000

Fort Worth Star-Telegram
400 W 7th St (76102)
PO Box 1870
Ft Worth TX 76101
817-390-7400; Fax: 817-390-7789
Circulation: 255,000; Sun: 356,000

Lisa Kestler, Arts/Entertainment Editor
Larry Swindell, Book Editor
Teresa McUsic, Business Book Reviews
Rex Seline, Business Editor
Jay Lewis, City Editor
Jennifer Packer, Education Editor
Debbie Price, Exec Editor
Holly Hansen, Feature Editor
Beverly Bundy, Food Editor
Carolyn Poirot, Health Editor
Leslie Gornstein, Hi-Tech Editor
Carol Nuckols, Hobby Editor
Julie Heaberlie, Lifestyle/Feature Editor
Dan Reed, News Editor
John Gravois, Political Editor
Kevin Dale, Sports Editor
Jerry Flemmons, Travel Editor

TCU Daily Skiff
Texas Christian Univ
2805 University Dr Moudy Bldg S
Ft Worth TX 76109-1379
817-921-7426; Fax: 817-921-7133
Circulation: 4,000

Gainesville Daily Register
306 E California St
Gainesville TX 76240-4006
817-665-5511; Fax: 817-665-0920
Circulation: 7,000; Sun: 8,800

Galveston County Daily News
8522 Teichman Rd
Galveston TX 77554-9119
409-744-3611; Fax: 409-744-7679
Circulation: 30,000; Sun: 30,000

The Greenville Herald Banner
2305 King St
Greenville TX 75401-3257
903-455-4220; Fax: 903-455-6281
Circulation: 12,000; Sun: 12,000

Valley Morning Star
PO Box 511
Harlingen TX 78551-0511
210-423-5511; Fax: 210-430-6204
Circulation: 30,000; Sun: 30,000

Henderson Daily News
1711 S Hwy 79
Henderson TX 75652-4509
903-657-2501; Fax: 903-657-2452
Circulation: 7,000; Sun: 8,000

Hereford Brand
313 N Lee
Hereford TX 79045-5341
806-364-2030; Fax: 806-364-8364
Circulation: 4,000; Sun: 4,600

The Daily Cougar
Univ of Houston
4800 Calhoun
Houston TX 77004-2610
713-743-5360; Fax: 713-743-5384
Circulation: 13,000

Daily Court Review
6807 Wynnwood
Houston TX 77008-5023
713-869-5434; Fax: 713-869-8887
Circulation: 3,000

Houston Chronicle
801 Texas Ave (77002)
PO Box 4260
Houston TX 77210-4260
713-220-7171; Fax: 713-220-6806
Circulation: 440,000, Sun: 840,000

Fritz Lanham, Book Editor
Scott Clark, Business Editor
Steve Jetton, City Editor
Chip Boisseau, Computer Editor
Jack Loftis, Editor-in-Chief
Melissa Aguilar, Entertainment Editor
Jane Marshall, Feature Editor
Ann Criswell, Food Editor
Madeleine Hamm, Home Editor
Renee Kientz, Lifestyle Editor
Tony Pederson, Managing Editor
Ruth Sorelle, Medical Editor
David Gerraughty, National Political Editor
Joe Doggett, Outdoor Editor
Carlos Byars, Science Editor
Dan Cunningham, Sports Editor
Harry Shattuck, Travel Editor

Southern Chinese News
12129 Bellaire Blvd
Houston TX 77072-2314
713-498-4310; Fax: 713-498-2728
Circulation: 25,000; Sun: 25,000

The Huntsville Item
1409 10th St
Huntsville TX 77340-3805
409-295-5407; Fax: 409-293-3909
Circulation: 7,000; Sun: 8,000

Jacksonville Daily Progress
PO Box 711
Jacksonville TX 75766-0711
903-586-2236; Fax: 903-586-0987
Circulation: 5,000; Sun: 6,000

Kerrville Daily Times
429 Jefferson
Kerrville TX 78028-4412
210-896-7000; Fax: 210-896-1150
Circulation: 10,000; Sun: 12,000

Kilgore News Herald
610 E Main St
Kilgore TX 75662-2612
903-984-2593; Fax: 903-984-7462
Circulation: 4,000; Sun: 5,000

Killeen Daily Herald
1809 Florence
Killeen TX 76541-8977
817-634-2125; Fax: 817-526-6397
Circulation: 22,000; Sun: 26,000

The Laredo Morning Times
111 Esperanza Dr
Laredo TX 78041-2607
210-728-2500; Fax: 210-723-1227
Circulation: 23,000; Sun: 25,000

Longview News-Journal
320 E Methvin
Longview TX 75601-7323
903-757-3311; Fax: 903-236-3874
Circulation: 34,000; Sun: 43,000

Lubbock Avalanche-Journal
PO Box 491
Lubbock TX 79408-0491
806-762-8844; Fax: 806-774-9603
Circulation: 70,000; Sun: 78,000

William E Kerns, Arts/Entertainment Editor
William E Kerns, Book Editor/Reviewer
Chris Van Wagenen, Business Editor
Hank Murphy, City Editor
Mike Lee, Education Editor
Randy Sanders, Exec Editor
Danette Baker, Food Editor
Danette Baker, Lifestyle Editor
Burle Pettit, Managing Editor
Doug Hensley, Sports Editor

The University Daily
Texas Tech Univ
103 Journalism Bldg
Lubbock TX 79409-4349
806-742-3388; Fax: 806-742-2434
Circulation: 14,000

Lufkin Daily News
PO Box 1089
Lufkin TX 75902-1089
409-632-6631; Fax: 409-632-6655
Circulation: 15,000

Beverly Johnson, Arts/Entertainment Editor
Jay Milner, Book Editor/Reviewer
Jackie Casper, Business Editor
Jeff Pownall, Computer Editor
Rhonda Marshall, Education Editor
Beverly Johnson, Food Editor
Beverly Johnson, Health/Medical Editor
Beverly Johnson, Home/Garden Editor
Beverly Johnson, Lifestyle/Feature Editor
Phil Latham, News Editor
Jackie Casper, Political Editor
Glen McCutchen, Publisher
Beverly Johnson, Religion Editor
Jack Stallard, Sports Editor
Jackie Casper, Travel Editor

Marshall News Messenger
309 E Austin
Marshall TX 75670-3475
903-935-7914; Fax: 903-935-6242
Circulation: 10,000; Sun: 12,000

The Monitor
1101 Ash St
McAllen TX 78501-4603
210-686-4343; Fax: 210-686-4370
Circulation: 32,000; Sun: 39,000

McKinney Courier-Gazette
4005 W University Ave
McKinney TX 75070-4801
214-542-2631; Fax: 214-548-7527
Circulation: 9,000; Sun: 8,300

Mexia Daily News
214 N Railroad St
Mexia TX 76667-2850
817-562-2868; Fax: 817-562-3121
Circulation: 3,000

Midland Reporter-Telegram
201 E Illinois St
Midland TX 79701-4852
915-682-5311; Fax: 915-682-3793
Circulation: 27,000; Sun: 30,500

Mineral Wells Index
300 SE 1st St
Mineral Wells TX 76067-5331
817-325-4465; Fax: 817-325-2020
Circulation: 5,000; Sun: 5,200

Mount Pleasant Daily Tribune
1705 Industrial Rd
Mount Pleasant TX 75455-2235
903-572-1705; Fax: 903-572-1705
Circulation: 7,000; Sun: 6,500

The Daily Sentinel
4920 Colonial Dr
Nacogdoches TX 75961-3021
409-564-8361; Fax: 409-560-4267
Circulation: 10,000; Sun: 12,500

New Braunfels Herald-Zeitung
707 Landa St
New Braunfels TX 78130-6113
210-625-9144; Fax: 210-625-1224
Circulation: 9,000; Sun: 10,200

The Odessa American
222 E 4th St
Odessa TX 79761-5122
915-337-4661; Fax: 915-333-7742
Circulation: 28,000; Sun: 35,000

The Orange Leader
200 Front St
Orange TX 77630-5802
409-883-3571; Fax: 409-883-6342
Circulation: 10,000; Sun: 13,000

Palestine Herald-Press
519 Elm St
Palestine TX 75801-2919
903-729-0281; Fax: 903-729-3380
Circulation: 10,000; Sun: 11,000

The Pampa News
403 W Atchison
Pampa TX 79065-6303
806-669-2525; Fax: 806-669-2520
Circulation: 7,000; Sun: 7,300

The Paris News
5050 SE Loop 286
Paris TX 75460-6576
903-785-8744; Fax: 903-785-1263
Circulation: 19,000; Sun: 15,000

Pasadena Citizen
PO Box 6192
Pasadena TX 77506-0192
713-477-0221; Fax: 713-477-9090
Circulation: 8,000; Sun: 14,000

Dana Darbin, Business Editor
Lora Bernard, Education Editor
Lisa Bass, Family/Food/Garden Editor
Lisa Bass, Lifestyle/Feature Editor
Mike Simmons, Managing Editor
Mike Simmons, News/Book Editor
Virginia Hahn, Religion Editor
Ed Bashinski, Sports Editor

Pecos Enterprises
324 S Cedar St
Pecos TX 79772-3211
915-445-5475; Fax: 915-445-4321
Circulation: 3,000; Sun: 4,500

Plainview Daily Herald
820 Broadway
Plainview TX 79072-7316
806-296-1300; Fax: 806-296-1315
Circulation: 8,000; Sun: 10,000

Plano Star Courier
801 E Plano Pky
Plano TX 75074-6746
214-424-6565; Fax: 214-578-0379
Circulation: 13,000; Sun: 15,000

Port Arthur News
549 4th St
Port Arthur TX 77640-6453
409-985-5541; Fax: 409-982-4903
Circulation: 23,000; Sun: 25,000

The Herald-Coaster
1902 S 4th St
Rosenberg TX 77471-5140
713-232-3737; Fax: 713-342-3219
Circulation: 9,000; Sun: 9,800

San Angelo Standard-Times
PO Box 5111
San Angelo TX 76902-5111
915-653-1221; Fax: 915-658-7341
Circulation: 37,000

Diane Murray, Arts/Entertainment Editor
Diane Murray, Book Editor
Diane Murray, Lifestyle/Feature Editor
Arlen Lohse, Managing Editor
Dennis Ellsworth, News Editor
Bill Miller, Regional Editor
Mike Lee, Sports Editor

Daily Commercial Recorder
6222 IH 10 W #101
San Antonio TX 78201-2014
210-736-4450; Fax: 210-736-5506
Circulation: 1,000

San Antonio Express-News
Ave E & 3rd St (78205)
PO Box 2171
San Antonio TX 78297-2171
210-225-7411; Fax: 210-229-9268
Circulation: 187,000; Sun: 278,000

Kristina Paledes, Arts Editor
Judith Rigler, Book Editor
Paul Hill, Business Editor
Linda Vaughn, Editor/Sunday Insight
Karen Haram, Food Editor
Don Finley, Health/Medical Editor
Rick Martinez, Higher Education Editor
Marsha Harlow, Lifestyle Editor
Denise Rios, Lower Education Editor
Robert Rivard, Managing Editor
Craig Thomason, News Editor
Mark MacDonald, Outdoors Editor
Ruth Davidson, Political Editor
Don Finley, Science Editor
Barry Robinson, Sports Editor
Julie Cooper, Travel Editor

San Marcos Daily Record
1910 Interstate Hwy 35 S
San Marcos TX 78666
512-392-2458; Fax: 512-392-1514
Circulation: 6,000; Sun: 8,400

The University Star
Southwest Texas State Univ
601 University Dr Old Main #102
San Marcos TX 78666-4616
512-245-3487; Fax: 512-245-3708
Circulation: 10,000

The Seguin Gazette-Enterprise
1012 Schriewer Rd
Seguin TX 78155-7473
210-379-5402; Fax: 210-379-8328
Circulation: 7,000; Sun: 8,000

Sherman Democrat
603 S Sam Rayburn Fwy
Sherman TX 75090-7258
903-893-8181; Fax: 903-868-1930
Circulation: 19,000; Sun: 22,000

Snyder Daily News
3600 College Ave
Snyder TX 79549-4637
915-573-5486; Fax: 915-573-0044
Circulation: 5,000; Sun: 6,000

Stephenville Empire-Tribune
590 S Loop
Stephenville TX 76401-4224
817-965-3124; Fax: 817-965-4269
Circulation: 5,000; Sun: 6,000

Sulphur Springs News-Telegram
401 Church St
Sulphur Springs TX 75482-2681
903-885-8663; Fax: 903-885-8768
Circulation: 7,000; Sun: 7,400

Sweetwater Reporter
PO Box 750
Sweetwater TX 79556-0750
915-236-6677; Fax: 915-235-4967
Circulation: 4,000; Sun: 4,200

Taylor Daily Press
211 W 3rd St
Taylor TX 76574-3518
512-352-8535; Fax: 512-352-2227
Circulation: 5,000

Temple Daily Telegram
10 S 3rd
Temple TX 76501-7619
817-778-4444; Fax: 817-778-4444
Circulation: 25,000; Sun: 27,000

The Terrell Tribune
1125 S Virginia
Terrell TX 75160-4556
214-563-6476; Fax: 214-563-6479
Circulation: 6,000; Sun: 6,200

Texarkana Gazette
315 Pine St
Texarkana TX 75501-5683
903-794-3311; Fax: 903-794-3315
Circulation: 33,000; Sun: 36,000

Ethal Channon, Asst Managing Editor
Lynn Blackmon, Book Editor/Reviewer
Lisa Bose, Business Editor
Tisha Gilbert, Education/Religion Editor
Judy Morgan, Family/Food/Garden Editor
Carmen Jones, Health/Medical Editor
Les Minor, Managing Editor
Jim Horras, News Editor
Johnny Green, Sports Editor
Lynn Blackmon, Travel Editor

Texas City Sun
7800 Emmett F Lowry Expy
Texas City TX 77591-2456
409-945-3441; Fax: 409-935-0428
Circulation: 11,000; Sun: 11,000

Tyler Courier-Times
410 W Erwin St
Tyler TX 75702-7133
903-597-8111; Fax: 903-595-6470
Circulation: 5,000; Sun: 54,000

Tyler Morning Telegraph
410 W Erwin St (75702)
PO Box 2030
Tyler TX 75710
903-597-8111; Fax: 903-595-0335
Circulation: 44,000; Sun: 54,000

Terry Cannon, Arts/Entertainment Editor
Everett Taylor, Book Editor
Danny Mogle, Business Editor
Betty Waters, Education Editor
Jim Giametta, Exec Editor
Joyce Turner, Food Editor

Marvin Ellis, Health Editor
Joyce Turner, Lifestyle Editor
Steve Knight, Outdoors Editor
Phil Hicks, Sports Editor
Shelley Roark, Travel Editor

The Vernon Daily Record
3214 Wilbarger
Vernon TX 76384-7927
817-552-5454; Fax: 817-553-4823
Circulation: 5,000; Sun: 5,700

The Victoria Advocate
311 E Constitution
Victoria TX 77901-8140
512-575-1451; Fax: 512-574-1220
Circulation: 42,000; Sun: 45,000

The Lariat
Baylor University
PO Box 97353 BU
Waco TX 76798-7353
817-755-1711; Fax: 817-755-1490
Circulation: 8,000

Waco Tribune Herald
900 Franklin Ave
PO Box 2588
Waco TX 76702-2588
817-757-5757; Fax: 817-757-0302
Circulation: 47,000; Sun: 61,000

Carl Hoover, Arts/Entertainment Editor
Carl Hoover, Book Editor
Mike Copeland, Business Editor
Mike Wallace, Education Editor
Lynn Bulmahn, Environmental/Science
Lynn Bulmahn, Health/Medical Editor
Theresa Johnson, Lifestyle Editor
Barbara Elmore, Managing Editor
Paula Blesener, News Editor
Mark Masferrer, Political Reporter
Kim Gorum, Sports Editor

Waxahachie Daily Light
200 W Marvin
Waxahachie TX 75165-3040
214-937-3310; Fax: 214-937-1139
Circulation: 7,000; Sun: 6,500

The Weatherford Democrat
512 Palo Pinto
Weatherford TX 76086-4128
817-594-7447; Fax: 817-594-9734
Circulation: 6,000; Sun: 6,700

Times Record News
1301 Lamar (76301)
PO Box 120
Wichita Falls TX 76307-0120
817-767-8341; Fax: 817-767-1741
Circulation: 39,000; Sun: 49,000

Bridget Knight, Arts/Entertainment Editor
Mike Daugherty, Book Editor
Ted Buss, Business Editor
Alden Brown, Education Editor
Susan O'Bryan, Family Editor
Judith McGinnis, Food Editor
Susan O'Bryan, Garden Editor
Susan O'Bryan, Health/Medical Editor
Susan O'Bryan, Lifestyle Editor
Gary Schneeberger, Managing Editor
Pat Fortner, Political Editor
Bridget Knight, Religion Editor
Nick Gholson, Sports Editor
Susan O'Bryan, Travel Editor

UTAH

The Herald Journal
75 W 3rd North St
Logan UT 84321-3971
801-752-2121; Fax: 801-753-6642
Circulation: 15,000; Sun: 15,000

Standard-Examiner
455 23rd St
PO Box 951
Ogden UT 84402-0951
801-394-7711; Fax: 801-625-4299
Circulation: 63,000; Sun: 64,000

Vanessa Zimmer, Arts/Entertainment Editor
Vanessa Zimmer, Book Review Editor
Mike Marino, Business Editor
Wendy Ogata, City Assignment Editor
Bill Petty, Computer Editor
Cheryl Buchta, Education Editor
Vanessa Zimmer, Lifestyle/Feature Editor
Ron Thornberg, Managing Editor
Ralph Wakley, Political Editor
Randy Hollis, Sports Editor

The Daily Herald
1555 N 200 West
Provo UT 84604-2519
801-373-5050; Fax: 801-373-5489
Circulation: 32,000; Sun: 34,000

The Daily Universe
Brigham Young Univ
538 ELWC
Provo UT 84602-1050
801-378-2957; Fax: 801-378-2959
Circulation: 19,000

The Deseret News
PO Box 1257
Salt Lake City UT 84110
801-237-2100; Fax: 801-237-2121
Circulation: 62,000; Sun: 68,672

Jerry Johnston, Book Review Editor
Max Knudson, Business Editor
Richard Hall, City Editor
David Croft, Computer Editor
Marjorie Cortez, Education Editor
Karl Cates, Environmental Editor
Carma Wadley, Fashion/Feature Editor
Jean Williams, Food Editor
Carma Wadley, Lifestyle Editor
Don Woodward, Managing Editor
Joseph Bauman, Medical Editor
Jon Ringwood, News Editor
Bob Bernick Jr, Political Editor
Carrie Moore, Religion Editor
John Robinson, Sports Editor
Scott Pierce, Television Editor
Katie Clayton, Travel Editor

Salt Lake Tribune
143 S Main St
PO Box 867
Salt Lake City UT 84110-0867
801-237-2011; Fax: 801-521-9418
Circulation: 190,000; Sun: 225,000

Terry Orme, Arts/Entertainment Editor
Brandon Griggs, Book Editor
Cherrill Crosby, Business Editor
James Shelledy, Editor
Judy Rollins, Features Editor
Judith Selby, Food Editor

Genevieve Folson, Garden Editor
Tim Fitzpatrick, Health Editor
David Noyce, National Editor
Peggy Fletcher Stack, Religion Writer
Kurt Kragthorpe, Sports Editor
Tom McCarthey, Travel Editor

Utah Chronicle
Univ of Utah
240 Union Bldg
Salt Lake City UT 84112-1192
801-581-7041; Fax: 801-581-3299
Circulation: 20,000

Daily Spectrum
275 E St George Blvd
St George UT 84770-2954
801-674-8200; Fax: 801-674-6264
Circulation: 20,000; Sun: 21,000

VERMONT

Barre Times-Argus
540 N Main St
Barre VT 05641-2504
802-479-0191; Fax: 802-479-4032
Circulation: 15,000

Jim Lowe, Book Editor
Ann Gibbons, Managing Editor

The Bennington Banner
425 Main St
Bennington VT 05201-2141
802-447-7567; Fax: 802-442-3413
Circulation: 8,000

Brattleboro Reformer
Black Mountain Rd
Brattleboro VT 05301
802-254-2311; Fax: 802-257-1305
Circulation: 11,000

Burlington Free Press
191 College St
PO Box 10
Burlington VT 05402-0010
802-863-3441; Fax: 802-660-1802
Circulation: 55,000; Sun: 70,000

Joe Cutts, Arts/Entertainment Editor
Sally Pollak, Book Editor
Julie Warwick, Business Editor
Anne Geggis, Education Editor
Deb Salomen, Home Editor
Joe Cutts, Lifestyle/Feature Editor
Mickey Hirten, Managing Editor
Joe Henry, News Editor
Steve Locklin, Sports Editor
Steve Mease, Travel Editor

Newport Daily Express
347 Hill St
Newport VT 05855
802-334-6568; Fax: 802-334-6891
Circulation: 6,000

Rutland Daily Herald
27 Wales St
Rutland VT 05701-4027
802-775-5511; Fax: 802-775-2423
Circulation: 23,000

John Van Hoesen, Arts/Entertainment Editor
Lee Huntington, Book Critic
Bruce Edwards, Business Editor

Kevin O'Connor, Education Editor
Linda Skovira, Food Editor
Linda Skovira, Health/Medical Editor
Tim Clemens, Lifestyle/Feature Editor
John Van Hoesen, Managing Editor
John Van Hoesen, Political Editor
Tim Clemens, Religion Editor
John Van Hoesen, Science Editor
Dennis Jensen, Sports Editor
Sally Johnson, Travel Editor

St Albans Messenger
281 N Main St
St Albans VT 05478-2503
802-524-9771; Fax: 802-527-1948
Circulation: 5,000

Caledonian Record
25 Federal St
St Johnsbury VT 05819-2636
802-748-8121; Fax: 802-748-1613
Circulation: 12,000

VIRGINIA

Education Daily
1101 King St #444
Alexandria VA 22314-2944
703-739-6444; Fax: 703-739-6715
Circulation: N/A

Defense Daily
1111 N 19th St #503
Arlington VA 22209-1709
703-522-5655; Fax: 703-522-6448
Circulation: 10,000

Gas Daily
1616 N Ft Myer Dr #1000
Arlington VA 22209-3100
703-528-1244; Fax: 703-528-1322
Circulation: N/A

USA TODAY
1000 Wilson Blvd
Arlington VA 22229
703-276-3400; Fax: 703-276-5513
For info: 800-USA-0001
Circulation: 2059,000

Paul Hoversten, Aerospace Reporter
Micheline Maynard, Automotive Reporter
Keith Alexander, Aviation Reporter
Jon Saraceno, Boxing Reporter
Rhonda Richards, Business/Travel Reporter
David Patrick Stearns, Classical Music Report
Larry King, Columnist, Larry King's People
Daniel Kadlec, Columnist, Street Talk
Tom Weir, Columnist
Jeannie Williams, Columnist
Kevin Maney, Columnist, Info Hwy Report
David Zimmerman, Country Music Reporter
Gary Fields, Crime Reporter
Kitty Yancey, Dep Mg Editor/Life
Linda Kauss, Deputy Mg Editor/Life
Jack Williams, Editor, The Weather Page
Peter Johnson, Editor, Inside TV
Karen Jurgensen, Editorial Page Editor
Tamara Henry, Education Reporter
Patty Rhule, Entertainment Editor
Ann Oldenburg, Entertainment Reporter
David Mazzarella, Exec Editor

Elizabeth Snead, Fashion Reporter
Shawn Sell, Feature Editor
Katy Kelly, Feature Reporter
Jerry Shriver, Food/Wine Critic
Jerry Potter, Golf Reporter
Nancy Hellmich, Health/Nutrition Reporter, Right Bites Column
Mike Brehm, Hockey Editor
Kevin Allen, Hockey Reporter
Mike Snider, Home Tech Reporter
Bruce Schwartz, Home Technology Editor
Steve Wieberg, HS/College Sports Reporter
Carolyn White, HS/College Sports Reporter
James Cox, Intl Correspondent
Tony Mauro, Legal Issues Reporter
Judi Hasson, Legislative Reporter
Deirdre Schwiesow, Leisure Travel Reporter
Susan Weiss, Managing Editor, Life Section
John Hillkirk, Managing Editor/Money
Hal Ritter, Managing Editor/News
Gene Policinski, Managing Editor/Sports
Julie Nichols, Media Relations Coord
David Lieberman, Media Reporter
Paul Wiseman, Money Bookshelf Editor
Beth Tuschak, Motor Sports Reporter
Mike Clark, Movie Critic
Susan Wloszczyna, Movie Critic
Anne Ayers, Music Editor
Greg Boeck, NBA Reporter
Larry Weisman, NFC Reporter
Jarrett Bell, NFL Reporter
Mike Dodd, Olympic Reporter
Oscar Dixon, Page 3 Editor (Sports)
Walter Shapiro, Political Columnist
Richard Benedetto, Political Correspondent
Jefferson Graham, Programming Profiles Rp
James T Jones IV, Rap/Jazz/R&B Reporter
Dennis Kelly, Reporter
Anita Manning, Reporter, Earth Notes Dept
David Lynch, Reporter, Telecommunications Industry
Donna Rosato, Reporter, Business Transportation
Ellen Neuborne, Reporter, Retailing
John Waggoner, Reporter, Smart Investing
Michael Hiestand, Reporter, The Biz
Edna Gundersen, Rock Music Reporter
Tim Friend, Science Reporter
Jerry Langdon, Soccer Reporter
Richard Willing, Social Issues Reporter
Bryan Burwell, Sports Columnist
James Kim, Technology Reporter
Doug Smith, Tennis Reporter
Ron Schoolmeester, Travel Editor
Cathy Grossman, Travel Reporter
Craig Wilson, Travel Reporter
Cathy Hainer, Travel Reporter
Matt Roush, TV Critic
Alan Bash, TV Writer (New York)
Mark Memmott, WA Editor
Del Jones, Workplace Reporter

Bristol Herald Courier Virginia Tennessean
320 Morrison Blvd
Bristol VA 24201-3812
Circulation: 45,000; Sun: 48,000

The Cavalier Daily
Univ of Virginia
Newcomb Hall Basement
Charlottesville VA 22904
804-924-1086; Fax: 804-924-7290
Circulation: 10,000

The Daily Progress
685 W Rio Rd
Charlottesville VA 22901-1413
804-978-7200; Fax: 804-978-7252
Circulation: 32,000; Sun: 35,000

The University Journal
Univ of Virginia
Newcomb Hall PO Box 709
Charlottesville VA 22902-0709
804-924-1748; Fax: 804-924-1394
Circulation: 10,000

Virginian Review
128 N Maple Ave
Covington VA 24426-1545
540-962-2121; Fax: 540-962-5072
Circulation: 8,000

Star-Exponent
122 Spencer St
Culpeper VA 22701
540-825-0771; Fax: 540-825-0778
Circulation: 8,000; Sun: 8,200

Danville Register and Bee
700 Monument St
Danville VA 24541-1512
804-793-2311; Fax: 804-799-0595
Circulation: 25,000; Sun: 28,000

The Journal Newspapers
2720 Prosperity Ave
Fairfax VA 22034-1000
703-560-4000; Fax: 703-846-8366

Mary Ellen Webb, Book Review Editor
Brenda Bouser, Family Editor
Linda Schubert, Lifestyle Editor
Jane Touzalin, Managing News Editor
Paul Bergeron, Sports Editor

**The following six newspapers all have the same editors, address and phone.

Alexandria Journal
Circulation: 5,000

Arlington Journal
Circulation: 8,000

Fairfax Journal
Circulation: 55,000

Montgomery Journal
Circulation: 30,000

Prince George's Journal
Circulation: 30,000

Prince William Journal
Circulation: 25,000

Northern Virginia Sun
2710-C Prosperity Ave
Fairfax VA 22031-4320
703-204-2800; Fax: 703-204-3455
Circulation: 2,000

The Free Lance-Star
616 Amelia St
Fredericksburg VA 22401-3887
540-373-5000; Fax: 540-373-8450
Circulation: 43,000; Sat: 46,000

Daily News-Record
231 S Liberty
Harrisonburg VA 22801-3621
540-574-6200; Fax: 540-433-9112
Circulation: 33,000

The Hopewell News
516 E Randolph Rd
Hopewell VA 23860-2652
804-458-8511; Fax: 804-458-7556
Circulation: 8,000

The News and Daily Advance
101 Wyndale Dr
Lynchburg VA 24501-6710
804-385-5400; Fax: 804-385-5511
Circulation: 38,000; Sun: 41,000

Journal Messenger
9009 Church St
Manassas VA 22110-5410
703-368-3101; Fax: 703-368-9017
Circulation: 10,000

Martinsville Bulletin
204 Broad St
Martinsville VA 24112-3704
540-638-8801; Fax: 540-638-4153
Circulation: 19,000; Sun: 21,000

Daily Press
7505 Warwick Blvd
PO Box 746
Newport News VA 23607-0746
804-247-4600; Fax: 804-245-8618
Circulation: 105,000; Sun: 124,000

Stephen Arnold, Arts/Entertainment Editor
Will Molineux, Book Editor
Michael Toole, Business Editor
Will Corbin, Exec Editor
Cheryl Segal, Family Editor
Cheryl Segal, Family/Charity/Religion
Maryann Hakowski, Managing Editor
Marguerite Hargreaves, Metro Editor
Ed Moore, Sports Editor

The Progress-Index
15 Franklin St
Petersburg VA 23803-4514
804-732-3456; Fax: 804-861-9452
Circulation: 20,000; Sun: 19,700

Virginian-Pilot
150 W Brambleton Ave
Norfolk VA 23510-2018
804-446-2000; Fax: 804-446-2414
Circulation: 250,000; Sun: 275,000

Roberta Vowell, Arts/Entertainment Editor
Ann Sorjesma, Book Editor
Joe Coccaro, Business Editor
Debra Adams, Education Editor
Ruth Fantasia, Food Editor
Esther Diskin, Health/Medical Editor
Marcia Cronin, Home Editor
Roberta Vowell, Lifestyle/Feature Editor
Cole Campbell, Managing Editor
Dale Eiseman, Political Editor
Esther Diskin, Religion Editor
Chic Reibel, Sports Editor

The Southwest Times
34 5th St NE
Pulaski VA 24301-4608
540-980-5220; Fax: 540-980-3618
Circulation: 8,000; Sun: 8,500

Richmond Times Dispatch
PO Box 85333
Richmond VA 23293
804-649-6000; Fax: 804-775-8059
Circulation: 212,000; Sun: 255,000

Cindy Creasy, Arts/Entertainment Editor
Ann L Merriman, Book Editor
Andrew Taylor, Business Editor
Andrew Taylor, Computer Editor
Ruth Intress, Education Editor
Bob Walsh, Feature Editor
Louis Mahoney, Food Editor
Beverly Orndorff, Health Editor
Betsy Mullen, Home Editor
Louise Seals, Managing Editor
Paul Gregory, News Editor
Tyler Whitley, Political Writer
Ed Briggs, Religion Editor
Jack Berninger, Sports Editor
Katherine Calos, Travel Editor

Roanoke Times
201 Campbell Ave SW
PO Box 2491
Roanoke VA 24010-2491
540-981-3100; Fax: 540-981-3391
Circulation: 105,000; Sun: 125,000

Jeff DeBell, Arts Editor
Mary Ann Johnson, Book Editor
John Levin, Business Editor
Joel Turner, Education Writer
Jeff DeBell, Feature Editor
Almena Hughes, Food Editor
Marty Horne, Home Editor
Rich Martin, Managing Editor
Sue Lindsey, Metro Editor
Dwayne Yancy, Political Editor
Bill Bern, Sports Editor
Caroline Daugherty, Travel Editor

The Daily News Leader
11 N Central Ave
Staunton VA 24401-4212
540-885-7281; Fax: 540-885-1904
Circulation: 19,000; Sun: 24,000

Northern Virginia Daily
120 N Holliday
Strasburg VA 22657-1418
540-465-5137; Fax: 540-465-9388
Circulation: 15,000

Suffolk News-Herald
130-132 S Saratoga St
Suffolk VA 23434-5323
804-539-3437; Fax: 804-539-8804
Circulation: 7,000; Sun: 6,900

The News-Virginian
544 W Main St
Waynesboro VA 22980-4527
540-949-8213; Fax: 540-942-4542
Circulation: 11,000

The Winchester Star
2 N Kent St
Winchester VA 22601-5038
540-667-3200; Fax: 540-667-0012
Circulation: 22,000

Potomac News
PO Box 2470
Woodbridge VA 22193-9070
703-878-8000; Fax: 703-878-3993
Circulation: 30,000; Sun: 31,000

WASHINGTON

The Daily World
315 S Michigan
Aberdeen WA 98520-6037
360-532-4000; Fax: 360-533-1328
Circulation: 17,000; Sun: 17,595

Journal-American
PO Box 90130
Bellevue WA 98009-9230
206-455-2222; Fax: 206-635-0603
Circulation: 32,000; Sun: 36,000

The Bellingham Herald
PO Box 1277
Bellingham WA 98227-1277
360-676-2600; Fax: 360-647-9260
Circulation: 27,000; Sun: 35,000

The Sun
545 Fifth St
PO Box 259
Bremerton WA 98337
360-377-3711; Fax: 360-479-7681
Circulation: 41,000

Jeff Brody, Asst News Editor
Jack Swanson, Business Editor
Chris Dungaden, Health/Medical Editor
Marty Bouvechio, Managing Editor
Chuck Stark, Sports Editor
Ken Martin, Travel Editor

The Daily Chronicle
321 N Pearl St
Centralia WA 98531-4323
360-736-3311; Fax: 360-736-1568
Circulation: 16,000

Daily Record
401 N Main St
Ellensburg WA 98926-3107
509-925-1414; Fax: 509-925-5696
Circulation: 6,000

Everett Herald
Grand & California Aves
PO Box 930
Everett WA 98206-0930
206-339-3000; Fax: 206-339-3049
Circulation: 55,000; Sunday 62,000

Mike Murray, Arts/Travel Editor
Diane Wright, Book Editor
Jeff Standaert, Economy Editor
Pam McGiffin, Education Writer
Leslie Moriarty, Environment/Medical Editor
Stan Strick, Exec Managing Editor
Julie Muhlstein, Feature Editor
Mike Benbow, Metro Editor
Kirby Arnold, Sports Editor
Jim Muhlstein, Topics Editor

Valley Daily News
600 S Washington
Kent WA 98032-5708
206-872-6600; Fax: 206-854-1006
Circulation: 32,000; Sun: 33,000

The Daily News
770 11th Ave
Longview WA 98632-2412
360-577-2500; Fax: 360-577-2536
Circulation: 25,000

Columbia Basin Herald
813 W 3rd Ave
Moses Lake WA 98837-2008
509-765-4561; Fax: 509-765-8659
Circulation: 10,000

Skagit Valley Herald
1000 E College Way
Mount Vernon WA 98273-5624
360-424-3251; Fax: 360-428-0400
Circulation: 21,000

The Olympian
1268 Fourth Ave E
PO Box 407
Olympia WA 98507-4212
360-754-5400; Fax: 360-357-0202
Circulation: 39,000; Sun: 43,000

Virginia Painter, Arts/Entertainment Editor
Jeff Smith, Business Editor
Linda Green, City News Editor
Frieda Bush, Education Editor
Jerre Redecker, Feature Editor
Filiz Satir, Health/Medical Editor
Len Bruzzese, Managing Editor
Mike Burgess, Sports Editor

Tri-City Herald
PO Box 2608
Pasco WA 99302-2608
509-582-1500; Fax: 509-582-1510
Circulation: 40,000; Sun: 43,000

Peninsula Daily News
305 W 1st Ave
Port Angeles WA 98362-2205
360-452-2345; Fax: 360-417-3521
Circulation: 15,000; Sun: 17,800

The Evergreen
Washington State Univ
PO Box 2008 CS
Pullman WA 99165-2510
509-335-4573; Fax: 509-335-7401
Circulation: 14,000

Daily of the Univ of Washington
Univ of Washington
144 Comm Bldg Box 353720
Seattle WA 98195-0001
206-543-7666; Fax: 206-543-2345
Circulation: 18,000

The Electricity Daily
1501 Western Ave #100
Seattle WA 98101-1570
206-382-0195; Fax: 206-382-0098
Circulation: 1,000

Seattle Daily Journal of Commerce
83 Columbia St
Seattle WA 98104-1430
206-622-8272; Fax: 206-622-8416
Circulation: 7,000

Seattle Post-Intelligencer
101 Elliot Ave W
Seattle WA 98119-4220
206-448-8000; Fax: 206-448-8166
Circulation: 203,000; Sun: 504,000

Gina Hills, Arts Editor
John Marshall, Book Reviewer
John Levesque, Business Editor
Sam Sperry, City Editor
Pete McConnell, Education Editor
Rob Taylor, Environmental Editor
Cecilia Goodnow, Family Editor
Janet Grimley, Feature Editor
Tom Sietsema, Food Editor
Susan Phinney, Home Editor
Bob Schnett, National Editor
Greg Johnston, Outdoor Editor
Rita Hibbard, Political Editor
Tom Paulson, Science Editor
Susan Phinney, Society Editor
Glen Drosendahl, Sports Editor
Susan Phinney, Style Editor
Duston Harvey, Travel Editor

Seattle Times
PO Box 70
Seattle WA 98111
206-464-2111; Fax: 206-464-2261
Circulation: 239,000; Sun: 500,000

Jan Even, Arts Editor
Donn Fry, Book Editor
Rob Weisman, Business Editor
Rich Buck, Computer Editor
Bill Ristow, Education Editor
Sharon Lane, Food Editor
Warren King, Health Editor
Terry Tazioli, Lifestyle Editor
Alex MacLeod, Managing Editor
Ron Judd, Outdoor Editor
Tom Brown, Political Editor
Lee Moriwaki, Religion Editor
Bill Detrich, Science Editor
Cathy Henkel, Sports Editor
Mary Cronin, Style Editor
Jim Molnar, Travel Book Reviewer
John Macdonald, Travel Editor

Spokesman-Review
999 W Riverside
PO Box 2160
Spokane WA 99210
509-459-5413; Fax: 509-459-5482
Circulation: 110,000; Sun: 150,000

Dan Webster, Book Editor/Reviewer
Mark Hester, Business Editor
Carla Johnson, Education Editor
Jim Kershner, Entertainment Editor
Rick Bonino, Food Editor
Jeanette White, Health Editor
Mike Guifoil, Home Editor
Kathryn J DeLong, Lifestyle/Feature Editor
Chris Peck, Managing Editor
Jim Camden, Political Reporter
Chris Wille, Religion Editor
Jeff Jordan, Sports Editor
Graham Vink, Travel Editor

Sunnyside Daily Sun News
520 S 7th St
Sunnyside WA 99944-2215
509-837-4500; Fax: 509-837-6397
Circulation: 4,000

The Morning News Tribune
1950 S State St
Tacoma WA 98405-2817
206-597-8686; Fax: 206-597-8274
Circulation: 120,000; Sun: 140,000

The News Tribune
1950 S State St
Tacoma WA 98405-2817
206-597-8686; Fax: 206-597-8274
Circulation: 120,000; Sun: 140,000

Don Ruiz, Arts Editor
Don Ruiz, Book Review Editor
Chris Carson, Business Editor
Don Ruiz, Entertainment Editor
Sandi Doughton, Environmental Editor
David Zeezk, Exec Editor
Don Ruiz, Fashion Editor
Graham Fysh, Financial Editor
Gary Jasinek, Food Editor
Caroline Ullman, Health/Medical Editor
Don Ruiz, Home Editor
Robert Mottram, Outdoor Editor
Mike Gilbert, Political Editor
Steve Maynard, Religion Editor
Glen Crevier, Sports Editor
Cynthia Flash, Technology Editor
Don Ruiz, Travel Editor

The Northwest Dispatch
1108 S 11th St
Tacoma WA 98405-4017
206-272-7587; Fax: 206-272-4418
Circulation: 15,000

The Tacoma Daily Index
718 Pacific Ave
Tacoma WA 98402-5208
206-627-4853; Fax: 206-627-2253
Circulation: 1,000

Vancouver Columbian
PO Box 180
Vancouver WA 98666-0180
360-694-3391; Fax: 360-699-6033
Circulation: 52,000; Sun: 62,400

Lynn Matthews, Arts/Entertainment Editor
Roger Sullivan, Book Editor
Jen Steele, Business Editor
Julia Anderson, City Editor
Tom Vogt, Education Editor
Bob Sisson, Health/Medical Editor
Don Chandler, Lifestyle/Features Editor
Brian Willoughby, Religion Editor
Loretta Callahan, Science Editor

Walla Walla Union-Bulletin
First & Poplar Sts
PO Box 1358
Walla Walla WA 99362-1358
509-525-3300; Fax: 509-525-1232
Circulation: 16,000

Richard Clayton, Arts/Entertainment Editor
Anne Charnley, Book Editor
Rick Doyle, Managing Editor
Bob Crider, News Editor
Becky Kramer, Science/Environment Editor
Jim Buchan, Sports Editor

Wenatchee World
14 N Mission St
Wenatchee WA 98801-2250
509-663-5161; Fax: 509-663-5413
Circulation: 28,000; Sun: 32,000

Yakima Herald-Republic
114 N Fourth St (98901)
PO Box 9668
Yakima WA 98909
509-248-1251; Fax: 509-577-7767
Circulation: 41,000; Sun: 44,000

Terry Campbell, Book Review Editor
Briar Dudley, Business Editor
Spencer Hatton, City Editor
Spencer Hatton, Education Editor
Terry Campbell, Family/Food/Garden Editor
Joy Redfield, Lifestyle/Feature Editor
Kathleen Gillagan, Managing Editor
Jim Scoggins, Sports Editor
Karen Troianello, Travel Editor

WEST VIRGINIA

The Register-Herald
801 N Kanawha St
Beckley WV 25801-3822
304-255-4400; Fax: 304-256-5611
Circulation: 35,000; Sun: 35,000

Bluefield Daily Telegraph
928 Bluefield Ave
Blufield WV 24701-2744
304-327-2800; Fax: 304-327-6179
Circulation: 26,000; Sun: 28,000

Charleston Daily Mail
1001 Virginia St E
Charleston WV 25301-2816
304-348-5140; Fax: 304-348-4847
Circulation: 50,000

Susan Jones, Book Editor/Reviewer
Chris Stadelman, Business Editor
Juliann Kemp, Lifestyle/Feature Editor
David J Greenfield, Managing Editor
Don Hager, Sports Editor

Charleston Gazette
1001 Virginia St E
Charleston WV 25301-2816
304-348-5140; Fax: 304-348-1233
Circulation: 53,000; Sun: 108,000

Jim Balow, Asst City Editor
Patty Vandergrift, City Editor
Jim Haught, Editor-in-Chief
Dalmer Robinson, Food Editor
Doug Imbrogno, Lifestyle/Feature Editor
Rosalie Earle, Managing Editor
Fanny Seiler, Political Editor
Danny Wells, Sports Editor

Clarksburg Exponent
324-326 Hewes Ave
Clarksburg WV 26301
304-624-6411; Fax: 304-624-4188
Circulation: 8,000

Pam Kendall, Business Editor
Edwin Sweeney, Managing Editor
Pam Marra, Page One Editor
Darlene Taylor, Society Editor
John Miller, Sports Editor

Clarksburg Telegram
324-326 Hewes Ave
Clarksburg WV 26301
304-624-6411; Fax: 304-624-4188
Circulation: 16,000

Bob Stealey, Arts/Entertainment, Managing, News, and Political Editor
Greg Talkington, Business/Religion/Travel
Bill Byrd, Education Editor
Roseanne Hurst, Family, Food, Garden, Lifestyle, Feature, People, Society Editor

Robert Billingsley, Sports, Outdoor, and Recreation Editor

The Inter-Mountain
520 Railroad Ave
Elkins WV 26241-3861
304-636-2121; Fax: 304-636-8252
Circulation: 13,000

Times-West Virginia
Quincy & Ogden
Fairmont WV 26554
304-367-2500; Fax: 304-367-2569
Circulation: 17,000

Herald-Dispatch
946 Fifth Ave
Huntington WV 25701-2004
304-526-4000; Fax: 304-526-2857
Circulation: 42,000; Sun: 48,000

Arlinda Smith, Book Editor/Reviewer
Fran Allread, City Editor
Brenda Lucas, Food Editor
Arlinda Smith, Lifestyle Editor
Micky Johnson, Managing Editor
Dave Wellman, Sports Editor

Mineral Daily News Tribune
24 Armstrong St
Keyser WV 26726-3202
304-788-3333; Fax: 304-788-3398
Circulation: 5,000

The West Virginia Daily News
200 S Court St
Lewisburg WV 24901-1310
304-645-1206; Fax: 304-645-7104
Circulation: 5,000

The Logan Banner
435 Stratton St
Logan WV 25601-3913
304-752-6950; Fax: 304-752-1239
Circulation: 10,000; Sun: 11,000

The Morning Journal
207 W King St
Martinsburg WV 25401-3211
304-263-8931; Fax: 304-263-8058
Circulation: 18,000; Sun: 19,232

Daily Athenaeum
West Virginia Univ
284 Prospect St
Morgantown WV 26505-5021
304-293-5092; Fax: 304-293-6857
Circulation: 15,000

Dominion-Post
1251 Earl L Core Rd
Morgantown WV 26505-5881
304-292-6302; Fax: 304-291-2326
Circulation: 22,000; Sun: 28,000

Moundsville Daily Echo
715 Lafayette Ave
Moundsville WV 26041-2143
304-845-2660; Fax: 304-845-2661
Circulation: 5,000

The Parkersburg News
519 Juliana St
Parkersburg WV 26101-5135
304-485-1891; Fax: 304-422-7134
Circulation: 34,000; Sun: 43,000

The Parkersburg Sentinel
519 Juliana St
Parkersburg WV 26101-5135
304-485-1891; Fax: 304-422-7134
Circulation: 14,000

Point Pleasant Register
200 Main St
Point Pleasant WV 25550-1030
304-675-1333; Fax: 304-675-5234
Circulation: 6,000

Weirton Daily Times
114 Lee Ave
Weirton WV 26062-4619
304-748-0606; Fax: 304-748-2202
irculation: 8,000; Sun: 9,000

The Welch Daily News
125 Wyoming St
Welch WV 24801-2220
304-436-3144; Fax: 304-436-3146
Circulation: 6,000

Intelligencer
1500 Main St
Wheeling WV 26003
304-233-0100; Fax: 304-232-5718
Circulation: 24,000

Bob Kelly, Managing Editor

Wheeling News Register
1500 Main St
Wheeling WV 26003
304-233-0100; Fax: 304-233-0327
Circulation: 24,000; Sun: 65,000

Margaret Beltz, Book Review Editor
Judy Tarowsky, Lifestyle/Family Editor
Mike Myer, Managing Editor
Nick Bedway, Sports Editor

Williamson Daily News
100 E 3rd Ave
Williamson WV 25661-3620
304-235-4242; Fax: 304-235-0730
Circulation: 12,000

WISCONSIN

Antigo Daily Journal
612 Superior St
Antigo WI 54409-2049
715-623-4191; Fax: 715-623-4193
Circulation: 7,000

Appleton Post Cresent
306 W Washington St
PO Box 59
Appleton WI 54912
414-733-4411; Fax: 414-733-1945
Circulation: 60,000; Sun: 70,000

Ed Berthiaume, Arts/Entertainment Editor
Maureen Blaney, Book Editor
Arlen Boardman, Business Editor
Maija Penikis, Education Editor
Ed Berthiaume, Lifestyle/Feature Editor
Bill Knutson, Managing Editor
Dan Flannery, News Editor
Maija Penikis, Religion Editor
Larry Gallup, Sports Editor
Myrna Collins, Travel Editor

The Daily Press
122 W 3rd St
Ashland WI 54806-1620
715-682-2313; Fax: 715-682-4699
Circulation: 8,000

News Republic
219 1st St
Baraboo WI 53913-2526
608-356-4808; Fax: 608-356-0344
Circulation: 4,000; Sun: 4,800

Daily Citizen
805 Park Ave
Beaver Dam WI 53916-2205
414-887-0321; Fax: 414-887-3137
Circulation: 12,000

Beloit Daily News
149 State St
Beloit WI 53511-6233
608-365-8811; Fax: 608-365-1420
Circulation: 17,000

Chippewa Herald-Telegram
321 Frenette Dr
Chippewa Falls WI 54729-3372
715-723-5515; Fax: 715-723-9644
Circulation: 8,000; Sun: 8,000

Leader-Telegram
701 S Farwell St
Eau Claire WI 54701-3831
715-833-9208; Fax: 715-833-9201
Circulation: 32,000; Sun: 42,000

Fond du Lac Reporter
33 W 2nd St
Fond du Lac WI 54935-4140
414-922-4600; Fax: 414-922-5388
Circulation: 20,000; Sun: 40,000

Daily Jefferson County Union
28 W Milwaukee Ave
Ft Atkinson WI 53538-2018
414-563-5553; Fax: 414-563-7298
Circulation: 10,000

The Green Bay News-Chronicle
Box 2467
Green Bay WI 54306-2467
414-432-2941; Fax: 414-432-8581
Circulation: 10,000; Sun: 65,000

Green Bay Press-Gazette
435 E Walnut
PO Box 19430
Green Bay WI 54307-9430
414-435-4411; Fax: 414-431-8379
Circulation: 60,000; Sun: 87,000

Warren Gerds, Arts/Entertainment Editor
Warren Gerds, Book Editor/Reviewer
Tom Content, Business Editor
Barb Uedelacker, City Editor
Lori Higgens, Education Editor
Claude Werder, Exec Editor
Jeff Ash, Family Editor
Dian Page, Food Editor
Lori Holloway, Managing Editor
Roger Schneider, Science Editor
Tony Walter, Sports Editor

The Janesville Gazette
1 South Parker Dr
Janesville WI 53545-3928
608-754-3311; Fax: 608-754-8179
Circulation: 28,000; Sun: 29,000

Kenosha News
715 58th St
Kenosha WI 53140-4136
414-657-1000; Fax: 414-657-8455
Circulation: 29,000; Sun: 31,000

La Crosse Tribune
401 N 3rd St
La Crosse WI 54601-3267
608-782-9710; Fax: 608-782-8540
Circulation: 38,000; Sun: 43,500

Badger Herald
Univ of Wisconsin
550 State St
Madison WI 53703-1011
608-257-4712; Fax: 608-257-6899
Circulation: 17,000

Daily Cardinal
Univ of Wisconsin
821 University Ave
Madison WI 53706-1412
608-262-5857; Fax: 608-262-0404
Circulation: 17,000

Madison Capital Times
1901 Fish Hatchery Rd
Madison WI 53713-1297
608-252-6400; Fax: 608-252-4445
Circulation: 24,000

Kevin Lynch, Book Editor
Jacob Stockinger, Lifestyle/Feature Editor
David Zwefel, Managing Editor
Joe Hart, Sports Editor

Wisconsin State Journal
1901 Fish Hatchery Rd
PO Box 8058
Madison WI 53708-8058
608-252-6100; Fax: 608-252-6119
Circulation: 90,000; Sun: 165,000

Brian Howell, Arts/Entertainment Editor
Phil Glende, Assignment Editor
Jennifer Sereno, Business/Political Editor
Phil Brinkman, Education Editor
Sandy Kallio, Food Editor
Cliff Behnke, Managing Editor
William Wineke, Medical/Religion Editor
Ron Seely, Science Editor
William Brophy, Sports Editor
Anita Clark, Travel Editor

Herald-Times-Reporter
902 Franklin
Manitowoc WI 54220-4514
414-684-4433; Fax: 414-684-4416
Circulation: 18,000; Sun: 18,800

Eagle Herald
1809 Dunlap Ave
Marinette WI 54143-1706
715-735-6611; Fax: 715-735-0229
Circulation: 10,000

Marshfield News-Herald
111 W 3rd St
Marshfield WI 54449-2811
715-384-3131; Fax: 715-387-4175
Circulation: 16,000

The Daily Reporter
207 E Michigan St #420
Milwaukee WI 53202-4905
414-276-0273; Fax: 414-276-8057
Circulation: 2,000

Milwaukee Journal Sentinel
333 W State St
PO Box 371
Milwaukee WI 53203-1506
414-224-2000; Fax: 414-224-2049
Circulation: 320,000

Jim Higgins, Arts Editor
Gerry Hinkley, Asst Managing Editor
Lois Blinkhorn, Book Editor
George Stanley, Business Editor
Danyel Hooker, Education Editor
Nancy Stohs, Food Editor
Heidi Reuter, Lifestyle/Feature Editor
Marty Kaiser, Managing Editor
Jo Sandin, Religion Editor
Joe Manning, Science Editor
Bill Windler, Sports Editor
Bruce Gill, State Editor
Nancy Curtis, Travel Editor

Monroe Evening Times
1065 4th Ave W
Monroe WI 53566-1318
608-328-4202; Fax: 608-328-4217
Circulation: 7,000

The Northwestern
224 State St
Oshkosh WI 54901-4839
414-235-7700; Fax: 414-235-1316
Circulation: 25,000; Sun: 28,000

Portage Daily Register
309 DeWitt St
Portage WI 53901-2113
608-742-2111; Fax: 608-742-8346
Circulation: 5,000; Sun: 7,000

The Journal Times
212 4th St
Racine WI 53403
414-634-3322; Fax: 414-634-9194
Circulation: 36,000; Sun: 37,000

Laura Summer-Coon, Business Editor
Mick Burke, Education Editor
Dave Kramer, General Information
Barb Schuetz, Lifestyle/Feature
Steve Lovejoy, News Editor
Susan Shacmanske, Sports Editor

The Daily News
314 Courtney St
Rhinelander WI 54501-3355
715-365-6397; Fax: 715-365-6367
Circulation: 7,000; Sun: 7,500

Shawano Leader
1464 E Green Bay St
Shawano WI 54166-2258
715-526-2121; Fax: 715-524-3941
Circulation: 7,000; Sun: 7,000

The Sheboygan Press
632 Center Ave
Sheboygan WI 53081-4621
414-457-7711; Fax: 414-457-0178
Circulation: 27,000; Sun: 29,000

Stevens Point Journal
1200 3rd Court
Stevens Point WI 54481-2855
715-344-6100; Fax: 715-344-7229
Circulation: 15,000

The Daily Telegram
1226 Ogden Ave
Superior WI 54880-1516
715-394-4411; Fax: 715-394-9404
Circulation: 11,000

Watertown Daily Times
,113-115 W Main St
Watertown WI 53094-7623
414-261-4949; Fax: 414-261-5102
Circulation: 10,000

Waukesha County Freeman
801 N Barstow St
Waukesha WI 53186-4801
414-542-2501; Fax: 414-542-6082
Circulation: 24,000

The Wausau Daily Herald
800 Scott St
Wausau WI 54403-4951
715-842-2101; Fax: 715-848-9360
Circulation: 26,000; Sun: 32,000

West Bend Daily News
100 S 6th Ave
West Bend WI 53095-3309
414-338-0622; Fax: 414-338-1984
Circulation: 11,000

Daily Tribune
220 1st Ave S
Wisconsin Rapids WI 54495-4154
715-423-7200; Fax: 715-421-1545
Circulation: 14,000

WYOMING

Casper Star Tribune
PO Box 80
Casper WY 82602
307-266-0500; Fax: 307-266-0568
Circulation: 36,000

Dan Whipple, Book Editor
Tom Morton, Business Editor
Dan Whipple, Education Editor
Ann McKinnon, Managing Editor
Tom Rea, News City Editor

Wyoming Eagle
702 W Lincolnway
Cheyenne WY 82001-4359
307-634-3361; Fax: 307-728-7163
Circulation: 17,000; Sun: 20,431

Melissa Jones, Book/Lifestyle Editor
Mary Woolsey, Editor
C J Putnam, Family/Food/Garden Editor
Ken Pompanio, Sports Editor

News-Record
1201 W 2nd St
Gillette WY 82716-3301
307-682-9306; Fax: 307-686-9306
Circulation: 7,000

The Branding Iron
Univ of Wyoming
Box 4238 University Sta
Laramie WY 82071-4238
307-766-6190; Fax: 307-766-4027
Circulation: 8,000

Laramie Daily Boomerang
314 S 4th St
Laramie WY 82070-3702
307-742-2178; Fax: 307-721-2973
Circulation: 8,000; Sun: 8,200

Rawlins Daily Times
6th & Buffalo Sts
Rawlins WY 82301
307-324-3411; Fax: 307-324-2797
Circulation: 4,000

The Riverton Ranger
421 E Main St
Riverton WY 82501-4438
307-856-2244; Fax: 307-856-0189
Circulation: 7,000

Daily Rocket-Miner
215 D St
Rock Springs WY 82901-6234
307-362-3736; Fax: 307-382-2763
Circulation: 9,000

The Sheridan Press
144 Grinnell St
Sheridan WY 82801-3933
307-672-2431; Fax: 307-672-7950
Circulation: 7,000

Northern Wyoming Daily News
201 N 8th St
Worland WY 82401-2614
307-347-3241; Fax: 307-347-4267
Circulation: 4,000

CANADA

ALBERTA

Calgary Herald
215 16th St SE
PO Box 2400 Sta M
Calgary AB Canada T2P 0W8
403-235-7100; Fax: 403-235-7379
Circulation: 137,000; Sun: 139,607

Ken McGoogan, Book Editor
Ken Hull, Business Editor
Ron Nowell, City Editor
Crosbie Cotton, Editor
Al Rach, Entertainment Editor
Vicki Barnett, Environmental Editor
Beth Burgess, Fashion, Home Editor/Special Section, Garden Editor
Cinny Willet, Food Editor
Steve Roberts, Managing Editor
Gordon Legge, Religion Editor
Mark Lowey, Science Editor
Mark Trembley, Sports Editor
Debrah Cummings, Travel Editor

Calgary Sun
2615 12th St NE
Calgary AB Canada T2E 7W9
403-250-4200; Fax: 403-291-4116
Circulation: 90,000; Sun: 97,000

Geoffrey Scotton, Business Editor
Bob Poole, Editor-in-Chief
David Vietch, Entertainment Editor
Lescia Corbella, Fashion Editor
Willie Fitzpatrick, Food Editor
Liscia Corbella, Lifestyle Editor
Chris Nelson, Managing/Book Editor
Martin Hudson, News Editor
Kit Poole, Special Sections Editor
Bill Davidson, Sports Editor
Roy Clancy, Sunday Editor
Jennifer Worley, Travel Editor

Edmonton Journal
10006 101st St
PO Box 2421
Edmonton AB Canada T5J 2S6
403-429-5100; Fax: 403-429-5500
Circulation: 171,000; Sun: 156,000

Bob Remington, Arts/Entertainment Editor
Gordon Morash, Book Editor
Peter Collum, Business Editor
Barb Wilkinson, Lifestyle/Feature Editor
Sheila Pratt, Managing Editor
Wayne Moriarty, Sports Editor

Edmonton Sun
4990 92 Ave
Edmonton AB Canada T6B 3A1
403-468-0100; Fax: 403-468-0139
Circulation: 90,000

Jeff Craig, Arts/Entertainment Editor
Tom Elsworthy, Book/Feature Editor
Dan Healing, Business Editor
Erik Floren, City Editor
Tim Leriche, Education Editor
Philip Joy, Food Editor
Jeff Craig, Lifestyle Editor
Donna Harker, News Editor
Scott Haskins, Sports Editor
Guy Demarnio, Travel Editor

Fort McMurray Today
Darrell Skidnuk, Managing Editor
Bag 4008
8550 Franklin Ave
Ft McMurray AB Canada T9H 3G1
403-743-8186; Fax: 403-790-1006
Circulation: 9,000

Daily Herald Tribune
10604 - 100 St Bag 3000
Grande Prairie AB Canada T8V 6V4
403-532-1110; Fax: 403-532-2120
Circulation: 8,000

Don Moon, City Editor
David Laffner, Managing Editor
Jeff McCoshen, Sports Editor

Lethbridge Herald
504 - 7th St S
Lethbridge AB Canada T1J 3Z7
403-328-4411; Fax: 403-328-4536
Circulation: 28,000

Gord Smiley, Business Editor
Sherry Gallant, Education Editor
Trish Brayne, Lifestyle Editor
Bill Whitelow, Managing Editor
Leona Flim, Religion Editor
Randy Jensen, Sports Editor

Medicine Hat News
3257 Dunmore Rd SE
Medicine Hat AB Canada T1A 7E6
403-527-6029
Circulation: 14,000

Alan Poirier, Asst Editor
Angela Stubbs, Lifestyle Editor
Gordon Wright, Managing Editor

Red Deer Advocate
2950 Bremner Ave
PO Bag 5200
Red Deer AB Canada T4N 5G3
403-343-2400; Fax: 403-341-6560
Circulation: 21,000; Sun: 23,000

Penny Caster, Arts/Entertainment Reporter
Pat Roche, Business Editor
Lana Michelin, Health/Medical Reporter
Joe McLaughlin, Managing Editor

BRITISH COLUMBIA

Cranbrook Daily Townsman
822 Cranbrook St N
Cranbrook BC Canada V1C 3R9
604-426-5201; Fax: 604-426-5003
Circulation: 4,000

David Sands, Editor

Peace River Block News
901 100th Ave
Dawson Creek BC Canada V1G 1W2
604-782-4888; Fax: 604-782-6770
Circulation: 2,000

Jeremy Hainsworth, Managing Editor

Alaska Highway News
9916 98th St
Fort St John BC Canada V1J 3T8
604-785-5631; Fax: 604-785-3522
Circulation: 32,000

Janelle Lake, Editor

Kamloops Daily News
393 Seymour St
Kamloops BC Canada V2C 6P6
604-372-2331; Fax: 604-374-3884
Circulation: 22,000

Mel Rothenburger, Editor

The Daily Courier
550 Doyle Ave
Kelowna BC Canada V1Y 7V1
604-762-4445; Fax: 604-762-3866
Circulation: 22,000

Andre Wettjen, Arts/Entertainment Editor
Pat Bulmer, Environmental Editor
Karen Maltby, Family Editor
Karen Maltby, Food Editor
Karen Maltby, Garden Editor
Andre Wettjen, Lifestyle/Feature Editor
Al Hogan, Managing Editor
Lorne White, Sports Editor

Kimberley Daily Bulletin
335 Spokane St
Kimberley BC Canada V1A 1Y9
604-427-5333; Fax: 604-427-5336
Circulation: 25,000

Christalee Douan, Editor

Nelson Daily News
266 Baker St
Nelson BC Canada V1L 4H3
604-352-3552; Fax: 604-352-2418
Vern Shaull, Publisher
Circulation: 5,000

David Howe, Managing Editor

Penticton Herald
186 Nanaimo Ave W
Penticton BC Canada V2A 1N4
604-492-4002; Fax: 604-492-2403
Circulation: 11,000

John Moorehouse, Business Editor
John Moorehouse, City Editor
John Moorehouse, Education Editor
Dave Duncan, Family Editor
Dave Duncan, Food Editor
Dave Duncan, Garden Editor
Dave Duncan, Health/Medical Editor
Dave Duncan, Lifestyle/Feature Editor
Mike Turner, Managing Editor
Dave Crompton, Sports Editor

Alberni Valley Times
4918 Napier St
Port Alberni BC Canada V9Y 7N1
604-723-8171; Fax: 604-723-0586
Circulation: 7,000

Rob Diotte, Editor

Prince George Citizen
PO Box 5700
Prince George BC Canada V2L 5K9
604-562-2441; Fax: 604-562-7453
Circulation: 22,000

Mark Allan, City Editor
Roy Nagel, Editor-in-Chief

Daily News
801 W 2nd Ave
Prince Rupert BC Canada V8J 1H6
604-624-6781; Fax: 604-624-2851
Send all info to Scott
Circulation: N/A

Scott Crowson, Managing Editor

Trail Times
1163 Cedar Ave
Trail BC Canada V1R 4B8
604-368-8551; Fax: 604-368-8550
Circulation: 7,000

Nancy Rode, Arts/Entertainment
   ood/Garden, Health/Medical,
   Lifestyle/Family, People/Society Editor
Tracy Konshuk, Business, Managing, and
   News Editor
Ray Masleck, Education Editor
Guy Bertrand, Sports Editor

Vancouver Province
2250 Granville St
Vancouver BC Canada V6H 3G2
604-732-2222; Fax: 604-732-2720
Circulation: 491,000; Sun: 460,000

Peter Clough, Arts/Entertainment Editor
Jarvis Whitney, Book Review Editor
Lorne Smith, Business Editor
Fabian Dawson, City Editor
Pete Clough, Lifestyle/Feature Editor
Neil Graham, Managing Editor
Lowell Ullrich, Sports Editor
Joseph Kula, Travel Editor

Vancouver Sun
2250 Granville St
Vancouver BC Canada V6H 3G2
604-732-2121; Fax: 604-732-2323
Circulation: 460,000; Sun: 550,000

Bart Jackson, Arts/Entertainment Editor
Graham Rockingham, Assignment Editor
Mark Andrews, Book Editor
Gerald Prosalendis, Business Editor
Gary Mason, City Desk
Valerie Casselton, FYI Editor
Rebecca Wigod, Health/Medical Editor
Steve Whysall, Home Editor
Shelley Fralic, Managing Editor
Douglas Todd, Religion Reporter
Brad Ziemer, Sports Editor
Miquel Moya, Travel Editor

Vernon Daily News
Thompson Newspaper
4301 -27th St
Vernon BC Canada Z1T 4Y5
604-545-0671; Fax: 604-545-7193
Send all info to Newsroom
Circulation: 8,000

Bill McIntyre, Managing Editor

Times-Colonist
2621 Douglas
PO Box 300
Victoria BC Canada V8W 2N4
604-380-5211; Fax: 604-380-5353
Circulation: 80,000

Liz Pogue, Arts/Entertainment Editor
Norman Gidney, Business Editor
Jack Knox, City Desk
Denise Helm, Education Editor
Carolyn Heiman, Food Editor
Helen Chestnut, Garden Editor
Jerry Young, Health/Medical Editor
Carolyn Heiman, Lifestyle/Feature Editor
David Brown, Managing Editor
Stan Cooper, Religion Editor
Patrick Murphy, Science Editor
Dave Senick, Sports Editor
Ron Joiner, Travel Editor

MANITOBA

Brandon Sun
501 Rosser Ave
Brandon MB Canada R7A 0K4
204-727-2451; Fax: 204-727-0385
Circulation: 20,000

Ken Coleman, Arts/Entertainment Editor
Jeffrey Lewis, Business Editor
Ken Coleman, Lifestyle/Feature Editor
Brian Marshall, Managing Editor
Mike Jones, Sports Editor

Flin Flon Reminder
10 N Ave
Flin Flon MB Canada R8A 0T2
204-687-3454; Fax: 204-687-4473
Circulation: 4,000

Rich Billy, Editor
Sharon Salthammer, Lifestyle/Feature
   Editor

Daily Graphic
PO Box 130
Portage La Prairie MB Canada R1N 3B4
204-857-3427; Fax: 204-239-1270
Circulation: 5,000

Simon Blake, Editor

Winnipeg Free Press
1355 Mt Ave
Winnipeg MB Canada R2X 3B6
204-697-7292; Fax: 204-697-7412
Circulation: 170,000; Sun: 155,000

Morley Walker, Book Review Editor
John Douglas, Business Editor
Maureen Fitzhenry, City Editor/Lifestyle
Aldo Santin, Education Editor
Morley Walker, Entertainment Editor
Duncan McMonagle, Managing Editor
Julian Rachey, Sports Editor
Mike Ward, Travel Writer

Winnipeg Sun
1700 Church Ave
Winnipeg MB Canada R2X 3A2
204-694-2022; Fax: 204-632-8709
Circulation: 45,000; Sun: 59,500

Ross McClennan, City Editor
Jim Kendle, Lifestyle/Feature Editor
Pat Doyle, Sports Editor

NEW BRUNSWICK

Daily Gleaner
PO Box 3370
Fredericton NB Canada E3B 5A2
506-452-6671; Fax: 506-452-7405
Circulation: 33,000

Sterling Kneebone, Arts/Entertainment
   Editor
Christy English, Book Editor
Anne Mooers, Business Editor
Kathy Jenkins, Education Editor
Christy English, Food Editor
Bill Witcomb, Managing News Editor
Forrest Orser, Political Editor
Sterling Kneebone, Religion Editor
Dave Ritchie, Sports Editor
Kathy Jenkins, Travel/City Editor

Telegraph-Journal/Times-Globe
210 Crown & Union Sts
PO Box 2350
St John NB Canada E2L 3V8
506-632-8888; Fax: 506-648-2652
Circulation: 30,000

Douglas Hughes, Arts/Entertainment
   Editor
John Morrissey, Business Editor
Darlene Godfrey, Lifestyle/Feature Editor
Scott Anderson, Managing Editor
Peter McGuire, Sports Editor
Mike Mullen, Religion Editor

NEW FOUNDLAND

Western Star
PO Box 460
Corner Brook NF Canada A2H 6E7
709-634-4348; Fax: 709-634-9824
Circulation: 13,000

Don Bradshaw, Arts/Entertainment Editor
Ray Sweetapple, Business Editor
Connie Murley, Family Editor
Connie Murley, Food Editor
Connie Murley, Garden Editor
Connie Murley, Health/Medical Editor
Connie Murley, Lifestyle/Feature Editor
Richard Williams, Managing Editor
Connie Murley, Religion Editor
Ray Sweetapple, Science Editor
Don Bradshaw, Sports Editor

Evening Telegram
Columbus Dr
PO Box 5970
St John's NF Canada A1C 5X7
709-364-6300; Fax: 709-364-3939
Circulation: 40,000; Sun: 65,000

Pat Doyle, Business Editor
Ted Warren, City Editor
Deanna Stokes-Sullivan, Education Editor
Lynn Brater, Family Editor
Peter Jackson, Garden Editor
Tray Barron, Health/Medical Editor
Joe Walsh, Managing Editor
Craig Jackson, Political Editor
Robin Short, Sports Editor

ONTARIO

Barrie Examiner
PO Box 370
Barrie ON Canada L4M 4T6
705-726-6537; Fax: 705-726-7245
Circulation: 14,000

Wayne Doyle, Arts/Entertainment Editor
Donna Danyluck, Book Editor
Donna Danyluck, Food Editor
Margaret Bruineman, Health Editor
Donna Danyluck, Lifestyle/Feature Editor
Mike Beaudin, Managing Editor
Steve Hardy, Sports Editor

Belleville Intelligencer
PO Box 5600
Belleville ON Canada K8N 5C7
613-962-9171; Fax: 613-962-9652
Circulation: 18,000

Jack Evans, Arts/Entertainment Editor

Chris Mallette, Book Editor
Jack Evans, Business Editor
Henry Bury, Education Editor
Linda O'Connor, Food Editor
Linda O'Connor, Lifestyle/Feature Editor
Nick Palmer, Managing Editor
Chris Mallette, Political Editor
Ady Voss, Sports Editor

The Expositor
53 Dalhousie St
Brantford ON Canada N3T 5S8
519-756-2020; Fax: 519-756-9481
Circulation: 32,000

Dennis Marcella, Arts/Entertainment Editor
Dennis Marcella, Book Editor
Mary Ann Davies, Lifestyle/Feature Editor
David Schultz, Managing Editor
Peter Fitzpatrick, Political Editor
Editor O'Leary, Sports Editor

Brockville Recorder & Times
Perry Beverley, Editor
23 King St W
PO Box 10
Brockville ON Canada K6V 5T8
613-342-4441; Fax: 613-342-4456
Circulation: 17,000

Cambridge Reporter
26 Ainslie St S
Box 1510
Cambridge ON Canada N1R 5T2
519-621-3810; Fax: 519-621-8239
Circulation: 15,000

Gordon Paul, Business Editor
Clyde Warrington, City Editor
Cheryl Long, Lifestyle/Feature Editor
Christina Jonas, Managing Editor
Brent Long, Sports Editor

Daily News
PO Box 2007
Chatham ON Canada N7M 5M6
519-354-2000; Fax: 519-436-0949
Circulation: 17,000

Randy Coote, Arts/Entertainment Editor
Randy Coote, Book Editor
Rod Hilts, Business Editor
Bill Reddick, Food Editor
Bill Reddick, Health/Medical Editor
Bill Reddick, Lifestyle/Feature Editor
Jim Blake, Managing Editor
Mike Bennett, Sports Editor

Cobourg Daily Star
415 King St W
PO Box 400
Cobourg ON Canada K9A 4L1
905-372-0131; Fax: 905-372-4966
All info goes to J T
Circulation: 6,000

J T Grossmith, Editor

Cornwall Standard-Freeholder
44 Pitt St
Cornwall ON Canada K6J 3P3
613-933-3160; Fax: 613-933-3664
Circulation: 19,000

Alf Lafave, Book Editor
Claude Laroche, Business Editor
Claudia Peel, Food Editor
Claudia Peel, Lifestyle/Feature Editor
Craig Elson, Managing Editor
Craig Elson, News Editor
Claude Laroche, Political Editor

Guelph Mercury
8 - 14 McDonnell St
Guelph ON Canada N1H 6P7
519-822-4310; Fax: 519-767-1681
Circulation: 17,000

Ed Cassavoy, Managing Editor

Hamilton Spectator
44 Frid St
Hamilton ON Canada L8N 3G3
905-526-3333; Fax: 905-521-8986
Circulation: 140,000

Dan Kislenko, Book Editor
Jill Morison, Book Editor
Steve McNeil, Business Editor
Steve Buist, District News Editor
Christine Cox, Education Editor
Suzanne Bouriet, Food Editor
Michelle Steeves, Lifestyle Editor
John Gibson, Managing Editor
Dana Robbins, Metro News Editor
Casey Korstan, Religion Editor
Tim Doyle, Sports Editor
Dan Kislenko, Travel Editor

Daily Miner & News
33 Main St
PO Box 1620
Kenora ON Canada P9N 3X7
807-468-5555; Fax: 807-468-4318
Circulation: 5,000

Ruth Bowiec, Book Editor
Ruth Bowiec, Lifestyle/Feature Editor
Fred Rinne, Managing Editor/News Editor

Kingston Whig-Standard
306 King St
Kingston ON Canada K7L 4Z7
613-544-5000; Fax: 613-530-4118
Circulation: 36,000

Tim Gordauier, Arts/Entertainment Editor
Lynn Messerschmidt, Associate Editor
Tim Gordauier, Book Editor
Bill Reid, Business Editor
Lynn Messerschmidt, Managing Editor
Tim Gordauier, Sports Editor

The Record
225 Fairway Rd S
Kitchner ON Canada N2G 4E5
519-894-2231; Fax: 519-894-3829
Circulation: 74,000

Philip Bast, Art/Entertainment Editor
Darach MacDonald, Book Editor
Ian Darling, Business Editor
Carol Jankowski, Food Editor
Kevin Crowley, Home Editor
Carol Jankowski, Lifestyle/Feature Editor
Don McCurdy, Managing Editor
John Harder, News Editor
Donna Shea, Religion Editor
Micky Mowbray, Sports Editor
Malcom Aird, Travel Editor

Lindsay Daily Post
Joe Hornyak, Managing Editor
Jamie Milne, Publisher
15 William St N
Lindsay ON Canada K9V 3Z8
705-324-2114; Fax: 705-324-0174
Circulation: 10,000

London Free Press
369 York St
PO Box 2280
London ON Canada N6A 4G1
519-679-1111; Fax: 519-667-4528
Circulation: 124,000; Sun: 144,000

Mary Nesbitt, Book Editor
Norman DeBona, Education Writer
Tony Pembridge, Executive Editor
Mary Jane Egan, Health/Medical Editor
Clare Dear, Home Editor
Tom Ruscitti, Labor Editor
Tess Kalinowski, Lifestyle Editor
Tess Kalinowski, Our Times Editor
Peter Geigen-Miller, Science Editor
James Reaney, Sports Editor
Doug English, Travel Editor

Niagara Falls Review
4801 Valley Way
Niagara Falls ON Canada L2E 6T6
905-358-5711; Fax: 905-374-0461
Circulation: 24,000

Steven Fields, City Editor
Leigh Williams, Lifestyle/Feature Editor
Michael Brown, Managing Editor
Dave Claydon, News Editor
Dave Rigby, Sports Editor
Leigh Williams, Travel Editor

North Bay Nugget
259 Worthington St W (P1B 3B5)
PO Box 570
North Bay ON Canada P1B 8J6
705-472-3200; Fax: 705-472-5128
Circulation: 25,000

Bruce Cowan, City Editor
Marlene Horner, Lifestyle/Feature Editor
Dave McClellan, Managing Editor
Gary Hogg, Week-End Editor

Daily Packet & Times
31 Colborne St E
PO Box 220
Orillia ON Canada L3V 6J5
705-325-1355; Fax: 705-325-7691
Circulation: 11,000

Randy Richman, City Editor
Joella Sidhu, Lifestyle/Feature Editor
Jeff Day, Managing Editor

The Sun Times
PO Box 200
Owen Sound ON Canada N4K 5P2
519-376-2250; Fax: 519-376-7190
Circulation: 25,000

Dan Harrison, Business Editor
Scott Dunn, Education Editor
Lise Thorbjornsen, Food Editor
Lise Thorbjornsen, Garden Editor
Lise Thorbjornsen, Health/Medical Editor
Jim Merriam, Managing Editor
Dan Harrison, News Editor
Dan Hanson, Sports Editor

The Examiner
400 Water St
PO Box 3890
Peterborough ON Canada K9J 8L4
705-745-4641; Fax: 705-743-4581
Circulation: 27,000

Scott Whalen, Arts/Entertainment Editor
Heather Dolman, Business Editor
John Driscoll, Education Editor
Janet Baal, Family Editor

Janet Baal, Food Editor
Jim Hendry, Health/Medical Editor
Janet Baal, Home Editor
E N Arnold, Managing Editor
Jim Hendry, News Editor
Janet Baal, People/Society Editor
Jim Hendry, Political Editor
Bob Seaver, Sports Editor

Evening Guide
PO Box 296
Port Hope ON Canada L1A 3W4
905-885-2471; Fax: 905-885-7442
Circulation: 4,000

Peggy Foster, Book Editor
J T Grossmith, Editor-in-Chief
Peggy Foster, Lifestyle/Feature Editor
Katherine Sedgwick, Managing Editor
Brian McNair, Sports Editor

Observer
140 S Front St
Sarnia ON Canada N7T 7M8
519-344-3641; Fax: 519-332-2951
Circulation: 25,000

Bruce Langer, Arts/Entertainment Editor
Bruce Langer, Book Editor
Bruce Langer, Business Editor
Brian Bolt, City Editor
Brian Bolt, Education Editor
Yvette Vanbergen, Food Editor
Yvette Vanbergen, Health/Medical Editor
Brian Bolt, Religion Editor
Brian Bolt, Science Editor
Dave Borody, Sports Editor

Sault Star
145 Old Garden River Rd
Sault St Marie ON Canada P6A 5M5
705-759-3030; Fax: 705-759-0102
Circulation: 27,000

John Halucha, Managing Editor

Simcoe Reformer
105 Donly Dr S
PO Box 370
Simcoe ON Canada N3Y 4L2
519-426-5710; Fax: 519-426-9255
Circulation: 10,000

Lisa Marr, Book Editor
Mike Bauslaugh, Business Editor
Gregg McLachlan, City Editor
Cheryl Bauslaugh, Family Editor
Lisa Marr, Food Editor
Lisa Marr, Garden Editor
Kim Novak, Managing Editor
Pete Kehoe, Sports Editor

The Standard
17 Queen St
St Catharines ON Canada L2R 5G5
905-684-7251; Fax: 905-684-6032
Circulation: 50,000

Kevin Cavanagh, Managing Editor

St Thomas Times-Journal
16 Hincks St
St Thomas ON Canada N5R 5Z2
519-631-2790; Fax: 519-631-5653
Circulation: 10,000

Amber Ogilvie, Book Reviewer
Mark Butterwick, City Editor
Ross Porter, Managing Editor

Beacon Herald
PO Box 430
Stratford ON Canada N5A 6T6
519-271-2220; Fax: 519-271-1026
Circulation: 14,000

Larke Turnbull, City Editor
Larke Turnbull, Lifestyle/Feature Editor
Ron Carson, Managing Editor
Larke Turnbull, Outdoor/Recreation Editor
Larke Turnbull, People/Society Editor
Larke Turnbull, Religion Editor
Larke Turnbull, Science Editor
John Kastner, Sports Editor

Sudbury Star
33 Mackenzie St
Sudbury ON Canada P3C 4Y1
705-674-5271; Fax: 705-674-6834
Circulation: 30,000; Sun: 30,000

Don McDonald, Book Editor
Boris Hrybinsky, Business Editor
Boris Hrybinsky, Education Editor
Lori Horner, Family Editor
Lori Horner, Food Editor
Lori Horner, Garden Editor
Lori Horner, Health/Medical Editor
Boris Hrybinsky, Managing Editor
Boris Hrybinsky, Religion Editor
Boris Hrybinsky, Science Editor
Norm Mayer, Sports Editor

Chronicle-Journal
75 S Cumberland St
Thunderbay ON Canada P7B 1A3
807-343-6200; Fax: 807-343-9409
Circulation: 30,000; Sun: 34,000

Linda Turk, Book Editor
Howard Partnoy, Business Editor
John Ayearst, City Editor
Jim Kelly, Health/Medical Editor
Colleen Baxter, Lifestyle/Feature Editor
Peter Haggert, Managing Editor
Bud Tolman, Sports Editor

The Daily Press
187 Cedar St S
PO Box 560
Timmins ON Canada P4N 7G1
705-268-5050; Fax: 705-268-7373
Circulation: 14,000

Donna Rescorla, Book Review Editor
Dave McGee, Managing Editor
Tom Perry, News Editor

The Globe & Mail
444 Front St W
Toronto ON Canada M5V 2S9
416-585-5000; Fax: 416-585-5085
Circulation: 330,000

Kathryn Ashenberg, Arts/Entertainment Editor
Peggy Wente, Business Editor
William Thorsell, Editor-in-Chief
Jennifer Lewington, Education Editor
Robert Matas, Environmental Bus Editor
Joanne Cates, Food Editor
Paul Taylor, Health Editor
Stephen Strauss, Science Editor
David Langford, Sports Editor
Les Buhasz, Travel Editor

Toronto Star
1 Yonge St
Toronto ON Canada M5E 1E6
416-367-2000; Fax: 416-869-4328
Circulation: 482,000; Sun: 484,156

Judy Stoffman, Book Editor
Fred Kuntz, Business Editor
David Ellis, City Editor
Rita Daly, Education Reporter
Kathleen Kenna, Entertainment Editor
Marian Kane, Food Editor
Carola Vyhnak, Lifestyle/Feature Editor
Lou Clancy, Managing Editor
Alan Christie, National Editor
Dennis Morgan, Saturday Editor
Joe Hall Sr, Science Writer
Dave Perkins, Sports Editor
Leslie Scrivener, Sr Faith & Ethics Rep
Mitch Smith, Travel Editor

Toronto Sun
333 King St E
Toronto ON Canada M5A 3X5
416-947-2222; Fax: 416-361-1205
Circulation: 300,000; Sun: 470,000

Kathy Brooks, Arts/Entertainment Editor
Heather Mallick, Book Editor
Linda Letherdale, Business Editor
Srobhan Moore, City Editor
Cynthia David, Food Editor
Sharon Lem, Health/Medical Editor
Ken Winlaw, Home Editor
Marilyn Linton, Lifestyle/Feature Editor
Scott Morrison, Sports Editor
Jill Rigby, Travel Editor

Tribune
228 E Main St
PO Box 278
Welland ON Canada L3B 5P5
905-732-2411; Fax: 905-732-4883
Send all info to Gary
Circulation: 18,000

Gary Manning, Managing Editor

Windsor Star
167 Ferry St
Windsor ON Canada N9A 4M5
519-255-5711; Fax: 519-255-5515
Circulation: 121,000

Marty Gervais, Arts/Entertainment Editor
Marty Gervais, Book Editor
Robert Meyer, Business Editor
Dave Battagello, Education Editor
Ted Whipp, Food Editor
Rob Van Nie, News Editor
Richard Brennan, Political Editor
Doug Schmidt, Science Editor
Mark Falkner, Sports Editor
Marie Claire Simmonetti, Travel Editor

The Daily Sentinel-Review
PO Box 1000
Woodstock ON Canada N4S 8A5
519-537-2341; Fax: 519-537-3049
Circulation: 10,000

George Czerny, Publisher

PRINCE EDWARD ISLAND

Guardian Evening Patriot
165 Prince St
Charlottetown PE Canada C1A 4R7
902-629-6000; Fax: 902-566-3808
Circulation: 24,000

Doug Gallant, Arts/Entertainment Editor
Ron Ryder, Book Editor
Carolyn Drake, Lifestyle/Feature Editor
Gary MacDougall, Managing Editor
Garth Hurley, Sports Editor
Jim Palmateer, Television Editor

Summerside Journal-Pioneer
4 Queen St
PO Box 2480
Summerside PE Canada C1N 4K5
902-436-2121; Fax: 902-436-0784
Circulation: 12,000

Darlene Shea, Education Editor
Gertrude Deighan, Family/Food Editor
Gertrude Deighan, Health/Medical Editor
Wayne Young, Managing Editor
Gertrude Deighan, News Editor
Gertrude Deighan, Religion Editor
Bill Semple, Sports Editor

QUEBEC

Le Nouvelliste
1920 Belle Feuille St
Trois-Riveres
G9A 5J6 PQ Canada Canada
819-376-2501; Fax: 819-376-0946
French language; Circulation: 50,000

Andre Poitras, Dir de l'information

Journal of Commerce & Commercial
Aviva Freudman, Editor--Canada Bureau
231 St Jacques St #880
Montreal PQ Canada H2Y 1M6
514-931-6611; Fax:
Circulation: 23,000

Montreal Gazette
250 St Antoine St W
Montreal PQ Canada H2Y 3R7
514-987-2222; Fax: 514-987-2399
Circulation: 276,000; Sun: 278,000

Ann Duncan, Arts/Entertainment Editor
Bryan Demchensky, Book Editor
Jim Ferrabee, Business Editor
Katherine Wallace, City Editor
Irwin Block, Education Editor
Julian Armstrong, Food Editor
Jeff Heinrich, Health Editor
Annabelle King, Home Editor
Cecelia McGuire, Lifestyle Editor
Jennifer Robinson, Political Editor
Bryan Demchensky, Science Editor
Jack Romanelli, Sports Editor
Paul Waters, Travel Editor

Montreal La Presse
7 Ouest rue St Jacques
Montreal PQ Canada H2Y 1K9
514-285-7306; Fax: 514-285-6808
Circulation: 195,000; Sun: 327,000

Roger Lendry, City Editor

Quebec Le Soleil
925 Sd-Louis Rd (CP1 547)
Quebec PQ Canada G1K 7J6
418-686-3270; Fax: 418-686-3374
Circulation: 78,000; Sun: 78,000

Jaques Samson, Arts/Entertainment Editor
Jacques Samson, Book Editor
Jilles Ouellet, Business Editor
Andre Forgues, Directeur/l'informat
Vincent Cliche, Education Editor
Jacques Samson, Food Editor
Andre Forgues, Managing Editor
Berthold Landry, News Editor
Jilles Ouellet, Science Editor
Maurice Dumars, Sports Editor
Vianney Duchesne, Travel Editor

SASKATCHEWAN

Prince Albert Daily Herald
30 Tenth St E
PO Box 550
Prince Albert SK Canada S6V 5R9
306-764-4276; Fax: 306-763-3331
Circulation: 10,000

Wayne Roznowsky, Editor

Regina Leader Post
1964 Park St
PO Box 2020
Regina SK Canada S4P 3G4
306-565-8211; Fax: 306-565-2588
Circulation: 80,000

Patrick Davitt, Arts Editor
Pat Carlson, Book Editor
Bruce Johnstone, Business Editor
Irene Seiberling, Lifestyle Editor
Gregg Drinnan, Sports Editor

The StarPhoenix
204 Fifth Ave N
Saskatoon SK Canada S7K 2P1
306-652-9200; Fax: 306-664-0437
Circulation: 60,000

Pat Macsymic, Arts/Entertainment Editor
Ted Hainworth, Book Editor
Gord Struthers, Business Editor
Cam Hutchinson, Editor
Pat Macsymic, Food Editor
Ted Hainworth, Lifestyle/Feature Editor
Doug McConachie, Sports Editor
Jens Nielson, Travel Editor

Other Newspaper Editors and Book Reviewers

There are many other newspapers that are weekly. While we can't list them all, we've listed addresses and phone numbers of several here in the United States and Canada. Besides the book editors, we've also listed the editors of other sections.

Alaska

Homer News
3482 Landing St
Homer AK 99603
907-235-7767; Fax: 907-235-4199
Circulation: 5,000

Jan O'Meara, Arts/Entertainment Editor
Jan O'Meara, Book Editor/Reviewer
Mark Turner, Lifestyle/Feature Editor
Mark Turner, News Editor
Doug Loshbaugh, Sports Editor

Arizona

Ahwatukee Foothills News
10631 S 51st St
Phoenix AZ 85044
602-496-0665; Fax: 602-893-1684
Circulation: N/A

Patty McCormack, Editor

Phoenix New Times
1201 E Jefferson (85034)
PO Box 2510
Phoenix AZ 85002
602-271-0040; Fax: 602-340-8806
Circulation: 132,000

Scott Verbout, Clubs Editor
John Mecklin, Editor
M V Moorhead, Film Reviews
Jeremy Voas, Managing Editor
David Holthouse, Music Editor
Clay McNear, Thrills Editor (Events)

Red Rock News
298 Van Deren (86336)
PO Box 619
Sedona AZ 86339
520-282-7795; Fax: 520-282-6011
Circulation: 8,000; Published on Wed & Fri

Pam Horton, Arts/Entertainment Editor
Lois Marck-Stalvey, Book Reviewer
John Conway, Business/Education Editor
John Cowan, Garden Editor
Niki Hale, Lifestyle/Feature Editor
Tom Brossart, Managing Editor
Joani Knowles, Political Editor
Jason Stevens, Sports Editor
Pam Horton, Travel Editor

The Current
325 E Broadway Rd
Tempe AZ 85282
602-967-3880; Fax: 602-275-3279
Circulation: 13,000

John Eichenauer, Contact

Tucson Weekly
201 W Cushing
Tucson AZ 85701
520-792-3630; Fax: 520-792-2096
Circulation: 40,000

Margaret Regan, Book Editor
Douglas Biggers, Editor

California

Anaheim Bulletin
1771 S Lewis St
Anaheim CA 92805-6498
714-634-1567; Fax: 714-704-3714
Circulation: 66,000

John Swanson, City Editor
Frank Mickadeit and Rick Arthur, Executive Editors

The Daily Californian
600 Eshelman
Berkeley CA 94720
510-849-2482
Circulation: 25,000; Published on Tues & Fri

East Bay Express
931 Ashvy Ave (94710)
PO Box 3198
Berkeley CA 94703
510-540-7400; Fax: 510-540-7700
Circulation: 64,000

Michael Covino, Books Editor
Brady Kahn, City Editor
John Raeside, Editor
Melanie Curry, Managing Editor
Lee Hildebrand, Music Editor

Beverly Hills Courier
8840 W Olympic Blvd
Beverly Hills CA 90211
310-278-1322; Fax: 310-271-5118
Circulation: 48,000

March Schwartz, Editor

San Mateo Weekly
824 Cowan Rd
Burlingame CA 94010
415-692-9406; Fax: 415-692-7587
Circulation: 29,000

Grant DuBois, Editor
Marc Burkhardt, Managing Editor

Chico News and Review
353 E Second St
Chico CA 95928
916-894-2300; Fax: 916-894-0143
Circulation: 60,000

Elizabeth Kieszkowski, Book Reviewer
Bob Speer, Lifestyle/Feature/News Editor

Claremont Courier
PO Box 820
Claremont CA 91711
909-621-4761
Circulation: 6,000

Patricia Yarborough, Managing Editor

Clearlake Observer American
PO Box 6328
Clearlake CA 95422
707-994-6444; Fax: 707-994-5335
Circulation: 5,000; Published Wed & Sat

Dave Stoneberg, Editor

Corona-Norco Independent
823 S Main St
Corona CA 91720
909-737-1234; Fax: 909-737-1572
Circulation: 23,000

John Orr, Managing Editor

OC Weekly
151 Kalmus Dr #H10
Costa Mesa CA 92626
714-708-8400; Fax: 714-708-8410
Circulation: 50,000

Will Swaim, Editor

Cupertino Courier
20465 Silverado Ave
Cupertino CA 95014
408-255-7500; Fax: 408-252-3381
Circulation: 18,000

Mike DeGive, Editor

Desert Sentinel
PO Box 338
Desert Hot Springs CA 92240
619-329-1411; Fax: 619-329-3860
Circulation: 8,000

John Waters, Editor

Imperial Valley Press
205 N 8th St
PO Box 2770
El Centro CA 92244
619-352-2211; Fax: 619-353-3003
Circulation: 19,000

Don Quinn, Arts/Entertainment Editor
Don Quinn, Book Editor/Reviewer
Bret Kofferd, City News Editor
Susan Giller, Managing Editor

El Segundo Herald
312 E Imperial Ave
PO Box 188
El Segundo CA 90245
310-322-1830; Fax: 310-322-2787
Circulation: 15,000

Heidi Maerker, Editor

Metronews
1296 N Wishon
Fresno CA 93728
209-445-4131; Fax: 209-445-0854
Circulation: N/A

Lou Adams, Managing Editor

Orange County News
9872 Chapman Ave #108
Garden Grove CA 92641
714-530-7622; Fax: 714-530-7142
Circulation: 45,000; Published Wed & Fri

John Seymour, City Editor
Dave Roque, Editor-in-Chief

Easy Reader
832 Hermosa Ave
Hermosa Beach CA 90254
310-372-4611; Fax: 310-318-6292
Circulation: 60,000

Kevin Cody, Editor

Hollywood Citizen News
PO Box 931149
Hollywood CA 90093-1149
213-463-3400
Circulation: N/A

Robert Gilbert, Managing Editor

Irvine World News
PO Box C-19512
Irvine CA 92713-9512
714-261-2435; Fax: 714-261-2623
Circulation: 48,000

Peggy Blizzard, Arts/Entertainment Editor
Chuck Loos, Business/Religion Editor
Patrick Larkin, Education Editor
Don Dennis, Health/Science Editor
Don Dennis, Managing Editor
Chuck Loos, Political Editor
Tim Burt, Sports Editor

La Jolla Light
450 Pearl St
PO Box 1927
La Jolla CA 92038
619-459-4201; Fax: 619-459-5507
Circulation: 8,000

Pat Broderick, Business Editor
Cynthia Queen, Editor-in-Chief
Jennifer Poyen, Education Editor
Jennifer Poyen, Health/Medical Editor
Arion Collins, Managing/Religion Editor
Jeff Ferrantino, Sports Editor

Capistrano Valley News
22481 Aspan
Lake Forrest CA 92630
714-768-3631; Fax: 714-454-7354
Circulation: 9,000

Steve Silberman, Editor

Desert Mailer News
741 East Ave I
Lancaster CA 93535
805-945-8671; Fax: 805-942-6418
Circulation: 15,000

Gen Fortis, Editor

Los Altos Town Crier
Select Communications Inc
138 Main St
Los Altos CA 94022
415-948-9000; Fax: 415-948-6647
Circulation: 20,000

Bruce Barton, Editor

Civic Center NewSource
210 S Spring St
Los Angeles CA 90012
213-628-4384; Fax: 213-687-6509
Circulation: 9,000

Roger M Grace, Editor-in-Chief

Downtown News
1264 W 1st St
Los Angeles CA 90026
213-481-1448; Fax: 213-250-4617
Circulation: 47,000

Toni Page Birdsong, Calendar Editor
Jack Skelley, Managing Editor

Drama-Logue
PO Box 38771
Los Angeles CA 90038
213-464-5079
Circulation: 18,000

Faye Bordy, Editor

Los Angeles Business Journal
5700 Wilshire Blvd
Los Angeles CA 90036
213-549-5225; Fax: 213-549-5262
Circulation: 125,000

Anne Rackham, Business Editor
Tim Deady, Computer/Science Editor
Benjamin Cole, Finance
Ron Shinkman, Health Editor
Marty Ahern, Managing Editor
Doug Young, News Editor

Los Angeles Reader
The Burnside Group
5550 Wilshire Blvd #301
Los Angeles CA 90036-3889
213-965-7430; Fax: 213-933-0281
Circulation: 90,000

David Ulin, Book Editor
Andy Klein, Film Editor
Erik Himmelsbach, Managing Editor
Natalie Nichols, Music Editor
Michael Frym, Theater Editor

Los Angeles Sentinel
38 Crenshaw Blvd
Los Angeles CA 90008
213-299-3800; Fax:
Circulation: 39,000

Marshall Lowe, Editor

Los Angeles View
2342 Sawtelle Blvd
Los Angeles CA 90064
310-477-0403; Fax: 310-477-8428
Circulation: 75,000

Alex Demyanenko, Editor

Los Gatos Weekly-Times
245 Almendra Ave
Los Gatos CA 95030
408-354-3110; Fax: 408-354-3917
Circulation: 19,000

Dale Bryant, Editor

Country Almanac
855 Oak Grove #101
Menlo Park CA 94025
415-328-1600; Fax: 415-328-9670
Circulation: 21,000

Jane Knoerle, Art/Entertainment Editor
Richard Hine, Managing Editor

Pacific Sun
21 Corte Madera Ave
PO Box 5553
Mill Valley CA 94941
415-383-4500; Fax: 415-383-4159
Circulation: 43,000

Kay McNamara, Associate Editor
Elizabeth Stewart, Book Editor
Steve McNamara, Editor
Linda Xiques, Managing Editor

Orange County Business Journal
4590 Mac Arthur Blvd #100
Newport Beach CA 92660
714-833-8373; Fax: 714-833-8751
Circulation: 21,000

Jerry Sullivan, Arts/Entertainment Editor
Jerry Sullivan, Business Editor
Mike Lyster, Education Editor
Howard Fine, Environmental Editor
Anne Bannon, Feature Editor
Fifi Chal, Food Editor
Mike Lyster Adam Steinhauer,
  Health/Medical Editors
David Whiteside, Managing Editor
Peter Hund, People/Society Editor
Jerry Sullivan, Sports/Travel Editor

Palo Alto Weekly
703 High St (94302)
PO Box 1610
Palo Alto CA 94302
415-326-8210; Fax: 415-326-3928
Circulation: 50,000

Monica Hayde, Arts/Entertainment Editor
Paul Gullixson, Book Reviewer
Paul Gullixson, Managing Editor
Keith Peters, Sports Editor

Pasadena Weekly
50 S Delacey Ave #200
Pasadena CA 91105
818-584-1500; Fax: 818-795-0149
Circulation: 105,000

Bill Evans, News Editor

Book Publishing Resource Guide   Page 351

Palos Verdes Peninsula News
4010 Palos Verdes Dr N #208
PO Box 2609
Rolling Hills Est CA 90274
310-377-6877; Fax: 310-544-4322
Circulation: 18,000; Published Thurs and Sat

Frank Brown, Arts/Entertainment Editor
Nancy Forrest, Education Editor
Frank Brown, Lifestyle/Feature Editor
Alan Gafford, News Editor
Nancy Forrest, Religion Editor
Brian Arthurs, Sports Editor

Sacramento News & Review
1015 20th St
Sacramento CA 95814
916-498-1234; Fax: 916-498-7920
Circulation: 85,000

Rachel Orvino, Arts/Entertainment Editor
Nick Budnick, Business Editor
Melinda Welsh, Editor
Rachel Orvino, Education/Food Editor
Nick Budnick, Political/Sports Editor

San Diego Reader
PO Box 85803
San Diego CA 92186-5803
619-235-3000; Fax: 619-231-0489
Circulation: 134,000

Leslie Venolia, Arts/Entertainment Editor
Judith Moore, Book Reviewer
Jim Holman, Editor
Leslie Venolia, Events Editor
Eleanor Widmer, Food Editor
Matt Potter, Political Editor

San Francisco Bay Guardian
520 Hampshire St
San Francisco CA 94110-1417
415-255-3100
Circulation: 139,000

J H Tompkins, Arts Editor
Miriam Wolf, Lifestyle/Feature Editor
Tim Redmond, Managing/Political Editor

San Francisco Business Times
275 Battery St #940
San Francisco CA 94111
415-989-2522; Fax: 415-398-1895
Circulation: 15,000

Jim Gardner and Steve Symanovich,
   Managing Editors
Michael Console, News Editor

San Francisco Independent
1201 Evans Ave
San Francisco CA 94124
415-826-1100; Fax: 415-826-537
  Circulation: 500,000; Published Tues, Fri & Sun

Susan Herbert, Book Editor
Pat Christanson, Business Editor
Anita Katz, Family/Feature Editor
Anita Katz, Food/Garden Editor
Susan Herbert, Managing Editor
Joe Strupp, Political Editor
Greg Watkins, Sports Editor

SF Weekly
425 Brannan St
San Francisco CA 94107
415-541-0700; Fax: 415-777-1893
Circulation: 90,000

Dirk Olin, Editor

Metro
550 South 1st
San Jose CA 95113
408-271-3500; Fax: 408-298-0602
Circulation: 125,000

Judi Blackwell, Calendar Editor
Dan Pulerano, Main Editor
Corrine Asturias, Managing Editor
Todd Inoue, Music Critic

San Luis Obispo New Times
197 Santa Rosa St
San Luis Obispo CA 93405
805-546-8208; Fax: 805-546-8641
Circulation: 42,000

Steve Moss, Editor

Random Lengths News
1117 S Pacific Ave
San Pedro CA 90731
310-519-1442; Fax: 310-832-1000
Circulation: 30,000

J P Griscol, Editor

Santa Barbara Independent
1221 State St #200
Santa Barbara CA 93101-2616
805-965-5205; Fax: 805-965-5518
Circulation: 40,000

D J Palladino, Book Editor
Martha Sadler, City Editor
Marianne Partridge, Editor
Rebecca Moody, Entertainment Editor
Audrey Berman, Features Editor
Laurence Hauben, Food Editor
Audrey Burman, Managing Editor
Nick Welsh, News Editor

Metro Santa Cruz
111 Union St
Santa Cruz CA 95060
408-457-9000; Fax: 408-457-5828
Circulation: 30,000

Buz Bezore, Editor

Sonoma County Independent
540 Mendocino Ave
Santa Rosa CA 95401
707-527-1200; Fax: 707-527-1288
Circulation: 90,000

Greg Cahill, Editor

Coast Weekly
668 Williams Ave
Seaside CA 93955
408-394-5656; Fax: 408-394-2909
Circulation: 42,000

Chuck Thurman, Associate & Book Editor
Chuck Thurman, Editor
Bradley Zeve, Managing Editor
Jill Duman, News Editor

Santa Ynez Valley News
423 Second St
PO Box 647
Solvang CA 93463
805-688-5522; Fax: 805-688-7685
Circulation: 8,000

Pam Mowry, Arts/Entertainment Editor
Bart Ortberg, Business/Education Editor
Bart Ortberg, Health/Medical Editor
Pam Mowry, Lifestyle/Feature Editor
Bart Ortberg, News/Managing Editor
Bart Ortberg, Political/Religion Editor

St Helena Star
PO Box 346
St Helena CA 94574
707-963-2731; Fax: 707-963-8957
Circulation: 4,000

Kerry Benefield, Managing Editor

Azusa Herald Press
1210 N Azusa Canyon Rd
West Covina CA 91790
818-854-8700; Fax: 818-854-8719
Circulation: 12,000

Rick Krzyanowski, Executive Editor

The Acorn
960 S Westlake Blvd #207
Westlake Village CA 91361
805-379-0266; Fax: 805-379-2164
Circulation: 35,000

Ron Latimore, Editor

Colorado

Boulder Weekly
690 S Lashley Ln
Boulder CO 80303
303-494-5511; Fax: 303-494-2585
Circulation: 25,000

Joel Dyer, Editor

Colorado Springs Independent
121 E Pikes Peak #455
Colorado Springs CO 80903
719-577-4545; Fax: 719-577-4107
Circulation: 27,000

Kathryn Eastburn, Editor

Denver Business Journal
1700 Broadway #515
Denver CO 80290
303-837-3500; Fax: 303-837-3535
Circulation: 20,000

Henry Durboff, Editor

Up the Creek
5670 E Evans #210
Denver CO 80222
303-758-5105
Downstream Notes cover books
Circulation: N/A

Stan Janiak, Publisher/Editor

Westword
1621 18th St #150
Denver CO 80202
303-296-7744; Fax: 303-296-5416
Circulation: 110,000

Patricia Calhoun, Editor

Sentinel Newspapers
1224 Wadsworth Blvd
Lakewood CO 80215
303-239-9890; Fax: 303-239-9808
Circulation: 19,000

Ben Miller, News Editor

Connecticut

Hartford Advocate
100 Constitution Plz
Hartford CT 06106
860-548-9300; Fax: 860-548-9335
Circulation: 60,000

Russ Hoyle, Editor

New Haven Advocate
1 Long Wharf Dr
New Haven CT 06511
203-789-0010; Fax: 203-787-1418
Circulation: 55,000

Josh Mamis, Editor

Litchfield County Times
32 Main St
New Milford CT 06776
203-355-4121; Fax: 203-354-8706
Circulation: 17,000

Ken Paul, Editor

Fairfield County Weekly
One Dock St 5th Fl
Stamford CT 06902
203-406-2406
Circulation: 80,000

Lorraine Gengo, Editor

Delaware

The Dialogue
1925 Delaware Ave
PO Box 2208
Wilmington DE 19899-2208
302-573-3109; Fax: 302-573-2397
Circulation: 48,000

Robert Johnston, Editor
Daniel Medinger, General Manager
Patricia Morrison, Managing Editor

District of Columbia

Human Events
422 First St SE
Washington DC 20003-1871
202-546-0856; Fax: 202-546-9579
Circulation: 30,000

John Gizzi, Asst Political Editor
Allan Ryskind, Capitol Hill Editor
Thomas S Winter, Editor
Jennifer Rausch, Managing Editor

Roll Call: The Newspaper of Capital Hill
900 Second St NE #107
Washington DC 20002
202-289-4900; Fax: 202-289-5377
Circulation: 17,000, Published Mon & Thurs

Stacey Mason, Editor
Morton Kondracke, Exec Editor
Laurie Battaglia, Publisher

Washington City Paper
2390 Champlain St NW
Washington DC 20009
202-332-2100; Fax: 202-462-8323
Circulation: 93,000

Nicole Arthur, Arts Editor, City Lights
Nathalie Op De Beeck, Book Reviewer
David Carr, Editor
Mark Jenkins, Film Critic

Florida

Boca Monday
601 Fairway Dr
Deerfield Beach FL 33441
305-563-3311; Fax: 305-429-1207
Circulation: 2,600

Rick Hayden, Editor

The Eastsider
3115 NW 10th Ter #105
Fort Lauderdale FL 33309
305-563-3311; Fax: 305-563-4230
Circulation: 29,000

Rick Hayden, Editor

Jewish Journal-Broward
601 Fairway Pl
Deerfield FL 33441-1867
305-698-3957; Fax: 305-663-4230
Circulation: 27,000

Andrew Polin, Editor

West Boca Times
601 Fairway
Deerfield Beach FL 33441-1867
305-698-6397
Circulation: 20,000

Rick Hayden, Editor

Hi-Riser
3115 NW 10 Ter
Ft Lauderdale FL 33309
305-563-3311; Fax: 305-663-4230
Circulation: N/A

Candi Calkins, Editor

Digest
224 S Dixie Hwy
PO Box 1310
Hallandale FL 33009-0785
305-457-8029; Fax: 305-457-1284
Circulation: 45,000

Peter Bluesten, Editor
Larry Bluestein, Managing Editor

Folio Weekly
9456 Phillips Hwy #11
Jacksonville FL 32256
904-260-9770; Fax: 904-260-9773
Circulation: 35,000

Bob Snell, Editor

Bay Bulletin
Florida Today
PO Box 419000
Melbourne FL 32941-9000
407-242-3801; Fax: 407-242-6620
Circulation: 31,000

Harry McNamara, Editor

Miami New Times
330 Biscayne Blvd 10th Fl #1000
PO Box 011591
Miami FL 33132
305-372-0004; Fax: 305-579-1590
Circulation: 100,000

Jim Mullin, Editor
Tom Finkel, Managing Editor
Greg Baker, Music Editor
Michael Lewis, Editor

Pinellas News
533 4th St N
St Petersburg FL 33701
813-894-2411; Fax: 813-894-2522
Circulation: 10,000

Robert Potter, Publisher/Editor

Weekly Planet
402 Reo St #218
Tampa FL 33602
813-286-1600; Fax: 813-289-8010
Circulation: 75,000

Susan Tibbits, Managing Editor

Orlando Weekly
807 S Orlando Ave #R
Winter Park FL 32789
407-645-5888; Fax: 407-645-2547
Circulation: 50,000

Jeff Truesdell, Editor

Flagpole Magazine
112 S Foundry St
Athens GA 30603
706-549-9523; Fax: 706-548-8981
Circulation: 15,000

Pete McCommons, Editor

Georgia

Atlanta Bulletin
1655 Peachtree St NE #1102
PO Box 92095
Atlanta GA 30314
404-874-1968; Fax: 404-874-1950
Circulation: 50,000

David Smith, Business Editor
Willie Hunter, Entertainment Editor
Carl Millender, Feature Editor
Diona McKenzie, Managing Editor
David Alexander, Sports Editor

Atlanta Daily World
145 Auburn Ave NE
Atlanta GA 30335
404-659-1110
Circulation: 18,000; Published Tues, Thurs, and Sun

Portia Scott, Book Editor
Lloyd Smith, Business Editor
Della Pulliam, Education Editor
Ruth Scott, Food/ Lifestyle/Feature Editor
William Fowlkes, Health/Medical Editor
Portia Scott, Managing Editor

Creative Loafing
750 Willoughby Way NE
Atlanta GA 30312
404-688-5623; Fax: 404-522-1532
Circulation: 180,000

Tony Paris, Editor

Southern Voice
1095 Zonolite Rd (30306)
PO Box 18215
Atlanta GA 30316
404-876-1819; Fax: 404-876-2709
Circulation: 20,000

Devon Clayton, Editor
Christina Cash, Exec Editor

Decatur DeKalb News Era
739 DeKalb Industrial Way
Decatur GA 30033
404-292-3536; Fax: 404-299-3218
Circulation: 11,000

John Sell, Editor-in-Chief
Phil Hermann, Managing Editor

Hawaii

Honolulu Weekly
1200 College Walk #214
Honolulu HA 96817
808-528-1475; Fax: 808-528-3144
Circulation: 40,000

Christine Whalen, Editor

Pacific Business News
863 Halekauwila St (96813)
PO Box 833
Honolulu HI 96808
808-596-2021; Fax: 808-591-2321
Circulation: 15,000

Chuck Davis, Asst News Editor
Michelle Yamaguchi, Editor

Idaho

Boise Weekly
280 N 8th St #30
Boise ID 83702
208-344-2055; Fax: 208-342-4733
Circulation: 13,000

David Madison, Editor

Illinois

Belleville Journal
219 N Illinios
Belleville IL 62220
618-277-7000; Fax: 618-277-7018
Circulation: 36,000; Published Wed and Sat

Scott Queen, Editor

Chicago Northwest Press
4941 N Milwaukee Ave
Chicago IL 60630-2114
312-286-6100
Circulation: 60,000

Randy Erickson, Editor

Chicago Reader
11 E Illinois St
Chicago IL 60611
312-828-0350; Fax: 312-828-9926
Circulation: 137,000

Alison True, Editor
Tom Terranova, Editorial Assistant
Michael Lenehan, Exec Editor

Chicago Weekly
770 N Halsted #208
Chicago IL 60622
312-243-8786; Fax: 312-243-8802
Circulation: 64,000

Brian Hieggelke, Editor

Inside
Inside Publications
4710 N Lincoln Ave
Chicago IL 60625-2010
312-878-7334; Fax: 312-878-0959
Circulation: 48,000

Nancy Amdur, Managing Editor
Joseph Cunniff, Music Writer

NewCity
New City Communications
770 N Halsted #208
Chicago IL 60622
312-243-8786; Fax: 312-243-8802
Circulation: 65,000

Brian Hieggelke, Editor
Frank Sennett, News Editor

North Loop News
1332 N Halsted St
Chicago IL 60622
312-787-5396; Fax: 312-787-1616
Circulation: 2,000

Debby Madden, Features Editor

Spotlight Chicago
Leader Papers
6010 W Belmont Ave
Chicago IL 60634-5195
312-283-7900; Fax: 312-283-7761
Circulation: 25,000

Patrice Raia, Managing Editor

Windy City Times
Sentury Publications
970 W Montana 2nd Fl
Chicago IL 60614
312-935-1974; Fax: 312-935-1853
Circulation: 22,000

Roy De La Mar, Managing Editor
Lawrence Bommer, Theater Editor

Illinois Times
610 S 7th St
Springfield IL 62708
217-753-2226; Fax: 217-753-2281
Circulation: 33,000

Fletcher Farrar, Jr, Editor

Indiana

Bloomington Voice
3902B Old S State Rd 37
Bloomington IN 47401
812-331-0963; Fax: 812-337-3308
Circulation: 17,000

Diane Aden-Hayes, Editor

NUVO
811 E Westfield Blvd
Indianapolis IN 46220
317-254-2400; Fax: 317-254-2409
Circulation: 54,000

Harrison Ullmann, Editor

Iowa

Herald
PO Box 427
Altoona IA 50009-0427
515-967-4224;
Circulation: 3,000

Margaret Ludington, Arts/Entertainment Editor
Amy Duncan, Editor
Denise Edgington, News Editor

Herald Journal
Page County Newspapers Inc
Box 278
Clarinda IA 51632-0278
712-542-2181; Fax: 712-542-5424
Circulation: 4,000

Elaine Armstrong, Lifestyles/Features Editor
Wayne Matheny, Publisher
Heidi Lowthorp, Sports/Religion Editor

Times-Republican
205 W Jackson
PO Box 258
Corydon IA 50060-0258
515-872-1234; Fax: 515-872-1965
Circulation: 3,500

Tammy Courter, News Editor

The Decorah Journal
107 E Water St
PO Box 350
Decorah IA 52101
319-382-4221; Fax: 319-382-5949
Circulation: 6,000

Ken Eide, Advertising Manager
Patrick Maloney, Executive Editor
Rick Fromm, Managing Editor
Randy Uhl, News Editor

Cityview
The Depot at Fourth
100 Fourth St
Des Moines IA 50309
515-288-3336; Fax: 515-288-0309
Circulation: 30,000

Jeff Inman, Arts/Entertainment Editor
Pete Kotz, Editor
Steve McIntire, Film Critic
Steve McIntire, Theater Critic

Dyersville Commercial
153 First Ave E
PO Box 128
Dyersville IA 52040-1102
319-875-7131; Fax: 319-875-2279
Circulation: 4,000

Robert LeMay, Editor

Fairfield Weekly Reader
607 W Broadway #130
PO Box 2426
Fairfield IA 52556-3202
515-472-8282; Fax: 515-469-5826
Circulation: 3,000

Hilary Kurtz, Editor-in-Chief

Summit
Summit Printing Co
Box 350
Forest City IA 50436-0350
515-582-2112; Fax: 515-582-4442
Circulation: 4,000

Ann Carter, Editor

Opinion-Tribune
Landmark Comm Newspapers Inc
PO Box 191
Glenwood IA 51534-0191
712-527-3191; Fax: 712-527-3193
Circulation: 4,000

Joe Foreman, Editor

Free Press (Adair County)
Kenneth Sidoy, Managing Editor
108 E Iowa St
PO Box 148
Greenfield IA 50849-0148
515-743-6121; Fax: 515-743-6122
Circulation: 3,000

Register
Deb Werkman, Managing Editor
Register Printing Co
601 G Ave
Grundy Center IA 50638-1549
319-824-6958; Fax:
Circulation: 3,000

Hedrick Journal
Dee Emry, Managing Editor
Burdell Hensley, Sports Editor
Mother Wit Publishing Co
PO Box 215
Hedrick IA 52563-0215
515-653-2344; Fax: 515-653-4708
Circulation: 350

Ida County Courier
Beth Wolterman, News Editor
Mike Thornhill, Sports Editor
Box 249
Ida Grove IA 51445-0249
712-364-3131; Fax: 712-364-3010
Circulation: 3,000

Record-Herald/Indianola Tribune
Deb Belt, Managing Editor
Rex Troute, Sports Editor
203 W Salem Ave
PO Box 259
Indianola IA 50125-0259
515-961-2511; Fax: 515-961-4833
Circulation: 6,000

Icon
Icon Publishing
PO Box 3002
Iowa City IA 52244-3002
319-351-1531; Fax: 319-351-0255
Circulation: 30,000

Matt Hornaday, Arts/Entertainment Editor
Michelle Rubin, Managing Editor

Osceola Sentinel-Tribune
Clarke County Publishing
115 E Washington
Osceola IA 50213-2060
515-342-2131; Fax: 515-342-2060
Circulation: 4,000

Frank Morlan, Editor

Valley News Today
Valley Publications
Box 369
Shenandoah IA 51601
712-246-3097; Fax: 712-246-3099
Circulation: 4,000

Julia Dinville, News Editor
Kalani Simpson, Sports Editor

Tri-County Times
Box 237
Slater IA 50244-0237
515-685-3412
Circulation: 5,000

Sharon Rood, Arts/Entertainment Editor
Edwin Rood, Editor
Dianne Nelson, Religion Editor
Darren Tromblay, Sports Editor

Sioux City Herald
423 Broad Box 233
Story City IA 50248-1607
515-733-4318; Fax: 515-733-4319
Circulation: 2,000

Eloise Thorson, Managing Editor

News-Herald
Tama County Newspapers Inc
220 W 3rd St
Tama IA 52339-2308
515-484-2841; Fax: 515-484-5705
Circulation: 7,000

Nancy Dostal, Editor

Tipton Conservative
124 W 5th St
PO Box 271
Tipton IA 52772-0271
319-886-2131; Fax: 319-886-0271
Circulation: 5,000

Mary Wethington, Arts/Entertainment Editor
Bev Hancock, Family/People/Society
Sally Taylor, Lifestyle/Features Editor
Stuart Clark, News Editor
H E Clark, Publisher
Darren Miller, Sports Editor

Waukon Standard
15 1st St NW
Waukon IA 52172-1621
319-568-3431
Circulation: 4,000

Sherry Jenkins, Family Editor
Tom Johnson, Managing Editor
Dick Schilling, News Editor
Jeremy Troendle, Sports Editor

Franklin Sun
Hanna Publishing Co
Box 550
Winnsboro IA 71295-0550
319-435-4521; Fax: 319-435-9220
Circulation: 6,000

Leslie Young, News Editor

Madisonian
Chris Dorsey, News Editor
112 W Court Ave
Box 350
Winterset IA 50273-0350
515-462-1577; Fax: 515-462-1577
Circulation: 4,000

Ted Gorman, Managing Editor

Kansas

College Boulevard News
Sun Publications
7373 W 107th St
Overland Park KS 66212
913-381-5755; Fax: 913-381-9889
Circulation: 30,000

Liz Irwin, Managing Editor

Wichita Metro News
400 N Woodlawn #201
Wichita KS 67208
316-684-3699;
Circulation: N/A

Tom Lewis, Editor

Kentucky

Louisville Eccentric Observer
3900 Shelbyville Rd #14A
Louisville KY 40207
502-895-9770; Fax: 502-895-9779
Circulation: 35,000

John Yarmuth, Editor

Louisana

Times of Acadiana
201 Jefferson St
Lafayette LA 70502
318-237-3560; Fax: 318-233-7484
Circulation: 32,000

Richard Baudouin, Editor

Gambit Weekly
3923 Bienville St
New Orleans LA 70119
504-486-5900; Fax: 504-488-7263
Circulation: 40,000

Clancy DuBos, Executive Editor

Maryland

Baltimore City Paper
812 Park Ave
Baltimore MD 21201
410-523-2300; Fax: 410-523-2222
Circulation: 91,000

Andy Markowitz, Editor

Gaithersburg Gazette
1200 Quinee Orchard Blvd
Gaithersburg MD 20878
301-948-3120; Fax: 301-670-7183
Circulation: 250,000

Georgia McDonald, Managing Editor

Montgomery Sentinel
615 S Fredrick Ave #303
Gaithersburg MD 20877
301-417-1200; Fax: 301-417-1210
Circulation: 27,000

Margo Turner, Main Editor

Mariland Gazette
PO Box 567
Glen Burnie MD 21060-0040
410-766-3700; Fax: 410-766-7031
Circulation: 34,000; Published Wed & Sat

Robert Mosier, Managing Editor

Maine

Casco Bay Weekly
561 Congress St
Portland ME 04101
207-775-6601; Fax: 207-775-1615
Circulation: 30,000

Sarah Goodyear, Editor

Maine Times
561 Congress St
Portland ME 04101
207-828-5432; Fax: 207-828-5438
Circulation: 15,000

Doug Rooks, Editor

Massachusetts

Brookline Citizen Journal
101 N Beacon
Allston MA 02134
617-232-7000; Fax: 617-254-5081
Circulation: 12,000

David Exum, Editor

Worcester Phoenix
314 Washington St
Auburn MA 01501
508-832-9800; Fax: 508-832-5510
Circulation: 40,000

Clif Garboden, Editor

Bay State Banner
68 Fargo St #5811
Boston MA 02210-2122
617-357-4900; Fax: 617-542-7119
Circulation: 11,000

Melvin Miller, Editor
Robin Washington, Lifestyle/Feature Editor
Robin Washington, Managing Editor

Boston Phoenix
126 Brookline Ave
Boston MA 02115
617-536-5390; Fax: 617-859-8201
Circulation: 135,000

Jeffrey Gantz, Arts/Entertainment
Robert Sullivan, Book Editor/Reviewer
Peter Kadzis, Editor
Tom DeKay, Editor, Literary Section
Tim Sandler, Environmental Editor
Caroline Knepp, Family Editor
Robert Nadeau, Food Editor
Tom deKay, Lifestyle/Feature Editor
Vicki Sanders, News Editor
Caroline Knepp, People/Society Editor
Al Giordano, Political Editor

The Valley Advocate
87 School St
Hatfield MA 01038
413-247-9301; Fax: 413-247-5439
Circulation: 27,000

Dan Caccavaro, Managing Editor

North Shore Community Newspapers
PO Box 192
Ipswich MA 01938-0292
508-356-5141; Fax: 508-356-9188
Circulation: N/A

Janet MacKay Smith, Managing Editor

The Valley Optimist
Optimist Publications
13 Old South St
Northampton MA 01060
413-586-7070; Fax: 413-586-0412
Circulation: 17,000

Karen Shaffner, Arts Editor
Sarah Shoemaker, Editor-in-Chief
Ben Geman, News Editor

South Shore News
Marc Songini, Editor
65 Grove St
Rockland MA 02370-2314
617-878-5100; Fax: 617-878-1318
Circulation: 70,000

The Jewish Weekly News
99 K Mill St
PO Box 1569
Springfield MA 01101
413-739-4771; Fax: 413-739-7099
Circulation: 15,000

Mark Auerback, Arts Editor
Kenneth G White, Editor
Gail G White, Judaica Editor

Springfield Advocate
1127 Main St
Springfield MA 01103
413-781-1900; Fax: 413-781-1906
Circulation: 38,000

Dan Caccavaro, Editor

The Armenian Weekly
80 Bigelow Ave
Watertown MA 02172
617-926-3974; Fax: 617-926-1750
Circulation: 3,000

Viken Aprahamian, Editor

Worcester Magazine
172 Shrewsbury St
Worcester MA 01604
508-755-8004; Fax: 508-755-8860
Circulation: 40,000

Walter Crockett, Editor

Michigan

Metro Times
733 St Antoine
Detroit MI 48226
313-961-4060; Fax: 313-961-6598
Circulation: 100,000

Thom Jurek, Arts Editor
Desiree Cooper, Managing Editor

The Lake Country Gazette
Fen's Rim Publications
PO Box 885
Elk Rapids MI 49629-0885
616-264-6800; Fax: 616-264-6890
Circ is seasonal: winter 15,000
Frequency: 26; Circulation: 25,000

Greg Reisig, Editor

Detroit Monitor
33490 Groesbeck
Fraser MI 48026
810-296-6007; Fax: 810-296-6072
Circulation: 47,000

Horst Mann, Book Reviewer
Horst Mann, Managing Editor
George Eichorn, Sports Editor

Clarkston Reminder
United Way Blvd
50 Wayne #201
Pontiac MI 48432
810-253-9938; Fax: 810-338-4740
Circulation: 119,000

Pauline Averbach, Managing Editor

Fenton Independent
PO Box 497
Swartz Creek MI 48473
810-733-2239; Fax: 810-733-2688
Circulation: 15,000

Dennis Setter, Managing Editor

Minnesota

Ojibwe News
Native American Press
1819 Bemidji Ave
Bemidji MN 56601
218-751-1655; Fax: 218-751-0650
Circulation: 6,000

William Lawerence, Editor

Minneapolis Sun Publication
7831 E Bush Lake Rd
Bloomington MN 55439
612-831-1200; Fax: 612-896-4728
Circulation: 30,000

Yvonne Klinnert, Sr Managing Editor

City Pages
401 N Third St #550 (55401)
PO Box 59183
Minneapolis MN 55459-0183
612-375-1015; Fax: 612-372-3737
Circulation: 100,000

Will Hermes, Arts/Entertainment Editor
Will Hermes, Book Editor
Will Hermes, Music Editor
Steve Perry, News Editor

Skyway Publications
15 S 5th St #800
Minneapolis MN 55402
612-375-9222; Fax: 612-375-9208
Circulation: 55,000

Greg Erickson, Editor

Twin Cities Reader
Bibliofile
105 5th St #200
Minneapolis MN 55402
612-321-7300; Fax: 612-321-7333
Circulation: 100,000

Claude Peck, Managing Editor

Asian American Press
417 University Ave W
St Paul MN 55103
612-224-6570; Fax: 612-224-7032
Circulation: 15,000

Tom Morley, Book & TV Review Editor
Nghi Huynh, Editor

Missouri

The New Times
New Mirror Publishing
207 Westport Rd #201
Kansas City MO 64111
816-753-7880; Fax: 816-561-6252
Circulation: 50,000

Tony Allard, Art Editor
Ron Vuturo, Book Editor
Melissa Blazek, Calendar Editor
Dan Cherrington, Food Editor
C J Janovy, Managing Editor
David Cantwell, Music Editor
Steve Walker, Theater Editor

Pitch Weekly
3535 Broadway
Kansas City MO 64111
816-561-6061; Fax: 816-756-0502
Circulation: 85,000

Bruce Rodgers, Editor
Charles Cowdrick, Art Editor
Darla McFarland, Book Editor
Bruce Rodgers, Editor
D A Arneson, Food Writer
Jon Niccum, Music Editor
Terry Erbe, Theatre Editor

Wednesday Magazine
Townsend Communications Inc
20 E Gregory
Kansas City MO 64114
816-361-0616; Fax: 816-822-1856
Circulation: 34,000

David Knopf, Contact

Liberty Tribune
Townsend Communications Inc
104 N Main
Liberty MO 64068
816-781-4941; Fax: 816-781-0909
Circulation: 10,000

Angie Borgedalen, Contact

Kansas City Dispatch
Townsend Publications
PO Box 12338
North Kansas City MO 64116-0338
816-454-9660; Fax: 816-454-7523
Circulation: 58,000

Jack Miles, Assistant Editor
Sandra Swofford, Lifestyles Editor
Lynn Brown, Managing Editor
Scott Wogoman, Sports Editor

Raytown Tribune
Townsend Communications Inc
10227 E 61st St
Raytown MO 64133
816-358-6397; Fax: 816-358-5141
Circulation: 21,000

Don Ledford, Editor

Community News
5748 Helen
St Louis MO 63136
314-261-5555; Fax: 314-261-2776
Circulation: N/A

Charles Bockskopf, Editor

The Riverfront Times
Hartmann Publishing
1221 Locust St #900
St Louis MO 63103
314-231-6666; Fax: 314-231-9040
Circulation: 100,000

Cliff Froelich, Exec Editor
Saffir Ahmed, Managing Editor
Thomas Crone, Sports Editor

St Louis American
4144 Lindell Blvd
St Louis MO 63108
314-533-8000; Fax: 314-533-0038
Circulation: 65,000

Eric Clark, Managing Editor

Montana

Missoula Independent
115 South 4th W
Missoula MT 59801
406-543-6609; Fax: 406-543-4367
Circulation: 15,000

Eric Johnson, Editor

Nevada

Reno News and Review
900 W First St #102
Reno NV 89503
702-324-4440; Fax: 702-324-4572
Circulation: 25,000

R V Scheide, Editor

New Hampshire

New Hampshire Sunday News
100 William Loeb (03103)
PO Box 9555
Manchester NH 03108
603-668-4321; Fax: 603-668-0382
Circulation: 100,000

Barry Palmer, Book Editor
Bill Regan, Business Editor
Barry Palmer, Entertainment Editor
Charles Perkins, Executive Editor
Ellie Ferriter, Home Editor
Ellie Ferriter, Lifestyle Editor
Jim Linehan, Managing Editor
Dave Johnson, Sports Editor

Monadnock Ledger
20 Grove St
PO Box 36
Peterborough NH 03458-2420
603-924-7172; Fax: 603-924-3681
Circulation: 7,000

Jane Eklund, Co-Editor

New Jersey

Bellville Post
266 Liberty St
PO Box 110
Bloomfield NJ 07003
201-743-4040; Fax: 201-680-8848
Circulation: 3,300

Russell Roemmele, Editor

Bloomfield Independent Press
266 Liberty St
PO Box 110
Bloomfield NJ 07003
201-743-4040; Fax: 201-680-8848
Circulation: 8,000

Russell Roemmele, Editor

Glenridge Paper
266 Liberty St
PO Box 110
Bloomfield NJ 07003
201-743-4040; Fax: 201-680-8848
Circulation: 2,000

Russell Roemmele, Editor

Nutley Journal
266 Liberty St
PO Box 110
Bloomfield NJ 07003
201-743-4040; Fax: 201-680-8848
Circulation: 6,000

Russell Roemmele, Editor

Dateline Journal
10 Park Pl
Butler NJ 07405
201-365-3000; Fax: 201-838-1495
Circulation: 38,000; Published Wed & Sun

Nancy Rubenstein, Executive Editor
Albina Sportelli, Managing Editor

The Suburbanite
231 Herbert Ave Bldg 2
Closter NJ 07624
201-784-0266; Fax: 201-784-2592
Circulation: 50,000

David Savastano, Main Editor

Hacketstown Forum
PO Box 500
Hacketstown NJ 07840-0500
908-852-1212; Fax: 908-852-9320
Circulation: 36,000

Dan Hirshberg, Editor

Maplewood News-Record
463 Valley St
PO Box 158
Maplewood NJ 07040
201-763-0700; Fax: 201-763-2557
Circulation: 8,000

Rose Manzo, Managing Editor

Criterion News Advertiser
PO Box 4278
Metuchen NJ 08840
908-548-8300
Circulation: 45,000

William Crane, Editor

Essex Journal
Worral Publications
PO Box 849
Orange NJ 07051-0849
201-674-8000; Fax: 201-674-2038
Circulation: 40,000

Anthony Venutolo, Editor
Anthony Puglisi, Regional Editor
Worral Publications

Bergen News
PO Box 616
Palisades Park NJ 07650
201-947-5000; Fax: 201-947-6968
Circulation: 40,000

Eleanor Marra, News Editor

Suburban News
PO Box 2309
Westfield NJ 07091-2309
908-396-4500; Fax: 908-396-4770
Circulation: 130,000

Ellen Fox, Editor

New Mexico

Weekly Alibi
2118 Central Ave SE #151
Albuquerque NM 87106-4004
505-268-8111; Fax: 505-256-9651
Circulation: 37,000

Micheal Henningsen, Editor

Rio Grande Sun
238 N Railroad Ave
PO Box 790
Espanola NM 87532
505-753-2126; Fax: 505-753-2140
Circulation: 11,000

Robert Trapp, Editor/Publisher

Las Cruces Bulletin
1210 E Madrid (88001)
PO Box 637
Las Cruces NM 88004
505-524-8061
Circulation: 20,000

Stephen Klinger, Editor
Lynn Nusom, Food Editor
Cheryl Thornburg, TeenBeat Editor

Santa Fe Reporter
132 E Marcy
PO Box 2306
Santa Fe NM 87504-2306
505-988-5541; Fax: 505-988-5348
Circulation: 25,000

Tom Collins, Arts/Book Editor
Julia Goldberg, Calendar Editor
Hope Aldrich, Editor
Robert Mayer, Managing Editor

New York

Capitol District Business Review
PO Box 15081
Albany NY 12212
518-437-9855; Fax: 518-438-9219
Circulation: 8,000

Marlene Kennedy, Editor

Metroland Magazine
4 Central Ave 4th Fl
Albany NY 12210
518-463-2500; Fax: 518-463-3712
Circulation: 33,000

Stephen Leon, Editor

Afro Times
1360 Fulton St
Brooklyn NY 11216-2600
718-636-9500; Fax: 718-857-9115
Circulation: 60,000

Andre Penix-Smith, Managing Editor

Bay Ridge Paper
26 Court St
Brooklyn NY 11242
718-834-9350; Fax: 718-834-9278
Circulation: 27,000

Diane Webber, New Editor

Brooklyn Paper Publications
26 Court St
Brooklyn NY 11242
718-834-9350; Fax: 718-834-9278
Circulation: N/A

Tracy Connor, Editor

Brooklyn Spectator
8723 Third Ave
Brooklyn NY 11209
718-238-6600; Fax: 718-238-6630
Circulation: 10,000

Sarah Otey, Managing Editor
Frank Griffin, Publisher

Home Reporter
8723 Third Ave
Brooklyn NY 11209
718-238-6600; Fax: 718-238-6630
Circulation: 10,000

Sarah Otey, Managing Editor
Frank Griffin, Publisher

Jewish Press
338 Third Ave
Brooklyn NY 11215-1879
718-330-1100; Fax: 718-935-1215
Circulation: 174,000

Sholom Klass, Editor

New American
1360 Fulton St
Brooklyn NY 11216-2600
718-636-9500; Fax: 718-857-9115
Circulation: 70,000

Eleanor Branch, Managing Editor

Park Slope Paper
Editor
26 Court St
Brooklyn NY 11242
718-834-9350; Fax: 718-834-9278
Circulation: 36,000

Yankee Trader
1 Glenmere Ln
Coram NY 11727
516-331-3300; Fax: 516-331-3481
Circulation: 185,000

Caroline P Thorenz, Managing City Editor
John Sutter, Managing Editor

Queens Tribune
174-15 Horace Harding Expy
Fresh Meadows NY 11365
718-357-7400; Fax: 718-357-9417
Circulation: 146,000

David Oatss, Main Editor

Ithaca Times
109-111 N Cayuga St
Ithaca NY 14851
607-277-7000; Fax: 607-277-1012
Circulation: 20,000

Jay Wrolsted, Editor

The Herald
PO Box 537
New Paltz NY 12561
914-679-7363; Fax: 914-255-7005
Circulation: 3,500

Julie O'Corozine, Managing Editor

Downtown Resident
215 Lexington Ave 13th Fl
New York NY 10016
212-679-1850; Fax: 212-679-4886
Circulation: 50,000

Carin Smilk, Editor-in-Chief

Mid Side Resident
215 Lexington Ave 13th Fl
New York NY 10016
212-679-1850; Fax: 212-679-4886
Circulation: 50,000

Carin Smilk, Editor-in-Chief

The Militant
410 West St
New York NY 10014
212-243-6392; Fax: 212-924-6040
Circulation: 8,000

Steve Clark, Editor

New York Observer
54 E 64th St
New York NY 10021
212-755-2400; Fax: 212-688-4889
E-mail: observe@interport.net
Circulation: 50,000

Lisa Chase, Book Editor

Celia McGee, Publishing Columnist
NY Observer Publishing Columnist
320 Riverside Dr
New York NY 10025
212-755-2400; Fax: 212-961-0981

New York Press
The Puck Bldg
295 Lafayette St 9th Fl
New York NY 10012-2772
212-941-1130; Fax: 212-941-7824
Circulation: 95,000

Russ Smith, Editor
Sam Siftom, Editor
Godfrey Cheshire, Film Critic
Adam Heimlich, Listings Editor
J R Taylor, Music Writer
Jessica Willis, Music Writer

Upper East Side Resident
Carin Smilk, Editor-in-Chief
Resident Publications
215 Lexington Ave 13th Fl
New York NY 10016
212-679-1850; Fax: 212-679-4886
Circulation: 50,000

Upper West Side Resident
Resident Publications
215 Lexington Ave 13th Fl
New York NY 10016
212-679-1850; Fax: 212-679-4886
Circulation: 50,000

Carin Smilk, Editor-in-Chief

The Village Voice
36 Cooper Square
New York NY 10003-4846
212-475-3300; Fax: 212-475-8473
http://www.villagevoice.com
Circulation: 235,000

Jeff Weinstein, Arts/Entertainment Editor
Lee Smith, Book Review Department
Andy Hsiao, City Editor
Karen Durbin, Editor
Doug Simmons, Features Editor
Robert Sietsema, Food Editor
Doug Simmons, Managing Editor
Richard Goldstein, Metro Editor
Robert Hennelly, Science Editor
Jeff Klein, Sports Editor

The Villager
80 Eighth Ave
New York NY 10011
212-229-1890; Fax: 212-229-2790
Circulation: 10,000

Michael Haferman, Assistant Editor
Tom Butson, Editor

Hudson Valley Black Press
PO Box 2160
Newburg NY 12550
914-562-1313
Circulation: 32,000

Chuck Stewart, Editor/Publ

Suffolk Life
PO Box 167
Riverhead NY 11901-0101
516-369-0800
Circulation: 488,000

Lou Grasso, Managing Editor

City Newspaper
250 N Goodman St
Rochester NY 14607
716-244-3329; Fax: 716-244-1126
Circulation: 30,000

Mary Anna Towler, Editor

Syracuse New Times
1415 W Genesee St
Syracuse NY 13204
315-422-7011; Fax: 315-422-1721
Circulation: 45,000

Bill Delapp, Book Editor
Mike Greenstein, Editor-in-Chief

Southern Dutchess News
84 E Main St
Wappingers Falls NY 12590
914-297-3723; Fax: 914-297-6810
Circulation: 26,000

John Darcy, Assistant Editor
Bill Parsons, Managing Editor

Woodstock Times
Ulster Publishing
PO Box 808
Woodstock NY 12498
914-679-7363; Fax: 914-679-2841
Circulation: 9,000

Lee Reich, Columnist
Mikhail Horowitz, Cultural Czar
Parry D Teasdale, Managing Editor

North Carolina

Mountain Xpress
PO Box 144
Ashville NC 28802
704-251-1333; Fax: 704-251-1311
Circulation: 20,000

Jeff Fobes, Editor

The Independent Weekly
PO Box 2690
Durham NC 27715
919-286-1972; Fax: 919-286-4274
Circulation: 50,000

Bob Moser, Arts/Editor
Karen Mann, Calendar Editor
Gillian Floren, Editor

Times-Inquirer
1201 C Wayne Memorial Dr
Goldsboro NC 27533
919-734-5444; Fax: 919-734-0290
Circulation: 30,000

Ken Plummer, Managing Editor

Mount Olive Tribune
301 NC Hwy 55 West
PO Box 709
Mount Olive NC 28365-0709
919-658-9456; Fax: 919-658-9559
Circulation: 5,000

Steve Herring, Managing Editor

Ohio

Athens News
14 N Court St
Athens OH 45701
614-594-8219; Fax: 614-594-5695
E-mail: 71621,21@compuserv.com
Circulation: 17,000

Terry Smith, Editor

Bedford Sun Banner
Sun Newspapers
3355 Richmond Rd #171
Beachwood OH 44122
216-464-6397; Fax: 216-464-8816
Circulation: N/A

Mark Morilak, Editor

Chagrin Herald Sun
Sun Newspapers
3355 Richmond Rd #171
Beachwood OH 44122
216-464-6397; Fax: 216-464-8816
Circulation: N/A

Mary Jane Skala, Editor

Euclid Sun Journal
Sun Newspapers
3355 Richmond Rd #171
Beachwood OH 44122
216-464-6397; Fax: 216-464-8816
Circulation: 13,000

Mark Morilak, Editor

Solon Herald Sun
Sun Newspapers
3355 Richmond Rd #171
Beachwood OH 44122
216-464-6397; Fax: 216-464-8816
Circulation: 4,000

Mary Jane Skala, Editor

The Sun Messenger
Sun Newspapers
3355 Richmond Rd #171
Beachwood OH 44122
216-464-6397; Fax: 216-464-8816
Circulation: 15,000

Mark Morilak, Editor

The Sun Press
Sun Newspapers
3355 Richmond Rd #171
Beachwood OH 44122
216-524-0830; Fax: 216-464-8816
Circulation: 200,000

Joann Draus-Klein, Arts/Entertainment
   and People/Society Editor
Stan Urankar, Book, Family, Lifestyle, and
   Feature Editor
Mary Jane Skala, Editor
John Urbancich, Exec Editor
Barbara Collier, Food Editor
Susan McClure, Garden Editor

Sun Scoop Journal
Sun Newspapers
3355 Richmond Rd #171
Beachwood OH 44122
216-464-6397; Fax: 216-464-8816
Circulation: 5,000

Mark Morilak, Editor

West Geauga Sun
Sun Newspapers
3355 Richmond Rd #171
Beachwood OH 44122
216-464-6397; Fax: 216-464-8816
Circulation: 8,000

Mary Jane Skala, Editor

The News Sun
Sun Newspapers
32 Park Dr
Berea OH 44017
216-243-3725; Fax: 216-243-4905
Circulation: N/A

Linda Kinsey, Editor

Parma Sun Post
Sun Newspapers
32 Park Dr
Berea OH 44017
216-243-3725; Fax: 216-243-4905
Circulation: N/A

Linda Kinsey, Editor

The Sun Star
Sun Newspapers
32 Park Dr
Berea OH 44017
216-243-3725; Fax: 216-243-4905
Circulation: N/A

Linda Kinsey, Editor

Cincinnati CityBeat
23 E 7th St #617
Cincinnati OH 45202
513-665-4700; Fax: 513-665-4369
Circulation: 33,000

John Fox, Editor

Cincinnati Downtowner
Carri Bostian, Managing Editor
128 E Sixth St 8th Fl
Cincinnati OH 45202
513-241-9906
Circulation: 24,000

EveryBody's News
Goodwin Communications
1310 Pendleton #700
Cincinnati OH 45202
513-381-2606; Fax: 513-287-8643
Circulation: 41,000

Randy Katz, Editor

Press Community Newspapers
5552 Cheviot Rd
Cincinnati OH 45247
513-923-3111; Fax: 513-923-1806
Circulation: 250,000 (16 versions)

Nancy Daily, Managing Editor

Brooklyn Sun Journal
Sun Newspapers
5510 Cloverleaf Pky
Cleveland OH 44125
216-524-0830; Fax: 216-524-7792
Circulation: 10,000

Carol Kovach, Editor

Call & Post
1949 E 105th St
Cleveland OH 44106
216-791-7600; Fax: 216-791-6568
Circulation: 65,000

Shelly Shockley, City Editor
Kamala Bustamante, Entertainment Editor
Tuan Bustamante, Managing Editor
John Lenear, Senior Editor
Grover Creighton, Sports Editor

Cleveland Free Times
1846 Coventry Rd #100
Cleveland OH 44118
216-321-2300; Fax: 216-321-4456
Circulation: 40,000

Cindy Barber, Edutor

Cleveland Jewish News
3645 Warrensville Ctr Rd #230
Cleveland OH 44122-5294
216-991-8300; Fax: 216-991-2088
Circulation: 16,000

Cynthia Dettelbach, Editor

Garfield-Maple Sun
Sun Newspapers
5510 Cloverleaf Pky
Cleveland OH 44125
216-524-0830; Fax: 216-524-7792
Circulation: 11,000

Carol Kovach, Editor

Nordonia Hills Sun
Sun Newspapers
5510 Cloverleaf Pky
Cleveland OH 44125
216-524-0830; Fax: 216-524-7792
Circulation: N/A

Carol Kovach, Editor

The Sun Courier
Sun Newspapers
5510 Cloverleaf Pky
Cleveland OH 44125
216-524-0830; Fax: 216-524-7792
Circulation: 7,000

Carol Kovach, Editor

The Twinsburg Sun
Sun Newspapers
5510 Cloverleaf Pky
Cleveland OH 44125
216-524-0830; Fax: 216-524-7792
Circulation: 5,000

Carol Kovach, Editor

Columbus Alive
PO Box 15309
Columbus OH 43215-0309
614-221-2449; Fax: 614-221-2456
Circulation: 33,000

Sally Crane MacPhail, Editor

Columbus Guardian
400 Dublin Ave #100
Columbus OH 43215
614-469-1510; Fax: 614-469-1508

Mimi Morris, Editor

Dayton Voice
1927 N Main St
Dayton OH 45405
513-275-8855; Fax: 513-275-6056
Circulation: 24,000

Marrianne McMullen, Editor

EastSide Weekend Newsmagazine
Weekend Publications
4700 Duke Dr #130
Mason OH 45040
513-459-1711; Fax: 513-459-1722
Circulation: 50,000

Susan McHugh, Publisher

Brunswick Sun Times
Sun Newspapers
2795 Medina Rd
Medina OH 44256
216-725-1147; Fax: 216-725-2314
Circulation: 6,100

Glenn Wojciak, Editor

The Medina Sun
Sun Newspapers
2795 Medina Rd
Medina OH 44256
216-725-1147; Fax: 216-725-2314
Circulation: N/A

Glenn Wojciak, Editor

Sun Banner Pride
Sun Newspapers
2795 Medina Rd
Medina OH 44256
216-725-1147; Fax: 216-725-2314
Circulation: 4,500

Charles Aukerman, Editor

Lakewood Sun Post
Sun Newspapers
2889 S Lorain Rd
North Olmsted OH 44070
216-777-3800; Fax: 216-777-8423
Circulation: 13,000

The Sun Herald
Kevin Burns, Editor
Sun Newspapers
2889 S Lorain Rd
North Olmsted OH 44070
216-777-3800; Fax: 216-777-8423
Circulation: 18,000

Kevin Burns, Editor

The Sun
Sun Newspapers
2889 S Lorain Rd
North Olmsted OH 44070
216-777-3800; Fax: 216-777-8423
Circulation: N/A

Kevin Burns, Editor

West Side Sun News
Sun Newspapers
2889 S Lorain Rd
North Olmsted OH 44070
216-777-3800; Fax: 216-777-8423
Circulation: 17,500

Kevin Burns, Editor

Oklahoma

Oklahoma Gazette
801 NW 36th St
Oklahoma City OK 73154-1649
405-528-6000; Fax: 405-528-4600
Circulation: 46,000

Mike Easterling, Editor

Oregon

Albany Democrat-Herald
600 Lyon St
Albany OR 97321-2919
503-926-2211; Fax: 503-926-5298
Circulation: 99,000

Eugene Weekly
1251 Lincoln
Eugene OR 97401
541-484-0519; Fax: 541-484-4044
Circulation: 26,000

Degra Gwartney, Editor

Willamette Week
822 SW 10th Ave
Portland OR 97205
503-243-2122; Fax: 503-243-1115
Circulation: 75,000

Audrey Van Buskirk, Arts/Entertainment Editor
Audrey Van Buskirk, Book Editor/Reviewer
Audry Van Buskirk, Business Editor
Audry Van Buskirk, Education Editor
Mark Schrag, Health/Medical Editor
Chris Ludgate, Lifestyle/Feature Editor
John Schrag, Managing Editor
Mark Zusman, News/Political Editor

Pennsylvania

Montgomery Post
Montgomery Publishing
416 Egypt Rd
Norristown PA 19403
610-630-6200; Fax: 610-630-9765
Circulation: 14,000

Lisa Lombardo, Managing Editor

German Town Paper
2385 W Ccheltanham Ave
Philadelphia PA 19150
215-885-4111; Fax: 215-885-0226
Circulation: 15,000

Marshall Rothman, Managing Editor

Girard Home News
250 W Girard Ave
Philadelphia PA 19123
215-925-7768; Fax: 215-925-2339
Circulation: 16,000

Frank Silverman, Editor

The Lane Leader
2385 W Ccheltanham Ave
Philadelphia PA 19150
215-885-4111; Fax: 215-885-0226
Circulation: 29,000

Marshall Rothman, Managing Editor

Philadelphia City Paper
206 S 13th St
Philadelphia PA 19107
215-732-5542; Fax: 215-732-9033
Circulation: 95,000

Howard Altman, Managing Editor

Philadelphia Northeast Times
Smylie Times Bldg #501
8001 Roosevelt Blvd
Philadelphia PA 19152
215-332-3300; Fax: 215-355-4812
Circulation: 117,000

John Scanlan, Editor

Philadelphia Weekly
1701 Walnut St
Philadelphia PA 19103
215-563-7400; Fax: 215-563-6799
Circulation: 120,000

Tim Whitaker, Editor

Star Newspaper Group
250 W Girard Ave
Philadelphia PA 19123
215-925-7768; Fax: 215-925-2339
Circulation: 12,000

Deborah Szumowski, News Editor

In Pittsburgh Newsweekly
2100 Wharton St #300
Pittsburgh PA 15203
412-488-1212; Fax: 412-488-1217
Circulation: 55,000

Andy Newman, Editor

Rhode Island

Providence Phoenix
150 Chestnut St
Providence RI 02903
401-273-6397; Fax: 401-273-0920
Circulation: 60,000

Lou Papineau, Editor

Tennessee

Metro Pulse
505 Market St
Knoxville TN 37902
423-522-5399; Fax: 423-522-2955
Circulation: 26,000

Bill Dockery, Editor

Memphis Flyer
460 Tennessee St
PO Box 687
Memphis TN 38101
901-521-9000
Circulation: N/A

Linda Willis, Calendar Editor
Dennis Freeland, Editor
John Branston, News Editor
Jackson Baker, Politics Editor

Nashville Scene
209 10th Ave S #222
Nashville TN 37203-4101
615-244-7989; Fax: 615-244-8578
Circulation: 153,000

Bruce Dobie, Editor

Texas

Austin Chronicle
PO Box 49066
Austin TX 78765
512-454-5766; Fax: 512-458-6910
E-mail: barvaro@auschron.com
Circulation: 80,000

Louis Black, Editor

Texas Observer
307 W 7th St
Austin TX 78701-2917
512-477-0746; Fax: 512-474-1175
Circulation: 7,000

Louis Dubose, Editor

The Newspaper
5160 Spruce
Bellaire TX 77401
713-668-9293; Fax: 713-668-9453
Circulation: 40,000

Kathleen Ballanfant, Editor

Houston Community Papers
PO Box 280
Channelview TX 77530-0280
713-452-0530; Fax: 713-860-5332
Circulation: 385,000

Edwin Henry, Managing Editor

Dallas Observer
2130 Commerce
Dallas TX 75201
214-757-9000; Fax: 214-757-8593
Circulation: 100,000

Julie Lyons, Editor

Houston Press
2000 W Loop S #1900
Houston TX 77027
713-624-1400; Fax: 713-623-1444
Circulation: 80,000

Ed Simmon, Editor
Mitchel Shields, Managing Editor

Public News
2038 Lexington
Houston TX 77098
713-520-1520; Fax: 713-520-9390
Circulation: 45,000

Mark Frohman, Art Editor
Michael Bergeron, Film Editor
Bobette Riner, Food Editor
Patrick Griggs, Managing Editor
Kim Stoilis, Music Editor
Bert Woodall, Political Editor
Red Connelly, Sports Editor
Glenna Bell, Theater Editor

San Antonio Current
8750 Tesoro Dr #1
San Antonio TX 78217
210-828-7660; Fax: 210-828-7883
Circulation: 32,000

Mike Hood, Editor

Utah

Private Eye Weekly
60 W 400 S
Salt Lake City UT 84101
801-575-7003; Fax: 801-575-6106
Circulation: 50,000

Tom Walsh, Editor

Virginia

Maryland Express
The Journal Newspapers
2720 Prosperity Ave
Fairfax VA 22034-1000
703-560-4000; Fax: 703-846-8366
Circulation: 226,000

Mary Ellen Webb, Book Review Editor
Brenda Bouser, Family Editor
Linda Schubert, Lifestyle Editor
Jane Touzalin, Managing News Editor
Paul Bergeron, Sports Editor

Mongomery Express
The Journal Newspapers
2720 Prosperity Ave
Fairfax VA 22034-1000
703-560-4000; Fax: 703-846-8366
Circulation: 115,000

Mary Ellen Webb, Book Review Editor
, Business Editor
Brenda Bouser, Family Editor
Linda Schubert, Lifestyle Editor
Jane Touzalin, Managing News Editor
Paul Bergeron, Sports Editor

Prince George's Express
The Journal Newspapers
2720 Prosperity Ave
Fairfax VA 22034-1000
703-560-4000; Fax: 703-846-8366
Circulation: 111,000

Mary Ellen Webb, Book Review Editor
Brenda Bouser, Family Editor
Linda Schubert, Lifestyle Editor
Jane Touzalin, Managing News Editor
The Journal Newspapers
Paul Bergeron, Sports Editor

Prince William Weekly-Potomac
The Journal Newspapers
2720 Prosperity Ave
Fairfax VA 22034-1000
703-560-4000; Fax: 703-846-8366
Circulation: 27,000

Mary Ellen Webb, Book Review Editor
, Business Editor
Brenda Bouser, Family Editor
Linda Schubert, Lifestyle Editor
Jane Touzalin, Managing News Editor
Paul Bergeron, Sports Editor

Virginia Express
The Journal Newspapers
2720 Prosperity Ave
Fairfax VA 22034-1000
703-560-4000; Fax: 703-846-8366
Circulation: 142,000

Mary Ellen Webb, Book Review Editor
Brenda Bouser, Family Editor
Linda Schubert, Lifestyle Editor
Jane Touzalin, Managing News Editor
Paul Bergeron, Sports Editor

Federal Times
6883 Commercial Dr
Springfield VA 22159
703-750-8656; Fax: 703-750-8602
Circulation: 40,000

Maryann Lester, Editor

Times Journal Company
6883 Commercial Dr
Springfield VA 22159-0180
703-750-8646; Fax: 703-750-8622
Nprs for Army/Navy/Airforce
Circulation: N/A

Jim Doyle, Editor

Washington

The Seattle Weekly
1008 Western Ave #300
Seattle WA 98104
206-467-4370; Fax: 206-467-4377
Circulation: 34,000

Sumi Hahn, Art/Entertainment Editor
Katherine Koberg, Book Editor
Sumi Hahn, Food Editor
Katherine Koberg, Managing Editor
David Brewster, Editor

The Stranger
1202 E Pike #1225
Seattle WA 98122-3934
206-323-7101; Fax: 206-323-7203
Circulation: 52,000

Emily White, Editor

The Pacific Northwest Inlander
W 1702 Dean
Spokane WA 99201
509-325-0634; Fax: 509-325-0638
Circulation: 101,000

Ted McGregor, Jr, Editor

Wisconsin

Isthmus
101 King St
Madison WI 53703-3313
608-251-5627; Fax: 608-251-2165
Circulation: 51,000

Dean Robbins, Book Editor/Reviewer
Marc Eisen, Editor
Judy Davidoff, Feature Editor
Bill Leuders, Political Editor
Andy Cohen, Sports Editor

Shephard Express
1123 N Water St
Milwaukee WI 53202
414-276-2222; Fax: 414-276-3312
Circulation: 55,000

Scott Kerr, Editor

CANADA

British Columbia

Monday Magazine
1609 Blanshard St
Victoria BC Canada V8W 2J5
604-382-6188; Fax: 604-382-6014
Circulation: 40,000

James MacKinnon, Editor

Quebec

The Chronicle
15 Cartier
Pointe Claire PQ Canada H9S 4R7
514-630-6688; Fax: 514-694-7620
Circulation: 30,000

Brenda O'Farrell, Business Editor
Brenda O'Farrell, Editor
Donald McGowan, Lifestyle/Feature Editor
John Austen, Sports Editor

Saskatchwan

Lloydminster Times
Doug Collie, Editor
4828 44th St
Lloydminster SK Canada S9V 0G8
306-825-5522; Fax: 306-825-3207
Circulation: 13,000; Published Sun and Wed

Subject Category Codes

10 **General Non-Fiction**
11 **Fine Arts**
    11P   Photography
12 **Architecture / Construction**
    12A   Architecture
    12B   Building / Construction
13 **Alternative Social Issues**
14 **Performing Arts**
    14D   Dance
    14M   Music
    14T   Theatre / Drama
15 **Animals / Pets**
16 **Transportation**
    16A   Automobiles
    16R   Railroads
17 **Biographies / Celebrities**
    17B   Biographies
    17C   Celebrities
    17P   Real People
19 **Business / Economics**
    19A   Accounting
    19B   Banking
    19C   Careers / Labor
    19E   Economics
    19F   Fund-raising / Non-profits
    19G   Management
    19H   Real Estate / Home
    19I   Investment
    19L   Law
    19M   Marketing / Sales
    19O   Opportunity Seekers
    19P   Purchasing
    19R   Retail Sales
    19S   Small Business
    19X   Industrial / Production
21 **Children's Interests**
    21T   Teenagers
23 **Computers / Technology**
    23C   Computers
    23E   Home Electronics
    23T   Technology
24 **Engineering**
25 **Consumer Issues**
    25T   Consumer Taxes
27 **Cooking / Food / Nutrition**
28 **Collectibles / Antiques**
29 **Crafts / Hobbies / How-to**
    29C   Crafts
    29H   Hobbies and How-to
31 **Education / Child Development**
    31C   Child Development
    31E   Education / Teaching
    31P   Parenting
33 **Entertainment / Movies / Humor**
    33C   Comics / Comedy
    33H   Humor
    33M   Movies
    33T   Television / Radio

35 **Family / Marriage / Retirement**
    35A   Aging Issues / Retirement
    35F   Family
    35M   Marriage
    35R   Relationships / Romance
    35S   Sexual Issues
36 **Lifestyle/Feature**
37 **Gay / Lesbian**
39 **Health / Medicine / Exercise**
    39D   Disabilities
    39E   Exercise
    39H   Holistic Health
    39M   Medicine / Doctors
    39R   Recovery / Drug Abuse
40 **Beauty / Fashion**
    40B   Beauty
    40F   Fashion
41 **History**
    41A   American History
    41G   Genealogy / Family History
    41W   World History
43 **House / Garden**
    43D   Home Decorating
    43G   Gardening
    43H   House and Home
44 **International Issues and News**
    44A   Asia
    44E   Europe
    44F   Africa
    44S   South America
    44Z   Australia / New Zealand
45 **Languages**
    45X   Linquistics
    45W   Words
47 **Literature / Humanities**
48 **Military**
49 **Minority Issues and Studies**
    49A   Native American
    49B   Black
    49H   Hispanic / Chicano
    49O   Other
51 **Nature / Ecology / Conservation**
    51A   Agriculture / Farming
    51B   Biology / Botany
    51E   Environmental Issues
    51N   Nature
53 **New Age / Astrology**
54 **Philosophy / Metaphysics**
    54M   Metaphysics
    54P   Philosophy
55 **Politics / Government**
    55C   Crime / Police Work
    55G   Government
    55L   Law
    55P   Politics

56 **Publishing / PR / Writing**
    56M   Media / Publicity
    56P   Publishing
    56W   Writing
    56X   Printing
57 **Psychology / Self-Help**
    57B   Behavior
    57P   Psychology / Therapy
    57S   Self-Help / Advice
59 **Reference Books**
61 **Regional Issues and Interests**
63 **Religions**
    63C   Catholic
    63E   Eastern Religions
    63J   Jewish
    63M   Muslim
    63O   Other Religions
    63P   Protestant
65 **Sociology / Anthropology**
    65A   Anthropology
    65S   Social Issues
67 **Science / Mathematics**
    67A   Astronomy / Space
    67M   Mathematics
    67S   Science
69 **Sports / Games / Recreation**
    69G   Games
    69H   Hunting / Fishing
    69R   Recreation / Hiking
    69S   Spectator Sports
70 **Nautical / Aviation**
    70A   Aviation
    70N   Nautical / Sailing
71 **Travel / Geography**
    71D   Domestic Travel
    71F   Foreign Travel
    71G   Geography
73 **Women's Issues**

75 General Fiction

76 **Children's Stories**
77 **Contemporary Novels**
78 **Ethnic / Minority Literature**
79 **Folklore / Fairy Tales**
80 **Foreign Literature**
81 **Historical Novels**
82 **Horror Novels**
83 **Literary Novels**
84 **Mysteries / Detective Novels**
85 **Romances / Gothic Romances**
86 **Science Fiction / Fantasy**
87 **Suspense / Adventure Novels**
88 **Westerns**
89 **Young Adult Novels**
90 **Short Stories / Anthologies**
95 **Poetry**

97 News / Current Events

99 General Interest

Section IV:

Marketing Services

365   **Publicity Services**

373   **Marketing Services and Publishing Consultants**

377   **Speakers Bureaus**

379   **Cooperative Marketing Services**

383   **Card Decks or Card Packs**

393   **Mailing List Brokers and Managers**

415   **Trade Shows, Book Fairs, and Conventions**

       415   Book Shows
       417   Foreign Book Shows
       418   Other Trade Shows
       419   Trade Show Directories
       419   Exhibit Services

421   **Publishing Associations**

       421   Author's Associations
       424   Booksellers Associations
       425   Publishers Associations
       430   Other Associations of Interest

432   **Publishing Institutes, Courses, and Conferences**

434   **Miscellaneous Marketing Resources**

Section IV: Services

This section features a variety of services for book publishers and other marketers. These services are divided into the following sections:

- **Publicity services** — including public relations services, author escorts, news release distributors, news feature services, satellite interviews, and more.
- **Marketing services** — book marketing services, publishing consultants, telemarketing services, marketing researchers, special markets consultants, advertising agencies.
- **Speaker's bureaus** — companies and associations that help authors and other speakers to book engagements.
- **Cooperative marketing services** — co-op mailings to libraries and booksellers insert programs, paid placements in publicity directories and newsletters, game show placements, per inquiry catalog listings, and other co-op marketing programs.
- **Card packs** — card packs that feature some books; also directories of card packs.
- **Mailing list sources** — mailing list brokers, mailing list managers, and directories of mailing lists sources.
- **Trade shows** — book shows, book fairs, and conventions; foreign book shows; other trade shows important to book publishers; trade show directories; and exhibit services that can display your books at conventions and conferences where you cannot attend.
- **Publishing associations** — associations for authors, booksellers, and publishers, including regional and special-interest associations.
- **Publishing institutes** — book publishing institutes, courses, conferences, and other educational opportunities.
- **Miscellaneous marketing resources** — all sorts of sources and resources to help you market your books better, everything from audio duplication services to bar code suppliers, from clipping bureaus to indexers, from toll-free phone numbers to typesetters, from proofreaders to publishing lawyers, and much, much more.

Use these marketing services to help you market your books, either as an adjunct to your own in-house staff and/or as supplements your other marketing programs. For example, you might want to use an outside publicity agency for a special title where you might not have the time to give it the attention it deserves. Or you might join in a co-op mailing to libraries as a supplement to your other direct marketing and distribution efforts. Or call on a list broker to help you locate the best list for a new book promotion. And definitely join at least one publishing association so you can learn from the experiences of your fellow publishers.

Don't think that you can always do everything yourself. Learn to delegate some of the jobs that need to be done. These outside services and programs can serve to lessen your load and allow you to focus on those things you do best.

Publicity Services

The following companies offer various publicity services for books, authors, and other products or services. If you decide not to do your own publicity work, these people can help you reach a wider audience.

A

Accent on Broadcasting
Randie Levine
165 West 66th St
New York NY 10023-6538
212-362-3616; Fax: 212-362-6182
Subjects: 99
Service: Author tours

The Alexander Company
Roy Alexander
239 East 32nd St
New York NY 10016
212-684-0340; Fax: 212-684-0342
Subjects: 99

Alice B Acheson
PO Box 735
Friday Harbor WA 98250
360-378-2815; Fax: 360-378-2841
Subjects: 99
Service: PR/author tours/sub rights sales

Allen Communications Services
Alice Allen
136 E 57th #1500
New York NY 10022
212-755-4545; Fax: 212-755-9743
Subjects: 99
Service: PR, marketing, seminars, media relations

The Alternative
Nancy Colson
Media Placement Specialists
330 West 56th St
New York NY 10019
212-246-1580; Fax: 212-956-3728
Subjects: 53-99
Service: Media placement

Anita Halton Public Relations
Anita Halton
559 Alta Vista Way
Laguna Beach CA 92651
714-494-8564; Fax: 714-494-1651
Subjects: 99(West coast tours)
Service: Book publicity/author escort

Anita Helen Brooks Associates
Anita Brooks
155 East 55th St Apt 10G
New York NY 10022-4038
212-755-4498
Subjects: 99
Service: All publicity services

Anne Berg Public Relations
Anne Poland Berg
10 Piedmont Ctr #802
Atlanta GA 30305
404-262-2266
Subjects: 61(SE US)-99
Service: PR

Anne Hardy Public Relations
Anne Hardy, Pres
137 West 75th St
New York NY 10023
212-496-6585; Fax: 212-496-6840
Subjects: 40-99
Service: Book publicity

Azen Bitner Pierson
1330-B SE Fourth Ave
Fort Lauderdale FL 33316-1958
305-522-0022; Fax: 305-522-2847
Subjects: 99
Service: PR, marketing, graphic communications

B

Bacon's Publicity Distribution
Bacon's Mailing Service
R H Bacon Co
332 S Michigan Ave
Chicago IL 60604-4301
312-922-2400; 800-621-0561;
    Fax: 312-922-3127
Subjects: 99
Service: General news release distribution

Barbara J Hendra Associates
Barbara J Hendra
142 Sterling Pl
Brooklyn NY 11217-3307
212-947-9898; Fax: 212-622-3322
Subjects: 99
Service: Book publicity
Memo: Specialist in book publicity with an excellent track record with business books.

Bender Goldman & Helper PR
11500 West Olympic Blvd #655
Los Angeles CA 90064
310-473-4147; Fax: 310-478-4727
Subjects: 99
Service: PR & marketing communications

Betty Marks Public Relations
Betty Marks
176 East 77th St
New York NY 10021-1909
212-535-8388
Subjects: 99
Service: Book publicity

The Bishopric Agency
Susan Bishopric
400 Viscaya Ave
Coral Gables FL 33134-7160
305-448-3222
Subjects: 28-33-99
Service: Publicity

The Blaine Group Inc
Devon Blaine
7465 Beverly Blvd
Los Angelos CA 90036-2749
213-938-2577; Fax: 213-939-7701
Subjects: 99
Service: Book Publicity

The Bohle Co
1999 Ave of the Stars #550
Los Angeles CA 90067-6022
310-785-0515; Fax: 310-785-0459
Service: Publicity

The Bookers
Morton Wax
200 W 51st St
New York NY 10019-6208
212-302-5360; Fax: 212-302-5364
Subjects: 99
Service: Book publicity

Brad Pappas & Associates
Brad Pappas, Pres
322 First Ave S #201
Minneapolis MN 55401-1618
612-375-0141; Fax: 612-375-0143
Subjects: 99
Service: Product sampling and publicity

Britt & Associates
Trisha Britt
1980 Washington St #106
San Francisco CA 94109
415-474-0326; Fax: 415-776-3883
Subjects: 39-99
Service: PR for surgeons, authors, etc

Brody Public Relations
Beth Brody
145 Kingwood Stockton Rd
Stockton NJ 08559
609-397-3737; Fax: 609-397-3666
Subjects: 12B-19H-19R-23C-31E-39-99
Service: Book and author publicity
Memo: Beth has done publicity in the following fields: health care, education, real estate/construction, retail, computers, and publishing (including Bantam, Doubleday Dell, Berkley, Peterson's Guides, Reed Reference, Westcliffe, Villard, and Jolly Learning). Ask for a free copy of the Brody PR Newswire Newsletter with valuable PR tips.

BSK Communications & Associates
PO Box 554
Oradell NJ 07649
201-262-3277; Fax: 201-262-3277
Subjects: 56W(freelance writers)
Service: Publicity
Memo: Publishers of "The Prolific Freelancer" & "The Paperless Planet".

Business Wire
44 Montgomery St 39th Fl
San Francisco CA 94104-4774
415-986-4422; Fax: 415-788-5335
Subjects: 19
Service: Electronic transmission of news

C

Cade Communications
Lisl Cade
172 West 79th St
New York NY 10024-6402
212-595-6225; Fax: 212-877-3241
Subjects: 99
Service: Book publicity

Canaan Communications
Lee Canaan, Pres
301 E 47th St
New York NY 10017-2302
212-223-0100
Subjects: 99
Service: All media

Capener/Walcher
620 C St 6th Fl
San Diego CA 92101
619-238-8500; Fax: 619-238-8505
Subjects: 99
Service: PR

Caroline O'Connell PR
Caroline O'Connell
8439 Sunset Blvd #104
Los Angeles CA 90069
213-654-5775; Fax: 213-656-2647
Subjects: 99
Service: Author tours/book publicity

Carolyn Anthony Public Relations
Carolyn Anthony
213 St Johns Pl
Brooklyn NY 11217-3405
718-638-1822; Fax: 718-622-8373
Subjects: 99
Service: PR services, subsidiary rights

Caruba Organization
Alan Caruba
PO Box 40
Maplewood NJ 07040
201-763-6392; Fax: 201-763-4287
Subjects: 99
Service: Radio, TV, print publicity

Cassidy Brown Public Relations
Cassidy Brown
350 Essex Ave
Gloucester MA 01930-2352
508-281-3102
Subjects: 99
Service: National publicity

Celebrity Guide of California
Darlene La Madrid, Dir
535 Madrona Ave
Chula Vista CA 91910
619-426-2332; Fax: 619-476-0263
Subjects: 99
Service: Author tours, escort services

Celia Rocks Communications
Celia Rocks, Pres
1015 2nd St NE #215
Hickory NC 28601
704-322-3111; Fax: 704-322-1839
Subjects: 99
Service: Books & authors only
Memo: Personalization & persistence: the two simple secrets to successful book publicity from Celia Rocks.

Colorado Voice Productions
L Platts
1255 Ogden St #604
Denver CO 80218-1948
303-837-1656
Subjects: 99
Service: PR

The Communications Center
538 Street Rd
Southhampton PA 18966-3790
215-396-0610
Subjects: 99
Service: Media release service

Community Media Workshop
Veronica Drake, Newsdesk Mgr
CMW
600 S Michigan Ave
Chicago IL 60605
312-663-3225; Fax: 312-663-3227
Subjects: 56M
Memo: Publish "Getting On the Air & Into Print: A Citizen's Guide to Chicago-Area Media". West side office: Community Media Workshop, c/o Malcom X College, 1900 W Van Buren, Rm 2519, Chicago, IL 60612; phone: 312-850-7321; FAX: 312-850-7323; President: Thom Clark; Vice President of company is Hank DeZutter.

D

D W J Associates Inc
1 Robinson Lane
Ridgewood NJ 07450-2258
201-445-1711
Subjects: 99
Service: VNR production

Daily Business Satellite
Potomac Television/Communication
500 North Capitol St NW #800
Washington DC 20004
202-783-8000
Subjects: 19-25-39
Service: VNR distribution and tracking

David X Manners Company
Tim Manners
4 Landmark Sq
Stamford CT 06901-2502
203-353-1212
Subjects: 19M
Service: Marketing services, PR

DeChant & Huges Assoc Inc
Carol DeChant, Pres
2930 N Commonwealth Ave
Chicago IL 60657
312-935-7116; Fax: 312-525-0231
Subjects: 99
Service: Book publicity, author tours

Derus Media Service
500 N Dearborn St
Chicago IL 60610-4901
312-644-4360; Fax: 312-644-9192
Subjects: 27-43-99
Service: New release
Memo: A typical 1-column release costs $1,200 for 1,000 editors.

Diane Glynn Publicity and PR
Diane Glynn, Pres
310 Madison Ave #1711
New York NY 10017-6009
212-983-8700; Fax: 212-949-1543
Subjects: 99
Service: Full service

Dorf & Stanton
Bob Dorf and Alex Stanton
111 Fifth Ave
New York NY 10003-1005
212-420-8100; Fax: 212-505-1397
Subjects: 99
Service: Book publicity

Dougherty and Associates
Michael J Dougherty
8707 Falmouth Ave #325
Playa del Rey CA 90293-8601
310-827-9190
Subjects: 19M
Service: Marketing, events production

The Dresback Company
8019 1/2 Melrose Ave #1
Los Angeles CA 90046-7032
213-658-9070; Fax: 213-658-7050
Subjects: 14-33-99
Service: Radio promos/entertainment industy

E

E Bruce Harrison Co
Jeff Conley
1440 New York Ave NW
Washington DC 20005
202-638-1200
Subjects: 51E-55(public affairs/PR)
Service: Public affairs, PR

F

Family Features Editorial Serv
8309 Melrose Dr
Shawnee Mission KS 66214-1629
913-888-3800
Subjects: 27-99
Service: Full-color newspaper releases

First Impressions
Tena Spears, Publicist
2755 SE 32nd
Portland OR 97202
503-233-4066
Subjects: 99
Service: Book publicity

Fortson Communications
2217 Stanley Hills Dr
Los Angeles CA 90046-1531
213-654-4059
Subjects: 99
Service: Tours and PR for books

Frank Promotion Corp
Ben Frank, Pres
60 East 42nd St #2119
New York NY 10165
212-687-3383; Fax: 212-986-5956
Subjects: 99
Service: Radio, TV publicity, and more

Fred Rosen Associates
Fred Rosen
730 Columbus Ave
New York NY 10025-6658
212-316-9023
Subjects: 99
Service: Book publicity

G

Gaia Communications
Janet Bridgers & Catherine Leach
PO Box 69193
West Hollywood CA 90069
310-274-1456
Subjects: 51E
Service: PR for environmental products

Gail Leondar Public Relations
Gail Leondar
18 Linwood St
Arlington MA 02174-6608
617-648-1648
Subjects: 13-65-73-99
Service: Publicity for authors

Gaughen Public Relations
Barbara Gaughen
226 East Canon Perdido #B
Santa Barbara CA 93101-2234
805-965-8482; Fax: 805-965-6522
Subjects: 99
Service: Book publicity

Goldmark Media Escorts
Kathi Kamen Goldmark
2259 14th Ave
San Francisco CA 94116-1842
415-664-3333; Fax: 415-664-0517
Subjects: 99
Service: Author escorts

Greenberg Public Relations
Susannah Greenberg, Pres
2166 Broadway #9E
New York NY 10024
212-496-7581; Fax: 212-496-5661
E-Mail: booknews@pipeline.com
Subjects: 99
Service: Publicity for books

H

Haddon Lynch & Baughman PR
Kathy Baughman
875 N Michigan Ave #1330
Chicago IL 60611
312-649-0371; Fax: 312-649-1119
Subjects: 99
Service: Book publicity

Hal Copeland Company
Hal Copeland
5646 Milton St
Meadows Building #336
Dallas TX 75206
214-361-8788
Subjects: 11-15-19-27-33-39
Service: Independent publicist

Hansen & Young PR Consultants
M W Hansen
183 East 94th St #1A
New York NY 10128-2106
212-534-2676; Fax: 212-534-3069
Subjects: 99
Service: Publicity for some authors

Health Professionals Media Network
315 E 56th St #2H
New York NY 10022
800-871-8071; Fax: 212-752-2788
Subjects: 39H-39M
Service: PR for health & wellness books

Hi-Tech Public Relations
Gail Anderson
444 DeHaro St #207
San Francisco CA 94105
415-904-7000; Fax: 415-904-7025
Subjects: 23
Service: PR

Hill & Knowlton
Robert Stone
420 Lexington Ave
New York NY 10170-0002
212-697-5600; Fax: 212-210-8866
Subjects: 99
Service: Publicity for books/products

Hilsinger-Mendelson Inc
Judy Hilsinger
8436 W Third St #750
Los Angeles CA 90048
213-658-1022
Subjects: 99
Service: National author tours

Hilsinger-Mendelson Inc
Sandi Mendelson
149 5th Ave
New York NY 10010-6801
212-387-8383
Subjects: 99
Service: National author tours

Hohenstein Public Relations
Nan Hohenstein
250 Columbus Ave #211
San Francisco CA 94133-4536
415-989-7355; Fax: 415-989-5311
Subjects: 23-31-99
Service: PR for education/software/books

Howard J Hall & Associates
Howard J Hall
5 Hillcrest Dr
Chelmsford MA 01824
508-250-5915; Fax: 603-425-2197
Subjects: 19I-23
Service: Investor relations/high tech

I

Images International
Frida Greene & Judith Jacovitz
6624 Newcastle Ave
Reseda CA 91335
818-344-5279
Subjects: 56-99
Service: Book publicity

Inside Track Publicity
Camilla Englund
3603 NE Hassalo St
Portland OR 97232
503-238-1493
Subjects: 99
Service: PR

Irene Reichbach
254 East 68th St
New York NY 10021
212-988-1770; Fax: 212-988-6313
Subjects: 99
Service: Book publicity

J

Jane Wesman Public Relations
Jane Wesman
928 Broadway #903
New York NY 10010-6008
212-598-4440; Fax: 212-598-4590
Subjects: 99(book publicity/spec events)
Service: Author & satellite tours

Jeanne-Marie Phillips Assoc
Jeanne-Marie Phillips
225 5th Ave
New York NY 10178
212-696-4822
Subjects: 99
Service: PR

Jericho Promotions
Kim Morgan or Greg Mowery
924 Broadway
New York NY 10010-6007
212-260-3744; Fax: 212-260-4168
Subjects: 99
Service: Publicity for book publishers

Jimmy Booth Public Relations
Jimmy Booth, Pres
14 Eastbrook Bnd
Peachtree City GA 30269-1530
770-487-2477; Fax: 770-487-9225
Subjects: 19-39-99
Service: 99

Joan Robbins, Media Escort
Joan Robbins
4000 Island Blvd #2901
North Miami Beach FL 33160-2593
305-933-9793
Subjects: 61(FL)
Service: Media escorts

Joe Vitale Agency
Joe Vitale, Copywriter
412 N Coast Hwy #380
Houston TX 77230-0792
713-999-1110; Fax: 713-999-1313
E-Mail: mrfire@blkbox.com
Subjects: 99
Service: PR services

K

Karen Teitelbaum PR
Karen Teitelbaum
103 Carleton Rd
Wallingford PA 19086-6116
215-892-9192; Fax: 215-892-9424
Subjects: 99
Service: PR services

Kathlene Carney & Associates
Kathlene Carney
1926 Castle Dr
Petaluma CA 94954
707-765-1234; Fax: 707-765-0816
Subjects: 99
Service: Author tours, regional/national

KEF Media Associates
213 W Institute Pl #405
Chicago IL 60611
312-951-5894; Fax: 312-951-5893
Subjects: 99
Service: Video news releases

Kerr Kelly Inc
One Sound Shore Dr
Greenwich CT 06830-7251
203-622-1723; Fax: 203-622-1728
Subjects: 99
Service: PR

KSB Promotions
Kate Siegel Bandos
55 Honey Creek NE
Ada MI 49301
616-676-0758; Fax: 616-676-0759
Subjects: 71-99
Service: PR (small press)

KSK Communications
Karla Masters, Acct Coordinator
Kaleidoscope Newsletter
8618 Westwood Ctr Dr #400
Vienna VA 22182-2280
703-734-1880; Fax: 703-821-2756
Subjects: 99
Service: Publicity and advertising

L

Ladd Ltd
Parker Ladd
1 Beekman Pl
New York NY 10022-8057
212-486-1112
Subjects: 56
Service: Project managing and consulting

Lawrence Communications
Bonnie Lawrence
1515 Beverly Pl
Albany CA 94706-2507
510-525-0544
Subjects: 99
Service: PR/writing for non-profits/books

Levinson Associates
1440 Veteran Ave #650
Los Angeles CA 90024-4838
213-460-4545; Fax: 213-663-2820
Subjects: 99
Service: Book publicity

Lisa Ekus Public Relations
Lisa Ekus
57 North St
Hatfield MA 01038-9748
413-247-9325; Fax: 413-247-9873
Subjects: 27
Service: PR for cookbooks and food events

Lobsenz-Stevens
Amelia Lobsenz & Art Stevens
460 Park Ave S
New York NY 10016-7301
212-684-6300; Fax: 212-696-4638
Subjects: 99
Service: Book publicity

M

M Lande Promotions
Stephanie Rowden
44 Prospect Park W
Brooklyn NY 11215-2363
212-344-0930; Fax: 212-344-0930
Subjects: 99
Service: Book publicity

Manning Selvage & Lee
James O Ahtes
3 Illinois Ctr
303 E Wacker Dr #440
Chicago IL 60601
312-819-3535; Fax: 312-819-3578
Subjects: 99
Service: Book publicity

Martin Kane Public Relations
Martin Kane
3345 Wilshire Blvd #603
Los Angeles CA 90010-1873
213-388-1208
Subjects: 99
Service: PR

Martin Pine Associates
Martin Pine
2073 Gerritsen Ave
Brooklyn NY 11229-3705
718-339-1417
Subjects: 99
Service: Radio/TV talk show arrangements

Mazza Marketing Group
Bob Mazza
2730 Wilshire Blvd
Santa Monica CA 90403-4743
310-829-4401
Subjects: 99
Service: Book publicity

McCurdy Communications
Michael J McCurdy, Pres
1360 York Ave
New York NY 10021-4030
212-288-6994
Subjects: 99
Service: TV production and syndication

Media Distribution Services
Dan Cantelmo Jr, Pres
307 W 36th St
New York NY 10018-6403
212-279-4800; Fax: 212-239-8308
Subjects: 99
Service: Distribution to all media

Media Relations
Christopher Glenn
1550 E 78th St
Minneapolis MN 55423-4644
612-798-7200
Subjects: 99
Service: Radio & TV placements in U S

Medialink
708 Third Ave
New York NY 10017
212-682-8300; Fax: 212-682-2370
800-843-0677
Subjects: 99
Service: Video news releases and distribution

Meg Cullar Public Relations
Meg Cullar
125 Karem Rd
Waco TX 76710-6513
817-754-6513
Subjects: 57-63
Service: Religious/inspirational authors

Metro Creative Graphics
Beth Baynum, Sales Dir
Metro Publicity Services
33 West 34th St
New York NY 10001-3099
212-947-5100; Fax: 212-714-9139
800-223-1600
Subjects: 99(newspaper features/sections)
Service: New service: Book Beat which will go to 7,000 newspapers. Cost: $126 per column inch

Michael Druxman Public Relations
Michael Druxman
PO Box 8086
Calabasas CA 91302-8086
818-591-1963; Fax: 818-876-0069
Subjects: 99
Service: PR for books/businesses/movies

Michael Kassin Public Relations
Michael Kassin
210 East 15th St
New York NY 10003-3922
212-529-8832; Fax: 212-529-8912
Subjects: 99
Service: Book publicity

N

Name That Book
239 East 32nd St
New York NY 10016-6393
212-684-0340
Subjects: 99
Service: PR for books

Nathana Josephs PR
Nathana Josephs, Pres
205 West End Ave #19A
New York NY 10023-4805
212-769-2198
Subjects: 27
Service: PR for food products, restaurants

News Broadcast Network
Lee Shepard
7309 Idylwood Ct
Falls Church VA 22043
703-893-4577; Fax: 703-893-6967
Subjects: 99(radio/TV)
Service: Releases/satellite tours/etc

News Broadcast Network
Bob Kimmel
149 Madison Ave #804
New York NY 10016-6778
212-889-0888; Fax: 212-696-4611
Subjects: 99
Service: Releases, radio/TV, satellite tours, etc

News USA
Richard Smith, Pres
8300 Boone Blvd #810
Vienna VA 22182
703-827-5800; Fax: 703-827-5811
800-355-9500
Subjects: 99
Service: Newspaper features, sections

News/Broadcast Network
News/Radio Network
9431 W Beloit Rd
Milwaukee WI 53227
414-321-6210; Fax: 414-321-3608
Subjects: 99
Service: Radio newsfeeds, PSA's, tapes, etc

The Nolan-Lehr Group
Betsy Nolan and Donald Lehr
224 West 29th St
New York NY 10001-5204
212-967-8200
Subjects: 99
Service: Book publicity: specialize in cross country tours

North American Network
Radio News Services
7910 Woodmont Ave #1400
Bethesda MD 20814-3015
301-654-9810; Fax: 301-654-9828
Subjects: 99
Service: Radio publicity, newsfeed, fax service, PSAs, etc
Memo: Send for their free Official RadioTour Handbook on how to book and handle a radio interview tour.

North American Precis Syndicate
201 East 42nd St
New York NY 10017-5704
212-867-9000
Subjects: 99
Service: PR distribution, multi-media releases, camera-ready releases

North American Precis Syndicate
1901 Avenue of the Stars
Los Angeles CA 90067-6001
310-552-8000
Subjects: 99
Service: PR distribution, multi-media releases, camera-ready releases

North American Precis Syndicate
333 N Michigan Ave
Chicago IL 60601
312-856-9000
Subjects: 99
Service: PR distribution, multi-media releases, camera-ready releases

North American Precis Syndicate
1101 14th St NW
Washington DC 20005-5601
202-347-5000
Subjects: 99
Service: PR distribution, multi-media releases, camera-ready releases

O

On the Scene Productions
Sally Jewett
5900 Wilshire Blvd
Los Angeles CA 90036-5013
213-930-1030; Fax: 213-930-1840
Subjects: 99
Service: Satellite and video interviews

On the Scene Productions/NY
Mark Haefeli, Mg Partner
475 Park Ave S 10th Fl
New York NY 10016-6901
212-983-0123
Subjects: 99
Service: Satellite and video interviews

One Potata Productions
Diane Mancher
80 E 11th St
New York NY 10003-6000
212-353-3478
Subjects: 56
Service: Specialize in promotion of books and authors

P

P & F Communications
Barbara Pflughaupt
12 East 86th St
New York NY 10028-0506
212-861-2100; Fax: 212-249-0355
Subjects: 21-33
Service: PR

Padilla Speer Beardsley
Selden Sutton
950 Third Ave #1600
New York NY 10022-2705
212-752-8338; Fax: 212-752-6082
Subjects: 99
Service: Book publicity

Pat Rose & Associates
Pat Rose
414 Mason St
San Francisco CA 94102-1708
415-433-3232
Subjects: 56
Service: Public relations and marketing

PDK Communications
Paula DuPont-Kidd, Pres
PO Box 52202
Philadelphia PA 19115
215-289-5615
Subjects: 99
Service: Writing, editing, promoting

Peggy Tagliarino PR
Carolyn Gross
105 5th Ave
New York NY 10003-1010
212-741-0079; Fax: 212-741-7433
Subjects: 99
Service: Book publicity

PIMS New York
1133 Broadway #423
New York NY 10010-8001
212-645-5112; Fax: 212-645-5217
Subjects: 99
Service: NR distribution, faxing, etc

Planned Communications Service
12 E 46th St
New York NY 10017-2418
212-697-2765; Fax: 212-445-2820
Subjects: 99
Service: Radio

Planned Television Arts
Rick Frishman
301 E 57th St
New York NY 10022
212-593-5845; Fax: 212-715-1664
Subjects: 99
Service: TV/radio interviews
Memo: In June 1996, PTA launched a new cookbook division under the leadership of Suzanne Chase (who had previously been an independant cookbook publicist). Call Suzanne at 212-989-1988.

Porter/Novelli
John Porter & William Novelli
437 Madison Ave
New York NY 10022-7001
212-872-8000; Fax: 212-872-8107
Subjects: 99
Service: Book publicity

PR Newswire
1515 Broadway 32nd Fl
New York NY 10036
212-832-9400; Fax: 800-793-9319
Subjects: 16A-19-21-23E-27-39-43-69-71-99
Service: News release distribution
Memo: Also does feature packages for newspapers that use camera-ready copy.

PTA Interactive
Adam Grossberg
Planned Television Arts
301 E 57th St
New York NY 10022
212-593-5820; Fax: 212-715-1664
E-Mail: ptactive@aol.com
Subjects: 99
Service: Promotes authors, books, & speakers in cyberspace

Public Relations Services
Abby Brown
350 Essex Ave
Gloucester MA 01930
508-281-3102
Subjects: 99
Service: Book publicity

Publicity to Go
Judith Erdmann, Pres
1485 Sargent Ave
St Paul MN 55105
612-690-5552
Subjects: 99
Service: PR Specialty: independent publishers

Publishers Support Services
Linda Radke
Five Star Publications
4696 West Tyson St
Chandler AZ 85226-2903
602-940-8182; Fax: 602-940-8787
Subjects: 19-19L-31E-39-55L-63J
Service: MDs/lawyers/hospitals/educators
Memo: New co-op ad package to Jewish markets (gift shops, bookstores, social services, etc).

Pyle & Associates
Jeanne Louise Pyle
PO Box 58792
Seattle WA 98138
206-282-2970
Subjects: 99
Service: Publicity, marketing, media escort

R

The Raleigh Group
Raleigh Pinskey, Pres
1223 Wilshire Blvd #502
Santa Monica CA 90403-5400
310-998-0055; Fax: 310-998-0034
Subjects: 14-17C-33
Service: Entertainment PR

Ravelle Brickman Public Relations
Ravelle Brickman, Pres
53 Horatio St
New York NY 10014-1510
212-924-1254
Subjects: 99
Service: Publicity/public relations
Memo: Consumer products, business-to-business, and non-profits.

Re:Sources
Betty Levine
194 Grant Ave
Newton Centre MA 02159
617-244-1874
Subjects: 99
Service: PR services for books/products

Rentsch Associates
Gail Rentsch
1841 Broadway
New York NY 10023-7603
212-397-7341; Fax: 212-397-7381
Subjects: 99
Service: Book publicity

Romer Communications Inc
Karen Romer, Pres
135 E 57th St
New York NY 10022-2009
212-575-1892; Fax: 212-869-6584
Subjects: 99
Service: TV/radio/print Interviews
Memo: Special $5,000 five-city media tour.

Ron Marin Associates
Ron Marin
9 Union Pl
Newton NJ 07860-1817
201-579-3369
Subjects: 99
Service: Publicity services

Roskin/Friedman
Linda Clark
8425 West 3rd St #309
Los Angeles CA 90048
213-653-5411; Fax: 213-653-3663
Subjects: 99
Service: Book publicity

Ruder Finn
David Finn
301 East 57th St 3rd Fl
New York NY 10022
212-593-6400; Fax: 212-593-6398
Subjects: 99
Service: Book publicity

Russ Fons Public Relations
Las Vegas NV 89130
702-658-7654
Subjects: 99
Service: Book publicity

S

S&S Public Relations
Lisa Freed and Jill Schmidt
40 Skokie Blvd #430
Northbrook IL 60062-1617
708-291-1616; Fax: 708-291-1758
Subjects: 99
Service: PR

Savvy Management
Anthony Staffieri
80 4th Ave #800
New York NY 10003-5226
212-477-1717; Fax: 212-477-1736
Subjects: 99
Service: All services

The Sayles Organization
Nancy Sayles
5321 Coldwater Canyon Ave
Sherman Oaks CA 91401-6110
818-769-4466
Subjects: 99
Service: Book publicity

Selma Shapiro Public Relations
Selma Shapiro, Pres
271 Madison Ave
New York NY 10016-1001
212-867-7038; Fax: 212-867-8641
Subjects: 99
Service: Book review media, radio, TV

SES Media Management
Steve Urevith
9 Diana Ct
Ramsey NJ 07446
201-934-8940; Fax: 201-934-0839
800-989-4405
Subjects: 56M
Service: This company takes authors on radio and TV tours

Shapian and Associates
Betty Shapian, Pres
5900 Wilshire Blvd #1400
Los Angeles CA 90036-5013
213-937-3611; Fax: 213-930-1840
Subjects: 99
Service: PR
Memo: See also On the Scene Production.

Sharp PR
Denise Sharpton, Pres
PO Box 710452
Dallas TX 75371
214-821-9000; Fax: 214-826-8802
Subjects: 11-33-49-56W
Service: PR

The Shepard Agency
Jean Shepard
SE Plaza
Pawling Savings Bank Bldg #3
Brewster NY 10509
914-279-2900; Fax: 914-279-3239
Subjects: 99
Service: PR

Shepard Public Relations
Sally Jean Shepard
100 Avenida Miraflores
Belvedere Tiburon CA 94920-1404
415-435-3571; Fax: 415-435-9257
Subjects: 11-27-71-99
Service: Food/art/travel/book publicity

Sheridan-Elson Communications
30 West 86th St
New York NY 10024-3644
212-239-2000; Fax: 212-629-4417
Subjects: 99
Service: Radio/TV

Sheryn Hara & Associates
Sheryn Hara, Pres
4208 198th SW #105
Lynnwood WA 98036
206-775-7868; Fax: 206-776-1664
Subjects: 99
Service: Publicity and promotion services for authors, speakers, and trainers

Sotres Link
Joanne Sotres
244 Madison Ave
New York NY 10016-2817
212-532-4164
Subjects: 99
Service: Book publicity

Souder & Bertone Association
Rosemary Souder
2214 NE 8th St
Gainesville FL 32609
904-376-7529
Subjects: 99
Service: Book publicity-literary agent

Strictly Book Promotions
Dan Vojir
21 Isis St #102
San Francisco CA 94103
415-626-2665; Fax: 415-431-4425
E-mail: strictly@bookpromo.com
Web: http://www.bookpromo.com
Services: Book publicity

Susan Fassberg Communications
Susan Fassberg
431 1/2 N Hayworth St
Los Angeles CA 90048
213-655-3647
Subjects: 61(CA)-99
Service: PR

Susan Friedman Public Relations
Susan Friedman, Pres
6861 Yellowstone Blvd #210
Forest Hills NY 11375-3313
718-520-8829; Fax: 212-989-7178
Subjects: 99
Service: PR for authors and publishers

Susan Magrino Agency
Susan Magrino, Pres
167 East 73rd St
New York NY 10021-3510
212-744-2004; Fax: 212-744-3304
Subjects: 11-27-43-75-99
Service: Book publicity

Susan Ostrov Associates
Susan Ostrov
32 Valleywood Rd
Cos Cob CT 06807
203-629-4416; Fax: 203-629-5759
Subjects: 99
Service: Book PR

Suzy Strauss & Associates
Suzy Strauss
3230 Octavia St
San Francisco CA 94123-2211
415-673-4773; Fax: 415-673-4757
Subjects: 99(books/theatre/retail stores)
Service: PR and advertising

Syntax
Cynthia Kirk
326 Cumberlain
Brooklyn NY 11238
718-875-3502; Fax: 718-875-2954
Subjects: 99
Service: Book publicity

T

Talk Radio
Video Marketing of Minneapolis I
7850 Metro Pky #206
Bloomington MN 55425-1521
612-851-8710; Fax: 612-851-8706
Subjects: 99
Service: Gets authors on talk radio shows

Targetron Inc
220 5th Ave
New York NY 10001-7708
212-889-2323
Subjects: 99
Service: Video news releases production and distribution

Ted Barkus, Publicist
1512 Spruce St
Philadelphia PA 19102-4524
215-545-0616; Fax: 215-545-7976
Subjects: 99
Service: Book publicity

Television Communicators Media
Robert D Wechter
Communication Service
4626 Davenport St NW
Washington DC 20016-4418
202-966-6616
Subjects: 99
Service: Help for TV PR: TV media, interview training, spokesperson, press consultant, court testimony, full service media communication and will help with speaking and writing speeches

Thomas P Seigenthaler PR
Beth Seigenthaler
2909 Poston Ave
Nashville TN 37203-1346
615-327-7999; Fax: 615-327-8093
Subjects: 99
Service: Book publicity

Toni Werbell Public Relations
Toni Werbell
5 West 86th St
New York NY 10024-3603
212-662-5450; Fax: 212-662-5450
Subjects: 99
Service: PR for books, public policy, etc

V

V M Frantz & Company
Ginna Frantz
271 Madison Ave
New York NY 10016-1001
212-697-4288; Fax: 212-687-0564
Subjects: 99
Service: Book publicity

Valerie Ryan Media Services
Valerie Ryan
1352 NE 62nd St
Seattle WA 98115
206-524-1795; Fax: 206-523-5740
Subjects: 61(WA)-99
Service: Publicist/media escort

Vantage Point Publicity
Victoria Sutherland
2389 Cherry Ln
Cedar MI 49621-9411
616-228-6260; Fax: 616-228-6260
Subjects: 99
Service: Book publicity

Vicki Eisenberg Agency
Vicki Eisenberg
929 Fernwood Dr
Richardson TX 75080-4935
214-918-9593; Fax: 214-918-9976
Subjects: 99
Service: Multi-city tours TV and radio

W

Warburg & Associates
Sue Rayner Warburg
2390 Powell St #407
San Francisco CA 94133-1446
415-921-0461; Fax: 415-362-9747
Subjects: 99
Service: PR for books, authors,
 non-profits, and special events

Watermark Communications
Barbara Caswell
PO Box 2959
Petaluma CA 94953-2959
707-763-0252; Fax: 707-769-9616
Subjects: 99
Service: Book publicity

Weintraub & FitzSimons
Louis Weintraub
488 Madison Ave
New York NY 10022
212-688-1932
Subjects: 99
Service: Book publicity

Weston Communications
10280 County Rd 18
Eden Prairie MN 55347-5100
612-941-3090; Fax: 612-941-3090
Subjects: 99
Service: Book publicity
:

Abbreviations Used

Territory

CN	Canada
IT	International
MX	Mexico
OT	Other
US	United States with some state abbreviations for the different states

Markets

BK	Bookstores
CO	Colleges
JB	Jobbers
MM	Mass Markets
NS	Newsstands
OT	Other
PL	Public Libraries
RO	Retail Outlets
SC	Schools
SL	Special Libraries

Items

CA	Calendars
CO	Comics
CR	Craft Items
GA	Games
GC	Greeting Cards
GI	Gifts
HC	Hardcovers
MA	Maps and Atlases
MG	General / Special Magazines
ML	Literary Magazines
MM	Mass Market Books
NP	Newspapers
OP	Out of Print Books
OT	Other Items
PB	Trade Paperbacks
PO	Posters
RC	Records
RM	Remainders
SB	Stickers/Bookmarks
ST	Stationery
SW	Software
TA	Tapes, Audio
TO	Toys
TV	Tapes, Video
TX	Textbooks
US	Used books

Marketing Services and Publishing Consultants

The following individuals and companies can provide advice and/or services to help you market your books.

A

AAB Communications
Joan Tharp
2809 Wayzata Blvd
Minneapolis MN 55405
612-374-4888; 800-243-9712;
 Fax: 612-374-9642
Subjects: 99

About Books
Marilyn Ross
425 Cedar St
PO Box 1500
Buena Vista CO 81211-1500
719-395-2459; Fax: 719-395-8374
Subjects: 99
Service: Complete PR & marketing services

Alan C Hood & Company
Alan C Hood Jr, Pres
PO Box 775
Chambersburg PA 17201-2509
717-267-0867; Fax: 717-267-0572
Subjects: 99
Service: Publishing consultant

Alpha Answering Service
Dan L'Heureux, Pres
1310 West 98th St
Minneapolis MN 55431-2614
612-884-1111; Fax: 612-888-9868
Subjects: 99
Service: They do various tasks, message taking, voice mail, etc

American Media Group
Michael Patrick, Acct Exec
7300 W 110th St #960
Overland Park KS 66210
913-345-9987; Fax: 913-345-8797
Subjects: 99
Service: Marketing products on TV

American Passage Media Corp
6211 W Howard St
Niles IL 60648-4114
206-282-8111
Subjects: 31-48-99
Service: Places ads in military weeklies and college locations

American Passage Media Corp
215 W Harrison
Seattle WA 98119
800-426-5537; Fax: 206-282-1280
Subjects: 31-48-99
Service: Places ads in military weeklies and college locations

Anthony Schulte, Consultant
Anthony Schulte
488 Madison Ave #1120
New York NY 10022-5702
212-751-1029; Fax: 212-826-9496
Subjects: 99
Service: Financial consultant

Atlantic Accord
Arjaan Everts
1229 19th St NW
Washington DC 20036
202-659-5714; Fax: 202-429-4912
Subjects: 99
Service: Mergers, acquistions, sales (publishing companies)

Authentic Information Center
Kwaku Kushindana
PO Box 52916
Baton Rouge LA 70892-2916
504-356-0076
Subjects: 49(non-fiction only)
Service: Editorial assistance, marketing plans, promotional tours, interviews, etc, for self-publishers, authors, and small publishers

B

Berkery Noyes & Co
Joseph W Berkery, Pres
50 Broad St
New York NY 10004-2307
212-668-3022
Subjects: 99
Service: Investment banker

Nat Bodian, Consultant
5 Henley Ave
Cranford NJ 07016
908-272-5810
Subjects: 56-99
Service: Scholarly/technical books

Booksales Marketing
Robert Morris
407 East 100th St
Minneapolis MN 55420
612-884-2294
Subjects: 39R-99
Service: Sets up national sales forces

Brady & Paul Communications
John Brady & Greg Paul
63 Hill Side Ave
Melrose MA 02176
617-665-4941
Subjects: 99
Service: Magazine consultants design, edit

Business Marketing Consultants
Stephen Kerr, Pres
2588-D El Camino Real #287
Carlsbad CA 92008
619-967-7916; Fax: 619-967-6806
Subjects: 99
Service: Mergers & acquisitions (book & magazine publishers)

C

Carla Ruff
666 29th St
San Francisco CA 94131-2206
415-826-9008
Subjects: 99
Service: Sales/marketing/PR

Catalog Solutions
Jess F Clarke Jr, Pres
521 Riverside Ave
Westport CT 06880-5703
203-454-1919; Fax: 203-226-7333
Subjects:99
Service: Catalog products, especially TV top sellers

Christine Hopf-Lovette
1345 Edgewood Rd
Redwood City CA 94062-2730
415-369-6286
Subjects: 99
Service: Sales/marketing/PR for books

Clifford Publishing Services
Anna Clifford, Pres
96 Ingram Hill
Essex CT 06426
203-767-7662; Fax: 203-767-7662
Subjects: 71-99
Service: Marketing/sales/promotional

Cole & Associates
John Cole, Pres
1780 Daniel Bray Hwy
Stockton NJ 08559
609-397-2699; Fax: 609-397-2606
Subjects: 23-99
Service: Multimedia, database publishing

Cole Associates
David and Mary Lee Cole
721 Creston Rd
Berkeley CA 94708
510-525-6902; Fax: 510-528-0842
E-Mail: dcole@well.com
Subjects: 99(book publicity & marketing)
Service: Business planning, staff training, sales management, direct mail management, marketing plans, etc

Connie Goddard Book Development
Connie Goddard
203 N Wabash Ave
Chicago IL 60601-2406
312-759-5822
Subjects: 99

Cowan Liebowitz & Latman PC
Martin P Levin, Counsel
605 Third Ave
New York NY 10158
212-503-6200
Subjects: 99
Service: Legal assistance, acquisition advice

Creative Learning Products
Dir of Marketing
150 Morris Ave
Springfield NJ 07081-1315
201-467-0266
Subjects: 21-31-76-79
Service: Children's toy/book/video/games

Cross River Publishing Consultants
Thomas Woll, Pres
3 Holly Hill Ln
Katonah NY 10536-2405
914-232-6708
Subjects: 99
Service: Book publishing consultant

Crouch International
1156 Ave of the Americas #710
New York NY 10000
212-944-2113
Subjects: 99
Service: Management consultants

D

D L Blair
1051 Franklin Ave
Garden City NY 11530-2907
516-746-3700; Fax: 516-746-3889
Subjects: 99
Service: Sweepstakes consultants

Darian Direct
Vivian Darian Sudhalter
4 Judkins Ct
Merrimac MA 01860-1513
508-346-9682
Subjects: 23-99

David R Replogle and Assoc
David Replogle, Pres
75 Terry Dr #223
Hingham MA 02044-0001
617-749-1988
Subjects: 99
Service: Specializing in new technology

Don Jagoda Associates
4370 Tujunga Ave #150
Studio City CA 91604-2776
818-508-3000; Fax: 818-508-3034
Subjects: 99
Service: Sweepstakes and games

Don Jagoda Associates
100 Marcus Dr
Melville NY 11775-0002
516-454-1800; Fax: 516-454-1833
Subjects: 99
Service: Sweepstakes and games

Doyen Literary Service
B J Doyen
19005 660th St
Newell IA 50568-9801
712-272-3300
Subjects: 99

E

EBSCO Telemarketing
Bob Cortellino
1707 69th St #201
North Bergen NJ 07047
800-373-0533; Fax: 201-854-3174
Subjects: 19-19M
Service: Telemarketing

Elkay Publishing Services
Linda Kahn
239 East 79th St
New York NY 10021-0810
212-288-6188; Fax: 212-935-4172
Subjects: 12-19-31E-51E
Service: Consults in sales, marketing, and distribution of professional books

F

FAC Services Group
501 Indust Dr
Bensenville IL 60106-1320
708-238-4130
Subjects: 99
Service: Sweepstakes/games

G

Game-Show Placements
Bob Robertson, Pres
7011 Willoughby Ave
Hollywood CA 90038-2332
213-874-7818; Fax: 213-874-0643
E-Mail: gsp@ix.netcom.com
Subjects: 33-99
Service: Offers 5 programs to get your books featured on TV, the Internet, & movies: Game-Show Placements, Sports Price Network, Products-In-Film Registry, Cable Network 800# Showcase, & Internet Game Placements. About $195.00 per placement.

Gilpin Publishing Consultant
Wayne Gilpin
PO Box 597
Alliston ON Canada L0M 1A0
705-424-6507; Fax: 705-435-7369
Subjects: 61(Canada)
Service: Marketing, distribution, info, etc

H

Hallenbook
Leo Hallen, Pres
County Route 9
PO Box 357
Chatham NY 12037
518-392-4526; Fax: 518-392-4557
Subjects: 99
Service: Sales/marketing for publishers

Hill/Martin Associates
Duke Hill
756 Collier Dr
San Leandro CA 94577
510-483-2939
Subjects: 99
Service: Sales/marketing of books

The Huenefeld Company
John Huenefeld, Editor
The Huenefeld Newsletter
41 North Road #201
Bedford MA 01730-1037
617-275-1070; 800-441-6224
Subjects: 56-99
Service: Consulting

I

InfoCision Management
Alisa Getzinger
325 Springside Dr
Akron OH 44333
216-668-1400
Subjects:99
Service: Outbound telemarketing
Memo: Free newsletter called: "TeleResponse"

INTERPUB
Cliff Martin, Pres
1215 Fir Ln
PO Box 50123
Eugene OR 97405
541-342-6901; Fax:541-342-6901
E-Mail: cliffmar@efn.org
Subjects: 56-99
Service: Special markets consultant

Irene Handberg International
Irene Handberg, Consultant
300 East 93rd St
New York NY 10128
212-996-5983
Subjects: 21-23-31E-76
Service: Consulting in distribution, product development, and forming strategic partnerships.

Book Publishing Resource Guide   Page 375

J

Jameson Advertising Inc
Roland Grybauskas, Pres
96 Morton St
New York NY 10014-3326
212-645-4646
Subjects: 99
Service: Marketing, product development

Jane Williams Consultant
Bluestocking Press
3333 Gold Country Dr
PO Box 1014
Placerville CA 95667-1014
916-622-8586
Subjects: 31(educational markets)
Service: Home schooling consultant

K

Kaufmann & Associates
Deborah Kaufmann
3422 E Howell
Seattle WA 98122
206-324-4258; Fax: 206-324-2392
Subjects: 73-99
Service: Marketing/promotion services

L

Laing Communications
Christine Laing, Editorial Dir
Management Update Newsletter
16250 NE 80th St
Redmond WA 98052
206-869-6313; Fax: 206-869-6318
Subjects: 56P

M

Marden-Kane Inc
36 Maple Pl
Manhasset NY 11030-1927
516-365-3999; Fax: 516-365-5250
Subjects:99
Service: Contests, games, incentives, sweepstakes
Memo: Chicago: 312-266-4919; Los Angeles: 310-578-5802; San Francisco: 415-771-2489.

Margaret Liddiard
Marketing Communications for Publishers
15823 OK Mill Rd
Snohomish WA 98290-7731
206-335-1279; Fax: 206-335-5973
Subjects: 99
Service: Marketing and publicity campaign

Marketing Directions Inc
Brian Jud
PO Box 715
Avon CT 06001-9965
203-675-1344
Subjects: 99(for self-published authors)
Service: Distribution network creation, also pricing strategies, promotion ideas, talk shows

McHugh Publishing Reports
John B McHugh, Consultant
5747 N Ames Ter
Glendale WI 53209
414-351-3056; Fax: 414-351-0666
Subjects: 56-99
Service: Specialties: educational, professional, and association sales

Media Weavers
Linny and Dennis Stovall
Blue Heron Publishing
24450 NW Hansen Rd
Hillsboro OR 97124-8355
503-621-3911; Fax: 503-621-9826
Subjects: 61(NW US)-99
Service: Production/promotion consultants

Medianet
Amy Plummer
PO Box 1087
Carlisle PA 17013
717-243-4285; Fax: 717-243-1810
Subjects:99
Service: Distributes editorial requests
Memo: E-Mail: USLifeLine@aol.com or 71344.2761@compuserve.com.

MGP Direct
Roberta Rosenberg, Pres
PO Box 841
Bowie MD 20718-0841
301-464-9423; Fax: 301-262-7919
Subjects: 19M-56
Service: Direct marketing/adverstising
Memo: DM agency specializing in books, magazines, newsletters, electronic publishing. List brokerage, media placement,copywriting, strategic planning, etc.

Moseley Associates
270 Madison Ave #1207
New York NY 10016-0601
212-213-6673; Fax: 212-213-6675
Subjects: 99
Service: Management consultants

N

New Editions International Ltd
Gerry White, Editor
PO Box 2578
Sedona AZ 86339
602-282-9574; Fax: 602-282-9730
E-Mail: neweditions@sedona.net
Subjects: 39H-53
Service: Consulting
Memo: Formerly First Editions

North/SW Publishers Consortium
Lynette and Arthur Horn
6101 Truck Village Dr
PO Box 1632
Mount Shasta CA 96067
916-938-2353; Fax: 916-938-6343
Subjects: 99
Service: Publicity/exhibits/representing

P

Partnership Book Services
Stanley Thiessen, Pres
PO Box L
Hillsboro KS 67063
800-442-1670; Fax: 316-947-3392
Subjects: 21-21T-27-75
Service: Most of our published work falls under the "subsidy" catagory,but we do offer distribution/fulfillment & marketing services

Paz & Associates
Donna Paz
212 Sloan Rd
Nashville TN 37209-4612
615-298-2303; Fax: 615-298-9864
Subjects: 99
Service: Consults booksellers/publishers

Penton Publishing
Penton Press
1100 Superior Ave
Cleveland OH 44114-2543
216-243-5700; 800-321-7003; Fax: 216-243-4265
Subjects: 99
Service: Research Services

PMA Literary & Film Management
Peter Miller
220 W 19th St #501
New York NY 10011-4035
212-929-1222
Subjects: 56
Service: Representation, packaging, writing

PMC Partnership Ltd
90 Post Rd West
Westport CT 06880-4208
203-227-8478
Subjects: 99
Service: Sweepstakes, games, and contests; Send for brochure

PrimeLife
127 S Olive St
Orange CA 92666-9942
714-744-1291; 800-284-3140
Subjects: 35A(mature market)
Service: Advertising, PR, DM, promotions

Professional Publishers Group
Al Robertson
Brentwood House Ctr
127 Franklin Rd #310
Brentwood TN 37027
615-371-8097; 800-869-6969
Subjects: 19B-19L-39-55L
Service: Telemarketing

The Publisher's Consultant
Robert Avery
15 Chapman Pl
PO Box 737
Redding CT 06896-0737
203-938-9162
Subjects: 99
Service: Mass market sales, distribution

R

R L Silver Associates
Ronald Silver, Pres
386 Park Ave S
New York NY 10016-8804
212-684-0560; Fax: 212-685-9468
Subjects: 99
Service: PR, advertising, graphics

Reid Resources
W Kathleen Reid
454 West 23rd St
New York NY 10011-2138
212-206-0035; Fax: 212-206-8507
Subjects: 31
Service: School, education markets, also home education market

Sarris Bookmarketing Service
Shirley Sarris, Pres
Tools of the Book Trade list
315 West 23rd St #10C
New York NY 10011-2247
212-229-1690
Subjects: 56-99
Service: Marketing

Scott/Satz Group
Louis Satz and Gloria Scott
539 Monarch Ridge
Walnut Creek CA 94596-2955
510-934-2919; Fax: 510-930-8918
Subjects:99
Service: Sales and marketing consultants

Selling Your Business
Jim Martin, Pres
James Martin & Assoc
3061 Cranston Dr PO Box 798
Dublin OH 43017
614-889-9747; Fax: 614-889-2659
Subjects:99
Service: Publishing merger, acquisition, and financial services

Sensible Solutions
Judith Appelbaum
271 Madison Ave #1007
New York NY 10016
212-687-1761; Fax: 212-867-8641
Subjects: 99
Service: General marketing services

Sid Gross & Associates
Sid Gross
10 E End Ave
New York NY 10021-1106
212-988-3251
Subjects: 99
Service: Advice on marketing books to bookstores

The Sweepstakes Center
2290 East Ave
Rochester NY 14610-2515
716-256-0080
Subjects: 99(
Service: Custom or shared sweepstakes, from concept through fulfillment

T

Tudor Publishers Inc
Eugene E Pfaff Jr/Martin Hester
PO Box 38366
Greensboro NC 27438
910-282-5907
Subjects: 31-35-55-57-63-65
Service: Social workers, counselors, pastor

V

Ventura Associates
Lisa K Manhart, VP
1211 Ave of the Americas
New York NY 10036
212-302-8277; Fax: 212-302-2587
Subjects:99
Service: Sweepstakes Consultants
Memo: Marla Altberg, Sr VP, Marketing

Veronis Suhler & Associates
Martin Maleska
350 Park Ave
New York NY 10022
212-935-4990
Subjects: 99
Service: Venture capitalists, M&A, investment bankers for all media

Video Enterprises
13340 Olympic Blvd #365
Los Angeles CA 90064-1608
310-312-1500; Fax: 310-312-1568
Subjects: 33-99
Service: Game show placements

Vocational Marketing Services
Michael S Walsh
17600 S Williams St #6
Thornton IL 60476
708-877-2814
Subjects: 19C-31
Service: Vocational education, books, AV, software, materials

W

Williams College Marketing
Susanne K Williams
49 Sidney Pl
Brooklyn NY 11201-4645
718-802-1407
Subjects: 31-65-99
Service: College adoptions

Wittman Associates
Allan Wittman, Pres
150 Fifth Ave
New York NY 10011-4311
212-627-0799; Fax: 212-633-6294
Subjects: 99
Service: Management consultants, business plans, mergers and acquisitions, and sales

The Write Place
Pat Sabiston
4412 Fletcher St
Panama City FL 32405-1017
904-769-4345; Fax: 904-769-4348
Subjects: 99
Service: Marketing/promo for small press

Writers & Research Inc
4810 St Paul Blvd
Rochester NY 14617-1744
716-266-4630; Fax: 716-544-1838
Subjects: 99

Speaker's Bureaus

The following associations and companies help authors and other speakers to book engagements. One of the best ways to promote your books is to encourage your authors to get out and speak to groups around the country. These bureaus may be open to representing your authors as speakers.

American Program Bureau
Ms Chris Harris
36 Crafts St
Newton MA 02158-1249
617-965-6600
Subjects: 69-99

Authors Unlimited
Arlynn Greenbaum, Pres
31 East 32nd St #300
New York NY 10016-5509
212-481-8484
Subjects: 99
Service: Directory of authors (paid list)
Memo: Arranges lectures at colleges, conventions, churches, conferences, corporations, museums, libraries, bookstores, etc.

B K Nelson Lecture Bureau
Bonita K Nelson
84 Woodland Rd
Pleasantville NY 10570
914-741-1322; Fax: 914-741-1324
Subjects: 19-57-99
Memo: Some of the authors she represents via her lecture bureau include Steve Garvey, Roger Ailes, Charles Scribner III, Robert Bly, Edward Taub, and Elliot Katt. Also a literary agent.

BG Speakers Bureau
1362 N Dohney Dr
Los Angeles CA 90069-1725
310-858-1944; Fax:
Subjects: 19-19M-39-57-69
Memo: Specializes in authors, business, financial, health care, marketing, media, sales motivation, and sports personalities.

Briarwood Writers' Alliance
Bill Thompson
61 Briarwood Cir
Needham Heights MA 02194-1829
617-449-7638
Subjects: 75-90-95-99
Service: Speaker's bureau for college, library (Literary & authors only)

Burns Sports Celebrity Serv Inc
David Burns
230 N Michigan Ave #1010
Chicago IL 60601
312-236-2377
Subjects: 69-99

Capital Speakers Inc
807 National Press Bldg
Washington DC 20004
202-393-0772
Subjects: 17-55-69-99
Memo: This company advises organizations on which speakers will best suit their needs and then helps them to establish contacts with the appropriate agents.

Celebrity Endorsement Network
Noreen Jenney, Pres
Canoga Park CA 91303
818-704-6709; Fax: 818-704-8567
Subjects: 33-69-99(celebrities)
Memo: This company finds celebrities to endorse products or act as spokespeople on TV, infomercials, and other advertising and promotional campaigns. They have found celebrities for Revlon, Denny's, Anhauser-Busch, and others.

The Chelsea Forum
Jane Pasanen
420 West 23rd St #5D
New York NY 10011-2172
212-243-4400
Subjects: 99
Service: Author lecture bureau

CLASS -- Speakers
Authors, and Speakers Services
1645 S Rancho Sante Fe Rd #102
San Marcos CA 92069-5188
619-471-1722
Subjects: 63-99

Eagles Talent Associates
30 Westfield Rd
PO Box 859
Short Hills NJ 07078-1224
201-376-3737; 800-345-5607
Subjects: 99(speakers and entertainers)

Five Star Speakers Trainers & Consultants
Nancy Lauterbach
8685 W 96th St
Shawnee Mission KS 66212-3316
913-648-6480
Subjects: 99

Global Issues Speakers Bureau
Lois Hoffmann, Dir
PO Box 15250
Washington DC 20003
202-546-3950; 800-428-3927
Subjects: 41-44-55-65

Goodman Speakers Bureau
Diane Goodman
56 Arbor St
Hartford CT 06106-1201
860-233-0460; Fax: 860-236-6674
Subjects: 99

Greater Talent Network
150 Fifth Ave
New York NY 10011-4311
212-645-4200; Fax: 212-627-1471
Subjects: 99
Memo: Represents Olympia Dukakis, Carol Beck, and Gail Sheehy (author of Passages and The Silent Passage).

Harry Walker Agency
One Penn Plz #2400
New York NY 10118-2491
212-563-0700; Fax: 212-629-7958
Subjects: 55-99
Memo: Represents George Bush, Dick Cheney, Lynn Martin, and Marlin Fitzwater.

Hilton Memory Seminar
Joseph Kessler
Kessler Management Intl
10747 Wilshire Blvd #807
Los Angeles CA 90024-4455
213-824-3333; 800-447-9272; Fax: 213-470-2111
Subjects: 19-57-99

Inc Speakers Bureau
Ken Eisenstein
American Program Bureau
36 Crafts St
Newton MA 02158
617-965-6600; Fax:
Subjects: 19-57

International Management Group
Cuyahoga Savings Bldg
Cleveland OH 44100
216-522-1200
Subjects: 69
Service: Sports stars managers

Jodi F Soloman Speakers Bureau
325 Huntington Ave #112
Boston MA 02115-4546
617-266-3450; 800-669-2857; Fax: 617-266-5660
Subjects: 99
Memo: Represents Sarah Weddington (attorney who argued Roe vs. Wade).

Key Seminars Speakers Bureau
18885 Valley View Rd
Eden Prairie MN 55346-3942
612-949-8833; Fax: 612-835-9488
Subjects: 19-33-69-99

Keynote Inc
1201 Grand Ave
West Des Moines IA 50265-3523
515-223-5606
Subjects: 19M-56

Keynote Speakers Inc
425 Sherman Ave
Palo Alto CA 94306-1823
415-325-9711
Subjects: 99

Leigh Bureau
11900 W Olympic Blvds #619
Los Angeles CA 90064-1151
310-442-9898
Subjects: 99

Leigh Speakers Bureau
50 Division St #200
Somerville NJ 08876-2943
908-253-8600; Fax: 908-253-8601
Subjects: 99
Memo: Represents Patricia Aburdene (author of Megatrends for Women), Frances Hesselbein (President of Peter Drucker Foundation), and Anita Hill.

MasterMedia Speakers Bureau
Ken Goody, Dir
134 Hillsborough Rd
Belle Mead NJ 08502-2707
908-359-1647; Fax: 212-348-2020
Subjects: 19-55-57-65
Memo: 800-453-2873; 212-260-5600

National Speakers Bureau
222 Wisconsin Ave
Lake Forest IL 60045-1735
708-295-1122; 800-323-9442; Fax: 708-295-5292
Subjects: 99

National Speakers Forum
5028 Wisconsin Ave NW #301
Washington DC 20016-1735
202-244-1789
Subjects: 55-99

Nationwide Speakers Bureau
130 El Camino Dr
Beverly Hills CA 90212-2600
310-273-8807; Fax: 310-273-5928
Subjects: 99
Memo: Represents Tracy Austin, Rita Davenport (author of Making Time / Making Money), and Faith Popcorn (author of The Popcorn Report).

New Directions Speakers/Programs
Gail Larsen
78 Old Kings Hwy
Sandwich MA 02563-1864
508-888-6702
Subjects: 99
Service: Represents 30 speakers
Memo: Represents Susanne Sims (environmental marketing consultant), Beth Jarman (author of Break Point and Beyond), and Jennifer James (cultural anthropologist).

PAS Speakers Bureau
Molly Burns, Dir
Publ Assn of the South
PO Box 43533
Birmingham AL 35243
205-967-4387; Fax: 205-967-0580
Subjects: 61(South)-99
Service: Features PAS writers/publishers

Portland Speakers Bureau
Carly Holliday
703 Broadway
Portland OR 97201
503-241-2411
Subjects: 61(OR/WA)-99
Service: World wide with any subjects

Professional Business Speakers
Jeanine Anderson
8015 Holland Ct #C
Arvada CO 80005-2272
303-425-9652
Subjects: 19
Service: Primarily to business audiences

Promotional SportsStars SpeakerB
130 El Camino Dr
PO Box 3768
Beverly Hills CA 90212-2700
310-273-8807; Fax: 310-273-5928
Subjects: 17-69

Results Unlimited
Helen Trautman
421 Cochran Rd #205
Pittsburgh PA 15228-1255
412-344-7477; Fax: 412-343-3883
Subjects: 99(speakers & program planning)

Sisters in Crime Speakers Bureau
Elaine Raco Chase, Dir
4333 Majestic Ln
Fairfax VA 22033-3538
Subjects: 56W-84
Service: For women mystery writers

Southwest Speakers Bureau Inc
5485 Belt Line Rd
Dallas TX 75240-7655
214-458-1627; Fax: 214-458-0386
Subjects: 99
Memo: Answering machine correction.

SpeakerConnect USA
Atlanta Speakers Bureau
2859 Paces Ferry Rd #1830
Atlanta GA 30339-5701
404-432-1394; Fax: 404-432-3528
Subjects: 99
Memo: Represents M Kay duPont (author of Business Etiquette and Professionalism).

The Speakers Network
Sandra Roork
2727 Rothwood Dr
PO Box 15222
Charlotte NC 28211-2621
704-364-7461; Fax: 704-364-4981
Subjects: 99

Walters Speakers Services
Dottie Walters
PO Box 1120
Glendora CA 91740
818-335-8069; Fax: 818-335-6127
Dottie@SpeakAndGrowRich.com
Subjects: 99

Washington Speakers Bureau
310 S Henry St
Alexandria VA 22314-3524
703-684-0555; Fax: 703-684-9378
Subjects: 99
Memo: Represents Nancy Austin (co-author of A Passion for Excellence), Dan Quayle, General Norman Schwarzkopf, John Sununu, and Jack Kemp.

Cooperative Marketing Services

The following companies and associations offer co-op marketing and publicity opportunities for book publishers. Co-op marketing programs provide an inexpensive way to test the potential of new markets.

1-800-BOOKSTORE
2680 Apple Way
Ann Arbor MI 48104-1802
313-998-0401
Subjects: 99
Service: Bookstore 800 system

African-American Value Pack
Andrew Morrison, Pres
NIA Publishing
139 Fulton St #804
New York NY 10038-2594
212-285-0865; 800-542-5578;
    Fax: 212-285-0282
Subjects: 49B
Service: Card pack

Amalgamated Publishers
Isaac Lester
350 W Ontario
Chicago IL 60610-4040
312-943-2033; Fax: 312-943-1478
Subjects: 49B(Black newspapers)
Service: 12,600,000 readers

Amalgamated Publishers
Michael House
45 W 45th St
New York NY 10036-4602
212-869-5220; Fax: 212-302-9406
Subjects: 49B(Black newspapers)
Service: 12,600,000 readers

Amalgamated Publishers
Michael Green
3200 Wilshire Blvd
Los Angeles CA 90010-1333
213-292-2456; Fax: 213-292-2034
Subjects: 49B(Black newspapers)
Service: 12,600,000 readers

Amalgamated Publishers
Alexandra Cantor, Dir
ASJA Newsletter
1501 Broadway #302
New York NY 10036-5501
212-997-0947; Fax: 212-768-7414
Subjects: 56W-99
Service: Professional writers

American Publishing Company
Susan Smith-Welch
dba The Kirksville Crier
506 W Potter Ave PO Box 1049
Kirksville MO 63501-1166
816-665-4663; 800-748-8249;
    Fax: 816-665-7794
Subjects: 99(newspaper classified ads)
Service: 260 local pubns

Books for Review
Jan Nathan, Dir
Publishers Marketing Assoc
2401 Pacific Coast Hwy #102
Hermosa Beach CA 90254-2734
310-372-2732; Fax: 310-374-3342
E-mail: PMAonline@aol.com
Subjects: 10
Service: Co-op mailing to reviewers

Bookseller Program
c/o Publishers Marketing Assn
2401 Pacific Coast Hwy #102
Hermosa Beach CA 90254-2734
310-372-2732; Fax: 310-374-3342
Subjects: 99
Service: Mailings to bookstores

CableMail
Robert Kweller
c/o ERS Media Services
24009 Ventura Blvd #230
Calabasas CA 91302-1418
818-591-7600; Fax: 818-591-7659
Subjects: 99
Service: Inserts in cable TV bills

Carol Wright Co-op
Donnelley Marketing
70 Seaview Ave
PO Box 10250
Stamford CT 06904
203-357-7277; 800-433-list;
    800-67-TARGET
Subjects: 35A-99
Service: Co-op mailings

Carol Wright Hispanic Co-op
Donnelley Marketing
70 Seaview Ave
PO Box 10250
Stamford CT 06904
203-357-7277; 800-433-list;
    800-67-TARGET
Subjects: 45(Spanish)-49(Hispanic)-99
Service: Co-op mailings

Cata-List Catalog Directory
c/o Venture Communications
60 Madison Ave 3rd Fl
New York NY 10010-1600
212-684-4800; Fax: 212-576-1129
Subjects: 99
Service: Inquiry postcards

CMP Executive Women Co-op
CMP Direct Marketing Services
One Jericho Plz
Jericho NY 11753
516-733-6801
Subjects: 19-73(business women)
Service: Co-op mailings

College Library Program
c/o Publishers Marketing Assn
2401 Pacific Coast Hwy #102
Hermosa Beach CA 90254-2734
310-372-2732; Fax: 310-374-3342
Subjects: 31E
Service: Mailings to colleges/univ

College Students Co-op
Ray Lewis, Marketing VP
Larry Tucker Inc
188 Broadway
Westwood NJ 07675-9865
201-307-8888; Fax: 201-307-1200
Subjects: 99
Service: College students

Conscious Products for Conscious
Steve Petterson, Pres
Excaliber Publishing Co
8190E Mira Mesa Blvd #323
San Diego CA 92126-2602
619-695-3091; Fax: 619-578-4445
Subjects: 39H-39R-53-54-57
Service: 10M(new age/2M recovery stores)
Memo: Conscious Products for
    Conscious People.

The Contact Sheet
Alexis Paarks, Publisher
Media Syndicate
PO Box D
Eldorado Springs CO 80025-0016
303-499-8358; Fax: 303-494-3330;
    800-533-2324
Subjects: 99
Service: Media contact sheet

Cosmic Connection TV
Catherine Masters, Exec Producer
EMA Inc
115 Church St
Decatur GA 30030-3326
404-371-1103
Subjects: 53-54
Service: A metaphysical TV ad channel
Memo: This metaphysical commercial
    program airs twice a week Tuesdays,
    7:30pm, and Fridays, 11:30pm) over
    cable TV to 240,000 homes in the
    Atlanta area.

DDDD Publications
Dee Francses
9715 Foster #A
St Louis MO 63114-2813
314-427-3329; 800-723-4077
E-Mail: dpoet@inlink.com
Subjects: 99
Service: Co-op mailings

Denali Press Co-op Mailings
The Denali Press
PO Box 021535
Juneau AK 99802-1535
907-586-6014; Fax: 907-463-6780
Subjects: 45-49(Hispanic)-78-80-99
Service: Libraries/bookstores/etc

Disability Marketing Group
EKA Marketing & Distribution
202-296-1488; Fax: 202-861-1645
Subjects: 39D
Service: Co-op
Memo: A subsidiary of Evan Kemp Associates Inc.

Elementary Co-Op
Ray Lewis, Marketing VP
Larry Tucker Inc
188 Broadway
Westwood NJ 07675-9865
201-307-8888; Fax: 201-307-1200
Subjects: 21-31-76-79
Service: Co-op

Excaliber Publishing Company
Karen Delia, Mktg Dir
8190E Mira Mesa Blvd #323
San Diego CA 92126-2602
619-695-3091; Fax: 619-578-4445
Subjects: 99
Service: Co-op

First Editions Coop Mailings
Sophie Tarila, Dir
2855 Southwest Dr #1
PO Box 2578
Sedona AZ 86336-3773
602-282-9574; Fax: 602-282-9730
Subjects: 39H-53-54
Service: 4344 retailers/950 music stores
Memo: Also 450 publications, 1,100 publishers, and 425 audio producers.

FYI Directory of News Sources
Julia Stocks Corneal, Publ
2 Evergreen Rd #2A
PO Box 868
Severna Park MD 21146-0868
410-647-1013; Fax: 410-647-9557
Subjects: 99
Service: Sent to 20,000 jouralists
Memo: FYI Directory of News Sources and Information is also available on computer disk.

Heritage Book News
Laird C Towle, Pres
c/o Heritage Books
1540 Pointer Ridge Pl
Bowie MD 20716-1800
301-390-7709
Subjects: 41G-98
Service: Genealogy co-op mailings

High School Students Co-op
Ray Lewis, Marketing VP
Larry Tucker Inc
188 Broadway
Westwood NJ 07675-9865
201-307-8888; Fax: 201-307-1200
Subjects: 99
Service: High school students

IBIS Information Services
Attn: Co-op Mailings
245 W 17th St
New York NY 10011-5300
212-779-1344
Subjects: 44-99
Service: Foreign libraries/bookstores

Imprint Catalog
13214 Shaker Square
Cleveland OH 44120-2315
216-751-9100
Subjects: 99
Service: University press books

International Publisher Alliance
c/o Powell Productions
11337 Starkey Rd #G2
Largo FL 33773-4701
813-391-3958; Fax: 813-391-4598
Subjects: 99
Service: Co-op exhibits-trade shows)

Interviews & Reviews
2218 Bamboo St
Mesquite TX 75150-3735
214-613-4033; Fax: 214-613-2244
Subjects: 99
Service: PR ads to broadcasters/eds

K-12 Library Program
c/o Publishers Marketing Assn
2401 Pacific Coast Hwy #102
Hermosa Beach CA 90254-2734
310-372-2732; Fax: 310-374-3342
Subjects: 31E
Service: Mailings to school libraries
Memo:

Leading Edge Review
Sheila Grams, Publisher
5133 Russell Ave S (55410)
PO Box 24068
Minneapolis MN 55424
612-929-9534; 800-729-9504
Subjects: 39H-53-54-57
Service: Book review co-op newsletter to bookstores and media.

LeadNet Card
Michael Gilbert
Skyline Communications
36 Court St PO Box 336
Geneseo NY 14454-1050
800-475-9266
Subjects: 99
Service: Free inquiry postcards

Leisure Years Co-Op
Ray Lewis, Mktg VP
Larry Tucker Inc
188 Broadway
Westwood NJ 07675-9865
201-307-8888; Fax: 201-307-1200
Subjects: 35A(retirement)-99
Service: Co-op

Literary Resource Quarterly
Paul Hensler, Editor
AYCS Productions
4401 Capitola Rd #5
Capitola CA 95010
800-995-1483; Fax: 800-995-1487
Subjects: 99
Service: Sent to 30,000 bookstores
Memo: This quarterly magazine format co-op mailing is sent to 30,000 bookstores and film and television rights buyers. Rates:$400/issue (8 issues) to $750/issue (1 issue) for a 4-color 1/9th page ad.

Mailing List Co-op Program
Brian Smart, Owner
ESA Publications
RR 1 Box 118AA
Archie MO 64725
816-293-5289; Fax:
Subjects: 83-86-90-95-99
Service: Small press publishers
Memo: Co-op mailing list program, merging mailing lists from small publishers. Also Small Presses Publications Catalog co-op book catalog.

Mardev
Robert Howells
245 W 17th St
New York NY 10011-5300
212-924-4490; Fax: 212-924-1440; 800-545-8517
Subjects: 99
Service: Mailings to foreign libr/bkstore

MarketSource
10 Abeel Rd
Cranbury NJ 08512
609-655-8990; Fax: 609-395-0737
Subjects: 21-31-76-99
Service: College/teen/golf co-ops

Mature Market Co-Op
Meg Traylor or Rick Frazier
Response Media Products
2323 Perimeter Park Dr #200
Atlanta GA 30341-1339
770-451-5478; Fax: 770-451-4929
Subjects: 35A-99
Service: Co-op mailings 500,000 annually

Metaphysical Co-Op Advertising
Steve Petterson, Pres
Excaliber Publishing Co
7954 Westbury Ave
San Diego CA 92126-2132
619-695-3091
Subjects: 39H-53-54
Service: Metaphysical bookstores

Metaphysical Reviews
Richard Fuller, Sr Editor
804 Perkins Ave NE
Grand Rapids MI 49505-5900
616-235-3095; Fax:
Subjects: 53-54(truth/love/integrity)
Service: Sent to 200 New Age mags
Memo: Reviews are sent quarterly to 200 New Age magazines plus placed on the Internet. Cost: $400.00 per year per title (for major publishers) and $300 per year per title (for smaller publishers).

Music Print Media Co-op
Bob Baker
Spotlight Publications
7350 Manchester #200
St Louis MO 63143-3108
314-781-0400; Fax: 314-781-0287
E-Mail: Bob101Ways@aol.com
Subjects: 14M-56M
Service: 700 music magazines & newspapers.

National Response Corporation
Philip Kratzer, Pres
Inwood Plz
2442 Cerrillos Rd #45
Santa Fe NM 87505-3262
Subjects: 99(newspaper classified ads)
Service: Network of 5,000 newspapers

National Suburban Marketing
Jim Cunningham, Sr VP
US Suburban Press
420 Lexington Ave #2150
New York NY 10170-0002
212-687-8425
Subjects: 99 FSIs
Service: Inserts in suburban newspapers

National Syndications
Lynn Hamlin, Book Mgr
230 Fifth Ave #2010
New York NY 10001-7704
212-686-8680; Fax: 212-889-1146
Subjects: 99
Service: Book ads in Parade & USA Weekend

New Age Cooperative Mailings
c/o New Editions Intl
2855 Southwest Dr #1
Sedona AZ 86336-3773
520-282-9574; Fax: 520-282-9730
Subjects: 39H-53-54-57
Service: Bookstores/retail outlets
Memo: Co-op mailings to bookstores & retail outlets.

New Book Showcase
Bruce Fisher
4123 N Longview
Phoenix AZ 85014-4949
800-880-9091; Fax: 602-279-6901
Subjects: 99
Service: A bi-monthly video trade magazine for booksellers featuring new books (paid listings), industry news, book fairs, book buying trends, etc.

New Parents Co-Op
Ray Lewis, Mktg VP
Larry Tucker Inc
188 Broadway
Westwood NJ 07675-9865
201-307-8888; Fax: 201-307-1200
Subjects: 21-31-35-76-79
Service: Co-op mailing

Newsmaker Interviews
8217 Beverly Blvd
Los Angeles CA 90048-4530
213-655-2793; Fax: 310-271-6073
Subjects: 99
Service: Radio/TV publicity directory

NPC Directory of News Services
Anne Schwartz
Natl Press Club Directory
529 14th St NW
Washington DC 20045-1000
202-662-7525; Fax: 202-662-7512
Subjects: 99

One-Stop Catalog Shop
c/o Visual Horizons
180 Metro Park
Rochester NY 14623-2610
716-424-5300; Fax: 716-424-5313
Subjects: 99
Service: Generates leads for catalogs & business services thru direct mail & Internet for 45 cents a lead.

Paisley Publishing
Susan Robuck
2604 Ashmore Ave
Chattanooga TN 37415-6353
615-870-8890
Subjects: 21

Perspectives Press Co-op Mailing
Pat Johnston, Publisher
Perspectives Press
PO Box 90318
Indianapolis IN 46290-0318
317-872-3055
Subjects: 31-35(adoption/infertility)
Service: Families/professionals/agencies

PMA Co-op Mailings
Jan Nathan, Dir
Publishers Marketing Assn
2401 Pacific Coast Hwy #102
Hermosa Beach CA 90254-2734
310-372-2732; Fax: 310-374-3342
E-mail: PMAonline@aol.com
Subjects: 10
Service: Co-op mailing to libraries/etc

Pre-School Co-op
Ray Lewis, Marketing VP
Larry Tucker Inc
188 Broadway
Westwood NJ 07675-9865
201-307-8888; Fax: 201-307-1200
Subjects: 21-31-76-79
Service: Co-op

Product Movers
297 State St
Norht Haven CT 06473-2131
203-287-0838; Fax:
Subjects: 99 FSIs
Service: Newspaper advertising supplement

Public Library Program
c/o Publishers Marketing Assn
2401 Pacific Coast Hwy #102
Hermosa Beach CA 90254-2734
310-372-2732; Fax: 310-374-3342
Subjects: 99
Service: Mailings to public library

Publicity Express
Barry Phillips
2966 Diamond St #442
San Francisco CA 94131
415-526-2974; 800-541-2897
Subjects: 99(interview directory)

Publishers Support Services
Linda F Radke
Five Star Publications
4696 W Tyson St
Chandler AZ 85226-2903
602-940-8182; Fax: 602-940-8787
Subjects: 19-19C-19L-27-31E-39-55L
Service: Doctors/lawyers/hospitals
Memo: PSS is sponsoring two new co-op mailings: 1100 Arizona libraries ($129.00 for full-page flyers) and a mailing to 10,000 vocational educators, career counselors, home economics teachers, etc.(cost: $160.00 per 1000 flyers).

QBI Library Conference Displays
Vendor Book Exhibit
Quality Books
918 Sherwood Dr
Lake Bluff IL 60044-2204
708-295-2010; Fax: 708-295-1556
Subjects: 99
Service: Library conferences

Quad Marketing
104 Holmes Dl
Albany NY 12208-1448
212-603-6000
Subjects: 99 FSIs
Service: Newspaper advertising supplement

Radio/TV Interview Report
Bradley Communications
135 E Plumstead Ave
PO Box 1206
Lansdowne PA 19050-8206
610-259-1070; Fax: 610-284-3704
Subjects: 99(radio interview pd listings)
Service: Sent to 4,700 radio/TV producers

Rights from USA Review
Jan Nathan, Dir
Publishers Marketing Assn
2401 Pacific Coast Hwy #102
Hermosa Beach CA 90254-2734
310-372-2732; Fax: 310-374-3342
E-Mail: PMAonline@aol.com
Subjects: 99
Service: Foreign rights co-op mailing

Select Information Exchange
SIE Sales Lead Program
244 W 54th St 6th Fl
New York NY 10019-5502
212-247-7238; Fax: 212-787-4269
Subjects: 99
Service: Free inquiry postcards

Sourcebooks Review
Dominique Raccah, Publ
Financial Sourcebooks
PO Box 372
Naperville IL 60566-0372
708-961-2161
Subjects: 19B-19I-19M(banking/insurance)
Service: 1000 editors and 3000 libraries

Southern Media Ventures
Shannon Smith, Mktg Dir
PO Box 41695
Nashville TN 37204-1695
Subjects: 99
Service: They will be doing periodic co-op mailings to libraries, bookstores, and almost any other place that sells books (garden centers, craft stores, bakeries, schools, hardware stores, etc).

Spanish Health and Women's Books
Ruth Gottstein
Volcano Press
PO Box 270
Volcano CA 95689
209-296-3445
Subjects: 39-45(Spanish)-73-78-80(Spanish)
Service: Also co-op mailings

Strawberry Patch
Diane Pfeifer
Gift Store Marketing Mailings
PO Box 52404
Atlanta GA 30355-0404
404-261-2197; Fax: 404-841-9586
Subjects: 21-27-31D-99(general gift)
Service: Cookbooks, baby/maternity books
Memo: Co-op mailings to genre-specific gift shop buyers.

Target Catalog Mailings
c/o Publishers Marketing Assn
2401 Pacific Coast Hwy #102
Hermosa Beach CA 90254-2734
310-372-2732; Fax: 310-374-3342
Subjects: 99
Service: Mailings to Libr/reviewers/store

Twin Peaks Press
PO Box 129
Vancouver WA 98666-0129
360-694-2492; Fax: 360-696-3210
Subjects: 99
Service: Co-op mailings

US Suburban Press
c/o National Home Delivery
420 Lexington Ave #453
New York NY 10170-0499
212-986-8986; Fax: 212-986-8033
Subjects: 99
Service: Inserts in suburban newspapers

Val-Pak Direct Marketing Systems
8605 Largo Lakes Dr
Largo FL 33773-4912
813-393-1270; Fax: 813-393-5003; 800-282-5725
Subjects: 99
Service: Direct marketing

Visual Horizons
One-Stop Catalog Shop
180 Metro Park
Rochester NY 14623-2666
716-424-5300; Fax: 716-424-5313
Subjects: 99
Service: Free inquiry postcards

VMS Co-op Mailing
Durward Humes
Visual Management Systems
PO Box 484
Wilmette IL 60091-0484
847-251-8880; Fax: 847-251-1919
Subjects: 19G
Service: Co-op

Yearbook of Experts, Authorities
and Spokespersons
Broadcast Interview Source
2233 Wisconsin Ave NW
Washington DC 20007-4104
202-333-4904; Fax: 202-342-5411
E-Mail: Yearbook@delphi.com
Subjects: 99
Service: Authors available for interview

Abbreviations Used

Territory

CN	Canada
IT	International
MX	Mexico
OT	Other
US	United States with some state abbreviations for the different states

Markets

BK	Bookstores
CO	Colleges
JB	Jobbers
MM	Mass Markets
NS	Newsstands
OT	Other
PL	Public Libraries
RO	Retail Outlets
SC	Schools
SL	Special Libraries

Items

CA	Calendars
CO	Comics
CR	Craft Items
GA	Games
GC	Greeting Cards
GI	Gifts
HC	Hardcovers
MA	Maps and Atlases
MG	General / Special Magazines
ML	Literary Magazines
MM	Mass Market Books
NP	Newspapers
OP	Out of Print Books
OT	Other Items
PB	Trade Paperbacks
PO	Posters
RC	Records
RM	Remainders
SB	Stickers/Bookmarks
ST	Stationery
SW	Software
TA	Tapes, Audio
TO	Toys
TV	Tapes, Video
TX	Textbooks
US	Used books

Card Decks or Card Packs

Card decks (also known as card packs) are collections of advertising postcards mailed to target groups of businesses, professionals, or consumers. Here are some of the card packs in which publishers have advertised their books.

A

The Aardvark Group
Peggy Redlin
38W183 Joan Dr
St Charles IL 60175-6053
708-513-5181; Fax: 708-513-5127
Subjects: 99

Aardvark Party Pack
Peggy Redlin
The Aardvark Group
41W067 Kings Mill Dr
Medinah IL 60157
708-513-5181; Fax: 708-513-5127
Subjects: Deals w/anything for a party

Abelow Response
David Schwartz, Pres
2 Dubon Ct
Farmingdale NY 11735-1008
516-293-8550; Fax: 516-791-7429
Subjects: 19-99

Adults 50-65
Larry Tucker Inc
188 Broadway
Westwood NJ 07675-9865
201-307-8888; Fax: 201-307-1200
Subjects: 99

Adults 60 Up
Larry Tucker Inc
188 Broadway
Westwood NJ 07675-9865
201-307-8888; Fax: 201-307-1200
Subjects: 99

Advertising Sales & Mktg Pros
Card Pack Division
Venture Communications
60 Madison Ave 3rd Fl
New York NY 10010-1600
212-684-4800; Fax: 212-576-1129
Subjects: 19M

Agri Mart Postcard Mailings
John Machalek
Machalek Communications
1401 W 76th St #440
Minneapolis MN 55423
612-798-5520; Fax: 612-798-4814
Subjects: 99

American Printer Card Deck
Lauren Knapp
Maclean Hunter Publ Co
29 N Wacker Dr
Chicago IL 60606-3203
312-726-8202
Subjects: 56X

ApparelPak
The Salesman's Guide
Reed Reference Publishing
121 Chanlon Rd PO Box 31
New Providence NJ 07974
908-665-2818; Fax: 908-665-6688;
  800-223-1797
Subjects: 40(clothing buyers)

Art & Design News
6330 E 75th St #212
Indianapolis IN 46250-2700
317-849-6110; Fax: 317-576-5859
Subjects: 11

Attorney Card Pack
Clark and Pfingstein
155 E Road St
Deerfield IL 60015
800-323-1336; Fax: 708-948-9340
Subjects: 19L-55L

B

Baptist-Pak
Sue Hair or Debbie Whelan
Ed-Pak Publishing
PO Box 1132
Canyon TX 79015-1132
806-655-1207; Fax: 806-655-3601;
  800-654-1764
Subjects: 63P(Baptist churches)

Beach List Services
4302 Harding Pl
Nashville TN 37205-4529
615-665-9003; Fax: 615-665-4442
Subjects: 19-73
Service: Home-based women's businesses

Black Families
Larry Tucker Inc
188 Broadway
Westwood NJ 07675-9865
201-307-8888; Fax: 201-307-1200
Subjects: 49-7897-99

Bloomfield Publications
5850 Lorac Dr #M
Clarkston MI 48346-2915
313-620-2165
Subjects: 99

Book & Resource Buyers Edition
Bill Burns
Resource Publications
160 E Virginia St #290
San Jose CA 95112-5848
408-286-8505; Fax: 408-287-8748
Subjects: 99

Bookstore Journal Action Cards
Christian Booksellers Assn
2620 Venetucci Blvd
Colorado Springs CO 80906-4003
719-576-7880; Fax: 719-576-0795
Subjects: 63-99

Building Operating Management
Hot Line Pack
2100 W Florist Ave
PO Box 694
Milwaukee WI 53209-3721
414-228-7701; Fax: 414-228-1134
Subjects: 12B

Business Buyer Resource Deck
Arlence Ciparro
The Economics Press
12 Daniel Rd
Fairfield NJ 07004-2575
800-526-2554; Fax: 201-227-3558
Subjects: 19C-19G
Service: Subscribers to Bits & Pieces

Business Buyers' Action Pack
Arlene Ciparro
The Economics Press
12 Daniel Rd
Fairfield NJ 07004
800-526-2554
Subjects: 19C-19P
Service: Purchasers of business products

Business Marketing Action Cards
Curtis Moore
Business Marketing Magazine
740 Rush St
Chicago IL 60611-2525
312-649-7811; Fax: 312-649-5462;
  800-678-2724
Subjects: 19M

Business Performance Pack
Arlence Ciparro
The Economics Press
12 Daniel Rd
Fairfield NJ 07004
800-526-2554; Fax:
Subjects: 19C-19G
Service: Canadian subs to Bits & Pieces

Business Technology Exec-Cards
Hughes Communications
211 W State St
PO Box 197
Rockford IL 61101-1111
815-963-4000; Fax: 815-963-7773;
 800-435-2937
Subjects: 23

Byte Deck
Ed Ware
1 Phoenix Mill Ln
Peterborough NH 03458-1434
603-924-9281; Fax: 603-924-2683
Subjects: 23

C

Caddylak Systems
Direct Media Card Decks
200 Pemberwick Rd
PO Box 4565
Greenwich CT 06830
203-532-1000; Fax: 203-531-1452
Subjects: 19-55

Campus Life Card Deck
Christianity Today
465 Gunderson Dr
Carol Stream IL 60188-2415
708-260-6200; Fax: 708-260-0111
Subjects: 63-89
Service: Subscribers to Campus Life

Campus Life Regional Friends
Card Pack Director
Christianity Today
465 Gunderson Dr
Carol Stream IL 60188-2415
708-260-6200; Fax: 708-260-0111
Subjects: 63-89
Memo: 2 times per year (February & November). Jr and Senior High Schools.

Card Deck Customer Directory
Bolt Publishing Co
449 E 1st St
Tustin CA 92780-3311
714-832-8315; Fax: 714-832-3476
Subjects: 19
Service: 800 advertisers in card packs
Memo: Also features most major card packs.

Card Deck Rates and Data
Standard Rate & Data Service
1700 E Higgins Rd
Des Plaines IL 60018-5621
708-375-5068; Fax: 708-375-5009
Subjects: 19-99
Service: 700 card decks/500 co-ops/insert

Card Pack Media Directory
Solar Press
1120 Frontenac Rd
Naperville IL 60563-1749
708-983-1400; Fax: 708-983-6125;
 800-323-2751
Subjects: 99

Career Resources
Intercristo
19303 Fremont Ave N
Seattle WA 98133-9986
206-546-7330; 800-426-1343
Subjects: 19C-63

Catholic Church/School Market
Ned Watts
43 Zurich Way
Tell City IN 47586-2099
812-547-8516; Fax:
Subjects: 63(Catholic)-99
Service: Catholic churches and schools

CD-ROM Gold Pak
Chris Withers
Pemberton Press
462 Danbury Rd
Wilton CT 06897-2126
203-761-1466; Fax: 203-761-1444;
 800-248-8466
Subjects: 23C(CD-ROM users & developers)
Memo: Formerly DC-ROM Gold Pak.

Chartsearch Card Decks
14 Willow St
London EC2B 2XY England
71-638-4937; Fax: 71-739-2760
Subjects: 44(Great Britain)

Chilton's Execu-Deck
George Furyga
Chilton Co
4th Floor
Wayne PA 19089-0001
800-274-2207; Fax: 214-964-1888
Subjects: 19

Christian Family Shopper
Tri-Media Publications
2825 Bledsoe St
Fort Worth TX 76107-2901
708-673-4440
Subjects: 35F-63P

Christian Shoppers Card-A-Log
Donna Fisher
Strang Communications
600 Rinehart Rd
Lake Mary FL 32746-4872
407-260-0306; Fax:
Subjects: 63P-99
Service: Subscribers to Charisma

Church Product Alert Card Pack
Christianity Today
465 Gunderson Dr
Carol Stream IL 60188-2415
708-260-6200; Fax: 708-260-6200
Subjects: 63
Service: Church decision makers

Church Resource Packet
Keener Marketing
124 E Main
Dayton TN 37321-1319
615-775-3300; Fax: 615-775-3380
Subjects: 63
Service: Pastor/youth educator/music dir

Clement Communications ActionPac
Card Pack Division
Venture Communications
60 Madison Ave 3rd Fl
New York NY 10010-1600
212-684-4800; Fax: 212-576-1129
Subjects: 19M-57(sales/inspiration)

CMP InformationWeek/MIS Deck
CMP Direct Marketing Services
One Jericho Plz 2nd Fl Wing A
Jericho NY 11753
516-733-6700; Fax: 516-733-6820;
 800-972-5544
Subjects: 23C
Memo: Also other decks: CMP Varbusiness Executive Card Deck (80,000 resellers), CMP Computer Reseller News Card Deck (90,000 resellers), CMP Network Computing Client-Server Card Deck (130,000), CMP Open Systems Today Card Deck (100,000 UNIX buyers), CMP CommunicationsWeek Card Deck (100,000 high-level managers).

CMP Sales & Marketing Power Deck
CMP Direct Marketing Services
1 Jericho Plz 2nd Fl Wing A
Jericho NY 11753
516-733-6700; Fax: 516-733-6820;
 800-972-5544
Subjects: 19M-23-24-71

Community Cardpack
Sean Strub
Strub Media Group
Old Chelsea Sta Box 1274
New York NY 10113-1274
212-242-1900; Fax: 212-242-1963
Subjects: 37
Service: Gay male households

CompuDeck
PO Box 55886
Birmingham AL 35255-5886
Subjects: 19-23

Computer Owners Action Pac
Card Pack Division
Venture Communications
60 Madison Ave 3rd Fl
New York NY 10010-1600
212-684-4800; Fax: 212-576-1129
Subjects: 23

Computerworld Response Directory
PO Box 9171
Framingham MA 01701-9171
508-879-0700; Fax: 508-620-7739
Subjects: 23

Construction Resources Cards
Craftsman Book Co
6058 Corte Del Cedro
PO Box 6500
Carlsbad CA 92009-1514
619-438-7828; Fax: 619-438-0398;
  800-829-8123.
Subjects: 12-43(home)
Service: Building/remodeling contractors

Country Family Card Pack
Select Publishing
10 Odana Ct
Madison WI 53719-1109
608-277-5787; Fax: 608-277-9001
Subjects: 35F
Service: 200,000 rural/suburban families

Craft Market Action Cards
Phil Hipshman
Total Media Concepts
222 Cedar Ln #201
Teaneck NJ 07666
201-692-0018; Fax: 201-692-9817
Subjects: 29
Service: Women who buy craft kits

Current Contents Action Pack
Institute for Scientific Info
3501 Market St
Philadelphia PA 19104-3302
215-386-0100; Fax: 215-386-6362;
  800-336-4474
Subjects: 39-51-67(research scientists)

Curriculum Leaders Action Deck
MGI Decks
Marketing General Inc
1613 Duke St
Alexandria VA 22314-3406
703-549-4420; Fax: 703-549-6057;
  800-899-4420
Subjects: 31
Memo: Members of the Association for
  Supervision and Curriculum
  Development.

D

Designer Direct Returns
Phyllis Hurdleston
North American Publishing
401 N Broad St
Philadelphia PA 19108-1001
215-238-5342
Subjects: 12-43
Service: Interior designers/architects
Memo: Main Office: 215-238-5342; Home
  Office: 609-235-4197

Direct Male Card Pack
Andrew Isen
Winmark Concepts
1711 Connecticut Ave NW #300
Washington DC 20009-1139
202-483-1300
Subjects: 37
Service: Gay male households

Directors of Religious Education
Bill Burns
Resource Publications
160 E Virginia St #290
San Jose CA 95112-5848
408-286-8505; Fax: 408-287-8748
Subjects: 63
Memo: January, May, September.

Directory of Insert Programs
Direct Media
200 Pemberwick Rd
PO Box 4565
Greenwich CT 06830
203-532-2371; Fax: 203-531-1452
Subjects: 99
Memo: A directory of all their managed
  insert programs.

Doctor's Practice Card Deck
Card Deck Division
Leon Henry Inc
455 Central Ave #315
Scarsdale NY 10583
914-723-3176; Fax: 914-723-0205
Subjects: 39

Duke Communications Intl
165 S Union Blvd #315
Lakewood CO 80228-2211
800-445-1198
Subjects: 99

E

Early Childhood Special Needs
Vicki Peterson
11924 W Washington Blvd
Los Angeles CA 90066-5867
310-398-2754; Fax: 310-397-4980;
  800-445-2089
Subjects: 21-31-76
Memo: Mailed to preschools, head starts,
  clinics, and institutions serving
  children, birth to 8-years-old.

Ed-Pak Publishing
PO Box 1132
Canyon TX 79015-1132
800-654-1764; Fax: 806-655-3601
Subjects: 21-31-76-79
Service: School principals

Entrepreneur Response Path
Card Pack Division
Venture Communications
60 Madison Ave 3rd Fl
New York NY 10010-1600
212-684-4800; Fax: 212-576-1129
Subjects: 19O-19S-19
Service: Subscribers to Entrepreneur

Executive Action Card Deck
Sue Cariato
Dartnell Publishing
4660 Ravenswood Ave
Chicago IL 60640-4510
800-621-5463; Fax: 312-561-3801
Subjects: 19

Executive Merchandise Card Pack
Simon Direct
S-4 Brier Hill Ct
East Brunswick NJ 08816
908-651-7222
Subjects: 19
Service: Buyers of binders, etc

Executive Products & Services
Direct Response Marketing Dept
The Interface Group
300 1st Ave
Needham MA 02194-2703
617-449-6600; Fax: 317-449-6953
Subjects: 19-23

F

F.I.S. Marketing Inc
Ray Allen, Publisher
155 River Rd
North Arlington NJ 07031
201-991-7800; 800-238-2862;
  Fax: 201-997-9885
Subjects: 19M-19X
Service: Marketing promotion cards

Facilities Management Deck
Mike Spring, Publisher
North American Publishing
401 N Broad St
Philadelphia PA 19108-1001
609-235-4197
Subjects: 12-19X
Service: Buyers of business products

Fidelity Products
Direct Media Card Decks
200 Pemberwick Rd
PO Box 4565
Greenwich CT 06830
203-532-1000; Fax: 203-531-1452
Subjects: 19
Service: Office supply buyers

Financial Automation Technology
Card Deck Mgr
Dealers' Digest
2 World Trade Ctr 18th Fl
New York NY 10048-0203
212-227-1200; Fax: 212-432-1039
Subjects: 19B-19I

Financial Planners Card Pack
Market/Media Associates
1150 Wilmette Ave
Wilmette IL 60091-2642
708-251-2541
Subjects: 19I

Financial World Response Pack
MGA Marketing
930 Turret Ct
Mundelein IL 60060-3821
708-566-9450; Fax: 708-566-9519
Subjects: 19
Service: Financial World subscriptions

First Wall Streeter
Harvey Krumholz
Doyle Publishing Corp
PO Box 1977
Ponte Vedra FL 32004-1977
Subjects: 19I

Focus On Books Card Pack
Caddylak Systems
131 Heartland Blvd
Brentwood NY 11717-8315
516-254-2000
Subjects: 19

Folio: Action Cards
Folio Publishing Co
911 Hope St
Stamford CT 06907-0949
203-358-9900; Fax: 203-357-9014
Subjects: 11(graphics)-56(publishing)
Service: Folio subscribers

Food Service Action Cards
Direct Action Postcards
4763 S Packard Ave
PO Box 494
Cudahy WI 53110-1446
414-744-6265; Fax: 414-744-6844
Subjects: 19-27
Service: Restaurant owners/food service

G

Gardener's Marketplace
Judith Evrard
Schoolhouse Rd
Pownal VT 05261
802-823-5811
Subjects: 43G
Memo: Bound Card Deck - 20 years in business.

Grade Sch & High Sch Students
Larry Tucker Inc
188 Broadway
Westwood NJ 07675-9865
201-307-8888; Fax: 201-307-1200
Subjects: 99
Service: Grade and high school students

Graphic Arts Monthly Ad Cards
Graphic Arts Monthly
243 W 17th St
New York NY 10011-5300
212-463-6834; Fax: 212-463-6530
Subjects: 11(graphics)-56(printing)

Great Outdoors-Dek
Jon Machalek
Machalek Publishing
15 S 9th St
Minneapolis MN 55402-3108
612-332-1236; Fax:
Subjects: 43G-69R
Service: Landscapers/recreation parks
Memo: Sends three different 30M decks to park and recreation directors, landscape professionals, and school ground maintenance professionals.

Greeting Card Retailers Cards
John Jarema, Publisher
The Aardvark Group
9380 Hidden Lake Cir
Dexter MI 48130-9519
313-426-5755; Fax: 313-426-8109
Subjects: 11-33-99
Service: Retailers

H

Hard Money Digest
2201 Big Cove Rd SE
Huntsville AL 35801-1349
205-534-1535
Subjects: 19I

Harrowsmith Card Pack
Ferry Rd
Charlotte VT 05445
802-425-3961; Fax: 802-425-3307
Subjects: 43

Health & Natural Healing Card Pk
Prentice Hall Direct
Target Mkt Card Decks
113 Sylvan Ave
Englewood Cliffs NJ 07632-3502
800-937-9970; Fax: 201-592-2950
Subjects: 39-57S
Service: 150,000 buyers

Health & Safety Card Deck
Linda Scarborough, Sales Mgr
Stevens List Management
225 N New Rd
Waco TX 76710-6931
817-776-9000; Fax: 817-776-9018
Subjects: 39

Health Pack
Bob Aronson
Market & Media Analysis Inc
4411 Bee Ridge Rd #284
Sarasota FL 34233-2514
813-378-4919; Fax:
Subjects: 39H-53-54-57
Memo: Formerly called Heal*Pak.

Health/Physical Education
MGI Decks
Marketing General Inc
1613 Duke St
Alexandria VA 22314-3406
703-549-4420; Fax: 703-549-6057;
    800-899-4420
Subjects: 39

High Tech Times
117 W Micheltorena
Santa Barbara CA 93101-3035
805-966-3353
Subjects: 19-23

Hispanic
Larry Tucker Inc
188 Broadway
Westwood NJ 07675-9865
201-307-8888; Fax: 201-307-1200
Subjects: 44-45-49-78-97-99

Hotline Education Responders
MGI Decks
Marketing General Inc
1613 Duke St
Alexandria VA 22314-3406
703-549-4420; 800-899-4420;
    Fax: 703-549-6057
Subjects: 31

Hotline Postcard Deck
Building Operating Management
2100 W Florist Ave
PO Box 694
Milwaukee WI 53209-3721
414-228-7701; Fax: 414-228-1134
Subjects: 12(building)-24

HR Action Cards
Sue Montgomery
Society for Human Resource Mgmt
606 N Washington St
Alexandria VA 22314-1943
703-548-3440; Fax: 703-836-0367
Subjects: 19C

Human Resources Performance Pac
Card Pack Division
Venture Communications
60 Madison Ave 3rd Fl
New York NY 10010-1600
212-684-4800; Fax: 212-576-1129
Subjects: 19C-57(personnel/training)

Hunter's Card Pack
North American Hunting Club
Marketshare Publications
5750 W 95th St #300
Shawnee Mission KS 66207-2969
800-345-1542; Fax: 913-649-7200
Subjects: 69(hunting)
Service: Club members

I

IEN Direct Response Cards
Penn Plz
5 Thomas St
New York NY 10007-1106
212-629-1508
Subjects: 19X-24
Service: Industrial Equipment News subs

Impact Postcard Deck
Invester Co-op Booklet
PO Box 411128
Kansas City MO 64141-1128
816-471-3862
Subjects: 19I
Service: Investors/stock traders
Memo: Newsletter

Indian America Postcard Deck
Fred Snyder, Editor
Natl Native American Co-op
PO Box 1000
San Carlos AZ 85550-1000
602-622-4900
Subjects: 49A

Insurance Mktg & Mgmt Services
Gordon Levy
MGA Marketing
930 Turret Ct
Mundelein IL 60060-3821
708-566-9450; Fax: 708-566-9519
Subjects: 19M
Service: Insurance agents

International Marine Deck
Card Pack Division
Venture Communications
60 Madison Ave 3rd Fl
New York NY 10010-1600
212-684-4800; Fax: 212-576-1129
Subjects: 70N
Service: Book buyers

Investor's Advantage Action Card
Card Pack Division
Venture Communications
60 Madison Ave 3rd Fl
New York NY 10010-1600
212-684-4800; Fax: 212-576-1129
Subjects: 19I

ITC Industrial Response Deck
ITC Publishers Service
63 Hemlock Dr
Hempstead NY 11550
516-485-1000;800-336-1818
Subjects: 19P-19X
Service: Buyers List

J

Jeffrey Lant's SuccessDek
PO Box 38-2767
Cambridge MA 02238-2767
617-547-6372; Fax: 617-547-0061
Subjects: 19M

Jewish Education Card Deck
David Rubin or Jill Cohen
RC Direct
200 S Water St
Milwaukee WI 53204-1450
414-271-3313; Fax: 414-271-4244
Subjects: 31-63J
Service: Principals and rabbis

K

K-8 Librarian Card Pack
Media Services Inc
107 S West St #114
Alexandria VA 22314-2891
800-950-6211
Subjects: 31E
Service: 65,000 K-8 librarians

L

Lan Times
1900 O'Farrell St #200
San Mateo CA 94403
415-513-6800
Subjects: 19-23

Learning Action Pac
Springhouse Corp
1111 Bethelem Pike
Spring House PA 19477-1114
215-646-8700; Fax: 215-646-4399
Subjects: 31
Service: Learning subscribers

M

Mac Times
Production Mgr
Top Floor
117 W Micheltorena
Santa Barbara CA 93101-2586
805-966-3353; Fax: 805-963-1143
Subjects: 23(McIntosh)

Machalek Communications Inc
Dick Powell, Exec VP
1401 W 76th St #440
Minneapolis MN 55423
800-846-5520; Fax: 612-798-4814
Subjects: 99

Manager's Answer Cards
Doris Getharde
Abarth Associates
357 Asbury Rd
Farmingdale NJ 07727
908-938-6116; Fax: 908-938-4419
Subjects: 19G
Service: Buyers of business products

Managers' Resource Deck
Arlence Ciparro
The Economics Press
12 Daniel Rd
Fairfield NJ 07004-2575
800-526-2554; Fax: 201-227-3558
Subjects: 19C-19G
Service: Subscribers to Bits & Pieces

Manufacturing Management Product
Laura Malanga
Chilton Company
1 Chilton Way
Radnor PA 19089-0001
215-964-4365; Fax: 215-964-1888
Subjects: 19P-19X
Service: 800-274-2207

Marketing Manager Sales Ideas
Harvey Krumholz
Doyle Publishing Corp
2101 Resford Rd #172W
Charlotte NC 28211
704-364-0719; 800-327-6970;
   Fax: 704-362-1733
Subjects: 19M

Marketing Platinum Card Pack
Scott Goldman
Eaton Hall Publishing
123 Columbia Turnpike
Florham Park NJ 07932
201-514-5900
Subjects: 19M
Service: Sales executives

Marketing Promotion Cards
Ray Allen, Publ
155 River Rd
PO Box 520
North Arlington NJ 07031
201-991-7800; 800-238-2862;
   Fax: 201-997-9885
Subjects: 19M

Math-Micro Action Deck
MGI Decks
Marketing General Inc
1613 Duke St
Alexandria VA 22314-3406
703-549-4420; 800-899-4420;
   Fax: 703-549-6057
Subjects: 23-67
Memo: Secondary math teachers.

Maxwell Macmillan Tax Pack
Trump Card Marketing
222 Cedar Ln
Teaneck NJ 07666
201-833-8844; 800-88-TRUMP
Subjects: 19A-19F-25T

McGraw-Hill Architecture Deck
Card Pack Division
Venture Communications
60 Madison Ave 3rd Fl
New York NY 10010-1600
212-684-4800; Fax: 212-576-1129
Subjects: 12-43
Service: Architects/builders

McGraw-Hill Business & Marketing
Card Pack Division
Venture Communications
60 Madison Ave 3rd Fl
New York NY 10010-1600
212-684-4800; Fax: 212-576-1129
Subjects: 19-19M
Service: Business leaders

McGraw-Hill Engineering Decks
Card Pack Division
Venture Communications
60 Madison Ave 3rd Fl
New York NY 10010-1600
212-684-4800; Fax: 212-576-1129
Subjects: 24
Memo: Civil Engineering, Electrical
   Construction, Electronic Design
   Engineering, and Mechanical
   Engineering decks.

McGraw-Hill Human Resources Deck
Card Pack Division
Venture Communications
60 Madison Ave 3rd Fl
New York NY 10010-1600
212-684-4800; Fax: 212-576-1129
Subjects: 19C-57

McGraw-Hill Prof Computing Deck
Card Pack Division
Venture Communications
60 Madison Ave 3rd Fl
New York NY 10010-1600
212-684-4800; Fax: 212-576-1129
Subjects: 19-23
Service: Computer users

McGraw-Hill Real Estate Deck
Card Pack Division
Venture Communications
60 Madison Ave 3rd Fl
New York NY 10010-1600
212-684-4800; Fax: 212-576-1129
Subjects: 19H

MedDeck
428 E Preston St
Baltimore MD 21202-3923
800-222-3790; 800-222-3790;
    Fax: 410-528-4312
Subjects: 39
Service: Neurology/urology

Media Horizons Inc
Alan Kraft, Pres
94 East Ave
Norwalk CT 06851
203-857-0770; Fax: 203-857-0296
Subjects: 19-25
Service: Card decks/inserts/co-op mailing
Memo:

Media Management
PO Box 21433
Roanoke VA 24018-0145
800-842-6842; Fax: 703-989-5890
Subjects: 63

Media Services Inc
107 S West St #114
Alexandria VA 22314-2891
703-751-6246; 800-950-6211;
    Fax: 703-751-0474
Subjects: 31

Ministries Today Card-a-Log
Strang Communications
600 Rinehart Rd
Lake Mary FL 32746-4872
407-260-1135
Subjects: 63
Service: Pentacostal/chrismatic pastors

Ministry Values/Growing Churches
Media Management
PO Box 21433
Roanoke VA 24018-0145
800-842-6842; Fax: 703-989-5809
Subjects: 63P
Service: 703-989-1330 churches

Moller & Associates
2274 E Sunshine St
Springfield MO 65804-1856
417-886-2200; Fax: 417-882-7919

Music Information Cards
Tri-Media Publications
2825 Bledsoe St
Fort Worth TX 76107-2901
708-673-4440
Subjects: 14M-63P

N

Nation's Business Executives Pac
Card Pack Division
Venture Communications
60 Madison Ave 3rd Fl
New York NY 10010-1600
212-684-4800; Fax: 212-576-1129
Subjects: 19(magazine subscribers)
Service: Nation's Business

National Law Journal Card Pack
National Law Journal
111 8th Ave #900
New York NY 10011-5201
212-741-8300
Subjects: 19L-55L

National Pen Company
Direct Media Card Decks
200 Pemberwick Rd
PO Box 4565
Greenwich CT 06830
203-532-1000; Fax: 203-531-1452
Subjects: 19M

National Seminars Executives
Direct Media Card Decks
200 Pemberwick Rd
PO Box 4565
Greenwich CT 06830
203-532-1000; Fax: 203-531-1452
Subjects: 19

Natl Assn of Female Executives
Direct Media Card Decks
200 Pemberwick Rd
PO Box 4565
Greenwich CT 06830
203-532-1000; Fax: 203-531-1452
Subjects: 19-73
Service: NAFE association members

New Age Journal Card Deck
Card Pack Division
Venture Communications
60 Madison Ave 3rd Fl
New York NY 10010-1600
212-684-4800; Fax: 212-576-1129
Subjects: 39H-53

New Businesses-Dek
Jon Machalek
Machalek Publishing
15 S 9th St
Minneapolis MN 55402-3108
612-332-1236
Subjects: 19
Service: New businesses

New Parents Value Pack
Trump Card Marketing
222 Cedar Ln
Teaneck NJ 07666
201-836-8000; 800-88-TRUMP;
    Fax: 201-836-5383
Subjects: 21-31P-35F(new parents)

New Products for Church Leaders
Gospel Light Publications
2300 Knoll Dr
PO Box 3875
Ventura CA 93006-3875
805-644-9721; 800-235-3415;
    Fax: 805-650-8713
Subjects: 63(Protestant)
Service: Buyers of Gospel Light products

NursePac
Card Pack Division
Venture Communications
60 Madison Ave 3rd Fl
New York NY 10010-1600
212-684-4800; Fax: 212-576-1129
Subjects: 39(nurses)
Service: Subscribers to Nursing Journal

O

Office Managers Information Pack
Simon Direct
F-4 Brier Hill Ct
East Brunswick NJ 08816
908-651-7222; Fax: 908-651-7559
Subjects: 19P
Service: American Office Managers Assn

Office Systems Action Pack
Springhouse Corp
1111 Bethelem Pike
Spring House PA 19477-1114
215-646-8700; Fax: 215-646-4399
Subjects: 19-23
Service: Office Systems subscribers

On-Target Postcard Deck
Carol Valaitis
North American Publishing
401 N Broad St
Philadelphia PA 19108-1001
215-238-5342
Subjects: 19M
Memo: Main Office: 215-238-5342; Home Office: 609-235-4197 (both phone numbers checked).

One Minute Catalog for Dentist
SYCOM
PO Box 7947
Madison WI 53791-0001
800-356-8153
Subjects: 39(dentists)

Opportunity Seekers Card Pack
Trump Card Marketing
222 Cedar Ln
Teaneck NJ 07666
201-833-8844; 800-88-TRUMP
Subjects: 19O

P

P-H Business Computing Pac
Card Pack Division
Venture Communications
60 Madison Ave 3rd Fl
New York NY 10010-1600
212-684-4800; Fax: 212-576-1129
Subjects: 23

P-H Business Management Cards
Card Pack Division
Venture Communications
60 Madison Ave 3rd Fl
New York NY 10010-1600
212-684-4800; Fax: 212-576-1129
Subjects: 19G

P-H Financial Management Cards
Card Pack Division
Venture Communications
60 Madison Ave 3rd Fl
New York NY 10010-1600
212-684-4800; Fax: 212-576-1129
Subjects: 19A-19E

P-H Health & Fitness Action Pac
Card Pack Division
Venture Communications
60 Madison Ave 3rd Fl
New York NY 10010-1600
212-684-4800; Fax: 212-576-1129
Subjects: 39(Prentice-Hall book buyers)

P-H Lawyers Action Cards
Card Pack Division
Venture Communications
60 Madison Ave 3rd Fl
New York NY 10010-1600
212-684-4800; Fax: 212-576-1129
Subjects: 19L-55L

P-H Music Educators Action Cards
Card Pack Division
Venture Communications
60 Madison Ave 3rd Fl
New York NY 10010-1600
212-684-4800; Fax: 212-576-1129
Subjects: 14(music)-31
Service: Prentice-Hall book buyers

P-H Sports & Coaching Action Pac
Card Pack Division
Venture Communications
60 Madison Ave 3rd Fl
New York NY 10010-1600
212-684-4800; Fax: 212-576-1129
Subjects: 69(Prentice-Hall book buyers)

Package Insert & Co-op Directory
Harriet Rosen, VP
20 Lake Dr
PO Box 930
Hightstown NJ 08520-0930
609-443-1298; Fax: 609-443-0397
Subjects: 99(Directory of Card Packs)
Service: Package inserts & co-op mailings

Parents of Infants & Toddlers
Larry Tucker Inc
188 Broadway
Westwood NJ 07675-9865
201-307-8888; Fax: 201-307-1200
Subjects: 21-31-35-76-79

Parish Pastor Edition
Bill Burns
Resource Publications
160 E Virginia St #290
San Jose CA 95112-5848
408-286-8505; Fax: 408-287-8748
Subjects: 63
Memo: January, May, September.

Pastors Information Cards
Tri-Media Publications
2825 Bledsoe St
Fort Worth TX 76107-2901
708-673-4440
Subjects: 63P

PC Network Package Inserts
Direct Media Insert Management
200 Pemberwick Rd
PO Box 4565
Greenwich CT 06830
203-532-1000; Fax: 203-531-1452
Subjects: 23
Service: $45/M

PC World Action Cards
Kevin Normandeau
CW Communications
492 Old Connecticut Path
Framingham MA 01701-4584
508-820-8113; Fax: 508-651-1853
Subjects: 23C(IBM)

PD&D Post Pack
Laura Malanga
Chilton Co
1 Chilton Way
Wayne PA 19089-0001
215-964-4365; 800-274-2207;
    Fax: 215-964-4947
Subjects: 19P-19X-24

Penton Publishing
Laurel Hirkala
Postcard Packs
1100 Superior Ave
Cleveland OH 44114-2543
216-696-7000; Fax: 216-696-4369
Subjects: 99

Pet-Dek
Machalek Communications
1401 W 76th St #440
Minneapolis MN 55423
800-846-5520; Fax: 612-798-4814
Subjects: 15
Service: 22,500 pet product retailers

Physician ActionPac
Linda Scarborough, Sales Mgr
Stevens List Management
225 N New Rd
Waco TX 76710-6931
817-776-9000
Subjects: 39
Service: Doctors/osteopaths

Plane Talk: Good Ideas
for Aircraft Owners
Trump Card Marketing
222 Cedar Ln
Teaneck NJ 07666
201-837-1093; Fax: 201-833-9243
Subjects: 70A
Service: Owners of corporate pilots

Police & Security Action Pack
Direct Action Postcards
4763 S Packard Ave
PO Box 494
Cudahy WI 53110-1446
414-744-6265; Fax: 414-744-6844
Subjects: 55C(law enforcement)
Service: Security agencies

Prentice-Hall Direct
Catherine Rogers
Card Deck Division
113 Sylvan Ave
Englewood Cliffs NJ 07632-3502
800-937-9970; Fax: 201-592-2950
Subjects: 99
Service: 21 target market card decks

Prentice-Hall Direct
Target Market Card Decks
113 Sylvan Ave
Englewood Cliffs NJ 07632-3502
800-937-9970; Fax: 201-592-2950
Subjects: 31(faculty)

Presidents Exec-Cards
Hughes Communications
211 W State St
PO Box 197
Rockford IL 61101-1111
815-963-4000; 800-435-2937;
    Fax: 815-963-7773
Subjects: 19

Primary K-3 Education Card Pack
Marsha Brown, Publisher
Media Services
510-C S Van Dorn St
Alexandria VA 22304-4612
703-751-6246; Fax: 703-751-0474
Subjects: 21-31C-31E
Service: K-3 teachers and administrators

Principals Action Deck
MGI Decks
Marketing General Inc
1613 Duke St
Alexandria VA 22314-3406
703-549-4420; 800-899-4420;
    Fax: 703-549-6057
Subjects: 21-31

Print Cards
Phyllis Hurdleston, Sales Mgr
North American Publishing
401 N Broad St
Philadelphia PA 19108-1001
609-235-4197
Subjects: 11(graphics)-56(printing)

Programmer's Power Card Pack
M&T Publishing
411 Borrel #100
San Mateo CA 94402
415-358-9500
Subjects: 23

PTO-Pak
Sue Hair or Debbie Whelan
Ed-Pak Publishing
PO Box 1132
Canyon TX 79015-1132
806-655-1207; 800-654-1764;
    Fax: 806-655-3601
Subjects: 21-31-35F(parent-teacher org)

Public Library Card Pack
Dale Lear
4-D Video Productions
848 2nd Ave
Gallipolis OH 45631-1635
614-446-8040; Fax: 614-441-0329
Subjects: 99
Service: Libraries

R

R S Means
100 Constitution Dr
Plymouth MA 02360-3206
800-448-8182; Fax: 617-585-7466
Subjects: 99

Real Estate Response Cards
22720 Savi Ranch Pky
Yorba Linda CA 92887-4608
714-921-2799; 800-854-8075
Subjects: 19H

Reseller Mgt Card Pack
Gordon Action Cards
301 Gibralter Dr
Morris Plains NJ 07950
800-222-0289; Fax: 201-292-0083
Subjects: 23
Service: Computer Dealer: 201-361-9060

Resources Action Cards
Bill Burns
Resource Publications
160 E Virginia St #290
San Jose CA 95112-5876
408-286-8505; Fax: 408-287-8748
Subjects: 63(primarily Catholic)
Service: Religious leaders
Memo: January, May, September.

Retired Military Market Pack
Simon Direct
F-4 Brier Hill Ct
East Brunswick NJ 08816
908-651-7222; Fax: 908-651-7559
Subjects: 35A-48
Service: Retired military officers

Rodale Books Cookbook Buyers
Joel Katz, Publ
Leon Henry Card Deck Div
455 Central Ave #315
Scarsdale NY 10583
914-723-3176; Fax: 914-723-0205
Subjects: 27

Rose Printing Co Inc
Rose Building
2503 Jackson Bluff Rd
Tallahassee FL 32304-4405
800-CARD-PAK
Subjects: 99

S

S&P's Investment Forum
Trump Card Marketing
222 Cedar Ln
Teaneck NJ 07666
201-833-8000
Subjects: 19I

Sales & Marketing Exec-Cards
Hughes Communications
211 W State St
PO Box 197
Rockford IL 61101-1111
815-963-4000; 800-435-2937;
    Fax: 815-963-7773
Subjects: 19M
Memo: Also publish Sales & Marketing Strategies & News Action Pak.

Sales & Marketing Success Deck
Jeffrey Lant
JLA Associates
50 Follen St #507
Cambridge MA 02138-3507
617-547-6372
Subjects: 19-57

Sapphile Card Pack
Sean Strub
Strub Media Group
Old Chelsea Sta Box 1274
New York NY 10113-1274
212-242-1900; Fax: 212-242-1963
Subjects: 37-73
Service: Lesbian households

Schmidt Printing
1101 Frontage Rd NW
Byron MN 55920-1386
507-775-6400; Fax: 507-775-6655
Subjects: 99
Memo: Printer of card packs, insert cards, cover wraps, newsletters, and direct mail packages.

School Libraries in Technology
MGI Decks
Marketing General Inc
1613 Duke St
Alexandria VA 22314-3406
703-549-4420; 800-899-4420;
    Fax: 703-549-6057
Subjects: 23-31

Science Teachers Action Deck
MGI Decks
Marketing General Inc
1613 Duke St
Alexandria VA 22314-3406
703-549-4420; 800-899-4420;
    Fax: 703-549-6057
Subjects: 23-24-39-51-67
Memo: Members of the National Science Teachers Association.

Select Deck
Simon Direct
F-4 Brier Hill Ct
East Brunswick NJ 08816
908-651-7222
Subjects: 23(IBM)

Seton Name Plate
Direct Media Card Decks
200 Pemberwick Rd
PO Box 4565
Greenwich CT 06830
203-532-1000; Fax: 203-531-1452
Subjects: 19
Service: Office supply buyers

SFG
999 N Main St #103
Glen Ellyn IL 60137-3572
203-532-1000; Fax: 203-531-1452
Subjects: 23
Service: Computer supply buyers

Shop-At-Home Directory
650 S Cherry St #440
Denver CO 80222-1806
303-758-1414
Subjects: 99
Service: Mail order catalog buyers

Social Studies Action Deck
MGI Decks
Marketing General Inc
1613 Duke St
Alexandria VA 22314-3406
703-549-4420; 800-899-4420; Fax: 703-549-6057
Subjects: 13-31-41-44-49-55-65
Memo: Members of the National Council for the Social Studies.

Solar Press Inc
1120 Frontenac Rd
Naperville IL 60563-1799
800-323-2751; Fax: 708-983-6125
Subjects: 99(media directory)
Service: 708-983-1400

Special Education Action Deck
MGI Decks
Marketing General Inc
1613 Duke St
Alexandria VA 22314-3406
703-549-4420; 800-899-4420;
    Fax: 703-549-6057
Subjects: 31

Storey's Publishers Marketplace
Storey Communications Inc
Schoolhouse Road
Pownal VT 05261
800-827-5622; Fax: 802-823-5818
Subjects: 27-29-39-43-51-73

Success! Action Pac
Card Pack Division
Venture Communications
60 Madison Ave 3rd Fl
New York NY 10010-1600
212-684-4800; Fax: 212-576-1129
Subjects: 19
Service: Success magazine subscribers

Successful Retailers Action Card
G L Hoffman
3800 Annapolis Ln
Minneapolis MN 55447-5441
612-553-3200; Fax: 612-553-3222
Subjects: 19R-99
Service: Independent single-store retails

Supt/Dist Administrators Action
MGI Decks
Marketing General Inc
1613 Duke St
Alexandria VA 22314-3406
703-549-4420; 800-899-4420;
Fax: 703-549-6057
Subjects: 31

T

TAB Electronic Pack
Card Pack Division
Venture Communications
60 Madison Ave 3rd Fl
New York NY 10010-1600
212-684-4800; Fax: 212-576-1129
Subjects: 23

Tak-Pak
Sue Hair
Ed-Pak Publishing
PO Box 1132
Canyon TX 79015-1132
806-655-1207; 800-654-1764;
Fax: 806-655-3601
Subjects: 15(horses)-69R(horseback riding)

Teaching Pre K-8 Action Pac
Card Pack Division
Venture Communications
60 Madison Ave 3rd Fl
New York NY 10010-1600
212-684-4800; Fax: 212-576-1129
Subjects: 21-31-76
Service: Highlights Magazine

Tech Talk
Harvey Krumholz
Doyle Publishing Corp
2101 Rexford Rd #172W
Charlotte NC 28211-3477
704-364-0719; 800-327-6970;
Fax: 704-362-1733
Subjects: 23

Thos Oak & Sons Package Inserts
Direct Media Insert Management
200 Pemberwick Rd
PO Box 4565
Greenwich CT 06830
203-532-1000; Fax: 203-531-1452
Subjects: 39
Service: Health care and safety buyers

Today's Business Woman Cards
Direct Media Card Decks
200 Pemberwick Rd
PO Box 4565
Greenwich CT 06830
203-532-1000; Fax: 203-531-1452
Subjects: 19-73
Service: From DMI database

Today's Catholic Teacher Pack
Peter Li Inc
330 Progress Rd
Dayton OH 45449-2322
513-847-5900; 800-523-4625 inserts
Subjects: 63(Catholic)

Today's Christian Woman Card Pak
Christianity Today
465 Gunderson Dr
Carol Stream IL 60188-2415
708-260-6200; Fax: 708-260-6200
Subjects: 63
Service: Pastor's wives

Today's Factory Pack
Gordon Action Cards
301 Gibralter Dr
Morris Plains NJ 07950
201-361-9060; 800-222-0289;
Fax: 201-292-0083
Subjects: 19X

Tools for Business Success Pac
Card Pack Division
Venture Communications
60 Madison Ave 3rd Fl
New York NY 10010-1600
212-684-4800; Fax: 212-576-1129
Subjects: 19

Tour & Travel Marketplace
Nancy Carino, Natl Sales Rep
CMP Publications
600 Community Dr
Manhasset NY 11030-3847
516-562-5961; Fax: 516-562-5465
Subjects: 71
Service: Features hotels

Travel Agents Marketplace
Claudia Hirsch, Sales Mgr
Miller-Freeman Publications
1515 Broadway
New York NY 10036-8901
212-869-1300
Subjects: 71
Service: Features hotels

Treasured Portraits Hotline Coop
RMI Direct Marketing Inc
4 Skyline Dr
Hawthorne NY 10532-2120
914-347-4949; Fax: 914-347-2954
Subjects: 21-76-99
Service: Mailings to young parents

Trucker Card Deck
Jesse Drummon, Creative Dir
Ad Man
12631 E Imperial Hwy #117B
Santa Fe Springs CA 90670-4754
310-929-3349; Fax:
Subjects: 16A
Service: For truckers in California

Trump Card Marketing Inc
222 Cedar Ln
Teaneck NJ 07666
201-836-8000; Fax: 201-836-5383
Subjects: 99

V

Vet-Dek Card Pack
Machalek Publishing
15 S 9th St
Minneapolis MN 55402-3108
612-332-1236
Subjects: 15
Service: Veterinary Product News subs

Virtue Value Pak
Carlton Dunn & Assoc
36 S Broadway
Pitman NJ 08071
609-582-0690; Fax: 609-582-1206
Subjects: 63
Service: Evangelical women

Visual Horizon's Products
Direct Media Card Decks
200 Pemberwick Rd
PO Box 4565
Greenwich CT 06830
203-532-1000; Fax: 203-531-1452
Subjects: 19

VNR Architecture Action Pac
Card Pack Division
Venture Communications
60 Madison Ave 3rd Fl
New York NY 10010-1600
212-684-4800; Fax: 212-576-1129
Subjects: 12
Service: Van Nostrand Reinhold book buyer

VNR Electronic Engineering Pac
Card Pack Division
Venture Communications
60 Madison Ave 3rd Fl
New York NY 10010-1600
212-684-4800; Fax: 212-576-1129
Subjects: 24
Service: Van Nostrand Reinhold book buyer

VNR Hospitality/FoodService Pac
Card Pack Division
Venture Communications
60 Madison Ave 3rd Fl
New York NY 10010-1600
212-684-4800; Fax: 212-576-1129
Subjects: 27
Service: Van Nostrand Reinhold book buyer

W

Wee-Pak
Sue Hair or Debbie Whelan
Ed-Pak Publishing
PO Box 1132
Canyon TX 79015-1132
806-655-1207; 800-654-1764;
Fax: 806-655-3601
Subjects: 21-31(day care center directors)

WG & L Action Card Decks
1 Penn Plz 42nd Fl
New York NY 10119-0002
212-971-5000

What's New in Home Economics
Susan Dion
North American Publishing
1429 Walnut
Philadelphia PA 19102-3218
215-563-3501
Subjects: 27-31
Service: Home economist/extenstion agents

What's NEW in Mature Marketing
Nora Coxon
American Custom Publishing
621 E Park Ave
Libertyville IL 60048-2904
708-816-8660; Fax: 708-816-8662
Subjects: 35A
Service: Directors of mature marketing

Wiley Accounting/Finance Pac
Card Pack Division
Venture Communications
60 Madison Ave 3rd Fl
New York NY 10010-1600
212-684-4800; Fax: 212-576-1129
Subjects: 19A

Wiley Agriculture Card Deck
Card Pack Division
Venture Communications
60 Madison Ave 3rd Fl
New York NY 10010-1600
212-684-4800; Fax: 212-576-1129
Subjects: 51A

Wiley Business & Management
Card Pack Division
Venture Communications
60 Madison Ave 3rd Fl
New York NY 10010-1600
212-684-4800; Fax: 212-576-1129
Subjects: 19-19G

Wiley Business/Computer Deck
Card Pack Division
Venture Communications
60 Madison Ave 3rd Fl
New York NY 10010-1600
212-684-4800; Fax: 212-576-1129
Subjects: 19-23

Wiley Computers & Data Proc Pac
Card Pack Division
Venture Communications
60 Madison Ave 3rd Fl
New York NY 10010-1600
212-684-4800; Fax: 212-576-1129
Subjects: 23

Wiley Electrical & Electronics
Card Pack Division
Venture Communications
60 Madison Ave 3rd Fl
New York NY 10010-1600
212-684-4800; Fax: 212-576-1129
Subjects: 23E-24

Wiley Engineers' Action Cards
Card Pack Division
Venture Communications
60 Madison Ave 3rd Fl
New York NY 10010-1600
212-684-4800; Fax: 212-576-1129
Subjects: 23-24-57
Memo: Also Mechanical Engineers and Chemical Engineering.

Wiley Financial Executive's Card
Card Pack Division
Venture Communications
60 Madison Ave 3rd Fl
New York NY 10010-1600
212-684-4800; Fax: 212-576-1129
Subjects: 19A-19I

Wiley Geology Card Deck
Card Pack Division
Venture Communications
60 Madison Ave 3rd Fl
New York NY 10010-1600
212-684-4800; Fax: 212-576-1129
Subjects: 67(geology)

Wiley Law Decks
Card Pack Division
Venture Communications
60 Madison Ave 3rd Fl
New York NY 10010-1600
212-684-4800; Fax: 212-576-1129
Subjects: 19L-55L
Memo: General Law, Construction Law, and Trial Law decks.

Wiley Mathematics/Statistics
Card Pack Division
Venture Communications
60 Madison Ave 3rd Fl
New York NY 10010-1600
212-684-4800; Fax: 212-576-1129
Subjects: 67(mathematics)

Wiley Psychology Card Pack
Card Pack Division
Venture Communications
60 Madison Ave 3rd Fl
New York NY 10010-1506
212-684-4800; Fax: 212-576-1129
Subjects: 57(psychology)

Wiley Real Estate Pack
Card Pack Division
Venture Communications
60 Madison Ave 3rd Fl
New York NY 10010-1506
212-684-4800; Fax: 212-576-1129
Subjects: 19H

Windows World Direct Card Pack
Direct Response Marketing Dept
The Interface Group
300 First Ave
Needham Heights MA 02194
617-449-6600; Fax:
Subjects: 23(windows)
Service: Attendees to Windows World

WinMark Concepts
2339 Ashmead Pl NW #2
Washington DC 20009-1427
203-483-1300

Wood Magazine Card Pack
Better Homes & Gardens
750 3rd Ave
New York NY 10017-2703
212-551-7158; Fax: 212-551-7115
Subjects: 29-43(woodworking)
Service: Subscribers

Working Woman Exec-Deck
Card Pack Division
Venture Communications
60 Madison Ave 3rd Fl
New York NY 10010-1600
212-684-4800; Fax: 212-576-1129
Subjects: 19-73
Service: Subscribers to Working Woman

World Communications Inserts
Direct Media Insert Management
200 Pemberwick Rd
PO Box 4565
Greenwich CT 06830
203-532-1000; Fax: 203-531-1452
Subjects: 39(diets)
Service: Buyers of diet products

Y

Youth Ministry Resource Pack
2890 N Monroe
PO Box 481
Loveland CO 80538-3274
303-669-3836
Subjects: 31-63
Service: Youth ministers

Mailing List Brokers and Managers

The following companies can provide you with specialized mailing lists for your direct mail promotions.

A

21st Century Marketing
David Schwartz
2 Dubon Ct
Farmingdale NY 11735-1012
516-293-8550; Fax: 516-293-8974
Subjects: 21-23-35F-76-99

360 Group
Allan Euphrat
700 5th Ave
San Rafael CA 94901
415-485-5478; Fax: 415-485-0939
Subjects: 19-25-43(homeowners)

5M List Co
Douglas Lee, Pres
2525 Wilson Blvd
Arlington VA 22201
703-528-6688; Fax: 703-528-2763
Subjects: 19F-55P(conservative)

A B Data Ltd
Connie Eastman, List Broker
8050 N Port Washington Rd
Milwaukee WI 53217
414-352-4404; 800-558-6908; Fax: 414-352-3994
Subjects: 11-19-44-56-63J-99

A H Direct Marketing
Audrey V Campbell, Mktg VP
360 W 22nd St 11th Fl
New York NY 10011
212-242-6652; 800-842-6336; Fax: 212-463-8526
Subjects: 51E-55L-99

A H Direct Marketing Inc
Anthony Hallock, Pres
3936 Central Ave
St Petersburg FL 33711
813-327-5229; Fax: 813-327-5411
Subjects: 19 (general business & consumer lists)

A-A-C-S Inc/AccuData America
1326 Cape Coral Pky
Cape Coral FL 33904-9889
800-732-1111; Fax: 813-540-0310
Subjects: 19

AAA Best Mailing Lists Inc
Herbert Kirsch
888 S Craycroft Rd
Tucson AZ 85711
800-692-2378; Fax: 602-745-3800
Subjects: 19

The Abadi Group Inc
Charles Abadi, Pres
1312 Allenhurst Ave
Ocean NJ 07712
908-531-7557; Fax: 908-517-1332
Subjects: 19F-19O-31-39

ABC-Advanced BusinessCompilation
Kevin Muth, VP Sales
2101 Corporate Blvd
Boca Raton FL 33431
407-241-4414; 800-777-5478; Fax: 407-241-5878
Subjects: 19

Abelow Response
David Schwartz, Pres
Twenty-First Century
2 Dubon Ct
Farmingdale NY 11735
516-293-8550; Fax: 516-791-7429
Subjects: 19-99

Abelson Comm Inc
Susan Kaplan, Co-Owner
43 D Rocklyn Ave
Lynbrook NY 11563
516-596-9610; Fax: 516-596-9618
Subjects: 23 (PC based)

Abingdon Associates
Rosanne Vallar
87 Montgomery St
Scarsdale NY 10583
914-472-0650
Subjects: 19-19X

Abstract/Records Service Inc
Joanne Zapata, Admin Mgr
20450 Walnut Dr
Walnut CA 91789
909-598-1961; Fax: 909-598-2370
Subjects: 19-25

Accountants Post Card Shopper
Rick Villines
Mostad & Christensen
PO Box 1709
Oak Harbor WA 98277
360-679-4164; Fax: 360-679-4167
Subjects: 19A (CPA firms)

AccuData America
Paul Terriot, National Sales Manager
1625 Cape Coral Pky
Cape Coral FL 33904-9617
941-549-1111; 800-732-6680; Fax: 941-540-1400
Subjects: 16A-19-25

ACM
Cynthia Ryan
1515 Broadway 17th Fl
New York NY 10036
212-869-7440
Subjects: 99
Memo: Affiliated with Rubin Response in IL; 708-619-9800 ask for Darlene Ellman, List Manager.

ACT ONE Mailing List Serv Inc
Jeffrey Lichtenstein
118 Pleasant St #4
Marblehead MA 01945
800-228-5478; Fax: 617-639-2733
Subjects: 19-25

Action List Service Inc
Lynnda Martin, VP
1 Kalisa Way
Paramus NJ 07652-3508
201-818-1881; Fax: 201-818-1996
Subjects: 19-19O-25

Action Markets
School Lists Mailing Corp
1710 Hwy 35
Oakhurst NJ 07755
908-531-2212; Fax: 908-531-4640
Subjects: 14-21-31-76-99 (Sschools/teachers/etc)

Acton Direct
Sue Burger/Justin Norblade
4901 N 57th St
PO Box 5059
Lincoln NE 68507
402-466-8400; Fax: 402-466-9074
Subjects: 19-39-55L-99
Memo: Sue and Justin are List Managers.

Ad-Lib Lists
Marie Kiefer, Owner/Publisher
Ad-Lib Publications
51 1/2 West Adams St
Fairfield IA 52556
515-472-6617; Fax: 515-472-3186
E-Mail: Adlib100@aol.com
Subjects: 56(book publishers, printers, publicity outlets, wholesalers)-99

ADC Direct Marketing
Samantha Allen, Services Mgr
266 Mobile Ave #205
Camarillo CA 93010
805-987-3466; 800-445-4787; Fax: 805-987-3522
Subjects: 99

ADCO List Management Services
Mark Berry, VP
Div of Alan Drey Co Inc
333 N Michigan Ave
Chicago IL 60601
312-236-8508; Fax: 312-346-5834
Subjects: 19-25

Addressing Unlimited Inc
Robert Meyer, Pres
14621 Titus St
Van Nuys CA 91402
818-873-4214; Fax: 818-787-0619
Subjects: 19-25-43H

Addressing Your Needs
Liz Cook, Sales Dir
2324 Ridgepoint Dr #A
Austin TX 78754
512-933-0007; Fax: 512-919-5200
Subjects: 19-25

Advanced List Marketing Assoc
Beth Fisher-Bell, List Mgr
12700 Fair Lakes Cir #340
Fairfax VA 22033
703-803-9662; Fax: 703-803-9669
Subjects: 19F-31-39-55P

Advanced Mail Inc
Gary Dreher, Pres
1825 Oxford Ave
Eau Claire WI 54701
715-839-8801; Fax: 715-839-8906
Subjects: 19-25-43H

Advanced Technology Marketing
Marilyn Martin
6053 W Century Blvd 2nd Fl
PO Box 45028
Los Angeles CA 90045
800-624-4303; Fax: 310-337-0434
Subjects: 19-23T

Advantage Direct Marketing Group
Robert Perez, Pres
450 Seventh Ave #1806
New York NY 10123-1806
212-967-4468; Fax: 212-967-4562
Subjects: 25

ADVO Inc
Tricia Vachon, Service Rep
One Univac Ln
PO Box 755
Windsor CT 06095-0755
203-285-6100; Fax: 203-244-2976
Subjects: 99(demographic)

Advon Distributors Inc
Sandi Birch
640 S State
Shelley ID 83274
208-357-7391; Fax: 208-357-5317
Subjects: 19-25

Affinity Marketing Group
Janice Payne, List Mgr
9663 C St (22032)
PO Box 2409
Fairfax VA 22031
703-978-4927; Fax: 703-978-7832
Subjects: 99 (liberal/humanitarian donors)
Memo: Jennifer Krause, List Manager also.

Aggressive List Management Inc
Pam McFeely, Mktg VP
18-2 E Dundee Rd #101
Barrington IL 60010
708-304-4030; Fax: 708-304-4032
Subjects: 19-25

Alan Drey Co Inc
Brian Hoika/Allen Schonwald
333 N Michigan Ave
Chicago IL 60601
312-346-7453; Fax: 312-346-5834
Subjects: 19-25-99
Memo: Also offices in New York, California, & Pennsylvania.

All American List Corp
Debbie Goddard, Acct Rep
2841 Harland Rd #403
Falls Church VA 22043
703-204-1422; Fax: 703-204-1022
Subjects: 19F-39(health)-63(Catholic)
Memo: Mr Hawley Van Wyck, President of ALC.

AllMedia Inc
Rick Becker/Mary Laefler
4965 Preston Park Blvd #300
Plano TX 75093
214-985-4060; Fax: 214-985-4061
Subjects: 19-25

ALM - Applied List Management
Roland Outar, List Broker
1801 Lee Rd #301
Winter Park FL 32789
407-628-5700; 800-333-5697;
   Fax: 407-628-0807
Subjects: 19

Alpha Marketing & Consulting
Gerry L Ginsburg
800 Summer St #315
Stamford CT 06901
203-359-2420; Fax: 203-325-4443
Subjects: 19

Amer Institute/Aeronautics/Astro
Leonard Rosenberg
370 L'Enfant Promenade SW
Washington DC 20024-2518
202-646-7466; Fax: 202-646-7508
Subjects: 24-48-70A(aerospace)
Memo: Full name: American Institute of Aeronautics & Astronautics.

Amer Institute/Chemical Engineer
Miriam Serrano, List Mgr
345 E 47th St
New York NY 10017
212-705-7338; 800-242-4363;
   Fax: 212-752-3294
Subjects: 24(chemical engineers)

America Direct Inc
Carla Nelson, List Mgr
9606 Blincoe Ct
Burke VA 22015
703-764-0491; Fax: 703-764-0050
Subjects: 19F-55P

American Baby Direct Mail
James Long, Mgr
Cahners Publ/Reed Publ USA
249 W 17th St
New York NY 10011
212-337-7167; 800-537-7930;
   Fax: 212-463-6631
Subjects: 25-31P-35F(new parents)

American Bar Association
Attn: List Manager
Lawyer Lists
541 N Fairbanks Ct 13th Fl
Chicago IL 60611
312-988-LIST; Fax: 312-988-5455
Subjects: 19L-55L

American Booksellers Association
Bernard E Rath, Exec Dir
828 S Broadway
Tarrytown NY 10591
914-591-2665; Fax: 914-591-2720
Subjects: 99
Service: Trade assn for retail bookseller

American Business Lists
Vin Gupta, Chairman/CEO
5711 S 86th Cir
PO Box 27347
Omaha NE 68127
402-592-9000; Fax: 402-331-1505
Subjects: 19(Lists of 11 million businesses)
Memo: A division of American Business Information Inc. NASDAQ symbol: ABII.

American Church Lists
Cindy Schoen, Client Services
PO Box 1544
Arlington TX 76004-1544
817-261-6233; 800-433-5301;
   Fax: 817-861-0167
Subjects: 63

American Computer Institute
111 Lynn Ave
Ames IA 50014
800-558-2864
Subjects: 19-23

American Correctional Assn Lists
Gabby Daley
4380 Forbes Blvd
Lanham MD 20706-4322
800-222-5646; Fax: 301-918-1900
Subjects: 55(prisoners)

American Data Consultants
Scott Howard/Chris Wilson
1010 Washington Blvd
Stamford CT 06901
203-358-9909; 800-634-2547;
   Fax: 203-358-9882
Subjects: 69H

American Data Resources
John Scammon, Natl Sales Mgr
24551 Raymond Way #110
Lake Forest CA 92630
800-541-0099; Fax: 714-588-0613
Subjects: 43H(homeowners)

American Direct Mkg Service
1120 Empire Central Pl #300
Dallas TX 75247
314-634-2361; 800-527-5080;
    Fax: 314-630-7528
Subjects: 19

American Fund Raising Lists Inc
Sue McKenzie, Dir
600 Winter St
Waltham MA 02154
617-890-2870
Subjects: 19F

American Health Consultants List
Lauren Dreyfuss
3525 Piedmont Rd NE
Six Piedmont Ctr #400
Atlanta GA 30305
800-688-2421; Fax: 800-284-3291 or
    404-262-7837
Subjects: 39M(doctors, hospital, nurses, firms, and consultants)

The American Law Institute
Deborah Rubino
4025 Chestnut St
Philadelphia PA 19104-3099
215-243-1662; Fax: 215-243-1664
Subjects: 19L

American Library Association
Attn: Wanda Saez
50 E Huron St
Chicago IL 60611
312-944-6780; 800-545-2433;
    Fax: 312-440-9374
Subjects: 99
Memo: Wanda's ext: 2460.

American List Counsel
Fran Green, List Mgmt Dir
88 Orchard Rd CN-5219
Princeton NJ 08543
800-822-LIST; Fax: 908-874-4433
Subjects: 99 (classic mailing lists)
Memo: Catalog available.

American Mailing Lists Corp
Rick Gorsky, List Mgr
12500 Fair Lakes Cir #155
Fairfax VA 22033-3804
703-893-2340; Fax: 703-847-9715
Subjects: 19F-27-35A-56P

American Mktg/CommunicationsCorp
1680 E Gude Dr
Rockville MD 20850
301-738-5787; Fax: 301-762-5887
Subjects: 99

American Student List Co
Attn: List Manager
330 Old Country Rd
Mineola NY 11501
516-248-6100; Fax: 516-248-6364
Subjects: 21-21T-31-76-89-99 (student lists, all grades)

American Vocational Assn
Kathryn Argy
1410 King St
Alexandria VA 23214
703-683-3111; Fax: 703-683-7424
Subjects: 19M-19X-31E-56M

Amtower & Co
Mark Amtower, Pres
PO Box 339
Ashton MD 20861
301-924-0058
Subjects: 55G (government officials lists)

Ancona Lists
Barry Ancona
101 W 12th St #9J
New York NY 10011
212-366-9051; Fax: 212-366-9043
Subjects: 19

Antigone Associates Ltd
Jo Ann D Alberts, Pres
801 West St Rd #1
Feasterville PA 19053-7383
215-357-9267; Fax: 215-357-2039
Subjects: 19-21-25-27-29-51A-98

Apartment Owners/Mgrs Assn of US
Robert McGough, Pres
65 Cherry Plz
Watertown CT 06795
203-274-2589; Fax: 203-274-2580
Subjects: 19H

Applied Computer Research Inc
Alan Howard
PO Box 82266
Phoenix AZ 85071
800-234-2227; Fax: 602-995-0905
Subjects: 23 (computer installation execs)

Argus Direct Business Lists
Diane
404-618-0391; Fax: 404-618-0347
Subjects: 19

Art Network
Sarah Meyer
PO Box 369
Renaissance CA 95962
916-692-1355; Fax: 916-692-1370
Subjects: 11(art schools, museums, artist, etc)

Asia Marketing & Management
James Chann
2014 Naudain St
Philadelphia PA 19146-1317
215-735-7670; Fax: 215-735-9661
Subjects: 23-24-38-44(Chinese)-67 (institutional buyers)

ASID Service Corp
Rosemarie Franz
608 Massachusetts Ave NE
Washington DC 20002
202-546-3480; Fax: 202-546-3240
Subjects: 43D

Asset Inernational Inc
125 Greenwich Ave
Greenwich CT 06830
203-629-5014; Fax: 203-629-5024
Subjects: 99

Assn of Trial Lawyers of America
Cynthia Connelly/Elsa Riemer
1050-31st St NW
Washington DC 20007
800-424-2725; Fax: 202-298-6849
Subjects: 19L-25

Association Growth Enterprises
Kevin McKenzie
1101 Mercantile Ln #100
Landover MD 20774
301-925-1420; Fax: 301-925-1429
Subjects: 48 (retired military & reservists)

Atlantic List Co Inc
Edward Krug, Pres
1525 Wilson Blvd #1225
Arlington VA 22209
703-528-7482; Fax: 703-528-7492
Subjects: 19-19F-23-35A-55P-56

ATP Mailing List Center
Christopher Stoney, Gen Mgr
Div/ALPHA-Intl Tech Professional
345 N Bartlett #202
Medford OR 97501
503-770-3366; 800-548-5478;
    Fax: 503-770-5444
Subjects: 19-25-36

Audio Response Inc
Howard Linzer/George Collins
250 W 57th St
New York NY 10019
212-489-8610; Fax: 212-262-3474
Subjects: 19-25

Aus-Tex Printing & Mailing
Cheryl Amato, Supv
501 W 3rd St
Austin TX 78701-3807
512-476-7581; Fax: 512-476-0092
Subjects: 19-25

AVANTI! Direct Marketing
Mike Buoncristiano
450 Seventh St
Hoboken NJ 07030
201-222-0404; Fax: 201-222-5535
Subjects: 25(general consumer lists)

AZ Marketing Services Inc
Arlene Clanny, VP List Mgmt
31 River Rd
Cos Cob CT 06807
203-629-8088; Fax: 203-661-1068
Subjects: 19-19F-25

B

Backroads Bicycle Touring
1516 5th St
Berkeley CA 94710-1713
415-527-1555; Fax: 415-527-1444
Subjects: 69

Bacon's Media Lists
332 S Michigan Ave #900
Chicago IL 60604
312-922-2400; Fax: 312-922-3127
Subjects: 19M-56M

Barry Ancona List Management
Barry Ancona, Pres
101 W 12th St 9J
New York NY 10011
212-366-9051; Fax: 212-366-9043
Subjects: 19-99

Behavior Bank
Metromail
529 Fifth Ave
New York NY 10017-4674
212-599-2616; Fax: 212-557-5259
Subjects: 99

Bernice Bush Springdale Lists
Beth Ann Thompson
15052 Springdale St
Huntington Beach CA 92649
714-891-3344; Fax: 714-897-0650
Subjects: 14M-19F-63

Best Business Services
Douglas Gregory, List Mgr
1800 S Robertson #58
Los Angeles CA 90035
310-836-5530; Fax: 310-204-5642
Subjects: 19-25-31E(college students)

Best List Managers Inc
Nancy Brown, Sales Mgr
5030 Champion Blvd #6240
Boca Raton FL 33496
407-496-1086; Fax: 407-496-1432
Subjects: 25-28

The Best Lists Inc
Leyla Uzer, List Mgr
Div of Response Dynamics Inc
2070 Chain Bridge Rd #400
Vienna VA 22180
703-442-7595; Fax: 703-790-8564
Subjects: 19F (telemarketing)

Best Mailing Lists Inc
Karen J Kirsch, CEO
888 South Craycroft Rd
Tucson AZ 85711
602-745-0200; 800-692-2378;
   Fax: 602-745-3800
Subjects: 19-99

Bethesda List Center Inc
David James, Pres
4424 Montgomery Ave #305
Bethesda MD 20814
301-986-1455; Fax: 301-907-4870
Subjects: 19

Better List Brokerage/Mgmt Corp
Jon Martin, Sales Mgr
5030 Champion Blvd #6240
Boca Raton FL 33496
407-496-1086; Fax: 407-496-1432
Subjects: 25-28 (card holders/mail order buyers)

Better Lists Inc
Tim Rath, Pres
16 Liberty St
Stamford CT 06902
203-324-4171
Subjects: 19-25

Bick International
Israel Bick, Pres
PO Box 854
Van Nuys CA 91408
818-997-6496; Fax: 818-988-4337
Subjects: 19-25

Billian Publishing Inc
Cathy Parker
2100 Powers Ferry Rd
Atlanta GA 30339
404-955-8484; Fax: 404-955-8485
Subjects: 23-39 (Healthcare Blue Book database)

BMI Medical Information Inc
Linda Dorman, VP Sales/Mktg
2101 S Arlington Heights Rd #195
Arlington Heights IL 60005
800-888-8717; Fax: 708-228-9424
Subjects: 39M (medical/professional lists)

Boardroom Lists
Charles Teller/Peter Leeds
330 W 42nd Stve
New York NY 10036
212-239-9000
Subjects: 99 (book buyers/subscriber lists)

Bocca Direct Marketing
Richard Bonvicino, Dir
Snug Harbor Sta
PO Box 83
Duxbury MA 02332
800-356-5478
Subjects: 19-25

Bowker Mailing Lists
John Panza
Connors Direct Mail Service
245 West 17th St
New York NY 10011
212-337-7164; Fax: 212-463-6532
Subjects: 99
Service: Bookstores, libraries, publishers

The Broadmore Group
3431B Date Palm Dr #186
Cathedral City CA 92234
619-324-3072; Fax: 619-321-5314
Subjects: 99

Brooks Mann Inc
Rita Vizzini, List Rep
1350 W 9th St #230
Cleveland OH 44113
216-696-5588; Fax: 216-241-2810
Subjects: 19-25

Bruckenthal Associates Inc
Robert Bruckenthal, Pres
47 Byron Pl
Scarsdale NY 10583
914-723-8321; Fax: 914-723-8340
Subjects: 19-25

The Bureau Inc
Resa Arnold, Pres
2555 SE Bonita St
Stuart FL 34997
407-283-8850
Subjects: 19-25

Burlington Marketing
Bob Goldstein, Pres
14 Vincent Rd
Burlington MA 01803
617-272-3432; Fax: 617-272-7715
Subjects: 19-25-35F

Business Digest Mail
Bev Valera, Mgr
72 Winter St
Hyannis MA 02601
508-778-5042; Fax: 508-778-5063
Subjects: 19-35A-56P

Business News Publishing Co
Jesse Piper
PO Box 2600
Troy MI 48007
800-837-7370; Fax: 810-362-4932
Subjects: 19

Business Research Publications
Vijay Thakkar
65 Bleeker St 5th Fl
New York NY 10012
212-673-4700; Fax: 212-475-1790
Subjects: 19-19X-39

Business Research Services Inc
Sharon Washington
4201 Connecticutt Ave NW #610
Washington DC 20008
800-845-8420; Fax: 202-686-3228
Subjects: 19-49-73 (minority and women-owned businesses)

C

CAF List Co
Wesley Richardson, Broker
PO Box 189
Washington Grove MD 20880
202-547-0200; Fax: 202-547-5035
Subjects: 43(residential)-55P-63

Cahners Direct Marketing Service
R R Bowker/Reed Publ
1350 E Touhy Ave Box
Des Plaines IL 60018
847-390-2361; 800-323-4958;
   Fax: 847-390-2779
Subjects: 12B-19-23-27-31E-56P-71

Cambridge Career Products
Lesley Benson
PO Box 2153
Charleston WV 25328-2153
800-468-4227
Subjects: 31E

Canadian List Services
Coral Gifkins/Nola Ferguson
494 McNicoll Ave #201
Willowdale ON Canada M2H 2E1
416-494-7974; Fax: 416-492-4173
Subjects: 25-35A(telemarketing)

The Capable Mind
10 Soundview Gardens Unit D
Port Washington NY 11050
516-883-2343; Fax: 516-883-5119
Subjects: 99

Capitol Publications
Edna Flynn
1101 King St #444
Alexandria VA 22314
703-739-6441; Fax: 703-739-6501
Subjects: 31E-39

Capstone Lists Inc
Bessie Thibodeaux, List Mgr
2900 Eisenhower Ave #201
Alexandria VA 22314
703-329-9775; Fax: 703-329-0677
Subjects: 19F

Cardinal Mailing Services Ltd
C Scott May
552 N Nimitz Hwy
Honolulu HI 96817
808-538-3884; Fax: 808-521-1419
Subjects: 19(execs)-43(residenttial)

Carnegie Marketing Associates
Mary Thompson, List Mgr
3878 Carson St #220
Torrance CA 90503
310-540-4757; Fax: 310-540-7407
Subjects: 19I-55P (mail order buyers, subscribers)

Carney Direct Marketing (CDM)
Guy Connor/Michael Carney
15530-B Rockfield Blvd #3
Irvine CA 92718
714-581-5100; 800-240-3349;
   Fax: 714-581-4564
Subjects: 19-25-99

Carol Enters List Co
Jerry Hopkins, Acct Exec
9663C Main St
Fairfax VA 22032
703-452-0052; Fax: 703-425-0056
Subjects: 19F

CAS Marketing Inc
Kent Stormberg, Pres
616 S 75th St
Omaha NE 68114-4624
402-393-0313; 800-524-0908;
   Fax: 402-390-9497
Subjects: 19-99

Catalyst Direct Marketing Inc
Becky Santaniello, Acct Exec
301 Godwin Ave
Midland Park NJ 07432
201-612-0909; Fax: 201-612-9721
Subjects: 19-19O-21-40F

Catholic Lists
Barbara Coto
22 W First St #511
Mount Vernon NY 10550
914-668-7320; Fax: 914-668-9188
Subjects: 63(Catholics)

CCS Direct Inc
Theresa Smith, Acct Rep
3240 S Dodge Blvd #2
Tucson AZ 85713-5478
800-422-5478; Fax: 602-747-3407
Subjects: 19-25-99

Certified Mailing Lists Co
Hugh Chewning, Pres
4 Candlebush
Irvine CA 92715
714-854-2942; Fax: 714-854-5401
Subjects: 19F-56(book buyers)

Channing L Bete Co
Attn: List Manager
200 State Rd
South Deerfield MA 01373
413-665-7611; Fax: 413-665-2671
Subjects: 19-31-39-55-63
Service: Leaders in all fields

Charles Crane Associates Inc
Eugene Adoff, Sales Mgr
2050 Center Ave
Fort Lee NJ 07024
201-944-2240; Fax: 201-944-7119
Subjects: 19-25-99

Charles Moore Assoc Inc
Charles Moore
Box 6 Stump Rd
Southhampton PA 18966
215-355-6084; Fax: 215-364-2212
Subjects: 19-25

Chesapeake Direct Inc
Rory Brennan, Pres
201 Balsam Dr Box 1323
Severna Park MD 21146
410-544-5880; Fax: 410-544-5602
Subjects: 19F-25-44-55P

Chester Mailing List Consultants
Barbara Goodwin, List Broker
3251 Old Lee Hwy #504
Fairfax VA 22030
703-934-2700; Fax: 703-934-2705
Subjects: 19F-25-35A-39-48(veterans)

Chilcutt Direct Marketing
Mkg Coordinator
9301 Cedar Lake Ave
PO Box 14890
Oklahoma City OK 73113
405-478-7245; Fax: 405-478-2984
Subjects: 15-51-69H-69R (hunters and fishers)

Chilcutt Direct Mktg/Outdoor Lis
Stephanie Lamamma, VP/ListSales
9301 Cedar Lake Ave
PO Box 14890
Oklahoma City OK 73113
405-478-7245; Fax: 405-478-2984
Subjects: 28-43G-69 (Mail order buyers)

Chilton Direct Mktg/List Mgmt
Bob Cronin, Dir
One Chilton Way
Radnor PA 19089
800-274-2207; Fax: 610-964-1888
Subjects: 19-99 (Industrial/professional lists)

Christopher Resources Inc
Marty Fabish/Melissa Maori
PO Box 488
Frankfort IL 60423-0488
800-332-3441; Fax: 815-485-2499
Subjects: 19X (US and international specialty industries)

Chronicle of Higher Education
Marianne Jacobs
1255 23rd St NW #700
Washington DC 20037
202-466-1000; Fax: 202-296-2691
Subjects: 31E

The Chronicle of Philanthropy
Kristen Pedisich
1255 23rd St NW
Washington DC 20037
202-466-1234; Fax: 202-296-2691
Subjects: 19F

Clark Boardman Callaghan/CBC
Nicholas Englezos
375 Hudson St
New York NY 10014-9986
800-422-2101; Fax: 212-206-8312
Subjects: 19L (CBC Legal and Taxation Book Buyers File. also reference publications, newsletters, prof associations, seminars, credit cards, software, high ticket items, & fundraising)

Clothing Manufacturers Assn/USA
Alice Austria
1290 Ave of the Americas #1061
New York NY 10104
212-757-6664
Subjects: 19X(apparel)

CMC List Capital
Bob Borzage
1823 Montgomery Rd
Thousand Oaks CA 91360
805-373-0882; Fax: 805-373-9812
Subjects: 19-25-99

CMG Information Services
John Hood, Sr VP
187 Ballardvale St #B110
PO Box 7000
Wilmington MA 01887-7000
508-657-7000; 800-677-7959;
   Fax: 508-988-0046
Web: http://www.cmgi.com
E-mail:Kbello@cmgi.com
Subjects: 19-31-39-41-44-55-57-59-65-67 -99 (college marketing group, college faculty, mail order book buyers, libraries, schools)

CMP Direct Marketing Services
Margaret Mathison
1 Jericho Plz 2nd Fl Wing A
Jericho NY 11753
516-733-6700; 800-972-5544;
   Fax: 516-733-6820
Subjects: 19-23

Cody Associates Inc
100 Aviation Dr S #201
Naples FL 33942
941-434-4121; Fax: 941-434-4122
Subjects: 99

College Bookstores List
Robert Oman
204 Fair Oaks Park
Needham MA 01890
617-444-7455
Subjects: 99 (publishing list, college bkstores)

Columbia Dir Mktg/List Division
Tracy Olsen, List Broker
60 West St #405
Annapolis MD 21401
410-268-8881; Fax: 410-268-8999
Subjects: 19F-51E

Columbia House Lists
Evelyn Deitz
Columbia House
1221 Ave of the Americas
New York NY 10019-6101
212-596-2421
Subjects: 14(records and tapes)
Service: Lists and package insert program

Command Productions
Warren Weagant
PO Box 26348
San Francisco CA 94126-6348
415-332-3161
Subjects: 99 (radio/TV stations)

Commercial Mailing Lists Inc
Bruce Forman
PO Box 951
Framingham MA 01701-0373
508-879-2647; Fax: 508-879-2911
Subjects: 19-25-99

Commonwealth List Co
Debbie McGinty, List Mgr
4401 Fairlakes Ct #400
Fairfax VA 22033
703-802-4545; Fax: 703-802-2651
Subjects: 19F-39-51E-55P

Compass Publications
David Hertzig
1117 N 19th St #1000
Arlington VA 22209-1725
703-524-3136; Fax: 703-841-0852
Subjects: 24-67(underwater industries)

Compiled Solutions Inc
Leland Kroll
666 Plainsboro Rd #540
Plainsboro NJ 08536
609-275-6452; Fax: 609-936-1918
Subjects: 99
Service: List compilers

Compilers Plus
Ed Mallin
466 Main St
New Rochelle NY 10801
914-633-5240; 800-431-2914;
    Fax: 914-633-5261
Subjects: 99
Service: Catalog available

CompuName Inc
Tom Miller, VP/Group Mktg Mgr
411 Theodore Fremd Ave
Rye NY 10580-1497
914-925-2401
Subjects: 19-25-99

Computer Economics Inc
5841 Edison Pl
Carlsbad CA 92008
619-438-8100; Fax: 619-431-1126
Subjects: 19-23

Conrad Direct Inc
Barbara Schonwald
300 Knickerbocker Rd
Cresskill NJ 07626
201-567-3200; Fax: 201-567-1530
Subjects: 19-71-99

Consolidated Mailing Service
Max Bradbard
Div of Two Star Films
PO Box 495
St James NY 11780
516-584-7283
Subjects: 31E-39

Consumers Digest
5705 N Lincoln Ave
Chicago IL 60659
312-275-3590; Fax: 213-275-7273
Subjects: 99

Consumers Marketing Research Inc
Norman Nelson, Pres
600 Huyler St
S Hackensack NJ 07606
201-440-8900; Fax: 201-440-2168
Subjects: 19-19F-25-49-63

Coolidge Company Inc
Richard Steeg
25 West 43rd St
New York NY 10036
212-642-0300; Fax: 212-642-0347
Subjects: 19-25-99

Cornerstone List Managers Inc
Don Lange, List Mgr
2300 Yonge St #2005
PO Box 2465
Toronto ON M4P 1E4
416-932-9555; Fax: 416-932-9566
Subjects: 19-19F-51N-73-99(Canadian)

CorpTech
12 Alfred St #200
Woburn MA 01801
617-932-3939; 800-333-8036;
    Fax: 617-932-6335
Subjects: 23(high-tech manufacurers)

Country Marketing Ltd
List Management
176 E Main St
Ilion NY 13357
315-895-7737; Fax: 315-895-7392
Subjects: 25-39-40B

County Data Corp
Michael Allen
PO Box 416
Winooski VT 05404
802-655-5888; Fax: 802-655-5005
Subjects: 19-19H-43(new homeowners)

Cowles Media Inc
911 Hope St Box 4949
Stamford CT 06907-0949
203-358-9900
Subjects: 99

Craftsman Book Company
Amy Hall, Mktg Asst
6058 Corte Del Cedro
PO Box 6500
Carlsbad CA 92018-9974
619-438-7828; 800-829-8123;
    Fax: 619-438-0398
Subjects: 12B

Craver Mathews Smith & Co
300 N Washington St #200
Falls Church VA 22046
703-237-0600; Fax: 703-237-0622
Subjects: 99

Creative Access
John Butsch
415 W Superior
Chicago IL 60610
800-422-2377; Fax: 312-440-1110
Subjects: 19-19M(advertising)

Creative List Services Inc
Aileen Neill, List Mgr
Div/The Direct Marketing Group
40 Daniel St
Farmingdale NY 11735
516-752-9500
Subjects: 19-25-99

Cromwell Lists
Bill Buchler, List Mgr
Affiliate of Leichtung
4944 Commerce Pky
Cleveland OH 44128
216-831-6193
Subjects: 99(mail-order buyers lists)

Crosslists Co
Pamela Jarson, VP/Gen Mgr
11370 Manchester Rd
St Louis MO 63122
314-821-1994; Fax: 314-965-0613
Subjects: 19-19F-25-43H-63

Custom List Services Inc
Cori Reider, List Serv Mgr
3 Metro Plz #107
8300 Professional Pl
Landover MD 20785
301-459-9885
Subjects: 19F

Custom Mailing Services
Bruce Ellis, Acct Rep
145 Grove St Ext
Peterborough NH 03458
603-924-9442; Fax: 603-924-9441
Subjects: 19-25-99

Customer Insight Company
6855 S Havana St 4th Fl
Englewood CO 80112-3841
303-790-7002
Subjects: 99
Memo: A Metromail/R R Donnelley & Sons Co.

CW Lists
Deb Goldstein, List Mgr
Computer World
Box 880
Framingham MA 01701
800-343-6474; Fax: 617-879-0700
Subjects: 23

D

D-J Associates
Carol Forbes, List Mgr
77 Danbury Rd
PO Box 2048
Ridgefield CT 06877
203-431-8777; Fax: 203-431-3302
Subjects: 19F-21-23-25-31-35-40F-99

Daniel Publishing Group
Joseph Daniel
713 Pearl St
Boulder CO 80302
303-442-2609; Fax: 303-442-2399
Subjects: 99

Dartnell
John Morrison, List Mgr
4660 Ravenswood Ave
Chicago IL 60640
800-621-5463; Fax: 312-561-4000
Subjects: 99(customer/mail-order buyers)

Dasher Inc
Beverly Lesher/Marsha Davis
1660 S Cameron St
Harrisburg PA 17104-3145
717-234-3274; Fax: 717-234-6092
Subjects: 19-25-43(residential)

Data Based Lists
Rebecca Hitchcock, List Mgr
4010 Morena Blvd #200
San Diego CA 92117
800-336-6060; Fax: 619-483-9851
Subjects: 23(computer magazines)

Data Marketing Group Ltd
1983 Marcus Ave #124
Lake Success NY 11042
516-775-3400; Fax: 516-775-7900
Subjects: 99

Database America Companies Inc
Jule Albanese, Natl List Sales
100 Paragon Dr
Montvale NJ 07645
201-476-2300; 800-223-7777;
 Fax: 201-476-2405
Subjects: 19-25-99

Database Management
Cindy Lin
304 Park Ave S
New York NY 10010
212-388-8830; Fax: 212-388-8890
Subjects: 45(Spanish)-49H-49O(Asian)

Database Publishing Co
Diane Pearce, VP Sales
1590 S Lewis St
Anaheim CA 92805
800-888-8434; Fax: 714-778-8611
Subjects: 19X-61(AZ/CA-OR-WA)

Datapulse
2 Executive Dr
Fort Lee NJ 07024-3393
201-592-0700; Fax: 201-592-8052
Subjects: 99
Memo: Catalog available.

Davison Publishing Co Inc
Bruce Nealy
PO Box 477
Ridgewood NJ 07451
201-445-3135; Fax: 201-445-4397
Subjects: 19X(apparel)

DCC Data Service Inc
David Cromartie/Kay Efron
1200 18th St NW #704
Washington DC 20036
202-452-1419
Subjects: 19-25-48-70N

DCI List Management
Alan Zamchick
Div/Diamandis Communications Inc
1633 Broadway
New York NY 10019
212-767-6677; Fax: 212-767-5605
Subjects: 99(subscriber lists)

The Denali Press
Sally Silvas-Ottumwa
PO Box 021535
Juneau AK 99802-1535
907-586-6014; Fax: 907-463-6780
Subjects: 31E-49H-59(libraries)

Dependable Lists Inc
Tamara Stankoven, Dir/List Mgmt
950 S 25th Ave
Bellwood IL 60104
708-544-1000; Fax: 708-544-1094
Subjects: 99

Direct Communications Corp
Christopher Mayka, VP
24 Wales St
Rutland VT 05701
802-747-3322; Fax: 802-747-3376
Subjects: 19-25-56-99

Direct Mail Advertising Corp
Jack Hurley/Len Himsworth, Reps
5870 Miami Lakes Dr
Miami Lakes FL 33014
305-557-4153; Fax: 305-825-8804
Subjects: 19-25-43(residential)

Direct Marketing Assn
Shirley Chen/Pauletta Peach
11 W 42nd St 25th Fl
New York NY 10036
212-768-7277; Fax: 212-599-1268
Subjects: 19M-telemarketing

Direct Marketing Enterprises Inc
Mark Scheifley, Pres
374 Circle of Progress
Pottstown PA 19464
610-326-4966; Fax: 610-326-4967
Subjects: 19X

Direct Marketing List Source
Standard Rate & Data Service
1700 Higgins Rd
Des Plaines IL 60018
708-375-5068; 800-851-7737;
 Fax: 708-375-5009
Subjects: 19-99(direct mail lists)
Memo: Formerly Direct Mail List Rates & Data.

Direct Marketing Technology Inc
955 American Ln
Schaumburg IL 60173-4998
708-517-5600
Subjects: 25(consumer lists)

Direct Media Inc
200 Pemberwick Rd
Greenwich CT 06830
203-532-1000; Fax: 203-531-1452
Subjects: 19-19F-25-99

Directors Guild Lists
Constance Franklin, Mgr
Directors Guild Publishers
13284 Rices Crossing #3 POB 369
Renaissance CA 95962
800-383-0677; Fax: 916-692-1370
Subjects: 11

Directory of Mailing List Co
Barry T Klein, Editor
Todd Publications
PO Box 301
West Nyack NY 10994
914-358-6213
Subjects: 99 (mailing houses)

Dirmark Business Lists
Michael A Newton Jr, VP
9582 Tara Blvd
Jonesboro GA 30236
404-477-7797; 800-950-5478;
 Fax: 404-477-0417
Subjects: 19

Disability Marketing Group
Marsha Sussman, Mktg Dir
1050 Connecticut Ave NW #1250
Washington DC 20036
202-296-1488; Fax: 202-861-1645
Subjects: 39D

DM News
19 W 21st St
New York NY NY 10010
212-741-2095
Subjects: 19-99 (subscriber lists)

DMCA Direct
Joy Weiss/Mary Hulbert
1 Corporate Woods Dr
Bridgeton MO 63044
314-344-8000; Fax: 314-344-8080
Subjects: 19-19L-23-25-43(occupant lists)

DMG Lists Ltd
Margaret Hoerres
1981 Marcus Ave #214
Lake Success NY 11042
516-775-3400; Fax: 516-775-7900
Subjects: 99

Donnelley Marketing
70 Seaview Ave
Stamford CT 06902
203-353-7000; 800-433-5478
Subjects: 35A-99(senior lifestyle lists)

Doubleday List Marketing
Eileen Fagan
Subs/Doubleday Bk & Music Clubs
501 Franklin Ave
Garden City NY 11530
516-873-4477; Fax: 516-873-4774
Subjects: 99 (book buyers lists)

Doug Ross Communications
3225 S Hardy Dr #101
Tempe AZ 85282
602-966-1744; Fax: 602-894-1770
Subjects: 99

Doyle Publishing Corp
Ken Self/John Vaccaro
2101 Rexford Rd #172W
Charlotte NC 28211
704-364-0719; Fax: 704-362-1733
Subjects: 19-19O

DP Directory Inc
525 Goodale Hill Rd
Glastonbury CT 06033
203-659-1065
Subjects: 23-99

Dresden Direct Inc
1200 High Ridge Rd
Stamford CT 06905
203-329-3030; Fax: 203-322-6107
Subjects: 99

DSD List Services
Karen Gallion, List Mgr
125 E Sir Francis Drake Blvd #200
Larkspur CA 94939
415-461-6202; Fax: 415-461-7953
Subjects: 19F

Dun's Educational Directory
Dun's Marketing Services
3 Sylvan Way
Parsippany NJ 07054
201-455-0900
Subjects: 31E

Dunhill International List Co
Robert Dunhill
1951 NW 19th St
Boca Raton FL 33431-7344
407-347-0200; Fax: 407-347-0400
Subjects: 19-35-44-57

Dustbooks Mailing Lists
Len Fulton
Dustbooks Publishing Co
PO Box 100
Paradise CA 95967
916-877-6110; Fax: 916-877-0222
Subjects: 99(small press)mail-order
    buyers/publ lists)

E

Eagle Publications
42400 9 Mile-B
Novi MI 48375
313-347-3490; Fax: 313-347-3492
Subjects: 19X-51E

Eagle Publishing List Marketing
Rosann Garber, List Mgr
Div of Phillips Publishing Intl
422 First St SE
Washington DC 20003
202-546-5005; Fax: 202-546-8759
Subjects: 19F-55P-56P

East-West List Corp
Donald Hiner, List Mgr
5203 Leesburg Pike #307
Falls Church VA 22041
703-578-2900; Fax: 703-578-2905
Subjects: 48-55-99

Eastern Direct Marketing Inc
Leigh Slayden, Prod Mgr
100 N Washington St #232
Falls Church VA 22046
703-241-0600; Fax: 703-241-0603
Subjects: 11-19(charities, professional &
    trade association lists)

Ed Burnett Consultants
John Kehoe, Dir
Database America Companies
100 Paragon Dr
Montvale NJ 07645
800-223-7777; Fax: 201-476-2411
Subjects: 19-19F-23-25

Edith Roman Associates
Lee Roberts
253 W 35th St
New York NY 10001
212-695-3836; 800-223-2194;
    Fax: 212-629-5924
Subjects: 99(catalog available)

Editor and Publisher Co
H K Vos
11 West 19th St
New York NY 10011-4236
212-675-4380; Fax: 212-929-1259
Subjects: 56P(publishing lists)

Edmaro's Inc
W T O'Shields, Dir
301 Wilcrest #3305
Houston TX 77042
713-784-4606
Subjects: 69R (recreation/leisure/outdoors
    list)

Education Data Services
601 E Marshall St
Sweet Springs MO 65351-0295
800-671-9813; Fax: 816-335-4157
Subjects: 31E

Education Mailings Clearinghouse
601 E Marshall St
Sweet Springs MO 65351
816-335-6373
Subjects: 31E (educational lists)

Educational Directories Inc
Linda Sanchez
PO Box 199
Mount Prospect IL 60056-0199
708-459-0605; Fax: 708-459-0608
Subjects: 31E
Service: Public/private schools

EEI List Services
Eleanor Johnson
66 Canal Ctr Plz #200
Alexandria VA 22314-5507
703-683-0683; Fax: 703-683-4815
Subjects: 19-56

Eleanor L Stark Co Inc
Eleanor L Stark, Pres
515 Madison AVe #2300
New York NY 10022
212-838-1935; Fax: 212-751-2024
Subjects: 19-44

ELS (Estee List Services Inc)
270 N Ave #805
New Rochelle NY 10801
914-235-7080; Fax: 914-235-6518
Subjects: 99

Elsevier Business Lists
Val DeGeiso, VP
Div of Gordon Publications Inc
301 Gibralter Dr Box 650
Morris Plains NJ 07950
201-292-5100; Fax: 201-898-9281
Subjects: 19-23-39-67

Enertex Marketing
Naomi Gross, List Mgr
99 Madison Ave
New York NY 10016
212-532-3115; Fax: 212-532-1878
Subjects: 19F-19M-33

Essential Lists
Joanne Chevrier
263 Ave Labrosse
Pointe-Clair PQ H9R 1A3
514-695-8218; Fax: 514-695-5988
Subjects: 19-19F-25-44-56

Estee List Services Inc
Chris Ragusa, Pres
PO Box 1765
New Rochelle NY 10802
914-235-7080; Fax: 914-235-6518
Subjects: 19F-49H-56

ETR Associates
Mary Nelson
PO Box 1830
Scotts Valley CA 95062
408-438-4060; Fax: 408-438-4284
Subjects: 31E-35F-39

Evergreen Marketing
Evawn Lewis, Pres
Rd 1 Box 812
Landisburg PA 17040
717-789-4899; Fax: 717-789-4047
Subjects: 25-44(British)-69H

Executive Enterprises Inc
Alice Bello
List Sales Div
22 West 21st St
New York NY 10010-6990
212-645-7880; Fax: 212-366-9708
Subjects: 19

F

Fairfield Marketing Group
Ed Washcilla Jr, Pres
830 Sport Hill Rd
Easton CT 06612-1241
203-261-5585; Fax: 203-261-0884
Subjects: 21-31E(educational lists)

Fasano & Associates
Franchesca Wollmann, VP Sales
3599 Cahuenga Blvd W 4th Fl
Los Angeles CA 90068
213-874-4400; Fax: 213-874-0230
Subjects: 21-40F-69-99

FDR List Management
Linda Duguid
62 Spring Hill Rd
Trumbull CT 06611
203-452-1919; Fax: 203-452-1039
Subjects: 27-29-31-35-39

First Editions Mailing Lists
Sophie Tarila, Dir
First Editions
80 N Payne Pl PO Box 2578
Sedona AZ 86339-2578
602-282-9574; Fax: 602-282-9730
Subjects: 39H-53-54
Memo: 4344 retailers, 950 music stores, 450 publications, 1,100 publishers, and 425 audio producers.

First Financial Response
Bob Borzage
587 N Ventu Park Rd #F-231
Newbury Park CA 91320
805-339-2539; Fax: 805-339-0959
Subjects: 19-25
Service: Telemarketing/direct response

Firstmark
Michael Pomerantz, Pres
34 Juniper Ln
Newton Center MA 02159
617-965-7989; 800-729-2600;
  Fax: 617-965-8510
Subjects: 19-23T-25-39

Fleetwood Communications
PO Box 2134
Blaine WA 98230
604-278-2560
Subjects: 31E
Service: Canadian high schools/colleges

Flynn Direct Response Inc
62 Spring Hill Rd
PO Box 759
Trumbull CT 06611
203-452-1919; Fax: 203-452-1039
Subjects: 25-44(Canada)-56P-99

FMP List Services Inc
Dave Irwin, Acct Exec
1019 W Park Ave
Libertyville IL 60048
708-816-1919; Fax: 708-816-1969
Subjects: 25-43H(new homeowners, credit card shoppers, new movers)

Focus USA
Meg Kimball
63 Grand Ave
River Edge NJ 07661
201-489-2525; Fax: 201-489-4499
E-Mail: focususa@carroll.com
Subjects: 49B-49H (ethnic lists)

Franklin Distributors Corp
Allan Gill
PO Box 320
Denville NJ 07834
201-267-2710; Fax: 201-663-1305
Subjects: 11P-55 (mail-order buyers)

Fred E Allen Inc
JoDana Cargile
2756 W Ferguson Rd
Mt Pleasant TX 75455
903-572-1701; Fax: 903-572-1703
Subjects: 19-25

Fred Singer Direct Marketing Inc
Sandra Roscoe, VP Mgmt
1329A North Ave #102
New Rochelle NY 10804
914-636-0020; Fax: 914-235-0970
Subjects: 19-25-99

Fred Woolf List Co Inc
110 Corporate Park Dr
White Plains NY 10604-3800
914-694-4466; 800-431-1557;
  Fax: 914-694-1710
Subjects: 99(catalog available)

G

GaleLists
Chris Miller
Gale Research Inc
645 Griswald
Detroit MI 48226
800-877-4253; Fax: 313-961-6083
Subjects: 19-99(libraries, assns, and companies(lists from their directories)

Garrett Park Press Mailing Lists
Robert Calvert Jr, Pres
Garrett Park Press
PO Box 190
Garrett Park MD 20896
301-946-2553
Subjects: 49-73 (minority and women's groups)

George D Hall Co
Carol Nastasia
50 Congress St
Boston MA 02109
800-446-1215; Fax: 617-523-4862
Subjects: 19X-25-31E-39-43H(residential)

George Sterne Agency
George Sterne, Pres
254 E Grand Ave
Escondido CA 92025
619-432-6913; Fax: 619-432-7950
Subjects: 19-19O

George-Mann Associates Inc
George Sharoff, Pres
569 Abbington Dr #B
PO Box 930
Hightstown NJ 08520-0930
609-443-1330; Fax: 609-443-0397
Subjects: 19-25-99

Gerald L Lewis Direct Mktg
2204 N 184th St
Shoreline WA 98133
206-363-0720; Fax: 206-363-0729
Subjects: 99

Get-List
Steve Waxman, Pres
7500 Frankfort Rd Box 606
Versailles KY 40983
606-873-9229; Fax: 606-873-4216
Subjects: 19-25-48

Global Direct Marketing Inc
Martin Freundlich, VP
189 Knickerbocker Rd
Closter NJ 07624
201-767-6088; Fax: 201-767-6091
Subjects: 19-25-44-99 (international business, consumer lists)

Global Success Corp
Jody Statile
2400 Ninth St #450
Naples FL 33940
813-261-4335; Fax: 813-261-6713
Subjects: 99

GMI/Uni-Mail Commercial
Kay Cassidy
352 Park Ave S 14th Fl
New York NY 10010-1709
212-679-7655; Fax: 212-679-7590
Subjects: 99(mail order/subscriber lists)

Gnames Enterprises
Kim Jackson, List Mgr
6642 W Ida Dr #223
Littleton CO 80123
303-798-4819; Fax: 303-798-4721
Subjects: 99

Gold Medal Hair Products
Rick Laban, List Mgr
1 Bennington Ave
Freeport NY 11520
516-378-6900; Fax: 516-378-0168
Subjects: 40B

Good Fortune Marketing Inc
Sue Perry, Mktg Dir
210 Commerce Blvd
Round Rock TX 78664-2189
512-255-6014; Fax: 512-255-7532
Subjects: 19-73

Great Lakes Fulfillment
List Management Division
PO Box 3670
Erie PA 16508
800-964-5478; Fax: 814-455-1942
Subjects: 99(sweepstakes entrants)

Greenwich Consultants
Tony Vercillo
15821 Feklock Ln
Chino Hills CA 91709
909-393-0855; Fax: 909-393-9405
Subjects: 16-19O (credit repair seekers)

Greystone Services Inc
Catherine Armao
PO Box 482
Beverly MA 01915
508-927-0188; Fax: 508-921-5120
Subjects: 19-25-99

Group 1 Software
Lisa Mills
4200 Parliament Pl #600
Lanham MD 20706
800-368-5806; Fax: 301-731-0360
Subjects: 19-25-99

H

Hachette Magazines/List Mgmt
Lynn Martusciello, List Sales Mg
1633 Broadway 43rd Fl
New York NY 10019
212-767-6677; Fax: 212-767-5605
Subjects: 21-25-56P

Hank Marshall Marketing Co
Hank Marshall, Pres
PO Box 2729
Laguna Hills CA 92654
714-581-5856; Fax: 714-581-5858
Subjects: 19-19O-57S-56P
Service: Also package insert programs

Harris Publishing Co
Robert Harris, Pres
2057 Aurora Rd
Twinsburg OH 44087
216-485-9000; 800-888-5900;
   Fax: 216-963-6355
Subjects: 19X

Harrison Publishing Co Inc
Tim Harrison, Gen Mgr
624 Patton Ave
Asheville NC 28806-3890
800-438-5829; Fax: 800-645-5909
Subjects: 19-25-99

Harvard Professional Lists Inc
955 Massachusetts Ave #306
Cambridge MA 02139
617-661-0617; Fax: 617-661-1531
Subjects: 39(mental health)
Service: List brokers

Hauser List Services Inc
David Hauser
10 Commercial St
Hicksville NY 11801
516-735-1680; Fax: 516-735-1797
Subjects: 99
Service: List rental security/database

Hearst Business Lists Rentals
Terry Curatolo, List Mgr
645 Stewart Ave
Garden City NY 11530
516-227-1300; Fax: 516-227-1901
Subjects: 19

Heartland Ag-Business Group
Shannon Bushman, List Mgr
1003 Central Ave
Ft Dodge IA 50501
800-247-2000; Fax: 515-955-6108
Subjects: 51A

Heldref Publications
Susan Bindman
4000 Albemarle St NW
Washington DC 20016
202-362-6445; Fax: 202-537-0287
Subjects: 31E-56P

Hemisphere Marketing Inc
Edwin Okamura
100 Spear St #430
San Francisco CA 94105
415-777-1171; Fax: 415-777-2371
Subjects: 19-25-44

HFM List Management
Alan Zamchick/Lynn Martusciello
1633 Broadway 43rd Fl
New York NY 10019
212-767-6677; Fax: 212-767-5605
E-Mail: HFMListMan@aol.com
Subjects: 11P-16A-27-35-40-43-70N-73-99
Memo: Lynn's phone: 212-767-6237.

Highlights (For Children)
Sue Iams/Barbara Brenke
2300 W Fifth Ave Box 269
Columbus OH 43216-0269
614-486-0631; Fax: 614-486-0762
Subjects: 21-31E

HMI Associates Inc
Alex Solomon, Key Accts Mgr
1724 W 10th Pl #1
Tempe AZ 85281
602-921-3220; 800-921-7402;
   Fax: 602-921-3228
Subjects: 19-25-99

Hoke Communications Inc
Amy Lader
224 7th St
Garden City NY 11530
800-229-6700; Fax: 516-294-8141
Subjects: 19-19F (magazine subscribers)

Homeowners Marketing Services
Bernie Davis
12444 Victory Blvd #316
North Hollywood CA 91609
800-232-2134; Fax: 818-505-9729
Subjects: 19-43H(homeowners)

HR Direct Inc
David Hawthorne, Pres
508 N Second St
Fairfield IA 52556-2464
515-472-7188; Fax: 515-472-5729
Subjects: 19-25-36-56
Memo: Favors smaller publishers.

Hughes Communications Inc
Bruce Ericson
211 W State St
Rockford IL 61101
800-435-2937; Fax: 815-963-7773
Subjects: 19I-19M (business executives)

Human Resources Exec Magazine
PO Box 980
Dresher PA 19044
215-784-0910; Fax: 215-784-0317
Subjects: 19

Huntsinger & Jeffer List Service
Joy Kaulfers Beggs, Mgr
809 Brook Hill Cir
Richmond VA 23227
804-266-2499; Fax: 804-261-4864
Subjects: 19F-39-47-55P-63

HVB List Promotions Inc
Renee Radics, Gen Mgr
PO Box 1832
Middleburg VA 22117
703-592-3087; Fax: 703-592-3088
Subjects: 19F-55P-44(international lists)

I

IBIS International Direct
Laura Williams/Mark Pow, Accts
249 W 17th St 10th Fl
New York NY 10011-5300
800-433-6226; Fax: 212-779-1344
Subjects: 19-31E-44-99

IDG List Services
Deb Goldstein
PO Box 9151
Framingham MA 01701
508-370-0820; Fax: 508-370-0020
Subjects: 23

IGL Direct
Becky Colbert, Mgr
4901 N 57th St
Box 5059
Lincoln NE 68505
402-466-8400; Fax: 402-466-9074
Subjects: 15-19-19L-31E-39

IMPCO Direct Response
Nancy Budinger, List Broker
100 Rockwood St
Rochester NY 14610
716-473-1432
Subjects: 19-25-99

InfoBase (Data Enhancement Serv)
Denise Rose
301 Industrial Blvd
Conway AR 72032
800-768-3282
Subjects: 99

Infocore Inc
Mark Irace, Acct Exec
285 N El Camino Real #214
Encinitas CA 92024
619-634-5064; Fax: 619-634-2669
Subjects: 19-25-44

Infocus Lists
Beverly Young, List Mgr
341 Victory Dr
Herndon VA 22070
703-834-0100; Fax: 703-834-0110
Subjects: 19-19F-25-55P

Infolists Inc
Katy Swain, Gen Mgr
1730 Stickney Point Rd #200
Sarasota FL 34231-8845
813-923-1449; Fax: 813-923-2374
Subjects: 19(seminars)-31E

InfoMat Inc
Brandy Carpenter, List Mgr
1815 West 213th St #210
Torrance CA 90501
310-212-5944; Fax: 310-212-5773
Subjects: 19-19F-25-39-55P

Informat Inc
Brandy Carpenter/Brenda Stanley
1815 W 213th St #210
Torrance CA 90501
310-212-5944; Fax: 310-212-5773
Subjects: 71 (New Guinea Tours list)

Information Marketing Services
8130 Boone Blvd #310
Vienna VA 22182
703-821-8130; Fax: 703-821-8243
Subjects: 19-31E-39-44-55

Initio List Marketing Inc
Mary Sachariah, Dir/Sales/Mktg
725 Dell Rd
Carlstadt NJ 07072
201-935-2450; Fax: 201-935-8978
Subjects: 25-40F

Innovative Management Serv Inc
441 Lexington Ave
New York NY
212-983-0100; Fax: 212-983-0107
Subjects: 19M

Institute Lists
Debra Goldfarb, Dir/List Service
29 W 35th St 5th Fl
New York NY 10001-2299
212-244-0360; Fax: 212-564-0465
Subjects: 19-99

Institute of Real Estate Mgmt
Pat Hoffman
430 N Michigan
Chicago IL 60610
312-661-1953; Fax: 312-661-0217
Subjects: 19H-56P

Integrated Business Services
Int Business List
PO Box 606
Hudson OH 44236
216-656-1100; Fax: 216-656-1106
Subjects: 39M (doctors, hospitals, companies)

International Business Lists Ltd
Gary Walter, Owner
162 N Franklin St #300
Chicago IL 60606-1895
312-236-0350; 800-535-0350;
   Fax: 312-236-4092
Subjects: 19-43(residential)(US & Canada)

International Direct Response
Cathy Stiebritz, Acct Mgr
60 Chestnut Ave #100
Devon PA 19333
215-688-6868; Fax: 215-688-7260
Subjects: 19-25-31E-55

Investment Information Services
Diane Rebetti
1050 W Pipeline Rd #200
Hurst TX 76053
800-645-2131; Fax: 817-595-2746
Subjects: 19I-19F-19H

IRA (I Rent America)
Michael Hall, Pres
701 N Plano Rd
Richardson TX 75081
800-548-9959; Fax: 214-705-2797
Subjects: 25-35A (Mail-order buyers, consumer lists)

ITTP Direct
Susan Frederick, Dir
Div/Intl Thomson Transport Press
424 W 33rd St
New York NY 10001
212-714-3198; Fax: 212-695-5025
Subjects: 19(executives)(industrial, commercial traffic)

J

J F Glaser Inc
Bill Parbs, List Mgr
999 Main St #103
Glen Ellyn IL 60137
708-469-2075; Fax: 708-790-5244
Subjects: 19-23-25-99

J R Direct Marketing Inc
Sheryl Storey, List Mgmt
4703 51st St #1
Delta BC V4K 2W1
604-940-0277; Fax: 604-946-1419
Subjects: 19-25-99

James B Kinkead & Assoc
Lorna Kinkead, VP
PO Box 906
Scottsdale AZ 85252
602-947-5478; Fax: 602-970-1525
Subjects: 19-25-99

James Chan
2014 Naudain St
Philadelphia PA 19146
215-735-7670; Fax: 215-735-9661
Subjects: 23-24-39-44(Chinese)-67 (institutional buyers)

JAMI Marketing Services Inc
Fran Golub, List Mgr
1 Blue Hill Plz
Pearl River NY 10965
914-620-0700; Fax: 914-620-1885
Subjects: 19-25-99

JAMI/Hotline List Division
Ronni Potenza, List Mgr
535 Fifth Ave
New York NY 10017
212-490-1590; Fax: 212-286-0960
Subjects: 28-27(diet)

JBW Direct
Sherry Kuroda, List Mgr
1 Madison Ave
PO Box 449
Grand Junction TN 38039
901-764-2651
Subjects: 19-25-69

JDA (Johnson Direct Advertising)
212 High St
Palo Alto CA 94301
415-321-3777; Fax: 415-321-1862
Subjects: 99

JF Direct Marketing Inc
73 Croton Ave #106
Ossining NY 10562
914-762-8633; Fax: 914-762-9247
Subjects: 61(people/new movers)

JHL Mail Marketing Inc
Joseph Leek, Pres
3100 Bortham Ave
Stevens Point WI 54481
715-341-0581; Fax: 715-341-9645
Subjects: 15-19-25

Johnson & Associates
802 W 16th Box 648
Mt Pleasant TX 75455
214-572-1231
Subjects: 48-69

Johnson Direct Advertising
Dax Parreno, List Mgr
400 Seaport Ct #100
Redwood City CA 94063
415-306-1537; Fax: 415-306-1546
Subjects: 19-25

Johnson Hill Press Inc
Maria LaRosa Turner
1233 Janesville Ave
Ft Atkinson WI 53538
414-563-6388; Fax: 414-563-1701
Subjects: 24-19X-51A

Joncas Postexperts Inc
Susan Higgins/Lucie Lacelle
7875 Transcanadienne
Ville St Laurent PQ Canada H4S 1L3
514-333-7480; Fax: 514-332-6915
Subjects: 99(Quebec & Canadian lists)

Jordan Direct
Tom & Dori Jordan, Owners
959 W Partridge Dr
Palatine IL 60067
708-776-9394; Fax: 708-776-9396
Subjects: 25(mostly female)-29C

Junction List Services
269 Middlesex Rd
Buffalo NY 14216
716-876-2375; Fax: 716-876-2324
Subjects: 99

Junction List Services Inc
Tami Toal, Bus Div Mgr
820 N Orleans #410
Chicago IL 60610
312-944-5094; Fax: 312-944-6819
Subjects: 99

K

K M Lists Inc
E Jen McBride, Pres
628 S Rt 73 Box 609
Berlin NJ 08009
800-635-5833; Fax: 609-768-8375
Subjects: 19-25-39

K-III Press Inc
Susan Frederick/John Choi
424 W 33rd ST
New York NY 10001
212-714-3198; Fax: 212-268-0266
Subjects: 16-19-56P

The Kaplan Agency
Siobhan Caragine
1200 High Ridge Rd
Stamford CT 06905
203-968-8800; Fax: 203-968-8871
Subjects: 28

The Kaplan Agency
Dick Calvin
1200 High Ridge Rd
Stamford CT 06905
203-968-8800; Fax: 203-968-8871
Subjects: 99

The Kaplan Agency
Siobhan Caragine
1200 High Ridge Rd
Stamford CT 06905
203-968-8800; Fax: 203-968-8871
Subjects: 43G (Wayside Gardens List)

The Kaplan Agency
Robin Black, Dir/New Bus Dev
1200 High Ridge Rd
Stamford CT 06905
203-968-8800; Fax: 203-968-8871
Subjects: 99 (direct response, mail-order buyers)

Karl Business Lists
Alfred Carlson
One American Ln
Greenwich CT 06831
203-552-0501; 800-394-0294; Fax: 203-552-6799
Subjects: 19-19X-24-67S

Kelk & Assoc
Gerry Kelk, Pres
36 Ferndale Rd
Deer Park IL 60010-3666
708-381-0009; Fax: 708-381-3221
Subjects: 19-25-99

Ken Ecrit Lists
PO Box 231
Decatur IL 62525
217-422-5020
Subjects: 19O

Kennedy Publications
Bonnie Partridge
Templeton Rd
Fitzwilliam NH 03447
800-531-0007; Fax: 603-585-9555
Subjects: 19C-19G-73

Key Contacts & Communications
William/Monica Spence
911 First St
Rockville MD 20850
301-340-9197
Subjects: 19-19I-25 (mail-order buyers)

KJ Direct
3405 N Kennicott Ave
Arlington Heights IL 60004-1431
708-342-5050; Fax: 708-342-5059
Subjects: 61 (registered voter list)

The Kleid Company Inc
Michael Manzari, Pres/CEO
530 Fifth Ave 17th Fl
New York NY 10036-5198
212-819-3400; Fax: 212-719-9727
Subjects: 99 (catalog available)

L

L.I.S.T. Inc
Glenn Freedman, Pres
320 Northern Blvd
Great Neck NY 11021
516-482-2345; Fax: 516-487-7721
Subjects: 19-19M-23T (publications, seminars)

Ladd Associates Inc
Jack Ladd, Pres
2527 Fillmore St
San Francisco CA 94115
415-921-1001; Fax: 415-921-2311
Subjects: 19-19F-19I-56P

The Lake Group
Joyce P Lake
CompuName Inc
411 Theodore Fremd Ave
Rye NY 10580
914-925-2401; Fax: 914-925-2499
Subjects: 99

The Lake Group
Henry M DiSciullo
Names In The News Inc
411 Theodore Fremd Ave
Rye NY 10580
914-925-2400; Fax: 914-925-2499
Subjects: 99

Lake Publishing Corp
Nancy Toberman, List Rental Mgr
17730 W Peterson Rd Box 159
Libertyville IL 60048
708-362-8711; Fax: 708-362-3484
Subjects: 23-24

Lakewood Lists
Paul Kolars, List Mgr
50 S Ninth St
Minneapolis MN 55402
612-340-4824; Fax: 612-333-6526
Subjects: 11-19-69-71 (subscribers to trade magazines)

Lambda Rising
L Page Maccubbin
1625 Connecticut Ave NW
Washington DC 20009
202-462-6969; Fax: 202-462-7257
Subjects: 37 (book buyers/mail-order buyers)

Larimer Creative Marketing Inc
6500 Greenville Ave #520
Dallas TX 75206
214-987-9194; 800-487-1384; Fax: 214-987-2237
Subjects: 99

Lawyer's Register Publishing Co
Roger Perlmuter/Meg Schultz
30700 Bainbridge Rd #H
Solon OH 44139
216-248-0135; Fax: 216-349-5879
Subjects: 19L (legal lists)

The Lead Sheet
Brian O'Connell, VP
136 W Canal St
Winooski VT 05404
800-545-3237; Fax: 800-972-5919
Subjects: 19-44 (US & Canada/Responsive new bus formulations)

Lee & Associates
Cherie Niemeyer
8506 E 61st St #118
Tulsa OK 74133
918-252-7790
Subjects: 69 (soccer players/coaches)

The Leland Company
Sue McDorman
1801 W Leland Ave
Chicago IL 60640-4595
312-561-4005; Fax: 312-561-3801
Subjects: 19

Len Mor Publications
Nora Champion, Circ Dir
PO Box 75035
Washington DC 20013
202-488-8879
Subjects: 39-49-55

Leon Henry Inc
Gail Henry, Gen Mgr
455 Central Ave
Scarsdale NY 10583
914-723-3176; Fax: 914-723-0205
Subjects: 19-25-99

Leonard & Assoc
Sarri Dorfman, List Mgr
603 Horsham Rd #4 Box 220
Horsham PA 19044
215-675-9133; Fax: 215-675-9376
Subjects: 19F (non-profit)-39

LH Management
Debra Goldstein, Mgr
Div of Leon Henry Inc
455 Central Ave
Scarsdale NY 10583
914-723-3176; Fax: 914-723-0205
Subjects: 19-25-99
Service: Also package insert programs

Lifecycle Learning
Michael Larson, Database Mgr
44 Oak St
Newton Upper Falls MA 02164
617-964-5057; Fax: 617-965-5054
Subjects: 39-57

Lifestyle America
45 Legion Dr
Cresskill NJ 07626
201-894-8300; Fax: 201-894-8996
Subjects: 25 (mail-order buyers)

Lifestyle Change Communications
1700 Water Pl #150
Atlanta GA 30339
404-984-1100; Fax: 404-984-8111
Subjects: 99 (National Household Index file)

Lifestyle Selector
April Liske, Acct Mgr
1621 18th St #300
Denver CO 80202
303-292-5000; 800-525-3533;
   Fax: 303-294-9628
Subjects: 25-99
Memo: 18 million name consumer list database.

Lighthouse List Co
6499 NW 9th Ave #206
Ft Lauderdale FL 33309
305-489-3008; Fax: 305-489-3040
Subjects: 69-99

Lillian Vernon Corp
Joy Contreras, List Mgr
543 Main St
New Rochelle NY 10801
914-576-6400; Fax: 914-637-5740
Subjects: 25 (catalog buyers list)
Memo: Over 3 million names.

List America Inc
Katrina Reyes/Tom Mays, Acct Mgr
1202 Potomac St NW
Washington DC 20007
202-298-9206; Fax: 202-338-9048
Subjects: 19-19F-25-55P-63-99
   (charitable/donor lists)

The List Authority
Fred Kallet, VP
192 3rd Ave
Westwood NJ 07675
201-666-0100; Fax: 201-358-2395
Subjects: 25 (mail-order, subcribers, inquirers)

List Bank
Steve Krug, List Rep
500 Davis Ctr #1010
Evanston IL 60201
708-864-0550; Fax: 708-864-0765
Subjects: 25

The List Connection Inc
Elaine Cantor, Pres
540 W Boston Post Rd
Mamaroneck NY 10543
914-381-2010; Fax: 914-381-2163
Subjects: 19-25-73-99

List Counsellors Inc
Liz Barnes, List Mgr
3 S Main St
PO Box 546
Allentown NJ 08501
609-259-0600; Fax: 609-259-7753
Subjects: 99

List Dimensions
2245 Midland Ave
Toronto ON M1P 4P9
416-297-4058; Fax: 416-297-7984
Subjects: 99

The List Emporium Inc
Rich Retzer, List Mgr
2000 Shawnee Mission Pkwy #235
Westwood KS 66205
913-236-6830; Fax: 913-236-4842
Subjects: 19-31E-57S

List Locators & Managers Inc
Nancy Brown, List Mgr
10020 King St #400
Overland Park KS 66210
913-338-5055; Fax: 913-338-1078
Subjects: 19-29-43G-69R-71

List Logic
Thomas Zambraski, Broker
33 S Parliman Rd
LaGrangeville NY 12540
914-223-5178; Fax: 914-223-3975
Subjects: 19-19L-39-51E

List Marketing Limited
Bob Albert, Pres
1037 E Putnam Ave
Riverside CT 06878
203-637-6700; Fax: 203-637-4755
Subjects: 19-19F-25 (mag subscribers, seminars)

List Masters Inc
Jack Newman, List Mgr
4124 Fields Dr
Lafayette Hill PA 19444
215-233-2890; Fax: 215-836-5859
Subjects: 19-25

List Pro of America
Diane O'Brien, Pres
3089-C Clairmont Dr #267
San Diego CA 92117
619-483-1410; Fax: 619-270-6669
Subjects: 19-25-53

List Services Corp
6 Trowbridge Dr
PO Box 516
Bethel CT 06801-0516
203-791-4418; Fax: 203-778-4299
Subjects: 99

The List Source Inc
Allan Bilofsky, Pres
1415 Rte 70 E #100
Cherry Hill NJ 08034
609-795-3344
Subjects: 19-25-99

List Strategies Inc
Joel Cooper, Pres
1290 Ave of the Americas
New York NY 10104
212-767-1000; Fax: 212-541-4408
Subjects: 19-23T-25-31E

List Technology Systems Group
Barbara Jiminez, List Mktg
1001 Ave of the Americas
New York NY 10018
212-719-3850; Fax: 212-719-1878
Internet: listtech@haven.ios.com
Subjects: 19-23

Listco Mailing Lists
Fay Epstein, Service Mgr
620 Frelinghuysen Ave
Newark NJ 07114
201-802-1229; Fax: 201-802-1702
Subjects: 11P-19O-19F-39-53-63(Jewish)

Listline
Liz Lang, Acct Mgr
187 Ballardvale St #B110
Wilmington MA 01887
508-657-6161; Fax: 508-657-5700
Subjects: 19-19L-23T-25-31E-39

Listmart Inc
Ellen Helmich
1900 Erie #203-3
North Kansas City MO 64116
816-471-7333; 800-471-5478;
   Fax: 816-471-7747
Subjects: 99
Memo: Call, and they will give you at least three new list ideas for your next mailing or telemarketing campaign.

Listmaster
Ted Shuel, Pres
700 Fifth Ave
San Rafael CA 94901
415-485-5478; Fax: 415-485-0939
Subjects: 19-25-43(residential)-61(CA) (upscale lists)

The Listworks Corp
Robin LaScola, List Mgr
1 Campus Dr
Pleasantville NY 10570
914-769-7100; Fax: 914-769-8070
Subjects: 19-19F-25

LLM-List Locators & Managers Inc
Nancy Brown, List Mgr
11020 King St #400
Overland Park KS 66210
913-338-5055; Fax: 913-338-1078
Subjects: 19-28-29-43D-43G-69R-71

LR Direct Ltd
Richard Cueba, List Broker
972 Post Rd
Darien CT 06820
203-656-1879; Fax: 203-656-1916
Subjects: 19-25-99

LTN Partners
Theresa Navarro
134 98th Ave
Oakland CA 94603
510-568-6047; Fax: 510-568-6040
Subjects: 19-19F-25-31E

M

M & T International Marketing
411 Borel Ave #100
San Mateo CA 94402
415-358-9500; Fax: 415-358-0743
Subjects: 23-44E
Service: Windows users in France

M/D/A List Management Inc
John Papalia, VP/List Mgr
Div of Trinet Direct Group
Hardscrabble Rd
Croton Falls NY 10519
914-277-5558
Subjects: 19-25-99

The MacFarland Co
Harriet Walker
PO Box 116
Whitehouse Station NJ 08889-0116
908-236-0533; Fax: 908-236-0633
Subjects: 99

Maclean-Hunter DM Services
Veronica White, Mgr
777 Bay St
Toronto ON Canada M5W 1A7
416-596-5040; Fax: 416-593-3310
Subjects: 19-19X

Macro Mark Inc
65 W 96th St
New York NY 10025
212-662-1170; Fax: 212-662-1195
Subjects: 99

Magazine Marketing Inc
Scott MacAdam, Dir/Acct Mgt
191 Clarksville Rd
Lawrenceville NJ 08002
609-452-1633; Fax: 609-520-1663
Subjects: 19-23-25

Mail Marketing Guild
Hal Roberson, Pres
171 Terrace St
Haworth NJ 07641-1899
201-387-1010; Fax: 201-387-2976
Subjects: 19-25-56P

Mail Marketing Resources
Vicki White, Dir
Div of Chain Store Guide
425 Park Ave
New York NY 10022
212-371-9400; Fax: 212-826-6390
Subjects: 19-19R (executives)

Mailing Lists Asia
Carolyn Boulter, List Res Mgr
6/F #C-E Ho Lee Commerical Bldg
PO Box 38 D'Aquilar St
Central Hong Kong
852-526-1208; Fax: 852-524-9177
Subjects: 44(international lists)-99

Mailing Lists Plus Inc
Carol Kollmann, Pres
1239 120th Ave NE #H
Bellevue WA 98005
206-451-3335; Fax: 206-646-4485
Subjects: 19-19H-25-35A

Mailings Clearing House
Lois Campbell/Barbara Clemmons
Div of Roxbury Press
601 E Marshall St
Sweet Springs MO 65351-0295
800-776-6373; Fax: 816-335-4157
Subjects: 19-31-39-55-63 (schools and teachers; low cost)

Main Street Agency
Guy Reffett
934 N Main St
Rockford IL 61103
815-964-5813; Fax: 815-964-9403
Subjects: 11-35A-63 (subscriber lists)

Mal Dunn Associates Inc
Russell Dunn, VP
Hardscrabble Rd
Croton Falls NY 10519
914-277-5558; Fax: 914-277-5636
Subjects: 19-25-99

Mardev USA
Mark Bridges, Sales Dir
245 West 17th St
New York NY 10011
212-924-4490; Fax: 212-924-1440
Subjects: 19-25-44

Market Data Retrieval
Attn: List Manager
475 Sansome St #17005
San Francisco CA 94111
415-732-5100; Fax:
Subjects: 19-21-23-31-63-76-89 (schools, librariries, college, day care)

Market Data Retrieval
Attn: List Manager
55 W Monroe St #2640
Chicago IL 60603
312-263-4169; Fax: 312-345-4360
Subjects: 19-21-23-31-63-76-89 (schools, librariries, college, day care)

Market Data Retrieval Inc
Jim Holt, VP/Sales
16 Progress Dr
Shelton CT 06484
800-333-8802; Fax: 203-929-5253
Subjects: 19-21-23-31E-44(schools, librariries, college, day care)

Market Identification Inc
Francis King, Pres
20 N Wacker Dr #1734
Chicago IL 60606
312-782-5583; Fax: 312-782-3886
Subjects: 51A

Market Motivators Inc
Lawrence Pentler, Pres
5201 W Donges Bay Rd N104
Mequon WI 53092
414-242-9800
Subjects: 99
Service: List/database management

Marketing Communications Inc
Chris Campbell, Sales Dir
10605 W 84th Terr
Lenexa KS 66214
913-492-1575
Subjects: 19-25-99

Marketing Direct Associates
1291A S Powerline Rd #326
Pompano Beach FL 33069
305-784-9050; Fax: 305-784-0112
Subjects: 69-99

Marketing General Inc
Terri Bolen, List Mgr
105 Oronoco St
Alexandria VA 22314-2015
800-899-4420; Fax: 703-549-0697
Subjects: 31E
Memo: American Association of School Administrators-Superintendents file.

Marketing III Direct Response
Anne Marie Carroll, Sales Rep
Maple Hill Dr #44
Mahopac NY 10541
914-628-8772; Fax: 914-628-8766
Subjects: 19S-19F-39

The Marketing Information Bureau
135 Brian Dr
North York ON M2J 3Y8
516-333-9480; Fax: 516-333-9483
Subjects: 17P(homeowner lists)

Marketing Services International
Sarrell Veracka, VP/List Mgmt
625 N Michigan Ave #1920
Chicago IL 60611
312-642-1620; Fax: 312-642-0679
Subjects: 19(financial)-25-(consulting)

Marketry Inc
Greg Swent/Linda Linderman
2020 116th Ave NE #100
Bellevue WA 98004-3017
206-451-1262; 800-346-2013;
    Fax: 206-451-1941
Subjects: 19-25(mail-order lists)

Mary Elizabeth Granger Assoc Inc
Bonnie Granger, Pres
110 West Rd #355
Baltimore MD 21204
410-296-5151; Fax: 410-296-3115
Subjects: 19F-25-99

Master Lists
Phelon, Sheldon & Marsar Inc
15 Industrial Ave
Fairview NJ 07022
201-941-8804; 800-234-8804
Subjects: 19(many business lists)

Master Response List Division
David Tweedy, Acct exec
1600 Airport Freeway #506
Bedford TX 76022
817-545-9494; Fax: 817-283-9395
Subjects: 19-25-99

Matt Brown & Associates
Matt Brown, Pres
2769 Orchard Run Rd
Dayton OH 45449
513-434-3949; Fax: 513-434-6272
Subjects: 19-25

McGraw-Hill List Management Ctr
Howard Flood, Gen Mgr
Subs of McGraw-Hill Inc
Princeton Rd
Hightstown NJ 08520
609-426-5695; Fax: 609-426-5096
Subjects: 99 (book buyers lists)

McIntyre & Dodd Marketing Inc
Suzanne Mhanna
3049B rue Deacon
Dollard desOrmeaux PQ Canada H9B 2M5
Subjects: 19-25-99

The McNichols Group Inc
Dorothy McNichols, VP
51 Sherwood Terr #L
Lake Bluff IL 60044-2232
708-295-0300; Fax: 708-295-0334
Subjects: 19-25-99

MEC List Management
Gail Emery
PO Box 3727
Santa Monica CA 90408
213-450-0500; Fax: 213-450-0132
Subjects: 19-23-24-25-39-51E

MEDEC List Marketing
Medical Economics Co
5 Paragon Dr
Montbelle NJ 07645
201-358-7200; Fax: 201-573-4956
Subjects: 39-99 (international mailing lists)

Media Horizons Inc
Alan Kraft, Pres
94 East Ave
Norwalk CT 06851
203-857-0770; Fax: 203-857-0296
Subjects: 19-25

Media Index Publishing Inc
James Baker
PO Box 24365
Seattle WA 98124-0365
206-382-9220; Fax: 206-382-9437
Subjects: 19-25-56M(film/video)

Media Management Group
Lee Kroll, Pres
666 Plainsboro Rd #540
Plainsboro NJ 08536
609-275-0050; Fax: 609-275-6606
Subjects: 99
Memo: Kroll Direct Marketing Inc is an affiliate.

Media Marketplace Inc
Tom Kellogg
140 Terry Dr
PO Box 500
Newtown PA 18940
215-968-5020; Fax: 215-968-9410
Subjects: 21-27-56(writing)-76-99

Media Mart
Lisa Walter Donnelly
1101 King St #902
Alexandria VA 22314
703-548-2400; Fax: 703-548-9387
Subjects: 19-99
Memo: Division of KCI Inc.

Media Masters Inc
275 Madison Ave 25th Fl
New York NY 10016
212-681-1885; Fax: 212-681-9716
Subjects: 99
Service: Lists and package inserts

Media Weavers Lists
Dennis Stovall
Blue Heron Publishing
24450 NW Hansen Rd
Hillsboro OR 97124
503-621-3911; Fax: 503-621-9826
Subjects: 56P-56W-61(NW US)-99 (libraries, stores, media, writers)

Medical Marketing Services Inc
Greg Hill, VP/Sales
185 Hansen Ct #110
Wood Dale IL 60191
800-MED-LIST; Fax: 708-350-1896
Subjects: 39M(doctors, dentists, pharmacists, long-term, managed care)

Mega Lists
Jules Leib, Dir
521 E 86th Ave #V
Merrillville IN 46410
219-756-6071; Fax: 219-756-6072
Subjects: 19-19O-31E-57S (credit cards, home study, cassettes)

Mega Media Assoc Inc
Aileen Geslin, Sales Mgr
PO Box 4259
Newport Beach CA 92661
714-673-2290
Subjects: 19O-56P (mail-order buyers)

Meredith List Marketing
Ron Davis, VP
1716 Locust St
Des Moines IA 50309-3023
515-284-2891; Fax: 515-284-3878
Subjects: 27-29-35-39-43-51A-69

Metro Direct Marketing
Tom Soukup
333 Seventh Ave
New York NY 10001
212-594-7688; Fax: 212-465-8877
Subjects: 11-19-19F

Metromail Corp
James McQuaid, Pres
R R Donnelley & Sons Co
360 E 22nd St
Lombard IL 60148
800-541-0524; Fax: 800-426-8901
Subjects: 99(homeowners, new parents, students)(over 80 million names)

Metromail/Donor List Mangement Group
Phil Wagner, List Mgr
R R Donnelley & Sons Co
529 Fifth Ave
New York NY 10017
212-856-5301; Fax: 212-370-0827
Subjects: 19F-99 (non-profit donor lists)

MGI Lists
Ray Kosby/Amy Lewis
105 Oronoco St
Alexandria VA 22314
703-739-1000; Fax: 703-549-0697
Subjects: 21-31E-39 (non-profit organizations, associations)

MGM Mailing Lists & Consulting
Mark Linse
39 S Precinct Rd
Centerville MA 02632
508-420-4043; Fax: 508-420-0726
Subjects: 43H

MGT Associates Inc
Marjorie Webb, Pres
11111 Santa Monica Blvd
Los Angeles CA 90025
310-473-7550; Fax: 310-473-1616
Subjects: 25-99 (direct response consumer lists)

Midwest Direct Marketing Inc
PO Box 6313
Kansas City KS 66106
913-596-1300; Fax: 913-596-1325
Subjects: 16A(truck owners)

Midwest Lists & Media
Harriet Coffelt, List Mgr
9301 N Milwaukee Ave
Niles IL 60648
708-966-2485; Fax: 708-966-8207
Subjects: 19insurance)-28-57S
Service: Consulting

Mike Wilson List Counsel
Wilson Marketing Group
11924 W Washington Blvd
Los Angeles CA 90066-5502
310-398-2754; Fax: 310-397-4980
Subjects: 21-31-35-76-99

The Millard Group Inc
Linda McAleer
10 Vose Farm Rd
PO Box 890
Peterborough NH 03458-0890
603-924-9262; Fax: 603-924-7810
Subjects: 99

Milwaukee Direct Marketing
Ron Davis
240 Regency St
Waukesha WI 53186
414-789-2240; Fax: 414-789-2250
Subjects: 19-25-31(school)
Service: Special interest list

MJH Group Inc
Debbie Kolnberger, List Mgr
1983 Marcus Ave #120
Lake Success NY 11042
516-358-7885; Fax: 516-328-9584
Subjects: 19-21-25-40B

MLR Publishing Co
Janet Carroll, List Mgr
229 S 18th St
Philadelphia PA 19103
215-790-7000; Fax: 215-790-7005
Subjects: 39

MMS Inc(Medical Marketing Lists)
Sandy Ksycki, List Supv
700 N Wood Dale Rd #W
Wood Dale IL 60191
708-350-1199; 800-633-5478;
   Fax: 708-350-1896
Subjects: 19-39 (mail-order buyers)

Mokrynski & Associates Inc
Marlies Fuchs
401 Hackensack Ave
Hackensack NJ 07601
201-488-5656; Fax: 201-488-3174
Subjects: 99
Memo: Over 100 upscale catalog lists.

Monarch Accounting Supplies
William Grierson, Pres
PO Box 4066
Bridgeport CT 06607
800-828-6718; Fax: 203-381-0310
Subjects: 19A (accounting firms)

Morris Direct Marketing Inc
Ken Morris, Pres
300 W 55th St #19D
New York NY 10019
212-757-7711; Fax: 212-757-2126
Subjects: 19(executives)-23

Mountainside Publishing Co Inc
Ann Dougherty
PO Box 8330
Ann Arbor MI 48107
313-662-3925; Fax: 313-662-4450
Subjects: 56P

MPG List Co
Sandy Brill-Bassett, List Coord
115 S Union St #308
Alexandria VA 22314
703-683-7755; Fax: 703-683-5592
Subjects: 19F-56P

MSC Lists Inc
Maureen Lance, Pres
450 Los Verdes Dr
Santa Barbara CA 93111
805-967-5394; Fax: 805-964-1702
Subjects: 99 (special interest magazine lists)

The MTA Group
John Utz, Dir/Bus Dev
12 Telva Rd
Wilton CT 06897-3732
203-762-2566; Fax: 203-762-7466
Subjects: 19-25

Muldoon List Center
Fabiola Molina, Acct Exec
300 Park Ave S 7th Fl
New York NY 10010
212-979-8193; Fax: 212-477-2470
Subjects: 19-19F-25-56P (mail-order, publishers lists-US & CN)

Murdoch Magazines Travel Lists
Robin Rosenfeld, Sales Mgr
Div of News Group Publications
500 Plaza Dr
Secaucus NJ 07094
201-902-1862
Subjects: 71

N

N M Direct
Tina Carter
5800 E Campus Circle Dr #101
Irving TX 75063
214-714-3205; Fax: 214-714-3192
Subjects: 99

NAM - New Age Mailing Lists
Debbie Sanchez
PO Box 970
Santa Cruz NM 87567
505-753-5086; Fax: 505-753-9249
Subjects: 13-27-39-53
Service: Bookstores/publishers

The Name Exchange
226 4th St NE
Washington DC 20002
202-543-7084; Fax: 202-543-6729
Subjects: 99

Name Finders Lists Inc
Darlene Johnson, List Mgmt Serv
160 Sansome St #400
San Francisco CA 94104
415-955-8585; 800-221-5009;
   Fax: 415-955-8580
Subjects: 19-25-99

Namebank International Inc
Brace Ford/Larry Reinhart, Mgrs
14 W Mt Vernon Pl
Baltimore MD 21201
410-783-8460; Fax: 410-783-8484
Subjects: 19(finance)-25-39-44-71

Names and Addresses Inc
Lisa Osbourne
List Management Div
160 E Marquardt Dr
Wheeling IL 60090-6428
708-465-1500; Fax: 708-465-1521
Subjects: 19(execs)-19M-25-28

Names in the Mail Inc
Judy Ashley
10710 Shiloh Rd
Dallas TX 75228
800-688-5701; Fax: 214-686-4679
Subjects: 19-25-99

Names in the News California
One Bush St #300
San Francisco CA 94104
415-989-3350; Fax: 415-433-7796
Subjects: 13-15-39-51-55-65-73-99
   (progressive non-profit assns)

Names in the News Inc
Richard Holpp, Gen Mgr
411 Theodore Fremd Ave
Rye NY 10580
914-925-2400; Fax: 914-925-2498
Subjects: 19-19F-23T-25-56P

National Assn of Home Builders
Leann Cardillo, List Mgr
1201 15th St NW
Washington DC 20005-2800
202-861-2125; Fax: 202-822-0559
Subjects: 43(home builders membership lists)

National Fundraising Lists Inc
Patti Loescher
1682 Village Green
Crofton MD 21114
301-721-5700; Fax: 301-858-0107
Subjects: 19F-19M

National League for Nursing
Wendy Lund
350 Hudson St
New York NY 10014
212-989-9393; Fax: 212-989-3710
Subjects: 31E-39 (Book buyers)

National List Council Inc
Leslie Hensley
7033 Stapoint Ct #A
Winter Park FL 32792
407-677-5478; Fax: 407-678-6094
Subjects: 19-19H-23-25

National List Exchange Inc
Karen Sinisi/Bryan Borower, Mgrs
26750 US Hwy 19N #400
Clearwater FL 34621
813-799-0008; Fax: 813-791-9682
Subjects: 19-19F

National Response List Mktg Inc
Kelly Ransbottom, List Mgr
805 King St #400
Alexandria VA 22314
703-519-0717; Fax: 703-519-8526
Subjects: 19F(political & Catholic)

National Technical Info Service
Lorraine Schrock, List Mgr
5285 Port Royal Rd
Springfield VA 22161
703-487-4812; Fax: 703-321-8547
Subjects: 19H-55G

National Women's Mailing List
Jill Lippitt
PO Box 68
Jenner CA 95450
707-632-5763; Fax: 707-632-5589
Subjects: 73 (individuals/organizations)

Nations Care Direct Marketing
Greg Fox, Pres
6931 Arlington Rd
Bethesda MD 20814
301-215-7400; Fax: 301-215-7314
Subjects: 19-25

Natl Advertising/Mktg Enterprise
J A Gatlin, Pres
7323 N Figueroa St
Los Angeles CA 90041
213-748-2241; Fax: 213-255-1098
Subjects: 19-25-99

NCRI List Management
Div of Select Marketing Inc
45 Legion Dr
Cresskill NJ 07626-2100
201-894-8300; Fax: 201-894-8996
Subjects: 25 (mail-order buyers lists)

NDL/The Lifestyle Selector
Tony White, Sr VP
1621 18th St
Denver CO 80202
303-292-5000; 800-525-3533;
   Fax: 303-294-9628
Subjects: 25

Neiman Marcus List Management
Tina Carter, List Rental Mgr
13800 Diplomat Dr
Dallas TX 75234
214-888-9815; Fax: 214-888-9912
Subjects: 25 (mail-order buyers)

Network Communications Inc
Barry Dennis, Pres
PO Box 398
Timonium MD 21094
410-296-0113
Subjects: 19-25

New Age Mailing Lists
G K Khalsa, Service Mgr
PO Box 970
Santa Cruz CA 87567
505-753-5086; Fax: 505-753-9249
Subjects: 19-31E-39-53-54-57S-69 (book buyers, seminars)

New Alternatives for Publishing, Retailing and Advertising--NAPRA
Marilyn McGuire, Dir
PO Box 9
Eastsound WA 98245
206-376-2702; Fax: 206-376-2704
E-Mail: napra@aol.com or napra@pacificrim.net
Subjects: 39H-53-54-56P (New Age bookstores & publishers)

New Customer Acquisition
Bob Karl, Pres
Div of John Jay Corp
620 Franquette St
Medford OR 97501
503-779-9999
Subjects: 19-25

New Resi Data Marketing Inc
136 Kinderkamack Rd
Park Ridge NJ 07656
201-476-1800; Fax: 201-476-1847
Subjects: 99

Newport Marketing
1400 Quail St #180
Newport Beach CA 92660
714-752-2577; Fax: 714-752-5259
Subjects: 19-25

NM Direct
Shelita Sneed
5800 Campus Circle Dr #101
Irving TX 75063
214-714-3205; Fax: 214-714-3192
Subjects: 19R (upscale dept store)

North American Communications
Rick Field, Contact
1330 30th St
San Diego CA 92154
619-575-4700; Fax: 619-575-4998
Subjects: 19-25

North Shore Direct
708 Church St #231
Evanston IL 60201
708-328-0966
Subjects: 99

Novus Marketing Inc
Chuck Hengel
601 Lakeshore Pky
Minnetonka MN 55305
612-476-7719; Fax: 612-476-7725
Subjects: 99 (direct mail customer aquisition)

Novus Marketing Inc
List Management Div
245 Saw Mill River Rd
Hawthorne NY 10532
914-742-2200; Fax: 914-742-2201
Subjects: 23-39-43-69-99 (magazine list manager)

NRL Brokerage
Stephen D Bogner, Pres
100 Union Ave
Cresskill NJ 07626
201-568-0707; Fax: 201-568-9893
Subjects: 19-23E-25

NYNEX Telemarketing Services
Susan Worden, Sr Mgr
100 Church St 17th Fl
New York NY 10007
212-513-9542
Subjects: 19-25-99

Old Colony Advertising, Inc
120 North Meadows Rd
Medfield MA 02052
508-359-4649; Fax: 508-359-7215
Subjects: 73-99

Old Dominion List Co Inc
James Carroll, List Mgmt Dir
Div of H J Inc
809 Brook Hill Cir
Richmond VA 23227
804-266-4941
Subjects: 19F
Memo: Joy Kauffers Beggs, List Brokerage Dir.

Omega Direct
5582 Peachtree Rd #101
Atlanta GA 30341
404-936-9570; Fax: 404-936-0149
Subjects: 19(taxes/State Taxation Institute Newsletter subscriber file)

Omega List Co
Mike Hiban, List Mgr
Eberle Dir Marketing Group
1420 Spring Hill Rd #490
McLean VA 22102-3006
703-821-1890; Fax: 703-821-0920
Subjects: 19F-55P-63

On-Line Resources
Nicolas Matar, List Broker
20540 E Arrow Hwy #N2
Covina CA 91724
818-332-8879; Fax: 818-331-1290
Compuserve 70372,3302
Subjects: 23

Oregon List/Group
Allen Nelson, Gen Mgr
9055 SW 130th Ave
Beaverton OR 97008
503-524-6820; Fax: 503-524-5741
Subjects: 19F-55P-56P

Orion Direct Marketing
Mike Spenser, List Strategy Spec
360 Herndon Pkwy #900
Herndon VA 22070
703-471-7700; Fax: 703-471-6464
Subjects: 25(non-profit)-23T

Oryx Press Mailing Lists
Oryx Press
2214 N Central at Encanto
Phoenix AZ 85004
602-254-6156; Fax:
Subjects: 99(book buyers lists)

The Other List Company Inc
Ernie Tacinelli
PO Box 286
Matawan NJ 07747
908-591-1180; Fax: 908-591-8472
Subjects: 15-99

Oxbridge Communications Inc
Ken Njenga
150 Fifth Ave #302
New York NY 10011
212-741-0231; Fax: 212-633-2938
Subjects: 99 (publishing lists, periodicals)

Pacific Lists Inc
Paula Huntley
100 Tamal Plz #50
Corte Madera CA 94925
415-945-9450; Fax: 415-945-9451
Subjects: 99

Pacific Media Concepts
Lisa Truelove, List Mgr
2100 Main St #300
Huntington Beach CA 92648
714-536-7996
Subjects: 99

Paragon Direct Marketing
Eric Silverman, Pres
1482 Westgate Dr
Fort Lee NJ 07024
201-224-8029; Fax: 201-224-6914
Subjects: 19-25-99

ParaLists
Dan Poynter, Pres
Para Publishing
PO Box 8206
Santa Barbara CA 93118
805-968-7277; 800-727-2782;
    Fax: 805-968-1379
E-Mail: DanPoynter@ParaPublishing.com
Subjects: 69(parachuting)-70A-99 (variety of lists)

Parent's Mailing Lists
18235 Minnetonka Blvd #425
Deephaven MN 55391
800-255-3379
Subjects: 99(subscriber lists)

Parrish Associates Inc
Charles Parrish, Pres
721 Olive St #1200
St Louis MO 63101
314-241-5410; Fax: 314-241-6125
Subjects: 19-25-99

Parsons Technology Inc
1 Parsons Dr
Hiawatha IA 52233
319-395-9626; Fax: 319-395-7606
Subjects: 19-23

Pennwell Publishing Co
1421 S Sheridan Rd
Tulsa OK 74112
800-331-4463; Fax: 918-832-9348
Subjects: 99

Penton Publishing
Ilene Schwartz
Penton Lists
1100 Superior Ave
Cleveland OH 44114-2543
216-696-7000; Fax: 216-696-6662
Subjects: 12-19C-19G-19X-23T-24-27-55G-56M
Memo: Min order: 5,000 names.

Performance Marketing
Roger Henebry
3120 Cottonwood Dr (98029)
PO Box 32699
Laughlin NV 89028-2699
702-299-0111; Fax: 702-299-0224
E-Mail: mailings@accessnv.com.
Subjects: 39-19-23T-51A-43D-29-69(gifts) 21-63-51

Peter LI Education Group
Deborah Paxson/Rosemary Walker
330 Progress Rd
Dayton OH 45449
513-847-5900; Fax: 513-847-5910
Subjects: 23-31E-63(Catholic)

Phelon, Sheldon & Marsar Inc
15 Industrial Ave
Box 517
Fairview NJ 07022
201-941-8804; Fax: 201-941-5515
Subjects: 11P (cameras, film, books, and video tapes for photo enthusiasts & working photographers)

Phillips Business InformationInc
Susan Katz, Contact
1201 Seven Locks Rd
Potomac MD 20854
301-340-1520
Subjects: 19(hi-tech)

Phillips Publishing List Mktg
John Baldwin
7811 Montrose Rd
Potomac MD 20854
301-340-2100; Fax: 301-294-1307
Subjects: 99

Pinnacle List Co
2800 Shirlington Rd #401
Arlington VA 22206-3601
703-379-4394; Fax: 703-379-5312
Subjects: 19-25-99

Pioneer Pacific List Mktg Inc
Jan Ackert, List Mgr
3575 Cahuenga Blvd W #330
Los Angeles CA 90068-1358
213-878-2870; Fax: 213-878-2882
Subjects: 19-25-33

PMM Marketing Inc
999 18th St #2420
Denver CO 80202
800-221-0223; Fax: 303-295-1166
Subjects: 99

Polaris Communications
Keith Barnett, Pres
6001 Chapel Hill Rd #112
Raleigh NC 27607
919-851-3434; Fax: 919-851-3822
Subjects: 19-25-99

Political Resources Inc
Carol Hess, Pres
PO Box 3177
Burlington VT 05401
800-423-2677; Fax: 802-864-9502
Subjects: 55P

Polk Direct
Niches Consumer Lists
R L Polk & Co
2340 Des Plaines Ave #414
Des Plaines IL 60018-3225
847-297-4210; Fax: 847-297-1629
Subjects: 99

Postal Promotions
1100 Birchmount Rd
Scarborough ON Canada M1K 5H9
416-752-8100; Fax: 416-752-8239
Subjects: 61(Canadian)-99

Potomac List Co Inc
Danielle Bartoe
1015 18th St NW #702
Washington DC 20036
703-904-0909; Fax: 703-904-0101
Subjects: 69R(golf) (Alien Sport file)

Practical Management Inc
Kevin Amuzegar, List Mgr
23801 Calabasas Rd #2026 Box8789
Calabasas CA 91372-8789
818-348-9101; Fax: 818-348-0256
Subjects: 19(seminars)-31E

Praxis Publications Lists
Elizabeth Johanna, Contact
3111 E Washington Ave #4
Madison WI 53704
608-244-5633; Fax: 608-244-3255
Subjects: 49B

Preferred Lists
Rhonda Bell
5201 Leesburg Pike #1007
Falls Church VA 22041-3203
703-931-8000; Fax: 703-931-3800
Subjects: 99

Prestige Mailing Lists Inc
Debbie Hile, Pres/List Mgr
1539 Sawtelle Blvd #1
Los Angeles CA 90025
310-473-7116; Fax: 310-477-3217
Subjects: 25 (direct response/mail-order)

Print Mail of Maine
Ronald Nevers, Pres
75 Bishop
Portland ME 04101
207-878-8000; Fax: 207-878-7790
Subjects: 31E-35F (home-schooling families)

Professional Direct & Advanced
Business Compilation
2101 Corporate Blvd
Boca Raton FL 33431
800-777-LIST; Fax: 407-241-5878
Subjects: 25(exec/professionals lists)

Professional Mktg Communications
Sherry Hang, Mgr/Acct Services
PO Box 1315
Dayton OH 45401
513-252-1122; Fax: 513-847-7449
Subjects: 19

Profile America List Co
45 Legion Dr
Cresskill NJ 07626
201-569-7272; Fax: 201-569-5552
Subjects: 44(foreign members list)

Prospects Unlimited
Nancy Sprague
330 Front St W #1100
Toronto ON M5V 3B7
416-581-1273; Fax: 416-581-0258
Subjects: 21-27-29-35A-43-69-76
Memo: Canadian consumers, Sports Base, Do It Yourself Base, etc.

Publisher's Mail Service Inc
Marc Brenard, Contact
10545 W Donges Ct
Milwaukee WI 53224
414-354-1423; Fax: 414-354-9338
Subjects: 19-25-99

Publishers List Exchange Inc
Dick Mueller, Program Dir
951 Broken Sound Pkwy NW Bldg190
PO Box 3012
Boca Raton FL 33431-0912
Fax: 407-998-9830
Subjects: 99 (catalog buyers database)

Q

Qualified Lists Corp
Dick Mitchell, Pres
Div of Walter Karl Co
135 Bedford Rd
Armonk NY 10504
914-273-6606; Fax: 914-273-6537
Subjects: 19-19F-19M-43(residential)

Quality Education Data
Attn: List Manager
1700 Lincoln Street #3600
Denver CO 80203-4536
303-860-1832; Fax: 303-860-0238
E-mail: Lzawacki@qeddata.com
Subjects: 31-39-63-69-99
Memo: New Response Database of teachers, school districts, and other professionals who have purchased educational products.

QW Communications
PO Box 6591
Concord NH 03303-6591
603-648-2629
Subjects: 99
Service: Conference & seminar attendees

R L Polk & Co
Jerry Helmicki, Mgr
List Services
6400 Monroe Blvd Box 1521
Taylor MI 48180
313-292-3200; Fax: 313-292-6249
Subjects: 19-25-99

RAD Marketing & RadioBase
167 Crary-on-the-Park
Mt Vernon NY 10550
914-668-3563; Fax: 914-668-4247
Subjects: 99

RC Direct Inc
200 S Water St
Milwaukee WI 53204
414-271-3313; Fax: 414-271-4244
Subjects: 63J
Memo: Small lists as few as 2500.

Regional Readers Database
American List Council
88 Orchard Rd CN5219
Princeton NJ 08543
800-ALC-LIST; Fax: 908-874-4433
Subjects: 99
Memo: 690,000 magazine subscribers.

Religious Booksellers List
Christian Booksellers Assn
2620 Venetucci Blvd
Colorado Springs CO 80909
719-576-7880
Subjects: 63-99

Religious Lists
Marty Sass, Pres
86 Maple Ave
New City NY 10956
914-634-8724; Fax: 914-634-3609
Subjects: 19F-63

Research & Response Intl Inc
George Collins, Pres
250 W 57th St #1610
New York NY 10107
212-489-8610; Fax: 212-262-3474
Subjects: 19-25-99

Research Projects Corp
List Manager
95 Glen Ln
Southbury CT 06488-1885
203-263-0100; 800-243-4360; Fax: 203-263-0132
Subjects: 19-25-99

Resource & Development Group Inc
Ronald Benjamin, Pres
8416 Melrose Dr
Lenexa KS 66214
913-888-6222; Fax: 913-888-2493
Subjects: 19-19F-25

Response Innovations
Jennifer Charron, List Broker
50 S 9th St #200
Minneapolis MN 55402
612-332-1762; Fax: 612-332-1511
Subjects: 19-19L-31E

Response Mailing Lists
Sue Polan
Mktg Div of Response Group Inc
20200 NE 10th Pl
Miami FL 33179-2510
305-652-4610; Fax: 305-770-1470
Subjects: 19-19F-19H-19I-25-51A-63-69

Response Media Products
2323 Perimeter Park Dr #200
Atlanta GA 30341-1335
404-451-5478; Fax: 404-451-4929
Subjects: 99
Service: Newspaper inserts

Response Unlimited
The Old Plantation
RR 5 Box 251
Waynesboro VA 22980-9111
703-943-6721; Fax: 703-943-0841
Subjects: 63-99

Revolution Software Inc
20 Chester Woods Dr
Chester NJ 07930-2828
908-879-7038; Fax: 908-879-6297
Subjects: 23C (software buyers, publishers lists)

Rickard List Marketing
5512 Merrick Rd
Massapequa NY 11758
516-795-6466; Fax: 516-541-6435
Subjects: 19-25-99

Riffkin Direct Inc
Ed Fishman & Brad Halfond
64 Appletree Ln
Roslyn Heights NY 11577-2432
516-621-1076; Fax: 516-621-7127
Subjects: 19-25-99

The Right Lists Corp
Patty Anderson, List Mgr
3554 Chain Bridge Rd #301
Fairfax VA 22030
703-691-0808; Fax: 703-273-4514
Subjects: 55P
Memo: Conservative/political lists.

Ring Mailing Lists
PO Box 15061
Ft Lauderdale FL 33318
954-742-9519; Fax: 954-742-7882
Subjects: 19O (opportunity seekers)

RMI Direct Marketing Inc
Laura Smith
4 Skyline Dr
Hawthorne NY 10532
914-347-4949; Fax: 914-347-2954
Subjects: 19-99

The Rockford Institute
Rochelle Frank
934 N Main St
Rockford IL 61103
815-964-5813; Fax: 815-965-1826
Subjects: 11-35F-55-63

Rubin Response Services Inc
Darlene Ellman, List Mgr
Supervisor of Dept
1111 Plaza Dr
Schaumburg IL 60173
708-619-9800; Fax: 708-619-0149
Subjects: 99
Service: Affiliated with ACM: 212-869-7440

Saavoy List Management
Jane McAveney
Mack Centre VI
PO Box 1765
Paramus NJ 07652
201-967-5777; Fax: 201-967-5051
Subjects: 99

Sage Information Services
Roger Hurlbert, Pres
414 Clement St
San Francisco CA 94118
415-221-0414
Subjects: 43 (residential/home owners list)

The Salesman's Guide Inc
Ed Blank, Dir/List Sales
Reed Reference Publ Lists
121 Chanlon Rd
New Providence NJ 07974
800-223-1797; Fax: 908-665-3560
Subjects: 21-40F-71

SanMar Associates Inc
177 Main St #332
Fort Lee NJ 07024
201-488-7797; Fax: 201-488-7765
Subjects: 69R
Service: Country Walkers Vacations file

SBA Lists Inc
Martin Svigir, Gen Mgr
420 Madison Ave
New York NY 10017
212-755-4440; Fax:
Subjects: 25 (subscriber lists)

Select List Corp
PO Box 414
Glenwood Landing NY 11547-0414
516-676-7831; Fax: 516-676-9746
Subjects: 19-19X-25-99

Senior Citizens Unlimited
Carol Garfield, List Mgr
711 Westchester Ave
White Plains NY 10604
800-431-1712; Fax: 914-997-8065
Subjects: 35A

The Senior Source
Patty Kondub
50 Main St #1000
White Plains NY 10606
800-882-9930; Fax: 914-682-2149
Subjects: 35A-99

Shopsmith Inc
Jane Miller, List Mgr
3931 Image Dr
Dayton OH 45414-2591
513-898-6070
Subjects: 25 (consumer, retail, mail order)

Silverback Communications Inc
Bart Walters
56 E Pine St #100
Orlando FL 32801
407-422-2299; Fax: 407-425-6441
Subjects: 19

Simon Direct Inc
Dana Simon Sr, VP
4 Cornwall Dr #102
East Brunswick NJ 08816
908-651-7222; Fax: 908-651-7559
Subjects: 19-25-99

SK&A Research Inc
2601 Main St #650
Irvine CA 92714-6220
714-476-2051; Fax: 714-476-2168
Subjects: 39(health care professionals)

Snow Business Lists
Gregory Popp, Gen Mgr
2360 Congress St
Clearwater FL 34623
813-789-3900; Fax: 813-787-1904
Subjects: 23-99

Society of Prof Journalists
Cindy Storer, Mktg Dir
16 S Jackson St Box 77
Greencastle IN 46135-0077
Fax: 317-653-4631
Subjects: 56P

Sorkins' Directories Inc
Shannon Gelven, Mgr
1350 Elbridge Payne Rd #101
St Louis MO 63017
800-758-3228; Fax: 800-721-5478
Subjects: 19(execs)-61(MO/KS/IL)

Southam Business Lists
1450 Don Mills Rd
Don Mills ON Canada M3B 2X7
416-442-2299; 800-387-0273;
    Fax: 416-442-2240
Subjects: 19-39-61(Canada)-99

Southwest Mail Advertising
John Gravel & Tony Correnti Jr
12770 Commonwealth Dr
Ft Myers FL 33913
813-278-5778; Fax: 813-278-0597
Subjects: 19-25-99

Special Libraries Association
Steve Jones, Sales Mgr
1700 18th St NW
Washington DC 20009
202-234-4700; Fax: 202-265-9317
Subjects: 31E

The Specialists Ltd
Andrew Ostroy, VP
1200 Harbor Blvd 9th Fl
Weehawken NJ 07087
201-865-5800; Fax: 201-867-2450
Subjects: 19-25-27-99

Springdale Lists
Bernice Bush, Pres
15052 Springdale ST #A
Huntington Beach CA 92649
714-891-3344; Fax: 714-897-0650
Subjects: 19F-21(donor/mail order buyers)

Springhouse List Management
Joe Andres
Springhouse Corp
1111 Bethelem Pike
Springhouse PA 19477
215-646-8700; Fax: 215-646-4399
Subjects: 19-31-39

SRDS Direct Marketing List Source
Tom Drouillard, VP of Circ
1700 Higgins Rd
Des Plaines IL 60018
800-851-7737; Fax: 847-375-5001
Subjects: 99
Memo: Published bimonthly, 14,000 business, consumer and agri-market lists in 220 market classifications plus categories of service and supplier companies at your fingertips.

Statlistics
John Papalia
11 Lake Ave Ext
Danbury CT 06811
203-778-8700; Fax: 203-778-4839
Subjects: 99

Stevens List Management Center
Nan Senn, List Mgr
Stevens Publishing
225 N New Rd
Waco TX 76710-6931
817-876-3360
Subjects: 19-25-99

Stevens-Knox List Management
Ralph Stevens, Pres
304 Park Ave S
New York NY 10010
212-388-8800; Fax: 212-388-8890
Subjects: 99
Service: List management

The Strub Media Group Inc
Charles Chin
Old Chelsea Sta
PO Box 1274
New York NY 10113-0920
212-242-1900; Fax: 212-242-1963
Subjects: 37

Super Sportsmen Action Pack
Firearms Marketing Group
591 Camino de la Reina #200
San Diego CA 92108
619-297-8520; Fax: 619-297-5353
Subjects: 15-51-69 (outdoor merchandise consumers)

The Swiss Colony
1112 7th Ave
Monroe WI 53566
608-328-8400; Fax: 608-324-4503
Subjects: 27 (food/gift mailing lists)

T

TAB Direct
3133 Connecticut Ave NW #32
Washington DC 20008-5147
202-319-9866; Fax: 202-319-9867
Subjects: 99

The Taft Group
Wendy Muldauer, Mktg Mgr
12300 Twinbrook Pkwy #450
Rockville MO 20852
301-816-0210; Fax: 301-816-0811
Subjects: 19F

Taybi Direct Inc
Paul Taybi
10468 San Pablo Ave
El Cerrito CA 94530
510-525-1500; Fax: 510-525-7225
Subjects: 19-23

Taybi Direct List Management
Jane Nagatoshi
10468 San Pablo Ave
El Cerrito CA 94530
510-525-1500; Fax: 510-525-7225
Subjects: 19(business to business lists)

TCI List Management
5511 Laurel Canyon Blvd
Valley Village CA 91607
818-752-1800; Fax: 818-752-1808
Subjects: 19-69-70N-99

Technical List Computing Inc
221 E 1st St
Ferdinand IN 47532-0027
812-367-2545; Fax: 812-367-2546
Subjects: 99
Service: TLC - a computer service co

Technimetrics Inc
Patricia Friedman, VP
80 South St
New York NY 10038
212-509-5100; Fax: 212-363-3971
Subjects: 19 (financial databases)

Thomas Publishing Co
Donna Hamilton
5 Penn Plz
New York NY 10119
212-290-7224; Fax: 212-290-7202
Subjects: 19

Book Publishing Resource Guide
Page 413

Thomas Stuart Media Management
44 Franklin ST Box 2002
Nashua NH 03061-2002
603-880-2478; Fax: 603-880-2309
Subjects: 19-25-99

Times Direct Marketing USA
Chris Peterson, Dir
665 3rd St #240
San Francisco CA 94107-1923
415-247-2880; Fax: 415-247-2884
Subjects: 23T(high-tech-44(international)

Total Media Concepts Inc
Phil Hipshman, VP
185 Walnut St
Teaneck NJ 07666
201-692-0018; Fax: 201-692-9817
Subjects: 25-29 (mail order buyers)

Tower Publishing
Margaret Van Note, Mktg Dir
34 Diamond St Box 7220
Portland ME 04112
207-774-9813; Fax: 207-775-1740
Subjects: 19L-19I

Travel & Family-Related Lists
Carousel Press
PO Box 6061
Albany CA 94706-0061
510-527-5849; Fax:
Subjects: 21-31-35F-71-76
Service: Media, bookstores, families: 20,000 travelling families, 325 family-oriented publications and writers, 300 travel publications and writers, 305 travel writers at newspapers, 40 Canadian travel media, and 155 travel bookstores

Tri-Media Marketing Serv Inc
5200 Main St #205
Skokie IL 60077-2158
800-874-0338; Fax: 708-673-4469
Subjects: 14M-63

Tri-Media Marketing Services
Fran Horvath, List Broker
1600 W 7th St #700
Ft Worth TX 76102-2505
800-874-0338
Subjects: 19-21-25-63

Triangle Marketing Services
John Knoebel
80 Eighth Ave #305
New York NY 10011
212-242-4040; Fax: 212-242-1344
Subjects: 99

Trumbull Marketing Group Inc
Michael Nevins, Owner
105 Beacon St
Black Rock CT 06605
203-333-5478; Fax: 203-261-7423
Subjects: 19-31E-39

TRW Real Estate Marketing Info
1330 Cooley Dr #300
Colton CA 92324
800-247-8019; Fax: 714-422-0206
Subjects: 19H

TRW Target Marketing Services
Consumer List Division
701 TRW Pky
Allen TX 75002
800-527-3933
Subjects: 99

Turner Marketing Systems
Ken Turner, Pres
34768 Hwy 79 S
Warner Springs CA 92086-9618
800-867-5273; Fax: 619-782-3207
Subjects: 19H

Twin Peaks Press Lists
Helen Hecker
PO Box 129
Vancouver WA 98666
360-694-2492; Fax: 360-696-3210
Subjects: 39-56P-71

U

U S West Lists
U S West Marketing Resources
3190 S Vaughn Way 2 N
Aurora CO 80014-3506
800-999-4630
Subjects: 43H(new movers)

Unarius Academy of Science
Carol Robinson, Office Mgr
145 S Magnolia Ave
El Cajon CA 92020
619-444-7062; 800-824-6741;
    Fax: 619-444-9637
Subjects: 53(seminar attendees)

Uni-Mail Business List Managemt
1701 E Lake Ave
Glenview IL 60025
708-998-8990; Fax: 708-998-1801
Subjects: 19

Uni-Marketing
352 Park Ave S
New York NY 10010-1709
212-685-6191; Fax: 212-679-7590
Subjects: 99
Memo: International lists.

Unimail List Corp
352 Park Ave S 14th Fl
New York NY 10010
212-679-7000; Fax: 212-679-7590
Subjects: 39
Memo: 500,000 doctors; 680,000 others.

United Communications Group
Barbara Kaplowitz, List Mgr
Government Contractors List
11300 Rockville Pike #1100
Rockville MD 20852
301-816-8950; Fax: 301-816-8945
Subjects: 19-55(government contractors)

Urner Barry Publications inc
Paul Brown Jr
PO Box 389
Toms River NJ 08754
908-240-5330; Fax: 908-341-0891
Subjects: 19(wholesalers)-27

US Comm for Scholastic Assistanc
List Manager
College Bound
PO Box 668
O'Fallon IL 62269
Subjects: 31(College Scholarship Lists)

US Monitor
86 Maple Ave
New City NY 10956-9810
914-634-1331; 800-767-7967;
    Fax: 914-634-9618
Subjects: 99
Memo: This company monitors mailings lists as to timely delivery, if items have been delivered, and monitors against unauthorized uses of your lists.

US West Marketing Resources
Sandy Rhone, Natl Sales Mgr
Subs of US West
10375 E Harvard Ave #201
Denver CO 80231
800-999-4630; Fax: 303-369-1377
Subjects: 25-99

Valerie Davis & Assoc
Valerie Davis, Pres
500 N Commercial St 4th Fl
Manchester NH 03101
603-624-9220; Fax: 603-624-9229
Subjects: 19-56P(mail-order buyers)

Venture Communications
Bette Anne Keane, VP
60 Madison Ave 3rd Fl
New York NY 10010
212-684-4800; Fax: 212-545-1680
Subjects: 99
Service: Free list appraisal

W

W S Ponton Inc
Marianne Rabinowitz, Gen Mgr
The Ponton Bldg
5149 Butler St
Pittsburgh PA 15201
412-782-2360; 800-628-7806;
    Fax: 412-782-1109
Subjects: 19-25-99

Wall Street Lists
George Schlieben, Owner
PO Box 372
Yardley PA 19067
215-493-6783
Subjects: 19-25-99

Walter Karl List Management
Brian Hade
1 American Ln
Greenwich CT 06831
203-552-6700; Fax: 203-552-6799
Subjects: 19-21-39-51E-61-63-97

Warren Gorham & Lamont Inc
Mary Kay, Mgr
1 Penn Plz 42nd Fl
New York NY 10119
212-971-5151; Fax: 212-971-5444
Subjects: 19-56P

Water Pollution Control Fedrn
601 Wythe St
Alexandria VA 22314-1994
703-684-2400; Fax: 703-684-2492
Subjects: 24-51E
Memo: Also card deck mailings.

Watts List Management
455 Horner Ave
Toronto ON M8W 4W9
416-252-7741; Fax: 416-252-0037
Subjects: 69S(auto racing)
Memo: 6,000 names.

Wayne C Johnson & Assoc Inc
David Bauer/Kurt Snow, List Mgrs
400 Capitol Mall #1560
Sacramento CA 95814
916-446-8866; Fax: 916-446-9029
Subjects: 19F-55P(conservative)

Weiss Publishing & Marketing Inc
Angela Leonard, List Broker/Mgr
4176 Burns Rd
Palm Beach Gardens FL 33410
407-627-3310; Fax: 407-625-6685
Subjects: 19I (financial/investor lists)

Western Mailing Lists
Jean Vogel, Exec VP
14621 Titus St
Van Nuys CA 91402
818-781-8076; Fax: 818-781-5113
Subjects: 19-19O-25

William-Neil Associates
Emil Assad, Acct Exec
1316 Illinois
Sidney NE 69162
308-254-6019; Fax: 308-254-6102
Subjects: 51

Williams Direct
Carolyn Williams, VP
PO Box 205
Burlington KS 66839-0205
316-364-8431; Fax: 316-364-8432
Subjects: 14M(gospel)-49B-63

Williams-Sonoma Mailing Lists
Bonnie Allen Carpender
100 North Point
San Francisco CA 94133
415-421-7900; Fax: 415-434-0881
Subjects: 99 (mail order buyers)

Willowood Lists
Willowood Press
PO Box 1846
Minot ND 58702-1846
800-253-2890; Fax: 701-838-3933
Subjects: 31-99 (libraries, schools, English Depts)

Wilson Marketing Group Inc
Vicki Peterson, VP
11924 W Washington Blvd
Los Angeles CA 90066
310-398-2754; 800-445-2089;
    Fax: 310-397-4980
Subjects: 99

Wine Mailing Lists
International Wine Review
227 Enfield Falls Rd Box 285
Ithica NY 14850-8797
607-273-6071
Subjects: 27(food and wine)

Winterbourne Travel Lists
Elaine O'Gara
Winterbourne Press
7301 Burnet Rd #102-179
Austin TX 78757
512-419-1334
Subjects: 71
Service: 900 tourist bureaus/600 writers

Winthill List Management
Katia Segre Cohen, List Mgr
801 Wayne Ave #205
Silver Spring MD 20910
301-585-3951; Fax: 301-587-3726
Subjects: 31E-39
Service: Nurses/mental health specialties

William Stroh Inc
William Stroh III
568 54th St
W New York NY 07093
201-864-4800; Fax: 201-864-2956
Subjects: 19-25-99

Word Perfect Publishing Corp
Ian Gilbert
270 W Center
Orem UT 84057-4637
Fax: 801-226-8804
Subjects: 23

World Innovators Inc
72 Park St
New Canaan CT 06840
203-966-0374; Fax: 203-966-0926
Subjects: 11-19-23-44-67-99

World Wide Mailing Inc
Kathy Greiner, Sales Admin
1216 11th Ave
Altoona PA 16601-3416
814-942-5055; Fax: 814-942-6166
Subjects: 25-43(resident, game, contests, puzzles lists)

Worldata
Helene Schwedelson
5200 Town Ctr Cir
Boca Raton FL 33486
407-393-8200; Fax: 407-368-8345
Internet: helene@worldata.com
Subjects: 23-99

Worldwide Media Group Ltd
Linda Kimbrough (USA)
Eton Place
64 High St, Burnham
Buckinghamshire EN SL1 7JT
206-933-3005; Fax: 206-933-0252
Subjects: 19-23-99 (business names across Europe)
Memo: Linda is the US representative.

Y

Yankee List Marketing
Chip Hetzel, Pres
1010 Palmer Rd #1
Ft Washington MD 20744
301-248-7655; Fax: 301-248-1188
Subjects: 19F-55P

Yost List Co
Catherine Yost, Pres
3 Jordan East
Irvine CA 92715
714-786-8404; Fax: 714-786-3683
Subjects: 19-19F-25-55P-61

Z

Zed Marketing Group
3100 Cactus Dr #200
Edmond OK 73013
405-348-8145; Fax: 405-348-5541
Subjects: 25 (horticulture, outdoor activities)

Zeller List Corp
Christy Karl, Gen Mgr
15 E 26th St
New York NY 10010
212-685-7512; Fax: 212-213-3042
Subjects: 99
Catalog #: 800-221-4112
Memo: Merger of: Zeller & Letica, Research Projects, & Alvin B Zeller.

Zenith Mailing List Co
124 Washington Ave #B
Point Richmond CA 94801
415-554-0532; Fax: 415-554-0516
Subjects: 39

Ziff-Davis List Services
1 Park Ave
New York NY 10016
800-999-LIST
Subjects: 99
Memo: 380,000 active subscribers.

Zip Along Associates Inc
Arthur Yourish, Pres
311 Woods Ave
Oceanside NY 11572
516-536-6160
Subjects: 19-25-99

Trade Shows, Book Fairs and Conventions

This section is divided into five units: 1) book shows in the US and Canada, 2) book shows in other countries, 3) other trade shows where publishers exhibit their books (this is a short select list of possibilities), 4) a bibliography of trade show directories, and 5) exhibit services (companies which will exhibit one or more titles for you at selected shows).

Book Shows

AASL Conference
Cheryl Vargas x1393
Amer Assn of School Librarians
50 E Huron St
Chicago IL 60611-2729
312-944-6780; Fax: 312-664-7459
Subjects: 21-31-76-79
Dates: Next conference is in Portland, April 2-6th 1997.

Book Expo American
Director
American Booksellers Assn
828 S Broadway
Tarrytown NY 10591-6603
914-591-2665; 800-637-0037;
Fax: 914-591-2720
Subjects: 99
Dates: Late May-Early June.

Buckeye Book Fair
Jackie Harris (Ext 317)
Wooster Daily Record
212 E Liberty St
Wooster OH 55691
800-686-2958
Subjects: 99
Dates: Nov 2. Authors are selected by committee for participation in this fair.

Bumbershoot: Seattle Arts Festival
Judith Roche, Literary Arts Dir
Bumbershoot Festival Commission
PO Box 9750
Seattle WA 98109-0750
206-281-7788; Fax: 206-281-7799
Subjects: 99
Dates: Sept 20 to Oct 2.

Campus Market Expo
Natl Assn of College Stores
528 E Lorain St
Oberlin OH 44074-1238
216-775-7777
Subjects: 99
Service: College bookstores convention
Dates: April.

Canadian Booksellers Convention
Manager
Canadian Booksellers Assn
301 Donlands Ave
Toronto ON Canada M4J 3R8
416-467-7883
Subjects: 61(CN)-99
Dates: July.

CBA Convention
Convention Manager
Christian Booksellers Assn
2620 Venetucci Blvd
Colorado Springs CO 80906-4003
719-576-7880; Fax: 719-576-0795
Subjects: 63-99
Service: 6800 bookstores
Dates: July.

DMA Annual Conference/Exhibition
Direct Marketing Assn
1120 Ave of the Americas 14th Fl
New York NY 10036-6700
212-790-1500; Fax: 212-790-1400
Internet: http://www.the-dma.org
Subjects: 99

DMB National Conference
Direct Marketing to Business
535 Connecticut Ave
Norwalk CT 06854
203-857-5660; Fax: 203-857-5654
Subjects: 19M
Service: Sponsor: Dun & Bradstreet

Great Midwestern Bookshow
430 Oak Grove #B6
Minneapolis MN 55403-3228
612-872-7734
Subjects: 75-95-99(small press)

International Festival of Author
International Readings Dept
Harbourfront Corp
410 Queens Quay West
Toronto ON Canada M5V 2Z3
416-973-4600
Subjects: 75-90-95
Dates: October.

Madison Book Fair
Hank Luttrell, Vendor Mgr
20th Century Books
108 King St
Madison WI 53703-3314
608-251-6226
Subjects: 99
Dates: Sept 7. Sponsored by the Madison Area Independent Booksellers and the Dan County Library Service.

Miami Book Fair International
Alina Interian, Exec Dir
Miami Dade Community College
300 NE 2nd Ave #1501
Miami FL 33132-2297
305-237-3258; Fax: 305-237-3796
Subjects: 99
Service: Annual consumer book fair
Dates: Nov 17-24. 325 exhibitors. Booth cost: $550.00.

Mid-South Booksellers Association Convention
Mark Zumpe, Pres
Mid-South Booksellers Assn
PO Box 750043
New Orleans LA 70175-0043
504-865-8310
Subjects: 99
Dates: Sept 6-8.

Mountains/Plains Booksellers Trade Show
Lisa Knudsen, Exec Dir
805 LaPorte Ave
Ft Collins CO 80521-2520
303-484-5856; Fax: 303-484-5856
Subjects: 99
Dates: Sept 27-29 in Denver, CO.

MuseumStore Association Convention
Museum Store Assn
501 S Cherry St #460
Denver CO 80222-1327
303-329-6968; Fax: 303-329-6134
Subjects: 11-29-41-65-99
Service: Museums

NCDM Conference & Exposition
Ed Berkowitz
National Ctr for Database Mkg
Box 4232
Stamford CT 06097-0232
203-358-9900; Fax:
Subjects: 23-99(database marketing)
Dates: Dec 10-12, 1995 in Orlando, FL, 16th National Conference & Exposition.

New England Booksellers Association Trade Show
Rusty Drugan, Dir
New England Booksellers Assn
847 Massachusetts Ave
Cambridge MA 02139-3001
617-576-3070; 800-466-8711;
    Fax: 617-476-3091
Subjects: 99
Dates: Sept 28-29 at the World Trade Center in Boston. 1,800 attendees. Tables: $285.00.

New York Book Fair
Kathy McAuley, Development Dir
Goddard Riverside Community Ctr
593 Columbus Ave
New York NY 10024-1904
212-873-4448
Subjects: 99
Dates: Nov 23-24. Volunteer book fair to help inner-city kids, low-income elderly, and the homeless.

New York is Book Country
Linda Exman
Time Inc Books
1271 Ave of the Americas
New York NY 10020-1300
212-522-3043
Subjects: 99
Dates: Sept 27-29.

Northern CA Booksellers Trade Show
Ginie Thorp, Exec Dir
Northern California Booksellers
5643 Paradise Dr #12
Corte Madera CA 94925
415-927-3937; Fax: 415-927-3971
E-Mail: nciba@aol.com
Subjects: 99
Dates: Oct 4-7 in Oakland, CA.

Northwest Bookfest
Kitty Harmon, Dir
2208 NW Market St #300
Seattle WA 98107
206-789-9868; Fax: 206-784-5316
E-Mail: bfestival@aol.com
http://www.speakeasy.org/nwbookfest
Subjects: 99
Dates: Oct 26-27 at Pier 48 in downtown Seattle.

NYNJBA/MABA Combined Trade Show
Larry Robin, Convention Dir
Mid-Atlantic Booksellers Assn
108 S 13th St
Philadelphia PA 19107-4532
215-735-9600; Fax: 215-735-2670
Subjects: 99
Dates: Oct 6-7 in Atlantic City, NJ.

Omaha New Media Expo
Univ of Nebraska at Omaha
NE Business Development Ctr
1313 Farnam #132
Omaha NE 68102-1836
402-595-2381; Fax: 402-595-2385
Subjects: 19-31E-56
Dates: January, Mid-America's Premier Interactive Multimedia Conference.

Pacific NW Booksellers Assn Trade Show
Thom Chambliss, Dir
1510 Mill St
Eugene OR 97401-4258
503-683-4363; Fax: 503-683-4363
Subjects: 99
Dates: Sept 20-23
Memo: For more info, contact: Marc LePine, PO Box 1254, Springfield, OR 97477: 503-747-5613.

PLA National Conference
Sandy Donnelly, Exhibits Mgr
Public Library Assn - ALA
50 E Huron St
Chicago IL 60611-2729
312-944-6780; Fax: 312-440-9374
Subjects: 99
Dates: Conference is every 3-4 yrs.

Poetry Publication Showcase
Lee Briccetti, Dir
Poets House
72 Spring St 2nd Fl
New York NY 10012-4019
212-431-7920
Subjects: 95

Printer's Row Book Fair
Judy Weisman, Dir
Burnham Park Planning Board
1727 S Indiana Ave #104
Chicago IL 60616-1345
312-987-1980
Subjects: 99
Dates: June

Puerto Rico International Book Fair '97
The Rodd Group
200 Varick St 11th Fl
New York NY 10014-4810
718-518-4195; Fax: 718-518-4290
Subjects: 56

Quebec International Book Fair
M Lorenzo Michaud, Dir
2590 Blvd Laurier #860
Sainte-Foy PQ Canada G1V 4M6
418-658-1974
Subjects: 99
Service: Canadian foreign rights

Rocky Mountain Book Festival
Kimberly Taylor, Dir
Colorado Ctr for the Book
201 E Colfax #309 PO Box 360
Denver CO 80201
303-273-5933; Fax: 303-273-5935
E-Mail: 103332.1376@compuserve.com
Web:http://www.aclin.org/code/cfb
Subjects: 99
Dates: Oct 5-6, Booth cost: $395.00.

Sacramento Reads!
Julie Dittmar
Sacramento Literacy Coalition
PO Box 15779
Sacramento CA 95852
916-321-1790; Fax: 916-321-1783
Subjects: 99
Dates: Sept 28-29. Sponsored by the Sacramento Bee. Contact Terry Debencik at 916-443-6223 for exhibiting.

Salon du livre de Montreal
Attn: Manager
Salon du Livre
1151 rue Alexandre de Seve
Montreal PQ Canada H2L 2T7
Subjects: 99

San Antonio Inter-American Fair
Bryce Mulligan, Dir
Guadalupe Cultural Arts Ctr
1300 Guadalupe St
San Antonio TX 78207-5519
210-271-3151; Fax: 210-271-3480
Subjects: 45(Spanish)-49-61(TX)-78-99
Dates: Oct 31 to Nov 4.

Scholastic Book Fairs
Suzanne Harrold, Buyer
14300 E 35th Pl #105
Aurora CO 80011-1630
303-934-0786; Fax: 303-371-6170
Subjects: 99
Dates: Several.

SE Booksellers Association Convention
Wanda Jewell, Exec Dir
3806 Yale Ave
Columbia SC 29205-3550
803-252-7755; Fax: 803-252-8589
Subjects: 99
Dates: Sept 27-29. Opryland in Nashville, TN; 340 exhibits - 800booksellers.

Secrets of Successful Subscription Marketing
Blue Dolphin Communications
83 Boston Post Rd
Sudbury MA 01776-2450
508-443-6363; Fax: 508-443-9728
Subjects: 19M-56M
Dates: Oct 1-3, 1996, New York, NY.

SF Bay Area Book Festival
Elizabeth Whipple, Dir
123 Townsend St #260
San Francisco CA 94107
415-908-2833; Fax: 415-908-2839
Web: http://www.sfbook.org
Subjects: 61(CA)-99
Dates: Open to the public. 330 exhibitors. Booth fee: $325.00.

Small Press Book Fair
Karin Taylor, Dir
Small Press Ctr
20 W 44th St
New York NY 10036-6604
212-764-7021; Fax: 212-354-5365
Subjects: 75-83-95-99
Dates: Sept 28-29.

Southern Festival of Books
Marilyn Friendlander, Coord
Tennessee Humanities Council
1003 18th Ave S
Nashville TN 37212-2104
615-320-7001
Subjects: 99
Dates: Oct 11-13 at Legislative Plz in Nashville.

Upper Midwest Booksellers Tradeshow
Susan Walker Wood, Dir
Upper Midwest Bksellers Assn
4018 W 65th St
Minneapolis MN 55435-1728
612-926-4102; Fax: 612-925-5876
Subjects: 99
Dates: Oct 11-13 at the Hyatt Regency Hotel in Minneapolis, MN. 200 exhibits - 450 booksellers.

Foreign Book Shows

Beijing International Book Fair
Ling Huaying
China National Publications
PO Box 88
Beijing China
408-2645
Subjects: 99

Bologna Children's Book Fair
Luciano Chicchi, Dir
Fiera del libro per ragazzi
Piazza Constituzione 6
Bologna 40128 Italia
051-282.111
Subjects: 21-76-89
Service: Major children's book fair

Brasil Internacional do Livro
Attn: Manager
Camara Brasileira do Livro
Avenida Ipiranga 1267, 10' andar
01039 Sao Paulo SP Brasil
Subjects: 99
Service: Biennial

Brussels International Book Fair
Willy Vandermeulen, Dir
321 Avenue des Volontaires
B-1150
Brussels Belgium
Subjects: 99
Service: French/Flemish foreign rights

Buenos Aires Book Fair
Fundacion El Libro
Avda Cordoba 875 - 1054
Buenos Aires Argentina
541-311-6761
Subjects: 99
Service: International book fair

Cairo International Book Fair
Samir Saad Khalil, Dir
General Egyptian Book Org
Corniche El Nil, Bolac
Cairo Egypt
00202-775371
Subjects: 99
Service: Egyptian foreign rights

Cairo Intl Children's Book Fair
Samir Saad Khalil, Dir
General Egyptian Book Org
Corniche El Nil, Bolac
Cairo Egypt
00202-775371
Subjects: 21-31-76-89
Service: Open to the public

Calcutta Book Fair
B K Dhur, Dir
5A, Bahwani Dutta Ln
Calcutta 700 073 India
31-1541
Subjects: 99

Colombo Children's Book Fair
Attn: Manager
Children's Book Fair
415 Galle Rd
Colombo 4 Sri Lanka
Subjects: 21-76

Frankfurt Book Fair
Peter Weidhaas, Dir
PO Box 10 01 16
D6000 Frankfurt 1 W Germany
4969210-2217; Fax: 4969210-2227
Subjects: 44-99(major foreign rights fair)
Service: Fax: 011-4969-210-2227

Geneva International Fair
for Books and the Press
Pierre-Marcel Favre
PO Box 3569
CH-1002 Lausanne Switzerlnd
Subjects: 99
Service: New book fair

Guadalajara Intl Book Fair
Maricarmen Canales
Hidalgo 1417
A Postal 39-130
Guadalajara 44170 Mexico
36-25-28-17; Fax: 36-25-73-59
Subjects: 44-45-78-80-99

Hong Kong International BookFair
Hong Kong Trade Development
36th-39th Fl Office Tower
Convention Plz 1 Harbour Rd
Wanchai Hong Kong
852-833-4333; Fax: 852-824-0249
Subjects: 44-99

Ife Book Fair
Attn: Manager
Univ of Ife Bookshop
Ile-Ife
Oyo State Nigeria
Subjects: 99

International Book Fair/Belgrade
Vojislav Vujovic
Assn of Yugoslavia Publishers
Kneza Milosa 25
Belgrade 11000 Yugoslavia
011-642-248
Subjects: 99

International Children Book Fair
SEP-Direccion General de Publicaciones y Medios
Avda Revolucion 10 Piso PB20-650
Villa Obregon DF Mexico
Subjects: 21-45(Spanish)-76-80-89

Intl Book Fair of Mexico
Sergio Tirado Ledesma, Dir
Tacuba 5
Apartado Postal 20-515
Mexico D.F. 06000 Mexico
905-548-5535
Subjects: 99
Service: Latin American foreign rights

Jerusalem Intl Book Fair
Zev Birger
212 Jaffa Rd
PO Box 1241
Jerusalem 94383 Israel
02-380896
Subjects: 99
Service: Israeli foreign rights

Liber 90 (Barcelona Book Fair)
Evelyn Del'Epine, Dir
Federation of Spanish Publishers
Paseo de la Castellana 82
Madrid 28036 Espana
91-457-44-04; Fax: 93-423-86-51
Subjects: 45(Spanish)-80-99

London Book Fair
Director
Oriel House, 26 the Quadrant
Richmond-Upon-Thames
Surrey TW9 1DL UK England
4481-9489933; Fax: 4481-9489930
Subjects: 99
Service: English language foreign rights

Manila International Book Fest
Attn: Manager
PHILCITE, CCP Complex
PO Box 598
Manila Philippine
Subjects: 99

Middle East Bookfair
Overseas Exhibition Services
11 Manchester Square
London WIM 5AB UK England
Subjects: 99
Service: Bahrein

Moscow International Book Fair
Vladislav Shevchenko, Dir
C C C P Goskomisdat
16 Chekhov St
Moscow 103006 U S S R
Subjects: 99
Service: Russian foreign rights/biennial

Salon International du Livre et
de la Presse a Geneve
SILPG
CP#125, CH-1211
Geneve 4 Schweiz
Subjects: 99

Saudi Bookfair
Overseas Exhibition Services
11 Manchester Square
London WIM 5AB UK England
Subjects: 99
Service: Riyadh, Saudi Arabia

Scientific & Technical Book Fair
Editrice Bibliografica
Viale Vittorio Veneto, 24
20124 Milano Italia
193926597950
Subjects: 23-67-99(professional)

Singapore Festival of Books
N T S Chopra, Dir
Festival of Books Singapore
865 Mountbatten Rd #05-28
Singapore 1543 Singapore
344-1495; Fax: 344-0180
Subjects: 99

Sofia International Book Fair
Attn: Manager
Department of Exhibitions
11 Slaveikov Square
Sofia Bulgaria
Subjects: 99

Swedish Book Fair
Urban Hagman, Congress Ctr
Stockholmsmassan AB
S-125-80
Stockholm Sweden
Subjects: 99
Service: Scandanavian foreign rights

Tianjin International Book Fair
Attn: Manager
International Exhibits
57 Wyndham St 1st Fl
Central Hong Kong
Subjects: 99

Tokyo International Book Fair
Carlos Jimenez
Cahners Exposition Group
999 Summer St PO Box 3833
Stamford CT 06905-0833
203-964-0000; Fax: 203-964-9209
Subjects: 99

Tokyo International Book Fair
Reed Exhibitions Japan Ltd
18F Shinjuku-Nomura Bldg
1-2602 Nishi-Shinjuku
Shinjuku-ku, Tokyo 163-05
  81-3-3349-8501; FAX: 81-3-3349-8501

Torino National Book Fair
Erica Giacosa, Director
Salone Del Libro Torino
Largo Regio Parco 9
10152 Torino Italia
011-859133; Fax: 011-859479
Subjects: 44-99

Warsaw International Book Fair
Wladyslaw Bienkowski, Dir
Krakowskie Przedmiescie 7
PO Box 1001
Warsaw Poland
17-86-41
Subjects: 99
Service: Polish foreign rights

Other Trade Shows

American International Toy Show
Toy Manufacturers of America
200 Fifth Ave
New York NY 10010-3302
212-675-1141; Fax: 212-633-1429
Subjects: 21-76(toys)
Held in New York.

Art Materials Trade Show
Natl Art Materials Trade Assn
178 Lakeview Ave
Clifton NJ 07011-4099
201-546-6400; Fax: 201-546-0393
Subjects: 11-29(arts and crafts)

Comdex
The Interface Group
300 1st Ave
Needham MA 02194-2703
617-449-6600; Fax:
Subjects: 23(computer show)
Held in various locations.

Consumer Electronics Show
2001 Pennsylvania Ave NW
Washington DC 20006-1850
202-457-8700
Subjects: 23-24-33(consumer electronics)

Craft, Model & Hobby Show
Hobby Industries of America
319 E 54th St
PO Box 348
Elmwood Park NJ 07407-2712
201-794-1133
Subjects: 16-28-29-43

EDSA Trade Show
Dawn Mancuso
Educational Dealers & Suppliers
711 W 17th St #J-5
Newport Beach CA 92663
714-642-3986; 800-654-7099;
   Fax: 714-642-7960
Subjects: 21-31-76-89

Food Marketing Inst Convention
Food Marketing Institute
800 Conn Ave NW
Washtington DC 20036
202-452-8444; Fax: 202-429-4519
Subjects: 19M-27

The Gourmet Show
George Little Management
577 Airport Blvd 4th Fl
Burlingame CA 94010-2020
415-344-5171; Fax: 415-344-5270
Subjects: 27(gourmet food)
Held in San Francisco.

INPEX
Invention/New Product Expo
217 9th St
Pittsburgh PA 15290
412-288-1343; Fax: 412-288-1354
Subjects: 99

International Housewares Expo
National Housewares
Manufacturers Assn
6400 Shafer Ct
Rosemont IL 60018
708-292-4900
Subjects: 27-29-43

Luggage & Leather Goods Show
Luggage & Leather Goods Mfgs Asn
350 Fifth Ave #1317
New York NY 10118-1399
212-695-2340
Subjects: 71

Mail Order Merchandise Show
Marketing Resources Group
1254 Highway 27
North Brunswick NJ 08902
908-246-2212; Fax: 908-246-3939
Subjects: 99
Held in New York.

Marine Retailers Association Trade Show
Marine Retailers Assn
150 E Huron St
Chicago IL 60611-2912
312-944-5080
Subjects: 70(recreational boating)

The MoGo Show
Western Premium & Incentive Show
AMC Trade Shows
240 Peachtree St SW #2200
Atlanta GA 30303-3714
404-220-2201
Subjects: 19-71-99(P&I/motivation/travel)
Held in Los Angeles.

National Back-to-School Show
Thalheim Expositions
42 Bayview Ave
PO Box 4200
Manhasset NY 11030-1806
516-627-4000
Subjects: 21-31-76-79
Held in New York.

National Fitness Nutrition and Sports Exposition
George Little Management
10 Bank St
White Plains NY 10606-1952
914-948-6070; Fax: 212-685-6598
Subjects: 27-39-69
Held in Chicago.

National Merchandise Show
Thalheim Expositions
42 Bayview Ave
PO Box 4200
Manhasset NY 11030-1806
516-627-4000
Subjects: 99
Held in New York.

National Premium/Incentive Show
Hall-Erickson
150 Burlington Ave
Clarendon Hills IL 60514-1203
800-752-6312; 708-850-7770
Subjects: 19-27-43-99
Held in Chicago.

National Stationery Show
George Little Management
10 Bank St #1100
White Plains NY 10606-1952
914-948-6070
Subjects: 99

New York International Gift Fair
George Little Management
10 Bank St
White Plains NY 10606-1952
914-948-6070
Subjects: 99(gifts)
Other shows in Chicago and DC.

NOPA Convention
National Office Products Assn
301 N Fairfax St
Alexandria VA 22314-2633
703-549-9040; 800-542-6672;
    Fax: 703-683-7552
Subjects: 19

NSSEA Convention
Natl School Supply/Equipment Asn
8300 Colesville Rd #250
Silver Springs MD 20910-3243
301-495-0240; 800-395-5550;
    Fax: 301-495-3330
Subjects: 21-31-76-89
Memo: National School Supply & Equipment Association.

Pet Industry Trade Show
Pet Industry Distributors Assn
5024 Campbell Blvd
Baltimore MD 21236-5908
410-931-8100
Subjects: 15

Premium Incentive Show
Thalheim Expositions
42 Bayview Ave
PO Box 4200
Manhasset NY 11030-1899
516-627-4000; Fax: 516-365-5844
Subjects: 19-27-43-99
Held in New York.

Retail Hardware Trade Show
National Retail Hardware Assn
5822 W 74th St
Indianapolis IN 46278-1787
317-290-0338
Subjects: 16-29-43(hardware)

Variety Merchandise Show
Thalheim Expositions
42 Bayview Ave
PO Box 4200
Manhasset NY 11030-1806
516-627-4000
Subjects: 27-29-43-99
Held in New York.

World Sports Expo
National Sporting Goods Assn
1699 Wall St
Mount Prospect IL 60056-6213
312-439-4000
Subjects: 69

Trade Show Directories

Association Meeting Directory
PO Box 644
Millersville MD 21108-0644
410-987-4847; 800-541-0663
Subjects: 19-99(meeting sites & dates)

California Festivals & Events
Landau Communications
Tahoe City CA 96145
916-583-5605
Subjects: 61(CA)-99
Service: 300 off-beat festivals

Directory of Festivals, Sports & Special Events
International Events Group
213 W Institute Pl #303
Chicago IL 60610-3125
312-944-1727; Fax: 312-944-1897
Subjects: 69
Service: Sports and other special events

Directory of North American Fairs, Festivals and Expositions
Amusement Business
PO Box 24970
Nashville TN 37202-4970
615-321-4250; Fax: 615-327-1575
Subjects: 33-99
Service: Fairs more than three days

Exhibits Directory
Assn of American Publishers
71 5th Ave
New York NY 10003-3004
212-255-0200
Subjects: 99
Service: Libraries, booksellers, education

Intl Tradeshow Week Data Book
Tradeshow Week
R R Bowker Co
121 Chanlon Rd PO Box 31
New Providence NJ 07974
908-665-2818; Fax: 908-665-6688
Subjects: 19-99
Service: International trade shows

Sources of Information About Trade Shows and Expositions
Ctr for Exhibition Industry
4350 East West Hwy #401
Bethesda MD 20814-4426
301-907-7626; Fax: 301-907-0277
Subjects: 19-99
Service: Assns, media, books, tapes, and software

Technology Events Calendars
Tech Trade Events
769 Blvd East
Union City NJ 07087
201-941-3675; Fax: 201-392-1972
Subjects: 23C-23T
Service: 400 high-tech trade shows

Trade Shows Worldwide
Editor
Gale Research Co
835 Penobscot Bldg
Detroit MI 48226
313-961-2242; Fax: 313-961-6083
Subjects: 99
Service: Exhibits and conventions

Tradeshow Week Data Book
Tradeshow Week
R R Bowker Co
121 Chanlon Rd PO Box 31
New Providence NJ 07974
908-665-2818; 800-521-8110;
    Fax: 908-665-6688
Subjects: 19-99(international trade shows)

TradeShows & Exhibits Schedule
Successful Meetings
SM/Databank
355 Park Ave S
New York NY 10010-1706
800-253-6708
Subjects: 99(exhibits/conventions)
Service: 215-630-1462

Exhibit Services

Academia Book Exhibits
Bruce Davis
3925 Rust Hill Pl
Fairfax VA 22030-3921
703-716-5537; Fax: 703-691-2422
Service: Academic conferences

Association Book Exhibit
Mark Trocchi, Exhibits Mgr
639 S Washington St
Alexandria VA 22314-4109
703-519-3909; Fax: 703-519-7732
Subjects: 99
Service: Exhibits at 50

Baker & Taylor Exhibit Service
Patricia Bostelman
Baker & Taylor
50 Kirby Ave
Somerville NJ 08876-3100
908-722-8000
Subjects: 99
Service: International exhibits

Center for Thanatology Research and Education
Roberta Halporn
391 Atlantic Ave
Brooklyn NY 11217-1701
718-858-3026;
Subjects: 39(death)
Service: Meetings: death-related topics

Chickadee Books
Roy & Sharon Terry, Owners
325 Dry Bridge Rd
Mexico NY 13114-3331
315-298-6473
Subjects: 21-43G-51E-51N
Service: HC-PB
Memo: Exhibits & sells at conventions & schools.

Combined Book Exhibit
277 White St
Buchanan NY 10511-1607
914-739-7500; Fax: 914-739-7575
Subjects: 59-99
Service: Library, education, bookselling

Conference Book Service
80 S Early St
Alexandria VA 22304-6350
703-823-6968
Service: Book shows, professional conferences

ECA Co-op Publishers Exhibits
Mwalimu Mwadilifu, Pres
ECA Associates
Great Bridge Station PO Box 15004
Chesapeake VA 23328-5004
804-547-5542; Fax:
Subjects: 49(Black)-78-80
Service: Exhibits at 50 events
Memo: Exhibits of African heritage books at London Small Press Fair as well as other book fairs in West Africa and the US.

Exhibit Promotions Plus
11620 Vixens Path
Ellicott City MD 21042-1541
410-596-3028; Fax: 410-997-0764
Subjects: 19-31-35-55-57-63-65-99
Service: Professional & scholarly

FRC Combined Book Exhibit
The Family Resource Coalition
200 S Michigan Ave #1520
Chicago IL 60604-2404
312-341-0900
Subjects: 31-35
Service: Annual conference with exhibit

Independent Publishers Service
Ruth Gottstein, Volcano Press
21326 Consolation St
PO Box 135
Volcano CA 95689
209-296-7989; Fax: 209-296-4515
Subjects: 21-73-76
Service: Bologna Fair only

International Titles
Loris Essary, Dir
931 E 56th St
Austin TX 78751-1724
512-451-2221; Fax: 512-467-1330
E-Mail: leint@eden.com
Subjects: 99
Memo: Exhibits books at book fairs in London, Frankfurt, Taipei, and several other locations.

Joint Promotions
17 Stanley Hill Ave
Amersham, Bucks
HP7 PBB England
02403-7867
Subjects: 99
Service: International book fairs

Mainly Meetings
Linda C Cutrupi
One Bridge Plz #400
Fort Lee NJ 07024
201-592-5899; Fax: 201-568-5415
Subjects: 27-39-43G-35-61-51E

New American Writing
Sarah Stonich
311 Ramsey St
St Paul MN 55102-2323
612-228-0577
Subjects: 11-47-49-75-83-90-95-99
Service: Small press titles to Frankfurt

New Pages Exhibiting Service
Casey Hill
New Pages Press
PO Box 438
Grand Blanc MI 48439-0438
313-743-8055
Subjects: 13-37-49-53-73-99
Service: Library, bookseller, other fairs

PMA Display Service
Jan Nathan
Publishers Marketing Assoc
2401 Pacific Coast Hwy #102
Hermosa Beach CA 90254-2734
310-372-2732; Fax: 310-374-3342
E-mail: PMAonline@aol.com
Subjects: 10
Service: Many co-op exhibits

Publishers Book Display
John Money
Special Libraries Book Service
Old Malt House St Johns Rd
Banbury OX16 8HX OX England
1-0295-68301
Subjects: 99
Service: Conferences in England

Publishers Book Exhibit
Jon E Malinowski
277 White Buchnan
Peekskill NY 10566
914-739-7500; Fax:
Subjects: 99(academic/science/education)
Service: Book fairs and conferences

The Reference Shelf
Susan Kurpeski, Mgr
593 Pleasant St
Hanson MA 02341-1911
617-293-2194; Fax: 617-294-4153
Subjects: 59(directories)
Service: Co-op displays at library shows

Trade Show Marketing Services
3800 Wilson Ave SW #B
Cedar Rapids IA 52404-6347
319-396-5356; Fax: 319-396-4620

USA Book-Expo
Ed Malinowski
ABA Calendar Exhibit
46 Willow Dr
Briarcliff Manor NY 10510-1228
914-762-2422
Subjects: 99
Service: Calendars

Publishing Associations

While the following lists include most current bookseller and publisher associations, the list of writer's associations is just a small selection of the local and national associations for writers. Encourage your authors to join the appropriate author's associations and, Since many of these associations include journalists, you might also want to join as a way of making more contacts with media personnel. To keep in touch with the needs and desires of independent booksellers, join your regional booksellers association. Finally, join your regional publishers association, at least one national association, and any subject-specific associations appropriate for your books.

Author's Associations

Academy of American Poets
Director
Poetry Pilot Newsletter
584 Broadway
New York NY 10012-3229
212-427-0343
Subjects: 56W-95
Focus: Poetry writers

Alaska Center for the Book
Director
3600 Denali St
Anchorage AK 99503-6093
 Fax: 907-278-8839
E-Mail: akctrbk@aonline.com
Subjects: 61(AK)
Focus: Alaskan writers

American Agricultural Editors Association
President
ByLine Newsletter
1629 K St NW #1100
Washington DC 20006-1602
202-785-6709; Fax: 202-331-4212
Subjects: 51A-56M
Focus: Magazine/newsletter editors

American Auto Racing Writers and Broadcasters
Director
922 N Pass Ave
Burbank CA 91505-2703
818-842-7005
Subjects: 16A-56W-69S
Focus: Auto racing writers

American Black Book Writers Association
President
PO Box 10548
Marina Del Rey CA 90295-6548
310-822-5195
Subjects: 49B-56W-78-80
Focus: Black book writers

American Literary Translators Association
Rainer Schulte, Director
Univ of Texas at Dallas
PO Box 830688
Richardson TX 75083-0688
214-883-2093; Fax: 214-883-6303
Subjects: 45-99(translators)
Memo: Dr Eileen Tollett, Exec Secretary.

American Medical Writers Association
Director
AMWA Journal
9650 Rockville Pike
Bethesda MD 20814-3998
301-493-0003; Fax: 301-493-6384
Subjects: 39-56W
Focus: AMWA Freelance Directory

American Society of Business Press Editors
Jeanne Ribinskas, President
4445 Gilmer Ln
Cleveland OH 44143-2611
216-531-8306
Subjects: 19-56M-56W
Focus: Business press editors

American Society of Journalists & Authors
Director
ASJA Newsletter
1501 Broadway #302
New York NY 10036-5501
212-997-0947; Fax: 212-768-7414
Subjects: 56W-99
Focus: Professional writers

American Writers of Color Literary Agency
Marsha-Anne Tanksley
PO Box 282
Jamaica NY 11434-0282
718-529-5261
Subjects: 49B-78
Focus: Specializes in unpub writers

American Translators Association
Director
ATA Chronicle
1800 Diagonal Rd #220
Alexandria VA 22314-2840
Subjects: 45-99

Arizona Authors Association
Gerry Benninger
Newsletter Editor
11801 N Tatum Blvd #2
Phoenix AZ 85028-1613
602-996-9706;
Subjects: 56W
Focus: Arizona Authors

Asian American Journalists Association
Director
AAJA Newsletter
1765 Sutter St #1000
San Francisco CA 94115
413-346-2051
Subjects: 99
Focus: Founded 1981
Memo: Student development, job referrals, fellowship and internship reports.

Association of Professional Consultants
Director
17621 Irvine Blvd
Tustin CA 92680-3114
714-535-7530
Subjects: 99
Focus: American Association of Professional Consultants

Associated Business Writers of America
Director
Flash Market News
1450 S Havana #620
Aurora CO 80012-4032
303-751-7844
Subjects: 19-56W
Focus: Business writers

Associated Press Managing Editor
Susan Clark, President
50 Rockefeller Plz
New York NY 10020-1605
212-621-1500
Subjects: 56W
Focus: Members are executives of Associated Press Newspapers.

Austin Writer's League
Carmen Kelpner, Editor
Austin Writer Newsletter
1307 Kenny Ave #105
Austin TX 78704
512-440-1049; Fax: 512-499-0441
Subjects: 56W
Focus: Writers
Memo: Angela Smith, Director, 1501 W 5th St #E-2, Austin TX, 78703;512-499-8914. Ricki Ratliff, Columnist, Writer's Insider, 6205 Bull Creek Rd, Austin, TX 78757; 512-451-6555.

The Authors Guild
Director
Authors Guild Bulletin
330 W 42nd St, 29th Floor
New York NY 10036-6912
212-593-5904; Fax: 212-564-5363
Subjects: 56W
Focus: Authors

The Authors League of America
Director
330 W 42nd St
New York NY 10036-6902
212-564-8350
Subjects: 14-56W
Focus: Authors, dramatists

The Authors Resource Center
Executaive Director
TARC Newsletter
4725 E Sunrise Dr #219
Tucson AZ 85718-4534
502-325-4733
Subjects: 56W
Focus: Arizona authors

Aviation/Space Writers Association
President
17 S High St #1200
Columbus OH 43215
614-221-1900; Fax: 614-221-1989
Subjects: 67A-67
Focus: The communications network for aviation and aerospace. Aim is to foster quality communications and to promote accurate and authoritative writing

Brooklyn Writers' Network
Director
Pen in Hand Newsletter
2509 Ave K
Brooklyn NY 11210-3717
718-377-4945
Subjects: 99
Focus: Brooklyn NY writers

California Writers' Club
Director
California Writers Club Bulletin
2214 Derby St
Berkeley CA 94705
510-841-1217
Subjects: 56W-61(CA)
Focus: California writers

Canadian Authors Association
Director
Canadian Author & Bookman
275 Stater St #500
Ottawa ON Canada K1P 5H9
613-233-2846
Subjects: 61(CN)-99
Focus: Canadian authors

Christian Writers Guild
Chairman
Quill o' the Wisp Newsletter
260 Fern Ln
Hume CA 93628
209-335-2333
Subjects: 56W-63P-99
Focus: Christian writers

Computer Press Association
Galen Gruman, President
529 18th Ave
San Francisco CA 94121
415-750-9281
Subjects: 23-56W
Focus: CPA members are writers and editors regularly covering the computer industry

Connecticut Authors Association
Brian Jud
50 Lovely St
PO Box 715
Avon CT 06001-0715
203-675-1344; 800-562-4357
Subjects: 56W
Focus: Connecticut writers

Construction Writers Association
Secretary
Construction Writer Newsletter
PO Box 70835
Chevy Chase MD 20815
Subjects: 12B-19H-56W
Focus: Construction writers

Council of Biology Editors
Editor, CBE Views
11 S LaSalle St
Chicago IL 60601-1203
312-201-0101
Subjects: 39M-51(biology)-56W
Focus: Biology editors

Creative Screenwriters Group
CS Newsletter
6615 Franklin Ave Apt S4
Hollywood CA 90028-4788
Subjects: 33M-56W
Focus: Quarterly publication

Dog Writers Association of America
Mary Ellen Tarman
PO Box F
Hummelstown PA 17036-0200
717-566-9843
Subjects: 15(dogs)-56W
Focus: Dog writers

Editoral Freelancers Association
Newsletter Editor
71 W 23rd St
New York NY 10010-4102
212-929-5400
Subjects: 99
Focus: Editors, profreaders

Education Writers Association
Bert Menninga, Editor
Education Reporter Newsletter
1331 H St NW #307
Washington DC 20005-4706
202-429-9680
Subjects: 31-56W
Focus: Education writers

Florida Freelance Writers Association
Dana Cassell, Director
Cassell Communications
Main St PO Box A
North Stratford NH 03590-0167
603-922-8338; 800-351-9278; Fax: 603-922-8339
E-Mail: FJWX43B@prodigy.com
Subjects: 56W-61(FL)-99
Focus: Florida writers

Football Writers Association of America
Director
Fifth Down Newsletter
213 N Sheffield Dr
Bloomington TN 47408-3138
Subjects: 56W-69S(football)
Focus: Football writers

Garden Writers Association
Brian Ford, Editor
Garden Writers Bulletin
10210 Leatherleaf Ct
Manassas VA 20111-4245
703-257-1032; Fax: 703-257-0213
Subjects: 43G-56W
Focus: Garden writers

Gay & Lesbian Press Association
R J Curry, Exc Director
PO Box 8185
Universal City CA 91618-8185
818-902-1476
Subjects: 37-56W
Focus: Dedicated to the improvement of gay and lesbian press media.

Georgia Freelance Writers Association
Dana Cassell, Director
Cassell Communications
Maple Ridge Rd
North Sandwich NH 03259
603-284-6367; 800-351-9278; Fax: 603-284-6648
Subjects: 56W-61 (GA)-99
Focus: Georgia writers

Golf Writers Association of America
Director
25882 Orchard Lake Rd
Farmington Hills MI 48336-1269
810-442-1481
Subjects: 56W-69(golf)

Horror Writers Association
Virginia Aalko, Secy
5336 Reef Way
Oxnard CA 93055
Subjects: 56W-82
Focus: Horror writers

Independent Black Writers Association
Gloria Taylor-Edwards
PO Box 27504
Richmond VA 23261-7504
Subjects: 49B-56W
Focus: Black writers

International Association of Business Communicators
Norman G Leaper, Director
1 Hallidie Plz #600
San Francisco CA 94102
415-433-3400; 800-776-4222
Subjects: 19-56W
Focus: Business writers

International Black Writers
Rachel McMillan, Secy
Black Writer Magazine
PO Box 1030
Chicago IL 60690-1030
312-924-3818
Subjects: 49B-56W-78-80
Focus: Black writers

International Food, Wine, and Travel Writers Association
PO Box 13110
Long Beach CA 90803-8110
310-433-5969; Fax: 310-438-6384
Subjects: 27-71
Focus: Food, travel writers

International Association of Consultants
Donald Kaplan, President
1661 Williamsburg Sq
Lakeland FL 33803-4279
813-644-1991; Fax: 813-648-4768
Subjects: 99
Focus: Professional consultants

International Association of Crime Writers
Director
Border Patrol Newsletter
PO Box 1500
New York NY 10116-1500
212-757-3915
Subjects: 55C-56W-84
Focus: Crime and mystery writers

International Women's Writing Guild
Director
Gracie Sta, PO Box 810
New York NY 10028-0082
212-737-7536
Subjects: 56W-73
Focus: Women writers and publishers

League of Vermont Writers
Newsletter Editor
PO Box 1058
Waitsfield VT 05673-1058
802-496-3271
Subjects: 56W-61(VT)
Focus: Writers in Vermont

Media Alliance
Director
MediaFile Newsletter
814 Mission St #205
San Francisco CA 94103-3018
415-546-6334
Subjects: 56W
Focus: Media writers

Midwest Romance Writers
Director
MARA Newsletter
PO Box 32186
Kansas City MO 64171-5186
816-453-6296
Subjects: 56W-81-85
Focus: Romance writers

Mystery Writers of America
Editor
Third Degree Newsletter
17 E 47th St 6th Fl
New York NY 10017-1920
212-255-7005
Subjects: 56W-84
Focus: Mystery

National Association for Young Writers
NAYW News
5 Bonito Rd
Santa Fe NM 87505-8793
505-982-8596
Subjects: 21-56W-76
Focus: Young writers

National Press Club
Harry Bodaan, President
529 14th St NW
Washington DC 20045-1000
202-662-7500
Subjects: 99
Memo: A private organization composed of professional journalists who are directly related to the media. Persons must qualify to be admitted.

National Sportscasters & Sportswriters Association
Barbara Lockert, President
PO Box 559
Salisbury NC 28145-0559
704-633-4275
Subjects: 33T-56W-69
Focus: Sports writers and broadcasters

The National Writers Club
Director
NWC Newsletter
1450 S Havana St #620
Aurora CO 80012-4032
303-751-7844; Fax: 303-751-8593
Subjects: 56W
Focus: Writers

National Writers Union
Director
American Writer Magazine
873 Broadway
New York NY 10003
212-254-0279
Subjects: 56W
Focus: Writers

Native American Journalists Association
Director
230 Tenth Ave S #301
Minneapolis MN 55415
612-376-0441; Fax: 612-348-8724
Subjects: 49A(Native American)-56W
Focus: 40 newspapers

National Association of Professional Environmental Communicators
NAPEC Quarterly
PO Box 194643
San Francisco CA 94119-4643
Subjects: 51E-56W
Focus: Environmental communicators

National Association of Science Writers
Director
NASW Newsletter
PO Box 294
Greenlawn NY 11740-0294
516-757-5664
Subjects: 23-24-39-51-56W-67
Focus: Science Writers

National Federation of Press Women
Rosemary Carroll, President
4510 W 89th St #110
Shawnee Mission KS 66207-2292
913-341-0165
Subjects: 99
Focus: Women of the Press

National League of American Pen Women
Judith LaFourest, Editor
The Pen Woman Magazine
401 W 46th St
Washington DC 20036
202-785-1997
Subjects: 56W-73
Focus: Women writers

New Jersey Romance Writers
Director
PO Box 646
Old Bridge NJ 08857
Subjects: 56W-81-85
Focus: New Jersey romance writers

Outdoor Writers Association of America
James W Rainey, Exc Director
2017 Cato Ave #101
State College PA 16801-2765
814-234-1011
Subjects: 15-51-56W-69
Focus: Founded 1927
Memo: A nonprofit, international organization representing over 2000 professional outdooor communicators who report on diverse interests in the outdoors.

Pacific NW Writers Conference
Director
17345 Sylvester Rd SW
Seattle WA 98166
206-242-9757
Subjects: 56W-61(WA)
Focus: NW writers

PEN American Center
568 Broadway
New York NY 10012-3225
212-334-1660
Subjects: 56W-75-83-95-99
Focus: Poetry, fiction writers

Philadelphia Writer Organization
President
PWO Newsletter
PO Box 42497
Philadelphia PA 19101-2497
215-387-4950
Subjects: 56W-61(PA)
Focus: Philadelphia area writers

Poetry Society of America
Director
15 Gramercy Park S
New York NY 10003-1705
212-254-9628
Subjects: 56W-95
Focus: Poetry writers

Poets & Writers
Elliot Figman, Director
Poets & Writers Magazine
72 Spring St
New York NY 10012-4019
212-226-3586; Fax: 212-226-3963
Subjects: 47-56W-75-90-95-99
Focus: Poetry, fiction writers

Romance Writers of America
Catherine Carpenter, Editor
Romance Writers Report
13700 Veterans Memorial Dr #315
Houston TX 77014-1023
713-440-6885
Subjects: 56W-81-85
Focus: Historical and romance novelists

Sisters in Crime
PO Box 10111
Blacksburg VA 24062-0111
913-842-1325
Subjects: 56W-84
Focus: For women mystery writers

Small Press Writers & Artists
SPWAO Newsletter
167 Fox Glen Ct
Ormand Beach Fl 32174-4870
904-672-3085
Subjects: 56W-90-95-99(small press)
Focus: Small press writers

Society for Technical Communication
Intercom Newsletter
901 N Stuart St
Arlington VA 22203-1821
703-522-4114; Fax: 703-522-2075
Subjects: 23-24-39-56W-67
Focus: Technical writers, editors, educators, documentation managers, freelancers, consultants, illustrators, audiovisual specialists, etc

Society of American Business Editors & Writers
Janine Latus-Musick, Exec Director
University of Missouri
Box 838
Columbia MO 65205-0838
314-882-7862
Subjects: 19
Focus: Members are financial and economic news writers and editors

Society of American Travel Writers
President
1155 Connecticut Ave NW
Washington DC 20036-4306
202-429-6639
Subjects: 56W-61-71
Focus: Travel writers

Society of Children Book Writers
Editor
SCBW Bulletin
2273 Vanowen St #106
West Hills CA 91307-2650
818-888-8760
Subjects: 21-56W-76
Focus: Chidlren's book writers
Memo: Society of Children Book Writers and Illustrators. SCWBI, 435 N Maple Dr, Beverly Hills CA 90210.

St Louis Writers Guild
Richard Fischer, Editor
PO Box 7245
St Louis MO 63177-7245
Subjects: 56W-61(MO)
Focus: St Louis area writers

Tennessee Writers Alliance
President
PO Box 120396
Nashville TN 37212-0396
Subjects: 56W-61(TN)
Focus: Tennessee writers

Texas Freelance Writers Association
Dana Cassell, Director
Cassell Communications
Main St PO Box A
North Stratford NH 03590-0167
603-922-8338; 800-351-9278;
   Fax: 603-922-8339
E-Mail: FJWX43B@prodigy.com
Subjects: 56W-61(TX)-99
Focus: Texas writers

Texas Writers Association
Director
Writer's News
25 Highland Park
Dallas TX 75205-2789
214-363-9979
Subjects: 56W-61(TX)
Focus: Texas writers

Text and Academic Authors Association Inc
Editor
The Academic Editor
PO Box 7146
Grand Forks ND 58202-7146
Subjects: 19E-31-39-41-55-56W-57-65-67-99
Focus: Textbook autors

Textbook Authors Association
Norma Hood, Director
The TAA Report
PO Box 535
Orange Springs FL 32182-0535
904-546-5419
Subjects: 19E-31-39-41-55-56W-57-65-67-99
Focus: Textbook authors

Washington Independent Writers
Director
Woodward Bldg
733 15th St NW #220
Washington DC 20005-2112
202-347-2005
Subjects: 56W-61(DC)
Focus: Independent writers

Western Writers of America
WWA Newsletter
416 Bedford Rd
El Paso TX 79922-1204
915-584-1001
Subjects: 56W-88
Focus: Western writers

Willamette Writers
Director
9045 SW Barbur Blvd #5-A
Portland OR 97219
503-452-1592
Subjects: 56W-61(OR)
Focus: Willamette area writers

Women in Communications
Editor
The Professional Communicator
3717 Columbia Pike #3
Arlington VA 22204-4255
703-930-5555; Fax:
Subjects: 19M-56W-73
Focus: Publicity/advertising/journalism

Writers Connection
1610 Blossom Hill Rd
San Juan CA 95124-6349
408-445-3600
Subjects: 56W-61(CA)

Writers Guild of America West
Editor
The Journal
8955 Beverly Blvd
West Hollywood CA 90048-2420
213-550-1000
Web: http://www.wga.org
Subjects: 56W
Focus: Writers

Booksellers Associations

American Booksellers Association
Director
828 S Broadway
Tarrytown NY 10591-6600
914-591-2665; 800-637-0037;
   Fax: 914-591-2720
Subjects: 99
Focus: Retail bookstores

American Wholesale Booksellers Association
John Michel
FEP Inc
5405 Boran Dr
Tampa FL 33610-2012
813-621-6085; Fax: 813-626-9782
Subjects: 99
Focus: Regional book wholesalers

Association of Booksellers for Children
Caron Chapman
Building Blocks Newsletter
4412 Chowen Ave S #303
Minneapolis MN 55410
612-926-6650
Subjects: 21-76
Focus: 800 children's booksellers

Christian Booksellers Association
Bill Anderson, President
Box 200 Venetucci Blvd
Colorado Springs CO 80901-0200
719-576-7880; Fax: 719-576-0795
Subjects: 63-99
Focus: Christian retail stores

Feminist Bookstore Network
Carol Seajay
PO Box 882554
San Francisco CA 94188
415-626-1556; Fax: 415-626-8970
Subjects: 56P-73
Focus: Feminist bookstores

Great Lakes Booksellers Association
Jim Dana, Exec Director
PO Box 901
Grand Haven MI 49417
616-847-2460; 800-745-2460;
    Fax: 616-842-0051
Subjects: 61(MI)-99
Focus: Booksellers in IIL, IN, WI, MI

Intermountain Booksellers Association
Elizabeth Burton, Director
The King's English
1511 South 15th E
Salt Lake City UT 84105
801-484-9100
Subjects: 61(West)-99
Focus: Booksellers in CO, ID, NV, UT

Mid-Atlantic Booksellers Association
Larry Robin, Exec Director
Robin's Bookstore
108 S 13th St
Philadelphia PA 19017
215-735-9600; Fax: 215-735-2670
Subjects: 61(Mid-Atlantic)-99
Focus: Mid-Atlantic booksellers

Midwest Booksellers Association
Phil Black, President
The Bookworm
120 Regency Pky
Omaha NE 68114-4301
402-392-2877
Subjects: 61(NE/IA/KS/SD/ND)
Focus: Booksellers in Ne, IA, KS, SD, ND

Mountains & Plains Booksellers
Lisa Knudson
805 LaPorte Ave
Fort Collins CO 80521-2520
907-484-5856; 800-752-0249;
    Fax: 907-484-5856
Subjects: 61(Rocky Mountains)
Focus: Booksellers in Rocky Mt area

National Association of College Stores
Brenda Kitts
500 E Lorain St
Oberlin OH 44074-1294
216-775-7777; Fax: 216-775-4769
E-Mail: bkitts@nacs.org
Subjects: 31-99
Focus: College stores

New England Booksellers Association
Rusty Drugan, Director
847 Massachusetts Ave
Cambridge MA 02139
617-576-3070; 800-466-8711;
    Fax: 617-576-3091
Subjects: 61(New England)-99
Focus: New England booksellers

New Orleans/Gulf South Booksellers
Mary Francis Price, President
Beaucoop Books
5414 Magazine St
New Orleans LA 70115-3150
504-525-1846
Subjects: 61
Focus: Booksellers in MS, AL, NO

New York/New Jersey Booksellers
Cyd Rosenberg, Director
397 Arbuckle Ave
Cedarhurst NY 11516-1303
516-295-1004
Subjects: 61(NY/NJ)
Focus: Booksellers in NY, NJ

Northern California Independent
Ginie Thorp, Exec Director
Booksellers Association
5643 Paradise Dr #12
Corte Madera CA 94925-1815
415-927-3937; Fax: 415-927-3937
E-Mail: nciba@aol.com
Subjects: 61(CA)-99
Focus: California booksellers

Oklahoma Independent Booksellers
Lee Bollinger, President
Bollinger Books
10505 N May Ave
East Troy WI 53120
405-755-0020; Fax: 405-755-5513
Subjects: 61(OK)
Focus: Oklahoma booksellers

Pacific Northwest Booksellers
Thom Chambliss, Director
1510 Mill St
Eugene OR 97501-4258
503-683-4363; Fax: 503-683-4363
Subjects: 61(Pacific NW)-99
Focus: Booksellers in Pacific NW

San Diego Booksellers Association
Joe Tabler, President
Gaskamp Books
5650 Riley St
San Diego CA 92110-2505
619-291-3253
Subjects: 61(CA)
Focus: Booksellers in San Diego area

South Central Booksellers Association
Richard Howorth, Director
Square Books
1126 Van Buren Ave
Oxford MS 38655-3998
601-236-2262
Subjects: 61(South)-99
Focus: Booksellers in AL, AR, MS, TN

Southeast Booksellers Association
Wanda Jewell, Exec Director
3806 Yale Ave
Columbia SC 29205-3550
803-252-7755; 800-331-9617;
    Fax: 803-252-8589
Subjects: 61(South)-99
Focus: Southeastern booksellers

Southern California Booksellers
Lisa Friedman, President
Dutton's Brentwood Cookstore
PO Box 4176
Culver City CA 90231-4176
310-476-6263; Fax: 310-471-0399
Subjects: 61(CA)
Focus: California booksellers

Southwestern Booksellers Association
Marvin Steakley, President
PO Box 8362
Dallas TX 75205-0362
214-692-2436
Subjects: 61(TX)
Focus: Booksellers in TX, AZ, NM

Upper Midwest Booksellers Association
Susan Walker Wood, Director
UMBA Newswire
4018 W 65th St
Minneapolis MN 55435-1727
612-926-4102; Fax: 612-922-0076
Subjects: 61(Midwest)-99
Focus: Midwest booksellers in IA, IL, MN, ND, SD, WI

Publishers Associations

AAUP - Association of American University Presses
Peter Grenquist, Exec Director
584 Broadway #410
New York NY 10012-3264
212-941-6610; Fax: 212-941-6618
Web:
    http://aaup.princeton.educentral/homepage.html
Subjects: 99(university presses)
Focus: University Presses

American Book Producers Association
Stephen Ettlinger, President
160 Fifth Ave #625
New York NY 10010
212-645-2368; 800-209-4575;
 Fax: 212-989-7542
E-Mail: 4164812@ mcimail.com
Subjects: 99
Focus: Book producers

American Horse Publications
3846 Carriage Dr
South Daytona FL 32119
940-760-7743; Fax: 940-760-7728
Subjects: 15(horse magazines)
Focus: Horses

American Medical Publishers Association
Jill Rudansky, Exec Director
14 Fort Hill Rd
Huntington NY 11743-2202
516-423-0075; Fax: 516-423-0075
Subjects: 39-56
Focus: Medical publishing field

American Telemarketing Association
444 N Larchmont Blvd #200
Los Angeles CA 90004
800-441-3335; Fax: 213-462-3372
Subjects: 19M
Focus: Telemarketing

Arizona Book Publishing Association
Michele Stroup, Editor
Southwest Signature
7339 E Acoma Dr #7
Scottsdale AZ 85260-3119
602-483-0192
Subjects: 56W-61(AZ)
Focus: Arizona publishers
Memo: Mailing office for membership:
 PO Box 40105, Phoenix, AZ 85067;
 602-274-6264.

Association of Alternative Newsweeklies
1001 Connecticut Ave NW #822
Washington DC 20036
202-822-1955; Fax: 202-822-0929
Subjects: 56M-75
Focus: Alternative newsweeklies

Association of American Publishers
Nicholas Veliotes, Exec Director
71 Fifth Ave
New York NY 10003-3004
212-689-8920
Subjects: 56
Focus: American publishers

Association of Business Publishers
Terilyn McGovern, Director
675 Third Ave #400
New York NY 10017-5704
212-661-6360
Subjects: 19(periodicals)
Focus: Business publications

Association of Canadian Publishers
Genny Urquhart, Director
Canadian Book Marketing Centre
2 Gloucester St #301
Toronto ON Canada M4Y 1L5
416-413-4930; Fax: 416-413-4920
Subjects: 56-61(CN)
Focus: 150 Canadian book publishers
Memo: Formerly Canadian Book
 Information Centre.

Association of College & University Presses
California State Long Beach
1250 N Bellflower Blvd
Long Beach CA 90840-0006
310-985-4501
Subjects: 56X
Focus: College and university presses

Association of Desktop Publishers
Director
4507-30th
San Diego CA 92104
619-563-9714; Fax: 619-280-3778
Subjects: 23-56
Focus: For desktop publishers

Association of Directory Publishers
Carol C Hill, Exec Director
PO Box 157
Wrentham MA 02093-0157
508-883-3688; Fax: 508-883-3717
Subjects: 56M
Focus: Link to telephone directory industry

Association of Jewish Book Publishers
Rabbi Elliot Stevens, Exec Director
192 Lexington Ave
New York NY 10016-6823
212-684-4990
Subjects: 63J
Focus: Jewish book publishers

Association of Shareware Professionals
545 Grover Rd
Muskegon MI 49442-9427
616-788-5131; Fax: 616-788-2765
CompuServe: 72050,1433
Subjects: 23C-99(shareware software)
Focus: Shareware

Association of Utah Publishers
Utah State Univ Press
Logan UT 84322-0001
801-797-1200
Subjects: 61(UT)
Focus: Utah publishers

Audio Publishers Association
Jan Nathan, Newsletter Editor
APA Newsletter
2401 Pacific Coast Hwy #102
Hermosa Beach CA 90254-5414
310-372-0546; Fax: 310-374-3342
E-mail: apaonline@aol.com
Web: http://www.audiopub.org/apa
Subjects: 99(audiotapes)
Focus: Audiotape publishers
Memo: To join the Internet discussion list,
 send an E-Mail message to:
 Listserv@hslc.org. Send this message:
 Subscribe audiobooks.

Bay Area Publisher Network
Patrick Fanning
New Harbinger Press
5674 Shattuck Ave
Oakland CA 94609
510-652-0215
Subjects: 61(CA)-99
Focus: San Francisco area

Book Publicists of S California
Irwin Zucker, Director
6464 Sunset Blvd #580
Los Angeles CA 90028-8007
213-461-3921; Fax: 213-461-0917
Subjects: 56-61(CA)
Focus: California book pubiicists

Book Publishers Northwest
Thom Votteler, Newsltr Editor
PO Box 45628
Seattle WA 98145-0628
206-633-3774; Fax: 206-633-3815
E-Mail: votteler@pminc.com
Subjects: 56-61(NW US)
Focus: Northwest book publishers
Memo: Main address: PO Box 99642,
 Seattle, WA 98199.

Book Publishers of Texas
Dawn Albright, Editor
Publishers Digest Newsletter
4330 Bull Creek Rd #118
Austin TX 78731-5906
512-450-0340
Subjects: 56-61(TX)
Focus: Texas book publishers

Bookbinders' Guild of New York
181 Sargeant Ave
Clifton NJ 07013
212-490-8700
Subjects: 56P-56X
Focus: For production people/printers
Memo: For more info, contact Paul
 Stanley, Courier Companies, 60 East
 42nd Street #864, New York, NY
 10165-0864; phone above.

Bookbuilders of Boston
JoAnn D'Espinosa
Pages Newsletter Editor
27 Wellington Dr
Westwood MA 02090-2918
617-461-0298
Subjects: 56-61(MA)
Focus: New England publishers and
 printers

Bookbuilders of Washington
Robert Elwood, Editor
Graphic Composition Inc
47 Bushwood Rd
Bushwood MD 20618-9707
301-843-8277
Subjects: 56-61(DC)
Focus: DC publishers and printers
Memo: Association address: PO Box
 23805, Washington, DC 20026. Patricia
 Upchurch, President (202-287-3738;
 ext 378).

Bookbuilders West
Brooks Vitalone
PO Box 7046
San Francisco CA 94120-9727
510-226-1137
Subjects: 56-61(CA)-99
Focus: 150 companies

Calendar Marketing Association
Carol Peske, Editor
Calendar News Newsletter
621 E Park Ave
Libertyville IL 60048
708-816-8660; 800-828-8225;
    Fax: 708-816-8662
E-mail: calanders@aol.com
Web:
    http://www.acpinc.com/calendars.html.
Subjects: 99
Focus: Calendars

Catholic Press Association
Owen McGovern, Director
CPA Newsletter
3555 Veterans Memorial Hwy #0
Ronkonkoma NY 11779
516-471-4730
Subjects: 63(Catholic)
Focus: Catholic Newspapers, magazines

CD-I Association of North America
Laura Foti Cohen, Director
Inside CD-I Newsletter
11111 Santa Monica Blvd #700
Los Angeles CA 90025
310-444-6619; Fax: 310-479-5937
Subjects: 23C-99
Focus: CD-a

Chicago Women in Publishing
Jennifer Healy
325 W Huron St #403
Chicago IL 60610-3617
312-645-0083
Subjects: 56P-61(IL)-73
Focus: Chicago area women in publishing

Children's Book Council
David Riederman, Program Director
568 Broadway #404
New York NY 10012-5497
212-966-1990; 800-666-7608;
    Fax: 212-966-2073
Web: http://www.cbcbooks.org
Subjects: 21-31-56-76-79
Focus: Children's books

Christian Science Publishing Society
Annetta Douglass, Exec Director
1 Norway St
Boston MA 02115-3195
617-450-2000
Subjects: 63
Focus: Research library/broadcasts

CLMP (Council of Literary Magazines and Presses)
Jim Sitter, Director
CLM Pages
154 Christopher St #3C
New York NY 10014-2839
212-741-9110; Fax: 212-741-9112
Subjects: 47-56P-75-83-90-95
Focus: Literary publishers & magazines

Colorado Independent Publishers
Evelyn Kaye, President
CIPA Newsline
3031 5th St
Boulder CO 80304-2501
303-449-8474; Fax: 303-449-7525
Subjects: 56P-61(CO)
Focus: Colorado publishers

Comics Magazine Association of America
Peter Rush, Director
355 Lexington Ave 17th Fl
New York NY 10017
212-661-4261; Fax: 212-370-9047
Subjects: 33C
Focus: Comic magazines

Consortium of Northern Publishers
CNP
PO Box 60529
Fairbanks AK 99706
Subjects: 56P
Focus: Alaskan publishers

Council for Periodical Distributors Associations
60 East 42nd St #2134
New York NY 10165
212-818-0234
Subjects: 56
Focus: Magazine distributors, methods, PR, and improvements

Directory Publishers Alliance
Roxanne Christensen
Morgan Rand Publishing Co
2200 Sansom St
Philadelphia PA 19103
215-557-6794; 800-677-3839;
    Fax: 215-557-8414
Subjects: 59-99
Focus: Director publishers

Directory Publishers Forum
150 Fifth Ave #302
New York NY 10011
212-838-8640
Subjects: 19-59-99
Focus: Self-help and management of info services

Educational Paperback Association
Marilyn Abel, Exec Secretary
EPA Newsnetwork
PO Box 1399
East Hampton NY 11937-0709
212-879-6850
Subjects: 21-31E-76
Focus: Wholesellers selling to schools; includes distributors of paperback books to school, college, and library markets

Educational Press Association
Donald Stoll, Exec Director
Rowan College of New Jersey
201 Mullica Hill Rd
Glassboro NJ 08028-1700
609-863-7349; Fax: 609-863-5012
Subjects: 31-56-99
Focus: Educational magazines, books, etc

Electronic Media Marketing Association
New York NY
212-408-9100; Fax:
Subjects: 19M-23-23E-33T
Focus: Electronic marketing

Evangelical Christian Publishers
Doug Ross, Director
Footprints Newsletter
1969 E Broadway Rd #2
Tempe AZ 85282-1731
602-966-3998; Fax: 602-966-1944
Subjects: 56-63
Focus: Christian publishers

Florida Magazine Association
PO Box 10523
Tallahassee FL 32302
904-222-1907
Subjects: 56M-61
Focus: Florida magazine publishers

Florida Publishers Association
Christopher Carroll, Editor
Sell More Books! Newsletter
PO Box 20603
Bradenton FL 34204-0603
941-739-4800; Fax: 941-351-2533
E-Mail: naip@aol.com
Subjects: 56-61(FL)
Focus: Florida publishers

Game Inventors of America
Director
World Trade Ctr
Box 58711
Dallas TX 75258
214-331-4587; Fax: 214-330-9097
Subjects: 33-69(games)
Focus: Games

Greeting Card Association
Director
1200 E jSt NW
Washington DC 20005-3814
202-393-1778; Fax: 202-393-0336
Subjects: 99
Focus: Greeting card publishers

Houston Publishers & Author Association
Joe Vitale
303 Mill Stream Ct (77060)
PO Box 300792
Houston TX 77230-0792
713-999-1110; Fax: 713-999-1313
E-Mail: mrfire@blkbox.com
Subjects: 56P-61(TX)-99
Focus: Houston area publishers/authors

Independent Travel Publishers
Anna Clifford, Director
96 Ingham Hill Rd
Essex CT 06426
203-767-1799
Subjects: 61-71
Focus: Travel publishers
Memo: Contact her at: Globe Pequot Press (800-243-0495, Ext 322).

Industrial Directory Association
Grand Central Sta
PO Box 1515
New York NY 10163
212-972-3091
Subjects: 19-56-59-99
Focus: Industry

Information Industry Association
Paul Zurkowski, President
Information Times
555 New Jersey Ave NW #800
Washington DC 20001-2082
202-639-8262; Fax: 202-638-4403
Subjects: 19-59-99
Focus: Reference books and serials

Interactive Multimedia Association
Philip Dodds, Managing Director
Interactive Industry News
3 Church Cir #800
Annapolis MD 21401-1933
410-626-1380; Fax: 410-263-0590
Subjects: 23C-56M
Focus: Multimedia producers
Memo: Originally established in 1988 as the Interactive Video Industry Association.

International Interactive Communications Society
Editor-Reporter
PO Box 1862
Lake Oswego OR 97035
503-649-2065; Fax: 503-649-2309
Subjects: 23C-56M
Focus: Multimedia producers
Memo: The largest membership organization serving interactive developers, communicators, and artists.

International Map Trade Association
Linda Mickle, Editor
The Map Report
105 E Court St, PO Box 1789
Kankakee IL 60901
815-939-4627; Fax: 815-933-8320
E-mail: maptrade@aol.com
Web:http://www.maptrade.org/maptrade
Subjects: 71
Focus: Maps

International Communications Industries Association
Director
3150 Spring St
Fairfax VA 22031-2399
703-273-7200; Fax: 703-278-8082
Subjects: 23C-56M
Focus: Industry

International Publishing Management Association
Larry E Aaron, Exec Director
1205 W College St
Liberty MO 64068-1035
816-781-1111; Fax: 816-781-2790
Subjects: 56P-56X
Focus: International publishing

Jewish Book Council of The Jewish Community Center
Leonard Gold, President
15 E 26th St
New York NY 10010-1505
212-532-4949
Subjects: 63(Jewish)-99
Focus: Jewish bookstores, publishers, and centers

Licensing Industry Merchandisers Association
Director
350 Fifth Ave #6210
New York NY 10118
212-244-1944
Subjects: 19M(licensing)
Focus: Licensing merchandisers

Magazine Publishers of America
Donald Kummerfeld, President
919 Third Ave 22nd Fl
New York NY 10022-3902
212-872-3700; Fax: 212-888-4217
Subjects: 56M
Focus: Magazine publishers

Maine Publisher/Writer Alliance
Harriet Mosher, Director
Maine in Print
12 Pleasant St
Brunswick ME 04011-2201
207-729-6333
Subjects: 56-61(ME)

Marin Small Publishers Association
SPEX--Small Publishers Exchange
PO Box E
Corte Madera CA 94975
415-927-0523; Fax:
Subjects: 56-61(Bay area)
Focus: Bat area publishers

Mid-America Publishers Association
Deborah Eisloeffel, Editor
MAPA Newsletter
726 S 30th St
Lincoln NE 68510-1428
402-435-0976; Fax: 402-421-9093
Subjects: 56P-61(Midwest)
Focus: Midwest book publishers
Memo: Jerry Kromberg, Director, MAPA, 7301 Holdrege St, PO Box 30242, Lincoln, NE 68503-0242; 402-421-9666.
E-mail: 74352.472@compuserv.com.

MidAtlantic Publishers Association
Mary Hagy, President
The Dracon Bldg
318 Fitzwater St
Philadelphia PA 19147-3204
215-625-3740; Fax: 215-829-0064
Subjects: 56P-61
Focus: NJ, PA, DE, MD publishers

Midwest Independent Publishers
Pat Bell, Exec Editor
MIPA Newsletter
9561 Woodridge Cir
Eden Prairie MN 55347-2744
612-941-5053; Fax: 612-490-1182
Subjects: 56-61
Focus: Midwest self-publishers

Minnesota Publishers Roundtable
John Erwin Jr, President
59 Seymour Ave SE
Minneapolis MN 55414
612-378-9076 (Home phone/address)
Subjects: 56-61(MN)
Focus: Minnesota publishers

Multicultural Publishing and Education Council
Rennie Mau, President
2280 Grass Valley Hwy #181
Auburn CA 95603
916-888-0690; Fax: 916-888-0690
E-Mail: mpec@aol.com
Web:
   http://www.quiknet.com/mbt/mpec/mpec.html
Subjects: 13-49-65-73-78-80
Focus: Publishers of multicultural books

Multimedia Development Group
2601 Mariposa St
San Francisco CA 94110
415-553-2300; Fax: 415-553-2403
Subjects: 23C-56M
Focus: Multimedia producers
Memo: Members include Apple, IBM, AT&T, Adobe, Colossal Pictures, Hewlett-Packard, Intel, Kaleida, KQED, Microsoft, Macromedia, Tandem, and others.

National Association of Desktop Publishers
Susan Sigel, Membership Director
462 Old Boston Rd #8
Topsfield MA 01983
508-887-7900; 800-874-4113;
   Fax: 508-887-6117
Subjects: 23-56
Focus: Desktop publishing

National Association of Hispanic Publications
Tina Duran, Exec Director
301 S Frio St #102
San Antonio FL 78207
512-270-4590; Fax: 512-270-4591
Subjects: 45(Spanish)-49-56-78-80
Focus: Promotes Hispanic print media

National Association of Independent Publishers
Betty Lampe, Exec Director
PO Box 430
Highland City FL 33846-0430
813-648-4420; Fax: 813-648-4420
Subjects: 56P
Focus: For publishers starting out

National Association of Self-Published Food Writers
Joanna Lund, Healthy Exchanges
PO Box 124
DeWitt IA 52742-0124
319-659-8234
Subjects: 27-56P
Focus: Self-published food writers

National Association of Women's Yellow Pages
Ida Bialack, President
7358 N Lincoln Ave
Chicago IL 60646
708-679-7800; Fax: 708-679-7845
Subjects: 19-73-99
Focus: Women's yellow pages

National Association of Black Book Publishers
Gina Weldon, Exec Director
PO Box 22080
Baltimore MD 21203-4080
410-358-0980; Fax: 410-358-0987
Subjects: 49B-56P-99
Focus: Black book publishers

National Infomercial Marketing
Association Director
1201 New York Ave NW #1000
Washington DC 20005-3917
202-962-8342; 800-962-9796;
    Fax: 202-962-8300
Subjects: 19M-33T
Focus: Infomercials

National Mail Order Association
John Schulte, Director
Mail Order Digest
2807 Polk St
Minneapolis MN 55418-2954
612-788-1673; Fax: 612-788-1147
Web: http://www.nmoa.org
Subjects: 19M
Focus: Mail order

Native American Publishers Group
Gaye Brown, Director of Publ
National Museum of American Indian
470 L'Enfant Plz SW #7102
Washington DC 20560-0001
202-357-1300
Subjects: 49A
Focus: Native Americans

New Age Publishing/Retailing Alliance
Marilyn McGuire, Exec Director
PO Box 9
Eastsound WA 98245
206-376-2702; Fax: 206-376-2704
Subjects: 56P
Focus: New Age

New Hampshire Writers/Publishers
Cheryl Kimball, Editor
Ex Libris Newsletter
PO Box 150
Portsmouth NH 03802-0150
603-430-9475
Subjects: 56-61(New England)
Focus: Bimonthly newsletter

NIMA International
Association Director
1201 New York Ave NW #1000
Washington DC 20005-3917
202-962-8342; 800-962-9796
    Fax: 202-962-0603
Subjects: 19M-33T(infomercials)
Focus: Information marketing
Memo: Formerly: National Informational Marketing Association.

Northeastern Ohio Publishers Grp
Dr Peter Gail, Editor
The Western Reserve Publisher
2000 Lee Rd #23
Cleveland OH 44118-2559
216-932-2145; Fax: 216-491-0251
Subjects: 56P-61(OH)
Focus: Northern Ohio publishers
Memo: Formerly Cleveland Publishers Group.

Northern California Book Publicists Association
Laura Simonds, NCBPA News Ed
Jossey-Bass Inc
350 Sansome St
San Francisco CA 94104
415-433-1740; Fax: 415-433-0499
Subjects: 61(West)-99
Focus: Book publicity

Northwest Association of Book Publishers
Sharon Carrigan, Editor
Publishers' Focus Newsletter
19500 Hidden Springs Rd #25
West Linn OR 97068
503-636-7580
Subjects: 56-61(NW US)
Focus: Northwest book publishers

Optical Publishing Association
Richard Bowers, Exec Director
PO Box 21268
Columbus OH 43221
614-442-8805; Fax: 614-442-8815
Subjects: 23C-56P CD-ROMs
Focus: Optical & digital publishing

Orange County Publishers Network
William Gordon, President
North Ridge Books
818 N Via Alhambra
Laguna Hills CA 92653-4874
714-855-0640; Fax: 714-855-4860
Subjects: 56P-61(CA)
Focus: Orange County Publishers

Periodical & Book Association of America
Michael Morse, Director
120 E 34th St #7-K
New York NY 10016
212-689-4952; Fax: 212-545-8328
Subjects: 56M-56P-99
Focus: Periodical publishing
Memo: Trade show in Mid-June.

Philadelphia Publishers Group
Amy Blake, Editor
Bulletin Board Newsletter
PO Box 42681
Philadelphia PA 19101-2681
215-732-1863
Subjects: 56-61(PA)
Focus: Philadelphia area publishers

Publishers Association of South
Molly Burns, Director
700 S 28th St
Birmingham AL 35233-3417
205-322-4579; Fax: 205-326-1012
Subjects: 56P-61(South)
Focus: Southern publishers

Publishers Marketing Association
Jan Nathan, Exec Director
2401 Pacific Coast Hwy #102
Hermosa Beach CA 90254-2734
213-372-2732
Subjects: 19M-56
Focus: Assists in mktg & sale of books for publishers

Publishers' Publicity Association
Helen Atwan, Secy
Farrar Straus and Giroux
19 Union Square W
New York NY 10003
212-206-5323
Subjects: 56-99
Focus: Publisher's

Publishing Triangle
Eric Brandt, Editor
Thunder Mouth's Press
93 Greene St #2A
New York NY 10012-3856
212-226-0277
Subjects: 37(gay/lesbian)
Focus: Writers, booksellers, publishers of gay/lesbian material
Memo: Promotional kits available from: Michele Karlsberg, 47 Dongan Hills Ave, 1st Floor, Staten Island NY 10306.

Recovery Register Resource
Robert Morris
407 East 100th St
Bloomington MN 55420
612-884-2294
Subjects: 39R(bookstores & publishers)
Focus: Informal network for recovery

Religious Publishing Group
Charles Roth, Secy
Roth Advertising
333 Glen Head Rd
Old Brookville NY 11545
516-671-9292; Fax: 516-759-4227
Subjects: 56-63
Focus: Religious publishers

Rocky Mountain Book Publishers
Diane Borneman, Editor
The End St
2276 Pebble Beach Court
Evergreen CO 80439
303-670-0401; Fax: 303-670-0401
Subjects: 56-61(Rocky Mtns)
Focus: Rocky Mountain area book publishers
Memo: Alan Bernhard, Director, PO Box 19013, Boulder CO 80380; 303-499-9540; Fax: 303-499-9584.

San Diego Publishers Alliance
Claire Condra Arias
c/o Ellipsys Intl Pubns
4679 Vista St
San Diego CA 92116
619-280-8711; Fax: 619-280-8713
E-Mail: sdpa@ellipsys.com
Web: http://www.ellipsys.com
Subjects: 56-61(CA)
Focus: San Diego area publishers

Small Publishers Association of North America
Marilyn & Tom Ross, Directors
425 Cedar St
PO Box 1306
Buena Vista CO 81211-1306
719-395-4790; 800-331-8355;
   Fax: 719-395-8374
Subjects: 56P
Focus: Small publishers

Society for Scholarly Publishing
Editor
Scholarly Publishing Today
10200 West 44th Ave #304
Wheat Ridge CO 80033
303-422-3914; Fax: 303-422-8894
Subjects: 31-41-49-55-56P-57-65-99
E-Mail: Internet 5686814@mcimail.com
Focus: Scholarly books/magazines

Society of National Association Publications
Allison Parker, Exec Director
1735 N Lynn St #950
Arlington VA 22209
703-524-2000; Fax: 202-524-2303
Subjects: 56
Focus: Association publications

Software Publishers Association
Ken Wasch, Exec Director
1730 M St NW #700
Washington DC 20036
202-452-1600; Fax: 202-223-8756
Subjects: 23(software)
Focus: Principal trade assn of PC industry

Three Rivers Publishers Group
Dennis V Damp, Editor
3 Rivers Publishers Group News
401 Amherst Ave
Moon Township PA 15108
412-262-5578
Subjects: 56P-61(PA)
Focus: Pennsylvania publishers

Vermont Publishers Association
David Robinson, Newsletter Ed
Paradigm Press
278 College St
Burlington VT 05401
802-482-2988; Fax: 802-482-3125
Subjects: 56-61(VT)-99
Focus: Vermont publishers
Memo: VPA, c/o Upper Access, PO Box 457, Hinesburg, VT 05461; 802-482-2988; FAX: 802-482-3125.

Washington Directory Association
Dianne Johansson-Adams
Directory Publishing Resources
PO Box 19107 George Mason Sta
Alexandria VA 22320
703-329-8206; Fax: 703-960-9618
Subjects: 56P-59-61-99
Focus: Directory publishing

Western Publications Association
Mark Hanson, Exec Director
5000 Van Nuys Blvd #300
Sherman Oaks CA 91403
818-995-7338
Subjects: 56-61(West)
Focus: Magazine publishers

Wisconsin Authors & Publishers Alliance
Helen Ouimette, President
WAPA and Program Chairman
1209 S 36th St
Manitowoc WI 54220
414-682-4717
Subjects: 56-61(WI)
Focus: Wisconsin publishers

Wisconsin Publishers Production Club
Marty Ochs
PO Box 206
North Lake WI 53064
608-838-9899
Subjects: 56-61(WI)
Focus: Wisconsin publishers

Windows Prepublishing Association
Robb Kerr, President
1804 Hayes St
Nashville TN 37203
615-320-9473
Subjects: 23C-56P
Focus: Prepublishing

Women's National Book Association
Sandra Paul, Director
The Bookwoman
160 Fifth Ave #604
New York NY 10010
212-675-7805; Fax: 212-989-7542
E-Mail: 4164812@mcimail.com
Web: http://bookbuzz.com/wnba.htm
Subjects: 56W-73-99
Focus: Women book publishers

Yellow Pages Publishers Association
Janice Logan, President/CEO
340 E Big Beaver Rd
Troy NY 48083
313-680-8880; Fax: 313-680-1251
Subjects: 56M
Focus: Yellow pages publishing

Other Associations of Interest

American Association of School Librarians
American Library Association
50 E Huron St
Chicago IL 60611-2729
312-944-6780; Fax: 312-440-9374
Subjects: 21-31-76-79
Focus: School librarians

American Business Press
Willam Giacalone, VP/Mktg
675 3rd Ave #400
New York NY 10017-5704
212-661-6360
Subjects: 19-56
Focus: Business

American Consultants League
1290 N Palm Ave #112
Sarasota FL 34236-5604
813-952-9290; Fax: 813-379-6024
Subjects: 99
Focus: Consultants

American Library Association
Information Center
50 E Huron St
Chicago IL 60611-2795
312-944-6780; 800-545-2433;
   Fax: 312-440-9374
Subjects: 59-99
Focus: Librarians

American Seminar Leaders Association
Lynne Lindahl, Mg Editor
Up Front Newsletter
899 Blvd East
Weehawken NJ 07087
800-735-0511
Subjects: 99
Focus: Seminar leaders
Memo: Harriet Diamond, ASLA, 206 Sacramento St #205, Nevada City, CA 95959; 916-265-4535; Fax: 916-265-2338.

American Society of Indexers
ASI Newsletter
PO Box 386
Port Arkansas TX 78373-0386
512-749-4052
Subjects: 56(indexers)
Focus: Register of Indexers

Arcnet Trade Association
C Andrew Larsen, Exec Director
3365 N Arlington Hgts Rd
Arlington Heights IL 60004-7700
312-255-3003
Subjects: 56
Focus: Operates speakers bureaus/awards

Association of American Collegiate Literary Society
Andrew Smith, Governor
Philomathean Society
Box G College Hall
Philadelphia PA 19104
215-898-8907
Subjects: 99
Focus: Works with literary societies in the US to promote the creation of new societies, existing societies and reviving old societies

Association of Radio Talk Show Hosts
Carol Nashe, Exec Director
134 St Botolph St
Boston MA 02115-4819
617-956-3320; Fax: 617-956-2703
Subjects: 33T
Focus: Radio talk show hosts

Association of Professional Writing Consultants
3924 S Troost Ave
Tulsa OK 74105-3329
918-743-4793
Subjects: 45W-56W
Focus: Professional writing

Beatrice M Murphy Foundation
Beatrice M Murphy, Exc Director
2737 Devonshire Pl NW Apt 222
Washington DC 20008-3461
202-387-6053
Subjects: 99
Focus: Encourages reading, appreciation, and further production of black literature.

Before Columbus Foundation
Gundars Strads, Exec Director
660 13th St #203
Oakland CA 94612
415-268-9775
Subjects: 99
Focus: Participants are individuals interested in promoting contemporary American multicultural literature.

Church & Synagogue Library Association
Lorraine Burson, Director
Church & Synagogue Libraries
PO Box 19357
Portland OR 97280
503-244-6919
Subjects: 59-63
Focus: Religious libraries

College Media Advisors
MJ-300
University of Memphis
Memphis TN 38152-0001
901-678-2403; Fax: 901-678-4798
Subjects: 99
Focus: For persons who supervise/advise college media run by students

Copyright Society of the USA
Nadine Baker, Secy
435 W 116th St
New York NY 10027-7201
212-854-7696
Subjects: 14-33M-56
Focus: Copyright laws & rights

Council of Biology Editors
Editor, CBE Views
11 S LaSalle St
Chicago IL 60601-1203
312 201-0101
Subjects: 39M-51(biology)-56W
Focus: Biology

Editorial Freelancers Association
Laurie Lewis, President
71 W 23rd St
New York NY 10010-4102
212-929-5400
Subjects: 56(editors/proofreaders/etc)
Focus: Freelance editorial services for the communications and publishing industries.

Freelance Editorial Association
Carol Noble, President
PO Box 380835
Cambridge MA 02238-0835
617-643-8626
Subjects: 56(editors/indexers/writers)
Focus: Members are self-employed contractors or consultants with expertise in editorial functions such as copyediting, researching, indexing and proofreading, writing, illustrating, editing, project managing, desktop publishing, and translating.

International Platform Association
Director
PO Box 250
Winnetka IL 60093-0250
708-446-4321
Subjects: 56
Focus: Speaker's association

Investigative Reporters & Editor
Steve Weinberg, President
100 Neff Hall
Columbia MO 65211-0001
314-882-2042
Subjects: 99
Focus: Investigative reporting

Leap First
Lynn Rosen
123 W 92nd St #3
New York NY 10025-7577
212-864-3065; Fax: 212-866-0068
Subjects: 99
Focus: Social issues/fic/hist/science

Medical Library Association
Carla Funk, Exec Director
6 N Michigan Ave #300
Chicago IL 60602-4895
312-419-9094; Fax: 312-419-8950
Subjects: 39-59
Focus: Medical

NAEIR (National Association for Exchange of Industrial Resources)
560 McClure St
PO Box 8076
Galesburg IL 61401-4286
309-343-0704; Fax: 309-343-0862
Subjects: 19
Focus: Industry

National Book Critics Circle
Alida Becker, Sec
NBCC Journal
756 S 10th St
Philadelphia PA 19147-2742
215-925-8406
Subjects: 56W-56M-99
Focus: Book reviewers

National Newspaper Association
David Simonson, Exec VP
1525 Wilson Blvd #550
Arlington VA 22209-2411
202-466-7200; 800-829-4662; Fax: 202-331-1403
Subjects: 99
Focus: Newspapers

The National Rural Telecom Association
John O'Neal, Gen Counsel
1455 Pennsylvania Ave NW
Washington DC 20004-1008
202-628-0210
Subjects: 99
Focus: Rural telecommunications

National Speakers Association
Jihane Khawam, Editor
Speakout Newsletter
1500 S Priest Dr
Tempe AZ 85281-6203
602-968-2552; Fax: 602-968-0911
Subjects: 56(speaking)
Focus: Speaker's association

New Age World Services & Books
Victoria E Vandertuin, Owner
62091 Valley View Cir
Joshua Tree CA 92252-2548
619-366-2833
Subjects: 53-54M-57
Focus: New Age

Overseas Club of America
Sonya K Fry, Mgr
310 Maidson Ave Rm 2116
New York NY 10017-6009
212-983-4655; Fax: 212-983-4692
Subjects: 99
Focus: A media journalist organization

Professional and Technical Consultants Association
PO Box 4143
Mountain View CA 94040-4143
800-286-8703; Fax: 415-967-0995
Subjects: 23-24-67
Focus: Consultanting

Professional Editors Network of Minnesota
PEN Freelance Directory
PO Box 19265
Minneapolis MN 55149-0265
612-647-1210;
Subjects: 56W
Focus: Professional editors

Special Libraries Association
1700 18th St NW
Washington DC 20009-2514
202-234-4700
Subjects: 19-39-65-67-99
Focus: Special libraries

Toastmasters International
Director
PO Box 9052
Mission Viejo CA 92690-9052
714-858-8255; Fax: 714-858-1207
Subjects: 56W-99
Focus: Speaker's association

Publishing Institutes, Courses, & Conferences

Here are a few of the publishing institutes and courses available for those who want to enter publishing. Note that most of the publishing associations also offer monthly or annual seminars or conferences.

Book Publishing Institute
Graduate Publisher Newsletter
Howard Univ Press
PO Box 75374
Washington DC 20013-0374
202-686-6498
Subjects: 56W-56P
Focus: Summer publishing institute

Cape Cod Writers' Conference
Box 111
West Hyannisport MA 02672-0111
617-775-4811
Subjects: 56(writing)
Focus: Annual conference in August

Center for the Book
Director
Library of Congress room 605
101 Independence Ave SE
Washington DC 20541-4920
202-707-5221
Subjects: 56
Focus: Founded 1977

Certificate Program inPublishing
Richard Caramella, Coordinator
UC Berkeley Extension
2223 Fulton St
Berkeley CA 94720-1450
510-642-0462
Subjects: 56
Focus: Publishing

Chicago Book Clinic
Cindy Clark
11 S LaSalle St #1400
Chicago IL 60603-1211
312-553-2200
Subjects: 56P-61(IL)
Focus: Publishing

Children's Literature Assn
Norma Bagnall
22 Harvest Lane
Battle Creek MI 49015-7938
616-965-8180
Subjects: 21
Focus: Offers serious scholarship and research in the area of children's literature, provides and outlet for scholarship through conventions and publications

Colorado Center for the Book
Program Mgr
Colorado State Library
201 E Colfax Ave
Denver CO 80203-1704
303-866-6900
Subjects: 56
Focus: Publishing

Council on National Literatures
Annw Paolucci, President
PO Box 81
Flushing NY 11357-0081
212-767-8380
Subjects: 56-99
Focus: Founded 1974
Provides a forum for scholars concerned with comparative study of literature.

Cowles Business Media Inc
6 River Pl
Stamford CT 06907-1426
203-358-9900
Subjects: 56-99
Focus: Various conferences

Denver Publishing Institute
Suzanne Pfaff, Co-Dir
Univ of Denver
2075 S University Blvd
Denver CO 80210-4300
303-871-2711
Subjects: 56-99
Focus: Publishing

Design for Desktop Publishing
Lou Williams Seminars
180 N Stetson Ave #1500
Chicago IL 60601-6710
800-837-7123; Fax: 312-565-1770
Subjects: 56
Focus: Desktop design

Huenefeld Seminars
41 North Rd #201
Bedford MA 01730-1037
800-333-7716; Fax: 617-275-1713
Subjects: 56M-56P
Focus: 3 publishing seminars

Krause Library
John M Cinalli, Research Coord
American Booksellers Assn
828 S Broadway
Tarrytown NY 10591-6603
914-591-2665; 800-637-0037;
    Fax: 914-591-2720
Subjects: 56P-56W
Focus: Publishing

Magazine Career Institute
Office of Cabot Award
Graduate School of Journalism
Columbia University
New York NY 10027
212-854-4150
Subjects: 56(magazines)
Focus: Magazine publishing

Minnesota Center for Book Arts
24 N 3rd St
Minneapolis MN 55401-2164
612-338-3634
Subjects: 56(fine printing)
Focus: Papermaking/bookbinding/printing

New Communications Media
South Wind Publishing
8340 Mission Rd #106
Shawnee Mission KS 66206-1362
800-545-2647; Fax: 913-642-6611
Subjects: 23-56
Focus: Publishing

Newsletters
The Newsletter Factory
1000 Parkwood Cir SE #823
Atlanta GA 30339-2139
404-955-2002
Subjects: 56
Focus: Newsletter publishing

NYU Center for Publishing
New York University
48 Cooper Square Rm 108
New York NY 10003-9903
212-998-7100
Subjects: 56
Focus: Summer institutes/continuing ed

Pace Graduate Publishing Program
Dennis Hurley, Pace Univ
The Information Ctr
1 Pace Plz
New York NY 10038-1502
212-488-1531
Subjects: 56(books/magazines/video)
Focus: Master's graduate program, Information sessions also

Penton Publishing
Tina Vernon
Penton Education
1100 Superior Ave
Cleveland OH 44114-2543
216-696-7000; 800-321-7003;
    Fax: 216-696-4369
Subjects: 99
Focus: Publishing

Publishing Program
Ctr for Continuing Studies
Univ of Chicago
5835 S Kimbark Ave
Chicago IL 60637-1608
312-702-0539; Fax: 312-702-6814
Subjects: 99
Focus: Publishing

PubTech
Chicago Book Clinic
11 S LaSalle #1400
Chicago IL 60603-1211
312-553-2200; Fax: 312-201-0214
Subjects: 56
Focus: Publishing

Radcliffe Publishing Procedures
Lindy Hess
Radcliffe College
77 Brattle St
Cambridge MA 02138-3442
617-495-8678
Subjects: 56(magazines/books)
Focus: 6 week summer courses, Institute teaching book & magazine publishing & job placement

Small Press Center
Mary Bertschmann, Editor
Small Press Center News
20 W 44th St
New York NY 10036-6604
212-764-7021; Fax: 212-354-5365
Subjects: 56-83-99
Focus: Small press bibliography

Stanford Professional Publishing
Bill Muires, Dir
Bowman Alumni House
Stanford Univ
Stanford CA 94305-4005
415-725-1083
Subjects: 56
Focus: Summer institute

Vassar College Institute of
Publishing and Writing
Barbara Lucas, Dir
PO Box 300
Poughkeepsie NY 12602-0300
914-437-7000
Subjects: 56
Focus: Annual summer conference

Miscellaneous Resources

Many times when looking over some of the mail we receive we find something that might be interest to the people who use this book.

Ad/Advertising

Absolutely Advertising
PO Box 46
Eau Claire WI 54702-0046
800-358-2257
Service: Ad specialties catalog

AdWare
Chris Davis
Marketing
843 N Vista St
Los Angeles CA 90046
213-651-0191; Fax: 213-655-3438
Service: Advertising software

Eagle Creek X-Pressions
Calendar Sales
PO Box 53-2183
Indianapolis IN 46253-2183
317-297-7377
Service: Print ad specialties

Art/Design

Michael Barfield
407 Lilac Dr
St Charles MO 63303
314-947-6469
Service: Artwork: designs bookcovers and does some inside illustration

Jennifer Berman
PO Box 6614
Evanston IL 60204-6614
312-761-0104; Fax: 312-761-9047
Service: Artwork

Dover Pictorial Archive Catalog
Dover Publications Inc
11 East 2nd St
Mineola NY 11501
Service: Illustrations & designs for permission-free use

Gift Service Inc
3 Office Park Cir #310
Birmingham AL 35223
800-562-4448
Service: Trademark: "EdibleAdvertising"

Foster & Foster
104 S 2nd St
Fairfield IA 52556
515-472-3952; Fax: 515-472-3146
Service: Designer for books, etc

Idea Art
PO Box 291505
Nashville TN 37229-1505
800-433-2278; Fax: 800-435-2278
Service: Designs for flyers, brochures, newsletters, mailers, etc

Banking

Berkery Noyes & Co
Joseph W Berkery, Pres
50 Broad St
New York NY 10004
212-668-3022; Fax: 212-363-7077
Service: Investment bankers to the publishing, media, and comm industries

Barcode

Applied Image Inc
Donna Maronza
1653 E Main St
Rochester NY 14609
800-288-5989; Fax: 716-288-5989
Service: Bar-code needs

Bar Code Graphics Inc
875 N Michigan Ave #2640
Chicago IL 60611
312-664-0700; Fax: 312-664-4939
800-662-0701
Service: Bar code products

Film Masters Inc
Alan Curtis, Editor
2301 Hamilton Ave
Cleveland OH 44114
216-621-3456; Fax: 216-621-7908
800-621-2872
Service: Bar-coding in business

Symbology Inc
1039 10th Ave SE
Minneapolis MN 55414
800-328-2612; Fax: 612-331-3500
Service: Scan sheets & bar-coded menus

Binders

American Thermoplastic Company
622 Second Ave #709
Pittsburgh PA 15219-2086
800-456-6602; Fax: 412-642-7464
Service: Custom-imprinted binders

Business Cards

cardsNow
Div of Topitzes & Assoc Inc
4200 University Ave #2000
Madison WI 53705-2159
608-231-6100; Fax: 608-231-6116
800-233-9767
Service: Business cards

Echo Plastic Systems Inc
PO Box 69-4217
Miami FL 33269-1217
800-327-0693; Fax: 305-653-7745
Service: Plastic business cards

Royal Publishing
Michael Walters
PO Box 1120
Glendora CA 91740
818-335-8069; Fax: 818-335-6127
Service: Business cards

Clipping Bureau

American Press Clipping Service
119 Nassau St
New York NY 10038-2415
212-962-3797
Subjects: 99
Service: Clipping service

ATP Clipping Bureau
Israel Fleiss
5 Bleekman St
New York NY 10038
212-349-1177
Subjects: 99
Service: Clipping service

Bacon's Clipping Bureau
R H Bacon Co
332 S Michigan Ave
Chicago IL 60604-4301
312-922-2400; 800-621-0561;
  Fax: 312-922-3127
Subjects: 99
Service: Clipping service

Black Newspaper Clipping Bureau
68 E 121st St
New York NY 10035-2803
212-281-6000
Subjects: 49B-78-80
Service: Newspapers/radio/tv/magazines

Bowdens Information Services
1024 Birchmount Rd
Toronto ON Canada M1K 1S3
416-750-2220
Subjects: 61(Canada)-99
Service: Clipping service

Broadcast Newsclips--PR Newswire
970 E Hennepin Ave
Minneapolis MN 55414
612-331-7800
Subjects: 99
Service: Newsclips

Burrelles Press Clipping Service
75 E Northfield Rd
Livingston NJ 07039
201-992-6600; 800-631-1160
Subjects: 99
Service: Clipping service

Canadian Press Clipping Services
4601 Yonge St
Toronto ON Canada M2N 5L9
416-221-1660
Subjects: 61(Canada)-99
Service: Clipping service

Carolina Clipping Service
1115 Hillsborough St
Raleigh NC 27603-1500
919-833-2079
Subjects: 61(SC-NC)-99
Service: Clipping service

Clip Inc
1030 rue Cherrier
Montreal PQ Canada H2L 1H9
514-527-9391
Subjects: 61(Canada)-99
Service: Clipping service

Dynamic Graphics Inc
6000 N Forest Park Dr
PO Box 1901
Peoria IL 61656-9941
Subjects: 11-99
Service: Electronic clipper & clipper also on disc

Home Economics Reading Service
1341 G St NW
Washington DC 20005-3105
202-347-4763
Subjects: 27
Service: Clipping service

Kentucky Newsclip
1303 Clear Spring Trace #105
Louisville KY 40223-3860
502-339-7311
Subjects: 61(KY)-99
Service: Newsclips

Luce Press Clippings
42 South Ctr
Mesa AZ 85210-1306
602-834-6183; 800-628-0376
Subjects: 99(newspapers/magazines/TV)
Service: Press clipping

Luce Press Clippings
420 Lexington Ave
New York NY 10170-0002
212-889-6711; 800-628-0376
Subjects: 99(newspapers/magazines/TV)
Service: Press clipping

Magnolia Clipping Service
PO Box 12463
Jackson MS 39236-2463
601-956-4221
Subjects: 61(MS)-99
Service: Clipping service

Mature Market Clipping Service
Jo Slater, Admnstr
PO Box 90549
San Diego CA 92169-2549
619-272-2832
Subjects: 35A
Service: Clipping service

Nevada Press Clipping Service
PO Box 7057
Reno NV 89510-7057
702-322-7431
Subjects: 61(NV)-99
Service: Clipping service

New England Newsclip Agency
5 Auburn St
Framingham MA 01701-4879
617-879-4460
Subjects: 99
Service: Clipping service

Newsclip Clipping Bureau
Michael Buxbaum, Gen Mgr
213 W Institute Pl
Chicago IL 60610-3125
312-751-7300; 800-544-8433;
  Fax: 312-751-7306
Subjects: 99
Service: Clipping bureau

Pressclips Inc
1 Hillside Blvd
New Hyde Park NY 11040-4520
516-437-1047
Subjects: 99
Service: Clipping service

Radio TV Reports
RTV
Automated Broadcast Retrieval
41 E 42nd St
New York NY 10017-5202
212-309-1400
Subjects: 99
Service: Broadcast news monitoring

Collections

Allison, Jackson & Nichols
James A Rudloff, Acct Executive
410 River Street Ext
PO Box 1477
Oneonta NY 13820
607-432-9000; Fax: 607-432-8154
Service: Commercial collection service

Copyediting and Proofing

Carrollton Editing/Publishing
Doris M Knapp
171 Gallo Rd NW
Carrollton OH 44615
216-627-4289
Service: Copyediting/proofreading

Data

CAS Marketing Inc
Corporate Office
616 South 75th St
Omaha NE 68114-4624
402-393-0313; Fax: 402-390-9497
Service: Electronic data transmission

CD-ROM Technologies
5711 South 86th Cir
PO Box 27347
Omaha NE 68127-0347
402-593-4511; Fax: 402-331-6681
Service: Transfers info to CD-ROM format

CyberData
Jeff M Parness, VP
20 Max Ave
Hicksville NY 11801
516-942-8000; Fax: 516-942-0800
Service: Interactive fax and data services

Datasystem Solutions Inc
Lorna Linthacum Fenimore, VP
4350 Shawnee Mission Pky #179
Shawnee Mission KS 66205
913-362-6969; Fax: 913-362-6383
Service: In-house solution for circulation management

DMGT
Gale M Manning, Rep
141 Canal St
Nashua NH 03061
603-882-9500; Fax: 603-886-9686
Service: Credit card & information processing

IN-TOUCH Direct
PO Box 218
Sherborn MA 01770-0218
800-370-2693; Fax: 800-370-2694
Service: Business communication products

Karat Interactive Network Inc
1881 9th St #212
Boulder CO 80302-5148
800-947-5388; Fax: 303-440-9028
Service: FAX communications network

Knowledge IN Motion
Andrew Young, Pres
7878 Big Sky Dr #D
Madison WI 53719
609-829-3454; Fax: 608-829-3561
800-829-2459
Service: Conversion house

Delivery Service

Alternative Delivery Today!
Rick Barse & Cathy Sattler, Ed
PO Box 37
Kensington MD 20895
800-367-1525
800-547-0040
Service: Alternative delivery service

E-Fax Communications Inc
William Perell, VP Marketing
1611 Telegraph Ave Ste #555
Oakland CA 94612
510-836-6000; Fax: 510-836-8935
Service: Newsletter delivery by fax

Quick Link Information Services
Steve Solenzio, Sales Mgr
800-299-3773; Fax: 203-248-7116
Service: Broadcast FAX service

Direct Response

A+ Letter Service
Ray Finnegan
3245 Rt 35 North
PO Box 1248
Normandy Beach NJ 08739
908-830-1600; Fax: 908-830-5697
Service: Direct response/lettershops

Access Communications Systems
Janet Long
111 Executive Blvd
Farmingdale NY 11735
516-420-0770; Fax: 516-454-1720
Service: Direct response/lettershops

DRC Associates
Donald R Chinery, Pres
452 Hudson Terr
Englewood Cliffs NJ 07632
201-871-0081; Fax: 201-871-8664
Service: Agent for CDM Commercial Direct Mail Co-Hong Kong

Directories

American Business Directory
Bill Mattern, Sales Mgr
5711 S 86th Cir
PO Box 27347
Omaha NE 68127
402-593-4600; Fax: 402-331-5481
Service: State business directory

Displays

Abex Display Systems
7101 Fair Ave
North Hollywood CA 91605
800-537-0231
Service: Pop-up displays

Beemak Marketing Inc
PO Box 1045
Broomfield CO 80038
800-421-4393
Service: Displays

City Diecutting Inc
Eric De Vos
2 Babcock Pl
West Orange NJ 07052
201-736-1224; Fax: 201-736-1248
Service: Point of purchase displays

Downing Displays Inc
115 W McMicken Ave
Cincinnati OH 45210-1095
513-621-7888
800-883-1800
Service: Displays

Expand Display Information
Target Displays & Exhibits
9740 16th St North
St Petersburg FL 33716-4210
813-577-9335
Service: Modular pop-up tradeshow displays

Expo Concepts Inc
1130 East Mt Garfield Rd
Muskegon MI 49444
800-345-3196
Service: Portable displays

Exposure Display Systems
7101 Fair Ave
N Hollywood CA 91605
800-537-0231
Service: Displays

ExpoSystems
Corporate Headquarters
3203 Queen Palm Dr
Tampa FL 33619-1394
800-367-3976; Fax: 813-621-7904
Service: Displays

Featherlite Exhibits
7300 32nd Ave N
Minneapolis MN 55427
612-537-5533; 800-328-4827
Service: Exhibits

Foga Systems
Norman Ross, Sales Mgr
800 Del Norte Blvd
Oxnard CA 93030
805-988-3642; Fax: 805-988-1254
800-488-3642
Service: PVC tabletop displays

The Godfrey Group Inc
PO Box 30249
Raleigh NC 27622-0249
919-544-6504
Service: Displays

Hanna Design Rochester Inc
USA Division of Hanna Design
52 Marway Circle
Rochester NY 14624
716-247-6240
Service: Portable panel systems

Heritage Display Group
Jerre Miller
550 Vandalia St
St Paul MN 55114
612-646-7865
Service: Lightweight modular displays

Laarhoven Design
1790 Corporate Dr
Norcross GA 30093
800-825-2223
Service: Portable exhibits design

Magic Frame Display Systems
12700 SE Crain Hwy
Brandywine MD 20613
800-638-0980; Fax: 301-782-4051
Service: Merchandising displays

Literature Display Systems Inc
PO Box 501790
Indianapolis IN 46250
317-841-4398; Fax: 317-841-4391
800-669-4399
Service: Literature displays

Mountain Automation Corporation
Claude Wiatrowski
PO Box 2324
Fort Collins CO 80522-2324
800-487-3793; Fax: 303-493-6466
Service: Displays

Nomadic Display
Judy Watson, Pres
7400 Fullerton Rd
Springfield VA 22153
800-732-9395; Fax: 703-866-1869
Service: Display systems

Nomadic Instand
7400 Fullerton Rd #134
Springfield VA 22153
800-732-9395; Fax: 703-866-1869
Service: Portable displays

Perrygraf
19365 Business Center Dr
Northridge CA 91324-3552
818-993-1000; Fax: 818-993-7572
800-423-5329
Service: Pop-ups

Professional Displays
746 Arrow Grand Cir
Covina CA 91722-2198
818-967-1594; Fax: 818-966-4067
800-222-6838
Service: Displays

Randal Wood Displays
Debbie L Marrs
305 Laura Dr
Addison IL 60101
708-543-8030; Fax: 708-543-8096
Service: Manufacturer of merchandise fixtures

The Reference Shelf
593 Pleasant St
Hanson MA 02341
617-293-2194; Fax: 617-294-4153
Service: Specialized, face-out display services

Siegel Display Products
Marketing Manager
PO Box 95
Minneapolis MN 55440
800-626-0322; Fax: 800-230-5598
Service: Displays: acrylic, wire both counter and floor

Skyline Displays Inc
12345 Portland Ave
Burnsville MN 55337-1585
800-328-2725; Fax: 612-895-6318
Service: Trade show displays & graphics

TigerMark
21 Blandin Ave
Framingham MA 01701-7019
800-338-8465
Service: Wall-of-Light displays

Traverse Bay Display Company
George Smith
4366 Deerwood Dr
Traverse City MI 49686
800-240-9802; Fax: 616-938-3269
Service: Displays

Duplication

E-K Video Inc
Kris Barrigan, Sales Rep
892 Worcester St
Wellesley MA 02181
617-235-7260; Fax: 617-235-5312
800-729-4455
Service: Audio & video duplication service

PMR Productions
Preston Ransone, Exec Producer
PO Box 20405
Oxnard CA 93033
805-984-0122; Fax: 805-984-3262
Service: Books on tape

Univenture
Carrie Swank
4707 Roberts Rd
PO Box 28398
Columbus OH 43228
614-529-2100; Fax: 614-529-2110
800-992-8262
Service: CD packaging & storage

Vis
1111 Secaucus Rd
Secaucus NJ 07094
800-223-0433
Service: Top quality video duplication

Wings Digital Corp
Karen Michelini, Acct Rep
10 Commercial St
Hicksville NY 11801
516-933-2500; Fax: 516-933-2506
E-Mail: Wings@MCIMAIL.COM
Service: CD-ROM duplication facility

Envelopes

American Mail-Well Envelope
23 Inverness Way E
Englewood CO 80112
303-790-8023; Fax: 303-397-7409
Service: Envelopes

Atlantic Envelope Co
Jared Caplan
PO Box 741267
Atlanta GA 30374
800-833-9667; Fax: 404-609-8102
Service: Direct response/envelopes

Commercial Envelope Manufacturing Co
Pat Creditor, Sales Exec
900 Grand Blvd
Deer Park L.I. NY 11729
516-242-2500; Fax: 516-242-9588
800-327-7061
Service: Commercial envelope

Gam Printers
Charles D Grant, Pres
1102 W Church Rd
Sterling VA 22170
703-430-2813; Fax: 703-450-5311
Service: Letterhead envelopes

Nationwide Printing Inc
5906 Jefferson St
Burlington KY 41005
800-872-2902
Service: Direct response envelopes

Tension Envelope Corp
819 E 19th St
Kansas City MO 64108
816-471-3800
Service: Envelopes

Labels

Artistic Greetings
One Artistic Plz
Elmira NY 14925
Service: Personalized labels & "Fastamp" address stamps

Dispensa-Matic Label Dispensers
725 N 23rd St
St Louis MO 63103-9971
800-325-7303
Service: Label dispensers

Fae Labels
Fae Hakim
400 Budding Ridge
Cheshire CT 06410
203-272-3873
Service: Custom or blank labels, laser available

Grayarc
Gayle Anderson, Marketing Mgr
Greenwoods Industrial Park
PO Box 2944
Hartford CT 06104-2944
800-243-5250; Fax: 800-292-4729
Service: Advertising labels

Imprint Products
59 Court St Dept #33-3233
PO Box 1330
Binghamton NY 13902-1330
Service: Personalized mailing labels: self-stick; wet & stick

Interstate Label Company
1715 E Main St
PO Box 1239
Freeland WA 98249
800-426-3261
Service: Labels

Lancer Label
301 S 74th St
Omaha NE 68114
800-228-7074; Fax: 800-344-9456
Service: Business labels

Publishers Support Services
Linda Radke
PO Box 3142
Scottsdale AZ 85271-3142
800-545-STAR; 602-941-0770;
   Fax: 602-941-0069
Service: Labels

Wisconsin Label Group
MN Division
5218 12th Ave A
Minneapolis MN 55417
612-822-6979; Fax: 612-822-7091
Service: Labels

Mailing Service

Devan Direct Marketing Inc
Monte Mosher, Acct Exec
2900 Delaware Ave
Des Moines IA 50317-3893
515-265-3446; Fax: 515-265-2995
Service: Full-line mailing service

Dilley Manufacturing Co
211 E 3rd St
Des Moines IA 50309
515-288-7289; 800-247-5087
Service: Information packaging

John & Hayward
516-22 West 19th St
New York NY 10011-2876
212-675-4250; Fax: 212-924-3946
800-521-0080
Service: International mailings

Olwen Direct Mail Limited
Chris Flannery
1-2 Stafford Cross
Stafford Road
Croydon, Surrey CR9 4PD
81-688-7999; Fax: 81-668-1211
Service: Complete solution for European mailings

Royal Mail
Chris Powell, VP Sales/Mktg
152 Madison Ave #1603
New York NY 10016
800-803-1358
Service: International mail carrier

Trinity Marketing
Mr R Lamont
50 Barry Road
East Dulwich
London SE22 OHP
Service: Laser printing & mailing in Europe & UK

Publicity

Creative Ways
Marcia Yudin
PO Box 1310
Boston MA 02117
617-266-1613
Service: Media publicity

Kagan World Media Inc
126 Clock Tower Pl
Carmel CA 93923
408-624-1536; Fax: 408-625-3225
Service: Book of European television

R E Martin Public Relations
Renate Martin
14252 Culver Dr #A-240
Irvine CA 92714
714-786-5014
Service: Public relations

Spirit Marketing Co
202 East Magnolia St
Leesburg FL 34748
904-323-0777; Fax: 904-728-0581
800-888-4426
Service: Promotions & publicity

Software

DSD Associates Inc
330 S Magnolia Ave #204
El Cajon CA 92020
800-627-9032; Fax: 619-447-0901
Service: Accounting & business systems software

Dydacomp Development Corp
PO Box 641
Wayne NJ 07474-0641
800-858-3666
Service: Software to run your mail order business

Free Software Foundation
59 Temple Pl #330
Boston MA 02111-1307
617-542-5942; Fax: 617-542-2652
E-Mail: gnu@prep.ai.mit.edu
Service: Free software

Fulfillit
JSK Programming Service Inc
60 Surrey Ln
East Falmouth MA 02536-9909
508-457-5222; Fax: 508-457-5333
Service: Newsletter tracking software

Harvey International
1000 Elwell Ct
Palo Alto CA 94303-4306
415-961-2600; Fax: 415-961-4915
Service: Bookmaster Management Software

Imprint Enterprises Inc
Michael Gonski
1842 Centrepoint Dr
Naperville IL 60563
708-505-1700; Fax: 708-505-1511
800-433-4512
Service: KAO Infosystems

Inforonics Inc
Robin B Humes
550 Newtown Rd
PO Box 458
Littleton MA 01460
508-486-8976
Service: Database company provides services and software for publishing

Merlin's Medievel Market
The Haven Corp
1227 Dodge Ave
Evanston IL 60202-1008
708-869-3553
800-676-0098
Service: Business software

Publishers Business System
RH Communications Inc
PO Box 301177
Escondido CA 92030
619-480-5641; Fax: 619-739-9594
Service: Software for business management

Right's On
Sandy Paul
SKP Associates
160 Fifth Ave
New York NY 10010
212-675-7804; Fax: 212-989-7542
Service: Rights software

Software Diversified Services
Chantal Shreve, Natl Mkg Mgr
5155 East River Rd #411
Minneapolis MN 55421
612-571-9000; Fax: 612-572-1721
800-443-6183
Service: Computer service bureau

Special Paper

Artmaker Super Sheets
500 N Claremont Blvd
Claremont CA 91711
909-626-8065; Fax: 909-621-1323

Service: Extraordinary, professional paper, brochures, and report covers

BeaverPrints
305 Main St
Bellwood PA 16617
800-923-2837; Fax: 800-232-8374

Service: Pre-printed laser papers

CEM Paper Enterprises Inc
Vicki Parkin, VP/Sales
1169 Greenwood Ave
Jenkintown PA 19046
215-885-1111; Fax: 215-886-5769

Service: Full-service paper house

Weyerhaeuser Paper Company
Jeff Brundage, Natl Market Mgr
620m Lee Rd
Wayne PA 19087
215-251-9220

Service: Electronic imaging paper

Special Equipment

Autologic
1050 Rancho Conejo Blvd
Thousand Oaks CA 91320-1794
805-498-9611; Fax: 805-499-1167

Service: High-speed publishing technology, color scanners/laser imaging, proofers

Cummins-Allison Corp
One Cummins Ctr
Mt Prospect IL 60056
800-786-5528; Fax: 708-299-4939

Service: Paper shredders

Datalizer Slide Charts Inc
501 Westgate St
Addison IL 60101-4524
708-543-6000; Fax: 708-543-1616

Service: Slide charts

Direct Promotions
23935 Ventura Blvd
Calabasas CA 91302-1445
818-591-9010; Fax: 818-591-2071

Service: FIND-X cards

Special Services

Edit Ink
Bill Appel or Denise Sterrs
5907 Main St
Williamsville NY 14221
716-626-4431; Fax: 716-626-4388
800-259-6328

Service: A book-doctoring service

EMDS
MMTI
PO Box 234
Camden SC 29020
800-356-6684

Service: Manuscript marketing

Ideas Unlimited
1545 New York Ave NE
Washington DC 20002-1765
202-526-9696; Fax: 202-636-3992
800-345-2611

Service: 18 page publication for editors with features on every topic

Linguistic Systems
130 Bishop Richard Allen Dr
PO Box 31
Cambridge MA 02139
800-654-5006

Service: Language translations

Litle & Co
54 Stiles Rd
Salem NH 03079-4833
603-893-9333

Service: Credit card processing

MACS
Smith-Gardner & Assoc
1615 S Congress Ave
Delray Beach FL 33445-6368
407-265-2700; Fax: 407-265-2566

Service: Catalog fulfillment

Mexico Information Services Inc
PO Box 11770
Ft Worth TX 76110
800-446-0746; Fax: 817-924-9687

Service: Information products related to Mexico

Midwest Photo Co
4900 G Street (68117)
PO Box 686
Omaha NE 68101-0686
402-734-7200; Fax: 402-734-4319
800-228-7208

Service: Photos

The Nate Butler Studio Inc
Nate Butler
620 Richlmond Dr NE (87106-2149)
PO Box 27470
Albuquerque NM 87125-7470
505-268-6869; Fax: 505-260-0190

Service: Photos

National Book & Document
Roger Waynick/Ray Mullican
121 Seaboard Ln #11
Franklin TN 37067
800-809-9479; Fax: 615-221-4128

Service: Short-run book printing specialists

North of 49 D.M. Services Ltd
530 Coronation Dr #6
Scarborough ON Canada M1E 5C8
416-208-7822; Fax: 416-208-9221
800-667-8449

Service: Canadian lists, printing, lettershop, fulfillment, advice

Ornaal Color Photos
24 W 25th St
New York NY 10010
212-675-3850
800-826-6312

Service: Photographs

Pages Editorial Service
300 N State St #6021
Chicago IL 60610
312-222-9245; Fax: 312-222-9637

Service: Editorial service

PCS Mailing List Company
39 Cross St
Peabody MA 01960
508-532-7100; Fax: 508-532-9181
800-532-LIST

Service: Mailing list

PeopleSpeak
Sharon Goldinger
25342 Costeau Dr
Laguna Hills CA 92653
714-581-4958

Service: Speaking

Publishers' Photographic Service
10319 Pine Ridge Dr
Elliott City MD 21042
800-966-4880

Service: Photography for flyers, catalogs, ads, distrib, etc

Re:Search International
One Broadway 10th Fl
Cambridge MA 02142
; Fax: 617-577-9517
800-895-0212

Service: CD Search for Publishers/Div of Toronto Corp

RLS Associates Inc
250 Huron Ave
PO Box 5030
Port Huron MI 48061-5030
810-989-9500; Fax: 810-987-3562
800-842-8338

Service: Fulfillment services

Tony Saltzman
PO Box 7529
Grand Rapids MI 49510

Service: Specialized cartoons, gift cartoons for framing

Sports Select
Select Publishing
10 Odana Court
Madison WI 53719
608-277-5787; Fax: 608-277-9001
Service: Card decks

Stephen R. Ettlinger
225 E 28th St #1
New York NY 10016
212-683-0502
Service: Book doctor and editor

Teacher's Performance
Venture Communications
609 Madison Ave
New York NY 10010
212-684-4800; Fax: 212-576-1129
Service: Card decks

To the Point
Linda Singerle
1904 Sixty-First Court
Meridian MS 39305
601-693-4969; Fax: 601-693-4969
E-mail: point@cybertron.com
Service: Writing, editing, design, freelance

Tristar Productions
Keith Mirchandani (President)
1616 Duke St
Laureldale PA 19605
201-263-5002
Service: As seen on TV

USI Inc
33 Business Park Dr #5
Branford CT 06405-2944
800-243-4565; Fax: 203-481-7508
Service: Lamination

Wambtac
Claudia Suzanne
17300 17th St J-276
Tustin CA 92680
714-954-0580; Fax: 714-954-0793
800-641-3936
E-mail: claudiasu@aol.com
Service: Literary consultant & professional ghost writer

WEB Direct Marketing
401 S Milwaukee Ave
Wheeling IL 60090
708-459-0800; Fax: 708-459-7378
Service: New customer aquisition through alternative media - Mini-Books

West & Feinberg PC
Michael Gluckstern/Ronald West
4550 Montgomery Ave 7th Fl
Bethesda MD 20814
301-951-1500; Fax: 301-951-1525
Service: Legal & tax council in newsletter deals

Westlight
M Rogers
2223 S Carmelina Ave
Los Angeles CA 90099-4790
310-820-7077; Fax: 310-820-2687
800-622-2028
Service: Professional stock photography

Specialty Items

Appaloosa Custom Products Inc
PO Box 3156
Milford CT 06460
203-877-2919
Service: Pewter custom products

Badge A Minit
Dept MBB294 Box 800
LaSalle IL 61301
800-223-4103
Service: Pin-back button kits

Bannerland
431 W Blueridge Ave
Orange CA 92665
714-998-9646; Fax: 800-451-7853
800-654-0294
Service: Customized & ready-made display banners

Boscos Inc
PO Box 800
Boston MA 02123
800-926-7267
Service: Logo mugs

Britten Banners
4152 Cedar Run Rd
Traverse City MI 49684
616-941-8200; Fax: 616-941-8299
800-426-9496
Service: Banners for business, tradeshows, parties, etc

CeSan Limited
6662 Villa Sonrisa Dr #323
Boca Raton FL 33433
407-338-0721; Fax: 407-393-0060
Service: Custom printed plastic bags

Caere Corporation
Dean Hovey, VP/Bus Development
100 Cooper Ct
Los Gatos CA 95030
800-223-7346; Fax: 800-437-3299
Service: Omniform electronic forms

Carrot-Top Industries Inc
437 Dimmocks Mill Rd
PO Box 820
Hillsborough NC 27278
800-628-3524; Fax: 919-732-5826
Service: Flags, banners, decorations

Competitive Edge
2711 Grand Ave
Des Moines IA 50312
515-280-3343; Fax: 515-288-3343
800-458-3343
Service: Personalized coffee mugs

Convergence Corporation
1308 Continental Dr
Abingdon MD 21009
800-433-1782; Fax: 410-538-6121
Service: Counter mats

Creative Optics
708 Peterson St
Fort Collins CO 80524
303-484-6032; Fax: 303-484-5252
800-478-8008
Service: Custom imprinted sunglasses

Crestline
22 West 21st St
New York NY 10010
800-221-7797; Fax: 800-242-8290
Service: Custom imprinted products: exhibits, mugs, pens, buttons

Custom Mat Co Inc
PO Box 1009
Nashville TN 47448
812-988-6289; Fax: 812-988-6291
Service: Customized logo mats

Ecocenters Corporation
Frank R Piunno, VP/Sales
21111 Chagrin Blvd
Beachwood OH 44122-5395
216-991-9000; Fax: 216-752-8166
Service: Personalized & customized booklets, manuals, etc

Effective Promotions
Patricia O'Brien, Pres
670 Pawling Ave
Troy NY 12180
518-274-0291; Fax: 518-274-0290
Service: Custom-imprinted packaging

Folder Factory
PO Box 429
Edinburg VA 22824-0429
800-296-4321
Service: Folder designers kits

Golden Sea Graphics
704 Main
PO Box 36
Greenleaf KS 66943
800-535-5030; Fax: 913-747-2430
Service: Custom imprinted caps

Identity Watch
20909 East St
Southfield MI 48034-5934
800-875-5811; Fax: 810-354-6811
Service: Logo watches for gifts, premiums, incentives, awards

Image Watches Inc
Mr Colfer
9095 Telstar Ave
El Monte CA 91731-2809
818-312-2828
800-344-8050
Service: Full-color logos on watches

Imagica Imaging Magic
PO Box 4200
Ocala FL 34478-4200
904-840-0011
Service: Larger-than-life color prints

Jarrett & Associates
2355 Oakland Rd #2
San Jose CA 95131
800-343-7011
Service: Imprinted Combi pens & highlighters

Lands' End Corporate Sales
2 Lands End Ln
Dodgeville WI 53595-0001
800-338-2000
Service: Corporate sales catalog - clothing

Marco
4211 Elmerton Ave
Harrisburg PA 17109-9930
800-232-1121; Fax: 717-545-5672
Service: Heat sealed vinyl badge holders

Marketing Bulletin Board
117 W Micheltorena #C
Santa Barbara CA 93101
805-965-5858; Fax: 805-963-1143
Service: Customized lapel pins

Martguild Inc
576 Industrial Pky
PO Box 382
Chagrin Falls OH 44022
216-247-8978; Fax: 216-247-1107
Service: Logo in metal, pen sets, clocks, thermometers, etc

Nelson Marketing
210 Commerce St
PO Box 320
Oshkosh WI 54902-0320
414-236-7272; Fax: 414-236-7282
800-722-5203
Service: Logo mugs, promotional products

Northwestern Church Supply
PO Box 11011
Tacoma WA 98411-0011
800-228-0932; Fax: 800-248-0621
Service: Pens, ribbons, catalogs, promotions

PinSource
1233 Shelburne Rd
Pierson House
South Burlington VT 05403
800-678-9288; Fax: 802-865-3777
Service: Custom lapel pins

Positive Promitions
222 Ashland Pl
Brooklyn NY 11217
; Fax: 800-635-2329
800-635-2666
Service: Stik-Quik calendars

Renton's Intl Stationery Inc
4101 E Louisiana Ave #300
PO Box 22556
Denver CO 80222-9542
800-365-6644; Fax: 800-873-3060
Service: Stickers

The Ritz Company
7470 Wales Ave NW
N Canton OH 44720
216-494-9327; Fax: 800-968-4770
Service: Custom printed magnets

Sealed Air Corporation
301 Mayhill St
Saddle Brook NJ 07663
800-648-9093; Fax: 201-712-7019
Service: Packaging products division

Seton Name Plate Co
PO Box CD-1331
New Haven CT 06505-9984
800-243-6624
Service: Property ID plates

Shoreline Container
716 Mizar Ct
Traverse City MI 49684-8764
616-943-3022; Fax: 616-943-4634
800-628-1653
Service: Boxes, bags, packaging supplies

Solar Press
120 Frontenac Rd
Napperville IL 60563
Fax: 800-323-2751
Service: Trading cards

Southern Marketing Products
11371 Decimal Dr
Louisville KY 40299
800-266-5737; Fax: 502-266-7351
Service: Computerized logos on Polo shirts

Specialty Merchandise Corp
9401 De Soto Ave Dept 824-61
Chatsworth CA 91311-4991
Service: Provides catalogs for mail-order taking at home

Stephen G Fossler Company Inc
439 S Dartmoor Dr
Crystal Lake IL 60014
800-762-0030; Fax: 800-424-9292
Service: Anniversary seals

Sunmex Import Corp
11135 E Rush St #B
S El Monte CA 91733
818-580-7666; Fax: 818-580-7688
Service: Premium incentive gifts

Taymar Industries Inc
PO Box 12369
Palm Desert CA 92255-2369
619-341-6373; Fax: 619-341-6369
800-624-1972
Service: Promotional holders

U S Press
PO Box 640
Valdosta GA 31603-0640
800-227-7377
Service: Postcards

Universal Network Inc
10077 Grogan's Mill Rd Ste #200
The Woodlands TX 77380
713-363-4000; Fax: 713-364-8452
Service: Book Magic-a book clip and stand in one

Vinyl Industrial Products Inc
1700 Dobbs Rd
St Augustine FL 32086
800-874-0855; FL: 800-342-8324; Fax: 904-829-6903
Service: Custom-imprinted binders

Typesetting

Alphabet House
Ronnie Serr
139 Sweetzer Ave
Los Angeles CA 90084
213-655-7085; Fax: 213-6557828
E-mail: alphabethouse@artnet.net.
Service: Typesetting

LaserMaster Corp
6900 Shady Oak Rd
Eden Prairie MN 55344
612-944-9330
Service: Typesetters

Section V:

Bibliography

444 Bibliographies and Publishing Directories

    444   Directories of Authors
    444   Bibliographies
    446   Directories of Publishers

449 Marketing Directories

    449   Directories of Booksellers
    449   Directories of Mail Order Catalogs
    450   Directories of Companies
    451   Databases
    451   Editorial Calendar
    451   Fax Directories
    451   Directories of Libraries
    452   Media Directories
    456   Media Newsletters
    456   Directories of Organizations
    458   Directories of People
    460   Directories of Schools
    460   Directories of Wholesalers and Retailers

463 An Annotated Review of Books on Publishing

    463   General Publishing
    466   Careers in Publishing
    466   Specialized Publishing
    466   Publishing Periodicals
    467   Legal Guides to Publishing
    468   Marketing Your Books
    470   Advertising and Marketing
    472   Publicity and Speaking
    474   Editing, Design, & Printing
    475   Telemarketing
    476   General Business Guides
    476   Web Marketing and Research
    477   Book Publishing Anecdotes
    477   Out of Print Books

Section V: Bibliography

This bibliography features more than 500 directories and other books that can be useful in any book publishing and marketing program. The first two sections of this bibliography include directories that either feature books and publishers or can be used as information resources in targeting specific markets. The third part of this bibliography lists and reviews 250 books about publishing and marketing, letting you know which ones could serve your needs best.

The directories in the first section of this bibliography are divided into three categories:

- **Directories of authors** — Make sure your authors are listed in these directories, since most of these listings also feature the books written by the authors.
- **Bibliographies** — Make sure your books are listed in the appropriate bibliographies, so people in the book trade can locate your titles.
- **Directories of publishers** — Make sure your company is listed in these directories, since the marketplace listings can put you in contact with potential authors while the other directories will let librarians, bookstores, and other book buyers know how to order from you.

Use the directories in the second part of this bibliography to target buyers and other people who might be interested in your books.

- Use the directories of booksellers, mail order catalogs, libraries, schools, and wholesalers/retailers to locate potential buyers and resellers of your books.
- Use the directories of companies, organizations, and people to locate readers who might be interested in buying your book direct from you or working with you on a special markets sale.
- Use the media directories, databases, and newsletters to target media that might be interested in featuring your books or authors in stories or interviews. Besides general interest newspapers, magazines, and broadcast media, these directories also feature special interests (such as mature markets, colleges, minorities, religions, crafts, etc.) as well as local and regional media for all parts of the country and the world.

The final section of this bibliography features reviews of 250 books about publishing, printing, graphics, marketing, publicity, and other concerns of book publishers. Use these reviews to help you decide which books can best serve your information needs. This annotated review of books covers ten areas of publishing.

- **Publishing in general**, including self-publishing, management, history, and general how-to.
- **Specialized publishing**, including cookbooks, directories, and regional publishing.
- **Periodical publishing**, including the publishing of newsletters and magazines.
- **Legal guides to publishing**, covering copyrights, publishing law, trademarks, and more.
- **Book marketing**, featuring titles specifically about marketing books.
- **Advertising and marketing**, including direct marketing, copywriting, catalogs, and more.
- **Publicity**, including general PR, how to do TV and radio interviews, and speaking.
- **Book production**, including editing, design, graphics, layout, and printing.
- **Telemarketing, general business guides, web marketing and research**, books of interest
- **Book publishing anecdotes**
- **Out of print books**, featuring resource books that you might still find in your local library.

Bibliographies and Publishing Directories

Here are some of the major directories of authors, books, and book publishers. Be sure to see that your authors are listed in the major directories, your books listed in all appropriate bibliographies (especially *Books in Print*, which occurs automatically if you send in your Advance Book Information forms on time), and your own publishing company listed in the directories of publishers.

Directories of Authors

ASJA Directory
Director
Amer Soc of Journalists/Authors
1501 Broadway #302
New York NY 10036-5501
212-997-0947; Fax: 212-768-7414
E-Mail: 75227.1650@compuserve.com
Subjects: 56W-99()
Focus: Professional writers

Black Authors & Published Writer
Grace Adams, Editor
The Grace Company
PO Box 47
Rochester MI 48308
313-650-9450; 800-762-5799;
   Fax: 313-650-9450
Subjects: 49B-56W
Focus: Black Authors & Published Writers Directory. Lists major Black authors, book titles, editors, reviewers, playwrights, producers, publishers, and more

Children's Authors/Illustrators
Editors
Gale Research Co
835 Penobscot Bldg
Detroit MI 48226
313-961-2242; Fax: 313-961-6083
Subjects: 21-76
Focus: Illustrators/authors

Contemporary Authors
Editors
Gale Research Co
835 Penobscot Bldg
Detroit MI 48226
313-961-2242; Fax: 313-961-6083
Subjects: 17-99
Focus: Author biographies

Directory of American Poets and Fiction Writers
Poets & Writers
72 Spring St
New York NY 10012-4019
212-226-3586; Fax: 212-226-3963
Subjects: 75-77-83-90-95
Focus: Poets and fiction authors

International Authors & Writers Who's Who
Internationl Publications Serv
1900 Frost Rd #101
Bristol PA 19007-1519
800-821-8312; Fax: 215-785-5515
Internet: bkorders@tandpa.com
Subjects: 56W
Focus: Authors and writers

Who's Who in Editors & Poets in US & Canada
December Press
PO Box 302
Highland Park IL 60035-0302
708-940-4122
Subjects: 75-95-99
Focus: Authors who's who

Bibliographies

A to Zoo 4th Edition
R R Bowker
121 Chanlon Rd
New Providence NJ 07974
800-521-8110; Fax: 908-665-6688
Subjects: 21-76-79
Focus: 15,000 fiction/nonfiction titles

American Reference Book Annual
Anna Grace Patterson, Editor
PO Box 6633
Englewood CO 80155-6633
303-770-1220
Subjects: 59(reference books)
Focus: Annual directory

Association Publications in Print
R R Bowker Co
121 Chanlon Rd PO Box 31
New Providence NJ 07974
908-668-2818; Fax: 908-665-6688
Subjects: 19
Focus: Association books in print

Best Books/Videos/Video Games/ Music and Software for Children
ABC & F Press
PO Box 92
Bedford TX 76095-0092
800-528-3975
Subjects: 21-31P-76
Focus: 30 page report

Bibliographic Guide to Business and Economics
G K Hall
70 Lincoln St
Boston MA 02111-2661
617-423-3990
Subjects: 19
Focus: Business, economics

The Bookfinder
Editor
American Guidance Service
660 Publishers' Bldg
Circle Pines MN 55014
612-786-4343
Subjects: 21-31-76
Focus: Children's books

Books in Print
Cathy Conant
R R Bowker Co
121 Chanlon Rd PO Box 31
New Providence NJ 07974
800-521-8110; Fax: 908-665-6688
Subjects: 56
Focus: Books in print

Books in Print Database
ABI Information Office
R R Bowker Co
121 Chanlon Rd PO Box 31
New Providence NJ 07974
908-665-2818; Fax: 908-665-6688
Subjects: 99
Focus: Bibliographies for various areas

Building the Undergraduate Social Work Library
Dr Grafton Hull Jr, Editor
Univ of Wisconsin
Eau Claire WI 54702
715-836-4435; Fax:
Subjects: 57-65S(psychology/social work)
Focus: Sociology & human services

Business & Legal CD-ROMS in Print
Meckler Publishing
11 Ferry Ln West
Westport CT 06880
203-226-6967; Fax: 203-454-5840
Subjects: 19-19L-23C-55L(CD-ROMS)
Focus: CD-ROM/CD-I/CDTV/electronic book

CCBC Choices
Cooperative Children's Book Ctr
4290 Helen White Hall U of Wisc
600 N Park St
Madison WI 53706-1403
608-263-3720
Subjects: 21-21T-44-49-76-89
Focus: Children's books

CD-ROM Directory
Pemberton Press
462 Danbury Rd
Wilton CT 06897-2126
203-761-1466; Fax: 203-167-1444
Subjects: 23C-99
Focus: CD-ROMS

CD-ROMS in Print
Meckler Publishing
11 Ferry Ln West
Westport CT 06880
203-226-6967; Fax: 203-454-5840
Subjects: 23C-99(CD-ROMS)
Focus: CD-ROM/CD-I/CDTV/electronic book

Children's Books of the Year
The Child Study Book Committee
Bank Street College
610 W 112th St
New York NY 10025-1898
212-667-7200
Subjects: 21-76
Focus: Children's books

City & State Directories inPrint
Gale Research Co
835 Penobscot Bldg
Detroit MI 48226
313-961-2242; Fax: 313-961-6083
Subjects: 59-61
Focus: 5000 local directories

Computers and Computing
Information Resources Dir
Gale Research Co
835 Penobscot Bldg
Detroit MI 48226
313-961-2242; Fax: 313-961-6083
Subjects: 23
Focus: Periodicals/directories/books

Directories in Print
Editor
Gale Research Co
835 Penobscot Bldg
Detroit MI 48226
313-961-2242; Fax: 800-414-5043
Subjects: 19-59-99
Focus: Directories/databases

Directory of Business & Financial Information
Charles J Popovich, Editor
Ohio State Business Library
110 Page Hall 1810 College Rd
Columbus OH 43210
614-292-2136
Subjects: 19-19A-19E
Focus: Business

Directory of Publications Resources
Editorial Experts
66 Canal Center Plz #200
Alexandria VA 22314-1591
703-683-0683; Fax: 703-683-4915
Subjects: 56W
Focus: Books/magazines/programs/assns

Discrimination & Prejudice
Editors
Westerfield Enterprises
3043 Barnard St #1
San Diego CA 92110-5618
619-574-1132; Fax: 619-298-1589
Subjects: 49-55-65-73
Focus: Discrimination & Prejudice: An Annotated Bilbiography

E for Environment
Patti Sinclair, Editor
R R Bowker Co
121 Chanlon Rd PO Box 31
New Providence NJ 07974
908-665-2818; Fax: 908-665-6688
Subjects: 51
Focus: Nature and ecology books

Garden Literature: An Index
Garden Literature Press
398 Columbus Ave #181
Boston MA 02116-6008
617-424-1784; Fax: 617-424-1712
Subjects: 43G(magazine articles/bk review)
Focus: Indexes 100 magazines

Gardening: A Guide
Richard T Isaacson, Editor
Garland Publishing
136 Madison Ave 4th Fl
New York NY 10016-6711
212-686-7492
Subjects: 43G
Focus: Books/societies/periodicals

Gayellow Pages
Editor
Renaissance House
PO Box 292 Village Sta
New York NY 10014-0292
Subjects: 37
Focus: Bookstores/publications

Genealogical and Local History
Books in Print
6818 Lois Dr
Simpsonville MD 21150
Subjects: 41G
Focus: Genealogy

Guide to American Directories
Barry T Klein, Editor
Todd Publications
18 N Greenbush Rd #301
West Nyack NY 10994-2008
914-358-6213; Fax: 914-358-6213
Subjects: 59
Focus: Directories

Index of Desktop Publishing
Articles and Books
Brenner Information Group
13223 Black Mountain Rd #430
San Diego CA 92129-2659
Subjects: 23-56(desktop)
Focus: Desktop publishing books

Jewish Book Annual
Paula Gribetz Gottlieb, Dir
Jewish Book Council of America
15 E 26th St
New York NY 10010-1505
212-532-4949
Subjects: 63J
Focus: Jewish books

Just Cookbooks
Mary Barile, Editor
Heritage Publications
Church St PO Box 335
Arkville NY 12406-0335
914-586-3810
Subjects: 27
Focus: Cookbooks

Law & Legal Information
Directory
Gale Research Co
835 Penobscot Bldg
Detroit MI 48226
313-961-2242; Fax: 313-961-6083
Subjects: 19L-55L
Focus: Law assns/publications/etc

Learning AIDS
American Foundation
for AIDS Research
1515 Broadway #3601
New York NY 10036-8901
212-719-0033
Subjects: 37-39(AIDS)
Focus: Books/brochures/tapes/films

Native American Books in Print
Joe Ascione
Coyote Junction
7 Glenview Rd
Towaco NJ 07082
201-299-0506
COYOTEJUNC.@aol.com
Subjects: 49A-61(West and SW)
Focus: Native American books

Notable Children's Books
ALA - Association for Library
Services to Children
50 E Huron St
Chicago IL 60611-2729
312-944-6780; Fax: 312-440-9374
Subjects: 21-76
Focus: Children's books; This is a brochure

Notable Children's Trade Books
in the Field of Social Studies
Children's Book Council
568 Broadway #404
New York NY 10012-3225
212-254-2666; 800-666-7608
Subjects: 21-31-35-41-49-55-65-73-76
Focus: Children's books

Our Family/Our Friends/Our World
Editor
R R Bowker
121 Chanlon Rd PO Box 31
New Providence NJ 07974
908-665-2818; 800-521-8110;
  Fax: 908-665-6688
Subjects: 21-44-49-65
Memo: Focuses on books for children and teenagers about the cultures, identities, and histories of minority groups in the US and Canada as well as native cultures in the Third World. 25 contributors selected their top picks.

Outstanding Science Trade Books for Children
Children's Book Council
568 Broadway #404
New York NY 10012-3225
212-254-2666
Subjects: 21-23-24-39-51-67-76
Focus: Science books
Memo: National Science Teachers Association, 1742 Connecticut Avenue NW, Washington, DC 20009-1171; 202-328-5800.

Paperback Books for Young People: An Annotated Guide
American Library Assn
50 E Huron St
Chicago IL 60611-2729
312-944-6780; Fax: 312-440-9374
Subjects: 21-76
Focus: 800-545-2433
Memo: 1972 copyright. Co-author of this book is John T Gillespie. This book is out of print.

Portraying Persons w/ Disability
R R Bowker Co
121 Chanlon Rd PO Box 31
New Providence NJ 07974
908-665-2818; Fax: 908-665-6688
Subjects: 21-39D-76(children/teenagers)
Focus: Fiction and nonfiction

Real Estate Books & Periodicals in Print
Real Estate Publishing Co
PO Box 41177
Sacramento CA 95841-0177
916-677-3864
Subjects: 19H-43
Focus: Real estate books

Reference Sources for Small and Medium-Sized Libraries
ALA Reference & Adult Services
50 E Huron St
Chicago IL 60611-2729
312-944-6780; Fax: 312-440-9374
Subjects: 59
Focus: For libraries

Small Press Record of Books in Print
Len Fulton, Editor
Dustbooks 5826 Clark Rd
PO Box 100
Paradise CA 95967-0100
916-877-6110; Fax: 916-877-0222
Subjects: 99(small press)
Focus: Small press books

Sources: An Annotated Bibliograpy of Women's Issues
Rita McCollough, Editor
Knowlege, Ideas, & Trends
1311-0 Tolland Tpke #175
Manchester CT 06040
203-643-7831
Subjects: 73
Focus: Women's issues

Step-Parenting: Agencies, Books, Newsletters, to Help You Survive
ABC&F Press
PO Box 92
Bedford TX 76095-0092
800-528-3975
Subjects: 31P-35F-35M
Focus: Step-parenting

Subject Guide to Books in Print
Cathy Conant
R R Bowker Co
121 Chanlon Rd PO Box 31
New Providence NJ 07974
800-521-8110; Fax: 908-665-6688
Subjects: 56
Focus: Book subjects

Support Groups, Books, and Newsletters About Divorce
ABC&F Press
PO Box 92
Bedford TX 76009-0092
800-528-3975
Subjects: 35F-35M
Focus: Divorce, 3-page report

Trade Directories of the World
Croner Publications
21103 Jamaica Ave
Jamaica NY 11428-1532
718-464-0866
Subjects: 19-59
Focus: Trade directories

Universal Index
BiblioFile
The Library Corp
Research Park
Inwood WV 25428
304-229-0100; 800-624-0559;
  Fax: 304-229-0295
Subjects: 59
Focus: Indexes

The Video Source Book
Editor
Gale Research
835 Penobscot Bldg
Detroit MI 48226
313-961-2242; Fax: 313-961-6083
Subjects: 33-99(videos)
Focus: Video

Whole Again Resource Guide
Tim Ryan, Editor
Sourcenet
1728 N Moorpark Rd
Thousand Oaks CA 91360-5133
805-373-7123; Fax:
Subjects: 13-23T-51E-53
Focus: Magazines/directories/newspapers
Memo: Books on self-sufficiency, homesteading, preparedness, visions of the future, appropriate technology.

Words on Cassette
R R Bowker Co
121 Chanlon Rd PO Box 31
New Providence NJ 07974
908-665-2818; Fax: 908-665-6688
Subjects: 99(audiotapes)
Focus: Spoken word audiotapes only

Directories of Publishers

ABA Book Buyer's Handbook
Mary Ann Tennenhaus, Editor
American Booksellers Assn
828 S Broadway
Tarrytown NY 10591-6603
914-591-2665; Fax: 914-591-2720
Subjects: 99
Focus: For bookstore buyers

Alternative Publishers of Children's Books
Cooperative Children's Book Ctr
4290 Helen White Hall U of Wisc
600 N Park St
Madison WI 53706-1403
608-263-3720
Subjects: 13-21-49-76
Focus: Alternative children's publishers

American Publishers
K G Saur Inc
175 Fifth Ave
New York NY 10010-7703
212-982-1302
Subjects: 99
Focus: 71,000 US/CN book publishers

Arizona Marketplace for Writers
Carol Osman Brown
Golden West Publishers
4113 N Longview Ave
Phoenix AZ 85014-4949
602-265-4392
Subjects: 56-61(AZ)
Focus: Arizona magazines, newspapers, and publishers

Artist's & Graphic Designer Mkt
Stacie Berger
Writer's Digest Books
1507 Dana Ave
Cincinnati OH 45207-1056
513-531-2222
Subjects: 11
Focus: Book publishers using artists

Audiobook Reference Guide
Robin Whitten, Editor
AudioFile
PO Box 109
Portland OR 04112-0109
207-774-7563; 800-506-1212;
 Fax: 207-775-3744
E-mail: RAudioFile@aol.com
Subjects: 99
Focus: Spoken word audio

AV Market Place
Editor
R R Bowker Co
121 Chanlon Rd PO Box 31
New Providence NJ 07974
908-665-2818; 800-521-8110;
 Fax: 908-665-6688
Subjects: 99(audio/video suppliers/etc)

Business Organizations, Agencies and Publications Directory
Gale Research Co
835 Penobscot Bldg
Detroit MI 48226
313-961-2242; Fax: 800-414-5043
Subjects: 19
Focus: information services/publication

California and Hawaii Publishing Market Place
Writer's Connection
1601 Saratoga-Sunnyvale Rd #180
Cupertino CA 95014
408-973-0227; Fax: 408-973-1219
Subjects: 56-61(CA)-99
Focus: Newspapers/magazines/publishers

CD-ROM Market Place
Meckler Publishing
11 Ferry Ln West
Westport CT 06880
203-226-6967; Fax: 203-454-5840
Subjects: 23C-99(CD-ROMS)
Focus: CD-ROM/CD-I/CDTV/electronic book

Children's Book Market
Gailynn French, Asst Editor
95 Long Ridge Rd
Redding CT 06896
203-792-8600; Fax: 203-792-8406
Subjects: 21-76
Focus: Children's books

Children's Media Market Place
Editor
Neal-Schuman Publications
23 Leonard St
New York NY 10013-2914
212-925-8650
Subjects: 21-76
Focus: Publishers, clubs, stores, etc

Children's Writer's Market
Connie Eidenier, Editor
Writer's Digest Books
1507 Dana Ave
Cincinnati OH 45207-1056
513-531-2222
Subjects: 21-31-76-79
Focus: Book publishers/magazines

Children's Writer's Marketplace
S F Tomajczyk, Editor
Running Press
125 S 22nd St
Philadelphia PA 19103-4335
215-567-5080; Fax: 215-568-2919
Subjects: 21-31-76-79
Focus: Children's book publishers, magazines

Christian Writer's Markets Guide
Sally Stuart, Editor
Joy Publishing
PO Box 827
San Juan Capistran CA 92693-0827
714-493-8161
Subjects: 63(Christian)
Focus: Book publishers, magazines, etc

Colorado Book Guide
The Bloomsbury Review
1028 Bannock St
Denver CO 80204-4037
303-892-0620; Fax: 303-892-5620
Subjects: 56-61(CO)
Focus: Bookstores/libraries/publishers

Directory of College Stores Interested in Hosting Authors for Campus Appearances and Book Signings
National Assn of College Stores
528 E Lorain St PO Box 58
Oberlin OH 44074-1238
216-775-7777
Subjects: 99(college bookstores)
Focus: College stores

Directory of Little Magazines & Small Presses
Dustbooks
5826 Clark Rd
PO Box 100
Paradise CA 95967-0100
916-877-6110; Fax: 916-877-0222
Subjects: 99(small press)
Focus: Small press publishers

Directory of Poetry Publishers
Len Fulton, Editor
Dustbooks 5826 Clark Rd
PO Box 100
Paradise CA 95967-0100
916-877-6110; Fax: 916-877-0222
Subjects: 95
Focus: Book and magazine publishers

The Gardener's Book of Sources
Viking/Penguin
40 W 23rd St
New York NY 10010-5200
212-337-5200
Subjects: 43G
Focus: Companies/books/mags/societies

Guide to Alternative Presses
Elizabeth Gould, Editor
Writer's Resources
15 Margaret's Way
Nantucket MA 02554-4228
508-325-0041; Fax: 508-325-0667
Subjects: 13-53-54-63
Focus: Alternative presses

Guide to Literary Agents and Art/Photo Reps
Writer's Digest Books
1507 Dana Ave
Cincinnati OH 45207-1056
513-531-2222; Fax:
Subjects: 11-56W-99
Focus: Agents and reps

Guide to Publishers/Distributors Serving Minority Languages
Natl Clearinghouse/Bilingual Ed
5555 Wilson Blvd #605
Rosslyn VA 22205-1119
Subjects: 45-49
Focus: Publishers and distributors

Guide to Women Book Publishers
Clothespin Fever Press
5529 N Figueroa
Los Angeles CA 90042-4119
213-254-1373; Fax:
Subjects: 73-99
Focus: Publishing houses owned by women

Information MarketPlace
Kimberly Larson, Editor
Simba Information Directories
2200 Sansom St
Philadelphia PA 19103
800-355-1213; Fax: 215-557-8414
Subjects: 19-99(business/professional)
Focus: Information suppliers

Information Marketplace Director
SIMBA Information Inc
PO Box 7430
Wilton CT 06897
203-834-0033; Fax: 203-834-1771
E-Mail: simbainfo@simbanet.com
Subjects: 56P
Focus: Information marketing

Insider's Guide to Book Editors Publishers & Literary Agents
Prima Publishing
PO Box 1260
Rocklin CA 95677
916-624-5718
Subjects: 99
Focus: Book editors, literary agents

International Directory of Children's Literature
George Kurian Reference Books
PO Box 519
Baldwin Place NY 10505-0519
914-962-3287
Subjects: 21-76
Focus: Book clubs/stores/publishers/etc

International Directory of Little Magazines & Small Press
Dustbooks
5826 Clark Rd
PO Box 100
Paradise CA 95967-0100
916-877-6110; Fax: 916-877-0222
Subjects: 99(small press)
Focus: International magazines and small presses

International Literary MarketPlace
Editor
R R Bowker Co
121 Chanlon Rd PO Box 31
New Providence NJ 07974
908-665-2818; Fax: 908-665-6688
Subjects: 99
Focus: International publishers

Literary Market Place
Editor
R R Bowker Co
121 Chanlon Rd PO Box 31
New Providence NJ 07974
908-665-2818; Fax: 908-665-6688
Subjects: 99
Focus: Publishers, suppliers, etc

Market Guide for Young Artists
Kathy Henderson, Editor
Shoe Tree Press / Betterway
PO Box 219
Crozet VA 22932-0219
804-823-5661
Subjects: 11-21-31-76-79
Focus: Artists and photographers

Market Guide for Young Writers
Kathy Henderson, Editor
Shoe Tree Press / Betterway
PO Box 219
Crozet VA 22932-0219
804-823-5661
Subjects: 21-31-76-79
Focus: Young writers

NACS Book Buyer's Manual
Brenda L Henderson, Editor
Natl Assn of College Stores
528 E Lorain St PO Box 58
Oberlin OH 44074-1238
216-775-7777
Subjects: 99
Focus: Textbooks, college bookstores

New Choices for Writers
Elizabeth Gould, Editor
Writer's Resources
15 Margarets Way
Nantucket MA 02554-4228
508-325-0041; Fax: 508-325-0667
Subjects: 53-54-63(new age publishers)
Focus: Magazines and books

Northwest Publishing MarketPlace
Marjorie Gersh, Compiler
Writer's Connection
1601 Saratoga-Sunnyvale Rd #180
Cupertino CA 95014-5347
408-973-0227; Fax: 408-973-1219
Subjects: 56-61(OR-WA-ID-MT-WY-AK)-99
Focus: Newspapers/magazines/publishers

Novel & Short Story Writer's Mkt
Robin Gee, Editor
Writer's Digest Books
1507 Dana Ave
Cincinnati OH 45207-1056
513-531-2222
Subjects: 75
Focus: Book publishers

Photographer's Market
Editor
Writer's Digest Books
1507 Dana Ave
Cincinnati OH 45207-1056
513-531-2222
Subjects: 11-99
Focus: Photographers marketplace

Poet's Handbook
Lincoln B Young, Editor
Fine Arts Press
1311 Broadway PO Box 3491
Knoxville TN 37917-6502
Subjects: 95
Focus: Publishers of poetry

Poets Marketplace
Joseph J Kelly, Editor
Running Press
125 S 22nd St
Philadelphia PA 19103-4335
215-567-5080; 800-428-1111;
  Fax: 215-568-2919
Subjects: 95
Focus: Poets

Policies of Publishers: A Handbook for Order Librarians
Scarecrow Press
52 Liberty St
Metuchen NJ 08840
908-548-8600
Subjects: 99
Focus: Libraries

Publishers Directory
Editor
Gale Research Co
835 Penobscot Bldg
Detroit MI 48226
313-961-2242; Fax: 313-961-6083
Subjects: 56-99
Focus: Book publishers and others

Publishers Trade List Annual
Editor
R R Bowker Co
121 Chanlon Rd PO Box 31
New Providence NJ 07974
908-665-2818; Fax: 908-665-6688
E-mail:info@bowker.com
http://www.reedref.com
Subjects: 99
Focus: Publishers catalog —paid ads

Publishers' Catalogs Annual
Editor
Chadwyck-Healey
1101 King St
Alexandria VA 22314-2944
703-683-4890
Subjects: 99
Focus: Publishers catalog on microfilm

Publishers, Distributors and Wholesalers of the United States
R R Bowker
121 Chanlon Rd PO Box 31
New Providence NJ 07974
908-665-2818; Fax: 908-665-6688
Subjects: 56
Focus: Publishers/wholesalers

Southwest Publishing MarketPlace
Marjorie Gersh, Compiler
Writer's Connection
1601 Saratoga-Sunnyvale Rd #180
Cupertino CA 95014-5347
408-973-0227; Fax: 408-973-1219
Subjects: 56-61(AZ-NM-CO-TX-NV-UT)-99
Focus: Newspapers/magazines/publishers

Sports Market Place
Richard Lipsey, Editor
Sportsguide Inc
PO Box 1417
Princeton NJ 08542
Subjects: 69
Focus: Magazines/TV/assns/clubs/etc

Who's Who in African Heritage Book Publishing
Mwalimu Mwadilifu, Pres
PO Box 15004
Chesapeake VA 23328-5004
804-547-5542
Subjects: 49B-78-80
Focus: A Black literary marketplace

The Writer's Handbook
Sylvia K Burack, Editor
The Writer Inc
120 Boylston St
Boston MA 02116-4611
617-423-3157
Subjects: 56W-99
Focus: Book and magazine publishers

Writer's Market
Editor
Writer's Digest Books
1507 Dana Ave
Cincinnati OH 45207-1056
513-531-2222
Subjects: 56W-99
Focus: Book and magazine editors

Writer's Northwest Handbook
Linny & Dennis Stovall, Editors
Blue Heron Publishing
24450 NW Hansen Rd
Hillsboro OR 97124
503-621-3911; Fax: 503-621-9826
Subjects: 56-61(NW US)-99
Focus: OR/WA/ID/MT/BC media/publishers

Writers Resource Guide / Seattle
William R Griffin
Writers Publishing Service
1512 Western Ave
Seattle WA 98101
206-284-9954
Subjects: 56-61(WA)
Focus: Assns/newsletters/markets/etc

Writing for the Ethnic Markets
Editor
Writer's Connection
1601 Saratoga-Sunnyvale Rd #180
Cupertino CA 95014-5347
408-973-0227; Fax: 408-973-1219
Subjects: 49-56W-78-99
Focus: Newspapers/magazines/publishers

Marketing Directories

Use the following directories to help you target potential buyers for your books. This list is broken down into ten sections: 1) Booksellers, 2) Mail Order Catalogs, 3) Companies, 4) Fax Directories, 5) Libraries, 6) Media, 7) Organizations, 8) People, 9) Schools, and 10) Wholesalers and Retailers (other than bookstores).

Booksellers

Antiquarian Specialty and Used Book Sellers
Omnigraphics Inc
Penobscot Bldg
Detroit MI 48226
313-961-1340; Fax: 313-961-1383
800-234-1340; Fax: 800-875-1340
Subjects: 99
Focus: Used booksellers
Memo: Arranged by state. Indexed by subject, store name, and owner/manager's name.

Book Lover's Guide to Boston & Cape Cod
Lane Phalen, Editor
Brigadoon Bay Books
PO Box 957724
Hoffman Estates IL 60195-7724
847-884-6940; Fax: 847-884-6987
Subjects: 61(MA)-99
Focus: Bookstores in Boston
Memo: Also publish The Book Lover's Guide to Washhington, DC.

Book Marketing Profitcenter
Ad-Lib Publications
51 1/2 W Adams St
PO Box 1102
Fairfield IA 52556-1102
515-472-6617; Fax: 515-472-3186
E-Mail: MarieK7734@aol.com or Adlib100@aol.com
Subjects: 19M-56
Focus: Wholesalers/chains/clubs/more

New Book Lover's Guide to Chicagoland
Lane Phalen, Editor
Brigadoon Bay Books
PO Box 957724
Hoffman Estates IL 60195-7724
708-884-6940
Subjects: 61(IL)-99
Focus: Chicago area bookstores

New Marketing Opportunities
Sophie Tarila, Editor
New Editions
PO Box 2578
Sedona AZ 86339-2578
520-282-9574; Fax: 520-282-9730
Subjects: 39H-51E-53-54-57
E-mail: newedit@sedona.net
Focus: Publishers/stores/catalogs/media

San Diego Country Writers and Publishers Resource Guide
Red Book Press
3601 Main St PO Box 517
Ramona CA 92065-3862
619-789-0620
Subjects: 56-61(CA)-99
Focus: Publishers/media/other resources

Catalogs

Business to Business Catalogs
Grey House Publishing
Pocket Knife Square
PO Box 1866
Lakeville CT 06039-1866
860-435-0868; 800-562-2139;
  Fax: 860-435-0867
Subjects: 19
Focus: Mail order catalogs

Computer Catalogs
Barry T Klein, Editor
Todd Publications
PO Box 301
West Nyack NY 10994-0301
914-358-6213
Subjects: 23C
Focus: Catalogs and mail order firms

Cook's Mail Order Directory
Lynn Kerrigan, Editor
Page One Cooks
134 Eachus Ave PO Box 194
Bryn Mawr PA 19010-1313
610-527-5654; Fax: 610-527-5654
Subjects: 27
Focus: Cookbook and cooking catalogs

Directory of Mail Order Catalogs
Grey House Publishing
Pocket Knife Square
PO Box 1866
Lakeville CT 06039-1866
860-435-0868; 800-562-2139;
  Fax: 860-435-0867
Subjects: 19-99
Focus: Mail order catalogs

How to Sell to Mail Order Catalogs
Ad-Lib Publications
51 1/2 West Adams
PO Box 1102
Fairfield IA 52556-1102
515-472-6617; Fax: 515-472-3186
E-Mail: MarieK7734@aol.com
Subjects: 99
Focus: Mail order catalogs that carry books

Mail Order Business Directory
Bernard Klein
Todd Publications
PO Box 301
West Nyack NY 10994-0301
914-358-6213
Subjects: 19-99
Focus: Catalogs and mail order firms

National Dir of Mailing Lists
Oxbridge Communications
150 Fifth Ave #302
New York NY 10011-4311
212-741-0231; Fax: 212-633-2938
Subjects: 99
Focus: Mailing lists

National Directory of Catalogs
Catalog Data Center
Oxbridge Communications
150 Fifth Ave #302
New York NY 10011-4311
212-741-0231; Fax: 212-633-2938
E-mail: info@oxbridge.com
Subjects: 19M-99 catalogs
Focus: Catalogs

New Fiberworks Sourcebooks
Bobbi McRae
Fiberworks Publications
PO Box 49770
Austin TX 78765-9770
512-343-6112
Subjects: 29
Focus: Thousands of mail order sources for weaving, knitting, spinning, crochet, needlework, basketry, papermaking, quilting, lacemaking and more, including books

The Wholesale-by-Mail Catalog
HarperCollins Publishers
10 E 53rd St
New York NY 10022-5244
212-207-7000; 800-242-7737
Subjects: 99
Focus: Features wholesale catalogs for consumer in most interest areas

Companies

Adweek Agency Directory
Mitch Tebo, Dir/Operations
Adweek Directories
1515 Broadway 12th Fl
New York NY 10036-8901
212-536-5336; Fax: 212-536-5321
Subjects: 19M-56
Focus: Advertising/PR agencies

Best Directory of Recruiters
The Original Resume Co
1105 Lakeview Ave
Dracut MA 01826-4762
508-957-6600; Fax: 508-957-6605
Subjects: 19C
Focus: 16,100 recruiters in all areas
Memo: 800+ job & industrial specialties.

The CD-ROM Finder
James Shelton, Editor
Learned Information
143 Old Marlton Pike
Medford NJ 08055-8750
609-654-6266; Fax: 609-654-4309
Subjects: 99
Focus: CD-ROM products

The Corporate Address Book
Perigee/Putnam Books
200 Madison Ave
New York NY 10016-3903
212-576-8900; 800-631-8571
Subjects: 19
Focus: Corporations

The Corporate Yellow Book
Leadership Directory
104 Fifth Ave 2nd Fl
New York NY 10011
212-627-4140; Fax: 212-645-0931
Subjects: 19
Focus: Corporations/officers

Directory of Video, Multimedia & Audio Visual Equipment
ICIA
11242 Waples Mill Rd #200
Fairfax VA 22030-6079
703-273-7200; Fax: 703-278-8082
Subjects: 23C-56M
Focus: Video, multimedia, and audio visual equipment

Directory of Business Information Resources
Grey House Publishing
PO Box 186
Lakeville CT 06039-0186
203-435-0868; 800-562-2139;
    Fax: 203-435-0867
Subjects: 19
Focus: Business information

Directory of Online Databases
Gale Directory of Databases
835 Penobscot Bldg
Detroit MI 48226
313-961-2242; Fax: 313-961-6083
Subjects: 99
Focus: Online, portable databases

Directory of Portable Databases
Gale Directory of Databases
835 Penobscot Bldg
Detroit MI 48226
313-961-2242; Fax: 313-961-6083
Subjects: 99
Focus: Portable databases

Directory of Printers
Ad-Lib Publications
51 1/2 W Adams
PO Box 1102
Fairfield IA 52556-1102
515-472-6617; 800-669-0773;
    Fax: 515-472-3186
E-Mail: MarieK7734@aol.com or
    AdLib100@aol.com
Subjects: 56X
Focus: Book printers

Graphic Arts Blue Books
A F Lewis & Co
245 Fifth Ave
New York NY 10016-8728
212-679-0770; Fax: 212-545-7963
Subjects: 56
Focus: Graphic arts

Green Company Resource Guide
John Wasik
The New Consumer Institute
PO Box 51
Wauconda IL 60084-0051
708-526-0522; Fax: 708-526-1174
Subjects: 51E
Focus: Lists all trade groups, consultants, government agencies, articles, and related information on green products

Journal of Business Strategies
Faulkner & Gray
106 Fulton St
New York NY 10038-2708
800-535-8403
Subjects: 19-44E
Focus: Business

Lexicon-MTA
Jerry G Guttman, Pres
15 E Putnam Ave #274
Greenwich CT 06830-9726
800-328-8777
Subjects: 56
Focus: Directory of consulting services
Memo: Consultants located in New York, Los Angeles, Washington, DC, Toronto, & Mexico City.

Licensing Business Sourcebook
EPM Communications
160 Mercer St 3rd Fl
New York NY 10012-3208
212-941-0099; Fax: 212-941-1622
Subjects: 19M
Focus: Licensors/agents/licensees/etc

MacRae's Blue Book
Editor
65 Bleecker St
New York NY 10012-2420
212-673-4700; Fax: 212-475-1790
Subjects: 19
Focus: 50,000 businesses

O'Dwyer's Directory of Corporate Communications
J R O'Dwyer Co
271 Madison Ave
New York NY 10016-1001
212-679-2471; Fax: 212-683-2750
Subjects: 56M
Focus: Corporate

O'Dwyer's Directory of PR Exec
J R O'Dwyer Co
271 Madison Ave
New York NY 10016-1001
212-679-2471; Fax: 212-683-2750
Subjects: 56M
Focus: PR Executives

O'Dwyer's Directory of PR Firms
J R O'Dwyer Co
271 Madison Ave
New York NY 10016-1001
212-679-2471; Fax: 212-683-2750
Subjects: 56M
Focus: PR firms

O'Dwyer's Media Placement Guide
J R O'Dwyer Co
271 Madison Ave
New York NY 10016
212-679-2471; Fax: 212-683-2750
Subjects: 33M-33T
Focus: For PR people

Premium Incentive & Travel Buyer
The Salesman's Guide
Reed Reference Publishing
121 Chanlon Rd PO Box 31
New Providence NJ 07974
908-665-2818; 800-223-1797;
    Fax: 908-665-6688
Subjects: 99
Focus: Premium buyers – 20,000 buyers from 11,000 companies

The Textile Redbook
Billian Publishing
2100 Powers Ferry Rd
Atlanta GA 30339-5014
770-955-5656; Fax: 770-955-8485
Subjects: 19X
Focus: Over 6,100 textile mills in the US, Canada, & Mexico

Thomas Registry of American Manufacturers
Thomas Publishing
1 Penn Plz
New York NY 10119-0103
212-290-7225; Fax: 212-290-7206
Subjects: 19-49-73
Focus: Manufacturers by product

Databases

Accounting Professionals CPE Ins
Judy Marshall, List Mgr
4965 Preston Park Blvd #300
Plano TX 75093-5153
214-985-4060; Fax: 214-985-4061
Subjects: 19A
Focus: Accounting software

All-in-One Directory
Amalia Gebbie, Publisher
Gebbie Press
PO Box 1000
New Paltz NY 12561-0017
914-255-7560
Subjects: 99(
Focus: Media
Memo: PC diskettes: newspapers, radio/TV, magazines.

Computer Lifestyle
999 Main St
Glen Ellyn IL 60137-5832
708-469-2075; Fax: 708-790-5244
Subjects: 23
Focus: MacIntosh owners

Database Management
Cindy Lin
304 Park Ave S
New York NY 10010
212-388-8830; Fax: 212-388-8855
Subjects: 99
Focus: Database management

Edith Roman Assoc Inc Database
875 Ave of the Americas
New York NY 10001
212-695-3836; 800-223-2194;
 Fax: 212-629-5924
Subjects: 99
Focus: Database

Internet Business Advantage
Attn: Diane Jackson
1866 Colonial Village Ln
PO Box 10488
Lancaster PA 17601-6704
800-638-1639; Fax: 717-393-5752
E-Mail: success@wentworth.com
Subjects: 19-23
Focus: Business

Mediamatic System -- Targeter
Hymen Wagner, Pres
Media Distribution Services
307 W 36th St
New York NY 10018-6403
212-279-4800; Fax: 212-714-9092
Subjects: 99
Focus: 40,000 TV/radio/newspapers

Power Media Selects
Mitchell P Davis
Broadcast Interview Source
2233 Wisconsin Ave #301
Washington DC 20007-4104
202-333-4904; 800-955-0311;
 Fax: 202-342-5411
Subjects: 99
Focus: Influential media people

Memo: 834 news organizations: radio networks, 100 daily newspapers, leading TV talk shows, top 25 radio talk shows, trade magazines, major newsletters, new syndicates, topical magazines.

PR ProfitCenter Database
Ad-Lib Publications
51 1/2 W Adams St
PO Box 1102
Fairfield IA 52556-1102
515-472-6617; 800-669-0773Fax:
 515-472-3186
E-Mail: MarieK7734@aol.com or
 AdLib100@aol.com
Subjects: 99(print and broadcast media)
Focus: Magazines, newspapers, radio, TV, syndicated columnists

Reed Reference Publishing
PO Box 31
New Providence NJ 07974-9903
800-521-8110; Fax: 908-665-6688
Subjects: 99
Focus: Media

Talk Show Selects
Mitchell P Davis
Broadcast Interview Source
2233 Wisconsin Ave NW #540
Washington DC 20007-4104
202-333-4904; 800-955-0311;
 Fax: 202-342-5411
Subjects: 99
Focus: Radio/TV talk show producers

Editorial Calendar

Media Calendar Directory
Bacon's Information
332 S Michigan Ave #900
Chicago IL 60604-4304
312-922-2400; 800-621-0561;
 Fax: 312-922-3127
Subjects: 99
Focus: Editorial calendars

Fax Directories

Facsimile Users' Directory
Robert C Townsend
Monitor Publishing
104 Fifth Ave 2nd Fl
New York NY 10011-6901
212-627-4140; Fax: 212-645-0931
Subjects: 19-55-99
Focus: 34,000+ fax machines

Fax USA
Omnigraphics Inc
Penobscot Bldg
Detroit MI 48226
800-234-1340; Fax: 313-961-1383 33
Subjects: 19-59-99
Focus: Businesses/associations

Fred F Rapaport Convert Printed Directories
QuickTel Software Publ
18 E 48th St #902
New York NY 10017-1014
212-750-7300; Fax: 212-750-7302
Subjects: 19-55-99
Focus: 25-30 distributors

National Fax Directory
Gale Research Co
835 Penobscot Bldg
Detroit MI 48226-4094
313-961-2242; Fax: 800-414-5043
Subjects: 19-55-99
Focus: Corporations, organizations, and government

Libraries

American Library Directory
R R Bowker Co
121 Chanlon Rd PO Box 31
New Providence NJ 07974
908-665-2818; 800-521-8110;
 Fax: 908-665-6688
Subjects: 99
Focus: Libraries

Authors in Libraries Directory
Mary Shapiro, VP Mkt Planning
Baker & Taylor
652 E Main St PO Box 6920
Bridgewater NJ 08807-0920
908-218-0400
Subjects: 99
Focus: Author readings in libraries)

Directory of Federal Libraries
Oryx Press
4041 N Central at Indian School
Phoenix AZ 85012-3399
602-265-2651; Fax: 602-265-6250
Subjects: 55-99
Focus: Government libraries

Directory of Special Libraries and Information Centers
Gale Research Co
835 Penobscot Bldg
Detroit MI 48226
313-961-2242; Fax: 313-961-6083
Subjects: 99
Focus: Special libraries

Media

1000 Worldwide Business Directory
Ken Albertsen, Mgr
Albertsen's
PO Box 339
Nevada City CA 95959
916-477-0915; Fax: 916-477-0915
Subjects: 19-44-59
Focus: Directories

1000 Worldwide Newspapers
Ken Albertsen, Manager
Albertsen's
PO Box 339
Nevada City CA 95959
916-477-0915; Fax: 916-477-0915
Subjects: 99
Focus: Newspapers

Advertising Options Plus
Standard Rate & Data Focus
1700 Higgins Rd
Des Plaines IL 60018-5621
847-375-5068; Fax: 847-375-5009
Subjects: 99
Focus: Advertising

Bacon's Media Directories
Bacon's Information Inc
332 S Michigan Ave
Chicago IL 60604-4301
312-922-2400; 800-621-0561;
   Fax: 312-922-3127
Subjects: 56M
Focus: Newspapers/radio/TV
Memo: Formerly known as Bacon's Publicity Checker. 1700 daily newspapers, 8100 weekly newspapers, 9400 business, trade, and consumer magazines. Bacon's Media Lists make these lists available on labels or diskettes.

Black American Information Dir
Gale Research Co
835 Penobscot Bldg
Detroit MI 48226
313-961-2242; Fax: 313-961-6083
Subjects: 49B-78-80
Focus: Assns/media/programs/agencies

Black Resource Guide
R Benjamin Johnson, Editor
501 Oneida Pl NW
Washington DC 20011-2038
202-291-4373; Fax: 202-291-4373
Subjects: 49-78-80
Focus: Includes book publishers/etc

Book Publishing Resource Guide
Marie Kiefer
Ad-Lib Publications
51 1/2 West Adams St
Fairfield IA 52556
515-472-6617; Fax: 515-472-3186
Subjects: 19M-56
Focus: Book marketing/publicity
Memo: E-Mail: MarieK7734@aol.com or Adlib100@aol.com

Broadcasting & Cable MarketPlace
R R Bowker Co
121 Chanlon Rd PO Box 31
New Providence NJ 07974
908-665-2818; 800-521-8110;
   Fax: 908-665-6688
Subjects: 99
Focus: Radio and TV stations
Memo: Formerly Broadcasting Yearbook.

Burrelle's Media Directories
75 E Northfield Rd
Livingston NJ 07039
201-992-6600; 800-876-3342;
   Fax: 800-898-6677
Subjects: 49
Focus: All media

Business & Financial News Media
Larriston Communications
PO Box 20229
New York NY 10025-1518
212-864-0150
Subjects: 19-19F-19I
Focus: Business and financial news media

Business Media Directory
Bacon's Information
332 S Michigan Ave
Chicago IL 60604-4301
312-922-2400; 800-621-0561;
   Fax: 312-922-3127
Subjects: 19
Focus: Business and financial editors, beat reporters, freelancers, and show producers

Business Publications Rates/Data
Standard Rate & Data Focus
1700 Higgins Rd
Des Plaines IL 60018-5621
847-375-5068; 800-851-7737;
   Fax: 847-375-5009
Subjects: 19-99
Focus: Business magazines

Celebrity Focus International Inc
Jeff Kormos, Mg Dir Operations
8833 W Sunset Blvd #401
W Hollywood CA 90069-2110
310-652-1700; Fax: 310-652-9244
Subjects: 17
Memo: The only international organization which provides clients with accurate, up-to-date information on the world's leading personalities, newsmakers, and famous folk. Has a variety of services and a data base of more than 500,000 names. Invaluable for PR firms as agencies, and news media, among others.

Celebrity Focus International Inc
Mark Kerrigan, Mg Dir of Oper
1780 Broadway #300
New York NY 10019-1414
212-245-1460; Fax: 212-397-4626
Subjects: 17
Focus: As above

Chittenden Press Focus
1277 National Press Bldg
Washington DC 20045-2200
202-737-4434; Fax: 202-737-4434
Subjects: 56
Focus: Press

College Media Directory
Debra Striplan, Editor
Oxbridge Communications
150 Fifth Ave #302
New York NY 10011-4311
212-741-0231; Fax: 212-633-2938
Subjects: 31E-99
Focus: Magazines, newspapers, and radio shows

Complete Directory for People with Disabilities
Grey House Publishing
Pocket Knife Square
PO Box 1866
Lakeville CT 06039-1866
860-435-0868; 800-562-2139;
   Fax: 860-435-0867
Subjects: 39D
Focus: Disabilities

Complete Directory for People with Learning Disabilities
Grey House Publishing
Pocket Knife Square
Lakeville CT 06039
203-435-0868; 800-562-2139;
   Fax: 203-435-0867
Subjects: 31E-39D
Focus: Learning disabilities

Consumer Magazines Rates & Data
Standard Rate & Data Focus
1700 Higgins Rd
Des Plaines IL 60018-5621
847-375-5068; 800-851-7737;
   Fax: 847-375-5009
Subjects: 99
Focus: General magazines

Convention Digest
Chicago Convention Bureau
2301 S Lakeshore Dr
Chicago IL 60616-1417
312-567-8500; Fax: 312-567-8533
Subjects: 61(IL)
Focus: Conventions

Creeyadio Services One-to-One
Jay Trachman
PO Box 9787
Fresno CA 93794
209-448-0100; Fax: 209-226-7481
Subjects: 56
Focus: Radio

Dial-An-Expert: The National Directory of Quotable Experts
Marc McCutcheon, Editor
American Media Services
87 Hamilton St
South Portland ME 04106-4453
207-799-5689; Fax: 207-799-5689
Subjects: 99(700 national experts)
Focus: University profs & authors
Memo: Aimed at helping authors who are looking for experts to quote in magazine articles.

Directories on CD-ROM
Bacon's Information
332 S Michigan Ave
Chicago IL 60604-4301
312-922-2400; 800-621-0561;
   Fax: 312-922-3127
Subjects: 99
Focus: CD-ROM

Directory of Aging Resources
Business Publishers Inc
951 Pershing Dr
Silver Spring MD 20910-4432
800-274-0122; Fax: 301-585-9075
Subjects: 35A
Focus: National associations and advocacy groups, government offices, funding sources

Directory of Alternative and Radical Publications
Alternative Press Institute
PO Box 33109
Baltimore MD 21218-0401
301-243-2471; Fax: 410-235-5325
Subjects: 13-53
Focus: Magazines

The Directory of Business Information Resources
Grey House Publishing
Pocket Knife Square
PO Box 1866
Lakeville CT 06039-1866
860-435-0868; 800-562-2139;
   Fax: 860-435-0867
Subjects: 19-99(assn/newsletter/mags/etc)
Focus: 85 major business areas, from accounting and advertising to transportation and wholesalers

Directory of Ethnic Periodicals
Matthew Manning
Oxbridge Communications
150 Fifth Ave #302
New York NY 10011-4311
212-741-0231; Fax: 212-633-2938
Subjects: 49
Focus: Minority magazines

Directory of Periodicals of Interest to the Health Industry
Quick Source Press
10 Pelham Ave
Manuet NY 10954-3428
914-627-6511; Fax: 914-627-6512
Subjects: 39
Focus: Periodicals/online databases

Directory of Periodicals Online
Nuchine Nobari, Editor/Publ
Library Alliance
264 Lexington Ave #4C
New York NY 10016-4182
212-685-5297
Subjects:
   19-19L-23-24-39-51-55L-56M-67-97
Focus: Magazines available online (either indexed, abstracted, or full-text) 4 editions: News, Law & Business; Science & Technology; Medical & Humanities

Directory of Political Newsletters
Lynn Helleburst, Editor
Government Research Focus
214 SW 6th Ave
Topeka KS 66603-3719
913-232-7720; 800-346-6898;
   Fax: 913-232-1615
Subjects: 13-55
Focus: US and state government newsletters

Editor and Publisher Yearbook
Editor
11 West 19th St
New York NY 10011-4236
212-675-4380; Fax: 212-691-7287
Subjects: 99
Focus: Newspapers

Encyclopedia of Associations – National
Gale Research Co
835 Penobscot Bldg
Detroit MI 48226-4094
313-961-2242; Fax: 313-961-6083
Subjects: 19-23-24-31-39-51-55-57-65-67-99
Focus: Newsletters/journals/magazines

Florida News Media Directory
News Media Directories
PO Box 316
Mount Dora FL 32757-0316
352-383-3023; Fax: 352-383-9233
Subjects: 56M-61(FL)
Focus: Florida media

Free Circulation Community Papers
Media Guide
Assn of Free Community Papers
401 N Michigan Ave
Chicago IL 60611-4212
312-644-6610
Subjects: 99
Focus: Free circulation newspapers

Gale Directory of Publications and Broadcast Media
Gale Research Co & Broadcasting
835 Penobscot Bldg
Detroit MI 48226-4094
313-961-2242; 800-877-4253;
   Fax: 800-414-5043
Subjects: 99(mags/newspapers/radio/TV)
Focus: 25,000 + print media, 10,000 broadcast media

Goldwyn's List of Wine Media
310 S Peoria #504
Chicago IL 60607-3534
312-226-7857; Fax: 312-226-7558
Subjects: 27(wine)
Focus: Writers/editors/retail/tourists

Guide to Disability Periodicals
Joseph Baird
Committee to Promote Writing
English Dept/Kent St Univ Rm 113
Kent OH 44242-0001
216-672-3000; Fax: 216-672-3152
Subjects: 39
Focus: Disability

Guide to Religious and Inspirational Magazines
Livia Fiordelisi, Editor
Writer's Resources
15 Margaret's Way
Nantucket MA 02554-4228
508-325-0041; Fax: 508-325-0667
Subjects: 56W-63
Focus: Religious and inspirational magazines

Hawaii All Media Publicity Guide
Avatar PR
1521 S King #401
Honolulu HI 96826
808-946-1641; Fax: 808-946-1641
Subjects: 61(HI)
Focus: Hawaii media

Hispanic Americans Information Directory
Gale Research Co
835 Penobscot Bldg
Detroit MI 48226-4094
313-961-2242; Fax: 313-961-6083
Subjects: 45(Spanish)-49H-78-80
Focus: Assns/media/programs/agencies

Hispanic Media and Markets
Standard Rate & Data Focus
1700 Higgins Rd
Des Plaines IL 60018-5621
847-375-5068; 800-851-7737;
   Fax: 847-375-5009
Subjects: 45(Spanish)-49-78-80
Focus: Hispanic Media

Hispanic Media USA
Ana Veciana-Suarez
The Media Institute
1000 Potomac St NW #301
Washington DC 20007-3547
202-298-7512; Fax: 202-337-7092
Subjects: 45(Spanish)-49(Hispanic)-78
Focus: Hispanic print/broadcast media

Hudson's Subscription Newsletter Directory
Joan W Artz, Editor
The Newsletter Clearinghouse
44 W Market St PO Box 311
Rhinebeck NY 12572-1403
914-876-2081; 800-572-3451;
   Fax: 914-876-2561
Subjects: 99
Focus: Subscription newsletters

Hudson's Washington News Media
The Newsletter Clearinghouse
PO Box 311
44 W Market St
Rhinebeck NY 12572-0311
914-876-2081; Fax: 914-876-2561
Subjects: 99
Focus: DC news media contacts

Hudsons State Capital News Media
The Newsletter Clearinghouse
PO Box 311
44 W Market St
Rhinebeck NY 12572-0311
914-876-2081; Fax: 914-876-2561
Subjects: 99
Focus: State capital news contacts

International Media Directory
Bacon's Information
332 S Michigan Ave
Chicago IL 60604-4301
312-922-2400; 800-621-0561;
　Fax: 312-922-3127
Subjects: 44-99
Focus: International media

Jewish Press in America
Joseph Jacobs Organization
60 E 42nd St
New York NY 10165-0006
212-687-6234; Fax: 212-687-9785
Subjects: 63J
Focus: Jewish publications

Magazines for Young People
Bill Katz & Linda Katz, Editors
R R Bowker
121 Chanlon Rd PO Box 31
New Providence NJ 07974
908-665-2818; 800-521-8110;
　Fax: 908-665-6688
Subjects: 21-21T-31-76-89
Memo: 800 magazines for children and young adults. 200 magazines for teachers, librarians, and other educators. 80 subject categories

Major College Newspapers
Charles Dalley Oliver, Publ
Oliver Communications
9 Cannon St
Norwalk CT 06851
508-428-7287
Subjects: 31-99
Focus: College newspapers

Matthews Media Directory
Canadian Corporate News
25 Adelaide St E
Toronto ON Canada M5C 3A1
416-362-5739; Fax: 416-955-0705
Subjects: 99
Focus: Canadian magazine, radio, TV, and newspaper

Media Factbook
Communications Dept
United Way
95 M St SW #306
Washington DC 20024-3622
202-488-2060; Fax: 202-488-2099
Subjects: 61(DC/MD/VA)
Focus: Local print/broadcast media

Media Guide for Activists
Washington Peace Ctr
2111 Florida Ave NW
Washington DC 20008-1912
202-234-2000; Fax: 202-265-5233
Subjects: 99
Focus: Washington DC area

Media List
Sally Gary, Author
2726 Shelter Island Dr #94
San Diego CA 92106-2731
619-222-8489; Fax: 619-222-0772
Subjects: 61(CA)-99
Focus: Local/national talk shows & more

Metro California Media Directory
Public Relations Plus
PO Box 1197
New Milford CT 06776
203-354-9361; 800-999-8448;
　Fax: 203-355-8048
Subjects: 61(CA)-99
Focus: California media

Minnesota Media Directory
Jim Hayes, Editor
Burrelle's Media Directories
75 E Northfield Ave
Livingston NJ 07039
800-876-3342; Fax: 800-898-6677
Subjects: 99
Focus: Minnesota media

National Directory of Magazines
Barry Lee
Oxbridge Communications
150 Fifth Ave #302
New York NY 10011-4311
212-741-0231; Fax: 212-633-2938
Subjects: 99(
Focus: Magazines only
Memo: Also available in IBM-PC diskette format.

National Directory of Newspaper Op-Ed Pages
Communication Creativity
PO Box 909
Buena Vista CO 81211-0909
719-395-8659; 800-331-8355;
　Fax: 719-395-8374
Subjects: 99
Focus: Newspapers w/ op-ed section

National Media Directory
Jim Hayes, Editor
Burrelle's Media Directories
75 E Northfield Ave
Livingston NJ 07039
800-876-3342; Fax: 800-898-6677
Subjects: 99
Focus: All media

National News Media Yellow Book
Leadership Directories
104 Fifth Ave 2nd Fl
New York NY 10011-6901
212-627-4140; Fax: 212-645-0931
Subjects: 99(mags/newspapers/radio/tv)
Focus: 18, 000 journalists

National Religious Broadcasters
NRB
7839 Ashton Ave
Manassas VA 20109-2883
703-330-7000; Fax: 703-330-7100
Subjects: 56M-63
Focus: Religious broadcasters

New England Media Directory
Jim Hayes, Editor
Burrelle's Media Directories
75 E Northfield Rd
Livingston NJ 07039
800-876-3342; Fax: 800-898-6677
Subjects: 61(New England)
Focus: New England media

New Jersey Media Directory
Jim Hayes, Editor
Burrelle's Media Directories
75 E Northfield Rd
Livingston NJ 07039
800-876-3342; Fax: 800-898-6677
Subjects: 61(NJ)
Focus: New Jersey media

New York Media Directory
Jim Hayes, Editor
Burrelle's Media Directories
75 E Northfield Rd
Livingston NJ 07039
800-876-3342; Fax: 800-898-6677
Subjects: 61(NY)
Focus: NY media

New York Publicity Outlets
Public Relations Plus
PO Box 1197
New Milford CT 06776
203-354-9361; 800-999-8448;
　Fax: 203-355-8048
Subjects: 61(NY)-99
Focus: NY media

New York State Media Directory
Editor
Burrelle's Media Directories
75 E Northfield Rd
Livingston NJ 07039
201-992-6600; 800-631-1160;
　Fax: 201-992-1736
Subjects: 61(NY)
Focus: NY state media

Newsclip's Illinois Media
Newsclip
213 W Institute Pl
Chicago IL 60610-3125
312-751-7300; 800-544-8433;
　Fax: 312-751-7306
Subjects: 61(IL)-99
Focus: IL media

Newsletters in Print 1996
Gale Research Co
835 Penobscot Bldg
Detroit MI 48226-4094
313-961-2242; Fax: 313-961-6083
Subjects: 99
Memo: Newsletters & 11,500 authoritative sources of information

Newspaper Database-on-Diskette
Publishers Network
PO Box 3190
Vista CA 92085-3190
619-941-4100; Fax: 619-941-2295
Subjects: 99
Focus: Newspapers

Newspaper Rates & Data
Standard Rate & Data Focus
1700 Higgins Rd
Des Plaines IL 60018-5621
847-375-5068; 800-851-7737;
　Fax: 847-375-5009
Subjects: 99
Focus: Newspapers

No Nonsense E-Mail/Website Guide for Writers
Anthony Carr
New Earth Communications
PO Box 629
Herndon VA 20171
E-Mail: MrWriteVA@aol.com
Subjects: 56
Focus: All sorts of internet resources

North American Senior Media Directory
Gene & Adele Malott, Editors
Gen Publishing Group
250 E Riverview Cir
Reno NV 89509-1115
702-786-7419
Subjects: 35A
Focus: Senior media

Oxbridge Directory of Newsletters
Oxbridge Communications
150 Fifth Ave #302
New York NY 10011-4311
212-741-0231; Fax: 212-633-2938
Subjects: 99
Focus: Newsletters

Pennsylvania Media Directory
Jim Hayes, Editor
Burrelle's Media Directories
75 E Northfield Rd
Livingston NJ 07039
800-876-3342; Fax: 800-898-6677
Subjects: 61(PA)-99
Focus: PA media

Philadelphia Publicity Guide
Fund-Raising Institute
PO Box 365
Ambler PA 19002-0365
215-628-8729
Subjects: 61(PA)
Focus: Philadelphia media

PIMS European Media Directory
1133 Broadway #423
New York NY 10010-7988
212-645-5112; Fax: 212-645-5217
Subjects: 44(European media)
Focus: European media

Publishing for Professional Markets: Review, Trends, & Forecast
Claire Schoen, Editorial Dir
SIMBA Information Inc
PO Box 7430
Wilton CT 06897-7430
203-834-0033; Fax: 203-834-1771
Subjects: 56P
Focus: Publishing

Radio Phone Interview Shows
Ad-Lib Publications
51 1/2 West Adams
PO Box 1102
Fairfield IA 52556-1102
515-472-6617; 800-669-0773Fax: 515-472-3186
E-Mail: MarieK7734@aol.com or AdLib100@aol.com
Subjects: 99
Focus: Radio phone interview shows

Radio Yearbook
BIA Publications
14595 Avion Pky #500
Chantilly VA 20151-1102
703-818-2425; Fax: 703-803-3299
Subjects: 99
Focus: Radio information

Radio/TV Contacts Focus
Media News Keys
4029 27th St
Long Island City NY 11101-3814
718-937-3990
Subjects: 99(radio/TV programs)
Focus: Originating in New York City

San Diego Finder Binder
James Tuck, Editor
8546 Chevy Chase Dr
La Mesa CA 91941-5325
619-463-5050; Fax: 619-463-5097
Subjects: 61(CA)-99
Focus: All media in San Diego area
Memo: Other Finder Binder directories are franchised for Arizona, Cleveland, Dallas, Denver, Houston, Milwaukee, Oklahoma City, Pittsburgh, Portland, Saint Louis, and Seattle.

Senior Media Directory
Gem Publishing Group
250 E Riverview Cir
Reno NV 89509-1115
702-786-7419
Subjects: 35A
Focus: Newspapers, magazines, newsletters, syndicates, columnists, radio, and TV programs. Mailing lists available on labels.

Senior Media Guide
CD Publications
8204 Fenton St
Silver Spring MD 20910
301-588-6380; 800-666-6380; Fax: 301-588-6385
Subjects: 35A
Focus: Senior mediia

Smorgasbord of Cooks Periodicals
Lynn Kerrigan, Editor
Page One Cooks
134 Eachus Ave PO Box 194
Bryn Mawr PA 19010-1313
610-527-5654; Fax: 610-527-5654
Subjects: 27
Focus: Food-related publications, 130 mags/newsletters

Sports Advantage
Standard Rate & Data Focus
1700 Higgins Rd
Des Plaines IL 60018-5621
847-375-5068; 800-851-7737; Fax: 847-375-5009
Subjects: 69
Focus: Media, ad options, endorsements

Spot Radio Rates & Data
Standard Rate & Data Focus
1700 Higgins Rd
Des Plaines IL 60018-5621
847-375-5068; 800-851-7737; Fax: 847-375-5009
Subjects: 99
Focus: Radio stations

Spot Television Rates & Data
Standard Rate & Data Focus
1700 Higgins Rd
Des Plaines IL 60018-5621
847-375-5068; 800-851-7737; Fax: 847-375-5009
Subjects: 99
Focus: TV stations

Standard Periodical Directory
Matthew Manning
Oxbridge Communications
150 Fifth Ave #302
New York NY 10011-4311
212-741-0231; 800-955-0231; Fax: 212-633-2938
Subjects: 99
Focus: Magazines and newsletters

Talk Shows & Hosts on Radio
Whitefoord Press
806 Oakwood Blvd
Dearborn MI 48124-2319
313-274-1038; 800-972-2584; Fax: 313-274-9263
Subjects: 33R-99
Focus: Radio talk shows
Memo: Lists station addresses, owners, formats, markets, and power as well as show hosts, producers, times, subjects, and format. Does not list whether they do phone interviews. Arranged geographically.

Texas Media Directory
Jim Hayes, Editor
Burrelle's Media Directories
75 E Northfield Ave
Livingston NJ 07039
800-876-3342; Fax: 800-898-6677
Subjects: 99
Focus: Texas media

TIA International Travel News Directory
TIA Communications Dept
1100 New York Ave NW #450
Washington DC 20005-3934
202-408-8422; Fax: 202-408-1255
Subjects: 71
Focus: International travel

Top 200 TV News/Talk Shows
Ad-Lib Publications
51 1/2 West Adams
PO Box 1102
Fairfield IA 52556-1102
515-472-6617; 800-669-0773; Fax: 515-472-3186
E-Mail: MarieK7734@aol.com or AdLib100@aol.com
Subjects: 99
Focus: TV news/talk/magazines shows

Travel Leisure & Entertainment News Media Directory
Larriston Communications
PO Box 20229
New York NY 10025-1518
212-864-0150
Subjects: 11-14-27-33-35-40-43-71-99
Focus: Media contacts

Ulrich's International
Periodicals Directory
R R Bowker Co
121 Chanlon Rd PO Box 31
New Providence NJ 07974
908-464-6800; 800-521-8110;
 Fax: 908-665-6688
Subjects: 99
Focus: Magazines and other periodicals
Memo: Besides being available in a 5-volume set of books, Ulrich's is also available online, in microfiche, on CD-ROM, and on tape.

Vermont Media Directory
KSV Communaters
212 Battery St
Burlington VT 05401-5281
802-862-8261; Fax: 802-863-4724
Subjects: 61(VT)
Focus: Vermont Media

Washington Media Directory
The McConnell Co
200 1st Ave W #210
Seattle WA 98119
206-285-0140; Fax: 206-285-5073
Subjects: 61(NW US)
Focus: Washington state media

Working Press of the Nation
Reed Reference Publications
121 Chamlon Rd
New Providence NJ 07974
908-665-2818; 800-521-8110;
 Fax: 908-665-6688
Subjects: 99
Focus: All media

Writing in Ohio
Lavern Hall
Writer's World Press
PO Box 24684
Cleveland OH 44124-0684
216-481-8278; Fax: 216-481-2057
Subjects: 56W-61(OH)
Focus: Publishers/magazines/groups/etc

Media Newsletters

Book Marketing Update
John Kremer, Editor
Open Horizons Publishing Co
PO Box 205
Fairfield IA 52556-0205
515-472-6130; Fax: 515-472-1560
E-Mail: JohnKremer@aol.com
http://www.bookmarket.com
Subjects: 56-99
Focus: Media & book marketing contacts

Book Promotion Hotline
Marie Kiefer, Editor
Ad-Lib Publications
PO Box 1102
Fairfield IA 52556-1102
515-472-6617; Fax: 515-472-3186
E-Mail: MarieK7734@aol.com or
 Adlib100@aol.com
Subjects: 56-99
Focus: Media & book marketing contacts

Bulldog Reporter
Lori Kaplan
InfoComm Group
1250 45th St #200
Emeryville CA 94608
510-596-9300; 800-959-1059;
 Fax: 510-596-9331
Subjects: 56-99(media info)
Focus: Media
Memo: They have separate editions for Western, Eastern, and Central US.

Contacts Newsletter
Madeleine Gillis, Editor
CAP Communications
3520 Broadway
Long Island City NY 11106-1114
718-721-0508; Fax: 718-274-3387
Subjects: 99
Focus: Weekly media update newsletter
Memo: Deadline: Wednesday before the Monday edition.

Lifestyle Media Reporter
John Papageorge, Editor
InfoComm Group
1250 45th St #200
Emeryville CA 94608
510-596-9300; 800-959-1059;
 Fax: 510-596-9331
Subjects: 56M-99
Focus: Lifestyle media info

Media Resource Focus
Scientists Institute for Public Informationl
1328 Broadway #300
New York NY 10001
212-268-5279; 800-223-1730
Subjects: 23-24-39-67
Focus: Scientists.
Memo: This service specializes in putting journalists in touch with experts in the fields of science, medicine, and technology.

Newsletter Association
Frederick Goss, Exec Dir
15401 Wilson Blvd #403
Arlington VA 22209
703-527-2333
Subjects: 56
Focus: Newsletters

On the Internet: User Demographics and Trends
Tom Niehaus, VP
Simba Information Inc
PO Box 7430
Wilton CT 06897
203-834-0033; Fax: 203-834-1771
E-Mail:SIMBA99@aol.com
Subjects: 23-23T
Focus: Internet users

PartyLine Newsletter
Betty Yarmon
35 Sutton Pl
New York NY 10022-2464
212-755-3487; Fax: 212-755-3488
E-Mail: 102063.1571@compuserve.com
Subjects: 99
Focus: Biweekly media update newsletter

Print Publishing/School Market
SIMBA Information Inc
213 Danbury Rd PO Box 7430
Wilton CT 06897-7430
203-834-0033; Fax: 203-834-1771
Subjects: 31
Focus: School markets
Memo: E-Mail: SIMBA99@aol.com.

Profnet
Dan Forbush
State Univ of New York
Stony Brook
New York NY
800-776-3638
E-Mail: profnet@sunysb.edu
Subjects: 56M-99
Memo: This service electronically distributes editorial requests to hundreds of public info officers at colleges & universities around the world. Responses come back to your E-Mail address.

Specialty Directory Publishing: Market Analysis/Forecast
SIMBA Information Inc
PO Box 7430
Wilton CT 06897
203-834-0033; Fax: 203-834-1771
E-Mail: info@simbanet.com
Subjects: 19M
Focus: Directory publishing

Organizations

1001 Free Recipes
Lynn Kerrigan, Editor
Page One Cooks
134 Eachus Ave PO Box 194
Bryn Mawr PA 19010-1313
610-527-5654; Fax: 610-527-5654
Subjects: 27
Focus: 300 assns offering recipes

African-American Resource Guide
Anita Doreen Diggs, Author
Barricade Books
150 Fifth Ave #700
New York NY 10011-4311
212-627-7000; Fax: 212-627-7028
Subjects: 49B(books/videos/organizations)
Focus: Professional associations/etc
Memo: They send two catalogs out a year, spring and fall.

Alternative Access Directory
Jack Wieder
Catalyst Press
PO Box 462
Kentfield CA 94914-0462
Subjects: 13-53
Focus: Alternative organizations

American Art Directory
R R Bowker Co
121 Chanlon Rd PO Box 31
New Providence NJ 07974
908-665-2818; Fax: 908-665-6688
Subjects: 11(organizations/libraries)
Focus: Schools/museums/etc

Associations Canada
Gale Research Co
PO Box 33477
Detroit MI 48232-5477
313-961-2242; 800-877-4253;
   Fax: 313-961-6083
Subjects: 99
Focus: Canadian associations

Authentic Jane Williams' Home School Market Guide
PO Box 2030
Shingle Springs CA 95682
916-622-8586; 800-959-8586;
   Fax: 916-642-9222
Subjects: 31E
Focus: Home schooling families

Big Black Book
Unlimited Creative Enterprises
PO Box 400476
Brooklyn NY 11240-0476
718-638-9223; Fax: 718-857-5246
Subjects: 19-49B-61(New York City)
Focus: Black businesses, professionals, and organizations in metro New York City

Book Arts Directory
Page Two Inc
PO Box 77167
Washington DC 20013-7167
800-821-6604; Fax: 800-538-7549
Subjects: 59P
Focus: Books/caligraphy

Canadian Environmental Directory
Gale Research Co
PO Box 33477
Detroit MI 48232-5477
313-961-2242; 800-877-4253;
   Fax: 313-961-6083
Subjects: 51E(Canadian government/media)
Memo: Environmental government contacts, libraries, media, schools, events, products and services. Plus 2400 associations.

Conservation Directory
National Wildlife Federation
1400 16th St NW
Washington DC 20036-2217
202-797-6800; 800-432-6564;
   Fax: 202-797-6646
Subjects: 15-51-51E
Focus: Conservations

Direct Marketing Market Place
National Register Publishing
121 Chanlon Rd
New Providence NJ 07974
908-665-2818; Fax: 908-665-6688
Subjects: 99
Focus: Direct marketing

Directory of American Youth Organizations
Elizabeth Verdick
Free Spirit Publishing
400 1st Ave N #616
Minneapolis MN 55401-1724
612-338-2068; Fax: 612-337-5050
Subjects: 21-31-76-79-89
Focus: Youth organizations

Doctor's Complete Guide to Pediatric Hotlines and Resources
ABC&F Press
PO Box 92
Bedford TX 76095-0092
800-528-3975; Fax: 817-283-6357
Subjects: 31D-39
Focus: Pediatric resources

Encyclopedia of Associations
Natl Associations of the US
Gale Research Co
835 Penobscot Bldg
Detroit MI 48226
313-961-2242; Fax: 800-414-5043
Subjects: 99
Focus: Associations

Encyclopedia of Business Information Sources
Gale Research Co
835 Penobscot Bldg
Detroit MI 48226-4094
313-961-2242; Fax: 313-961-6083
Subjects: 19
Focus: Print/electronic sources

Encyclopedia of Health Information Sources
Gale Research Co
835 Penobscot Bldg
Detroit MI 48226-4094
313-961-2242; Fax: 313-961-6083
Subjects: 39
Focus: Directories/books/pubs/services

Encyclopedia of Medical Organizations and Agencies
Gale Research Co
835 Penobscot Bldg
Detroit MI 48226-4094
313-961-2242; Fax: 313-961-6083
Subjects: 39
Focus: Directories/books/pubs/services

Encyclopedia of Physical Science & Engineering Information Sources
Gale Research Co
835 Penobscot Bldg
Detroit MI 48226-4094
313-961-2242; Fax: 313-961-6083
Subjects: 23-24-67
Focus: Directories/books/services

Encyclopedia of Senior Citizens Information Sources
Gale Research Co
835 Penobscot Bldg
Detroit MI 48226-4094
313-961-2242; Fax: 313-961-6083
Subjects: 35(retirement)
Focus: Directories/books/services

Ferrari's Places for Men
Marianne Ferrari
Ferrari Publications
3542 W Calavar
Phoenix AZ 85023-5513
602-863-2408; Fax: 602-439-3952
Subjects: 37
Focus: Lists cruises, outdoor adventures, tours, festivals, events, B&B's, bars, nightlife, etc

Ferrari's Places for Women
Marianne Ferrari
Ferrari Publications
3542 W Calavar
Phoenix AZ 85023-5513
602-863-2408; Fax: 602-439-3952
Subjects: 37-73
Focus: Lists cruises, outdoor adventures, tours, festivals, events, B&B's, etc including women's bookstores

Government Assistance Almanac
Omnigraphics Inc
Penobscot Bldg
Detroit MI 48226
313-961-1340; 800-234-1340;
   Fax: 800-875-1340; Fax: 313-961-1383
Subjects: 55
Focus: Government assistance program

Hispanic Resource Directory
Editor
The Denali Press
PO Box 1535
Juneau AK 99802-1535
907-586-6014; Fax: 907-463-6780
Subjects: 45(Spanish)-49-78-80
Focus: Hispanic organizations

Hospital Blue Book
Sandra McBrager
Billian Publishing
2100 Powers Ferry Rd
Atlanta GA 30339-5014
770-955-5656; Fax: 770-952-0669
Subjects: 39M
Focus: Hospitals & medical schools

Information Industry Directory
Gale Research Co
835 Penobscot Bldg
Detroit MI 48226-4094
313-961-2242; Fax: 313-961-6083
Subjects: 99
Focus: Print/electronic sources

The Librarian's Yellow Pages
Raissa Formerand, Publisher
Garance Inc
2089 Boston Post Rd
Larchmont NY 10538-3701
914-834-7070; Fax: 914-833-3053
Subjects: 99(librarian supplies)
Focus: Circulated to 50,000 libraries.
Memo: Features book publishers as well as other library suppliers.

Long Distance Directory of Government Addresses and Phones
Omnigraphics Inc
Penobscot Bldg
Detroit MI 48226
313-961-1340; 800-234-1340;
Fax: 800-875-1340; Fax: 313-961-1383
Subjects: 55
Focus: Governement addresses

Macrocosm USA
Sandi Brockway, Editor
Macrocosm USA Inc
PO Box 185
Cambria CA 93428
805-927-8030; Fax: 805-927-1987
E-Mail: Brockway@macronet.org
Http://www.macronet.org/macronet/
Subjects: 13-49-51-55-65
Focus: Progressive political groups

Medical & Health Information Directory
Gale Research Co
835 Penobscot Bldg
Detroit MI 48226-4094
313-961-2242; Fax: 313-961-6083
Subjects: 39
Focus: Information for medical/health

Minority Organizations: A National Directory
Robert Calvert Jr, Pres
Garrett Park Press
PO Box 190
Garrett Park MD 20896-0190
301-946-2553
Subjects: 49
Focus: Minority organizations

National Directory of Addresses and Telephone Numbers
Omnigraphics Inc
Penobscot Bldg
Detroit MI 48226
313-961-1340; 800-234-1340;
  FAX: 800-875-1340; Fax: 313-961-1383
Subjects: 19-55-99
Focus: Addresses and telephone numbers
Memo: Also available on disc and CD-ROM.

National Directory of Nonprofit Organizations
The Taft Group
12300 Twinbrook Pky #450
Rockville MD 20852-1606
800-877-8238; Fax: 301-816-0811
Subjects: 99
Focus: Nonprofit groups

National Trade & Professional Associations of the U S
Columbia Books Publishers
1212 New York Ave NW #330
Washington DC 20005-3987
202-898-0662; Fax: 202-898-0775
Subjects: 19-99
Focus: Associations

Nostalgia Entertainment Sourcebook
Jordon Young
Moonstone Press
2019 E Center St
Anaheim CA 92806-3602
714-956-2246
Subjects: 14-14M-33-33M-33T-41A
Focus: Nostalgia
Memo: Sources for old movies, records, etc; fan clubs, festivals, nostalgia radio stations, revival cinemas, libraries, museums, record shops, film/video dealers, etc.

NW Gardener's Resource Directory
Stephanie Feeney
Whatcom in Bloom Garden Society
59 Strawberry Point
Bellingham WA 98226
Subjects: 43G
Memo: Features nurseries, growers, seed sources, garden shows, garden centers and shops, horticultural libraries, garden clubs, book shops, literature sources for the professional and amateur gardener.

Parapsychology, New Age, and the Occult: A Source Encyclopedia
Cheryl Lacoff, Editor
Reference Press Intl
17553 Fieldbrook Cir E
Boca Raton FL 33496-1563
407-994-3699
Subjects: 39H-53-54-57
Memo: Lists publications, associations, schools, stores, centers, producers, events, radio/TV shows, wholesalers, museums, etc, in the fields of metaphysics, parapsychology, unexplained phenomena, new age, spirituality, and holistic lifestyles and health

Religion & Public Affairs
The Rockford Institute
934 N Main St
Rockford IL 61103-7061
815-964-5053; Fax: 815-965-1826
Subjects: 55-65-63
Focus: 160 religious organizations/etc

Research Centers Directory
Gale Research Co
835 Penobscot Bldg
Detroit MI 48226-4094
313-961-2242; Fax: 313-961-6083
Subjects: 23-24-67
Focus: Research centers

Scientific and Technical Organizations and Agencies
Gale Research Company
835 Penobscot Bldg
Detroit MI 48226-4094
313-961-2242; Fax: 313-961-6083
Subjects: 23-24-67
Focus: Scientific and technical organizations

State & Regional Associations
Columbia Books
1212 New York Ave NW #330
Washington DC 20005-3987
202-898-0662
Subjects: 61-99
Focus: Associations

Think Tank Directory
Lynn Helleburst, Editor
Government Research Focus
214 SW 6th Ave #301
Topeka KS 66603-3719
913-232-7720; 800-346-6898;
  Fax: 913-232-1615
Subjects: 55-65-99
Focus: Public policy thinktank

Third World Resource Directory
Thomas Fenton & Mary Heffron
Orbis Books
Maryknoll NY 10545-9999
914-941-7590; Fax: 914-941-7005
Subjects: 13-55(international)-80
Focus: Organizations, publications, etc

Training and Development Organizations Directory
Gale Research Co
835 Penobscot Bldg
Detroit MI 48226-4094
313-961-2242; Fax: 313-961-6083
Subjects: 19C
Focus: Seminars/workshops

Visitor and Convention Bureaus
Open Horizons Publishing Co
209 S Main St #200
PO Box 205
Fairfield IA 52556-0205
515-472-6130; Fax: 515-472-1560
Subjects: 61-71
Focus: US/Canada visitor bureaus
Memo: Database on disk.

Volunteerism
Harriet Clyde Kipps, Editor
R R Bowker
121 Chanlon Rd PO Box 31
New Providence NJ 07974
908-665-2818; Fax: 908-665-6688
Subjects: 99(volunteer organizations)
Focus: Training/programs/publications

People

American Economic Foundation
Marcia Hurt
1370 Ontario St #1700
Cleveland OH 44113-1701
216-321-6547
Subjects: 19
Focus: Economics

American Medical Directory
American Medical Assn
515 N State St
Chicago IL 60610-4325
312-464-5000; Fax: 312-464-5600
Subjects: 39
Focus: US(doctors)

American Men & Women of Science
Reed Reference Publishing
121 Chanlon Rd PO Box 31
New Providence NJ 07974
908-665-2818; 800-521-8110;
  Fax: 908-665-6688
Subjects: 23-24-39-51-67
Focus: Men/women of science

American Speaker
Aram Bakshian Jr
Georgetown Publishing House
1101 30th St NW Dept SEJ106
Washington DC 20007-3708
800-915-0022; Fax: 202-337-1512
Subjects: 56M
Focus: Resource for public speakers

Association Meeting Planners Conference/Convention Directors
The Salesman's Guide
Reed Reference Publishing
121 Chanlon Rd PO Box 31
New Providence NJ 07974
908-665-2818; 800-223-1797Fax:
 908-665-6688
Subjects: 19-61-71
Focus: Meeting planners

ASTD Buyer's Guide/Consultant
Denise Bolos, Acct Exec
1640 King St
PO Box 1443
Alexandria VA 22313-2043
703-683-8175; Fax: 703-683-7259
Subjects: 19
Focus: Buyers
Memo: "American Society for Training and Development."

Cavalcade of Acts & Attractions
Amusement Business
PO Box 24970
Nashville TN 37202-4970
615-321-4250; Fax: 615-327-1575
Subjects: 11-14-17-33
Focus: Musicians/artists/circuses/etc

The College Publishing Market
Hope Mascott, Dir/Mktg Communica
CMG Information Services
187 Ballardvale St #B110
Wilmington MA 01887-1062
508-657-7000; Fax: 508-988-0046
Subjects: 56P
Focus: College text book publishers

Consultants and Consulting Organizations Directory
Gale Research Co
645 Griswold St #3480
Detroit MI 48226-4216
313-961-2926; Fax: 313-961-5919
Subjects: 17-99-19-55
Focus: Business & government consultant

Contact Book
Mark Kerrigan
Celebrity Focus
1780 Broadway #300
New York NY 10019-1414
212-757-7979; Fax: 212-397-4626
Subjects: 99
Focus: Authors

Corporate Meeting Planners
The Salesman's Guide
Reed Reference Publishing
121 Chanlon Rd PO Box 31
New Providence NJ 07974
908-665-2818; Fax: 908-665-6688
Subjects: 19-61-71
Focus: Meeting planners for corporations
Memo: Also indicates which companies use professional speakers for their meetings.

Directory of Health Care Strategic Management & Communications Consultants
American Hospital Assn
840 N Lake Shore Dr
Chicago IL 60611-2431
312-280-6000
Subjects: 19M-39-56(PR)
Focus: Health care strategic management & communications consultants

Directory of Medical Specialists
Marquis Who's Who
Reed Reference Publishing
121 Chanlon Rd PO Box 31
New Providence NJ 07974
908-665-2818; Fax: 908-665-6688
Subjects: 39
Focus: Doctors/medical specialists)

Literary Agents of North America
Leonie Rosenstiel, Dir
Author Aid / Research Assoc
340 E 52nd St
New York NY 10022-6728
212-758-4213
Subjects: 56W
Focus: Literary agents

Directory of Top Computer Executives
Applied Computer Research
PO Box 82266
Phoenix AZ 85071-2266
602-995-5929; 800-234-2227;
 Fax: 602-995-0905
Subjects: 23
Focus: Computer professionals

Madison Avenue Handbook
Michael Henry
Peter Glenn Publications
42 West 38th St Rm 802
New York NY 10018-6210
212-869-2020; Fax: 212-869-3287
Subjects: 11-19M
Focus: Sources for advertising pros

Pratt's Guide/Venture Capital Sources
Shauna Obergfell, Publicist
The Oryx Press
4041 N Central at Indian School
Phoenix AZ 85012-3330
602-265-2651; Fax: 602-265-6250
E-Mail: sobergf@oryxpress.com
Subjects: 19
Focus: Venture capital sources

Star Guide
Axiom Information Resources
PO Box 8015
Ann Arbor MI 48107-8015
313-761-4842
Subjects: 11-14-17-33-55-69
Focus: Celebrity stars: covers music, movie, TV, sports, and political celebrities

Who's Who Among Human Services Professionals
Marquis Who's Who
121 Chanlon Rd PO Box 31
New Providence NJ 07974
908-665-2818; Fax: 908-665-6688
Subjects: 35R-57-65
Focus: Human services professionals

Who's Who Among Young American Professionals
Marquis Who's Who
121 Chanlon Rd
New Providence NJ 07974
908-665-2818; Fax: 908-665-6688
Subjects: 19-35R-57-65
Focus: Young American professionals

Who's Who in Advertising
Marquis Who's Who
Reed Reference Publishing
121 Chanlon Rd PO Box 31
New Providence NJ 07974
908-665-2818; Fax: 908-665-6688
Subjects: 19M
Focus: Advertising professionals

Who's Who in America
Marquis Who's Who
Reed Reference Publishing
121 Chanlon Rd PO Box 31
New Providence NJ 07974
908-665-2818; Fax: 908-665-6688
Subjects: 99
Focus: General who's who

Who's Who in American Art
Reed Reference Publishing
121 Chanlon Rd PO Box 31
New Providence NJ 07974
908-665-2818; Fax: 908-665-6688
Subjects: 11-17
Focus: Art professionals

Who's Who in American Education
Marquis Who's Who
Reed Reference Publishing
121 Chanlon Rd PO Box 31
New Providence NJ 07974
908-665-2818; Fax: 908-665-6688
Subjects: 31
Focus: Education/teachers

Who's Who in American Law
Marquis Who's Who
Reed Reference Publishing
121 Chanlon Rd PO Box 31
New Providence NJ 07974
908-665-2818; Fax: 908-665-6688
Subjects: 19L-55L
Focus: Lawyers/judges/etc

Who's Who in American Nursing
Marquis Who's Who
Reed Reference Publishing
121 Chanlon Rd PO Box 31
New Providence NJ 07974
908-665-2818; Fax: 908-665-6688
Subjects: 39
Focus: Nursing

Who's Who in American Politics
Reed Reference Publishing
121 Chanlon Rd PO Box 31
New Providence NJ 07974
908-665-2818; Fax: 908-665-6688
Subjects: 13-44-48-55
Focus: American politicians

Who's Who in Finance & Industry
Marquis Who's Who
Reed Reference Publishing
121 Chanlon Rd PO Box 31
New Providence NJ 07974
908-665-2818; Fax: 908-665-6688
Subjects: 19
Focus: Decision makers

Who's Who of American Women
Marquis Who's Who
Reed Reference Publishing
121 Chanlon Rd PO Box 31
New Providence NJ 07974
908-665-2818; Fax: 908-665-6688
Subjects: 19-39-55-67-73-99
Focus: Career women

Who's Who of Emerging Leaders in America
Marquis Who's Who
121 Chanlon Rd
New Providence NJ 07974
908-665-2818; Fax: 908-665-6688
Subjects: 19-55-99
Focus: Emerging leaders

Schools

CIC School Directories
Market Data Retrieval
16 Progress Dr
PO Box 2117
Shelton CT 06484-9990
203-926-4800; 800-333-8802;
   CT: 800-435-3742; Fax: 203-926-0784
Subjects: 21-31-76-79-89
Focus: Schools

Directory of Post Secondary Inst
US Government Printing Office
Washington DC 20402-0001
202-512-1800; Fax: 202-512-2250
Subjects: 31
Focus: All colleges/universities

Guide to Art & Craft Workshops
Shaw Associates
PO Box 1295
New York NY 10023-1295
212-799-6464; Fax: 212-724-9287
Subjects: 11-29
Focus: Art and craft workshops

The Guide to Cooking Schools
Shaw Associates
PO Box 1295
New York NY 10023-1295
212-799-6464; Fax: 212-724-9287
Subjects: 27
Focus: Cooking schools

Guide to Golf Schools & Camps
Shaw Associates
PO Box 1295
New York NY 10023-1295
212-799-6464; Fax: 212-724-9287
Subjects: 69(golf)
Focus: Golf schools and camps

Guide to Photography Workshops
Shaw Associates
PO Box 1295
New York NY 10023-1295
212-799-6464; Fax: 212-724-9287
Subjects: 11P
Focus: Photography

The Guide to Writers Conferences
Dorene Kaplan, Editor
Shaw Associates
625 Biltmore Way #1406
Coral Gables FL 33134-7539
305-446-8888; Fax: 305-446-1837
Subjects: 56W
Focus: Writer's conferences

National Faculty Directory
Gale Research Co
835 Penobscot Bldg
Detroit MI 48226-4094
313-961-2242; Fax: 313-961-6083
Subjects: 31-99
Focus: Faculty at colleges/universities

Publishing for the College Market: Trends & Forecasts
Claire Schoen, Editorial Dir
213 Danbury Rd
PO Box 7430
Wilton CT 06897-7430
203-834-0033; Fax: 203-834-1771
Subjects: 31E-56P
Focus: College publishing

Wholesalers and Retailers

Automotive Aftermarket Suppliers
Chain Store Guides
3922 Coconut Palm Dr
Tampa FL 33619-1389
800-927-9292; Fax: 800-346-8047
Subjects: 16A
Focus: 1300+ chains
Memo: Published annually in September.

Building Products & Hardlines Distributors
Chain Store Guides
3922 Coconut Palm Dr
Tampa FL 33619-1389
800-927-9292; Fax: 800-346-8047
Subjects: 12B
Focus: 1800+ building products & hardlines distributors
Memo: Published annually in July.

Buyer's Directory
ARMY Times Publishing Co
6883 Commercial Dr
Springfield VA 22151-4202
703-750-9000; 800-369-5718 ext 810
   Fax: 703-750-8622
Subjects: 48(military)-99
Focus: Military buying

Chain Restaurant Operators
Chain Store Guides
3922 Coconut Palm Dr
Tampa FL 33619-1389
800-927-9292; Fax: 800-346-8047
Subjects: 27
Focus: 4688+ restaurant chains
Memo: Published in April.

Computer & Software Retail & Distributors
Chain Store Guides
3922 Coconut Palm Dr
Tampa FL 33619-1389
800-927-9292; Fax: 800-346-8047
Subjects: 23
Focus: Computer/software retailers
Memo: Published in October.

Craft Shop & Gallery Directory
Adele Patti, Ed/Publ
Front Room Publishers
PO Box 1541
Clifton NJ 07015-1541
201-773-4215; Fax: 201-815-1235
Subjects: 29
Focus: Craft stores/etc

The Cyclists' Yellow Pages
Adventure Cycling Assn
150 E Pine (59802)
PO Box 8308
Missoula MT 59807
406-721-1776; Fax: 406-721-8754
Subjects: 69(bicycling)
Focus: Bike shops/other resources

Department Stores/Mail Order Firms
Chain Store Guide Info Services
3922 Coconut Palm Dr
Tampa FL 33619-1389
800-927-9292; Fax: 800-346-8047
Subjects: 99
Focus: Lists over 5,700 stores
Memo: Published in November.

Directory of Funparks & Amusements
Amusement Business
PO Box 24970
Nashville TN 37202-4970
615-321-4250; Fax: 615-327-1575
Subjects: 15-33
Focus: Amusement, theme & water parks, zoos and other tourist attractions.

Discount & General Merchandise Stores
Chain Store Guide Info Services
3922 Coconut Palm Dr
Tampa FL 33619-1389
800-927-9292; Fax: 800-346-8047
Subjects: 99
Focus: 10,000+ discount store locations
Memo: Published in March.

Book Publishing Resource Guide

Page 461

Drug Store and HBC Chains
Chain Store Guide Info Services
3922 Coconut Palm Dr
Tampa FL 33619-1389
800-927-9292; Fax: 800-346-8047
Subjects: 39
Focus: 2,000+ drug store chains.
Memo: Published in June.

Foodservice Distributors
Chain Store Guide Info Services
3922 Coconut Palm Dr
Tampa FL 33619-1389
800-927-9292; Fax: 800-346-8047
Subjects: 27-39
Focus: 4,400+ food distributors
Memo: Published in May.

Gift, Housewares & Home Textiles
The Salesman's Guide
Reed Reference Publishing
121 Chanlon Rd PO Box 31
New Providence NJ 07974
908-665-2818; 800-223-1797;
    Fax: 908-665-6688
Subjects: 29-40-43-99
Focus: Retail stores
Memo: 25 types of retailers from department stores to home shopping TV networks, from catalog houses to membership warehouses. Provides name, addresses, phone numbers, and buyers (with product-line responsibilities).

High Volume Independent Drug Strores
Chain Store Guide Info Services
3922 Coconut Palm Dr
Tampa FL 33619-1389
800-927-9292; Fax: 800-346-8047
Subjects: 39
Focus: 7,800+ one-unit independent drug stores
Memo: Published in December.

Home Center & Hardware Chains
Chain Store Guide Info Services
3922 Coconut Palm Dr
Tampa FL 33619-1389
800-927-9292; Fax: 800-346-8047
Subjects: 43
Focus: Names of more than 20,000 key personnel
Memo: Published in July.

Home Furnishings Retailers and Distributors
Chain Store Guide Info Services
3922 Coconut Palm Dr
Tampa FL 33619-1389
800-927-9292; Fax: 800-346-8047
Subjects: 43
Focus: Lists over 17,500 stores
Memo: Published in March.

Major Mass Market Merchandisers
The Salesman's Guide
Reed Reference Publishing
121 Chanlon Rd PO Box 31
New Providence NJ 07974
908-665-2818; Fax: 908-665-6688
Subjects: 40(clothing)
Focus: Mass market firms
Memo: Buyers of clothing and accessories.

Men's & Boy's Wear Specialty Stores
Chain Store Guide Info Services
3922 Coconut Palm Dr
Tampa FL 33619-1389
800-927-9292; Fax: 800-346-8047
Subjects: 99
Focus: 3,000+ chains
Memo: Published in August.

New Pages Distributors Directory
New Pages Press
4426 S Belsay Rd
Grand Blanc MI 48439
313-743-8055; Fax: 313-743-2730
Subjects: 13-47-53-55-73-75-83-99
Focus: 100 distributors

Phelon's Discount Stores
Joseph R Marsar Jr
Phelon Sheldon & Marsar
15 Industrial Ave
Fairview NJ 07022
201-941-8804; 800-234-8804;
    Fax: 201-941-5515
Subjects: 99
Focus: 2,000 chains/5000 jobbers

Selling to the Other Educational Markets
Jane Williams
Bluestocking Press
PO Box 2030
Shingle Springs CA 95682
916-621-1123; Fax:
Subjects: 21-31-76(educational markets)
Focus: Books/catalogs/distributors/etc
Memo: Home school and private education market. This company also offers an exhibit service.

Sheldon's Retail
Phelon, Sheldon & Marsar
15 Industrial Ave
Fairview NJ 07022
201-941-8804; Fax: 201-941-5515
Subjects: 99
Focus: Department and women's stores

Single Unit Supermarket Operators
Chain Store Guides
3922 Coconut Palm Dr
Tampa FL 33619-1389
800-927-9292; Fax: 800-846-8047
Subjects: 27
Focus: 6000
Memo: Published in December.

Sloan's Green Guide to Antiques Dealers - New England
The Antique Press
105 Charles St #140
Boston MA 02114-3260
617-723-3001; Fax: 617-248-0815
Subjects: 28
Focus: New England antique dealers

Sporting Goods Buyers
The Salesman's Guide
Reed Reference Publishing
121 Chanlon Rd PO Box 31
New Providence NJ 07974
908-665-2818; 800-223-1797;
    Fax: 908-665-6688
Subjects: 69(sporting goods stores)
Focus: Stores that carry sporting goods equipment, clothing, and footwear. 12,400 buyers for over 87,000 locations.

Sporting Goods Register
Sporting Goods Dealer
1212 N Lindbergh Blvd
St Louis MO 63132-1704
314-997-7111; Fax: 314-993-7726
Subjects: 69
Focus: Wholesalers

Supermarket, Grocery, and Convenience Store Chains
Chain Store Guide Info Services
3922 Coconut Palm Dr
Tampa FL 33619-1389
800-927-9292; Fax: 800-346-8047
Subjects: 99
Focus: 3,700+ supermarket chains
Memo: Published in June.

Thomas Grocery Register
Thomas Publishing
1 Penn Plz
New York NY 10119-0103
212-290-7225; Fax: 212-290-7206
Subjects: 19-27
Focus: Food chains and wholesalers, etc

Value Added Resellers
Chain Store Guides
3922 Coconut Palm Dr
Tampa FL 33619-1389
800-927-9292; Fax: 800-846-8047
Subjects: 99
Focus: 4,000 resellers
Memo: Published in October.

Wholesale Grocers
Chain Store Guides
3922 Coconut Palm Dr
Tampa FL 33619-1389
800-927-9292; Fax: 800-846-8047
Subjects: 27
Focus: 1,800 wholesale grocers
Memo: Published in July.

Directory of Wholesale Reps for Craft Professionals
Sharon K Olson
Northwoods Trading Co
13451 Essex Ct
Eden Prairie MN 55347-1708
612-937-5275
Subjects: 29
Focus: Wholesaler reps

Womens' & Childrens' Wear Specialty Stores
Chain Store Guide Info Services
3922 Coconut Palm Dr
Tampa FL 33619-1389
800-927-9292; Fax: 800-346-8047
Subjects: 99
Focus: 5,200+ chains
Memo: Published in August.

An Annotated Review of Books on Publishing

The following pages present reviews of books about publishing, printing, graphics, publicity, and marketing. These reviews are derived from three editions of *The Independent Publisher's Bookshelf*, as well as John Kremer's "Book Previews" in *Book Marketing Update* newsletter, and John McHugh's *Book Publishing Contracts: An Introduction*.

Any book listed in bold letters may be ordered through the **Ad-Lib**. To order, just call toll-free, 800-669-0773, or write to Ad-Lib Publications, PO Box 1102, Fairfield, IA 52556-1102; (515) 472-6617; Fax: (515) 472-3186. All titles are usually in stock for fast, same-day shipment.

Please note that we give a 10% discount for orders of three or more books. We also accept VISA, MasterCard, and American Express credit cards. When ordering, add $5.00 postage and handling for the first book ordered and 50¢ for each additional book. Your satisfaction is guaranteed. If any book does not live up to your expectations, return it to us in good condition within 30 days for a full refund. No questions asked.

All other books reviewed here may be ordered from your favorite local bookseller, checked out at the library, or ordered direct from the publisher.

General Publishing

The following books are general introductions to self-publishing or mainstream publishing. While some books provide basic commentary, others describe step-by-step procedures or relate personal experiences in publishing books.

The two best books for those who want to learn how to publish their own books are *The Self-Publishing Manual* by Dan Poynter and *The Complete Guide to Self-Publishing* by Tom and Marilyn Ross. Both books are highly recommended.

And, before you get ready to market your books, be sure to read, *1001 Ways to Market Your Books — For Authors and Publishers*. While we're certainly biased, *1001 Ways* is the best book on the subject, bar none.

- Appelbaum, Judith, **How to Get Happily Published, Fourth Edition,** (New York: Harper & Row, 1992), 317 pages, softcover, $12.00.
  Intended primarily to educate writers on how to approach and work with established publishers, it also includes three chapters about the self-publishing option. It has an excellent annotated resources section of 75 pages. The section on how to be your own best salesperson is also superb.

- Bell, Patricia J, **The Prepublishing Handbook;** (Eden Prairie, MN: Cat's-Paw Press, 1992, 612-941-5053), 117 pages, softcover, $12.00.
  Should you publish your book yourself? With the information in this book, you can decide if publishing is for you. Learn about the process of producing a book, the hidden and open costs involved, the risks and rewards of publishing independently — before you publish.

- Bloomfield, Masse, *How to Publishing Your Own Book for Less Than $575*, (Masefield Books, 1995).
  This book describes how to publish a few copies of your book to test market it.

- Bower, Donald E., *The Professional Writers Guide,* (The National Writers Club, 1990) 152 pages, $16.95.
  This book is intended to assist the freelancer. It's step by step from beginning to your final draft. Also describes equipment and supplies you need for a successful and efficient writing career. Easy reading, very informative.

- Buchanan, Jerry, *Writer's Utopia Formula Report*, (Vancouver, WA: Towers Club, 1987; 206-574-3084), 85 pages, softcover, $12.95.
  Lots of inspirational hurrah! hurrah! to get your juices stirring. He does this cheerleading bit very well, and it alone is enough to make his entire report worth the $10.00 if you are a slow starter. Otherwise, you are better served with other books.

- Burgett, Gordon, **Publishing to Niche Markets,** (Santa Maria, CA: Communication Unlimited, 1995), 200 pages, softcover, $14.95.
  This book describes the pros and cons of self-publishing versus selling your book to a mainstream publisher. His conclusion? If you can write a book for a specific market, you will be better off publishing it yourself. If you are at a loss for a topic, he shows how to research a topic, find an audience, and test market the book.

- Cardoza, Avery, **The Complete Guide to Successful Publishing.** (Cardoza Publishing, 1995; 714-743-5229). $19.95.
  A great book on "how to create, print, distribute, and make money publishing books." A useful addition to the books on publishing.

- Cool, Lisa Collier, **How to Write Irresistible Query Letters,** (Cincinnatti, OH: Writer's Digest Books, 1990), 136 pages, softcover, $11.99.
  This popular books shows writers how to increase their chances of a sale by preselling the idea via a query letter. Clear, well organized guide to query letters.

- Davis, Kenneth, *Two-Bit Culture: The Paperbacking of America*, (Boston: Houghton-Mifflin, 1984), 430 pages, softcover, $18.95.

  A history of the mass-market paperback publishing industry.

- Dessauer, John P., *Book Publishing: A Basic Introduction, Third Edition*, (New York: Continuum, 1993), 260 pages, hardcover, $24.95.

  This is a new revision of the classic book about the publishing industry. The book is not a how-to manual, rather, it's a clear and systematic review of how books are published.

- Ensign, Paulette, *Turn Your Expertise into Cash: Learn How to Write and Sell Booklets*, (Organizing Solutions, 1993; 914-666-6414). $29.95.

  Describes how she sold 50,000 booklets without spending a penny on advertising.

- Follett, Robert J. R., **Financial Feasibility in Book Publishing**, (Oak Park, IL: Alpine Guild, 1988), 72 pages, saddle-stitched, $12.95.

  This manual is a step-by-step guide to the process of determining production costs, forecasting sales, and calculating revenues. Not only can it prevent you from making money-losing editorial decisions, but it can help you make better use of your marketing dollars (by planning reasonable budgets and sticking to them).

- Gallagher, Patricia C, *For All The Write Reasons*, (Worcester, PA: Young Sparrow Publishing, 1992), 398 pages, softcover: $24.95.

  Learn from the experiences of people just like you. If you like to write and wonder how to go about getting a book published, this is THE book you need to find a publisher or to self-publish. Patricia Gallagher and thirty nine other experts in their field offer a blend of realty and inspiration in this unique anthology.

- Geiser, Elizabeth, and Arnold Dolin, Editors, *The Business of Book Publishing*, (Boulder, CO: Westview Press, 1985; 303-444-3521), 360 pages, hardcover, $73.50.

  The book is a collection of articles distilled from the curriculum of the University of Denver Publishing Institute. The articles offer clear, detailed explanations of the many aspects of publishing: editing, production, and marketing. More recent developments (such as the paperback explosion, the rising importance of book chains, and new technology) are also covered.

- Henderson, Bill, *The Publish-It-Yourself Handbook, Third Edition*, (Wainscott, NY: Pushcart, 1987; 516-324-9300), 365 pages, softcover, $11.95.

  One of the first books on self-publishing, it is an anthology of autobiographical sketches written by people who chose to self-publish all or some of their writings. It is certainly one of the more entertaining books with its stories and anecdotes covering all phases of self-publishing. It is not, however, a handbook.

- Heine, Art and Jean, **Book Selling $101**, (J-Mart Press, 1995; 804-498-4060). $9.95.

  This primer focuses on the author's role in the marketing process.

- Howard, Lee, *How to Publish Your Own Book Successfully*, (Clearwater, FL: Selective Publishers, 1980; 813-447-0100), 80 pages, saddle-stitched, $15.00.

  This book is primarily fluff, with few details and fewer bits of useful information for the self-publisher.

- Huenefeld, John, **The Huenefeld Guide to Book Publishing, Revised Sixth Edition,** (Lexington, MA: Mills & Sanderson, Spring 1997), softcover.

  This book is probably the best overall guide for small and mid-size publishing companies which are expanding their operations. It also makes a superb training manual for new employees.

- Kavka, Dorothy, and Dan Heise, *The Successful Self-Publishinger: Produce and Market Your Own Best Seller,* (Evanston Publishing, 1996; 800-594-5190). $19.95.

  Another basic introduction to self-publishing. It's strength; interior design of the book.

- Lant, Jeffrey, **How to Make a Whole Lot More Than $1,000,000 Writing, Commissioning, Publishing and Selling How-To Information,** (Cambridge, MA: Jeffrey Lant Associates, 1990), 500+ pages, softcover, $39.95

  A packed, detailed book about creating and selling books, tapes, reports, and other information products. Loaded with publicity and marketing ideas.

- Larsen, Michael, **How to Write a Book Proposal**, (Cincinnati, OH: Writer's Digest Books, 1990), 136 pages, softcover, $12.99.

  Written by a literary agent who has successfully placed authors' manuscripts with more than sixty publishers, this book takes you through every step of writing a nonfiction book proposal.

- Marsh, Carole, *Publishing on Command: How to Publish & Print One Book at a Time—Profitably!*, (Atlanta, GA: Gallopade Publishing, 1994; 800-536-2438), 36 pages, $14.95, softcover; $19.95, hardcover; $29.95.

  This book describes the process of publishing books on demand, that is, printing and binding books as they are needed. Carole Marsh, publisher of 600 such books, describes her ten-step system for publishing on command.

- McHugh, John B., *McHugh Publishing Reports*, (Glendale, WI: McHugh Publishing Reports)

  These reports are brief practical guides intended primarily for small publishers, assocations which publish books as a sideline, and self-publishers. The advice is usually reliable, to the point and, most important, oriented towards creating a profitable operation without ignoring the realities of sound financial management. Below are just a few of the reports he publishes.

- *Book Publishing Contracts: An Introduction*, (Milwaukee WI: McHugh Consulting, 1995; 414-351-3056), 60 pages, $58.00.

  Provides insights as to how a book contract is used as an acquisition tool. The **business rationale** is explained for every book contract provision.

- *Electronic Rights for Publishers: Protecting Your Interests*, (Milwaukee WI: McHugh Consulting, 1995; 414-351-3056), 17 pages, $17.00.

  An introduction to electronic rights is presented in Electronic Rights for Publishers. While electronic publishing is rapidly evolving (and changing), publishers still have the **largest stake** in protecting their interest in the electronic rights of their publishing property.

- *Managing Book Acquistions: An Introduction,* (Milwaukee WI: McHugh Consulting, 1995; 414-351-3056), 65 pages, $48.00

  Managing Book Acquisitons provides an overview of the entire process of acquiring books. Each step in the acquisitions process is described. Written by an experienced publisher who has actually acquired and published books. A companion volumn for McHugh's **Book Publishing Contracts.**

- *Permissions Management for Requesters and Granters: Dealing with Copyright and Fair Use,* (Milwaukee WI: McHugh Consulting, 1995; 414-351-3056), 62 pages, $68.00

  A how-to approach for managing the process of permissions for both the requester and the granter. Permissions Management takes the position that there **is not** one "lock-step" method of managing permissions either for the requester or the granter. Rather, managing permissions requires **a special way of thinking** about copyright, fair use and permissions.

- Muckle, Jim, *Self-Publishing Success Story,* (Sebastopol, CA: K.S.J. Publishing, 1989; 800-356-9315), softcover, $5.00.

  A personal and fun recounting of how to publish books on a shoestring.

- National Writers Union, *Guide to Freelance Rates and Standard Practice* (Cincinnati, OH: Writer's Digest, 1995; 800-822-6339.

  Reviewed by John B McHugh ©1996

  A pro-author bias dominates this book. Contains 39 pages on book contracts. Provides valuable insights into the author's perspective on contracts and a wide variety of publishing matters.

- Ortman, Mark, **A Simple Guide to Self-Publishing, 2nd Edition,** (Wise Owl Books, 1996; 206-822-9699), $7.95

  A low-cost basic primer on self-publishing, now with Internet information.

- Poynter, Dan, **Business Letters for Publishers**, (Santa Barbara: Para Publishing, 1981), computer disk in various word-processing formats, $29.95.

  A collection of sample book publishing correspondence, from sales and promotion to order processing to collections to requests for information to trademark protection to manuscript rejections — 74 letters in all! An easy-to-use timesaver.

- Poynter, Dan, **The Self-Publishing Manual, 9th Edition,** Completely Revised. (Santa Barbara, CA: Para Publishing, 1996), 458 pages, softcover, $19.95.

  The most comprehensive and informative book about self-publishing on the market today. None better. If you can afford to buy only one book on publishing, buy this book. Dan Poynter has published over 20 books as a one-man publishing firm and has sold well over $2,000,000 worth. In this book, he takes you step by step from idea, through manuscript, printing, promotion, sales, and much more.

- Radke, Linda Foster, **The Economical Guide to Self-Publishing: How to Produce and Market Your Book on a Budget,** (Chandler, AZ: Five Star Publications, 1996, 602-940-8182), 196 pages softcover, $19.95.

  This book takes authors through all steps in manuscript preparation, printing, promotion and distribution, including establishing one's own business and sources of networking and cooperative markets.

- Ross, Tom and Marilyn, **The Complete Guide to Self-Publishing,** (Cincinnati, OH: Writers Digest Books, 1994), 406 pages, softcover, $18.99.

  One of the best books on self-publishing now available, this guide is loaded with marketing ideas.

  Now, when people ask me to recommend a book on self-publishing or publishing, I have to decide between Ross's **Guide** and Poynter's **Manual**. Both are superb. Ross' is easier and more enjoyable to read, but Dan's is more comprehensive. Ross' is tops on marketing and distribution, but Dan's is still better on most other points.

  So, what to do? Well, it should be obvious. Buy both. These two books, in my estimation, are the two best general books on publishing available anywhere at any price. Both books should be on the reference shelf of every publisher — whether large, small, or self-publisher.

- Salisbury, Linda and Jim, *Smart Self-Publishing: An Author's Guide to Producing a Marketable Book,* (Tabby House, 1995; 941-629-7646). $12.95.

  The best packaged book of all books on self-publishing. Nice looking. Easy to read. A good intro to self-publishing through a book packager (such as the authors).

- Seidman, Michael, *From Printout to Published, A Guide to the Publishing Process*, (New York, NY: Carroll & Graff, 1992; 800-788-3123), 105 pages, softcover, $10.95.

  This book gives writers an inside look at how a book is published. Since the book was written by the editor of Tor Books, it gives special attention to the production and marketing of mass-market genre novels.

- ShawGuides, *The Guide to Writers Conferences,* Coral Gables, FL: ShawGuides, Inc, 1992), 262 pages, softcover, $16.95.

  This is the only comprehensive source of detailed information about short-term programs for aspiring and professional writers. You can easily find the programs that fit your needs.

- Smith, Ronald Ted, *Book Publishing Encyclopedia, Second Edition,* (BookWorld, 1996; 800-444-2524). $14.95.

  A very basic introduction to publishing.

- Sutter, Jan, *Slinging Ink*, (Los Altos, CA: William Kaufman, 1982), 168 pages, softcover, $7.95.

  A practical guide for those interested in publishing ephemeral items such as newspapers or magazines. Teaches fundamental journalistic principles plus basic publishing skills.

- Suzanne, Claudia, **This Business of Books, 3rd Edition,** (Tustin, CA: Wambtac; 800-641-3936; E-mail: wambtac@aol.com) 256 pages, softcover, $19.95.

  This Business of Books is designed to "mentor" both laymen and professionals through the confusing, often contradictory process of conceptualizing, writing, editing, submitting, royalty or self-publishing, promoting and selling their first book. This realty-based guide provides clear explanations and frank discussions.

- Williams, Thomas, *Kitchen-Table Publisher: How to Start, Manage and Profit from Your Own Homebased Publishing Company,*(Venture Press, 1996; 800-360-4511; E-mail: publish@gate.net). $29.95.

  This book covers the publishing of magazines, travel guides, real estate buides, directories, weekly newspapers as well as books. A great idea stimulator for ways to expand your business or expertise.

- Writer's Digest Editors, *Getting It Published, A Beginners Guide to*, (Cincinnati, OH: Writers Digest Books, 1994), 208 pages, softcover, $16.99.
  A new writer may ask how to you get your work into print? This book is a collection of articles that identify who, where and takes the mystery out of getting published. Easy reading. Very well written.

Careers in Publishing

- Fry, Ronald, *Book Publishing Career Directory*, (Detroit, MI: Visible Inc, 1993-94 5th Edition), 292 pages, hardcover, $39.00.
  This directory features twenty short articles covering the major and minor job opportunities in book publishing. It also lists available job opportunities at 100 major publishing houses. Updated periodically.

Specialized Publishing

The following books describe how to publish cookbooks, directories, and other specialized books.

- Bold, Mary, *Publish Your Own Book: A Resource Book for Young Authors*, (Arlington, TX: Bold Productions, 1987; 817-468-9924), 36 pages, comb-bound, $6.95.
  A short booklet designed to help students self-publish from 10 to 200 copies of a book using their local copy shop.

- Boyer 3rd, Carl, *How to Publish and Market Your Family History, Fourth Edition*, (Newhall, CA: Carl Boyer, 1993; 805-259-3154), hardcover. $17.50.
  Describes how to research, organize, and publish family histories. Difficult to read because of its design, but full of information.

- Gregory, Howard, *Self-Publish Your Own Picture Book*, (Redondo Beach, CA: Howard Gregory Associates, 1989), 176 pages, hardcover, $23.95; softcover, $14.95.
  A conglomeration to tips on how to write, photograph, paste-up, and market a self-published photo book.

- Hastings, Gerald, *Publish Good News: A Resource Guide for Personal Publishing by Church Groups*, (Dallas: Stone Canyon Press, 1986), saddle-stitched, $6.50.
  A basic primer for church groups or other nonprofit groups interested in publishing a book.

- Kramer, Felix/Loraas, Maggie, *Desktop Publishing Success*, (Homewood, IL: Business One Irwin, 1991; 708-789-5480). 350 pages, softcover, $30.00.
  Required reading — for the entrepreneur, the novice or experienced. Desktop Publishing is a must. Straight forward advice. Very much recommended and quite inspiring.

- Moore, Marilyn, **The Self-Publishing Cook: How to Write, Publish and Sell Your Own Cookbook,** (Wooden Spoon Kitchen, 1995; 217-283-6883). $14.95.
  A basic guide to cookbook publishing, but it forgets to talk at all about testing — which is vital when publishing cookbooks. You must be able to answer the question: Can anyone read the recipe and successfully recreate the dish described?

- Perkins, Russell, *Directory Publishing: A Practical Guide, Third Edition*, (Philadelphia: Morgan Rand, Spring 1992; 215-938-5511), 178 pages, softcover, $39.95.
  This book covers all the important steps to publishing a directory: research, planning, editorial, production, circulation, sales promotion, fulfillment, and advertising.

- Ross, Marilyn and Tom, **How to Make Big Profits Publishing City & Regional Books**, (Buena Vista, CO: Communication Creativity, 1987), 221 pages, softcover, $14.95.
  There are plenty of publishing opportunities in your own backyard, everything from tourist guides and regional histories, to consumer directories and cookbooks. If you are looking for ways to expand your line of titles, read this book. It is packed with ideas and real-life examples.

- Townsend, Doris McFerran, *The Way to Write and Publish a Cookbook*, (New York, St. Martins, 1985; 800-877-5351), softcover, $8.95.
  Another guide to publishing cookbooks.

- Webber, Earlynne, *Your Life Story: How to Write, Publish and Sell It Yourself*, (Las Vegas, NV: Echo Publishing, 1984; 409-866-0997), 154 pages, softcover, $9.95.
  The first half of this book describes how to write your own autobiography or ghostwrite someone else's using the progressive writing method. The second half, a general guide to publishing your own books, does not cover anything new.

Publishing Periodicals

The following are some of the best books on the subject of publishing newsletters or magazines. Newsletters, especially, can be an effective way to market your books.

- Beach, Mark, **Editing Your Newsletter, Fourth Edition**, (Cincinatti, OH: Writers Digest Books, 1995), 160 pages, softcover, $22.99.
  This book is a superb overview of all the ins and outs of editing and designing a newsletter. It's a classic.

- Brigham, Nancy, **How to Leaflets, Newsletters and Newspapers**, (Cincinatti, OH: Writers Digest Books North Light Books, 1991), 176 pages, softcover, $14.95.
  A practical guide with step by step instructions and the latest on desktop publishing, legal rights computer services — mailing rules, rates — tells you everything.

- Compaine, Benjamin, *The Business of Consumer Magazines*, (Boston, MA: G.K. Hall, 1982, 617-423-3990), 198 pages, hardcover, $35.95.
  With plenty of statistics and stories, this book is a good introduction to magazine publishing. However, it is not a how-to book.

- Goss, Frederick D., *Success in Newsletter Publishing, Third Edition*, (Arlington, VA: Newsletter Association, 703-527-2333), 272 pages, hardcover, $37.50.
  Written by the director of the Newsletter Association, this book covers everything you would want to know about starting up a newsletter. The major difference between the Goss's book and Hudson's (described below), is that Hudson's book covers all sorts of newsletters from in-house to non-profit to subscription-based, while Goss's book focuses on publishing subscription-based newsletters for profit.

- Moen, Daryl R., *Newspaper Layout and Design, Third Edition*, (Ames, IA: Iowa State University Press, 515-292-0140), softcover, $31.95.
  For those interested in publishing newspapers or applying newspaper designs to newsletters and magazines, this book covers everything from layout and design to using photographs and packaging special sections. The book includes many examples taken from actual newspapers and magazines.

- Parnau, Jeffrey, *The Handbook of Magazine Production*, (Stamford, CT: Hansen Publishing, 1985, 203-358-9900), hardcover, $69.95.
  Describes all the typesetting, pre-press, printing, and binding procedures required to produce a magazine.

- Williams, Patricia A., *Creating and Producing the Perfect Newsletter*, (Glenview, IL: Scott, Foresman, 1989, 800-242-7737), 298 pages, hardcover, $17.95.
  While this book covers all areas of starting up an organizational newsletter, its strongest points are editorial and design.

Legal Guides to Publishing

The following are a few of the books that answer basic questions about copyrights, trademarks, contracts, libel, and other legal questions that can come up when writing and publishing books.

- Andorka, Frank H., *A Practical Guide to Copyrights & Trademarks*, (New York: Pharos Books, 1989, 212-692-3824), 96 pages, hardcover, $19.95.
  Provides a clear, basic understanding of the laws of copyright and trademarks. Shows how to protect new works and provides guidelines on how to use legally the works and ideas of others.

- Blue, Martha, *By the Book: Legal ABC's for the Printed Word*, (Flagstaff, AZ: Northland Publishing, 1989, 800-346-3257), 488 pages, hardcover, $45.00.
  A review of some basic publishing contracts plus a discussion of other legal questions that might come up during the process of publishing a book, newspaper, magazine, or other literary work. Directed at the smaller publisher rather than to lawyers, this book is one of the easier ones to read if you want to familiarize yourself with the ins and outs of publishing law.

- Blue, Martha, *Making It Legal: A Law Primer for Authors, Artists and Craftspeople*, (Flagstaff, AZ: Northland Publishing, 1988, 800-346-3257), 177 pages, softcover, $15.95.
  Provides advice for most legal questions that might crop up for a writer or artist, including legal status, business licenses, defamation, negligence and product liability, copyright, unfair competition, contracts, taxes, and more.

- Bunnin, Brad and Beren, Peter, *The Writer's Legal Companion*, (Addison Wesley, 1988; 800-822-6339).
  Publishing law including contracts. Bunnin is a publishing lawyer. It's pro-author.

- Clark, Charles, *Publishing Agreements: A Book of Precedents, Fourth Edition*, (New York, New Amsterdam Books, 800-366-2665), Hardcover, $75.00.
  Besides presenting sample publishing agreements (based on British publishing practice), this book provides many detailed notes and comments based on standard publishing practice.

- Crawford, Tad, **Business & Legal Forms for Authors & Self-Publishers**, (New York NY: Allworth Press, 1996, 800-247-6553), 192 pages, softcover, $19.95.
  Reviewed by John B McHugh ©1996
  Publisher Crawford, who is also a lawyer, has compiled a treasure-trove of contracts not only for authors but also contracts a publisher can use with book designers, printers, sales representatives, book distributors, etc. Crawford provides commentary on each legal form and sound practical advice. Has some pro-author bias. This outstanding resource belongs in your library!

- Fishman, Setphen, **The Copyright Handbook: How to Protect and Use Written Works, 2nd Edition** (Nolo Press, 1994; 800-922-6656).
  Reviewed by John B. McHugh ©1996
  This is the authoritative book on copyright! Attorney Fishman discusses every conceivable aspect of copyright. All necessary copyright forms are included with advice on completing copyright paperwork. Fishman writes from the perspective of the copyright owner, which should be the publisher.

- Killough, Harold P, *The Beginning Creator's Copyright Manual*, (Manhattan, KS: Harold P Killough, 1988), 179 pages, softcover, $14.00.
  A good overview of the copyright law for beginners, especially writers.

- Kirsch, Jonathan, **Handbook of Publishing Law** (Acrobat Books, 1995; 310-578-1055). $21.95.
  Reviewed by John B. McHugh © 1996.
  Lawyer Kirsch provides 96 pages on book contracts. He discusses everything about the subject and more. Every possible legal implication is discussed. Views the contract from the perspective of both author and publisher. Heavy emphasis on subsidiary rights and trade book contracts, which, reflects the author's location, Los Angeles and Hollywood. The Kirsch book is an outstanding survey of publishing law.

- Kozak, Ellen, *Every Writer's Practical Guide to Copyright Law*, (NY: Owlet Publishing 1997; 212-886-9200), softcover, $9.95.
  This booklet answers 50 of the most common questions writers ask about copyright laws, including writing under a pseudonym, using established characters (such as Scarlett O'Hara), and copyright protection for articles in a collective work.

- Levine, Mark, *Negotiating a Book Contract :A Guide for Authors, Agents and Lawyers,* Third Edition, (Wakefield RI: Moyer Bell, 1988; 401-789-0474).
  Reviewed by John B McHugh ©1996
  This excellent little book has a **pro-author** bias with an adversial edge against the publisher. If you deal regularly with agents and lawyers representing authors, you will gain many insitghts as to what the other party is thinking as you negotiate.

- Perle, E. Gabriel, and John Taylor Williams, *The Publishing Law Handbook*, (Frederick MD: Aspen Law, 1992; 800-234-1660), looseleaf, $180.00.

  Another of the looseleaf handbooks for lawyers, this one covers publishing law only (rather than the legal questions of the entire entertainment industry).

- Poynter, Dan, and Charles Kent, **Publishing Contracts on Disk**, (Santa Barbara, CA: Para Publishing, 1987), various word-processing formats for IBM-PC, Macintosh, or compatible computers, $29.95.

  These publishing contracts are designed to be used by smaller publishers as guidelines for developing their own legal contracts with minimal help from their lawyers. Besides publishing contracts for trade books and textbooks, this disk also includes agreements for co-publishing, sales representation, distribution, collaboration, translation, merchandising rights sales, releases, and more. The disk format makes it quick and easy to adapt the contracts to your special needs.

- Strong, William, *The Copyright Book, Fourth Edition*, (Cambridge, MA: MIT Press, 1993; 617-625-8569), softcover, $30.00.

  This guide, which is far more readable than anything put out by the copyright office, includes details on how to go about registering, transferring, and protecting a copyright. It also describes the ins and outs of fair use and infringement as well as tax treatments for copyrights.

- Taylor, Barbara Sieck, *Pressing Business*, (New York: VLA, 1984), softcover, $6.95.

  Describes how to set up a nonprofit corporation and gain tax-exempt status. Also answers other basic business questions for small literary presses.

- Young, Woody, *A Business Guide to Copyright Law: What You Don't Know Can Cost You*, (Fountain Valley, CA: Joy Publishing, 1988; 714-545-4321), 68 pages plus copyright forms, softcover, $14.95.

  This guide answers all the basic copyright questions a writer might have. Plus it includes copies of all the copyright forms a beginning writer would need to use.

Marketing Your Books

- Bodian, Nat G., *Book Marketing Handbook: Tips and Techniques, Volume One*, (New York: R. R. Bowker, 1980), 482 pages, hardcover, $64.95.

- Bodian, Nat G., *Book Marketing Handbook: Tips and Techniques, Volume Two*, (New York: R. R. Bowker, 1983), 607 pages, hardcover, $64.95.

  These two volumes are designed to be used by publishers of technical, professional, and scholarly books and journals, but they provide so many superb marketing tips and techniques that every publisher, large or small, should have a copy of both volumes. Highly recommended even though there is so much information packed into these books that you might well find that you never finish them. No harm done; even a little goes a long way.

- Bodian, Nat G., *How to Choose a Winning Title*, (Phoenix: Oryx Press, 1989), 176 pages, softcover, $25.00.

  If you've ever agonized over the title of a book, this new guide will provide you with all the tips, insights, and real-life examples you'll need to come up with selling titles. Absolutely fascinating reading!

- Bodian, Nat G., *The Publisher's Direct Mail Handbook*, (Phoenix: Oryx Press, 1987 (originally published by ISI Press), 256 pages, hardcover, $42.50.

  Another gem from Bodian, this book is a goldmine of ideas on how to sell books by mail. If you do any direct mail promotions for books, especially for professional or technical titles, this book will provide many inside tips based on years of experience.

- Carter, Robert A., *Trade Book Marketing: A Practical Guide*, (New York: R. R. Bowker, 1983), 320 pages, softcover, $24.95.

  A valuable introduction to publishing and marketing using the standard book marketing channels. It should give you some idea of the odds against you cracking the mass retailers or the bestseller lists.

- Davis, Sally Prince, *Marketing and Self-Promotion, The Graphic Artist's Guide to, Revised Edition*, (Cincinnati: North Light Book, 1991), 128 pages, softcover $19.95.

  Revised and updated, a step by step guide for the freelance graphic artist — focuses on marketing and self-promotion. Very well written and illustrated.

- Erbe, Jack, *How to Make Money Promoting and Selling Books, Crafts, Gifts and Other Small Products*, (Van Nuys, CA: Publishers Services, 1985; 818-785-8039), 74 pages, softcover, $10.00.

  This book includes 31 book publication, 39 publicity, 30 advertising, 33 marketing, and 31 merchandising ideas. Most are short and very general with few examples.

- Hill, David Cahpin, *Direct Marketing: Tracking Analysis & Forecasting* (dh Direct, 1996; 408-252-8565). $39.95.

  This book descibes how to forecast direct mail, catalog, and space advertising programs.

- Kiefer, Marie, and Kremer, John, **Book Marketing Profitcenter**tm, (Fairfield, IA: Ad-Lib Publications, 1996), 7000+ records available in various data file formats for IBM-PCs, Macintoshes, or compatibles, $150.00.

  These data files are continuously updated. You get the latest version on the day you order. Includes more than 2000 specialty booksellers, 318 distributors, 710 wholesalers, 240 paperback jobbers, 240 sales representatives, 39 fulfillment services, 285 chain store buyers, 483 top independent booksellers, 119 book clubs, 823 mail order catalogs, 45 remainder dealers, 200 mailing list sources, 250 publicity and marketing services, card packs, book fairs and conventions, publishing associations, and much, much more! No other book marketing database offers so much for so little cost — about 2¢ a contact.

- Kiefer, Marie and Kremer, John, **How to Sell to Mail Order Catalogs**, (Fairfield, IA: Ad-Lib Publications, 1996), 75 pages, report, $30.00.

  This report not only describes all the steps you need to follow to sell a book or other product to mail order catalog houses, but it also lists more than 550 catalogs that carry books, tapes, and other items. Current names, addresses, buyers, phone numbers, and subject interests are listed.

- Kremer, John, **1001 Ways to Market Your Books — For Authors and Publishers**, (Fairfield, IA: Open Horizons, April 1993), softcover, $19.95. New edition in 1997.

    This book features more than 1000 tips, techniques, and examples of how you can market your books more effectively. It covers traditional markets as well as special sales, subsidiary rights, direct mail, telemarketing, foreign sales, and much, much more. This book will help you to sell more books — and have fun doing it ... and make money doing it. This book includes two special chapters especially designed to help writers market their books and get the most out of the publication of their books.

- Landen, Hal, **Marketing with Video: How to Create a Winning Video for Your Small Business or Non-Profit**, (Oak Tree Press, 1996; 914-355-1400). $19.95.

    If you are thinking of using video to market your books, check this book out.

- McHugh, John, *College Publishing Market*, (Glendale, WI: McHugh Consulting, 1995, report, 50 pages, $48.00.

    The College Publishing Market presents a comprehensive overview of the business of college publishing. This standard reference discusses all aspects of publishing and selling to the college market. The entire life-cycle of the college publishing market is explained.

- Mladjenovic, Paul, *Zero-Cost Marketing* (Prosperity Network, 1996; 800-787-2829). $35.00.

    Lots of low-cost or no-cost ways to market anything.

- Nicholas, Ted, *How to Self-Publish Your Own Book and Make It a Best Seller!*, (Wilmington, DE: Enterprise Publishing, 1975; 302-654-0110), 200 pages, softcover, $6.95.

    This book is especially strong on promoting and marketing your books by mail. Nicholas gives many examples from his own experience in writing and publishing a half dozen bestsellers.

- Powers, Melvin, **How to Self-Publish Your Book and Have the Fun and Excitement of Being a Best-Selling Author**, (North Hollywood, CA: Wilshire Books, 1993), 176 pages, softcover, $20.00.

    This book is worthwhile for the section on selecting titles and cover designs for your books and the one describing innovative strategies for marketing your books through bookstores.

- Poynter, Dan, *Book Marketing: A New Approach*, (Santa Barbara, CA: Para Publishing, 1988), 61 pages, report, $14.95.

    Like everything Dan does, this report offers many tips and suggestions based on practical experience in marketing books to bookstores, libraries, and special markets.

- Poynter, Dan, *Book Reviews*, (Santa Barbara, CA: Para Publishing, 1988), 39 pages, report, $24.95.

    Describes in detail how to make galleys and structure a review program to ensure that your books are reviewed.

- Poynter, Dan, *Direct Mail for Book Publishers*, (Santa Barbara, CA: Para Publishing, 1988), 52 pages, report, $19.95.

    For publishers with a specific audience, direct mail can be the most effective way to reach buyers. This report covers the basics.

- Poynter, Dan, *News Releases and Book Publicity*, (Santa Barbara, CA: Para Publishing, 1988), 46 pages, report, $19.95.

    Describes how to write news releases, with many examples.

- Poynter, Dan, **Book Fairs: An Exhibiting Guide for Publishers, 4th Edition**, (Santa Barbara, CA: Para Publishing, 1986), 96 pages, softcover, $7.95.

    This book describes the ins and outs of displaying your books at conventions and fairs. It includes everything from selecting the most appropriate book fairs, to creating an effective display, to actually operating the booth. Essential for first-time exhibitors.

- Revoyr, Jack, *A Primer on Licensing, Second Edition* (Kent Press, 1995; 203-358-0848). $37.95.

    Provides the basics for establishing a trademark licensing program.

- Revoyr, Jack, *Licensee Survival Guide* (Kent Press, 1995; 203-358-0848).

    If you want to license a trademark, character, etc. for use in your book or marketing campaign, this book is for you.

- Sackheim, Maxwell, *Billion Dollar Marketing: Concepts and Applications* (Towers Club Press, 1995; 800-524-4045). $29.95. (includes free audio tape).

    Sackheim, the developer of the negative option plan and Book-of-the-Month Club, provides many examples on how to write ads that sell. An incredible book by an incredible man. If you plan to do any direct marketing, read this book.

- Schrello, Don, *How to Market Training & Information: Everything You Need to Know to Sell Seminars, Workshops, Conferences, Tapes, Videos, Books, Software and Other Self-Improvement or Continuing Education Products and Services* (Schrellol Direct Marketing, 1994; 800-367-6559). $69.95.

    If you want to expand your information publishing beyond books, this big book shows you how to sell many other information products.

- Shatzkin, Leonard and Mike, *The Business of Publishing: How to Survive and Prosper in the Publishing and Bookselling Industry* (Harvard Business School Press; 1996). $24.95.

    We haven't seen a review copy yet, but from the promotional material, it seems to have more to offer bookstores than book publishers. Focus for publishers is on the economics of publishing.

- Tarila, Sophia, *Flyers That Work: Promotion Products, Events, Services & More* (First Editions, 1994; 602-282-957). $10.95

    Describes how to write, design, print, and post flyers that sell.

Advertising and Marketing

The following books are only a few of the many excellent books about advertising, copywriting, and direct response marketing, but these alone would make a superb reference library for marketing any products.

Again, please note that the titles in **bold** are only a toll-free phone call away. To order, just call **800-669-0773**. Have your VISA, MasterCard, or American Express credit card handy. Or send a check or money order to Ad-Lib Publications, PO Box 1102, Fairfield, IA 52556-1102. Satisfaction guaranteed, or your money back!

- Bayan, Richard, **Words That Sell**, (Chicago: Contemporary, 1994), 127 pages, softcover, $13.95.
  If you have trouble finding the right words when you are writing catalog copy, advertisements, news releases, or book blurbs, this book is for you. It is a superb practical combination of a thesaurus and a course in advertising copywriting. Need help wording your guarantee, see page 87. Need a word to connote status or style, see pages 65 through 67. Want to reword your order form, see page 88. Have trouble making snappy transitions, see page 11.

- Bentley, Nancy, and Donna Guthrie, *How to Promote Your Children's Book on a Shoestring*, (Children's Book Insider, 1994; 800-807-1916), $15.95.
  A great book for authors who want to promote their children's book. Special strength: promoting author appearances at bookstores, schools, and libraries. Includes four pages of wonder clip art you can use.

- Bly, Robert, **The Copywriter's Handbook**, (New York: Henry Holt & Co, 1990), 354 pages, softcover, $13.95.
  This book presents lots of advice on how to write copy that sells, including 8 headlines that work, 11 ways to make your copy more readable, 15 ways to open a sales letter, and much more. Especially valuable for people seeking jobs as copywriters.

- Bly, Robert, **The Perfect Sales Piece**, (New York: John Wiley, 1994), 240 pages, softcover, $14.95.
  If you want to design and write better brochures, promotional literature, and catalogs, here's help. How to find and evaluate talent, how to use the 11 basic types of sales literature, how to write benefit-oriented ad copy, how to get the best price on printing — these are just a few of the many topics covered in this book.

- Bodian, Nat G., *NTC's Dictionary of Direct Mail and Mailing List Terminology*, (Lincolnwood IL: NTC, 800-323-4900), 320 pages, hardcover, $49.95.
  This book is essentially a dictionary of 1500 definitions of terms and concepts from the direct mail industry, everything from to A/B split to zig zag fold. If you are new to the industry and want to know what people are talking about, this book will tell you in clear and simple words.

- BrezenBlock, Tamara and Robinson, William A., *Sales Promotion Handbook, 8h Edition*, (Chicago: Dartnell, 1994), 910 pages, hardcover, $69.95.
  A standard in the field of sales promotion, this book is loaded with ideas, tips, examples, and much more — all showing you how to make better use of your sales promotions. Like the other Dartnell handbooks, this book cannot be digested in one reading.

- Brumbaugh, J. Frank, *Mail Order Made Easy*, (North Hollywood, CA: Wilshire Books, 1982), 208 pages, softcover, $20.00.
  Provides nuts-and-bolts know-how for mail order beginners. Contains chapters on choosing a product that sells, naming your price, using classified ads, choosing periodicals for advertising, designing and producing your sales package, and handling orders.

- Caples, John, **Tested Advertising Methods, New 5th Edition**, (New York: Prentice-Hall, 1996), 320 pages, softcover, $29.95.
  Everything you would want to know about writing ads that sell. The copywriter's bible, this book reveals proven selling techniques. Includes 20 formulas for writing winning headlines, 32 ways to increase inquiries, 20 ways to improve selling power, 17 ways to test your ads, and much more. Useful for writing your publicity releases and promotional brochures as well as advertisements.

- Chapman Jr., Edward A., **Exhibit Marketing: A Survival Guide for Managers**, (New York: McGraw-Hill), hardcover, $29.95.
  This book is an incredibly detailed guide to planning, designing, managing, and promoting exhibits at major trade shows. Includes all the forms you'll need to create a successful, selling exhibit of your books or other products.

- Clark, Silvana, *Taming the Marketing Jungle: 104 Marketing Ideas When Your Motivation Is High and Your Budget Is Low*, (Memory Makers, PO Box 19732, Seattle WA 98109). $6.95
  A great little book of marketing idea stimulators.

- Cohen, William A., **Building a Mail Order Business, 4th Edition**, (New York: John Wiley, 1996), 571 pages, hardcover, $39.95.
  A thorough guide for beginner and professional alike, this book details everything from financing and start up to the most sophisticated new mail order techniques. Over 150 illustrations, case histories, graphs, samples, and checklists show you exactly what to do. Highly recommended!

- Cossman, E. Joseph, **How I Made $1,000,000 in Mail Order**, (New York: Simon & Schuster, 1992), 270 pages, softcover, $13.00.
  Cossman is famous for his one-shot mail order promotions (ant farms, fish lures, etc.). This book presents a common sense, step-by-step procedure for promoting single items via mail order and some very creative direct marketing ideas!

- Davidson, Jeffrey P., **Marketing on a Shoestring: Low-Cost Tips for Marketing Your Products or Services**, (New York: John Wiley, 1988), 223 pages, softcover, $14.95.
  While aimed primarily at local small businesses, this book contains many practical, low-cost, low-hassle strategies for marketing any product or service. Among the tips discussed are yellow pages advertising, business directories, brochures, bulletin boards, speaking, and marketing via the telephone.

- Dobkin, Jeffrey, *How to Market a Product for Under $500!*, (Danielle Adams Publishing, 1996; 610-642-1000). $44.50.
  The focus of this book is on direct marketing using multiple exposures. The book features over 400 pages packed with direct marketing details. Good book.

- Fuller, Bruce, *Crank 'Em Up!!!* (Self-Counsel Press, 1995; 604-986-3366). $10.95.
  This book will show you how to motivate your sales reps, including creating sales manuals, training, making presentations, running sales meetings, and using sales contests.

- Gosden Jr., Freeman F., **Direct Marketing Success: What Works and Why**, (New York: John Wiley, 1985), 225 pages, hardcover, $17.95.

    If you've ever wondered why there are certain direct marketing rules (and when and why you can sometimes break them), this book will answer many of your questions. For example, it describes why long letters work, why teasers work, why picture captions are more important than pictures, why lift letters increase sales, why some lists do better than others, and much, much more.

- Hill, David Chapin, *Direct Marketing: Tracking Analysis & Forecasting*, (dh Direct, 1996; 408-252-8565). $39.95.

    This book describes how to forecast direct mail, catalog, and space advertising programs.

- Hodgson, Richard, *Direct Mail and Mail Order Handbook, Third Edition*, (Chicago: Dartnell, 1980), 1555 pages, hardcover, $49.95.

    A classic in the field so full of information that you won't be able to digest it all in just one reading. It's the kind of handbook you'll come back to again and again as you carry out your direct marketing promotions.

- Kremer, John, **Complete Direct Marketing Source Book**, (John Wiley), 288 pages, hardcover, $24.95.

    This book is an easy-to-use introduction to running a mail order operation. It includes worksheets, tables, sample letters, flow charts plus instructions to help anyone develop and carry out a successful direct response marketing program. This book makes all the time-consuming details so much easier to handle.

- Lant, Jeffrey, **Cash Copy**, (Cambridge, MA: Jeffrey Lant Associates, 1989), 480 pages, softcover, $35.00

    This book has quickly become my favorite guide to writing promotional copy that sells. Chapter 11 on selling solutions is alone worth the price of the entire book. If you have ever been stuck when writing a direct mail letter, brochure, news release, cover letter, catalog copy, or advertisement, this book will open up new possibilities for you. A superb book.

- Lant, Jeffrey, **Money Making Marketing**, (Cambridge, MA: Jeffrey Lant Associates, 1987), 268 pages, softcover, $35.00.

    Another of Lant's exhaustive books, this one presents hundreds of creative, inexpensive, opinionated, and effective marketing techniques. His emphasis is on creating repeat customers for your products. Packed with detailed, money-making information.

- Levinson, Jay Conrad and Seth Godin, *Guerilla Marketing: For the Home-Based Business*, (Boston: Houghton-Mifflin, 1985), 240 pages, softcover, $11.95.

    The book on marketing with a small budget. Packed with practical advice and tactics to get the most from your marketing budget — both in terms of time and money.

- Levy, Sydney, George Frericks, and Howard Gordon *Marketing Manager's Handbook*, 3rd Edition (Chicago: Dartnell, 1994; 312-561-4000), 1456 pages, hardcover, $69.95.

    A complete reference work for any marketing manager, this book covers everything from planning your marketing strategy to dealing with the resulting sales. This is one of several superb Dartnell handbooks on marketing and promotion. Since this book is huge, you will need several weeks (even years) to digest all its details.

- Lewis, Herschell G., **Direct Mail Copy That Sells**, (New York: Prentice-Hall, 1984), 258 pages, softcover, $14.95.

    This book gives specific techniques for writing irresistible copy, from attention-grabbing headlines to response-producing order forms. Also reveals dozens of common copy errors that can weaken the response to your ads and other promotional materials. These practical, high-impact ideas are presented with warmth and humor. Good reading.

- Nash, Edward, Editor, *The Direct Marketing Handbook*, (New York: McGraw-Hill, 1992), 827 pages, hardcover, $69.95.

    This is a classic in the field. It covers everything from planning to budgeting to design and production to execution to fulfillment.

- Playle, Ron, *Selling to Catalog Houses*, (Des Moines, IA: R & D Services, 1982), 48 pages, saddle-stitched, $12.00.

    A succinct manual for selling your books to major mail order catalog marketers. Includes sample letters, pricing guidelines, addresses, and more.

- Powers, Melvin, **How to Get Rich in Mail Order**, (North Hollywood, CA: Wilshire Books, 1985), 350 pages, softcover, $20.00.

    Melvin has been publishing books, both his own and others, for over 25 years (and sold millions of dollars worth of books). Although this book is about mail order, its primary focus is on selling information (books) by mail. The book is jam-packed with examples of successful mail order ads and promotional literature.

- Rice, Craig S., *Marketing without a Marketing Budget*, (Holbrook, MA: Bob Adams, 1989, 800-872-5627), 317 pages, softcover, $10.95.

    A potpourri of brief ideas to help you get the most from your marketing dollars, this book offers good basic advice. Not as good, however, as the similar do-less-and-accomplish-more books by Jay Levinson and Jeffrey Davidson.

- Robinson, William A., *Best Sales Promotions, Sixth Edition*, (Lincolnwood, IL: NTC Business Books, 1987), 372 pages, hardcover, $29.95

    If you've ever thought about using sales promotions (couponing, sampling, refunds, sweepstakes, continuity programs, premium packs, trade incentives, etc.) to promote your books, this book will stimulate your creative juices to overflowing. It describes and illustrates the most outstanding sales promotions of the past 10 years. Provides a real boost to your idea quotient!

- Schwab, Victor, *How to Write a Good Advertisement*, (North Hollywood, CA: Wilshire Books), 234 pages, softcover, $20.00.

    Presents 100 good headlines with explanations of why they have worked. Plus 22 ways to hold the reader's attention once you've attracted it. The book also includes details on all aspects of writing successful advertisements.

- Simon, Julian, **How to Start and Operate a Mail Order Business, 5th Edition**, (New York: McGraw-Hill, 1993), 538 pages, hardcover, $39.95.

    This book is a comprehensive manual packed with sound advice and basic mail order techniques to help anyone make money in mail order. It covers everything you need to know to start and operate a successful mail order business. This is a book to be read more than once. It should be kept on your reference shelf at all times for easy reference.

- Siskind, Barry, *The Successful Exhibitors's Handbook*, (Bellingham, WA: Self-Counsel Press, 1993), 256 pages, softcover, $10.95.

  This book discusses the whole process, from initial scouting of locations to the after-show review of your performance. Whether you are a newcomer looking for a primer or an old hand ready for a refresher course, you can benefit from this book.

- Sroge, Maxwell, *How to Create Successful Catalogs, 2nd Edition*, (Lincolnwood, IL: NTC Business Books, 1985), 460 pages, hardcover, $89.95.

  Sroge shows how to improve the design, artwork, and copy of your catalogs to create the most effective sales message. Special emphasis is given to the four major parts of any catalog: the front cover, the back cover, the order form, and the guarantee. Many examples and checklists make the information in this book easy to absorb and implement.

- Stilson, Galen, *59 Response/Profit Tips, Tricks, & Techniques to Help You Achieve Major Mail Order Success*, (Fort Worth, TX: Premier Publishers, 1984), 32 pages, saddle-stitched, $12.00.

  A brief but excellent collection of tips and techniques for any direct marketer. It actually includes many more than 59 tips (one tip alone lists 23 rules for increasing response to your ads — this list itself is worth the small price of this manual).

- Stone, Bob, **Successful Direct Marketing Methods, Sixth Edition**, (Lincolnwood, IL: NTC Business Books, 1996), 640 pages, hardcover, $49.95.

  The professional's direct marketing bible, this book is not for beginners. But for anyone with an iota of experience in direct marketing, this book will quickly pay its own way. A superb overview of the entire business of direct marketing. In my opinion, it is the best book on direct marketing available anywhere — comprehensive, readable, and authoritative. A book to keep on your reference shelf for easy use at all times.

- Stone, Bob, and John Wyman, *Successful Telemarketing*, (Lincolnwood, IL: NTC Business Books, 1985), 224 pages, softcover, $19.95.

  One of the best introductions to the new field of telemarketing. Read it carefully if you are considering using telephones to market your books (whether for outbound WATS calls or inbound 800 calls).

- Ulanoff, Stanley, *Handbook of Sales Promotion*, (New York: McGraw-Hill, 1985), 624 pages, hardcover, $63.50

  Like the Dartnell book on sales promotion, this one is an all-in-one-book compendium off sales promotion techniques and ideas. Very comprehensive. Useful if you are considering using sweepstakes, coupons, giveaways, rebates, or other promotional gimmicks.

- Voiles, Brian Keith, *Advertising Magic! The Complete Guide to Creating Hot Ads & Sales letters That Work!!!* (Brian Keith Publishing, 1995; 801-255-5548). $247.00.

  Includes two packed binders plus six audiotapes. This is a detailed course on how to write ads (and news releases) that get results. Written by a copywriter with a great heart. If you work his system, your promo writing will change.

Publicity and Speaking

The following titles are the best of the lot. Since most books are sold via publicity, reviews, and word of mouth, these books are invaluable reading for any publisher.

- Bly, Robert, **Targeted Public Relations: How to Get Thousands of Dollars of Dollars of Free Publicity for Your Product, Service, Organization, or Idea** (Owl Books, 1994). $14.95

  A good basic book on how to get publicity by targeting your pitch.

- Borden, Kay, **Bullet proof News Releases: Help at Last for the Publicity Deficient** (Franklin-Sarrett, 1994; 800-444-2524). $18.95.

  Focuses on how to get newspaper publicity — with tips from 135 editors!

- Brewer, Annie M and Brewer, Donald E, *Talk Shows and Host on Radio,* (Dearborn, MI: Whitefoord Press, 1996. 313-274-1038), 200 pages. softcover $40.00.

  A very informative directory — maked a great sourcebook. Incudes show titles, format, call letters/frequencies, biographical information on hosts and show locators.

- Burgett, Gordon, **How to Sell 75% of Your Freelance Writing**, (Santa Maria, CA: Communication Unlimited, 1995), 226 pages, softcover, $12.95.

  One overlooked means of getting free publicity is to sell magazine articles excerpted from or related to your books. Not only do these articles help to publicize the book and/or the author, but they are also a superb way for the author to earn extra income.

- Chase, Helen and Bill, *Chase's Annual Events*, (Chicago, IL: Contemporary Books, annual), softcover, $49.95. 1997 soon available

  This book is a publicist's dream! The latest edition lists more than 7000 weird and wonderful days, weeks, and months. With that many listings, you should be able to find at least 15 special events to plug each book you publish. Use these special days or weeks as news pegs to give a little boost to your publicity efforts or, better yet, use them to create a unique updated PR campaign for one of your older titles.

- Glenn, Peggy, **Publicity for Books and Authors**, (Huntington Beach, CA: Aames-Allen Publishing, 1985), 182 pages, softcover, $12.95.

  This is a superb, well-written, easy-to-use guide to obtaining publicity. Over half the book is devoted to handling author tours and public appearances — how to pack, what to wear, how to do radio and TV interviews, and more. An invaluable reference book for publishers and authors.

- Gaughen, Barbara, and Ernest Weckbaugh, **Book Blitz" Getting Your Book in the News** (Best-seller Books, 1994). $12.95.

  A great book on how to get more publicity for your books and authors.

- Goff, Christine Friesleben, Editor, *The Publicity Process, Third Edition*, (Ames, IA: Iowa State University Press, 1989), 305 pages, softcover, $22.95.

  Designed as a textbook for journalism students, this book provides a solid overview of the entire publicity process, from selecting the proper media to creating the news release and other material.

- Kelly, Kate, *The Publicity Manual*, (Larchmont, NY: Visibility Enterprises, 1984), 184 pages, softcover, $29.95.

    Designed to show you how to obtain free publicity without hiring a professional, this book presents a concise step-by-step approach to obtaining publicity. Well laid out and easy to use, but not as comprehensive as Lant's book.

- Kiefer, Marie and Kremer, John, **PR Profitcenter**tm, (Fairfield, IA: Ad-Lib Publications, 1996), 10,500 media records in various data formats for IBM-PC, Macintosh, or compatibles, $200.00.

    These data files provide key contact names, addresses, phone numbers, subject interests, and other important details for more than 15,500 media, including 5500 newspaper editors, 3550 magazine editors, 2400 radio shows, 900 TV shows, and 725 syndicated columns. The 10,500 records are available in a variety of data file formats to use with your favorite database program on the IBM-PC, Macintosh, or compatibles.

    A great time-saver. No other directory or database offers so much for so little cost (less than 1.5¢ per name!).

- Kiefer, Marie and Kremer, John, **Radio Phone Interview Shows: How to Do an Author Tour from Your Home**, (Fairfield: Ad-Lib Publications, 1996, updated annually), report, $40.00.

    This report lists more than 800 radio shows that feature phone interviews with authors and other experts. This report includes 25 pages of addresses formated to copy onto labels with any photocopy machine, plus 30 more pages of details about each show: radio station, show name, contact person, address, phone number, subject interests, hosts, times, and much more. Radio phone interviews are one of the most cost-effective ways to promote books and authors.

- Kiefer, Marie and Kremer, John, **The Top 200 National TV News / Talk / Magazine Shows**, (Fairfield, IA: Ad-Lib Publications, 1996, updated annually), report, $30.00.

    This report features 200 national television news, talk, and magazine shows — who to contact, how to book the show, what subjects the show is interested in, names of hosts, and other details. Indispensable for anyone wanting to book a guest appearance on a national TV talk show or place a story on the national news.

- Lant, Jeffrey, **Money Talks: The Complete Guide to Creating a Profitable Workshop or Seminar in Any Field**, (Cambridge, MA: Jeffrey Lant Associates, 1985), 310 pages, softcover, $35.00.

    It's subtitle describes this book perfectly. An excellent guide to promoting your authors or books through speaking engagements.

- Lant, Jeffrey, **The Unabashed Self-Promoter's Guide**, (Cambridge, MA: Jeffrey Lant Associates, 1983), 366 pages, softcover, $35.00.

    The best general book on publicity now available, it provides detailed advice for anyone having anything to promote whether it be a book, a new product, themselves, an event, an idea, or whatever. Describes how to gain contacts through networking, where to find media addresses, how to approach various media, and more. Contains many examples which will stimulate your creative juices. Plus sample letters and news releases for any occasion.

- Mallory, Charles, *Publicity Power: A Practical Guide to Effective Promotion*, (Los Altos, CA: Crisp Publications, 1989), 96 pages, softcover, $9.95.

    A short, inexpensive, basic guide to obtaining publicity especially designed for small local businesses. It packs a lot of practical and useful information into an easily accessible format.

- Parinello, Al, **On the Air: How to Get on Radio and TV Shows and What to Do When You Get There** (Prosperity Network, 1996; 800-787-2829), 120 pages, softcover, $24.95.

    This is both an enjoyable and informative book for anyone interested in becoming a talk show guest. Great advice for the novice or experienced. Easy to understand.

- Randall, Hal, *Publicity Photography*, (Twain Harte, CA: Studio Press, 1996), 106 pages, softcover, $17.50.

    While aimed primarily at professional photographers, this book has much to offer anyone who wants to get more mileage from their publicity efforts. Remember: A picture is worth a thousand words. This book shows how to produce the kind of publicity shots that editors want to see — photos that are interesting, informative, and exciting. Illustrated with hundreds of actual publicity photos that received wide news coverage, this book will have you brimming over with new ways to publicize your books and authors.

- Shafer, Ross, *How to Get Famous*, (Ross Shafer Productions, 1994; 800-747-1710). $49.95.

    Focuses on how to get booked on national TV shows. Plus what to do when you are on the show.

- Stauber, John, and Sheldon Rampton, *Toxic Sludge Is Good for You!: Lies, Damn Lies, and the Public Relations Industry*. (Common Courage Press, 1995; 207-525-0900. $16.95.

    Reveals how PR people can spin the news, organize "grass roots "groups, and conspire with politicians and lobbists to thwart democracy. You might learn something about how the big PR firms create the news.

- Vitale, Joe, *How to Get Front Page Coverage for Your Books* (Joe Vitale Agency, 1995; 713-999-1110; E-mail: mrfire@blkbox.com) $30.00.

    This short report provides examples of Joe's copywriting business showing how PR can increase business.

- Woodall, Marian K., **Thinking on Your Feet: How to Communicate under Pressure** 2nd Edition (Lake Oswego, OR: Professional Business Communication, 1988), 110 pages, softcover, $11.95.

    Every author who goes out on the talk show circuit should have this book. Practical, how-to suggestions when responding to tough questions for interviews, customer service, sales, presentation, managers, the opposite sex. Using on-target strategies and real life examples, here's help to improve your end of every conversation.

Editing, Design, & Printing

Before you can market your book, you must edit, design, typeset, and print a well-designed book. The following books will help you to do a better job producing your books.

- Adler, Elizabeth W, **Everyone's Guide to Successful Publications**, (Palo Alto, CA: Bull Publishing Co, 1991) 400 pages, softcover, $29.95.

    For the desktop publisher or for one who communicates on paper. A very well-written/illustrated book for writing, design and marketing.

- Barker, Malcom, **Book Design and Production**, (Londonborn, 1990) $24.95.

    A basic manual for the beginner, but with lots of useful illustrations for level of experience. Good book.

- Bann, David, *The Print Production Handbook,* (Cincinnati: Writer's Digest, 1985), 160 pages, hardcover, $16.95.

  This book describes all of today's new printing alternatives from offset lithography to flexography, ink jet printing, xerography, laser printing, letterpress, and thermography. It also analyzes the various typesetting systems then in use and which would best suit your needs.

- Beach, Mark; Steve Sheparo, and Ken Russon, **Getting It Printed: How to Work with Printers and Graphic Arts Services to Assure Quality, Stay on Schedule, and Control Costs**, (Cincinnati, OH: Writers Digest, 1993), 208 pages, $29.99.

  Of all the books on printing and graphics that I have read, this book is a standout. It is detailed, well-designed, and easy to use. It covers everything from planning the printing job, writing specifications, requesting quotations, working with typesetters, preparing camera-ready copy, proofing, and working with your printer to get the best job. Plus it provides specific criteria for checking every step of the process. If every printer and book publisher had this book, 90% of all printing problems would disappear.

- Beach, Mark; **Graphically Speaking**, (Manzanita, OR: Elk Ridge Publishing), 321 pages, softcover $29.50.

  Graphically Speaking brings the power of clear communication to every printing job that you produce.

- Beach, Mark, and Ryan, Kathleen, **Papers for Printing: How to Choose the Right Paper at the Right Price for Any Printing Job,** (Portland, OR: Coast to Coast Books, 1991), 44 sample sheets, 80 pages of text, softcover, $39.50.

  This booklet shows how to buy and specify paper for your various printing jobs. It includes 40 printed sample sheets, a chart that compares the costs of all 40 samples, a list of 678 paper brands, a list of 591 paper merchants, and a glossary of 214 paper terms.

- Bonura, Larry S., *Desktop Publisher's Dictionary,* (Plano, TX: Wordware Publishing, 1989, 800-229-4949), 300+ pages, hardcover, $21.95.

  This new dictionary includes definitions of more than 4000 words, phrases and abbreviations used in desktop publishing, typesetting, and graphics.

- Burke, Clifford, *Printing It: A Guide to Graphic Techniques for the Impecunious,* (Oakland, CA: Bookpeople, 1981), 127 pages, softcover, $5.95.

  A short guide that provides all the basics you need to know to prepare your own camera-ready copy for printers.

- *The Chicago Manual of Style,* (Chicago: University of Chicago Press, 1993, 312-568-1550), 936 pages, $40.00, hardcover.

  THE handbook of style for books. When you have questions about capitalization, punctuation, and usage, this book is the first place to look for answers. It will help you make the most acceptable choice when editing and copyediting your books.

- Collins, David, and Bob Cotton, *Basic Desktop Design & Layout,* (Cincinnati: North Light Books, 1989), 160 pages, hardcover, $27.95.

  A book for graphic designers who like to see what other people are doing in similar situations. Lots of samples of newsletters, brochures, magazines, and reports. Very graphic, but not a systematic how-to book for beginners.

- Doty, Betty, *Publish Your Own Handbound Books*, Redding, CA: The Bookery, 1980, 800-356-9315), hand-bound, $12.95.

  A charming little book that makes a persuasive case for producing your own limited edition books — write, typeset, print, and bind them yourself. It includes explicit instructions for binding books. Plus, Betty prodvies a kit of binding materials for your first attempt at doing it yourself.

- Graham, Walter B., **Complete Guide to Pasteup, Third Edition**, (Omaha, NE: Dot Pasteup Supply, 1987), 240 pages, softcover, $19.95.

  This is the classic book on how to prepare camera-ready copy for printing. If you are a newcomer to pasteup or have just hired a novice, this is the book to use. Very detailed and complete. Indeed, if this book has any faults, it would be the fact that it could very well overwhelm you with its details.

- Hill, Mary, and Wendell Cochran, *Into Print: A practical guide to writing, illustrating, and publishing*, (Los Altos, CA: William Kaufman, 1977, 415-323-6100), 175 pages, softcover, $12.00.

  Intended for the professional, scientist, engineer or educator who wants to produce a book. Includes a general discussion of how to get started, how to write, and how to arrange publication of your books and journals (with some suggestions on how to self-publish). Eight chapters detail how to prepare and choose illustrations, photos, graphs, maps, and so forth to accompany your written manuscript. It also includes a good section on how to prepare a useable index.

- Johnson, Christine Leslie, and Amy Christine Straayer, *A Book of One's Own*, (Chicago: Metis Press, 1979), 70 pages, softcover, $4.00.

  This book is the only one on self-publishing that gives tips on how to make your own printing plates — and do your own negatives, stripping, even printing. It could save you money if you would like to get involved in some or all steps of the book production process.

- Judd, Karen, **Copyediting: A Practical Guide**, (Los Altos, CA: Crisp Publications, 1990), 317 pages, hardcover, $17.95.

  When you have questions regarding the appropriate places to use numerals versus spelling out numbers, how to use the standard punctuation marks, how to mark changes in a manuscript (with standard proofreading symbols), how to typeset equations, how to format bibliographies or footnotes, look to this book for the answers. A very complete and easy-to-use guide. Highly recommended for your editors and copyeditors.

- Kiefer, Marie and Kremer, John, **Directory of Book Printers, 7th Edition**, (Fairfield, IA: Ad-Lib Publications, 1992), 390 pages, softcover, $14.95.

  This directory lists 781 printers of books, catalogs, magazines, and other bound publications. With this edition you can locate a quality printer who specializes in the quantities, sizes, and bindings you want to use — at a price you can afford.

- Laing, John, *Do-It-Yourself Graphic Design*, (New York: Macmillan, 1985, 800-223-2336), 156 pages, softcover, $15.00.

  A step-by-step guide to designing and producing any printed material — books, posters, brochures, letterheads, T-shirts, magazines, and more. Very detailed and well-designed. A delight to read and use. For the beginner, as well as the professional.

- Lem, Dean P., *Graphics Master, 5th Edition*, (Kihei Maui, HI: Dean Lem Associates, 1993), 3-ring binder, $54.50.

  A collection of planning and production aids to make all the technicalities of graphics production much easier. This workbook includes a chart of paper sizes, drawings (and names) of common brochure folds, a scaling wheel, and many other technical data charts and forms. A useful collection for anyone who spends a lot of time doing layouts and graphic design.

- Lippi, Robert, *How to Buy Good Printing & Save Money*, 144 pages, softcover, $14.50.

  A good, basic, easy-to-understand guide to buying printing services. While this book is a good book, it is not nearly as attractive, comprehensive, or detailed as Getting It Printed.

- McDarrah, Fred, *Stock Photo and Assignment Source Book, Third Edition*, (New York: Robert Silver Assn., 1989), 312 pages, softcover, $29.95.

  Lists sources for over 150,000,000 stock photos covering anything and everything — for every need from books and magazines to annual reports, brochures, publicity, ads, and more. A number of these sources provide free photos.

- Miles, John, *Design for Desktop Publishing: A Guide to Layout and Typography on the Personal Computer*, (San Francisco: Chronicle Books, 1987, 800-722-6657), 112 pages, spiral bound, $19.95.

  A good basic book on design, but the design of the book itself is too busy for me. I much prefer a more systematic, simpler design.

- Miller, Marlene, *Business Guide to Print Promotion*, (Laguna Beach, CA: Iris Communication Group, 1988), 220 pages, softcover, $19.95.

  A well-written, easy-to-grasp introduction to the entire process of creating business communications, from letterhead and business cards to brochures and advertisements. Covers basic copywriting, proofing, design, typography, printing, paper, and binding.

- Parker, Roger, **Looking Good in Print: A Guide to Basis Design for Desktop Publishing**, 3rd Edition(Chapel Hill, NC: Ventana Press, 1993), 428 pages, softcover, $24.95.

  Shows how to use computers to design and produce more effective brochures, newsletters, manuals, and catalogs. Also describes the common design pitfalls and how to avoid them.

- *Pocket Pal: A Graphics Arts Production Handbook*, (Memphis, TN, Pocket Pal Books, 1992), 216 pages, softcover, $7.25.

  A wonderful compendium of information on pre-press and printing processes. A basic reference book that still fits in your pocket!

- Poynter, Dan, **Publishing Short-Run Books, Fifth Edition**, Santa Barbara: Para Publishing, 1988), 144 pages, softcover, $5.95.

  A how-to book on preparing and reproducing small books using your local copy shop. It teaches how to set type inexpensively, pasteup camera-ready copy, print using your local copy shop, and bind your books yourself. A superb guide to producing your books and reports in short runs of 200 or less in a matter of days.

- Rice, Stanley, *Book Design: Systematic Aspects*, (New York: R. R. Bowker, 1978, 800-521-8110), 274 pages, hardcover, $34.95.

  A systematic and clear delineation of all the steps involved in producing a book, from editorial design decisions to printing and binding. Includes schedules, transmittal forms, press layouts, and other charts and forms to ensure that everything proceeds smoothly and efficiently. This books covers everything a book production manager needs to know to produce well-designed books on time and on budget. Highly recommended.

- Vandermeulen, Carl, *Photography for Student Publications*, (Orange City, IA: Middleburg Press, 1979), 160 pages, hardcover, $16.95; softcover, $12.95.

  This book should really be titled Photography for Small Publications because it is a good basic text for beginners of all kinds. It provides excellent advice on how to produce natural poses and better photos overall. It covers everything from handling cameras to setting exposures, composing photos, developing them, making prints, shooting for layouts, and much more.

- White, Jan V., *Graphic Design for the Electronic Age*, (NJ: Watson-Guptill, 1988, 800-451-1741), 224 pages, softcover, $27.50.

  This book has more to offer the book designer than the above book. It describes how to select a typeface and size, how to select a column style, how to handle illustrations, and how to put together and integrate a complete publication (front matter, text, and back matter).

Telemarketing

- Berger, David, *The Cheapest Way To Make Phone Calls, Send Faxes Or Use The Internet*. (Value Added Services, 1996; 313-741-8913; E-Mail: davidb@a2.com). $9.95.

  To promote his book, David is sending faxed press releases using a $1,000 free-month promotion offered by a long-distance provider.

- Langhoff, June, *Telecom Made Easy* (Aegis Publishing, 1995; 800-828-6961; E-Mail: aegis@aegisbooks.com). $19.95.

  Designed for businesses with five or less phone lines. Shows how to save money and work more efficiently using phone products and services.

- Langhoff, June, *The Telecommuter's Advisor: Working In The Fast Lane* (Aegis Publishing, 1996; 800-828-6961). $14.95.

  Work at home via computer.

- Mastin, Robert, *900 Know How: How To Succeed With Your Own 900 Number Business*, 3rd Edition (Aegis Publishing, 1996; 800-828-6961). $19.95.

  The book on using 900 numbers for sales and service.

General Business Guides

- Bautista, Velrisezar, *How To Build A Successful One-person Business, 2nd Edition* (Bookhaus, 1995; 800-807-6908). $24.95.
  Since many start-up book publishers start as a one-person business, this book should provide many with the basic information necessary to grow your business.

- Bryant, Hattie, *Small Business Today Guide To Beating The Odds* (Prima Publishing, 1996; 916-632-4400). $16.95.
  A companion book to the public TV series, Small Business 2000. How to start a business and make it a success.

- Damman, Gregory, *How To Form And Operate A Limited Liability Company: A Do-it-yourself Guide* (Self-Counsel Press, 1995; 604-986-3366). $16.95.
  For some publishers, this might be one way to protect your personal finances.

- Fellman, Henry Aiy'm, *How To Keep Your Hard-earned Money: The Tax Saving Handbook For The Self-employed* (Solutions Press, 1996; 800-211-0544). $17.95.
  Shows how self-employed people can take advantage of every legal tax deduction without getting into trouble with the IRS.

- King, Jan B., *Business Plans To Game Plans: A Practical System For Turning Strategies Into Action* (Merritt Publishing, 1994; 800-638-7597). $29.95.
  Includes more than 50 worksheets and exercises for making practical business decisions.

- Lonier, Terri, *Working Solo Sourcebook*, (Portico Press, 1995; 914-255-7165; E-Mail: lonier@aol.com). $14.95.
  A great resouce book for entrepreneurs and small businesses. Whatever you need to know, you can probably find it here.

- Pond, Michael, *How To Become A Credit Card Merchant Immediately Without Having To Apply At A Bank*, (MindBuilders, 1994; 800-255-4714). $19.95.
  Recounts how to use a fulfillment company to give you credit card merchant status.

- Sitarz, Daniel, *The Complete Book of Small Business Legal Forms, 2nd Edition,* (Carbondale, IL: Nova Publishing Co, 1996, 800-748-1175) 256 pages, softcover, $19.95, with Forms-on-Disk $29.95.
  This book allows entrepreneurs and businesses throughout the country to prepare and use dozens of standard legal documents without incurring huge legal fees. With this revised and updated edition, users can now edit and customize all of the legal forms on their own computers.

- Sitarz, Daniel, *Incorporate Your Business: The National Corporation Kit, 2nd Edition* (Carbondale, IL: Nova Publishing Co, 1996, 800-748-1175) 256 pages, softcover, $19.95, with Forms-on-Disk $29.95.
  This easily-understood business reference contains all of the legal forms and instructions necessary to start and operate a small business corporation.

Web Marketing and Research

- Brinson, J. Dianne, and Mark Radcliffe, *Multimedia Law Handbook,* (Ladera Press, 1994; 800-523-3721; E-Mail: laderapres@aol.com). $74.95. Contact them for the latest edition of this book.
  Covers copyright, trademark, contracts, clearing rights, complying with union rules, 15 sample contracts, and more.

- Castro, Elizabeth, *HTML For The World Wide Web* (Peachhpit Press, 1996; 510-548-4393; Web: http://www.peachpit.com). $17.95.
  A great introduction to writing HTML for the web.

- Emery, Vince, *How To Grow Your Business On The Internet*, 2nd Edition (Coriolis, 1996; 800-410-0192). $29.99.
  Gives detailed information on internal web servers, selling books on the Internet, and using strategic alliances to grow your business.

- Emery, Vince and Patrick Vincent, *Free Business Stuff From The Internet* (Coriolis, 1996; 800-410-0192). $19.99.
  Features free business resources you can get through the Internet that will help you make money, cut costs, build sales, and do research.

- Fahey, Mary Jo, and Jeffrey Brown. *Web Publisher's Design Guide: Master The Art Of Creating Awesome Web Pages* (Coriolis, 1995; 800-410-0192). $34.99. Includes a CD-ROM.
  Shows how to create web pages that stand out from the crowd.

- Glossbrenner, Alfred and Emily, *Making Money On The Internet* (McGraw-Hill, 1995; 800-822-8158). $19.95.
  A good starting book for those new to marketing via the Internet.

- Franks, Mike, *The Internet Publishing Handbook: For World-wide Web, Gopher, And Wais,* (Addison-Wesley, 1995; 617-944-3700). $22.95.
  You can view samples of this book at http://www.aw.com/devpress. Covers all the issues involved in publishing documents on the Internet.

- Gagnon, Eric, Editor, *What's On The Web* (Internet Media, 1996; 800-247-6553; E-Mail: gagnon@interramp.com). $23.95.
  Features all the best sites on the web - all available with a simple click via http://www.jumpcity.com.

- Gelormine, Vince, *Get 'em: How To Promote And Market Your Web Site* (Coriolis, 1996; 800-410-0192). $24.99.
  If you are not getting enough hits on your web site, this book includes 100's of tips to help you market your web site.

- Hoge Sr, Cecil. *The Electronic Marketing Manual: Integrating Electronic Media Into Your Marketing Campaign* (McGraw-Hill, 1994; 800-822-8158). $34.95.
  This 500-page manual covers TV, radio, telemarketing, audiotex, fax marketing, video catalogs and brochures, interactive computer discs, modem marketing, CD-ROM, kiosks, and other new technologies.

- *Internet Marketing, Print & Electronic Publishing Software Cd-Rom Mega-pak* (Powell Productions, 1995; Largo Florida). $29.90.

    57 shareware PC computer programs for publishing, internet marketing, accounting, contact lists, inventory control, and more.

- Janal, Daniel, *Online Marketing Handbook: How to Sell, Advertise, Publicize, and Promote Your Products and Services on the Internet and Commercial Online Systems* (New York, NY: VanNostrand Reinhold, 1995; 212-780-6128).

    Online Marketing Handbook guides you through the essentials of online marketing—from vital statistics on various online services to promotional devices that garner the best response rates. By learning how to take advantage of online technology, you can reduce costs, respond quickly to market conditions, and provide the convenience that your customers want.

- Keeler, Len, *Cyber Marketing*, (New York, NY: AMACOM Books, 1995; 212-586-8100; web: http://www.amanet.org). $24.95.

    A great reference for everything you need to know about getting online and maximizing your presence. It's easy to read.

- Lescher, John F., *Online Market Research: Cost Effective Search Ing Of The Internet And Online Databases*, (Addison-Wesley, 1995; 617-944-3700; web: http://www.aw.com). $19.95.

    This book will help you to save time and money in doing research via the Internet.

- Mudry, Jon, *Serving The Web* (Coriolis, 1995; 800-410-0192). $39.99 includes a CD-ROM with the software you need to set up a web site.

    This book and CD provide everything you need to set up and run a basic web site.

- Strangelove, Michael. *How To Advertise On The Internet* (Strangelove Press, 1994; 613-565-0982; E-Mail: Mstrange@fonorola.net), $49.50.

    Check to see if they have published an updated edition of this comprehensive manual by the publisher of The Internet Business Journal.

- Vitale, Joe, *Cyber Writing: How to Promote Your Product or Service Online (without being flamed)*, New York, NY: AMACOM, 1997, 212-586-8100, web: http://www.amanet.org). $18.95

    "If you want to write to sell online, and reap all the financial rewards of doing it right, then this is the book you want in your guerrilla arsenal. Reread it and reread it." Charles Rubin, coauthor of **Guerrilla Marketing Online** and **Guerrilla Marketing Online Weapons**.

Book Publishing Anecdotes

- Bodian, Nat, **The Joy Of Publishing** (Open Horizons, 1996; 800-796-6130; E-Mail: JohnKremer@aol.com). $29.95.

    An anecdotal history of book publishing with hundreds of real-life success stories.

- Burns, Eric, *The Joy Of Books: Confessions Of A Lifelong Reader*, (Prometheus Books, 1995; 800-421-0351). $24.95.

    Provides an informal history of books and reading.

- Gold, Jerome, *Publishing Lives: Interviews With Independent Book Publishers In The Pacific Northwest And British Columbia* (Black Heron Press, 1995; 206-363-5210). $22.85.

    The collective experience of these 31 publishers can provide you with many insights on what to do and what not to do in your own publishing business.

- Jennison, Keith, *The Best Of Times* (Marshall Jones, 1995; 800-258-1505). $14.95.

    A memoir of a career in book publishing..."when publishing was fun."

- Unwin, Sir Stanley, *The Truth About Publishing* (Lyons & Buford, 1995; 212-620-9580). $17.95.

    First published in 1926, this 1995 edition is a reprint of the final 1960 Allen & Unwin edition. Focused on publishing in the United Kingdom, this book describes some basic publishing truths that still hold for today.

Out of Print Books

The following books are either out of print, replaced by new editions, or no longer available from the publishers listed below. You may still find many of these in libraries, used-book shops, or in the homes or offices of your friends or co-workers.

- Annese, Lucius, *Write and Publish*, (Andover, MA: Charisma Press, 1980), 100 pages, hardcover, $10.00.

- Anonymous, *Home Publishing Careers* ($6.95)
    Secrets of Marketing Your Book ($10.00)
    Who's Getting Rich in Self-Publishing? ($10.00)

    The above three books were once offered by a mail order book dealer. I have not read the books. Nor do I know who their authors or publisher, or when the books were copyrighted.

- Anonymous, *Self-Publishing and Mail Order Book Selling Guide*, saddle-stitched, $5.95.

    I've seen this book advertised in several smaller mail order publications. It describes "how to turn paper and ink into tycoon mail order success."

- Armstrong, Donald R., *Book Publishing: A Working Guide for Authors, Editors and Small Publishers*, (Houston: D. Armstrong Company, 1979), 190 pages, hardcover, $10.00.

    A basic guide for self-publishers, with plenty of information on manuscript preparation and book design.

- Aronson, Charles N., *The Writer Publisher*, (Arcade, NY: Charles Aronson, 1976), 369 pages, softcover, $10.00.

    A wonderful, engaging book devoted primarily to an expose of vanity publishing. Aronson also presents a candid and sobering inside view of the realities of publishing a book yourself.

- Association of American University Presses, *One Book - Five Ways*, (Los Altos, CA: William Kaufman, 1978), 349 pages, hardcover, $19.95.

    It provides an inside look at how five university presses go about acquiring, designing, producing, and marketing a trade book (it actually shows how the five presses would go about publishing the **same** book in five remarkably **different** ways!). The many examples of the actual forms and procedures used by these publishers will save any growing publisher much time in organizing their own effective procedures.

- Baczynsky, Mark, *How I Make a Comfortable Living Writing and Publishing Short Miniguides*, (Kingston, NY: Embee Press, 1981), softcover, $9.95.

  Apparently a miniguide to miniguides. May be out of print. Embee did not respond to our request for a review copy.

- Balkin, Richard, *A Writer's Guide to Contract Negotiations*, (Cincinnati: Writer's Digest Books, 1985), 149 pages, softcover, $11.95.

  Plenty of advice for writers who want to negotiate their own magazine and book contracts. Useful for publishers who want to work closely with their authors to write a contract that both parties can live with.

- Barber, Hoyt L., *Copyrights, Patents & Trademarks: Protect Your Right Worldwide*, (Blue Ridge Summit: Liberty House, 1990), 258 pages, softcover, $15.95.

  The copyright information is basic, but the patent and trademark sections provide extensive listings on how to protect your rights state by state and country by country.

- Barnes, Jay, *How to Make Money Writing & Selling Simple Information*, (Fort Ann, NY: J. E. Barnes, 1981), 176 pages, softcover, $15.00.

  The book is a general manual on how to write and publish short how-to booklets and sell them through classified ads.

- Barhydt, James D., *The Complete Book of Product Publicity,* (New York: AMACOM, 1987), 308 pages, hardcover, $59.95.

  While much of this book is directed at public relations directors at large corporations, it covers two subjects so well that I have to recommend it.
  1) The chapter on broadcast media not only describes how to book interview shows, but also how to get on news shows. It describes when to use broadcast media, what makes a good TV news story, how to get the media's attention, and how to place a prepared story.
  2) If you are planning any media events to tie in with your trade show exhibits, the chapter on press conferences describes how to plan, organize, promote, and carry out such media events. To aid your planning, this chapter includes an action calendar, a budget checklist, facilities checklist, room layout, media contact log, and a complete 3-page media event checklist.

- Baskett, Robert, *Publish Your Book in Your Home Town*, (Las Vegas, NV: Baskett Associates, 1984), a course, $85.00.

  This was a course in self-publishing, with fourteen lessons plus two Idea Workship updates — for a cost of a little over $5.00 per lesson.

- Beahm, George, *How to Publish and Sell Your Cookbook*, (Hampton, VA: GB Publishing, 1985), 64 pages, softcover, $7.95.

  A short but superb introduction to publishing cookbooks.

- Beaumont, Joanna, *How to Do Your Own Publishing*, (Rozelle, Australia: Orlando Press, 1985), 90 pages, softcover, $15.00.

  For writers who want to self-publish a book in Australia or New Zealand.

- Bibeau, Simone, *Cash in on Today's Educational Market*, (Phoenix: Perception Publications, 1985), 246 pages, softcover, $14.95.

  This is a guide for teachers who want to make money outside the classroom. While part of the book covers other money-making opportunities such as writing magazine articles, speaking, and consulting, most of the book describes how to publish books for the school market.

- Bjorkman, David, *Write, Publish and Sell It Yourself*, (Leesburg, VA: Citizen's Law Library, 1979) or (Boulder, CO: Paladin Press, 1979), softcover, $9.95.

  For its time, not a bad introduction — but certainly eclipsed by books which have been published since that time.

- Bodian, Nat, *Bodian's Publishing Desk Reference*, (Phoenix: Oryx Press, 1988), 439 pages, hardcover, $49.00.

  It's subtitle describes it well: A Comprehensive Dictionary of Practices and Techniques for Book and Journal Marketing and Bookselling. It covers a little bit of everything, though it is weak when covering the independent publishing scene.

- Bodian, Nat G., *Copywriter's Handbook: A Practical Guide for Advertising and Promotion of Specialized and Scholarly Books and Journals*, (Phoenix: Oryx Press, 1984), 275 pages, softcover, $19.95.

  Even though this book is aimed at promoting professional and scholarly books, it still includes hundreds of copywriting tips and techniques of value to any book publisher, regardless of subject or audience.

- Bold, Mary, *The Decision to Self-Publish*, (Arlington, TX: Bold Productions, 1987), 250 pages, comb-bound, $14.95.

  Outlines the pros and cons of self-publishing, vanity publishing, and regular publishing. A useful guide for writers who want a basic overview of their book publishing options.

- Cain, Michael, *Book Marketing: A Guide to Intelligent Distribution*, (Paradise, CA: Dustbooks, 1981), 232 pages, hardcover, $12.50.

  A rather sobering review of the realities of the book sales system in 1980. Now outdated.

- Campbell, Alastair, *The Graphic Designer's Handbook: The reference manual for all designers — complete with four-color tint charts, Revised* Edition, (Philadelphia: Running Press, 1988), 192 pages, hardcover, $16.95.

  For a graphic designer's handbook, this book is poorly designed (not enough white space, too tight a gutter, too light a typeface). Nevertheless, this book is worth every cent of its $14.95 price just for its 28 pages of color tint charts, its glossary, and its other charts and tables.

- Carrey, Dixieann W., *Writer's Self-Publishing Procedures*, (Fort Lauderdale, FL: TIB Publications)

  The date of publication and price were not set when the 1982-83 and 1983-84 editions of **Books in Print** went to press. The book was not listed in the 1984-85 edition. Apparently the book was never published.

- Chambers, Wicke, and Spring Asher, **TV PR: How to promote yourself, your product, your service, or your organization on television**, (Rocklin, CA: Prima Publishing, 1986), 121 pages, softcover, $12.95.

  If you want to promote your books and authors via TV or radio, this book's for you. It describes how to develop TV contacts, pitch your ideas to producers, prepare for your appearance, and make the most of interviews.

- Chickadel, Charles, *Publish It Yourself*, revised edition, (San Francisco: Trinity Press, 1980), 207 pages, softcover, $5.95.

  I read this book after I had already read Poynter's **Manual**. It was a good introduction to self-publishing, but it just didn't compare to Poynter's book. It was not nearly as comprehensive or detailed.

- Corwin, Stanley J., *How to Become a Best-Selling Author*, (Cincinnati: Writer's Digest Books, 1984), hardcover, $14.95.

    This book is a superb manual on self-promotion. Its main purpose is to show authors how to promote their books to the bestseller lists. And that it does well. I recommend this book to any publisher or author looking to do more in the way of marketing their books.

- Cover & Text Paper Manufacturers, *The Cover & Text Book*, (New York: American Paper Institute, no date), 60 pages, $6.95.

    Primarily intended for printers, this book provides samples of paper stock for a variety of finishes and colors. It also demonstrates embossing, stamping, halftones, engraving, screen tints, die-cuts, and more. Plus examples of 2-color, 3-color, and 4-color typography, tints, halftones, and solids. If you don't know what some of these terms mean, you need this book. If you do know what they mean, then you will appreciate this one-stop creative stimulator of graphic ideas.

- Crook, Marion, and Nancy Wise, *How to Self-Publish and Make Money*, (Kelowna, BC: Sandhill Marketing, 1987), 136 pages, softcover, $12.95.

    A handbook for writers who want to self-publish in Canada.

- D'Aquilla, Thomas J., *How to Sell Information by Mail Successfully*, (Kensington, CT: Quality Book Company, 1976), 108 pages, softcover, $10.00.

    This book was out of date on how to obtain a copyright and on printing prices. But it included a detailed section on how to research and write informative booklets and manuals. The sections on classified advertising, ad testing, direct mail, and followup were also valuable for those wanting to market books in this way.

- Dible, Donald, *How to Write, Publish and Market Your Own Book*

    This book was listed in the Bibliography of one of the earlier editions of Poynter's **Manual**, but I have not been able to find any further information about this book. Apparently it is out of print.

- Doyle, A. C., *How to Be Your Own Publisher*, (Atlanta, GA: Bibliotheca Press) or (Houston, TX: Prosperity and Profits Unlimited), hardcover, $29.95; softcover, $19.95.

    The date of publication was not set at the time the 1982-83, 1983-84, or 1984-85 editions of **Books in Print** went to press. Apparently the book is still waiting to be published. In the meantime (between the three editions), the price for the hardcover increased by $40.00 (and then decreased by $30.00) and the softcover increased by $35.00 (and then decreased by the same amount).

- Doyle, Thomas Jr., Paul Thompson, & Herman Blackey, *Write Your Way to a Fortune*, (Van Nuys, CA: Creative Book Company, 1981), 125 pages, softcover, $15.00.

    This book is actually a collection of three shorter booklets on how to write, produce, and promote your self-published book. All three authors seem to know their subjects; however, for some reason, they glossed over the details.

- DuBoff, Leonard D., *Book Publishers' Legal Guide*, (Friday Harbor, WA: Copyright Information Service, 1984), 359 pages, hardcover, $24.95 (formerly $50.00).

    This book provides an extensive discussion of all the legal questions that might come up in a publishing business, from incorporation and financial contracts, to copyright law and censorship, to author and supplier contracts.

- Erbe, Jack, and Anitra Earle, *Successful Self-Publishing*, (Van Nuys, CA: Ondine Press, 1983), softcover, $20.00.

    This book is out of print.

- Feldman, Elane, *The Writer's Guide to Self-Promotion and Publicity*, (Cincinnati, OH: Writer's Digest Books, 1990), 214 pages, hardcover, $16.95.

    Here's a wealth of information and specific details on how to promote yourself as a writer — whether you're established or just starting out, whether you write books or for magazines or newspapers. Self-promotion and publicity are the best tools to help you do this, and this book is your best guide.

- Fidel, Stanley Leo, *Start-Up Telemarketing: How to Launch a Profitable Sales Operation*, (New York: John Wiley, 1987), 287 pages, softcover, $12.95.

    The best book on telemarketing — simple, direct, and to the point. Comes complete with a sample telemarketing manual including all the forms you'll need plus a phone presentation guide to answering questions and overcoming objections. Also has an extensive list of 700 resources, from automatic dialers to telemarketing consultants, from equipment suppliers to inbound and outbound services. If you are just getting started in telemarketing, this book is a must.

- Foster, Frank H., and Robert L. Shook, *Patents, Copyrights & Trademarks*, (New York: John Wiley, 1989), 256 pages, hardcover, $39.95.

    Another general guide to protecting your rights to inventions, writings, and trademarks.

- Frank, Susan, with Mindy N. Levine, *In Print: A concise guide to graphic arts and printing for small businesses and nonprofit organizations*, (New York: Prentice-Hall, 1984), 146 pages, softcover, $6.95.

    A well designed book — short but sweet, easy to read, pleasing to the eye. It is, however, aimed at designing flyers and brochures rather than bound publications. Also, perhaps it is too simple. It was designed to help you communicate with a professional graphic designer rather than do it yourself.

- Franklin, Walt, *Encyclopedia of Self-Publishing*, Revised Edition, (Alameda, CA: Media Unlimited, A-A-AA Publications, 1979), $24.95.

- Friedman, Leon, *Entertainment Industry Contracts: Book Publishing*, (Albany, NY: Matthew Bender, 1989), 4 volumes, $320.00 for the entire set.

    Unfortunately, in order to get the Book Publishing volume, you have to buy the complete set. Nonetheless, this volume does provide superb samples of the major book publishing contracts with comments. It includes contracts for trade and professional books, distributor agreements, reprint and other rights contracts, collaborator agreements, releases, permissions, licenses, and book club contracts.

- Fry, Ronald, *Internships, Volume 2 — Newspaper, Magazine, and Book Publishing*, (Hawthorne, NJ: Career Press, 1989), 284 pages, softcover, $26.95.

    A guide to internships available in the publishing industry.

- Griffin, Walter, *How to Publish Your Poems*, (Huntsville, AL: Strode Publications, 1984), 120 pages, softcover, no price set.

    I was unable to get a review copy of this book because the publisher's phone has been disconnected. Apparently they have moved.

- Goodman, Joseph V., *How to Publish, Promote and Sell Your Book*, 4th Edition, (Chicago: Adams Press, 1977), 63 pages, softcover, $4.00.

    Written by the owner of Adams Press (a book printing broker who specializes in self-published books), this book is a general, brief introduction to self-publishing.

- Gross, Martin, **The Direct Marketer's Idea Book**, (New York: AMACOM, 1989), 240 pages, hardcover, $19.95.

    Not for beginners, this book includes lots of tips and examples for direct marketing professionals, including such topics as how to identify your best prospects, how to create a better offer, how to head off buyer's objections, and much more.

- Hasselstrom, Linda M., *The Book Book: A Publishing Handbook*, (Hermosa, SD: Lame Johnny Press, 1981), 346 pages, softcover, $9.95.

    This book was organized like an encyclopedia — over 200 pages were devoted to the glossary of terms. This book made a good introduction to printing and publishing terms for the newcomer.

- Hill, Lawson T., *How to Build a Multi-Million Dollar Catalog Mail Order Business by Someone Who Did*, (New York: Simon & Schuster, 1984), 304 pages, softcover, $19.95.

    A practical handbook which describes the basic steps and principles for establishing a successful catalog business — how to gain market leadership, design effective layouts, prepare selling catalog copy, get quality printing, forecast sales, and much more.

- Holt, Robert Lawrence, *How to Publish, Promote, and Sell Your Own Book*, (New York: St. Martin's Press, 1985), 250 pages, hardcover, $16.95.

    A good basic book about self-publishing. Not as good as the Ross or Poynter books, but better than most, especially if you are considering self-publishing with the hopes of eventually selling reprint rights to a major publisher.

- Holtz, Herman, *Speaking for Profit*, (New York: John Wiley, 1993), 294 pages, softcover, $41.95.

    One of the most effective ways that authors can promote their books is to get out and speak to anyone and everyone who will listen. Why not get paid for it as well? This book shows you how. It describes everything you need to know to make it as a professional speaker: How to negotiate contracts. How to set fees. How to promote yourself. How to beat the fear of speaking. This book also includes a good listing of lecture bureaus, convention managers, and other resources.

- Hudson, Howard Penn, *Publishing Newsletters*, Revised Edition, (New York: Charles Scribner's Sons, 1988), 240 pages, softcover, $13.95.

    An excellent introduction and guide for anyone considering publishing a newsletter. Written by Howard Penn Hudson, editor of The Newsletter on Newsletters, this book reflects his long experience in publishing newsletters and his continuing contact with a wide variety of newsletters. Includes chapters covering all aspects of newsletter publishing: research, design, editorial, production, advertising, and subscription management. The book features a special chapter on how to find your editorial niche.

- Inverni, Claude, *How to Go into the Book Publishing Business on a Shoestring and Make a Huge Success of It*, (Albuquerque, NM: Institute for Economic and Financial Research, c/o American Classical College Press, 1980), 87 pages, $300.00.

    You would have to go into business on a shoestring after paying the price they asked for this 87-page book.

- Jacobson, Tom, *The Illustrated Guide to Self-Publishing for Profit*, (Albert Lea, MN: Reid Publishing, 1986?), softcover, $12.95.

    This book was announced but apparently was never published.

- Jones, Jo, *Adventure in Self-Publishng*, (Chesapeake, VA: Jo-Jo Publications, 1983), 450 pages, softcover, $9.95.

    When completed, this book was to have been a compilation of the experiences of self-publishers from around the United States. The book, however, was never published.

- Kiefer, Marie and Kremer, John, *How to Sell to Premium/Incentive Users*, (Fairfield, IA: Ad-Lib Publications, January 1993), 35 pages, report, $30.00.

    Besides showing how to approach premium/incentive users directly, this report describes how to use reps and promotion houses to sell your book or other product as a premium. The report provides detailed listings for premium sales reps and incentive promotion houses. Each listing includes names, addresses, key contacts, phone numbers, lines represented, markets served, and products they are looking to add to their lines.

- Kremer, John, *Book Marketing Made Easier*, (Fairfield, IA: Jay Fredricks Editions, 1991), 383 pages, softcover, $19.95.

    This new book is an extensive revision of the original FormAides for Successful Book Publishing. It now focuses on forms and procedures to help any publisher — large or small — to prepare and carry out an effective marketing plan. Over 70 forms help you through all the steps: preparing your marketing strategy ... planning your budget ... forecasting your sales ... copyrighting your book ... registering your books with the ISBN and CIP programs ... getting listed in the book publishing records ... researching the media ... sending out publicity releases ... obtaining reviews ... organizing author tours ... getting distribution ... setting up sales representation ... working with bookstores ... exhibiting your books ... submitting your books to catalogs ... granting subsidiary rights ... obtaining permissions and testimonials ... and dealing with authors. These forms take all the fuss out of book publishing.

    Note: Although this book covers book marketing, it does not cover direct marketing, which is already covered by Mail Order Selling Made Easier.

- Kremer, John; Marie Kiefer, and Bob McIlvride, *Book Marketing Opportunities: A Directory*, (Fairfield, IA: Ad-Lib Publications, 1986, 1987), 304 pages, softcover, $25.00.

    This invaluable directory has been incorporated into the book you are now reading.

- Kremer, John, *Directory of Short-Run Book Printers*, (Fairfield, IA: Ad-Lib Publications, 1983, 1984, 1986), 240 pages, softcover, $12.00.

    This directory has been expanded and retitled as **The Directory of Book, Catalog, and Magazine Printers**.now replaced by Marie Kiefer's **Directory of Printers.**

- Kremer, John, *FormAides for Successful Book Publishing*, (Fairfield, IA: Ad-Lib Publications, 1983), 52 pages, saddle-stitched, $5.95.

    This book was replaced by a new expanded version titled, **Book Marketing Made Easier**.

- Kremer, John, *The Independent Publisher's Bookshelf*, (Fairfield, IA: Ad-Lib Publications, 1986), 96 pages, softcover, $3.95.

    This book has been replaced by the Bibliography you are now reading.

- Kremer, John, *101 Ways to Market Your Books — For Publishers and Authors*, (Fairfield, IA: Ad-Lib Publications, 1986), 304 pages, hardcover, $19.95; softcover, $14.95.

  This book has been replaced by a revised and expanded version with a more truthful title, **1001 Ways to Market Your Books — For Authors and Publishers**.

- Kremer, John, *Self-Publishing Book Review*, (Fairfield, IA: Ad-Lib Publications, 1983), 28 pages, saddle-stitched, $3.00

  This book was replaced by **The Independent Publisher's Bookshelf**. (see above).

- LeFontaine, J. R., *Write Yourself a Fortune*, (Vashon Island, VA: Pegasus Press, 1982), 106 pages, hardcover, $19.95; softcover, $14.95.

- Lesly, Philip, *Lesly's Public Relations Handbook, 3rd Edition*, (New York: Prentice-Hall, 1983), hardcover, $42.50.

  A comprehensive manual for anyone involved in public relations work. Since it is a collection of articles, it does not have the clear focus and line of development as some of the other books reviewed here, but it does have a wealth of information.

- Lewis, Herschell G., *More Than You Ever Wanted to Know about Mail Order Advertising*, (New York: Prentice-Hall, 1983), 330 pages, softcover, $10.95.

  A readable, easy-to-use guide to mail order advertising. A great collection of tidbits, examples, and techniques. Plus 170 impact ideas, each alone worth the price of the book. Even experienced mail order professionals will benefit from this book. Don't put this book down until you've read it at least three times.

- Lindey, Alexander, *Lindey on Entertainment, Publishing and the Arts*, (New York: Clark Boardman, 1984, updated regularly), 4 volumes, $375.00.

  Like the Matthew Bender volumes, this set provides legal agreements and commentary for entertainment industry legal needs. Again, you cannot buy the book publishing agreements separately; the four volumes are sold only as a set.

- Manley, Edith, *Self-Publishing on a Shoestring: With Tax Angles*, (San Leandro, CA: Winicorp, 1984), 250 pages, softcover, $6.95.

  Listed in the 1983-84 **Books in Print**, the book was postponed by the author because of other commitments. As far as I know, it still has not been published.

- Mathieu, Aron, *The Book Market*, (New York: Andover Press, 1981), 474 pages, hardcover, $19.95.

  An excellent review of how conventional royalty publishers operate, including the ins and outs, ups and downs of traditional book marketing and distributing channels. Also discussed the self-publishing option.

- McFadyen, Barbara, and Marilyn G. Hoff, *Bring Out Your Own Book*, (Portland, OR: Godiva Press, 1980), 96 pages, softcover, $6.00.

  This book may no longer be in print since we did not receive a review copy when we requested one.

- Meeker, Charles A., *How to Print and Publish a Book Cheaply*, (Albuquerque, NM: Meeker Publications, ?) softcover, $25.50 or $14.75.

  The price of this book changed from $25.50 to $14.75 in the two years it was listed in **Books in Print**. Also the title was lengthened to: How to Manufacture and Distribute a Book for About 1/4 the Cost of What Is Normally Spent to Accomplish This (2 volumes, 4th edition). 4th edition? Where are the other three?

- Middletown, Tony, *A Desktop Publisher's Guide to Pasteup*, (Colorado Springs: PLUSware, 1987), 228 pages, softcover, $15.95.

  Not just for desktop publishers. Indeed, this book is one of the most readable books on how to lay out and paste up books, advertisements, and other printed items. A practical guide for preparing camera-ready copy for the printer.

- Millard, Bob, *Book Production on Your Kitchen Table*, (Nashville: Brevity Press, 1981), 51 pages, softcover, $4.95.

  A short guide to book production on a small scale. Not as comprehensive as Poynter's book listed below, but more personal and colloquial.

- Mogel, Leonard, **The Magazine: Everything You Need to Know to Make It in the Magazine Business, Second Edition**, (Chester, CT: Globe Pequot Press, 1988), 218 pages, softcover, $19.95.

  An excellent overview of the magazine business, this book provides detailed descriptions of all the functions required in producing a successful magazine (business staff, editorial, ad sales, design, production, circulation, and promotion). This book also outlines all the steps required to start up a new magazine (with case histories of 14 recent magazine startups, both successes and failures).

- Mogel, Leonard, *Making It in the Media Professions: A Realistic Guide to Career Opportunities in Newspapers, Magazines, Books, Radio, Television, the Movies, and Advertising*, (Chester, CT: Globe-Pequot Press, 1987), 292 pages, softcover, $15.95.

  Full of anecdotes, statistics, and plenty of practical advice, this book provides an insider's view of the various media. A joy to read.

- Mueller, L. W., *How to Publish Your Own Book*, Revised Edition, (Detroit, MI: Harlo Press, 1978), 180 pages, hardcover, $6.95; softcover, $4.95.

  This book is a good basic introduction to self-publishing, and one of the best (though not as comprehensive as Poynter's or Ross's). Its major plus: 24 pages illustrating the various effects possible with colored photos and line drawings.

- Muldoon, Katie, *Catalog Marketing: The Complete Guide to Profitability in the Catalog Business, Second Edition*, (New York: AMACOM, 1988), 410 pages, hardcover, $75.00.

  This book covers everything: how to get started, how to find your niche, how to select merchandise, how to create and produce a catalog, how to service your customers, and much more.

- Mulholland, Harry, *Guide to Self-Publishing*, (South Wirral, England: Mulholland-Wirral, 1984), 126 pages, 6 pounds.

  Subtitled an A to Z guide to self-publishing, this book was just recently brought to my attention. Obviously its focus is on self-publishing in England, but it might provide some interesting new angles for American publishers as well.

- Murray, Allis, *The Beginner's Guide to Profitable Publishing*, 70 pages, saddle-stitched, $14.95.

    I've seen this book advertised in several mail order publications. It is apparently another book on how to sell information reports; however, I am not sure, since no review copy was available.

- Owens, Bill, *Publish Your Photo Book*, (Owens Publishing), softcover, $8.95.

    A self-publishing book for photographers. Now out of print.

- Owen, Peter, Editor, *Publishing - The Future*, (Chester Springs, PA: Dufour Editions, 1989), 128 pages, hardcover, $21.00; softcover, $13.95.

    This book is a collection of articles describing the state of the book publishing industry in Great Britain. It includes special discussions about the future of books as a medium of expression.

- Palosaari, Charles, *7 Vital Steps to Writing & Publishing Reports*, (La Mesa, CA: American Bookdealers Exchange, 1981), 12 pages, saddle-stitched, $3.00

    Too basic and too general. In case you're wondering, here are the 7 basic steps: 1) generate ideas, 2) research, 3) write, 4) copyright, 5) decide whether to publish a report or a booklet, 6) typeset and print, and 7) advertise.

- Parkhurst, William, *How to Get Publicity*, (New York: Times Books, 1985), 245 pages, hardcover, $14.95.

    A superb book about getting publicity from a former book publicist for many major publishers. This book is clearer and easier to read than Lant's book, and almost as comprehensive. It provides detailed advice on how to work with major media to obtain free publicity. Now out of print.

- Philcox, Phil, *How to Publish Your Book and Make It a Best Seller!*, (Bend, OR: Maverick Publications, 1981), 88 pages, softcover, $6.95.

    This book does not cover production of books, but it does have good sections on marketing and selling your book without advertising. Good tips on how to market self-published novels and poetry. The book has wonderful cartoons by Phil Adams.

- Pitzer, Sara, *How to Write a Cookbook and Get It Published*, (Cincinnati, OH: Writers Digest Books, 1984), 253 pages, hardcover, $15.95.

    This book shows how to create or find recipes and then test them, how to write and organize the book, and how to illustrate and design the cookbook. Finally, it describes several different ways to sell your books to various markets. The section on testing recipes is essential reading for any serious cookbook author or published Now out of print.

- Polking, Kirk, **The Writer's Friendly Legal Guide**, (Cincinnati: Writer's Digest Books, 1989), 173 pages, hardcover, $16.95.

    A collection of articles covering the basic legal problems that can confront a writer, including invasion of privacy, fictional characters based on real people, libel, book contracts, model releases, copyright, and more.

- Potter, Clarkson N, **Who does What and Why in Book Publishing**, (New York, NY: Birch Lane, 1991), softcover, $12.95.

    This book describes the process from reading manuscripts, printing the book, selling to bookstores, negotiating a contract to advertising the product. An easy to read practical guide.

- Poynter, Dan, *Business Letters for Publishers*, (Santa Barbara, CA: Para Publishing, 1981), 80 pages, saddle-stitched, $14.95.

    A collection of sample letters for book publishing, from sales and promotion to order processing to collections to requests for information to trademark protection to manuscript rejections — 74 letters in all. This book is now available only as a computer disk.

- Poynter, Dan, *Publishing Forms*, (Santa Barbara, CA: Para Publishing, 1984), folder, $14.95.

    Still available in limited quantities.

- Raab, Susan, *An Author's Guide to Children's Book Promotion*, (Rose Valley, PA: Raab Associates, 1988), 58 pages, comb-binding, $9.95.

    A short collection of tips and ideas for authors who want to take a more active role in marketing children's books.

- Raeder, Nicholas, and Regina Longyear, *The Shoestring Publishers Guide*, Farmington, ME: Sol III Publications).

    Sol III has been out of business since 1975. The book is out of print.

- Rehmel, Judy, *So, You Want to Write a Cookbook!* (Richmond, IN: Judy Rehmel, 1982), 48 pages, saddle-stitched, $5.00.

    A concise yet complete description that should be required reading for any group wanting to make a profit on their fundraising cookbooks. Covers everything from planning what kind of cookbook to produce, collecting recipes, layout and typesetting, finding a printer, and selling the books once they are produced. The discussion of marketing, however, is very limited.

- Rice, Stanley, *Book Design: Text Format Models*, (New York: R. R. Bowker, 1978), 215 pages, hardcover, $29.95.

    An extensive collection of samples for typesetting standard text, lists, tables, poems, plays, footnotes, glossaries, bibliographies, captions, indexes, and more. These samples are a handy way to visualize the look of your book, choose the style you want, and specify the type.

- Richards, Pamela Spence, *Marketing Books and Journals to Western Europe*, (Phoenix: Oryx Press, 1985), 84 pages, softcover, $22.50.

    If marketing your books overseas (especially in Europe), you should read this book. It outlines the various approaches you could take to reach overseas markets, giving the strengths and weaknesses of each approach. This book, however, is too short; it could use a much more extensive resource section.

- Roberts III, Bobby, and Mack B. Morant, *Publish Your Own Book*, (Holly Hill, SC: R & M Publishing, 1982), 12 pages, saddle-stitched, $2.00.

    This book was nothing but a 12-page advertising pamphlet for a subsidy publishing firm. It certainly was not worth $2.00.

- Ross, Marilyn and Tom, *Book Promotion and Marketing*, (Buena Vista, CO: About Books, 1987), 6-tape audio album, $69.96.

    A great collection of ideas and suggestions (in an easily digestible format) for creating a successful sales and marketing program for your books. Put these tapes on while you drive to work or pack books or eat lunch.

- Ross, Marilyn and Tom, *The Encyclopedia of Self-Publishing*, (Buena Vista, CO: Communication Creativity, 1979), hardcover, $29.95.
  This book has been replaced by their new book, **The Complete Guide to Self-Publishing**, published by Writers Digest Books.

- Ross, Marilyn and Tom, *Marketing Your Books*, (Buena Vista, CO: Communication Creativity, 1990), 129 pages, softcover, $9.95.
  It's a good book.

- Ruggieri, Ford F., *The Poor Man's Guide to Self-Publishing*, (Olean, NY: Allegany Mountain Press, 1984), 152 pages, $24.95.
  They promised to send me a review copy, but failed to do so. Apparently, it is now out of print.

- Sanders, Norman, *Graphic Designer's Production Handbook*, (New York: Hastings House, 1982), 195 pages, softcover, no price on cover.
  This handbook covers 100 techniques for preparing mechanicals and other camera-ready copy for printing. Covers both basic as well as more advanced techniques.

- Schreiner-Yantis, Netti, *Publish It Yourself: A Manual*, (Springfield, VA: Genealogical Books In Print, ?), 200 pages, hardcover and softcover, price not set.
  Originally scheduled for publication in 1982, then rescheduled for 1984, this book may not yet be published.

- Sheafer, Silvia, *Write On: How to Write, Print, Publish & Market Your Own Book*, (Whittier, CA: Journal Publications, 1980), softcover, $7.95.
  Apparently the book is out of print. The forwarding order for the above address has expired.

- Sedges, Michael, *Selling Books to the Military Market*, (Owosso, MI: Strawberry Media, 1988), 20 pages, report, $20.00.
  Provides the basics to enable you to reach the military market through bookstores, sales representatives, publications, government buying offices, and military libraries.

- Shatzkin, Leonard, *In Cold Type: Overcoming the Book Crisis*, (Boston: Houghton Mifflin, 1982), 397 pages, softcover, $8.95.
  While this book focuses on the problems major publishers face in distributing and marketing their books, there is much here also for the smaller publisher. If nothing else, it demonstrates the incredible hurdles smaller publishers must overcome to sell their books in bookstores. Plus it provides some well-considered suggestions on how to improve the current distribution network which serves neither the publisher nor the bookseller.

- Sheldon, Harvey, *Publish, Promote and Profit with Your Own Book*, (El Cajon, CA: Automation Printing, 1981), $25.00.
  This edition is no longer available.

- Shinn, Duane, *How to Write & Publish Your Own Book, Song, Course, Slide Chart, or Other Printed Product*, (Medford, OR: Duane Shinn Publications, 1976), 200+ pages, looseleaf binder, $49.95.
  This binder presents ideas on how to develop a line of related products. It also includes a discussion of 9 basic marketing vehicles with plenty of examples (news releases, sales letters, brochures, etc.), plus 20 basic marketing channels. It is well-written, easy to read and understand, and practical. Includes samples of some of his other printed products.

- Sitarz, Dan, **The Desktop Publisher's Legal Handbook**, (Carbondale, IL: Nova Publishing, 1989), 240 pages, softcover, $19.95.
  This handbook is full of practical advice in plain English on how to recognize and avoid legal problems in publishing. It includes a clause-by-clause discussion of the pros and cons of a model book publishing contract.

- Smith, Keith, *Marketing for Small Publishers*, (London, England: Inter Action Centre, 1981), 131 pages, $25.00.
  I have not seen this book, but John Dawes of England rates this book as "the best book on selling books" in England.

- Spatz, Jake, *How to Write, Print, Bind and Publish Your Own Book, Revised Edition*, (Anderson, CA: Alert Publishers, 1982), 34 pages, saddle-stitched, $3.00.
  A nice little book for someone who wants to publish only 10 to 50 copies of a book, such as a genealogy. Describes how to print (using a photocopier) and bind your own books (using equipment you can make yourself). The section on binding is quite detailed.

- Tattan, L. A., *Publish Yourself Without Killing Yourself*, (Farmingdale, NJ: InPrint, 1981), 191 pages, softcover, $9.95.
  For those publishers who know little or nothing about how a book is typeset, pasted up, printed, and bound. More thorough than Burke's book, but not as readable.

- Tucker, Lloyd, *How to Start and Operate a Profitable Homemade Booklet Business*, (Woodville, TX: Modern Manuscripts, 1982), side-stitched, $25.00.
  I have not seen this book, but a friend ordered it and reports the following: "This book is 50 pages long, and didn't supply me with too much information of value except the idea that if he could sell this for $25.00, I ought to be able to do the same."

- Van Dusen, C. Raymond, *Self-Publishing: How to Cash in on Your Writing Ability Now!*, (Aberdeen, MS: Royal Court Reports, 1982), 50 pages, softcover, $3.95.
  This book tried to cover all phases of writing and publishing your own books in 50 small pages, 5 of which were cartoons and 10 of which were totally blank. The result: 35 pages of brief notes and surface treatments of 66 different aspects of self-publishing.

- Ward, Audrey and Philip, *The Small Publisher: A Manual and Case Histories*, (Cambridge, England: Oleander Press, 1979), hardcover, $25.00.
  This book covers the art and business of self-publishing and small press publishing in Great Britain. Of little practical value to U.S. publishers; of immense practical value to U.K. book publishers. Includes the case histories of over 50 small publishers in England.

- Weckesser, Bud, *Dollars in Your Mailbox*, (Dunkirk, NY: Green Tree, 1979), 80 pages, softcover, $10.00.
  This was a heavily promoted mail order book on selling information by mail. Like many of the others, it is too general. It lacks substance and detail.

- Weiner, Mike, *The Easiest Business on Earth*, (Chatsworth, CA: Allen Publishing, 1981), softcover, $12.95.
  I have not read this book, but according to its promotional literature it features the stories of Joe Karbo, Melvin Powers, and Jerry Buchanan.

- Weintz, Walter H., *The Solid Gold Mailbox,* (New York: John Wiley, 1987) 268 pages, hardcover, $22.95.

    An anecdotal, yet detailed account of how to create mail order campaigns that work — all based on the experiences of a man who created such campaigns for Reader's Digest as, Book-of-the-Month Club, Rodale Press, and many others. An interesting and informative book.

- Weinzoff, Warren, *So the Publisher Turned You Down,* (Glendale, CA: Great Western Publishing, 1982), 58 pages, softcover, free?

    Essentially a promo for Great Western Publishing, a subsidy publisher, this book answers some basic publishing and marketing questions.

- West, Celest, and Valerie Wheat, *The Passionate Perils of Publishing,* (San Francisco: Booklegger Press, 1978), softcover, $7.00.

    Essentially a guide to feminist and small presses. Not a handbook. It does, though, describe the experiences of some feminist presses.

- White, Jan V., *Editing by Design: A Guide to Effective Word-and-Picture Communication for Editors and Designers, Second Edition*, (New York: R. R. Bowker, 1982), 264 pages, softcover, $24.95.

    A graphic design guide for magazine editors and designers that shows how words and images can enhance each other and make for a more effective presentation. With the increasingly graphic nature of books today, this guide could help you to strengthen the visual impact of your books.

Index

1-800-BOOKSTORE, 379
1000 Worldwide Business Directory, 452
1000 Worldwide Newspapers, 452
1001 Free Recipes, 456
1996 Scripture Catalog, 129
1st Street Books, 98
21st Century Christian Bookstore, 114
21st Century Marketing, 393
21st Century Publications, 21
3 & 4 Wheel Action, 177
3-2-1 Contact Magazine, 177
33 Metalproducing, 233
360 Group, 393
4-H Catalog, 129
4-Wheel & Off Road, 177
4-Wheel Drive, 177
47th Street Photo, 129
57th Street Books, 104
5M List Co, 393
800-Software, 129
9th Avenue Books, 98

A

A & B Distributors, 21
A & B Smith Co, 21
A & M Church Supplies, 21
A A U W Outlook, 177
A B Data Ltd, 393
A H Direct Marketing, 393
A M Pierson, 21
A R E Press, 11
A to Z Comics, 109
A to Zoo 4th Edition, 444
A+ Letter Service, 436
A-A-C-S Inc/AccuData America, 393
A.R.E. Press, 129
A/E Monthly, 177
AAA Best Mailing Lists Inc, 393
AAA Going Places, 177
AAB Communications, 373
AAII Journal, 233
Aardvark Adventures, 129
Aardvark Books, 98
The Aardvark Group, 383
Aardvark Party Pack, 383
AASL Conference, 415
AB Bookman's Weekly, 173
ABA Book Buyer's Handbook, 446
ABA Convention, 415
Abacus, 177
The Abadi Group Inc, 393
Abafazi, 177
Abatis Books, 115
Abbeville Meridional, 301
Abbreviations list, 10, 54, 68, 79, 117, 123, 127, 168, 268, 372, 392
ABBWA Journal, 177
ABC Center, 112
ABC School Supply, 3
ABC-Advanced BusinessCompilation, 393
ABC-CLIO, 126
Abel Love Inc, 21, 169
Abelow Response, 383, 393
Abelson Comm Inc, 393

Abercrombie & Fitch, 94
Aberdeen American News, 331
Abex Display Systems, 436
Abilene Reflector-Chronicle, 298
Abilene Reporter-News, 333
Abingdon Associates, 393
The Aboard Group, 177
About Books, 373
Abracadata, 129
Abraham Associates, 69
Abranovic Associates, 21, 89
Abraxas, 177
Absolutely Advertising, 434
Abstract/Records Service Inc, 393
Abundant Life Seed Foundation, 129
Academe, 257
Academi-Text Medical Wholesalers, 21
Academia Book Exhibits, 419
Academic Book Center, 21
Academic Book Services Inc, 21
Accent on Broadcasting, 365
Accent on Living, 177
Accents Publications Service Inc, 21
Access Communications Systems, 436
Access Marketing, 69
Access to Computer Supplies Inc, 129
Accessory Merchandising, 233
Accountants Post Card Shopper, 393
Accounting Professionals CPE Ins, 451
Accounting Today, 233
Accoutrements, 129
AccuData America, 393
Ace Books, 126
ACM, 393
Acorn Naturalists, 129
The Acorn, 351
Acoustic Guitar, 177
The ACP Computer Hotline, 129
ACP Inc, 129
Acropolis Books, 11
Across the Board, 257
ACS Software, 129
ACT ONE Mailing List Serv Inc, 393
Action Computer Supplies, 129
Action List Service Inc, 393
Action Markets, 393
Active Home Video, 3
Activities Adaption & Aging, 257
Acton Direct, 393
Ad Age's Business Marketing, 269
Ad Astra Books, 51
Ad-Lib Lists, 393
Ad-Lib Publications, 81
Ad-Lib Recommended Books, 130
Ad/advertising, 434
Ada Evening News, 325
Adam and Eve, 130
Adams Avenue Bookstore, 98
Adams Book Company, 21
Adams Media Corporation, 11
Adams News Company Inc, 66
AdaptAbility, 130
ADC Direct Marketing, 393
ADCO List Management Services, 394
Adcock-Dean Associates, 69
AdcomNet, 269
Addressing Unlimited Inc, 394
Addressing Your Needs, 394
Adirondack Daily Enterprise, 318

Adler's Foreign Books, 21
Administration in Social Work, 257
Adobe Gallery, 130
Adoption Book Catalog, 130
Adoptive Families, 177
Adoptive Families of America, 130
ADS Publisher Services Inc, 21
Adults 50-65, 383
Adults 60 Up, 383
Advance Imaging, 233
Advanced Automation, 81
Advanced List Marketing Assoc, 394
Advanced Mail Inc, 394
Advanced Marketing Services, 22
Advanced Technology Marketing, 394
Advantage Computing, 130
Advantage Direct Marketing Group, 394
Adventure Bookstore, 106
Adventure Cyclists, 177
Adventure Publications, 11
Adventure Road, 177
Adventure West, 177
Adventures in Learning Catalog, 130
Advertiser-Tribune, 324
Advertising Age, 269
Advertising Options Plus, 452
Advertising Sales & Mktg Pros, 383
ADVO Inc, 394
Advocate, 285
Advocate-Messenger, 300
The Advocate, 178, 301, 324
Advon Distributors Inc, 394
AdWare, 434
Adweek, 269
Adweek Agency Directory, 450
Aerial, 178
Aerospace Daily, 286
Affilia: Journal of Social Work, 257
Affinity Marketing Group, 394
African American Heritage, 178
African American Review, 178
African-American Resource Guide, 456
African-American Value Pack, 379
Afro Times, 357
The Afro-Hispanic Review, 178
After Loss Bookshelf, 130
After the Stork, 130
Afterimage, 178
AG Consultant, 233
AgAccess, 130
Agada, 178
Agape Bookseller, 108
Agape Christian Bookstore, 92
Agent & Manager Magazine, 233
Aggressive List Management Inc, 394
Agincourt Press, 11
Aging Today, 233
Agni, 178
Agoura Book & Coffee Co, 98
Agri Marketing, 233
Agri Mart Postcard Mailings, 383
Ahwatukee Foothills News, 349
Aiken Standard, 331
Aim Magazine, 178
Aim Marketing, 81
AIMS International Books Inc, 3
Air & Space Smithsonian Magazine, 178
Air Craft Spruce & Specialty, 130
Air Force Magazine, 233

Air Land & Sea Catalog, 130
Air Line Pilot, 233
Air Transport World, 233
Air Travel Journal, 178
Airbrush Action, 233
Airlift Book Company, 10
Airliners Catalog, 130
Airport Business, 233
AIS Inc, 130
AKJ Book Fare Inc, 22
Akron Beacon Journal, 322
Akron Legal News, 322
Akwe: Kon Press, 178
Akwesasne Notes, 178
Al Gilly Associates, 69
Alabama Game & Fish, 178
Aladdin Books, 98
Alameda Times Star, 276
Alamo Square Distributors, 11
Alamogordo Daily News, 315
Alan C Hood & Company, 11, 373
Alan Drey Co Inc, 394
Alan Gordon Enterprises, 22
Alaska Airlines, 178
Alaska Highway News, 344
Alaska Magazine, 178
Alaska News Agency, 55
Alaska Northwest Books, 69
Alaskan Natural History Assn, 89
Albany Democrat-Herald, 326, 360
Albany Herald, 289
Albany Times-Union, 315
Albatross, 178
Alberni Valley Times, 344
Albert Lea Tribune, 307
Albion Recorder, 305
Albuquerque Journal, 315
Alcoholism Treatment Quarterly, 257
Alcuin Books, 98
Aldebaran Literary Magazine, 178
Aldus Add-Ons Catalog, 130
Aleene's Creative Living Magazine, 178
Alexander City Outlook, 273
The Alexander Company, 365
Alexanders Book Co Inc, 98
Alexandria Daily Town Talk, 301
Alexandria Journal, 339
Alfred Hitchcock Mystery Magazine, 178
Alhambra Book Store, 98
Alice B Acheson, 365
Alice Echo News, 333
All About Kids, 178
All America Distributors Corp, 22
All American List Corp, 394
All Art Products Inc, 69
All Chevy, 178
All Kids Considered, 178
All-in-One Directory, 451
Allan Davis & Associates, 69
Allegro New Media, 126
Allen Communications Services, 365
Alliance Review, 322
Alliance Times-Herald, 312
Allied Health & Nursing, 130
Allison, Jackson & Nichols, 435
AllMedia Inc, 394
Allure, 178
ALM - Applied List Management, 394
Alonso Book & Periodical Service, 66
Alpen Books, 22
Alpena News, 305
Alpha 10 Cycles Bookstore, 22
Alpha Answering Service, 373
Alpha Marketing & Consulting, 394
Alpha Products, 130
Alpha Supply, 130
Alphabet House, 441

Alpine News Distributors, 57
Alsto's Handy Helpers Catalog, 130
Alternative Access Directory, 456
Alternative Delivery Today!, 436
Alternative Medicine Digest, 179
Alternative Publishers of Children's Books, 446
The Alternative, 365
Altoona Mirror, 327
The Altus Times, 325
Altwerger Associates Inc, 69
Alva Review-Courier, 325
Alyson Publication, 11
Amalgamated Publishers, 379
Amarillo Globe-News, 333
Amarillo Periodicals Distributor, 65
Amazon Vinegar & Pickling Works, 130
Ambassador Book Service Inc, 22
Amcam Inc, 3
Amcorp Ltd, 22
Amer Institute/Aeronautics/Astro, 394
Amer Institute/Chemical Engineer, 394
Amer Jnl of Occupational Therapy, 233
America Direct Inc, 394
America Oggi, 314
America West Airlines Magazine, 179
America's Hobby Center, 22, 131
America's Network, 233
American Agent & Broker, 233
American Art Directory, 456
American Art Journal, 179
American Artist, 179
American Atheist, 179
American Baby, 179
American Baby Direct Mail, 394
American Banker, 317
American Bar Association, 394
American Bar Association Journal, 179
American Bicyclist, 179
American Book Center, 81
American Book Review, 179
American Bookseller, 173
American Booksellers Association, 394
American Buddhist Shim Gum Do, 22
American Bungalow, 179
American Business Directory, 436
American Business Lists, 394
American Cheerleader, 179
American Church Lists, 394
American City & County, 233
American Civil War, 179
American Civilization, 179
American Computer Institute, 394
American Computer Supply, 131
American Cooking Guild, 11
American Correctional Assn Lists, 394
American Craft, 234
American Dane, 179
American Data Consultants, 394
American Data Resources, 394
American Demographics, 234
American Direct Mkg Service, 395
American Druggist, 234
American Eagles Inc, 22
American Econo-Clad Services, 22
American Economic Foundation, 458
The American Enterprise, 179
American Family Publishers, 131
American Farrier, 234
American Forests, 179
American Fruit Grower, 234
American Fund Raising Lists Inc, 395
American Girl, 179
American Health, 179
American Health Consultants List, 395
American Heritage, 179
American Heritage of Invention, 179

American Historical Review, 179
American History, 179
American Hunter, 179
American Indian Art Magazine, 179
American Indian Books, 131
American Indian Quarterly, 180
American Industry, 180
American International Distrib, 81
American International Toy Show, 418
American Intl Distribution Corp, 3
American Iron Magazine, 180
American Journal of Nursing, 180
American Journalism Review, 180
The American Law Institute, 395
American Legacy, 180
The American Legion, 180
American Libraries, 173
American Library Association, 395
American Library Directory, 451
American List Counsel, 395
American Literature, 180
American Machinist, 234
American Mail-Well Envelope, 437
American Mailing Lists Corp, 395
American Marketplace, 269
American Media Corporation, 22
American Media Group, 373
American Media Library Books, 169
American Medical Directory, 458
American Medical News, 257
American Men & Women of Science, 458
American Metal Market, 317
American Mktg/CommunicationsCorp, 395
American Motorcyclist, 180
American Music Teacher, 257
American Nurseryman, 234
American Nurseryman Pub, 11
American Opinion Book Services, 22
American Opinion Bookstores, 91
American Orchid Society Catalog, 131
American Overseas Book Co, 22
American Passage Media Corp, 373
American Photo, 180
American Poetry Review, 180
American Police Beat, 234
American Press Clipping, 435
American Printer, 234
American Printer Card Deck, 383
American Program Bureau, 377
American Publishers, 446
American Publishing Company, 379
American Reference Book Annual, 444
American Regional Cookbooks, 131
American Rider, 180
American Rifleman, 180
American Rodder, 180
American Scholar, 180
American Scientist, 257
American Society for Mechanical Engineers, 131
American Society of Agronomy Inc, 22
American Society of Association Executives, 131
American Speaker, 458
American Student List Co, 395
American Survival Guide, 180
American Theater, 180
American Thermoplastic Company, 434
American Times, 180
American Vegetable Grower, 234
American Visions, 180
American Vocational Assn, 395
American Voice Magazine, 180
American Way Magazine, 180
American Woman, 180
American Woman Motorscene Magazine, 180

American Woodworker, 180
American Writer, 181
American Writers Review, 181
The Americas Review, 181
Americus Times-Recorder, 289
Ames Daily Tribune, 297
Ames News Agency, 59
Amherst Media, 11
Amicus Journal, 181
Amie's Books for Bakers, 131
AmigaWorld, 181
AMS Journal, 181
Amtower & Co, 395
Amtrak Express, 181
Amusement Business, 234
AMWA Journal, 181
The Anadarko Daily News, 325
Anaheim Bulletin, 349
Analog Science Fiction & Fact, 181
Ancestry, 131
Ancestry Inc, 22
Ancestry Magazine, 181
Anchorage Daily News, 274
Ancient Healing Ways, 22
Ancona Lists, 395
Andalusia Star News, 273
Anderson Herald-Bulletin, 294
Anderson Independent-Mail, 331
Anderson Merchandisers, 22
Anderson News, 22
Anderson News Company, 55, 57-60, 64-65
Anderson's Bookshop, 104, 109
Anderson-Crawford Associates, 69
Andrzejewski's Religious Goods, 23
Anemone, 181
Angelina Periodicals, 65
The Angelus, 181
Anglers Art-Books/Fly Fishermen, 131
Anglofile, 181
Animals Magazine, 181
The Animals' Voice, 181
Animation Magazine, 234
Anita Halton Public Relations, 365
Anita Helen Brooks Associates, 365
Ann Arbor News, 305
Anne Berg Public Relations, 365
Anne Hardy Public Relations, 365
Anne McGilvray & Company, 69
Annex Book Distributor, 23
Annie's Book Shop, 108
Anniston Star, 273
ANQ, 257
Answers Period Inc, 23
Antelope Valley Press, 279
Antheil Booksellers, 131
Anthony Schulte, Consultant, 373
Antigo Daily Journal, 342
Antigone Associates Ltd, 395
The Antioch Review, 181
Antipodes, 181
Antiquarian Specialty and Used Book Sellers, 449
Antique Doll World, 181
The Antique Trader Weekly, 181
Antiques & Auction News, 181
Antiques & Collectibles Magazine, 181, 234
Antiques & Collecting Hobbies, 181
Apalachee Quarterly, 181
Apartment Owners/Mgrs Assn of US, 395
Aperture, 181
Apollo Books, 11
Apothecary, 257
Appalachian Bible & Books, 23
Appalachian Bookstore, 104
Appaloosa Custom Products Inc, 440

Apparel Merchandising, 234
ApparelPak, 383
Appeal-Democrat, 278
Appearances, 182
Applause Theatre Book Catalog, 131
Applause Theatre Book Review, 182
Apple Book Co, 23
The Apple Catalog, 131
Apple Tree Book Shop, 110
Appleton Post Cresent, 342
Appliance, 234
Application Technology, 182
Applied Computer Research Inc, 395
Applied Image Inc, 434
Applied Mechanics Reviews, 257
Aqua Quest Publications, 131
Aquarium Fish Magazine, 182
ARA Services SBW-Mag & Book Div, 23
Arabian Horse Times, 182
Arabic & Islamic Univ Press, 23
Arachne, 182
Aramark, 56-57, 60-61, 63, 66-67
Arbit Books Inc, 23
Architectural Digest, 182
Architectural Record, 182
Architectural Specifier, 234
Architecture, 182
Archives of Environmental Health, 257
Archtype Press Inc, 11
Argonaut, 182
Argus Direct Business Lists, 395
Argus Leader, 332
Argus Observer, 327
Argus-Press, 307
Ariel Books, 11
Arizona Business Magazine, 257
Arizona Daily Star, 275
Arizona Daily Sun, 274
Arizona Daily Wildcat, 275
Arizona Highways, 182
Arizona Marketplace for Writers, 446
Arizona Periodicals, 55
Arizona Republic/Phoenix Gazette, 274
Arkansas Book Services Corp, 23
Arkansas Business, 182
Arkansas City Traveler, 298
Arkansas Democrat-Gazette, 276
Arkansas Sportsman, 182
ARL Newsletter, 173
Arlington Journal, 339
Armadillo & Company, 56
Armchair Detective, 182
The Armchair Sailor Bookstore, 91
Armchair Shopper, 131
Armenian Reference Books Co, 11
The Armenian Weekly, 355
Army Magazine, 234
Arrow Book Club, 119
Arrowhead Magazine Co Inc, 23
Art & Antiques, 182
Art & Auction, 182
Art & Design News, 383
Art Book Review Quarterly, 182
Art Business News, 234
Art Catalogues, 131
ART CONSULTING: SCANDINAVIA, 56
Art in America, 182
Art Materials Trade Show, 418
Art Network, 395
Art Network Catalog, 131
Art Reference Services Quarterly, 173
Art Sales Company, 23
Art Times, 182
Art/design, 434
Artesia Daily Press, 315
Arthritis Today, 182
Arthur Vanous Company, 23

Articles of War, 131
The Artilleryman, 182
Artist's & Graphic Designer Mkt, 446
Artist's Magazine, 182
Artistic Greetings, 437
Artmaker Super Sheets, 439
Artnews Magazine, 182
Arts Education Policy Review, 257
Artworx Software Co, 131
AS-UCLA Bookstore, 98
Asbarez Armenian Daily Newspaper, 277
Asbury Park Press, 314
ASCD Products, 131
ASHA Magazine, 234
Asheville Citizen-Times, 319
Ashgate Publishing Company, 12
Ashland Times-Gazette, 322
Asia Marketing & Management, 395
Asian Affairs: An American Review, 257
Asian American Press, 356
Asian World of Marial Arts, 131
ASID Service Corp, 395
ASJA Directory, 444
ASM International Software, 131
Aspen Bookshop, 104
Aspen Magazine, 182
Aspen Times Daily, 283
Aspen West Publishers, 23
Aspire Magazine, 182
Asset International Inc, 395
Assn of Trial Lawyers of America, 395
Associated Libraries Inc, 23
Associated Publishers Group, 3
Association Book Exhibit, 419
The Association Executive, 234
Association Growth Enterprises, 395
Association Management, 234
Association Meeting Directory, 419
Association Meeting Planners Conference/Convention Directors, 459
Association of Jewish Libraries Newsletter, 173
Association Publications in Print, 444
Association Trends, 257
Associations Book Distributors, 81
Associations Canada, 457
Assorted Book Company, 169
ASTA Agency Management, 234
ASTD Buyer's Guide/Consultant, 459
Astran Inc, 23
Atalanta's Music & Books, 98
Atchison Daily Globe, 299
Athens Banner-Herald, 289
Athens Daily News, 289
Athens Daily Review, 333
Athens Messenger, 322
Athens News, 358
Athens News Courier, 273
Athol Daily News, 303
Atlanta, 183
Atlanta Baby, 182
Atlanta Bulletin, 352
Atlanta Business Chronicle, 235
Atlanta Computer Currents, 182
Atlanta Daily World, 352
Atlanta Homes and Lifestyles, 183
Atlanta Journal & Constitution, 289
Atlanta Parent, 183
Atlanta Small Business Monthly, 235
Atlantic Accord, 373
Atlantic Book Learningland Ltd, 51
Atlantic City Press, 314
Atlantic Envelope Co, 437
Atlantic List Co Inc, 395
Atlantic Monthly, 132, 183
Atlantic News-Telegraph, 297
Atlantic Software Catalog, 132

Atlas News Agency, 60
ATP Clipping Bureau, 435
ATP Mailing List Center, 395
Atrium Publishing Group, 3, 69
Attachmate Corp, 132
Attitudes Catalog, 132
Attorney Card Pack, 383
Auburn Journal, 276
Auburn University Bookstore, 97
Auburndale Star, 286
Audacity: Magazine of Business Experience, 183
Audio, 183
Audio Book Club, 119
Audio Editions, 132
Audio Forum, 132
Audio Literature, 125
Audio Renaissance Tapes, 125
Audio Response Inc, 395
Audio rights buyers, 125
Audio Video Interiors, 183
Audio-Tech Business Book Summaries, 119
Audiobook Reference Guide, 447
AudioFile, 183
Audubon Court Books Ltd, 116
Audubon Magazine, 183
Audubon Workshop, 132
Augsburg Fortress Publishers, 12, 92
Augusta Chronicle, 289
Augusta Daily Gazette, 299
Augusta News, 59
Auntie's Bookstore, 115
Auromere Books & Imports, 23
Aurora Book Companions, 132
Auroria Book Center, 102
Aus-Tex Printing & Mailing, 395
Ausio Diversions, 23
Austad Company, 132
Austin & Nelson, 69
Austin American-Statesman, 333-334
Austin Child, 183
Austin Chronicle, 360
Austin Daily Herald, 307
Austin Management Group, 23
Austin News Agency, 65
Austin Periodical Services, 58, 64-65
Authentic Information Center, 373
Authentic Jane Williams' Home School Market Guide, 457
Authors in Libraries Directory, 451
Authors Unlimited, 377
Auto Racing Digest, 183
Auto Sound & Security, 183
Auto-Bound Inc, 23
Autologic, 439
Autom Wholesale, 132
Automated Fulfillment Corp, 81
Automated Resources Group, 81
Automotive Aftermarket Suppliers, 460
Autoweek, 183
AV Market Place, 447
AVANTI! Direct Marketing, 395
Avenue Books Inc, 98
Avenue Magazine, 183
Aviation Book Company, 23, 132
Aviation Daily, 286
Aviation History, 183
Aviation Week & Space Technology, 257
Aviator's Guild, 119
Avon Books, 126
Awareness & Health Unlimited, 23
AZ Marketing Services Inc, 395
Azen Bitner Pierson, 365
Aztec Bookstore, 98
Azusa Herald Press, 351

B

B B Kirkbride Bible Co Inc, 24
B Broughton Company, 9
B Dalton / Barnes & Noble, 91
B K Nelson, 126
B K Nelson Lecture Bureau, 377
B Klein, 132
B'nai B'rith Intl Jewish Monthly, 183
Baby Connection News Journal, 183
Baby Talk, 183
Babybug, 183
Back Home, 183
Backpacker Magazine, 183
Backroads Bicycle Touring, 395
Backroads Bicycling, 183
Backwoods Home Magazine, 183
Bacon's Clipping Bureau, 435
Bacon's Media Directories, 452
Bacon's Media Lists, 395
Bacon's Publicity Distribution, 365
Badge A Minit, 440
Badger Herald, 342
Badger Periodical, 24, 66
Baen Publishing Enterprises, 126
The Baggage Claim, 132
Bailey-Coy Books, 115
Baker & Baker Booksellers, 97
Baker & Taylor, 24
Baker & Taylor Exhibit Service, 419
Baker & Taylor International, 24
Baker Book House, 93
Baker Books, 107
Baker City Herald, 326
Bakers Books, 132
Bakersfield Californian, 276
Ball State Daily News, 296
Ballantine Books, 126
Balloon Life, 183
Balloons and Parties Today, 235
Baltimore Business Journal, 183
Baltimore City Paper, 355
Baltimore Magazine, 184
Baltimore Sun, 302
Baltimore's Child, 184
Balzekas Museum, 24
Bam: The California Music Magazine, 184
Bang-Knudsen Inc, 69
Bangor Daily News, 302
Bank Security Report, 235
Bank Systems & Technology, 235
Bankers Letter of the Law, 235
The Bankers Magazine, 235
Banking, 434
Banking Law Journal, 235
Banner of Truth, 24
Banner-Graphic, 295
Banner-News, 276
Bannerland, 440
Baptist Spanish Publishing House, 24
Baptist-Pak, 383
Bar Code Graphics Inc, 434
Barbara J Hendra Associates, 365
Barbara's Bookstore, 91
Barber's Bookstore, 114
Barcode, 434
Bargain Books, 103
Barjon's Books, 109
Barnes & Noble Catalog, 132
Barnett Books, 169
Baron Barclay Bridge Supplies, 12, 132
Barre Times-Argus, 338
Barrett & Co Booksellers, 114
Barrie Examiner, 345

Barron's National Business Financial Weekly, 184
Barry Ancona List Management, 395
Barry Bloom, Representative, 69
Bartleby's Books & Music, 115
Bascom Communications Company, 12
Baseball Digest, 184
Basic Crafts Co, 132
Basin Distributing, 61
Basin News Agency, 65
Basketball Digest, 184
Bassin' Magazine, 184
Bastrop Daily Enterprise, 301
Batavia Periodical Distributors, 61
Batesville Guard, 275
Baton Rouge Book Warehouse, 106
Baton Rouge Daily News, 301
The Battalion, 334
Battle Creek Enquirer, 305
Baudville Catalog, 132
Baxter Bulletin, 276
Baxter's Books, 108
Bay Area Parent Newsmagazine, 184
Bay Area Reporter, 184
Bay Books, 99
The Bay Bookstore, 110
Bay Bulletin, 352
Bay City Times, 305
Bay News Company, 63
Bay Ridge Paper, 357
Bay State Banner, 355
Bay to Bay Dist Inc, 3
Bayou Periodicals, 59
Baytown Sun, 334
BDK Books Inc, 12
BDL Homeware, 132
Beach List Services, 383
Beacon Herald, 347
The Beacon News, 291
Beardsley & Associates, 69
Beatrice Daily Sun, 312
The Beauford Gazette, 331
Beaumont Enterprise, 334
Beauregard Daily News, 301
Beauty Ed Book Catalog, 132
Beauty Inc, 235
Beaver County Times, 327
Beaver News, 59
Beavercreek News Current, 322
BeaverPrints, 439
Beck's Book Store, 93
Beckett Baseball Card Monthly, 184
Beckett Focus on Future Stars, 184
Beckett Football Card Monthly, 184
Beckett Hockey Monthly, 184
Bedford Books, 89
Bedford Daily Gazette, 327
Bedford Sun Banner, 358
Beechwood Global Publications, 24
Beekman Publishers, 12
Beemak Marketing Inc, 436
Beers Book Center, 99
Before & After, 235
Behavior Bank, 396
Behavioral & Social Sciences Lib, 173
Behavioral Health Management, 257
Behavioral Medicine, 258
Behind The Glass Cafe & Books, 97
Beijing Book Company Inc, 3
Beijing International Book Fair, 417
Beks Bookstore, 115
Believers Book Distributor, 132
Bell Magazine Agency Inc, 56
Bellefontaine Examiner, 322
Belles Lettres: A Review of Books by Women, 184
Belleville Intelligencer, 345

Belleville Journal, 353
Belleville News-Democrat, 291
Bellevue Gazette, 322
The Bellingham Herald, 340
Bellville Post, 356
Beloit Daily Call & Post, 299
Beloit Daily News, 342
Belvidere Daily Republican, 291
Ben Franklin Stores, 94
Ben Schrager, Representative, 69
Bender Goldman & Helper PR, 365
Benicia Herald, 276
The Benjamin Company Inc, 12
Benjamin de Wit Bookseller, 132
Benjamin News, 68
Bennett Marine Video, 132
Bennett Schneider Inc, 109
The Bennington Banner, 338
Benton County Daily Record, 275
Benton Courier, 275
Benton Evening News, 291
Berean Bookstores, 93
Bereavement, 184
Bergen News, 357
Berkeley Publishing, 126
Berkery Noyes & Co, 373, 434
Berkshire Eagle, 304
Berlin Daily Sun, 313
Berlin Reporter, 313
Bernan, 3
Bernice Bush Springdale Lists, 396
Best Bits & Bytes, 132
Best Books/Videos/Video Games/Music
  and Software for Children, 444
Best Business Services, 396
Best Continental Book Co Inc, 24
Best Directory of Recruiters, 450
Best List Managers Inc, 396
The Best Lists Inc, 396
Best Mailing Lists Inc, 396
Best Recipes, 184
The Best Seller, 115
The Best Software for Kids, 133
Bestseller, 111
BestSellers, 110
Bethany Fellowship Bookshop, 93
Bethesda List Center Inc, 396
Better Homes & Gardens, 184
Better Investing, 184
A Better Life For You, 177
Better List Brokerage/Mgmt Corp, 396
Better Lists Inc, 396
Better Nutrition for Today's Living, 184
A Better Tomorrow, 184
Betty Gaskill, Sales Rep, 69
Betty Marks Public Relations, 365
Beverly Books Inc, 24
Beverly Hills 213 Magazine, 184
Beverly Hills Courier, 349
Beverly Hills Today, 276
Beyda & Associates, 3
The BG News, 322
BG Speakers Bureau, 377
Bhaktivedanta Book Trust, 12
Bible Truth Publishers, 24
BiblioFile, 12
Bibliographic Guide to Business and
  Economics, 444
Bibliographies, 444-446
Bibliographies and publishing directories,
  444-448
Bibliotherapy for Children, 133
Bick International, 396
Bicycle Business Journal, 235
Bicycle Dealer Showcase, 235
Bicycle Posters & Prints, 133
Bicycle Retailer & Industry News, 235

Bicycle Tools & Small Parts, 133
Bicycling, 184
Big Black Book, 457
Big Blue Disk Software Catalog, 133
The Big Book of Software, 133
Big Books from Small Presses, 133
Big Colony News, 60
Big Horn Booksellers, 24
Big Sky Books, 109
Big Spring Herald, 334
Big Table Books, 106
Bikini, 184
Bilingual Educational Services, 24
Bilingual Publications, 3
Billboard, 235
Billian Publishing Inc, 396
Billings Gazette, 311
Billings News, 61
Binders, 434
Biobottoms Inc, 133
BioCycle, 184, 235
Biopeople, 235
Bioscience, 258
Biosoft Catalog, 133
Bird Breeder, 235
Bird Talk, 184
Bird Watcher's Digest, 133, 184
Bird's-Eye reView, 185
Birds & Blooms, 185
Birmingham Book Store Inc, 107
Birmingham News, 273
Birmingham Post Herald, 273
Bisbee Daily Review, 274
The Bishopric Agency, 365
Bismarck Tribune, 321
Bits & Pieces Catalog, 133
Biz Magazine, 185
Black American Information Dir, 452
Black Authors & Published Writers, 444
Black Beat, 185
Black Bond Books, 91
Black Books Bulletin, 185
Black Box Corporation, 133
Black Careers, 258
The Black Collegian, 185
Black Elegance, 185
Black Enterprise Magazine, 185
Black Families, 383
Black Health, 185
The Black Hills Pioneer, 332
Black Magazine Agency, 24
Black Moon Magazine, 185
Black Newspaper Clipping Bureau, 435
Black Resource Guide, 452
The Black Scholar, 258
Blacklist Mail Order, 133
Blackship Computer Supply, 133
Blacksmith Corporation, 133
Blackstone Audio, 24
Blackwell Journal-Tribune, 325
Blade Magazine, 185
Blade-Empire, 299
Bladen Journal, 320
The Blade, 324
The Blaine Group Inc, 365
Blockbuster Entertainment Corp, 95
Bloomfield Independent Press, 356
Bloomfield Publications, 383
Bloomington Voice, 353
The Bloomsbury Review, 185
Blue Chip Gifts, 133
Blue Hill Books, 107
Blue Ridge Country, 185
Blue Ridge News Co, 62
Blue Sky Marketing Inc, 4
Blue Springs Examiner, 309
Blue Star, 133

Bluefield Daily Telegraph, 341
Bluefield News Agency, 66
Blytheville Courier News, 275
BMI Educational Services, 24
BMI Medical Information Inc, 396
Boardroom Lists, 396
Boat/US Equipment Catalog, 133
Boating, 185
Bob Harman & Associates, 70
Bob Simmons & Associates, 70
Bob's Book Club, 119
Bobbin Magazine, 235
Boca Monday, 352
Boca Raton News, 286
Bocca Direct Marketing, 396
Body Mind & Spirit Magazine, 185
The Bohle Co, 365
Boing-Boing, 185
Boise Weekly, 353
Bolind Inc, 133
Bolivar Commercial, 308
Bologna Children's Book Fair, 417
Bomb Magazine, 185
Bomber Joe's, 51
Bon Appetit, 185
Bond Buyer, 317
Bonham Daily Favorite, 334
Bonner County Daily Bee, 291
Bonneville News, 66
Book & Company, 114
Book & Game Company Inc, 89, 115
Book & Resource Buyers Edition, 383
Book 'N Card Inc, 89
Book Alcove, 107
Book Arts Directory, 457
Book Bag Stores, 90
Book Buyers Bargains, 133
The Book Cellar, 102, 115
The Book Center, 99
Book clubs, 119-123
The Book Connection, 99
The Book Cottage, 114
Book Dealers World, 235
Book Distribution Center, 25
The Book Emporium, 90
The Book End, 110
Book Gallery, 87
Book Gallery West, 103
Book Hollow, 109
Book House of Stuyvesant Plaza, 111
The Book House, 25, 104
The Book Island, 98
Book Jobbers Hawaii, 25
The Book Lady, 164
Book Links, 173
Book Loft, 99
Book Lover's Guide to Boston & Cape
  Cod, 449
Book Margins Inc, 169
Book Market, 104
Book Marketing Plus, 25
Book Marketing Profitcenter, 449
Book Marketing Update, 456
Book Marketing Update Newsletter, 269
Book Nation, 105
Book Nook, 98, 115
Book Passage, 99
Book People Inc, 106, 114
The Book Place, 114
Book Promotion Hotline, 269, 456
Book Pros, 81
Book Publishing Company, 133
Book Publishing Report, 269
Book Publishing Resource Guide, 452
The Book Rack Ltd, 87
Book Rack Management, 91
Book Report, 173

Book Revue, 111
Book Sales Inc, 25
Book Service of Puerto Rico, 25
Book Shop at Brookside, 109
The Book Shop, 104-105
Book shows, 415-418
Book Soup, 99
The Book Stall at Chestnut Court, 104
Book Store, 106
The Book Store, 51, 114
Book Tech Distributing Inc, 25
Book Train, 102
Book Travellers West, 70
Book Tree, 133
The Book Tree, 108
The Book Vault, 113
Book Wholesalers Inc, 25
Book World Inc, 90, 110
Book-of-the Month Club, 119
Book/Mark, 185
Bookazine Company, 25
Bookberries, 111
The Bookcase at Wayzata, 108
Bookceller, 110
Bookcraft, 25
Bookends Bookstore, 99
The Bookers, 365
BookExpress, 51
Bookfairs By Toad Hall, 25
The Bookfinder, 444
Bookland Inc, 90
Bookland of Maine, 87
Bookland Stores, 169
The Booklegger, 25
Booklines Hawaii, 25
Booklink Distributors, 12
BookLink Inc, 70
Booklist, 173
Bookmargins, 25
Bookmarks, 111
The Bookmark, 105
BookMasters Inc, 81
The Bookmen Inc, 25, 169
Bookmen's Alley, 105
BookPage, 173
Bookpeople, 25
BookPeople of Moscow Inc, 104
Bookport Hingham Square, 107
Books & Books, 109
Books & Books Inc, 103
Books & Bytes Inc, 4
Books & Co For Kids, 112
Books & More, 114
Books & Things Newsland, 106
Books 'n Things, 111
Books About Cookbooks, 134
Books and Research Inc, 25
Books as donations, 170
Books Bohemian, 134
Books by Mail, 134
Books Connection, 87
Books Etc, 25, 113
Books Etc Inc, 98
Books for Animal Lovers, 134
Books for Asia Program, 170
Books for Business Inc, 134
Books for Financial Service Employees, 134
Books for Kids Foundation, 170
Books For Review, 379
Books for Your Business, 134
Books from Northwind Farms, 134
Books in Canada, 185
Books in Motion, 134
Books in Print, 444
Books in Print Database, 444
Books Inc, 90

Books International Inc, 66
Books N Things, 87
Books Nippan USA, 4
Books of Light, 119
Books of My Very Own, 119
Books of Paige's, 103
Books of Wall Street Catalog, 134
Books Off Berwyn, 105
Books on Tape, 125
Books to Grow On, 25
Booksales/Marketing, 373
Bookseller Program, 379
Booksellers (directories), 449
The Bookshelf, 113, 134
Bookshop Benicia, 99
Bookshop Santa Cruz, 99
The Bookshop, 104
Booksmith, 99
Booksmith Promotional Co, 26, 169
The Booksource, 26
The Bookstall, 107
Bookstore chains (and others), 87-96
The Bookstore Inc, 90
Bookstore Journal, 173
Bookstore Journal Action Cards, 383
The Bookstore, 97, 99, 106
Booktrader, 99
Bookviews, 269
Bookwise, 26
Bookworks, 99, 103, 111
Bookworks Inc, 113
The Bookworks, 109
Bookworld, 55, 87, 114
BookWorld Services, 4, 81
Bookworm, 26
The Bookworm, 99, 116
BookZeller, 105
Boonville Daily News & Report, 309
Bop Magazine, 185
Borders, 91
Borger News-Herald, 334
Borland International, 134
Boscos Inc, 440
The Boston Book Review, 185
Boston Business Journal, 185
Boston Globe, 303
Boston Herald, 303
Boston Magazine, 185
Boston Museum of Fine Arts, 134
Boston Music Company, 134
The Boston Parents' Paper, 185
Boston Phoenix, 355
Boston Review, 185
Boston Rite Book &..., 134
Boston Tab, 304
Bostonia, 185
Botanical Interests, 70
The Boulder Bookstore, 102
Boulder County Business Report, 186
Boulder Weekly, 351
Bound to Stay Bound Books, 26
Boundary 2, 186
Bountiful Books, 99
Bovine Veterinarian, 235
Bow & Arrow Hunting, 186
Bowdens Information Services, 435
Bowers & Merena Galleries Publ, 26
Bowhunter, 186
Bowker Mailing Lists, 396
Bowling Digest, 186
Boy's Life, 186
Bozeman Daily Chronicle, 311
Brace Books & More, 113
Bracket Racing U.S.A., 186
Brad Pappas & Associates, 365
Bradenton Herald, 286
Bradford Era, 327

Brady & Paul Communications, 373
Brainerd Daily Dispatch, 307
Brainstorms Catalog, 134
The Branding Iron, 343
Brandon Sun, 345
Branson Tri-Lakes Daily News, 309
Brasil Internacional do Livro, 417
Brattleboro Reformer, 338
Brauch Publishing Systems Inc, 81
Brazil Times, 294
Brazos Bookstore Inc, 114
Brazos Periodical Distributors, 65
Brazosport Facts, 334
Bread & Circus, 95
Breakaway, 186
Breakthrough Publications, 12
Breakwater Books Ltd, 20
Breeze Courier, 294
Brenham Banner-Press, 334
Brewer Sewing Supplies, 26
Briarwood Writers' Alliance, 377
Bridal Guide, 186
Bride's & Your New Home, 186
Bride's Magazine, 186
Bridge City Tool Works, 134
Bridge Street Books Ltd, 111
Bridge Works Publishing Co, 12
Bridge World, 134
Bridgeton Evening News, 313
Bright Horizons Specialty Dist, 4
Brilliance, 125
Brimar Publishing Inc, 20
Brio, 186
Bristol Herald Courier Virginia Tennessean, 338
Bristol Press, 285
British Heritage, 186
Britt & Associates, 365
Britten Banners, 440
Broadcast Engineering, 235
Broadcast Newsclips--PR, 435
Broadcasting & Cable, 235
Broadcasting & Cable MarketPlace, 452
The Broadmore Group, 396
Brockton Enterprise, 303
Brockville Recorder & Times, 346
Brodart, 26
Brodart Industries Ltd, 51
Broderbund Software Direct, 134
Brody Public Relations, 366
Broker World, 235
Brookings Register, 331
Brookline Booksmith, 107
Brookline Citizen Journal, 355
Brooklyn Bridge, 186
Brooklyn Paper Publications, 357
Brooklyn Spectator, 357
Brooklyn Sun Journal, 359
Brooks Mann Inc, 396
Brotherhood of Life Inc, 26
Brown Daily Herald, 331
Brown Wrapper Bookstore, 134
The Brownsville Herald, 334
Brownwood Bulletin, 334
Browse Awhile Books, 112
Browser Books, 99
Bruck W J Walsh, Representative, 70
Bruckenthal Associates Inc, 396
Brunner News Agency, 63, 87
Brunswick News, 289
Brunswick Sun Times, 359
Brussels International Book Fair, 417
Bryan Times, 322
Bryan-College Station Eagle, 334
Bryant Altman Map Inc, 26
BSK Communications & Associates, 366
Buckeye Book Fair, 415

Buckeye News, 26
Bucks County Courier Times, 329
Budget Book Service Div of LDAP, 26
Bueno Catalog, 134
Buenos Aires Book Fair, 417
Buffalo News, 316
Buffalo Spree, 186
Builder Magazine, 235
Builder's Booksource, 134
Building Operating Management, 383
Building Products & Hardlines Distributors, 460
Building Renovation, 236
Building the Undergraduate Social Work Library, 444
Bull's Head Bookshop, 112
Bulldog Reporter, 456
Bulldog Reporter Central Edition, 269
Bulldog Reporter Eastern Edition, 269
Bulldog Reporter Western Edition, 269
Bulletin & Review, 297
Bulletin of Bibliography, 258
The Bulletin, 326
Bumbershoot: Seattle Arts Festival, 415
Bunch of Grapes Bookstore, 107
Burch Inc, 81
Burdick Associates, 70
The Bureau Inc, 396
Burke's Book Store Inc, 114
Burlington Bookshop, 111
Burlington County Times, 314
Burlington Free Press, 338
Burlington Marketing, 396
Burns Archive Productions Ltd, 12
Burns News Agency, 62
Burns Sports Celebrity Serv Inc, 377
Burpee Garden, 135
Burrelle's Media Directories, 452
Burrelles Press Clipping Service, 435
Bus World, 236
Business & Career Books, 135
Business & Computer Bkstores Inc, 135
Business & Financial News Media, 452
Business & Health, 236
Business & Legal CD-ROMS in Print, 445
Business and Personal Success, 135
Business Books Network, 26
Business Buyer Resource Deck, 383
Business Buyers' Action Pack, 383
Business By Phone Catalog, 135
Business By The Book, 135
Business cards, 434
Business Communications Review, 236
Business Digest Mail, 396
Business Documents, 186
Business Education Forum, 258
Business Ethics, 236
Business Information Alert, 173
Business Insurance, 236
Business Marketing, 269
Business Marketing Action Cards, 383
Business Marketing Consultants, 373
Business Media Directory, 452
Business New Hampshire, 258
Business News, 186
Business News Publishing Co, 396
Business North Carolina, 258
The Business of Herbs, 236
Business Organizations, Agencies and Publications Directory, 447
The Business Owner, 186
Business Performance Pack, 384
Business Publications Rates/Data, 452
Business Reader, 135
Business Research Publications, 396
Business Research Services Inc, 396
Business Start-Ups, 186

Business Technology Exec-Cards, 384
Business to Business Catalogs, 449
Business Today, 186
Business trade magazines, 233-256
Business Venture Magazine, 186
Business Week, 186
Business Wire, 366
Butler Eagle, 327
Buttonwood Books & Toys, 107
Buyer's Directory, 460
Buzz Magazine, 186
By The Book, 99
Bye the Book Inc, 110
Byron Preiss Visual Publ Inc, 12
Byrrd Enterprises Inc, 26
BYTE, 186
Byte Deck, 384
Bytes and Pieces, 135

C & S News Agency, 65
C & W Zabel Company, 26
C H I P S Catalog, 135
C W Associates, 26
C/C++ Users Journal, 258
CA Magazine, 186
Cabbages and Kings Bookstore, 107
Cabela's, 135
Cabin Fever Books, 116
CabinetMaker, 236
Cable Avails, 236
Cable World, 236
CableMail, 379
Cablevision, 236
Caddylak Systems, 384
Cade Communications, 366
Cadillac Evening News, 305
Caere Corporation, 440
CAF List Co, 396
Cahners Direct Marketing Service, 396
Cairo International Book Fair, 417
Cairo Intl Children's Book Fair, 417
Cajun Country Distributors, 26
Cal-West Periodicals, 56
Calcutta Book Fair, 417
Caldor's Department Stores, 95
Caledonian Record, 338
Calgary Herald, 344
Calgary Sun, 344
California Aggie, 277
California and Hawaii Publishing Market Place, 447
California Digital Inc, 135
California Festivals & Events, 419
California Game & Fish, 187
California Horse Review, 236
California Kids History Catalog, 135
California Senior Citizen, 187
California Storytellers Catalog, 135
California Strategies, 187
Californian, 282
The Californian, 280
Call & Post, 359
Call Center, 236
Call-Leader, 294
Callaloo, 187
Callboard, 187
Calliope: World History for Young People, 187
The Call, 331
Camarillo Star, 276
Cambridge Career Products, 396
Cambridge Parenting Catalog, 135

Cambridge Reporter, 346
Cambridge University Press, 70
Camby & West Inc, 81
Camden Courier-Post, 313
Camden News, 275
CAMEX Inc, 169
Campaigns & Elections, 258
Camping & RV Magazine, 187
Camping Magazine, 258
Campus Bookstore, 97
Campus Life, 187
Campus Life Card Deck, 384
Campus Life Regional Friends, 384
Campus Market Expo, 415
Campus Store Queens College, 93
Can Technology International, 236
Can-Ed Media Ltd, 20
Canaan Communications, 366
Canadian Academic Technology, 135
Canadian Author, 258
Canadian Banker, 236
Canadian Booksellers Convention, 415
Canadian Business, 258
Canadian Dimension, 187
Canadian distributors, 9-10
Canadian Environmental Directory, 457
Canadian independent booksellers, 117
Canadian jobbers, 67-68
Canadian List Services, 396
Canadian Living, 187
Canadian News Company, 67
Canadian newspaper editors/book reviewers, 344-348
Canadian Press Clipping Services, 435
Canadian publishers, 20
Canadian Select Homes & Food, 187
Canadian weekly newspapers, 361
Canadian wholesalers, 51-54
Canav Books, 51
Cancer Fighters Bookshop, 135
Caners Sourcebook, 135
Canoe & Kayak Magazine, 187
Canon City Daily Record, 283
Canyonlands Natural History Assn, 90
Canyonlands Publications, 26
Capability's Books for Gardeners, 135
The Capable Mind, 396
Cape Cod Times, 304
Capener/Walcher, 366
Capistrano Valley News, 350
Capital City Comics, 27
Capital City Distribution, 27
Capital District Business Review, 258
Capital News, 60
Capital Speakers Inc, 377
The Capital, 302
Capitol Book and News, 97
Capitol District Business Review, 357
Capitol Hill Books, 102
Capitol News Agency, 66
Capitol Publications, 396
Capitola Book Cafe, 99
Capper's, 187
Capstone Lists Inc, 397
Car & Driver, 187
Car Craft, 187
Car Stereo Review, 187
Carann Distributors, 51
Card Deck Customer Directory, 384
Card Deck Rates and Data, 384
Card decks or card packs, 383-392
Card Pack Media Directory, 384
Cardinal Mailing Services Ltd, 397
cardsNow, 434
Career Aids, 135
Career Pilot, 236
Career Planning & Job Search, 136

Career Planning/Adult Development, 136
Career Press, 136
Career Resources, 384
Careers & Colleges, 187
Careers & the Disabled, 187
Cariad Ltd, 51
Caribbean Travel & Life, 187
Carl B Noelke Co, 27
Carl Fischer Music Distributor, 27
Carla Ruff, 373
Carleton College Book Store, 108
Carlsbad Current-Argus, 315
Carmi Times, 291
Carnegie Marketing Associates, 397
Carney Direct Marketing (CDM), 397
Carnival Book Club, 119
Carol Enters List Co, 397
Carol Wright Co-op, 379
Carol Wright Gifts, 136
Carol Wright Hispanic Co-op, 379
Carolan Craft Supplies, 136
Carole Purkey, Representative, 70
Carole Timkovich, Representative, 70
Carolina Biological Supply Co, 27, 136
Carolina Clipping Service, 435
Carolina News Co, 62
Carolina Parent, 187
Carolina Style, 187
Caroline O'Connell PR, 366
Carolyn Anthony Public Relations, 366
Carousel Press, 136
Carroll & Graf Publishers, 126
Carroll County Times, 303
Carroll Daily Times-Herald, 297
Carroll Reed Catalog, 136
Carrollton Editing/Publishing, 435
Carrot-Top Industries Inc, 440
Cars & Parts, 187
Carson Enterprises Book Catalog, 136
Carter & Carter, 20
Carthage Press, 309
Caruba organization, 366
CAS Marketing Inc, 397, 435
Casa Grande Dispatch, 274
Cascade News, 66
Casco Bay Weekly, 355
Casey Group, 70
Casper Star Tribune, 343
Cassette-of-the Month Club, 119
Cassidy Brown Public Relations, 366
Castner-Knott Dept Stores, 95
Casual Living USA, 136
Cat Fancy, 187
Cata-List Catalog Directory, 379
Catalist, 187
Catalog Age, 269
Catalog on a Disk, 136
The Catalog Shop, 136
Catalog Solutions, 373
Catalogs (directories), 449
Catalogue & Mail Order Business, 236
Catalogue from Golf House, 136
Catalyst Direct Marketing Inc, 397
Catechist, 188
Category codes, 80, 118, 232, 256, 272, 362
Catholic Answers Catalog, 136
Catholic Book & Supply Co, 27
Catholic Book Club, 119
Catholic Bookrack Service, 27
Catholic Church/School Market, 384
Catholic Digest Book Club, 119
Catholic Library World, 174
Catholic Lists, 397
Catholic Parent, 188
Catloging & Classification Qly, 173
Cats Cats and More Cats, 136

Cats Magazine, 188
Cavalcade of Acts & Attractions, 459
The Cavalier Daily, 339
CBA Convention, 415
CCBC Choices, 445
CCD Astronomy, 188
CCS Direct Inc, 397
CD Distributing Inc, 61
CD-ROM Directory, 445
The CD-ROM Finder, 450
CD-ROM Gold Pak, 384
CD-ROM Market Place, 447
CD-ROM Professional, 236
CD-ROM Technologies, 435
CD-ROM Today, 188
CD-ROMS in Print, 445
Cecchi News Agency, 62
Cecil Whig, 303
Cedar Fort Inc, 27
Cedar Valley Daily Times, 298
CEE News, 236
A Celebration Catalog, 129
Celebration Creations Catalog, 136
Celebrity Endorsement Network, 377
Celebrity Focus International Inc, 452
Celebrity Guide of California, 366
Celia Rocks Communications, 366
Cellular Business, 269
CEM Paper Enterprises Inc, 439
Center City News, 4
Center For Cuban Studies, 136
Center for Thanatology Research and Education, 419
Central Arizona Distributing, 55
Central Computer Products, 136
Central Daily, 278
Central Distribution Services, 81
Central Illinois Periodicals, 58
Central Maine Morning Sentinel, 302
Central News, 64
Central News Agency, 63
Central News Co Ltd, 68
Central News of Sandusky, 63
Centralia Sentinel, 291
Centrax Books and Distribution, 9
Centre Daily Times, 330
Ceramic Arts & Crafts, 188
Ceramics Monthly, 188
Certified Mailing Lists Co, 397
CeSan Limited, 440
Cessna Owner Magazine, 188
CFO, 258
CFO Library, 136
CFQ Bookshop, 136
CFW: Competitor for Women, 188
Chagrin Herald Sun, 358
Chain Restaurant Operators, 460
Chain Store Age Executive, 236
Challenge Magazine, 188
Chambers Catalog, 136
Chandler Arizonan Tribune, 274
Change, 236
Changes Magazine, 188
Changing Hands Bookstore, 98
Changing Men, 188
Channing L Bete Co, 397
Chanute Tribune, 299
Chapter 11, 87
Chapter One Bookstore, 105
Chapter Two Bookstore, 114
Chapters, 91
Chapters Bookshop, 105
Charisma, 188
Charles City Press, 297
Charles Crane Associates Inc, 397
Charles E Tuttle Company, 10, 12
Charles Levy Circulating Co, 58

Charles Moore Assoc Inc, 397
Charleston Daily Mail, 341
Charleston Gazette, 341
Charleston News Company Inc, 64
Charleston Post & Courier, 331
Charlotte Observer, 319
Charrette, 95
Chartsearch Card Decks, 384
Chassman & Bem Booksellers, 115
Chatelaine, 188
Chattanooga Free Press, 332
Chattanooga Times, 332
Cheatsheet Products Inc, 136
Cheboygan Daily Tribune, 305
Checkers Distributors, 27
Chef Magazine, 236
Chelsea, 188
The Chelsea Forum, 377
Chemical Engineers Book Club, 119
Chemical Week, 236
Chemists' Book Club, 119
Cheng & Tsui Company, 4, 27
Cheren Canada, 9
Cherokee Daily Times, 297
Cherry Lane Catalog, 137
Chesapeake & Hudson, 70
Chesapeake Bay Magazine, 188
Chesapeake Direct Inc, 397
Chess Life, 188
Chessler Books, 137
Chester Mailing List Consultants, 397
Chesterton Tribune, 294
Chevalier's Books, 99
Chevy High Performance, 236
Chicago Advertising & Media, 237
Chicago Books in Review, 237
Chicago Daily Law Bulletin, 291
Chicago Defender, 291
Chicago Law Book Company, 4
Chicago Lawyer, 237
Chicago Magazine, 188
Chicago Northwest Press, 353
Chicago Parent Newsmagazine, 188
Chicago Reader, 353
Chicago Sun-Times, 291-292
Chicago Tribune, 292
Chicago Tribune Gift Stores, 87
Chicago Weekly, 353
Chickadee Books, 419
Chickasha Daily Express, 325
Chickasha Star, 325
Chicken Boy Catalog, 137
Chico Enterprise-Record, 276
Chico News Agency Inc, 56
Chico News and Review, 349
Chilcutt Direct Marketing, 397
Chilcutt Direct Mktg/Outdoor List, 397
Child, 188
Child & Family Behavior Therapy, 258
Child & Youth Services, 188
Child Care Info Exchange, 258
Child Life, 188
Childbirth, 188
Childbirth Instructor, 188
Childcraft, 137
Children Book-of-the-Month Club, 120
Children's Authors/Illustrators, 444
Children's Book Insider, 188
Children's Book Market, 447
Children's Book Review, 189
Children's Books Catalog, 137
Children's Books of the Year, 445
Children's Bookstore, 51
Children's BookStore Dist, 51
Children's Business, 237
Children's Digest, 189
Children's Media Market Place, 447

Children's Ministry, 189
Children's Playmate, 189
Children's Writer's Market, 447
Children's Writer's Marketplace, 447
Childrens Small Press Collection, 4
Childsplay, 189
Childswork/Childsplay Catalog, 137
Chile Pepper Magazine, 189
Chillicothe Constitution-Tribune, 309
Chillicothe Gazette, 322
Chilton Direct Mktg/List Mgmt, 397
Chilton's Execu-Deck, 384
China Books & Periodicals Inc, 12
China Cultural Center, 27
China Daily, 317
China Tribune, 317
Chinaberry Book Service, 137
Chinese Christian Mission, 27
Chinese Times, 281
Chinese United Journal, 317
Chinook Bookshop, 102
Chip Chats, 237
Chippewa Herald-Telegram, 342
Chittenden Press Focus, 452
Chocolatier, 189
Choice, 174
Choice Books, 27, 51
Christian Armory, 93
Christian Book & Gift Shop, 93
Christian Book Distributors, 137
The Christian Century, 189
Christian Family Shopper, 384
Christian Literature Crusade, 27
Christian Parenting Today, 189
Christian Publications Inc, 27
Christian Science Monitor, 303
Christian Shoppers Card-A-Log, 384
Christian Supply Bookstore, 93
Christian Writer's Markets Guide, 447
Christianity Today, 189
Christie & Christie, 9
Christine Hopf-Lovette, 373
Christine Pegram Main Bookshop, 27
Christopher Resources Inc, 397
Christopher Ward & Co Inc, 70
Christopher's Books, 99
Chronicle, 285
Chronicle News, 284
Chronicle of Higher Education, 397
The Chronicle of Philanthropy, 237, 397
The Chronicle of the Horse, 189
Chronicle-Journal, 347
Chronicle-Tribune, 296
Chronicles, 189
The Chronicle, 319, 361
Chuck & Dave's, 107
Chuck Wagon Outfitters, 137
Church Product Alert Card Pack, 384
Church Resource Packet, 384
Churchill Livingstone, 137
CIC School Directories, 460
Cincinnati CityBeat, 359
Cincinnati Court Index, 322
Cincinnati Downtowner, 359
Cincinnati Enquirer, 322
Cincinnati Post, 322
Cineaste, 189
Cinefantastique, 189
Cinema Book Society, 120
Cinema Books, 137
Cinema City, 137
Cinema Guild, 4
Cinescape, 189
CIO Magazine, 258
Circa Publications Inc, 27
Circle Book Service, 27
Circle Craft Supply, 137

Circle Track & Racing Technology, 189
Circleville Herald, 322
Circulation Management, 237
Circulator's Book Shelf, 137
Circus Magazine, 189
Citizen, 189, 313, 315
Citizen Register, 319
Citizen Tribune, 333
Citizens' Voice, 330
Citrus County Chronicle, 286
City & State Directories in Print, 445
City Diecutting Inc, 436
City Family, 189
City Lights Booksellers & Publ, 99
City News Agency, 63
City Newspaper, 358
City Pages, 356
City Parent, 189
Cityview, 353
Civic Center NewSource, 350
Civil Engineering, 258
Civil Engineers' Book Club, 120
Civil War Times Illustrated, 189
Civilized Traveller, 90
CJR Periodical, 4
Claremont Courier, 349
Clarion Ledger, 309
Clark Boardman Callaghan/CBC, 397
Clarksburg Exponent, 341
Clarksburg Telegram, 341
Clarksdale Press Register, 308
Clarkston Reminder, 355
Class, 189
CLASS - Speakers, 377
Classic Auto Restorer, 189
Classic Gift Shoppe, 27
Classic Motorbooks, 137
Classic Toy Trains, 189
Classroom Reading Service Inc, 27
Claude M Diffusion Ltd, 9
Clavier, 237
Clay Center Dispatch, 299
Clay Today, 288
Clayton News/Daily, 289
A Clean Well-Lighted Place, 99
Cleaner Times, 237
The Clearing House, 258
Clearlake Observer American, 349
Cleburne Times-Review, 334
Clement Communications ActionPac, 384
Clergy Journal, 237
Cleveland Daily Banner, 332
Cleveland Free Press, 359
Cleveland Jewish News, 359
Cleveland Magazine, 189
Clifford Publishing Services, 373
Climbing, 189
Clint's Books & Comics, 95
Clinton Daily Democrat, 309
Clinton Daily Journal, 292
The Clinton Daily News, 325
Clinton Herald, 297
Clip Inc, 435
Clipper Ship Bookshop, 103
Clipping bureau, 435
Closing the Gap, 237
Clothing Manufacturers Assn/USA, 397
Clotilde Inc, 137
Clout, 190
Clovis News Journal, 315
Club MAC, 137
Club Management, 269
Clubhouse, 190
Clubhouse Jr, 190
Clyde Robin Seed Catalog, 137
CM Magazine, 190
CMA Magazine, 258

CMC List Capital, 397
CMG Information Services, 397
CMO Superstore & Catalog, 137
CMP Direct Marketing Services, 397
CMP Executive Women Co-op, 379
CMP InformationWeek/MIS Deck, 384
CMP Sales & Marketing Power Deck, 384
Coast to Coast, 190
Coast Weekly, 351
Cobblestone, 190
Cobourg Daily Star, 346
Cobras, 190
Cochran News Agency, 65
The Cockpit, 137
Cody Associates Inc, 397
Cody's Books Inc, 100
Coeur d'Alene Press, 290
CoffeeTalk, 237
Coffeyville Journal, 299
Cogan Books, 27
Coin, 190
Cokesbury, 93
Colborn School Supply Stores, 95
Colby Free Press, 299
Coldwater Creek, 138
Cole & Associates, 373
Cole Parmer Catalog, 138
Coliseum Books Inc, 111
Collecting Toys, 190
Collection Management, 174
Collections, 435
Collector Editions, 190
Collector's SportsLook, 190
Collectors News, 190
College & Research Libraries, 174
College bookstores, 93-94
College Bookstores List, 397
College Boulevard News, 354
College Connection, 321
College Library Program, 379
College Media Directory, 452
College Outlook, 190
The College Publishing Market, 459
College Store Journal, 237
College Students Co-op, 379
College Suppliers, 70
College Teaching, 190
Collegian, 284
Collision Magazine, 237
Colloquim Books, 114
Colombo Children's Book Fair, 417
Colonial Garden Kitchens, 138
Colonial Homes, 190
Colonial Williamsburg Foundation, 28
Color Publishing, 190, 237
Colorado Book Guide, 447
Colorado Homes & Lifestyles, 190
Colorado Periodical Distributors, 57
Colorado Springs Fine Arts Ctr, 28
Colorado Springs Independent, 351
Colorado Voice Productions, 366
Coloradoan, 284
Columbia Basin Herald, 340
Columbia County News Agency, 62
Columbia Daily Spectator, 317
Columbia Daily Tribune, 309
Columbia Dir Mktg/List Division, 397
Columbia House Audio Books, 120
Columbia House Lists, 398
Columbia House Music Club, 120
Columbia House Video Club, 120
Columbia Journalism Review, 190
Columbia Magazine, 190
Columbia Missourian, 309
Columbus Alive, 359
Columbus Daily Advocate, 299
Columbus Dispatch, 322

Columbus Guardian, 359
Columbus Ledger-Enquirer, 289
Columbus Republic, 294
Columbus Telegram, 312
Combined Book Exhibit, 420
Comdex, 418
The Comedy Magazine, 190
Comics Buyer's Guide, 190
Coming Attractions, 190
Command Productions, 398
The Commercial Appeal, 333
Commercial Dispatch, 308
Commercial Envelope Manufacturing Co, 437
Commercial Mailing Lists Inc, 398
Commercial News, 292
Commercial Review, 296
Common Market Inc, 103
A Common Reader, 138
Commonwealth List Co, 398
Commonwealth-Journal, 301
Communication Arts, 237
Communication World, 237
The Communications Center, 366
Communications Daily, 190, 286
Communications Data Services, 81
Communications Media, 111
Communications of the ACM, 190
Community & Junior College Libs, 174
Community Bookstore, 111
Community Cardpack, 384
Community Media Workshop, 366
Community News, 356
Community News Center, 87
Community Newscenter #1, 108
Como Sales Company Inc, 70
Companies (directories), 450
Compass Publications, 398
Competitive Edge, 440
Compiled Solutions Inc, 398
Compilers Plus, 398
The Compleat Strategist Inc, 95
Complete Directory for People with Disabilities, 452
Complete Directory for People with Learning Disabilities, 452
Complete Woman, 190
Comprehensive Health Education, 138
Compton's NewMedia, 4
Compuadd, 138
CompuBooks Online Bookstore, 138
Compuclassics Inc, 138
CompuDeck, 384
CompuName Inc, 398
CompuPower Corporation, 81
Compuser/Compudyne Direct, 138
Computability Consumer Electroni, 138
Computer & Software Retail & Distributors, 460
Computer Action Inc, 81
Computer Artist, 191
The Computer Book Club, 120
Computer Catalogs, 449
Computer Design, 191
Computer Discount Warehouse, 138
Computer Economics Inc, 398
Computer Gaming World, 191
Computer Life, 191
Computer Lifestyle, 451
Computer Literacy Bookshops Inc, 87
Computer Magazine, 191
Computer Owners Action Pac, 384
Computer Plus - Dealer Catalog, 138
Computer Professionals' Books Society, 120
Computer Publishing/Advertising, 270
Computer Reseller News, 237

Computer Shopper, 191
Computer Software & Tutorials, 138
Computer User, 191
Computer-Aided Engineering, 237
Computers and Computing, 445
Computers in Human Services, 191
Computerworld, 191
Computerworld Response Directory, 384
Conacher News Ltd, 67
Conceive Believe Achieve, 138
Concord Monitor, 313
Concord Tribune, 319
Conde Nast Traveler, 191
Conference Book Service, 420
Confrontation, 191
Congress Avenue Booksellers, 114
Congress Daily, 286
Congressional Monitor, 286
Conkey's Bookstore, 116
Connecticut Magazine, 191
Connecticut Post, 285
Connemara Trading Co, 28
Connersville News-Examiner, 294
Connie Goddard Book Development, 374
Conrad Direct Inc, 398
The Conroe Courier, 334
Conscious Products for Conscious People, 379
Consequences, 191
Conservation Directory, 457
Conservative Book Club, 120
Consolidated Mailing Service, 398
Consolino & Woodward, 70
Consortium Book Sales & Dist, 4
Construction Bookstore, 90, 138
Construction Resources Cards, 385
Constructive Playthings Catalog, 138
Consultants and Consulting Organizations Directory, 459
Consultants News, 270
Consulting Psychologists Press, 12
Consulting Specifying Engineer, 191, 258
Consumer Education Research Ctr, 138
Consumer Electronics Show, 418
Consumer Information Catalog, 138
Consumer Magazines Rates & Data, 452
Consumer Marketing Resources Inc, 138
Consumer Reports, 191
Consumers Digest, 191, 398
Consumers Marketing Research Inc, 398
Consumers Research, 191
Contact Book, 459
The Contact Sheet, 379
Contacts Newsletter, 456
Contemporary Arts Press, 12
Contemporary Authors, 444
Contemporary Long-Term Care, 237
Contemporary Pediatrics, 258
Contemporary Urology, 237
Continental Book Co, 28
Continental Profiles, 191
Contra Costa Times, 283
Contracting Business, 237
Controller Magazine, 237
Convene, 237
Convenience Store News, 237
Convention Digest, 452
Convergence Corporation, 440
Converting Magazine, 238
Conway Daily Sun, 313
The Cook's Garden, 139
Cook's Mail Order Directory, 449
The Cookbook Collection, 28
Cookbook Resources USA Ltd, 70
Cookbook Warehouse Div-Booklink, 28
Cooking Light, 191
Coolidge Company Inc, 398

Coolware Inc, 139
Cooperative Etudiante, 51
Cooperative marketing services, 379-382
Copper Electronics, 139
Copperfield & Company, 106
Copperfield's Books, 87
Copy Imaging & Reproduction, 238
Copyediting and proofing, 435
Cordee, 10
Cordele Dispatch, 289
Corel Magazine, 191
Corinth Films, 4
Cornell Daily Sun, 316
Corner Bookstore, 111
Cornerstone List Managers Inc, 398
Cornwall News Distributors, 68
Cornwall Standard-Freeholder, 346
Corona-Norco Independent, 349
Corporate & Incentive Travel, 238
The Corporate Address Book, 450
Corporate Book Resources, 28
Corporate Cashflow, 258
Corporate Cleveland Magazine, 238
Corporate Detroit Magazine, 259
Corporate Finance, 191
Corporate Fulfillment Systems, 81
Corporate Legal Times, 259
Corporate Meeting Planners, 459
Corporate Meetings & Incentives, 238
Corporate Report Minnesota, 191
Corporate Travel, 238
The Corporate Yellow Book, 450
CorpTech, 398
Corpus Christi Caller-Times, 334
Corradetti Enterprises, 169
Corric K's, 100
Corry Journal, 328
Corsicana Daily Sun, 334
Cortland Standard, 316
Corvallis Gazette-Times, 326
Corvette Fever, 191
Corvette Quarterly, 191
Coshochton Tribune, 323
Cosmic Connection TV, 379
Cosmopolitan, 192
Costco Wholesale, 95
Cottage Life, 192
Cotton Grower, 238
Cotton Patch, 139
Council Bluffs Nonpareil, 297
Council Grove Republican, 299
Countdown, 192
Country, 192
Country Accents, 192
Country Almanac, 192, 350
Country America, 192
Country Bookshelf, 109
Country Business, 192
Country Charm, 192
Country Connections, 192
Country Data Corp, 398
Country Decorating Ideas, 192
Country Family Card Pack, 385
Country Folk Art Magazine, 192
Country Handcrafts, 238
Country Home & Garden Book Club, 120
Country Inns/Bed & Breakfast, 238
Country Journal, 192
Country Living, 192
Country Marketing Ltd, 398
Country Victorian, 192
Country Woman, 192
Countryside Books, 28
Courier, 323
Courier Herald, 289
The Courier News, 292
Courier Post, 311

Courier-Democrat, 276
Courier-Express, 328
Courier-News, 313
Courier-Observer, 318
Courier-Times, 296
Courier-Tribune, 319
Court and Commercial Record, 295
Coutts Library Services Inc, 28
Covenant Communications, 28
Cover to Cover, 107
Cover to Cover Bookstore, 110
Covox Inc, 139
Cowan Liebowitz & Latman PC, 374
Cowboy Magazine, 192
Cowles Media Inc, 398
Cowley Distributing, 61
CQ-Radio Amateur's Journal, 192
Craft Business Books, 139
Craft King Inc, 139
Craft market Action Cards, 385
Craft Shop & Gallery Directory, 460
Craft Wholesalers, 28
Craft, Model & Hobby Show, 418
Crafter's Choice Book Club, 120
Crafts 'N Things, 192
Crafts Americana Group, 28
Crafts Magazine, 238
Craftsman Book Co, 12, 398
Craig E McCroskey Inc, 70
Crain's Chicago Business, 192
Crain's Detroit Business, 192
Crain's New York Business, 192
Crain's Small Business, 192
Cranbrook Daily Townsman, 344
Cranford Bookstore, 110
Crappie Magazine, 192
Crate & Barrel Catalog, 139
Craver Mathews Smith & Co, 398
Crawford-Peters Aeronautics, 139
Crayola Kids, 193
Crazy Bob's, 139
Creative Access, 398
Creative Classroom, 238
Creative Crafts Distributor, 28
Creative Exhibiting Techniques, 238
Creative Homeowner Press, 13
Creative Kids, 193
Creative Learning Products, 374
Creative List Services Inc, 398
Creative Loafing, 193, 352
Creative Machine, 139
Creative Needle, 139
Creative New Jersey, 193, 259
Creative Optics, 440
Creative Retirement, 238
Creative Selling, 270
Creative Ways, 438
Creativity Magazine, 238
Credit Card Management, 238
Credit Union Magazine, 238
Creeyadio Services One-to-One, 452
Crescent Books Catalog, 139
Crescent Imports & Publications, 4
Crescent International Inc, 28
Crescent-News, 323
Crestline, 440
Creston News-Advertiser, 297
Cricket, 193
Criminal Law Bulletin, 259
Crimson White, 274
Criterion News Advertiser, 357
Critic's Choice Video, 139
Critique:Studies in Contemp Fic, 193, 259
Critiques Livres, 79
Crochet Digest, 193
Crochet World, 193
Crochet World Specials, 193

Cromland, 28
Cromwell Lists, 398
Crone Chronicles, 193
Crookston Daily Times, 307
Cross Country Books, 52
Cross Country Skier, 193
Cross River Publishing Consultants, 374
Cross Stitcher, 193
Cross-Stitch Plus, 193
Crossings Book Club, 120
Crosslists Co, 398
Crouch International, 374
Crowley News, 66
Crowley Post-Signal, 301
Crown and Super Crown Books, 91
Crown Publications Inc, 52
Cruise Travel, 193
Cruises & Tours, 193
Cruising World, 193
Crutchfield Computer Catalog, 139
CSI Direct, 139
Cuban Boy's Spanish Books, 28
Cuda's Book Store, 108
Cullman Times, 273
Culpepper Hughes & Head, 139
Cultural Hispana, 4
Cumberland General Store, 139
Cumberland Times-News, 303
The Cummer Museum Shop, 103
Cummins News, 58
Cummins-Allison Corp, 439
CUP Services, 5
Cupertino Courier, 349
Curiosity Book Shop, 97
Current, 238
Current Books Magazine, 193
Current Contents Action Pack, 385
Current Inc, 139
The Current, 349
Curriculum Leaders Action Deck, 385
Curtis Circulation Co, 13
Cushing Daily Citizen, 325
Custom Home, 238
Custom List Services Inc, 398
Custom Mailing Services, 398
Custom Mat Co Inc, 440
Custom Rodder, 193
Customer Insight Company, 398
Cutting Edge Opportunities, 193
CW Lists, 398
CWC Software Inc, 81
CWI Products & Services, 139
CyberData, 436
Cyberspace PR Newsletter, 270
Cycle World, 238
Cycling USA, 193
The Cyclists' Yellow Pages, 460
The Cyclosource Catalog, 139
Cypress Book Co Inc, 28
Cypress House, 13
Cyrano's Bookstore & Cafe, 97

D & J Book Distributors, 28
D D L Books, 5
D L Blair, 374
D Magazine, 193
D Robbins & Company, 5
D W J Associates Inc, 366
D Young & Associates, 28
D-J Associates, 399
Daedalus Books Inc, 28, 169
Daily Advance, 320

Daily Advertiser, 301
Daily Advocate, 323
Daily American, 294, 330
Daily American Republic, 310
The Daily Ardmorette, 325
The Daily Astorian, 326
Daily Athenaeum, 341
Daily Aztec, 280
Daily Banner, 302
Daily Barometer, 326
The Daily Beacon, 333
Daily Breeze, 282, 286
Daily Bruin, 278
Daily Bulletin, 316
Daily Business Review, 287
Daily Business Satellite, 366
The Daily Californian, 349
Daily Camera, 283
Daily Campus, 285
The Daily Campus, 334
Daily Capital News, 310
Daily Cardinal, 342
Daily Chief-Union, 324
Daily Chronicle, 292
The Daily Chronicle, 340
Daily Citizen, 276, 342
Daily Citizen-News, 289
Daily Clay County Advocate-Press, 293
Daily Clintonian, 294
Daily Collegian, 277
The Daily Collegian, 330
Daily Comet, 302
Daily Commerce, 278
Daily Commercial, 287
Daily Commercial Record, 334
Daily Commercial Recorder, 336
Daily Construction Service, 280-281
Daily Corinthian, 308
The Daily Cougar, 335
Daily Courier, 320, 328
The Daily Courier, 344
Daily Court Reporter, 323
Daily Court Review, 335
Daily Democrat, 283, 298
Daily Democrat, 310
Daily Dispatch, 274
Daily Eastern News, 291
Daily Editor, 316
Daily Egyptian, 291
Daily Evening Item, 304
Daily Events, 310
Daily Forty-Niner, 278
Daily Free Press, 303
Daily Freeman-Journal, 298
Daily Gate City, 298
Daily Gazette, 294
The Daily Gazette, 318
Daily Gleaner, 345
The Daily Globe, 324
Daily Graphic, 345
Daily Guide, 311
Daily Hampshire Gazette, 304
The Daily Helmsman, 333
Daily Herald, 291, 321
Daily Herald Tribune, 344
The Daily Herald, 332, 337
Daily Home, 274
Daily Iberian, 302
Daily Illini, 294
Daily Independent, 280, 300, 320
Daily Inter Lake, 311
Daily Iowan, 298
Daily Iowegian, 297
Daily Item, 303, 319, 330
Daily Jefferson County Union, 342
Daily Jeffersonian, 322
Daily Journal, 284, 293, 295, 308, 310, 314

Daily Journal of Commerce, 301, 327
Daily Kent Stater, 323
Daily Leader, 293, 308
Daily Legal News, 302, 322, 324
Daily Local News, 330
Daily Mail, 303, 316
Daily Messenger, 316
Daily Midway Driller, 282
Daily Miner & News, 346
Daily Mining Gazette, 306
Daily Mississippian, 309
Daily Mountain Eagle, 273
Daily Nebraskan, 312
Daily News, 276, 280, 293, 299-301, 306, 310, 315, 319-321, 328-329, 332-333
Daily News (cont), 344, 346
Daily News Bulletin, 317
The Daily News Journal, 333
The Daily News Leader, 339
The Daily News Mercury, 304
Daily News of Newburyport, 304
Daily News Record, 317
Daily News Sun, 275
Daily News-Record, 339
Daily News-Tribune, 293
The Daily News, 340, 343
Daily Nexus, 282
Daily Northwestern, 292
The Daily O'Collegian, 326
Daily of the Univ of Washington, 340
Daily Orange, 318
Daily Pacific Builder, 281
Daily Packet & Times, 346
The Daily Pennsylvanian, 329
Daily Pilot, 276
Daily Planet, 140
Daily Post-Athenian, 332
Daily Press, 279, 283, 306, 330, 339
Daily Press & Dakotan, 332
The Daily Press, 342, 347
Daily Princetonian, 314
The Daily Progress, 339
Daily Quill, 311
Daily Racing Form, 314
Daily Record, 276, 300, 302, 310, 312, 314, 318-319, 324, 340
Daily Recorder, 280
Daily Reflector, 320
Daily Register, 293, 298
Daily Report, 289
Daily Reporter, 295-296, 298-299, 306, 312, 322
The Daily Reporter, 342
Daily Republican Register, 293
The Daily Republic, 332
Daily Reveille, 301
Daily Review, 301, 330
Daily Review Atlas, 293
Daily Rocket-Miner, 343
Daily Sentinel, 274, 318
Daily Sentinel Star, 309
The Daily Sentinel-Review, 347
Daily Sentinel-Tribune, 322
The Daily Sentinel, 324, 336
Daily Shipping News, 327
Daily Siftings Herald, 275
Daily Sitka Sentinel, 274
Daily Southerner, 321
Daily Southtown, 292
Daily Sparks Tribune, 313
Daily Spectrum, 338
Daily Standard, 322
Daily Star, 301, 318
Daily Statesman, 309
Daily Sun, 290
Daily Sun Post News, 280
Daily Sundial, 279

Daily Tar Heel, 319
Daily Targum, 314
Daily Telegram, 305
The Daily Telegram, 343
Daily Territorial, 275
The Daily Texan, 334
The Daily Tidings, 326
Daily Times, 293, 303, 315, 319
Daily Times Chronicle, 305
Daily Times Leader, 309
The Daily Times On Line, 284
Daily Times-News, 319
The Daily Times, 326
Daily Titan, 277
Daily Transcript, 283, 305
Daily Tribune, 307, 343
Daily Tribune News, 289
Daily Tribune-Matagorda County, 334
Daily Trojan, 278
Daily Union, 299
The Daily Universe, 337
Daily Variety, 278
Daily Vidette, 293
Daily Whale, 285
Daily World, 275, 302
The Daily World, 340
Daily Yomiuri, 317
DAK, 140
Dakota News Inc, 64
Dalhart Daily Texan, 334
Dallas Child, 193
Dallas Health & Fitness Magazine, 193
Dallas Morning News, 334
Dallas Observer, 360
The Dalles Chronicle, 327
Dan Semi, Representative, 70
Dance Book Club, 120
Dance Magazine, 238
The Dance Mart, 140
Dancing Dragon Catalog, 140
Dangerous Visions, 140
Daniel Publishing Group, 399
Daniel Smith Catalog, 140
Danner's Book End, 105
Danville News, 328
Danville News Agency, 66
Danville Register and Bee, 339
Darcy Williamson/South Cross Pub, 29
Darian Direct, 374
Darlin Library Book Services, 29
Dartek Computer Supply Catalog, 140
Dartmouth, 313
The Dartmouth Bookstore Inc, 110
Dartnell, 399
Das Book Haus, 113
Dasher Inc, 399
Data, 435-436
Data Based Advisor, 238
Data Based Lists, 399
Data Command, 140
Data Marketing Group Ltd, 399
Database America Companies Inc, 399
Database Management, 399, 451
Database Programming & Design, 259
Database Publishing Co, 399
Databases (directories), 451
Datalizer Slide Charts Inc, 439
Datamation, 193
The Datamation Bookshelf, 140
Datapulse, 399
Datasystem Solutions Inc, 81
Datasystem Solutions Inc, 436
Dateline Journal, 357
Dave Hoff & Associates, 70
David C Cook Dist, 52
David Lantzer, Representative, 70
David R Replogle and Assoc, 374

David X Manners Company, 366
Davidson College Bookstore, 112
Davidson School Catalog, 140
Davis Enterprise, 277
Davis-Kidd Booksellers, 87
Davison Publishing Co Inc, 399
Davka Hebrew/Judaic Software, 140
DAW Books, 126
Dawn Distributors, 52
Dawn Sign Press, 29
Day, 285
Dayton Daily News, 323
Dayton Voice, 359
Dayton-Hudson Book Depts, 95
dBase Advisor, 194
DBMS, 194
DBMS, 239
DCC Data Service Inc, 399
DCI List Management, 399
DDDD Publications, 380
De Queen Daily Citizen, 275
De Ru's Fine Art Books, 29
De Soto Sun Herald, 286
De Ville Books and Prints, 106
Dealernews, 239
Dealerscope Merchandising, 239
Dearborn Trade, 13
DEC Direct, 140
DECA Dimensions, 194
Decatur Daily, 273
Decatur Daily Democrat, 294
Decatur DeKalb News Era, 353
Decatur Herald & Review, 292
DeChant & Huges Assoc Inc, 366
Decision Data Direct, 140
Decor Magazine, 239
The Decorah Journal, 353
Decorative Artist's Workbook, 194
Decorative Arts Painting, 194
Decoy Magazine, 194
Defense Daily, 338
Dehoff Publications, 29
Del Rey Books, 126
Del Rio News-Herald, 334
Delaware County Daily Times, 327
Delaware Gazette, 323
Delaware State News, 285
Delicious, 194
Delivery service, 436
Dell Computer Corp, 140
Delphos Daily Herald, 323
Delta Democrat-Times, 309
Deming Headlight, 315
Democrat and Chronicle, 318
Democrat-News, 310
Democratic Left, 194
Denali Press Co-op Mailings, 380
The Denali Press, 399
Deneuve, 194
The Denison Herald, 334
Dental Economics & Proofs, 259
Denton Record-Chronicle, 334
Denver Business Journal, 351
Denver Post, 284
Department stores, 94-95
Department Stores/Mail Order Firms, 460
Dependable Lists Inc, 399
Depot Bookstore & Cafe, 100
Derby Square Bookstore, 107
Derrick, 329
Derry Dale Press, 29
Derus Media Service, 366
Des Moines Register, 297
Descant, 239
Deseret Book Club, 120
Deseret Book Company (Retail), 90
Deseret Book Distribution Center, 29

The Deseret News, 337
Desert Dispatch, 276
Desert Mailer News, 350
Desert Moon Periodicals, 29
Desert News, 55
Desert News Company, 56
Desert Sentinel, 349
Desert Skies, 194
Design Book Review, 194
Design Fax, 239
Design News, 239
Design Originals, 140
Designer Direct Returns, 385
Destination Discovery, 194
Destiny Image Catalog, 140
Details Magazine, 194
Detective Book Club, 120
Detroit Free Press, 306
Detroit Legal News, 306
Detroit Monitor, 355
Detroit Monthly, 194
Detroit News, 306
Devan Direct Marketing Inc, 438
Devils Lake Daily Journal, 321
DeVorss Book Distributors, 13
DG Direct, 140
Diabetes Self-Management, 194
Dial-An-Expert: The National Directory of Quotable Experts, 452
The Dialogue, 352
Diamond Art & Crafts, 29
Diamond Comic Distributors, 5
Diamondback, 303
The Diamond, 194
Diane Glynn Publicity and PR, 366
Diane Jackson, Representative, 70
Dianne's Do's and Don'ts, 194
Diario Las Americas, 287
Dick Blick Central, 140
Dickens Books Limited, 87
Dickinson Press, 321
Dickson's Bible Bookstores, 93
The Dictionary Catalogue, 140
Diesel: A Bookstore, 100
A Different Light Review, 141
Diffusion Dimedia Inc, 52
Diffusion Soussan Edilivre Inc, 52
Digest, 352
Digital PC Catalog, 141
Digital Video Magazine, 194
Dilley Manufacturing Co, 438
Dimension 5, 125
Dinosaur Times, 194
Dir of College Stores Interested in Hosting Authors for Campus.., 447
Dir of Health Care Strategic Mgmt/Communications Consultants, 459
Direct Communications Corp, 399
Direct Magazine, 239
Direct Mail Advertising Corp, 399
Direct Male Card Pack, 385
Direct Marketing, 270
Direct Marketing Assn, 399
Direct Marketing Enterprises Inc, 399
Direct Marketing Library, 141
Direct Marketing List Source, 399
Direct Marketing Market Place, 457
Direct Marketing Success Letter, 270
Direct Marketing Technology Inc, 399
Direct Media Inc, 399
Direct Media News, 270
Direct Micros, 71
Direct Promotions, 439
Direct Response Communication, 270
Directions, 194
The DirectLink Inc, 81

Directories in Print, 445
Directories of authors, 444
Directories of publishers, 446-448
Directories on CD-ROM, 453
Directors Guild Lists, 399
Directors of Religious Education, 385
Directory Marketplace, 141
Directory of Aging Resources, 453
Directory of Alternative and Radical Publications, 453
Directory of American Poets and Fiction Writers, 444
Directory of American Youth Organizations, 457
Directory of Business & Financial Information, 445
Directory of Business Information Resources, 450, 453
Directory of Ethnic Periodicals, 453
Directory of Federal Libraries, 451
Directory of Festivals, Sports & Special Events, 419
Directory of Funparks & Amusements, 460
Directory of Insert Programs, 385
Directory of Little Magazines & Small Presses, 447
Directory of Mail Order Catalogs, 449
Directory of Mailing List Co, 399
Directory of Medical Specialists, 459
Directory of North American Fairs, Festivals and Expositions, 419
Directory of Online Databases, 450
Directory of Periodicals of Interest to the Health Industry, 453
Directory of Periodicals Online, 453
Directory of Poetry Publishers, 447
Directory of Political Newsletters, 453
Directory of Portable Databases, 450
Directory of Post Secondary Inst, 460
Directory of Printers, 450
Directory of Publications Resources, 445
Directory of Special Libraries and Information Centers, 451
Directory of Top Computer Executives, 459
Directory of Video, Multimedia & Audio Visual Equipment, 450
Directory of Wholesale Reps for Craft Professionals, 461
Directory Strategies, 194
Directory World, 239
Dirmark Business Lists, 399
Disability Bookshop Catalog, 141
Disability Marketing Group, 380, 399
Discount & General Merchandise Stores, 460
Discount Boating Supplies, 141
Discount Master Animal Care, 141
Discount Store News, 239
Discoveries, 194
Discovery - Allstate Motor Club, 194
Discrimination & Prejudice, 445
Disk World Inc, 141
Diskette Gazette Catalog, 141
Disks & Labels To Go Inc, 141
Disney Adventures, 194
The Disney Catalog, 141
Dispatch, 277, 293, 320
Dispensa-Matic Label Dispensers, 437
Displays, 436-437
Distributed Art Publishers, 13
Distribution, 239
Distributors - exclusive and non-exclusive, 3-10
Distributors Nueva Vida, 29
The distributors, 29
Diversion, 195

Dixie News Co, 62, 64
Dixon Telegraph, 292
DM News, 270, 399
DMA Annual Conference/Exhibition, 415
DMA Publications Catalog, 141
DMB National Conference, 415
DMCA Direct, 399
DMG Lists Ltd, 399
DMGT, 436
DMR International, 29
DO-IT-YOURSELF-RETAILING, 239
Doctor's Complete Guide to Pediatric Hotlines and Resources, 457
Doctor's Practice Card Deck, 385
Doctors Foster & Smith Catalog, 141
Document Processing Technology, 239
Dodds Book Shop, 100
Dodge City Daily Globe, 299
Dodge Construction News, 292
Dodge Construction News Green Sheet, 279
The Dog & Cat Book Catalog, 141
Dog Fancy, 195
Dog World, 195
Doll Collector Price Guide, 195
Doll Reader, 195
Doll World, 195
Dolls, 195
Dollspart Supply Co Inc, 141
Dolphin Bookshop, 111
Dolphin Log, 195
Dominion-Post, 341
Don Jagoda Associates, 374
Don Olson Distribution, 29
Donnelley Marketing, 399
Doolco, 141
Doormouse Distributing, 52
Dorf & Stanton, 366
DOS Resource World, 195
Dot Gibson Distributors, 5
Dothan Eagle, 273
Doubleday Book Club, 120
Doubleday Childrens' Book Club, 120
Doubleday List Marketing, 399
Doubletake, 195
Doug Ross Communications, 400
Dougherty and Associates, 366
Douglas County Sentinel, 289
Dover News Agency, 29
Dover Pictorial Archive Catalog, 434
Dowagiac Daily News, 306
Down East Magazine, 195
Down Syndrome Today, 195
Downing Displays Inc, 436
Downtown Book Center Inc, 29, 103
Downtown News, 350
Downtown News & Books, 105
Downtown Resident, 357
Doyen Literary Service, 374
Doyle Publishing Corp, 400
DP Directory Inc, 400
Dr Dobbs Journal of Software, 195
Dr MAC, 141
Dragich Auto Literature, 141
Dragon Magazine, 195
Drama-Logue, 350
Draugas, 292
Drawing Board Computer Supply, 141
Drawing Board Full Line Catalog, 141
DRB Motors Catalog, 141
DRC Associates, 436
Dream Merchant Magazine, 195
Dream Network, 195
DreamHaven Books & Art, 13, 142
The Dresback Company, 366
Dresden Direct Inc, 400
Drown News Agency, 57

Drug Store and HBC Chains, 461
Drug Store News, 239
Drum Business, 239
Dryden Sales Company, 71
DSD Associates Inc, 438
DSD List Services, 400
DTP Direct, 142
Du Quoin Evening Call, 292
Dufour Editions, 13
Duke Communications Intl, 385
Duke Hill, Martin Associates, 72
Duluth News-Tribune, 307
Dun's Educational Directory, 400
The Duncan Banner, 325
Duncraft, 142
Dunhill International List Co, 400
Dunn's Supply, 142
Duplication, 437
Durango Herald, 284
Durant Daily Democrat, 325
Durham Herald Sun, 320
Durkin Hayes Publishing Ltd, 13, 125
Dustbooks Mailing Lists, 400
Dusty Hawkins & Associates, 71
Dutton & Associates, 71
Dutton's Books, 100
Dydacomp Development Corp, 438
Dyersville Commercial, 354
Dynamic Graphics Inc, 435

E

E & B Marine, 142
E A Prince & Son, 64
E Bruce Harrison Co, 367
E C S Publishing, 29
E F Schumacher Society, 142
E for Environment, 445
E Magazine, 195
E-Fax Communications Inc, 436
E-K Video Inc, 437
E/J Bloom Associates, 142
Eagle Books, 142
Eagle Creek X-Pressions, 434
Eagle Herald, 342
Eagle Publications, 400
Eagle Publishing List Marketing, 400
Eagle Times, 313
Eagle's View Publishing, 13
Eagle-Gazette, 323
Eagle-Tribune, 304
Eaglecrafts Inc, 29
Eagles Talent Associates, 377
Early American Life, 195
Early Childhood Catalog, 142
Early Childhood Special Needs, 385
Earth Guild Catalog, 142
Earth Magazine, 195
Earth Song Bookstore, 100
Earthlight Bookstore, 116
Earthling Bookshop, 100
Earthwatch Magazine, 195
Eas'l Publications, 29
East Bay Books, 100
East Bay Express, 349
East Kentucky News, 59
East Oregonian, 327
East Texas Distributing, 56, 65
East West Market Exchange, 142
East West Room, 29
East-West List Corp, 400
Eastern Book Company, 29
Eastern Direct Marketing Inc, 400
Eastern Mountain Sports, 95

Eastern Natl Park/Monument Assn, 90
Eastern News Distributors Inc, 5
Easton News Co, 64
Easton Star Democrat, 303
Eastside Records, 98
EastSide Weekend Newsmagazine, 359
The Eastsider, 352
Eastwind Books & Gallery, 30
The Eastwood Company, 142
Easy Reader, 350
Eating Well, 195
Eaton & Son Book Peddlers Inc, 90
Eaton's Department Stores, 95
Ebony, 195
EBS Book Service, 30
EBSCO Industries, 81
EBSCO Telemarketing, 374
ECA Co-op Publishers Exhibits, 420
Echo Plastic Systems Inc, 434
Ecocenters Corporation, 440
Ecological Book Club, 120
Economical Wholesale Co, 30
The Economist, 195
Ed Burnett Consultants, 400
Ed Hurt, Representative, 71
Ed-Pak Publishing, 385
Eddie Bauer, 142
Eden Daily News, 320
Edge, 196
Edges: Journal of American Knife Collecting, 196
EDI World, 239
Ediciones Universal, 30
Edinburg Daily Review, 335
Edit Ink, 439
Edith Roman Assoc Inc Database, 451
Edith Roman Associates, 400
Editor & Publisher, 239
Editor and Publisher Co, 400
Editor and Publisher Yearbook, 453
Editor's Choice Catalog, 142
Editor's Digest, 196
Editorial calendar, 451
Editorial Cernuda Corp, 30
Editorial Eye, 259
EDK Forecast, 270
Edmaro's Inc, 400
Edmond Evening Sun, 325
Edmonton Journal, 344
Edmonton Sun, 344
Edmund Scientific, 142
Edna Hibel Studio, 30
EDPACS: EDP Audit/Control/Security, 259
EDSA Trade Show, 418
Edu-Tech Corporation, 30, 169
Educalc, 142
Educated Traveler, 196
Education Daily, 338
Education Data Services, 400
Education Digest, 259
Education Mailings Clearinghouse, 400
Education Week, 239
Educational Book Distributors, 30
Educational Dealer, 239
Educational Development Corp, 30
Educational Directories Inc, 400
Educational Leadership, 259
Educational Marketer, 239
Educational Materials Catalog, 142
Educational Resources, 142
Educational Spectrums Catalog, 142
Educorp Software Catalog, 143
Edward Weston Graphics Inc, 30
Edwardsville Intelligencer, 292
EE Product News, 239
EEI List Services, 400
Eerdmans Publishing, 71

Effective Promotions, 440
Effingham Daily News, 292
Egghead Software, 143
Either/Or Bookstore, 100
El Cajon Daily Californian, 277
El Diario la Prensa, 317
El Dorado News-Times, 275
El Dorado Times, 299
El Heraldo de Brownsville, 334
El Manana Daily, 292
El Nuevo Herald, 287
El Paso Herald-Post, 335
El Paso Times, 335
El Qui-Jote Book Inc, 30
El Segundo Herald, 350
Elder's Bookstore, 30
Elderly Instruments, 143
Eldersong Publications, 143
Eldorado Daily Journal, 292
Eleanor Friede Books Inc, 13
Eleanor L Stark Co Inc, 400
Electric Consumer, 196
Electric Light & Power, 239
Electrical Wholesaling, 239
The Electricity Daily, 340
Electronic Arts Intermix, 5
Electronic Business Buyer, 239
Electronic Buyers News, 239
Electronic Design, 240
Electronic Distribution Today, 240
Electronic Engineering Times, 259
Electronic Entertainment, 196, 240
Electronic Information Report, 240
Electronic Media, 240
Electronic News, 240
Electronic Products, 259
Electronic Retailing, 240
Electronic Servicing/Technology, 240
Electronics, 240
Electronics Book Club, 120
Electronics Engineers' Book Club, 120
Elegant Bride, 196
Elementary Co-op, 380
Elizabeth City News, 62
Elizabethon Star, 332
Elk City Daily News, 325
Elkay Publishing Services, 374
Elkhart Truth, 294
Elko Daily Free Press, 312
Elks Magazine, 196
Elle, 196
Elle Decor, 196
Ellery Queen Mystery Magazine, 196
Elliott Bay Book Co, 116
Ellis Distributors, 30
Ellwood City Ledger, 328
ELS (Estee List Services Inc), 400
Elsevier Business Lists, 400
Ely Daily Times, 312
Elyria Chronicle, 323
EMDS, 439
Emergency Librarian, 174
Emery-Pratt Company, 30
Emmy Magazine, 196
Emory-Prosser-Seager, 71
Empire Books, 143
Empire News of Jamestown, 62
Empire Publishing Service, 5, 169
Empire State News, 61
Empire State Report, 196, 240
Employee Assistance Quarterly, 259
Emporia Gazette, 299
The Enchanted Doll House, 143
Encore Books, 52, 111
Encore Bookstore, 116
Encyclopedia of Associations, 457

Encyclopedia of Associations - National, 453
Encyclopedia of Business Information Sources, 457
Encyclopedia of Health Information Sources, 457
Encyclopedia of Medical Organizations and Agencies, 457
Encyclopedia of Physical Science/Engineering Information Sources, 457
Encyclopedia of Senior Citizens Information Sources, 457
Energy Daily, 286
The Energy Times, 196
Enertex Marketing, 400
Engineering Times, 259
The English Journal, 240
English Literature & Reading, 143
Enid News and Eagle, 325
The Ennis Daily News, 335
Enquirer-Journal, 320
Enterprise Communications, 196
Enterprise Ledger, 273
Enterprise Sun, 304
Enterprise-Journal, 309
Entertainment directories, 125
Entertainment Marketing Letter, 259
Entertainment Weekly, 196
Entrepreneur, 196
Entrepreneur Response Path, 385
Entrepreneur's Bookshop Catalog, 143
Envelopes, 437
Environment, 196
Environment Today, 240
Environmental Action, 196
Environmental Business Journal, 196
Environmental Media Corporation, 143
Environmental Protection, 240
EPI Fulfillment, 81
Epsilon Management Systems Inc, 81
Equal Opportunity Publications, 196
Erehwon Mountain Outfitters, 95
Eric Chaim Kline Bookseller, 30
Erickson Marketing, 71
Erie Times-News, 328
Errett Stuart Associates Inc, 71
ESCAPE, 196
Esquire, 196
Essence, 196
Essential Lists, 400
Essex Journal, 357
Estate Planning, 259
Estee List Services Inc, 400
Estherville Daily News, 297
ET Valueline, 143
ETD Gulf Coast Dist Div, 57
ETD Kromar, 65
ETD Mid-Atlantic Distributors, 30
Eternelle, 196
ETR Associates, 400
Ettlinger Editorial Projects, 13
Euclid Sun Journal, 358
Eugene Chernin Company, 30
Eugene Weekly, 360
Euro Sport Car, 197
European Book Company, 30
European Car, 197
Evangelical Book Club, 120
Evansville Courier, 294
Evansville Press, 295
Evening Guide, 347
Evening Herald, 330
The Evening Independent, 323
The Evening Leader, 324
Evening News, 307
The Evening News, 295

Evening Observer, 316
Evening Review, 323
Evening Star, 294
Evening Sun, 318, 328
Evening Telegram, 316, 345
Evening Times, 276, 316, 330
Evening Tribune, 316
Evening World, 294
Event Horizon Press, 13
Event World, 240
Everett Herald, 340
Evergreen Books, 107
Evergreen Marketing, 400
The Evergreen, 340
EveryBody's News, 359
Everyday Men, 197
EWA Miniature Cars USA, 143
Ex Libris, 100
Examiner-Enterprise, 325
The Examiner, 346-347
Excaliber Publishing Company, 380
Excalibur Hobbies Ltd, 30
Executive Action Card Deck, 385
Executive Books, 30
Executive Denver Magazine, 197
Executive Enterprises Inc, 400
Executive Excellence, 259
Executive Feedback, 197
Executive Female, 197
Executive Merchandise Card Pack, 385
Executive Products & Services, 385
Executive Summary/CA Education, 197
Exercise for Men Only, 197
Exhibit Promotions Plus, 420
The Exhibit Review, 270
Exhibitor Magazine, 270
Exhibits Directory, 419
Exhibits services, 419-420
Expand Display Information, 436
Expansion Management, 240
The Explicator, 259
Explorer, 197
Expo Concepts Inc, 436
EXPO-LIT, 143
The Expositer, 346
Exposure Display Systems, 436
Exposures Catalog, 143
ExpoSystems, 436
Express, 329
Express Book Freight, 82
Express Direct, 143
The Express-Times, 328
Expressions, 197
Eye On Education, 13
Eyecare Business, 240

F

F A O Schwartz Stores, 95
F.E.P. Inc, 31
F.I.S. Marketing Inc, 385
FAC Services Group, 374
Faces: The Magazine About People, 197
Facilities Design & Management, 240
Facilities management Deck, 385
Facilities Planning News, 240
Facsimile Users' Directory, 451
Fact & Fiction, 109
Facts and Fictions, 100
Fae Labels, 437
Faherty & Associates Inc, 71
Fair Street Productions, 13
Fairbanks News Agency, 55
Fairborn Daily Herald, 323

Fairchild Books & Visuals, 143
Fairfax Journal, 339
Fairfield Book Service Inc, 31
Fairfield County Weekly, 352
Fairfield County Woman, 197
Fairfield Daily Republic, 277
The Fairfield Ledger, 298
Fairfield Marketing Group, 400
Fairfield Weekly Reader, 354
The Faith Mountain Company, 143
FALCON Magazine, 197
Falcon Press Publishing, 13
Fall River Herald-News, 304
Fall River News, 60
Fallon Eagle Standard, 312
Family Bookstores, 91
Family Circle, 197
Family Features Editorial Serv, 367
Family Fun Magazine, 197
Family Handyman, 197
Family Life, 197
Family Motor Coaching, 197
Family Practice Management, 259
Family Software, 143
Family Times, 197
Family Travel Guides Catalogue, 143
FamilyFun, 197
Fancy Food Magazine, 240
Fangoria Horror in Entertainment, 197
Fantaco Enterprises Inc, 13
Fantasy & Science Fiction, 197
Fantasy Etc, 144
Far Corner Books, 13
Far West Book Service, 31
Fargo Forum, 321
Faribault Daily News, 308
Farley's Bookshop, 113
Farm Chemicals, 259
Farm Fresh Stores, 95
Farm Industry News, 240
Farm Journal, 240
Farmer's Digest, 240
Faro House, 169
Farrar Straus & Giroux, 14
Fasano & Associates, 401
FASHE Magazine, 197
Fashion Reporter, 197
Fat Girl Magazine, 198
FATE Magazine, 198
Fawcett Books, 126
Fax directories, 451
Fax USA, 451
The Faxon Company, 31
Faxon-SMS Canada, 52
Fay's Drug Stores, 95
Fayetteville Observer & Times, 320
FDA Consumer, 240
FDR List Management, 401
Featherlite Exhibits, 436
Federal Computer Week, 259
Federal Times, 361
Feedstuffs, 240
Fellow Travelers, 71
Feminist Bookstore News, 174
Fenton Independent, 355
Fergus Falls Daily Journal, 308
Ferrari's Places for Men, 457
Ferrari's Places for Women, 457
Fiarbanks Daily News-Miner, 274
Fiberarts, 198
Fickes Crime Fiction, 144
Fidelity Products, 385
Field, 198
Field & Stream, 198
Fig Garden Bookstore, 100
Filipinas, 198
Film Comment, 198

Film Directors Guide, 125
Film Masters Inc, 434
Film Producers Studios & Agents, 125
Film Quarterly, 198
Filmmakers Library, 5
Finance & Commerce, 308
Financial Automation Technology, 385
Financial Planners Card Pack, 385
Financial World, 198
Financial World Response Pack, 385
Find Catalog/SVP, 144
Fine Cooking, 198
Fine Gardening, 198
Fine Homebuilding, 241
Fine Print Distributors, 5
Fine Woodworking, 241
Finger Lake Times, 316
Firefighters Bookstore, 144
Firefly Book Club, 120
Firefly Books Ltd, 9
Fireside Bookstore, 116
Fireside Theatre, 120
First Editions Coop Mailings, 380
First Editions Mailing Lists, 401
First Financial Response, 401
First for Women, 198
First Glance Books, 14
First Impressions, 367
First Visit, 198
First Wall Streeter, 386
First Year of Life, 198
Firstmark, 401
Fisheries Product News, 241
Fitness, 198
The Five Owls, 198
Five Star Speakers Trainers & Consultants, 377
Flagpole Magazine, 352
Flannery Company, 31
Flash Magazine, 241
Flax Artists Materials, 144
Fleetwood Communications, 401
Fleming Museum, 31
Flin Flon Reminder, 345
Flint Journal, 306
FloraCulture International, 241
Floral Management, 241
Floral Mass Marketing, 241
Florence Morning News, 331
Florida Educational Paperbacks, 31
Florida Flambeau, 288
Florida Game & Fish, 198
Florida Living, 198
Florida News Media Directory, 453
Florida School Book Depository, 31
Florida Times Union, 287
Florida Today, 287
Florida Trend, 198
Flower & Garden, 198
Flower & Garden Book Service, 144
Flower News, 241
Fluid Power Service Center, 241
Fly Fisherman, 198
Flying, 260
Flynn & Talley Associates, 71
Flynn Direct Response Inc, 401
FMP List Services Inc, 401
Focus on Autistic Behavior, 260
Focus On Books Card Pack, 386
Focus on the Family, 198
Focus USA, 401
Foga Systems, 436
Folder Factory, 440
Folio Weekly, 352
Folio:, 241
Folio: Action Cards, 386
Follett College Stores, 93

Follett Library Resources, 31
Fond du Lac Reporter, 342
Font & Function Catalog, 144
Food & Beverage Marketing, 241
Food & Wine, 198
Food Arts, 241
Food Marketing Inst Convention, 418
Food Merchandising/Non-Food Retailing, 241
Food Products Press Catalog, 144
Food Service Action Cards, 386
FoodService Director, 241
Foodservice Distributors, 461
Football Digest, 198
Forbes, 199
Foreign book shows, 417-418
Foreign Trade Magazine, 241
Forest Sales & Distributing, 31
Forests and People, 241
Forever After, 100
Formula Magazine, 199
Forsyth Travel Library Inc, 5
Fort McMurray Today, 344
Fort Morgan Times, 284
Fort Myers News-Press, 287
Fort Scott Tribune, 299
Fort Wayne Journal-Gazette, 295
Fort Worth Child Magazine, 199
Fort Worth Commercial Recorder, 335
Fort Worth Star-Telegram, 335
Fortson Communications, 367
Fortune, 199
Forty-Eight States News Dist Co, 5
Forum of Women in Higher Education, 199
Forum Publishing Company, 14
Foster & Foster, 434
Foster's Daily Democrat, 313
Foundry Management & Technology, 241
Fountain Hills Bookstore, 98
Four Seasons Books at Carnegies, 116
Four Wheel Drive & Sport Utility, 199
Four Wheeler, 199
Four Winds Trading Company, 31
Fox & Sutherland Stationery, 111
FoxPro Advisor, 199
Foxwood International Ltd, 169
Francis Kuykendall's Press, 31
Franciscan Shops, SFSU, 100
Frank Mittermeier Catalog, 144
Frank Promotion Corp, 367
Frank Rizzo & Associates, 71
Frankfurt Book Fair, 417
Franklin Banner-Tribune, 301
Franklin Book Company, 31
Franklin Distributors Corp, 401
Franklin Marketeers, 71
Franklin Sun, 354
Fraser Management & Publications, 31
Frazier Mountain Books, 100
FRC Combined Book Exhibit, 420
Fred B Rothman and Co, 31
Fred E Allen Inc, 401
Fred F Rapaport Convert Printed Directories, 451
Fred L Saddy Books, 31
Fred Rosen Associates, 367
Fred Singer Direct Marketing Inc, 401
Fred Woolf List Co Inc, 401
Freddy's Feed & Read, 110
Frederick Leader, 325
Frederick News, 303
Frederick Post, 303
Free Circulation Community Papers, 453
Free Inquiry, 199
Free Lance, 277
The Free Lance-Star, 339

Free Press, 308
Free Press (Adair County), 354
Free Software Foundation, 438
Free Spirit Magazine, 199
Free Spirit Publishing, 14
Freebies, 199
Freeport Journal-Standard, 293
Fremont Argus, 277
Fremont Tribune, 312
French & European Publications, 31
Frequent Flyer, 199
Fresh Start, 199
Fresno Bee, 277
Frey Scientific, 144
Friendly Exchange, 199
The Friend, 199
Frog Tool Company, 144
Front Page Book & News, 108
Frontline Distribution Intl, 31
Fujii Associates, 71
Fulco Inc, 82
Fulfillit, 438
Fulfillment services, 81-83
Fuller Associates, 71
Fulmont News Company, 61
Fulton Sun, 309
Funaro Lufrano Associates, 82
Fund Raising Management, 241
Funny Side Up, 144
Funny Times, 199
Furniture/Today, 241
Future Visions Books, 144
Future World Corporation, 144
Futures Magazine, 241
Futurific Magazine, 241
Futurist Bookstore Catalog, 144
FYI Directory of News Sources, 380

G

G C T Catalog, 144
G Neil Companies Catalog, 144
Gaan Computer Supplies, 144
Gadsden Times, 273
Gage Distribution Co, 82
Gaia Communications, 367
Gail Leondar Public Relations, 367
Gainesville Daily Register, 335
Gainesville Sun, 287
Gainesville Times, 289
Gaithersburg Gazette, 355
Gale Directory of Publications and Broadcast Media, 453
Gale Research Catalog, 144
GaleLists, 401
Galesburg Register-Mail, 293
Galion Inquirer, 323
Gallery, 199
Gallery Bookshop, 100
Gallipolis Daily Tribune, 323
Gallup Distributing, 61
Gallup Independent, 315
Galveston County Daily News, 335
Gam Printers, 437
Gambit Weekly, 354
Gambler's Book Club, 144
Gamblers World Catalog, 145
Game Informer, 199
Game-Show Placements, 374
Games Magazine, 199
Gander Mountain, 145
Gannette Suburban Newspapers, 319
Gannon Distributing Co, 32
Garcia Street Books, 111

Garden City Telegram, 299
Garden Design, 199
Garden Gate Magazine, 199
The Garden Island, 290
Garden Literature: An Index, 445
The Garden of Beadin', 145
The Gardener's Book of Sources, 447
Gardener's Eden, 145
Gardener's Marketplace, 386
Gardener's Supply, 145
Gardening: A Guide, 445
Gardner News, 304
Garfield-Maple Sun, 359
Garrett Book Co, 32
Garrett Park Press Mailing Lists, 401
Gary and Riedel Co, 71
Gary Post-Tribune, 295
Gary Trim Associates, 72
Gas Daily, 338
Gaston Gazette, 320
Gateway Magazine, 199
Gaughen Public Relations, 367
Gay Bowles Sales, 32
Gay Community News, 199
Gayellow Pages, 445
Gaze, 199
Gazette Telegraph, 283
The Gazette, 297
Geary's Catalog, 145
Gem Guides Book Company, 14
Genealogical and Local History, 445
Genealogical Sources Unlimited, 5
General Aviation News & Flyer, 241
General News & Novelty Co Ltd, 68
General Publishing Company, 14
Genesee Country Museum, 112
Genesis, 199
Genesis Marketing Group, 72
Genetic/Soc/Gen Psych Monographs, 260
Geneva International Fair, 417
Genium Publishing Corp, 145
Genre Magazine, 200
Gent, 200
Gentlemen's Quarterly, 200
George D Hall Co, 401
George R Klein News, 63
George Scheer Associates, 72
George Sterne Agency, 401
George-Mann Associates Inc, 401
The Georgia Review, 200
Georgia Sportsman, 200
Georgia Trend, 200
Gerald L Lewis Direct Mktg, 401
Gerard Hamon Inc, 32
German Town Paper, 360
Germanic Review, 260
Gerold International Booksellers, 32
Gerry Sales Company, 72
Gessler Educational Software, 145
Gessler Publishing Company, 14
Get-List, 401
Gettysburg Times, 328
Gift & Stationery Business, 241
Gift Basket Review, 241
Gift Books Catalog, 145
Gift Service Inc, 434
Gift, Housewares & Home Textiles, 461
Gifted Child Today, 200
Gifts & Decorative Accessories, 242
Giftware News, 242
Gilbert Tribune, 274
Gilpin Publishing Consultant, 374
Giovanni's Room, 32
Girard Home News, 360
Girls' Life, 200
Girol Books Inc, 14
GJ's Wholesale Hobbies/Crafts Inc, 32

Glamour, 200
Glasgow Daily Times, 300
Gleaner, 300
Gleason Group Inc, 14
Glenbow Shop, 52
Glendale News-Press Leader, 277
Glenridge Paper, 356
Glenwood Post, 284
Global Computer Supplies, 145
Global Direct Marketing Inc, 401
Global Issues Speakers Bureau, 377
Global Success Corp, 401
Global Trading Post, 145
Global Turnkey Systems Inc, 82
The Globe & Mail, 347
Globe Books, 116
Globe Pequot Press Inc, 14
Globe-Gazette, 298
Gloucester County Times, 314
Gloucester Daily Times, 304
GLP International, 5
GMB Partnership, 145
GMI/Uni-Mail Commercial, 401
Gnames Enterprises, 401
Gnosis: Journal of Western Inner
 Tradition, 200
Godard Stationery Stores, 88
The Godfrey Group Inc, 436
Goerings' Book Center, 104
Gold Eagle Books, 126
Gold Medal Hair Products, 401
Golden Apple Bookstores, 100
Golden Gate National Parks Assn
 Bookstores, 90
The Golden Harp of Joel Andrews, 145
Golden Sea Graphics, 440
Golden Triangle Periodical Dist, 65
Golden-Lee Book Distributors, 32
Goldmark Media Escorts, 367
Goldmine, 200
Goldwyn's List of Wine Media, 453
Golf Digest, 200
Golf Magazine, 200
Golf Pro, 242
Golf Shop Operations, 242
Golf Traveler, 200
Golf World, 200
The Golfer, 200
GolfSmart Catalog, 145
Good 5 Cent Cigar, 330
Good Apple Newspaper, 200
The Good Cook, 121
Good Fortune Marketing Inc, 401
Good Housekeeping Magazine, 200
Good Medicine, 200
Good News Book & Gift, 106
Good News Magazine Distributors, 32
Good Old Days, 200
Good Old Days Special, 200
Good Times!, 200, 242
Goodman Speakers Bureau, 377
Gooseberry Patch, 145
Gordon Law & Associates, 72
Gordon Soules Book Publishers, 20
Gordon's Booksellers, 88
Goshen News, 295
Gospel Advocate Bookstores, 93
Gospel Mission, 32
Gourmet Guides, 145
Gourmet Magazine, 200
The Gourmet Show, 418
Government Assistance Almanac, 457
Government Computer News, 242
Government Executive, 242
Government Products News, 242
Government Publications, 145
Goyescas Corporation of Florida, 32

Grace Company, 5
Grade Sch & High Sch Students, 386
Graham Maughan Co, 32
Graham's Book & Stationery, 88
Grail Foundation of America, 32
Granary Books, 14
Grand Forks Herald, 321
Grand Haven Tribune, 306
Grand Junction Daily Sentinel, 284
Grand Rapids Business Journal, 200
Grand Rapids Parent, 201
Grand Rapids Press, 306
Grand Street, 242
Granta, 201
Grants Pss Daily Courier, 327
Graphic Artist's Book Club, 121
Graphic Arts Blue Books, 450
Graphic Arts Center Pub, 72
Graphic Arts Monthly, 242
Graphic Arts Monthly Ad Cards, 386
Graphic Design USA, 242
Grass Valley Union, 277
Gray Areas, 201
Grayarc, 437
Great Bend Tribune, 299
Great Christian Books, 145
Great Falls Tribune, 311
Great Games Products, 145
The Great Kids Company, 145
Great Lakes Fulfillment, 401
Great Midwestern Bookshow, 415
Great Northern Distributors Co, 64
Great Outdoors-Dek, 386
Great Pacific News, 67
Great Plains Game & Fish, 201
Greater Baton Rouge Business Rpt, 201
Greater Talent Network, 377
Greeley Tribune, 284
Green Apple Books, 100
The Green Bay News-Chronicle, 342
Green Bay Press-Gazette, 342
Green Company Resource Guide, 450
Green Gate Books, 14
Green Lion Books, 108
Greenberg Public Relations, 367
Greene Bark Press, 14
The Greeneville Sun, 332
Greenfield Daily Times, 323
Greenhaven Press Library, 145
Greenhouse Business, 242
Greenhouse Grower, 201, 242
Greensburg Daily News, 295
The Greenville Herald Banner, 335
The Greenville News, 331
Greenwich Consultants, 401
Greenwich Time, 285
Greenwood Commonwealth, 309
Greeting Card Retailers Cards, 386
Greetings Magazine, 242
Gregg Associates, 72
Grey Owl Indian Craft Sales, 32
The Greyhound Review, 242
Greystone Services Inc, 401
Griffin Daily News, 289
Grit, 201
Grocery Marketing, 242
Groom and Board, 242
Grounds for Murder Newsletter, 145
Grounds Maintenance, 242
Group 1 Software, 401
Group Practice Journal, 242
Group Tech Catalog, 146
The Group Travel Leader, 242
Grower Talks Bookshelf, 146
GrowerTalks, 242
Growing Edge, 242
Gryphon House Inc, 14

Guadalajara Intl Book Fair, 417
Guaranteed Irish, 32
Guardian Book Company, 32
Guardian Evening Patriot, 348
Guelph Mercury, 346
Guidance, 146
Guidance Associates, 146
Guide Light, 146
Guide to Alternative Presses, 447
Guide to American Directories, 445
Guide to Art & Craft Workshops, 460
The Guide to Cooking Schools, 460
Guide to Disability Periodicals, 453
Guide to Golf Schools & Camps, 460
Guide to Literary Agents and Art/Photo Reps, 447
Guide to Photography Workshops, 460
Guide to Publishers/Distributors Serving Minority Languages, 447
Guide to Religious and Inspsirational Magazines, 453
Guide to Women Book Publishers, 447
The Guide to Writers Conferences, 460
Guideposts Magazine, 201
Guild America Books, 121
The Guild, 93
Gulf Coast News, 55
Gulf States Educational Books, 32
Gunnison County Times, 284
Gurze Eating Disorders Bookshelf, 146
Guthrie Daily Leader, 325
Guzzardo's, 88

H

H A Kidd Company Ltd, 52
H H Marshall Ltd, 67
H Kauffman & Sons Book Dept, 146
H N Miller Books, 14
H P Kopplemann Inc, 32
Hachette Magazines/List Mgmt, 402
Hacker Art Books Inc, 146
Hacketstown Forum, 357
Hadassah Magazine, 201
Haddon Lynch & Baughman PR, 367
Hagstrom Map & Travel, 146
Hal Copeland Company, 367
Haley's Comics, 32
Half Price Books, 91
Hall of Cards & Books Inc, 90
Hallenbook, 374
Hallmark Data Systems, 82
Hamilton News Co, 33
Hamilton Spectator, 346
Hammacher Schlemmer Catalog, 146
Hammond Publishing Co Inc, 33
Hammond's Antiques, 109
Hampton Books Catalog, 146
Hancock House Publishers, 14
Hand Associates, 72
Handcraft Illustrated, 201
HandGunning, 201
Handleman Co, 169
Handleman National Book Dist, 33
Handwoven, 201
Hanford Sentinel, 277
Hank Marshall Marketing Co, 402
Hanna Design Rochester Inc, 436
Hannibal Courier-Post, 310
Hanover House Catalog, 146
Hansen & Young PR Consultants, 367
Happiness, 201
The Happy Booker, 100
The Happy Bookseller, 114

Haranbee Books & Crafts, 33
Hard Money Digest, 386
Hard-to-Find Needlework Books, 146
Hardware Age, 242
Harlan Daily Enterprise, 300
Harlan Tribune, 298
Harlequin Romances, 126
Harper Collins, 14
Harper Collins Audio, 125
Harper's, 201
Harper's Bazaar, 201
Harriet Carter Gifts, 146
Harris Publishing Co, 402
Harrisburg News Company, 64
Harrison Daily Times, 275
Harrison Fulfillment Services, 82
Harrison Publishing Co Inc, 402
Harrowsmith Card Pack, 386
Harry Collins, Representative, 72
Harry W Schwartz Bookshop, 116
Harry Walker Agency, 377
Harsand Financial Press, 14
Hartford Advocate, 352
Hartford Courant, 285
Harvard Associates Inc, 14
Harvard Bookstores Inc, 107
Harvard Business Review, 201
Harvard Coop, 94
Harvard Cooperative Society, 107
Harvard Crimson, 303
Harvard Magazine, 201
Harvard Professional Lists Inc, 402
Harvard University Art Museum, 33
Harvest Book Shoppe, 113
Harvey International, 438
Hasings Books Music & Video, 91
Haslam's Book Store Inc, 104
Hastings Tribune, 312
Hatch's Inc, 88
Hattiesburg American, 309
Haunted Bookshop, 98
Hauser List Services Inc, 402
Haven Corp, 146
Haverhill Gazette, 304
Havre Daily News, 311
Hawaii All Media Publicity Guide, 453
Hawaii Geographic Maps/Books, 33
Hawaii Hochi, 290
Hawaii Natural History Assn, 90
Hawaii Tribune Herald, 290
The Hawk Eye, 297
Hay & Forage Grower, 242
Hayward Daily Review, 277
Hazelden Educational Materials, 146
HB Fenn & Company, 9
Headline Business Computer Syst, 82
Heald Business College Stores, 94
Heald Technical College Store, 94
Health & Natural Healing Card Pk, 386
Health & Safety Card Deck, 386
Health Foods Business, 242
Health Magazine, 201
Health Master, 146
Health News & Review, 201
Health News Daily, 303
Health Pack, 386
Health Pages, 201
Health Professionals Media Network, 367
Health World Inc, 201
Health/Physical Education, 386
Healthcare Financial Management, 270
Healthcare Forum Journal, 260
Healthkit, 146
Healthline, 201
Healthy Kids, 201
The Hearing Review, 243
Hearlihy & Co, 146

Hearst Business Lists Rentals, 402
Heart & Soul, 201
Heart of America Press, 33
Heart Of The Lakes Publishing, 14
Hearth & Home, 243
Hearth Song Inc, 146
Hearthside Books, 97
Heartland Ag-Business Group, 402
Heartland USA, 202
Heating/Piping/Air Conditioning, 243
Hedrick Journal, 354
Heinecken & Associates Ltd, 72
Heizer Software, 146
Heldref Publications, 402
Hello Direct Catalog, 147
Hemet News, 281
Hemisphere Marketing Inc, 402
Hemispheres Magazine, 202
Hemmings Motor News, 147
Henderson Daily Dispatch, 320
Henderson Daily News, 335
Henry J Hubert, 72
Henryetta Daily Free-Lance, 325
Herald, 285, 300, 353
Herald and News, 327
Herald House Publishing, 33
Herald Journal, 296, 353
The Herald Journal, 337
Herald Star, 324
Herald Statesman, 319
Herald-Citizen, 332
The Herald-Coaster, 336
Herald-Dispatch, 341
Herald-Journal, 318-319
Herald-Palladium, 307
Herald-Standard, 330
Herald-Times-Reporter, 342
The Herald-Times, 294
The Herald, 295, 330-331, 357
The Herb Companion, 202
Herb Quarterly, 202
HerbalGram, 243
Herbko International, 33
Hereford Brand, 335
Heritage Book News, 380
Heritage Books Inc, 147
Heritage Display Group, 436
Heritage House Publishing Co, 52
Herr's Inc, 33
Herrington, 147
Hershey's Gift Catalog, 147
Hervey's Book Link, 33
HFM List Management, 402
HI Marketing, 79
Hi-Riser, 352
Hi-Tech Public Relations, 367
Hiawatha Daily World, 299
The Hibbert Group, 82
Hibbing Daily Tribune, 308
Hickory Daily Record, 320
High Country News, 202
High Performance Mopar, 202
High Performance Pontiac, 202
High Point Enterprise, 320
High School Students Co-op, 380
High Tech Times, 386
High Times, 243
High Volume Independent Drug Stores, 461
High Volume Printing, 243
Highlander Company, 147
The Highlander, 202
Highlights for Children, 147, 202, 402
Highsmith Microcomputer Catalog, 147
Highways, 202
Hill & Knowlton, 367
Hill-City News Agency, 66

Hill/Martin Associates, 374
Hillsdale Daily News, 306
Hilsinger-Mendelson Inc, 367
Hilton Memory Seminar, 377
Hinduism Today, 202
Hippocrates, 260
Hispanic, 202, 386
Hispanic Americans Information Directory, 453
Hispanic Books Distributors Inc, 33
Hispanic Business, 202
Hispanic Media and Markets, 453
Hispanic Media USA, 453
Hispanic Resource Directory, 457
Hispanic USA, 202
Historic Aviation Books, 33
Historic Aviation Catalog, 147
Historic Cherry Hill, 33
Historic Methods, 260
Historic Traveler, 202
History Book Club, 121
History of Political Economy, 260
History: Reviews of New Books, 260
HMI Associates Inc, 402
Hobbs Daily News-Sun, 315
Hobby Merchandiser, 243
Hobbyquest Marketing, 33
Hockey Digest, 243
Hockey Illustrated, 202
Hofcraft Catalog, 147
Hohenstein Public Relations, 367
Hoke Communications Inc, 402
Hokubel Mainchi, 281
Hokulele Distributors, 33
Holcomb's Educational Materials, 95
Hold Everything Catalog, 147
Holdenville Daily News, 325
Holdrege Daily Citizen, 312
Holiday Enterprises Inc, 33
Holistic Living, 202, 243
Holland Sentinel, 306
Hollywood Citizen News, 350
Hollywood Creative Directory, 125
Hollywood Reporter, 278
Holyoke News Company, 60
Home & Away, 202
Home Center & Hardware Chains, 461
Home Cooking, 202
Home Economics Reading Service, 435
Home Furnishings Executive, 260
Home Furnishings Retailers and Distributors, 461
Home Furniture, 202
Home Garden Magazine, 202
Home Gym & Fitness, 243
Home Health Care Services Quarterly, 260
Home Magazine, 202
Home Mechanix, 202
Home News & Tribune, 313
Home Office Computing, 202
Home PC, 202
Home Reporter, 357
Homecoming Magazine, 203
Homeowners Marketing Services, 402
Homer News, 349
Homes Magazine, 203
Homestead Book Company, 33
Hong Kong International BookFair, 417
Honolulu, 203
Honolulu Advertiser, 290
Honolulu Book Shops, 88
Honolulu Star-Bulletin, 290
Honolulu Weekly, 353
Hoover Brothers Inc, 91
Hoover's Educational Catalog, 147
Hope Farm Press & Bookshop, 33
Hope Magazine, 203

Hope Star, 275
The Hopewell News, 339
The Horchow Collection, 147
Horizon Books, 108, 115
Horizons Catalog, 147
Horn Book Guide, 174
Horse & Horseman Magazine, 203
Horse & Rider, 203
Horse Illustrated, 203
Horsemen's Yankee Pedlar Newspaper, 243
HorsePlay, 203
Horses All, 243
Horticulture, 203
The Hospice Journal, 260
Hospital Blue Book, 457
Hospital Topics, 243
Hospitality Design, 243
Hot Bike, 203
Hot Boat, 203
Hot Rod Magazine, 203
Hotels, 243
Hotho & Co, 33
Hotline Education Responders, 386
Hotline Newsletter, 270
Hotline Postcard Deck, 386
Houma Daily Courier, 301
The Hour, 285
House Beautiful, 203
House of 1776 Catalog, 147
House of Fabrics / So-Fro Fabric, 95
House of Tyrol, 147
HousePlant Magazine, 203
Houston Business Journal, 203
Houston Chronicle, 335
Houston Community Papers, 360
Houston Health & Fitness Sports, 203
Houston Metropolitan, 203
Houston Press, 360
HOW Magazine, 243
How to Sell More/Today's Market, 147
How to Sell to Mail Order Catalogs, 449
Howard J Hall & Associates, 367
Howard Ramer & Associates, 72
Howard's Bookstore, 105
HP Direct Computer Users Catalog, 147
HP Kopplemann Inc, 147
HPK Language Arts Catalog 6-12, 147
HPK Language Arts Catalog K-8, 148
HR Action Cards, 386
HR Direct Inc, 402
HRMagazine, 243
HRNews, 243
Hubbard Co, 34
Hubert NDiaye Book Co, 148
Hudson News, 88
Hudson Valley Black Press, 358
Hudson Valley News Dist Inc, 34
Hudson's Subscription Newsletter Directory, 453
Hudson's Washington News Media, 453
Hudsons State Capital News Media, 453
The Huenefeld Company, 374
Hughes Communications Inc, 402
Hugo Daily News, 325
Human Events, 352
Human Resources Exec Magazine, 402
Human Resources Performance Pac, 386
The Humanist, 203
HUMOResources Bookstore Catalog, 148
Humpty Dumpty's Magazine, 203
Hungry Mind Bookstore, 108
Hungry Mind Review, 174
Hunter's Card Pack, 386
Huntington Herald-Press, 295
Huntsinger & Jeffer List Service, 402
The Huntsville Item, 335

Huntsville News, 273
Huntsville Times, 273
Huron Daily Tribune, 305
Hurriyet, 317
Husker News Company, 59
Hutchins & Associates, 82
Hutchinson News, 299
HVB List Promotions Inc, 402
Hydraulics & Pneumatics, 243

I Love Cats, 203
I-5 Associates, 72
Iaconi Book Imports, 56
IBD Ltd, 34
IBIS Information Services, 380
IBIS International Direct, 402
ICD/Hearst Corporation, 6
ICN, 82
Icon, 354
ICS Books Inc, 148
Ida County Courier, 354
Idaho Press-Tribune, 291
Idaho State Journal, 291
Idaho Statesman, 290
Idea Art, 434
Ideal Foreign Books, 34
Ideal School Supply, 34
Ideas Unlimited, 439
Identity Watch, 440
IDG List Services, 402
IEEE Computer Graphics & Apps, 260
IEEE Design & Test of Computers, 260
IEEE Expert, 260
IEEE Micro, 260
IEEE MultiMedia, 243
IEEE Software, 260
IEN Direct Response Cards, 386
Ife Book Fair, 417
IFS-Independent Fulfillment Serv, 82
IGL Direct, 402
Il Literature, 100
Illinois Game & Fish, 203
Illinois News Service, 58
Illinois Times, 353
Image Club Graphics Inc, 148
Image Club Software Catalog, 148
Image Watches Inc, 440
Images International, 367
Images Media Corporation, 15
Imagica Imaging Magic, 440
Imaginarium Stores, 95
Impact Books, 34
Impact Postcard Deck, 386
IMPCO Direct Response, 402
Imperial Valley Press, 277, 350
Imported Books, 34
Imprint Catalog, 380
Imprint Enterprises Inc, 438
Imprint Products, 438
In Business, 203
In Fashion, 203
In Motion, 243
In Pittsburgh Newsweekly, 360
In These Times, 203
In-Fisherman, 203
In-Line, 204
In-Plant Printer, 243
IN-TOUCH Direct, 436
Inc Magazine, 204
Inc Speakers Bureau, 377
Incentive Magazine, 243
Income Opportunities, 243

Income Plus, 204
Incor Periodicals, 34
INCORP Periodicals Inc, 63
Independence Daily Reporter, 299
Independence Examiner, 310
Independent, 312
Independent Agent, 243
Independent Booksellers, 97-117
Independent Business, 204
Independent distributors (jobbers), 55-68
Independent Energy Magazine, 244
Independent Florida Alligator, 287
Independent Living, 204
Independent Music Association, 15
Independent Press Catalog, 148
Independent Publishers Group, 6
Independent Publishers Marketing, 6
Independent Publishers Service, 420
Independent Record, 311
The Independent Weekly, 358
Index of Desktop Publishing, 445
The Index-Journal, 331
Indian America Postcard Deck, 386
Indiana Business, 204
Indiana Daily Student, 294
Indiana Game & Fish, 204
The Indiana Gazette, 328
Indiana Periodicals, 88
Indiana Periodicals Distributors, 58
Indiana Review, 204
Indiana University Bookstore, 105
Indianapolis News, 295
Indianapolis Star, 295
The Indigo Sun, 204
Individual Investor, 204
Industrial Computer Master Srcbk, 148
Industrial Computing, 244
Industrial Purchasing Agents, 244
Industry Week, 244
Indy's Child, 204
Info Marketing Report, 270
Infobase (Data Enhancement Serv), 402
InfoCision Management, 374
Infocore Inc, 402
Infocus Lists, 402
Infolists Inc, 402
InfoMat Inc, 402
Infomax Trading Corp, 169
Informat Inc, 402
Information Industry Directory, 457
Information Marketing Services, 403
Information MarketPlace, 447
Information Marketplace Director, 447
Information Systems Management, 260
Information Technology & Library, 174
Information Today, 260
InformationWeek, 260
Inforonics Inc, 438
Infosource Inc, 148
Ingham Publishing Inc, 34
Ingram Distribution Group Inc, 6
Ingram Micro, 34
Ingram Periodicals Inc, 34
Initio List Marketing Inc, 403
Ink Projects, 15
Inland Valley Daily Bulletin, 279
INMAC, 148
Inner-City Express, 279
Innovative Management Serv Inc, 403
INPEX, 418
Input Culture Company, 34
Inside, 353
Inside Media, 244
Inside PR, 244
Inside Sports, 204
Inside Track Publicity, 367
Inside Triathlon, 204

Insider's Guide to Book Editors Publishers & Literary Agents, 447
Insight Magazine, 204
InSights, 204
Instant/Small Commercial Printer, 244
Institute Lists, 403
Institute of Real Estate Mgmt, 403
Institutional Distribution, 244
InStyle, 204
Insurance Mktg & Mgmt Services, 387
INTECH, 261
Integrated Business Services, 403
Integrated Distribution Services, 82
Intelletronics, 148
Intelligencer, 342
Intelligencer-Record, 328
Inter - Livres, 52
The Inter-Mountain, 341
Interact Direct, 148
InterActivity, 261
Intergalactic Trading Co Inc, 34
Interior Design Magazine, 261
Internal Auditing Alert, 261
International Authors & Writers Who's Who, 444
International Book Centre, 34
International Book Distrib Inc, 6
International Book Fair/Belgrade, 417
International Business Lists Ltd, 403
International Children Book Fair, 417
International Direct Response, 403
International Directory of Children's Literature, 447
International distributors, 10
International Festival of Author, 415
International Housewares Expo, 418
International Imports, 34
International Literary MarketPlace, 448
International Management Group, 377
International Marine Deck, 387
International Marine Publishing, 148
International Media Directory, 454
International Musician, 261
International Periodical Dists, 6
International Press Publications, 20, 169
International Publisher Alliance, 380
International publishers, 20
International Railway Journal, 244
International representatives, 79
International Specialized Books, 6
International Titles, 420
International Wealth Success, 148
Internet Business Advantage, 451
Internet World, 204
INTERPUB, 374
Interstate Book Stores Inc, 106
Interstate Distributors, 60
Interstate Label Company, 438
Interstate Periodicals Dist Inc, 59, 66-67
Interstate Textbook Co, 34
Intertech Marketing Inc, 148
Interviews & Reviews, 380
Intimate Bookshop Inc, 88
Intl Book Fair of Mexico, 417
Intl Tradeshow Week Data Book, 419
Intrepid Productions, 82
Inventor's Digest, 204
Investment Information Services, 403
Investor's Advantage Action Card, 387
Investor's Business Daily, 204, 278
Invisible Ink: Books on Ghosts, 148
Iola Register, 299
Iowa Book & Supply, 106
Iowa City Press-Citizen, 298
Iowa Game & Fish, 204
Iowa Periodicals Inc, 59
Iowa State Daily, 297

IPM Practitioner, 261
IPP Shipping & Warehousing, 82
IPS Associates Catalog, 148
IQRA Book Center, 148
IRA (I Rent America), 403
Iranbooks Inc, 15
Irene Handberg International, 374
Irene Reichbach, 367
Irish America Magazine, 204
Irish Books and Media, 34
Irish Family, 148
Ironside International Publisher, 34
Ironton Tribune, 323
Ironwood Book Shop, 105
Ironwood Daily Globe, 306
Irvine World News, 350
Irvington Publishers Inc, 15
Irwin Professional Publishing, 15
Irwin Publishing, 15
Isaac Asimov Science Fiction, 204
Islamic Book Service, 34
The Island Packet, 331
Island Parent Magazine, 204
The Island Ragpicker, 112
Islands Magazine, 204
Issues in Science and Technology, 261
Isthmus, 361
ITC Industrial Response Deck, 387
The Item, 331
Ithaca Journal, 316
Ithaca Times, 357
ITMB Publishing Ltd, 52
ITS World, 244
ITTP Direct, 403
IWA Catalog, 149

J

J & L Book Company, 34
J A Majors Company, 35
J A Majors Scientific Books, 35
J B Sales, 169
J C Penney Stores, 95
J C Strelow Christian Media Int, 35
J F Glaser Inc, 403
J G Sieve Periodicals Inc, 35
J K Gill, 90
J L Hammett's Learning World, 92
J L M Remainders, 35
J Levine Religious Supplies Inc, 35
J R Direct Marketing Inc, 403
J S Canner & Co Inc, 35
J S Ide Associates Inc, 73
J V West, 82
Jack & Jill, 204
Jack O'Dwyer's Newsletter, 244
Jackman Music Corporation, 6
Jackson Citizen Patriot, 306
Jackson County Floridan, 287
Jackson Sun, 332
Jacksonville Daily Progress, 335
Jacksonville Journal Courier, 293
Jacksonville Patriot, 275
JAM!!! (Junior America Magazine), 204
Jameco Electronics Catalog, 149
James & Law Company, 35
James B Kinkead & Assoc, 403
James Chan, 403
James L Evers Associates, 15
The James White Review, 205
Jameson Advertising Inc, 375
Jamestown Sun, 321
JAMI Marketing Services Inc, 403
JAMI/Hotline List Division, 403

Jane Wesman Public Relations, 368
Jane Williams Consultant, 375
Jane's Catalog, 149
The Janesville Gazette, 342
Japan Catalog, 149
Jarrett & Associates, 441
Java Monthly, 244
Jax Photo Books & Videos, 149
Jay R Benford, 35
Jaycees Magazine, 205
Jazz Times Magazine, 205
JBW Direct, 403
JCI Data Processing Inc, 82
JDA (Johnson Direct Advertising), 403
JDR Microdevices, 149
Jean Cohen Books, 35
Jeanne-Marie Phillips Assoc, 368
Jeff Herman Agency, 126
Jeffers Pet Catalog, 149
Jefferson City News & Tribune, 310
Jefferson News Co Inc, 55
Jeffrey Lant's SuccessDek, 387
Jennifer Berman, 434
Jennings Daily News, 301
Jensen Tools Inc, 149
Jericho Promotions, 368
Jerry Buchanan Bookstore, 149
Jerry Levy Associates, 73
Jerry's Catalog, 149
Jersey Journal, 314
Jerusalem Intl Book Fair, 417
Jessica's Biscuit Cookbooks, 149
Jet Magazine, 205
Jewish Action, 205
Jewish Book Annual, 445
The Jewish Book Club, 121
Jewish Education Card Deck, 387
Jewish Journal, 205
Jewish Journal-Broward, 352
Jewish Press, 357
Jewish Press in America, 454
The Jewish Weekly News, 355
JF Direct Marketing Inc, 403
JHL Mail Marketing Inc, 403
Jimmy Booth Public Relations, 368
Jive, 205
JLH Law Books Ltd, 52
Joan Robbins, Media Escort, 368
Joanna's Bookworm of Upland, 100
Jobs and Careers for the 90's, 149
Jodi F Soloman Speakers Bureau, 377
Joe Vitale Agency, 368
John & Hayward, 438
John Benjamins Publishing Co, 15
John Cole's Bookshop, 100
John Daly, Representative, 73
John Justice Book Wholesalers, 35
John K Sharpe Inc, 169
John Kooistra, Representative, 73
John Markham & Associates, 52
Johns Hopkins University Press, 73
Johnson & Associates, 403
Johnson City Press, 332
Johnson Direct Advertising, 403
Johnson Hill Press Inc, 403
Johnson News, 58
Johnson News Agency Inc, 58
Johnson-Smith Catalogs, 149
Johnstown Tribune Democrat, 328
Joint Promotions, 420
Joliet Herald-News, 293
Joncas Postexperts Inc, 403
Jonesboro Sun, 276
Joplin Globe, 310
Jordan Direct, 403
Joseph Agnelli, Representative, 73
Joseph Beth Booksellers, 106

Joseph S Ajlounty, Attorney, 127
Joseph T Reilly Co Inc, 35
Joshua's Christian Stores, 93
Journal, 308, 318
Journal Inquirer, 285
Journal Messenger, 339
The Journal Newspapers, 339
Journal of Academic Librarianship, 174
Journal of Accountancy, 261
Journal of Addictive Diseases, 261
Journal of Aging & Social Policy, 244
Journal of Agromedicine, 261
Journal of Ambulatory Care Management, 261
Journal of Analytic Social Work, 261
Journal of Applied Aquaculture, 261
Journal of Applied Biomechanics, 261
Journal of Arts Management & Law, 261
The Journal of Bank Taxation, 261
Journal of Blacks in Higher Education, 261
Journal of Business Strategies, 450
Journal of Business/Finance Librarians, 174
Journal of Cell Biology, 261
Journal of Chemical Dependency Treatment, 261
Journal of Child Sexual Abuse, 261
Journal of College & University Foodservice, 244
Journal of Commerce, 286
Journal of Commerce & Commercial, 292, 317, 348
Journal of Cost Management, 244
Journal of Couples Therapy, 261
Journal of Divorce & Remarriage, 261
Journal of East-West Business, 244
Journal of Economic Education, 261
Journal of Education for Business, 262
Journal of Educational Research, 262
Journal of Elder Abuse & Neglect, 262
Journal of Emotional/Behavioral, 262
Journal of Environmental Education, 262
Journal of Euromarketing, 262
Journal of Experimental Education, 244
Journal of Experimental Medicine, 262
Journal of Family Psychotherapy, 262
Journal of Family Social Work, 262
Journal of Feminist Family Therapy, 262
Journal of Food Products Marketing, 262
Journal of Gay & Lesbian Psychotherapy, 262
Journal of General Psychology, 262
Journal of Genetic Psychology, 262
Journal of Geriatric Drug Therapy, 262
Journal of Gerontological Social Work, 262
Journal of Global Marketing, 262
Journal of Group Psychotherapy, 262
Journal of Health Care Benefits, 244
Journal of Health/Social Policy, 262
Journal of Homosexuality, 262
Journal of Hospital Marketing, 244
Journal of Hospitality & Leisure Marketing, 244
Journal of Interlibrary Loan/Document, 174
Journal of International Consumer Marketing, 262
Journal of International Financial Markets/Inst, 244
Journal of International Food/Agribusiness Marketing, 262
Journal of Italian Food & Wine, 205
Journal of Library Administration, 174
Journal of Light Construction, 262
Journal of Marketing Channels, 244
Journal of Marketing for Higher Education, 244
Journal of Marketing Research, 263

Journal of Ministry in Addiction/Recovery, 263
Journal of Motor Behavior, 263
Journal of Multicultural Social Work, 244
Journal of Multinational Financial Management, 263
Journal of Musculoskeletal Pain, 263
Journal of Negro History, 263
Journal of Nonprofit/Public Sector Mkt, 263
Journal of Nutritional Immunology, 263
Journal of Offender Rehabilitation, 244
Journal of Organizational Behavior Management, 245
Journal of Partnership Taxation, 245
Journal of Petroleum Technology, 263
Journal of Pharmaceutical Care in Pain, 263
Journal of Pharmaceutical Care/HIV...., 263
Journal of Pharmaceutical Marketing & Management, 245
Journal of Pharmacoepidemiology, 263
Journal of Pharmacy Teaching, 263
Journal of Popular Film & TV, 205
Journal of Professional Services Marketing, 245
Journal of Promotion Management, 245
Journal of Psychology/Human Sexuality, 263
Journal of Psychosocial Oncology, 263
Journal of Rehabilitation, 263
Journal of Research on Computing in Education, 263
Journal of Social Psychology, 263
The Journal of Special Education, 263
Journal of Taxation of Employee Benefits, 245
Journal of Taxation of Exempt Organization, 245
The Journal of Taxation, 263
Journal of Teaching in Social Work, 263
Journal of Vegetable Crop Production, 263
Journal of Women & Aging, 263
The Journal Times, 343
Journal Tribune, 302
Journal-Advocate, 284
Journal-American, 340
Journal-News, 323
Journal-Register, 316
Journal-Review, 294
Journal-World, 299
Journalism Quarterly, 205
Judaica Book Club, 121
Junction List Services, 403
Juneau Empire, 274
Junior Scholastic, 205
Junius Book Distributors Inc, 35
Just Books, 103
Just Cookbooks, 445
Just CrossStitch Magazine, 205
Juvenile Merchandising, 245

K M Lists Inc, 403
K-12 Library Program, 380
K-8 Librarian Card Pack, 387
K-III Press Inc, 403
Ka Keo O Hawaii, 290
Kable Fulfillment Serv of Ohio, 82
Kable Fulfillment Services, 82
Kable News Company, 6
Kabyn Books, 35

Kagan World Media Inc, 438
Kalamazoo Gazette, 306
Kaleidoscope, 264
Kalispell News Agency, 61
Kalmin The Bookstore, 100
Kamloops Daily News, 344
Kampmann, Kump & Bell, 73
Kane County Chronicle, 293
The Kane Republican, 328
Kansas City Dispatch, 356
Kansas City Kansan, 299
Kansas City Periodical Dist Co, 59
Kansas City Star, 310
Kansas State Collegian, 299
The Kaplan Agency, 404
Kaplan School Supply Corp, 35
Karat Interactive Network Inc, 436
Karen Teitelbaum PR, 368
Karl Business Lists, 404
Kart Marketing International, 245
Kathlene Carney & Associates, 368
Kaufer Religious Supplies, 93
Kaufmann & Associates, 375
Kaye Distributors, 35
Kazi Publications Inc, 15
KC Publishing, 35, 149
KCMS, 82
Kearney Hub, 312
Keats Publishing Program, 149
Keene Sentinel, 313
Keepsake Quilting, 149
KEF Media Associates, 368
Keith Distributors, 35
Keithley-Data Acquis/Control, 149
Kelk & Assoc, 404
Kelly's Books, 100
Ken Ecrit Lists, 404
Kenet Media, 15
Kennebec-Journal, 302
Kennedy Publications, 404
Kenny's News Agency & Bookstore, 113
Kenosha News, 342
Kensington Books, 126
The Kent County Daily Times, 331
Kent News Agency Inc, 61
Kent State Univ Bookstores, 94
Kenton Times, 323
Kentucky Game & Fish, 205
Kentucky Kernel, 300
Kentucky New Era, 300
Kentucky Newsclip, 435
Kentucky Post, 300
Kerr Kelly Inc, 368
Kerrville Daily Times, 335
Ketab, 15
Ketchikan Daily News, 274
Ketterson's Old Market Bookstore, 110
Keven Monahan & Associates, 73
Key Contacts & Communications, 404
Key Seminars Speakers Bureau, 378
Key West Citizen, 287
Keynote Inc, 378
Keynote Speakers Inc, 378
KGB Magazine, 205
Kid City, 205
Kid's World, 205
The Kids' Place, 108
KidsBooks Inc, 35
KIDSRIGHT Catalog, 149
Kilgore News Herald, 335
Killeen Daily Herald, 335
Kimberley Daily Bulletin, 344
King Electronics Distributing, 35
The King's English, 115
Kingman Daily Miner, 274
Kingsport Times-News, 332
Kingston Daily Freeman, 316

Kingston News Service, 68
Kingston Whig-Standard, 346
Kinokuniya Bookstores of America, 35
Kinston Free Press, 320
Kipling Tyler Bookshop, 101
Kiplinger's Personal Finance, 205
Kirchen Brothers Catalog, 149
Kirksville Daily Express & News, 310
Kirkus Reviews, 174
Kit Car Illustrated, 205
Kitchen & Bath Business, 245
Kitchen Concepts, 73
Kitchener News Co Ltd, 68
Kitchenware News, 245
Kitplanes, 205
Kitrick Management Co, 36
Kiwanis Magazine, 205
KJ Direct, 404
KJ21 Bible Publishers, 15
The Kleid Company Inc, 404
Kleins of Westport, 103
Kliatt Paperback Book Guide, 174
Klockit Catalog, 150
Knives Illustrated, 245
Knowledge in Motion, 436
Knowledge Industries Inc, 36
Knox County Daily News, 294
Knoxville News-Sentinel, 333
Koala Books of Canada Ltd, 52
Kodiak Daily Mirror, 274
Koen Book Distributors, 36
Kokomo Tribune, 295
Kolb News Agency Inc, 57
Korea Herald, 317
Korea Times, 316
Kramerbooks, 103
Kreig's Books, 97
Krell Software, 150
Krikorian-Miller Associates, 73
Krotman & Berke, 73
KSB Promotions, 368
KSK Communications, 368
Kumquat Bookstore, 106
Kurtzman Book Sales Inc, 73
KWN Systems Inc, 150

L

L & W Book Sales, 15
L L Bean Catalog, 150
L L Company, 36
L-S Distributors, 36
L.I.S.T. Inc, 404
La Belle News Agency, 63
La Crosse Tribune, 342
La Grange Daily News, 289
La Jolla Light, 350
La Junta Tribune-Democrat, 284
La Moderna Poesia, 36
La Opinion, 278
LA Parent, 205
La Porte Herald-Argus, 295
Laarhoven Design, 436
Lab Safety Supply Catalog, 150
Labels, 437-438
Lacis Books, 36
Lacite, 36
Ladd Associates Inc, 404
Ladd Ltd, 368
Ladie's Home Journal, 205
Lady's Circle, 205
Ladybug, 205
Ladyslipper Inc, 36
Lafayette Journal & Courier, 295

Lahontan Valley News, 312
Laing Communications, 375
Laissez Faire Book Club, 121
Lake Charles American Press, 301
Lake City Register, 287
Lake Country Booksellers, 109
The Lake Country Gazette, 355
Lake County Record-Bee, 277
The Lake Group, 404
Lake Havasu City Herald, 274
Lake Publishing Corp, 404
Lake Sun Leader, 309
Lake Superior Magazine, 205
Lakeland Ledger, 287
Lakeport Distributors Inc, 64
Lakewood Lists, 404
Lakewood Sun Post, 359
Lamar Daily News, 284
Lambda Book Report, 206
Lambda Rising, 404
Lambda Rising News, 150
Lambert Book House Inc, 36
Lamppost Press Inc, 15
LAN Times, 206, 387
Lancaster County News Co, 64
Lancaster Intelligencer Journal, 328
Lancaster New Era, 328
Lancer Label, 438
Landmark Books International, 169
Lands' End Corporate Sales, 441
The Lane Leader, 360
Lansing State Journal, 306
Lantern, 322
Lapidary Journal, 245
Laramie Daily Boomerang, 343
The Laredo Morning Times, 335
Large Print Home Library, 121
Large print rights buyer, 126
The Lariat, 337
Larimer Creative Marketing Inc, 404
Larry Flynt Publications, 15
Larry Laster Old & Rare Books, 36
Larry's Book Nook, 101
Las Americas, 36
Las Cruces Bulletin, 357
Las Cruces Sun-News, 315
Las Vegas Daily Optic, 315
Las Vegas News Agency, 36
Las Vegas Review-Journal, 312
Las Vegas Sun, 312
LaserMaster Corp, 441
Laserstar, 150
Last Gasp, 36
Latin American Book Source Inc, 36
Latina Magazine, 206
Latina Style, 206
Latrobe Bulletin, 329
Laughter Works - The Warehouse, 150
Laurel Leader-Call, 309
Lauriat's, 36
Lauriat's and Royal Disc Bkstore, 90
Law & Justice Catalog, 150
Law & Legal Information, 445
Law Pak Inc, 36
The Law Works, 206
Lawn & Garden, 206
Lawrence Communications, 368
Lawrence Daily Record, 293
The Lawton Constitution, 325
Lawyer's Register Publishing Co, 404
Lay Renewal Ministries, 36
Le Diffuseur G Vermette Inc, 52
Le Mars Daily Sentinel, 298
Le Nouvelliste, 348
The Lead Sheet, 404
Leader-Herald, 316
Leader-Telegram, 342

Leader-Times, 328
Leaders Magazine, 264
The Leader, 316
Leading Edge Review, 380
LeadNet Card, 380
The Leaf-Chronicle, 332
Learn and Play Catalog, 150
Learning Action Pac, 387
Learning AIDS, 445
The Learning Co Software Catalog, 150
Learning Magazine, 264
Learning Tools Catalog, 150
Learning World Catalog, 150
Learningsmsith, 88
Lebanon Daily Record, 310
Lebanon Democrat, 333
Lectorum Publications, 36
Ledger Independent, 301
Ledger/Dispatch, 276
Lee & Associates, 404
Lee Collins & Associates, 73
Leesville Daily Leader, 301
Leff Brothers, 37
Left Bank Books, 109
Lefthanded Magazine, 206
Lefthanded Specialties, 150
Lefthanders Magazine Catalog, 150
Legacy Distributing, 37
Legal Intelligencer, 329
Legal News, 324
Legal Reference Services Qtly, 174
Leigh Bureau, 378
Leigh Speakers Bureau, 378
Leisure Books, 126
Leisure Years Co-op, 380
The Leland Company, 404
Lemstone Book Branch, 92
Lemuria Bookstore, 109
Len Mor Publications, 404
Lenoir News-Topic, 320
Leon Henry Inc, 404
Leonard & Assoc, 404
Leprechaun's Lair, 37
Les Cousins Books & Records Shop, 104
Les Editions Francaises, 20
Les Editions Heritage Inc, 52
Les Editions Levesque Publ, 52
Les Librairies Boyer, 90
Lesnick News Co Inc, 66
Lessiter Publications, 150
Let's Go Travel Publications, 150
Let's Live, 206
Let's Talk About Doll Making, 206
Lethbridge Herald, 344
Letter Arts Book Club, 150
Levinson Associates, 368
Levy Home Entertainment, 37, 58
Lewisburg Daily Journal, 329
Lewiston Morning Tribune, 290
Lexicon-MTA, 450
Lexington Herald-Leader, 300
LH Management, 404
Liber 90 (Barcelona Book Fair), 417
Liberation Distributors, 37
Liberties Fine Books & Music, 104
Liberty Hobby Distributors, 37
Liberty Tribune, 356
Libertyville Saddleshop Catalog, 150
Libido, 206
Libra Wholesale, 169
Librairie DeMarc, 88
Librairie Francaise Inc, 37
Librairie Papeterie Le Bouquin, 53
Librarian Friendly Comput Softwr, 150
The Librarian's Yellow Pages, 457
Libraries (directories), 451
Library & Archival Security, 174

Library Book Selection Service, 6
Library Hi Tech News, 175
Library Journal, 175, 206
The Library Ltd, 109
Library Sales Inc, 37
Library Talk, 175
Libreria Bereana, 37
Libreria Giron, 88
Libros de Espana Y America, 6
Licensing Business Sourcebook, 450
Life Cycle Books, 20
Life Magazine, 206
Lifecycle Learning, 404
Lifestyle America, 404
Lifestyle Change Communications, 404
Lifestyle Fascination Inc, 151
Lifestyle Media Reporter, 456
Lifestyle Media-Relations Report, 270
Lifestyle Selector, 405
Lifetime Books, 15
The Light Connection, 206
Light Impressions Catalog, 151
Light Impressions Corp, 37
The Lighter Side, 151
Lighthouse Books, 151
Lighthouse List Co, 405
Lilith Magazine, 206
Lillian Vernon Catalog, 151
Lillian Vernon Corp, 405
Lilly News, 55
Lilly's Kids Catalog, 151
Lilmur Publishing, 53
Lima News, 323
Limited Editions Club, 121
Lincoln Courier, 293
Lincoln Journal-Star, 312
Lincoln News Agency, 61
Lindsay Electrical Books Catalog, 151
Lindsay News, 37
Lindsey Daily Post, 346
Ling's International Books, 6
Lingua Franca, 245
Linguistic Systems, 439
Link Magazine, 206
Link-Up, 206
Links, 206
Linn's Stamp News, 206
Linton Daily Citizen, 295
The Lion, 206
Lisa Ekus Public Relations, 368
List America Inc, 405
The List Authority, 405
List Bank, 405
The List Connection Inc, 405
List Counsellors Inc, 405
List Dimensions, 405
The List Emporium Inc, 405
List Locators & Managers Inc, 405
List Logic, 405
List Marketing Limited, 405
List Masters Inc, 405
List of abbreviations, 10, 54, 68, 176
List Pro of America, 405
List Services Corp, 405
The List Source Inc, 405
List Strategies Inc, 405
List Technology Systems Group, 405
Listco Mailing Lists, 405
Listen USA!, 125
Listening Library, 125
Listline, 405
Listmart Inc, 405
Listmaster, 405
The Listworks Corp, 405
Litchfield County Times, 352
Literal Book Distributors, 37
Literary Agents of North America, 459

Literary Cavalcade, 206
Literary Guild of America, 121
Literary Market Place, 448
Literary Resource Quarterly, 380
The Literate Traveller, 151
Literature Display Systems Inc, 437
Litle & Co, 439
A Little Bit Crafty, 151
Little Book Shop Inc, 105
Little Professor Book Centers, 92, 104, 108, 110-114
Live Oak Media, 125
Live Steam, 206
Live!, 206
Living Batch Books, 111
Living Life!, 206
The Living Source, 151
Livingston Enterprise, 311
Llewellyn New Worlds, 206
Llewellyn Publications, 15
Llexell Fulfillment Services, 82
LLM-List Locators & Managers Inc, 405
Lloydminister Times, 361
Lobsenz-Stevens, 368
Local bookstore chains, 87-89
Locations, 207
Lodging, 245
Lodging Hospitality, 245
Lodi News-Sentinel, 277
Log Cabin Democrat, 275
Log Home Living, 207
The Logan Banner, 341
Logan Daily News, 323
Login Brothers Book Co, 37
Login Fulfillment Services, 82
Logos, 207
Lolly and Company, 73
Lompoc Record, 277
London Book Fair, 417
London Free Press, 346
Lone Star Comics/Science Fiction, 96
Long Beach Books Inc, 37
Long Distance Directory of Government Addresses and Phones, 457
Long Island Business News, 207
Long Island Parenting News, 207
Long's Drugs, 96
Longmont Daily Times-Call, 284
Longview News-Journal, 335
Look Japan, 207
Looking Glass Bookstore, 113
Loose Change, 207
Looseleaf Law Publications Inc, 37
Los Alamos Monitor, 315
Los Altos Town Crier, 350
Los Angeles Business Journal, 350
Los Angeles Daily Journal, 278
Los Angeles Daily News, 283
Los Angeles Magazine, 207
Los Angeles Reader, 350
Los Angeles Sentinel, 350
Los Angeles Times, 278
Los Angeles Times-Orange County, 276
Los Angeles View, 350
Los Gatos Weekly-Times, 350
Lost Treasure, 207
Lottery Players Magazine, 245
LottoWorld, 207
Lotus Light Distributing, 37
Lotus Notes Advisor, 207
Lotus Selects, 151
Louis Goldberg Library Books, 169
Louis L'Amour Western Magazine, 207
Louisiana Game & Fish, 207
Louisiana Periodicals, 59
Louisville Courier-Journal, 300
Louisville Eccentric Observer, 354

Louisville News Company, 59
Loveland Daily Reporter-Herald, 284
Loving More Magazine, 207
Lovington Daily Leader, 315
Lowell Sun, 304
Loyola Press Reader Catalog, 151
LPC Group, Login Trade Div, 6
LR Direct Ltd, 405
LTN Partners, 405
Lubbock Avalanche-Journal, 335
Lubbock News Co, 65
Luce Press Clippings, 435
Lucky Book Club, 121
Ludington Daily News, 306
Ludington News Co Inc, 60
Lufkin Daily News, 336
Luggage & Leather Goods Show, 418
Luminary Distributing, 37
Lushena Books, 15
The Lutheran, 207
Lyben Computer Systems, 151
Lynchburg Hardware/General Store, 151
Lynx Media Inc, 82
Lyons Daily News, 299

M

M & M News Agency Inc, 37
M & T International Marketing, 405
M Coy Books Inc, 116
M J Daniel Company, 73
M Lande Promotions, 368
M S News Company Inc, 59
M/D/A List Management Inc, 405
Ma'ayan Book Co, 37
MAC Line, 207
Mac Times, 387
The MAC Zone, 151
Mac's Backs Paperbacks, 112
MAC's Place, 151
MACAvenue, 151
MACBeat, 151
MACConnection, 151
The MacFarland Co, 406
MacGregor News Agency, 37
Machalek Communications Inc, 387
Machine Design, 245
MacHome Journal, 207
Mackin Book Co, 37
Maclean-Hunter DM Services, 406
MACMall, 151
Macomb Daily, 307
Macomb Journal, 293
Macon Chronicle-Herald, 310
Macon Telegraph, 289
MACProducts, 152
MacRae's Blue Book, 450
MacRae's Indian Book Distributor, 16
Macro Mark Inc, 406
Macrobiotic Book Catalog, 152
Macrocosm USA, 458
MACS, 439
MacUser, 207
MACWarehouse, 152
MacWeek, 207
MacWorld, 207
Mademoiselle, 207
Madera Tribune, 278
Madison Avenue Bookshop Inc, 112
Madison Avenue Handbook, 459
Madison Book Fair, 415
Madison Books & Computers, 97
Madison Capital Times, 342
Madison Courier, 296

Madison Daily Leader, 332
Madison Park Books, 116
Madison Press, 323
Madisonian, 354
Magazine & Bookseller, 175
Magazine book reviewers or editors, 177-231
Magazine Distributors, 38
Magazine Marketing Inc, 406
Magazines for booksellers, etc, 173-176
Magazines for Young People, 454
Magazines Inc, 59
Magee Publications, 38
Magic City, 6
Magic Frame Display Systems, 436
Magical Blend, 207
Magickal Childe Inc, 38
Magna Books, 170
Magnolia Bookshop, 104
Magnolia Clipping Service, 435
Mahoning Valley Distributors, 38
Mail Marketing Guild, 406
Mail Marketing Resources, 406
Mail Order Business Directory, 449
Mail Order Catalog, 152
Mail order catalogs that feature books, 129-168
Mail Order Merchandise Show, 418
Mail Tribune, 327
Mailer's Review, 245
Mailer's Software, 152
Mailing & Shipping Technology, 207
Mailing list brokers and managers, 393-414
Mailing List Co-op Program, 380
Mailing Lists Asia, 406
Mailing Lists Plus Inc, 406
Mailing service, 438
Mailings Clearing House, 406
Mailways International, 82
Main Street Agency, 406
Main Street Books, 107, 115
Main Street Marketing, 380
Maine Periodical Dist Inc, 38
Maine Times, 355
Maine Writers/Publ Alliance, 38
Mainly Meetings, 420
Mainstream, 207
Major College Newspapers, 454
Major Mass Market Merchandisers, 461
Major Reference Works, 152
Major Video Concepts, 6
Majors Scientific Books Inc, 88
Majors Scientific Bookstore, 96
Majors Scientific Distributors, 38
Mal Dunn Associates Inc, 406
Malibu Books & Co, 101
Malone Telegram, 316
Malvern Daily Record, 276
Manage Magazine, 207
Managed Healthcare, 245
Management Accounting, 208
Manager's Answer Cards, 387
Managers' Resource Deck, 387
Managing Office Technology, 245
Manderley, 152
Mangelsen's, 38
Manhattan Mercury, 299
Manhattan Publishing Co, 38
Manhatten Magazine, 208
Manila International Book Fest, 417
Manistee News-Advocate, 306
Manning Selvage & Lee, 368
Manson News Distributors, 62
Manteca Bulletin, 278
Manufacturing Management Product, 387
Many Feathers Books & Maps, 38

Many Hands, 208
Map Link, 38
Maplewood Crafts Catalog, 152
Maplewood News-Record, 357
Marboro Books, 169
Marcel Didier Inc, 53
Marco, 441
Marco Co, 38
Mardelva News, 60
Marden-Kane Inc, 375
Mardev, 380
Mardev USA, 406
Margaret Liddiard, 375
Margie's Book Nook, 101
Marginal Distribution, 53
Marietta Daily Journal, 289
Marietta Times, 323
Mariland Gazette, 355
Marin Independent Journal, 279
Marine Corps Gazette, 245
Marine Log, 245
Marine Retailers Association Trade Show, 418
Marine Supplies, 152
Marion Daily Republican, 293
Marion Star, 323
Marjen Books, 88
Mark Ziesing Bookseller, 152
Markair Magazine, 208
Market Data Retrieval, 406
Market Guide for Young Artists, 448
Market Guide for Young Writers, 448
Market Identification Inc, 406
Market Motivators Inc, 406
Market: Asia Pacific, 246
Market: Europe, 246
Market: Latin America, 246
Marketers Bookshelf, 152
Marketing Bulletin Board, 441
Marketing Communications Inc, 406
Marketing Computers, 264
Marketing Direct Associates, 406
Marketing Directions Inc, 375
Marketing directories, 449-462
Marketing General Inc, 406
Marketing III Direct Response, 406
The Marketing Information Bureau, 406
Marketing magazines, 269-271
Marketing Management, 264
Marketing Manager Sales Ideas, 387
Marketing Platinum Card Pack, 387
Marketing Power, 152
Marketing Promotion Cards, 387
Marketing services and publishing consultants, 373-376
Marketing Services International, 406
Marketing Technology Newsletter, 270
Marketing to Women, 270
Marketing Tools, 246
Marketplace Books, 113
Marketry Inc, 406
MarketSource, 380
Marquand Books Inc, 16
Marriage & Family Review, 264
Marriage Partnership, 208
Marshall Cavendish Corporation, 16
Marshall Chronicle, 307
Marshall Field's, 105
Marshall Independent, 308
Marshall News Messenger, 336
Marshall-Mangold Distributing Co, 38
Marshfield News-Herald, 342
Martguild Inc, 441
Martha Stewart Living, 208
Martin Beeman, Representative, 73
Martin Kane Public Relations, 368
Martin News Agency Inc, 65

Martin Pine Associates, 368
Martin/Osa Johnson Safari Museum, 38
Martinsville Bulletin, 339
Mary Elizabeth Granger Assoc Inc, 406
Mary Maxim Catalog, 152
Maryland Express, 361
Maryland News Distributing Co, 60
Marysville Journal-Tribune, 323
Maryville Daily Forum, 310
Maryville Daily Times, 333
Massachusetts Daily Collegian, 303
Massachusetts Review, 208
Mast, 208
Master Animal Care Catalog, 152
Master Lists, 406
Master Response List Division, 406
MasterMedia Speakers Bureau, 378
Masthead, 246
Material Handling Engineering, 246
Math Products Plus, 152
Math-Micro Action Deck, 387
Mathematics Teacher, 264
Matt Brown & Associates, 406
Matthews Media Directory, 454
Matthews Medical Books Co, 38
Mattoon Journal-Gazette, 293
Mature Market Clipping Service, 435
Mature Market Co-Op, 380
Mature Market Media, 380
Maurie's, 105
Maverick Mail Order Bookstore, 152
Maxis Software Toys Catalog, 152
Maxwell Macmillan Tax Pack, 387
Mayfield Messenger, 301
Maypop Books, 152
The Mazel Company, 170
Mazza Marketing Group, 368
MCA Home Video, 127
McAlester News-Capital/Democrat, 325
McBeth Corp, 53
McCall's, 208
McCook Daily Gazette, 312
McCormick Associates, 73
McCrory's Wholesale Books, 38
McCurdy Communications, 368
McCurtain Daily Gazette, 325
McDonough & Associates, 73
McDowell News, 320
McGraw-Hill Architecture Deck, 387
McGraw-Hill Business & Marketing, 387
McGraw-Hill Engineering Decks, 387
McGraw-Hill Human Resources Deck, 387
McGraw-Hill List Management Ctr, 406
McGraw-Hill Prof Computing Deck, 388
McGraw-Hill Real Estate Deck, 388
The McGuffey Writer, 208
McHugh Publishing Reports, 375
McIntyre & Dodd Marketing Inc, 406
McKinney Courier-Gazette, 336
McKinzey-White Booksellers, 102
McKnight Sales Inc, 38
McMahon Books Inc, 103
The McNichols Group Inc, 407
McPherson Sentinel, 299
McQueen Associates, 74
McQuerry Orchid Books, 152
Meader Book Distributing Co, 38
Meadville Tribune, 329
Meakin & Associates, 53
MEC List Management, 407
Mechanical Engineers' Book Club, 121
MedDeck, 388
MEDEC List Marketing, 407
Medford News, 63
Media & Methods, 246
Media (directories), 452-456
Media Calendar Directory, 451

Media Distribution Services, 368
Media Factbook, 454
Media Great, 152
Media Guide for Activists, 454
Media Horizons Inc, 388, 407
Media Index Publishing Inc, 407
Media List, 454
Media Management, 388
Media Management Group, 407
Media Marketplace Inc, 407
Media Mart, 407
Media Masters Inc, 407
Media newsletters, 456
Media Projects Inc, 16
Media Relations, 368
Media Resource Focus, 456
The Media Serivces Group Ltd, 82
Media Services Inc, 388
Media Weavers, 375
Media Weavers Lists, 407
Media Week, 246
Medialink, 368
Mediamatic System -- Targeter, 451
Medianet, 375
Medical & Health Information Directory, 458
Medical Economics, 264
Medical Equipment Designer, 246
Medical Marketing Services Inc, 407
Medical Reference Services Qly, 175
Medical Tribune for Family Phys, 264
Medicine Hat News, 344
Medina County Gazette, 323
The Medina Sun, 359
Meeting News, 264
Meeting Planners Computer Catalog, 152
Meetings & Conventions, 246
Meg Cullar Public Relations, 369
Mega Lists, 407
Mega Media Assoc Inc, 407
Mega-Books Inc, 16
Mellinger's Garden Catalog, 152
Melman-Moster Associates, 74
Melton Book Co Inc, 38
Memphis Flyer, 208, 360
Men's & Boy's Wear Specialty Stores, 461
Men's Fitness, 208
Men's Health Book Club, 121
Men's Journal, 208
Men's Perspectives, 208
Men's Style, 208
Mena Star, 276
Menasha Ridge Press Inc, 16
Mendon Associates Inc, 82
Mentor: The Resource for Men, 208
Merced News Co, 56
Merced Sun Star, 278
Mercedes Distribution Center, 82
Merchant Magazine, 246
The Mercury, 329
Meredith List Marketing, 407
Meriden Record-Journal, 285
Meridian Star, 309
Merisel Inc, 6
Merle Distributing, 38
Merlin's Medieval Market, 438
Merlyn's Pen, 208
Mervyn's California View, 208
Mesa Tribune, 274
Mesabi Daily News, 308
Messageries Dynamiques, 53
Messenger, 301
Messenger-Inquirer, 301
The Messenger, 298
Messing About in Boats, 208
Metacom Inc, 125
Metamorphous Press, 16

Metaphysical Co-Op Advertising, 380
Metaphysical Reviews, 381
Metlfax, 208
Metro, 351
Metro California Media Directory, 454
Metro Creative Graphics, 369
Metro Direct Marketing, 407
Metro Pulse, 360
Metro Santa Cruz, 351
Metro Times, 355
Metro Toronto News Co, 68
MetroKids Magazine, 208
Metroland Magazine, 357
Metromail Corp, 407
Metromail/Donor List Management Group, 407
Metronews, 350
MetroParent Magazine, 208
Metropolitan Home, 208
Metropolitan Museum of Art, 38, 153
Metropolitan News-Enterprise, 278
Metzger-Huset Associates, 74
Mexia Daily News, 336
Mexico Events /Mexico Update, 208
Mexico Information Services Inc, 439
Mexico Leader, 310
Meyer Religious Book Sales, 74
MGA Ltd, 16
MGI Lists, 407
MGM Mailing Lists & Consulting, 407
MGP Direct, 375
MGT Associates Inc, 407
MHW Distribution, 10
Miami Book Fair International, 415
Miami Books, 39
Miami Herald, 287
Miami New Times, 352
Miami News-Record, 325
Miami Valley Gateway Books, 112
Miami Valley News Agency Inc, 63
Micawber's Bookstore, 109
Michael Barfield, 434
Michael Bills, Representative, 74
Michael Carley, Representative, 74
Michael Druxman Public Relations, 369
Michael Kassin Public Relations, 369
Michael Wiese Productions, 153
Michael Wolff & Co Inc, 16
Michiana News Service Inc, 60
Michigan Church Supply Co, 39
Michigan Daily, 305
Michigan Florist, 208
Michigan Living, 208
Michigan Sportsman, 208
Mickler's Floridiana Inc, 39
Micro Computer Journal, 209
Micro Electronics Inc, 153
Micro Express, 153
Micro United, 7
Micromath Scientific Software, 153
Micronesia Media Dist Inc, 39
Microsoft Magazine, 209
MicroTimes, 209
Microwaves & R F, 209, 246
Mid Side Resident, 357
Mid-America Commerce & Industry, 246
Mid-Atlantic Game & Fish, 209
Mid-Penn Magazine Agency Inc, 64
Mid-South Booksellers Association Convention, 415
Mid-Western News Agency, 68
Middle Earth Bookshop, 153
Middle East & Islam Catalog, 153
Middle East Bookfair, 417
Middlesboro Daily News, 301
Middlesex Daily News, 304
Middletown Journal, 323

Middletown Press, 285
Midland Daily News, 307
Midland Reporter-Telegram, 336
Midnight Engineering, 264
Midpoint National, 82
Midpoint Trade Books, 74
Midstate Distributors, 63
Midtown Auto Books, 39
Midwest Computer Works, 153
Midwest Direct Marketing Inc, 407
Midwest European Publications, 39
Midwest Express Magazine, 209
Midwest Library Service, 39
Midwest Lists & Media, 407
Midwest Living, 209
Midwest Photo Co, 439
Might, 209
Mijerek's News & Bookstore, 106
Mike Wilson List Counsel, 407
Miles City Star, 311
Miles Kimball, 153
Milestone Publications, 20
Milford Daily News, 304
The Militant, 358
Military Book Club, 121
Military History, 209
Military History Catalog, 153
Military Lifestyle, 209
Military Review, 209, 264
Mill City Music Record Dist, 7
The Millard Group Inc, 407
Miller Harness Co, 39
Miller Trade Book Marketing, 74
Milligan News Company, 56
Millimeter, 246
Millville News, 313
Milton Daily Standard, 329
Milton Simpson Design, 16
Milwaukee Direct Marketing, 407
Milwaukee Journal Sentinel, 343
Milwaukee Magazine, 209
Mimi's Books & Paterns for the Serious
  Dollmaker, 153
Minden Press-Herald, 301
Mineral Daily News Tribune, 341
Mineral Land Publications, 39
Mineral Wells Index, 336
Miners Inc, 153
Mini Trucking, 209
Miniature Quilts, 209
Mining Journal, 306
Ministries Today Card-A-Log, 388
Ministry Values/Growing Churches, 388
Minneapolis Star Tribune, 308
Minneapolis Sun Publication, 356
Minnesota Daily, 308
Minnesota Media Directory, 454
Minnesota Monthly, 209
Minnesota Parent, 209
Minnesota Sports, 209
Minnesota Sportsman, 209
Minority Markets Alert, 246
Minority Organizations: A National
  Directory, 458
Minot Daily News, 321
Mirabella Magazine, 209
Mirth-Aid Catalog, 153
Miscellaneous resources, 434-441
Misco Power Up, 153
Mississippi Game & Fish, 209
Mississippi Library & Media Sup, 39
Mississippi Press, 309
Missoula Independent, 356
The Missoulian, 311
Missouri Game & Fish, 209
Misty Valley Books, 115
The Mix Bookshelf Catalog, 153

MJH Group Inc, 407
MKS Inc, 39
MLES Inc, 39
MLR Publishing Co, 407
MMS Inc(Medical Marketing Lists), 407
Moberly Monitor-Index/Democrat, 310
Mobile Office, 246
Mobile Press-Register, 273
Mobile Radio Technology, 264
Moby Dickens Bookshop, 111
Model Builder, 209
Model Railroader, 209
Model Retailer, 246
Modern Books & Crafts Inc, 7
Modern Bride, 209
Modern Drummer, 209
Modern Grocer, 246
Modern Healthcare, 264
Modern Maturity, 209
Modern Office Technology, 246
Modern Times Bookstore, 101
Modern Tire Dealer, 246
Moderna, 210
Modesto Bee, 278
Moe's Books Inc, 101
The MoGo Show, 418
Mohave Valley Daily News, 274
Mokrynski & Associates Inc, 407
Moller & Associates, 388
Monadnock Ledger, 356
Monahan Agencies Ltd, 67
Monarch Accounting Supplies, 407
Monarch Books of Canada, 53
Monday Magazine, 361
Monett Times, 310
Money Book Club, 121
Money Magazine, 210
Money Maker's Monthly, 246
Monitoring Times, 210
The Monitor, 336
Monk Magazine, 210
Monroe Evening News, 307
Monroe Evening Times, 343
Montana Kaimin, 311
Montana Magazine, 210
Montana Standard, 311
Monterey County Herald, 279
Montfort Publications, 39
Montgomery Advertiser-Journal, 273-274
Montgomery County Record, 328
Montgomery Express, 361
Montgomery Journal, 303, 339
Montgomery News Co Inc, 55
Montgomery Post, 360
Montgomery Sentinel, 355
Montreal Gazette, 348
Montreal La Presse, 348
Montrose Daily Press, 284
Moody Bookstores, 93
Moody Magazine, 210
Mook & Blanchard, 39
Moore County Citizen News-Record, 319
Moorpark Star, 279
Moorshead Publications, 153
Moose Magazine, 210
Mopar Muscle, 210
Morlock News, 62
The Morning Call, 327
Morning Herald, 303
Morning Journal, 323
The Morning Journal, 341
Morning News, 290, 328
Morning News Northwest Arkansas, 276
The Morning News Tribune, 340
Morning Sun, 300, 307
Morrill's New Directions, 153
Morris Costumes, 7

Morris Daily Herald, 293
Morris Direct Marketing Inc, 408
Morris Inc, 16
Mortgage & Real Est Exec Report, 264
Moscow International Book Fair, 417
Moscow-Pullman Daily News, 290
Moseley Associates, 375
Mother Earth News, 210
Mother Jones, 153, 210
Mother Lode News Company, 39
Mother O'Riley's Books, 112
Mothering, 210
Mothers' Mailpak, 381
Motherwear, 153
Motor Boating & Sailing, 210
Motor Trend, 210
Motorbooks International, 16
Motorcycle Consumer News, 210
Motorhome, 210
Motorland, 210
Moultrie Observer, 289
Moundsville Daily Echo, 341
Mount Airy News, 320
Mount Olive Tribune, 358
Mount Pleasant Daily Tribune, 336
Mount Pleasant News, 298
Mount Vernon Argus, 319
Mount Vernon News, 323
Mountain Ark Trader Catalog, 153
Mountain Automation Corporation, 437
Mountain Bike, 210
Mountain Democrat, 279
Mountain Lion Inc, 16
Mountain Living, 210
Mountain Mail, 284
Mountain N'Air Books, 16
Mountain Press, 16
The Mountain Press, 333
Mountain Rose Herbs, 153
Mountain Xpress, 358
Mountains/Plains Booksellers Trade
  Show, 415
Mountainside Publishing Co Inc, 408
Movie Entertainment Book Club, 121
Movie Marketplace, 210
Movieline, 210
Movies Unlimited, 154
Moving Books Inc, 39
MPG List Co, 408
Mpls-St Paul Magazine, 210
Mr Paperback, 39
Mr Paperback Stores, 88
Mr Paperback/Publishers News Co, 39
MRS Bulletin, 264
Mrs Gooch's Natural Foods, 96
Ms Magazine, 210
MSC Lists Inc, 408
The MTA Group, 408
Much Ado About Books, 101
Muldoon List Center, 408
Mullare News Agency Inc, 60
Multicultural Distributing Ctr, 39
MultiCultural Review, 210, 264
Multimedia Business Report, 270
Multimedia Merchandising, 246
Multimedia Producer, 210
MultiMedia Schools, 264
Multimedia World, 246
Mumford Library Book Sales, 39
Muncie Evening Press, 296
Muncie Star, 296
Murder Ink Ltd Catalog, 154
Murdoch Magazine Dist Inc, 40
Murdoch Magazines Travel Lists, 408
Murr's Library Service, 40
Murray Ledger and Times, 301
Muscatine Journal, 298

Muscle and Fitness, 210
Muscle Car Review, 211
Muscle Mustangs & Fast Fords, 211
The Muses, 112
Museum Store Association Convention, 415
Museums New York, 211
Music Book Service Corporation, 40
Music Book Society, 121
Music Connection, 246
Music for Little People, 154
Music Information Cards, 388
Music Print Media Co-op, 381
The Music Stand, 154
Musical Success Letter, 246
Musician, 247
Muskegon Chronicle, 307
Muskogee Daily Phoenix/Times Dem, 325
Mustang & Ford Magazine, 247
Mustang Daily, 281
Mustang Illustrated, 211
Mustang Monthly, 211
Mustard Seed, 40
Myron Kimnach Bookseller, 154
Mysteries By Mail, 154
The Mysterious Bookshop, 154
Mystery Guild, 121
Mystery Readers Journal, 211
Mystic Moon Magic Catalog, 154
Mystic Trader & Whole Life Products, 154

N

N L Associates, 40
N M Direct, 408
Na'amat Woman, 211
NACS Book Buyer's Manual, 448
NACSCORP Inc, 40
NAEIR - National Assn for Exchange of Industrial Resources, 170
NAFE Bookshelf, 154
Najarian Music Company, 40
NAM - New Age Mailing Lists, 408
The Name Exchange, 408
Name Finders Lists Inc, 408
Name That Book, 369
Namebank International Inc, 408
Names and Addresses Inc, 408
Names in the Mail Inc, 408
Names in the News California, 408
Names in the News Inc, 408
Nanci McCrackin, Sales Rep, 74
Nancy Suib & Associates, 74
Napa Valley Appellation, 211
Napa Valley Register, 279
Naples Daily News, 287
NAPRA ReVIEW, 175
Narrow Gauge Newsstand, 102
Nascar Super Truck Racing, 211
Nash Finch, 40
Nashua Express, 154
Nashville Banner, 333
Nashville Scene, 360
Nat Bodian, Consultant, 373
Natchez Democrat, 309
The Nate Butler Studio Inc, 439
Nathana Josephs PR, 369
Nation's Business, 247
Nation's Business Executives Pac, 388
Nation's Restaurant News, 247
National Assn of Home Builders, 408
National Association of Deaf, 40
National Back-to-School Show, 418
National Book & Document, 439

National Book Co Inc, 7
National Book Distributors, 40
National Book Network, 7, 74-75
National bookstore chains, 91-92
National Business Services, 82
National Business Woman, 211
National Catholic Reading Dist, 40
National Dipper, 247
National Dir of Mailing Lists, 449
National Directory of Addresses and Telephone Numbers, 458
National Directory of Catalogs, 449
National Directory of Magazines, 454
National Directory of Newspaper Op-Ed Pages, 454
National Directory of Nonprofit Organizations, 458
National Dragster, 211
National Faculty Directory, 460
National Fax Directory, 451
National Fire Protection Assn, 154
National Fitness Nutrition and Sports Exposition, 418
National Fulfillment Services, 82
National Fundraising Lists Inc, 408
National Gardening, 211
National Geographic, 211
National Geographic Traveller, 211
National Geographic World, 211
National Herald, 316
National Hog Farmer, 247
National Home Center News, 247
National Instruments, 154
National Jeweler, 247
National Journal, 211
National Lampoon, 211
National Law Journal, 264
National Law Journal Card Pack, 388
National League for Nursing, 408
National Learning Corp, 40
National Library Service, 170
National List Counsel Inc, 408
National List Exchange Inc, 408
National Media Directory, 454
National Merchandise Show, 418
National News Co Ltd, 68
National News Media Yellow Book, 454
National Parks Magazine, 211
National Pen Company, 388
National Plan Service, 154
National Premium/Incentive Show, 418
National Public Accountant, 247
National Real Estate Investor, 247
National Religious Broadcasters, 454
National Response Corporation, 381
National Response List Mktg Inc, 408
National Review, 211
National Rifle Assn, 40
National Seminars Executives, 388
National Speakers Bureau, 378
National Speakers Forum, 378
National Stationery Show, 419
National Storytelling Catalog, 154
National Suburban Marketing, 381
National Syndications, 381
National Technical Info Service, 408
National Trade & Professional Associations of the US, 458
National Training Center, 154
National Wildlife, 211
National Wildlife Federation, 154
National Women's Mailing List, 408
Nations Care Direct Marketing, 408
Nationwide Computer Distrib Inc, 154
Nationwide Printing Inc, 437
Nationwide Speakers Bureau, 378
The Nation, 211

Native American Books in Print, 445
Native American Distribution, 16
Native Peoples, 211
Natl Advertising/Mktg Enterprise, 408
Natl Assn of Female Executives, 388
Natural Choice Catalog, 154
Natural Foods Merchandiser, 211, 247
Natural Gardening Company, 154
Natural Health, 211
Natural History, 212
Natural Lifestyle Supplies, 155
Natural Science & Biology Books, 155
Naturally Magazine, 212
Nature Book Society, 122
The Nature Company, 96
Nature's Jewelry/Pyramid Books, 155
Naturegraph Publishers, 16
Nautical Book Club, 122
Naval Affairs, 247
NCDM Conference & Exposition, 415
NCFE Money-Book Store Catalog, 155
NCR Direct, 155
NCRI List Management, 408
NDL/The Lifestyle Selector, 408
NE Mississippi Daily Journal, 309
NEA Retired, 212
Nebraska Book Store, 94
Nebraska City News-Press, 312
Nebs Computer Forms & Software, 155
NEC Select Solutions, 155
Ned Ludd Books, 155
Negev Importing Company Ltd, 10
Neiman Marcus Catalog, 155
Neiman Marcus List Management, 408
Nelson Daily News, 344
Nelson Marketing, 441
Nelson News, 61
Nelson News Agency Inc, 59
Neo-Asian American Times, 316
Neodata Services Inc, 82
Neosho Daily News, 310
Nest Egg, 247
Netguide, 212
Network Administrator, 212
Network Communications Inc, 409
Network Computing Magazine, 212
Network Magazine, 212
The Network Marketer's Toolbox, 155
Network World, 212
Networking Solutions, 155
Nevada Appeal, 312
Nevada Daily Legal News, 313
Nevada Daily Mail/Sunday Herald, 310
Nevada Magazine, 212
Nevada Press Clipping Service, 435
New & Unique Videos, 155
New Age Cooperative Mailings, 381
New Age Entrepreneur, 155
New Age Journal Card Deck, 388
New Age Magazine, 212
New Age Mailing Lists, 409
New Age Marketing Opportunities, 270
New Age Retailer, 212, 247
New Alternatives for Publishing, Retailing and Advertising-NAPRA, 409
New American, 357
New American Library, 126
New American Writing, 420
New and Unique Videos, 7
New Bedford Standard Times, 304
New Beginnings, 212
New Book Lover's Guide to Chicagoland, 449
New Book Showcase, 381
New Books of Interest to Gay Men, 155
New Books of Interest to Women, 155
New Braunfels Herald-Zeitung, 336

New Businesses-Dek, 388
New Canaan Bookshop, 103
New Castle News, 329
New Century Communications, 16
New Choices for Writers, 448
New Concepts Book & Tape Distrib, 40
New Customer Acquisition, 409
New Directions Catalog, 155
New Directions Speakers/Programs, 378
New Editions International Ltd, 375
New Electric Railway Journal, 212
New England Book Sales Co, 75
New England Book Service Inc, 82
New England Booksellers Association Trade Show, 416
New England Bride, 212
New England Game & Fish, 212
New England Journal of Medicine, 264
New England Media Directory, 454
New England Mobile Book Fair, 40
New England Newsclip Agency, 435
New England Review, 264
New Equipment Digest, 247
New Era Publications, 7
The New Farm, 247
New Fiberworks Sourcebooks, 449
New Frontier Magazine, 212
New Hampshire College Bookstore, 94
New Hampshire Sunday News, 356
New Haven Advocate, 352
New Haven Register, 285
New Haven Regiter-Milford Edition, 285
New Horizons Book Shop Inc, 108
New Information Exchange, 155
New Jersey Book Agency, 40
New Jersey Books Inc, 40
New Jersey Herald, 314
New Jersey Media Directory, 454
New Leaf Distributing, 40
New Life Foundation, 40
New Living, 212
New Marketing Opportunities, 449
New Mexico Business Journal, 212
New Mexico Daily Lobo, 315
New Mexico Living, 212
New Mexico Magazine, 212
New Moon, 155
New Moon Parenting, 212
New Orleans Magazine, 212
New Pages Distributors Directory, 461
New Pages Exhibiting Service, 420
New Parents Co-Op, 381
New Parents Value Pack, 388
New Products for Church Leaders, 388
The New Republic, 212
New Resi Data Marketing Inc, 409
New Texas magazine, 212
New Thought, 264
The New Times, 356
New Volusian, 286
New Woman, 212
New Writer's Magazine, 212
New York Book Fair, 416
New York Daily Challenge, 316
New York Daily News, 317
New York Family, 213
New York Game & Fish, 213
New York International Gift Fair, 419
New York is Book Country, 416
New York Law Journal, 317
New York Magazine, 213
New York Media Directory, 454
New York Native, 213
New York Observer, 358
New York Periodical Dist Inc, 41
New York Post, 317
New York Press, 358

New York Publicity Outlets, 454
New York Review of Books, 175
New York State Media Directory, 454
New York Times, 317
New York University Book Center, 94
New Yorker, 213
Newark Book Center, 41
Newborn Enterprises Inc, 63
NewCity, 353
The Newman Group, 155
NewMedia Magazine, 213
Newport Daily Express, 338
Newport Daily Independent, 276
The Newport Daily News, 331
Newport Marketing, 409
News, 305
The News & Observer, 320-321
News & Record, 320
News 'N Novels, 88
The News and Daily Advance, 339
News Broadcast Network, 369
News Center West (Offices), 113
News Chief, 288
The News Depot Inc, 112
News From the Home Office, 247
News Future, 271
News Gazette, 291
News Herald, 288, 320, 324
News Journal, 323
The News Journal Company, 286
The News Journal, 286
News Republic, 342
News Shop, 107
News South Distributors, 57
The News Sun, 359
News Times, 285
News Tribune, 287
The News Tribune, 341
News USA, 369
News-Argus, 320
News-Banner, 294
News-Bulletin, 309
News-Dispatch, 296
News-Enterprise, 300
News-Gazette, 297
News-Herald, 293, 324, 328, 354
News-Item, 330
News-Messenger, 323
News-Pilot, 281
News-Press, 326
News-Record, 343
The News-Review, 327
The News-Sentinel, 295
The News-Star, 301
News-Sun, 294
The News-Sun, 295
News-Times, 295
News-Tribune, 305
The News-Virginian, 339
News/Broadcast Network, 369
Newsboy Books & Video, 88
Newsclip Clipping Bureau, 435
Newsclip's Illinois Media, 454
Newsday, 316-317
Newsdealers Supply Company, 55
Newsletter Association, 456
Newsletters in Print 1996, 454
Newsmaker Interviews, 381
Newsouth Distributor, 7
Newspaper Database-on-Diskette, 454
Newspaper editors and book reviewers, 273-348
Newspaper Rates & Data, 454
The Newspaper, 360
Newsouth Distributors Inc, 65
Newsweek, 213
Newton Daily News, 298

Newton Kansan, 299
Newton's Book Store, 112
Next Decade Catalog, 155
NexTech Systems Corp, 82
NG Hing Kee, 41
Niagara County News, 62
Niagara Falls Review, 346
Niagara Gazette, 318
Nichi Bei Times, 281
Nicholas Hoare Ltd, 53
Nichols Garden Nursery Catalog, 156
Nickleby's Book Store Cafe, 112
Nightengale-Conant Corporation, 7
Nihon Keizai Shimbun, 278
Niles Daily Star, 307
NJEA Review, 264
NM Direct, 409
No Nonsense E-Mail/Website Guide for Writers, 455
Nob Hill Gazette, 213
Noblesville Daily Ledger, 296
The Nolan-Lehr Group, 369
Noll's Educational Books, 41
Nolo News, 213
Nolo Press Bookstore, 156
Nomadic Display, 437
Nomadic Instand, 437
Non-Foods Merchandising, 247
Nonprofit World Journal, 213
NOPA Convention, 419
Nor'East Book Sales, 75
NorCal News Co, 56
Nordic Track Fitness Catalog, 156
Nordonia Hills Sun, 359
Norfolk Daily News, 312
The Norman Transcript, 325
North America Bookdealers Exchange, 41
North American Communications, 409
North American Fisherman, 213
North American Hunter, 213
North American Network, 369
North American Precis Syndicate, 369
North American Senior Media Directory, 455
North American Whitetail, 213
North Bay Nugget, 346
North Carolina Game & Fish, 213
North Carolina News Inc, 62
North Carolina School Book Dept, 41
North Cascades National Park, 41
North Central Book Distributors, 41
North Country Books Inc, 16
North County Times, 277
North East Wholesale Services, 41
North Hills News Record, 330
North Jersey Herald & News, 314
North Jersey Traveler, 213
North Light Book Club, 122
North Loop News, 353
North of 49 D.M. Services Ltd, 439
North Shore Community Newspapers, 355
North Shore Direct, 409
North Shore Distributors Inc, 58
North Shore Magazine, 213
North Shore News Company Inc, 60
North Texas Daily, 334
North Town Books, 101
North/SW Publishers Consortium, 375
Northern Arizona News Co, 55
Northern CA Booksellers Trade Show, 416
Northern Light Bookstore, 105
Northern News Company, 60
Northern Star, 292
Northern Sun Merchandising, 156
Northern Virginia Daily, 339
Northern Virginia Sun, 339
Northern Wyoming Daily News, 343

Northshire Bookstore, 115
NorthStyle Catalog, 156
Northwest Arkansas Times, 275
Northwest Bookfest, 416
Northwest Colorado Daily Press, 284
The Northwest Dispatch, 341
Northwest Florida Daily News, 287
Northwest Herald, 292
Northwest International Trading, 41
Northwest News, 67
Northwest News Co Inc, 63
Northwest News Company, 61
Northwest Publishing MarketPlace, 448
Northwest Travel, 213
Northwest-Signal, 324
Northwestern Church Supply, 441
Northwestern Products, 93
Northwestern University Press, 16
The Northwestern, 343
Norton News Agency Inc, 59
Norwalk Reflector, 324
Norwich Bookstore Inc, 115
Norwich Bulletin, 285
Nostalgia Entertainment Sourcebook, 458
Notable Children's Books, 445
Notable Children's Trade Books, 446
Noticias del Mundo, 317
Novalis, 53
Novel & Short Story Writer's Mkt, 448
Novoye Russkoye Slovo, 317
Novus Marketing Inc, 409
Nowy Dziennik Polish Daily News, 317
NPC Directory of News Services, 381
NRL Brokerage, 409
NRL Direct, 82
NSSEA Convention, 419
Nueces News Agency, 65
NUFAX, 156
Nugget, 213
NursePac, 388
Nursery Management & Production, 247
Nursing, 247
Nutley Journal, 356
Nutshell News, 213
NUVO, 353
NW Gardener's Resource Directory, 458
NYNEX Telemarketing Services, 409
NYNJBA/MABA Combined Trade Show, 416

O

O G Waffle Book Co, 41
O'Dwyer's Directory of Corporate Communications, 450
O'Dwyer's Directory of PR Exec, 450
O'Dwyer's Directory of PR Firms, 450
O'Dwyer's Media Placement Guide, 450
O'Reilley & Associates Inc, 17
Oak Park Book Center, 108
The Oak Ridger, 333
Oakland Community College, 94
Oakland Press, 307
Oakland Tribune, 279
Oasis, 213
Object Magazine, 247
Observer, 287, 296, 347
Observer-Dispatch, 319
Observer-News-Enterprise, 320
Observer-Reporter, 330
The Observer, 327
OC Weekly, 349
Ocala Star-Banner, 287
Occupational Hazards, 265

Occupational Health & Safety News, 265
Occupational Therapy in Health Care, 265
Ocean County Observer, 314
The Odessa American, 336
Odyssey Magazine, 213
Off Duty, 213
Off Our Backs, 213
Office Dealer Magazine, 247
Office Managers Information Pack, 388
Office Systems 95,
Office Systems Action Pack, 388
The Officer, 265
Ohio Game & Fish, 213
Ohio Periodical, 41
Ohio Periodical Distributors, 63
Oil Daily, 286
Ojibwe News, 355
Okeechobee News, 288
The Oklahoma Daily, 325
Oklahoma Game & Fish, 213
Oklahoma Gazette, 360
Oklahoma Journal Record, 325
Oklahoma Legislative Reporter, 325
Oklahoma Living, 214
Oklahoma Oil Reporter, 325
Oklahoma Today, 214
Oklahoman, 326
Okmulgee Daily Times, 326
Olathe News, 299
Old Cars Price Guide, 214
Old Colony Advertising Inc, 409
Old Dominion List Co Inc, 409
Old Harbor Books, 97
The Old House Antiques & Gifts, 156
Old Santa Fe Trail Books, 111
Old Time Crochet, 214
Old Town Book Merchant, 106
Olde Methuen Book Shoppe, 156
Olean Times Herald, 318
Oliver Gilliland, Representative, 75
Olivers Books, 117
Ollis Book Corp, 170
Ollis Book Corporation, 41
Olney Daily Mail, 293
Olson News Agency, 108
Olsson's Books & Records, 88
Olwen Direct Mail Limited, 438
The Olympian, 340
Omaha New Media Expo, 416
Omaha World Herald, 312
Omeda Communications, 82
Omega Direct, 409
Omega Engineering, 156
Omega List Co, 409
On the Internet: User Demographics and Trends, 456
On the Issues, 214
On the Scene Productions, 369
On the Scene Productions/NY, 369
On Three Inc, 156
On-Demand, 214
On-Line Resources, 409
On-Target Postcard Deck, 388
One Minute Catalog for Dentist, 388
One Potata Productions, 369
One-Stop Catalog Shop, 381
Oneida Daily Dispatch, 318
Online Access, 214
The Online Marketing Letter, 271
Online Time, 214
Online User, 214
Onondaga News Agency, 62
Ontario Craft, 214
Ontario Library Services Center, 53
Opelika-Auburn News, 274
Open Wheel Magazine, 214
The Opera Box Catalog, 156

Opera News, 214
Opinion-Tribune, 354
Opportunity Magazine, 214
Opportunity Seekers Card Pack, 388
Orange Coast Magazine, 214
Orange County Business Journal, 350
Orange County News, 350
Orange County Register, 281
The Orange Elephant, 156
The Orange Leader, 336
Orbis Books, 17
Orbit, 214
Orbit Books Corp, 41
The Order Fulfillment Group, 82
Oregon Business, 214
Oregon Coast Magazine, 214
Oregon Cycling, 214
Oregon Daily Emerald, 326
Oregon Historical Society, 75
Oregon List/Group, 409
The Oregonian, 327
Organic Agriculture Catalog, 156
Organic Gardening, 214
Organic Gardening Book Club, 122
Organica, 214
Organizations (directories), 456-458
Original Products DBA Jamil, 17
Original Publications, 17
Orion Direct Marketing, 409
Orion Magazine, 214
Orlando Magazine, 214
Orlando Sentinel, 288
Orlando Weekly, 352
Ornaal Color Photos, 439
Oroville Mercury Register, 279
Orr Books, 109
The Orvis Company Catalog, 156
Oryx Press Mailing Lists, 409
OS/2 Professional, 247
Osceola Sentinel-Tribune, 354
Oskaloosa Herald, 298
Other chains, 95-96
The Other List Company Inc, 409
Ottawa Valley News Agency Ltd, 68
Ottenheimer Publishers Inc, 17
Ottumwa Courier, 298
Our Children, 214
Our Family/Our Friends/Our World, 446
Our Kids & Teens Magazine, 214
Our Kids Houston, 214
Our Kids San Antonio, 215
Our Sunday Visitor, 215
Out, 215
Out Magazine, 215
Out West, 215
Outbound Traveler, 215
Outcry Magazine, 215
Outdoor Action, 215
Outdoor America, 215
Outdoor Life, 215
Outdoor Retailer, 247
Outlet Book Co, 170
The Outlook, 282
Outside Kids, 215
Outside Magazine, 215
Outstanding Science Trade Books for Children, 446
Owatonna People's Press, 308
Oxbridge Communications Inc, 409
Oxbridge Directory of Newsletters, 455
Oxfam America Catalog, 156
The Oxford American, 215
Oxford Book Stores, 88
Oxford Eagle, 309
Oxford University Press, 17
Oxnard Star, 279
Ozark News Agency Inc, 55

Ozark Periodicals Distrib Inc, 61

P

P & F Communications, 369
P-H Business Computing Pac, 389
P-H Business Management Cards, 389
P-H Financial Management Cards, 389
P-H Health & Fitness Action Pac, 389
P-H Lawyers Action Cards, 389
P-H Music Educators Action Cards, 389
P-H Sports & Coaching Action Pac, 389
P-O-P & Sign Design, 248
P-O-P Times, 248
Pacific Books, 41
Pacific Business News, 353
Pacific Crest, 41
Pacific Fishing, 248
Pacific Fulfillment Services, 83
Pacific Lists Inc, 409
Pacific Media Concepts, 409
Pacific Northwest Books, 41
The Pacific Northwest Inlander, 361
Pacific NW Booksellers Assn Trade Show, 416
Pacific Pipeline Inc, 41
Pacific Spirit WholeLife Catalog, 156
Pacific Sun, 350
Pack-O-Fun, 215
Package Fulfillment Center, 83
Package Insert & Co-op Directory, 389
Padilla Speer Beardsley, 369
Paducah Sun, 301
Pages Editorial Service, 439
Pages For All Ages Bookstore Inc, 105
Paint Horse Journal, 215
Paisley Publishing, 381
Paladin Press, 156
Palatka Daily News, 288
Palestine Herald-Press, 336
Palladium-Item, 296
Palladium-Times, 318
Palm Beach Daily News, 288
Palm Beach Post, 288
Palm Springs Desert Sun, 279
Palm Springs Life, 215
Palmer & Associates, 75
Palmer News, 59
Palmer Publications, 83
Palmer Video Magazine, 215
Palo Alto Weekly, 350
Palos Verdes Peninsula News, 351
The Pampa News, 336
Pan Asian Publications Inc, 53
Pandora Book Peddlers Catalog, 156
Pandora Distributors, 65
Panel World, 248
Pannonia Books, 53
Pantagraph, 291
Paper Boat Magazine, 215
Paper Collectors Marketplace, 215
The Paper Cutter, 96
Paper Industry, 248
Paperback Books for Young People: An Annotated Guide, 446
Paperback Previews, 156
Paperback rights buyer, 126
Paperbacks for Educators, 7
Parabola Magazine, 215
Parachute Press Inc, 17
Paragon Direct Marketing, 409
The Paragon, 157
Paragould Daily Press, 276
ParaLists, 409

Parameters: US Army War College, 248
Paraplegia News, 215
Parapsychology, New Age, and the Occult: A Source Encyclopedia, 458
Parent's Mailing Lists, 409
Parentguide News, 215
Parenting Magazine, 215
Parenting Press Catalog, 157
Parenting Resources Catalog, 157
Parents & Teenagers, 215
Parents Magazine, 215
Parents of Infants & Toddlers, 389
Parents of Teenagers, 216
Parents' Choice, 216
Parents' Press, 216
ParentSource, 216
Paris Daily Beacon News, 293
The Paris News, 336
The Paris Post-Intelligencer, 333
Paris Review, 216
Parish Pastor Edition, 389
Park Avenue Agents, 75
Park Books, 104
Park Slope Paper, 357
The Parkersburg News, 341
The Parkersburg Sentinel, 342
Parkplace Book Co, 116
Parks & History Assn Bookstores, 90
Parma Sun Post, 359
Parnassus, 97, 113
Parnassus: Poetry in Review, 216, 248
Parrish Associates Inc, 410
Parsons Sun, 300
Parsons Technology Inc, 410
Partisan Review, 216, 248
Partner Village Store, 157
Partners Book Distributing, 41
Partnership Book Services, 375
Party Source, 248
PartyLine Newsletter, 456
PAS Speakers Bureau, 378
Pasadena Citizen, 336
Pasadena Star-News, 279
Pasadena Weekly, 350
Pastors Information Cards, 389
Pat Rose & Associates, 369
Pathway Book Clubs, 122
Patricia Alfonsi, Representative, 75
Patricia Buck's Emporium, 107
The Patriot Ledger, 304
Patriot-News, 328
Paul & Company Publishers, 7
Pauline Books and Media, 93
Pauls Valley Daily Democrat, 326
Paxton Daily Record, 293
Paz & Associates, 375
PBD Inc, 83
PC America, 157
PC Computing, 216
PC Connection, 157
PC Gamer, 216, 248
PC Laptop, 216
PC Magazine, 216, 248
PC Network Package Inserts, 389
PC Novice, 216
PC Presentations Productions, 216
PC Techniques, 216, 248
PC Today, 216, 248
PC World, 216
PC World Action Cards, 389
PC World Lotus Edition, 216
PC Zone, 157
PCs ComIpeat, 157
PCS Data Processing, 83
PCS Mailing List Company, 439
PD&D Post Pack, 389
PDK Communications, 369

Peace River Block News, 344
Peaceful Living Publications, 20
Peaceful Valley Farm Supply, 157
Peachtree Magazine, 216
Pearl Publishing House, 17
Pecos Enterprises, 336
Pedigrees & R C Steele, 157
Pee Dee News Co Inc, 64
Pegasus Fantasy Books, 90
Peggy Tagliarino PR, 369
Pekin Daily Times, 293
Pen Notes, 17, 170
Pendar Book Company, 7
Pendragon Books, 101
Pendragon Software Library, 157
Penfield Press, 17
Penguin Books, 126
Penguin USA, 17
Peninsula Clarion, 274
Peninsula Daily News, 340
Peninsula News Co, 57
Penn News Co, 64
Pennsylvania Game & Fish, 216
Pennsylvania Magazine, 216
Pennsylvania Media Directory, 455
Pennwell Publishing Co, 410
Pensacola News Journal, 288
Pension Management, 248
Penthouse, 216
Penticton Herald, 344
Penton Publishing, 375, 389, 410
People (directories), 458-460
People Weekly, 216
People's Co-op Bookstore, 117
People's News and Book Mart, 89
PeopleSpeak, 439
Peoria Journal Star, 293
Perfect Response Co, 83
Performance Marketing, 410
Peribo, 79
Periodical Brokers, 7
Periodical Management Group, 90
Periodical Services Inc, 42
Perma-Bound Hertzberg New Method, 42
Perry Daily Journal, 326
Perrygraf, 437
Personal & Financial Source Book, 157
Personal Computing Tools, 157
Personal Selling Power, 248
Perspective, 248
Perspectives on Political Science, 216
Perspectives Press Co-op Mailing, 381
Peru Daily Tribune, 296
Pet Age, 248
The Pet Dealer, 248
Pet Food Express, 96
Pet Industry Trade Show, 419
Pet Product News, 248
Pet-Dek, 389
Peter Clark, Representative, 75
Peter Li Education Group, 410
Petoskey News-Review, 307
Pets Magazine, 216
Pharmaceutical/Medical Packaging, 265
Pharmacy Today, 248
Pharos-Tribune, 296
Phelon Sheldon & Marsar Inc, 410
Phelon's Discount Stores, 461
Philadelphia, 216
Philadelphia City Paper, 360
Philadelphia Daily News, 329
Philadelphia Gay News, 216
Philadelphia Inquirer, 329
Philadelphia Northeast Times, 360
Philadelphia Publicity Guide, 455
Philadelphia Weekly, 360
Phillips Business Information Inc, 410

Phillips Publishing List Mktg, 410
Phoenix, 329
Phoenix Books and Records, 101
The Phoenix Bookshop, 101
Phoenix Films & Video Inc, 7
Phoenix Home & Garden, 217
Phoenix Magazine, 217
Phoenix New Times, 349
The Phoenix, 101, 217
Photo District News, 248
Photo Techniques, 217
Photographer's Forum, 248
Photographer's Market, 448
A Photographer's Place, 157
Physical & Occupational Therapy, 265
Physician, 265
Physician ActionPac, 389
Physics Today, 265
PI Magazine, 265
Pic 'n' Save, 170
Picayune Item, 309
PieceWork: All This By Hand, 217
Piedmont News, 62
Pierre Capitol Journal, 332
The Pilot Log, 248
Pilot-News, 296
Pilot-Tribune, 298
PIMS European Media Directory, 455
PIMS New York, 370
Pine Bluff Commercial, 276
Pinellas News, 352
Pinnacle List Co, 410
PinSource, 441
Pioneer, 305
Pioneer Hi-Bred Intl, 157
Pioneer Pacific List Mktg Inc, 410
Pioneer/Advertiser, 307
Piper's Magazine, 217
Pipestone Indian Shrine Assn, 157
Piqua Daily Call, 324
Pitch Weekly, 356
The Pitt News, 329
Pittsburgh Business Times, 217
Pittsburgh Legal Journal, 329
Pittsburgh Magazine, 217
Pittsburgh Post Gazette, 329
Pittsburgh's Child, 217
Pittsfield News, 60
Pizza and Pasta, 248
Pizza Today, 248
PLA National Conference, 416
The Plain Dealer, 322
The Plainsman, 332
Plainview Daily Herald, 336
Plane & Pilot, 217
Plane Talk: Good Ideas, 389
Planetary Publications Catalog, 157
Planned Communications Service, 370
Planned Television Arts, 370
Planning For Excellence, 157
Plano Star Courier, 336
Plastic Canvas Crafts, 217
Plastic Canvas World, 217
Plastic News, 248
Plastics Engineering, 249
Plastics Technology, 249
Plastics World, 249
Platt's Oilgram News, 317
Play, 217
Play Fair Toys, 157
Playbill, 217
Playboy, 217
Players Library, 157
Playgirl, 217
Playthings, 249
Plough Publishing House, 17
Ploughshares: Journal of New Writing, 249

The Plow & Hearth, 158
PMA Co-op Mailings, 381
PMA Display Service, 420
PMA Literary & Film Management, 375
PMC Partnership Ltd, 375
PMM Marketing Inc, 410
PMR Productions, 437
Pocket Books, 126
Pocono Record, 330
Poet's Handbook, 448
Poetry Flash, 217
Poetry Publication Showcase, 416
Poets Marketplace, 448
Point Pleasant Register, 342
Polaris Communications, 410
Police & Security Action Pack, 389
Police Magazine, 249
Policies of Publishers: A Handbook for Order Librarians, 448
Polish-American Journal, 217
Political Resources Inc, 410
Politics and Prose, 103
Polk Direct, 410
Pollution Engineering, 249
Polybook Distributors, 42
Pomona Valley News Agency Inc, 56
The Ponca City News, 326
Poor Richards, 102
Popular Ceramics, 217
Popular Electronics, 217
Popular Hot Rodding, 217
Popular Mechanics, 217
Popular Photography, 249
Popular Science, 217
Popular Woodworking, 249
Port Arthur News, 336
Portage Daily Register, 343
Portales News-Tribune, 315
Porter's Photographic & Equip, 158
Porter/Novelli, 370
Portland News Company, 59
Portland Press Herald, 302
Portland Speakers Bureau, 378
Portrait of a Bookstore, 101
Portraying Persons w/ Disability, 446
Portsmouth Daily Times, 324
Portsmouth Herald, 313
Portsmouth News Agency, 63
A Positive Approach Inc, 217
Positive Bks/21st Century Kids, 158
Positive Promotions, 441
Post, 322
Post & Mail, 294
Post Register, 290
Post-Bulletin, 308
Post-Journal, 316
Post-Record, 281
The Post-Star, 316
Post-Tribune, 310
Postal Promotions, 410
The Poteau Daily News & Sun, 326
Potentials in Marketing, 271
Potomac List Co Inc, 410
Potomac News, 340
Potpourri, 218
The Potters Shop, 158
Pottery Barn, 158
Pottstown News Company, 64
Pottsville Republican, 329
Poughkeepsie Journal, 318
Powell's Book Store, 89, 105
Power Equipment Trade, 249
Power Media Selects, 451
Power Transmission Design, 249
Power Up! Software, 158
PR Newswire, 370
PR ProfitCenter Database, 451

PR Reporter, 271
PR Watch, 218
Practical Management Inc, 410
Prairie Fire, 218
Prairie House Books, 53
Prairie House Inc, 17
Prairie Lights Books, 106
Pratical Horseman, 249
Pratt Tribune, 300
Pratt's Guide/Venture Capital Sources, 459
Praxis Publications Lists, 410
Pre, 218
Pre Release Center, 170
Pre-School Co-op, 381
Preaching Magazine, 265
Preferred Lists, 410
Premiere Magazine, 218
Premium Incentive & Travel Buyer, 450
Premium Incentive Show, 419
Prentice Hall - Canada, 20
Prentice-Hall Direct, 389
Prepared Foods, 265
Prepress Direct!, 158
Prescott Courier, 275
Presidents Exec-Cards, 389
Presque Isle Wine Cellars, 158
Press & Sun Bulletin, 315
Press Community Newspapers, 359
Press Republican, 318
Press-Enterprise, 327
Press-Telegram, 278
Pressclips Inc, 435
Prestige Mailing Lists Inc, 410
Prevention, 218
Prevention Book Club, 122
Prevention in Human Services, 265
Prima Publishing, 7
Primary K-3 Education Card Pack, 389
Primary Sources & Original Works, 175
Prime, 218
PrimeLife, 375
Prince Albert Daily Herald, 348
Prince Books, 115
Prince George Citizen, 344
Prince George's Express, 361
Prince George's Journal, 303, 339
Prince William Journal, 339
Prince William Weekly-Potomac, 361
Princeton Book Company, 17
Princeton Daily Clarion, 296
Principals Action Deck, 389
Print, 265
Print & Sound, 75
Print Cards, 389
Print Mail of Maine, 410
Print Publishing/School Market, 456
Print/Graphic Design Bookstore, 158
Printed Circuit Design, 249
Printed Circuit Fabrication, 249
Printer's Row Book Fair, 416
Printers Inc Bookstore, 101
The Printers Shopper, 158
Printing Impressions, 249
Printing News Midwest, 249
Printing News/East, 249
Private Eye Weekly, 361
Private Pilot, 218
Produce Business, 249
Produce Merchandising, 249
Product Movers, 381
Productivity Programs, 158
Proe & Proe Associates, 75
Professional Boatbuilder, 249
Professional Book Center, 17
Professional Book Distributors, 42
Professional Business Speakers, 378
The Professional Communicator, 218

Professional Counselor, 249
Professional Direct & Advanced, 410
Professional Displays, 437
Professional magazines, 257-268
Professional Media Service Corp, 42
Professional Mktg Communications, 410
Professional Pilot, 265
Professional Publishers Group, 375
Professional Tool & Equip News, 249
Professional's Library, 42
Profile America List Co, 410
Profit: Info Tech for Entrepreneur, 249
Profnet, 456
Programmer's Power Card Pack, 389
The Programmer's Shop, 158
Progress, 327
The Progress-Index, 339
Progressive Architecture, 249
Progressive Distribution Service, 83
Progressive Grocer, 249
The Progressive Review, 218
The Progressive, 218
Proini, 316
The Prolific Freelancer, 218
Prologue Inc, 10
Promo, 271
Promotional Book Co, 53
Promotional SportsStars Speaker Bureau, 378
Propaganda Distributors Ltd, 79
Prospects Unlimited, 410
Provantage, 158
Providence Business News, 218
Providence Journal-Bulletin, 331
Providence Phoenix, 360
Provident Book Store, 122
Provident Bookstore, 93
Provincial News Company, 67
PsL Sourcebook, 158
Psychodrama & Sociometry, 265
Psychology Today, 218
Psychology Today Bookshelf/Tape, 158
Psychotherapy Book Club, 122
The PT Distributor, 249
PTA Interactive, 370
PTO-Pak, 390
Public Brand Software, 158
Public Citizen, 218
Public Library Card Pack, 390
Public Library Program, 381
Public News, 361
Public Opinion, 327
Public Relations News, 249
Public Relations Services, 370
Public Relations Tactics, 250
Publications Catalog, 158
Publications Services Inc, 83
Publicity, 438
Publicity Express, 381
Publicity service, 365-372
Publicity to Go, 370
Publish, 265
Publisher Inquiry Services, 158
Publisher Resources Inc, 7
Publisher's Clearinghouse, 158
The Publisher's Consultant, 376
Publisher's Intl Mktg Services, 42
Publisher's Mail Service Inc, 410
Publisher's Overstock, 158
Publisher's Toolbox, 159
Publishers Book Display, 420
Publishers Book Exhibit, 420
Publishers Business System, 438
Publishers Creative Systems, 83
Publishers Directory, 448
Publishers Distributing Company, 7
Publishers Distribution Center, 42

Publishers Distribution Service, 8
Publishers Group West, 8
Publishers List Exchange Inc, 410
Publishers Media, 42
Publishers Overstock Unlimited, 170
Publishers Resources Inc, 42, 83
Publishers Software System, 83
Publishers Storage & Shipping, 83
Publishers Support Services, 370, 381
Publishers Support Services, 438
Publishers Trade List Annual, 448
Publishers Weekly, 175
Publishers who also distribute books, 11-20
Publishers' Catalogs Annual, 448
Publishers' Photographic Service, 439
Publishers, Distributors and Wholesalers of the United States, 448
Publishing Entrepreneur, 218
Publishing for Professional Markets: Review, Trends & Forecast, 455
Publishing for the College Market: Trends & Forecasts, 460
Publishing Perfection, 159
Pudding House, 17
Pueblo Chieftain, 284
Pueblo To People Catalog, 159
Puerto Rico International Book Fair '97, 416
Pulley Learning Associates, 42
Pulp & Paper, 250
Pulse!, 218
Purchasing Magazine, 250
Purdue Exponent, 297
Pure, 218
Pure-Bred Dogs/American Kennel Gazette, 218
Puski-Corvin Hungarian Books, 42
Puss'N Books, 116
Putnam Book Center, 112
Putnam Reporter Dispatch, 319
PW Religion Bookline, 250
Pyle & Associates, 370
The Pyramid Collection, 159
Pyramid Film & Video, 8

QBI Library Conference Displays, 381
QST, 218
Quad City Times, 297
Quad Marketing, 381
Qualified Lists Corp, 410
Qualified Remodeler, 250
Quality Books Inc, 8
Quality Digest, 250
Quality Education Data, 411
Quality in Manufacturing, 250
Quality Paperback Book Club, 122
Quality Small Business Books, 159
The Quarter Horse Journal, 218
Quebec International Book Fair, 416
Quebec Le Soleil, 348
Queblo, 159
Queens Tribune, 357
Quest, 265
Quest Magazine, 265
Queue Inc, 159
Quick & Easy Crafts, 218
Quick & Easy Quilting, 218
Quick Link Information Services, 436
Quick Printing, 250
Quill & Quire, 250
Quill Corporation Catalog, 159

Quilt World, 218
Quilting International, 218
Quilting Today, 219
Quincy Herald-Whig, 293
Quinsept, 159
Quirks Marketing Research Review, 250
Quiz Control, 159
QVC Network, 159
QW Communications, 411

R & S Supply, 42
R & W Distribution Inc, 42
R B Walker Catalog, 159
R E Martin Public Relations, 438
R J Julia Booksellers, 103
R L Polk & Co, 411
R L Silver Associates, 376
R S Means, 390
Racquet Magazine, 219
RAD Marketing & RadioBase, 411
Radiance Magazine, 219
Radio Phone Interview Shows, 455
Radio Shack Catalog, 159
Radio TV Reports, 435
Radio Yearbook, 455
Radio/TV Contacts Focus, 455
Radio/TV Interview Report, 381
Rafu Shimpo, 278
Railroad Model Craftsman, 219
Railway Age, 250
Railway Track & Structures, 250
Rain, 219
Rainbow Bookstore, 116
The Rainbow Collection, 159
Rainbow West Christian Book, 93
Raincoast Book Distribution, 10
The Raleigh Group, 370
Raleigh News Agency Inc, 62
Ralin Wholesalers, 159
Ralph Curtis Books, 42
Randal Wood Displays, 437
Random House Audiobooks, 125
Random House Inc, 17
Random House Value Publishing, 170
Random House Video, 127
Random Lengths News, 351
Ranger Rick, 219
Ransom Hill Press, 42
Rapid City Journal, 332
Rapport, 219
Raritan Periodicals Sales Co, 42
Ratcliffe's Book & Office Supply, 96
Ravalli Republic, 311
Ravelle Brickman Public Relations, 370
Rawlins Daily Times, 343
Ray Gun, 219
Ray Wittrup, Representative, 75
Raytown Tribune, 356
Rayve Fulfillment, 83
RC Direct Inc, 411
Re:Search International, 439
Re:Sources, 370
RE:view, 265
Read News Agency, 55
Read On!, 111
Reader's Catalog, 159
Reader's Digest, 219
Reader's Digest Condensed Books, 122
Reading Circle, 42
Reading Eagle Times, 330
Reading Express Book Station, 108
Reading Peddler Book Fairs, 43

The Reading Teacher, 219
Reading's Fun Ltd, 43
Readme Agency, 83
Readmor Bookstores, 89
Readmore Academic Services, 43
Readmore Books, 91
Readmore Inc, 43
Readmore Magazines & Books, 89
Real Estate Books & Periodicals in Print, 446
The Real Estate Finance Journal, 219
The Real Estate Finance Journal, 250
Real Estate Response Cards, 390
Real Estate Review, 250
Real Goods Catalog, 159
Realtor News, 250
Reason, 219
Reasonable Solutions Software, 159
RECAP: Publications Inc, 17
Recipe Digest, 219
Reckon: Magazine of Southern Culture, 219
Record, 319
Record Gazette, 276
Record Herald/Indianola Tribune, 354
Record-Argus, 328
Record-Courier, 324
Record-Herald, 324, 330
Record-Searchlight, 280
Recorded Books, 125
Recorder, 280-281, 304, 315
The Record, 282, 313, 346
Recovery Shoppe, 101
Recreation News, 219
Recreation Resources, 250
Recreational Equipment Inc, 159
Recreational Gaming & Lottery, 159
Red & Black, 289
Red Deer Advocate, 344
Red Herring, 265
The Red Herring Mystery Magazine, 219
The Red Hot Company Catalog on Disk, 160
Red Rock Entertainment, 113
Red Rock News, 349
Red Rose Collection Catalog, 160
Red Rose Distributing, 56
Red Sea Press, 17
Redbook, 219
Redemption Digest & Securities, 317
Redlands Daily Facts, 280
Redwing Book Company, 43
Redwood Book Sales, 75
Reed Reference Publishing, 451
Reference Book Center Catalog, 160
Reference Books Catalog, 160
Reference Desk, 219
The Reference Librarian, 175
Reference Services Review, 175
The Reference Shelf, 420
The Reference Shelf, 437
Reference Sources for Small and Medium-Sized Libraries, 446
Reform Judaism, 219
Regent Book Company Inc, 43
Regina Leader Post, 348
Regina News Ltd, 68
Regina Ryan Publ Enterprises Inc, 18
Reginald Fennell Subscription, 43
Regional bookstore chains, 89-91
Regional Readers Database, 411
Register, 354
Register Citizen, 285
The Register Guard, 326
The Register-Herald, 341
Register-News, 293
Register-Star, 316

The Regulator Bookshop, 112
REI America, 8
Reid Resources, 376
Reidsville Review, 321
Reliable Corporation Catalog, 160
Religion & Public Affairs, 458
Religion Teacher's Journal, 265
Religious Booksellers List, 411
Religious bookstores, 92-93
Religious Lists, 411
Relix Magazine, 219
Remainder dealers, 169-170
Remarkable Products, 160
Remedial and Special Education, 266
Remember Magazine, 219
Reminisce, 219
Remodeling Magazine, 250
Renaissance Book Services, 43
Reno Gazette Journal, 313
Reno News and Review, 356
Renouf Publishing Co Ltd, 53
Rensselaer Republican, 296
Renton's Intl Stationery Inc, 441
Rentsch Associates, 370
Reporter, 295
Reporter Dispatch-Metro Edition, 319
Reporter Dispatch-Northern Edition, 319
The Reporter, 329
Repository, 322
Reprint Book Shop, 103
Reptiles, 219
Republican-Eagle, 308
Republican-Times, 311
Research & Response Intl Inc, 411
Research Alert Newsletter, 250
Research Books Inc, 43
Research Centers Directory, 458
Research Periodicals & Book Service, 43
Research Projects Corp, 411
Reseller Management, 250
Reseller Mgt Card Pack, 390
Residential Lighting, 250
Residential Treatment/Children.., 266
Resource & Development Group Inc, 411
Resource Recycling, 250
Resource Sharing & Info Networks, 175
ReSource: A Guide to Books/Audio, 160
Resources Action Cards, 390
Response Innovations, 411
Response Mailing Lists, 411
Response Media Products, 411
Response TV Magazine, 271
Response Unlimited, 411
Restaurant Business, 250
Restaurant Hospitality, 250
Restaurant Publicity News, 250
Restaurants & Institutions, 251
Results Unlimited, 378
Retail Hardware Trade Show, 419
Retail Store Image, 251
Retailing News, 251
Rethinking Schools, 266
Retired Military Market Pack, 390
The Retired Officer, 251
Retirement Life, 251
Reunions Magazine, 219
Review Times, 323
ReVISION Journal, 266
Revolution Software Inc, 411
Rhode Island Monthly, 220
The Rhode Island Parents' Paper, 220
Richard DeRose, Representative, 75
Richard Owen Roberts Wholesalers, 43
Richardson's Books Inc, 43
Richmond County Daily Journal, 321
Richmond Register, 301
Richmond Times Dispatch, 339

Rick O'Shea Associates, 76
Rickard List Marketing, 411
Rider, 220
Rider Circulation Services Inc, 43
Ridgeway Record, 330
Riffkin Direct Inc, 411
The Right Lists Corp, 411
Right On Programs, 160
Right On!, 220
Right's On, 438
Rights buyers, 125-127
Rights from USA Review, 381
Ring mailing Lists, 411
Rio Grande Book Co, 43
Rio Grande Sun, 357
Rittenhouse Book Dist Inc, 43
The Ritz Company, 441
River Oaks Bookstore, 114
River Road Recipes Cookbook, 43
The Riverfront Times, 356
Rivers and Mountains, 43
Riverside Book & Bible House, 43
Riverside Book Center, 101
Riverside Book Co Inc, 18, 170
Riverside Press Enterprise, 280
The Riverton Ranger, 343
Riverwalk Books Ltd, 116
Rizzoli International Bookstore, 43, 92, 105
RJV Computer Resources, 83
RLS Associates, 83
RLS Associates Inc, 439
RMI Direct Marketing Inc, 411
RN Magazine, 251
Road & Track, 220
Roanoke Times, 339
The Robb Report, 220
Robert Hale & Company, 43
Roberts Colonial House, 160
Robesonian, 320
Rochester News Co, 60
Rochester Sentinel, 296
Rock Bottom Remainders Inc, 170
Rock Island Argus, 294
Rockbottom Books, 44
Rockdale Citizen, 289
The Rockford Institute, 411
Rockford Register Star, 294
Rockland Journal-News, 319
Rockland-Catskill Inc, 62
Rockport Publishers, 18, 170
Rocks & Minerals, 266
Rocky Ford Gazette, 284
Rocky Mount Evening Telegram, 321
Rocky Mount News Agency, 62
Rocky Mountain Book Festival, 416
Rocky Mountain Game & Fish, 220
Rocky Mountain Natue Assn, 91
Rocky Mountain News, 284
Rocky Mountain Rider, 220
Rocky Mountain Sports Magazines, 220
Rod & Custom Magazine, 220
Rodale Books Cookbook Buyers, 390
Roghaar Associates, 76
Roig Spanish Books, 44
Roll Call: The Newspaper of Capital Hill, 352
Rolla Daily News, 310
Rolling Stone, 220
Romantic Times, 220
Romantic Times Books by Mail, 160
Rome News, 58
Rome News-Tribune, 290
Romer Communications Inc, 370
Ron Doussard & Associates, 76
Ron Marin Associates, 370
Ronald Columbus, Representative, 76
Rose Electronics, 160

Rose Printing Co Inc, 390
Roskin/Friedman, 370
Roswell Daily Record, 315
The Rotarian, 220
Roundhouse Books, 102
Roundtable Press Inc, 18
Routledge, 76
The Rower's Bookshelf, 160
Roy Derstine Book Co, 44
Roy Perry Associates, 76
Royal Mail, 438
Royal Publications, 44
Royal Publishing, 434
Rubber Ducky Magazine, 220
Rubin Periodicals Group, 62
Rubin Response Services Inc, 411
Ruder Finn, 370
Rug Hooking, 220
Runner's World, 220
Running Times, 220
Rushmore News Inc, 64
Rushville Republican, 296
Russ Fons Public Relations, 370
Russell Daily News, 300
Russia Book & Art Shop Inc, 44
Russian Life, 281
Ruston Daily Ledger, 302
Rutland Daily Herald, 338
RV Business, 251
Ryen Re Associates, 76
Ryukyu Martial Arts Co, 44

S

S & B Sales Associates, 76
S & L Sales Company, 44, 170
S & P of New York Budo, 160
S & S Arts & Crafts, 160
S & S Bookstore, 89
S & W Distributors Inc, 44
S&MSS (Sales & Mktg Sftwre Source), 160
S&P's Investment Forum, 390
S&S Computer Services Inc, 83
S&S Public Relations, 370
Saavoy List Management, 411
Sacramento Bee, 280
Sacramento News & Review, 351
Sacramento Reads!, 416
SafeSteps, 220
Sage Information Services, 411
Sagebrush Press, 44
Saginaw News, 307
SAIL Magazine, 220
Sailing Magazine, 251
Sailing World, 220
Sailors Bookshelf, 160
Saint Lawrence Nurseries Catalog, 160
Saint Mark's Bookshop, 112
Saks News, 63
Sal McLemore & Associates, 76
Salamanca Press, 318
Salem Evening News, 305
The Salem News, 324
Salem Statesman-Journal, 327
Sales & Marketing Exec-Cards, 390
Sales & Marketing Success Deck, 390
Sales and Mktg Strategies & News, 251
Sales Automation Survival Guide, 160
Sales Manager's Bulletin, 251
Sales representatives, 69-79
The Salesman's Guide Inc, 411
Salina Journal, 300
Salisbury Post, 321
Salon, 220

Salon du livre de Montreal, 416
Salon International du Livre, 417
Salon News, 251
Salt Lake Tribune, 337-338
Saltspring Software, 160
Salvation Army Supply Purchasing, 44, 93
Sam Borofsky Associates, 76
Sam Flax Inc, 96
Sam Tuo Book Center, 44
Sam Weller's Zion Books, 115
Sam's Wholesale Club, 44
The Sample Case, 220
Sampson Independent, 319
Samuel French Theatre/Film Bkshp, 160
Samuel Weiser Inc, 18
San Angelo Standard-Times, 336
San Antonio Current, 361
San Antonio Express-News, 336
San Antonio Inter-American Fair, 416
San Bernardino Sun, 280
San Diego Country Writers and
  Publishers Resource Guide, 449
San Diego Daily Transcript, 280
San Diego Family Press, 220
San Diego Finder Binder, 455
San Diego Museum of Art Store, 44
San Diego Parent Magazine, 220
San Diego Reader, 351
San Diego Union-Tribune, 280
San Francisciana, 44
San Francisco Bay Guardian, 351
San Francisco Business Times, 351
San Francisco Chronicle, 281
San Francisco Daily Journal, 281
San Francisco Examiner, 281
San Francisco Focus, 220
San Francisco Independent, 351
San Francisco Peninsula Parent, 221
San Francisco Review of Books, 221
San Gabriel Valley Daily Tribune, 276
San Jose Mercury News, 281
San Luis Obispo New Times, 351
San Marcos Daily Record, 336
San Mateo Times, 281
San Mateo Weekly, 349
Sandhill Book Marketing, 10
Sandhill Books, 106
Sandmeyer's Bookstore, 105
Sandpiper Gifts & Books, 160
Sandra Taylor Literary Ent, 18
Sandusky Register, 324
Sandy Mush Herb Nursery Catalog, 161
Sanford Herald, 288, 321
SanMar Associates Inc, 411
Santa Barbara Independent, 351
Santa Barbara Magazine, 221
Santa Barbara News Agency, 56
Santa Barbara News-Press, 282
Santa Cruz County Sentinal, 282
Santa Fe New Mexican, 315
Santa Fe Reporter, 357
Santa Maria Times, 282
Santa Rosa Press Democrat, 282
Santa Ynez Valley News, 351
Saphograph Corp, 44
Sapphile Card Pack, 390
Sapphire Systems, 83
Sapula Daily Herald, 326
Saraband, 18
Sarasota Herald Tribune, 288
Saratogian, 318
Sarris Bookmarketing Services, 376
Sassy, 221
Satellite Orbit, 221
Satellite TV Week, 221
Sathya Sai Book Center of Amer, 44
Saturday Evening Post, 221

Saudi Bookfair, 417
Sault Star, 347
Saunders Book Co, 53
Savannah News-Press, 290
Save Energy Catalog, 161
Saveur, 221
Savings & Community Banker, 266
Savvy Management, 370
Sax Arts and Crafts Catalog, 161
The Sayles Organization, 370
SBA Lists Inc, 411
SCB Distributors, 8
Scenario, 221
SCENTSITIVITY, 221
Schmidt Printing, 390
Schmul Publishing Co Inc, 44
Schoenhof's Foreign Books Inc, 44
The Scholar's Bookshelf, 44
Scholar's Choice Ltd, 53
Scholarly Book Service, 10
Scholastic Book Fairs, 45, 416
Scholastic Coach & Athletic Director, 266
Scholastic DynaMath, 221
Scholastic K-12 Educational Tech, 161
Scholastic Math Power, 221
Scholastic News, 221
Scholastic Scope, 221
Scholastic Update, 221
Scholium International, 18
School Aid Company, 45
School Book Fairs, 45
School Book Service Inc, 45
School Counselors Catalog 6-12, 161
School Counselors Catalog K-5, 161
School Libraries in Technology, 390
School Library Journal, 176
School Library Media Quarterly, 176
School Marketing Newsletter, 271
School Mates, 221
School Media Associates, 76
School of Metaphysics Natl Hdqt, 45
School Products Company, 8
School Works, 18
Schoolbell Books & Gifts Inc, 45
Schoolhouse Books Inc, 107
Schools (directories), 460
Schroeder's Book Haven, 45
Schuler Books Inc, 108
Schulze News Co Inc, 57
Science & Children, 266
Science & Technology Libraries, 176
Science Activities, 266
Science Books and Films, 251
Science Fiction Age, 221
Science Fiction Book Club, 122
Science Fiction Chronicle, 221
The Science Fiction Shop, 161
Science Magazine, 266
Science News, 251
Science News and Science News Books, 161
Science of Mind, 221
Science Spectra, 221
The Science Store, 104
Science Teacher, 266
Science Teachers Action Deck, 390
The Sciences, 221
Scientific & Medical Publication, 45
Scientific & Technical Book Fair, 417
Scientific American, 221, 266
Scientific and Technical Organizations
  and Agencies, 458
Scientific Computing/Automation, 221
SciTech Software for Science, 161
Scott Billyou, Representative, 76
Scott LePine, Representative, 76
Scott Stamp Monthly, 251

Scott's Book Shop Catalog, 161
Scott/Satz Group, 376
Scottsdale Progress, 275
Scouting, 221
The Scranton Times-Tribune, 330
SCS University Stores, 109
SE Booksellers Association Convention, 416
Sea Challengers, 45
Sea Challengers Catalog, 161
Sea Magazine, 221
Sea Mart Associates, 76
Seafood Business, 251
Sealed Air Corporation, 441
Searcher, 266
Season's Greetings, 221
Seasons Catalog, 161
Seattle Daily Journal of Commerce, 340
Seattle Magazine, 222
Seattle Post-Intelligencer, 340
Seattle Times, 340
The Seattle Weekly, 361
Seattle's Child, 222
Seaway News Co Ltd, 68
Secondary Mathematics Catalog, 161
The Secretary, 251
Secrets of Successful Subscription Marketing, 416
Securities Regulation Law Journal, 266
Security Management, 266
Sedalia Democrat, 310
See-Saw Book Club, 122
Seeds and Books Catalog, 161
The Seguin Gazette-Enterprise, 336
Select Deck, 390
Select Information Exchange, 382
Select List Corp, 411
Selected Booklist, 161
Selections Book Fairs Inc, 45
Selective Books Inc, 161
Self, 222
Self-Esteem Publishing, 18
Self-Help Warehouse, 161
SelfCare Catalog, 161
The Selling Advantage, 271
Selling Magazine, 266
Selling to Seniors, 266
Selling to the Other Educational Markets, 461
Selling Your Business, 376
Selma Shapiro Public Relations, 370
Selma-Times Journal, 274
Semiconductor International, 251
Seminary Cooperative Bookstore, 105
The Seminole Producer, 326
Semler News Agency, 66
Seneca News Agency, 61
Senior Citizens Unlimited, 412
Senior Media Directory, 455
Senior Media Guide, 455
The Senior Source, 412
Senior World of Los Angeles, 222
Sensible Solutions, 376
Sentinel, 308, 327, 329
Sentinel and Enterprise, 304
Sentinel Newspapers, 351
Sentinel Record, 275
Sentinel-Standard, 306
Sepher-Hermon Press Co, 61
Ser Padres (Being Parents), 222
Serendipity Courier News, 57
Serials Review, 176
Servatius News Agency Inc, 66
Service Merchandise, 96
Service News Co, 58, 60, 62
SES Media Management, 370
Sesame Street Magazine, 222

Seton Name Plate, 390
Seton Name Plate Co, 441
Seven Hills Book Distributors, 8
Seventeen Magazine, 222
Seventh Generation Catalog, 161
Sew News, 251
Sewanee Review, 222
Sewell Associates, 76
Sewing & Craft Supplies, 161
Sewing Bookshop, 161
Sewing Center Supply Company, 45
Sewing Decor, 222
Sewing Sampler, 162
Seybold Report on Public Systems, 251
Seymour Daily Tribune, 296
SF Bay Area Book Festival, 416
SF Weekly, 351
SFG, 390
Shakespeare & Co, 112
Shape Magazine, 222
Shapian and Associates, 370
Shareware Express, 162
Shareware Software for Apple/MAC, 162
Shareware Spectacular, 162
Sharing Ideas Newsmagazine, 222
Sharon News Agency, 64
Sharp PR, 371
Shawano Leader, 343
Shawnee News-Star, 326
The Sheboygan Press, 343
Shelby Report of the Southeast, 251
Shelby Star, 321
Shelbyville Daily Union, 294
Shelbyville News, 296
Shelbyville Times-Gazette, 333
Sheldon Wiener Sales Organization Inc, 76
Sheldon's Retail, 461
Shelter Publications Inc, 18
Shen's Books & Supplies, 45
The Shepard Agency, 371
Shepard Public Relations, 371
Shephard Express, 361
Sher Distributing, 45
The Sheridan Press, 343
Sheridan-Elson Communications, 371
Sherman Democrat, 336
Sheryn Hara & Associates, 371
Shinder's Readmore Bookstores, 89
Shirley Lewis Information Serv, 53
Shirley Robins & Associates, 76
Shofar Magazine, 222
Shooting Times, 222
Shop at Home Catalogs Directory, 162
Shop the World by Mail, 162
Shop-At-Home Directory, 390
Shopko Stores, 95
Shopping Center World, 251
Shopsmith Inc, 412
Shoreline Container, 441
The Shorthorn, 333
Shoshone News-Press, 290
Shreveport Times, 302
Shuey Book Search, 45
Shutterbug, 222
Sid Gross & Associates, 376
Siddall Associates, 76
The Sidney Daily News, 324
Sidney Kramer Books, 103
Sidney Telegraph, 312
Siegel Display Products, 437
Sierra Magazine, 222
Sierra News Company, 61
Sierra Vista Herald, 275
Signal, 251
Signals Catalog, 162
The Signal, 282
SignCraft, 251

Signs of the Times, 252
Silhouette Books, 126
Silo Inc, 8
Silver Burdett & Ginn Co, 45
Silver Circle Magazine, 222
Silver City Daily Press/Indep, 315
Silver Visions Publishing, 18
Silverback Communications Inc, 412
Simcoe Reformer, 347
Simi Valley Star, 282
Simon & Schuster Distribution, 18
Simon Direct Inc, 412
Sing Out! Magazine, 222
Sing Tao Daily, 317
Singapore Bank Bookstore, 108
Singapore Festival of Books, 418
The Single Family Home Plans, 222
The Single Parent, 222
Single Unit Supermarket Operators, 461
Single-Parent Family, 222
Sioux City Herald, 354
Sioux City Journal, 298
Sirak & Sirak Associates, 76
Sisk Fulfillment Service, 83
Siskiyou Daily News, 283
Sisters in Crime Speakers Bureau, 378
Sizzleware Shareware Library, 162
SK&A Research Inc, 412
Skagit Valley Herald, 340
The Skeptical Inquirer, 252
Ski Magazine, 222
Ski World of Orlando, 162
Skin Diver, 252
Skipping Stones, 222
Skis & Snowboard Repair Tools, 162
Sky and Telescope, 222
Sky Publications, 162
Skydiving Book Service, 162
Skyline Displays Inc, 437
Skyway Publications, 356
Skywriters, 222
Slidell Sentry-News, 302
Sloan's Green Guide to Antiques Dealers - New England, 461
Slow Lane Journal, 222
Small Business Controller, 252
Small Business Journal, 222
Small Changes, 45
Small Farm Today, 252
Small Magazine Review, 176
Small Press Book Fair, 416
Small Press Distribution Inc, 45
Small press literary agents, 126-127
Small Press Record of Books in Print, 446
Small World Books, 101
Smallwood & Stewart Inc, 18
SMART Computer & Software Retail, 252
Smart Electronics, 222
Smart Practice Book Club, 122
SmartKid, 223
SME Catalog, 162
Smith & Hawken, 92
Smith & Hawken Catalog, 162
Smith Books, 92
Smithmark Publishers, 170
Smithsonian, 223
Smithsonian Museum Shops, 96
Smorgasbord of Cooks Periodicals, 455
Snack Food, 252
Snow Business Lists, 412
Snow Country, 223
Snow Goer, 223
Snow Week, 223
Snowboarding, 223
Snowmass Village Book Shoppe, 102
Snowmobile Magazine, 223
Snyder Daily News, 336

Soap Opera Digest, 223
Sober Times, 223
Soccer Digest, 223
Social Education, 266
Social Science History Magazine, 266
Social Studies Action Deck, 390
Social Studies School Service, 8
The Social Studies, 266
Social Work in Health Care, 266
Social Work with Groups, 266
Society of Prof Journalists, 412
Sociology of Sport Journal, 266
Sofia International Book Fair, 418
Softcraft Font Catalog, 162
Softdisk Publishing, 162
Softshoppe Public Domain Shareware, 162
Software, 438
Software Add-Ons, 162
Software Development, 223
Software Diversified Services, 438
Software Engineering Strategies, 252
Software Excitement!, 162
Software Labs, 162
Software Magazine, 252
Software Solutions, 252
Software Source, 162
Software Spectrum, 163
SOHO America Newsletter, 252
Solana Periodicals, 56
Solar Light Books, 101
Solar Press, 441
Solar Press Inc, 390
Solar Today, 252
Soldier of Fortune, 223
Solomon Gundy's Book World, 110
Solon Herald Sun, 358
Solstice Catalog, 163
Solutions Catalog, 163
Somerville House Books Ltd, 20
Sonoma Co Daily Herald-Recorder, 282
Sonoma County Independent, 351
Sonshine Harbor Wholesale Books, 45
Sorkins' Directories Inc, 412
Sotres Link, 371
Souder & Bertone Association, 371
Sound & Image, 223
Sound & Video Contractor, 252
Sound Track Magazine, 252
Sounds True Catalog, 163
Source Books, 8
Sourcebooks Inc, 18
Sourcebooks Review, 382
Sources of Information About Trade Shows and Expositions, 419
Sources: An Annotated Bibliography of Women's Issues, 446
South Bend Tribune, 296
South Cantral Books, 45
South Carolina Bookstores Inc, 45
South Carolina Game & Fish, 223
South Eastern Book Co Inc, 46
South Florida Bride, 223
South Florida Magazine, 223
South Haven Daily Tribune, 307
South Idaho Press, 290
South Shore News, 355
Southam Business Lists, 412
Southeast Missourian, 309
Southeast News, 46
Southeast Periodical & Book Sale, 57
Southeastern Book Company, 46
Southeastern News Company, 46, 58
Southern Accents, 223
Southern Boating, 223, 252
Southern Book Service Inc, 46
Southern Chinese News, 335

Southern Dutchess News, 358
Southern Exposure, 223
Southern Festival of Books, 416
Southern Graphics, 252
Southern Illinoisan, 291
Southern Living, 223
Southern Living Vacations, 223
Southern Loggin' Times, 267
Southern Marketing Products, 441
Southern Media Ventures, 382
Southern Michigan News, 46
Southern Michigan News Co, 60
Southern Periodicals, 46
Southern Publishers Group, 46
Southern Territory Assoc Inc, 76-77
Southern Tier News Company, 61
Southern Voice, 353
Southern Wisconsin News Co, 46
Southwest Art, 223
Southwest Book Co, 46
Southwest Cookbook Distributors, 46
Southwest Daily News, 302
Southwest Daily Times, 299
Southwest Mail Advertising, 412
Southwest Natural/Cultural Herit, 46
Southwest Parks and Monuments, 91
Southwest Publishing MarketPlace, 448
Southwest School Book Depository, 46, 83
Southwest Speakers Bureau Inc, 378
Southwest Spirit, 252
Southwest Times Record, 275
The Southwest Times, 339
Souvenirs & Novelties, 252
Spanish & European Bookstore, 46
Spanish Health and Women's Books, 382
Spartan Daily, 281
Spartanburg Herald-Journal, 331
Speak Magazine, 223
Speaker's bureaus, 377-378
SpeakerConnect USA, 378
The Speakers Network, 378
Special Education Action Deck, 390
Special equipment, 439
Special Libraries Association, 412
Special paper, 439
Special services, 439-440
Special Services in the Schools, 267
Special Students, 163
The Specialists Ltd, 412
Specialty Directory Publishing: Market Analysis/Forecast, 456
Specialty Food Merchandising, 252
Specialty items, 440-441
Specialty Marketing Company, 58
Specialty Merchandise Corp, 441
Specialty Promotions Co Inc, 46
Speedimpex USA Inc, 8
Spencer Evening World, 296
Spencer Museum Publications, 46
Spider, 223
Spiegel Catalog, 163
Spike & Friends Collection, 163
Spin, 223
Spin-Off, 223
Spirit, 329
Spirit Marketing Co, 438
The Spirit of '76 Bookstore, 89
Spiritual Book Associates, 122
Splash, 223
Spokesman-Review, 340
Sport Chalet, 96
Sport Compact Car, 224
Sport Magazine, 224
Sport Truck Magazine, 224
Sporting Classics Magazine, 224
Sporting Goods Business, 252
Sporting Goods Buyers, 461

Sporting Goods Dealer, 252
Sporting Goods Register, 461
Sporting News, 224
SporTradition Publications, 18
Sports 'N Spokes, 224
Sports Advantage, 455
Sports Afield, 224
Sports Collectors Digest, 224
Sports Eye, 318
Sports Focus Magazine, 224
Sports Illustrated, 224
Sports Illustrated for Kids, 224
Sports Market Place, 448
Sports Select, 440
Sports Trend, 252
Sportsman's Guide Catalog, 163
SportStyle, 224
Spot Radio Rates & Data, 455
Spot Television Rates & Data, 455
Spotlight, 224
Spotlight Chicago, 353
Spring Arbor Distributors, 8
Springdale Lists, 412
Springfield Advocate, 355
Springfield News-Leader, 311
Springfield News-Sun, 324
Springfield Union News, 305
Springhouse List Management, 412
Square Books, 109
Square Deal Records Book Dept, 46
SRDS Direct Marketing List Source, 412
SRI Aurobindo Association, 46
St Albans Messenger, 338
St Anthony Messenger, 224
St Augustine Record, 288
St Charles Watchman, 309
St Cloud Times, 308
St Helena Star, 351
St Joseph Daily Courier, 311
St Joseph News Press, 311
St Louis American, 356
St Louis Countian, 311
St Louis Daily Record, 311
St Louis Post-Dispatch, 311
St Louis Small Business Monthly, 224
St Louis Watchman Advocate, 309
St Maries Gopher News, 60
St Martin's Press, 18, 77
St Paul Book & Stationery, 89
St Paul Legal Ledger, 308
St Paul Pioneer Press Dispatch, 308
St Petersburg Times, 288
St Thomas Times-Journal, 347
Stack & Company, 77
Stacks: The Network Journal, 252
Stacy Kaye, 77
Staff Development Catalog, 163
Stage Step Catalog, 163
Stamp Collector, 224
Stan V Wright Ltd, 67
Standard, 309
Standard & Poor's Daily News, 318
Standard & Poor's Dividend Record, 318
Standard Democrat, 310
Standard Observer, 328
Standard Periodical Directory, 455
Standard Publishing Co, 46
Standard-Examiner, 337
Standard-Speaker, 328
Standard-Star, 319
The Standard, 347
Stanford Bookstore, 101
Stanton & McDougall Ltd, 53
Staples & Charles Ltd, 18
Staples Direct, 163
Star, 319
Star Book Sales, 47

Book Publishing Resource Guide   Page 521

Star Guide, 459
Star Magazine, 224
Star Newspaper Group, 360
Star-Beacon, 322
Star-Courier, 293
Star-Exponent, 339
Star-Gazette, 316
Star-Herald, 312
Star-Journal, 311
Star-Ledger, 314
Stark Bros, 83
Stark Services, 83
Starkmann Book Service, 47
Starkville Daily News, 309
Starlite Inc, 8
Starlog, 224
The StarPhoenix, 348
Starr Fulfillment Corp, 83
Starscript Distributing Company, 47
Stash Tea Catalog, 163
State & Regional Associations, 458
State Gazette, 332
State Journal, 300
State Journal-Register, 294
State News, 306
State News Company, 62
State Press, 275
Staten Island Advance, 318
Staten Island Parent, 224
Statesboro Herald, 290
Statesville Record & Landmark, 321
The State, 331
Statford Publishing, 18
Statlistics, 412
STCS Inc, 83
Steamboat Today, 284
Steamboats, 163
Stearn Publishers Ltd, 18
Step-by-Step Graphics, 252
Step-Parenting: Agencies, Books,
    Newsletters to Help You Survive, 446
Stephen Berger-Sales Company, 77
Stephen G Fossler Company Inc, 441
Stephen James, Representative, 77
Stephen R Ettlinger, 440
Stephen Wilson, Representative, 77
Stephen Young & Associates, 77
Stephenville Empire-Tribune, 337
Stereo Review, 224
Sterling Rock Falls News Agency, 47
Stevens List Management Center, 412
Stevens Point Journal, 343
Stevens-Knox List Management, 412
Stillwater Gazette, 308
The Stitchery, 224
Stitches Magazine, 224
Stock Car Racing Magazine, 253
Stoll Multi-Media Services, 47
Stone & Thomas Dept Stores, 95
Stone Lion Bookstore, 102
Stone Soup, 224
Stonebridge Publishers Inc, 47
The Stonesong Press Inc, 19
Storey Communications Inc, 19
Storey's Publishers Marketplace, 390
Stories How to Books for Country, 163
Story House Corporation, 8
Storytelling Magazine, 224
Storytime Monthly, 224
Stover Landing Books, 101
The Stranger, 361
Strategic Simulations Products Catalog,
    163
Strauss Consultants, 77
Strawberry Patch, 382
Street & Smith's Sports Books, 224
Street Rod Action, 225

Street Rodder, 225
Strictly Book Promotions, 371
The Strub Media Group Inc, 412
Stuart Associates, 77-78
Stuart Brent Books, 105
Stuart News, 288
Studio Photography, 225
Studio Stores, 96
Sturgis Journal, 307
Stuttgart Daily Leader, 276
Style Weekly, 225
Subject Guide to Books in Print, 446
Suburban News, 357
The Suburbanite, 357
Success Spoken Here, 163
Success!, 225
Success! Action Pac, 390
Successful Black Parenting, 225
Successful Farming, 225
Successful Farming @griculture Online,
    225
Successful Meetings, 253
Successful Retailers Action Card, 390
Sudbury News Service Ltd, 68
Sudbury Star, 347
Sue Katz & Associates Inc, 19
Suffolk Life, 358
Suffolk News-Herald, 339
Sullivan Daily Times, 296
Sullivan Marketing, 382
Sulphur Springs News-Telegram, 337
Summerside Journal-Pioneer, 348
Summit, 225, 354
Summit Beacon International, 47
Summit Daily News, 284
Sun Banner Pride, 359
Sun Chronicle, 303
The Sun Courier, 359
Sun Herald, 286, 288, 308
The Sun Herald, 359
Sun Journal, 302, 320
The Sun Messenger, 358
Sun News, 331
The Sun Press, 358
Sun Remarketing, 163
Sun Scoop Journal, 359
The Sun Star, 359
The Sun Times, 346
Sun Wa Bookstore, 96
Sun-Sentinel, 287
Sun/Day Distributors Corporation, 47
Sunbelt Fulfillment Service, 83
Sunbelt Publications, 47
Sunbooks Catalog, 163
Sundance Books, 101
Sundance Bookstore, 110
Sundance Publishers & Dist, 47
Sunmex Import Corp, 441
Sunnyside Daily Sun News, 340
Sunset Magazine, 225
Sunshine Books, 101
The Sun, 225, 340, 359
Super Chevy, 225
Super Ford, 225
Super Sportsman Action Pack, 412
Super Stock & Drag Illustrated, 225
Superior Books, 47
Superior Fulfillment, 83
Supermarket Business, 253
Supermarket News, 253
Supermarket, Grocery, and Convenience
    Store Chains, 461
Supermart Book Distributors, 47
Support Groups, Books, and Newsletters
    About Divorce, 446
Supt/Dist Administrators Action, 391
Sure-Fire Business Success Cat, 163

Surgin & Sinclair Associates, 77
Surplus Software, 163
Surveillant: Acq for Intell Prof, 163
Susan Fassberg Communications, 371
Susan Friedman Public Relations, 371
Susan Herner Rights Agency, 126
Susan Magrino Agency, 371
Susan Ostrov Associates, 371
Susan's Card Co, 47
Suzy Strauss & Associates, 371
Svoboda, 314
Swan Technologies, 164
Swedish Book Fair, 418
Swedus Imports, 47
The Sweepstakes Center, 376
Sweet Celebrations Catalog, 164
Sweetwater Reporter, 337
The Swiss Colony, 412
Sybervision Catalog, 164
The Sycamore Tree, 164
Syl-la-bles Bookstore, 104
Symbology Inc, 434
Symphony Magazine, 225
Symposium, 267
Synergy Marketing Group Inc, 83
Syntax, 371
Syracuse New Times, 358
Syracuse Post Standard, 319
Sys Admin, 253

T

T B Hagstoz and Son Catalog, 164
T H E Journal, 253
T R Books, 47
T-V Library Assoc Wholesalers, 47
TAB Club, 122
TAB Direct, 412
TAB Electronic Pack, 391
Tack & Togs, 253
The Tacoma Daily Index, 341
The Taft Group, 412
Tahlequah Daily Pictorial Press, 326
Tahlequah Daily Times Journal, 326
Tahoe Daily Tribune, 282
Taj Book Service, 47
Tak-Pak, 391
Talas Catalog, 164
Talbot Associates, 78
Talk Radio, 371
Talk Show Selects, 451
Talk Shows & Hosts on Radio, 455
Talkers Magazine, 253
Talking Leaves, 112, 225
Tall Stories, 101
Tallahassee Democrat, 288
Talman Company, 8
Tampa Tribune, 288
Target Catalog Mailings, 382
Target Market News, 271
Target Marketing, 271
Target Stores, 96
Targetron Inc, 371
Taste of Home, 225
Tatnuck Bookseller, 47
Tatnuck Bookseller & Sons, 107
Tattered Cover Book Store, 103
Tattered Tales, 114
Taunton Daily Gazette, 305
Taxation for Accountants, 267
Taybi Direct Inc, 412
Taybi Direct List Management, 412
Taylor & Francis, 48
Taylor Daily Press, 337

Taylor Gifts Catalog, 164
Taylor Publishing Co, 19
Taymar Industries Inc, 441
TCI List Management, 412
TCU Daily Skiff, 335
Tea, 225
The Tea Leaf, 106
Teacher Magazine, 267
Teacher's Book Depository, 54
Teacher's Performance, 440
Teacher-Parent Store, 164
Teachers in Focus, 225
Teachers Treasures, 114
Teaching Children Mathematics, 267
Teaching Pre K-8, 267
Teaching Pre K-8 Action Pac, 391
Teaching Tolerance, 267
Tech Directions, 267
Tech Talk, 391
Technical Communication, 267
Technical Information Center, 164
Technical List Computing Inc, 412
Technical Services Quarterly, 176
Technimetrics Inc, 412
Technology and Learning, 267
Technology Events Calendars, 419
Technology in Government, 253
Technology Teacher, 267
Teck News Agency Ltd, 68
Ted Barkus, Publicist, 371
Ted Weinstein & Associate, 78
Teddy Bear and Friends, 225
Teen Magazine, 225
Telecom Library Catalog of Books, 164
Telecommunications Reports Int, 253
Telegram, 299
Telegram-Tribune, 281
Telegraph, 291, 312-313
Telegraph Herald, 297
Telegraph-Forum, 322
Telegraph-Journal/Times-Globe, 345
Telemarketing, 267
Telephony, 253
Television Communicators Media, 371
Tempe Daily News Tribune, 275
Temple Daily Telegram, 337
Temple News, 329
Tenex Computer Express, 164
The Tennessean, 333
Tennessee Sportsman, 225
Tennis Buyer's Guide, 253
Tennis Magazine, 225
Tennis Match, 225
Tension Envelope Corp, 437
The Terrell Tribune, 337
Terrific Titles for Young Reader, 54
Texarkana Gazette, 337
Texas Art Supply, 65
Texas Book Co, 48
The Texas Bookman, 170
Texas City Sun, 337
Texas Educational Paperbacks Inc, 48
Texas Highways, 225
Texas Library Book Sales, 48
Texas Media Directory, 455
Texas Monthly, 226
Texas Observer, 360
Texas People & Places, 226
Texas Sportsman, 226
Texoma News Agency, 65
The Textile Redbook, 450
That Bookstore in Blytheville, 98
That Patchwork Place Inc, 164
Theatre Communications Group, 9
Theodore Lucia, 78
Theodore Roosevelt Nature/History Assn Bkstores, 91

Theological Book Service, 122
Theos Resource Directory, 164
Thieme Med Publishrs Inc, 48
Think Tank Directory, 458
Thinkercisers, 164
Thinkers' Press, 19
Third World Resource Directory, 458
This Magazine, 226
The Thistle Book Shop, 116
Thomas Allen & Son Ltd, 78
Thomas Brothers Maps, 48
Thomas Grocery Register, 461
Thomas Murphy, Representative, 78
Thomas P Seigenthaler PR, 371
Thomas Publishing Co, 412
Thomas Reed Publications, 9
Thomas Registry of American Manufacturers, 450
Thomas Stuart Media Management, 413
Thomaston Books & Prints, 107
Thomasville Times-Enterprise, 290
Thomcomp, 83
Thompson Book & Supply, 96
Thompson Publishing Group, 83
Thos Oak & Sons Package Inserts, 391
Thousand Oaks Star, 282
Threads Magazine, 253
Thrifty Scholar, 105
Thunderbird Bookshops Inc, 101
TIA International Travel News Directory, 455
Tianjin International Book Fair, 418
Tiffin News Agency, 63
Tifton Gazette, 290
TigerMark, 437
Tigersoftware, 164
Tiller and Toiler, 299
Timber Harvesting, 267
Timberdoodle Catalog, 164
Time Distribution Services, 48
Time Magazine, 226
Time Out New York, 226
Time Warner Publisher Serv Intl, 62
Times, 289, 295
The Times and Democrat, 331
Times Daily, 273
Times Direct Marketing USA, 413
Times Georgian, 289
Times Herald, 307, 329
Times Herald-Record, 317
Times Journal, 273
Times Journal Company, 361
Times Leader, 330
Times News, 329
Times of Acadiana, 354
Times Record, 302
Times Record News, 337
The Times Recorder, 325
Times-Bulletin, 324
Times-Colonist, 345
Times-Courier, 291
Times-Herald, 275
Times-Illinois, 293
Times-Inquirer, 358
Times-Leader, 323
Times-Mail, 294
Times-News, 291, 320
The Times-Picayune, 302
Times-Press, 294
Times-Reporter, 324
Times-Republic, 294
Times-Republican, 298, 353
Times-Standard, 277
Times-Tribune, 300
Times-Union, 297, 318
Times-West Virginia, 341
The Times, 296, 331

Tipton Conservative, 354
Tipton County Tribune, 296
Tis Wholesale, 48
Title Books Inc, 48
TitleNet, 164
The Titusville Herald, 330
To the Point, 440
The Toadstool Bookshops, 110
The Toastmaster, 226
Today's Business Woman Cards, 391
Today's Catholic Teacher, 253
Today's Catholic Teacher Pack, 391
Today's Christian Woman Card Pak, 391
Today's Collector, 226, 271
Today's CPA, 267
Today's Factory Pack, 391
Today's News Herald, 274
Today's Old West Traveler, 226
Today's Parish, 267
Today's Sunbeam, 314
Tokyo International Book Fair, 418
Tole World, 253
Tom Shenk & Associates, 78
Tom Stouras, Representative, 78
Tonawanda News, 318
Toni Werbell Public Relations, 371
Tony Saltzman, 439
Tooling & Production, 253
Tools for Business Success Pac, 391
Tools for Exploration Catalog, 164
Top 200 TV News/Talk Shows, 455
Topeka Capital-Journal, 300
Toppan Company Ltd, 10
Tor Books, 126
Torino National Book Fair, 418
Toronto Star, 347
Toronto Sun, 347
Tortuga Books, 98
Total Circulation Services, 9
Total Health, 226
Total Information, 48
Total Media Concepts Inc, 413
Total Solutions, 164
Tour & Travel Marketplace, 391
Tour & Travel News, 253
Tout De Suite A La Microwave Inc, 48
Tow Ocean Books, 116
Tower Books, 101
Tower Hobbies Catalog, 164
Tower Publishing, 413
Tower Records & Books, 96
Town & Country, 226
Town Crier Inc, 106
Toys International, 89
Toys to Grow On Catalog, 164
Toys-R-Us Stores, 96
TR Wireless News, 253
Tracy Press, 282
Trade Directories of the World, 446
Trade show directories, 419
Trade Show Marketing Services, 420
Trade Shows Worldwide, 419
Trade shows, book fairs and conventions, 415-420
Tradeshow Week, 253
Tradeshow Week Data Book, 419
TradeShows & Exhibits Schedule, 419
Traditional Building, 253
Traditional Quilter, 226
Traditional Quiltworks, 226
Traffic World, 253
Trail Times, 345
Trailer Life, 226
Train of Thought, 165
Training, 226
Training and Development Organizations Directory, 458

Trains, 226, 253
Trans Pacific, 226
TransAllegheny Books, 48
TransAmerican & Export News Co, 9
Transbooks Inc, 48
Transcript, 304
Transmission & Distrubution, 253
Transportation & Distribution, 253
Travel & Family-Related Lists, 413
Travel & Leisure, 226
Travel 50 & Beyond, 226
Travel Agent Magazine, 253
Travel Agents Marketplace, 391
Travel America, 226
Travel Holiday, 226
Travel Leisure & Entertainment News Media Directory, 455
Travel Management Daily, 286
Travel Tech, 165
Travel Weekly, 253
Travel World News, 254
TravelAge, 254
Traveler Restaurant Bookseller, 48
Traveler's Checklist, 165
Travelhost, 226
Travelin' Magazine, 226
Traveller's Bookstore Catalog, 165
Travelwriter Marketletter, 271
Traverse Bay Display Company, 437
Traverse City Record Eagle, 307
Traverse Magazine, 226
Treasure Book Catalogue, 165
Treasure Chest, 254
Treasure Chest Books, 19
Treasure House Catalog, 165
Treasure Hunt Publications, 48
Treasure Valley News, 58
Treasured Portraits Hotline Coop, 391
Tree Frog Trucking Company, 48, 113
Tree of Life Inc, 48
Tree of Life Midwest, 48
Trend-Lines Catalog, 165
The Trenton Times, 314
The Trentonian, 314
Tri-City Herald, 340
Tri-County News Co Inc, 57
Tri-County Times, 354
Tri-fold Book Service, 48
Tri-Media Marketing Serv Inc, 413
Tri-State News Agency, 64
Tri-Valley Herald, 279
Trial Magazine, 267
Triangle Marketing Services, 413
Triangle News Company, 64
Tribune, 296, 347
Tribune Chronicle, 324
Tribune-Review, 328
Tribune-Star, 296
Trident Booksellers, 107
Trim Associates, 78
Trinity Marketing, 438
Triplicate, 277
Tristar Productions, 440
Troll Book Club, 122
Trolle Associates, 48
Tropical Fish Hobbyist, 226
Trover Shop Books, 89
Troy Daily News, 324
Troy Messenger, 274
Troyka Ltd, 54
Truck/Sport Utility High Performance, 254
Trucker Card Deck, 391
Truckin Classic Trucks, 254
Truckin', 254
True Detective, 226
True Love, 226
True Remainders Ltd, 54

Truepenny Books, 98
Trumble Greetings, 165
Trumbull Marketing Group Inc, 413
Trump Card Marketing Inc, 391
The Trumpeter, 254
TRW Real Estate Marketing Info, 413
TRW Target Marketing Services, 413
Tryon Daily Bulletin, 321
Tucson Citizen, 275
Tucson Lifestyle, 227
Tucson Weekly, 349
Tudor Publishers Inc, 376
Tufts Daily, 304
Tulare Advance-Register, 282
Tulare County News Agency Inc, 57
Tulsa Daily Commerce and Legal News, 326
Tulsa World, 326
Tunde Dada House of Africa, 48
Turlock Journal, 282
Turn of the Page, 113
Turner Company, 49
Turner Marketing Systems, 413
Turtle Magazine/Preschool Kids, 227
Tuscaloosa News, 274
Tustin Books, 102
TV Guide, 227
TWA Ambassador, 227
Twenty-Third Avenue Books, 113
TWICE, 254
Twin Cities Business Monthly, 254
Twin Cities Reader, 356
Twin City News Agency, 58
Twin Peaks Press, 382
Twin Peaks Press Lists, 413
Twin Peaks Speaks, 165
Twins Magazine, 227
The Twinsburg Sun, 359
Tyler Courier-Times, 337
Tyler Morning Telegraph, 337
Typesetting, 441
Tyrone Daily Herald, 330

U S Art Magazine, 254
U S Kids, 227
U S Press, 441
U S West Lists, 413
UAF Bookstore, 97
UARCO Computer Supplies Catalog, 165
Ubiquity, 9
UCLA Bookstore, 102
UCLA Magazine, 227
UFO Magazine, 227
Ukiah Daily Journal, 283
Ulrich's International, 456
Ultra Books Inc, 49
Unabridged Bookstore, 105
Unarius Academy of Science, 413
Unarius Educational Foundation, 49
Undercover Book Services, 165
Underground Books, 165
Uni-Mail Business List Mgmt, 413
Uni-Marketing, 413
Unicorn Books & Crafts Inc, 49
The Unicorn Textile Book Catalog, 165
Unimail List Corp, 413
Union City Daily Messenger, 333
Union Daily Times, 331
Union Democrat, 282
The Union Leader, 313
Union Plus, 227
Union-Recorder, 289

Union-Sun & Journal, 316
Unique Books, 9
Unique Hair & Beauty, 227
Unique Homes, 227
Uniquity Catalog, 165
United Chinese Press, 290
United Communications Group, 413
United Library Services Inc, 54
United News Co, 56
United News Wholesalers Ltd, 67
United Society of Shakers, 49
United Techbook Co, 49
Unity Bookstore, 109
Unity Magazine, 227
Univ of Cincinnati Bookstore, 94
Univ of Connecticut Co-Operative, 94
Univ of Minnesota Bookstores, 94, 109
Univ of Wisconsin Centers, 94
Univenture, 437
Universal Index, 446
Universal International, 170
Universal Network Inc, 441
Universal Sales & Marketing, 170
University Book Sales & Services, 54
University Book Store, 116
University Bookstore ID State Un, 104
University Daily Kansan, 299
The University Daily, 335
The University Journal, 339
University Marketing Group, 78
University of California Press, 78
University of Hawaii Bookstore, 94
University of New Mexico Press, 78
University of Oklahoma Press, 78
University of Texas Press, 78
University of Toronto Bookroom, 94
University of Washington Press, 9
The University Star, 336
University Supply Store, 94
UnixWorld, 254
Up the Creek, 351
Upchurch-Brown Booksellers, 102
UPCO Catalog for Birds Only, 165
UPCO Complete Pet Store Catalog, 165
Upper East Side Resident, 358
Upper Midwest Booksellers Tradeshow, 416
Upper West Side Resident, 358
Upscale Magazine, 227
Upside Magazine, 254
Upstart Crow Bookstore, 102
Uptown Book Co, 102
Urban Academic Librarian, 176
Urban Family Magazine, 227
Urban Forests, 267
Urbana Daily Citizen, 324
Urner Barry Publications Inc, 413
Urner Barry's Price-Current, 313
US Boat & Ship Modeler, 227
US Comm for Scholastic Assist, 413
US Games Systems Inc, 49
US Magazine, 227
US Monitor, 413
US News and World Report, 227
US Suburban Press, 382
US West Marketing Resources, 413
USA Book-Expo, 420
USA Fulfillment, 83
USA Gymnastics, 227
USA TODAY, 338
USA Weekend, 227
USA*Flex, 165
Useful Guide to Herbal Health, 165
USF Oracle, 288
USI Inc, 440
USTA Tennis Publications, 165
Utah Chronicle, 338

Utne Reader, 227
Utrecht Art & Drafting Supplies, 166

V

V & L Information Resources Corp, 54
V M Frantz & Company, 371
Vacations, 227
Vacaville Reporter, 283
Vail Daily, 284
Val Publishing Co, 49
Val-Pak Direct Marketing Systems, 382
Valassis Inserts, 382
Valdosta Daily Times, 290
Valerie Davis & Assoc, 413
Valerie Ryan Media Services, 371
Vallejo Times Herald, 283
The Valley Advocate, 355
Valley Book Center, 115
The Valley Bookstore Inc, 116
Valley City Times-Record, 321
Valley Courier-Alamosa, 283
Valley Daily News, 340
Valley Distributors Inc, 49
Valley Independent, 329
Valley Magazine, 227
Valley Morning Star, 335
Valley News, 313
Valley News Agency, 67
Valley News Company, 60
Valley News Dispatch, 330
Valley News Service Inc, 66
Valley News Today, 298, 354
Valley of the Sun, 166
The Valley Optimist, 355
Valley Times, 280
Valley-Times News, 273
Value Added Resellers, 461
Van Dyke News Company, 56
Van Khoa Bookstore, 49
Van W Keck, Representative, 78
Vancouver Columbian, 341
Vancouver Province, 345
Vancouver Sun, 345
Vanguard International Cinema, 166
The Vanguard, 327
Vanity Fair, 227
Vantage Magazine, 227
Vantage Point Publicity, 371
Vantage Sales & Marketing, 78
VAR Business, 254
Variety, 254
Variety Merchandise Show, 419
Vegetarian Gourmet, 228
Vegetarian Journal, 228
Vegetarian Resources, 166
Vegetarian Times, 228
Veggie Life, 228
VeloNews, 228
Ventura Associates, 376
Ventura Book Store, 102
The Ventura Companion, 166
Ventura County Star, 283
Venture Communications, 413
Verbatim Bookstore, 97
Verlinden Letterman & Stok, 166
The Vermont Book Shop Inc, 115
Vermont Country Store, 166
Vermont Life Catalog, 166
Vermont Life Magazine, 228
Vermont Media Directory, 456
Vernon Daily News, 345
The Vernon Daily Record, 337
Vero Beach Book Ctr, 104

Vero Beach Press-Journal, 288
Veronis Suhler & Associates, 376
Vesper Publishing Catalog, 166
Vet-Dek Card Pack, 391
Vet-Vax Catalog, 166
Vette, 228
VFW Magazine, 228
Vibe Magazine, 228
Vibrant Life, 228
Vic's Place, 113
Vicki Eisenberg Agency, 371
Vicksburg Evening Post, 309
Victor Hotho & Co, 170
The Victoria Advocate, 337
Victorian Video Productions, 166
Video Business, 254
The Video Collection, 166
Video Enterprises, 376
Video Magazine, 228
Video rights buyers, 127
The Video Source Book, 446
Video Store Magazine, 228
Video Systems, 254
VideoGames, 228
Vidette Times, 296
Vietnam Magazine, 254
Vietnam Opportunities, 271
Viking Discount Computer Supplies, 166
Village Book & Stationery, 110
Village Book Shop, 112
Village Book Store Inc, 110
Village Books, 116
The Village Bookshop, 103
Village Green Bookstores, 89
Village Software, 166
The Village Voice, 228, 358
The Villager, 358
Vim & Vigor, 254
Vincennes News Agency, 59
Vincennes Sun-Commercial, 297
Vindicator, 325
Vineyard & Winery Management, 254
Vinita Daily Journal, 326
Vintage Book Distributors, 49
Vintage Rails, 228
Vinyl Industrial Products Inc, 441
Virgin Nastertronic, 166
Virginia Express, 361
Virginia Game & Fish, 228
Virginia Review, 267
Virginian Review, 339
Virginian-Pilot, 339
Virtual Reality Special Report, 254
Virtual Reality World, 254
Virtue Magazine, 228
Virtue Value Pak, 391
Vis, 437
Visalia Times-Delta, 283
Vision Works, 49
Visitor and Convention Bureaus, 458
Vistabooks, 49
Visual Education Corporation, 19
Visual Horizon's Products, 391
Visual Horizons, 382
Vitality Distributors Inc, 49
Vitamin Shoppe Book Catalog, 166
VKH, 19
VMS Co-op Mailing, 382
VNR Architecture Action Pac, 391
VNR Electronic Engineering Pac, 391
VNR Hospitality/Food Service Pac, 391
Vocational Marketing Services, 376
Vogue, 228
Vogue Knitting, 228
Volcano Press, 19
Volunteer Energy ResourceCatalog, 166
Volunteerism, 458

Voyles News Agency Inc, 49
VQ Magazine, 228
Vroman's Book & Stationery, 102
VW Trends, 228

W

W Magazine, 228
W S Ponton Inc, 413
W T Cox Subscriptions Inc, 49
W W Norton & Co, 19
W W Wickel Co, 49
W Warner Book Distributors, 49
Wa Book Service Inc, 49
Wabash Plain Dealer, 297
Waco Tribune Herald, 337
Wahrenbrock's Books, 102
Wake Boarding, 228
Wakefield Daily Item, 305
Waking Owl Books, 115
Waldenbooks, 92, 170
Walking Magazine, 228
Wall Street Journal, 318
Wall Street Lists, 413
Walla Walla Union-Bulletin, 341
Wallace's Bookstores, 94
Walt's Hallmark, 96
Walter Karl List Management, 413
Walters Speakers Services, 378
Wambtac, 440
Wapakoneta Daily News, 324
Warburg & Associates, 372
Ward's Auto World, 254
Ward's Automotive International, 254
Ward's Automotive Reports, 255
Ward's Engine/Vehicle Tech Update, 255
Ward's Natural Science Catalog, 166
The Warm Store, 166
Warner Books, 126
Warner Press Inc, 50
Warner Publisher Services, 19
Warp Magazine, 228
Warren Gorham & Lamont Inc, 413
Warren Times-Observer, 330
Warsaw International Book Fair, 418
Warwick's Books, 102
Wasatch Book Distribution, 50
Washington Business Journal, 228
Washington City Paper, 352
Washington Daily News, 321
Washington Evening Journal, 298
Washington Flyer Magazine, 255
Washington Media Directory, 456
The Washington Monthly, 229
Washington Post, 286
Washington Post Magazine, 286
Washington Post Weekly, 229
Washington Speakers Bureau, 378
Washington Square News, 318
Washington Technology, 229
Washington Times, 286
Washington Times-Herald, 297
Washington Toy Company, 50
Washingtonian, 229
Watchung Booksellers, 111
Water Pollution Control Fedrn, 414
Water Ski, 229
Water Street Bookstore, 110
Waterbury Republican American, 285
Watercraft Business, 255
Waterloo-Cedar Falls Daily Courier, 298
Watermark Communications, 372
Waters Magazine, 255
Waterstone's Booksellers, 92

Watertower Books, 113
Watertown Daily Times, 319, 343
Watertown Public Opinion, 332
Watson-Guptill Distribution Ctr, 83
Watsonville Register-Pajaronian, 283
Watts List Management, 414
Waudesha County Freeman, 343
Waudon Standard, 354
The Wausau Daily Herald, 343
Waverly News Co Inc, 50
Waxahachie Daily Light, 337
Waycross Journal-Herald, 290
Wayfarer Publications Catalog, 167
Wayne C Johnson & Assoc Inc, 414
Wayne Donnell, Representative, 78
Wayne Finger Lakes Area, 50
The Wayne Independent, 328
Wearable Crafts, 229
Weatherford Daily News, 326
The Weatherford Democrat, 337
Weatherwise, 229
Weaving Works Catalog, 167
WEB Direct Marketing, 440
Wednesday Magazine, 356
Wee-Pak, 391
Weekend Woodcrafts, 229
Weekly Alibi, 357
Weekly newspaper editors/book reviewers, 349-361
Weekly Planet, 352
Weight Watchers Magazine, 229
Weintraub & FitzSimons, 372
Weirton Daily Times, 342
Weiss Publishing & Marketing Inc, 414
Welch Daily News, 342
Welcome Enterprises Inc, 19
Welding Design & Fabrication, 255
Wellington Daily News, 300
Wellsville Daily Reporter, 319
Welton Books, 19
Wenatchee News Agency Inc, 66
Wenatchee World, 341
Wessex Books and Records, 102
West & Feinberg PC, 440
West Bend Daily News, 343
West Boca Times, 352
West Central Tribune, 308
West Coast Video, 96
West Coast Woman, 229
West County Times, 280
West Geauga Sun, 359
West Hawaii Today, 290
West Side Sun News, 360
West Texas News Co, 65
The West Virginia Daily News, 341
West Virginia Game & Fish, 229
West Virginia Periodicals, 66
Westchester Family, 229
The Westerly Sun, 331
Western Christian Bookstores, 93
Western English World, 255
The Western Horseman, 229
Western Library Books, 50
Western Mailing Lists, 414
Western Marine Enterprises, 19
Western Michigan News Inc, 50
Western Outdoor News, 229
Western Outdoors, 229
Western Photographer, 229
Western Publishing, 50
Western Star, 345
Western Styles, 229
Westfield Evening News, 305
Westlight, 440
Weston Communications, 372
Westways, 229
Westword, 351

Wewoka Daily Times, 326
Weyerhaeuser Paper Company, 439
WG & L Action Card Decks, 392
What's New in Home Economics, 392
What's NEW in Mature Marketing, 392
What's Working in Sales Mgmt, 271
Wheeling News Register, 342
Whitaker House, 19
White Cap Books, 20
White Dove International, 19
White Flower Farm Catalog, 167
White Rabbit Books & Things, 89
White's Guide/Collect Figurines, 229
Whiting News Co Inc, 50
Whittier Daily News, 283
Who's Who Among Human Services Professionals, 459
Who's Who Among Young American Professionals, 459
Who's Who in Advertising, 459
Who's Who in African Heritage Book Publishing, 448
Who's Who in America, 459
Who's Who in American Art, 459
Who's Who in American Education, 459
Who's Who in American Law, 459
Who's Who in American Nursing, 459
Who's Who in American Politics, 460
Who's Who in Editors & Poets in US & Canada, 444
Who's Who in Entertainment, 125
Who's Who in Finance & Industry, 460
Who's Who of American Women, 460
Who's Who of Emerging Leaders in America, 460
Whole Again Resource Guide, 446
Whole Earth Access, 96
Whole Earth Provision Co, 114
Whole Earth Review, 229
Whole Foods, 255
The Whole Work Catalog, 167
Wholesale Art Materials, 50
Wholesale Distributors, 59
Wholesale Grocers, 461
The Wholesale-by-Mail Catalog, 449
Wholesalers, 21-54
Wholesalers and retailers (directories), 460-462
Wichita Eagle, 300
Wichita Metro News, 354
Wilcher Associates, 79
Wilcor International Book Dept, 50
Wild Earth Magazine, 229
Wild West Magazine, 229
Wilderness Books, 19
Wilderness Press, 19
Wildfowl Carving & Collecting, 255
Wildlife Art News, 229
Wiley Accounting/Finance Pac, 392
Wiley Agriculture Card Deck, 392
Wiley Business & Management, 392
Wiley Business/Computer Deck, 392
Wiley Computers & Data Proc Pac, 392
Wiley Electrical & Electronics, 392
Wiley Engineers' Action Cards, 392
Wiley Financial Executive's Card, 392
Wiley Geology Card Deck, 392
Wiley Law Decks, 392
Wiley Mathematics/Statistics, 392
Wiley Psychology Card Pack, 392
Wiley Real Estate Pack, 392
Wilkie News, 89, 113
Willamette Week, 360
William B Eerdmans Publishing, 126
William Hill, Representative, 79
William J Whitaker Associates, 79
William Korr Sales Company, 79

William S Hein & Co Inc, 50
William Schaeffer News Dist, 61
William Stroh Inc, 414
William Tricker Catalog, 167
William-Neil Associates, 414
Williams Booksellers, 114
Williams College Marketing, 376
Williams Direct, 414
Williams' Book Stores, 102
Williams-Sonoma Catalog, 167
Williams-Sonoma Mailing Lists, 414
Williams-Sonoma Stores, 96
Williamson Daily News, 342
Williamsport Sun-Gazette, 330
Williston Daily Herald, 321
Willmann-Bell Catalog, 167
Willowood Lists, 414
Wills Book Stores, 89
Wilmington Morning Star, 321
Wilmington News Journal, 324
Wilshire Book Co, 50
Wilson Daily Times, 321
Wilson Marketing Group Inc, 414
The Wilson Quarterly, 229
Wimmer Cookbook Distribution, 19
The Winchester Star, 339
Winchester Sun, 301
Wind in the Rigging Catalog, 167
Window Fashions Magazine, 255
Window Sources, 255
Windows NT, 267
Windows World Direct Card Pack, 392
Windows/DOS Developers Journal, 255
Windsor News, 54
Windsor Star, 347
Windsurfing, 229
Windy City Times, 353
Windy City Woman, 229
Wine Appreciation Guild, 20
Wine Enthusiast, 229
The Wine Enthusiast Company, 167
Wine Mailing Lists, 414
Wine Spectator, 230
Wines & Vines, 255
Winfield Daily Courier, 300
Wingra Woods Press, 20
Wings Digital Corp, 437
Wings Inc Catalog, 167
WinMark Concepts, 392
Winnipeg Free Press, 345
Winnipeg Sun, 345
Winona Daily News, 308
Winston-Derek Publ Group Inc, 20
Winston-Salem Journal, 321
Winterbourne Travel Lists, 414
Winterthur Museum Bookstore, 167
Winthill List Management, 414
Wired, 230
Wireless Catalog, 167
Wisconsin Label Group, 438
The Wisconsin Light, 230
Wisconsin Sportsman, 230
Wisconsin State Journal, 342
Wisconsin Trails, 230
Wisdom Publications, 167
Wise Owl Book Shoppe, 108
Wittman Associates, 376
Wolfe News Service, 62
The Woman Rebel, 230
Woman's Day, 230
Woman's Day Special Interest Publications, 230
Woman's World, 230
Women & Criminal Justice, 267
Women & Health, 267
Women & Politics, 267
Women & Therapy, 268

Women Circle, 230
Women in Business, 230
Women Today, 230
Women's Forum, 230
Women's History Catalog, 167
Women's Household Crochet, 230
Women's News, 230
Women's Sports and Fitness, 230
Women's Sports Traveler, 230
Women's Wear Daily, 255, 318
Womens' & Childrens' Wear Specialty Stores, 462
Womontyme Distribution Company, 50
Wood & Wood Products, 255
Wood Digest, 230
Wood Magazine Card Pack, 392
Woodcrafters Lumber Sales Inc, 50
Wooden Porch Books, 167
WoodenBoat Magazine, 230
The WoodenBoat Store, 167
Woodland Books, 20
Woodmen Magazine, 230
Woodshop News, 255
Woodsmith, 255
Woodstock Times, 358
Woodward News, 326
Woodwork, 255
Woodworker's Supply, 167
The Woodworkers' Store, 167
Woodworking Book Club, 123
Woodworking Unlimited Catalog, 167
Woolco Department Stores, 96
Worcester Magazine, 355
Worcester Phoenix, 355
Worcester Telegram & Gazette, 305
The Word For Today Inc, 50
Word of Life Distributors, 50
Word Perfect Publishing Corp, 414
Word Play, 106
WordPerfect Magazine, 230
Words on Cassette, 446
Wordsworth Bookstore, 108
Workbasket, 230
Workbench, 230, 255
Working Mother, 230
Working Press of the Nation, 456
Working Woman, 230
Working Woman Exec-Deck, 392
The World & I, 231
World Affairs, 268
World Art, 231
World Book Marketing, 50
World Broadcast News, 255
World Communications Inserts, 392
World Eye Bookshop, 108
World Innovators Inc, 414
World Journal, 319
World Life International USA, 50
World Literature Ministries, 20
World Literature Today, 268
World Press Review, 231
World Resources Institute, 167
World Sports Expo, 419
World University Bookstore, 50
World War II Magazine, 231
World Watch, 231
World Wide Mailing Inc, 414
World's Fair, 268
World's Greatest Gaming Catalog, 168
Worldata, 414
Worldwide Media Group Ltd, 414
Worldwide Media Service Inc, 79
The World, 326
Worship Leader Magazine, 231
Worthington Daily Globe, 308
WPL Associates Inc, 83
The Wright Group, 9

The Write Place, 376
Writer's Digest, 255
Writer's Digest Book Club, 123
Writer's Guidelines, 268
The Writer's Handbook, 448
Writer's Market, 448
Writer's Northwest Handbook, 448
Writer's Sorkshop Review, 231
Writers & Research Inc, 376
Writers House Inc, 127
Writers Resource Guide / Seattle, 448
Writers' Journal, 268
The Writer, 255
The Writewell Catalog, 168
Writing for the Ethnic Markets, 448
Writing in Ohio, 456
WVU Bookstores, 94
Wybel Marketing Group, 79
Wyoming Eagle, 343
Wyoming Periodical Distributors, 67

X

The Xenia Daily Gazette, 324
Xerox Office Supplies Catalog, 168

Y

Yachting, 231
Yakima Herald-Republic, 341
Yale Co-op, 103
Yale Daily News, 285
Yale Review, 255
Yang Sheng, 168
Yankee Book Peddler, 51
Yankee List Marketing, 414
Yankee Magazine, 231
Yankee News Company, 51
Yankee Trader, 357
Yard & Garden, 231
Yarn Tree Designs, 51
Yearbook of Experts Authorities and Spokespersons, 382
Yellow Brick Road, 106
Yellow Moon Press, 20
Yellowstone Art Center, 9
Yield House Catalog, 168
YM Magazine, 231
Yo! Youth Outlook, 231
Yoga International, 231
Yoga Journal, 231
Yoga Journal Book & Tape Source, 168
York Daily Record, 330
York Dispatch/York Sunday News, 330
York News-Times, 312
Yosemite Association Bookstore, 51
Yost List Co, 414
Young Adult/Teen Market Report, 271
Young Horizons Indigo, 231
Young Reader's Book Club, 123
Young Voices, 231
Young's News Agency Inc, 65
Your Company, 255
Your Health, 231
Your Home/Indoors & Out, 231
Your Money, 231
Your Pet, 231
Youth Markets Alert, 255
Youth Ministry Resource Pack, 392
Youthwalk, 231

Yuma Daily Sun, 275

Z

Zany Brainy, 91
ZCMI Department Stores, 95
Zed Marketing Group, 414
Zeller List Corp, 414
Zenith Books, 168
Zenith Mailing List Co, 414
Zeos Quarterly, 168
Zephyr Exclusive Software, 168
Ziff-Davis List Services, 414
Zillions, 231
Zillman Enterprises, 170
Zion Natural Historical Assn, 91
Zip Along Associates Inc, 414
Zone Magazine, 231
Zoo Review Catalog, 168